Where Are You
When I Need You?

Befriending God
When Life Hurts

ROBERT N. LEVINE

HarperSanFrancisco
An Imprint of HarperCollins*Publishers*

HarperCollins Web Site: http://www.harpercollins.com
HarperCollins®, ☰®, and HarperSanFrancisco™ are trademarks of
HarperCollins Publishers Inc.

FIRST EDITION

Library of Congress Cataloging-in-Publication Data

Levine, Robert N.
Where are you when I need you? : befriending God when life
hurts / Robert N. Levine. — 1st ed.
ISBN 0-06-251351-6 (cloth)
ISBN 0-06-251352-4 (pbk.)
1. Providence and government of God—Judaism. 2. Suffering—
Religious aspects—Judaism. 3. Theodicy. 4. Judaism—
Doctrines.   I. Title
BM645.P7L48   1996
296.3'11—dc20   95-25507

96 97 98 99 00 ❖ HAD 10 9 8 7 6 5 4 3 2 1

*To my parents, whose belief in me
inspired my belief in God.*

*To my wife and soul mate, Gina,
whose love makes all the rest possible.*

*To the men, women, and children of
Rodeph Sholom, whose searching minds
and caring hearts energized this effort to
answer their questions.*

CONTENTS

ACKNOWLEDGMENTS

All good teachers will tell you they have received more from their students than they have been able to give. That is precisely how I feel about the people I serve at Congregation Rodeph Sholom in New York City and have served at the United Jewish Center in Danbury, Connecticut. The wisdom and strength with which they challenge their own beliefs have made this book possible.

The clergy and staff with whom I work are fabulous colleagues and earn my continued respect. Particularly deep thanks go to my secretary, Marjorie Sachs, who gave me her counsel, help, and friendship every step of the way.

Warm gratitude is extended to my talented editor, Caroline Pincus, who continually inspires better work. Her fine assistant, Sue White, has been most helpful as well. I would also like to thank my temple president, Jack Levitt, for his sage comments and support of this endeavor; Mark Chimsky for his considerable help and guidance; my sister, Sheree Levine, for her keen insight; Carol Fass and Patti

Greenberg, who read the manuscript and made many helpful suggestions; and my agent, Dorothy Markinko, who has believed in this project from the start.

I want to express my deepest thanks to my wife, Gina, for her wisdom and support and to our three great children, Judah, Ezra, and Maya, who fill our lives with incredible joy every day.

Finally, I want to thank God for always being there and bestowing so many blessings upon me. This book is a small token of gratitude to my Eternal Friend.

I could not have written this book without the rusty old swing I visited often during my childhood. There I would sit in happy times and in sad times, too, and talk to God.

I didn't know what God looked like, I never heard God's voice, I did not even know what I expected of God. But there, among the trees and beneath the blue sky, I felt God above me, around me, within me. There I talked to God as a good, trusted friend.

When you talk out a problem with good friends, you don't always expect answers from them. You want a good listener, someone who will understand, who will feel a bit of what you are feeling, who will give you an idea you might not have had before or make you feel better. This was the God I met regularly in my backyard. Of course, I never actually saw God or heard God's voice. But I felt God's nearness, God's concern, and God's love.

When I was a kid, I sometimes needed a special friend. The doctors had told my parents that because of a muscle problem I was born with, I might not be able to walk. Thankfully, I proved those doctors wrong, but I did walk with a limp. Sometimes when I wasn't concentrating, my left arm didn't stay straight but curled up like a ball. I must have looked different from other kids in my class.

Some kids made fun of me; others did not want me as their friend. My parents were wonderful and understanding, but I still felt pretty lonely sometimes. I needed someone I could talk with and even cry with. I needed the Eternal Friend we call God.

How did I know God was there listening to me? Maybe this short story will help me explain: There once was a little girl, standing alone, holding a string. She held one end tightly in her hand, while the other end disappeared in a cloud bank. A man walked up to her and asked what she was doing. "Flying a kite," she said.

"I don't see any kite," he answered. "How do you know the kite is there?"

"Oh, that's easy," she replied. "I know it's there 'cause I can feel the tug."

I have felt the tug of God a lot, and it makes me feel happy and secure. Some thirty-five years since I first felt that tug, I want to introduce you to the God on the other end of the string, the God I have known all my life.

Today I am rabbi of a large New York City congregation. Many parents and kids, sometimes together, sometimes separately, come in to talk with me about God. They ask profound, sometimes troubling questions. They want to know why God would do bad things or let bad things happen to people. They ask if God really exists and if God is involved in our world.

To them God seems very powerful, very scary, and very far away. Too often they are quick to blame God for all that goes wrong in the world without thanking God for all that goes right. Too often they decide they can't believe in or love a God who makes people unhappy.

Theirs is not the God I have known all these years. I decided to write a book to introduce you to a different way of thinking about and relating to God: God as Eternal Friend.

One thing more. Lots of books about God are written only for adults; others are written for children. There are few that both parents and kids can read and discuss together. Feel free to do so with this book. When you're done, maybe parents can answer some of their kids' questions. And maybe kids can answer some of their parents' concerns as well.

CHAPTER I

If I Can't See God, How Do I Know God Exists?

Imagine, say the sages of old, two unborn babies inside their mother, aware only of what they can see. Pretend that somehow they can talk about what is going to happen to them in the future. One believes that good things lie ahead: life and love, maybe pizza and soda. The other thinks nothing good will happen down the road. Perhaps their argument sounds like this:

"What do you think has been going on for the last nine months? We wouldn't be growing like this if we weren't going somewhere!"

"Oh yeah? Where do you think you're going? If you leave this room and detach this cord, you'll be cut off from all food and nutrition. No, buddy, this is all there is, right here."

"I can't believe it. Too many wonderful things have happened to us already. There must be something beyond this."

"If you're so sure, tell me all about it. Tell me what is out there."

Of course, the happy one is stuck, unable to imagine breathing or eating or drinking. It seems the unhappy partner has won the argument.

And if the optimistic one goes down the birth canal first and starts to breathe, the roommate might hear a loud scream and think, "I knew it. I knew nothing good could exist beyond here." While at that very moment, loving parents are thrilled to hear the first cry of life from their newborn child.

Our world certainly is real, even though these unborn babies can't see it. So isn't it also possible that God is real, even though we can't actually see God?

I think so. I believe in God, but you don't have to take my word for it. Let's explore together. Think about the very first line of the Bible, in the story of creation. You might think the first sentence would tell us where God came from, to prove to the world that God exists. But the Bible starts with, "In the beginning God created the heavens and the earth." God wasn't made by something else, says the Bible. God always was and always will be; God is eternal.

We cannot actually see or hear or touch God. But we still can know God by looking at God's world and by seeing the results of God's work.

This has been true throughout history. Thousands of years later, after freeing the Israelites from Egyptian slavery, Moses led them to Mount Sinai. He then went up the mountain to receive the commandments from God. The people he left behind felt scared and alone. Afraid that he would not come back, they built a golden calf to worship instead of God.

When Moses came down from the mountain and saw what they had done, he was furious that the people had tried to build a god. So he threw the tablets at those who had built the calf.

Still shaken and angry, Moses went back up the mountain and demanded to see God face-to-face. He needed to know that God was still there on the mountain and that God, in fact, would be wherever Moses needed God. Listen to God's reply: "Nobody can see my face and live, but I will make all my goodness pass before you."

Moses could not actually see God back then, but Moses could see all that God did to help him and his people. You and I can't see God either. But we can know that God is around us because we are able to see God's goodness and maybe God's miracles. They may not be miracles like receiving the Ten Commandments on a mountaintop, the splitting of the Red Sea, or the birth of a child in a Bethlehem manger. But they may be miracles like the birth of a baby to someone you know or the beauty of autumn's leaves. You may sense God's presence whenever wonderful things happen around us that we cannot fully understand or explain.

God still works miracles every day. We just have to look for them. Often they are right in front of our eyes.

We know, for example, that the planets orbit the sun on course, but do we know why? We know that the pull of gravity keeps our feet on the ground, but do we know why? We know that when we are sick, forces within our bodies usually work overtime to make us well, but do we know why? The only answer that makes sense to me is that God is involved in this world and cares deeply about every one of us.

The story is told of a young fish who heard a word it didn't understand: *water*. Many older fish had heard the word, but they didn't believe there was any such thing. One day the young fish approached a wise old crab and asked, "What is water? Does it really exist?"

"Ah, yes, water," said the crab. "Water is that which surrounds us all. It is above us and below us. It flows all around us and within us. It enables us to keep going, and it gives us our lives. If there were no water, we would all die."

The young fish, though, swam away laughing, for it could not see the water.

God, too, is above us and below us, around us and within us, giving us life and a chance to grow and do many acts of kindness. We can see God, but only if we know how to look.

God's Big Bang

The sixth-grade class was waiting for me. They wanted to talk about God and had written some questions in advance.

"Let's do something different," I said. "You want to hear my views about God. But I also want to hear yours. Let's just talk together for a while."

"Okay," said Justin eagerly. "What I want to say is, 'I don't believe in God. I believe in science.'"

"You believe in science? So do I," I replied. "I believe God gave us the intelligence and imagination to explore the universe and see what we can learn. I do think there comes a point, though, when we can no longer answer all our questions. I'm not sure we can figure out, for example, how this universe functions in as orderly a way as it does. That's where God comes in."

"Well," Emily asked, "do you believe God created the universe, or do you believe in the Big Bang theory?"

"What do you mean by the Big Bang theory?" I asked.

"Well," said Emily, "out just beyond the solar system a bunch of matter was packed tightly together. As the molecules moved closer and closer together at greater and greater speeds, the temperature rose really quickly, and the whole thing exploded in a big bang. That's how the universe was formed."

"I can buy that," I replied.

"You can?" the kids asked, looking rather shocked.

"Yeah, the universe was formed probably ten to fifteen billion years ago, so I wasn't there. But that's as good a possibility as any. There's just one thing, though. In my view it didn't just happen by accident. I believe there was a blueprint, a plan for it all, and that God did the planning."

"But what about the Bible?" Tom wanted to know. "It says something different about how the world got started."

"The Bible tells us that in the beginning God created the heavens and the earth; the materials for this had to come from somewhere," I argued.

"But why do you think God was involved?" Emily asked.

"How could God *not* be involved?" I replied. "If there were an accidental explosion of tightly compressed molecules, I would expect the result to be a mess, not a magnificent solar system with planets orbiting the sun in set order, with the earth rotating on a fixed axis, and with gravity always keeping most of our feet on the ground—except maybe Michael Jordan's.

"I once read that the chances of an accidental Big Bang forming our world are the same as if there were an explosion in a print factory and all the letters lying around somehow collided and formed a dictionary. Or if a monkey grabbed a pencil, scribbled on a page, and the results turned out to be the Bible."

"But the Bible said God created the world in six days," Kevin chimed in.

"Yes," I replied. "The Bible also tells us that Noah lived 950 years, Abraham lived 175 years, and his wife Sarah lived for 127 years. Even if they ate only carrots and bean sprouts and laid off pizza and burgers, they wouldn't have lasted that long. A year in the Bible obviously is not the same as a year today, and a day didn't mean twenty-four hours.

"The Bible is telling us the world was created in six periods of time," I continued. "Each period could be millions of years. Yet the key point the Bible is making is that God did it all according to a plan and that God made the most sophisticated living creatures toward the end of creation. Human beings were made last, allowing us to take charge and take care of the earth."

"That sounds like evolution," Evan exclaimed.

"Yes it does," I assured the class. "If you ask me whether I believe in God's creation or in evolution, I say both. I think God planned the creation of the world, using evolution as the way to make the world work and to finally create us."

"I'm not sure I agree with you completely. I want to think about all this," said Rebecca.

"Good," I answered. "I hope you all do. Please don't accept my beliefs as the only way to look at how the world was formed. I want you to think for yourselves, to develop your own views. That's why God gave you the ability to think and even to argue."

"I just have one more question," said Jeremy. "Where did God come from?"

"Right there," I answered, pointing to the window. "And there," pointing to the sky. "I don't believe God was created as you and I were. If that happened, then God wouldn't be God.

"In the beginning," I continued, "God was everywhere, even right here where we're standing.

But God probably needed a world with living things, because it's lonely doing everything by yourself. It's also hard to make everything work by yourself. So God pulled back a little bit, making room for the world and for us.

"God didn't leave us here alone but gave us a lot of control over the planet and over our own lives, lots of opportunity to do wonderful things and chances to make mistakes, too. God wants us to learn from what we do wrong and try to do better the next time. That's how we grow and become better able to help other people. That's how we best accomplish what God wants us to do on this earth."

"We're here instead of God?" Wendy wanted to know.

"Not exactly," I said. "God is around, guiding the world and keeping an eye on the way people behave. But God doesn't swoop down like Superman and change everything bad that is going to happen. God can't, all alone, make this the best planet it can be. That's our job as well."

"So God needs us, like we need God," said Chad.

"That's right," I replied. "There's no magic wand up there to make everything all right. God works through people, inspiring us to do what we know is right. God really wants us to take responsibility for our lives and our world."

In fact, the sages tell the story that when God created Adam and Eve and put them in the Garden of Eden, God showed them around, pointing out to them the magnificent trees and plantings. God was letting them live in this beautiful garden, but God gave them a warning as well: "See my works, how beautiful they are. All that has been created is now given to you. But remember, you must never destroy the world I have made for you. For if you destroy it, there will be no one after you to fix it."

I think God is speaking to you and me as well, teaching us to do our part to take care of the world and not to destroy it. I think God is telling us that for this universe, one big bang—God's first big bang—is plenty. It's enough to last a lifetime—the world's lifetime.

CHAPTER 3

What Does God Look Like?

ake a piece of paper and draw a picture of God. Some of you will draw a figure of a large person. Others will picture a powerful wind or a spirit or a light that exists above us or around us.

If you have drawn a face on your God, think about whether it displays anger or kindness. Does it look more like a man or a woman?

We all have different views of what God might look like, and that is fine. Because we can't see God, we try to imagine what God looks like. People always have. But none of these could be God, because, according to the Bible, God was not created by someone or something else; God is the eternal creator of the world.

Think of it this way. If you could find the largest, brightest star in the sky with a very strong telescope, that would be just one of the stars God has made. Hard as we look, the best we can do is see what God does in the world. God really is too much, too awesome, for us to see with our own eyes.

But here is the good part. The God who made those huge stars and planets is also not so far away from us. After all, God made you and me and all the other people and animals that we love. So God has to be close enough to make all of us and care for us, too.

Of course, you might ask, "If God doesn't live on earth, how does God get here to do all this?" That's a good question. Many people, in fact, believe that God has helpers—angels sent to help God and to protect us. If you are Christian or Jewish, you might believe in angels. But many other people as well believe that some form of God comes very close to us. They may find God working in nature or sense God as a predictable force in the universe.

Christian people believe that Jesus is a form of God sent to the world to teach people about God and about how to live with one another. Many people feel close to God because they identify with and love Jesus.

Jewish people believe that Jesus was a wonderful person and teacher but not a form of God. But Jewish people also talk about a part of God that we can feel around us. It is called *sh'chinah* (*ch* like in *chanukah*, *i* like in *Easter*). It is the *sh'chinah* who is closest to us, who is most involved in our daily lives.

Jews and Christians have different ideas about how God shows up in the world and what exactly God wants from us. But it is important to know that for thousands of years both religions have shared a belief in the same God. We still do today. Because every one of us, including those who don't belong to a particular religious group, are children of one God, we should care about one another even more. The love we feel for God should translate into deeper love for all those God has created.

But, you may be asking, how does God communicate with people? I believe that God appears to us in ways we humans can understand, that God shows us as much of God as we need or can handle at any one time. If all of us see God in different ways, it may not be that we have a different God; it may be that we are experiencing different parts of God at different times.

The sages tell this story: When God wanted to appear to Moses in a burning bush, God thought for a long time about how to do it. Should it be in a loud booming voice? Moses could be frightened to death. How about a soft whispering voice? Maybe

Moses would hear nothing at all. So God chose to speak to Moses in a voice that Moses would recognize. God spoke to Moses in a voice that sounded just like Moses' father Amram.

You and I can see or hear God in different ways at different times. When we look at a beautiful sunset, we see the handiwork of God. When we do something kind for another person, we can sense God around us, urging us to do what is right. When we are troubled, we can feel God inside of us, helping us to feel better.

God is involved in our world and involved with us in many different ways. There may be days when you sense God is rather far away, helping, for example, the planets orbit the sun. On other days God will seem very close, giving you the support you need to make it through tough situations.

At times you may sense God in ways that are different from how other people do. You know what? Maybe God wants it that way.

CHAPTER 4

Why Did God Do This to Me?

*J*ackie twisted nervously in her chair. She was upset and had come to talk to me because she felt I was the only one who could answer her difficult question.

"Rabbi," she began, "I have to ask you something. Why is my father dead? My mom said that God must have had a reason, but she didn't know what it was. Do you? Why did God want my daddy?"

Jackie is searching for an answer to the question many of us ask: If there is a God, why do bad things happen? How could God let bad things happen to innocent people and to those we love the most?

Jackie is asking something people have been troubled about for thousands of years. In the Bible it is Job who asked the exact same thing. Job lived in the land of

Uz. He was a wonderful, kind person who loved God and was devoted to his wife and ten children. Job also was a rich man who had many servants and possessed much livestock.

One day everything Job loved was taken away from him: his family, his wealth, even his health. When all these terrible things happened to him, Job at first didn't respond; he was too shocked to say anything. Then he got angry, very angry, at God and wanted to know why such terrible things were happening to such a good person.

Then three friends came to try to help Job, but they ended up telling him that since God is always right and fair, the bad things happening must be Job's fault. Job must be the cause of his problems.

Job did not agree. He demanded to hear from God. Job knew he didn't deserve all his problems, so he wanted to hear God explain why he had them.

God answered him in a swirling whirlwind, a powerful twist of wind. There God taught Job that people can't always understand the great mysteries of the universe. We can't always understand how God works in our world.

But God said something to one of Job's friends, a man named Eliphaz, that we should think about, too: "I am angry at you, Eliphaz, and your two friends," God declared, "because you have not spoken of me in the right way, as my servant Job has."

So, according to the book of Job, the friends were wrong to think that we are always responsible when bad things happen. Job is right to ask questions. He is right to keep searching for the answer to the question "why."

The way I see it, God *wants* only good things to happen to us but can't always make them happen. Many people think God is all-powerful, but if God had *all* the power, wouldn't that mean we would be powerless? I don't think God is all-powerful; I believe we have a lot to say about what happens to us.

Don't we make important decisions every day, like whether to be kind or cruel to someone who annoys us? That's our choice, isn't it? Many of us will have to decide for ourselves whether to smoke cigarettes or drink alcohol or use drugs. Every day we face the dilemma of telling the truth or telling lies. With the money we have or earn, can't we decide how much we will spend on ourselves and how much we will give to someone less fortunate than we are?

God is kind, God is caring, God is powerful. But God may not be *all*-powerful. God may have decided not to be all-powerful so we would have the chance to use our brains and use our hearts to be the best people we possibly can be.

I'm not suggesting that God is weak. I believe that back when God created the first human being,

God decided not to do everything for us so that we could become God's partners on earth. God may not be able to stop all bad things from happening, but God will be able to help us deal with the problems we face in our world and will help us cope with the pain we all feel sometimes.

So, when we pray, we certainly can feel that God is listening. We can hope that God will give us the strength to do the right thing. But we can't think of God as some waiter sitting in heaven listening to our prayers, going to the back room and filling our orders, always giving us what we want.

I believe God always wants to be helpful. But the way God created the world and created human beings, giving us the ability to make our own decisions and to solve our own problems, means that God won't always be able to rush in and stop all bad things from happening.

Neither we nor God can take away all sickness, all hurt, all deaths in the world. But, we—God, you, and I—can bring more kindness and love into our families, into our world, into our schools, into our offices, everywhere. We can make things better than they are.

You have to remember that some things happen in this world that are not God's fault, and they're not our fault. They just happen. We can't always know why, and maybe God doesn't know why either. But we do know that we have the ability to work with God to make our world better than it is.

It is also true that if God can't always stop bad things from happening, God can help us make it hurt less. We can tell God what's on our minds and in our hearts and sense that God is there, making us feel better, giving us hope, reminding us that God will help until our burdens are eased.

When I finished explaining all this, Jackie nodded her head. Though she still didn't know why her father had died, she seemed relieved to hear that probably neither she nor God was responsible for the death.

But there was one more thing on Jackie's mind. "Where did my father go?" Jackie asked hopefully. "Is he in heaven?"

I told Jackie that there was a part of her father that could never die. In the Jewish tradition we believe that the soul leaves the body right after death, going to a special place that is as wonderful as the Garden of Eden. Others think that the soul floats freely between heaven and earth and can sense what is happening in the world.

Then I shared with Jackie the story of the two babies inside their mother who argued whether there was anything beyond what they could see.

"Just as this world exists even though those little ones couldn't see it yet," I said, "there very well might be a life after the one we know for the souls of people like your father."

After a long pause, Jackie slowly lifted her head and in a soft voice said, "Thanks. Now, when I think of my daddy, maybe I will be able to remember the ways he's still with me too."

Jackie put her hand on the door handle but turned around to say one more thing. "Rabbi," she said more confidently, managing a warm smile, "please thank God for me, too."

"I think you just did," I replied, returning the smile, "but I'll pass it along. God, too, can use a little gratitude."

CHAPTER 5

What Does God Expect of Us?

The old woman opened the door slowly. She seemed very quiet, very shy. But she agreed to tell the newspaper reporter a true story. Her name is Mary Smolinsky. During World War II she and her husband, both Catholic, owned a small farm. It was there that they saved a Jewish girl from being killed by the Nazis.

"Her parents used to buy vegetables and fruit from us," Mary explained. "They were wonderful, kind people. One day they showed up at our farm, not to take food from us, but to give us something terribly precious: their five-year-old daughter, Rivka.

" 'Please,' they begged, looking as scared as two deer being chased by hunters, 'take her in, hide her. The

Nazis want to kill all the Jews. We've lived a good life, but Rivka, she's so young, she has so much to live for. Please help her.'

"My husband looked at me and shook his head no," Mary added. "He knew we would be risking our lives. The Nazis would kill us, too, if they found out what we had tried to do.

"But," the woman slowly continued, "I pretended not to see him. I put my hand on the mother's shoulder and told her, 'Don't worry. Rivka will be safe with us.'"

"But why, why?" the reporter wanted to know. "Why were you willing to take that risk for people you hardly knew?"

"I looked into the face of that little child," Mary Smolinsky answered. "What I saw was the face of God. That told me what I had to do."

Mary Smolinsky believed God was telling her to save Rivka's life. Does God tell us what to do today? I believe that most people would want to follow God's teachings or commandments. But how can we find out what God wants us to do?

Many people believe that the Bible is God's way of letting people know what God wants from us. In the book of Exodus we read that thousands of people, recently freed from slavery, stood at the bottom of a mountain, Mount Sinai. Read the Bible's words

and try to picture how the people might have felt
back then, thousands of years ago:

> On the third day, as morning dawned, there was
> thunder and lightning, a dense cloud upon the
> mountain, and a very loud blast of a horn; all the
> people who were in the camp trembled. Now Mount
> Sinai was all in smoke, for God had come down upon
> it in fire; the smoke rose like the smoke of a furnace,
> the whole mountain shook violently. The blast of the
> horn grew louder and louder. As Moses spoke, God
> answered him in thunder. The Lord came down upon
> Mt. Sinai on the top of the mountain and Moses
> went up and received the tablets of the Law from
> God. (Exodus 19:16–20)

Many questions may come to mind as you read
this incredible story. Was God really there? Did God
really come down to the mountain in fire? Did God
write the tablets of Law (what we call the Torah)
and hand it over to Moses?

Of course you and I weren't standing at Mount
Sinai, but I will tell you what I think happened
there. Mount Sinai was like nothing the people had
ever seen or heard or felt before. They were amazed
at the incredible scenes unfolding before them.
Hearts pounding, they understood that God had
created these awesome experiences so that the
people would know that God was there and had

something important to teach them and future generations.

When I read these words I still feel a sense of awe and wonder, just like when I see a beautiful mountain or gorgeous sunset. When I see something incredible, I am particularly aware of God's ability to create beauty and miracles of many kinds.

So, yes, I believe God was there on top of that mountain, but I don't believe God spoke to Moses as you and I would speak to each other. Nor do I think God handed Moses the Torah as I might hand you this book.

Notice that the Bible says, "As Moses spoke, God answered him in thunder." The thunder may have been the way to prove that God was there. It was a sign, like the burning bush or the rainbow after Noah's flood.

But how did the people get the Torah if God didn't give it to Moses? Well, the thunder didn't tell Moses or anyone else what to put into the Torah. It just reminded Moses that God is around, that God who can seem so far away can be pretty close to us as well, and that God wants us to act in a certain way. I think that Moses heard what God wants us to do, not from some distant booming voice, but from deep inside himself. Maybe Moses heard a voice that sounded like his father's, as we discussed in chapter 3. Maybe the voice was no louder than a whisper.

Think about the last time you had a problem or a big decision to make. You thought about it all very carefully. You could make a good argument for deciding either way. But then you got a feeling inside, something that just told you what the right decision was. Is that your conscience? Is that God talking? Is it both?

One of my young students, Robbie, once said to me, "Sometimes I feel like there is a voice inside of me talking. But how can I be talking to myself? I guess that voice must be God's."

It very well might be. Maybe that was the voice Mary Smolinsky heard during World War II. Maybe you and I can hear that voice, too, if we listen not only with our ears, but with our hearts and minds at the same time.

CHAPTER 6

But It's Not Easy to Do the Right Thing!

f you read the last chapter, you may think that all you have to do is listen to that inner voice and you'll know exactly what to do. Sages of old tell us it might not be so easy.

They say that inside every one of us there is a kind of giant tug-of-war going on. On one side of the "rope" is the feeling rabbis of old called the evil inclination, a feeling buried deep inside, which tries to get us to behave as badly as we can. That's the side that comes out when we say hurtful things to people, when we cheat on a test, or when we cause pain for another person. Since not one of us is perfect, all of us have this evil inclination.

But just because we may be tempted to do obnoxious things, even though we may occasionally think bad thoughts, that doesn't mean we *have* to act on them.

Thankfully, there is another inclination inside of us, a different tug at the other end of that rope. It is what the rabbis call the good inclination. The good inclination urges us to reach out to someone who needs our help. It may move us to stop to help a stranger on the street, to want to give some of our hard-earned money to help people less fortunate than ourselves, even to give our brother or sister a break once in a while.

The good inclination and the evil inclination are not fighting each other all the time, but when they do fight, you feel it. That's why when you do something you know to be wrong, you feel bad. And when you do what you know is right, you may still wonder if you sacrificed some pleasure or popularity in the process. It's natural to wonder about this, but think also of what you have gained: When you act as good as you can, you not only please other people and probably God, you also satisfy your toughest critic, yourself.

People may be the only species created with the ability to choose between the good and bad inclinations. You can handle your evil inclination—you can control it—but you have to want to do so.

There is a story told of a man named Sussya who was getting old and thinking about the end of his life. "You know," he said, "when I die, if God wants to discuss what kind of life I've led, if God wants to know how well I've treated others, I won't worry about God asking, 'Sussya, why weren't you like Abraham or Moses or King David?' I know I could never be that wonderful or that great. The question I fear hearing from God is, 'Sussya, why weren't you Sussya? Why weren't you the best human being that you possibly could have been?'"

Sussya is reminding us that only we can make our good inclinations defeat our bad inclinations. Each of us has the ability to be incredibly kind and sensitive. But we also know that sometimes we can be pretty cruel and judgmental, particularly when people don't look or act exactly as we do. This next story shows what can happen when differences among people are feared rather than respected.

John Keller was a well-respected teacher at the Pinehurst School. Some of his students disliked him, because he gave a lot of homework and expected all the students to do the best they could. Mr. Keller was not married, and a couple of students in his class, Billy and John, started a rumor that he was gay, a "homo," as they put it.

One day Billy and John got into a real fistfight on the playground. Mr. Keller grabbed Billy and pulled the boys apart. "Young men," Mr. Keller exclaimed, "we're going to the office to call your parents!"

Billy's parents weren't home very much. They tried to make up for this by being Billy's pal whenever they were around. They pretty much believed Billy's side of the story every time and couldn't see that he often lied to cover his tracks, harming others in the process.

"Mom, John and I were just having a little fight, and Mr. Keller grabbed me in my private parts. He's a homo, you know. It must have felt good to him."

Billy's mom got angry and immediately telephoned his classmates' parents. "Do you know our children's teacher is a homosexual? He grabbed my son's penis, and I'm not going to let him get away with it!"

The next day a group of angry parents presented themselves to Mrs. Fletcher, the principal, demanding that Mr. Keller be fired.

These parents never bothered to find out what really had happened on the playground. Mr. Keller, in fact, was totally innocent and had just been doing his job. The parents also had no way of knowing whether their children's teacher was gay or straight, because Mr. Keller never discussed his personal life with his students. He simply wanted to be the best teacher he could be, and in fact he had become one of the school's very best.

The parents had let their worst prejudices come out. Without checking the facts, they had used their

words as weapons to hurt an innocent man, forgetting the Bible's Golden Rule, "You shall love your
neighbor as yourself." Together they had forgotten
that Mr. Keller wanted the same thing they did, the
best education for their children.

The evil inclination won out in this case, and a
wonderful teacher lost. Though he was cleared of all
wrongdoing, he felt he could no longer teach at that
school. But the rest of the students lost something,
too—a gifted teacher, the best they'd ever had. They
also saw something in their parents they did not expect to see: the same prejudices they sometimes felt,
the evil inclination winning out over the good inclination.

That night John Keller gathered his things in
his classroom. Tears streamed down his cheeks. He
was angry and hurt, feeling let down by the whole
school community.

Perhaps God felt terribly let down as well. If we
truly love God, we are supposed to show it by loving
everyone God created. Some people can't feel that
love because they are prejudiced against people who
seem different from them. And their evil inclination
may be powerful enough to persuade other people to
show prejudice as well.

In this story we saw how the evil inclination can
cause real pain to another person. If some parents
had stopped to think about what they were doing,

had let their good inclination overcome their fear, they might have defended John Keller against ignorance and prejudice.

God wants you to use the good inclination to do the right thing, even when peer pressure pushes you in the wrong direction. Your actions may not make you popular, but you will be able to look in the mirror and like the person you see. Perhaps it's only when you have earned self-respect that you will be able to earn God's respect.

In many situations one person can save a life, restore a reputation, or mend a broken heart. Maybe God wants you to be that person.

CHAPTER 7

What Will God Do If I Do Something Bad?

Everybody wanted to be like George Brown. He was the most popular student at Ridgeway High. Good student, captain of the basketball team, George was the type of guy who really cares about other people. Once a week, for example, he worked as a volunteer at the local hospital, visiting sick patients and seeing if they needed a magazine or candy bar.

George Brown seemed to be on top of the world. But one day everything changed. Just as if someone had turned off a faucet inside his head, George simply stopped talking. Sitting at his desk, he just stared off into space, as if he were a million miles away. He never went to the cafeteria anymore; basketball was a thing of the past.

Even good friends began to whisper: "Maybe he's on drugs, maybe he's sick." They all thought he was pretty weird. The strange thing is, no one really asked George what was wrong. They simply ignored him, afraid that what he had was catching. None of his schoolmates or anyone else who knew him took the time to ask George if they could help with whatever was bothering him.

Except Ernestine Jones. Ernestine worked in the hospital coffee shop from 3 to 11 P.M. For the last six months, George had come in for his dinner at 7 P.M. sharp, and Ernestine had been there to greet him. She would always try to get him to eat a piece of pie to "put some meat on those sorry bones."

"Thanks, Ernestine, but one mother is enough," George would joke, though he secretly liked her motherly ways.

Ernestine was one of the first to notice the changes in George, and she was worried. But she was not one to turn her head and walk away. Each day she came at him like a swarm of bees, demanding to know what was wrong.

"What is it, son?" Ernestine pleaded. "You can tell me. You can trust old Ernestine."

After about two weeks of this, George looked worse than ever. One day, burying his head in his hands, he suddenly blurted out, "All right, I'll tell you. I killed somebody."

54

"You what?" Ernestine's eyes looked like they were about to pop out of her head.

"Well, not exactly killed him," George explained slowly. "You see, there was this kid about nine or ten years old in the AIDS ward. He knew about me 'cuz he was a big basketball fan and had been to some of my games.

"Anyway, whenever I came to his room, I'd always stand at the door. He always looked so terrible, had these horrible marks on his face. He looked scary, and I, well, I just kept my distance. The kid wanted me to come in, talk sports, even give him an autograph.

"Then one day he just held out his hand like he really needed me to hold it. But I didn't, I just stayed at the door like always. I knew I couldn't catch AIDS from holding his hand, but I just froze. And you know what? That was the last time I saw him. He died the next day.

"It was the AIDS that killed him, I know that," George slowly whispered. "I know that it was his body that broke down, but I also think he had a broken heart. And I could have done something about that. But I didn't. I did nothing. *Nothing.*"

Now the tears were flowing freely down his cheeks.

"That's good, George. Crying's good, my love," Ernestine said softly. "I feel terrible for that poor child, and you might have made his last days happier. But I know that child's parents. They told me the only good thing about this hospital is you. They told me you took the time out of your busy life to come up and show some care for their son. I'm sure they forgive you for that last day. And I know God forgives you as well."

"God? God forgives me?" George's eyes widened. "How do you know that?"

"Let me tell you a story my pastor in church loves to tell," Ernestine continued, a warm smile now coming to her face. "It's a parable Jesus told about a prodigal son. You see, a man had two sons, and the younger took all his possessions, journeyed to a far-off land, and blew it all on wild living. When he had spent all he had, lo and behold a mighty famine came upon that land and, man, he was hungry.

" 'So,' he thought to himself, 'my father's servants have bread enough to spare, and I'm here dying of hunger. I will go back to my father and say to him, "Father, I have sinned against heaven and before you and am no longer worthy to be called your son; treat me as one of your servants." '

"While he was still a long way off, his father saw him and pitied him. As he drew near, his father threw his arms around him and kissed him. He told the servants, 'Bring out the best robe and put it on him. Put a ring on his hand and shoes on his feet. And bring the fattest calf and let us eat and be happy. For my son who was dead is alive again; he was lost and now is found. And we are very happy.'

"And when the other son heard what had happened, he got mad and said to his father, 'Lo these many years I have served you and never disobeyed you. But you never did this for me. But as soon as your son who used up all of his money for harlots and wild living returned, you have prepared for him the fattest calf.'

"'Son,' the father said to him, 'you are always with me, and all that I have is yours. It is right, though, that we should be happy now. For your brother was dead and now is alive. He was lost and now is found.'"

Ernestine wiped away her own tears and looked straight into George's eyes. "You've got to come back, too, Georgie, because God forgives you just like the son in the parable. Those parents forgive you, too. The only one who has a hard time forgiving you is you yourself."

George nodded his head, knowing she was right.

"Let me ask you something, George," Ernestine continued. "Is anyone else up there in that AIDS ward tonight?"

"Sure," George replied. "There's a guy who used to play college ball. He's six feet four inches tall."

"Go up there, George," Ernestine urged in a soft but firm voice. "Go up and talk to him. And hold his hand."

"God forgives," she called out as George got up from his stool to follow her advice. "God forgives even the sinners, even people who do a lot worse than you. But God wants us to do better next time."

George did a lot better next time. And every time after that, too.

CHAPTER 8

Bringing the
Messiah

One Sunday morning I went to church with the Thompson family. We all enjoyed the service. Their son Timmy listened closely to the minister's sermon.

When we arrived back at their house, Timmy ran to his room and quickly changed his clothes. "I'm Captain Terrific," he shouted, bursting into the den. "I'm here to help God save the world." This was something new to me—a Christian superhero. He certainly looked like one: He wore a cape and shiny boots, carried a sword, and wore a shiny cross around his neck.

But I was confused. "What do you mean, help God save the world? Can't God do it all alone?"

"Nope," Timmy replied, "it doesn't work that way. I need God to do the

really tough stuff. Miracles and all that. But God
needs me, too. We're partners!"

"How do you know God needs you? Did God
talk to you and tell you what to do?"

"Nope," Timmy said again. "Didn't have to. God
sent us Jesus, who told us good things to do. But
then the Roman army captured him and put him on
that cross. He looked really hurt and sad. If I was
there then, I woulda yelled, 'Captain Terrific to the
rescue,' and I would've saved Jesus."

Timmy wanted to save Jesus, but many Christians believe Jesus died on the cross for a reason—to
show God's love for people in pain and to help them
by forgiving all the things they've done wrong. They
believe that this terrible thing happened so that
people have a better chance of being good and kind
toward one another.

For Christians, furthermore, Jesus is the Christ,
the messiah or anointed one of God, sent to inspire
the world to love God and all humanity. They believe Jesus died and was resurrected and that he will
return as a permanent messiah sometime in the future. This will fulfill God's promise in the New Testament that the long-awaited kingdom of heaven
here on earth indeed has arrived.

Jews, too, have similar yearnings, but they don't
believe that Jesus of Nazareth is in fact the messiah.
When Jesus lived and taught, many people suffered

under the oppression of the Roman Empire. Unable to defeat Rome militarily, people looked heavenward for a savior.

Speculation about who the messiah would be and when he would come was intense and widespread. Some years after Jesus taught and inspired people, a prominent second-century rabbi named Akiba proclaimed that a man named Simeon bar Kosiba, called Bar Kochba, was the messiah. Sure that this "messiah" would lead them to victory, Akiba urged his followers to go to war against Rome. Thousands were killed in a crushing defeat, which proved to the people that Bar Kochba was a false messiah.

But messianic speculation has continued ever since. Some people hunger for a person who will appear as God's anointed one. Others hope not for a personal savior, but for a messianic age in which the entire world will live in peace and harmony.

Since so many people want this peace and harmony for our world, what can we do to make it happen? Some feel that strong belief will help turn messianic hopes into reality. Others believe that actions will be more important than the prayers and feelings in our hearts.

To God, however, this very well may be a silly distinction. How can you say you love God and not act as God wants you to in this world? Loving God must lead to love of humanity, or it is insincere, self-ish love at best.

Jews and Christians certainly disagree about who the messiah is, but they agree about the need for a messianic time. Most also agree that both belief and action are necessary to make this blessed age possible. We don't have to put on a cape and boots like Timmy, but we sure could use some of his enthusiastic commitment to help God and all of God's children.

The rabbis of old tell this instructive story: When a man asked Elijah the Prophet when the messiah would come, Elijah gave a surprising answer:

"Go and ask him yourself."

"Ask him myself? How? Where is he sitting?"

"He's over there by the door. He's sitting with the sick and the hurt. He's changing their bandages. He's changing them one by one."

I doubt that this wonderful person was the messiah. Probably he was an extremely caring human being who was doing his best to help others and was thus serving God.

All those who love God would do well to follow this man's example. Can you think of a better way to bring on the messiah?

CHAPTER 9

Does God Like One People Better Than Another?

The contestants are waving their signs, practicing their songs. They have been rehearsing a long time, and they know their stuff. Suddenly the lights go down, the spotlight shines, and it's time to begin.

Is this the Olympic Games, the Miss America Pageant? No, it's another edition of that famous game show *God Squad*. Tonight's subject is "God's Favorite Religion."

The finalists not only hope they are going to win. In their hearts they *know* they're going to win, because, though there are lots of other ways to pray to God, they have the *only* religion God still cares about. They are sure about that. And tonight, before the whole world, God is going to come down on that stage and beam a special light over the winner, proving what they have known all along: They and only they have the one true way to love and worship God.

"Well, folks," screams the announcer, "you can feel the excitement here tonight. Without further ado, let's start tonight's show!"

Suddenly a giant clock descends from the top of the stage. Contestants are each given one minute to tell the world why they and only they have God's favorite religion. Music, drum roll, "On your mark, get set. Go!"

Contestant Number 1 races to the front of the stage. "We're God's favorite religion and God's first religion. God chose us from all the other peoples and gave us God's most precious gift, the teachings called Torah."

"Not so fast," proclaims Contestant Number 2. "Yes, sure, you were the first, but God made a better agreement with us. To prove our special relationship, God came down to earth in the form of Jesus Christ to teach the world about faith and to tell us that the kingdom of heaven is near. This proves God loves us best."

"No, no, no," argues Contestant Number 3, "God is called Allah. And Allah be Praised sent the most perfect form of God's message to the prophet Muhammad. He, in turn, spread God's message, collected in our holy book called the Koran. Allah spoke to other people before us, to be sure, but they didn't understand and act on God's instructions as correctly and completely as we do."

"Well, thank you, contestants, for your wonderful presentations, each within one minute. Now, instead of the studio audience voting for the winner of God's Favorite Religion, we're going to let God decide. What we are hoping is that God will come down to this very stage, shine a big light over the winner, and knock the other two to the ground, so the whole world will know once and for all what is God's favorite religion. Are you ready, God?"

Of course God wasn't ready. Of course there's no show called *God Squad* and no contest to name God's favorite religion. So why this hokey game show idea? To make the point that competition among religions often becomes as silly as the idea of the *God Squad*. Too many people seem to believe that they have the only way of loving God, that God listens only to them and not to others.

Such people think they are important to God and other people are not. I don't think God wants us to have such a selfish attitude. To me the purpose of religion is to become less full of yourself and more full of God. The following story from the Bible seems to prove that is how God wants it, too.

At one time everyone spoke the same language. As people got together and learned more and more about building their world, they got pretty impressed with their own power. They said to each other, "Come, let's build a city with a tower to reach the sky, so everyone will know who we are. If we don't set ourselves up here in a big way, we might be scattered all over the world."

God came down to look at the city and tower the people had just built and was not happy. "If one people with one language tries to build a tower all the way up to me, they might think they are greater than me. Who knows what they will think of next?"

So God came down and mixed up their speech, and no single group could understand any other. God then scattered them and all people around the world as they are now.

Maybe God gave us different religions, then, so no one of them would become so powerful that it could say, "God loves me and doesn't love you." Maybe God made different religions not so they would fight to see which is best, but so people would find many different good ways to relate to God and to act the way God wants us to act.

Remember that when God made the first man and woman, God didn't give them a particular religion. The male was called Adam, a Hebrew word meaning "man" or "person." The female was first called "woman" and later named Havah or Eve, meaning "the mother of all who are living."

So all of us came from Adam and Eve. All of us—Jew, Christian, Muslim, and everyone else—are related to one another and are God's children, put on this earth to care about one another. Whenever people say they have God's favorite religion, are they speaking for God or for themselves and their own personal needs?

I believe God wants all of us to say, "I have a wonderful religion, a wonderful way to love God and other people as well. But so do you. Let's build together, but not great cities and towers that stretch to the sky. Let's build a world that treats people fairly, that takes care of people who can't always take care of themselves, that will put down its weapons and find ways to live in peace."

That's a world God will be proud to have created and to continue to love. That's a world worth working and praying for. You know what? If we prayed for that world together, I bet all of us would be able to hear God say, "Amen."

CHAPTER 10

Fighting
with God

mily Fester was angry. "I'm fit to be tied," she would tell anyone who would listen. "How can they do this? How can they take my baby away from me?"

Some weeks earlier Emily and her husband, Doug, had adopted an adorable baby girl named Christie. The baby seemed to take to her new parents instantly. For Emily and Doug this was a dream come true, a prayer that had been answered.

Life had never been happier, until the phone rang one night and the voice on the other end announced that the baby girl's birth mother had changed her mind and wanted Christie back. Long legal battles ensued; finally, a judge ruled that the birth mother had the legal right to get

Christie back. The Festers immediately appealed to a higher court, but even their own lawyer warned them not to be too hopeful.

"It seems like the whole world is against me," Mrs. Fester told a local television reporter. "The judge, the lawyers, the whole legal system—none of them cares about us or about Christie, either. I may be struck down for this, but I'm mad at God, too. In my prayers I had a big fight with God because I want to know how God could let this happen to our family."

I'm quite sure Mrs. Fester won't be struck down for arguing with God. The Bible shows us examples of heroic people arguing with God about issues of fairness and justice in our world.

Thousands of years ago, for example, God had decided to destroy two wicked cities but wanted Abraham to know about it first. When Abraham heard the news, he got so upset he forced himself to talk back to God.

"What if there are good people there, too? Will you kill them together with the wicked? What if there are fifty good people? Will you save the city for the sake of fifty? What about forty-five? Forty? Thirty? Twenty? What about ten? If there are ten good people there, will you save the city?"

Abraham was not struck down for disputing God's intentions. In fact, God listened to Abraham and said yes, God would save the city for the sake of ten good people.

Of course, we can't always get what we want by talking to God. It won't work for getting a raise or finding tickets to a sold-out concert. Even the most sincere, heartfelt prayer may not stop a divorce or secure an adoption.

Arguing with God also might not help a sick parent, grandparent, or close friend get well. This is because, in my judgment, God is not responsible for the illnesses or deaths of people we love. I believe God wants all of us to live long, healthy lives and is pained when any one of us dies.

God can't always change the bad things that happen to us and our families as much as God may want to. When creating the world, God gave us so much ability to solve our own problems that very likely God decided not to swoop down to earth every time we got into trouble. If God came to the rescue every time, people would stop trying to figure out solutions. They would simply stay home and wait for God to fix everything.

God remains very involved in the world, very concerned about all of us. But God doesn't want us to be so dependent on divine intervention that we stop using our God-given abilities to make this a better world. I believe God works very much through us, inspiring everyone to act godlike in relationship to others. So when we roll up our sleeves and demonstrate caring, we do so as God's representatives, perhaps God's partners here on earth.

Remember that in the biblical story God came to Abraham and told him about intending to destroy the truly evil people in those cities. Abraham immediately protested, challenging God not to ever purposely kill innocent people.

I think God was pleased with Abraham for standing up for good people and for what he believed in. After all, God immediately agreed with Abraham and promised not to kill the innocent men and women in those cities. I believe God was testing Abraham to see if Abraham would stand up for justice and fairness.

Before leaving so much of the responsibility for justice in the hands of people, God may have used Abraham as a test case to see if people could care for others enough to fight for them. Perhaps since Abraham passed his test, we might get the opportunity to pass ours: What will we do when we see injustice or cruelty? Will we just turn our heads and walk away, or will we try to do something that shows our concern?

This Bible story teaches that God wants us to speak out when people need help—our help or

God's help. Maybe God is waiting for us to argue or fight with God when we see things that we think are unjust or unfair.

Fight with God? How can people fight with God? Well, if God is our Eternal Friend, good friends are honest with each other. They like each other, but they don't always like everything the other does. God certainly might be critical of unkind remarks we make or selfishness we display. Similarly, when we don't understand what God is doing or think God isn't doing enough to right the wrongs we see around us, we have the right and duty to say so to God as we would to any other true friend.

Of course, we don't talk to God as we can talk to each other. But if it were possible to have such a conversation—if we could actually know what God was thinking or feeling at any time—I'm sure we would learn that God is not content with things as they are or too busy to care about human hurt.

In fact, God may feel pain when we do. The sages tell us that some years after the holy Temple was destroyed in Jerusalem and Jews had to leave their homes, the part of God closest to us, the sh'chinah, cried watching people in pain.

God would like to make things right all the time, but sometimes even God can't do that. If, for example, a person gets drunk, drives a car, and kills a child with that car, God probably won't be able to stop it from happening. But God will share in the sadness surrounding the death.

So God will not be upset with Emily Fester for asking questions and expressing anger to God. God certainly understands her feelings and probably respects her for expressing heartfelt emotions. Perhaps God shares her pain and wonders why people haven't yet come up with a system that is fairer to adopted children and their families. Maybe God will inspire us to work toward a better system of justice for all people.

God surely doesn't expect this of other creatures, but God does demand it of us. That's why God told Abraham what was going to happen in those cities. God wanted Abraham to speak up and show what a caring person he was and what a good friend to God he actually was.

I believe God wants us to do the same thing. After all, what are friends for?

CHAPTER 11

What If I Still Don't Know If There Is a God?

A friend of mine once said to me, "You know, with all that is happening in the world, it's hard to believe in God."

"With all that's happening in the world," I answered, "it's hard *not* to believe in God."

Maybe we're both right. If you sit and list all the reasons why there must be a God and all the reasons why there might not be a God, you would have a pretty long list on each side of the paper.

But it's not possible just to think our way to a relationship with God. To believe in God we have to use our hearts as well as our minds; we must *feel* the presence of God all around us and inside of us as well.

Most people very much want to discover the Eternal Friend we call God. But some of us have a hard time doing so, sometimes for different reasons. There are people who wonder if there is a God when so many bad things happen in this world.

We talked about this a lot in chapter 4. But think about this for a second: Bad things have happened to people for thousands of years, and human beings still continue to believe in God. That's because they have come to realize that God doesn't want bad things to happen but has given people a lot of power to decide what to do for themselves, even to make mistakes and try to do better next time.

They realize that God cannot simply wave a magic wand, and make everything all better. If that happened, we would not have the ability to fully use our brains and hearts to work together toward a better world. No, God works through *us*, giving us the ability not to make things perfect, but to make them better than they are.

The second problem I hear is, "Why isn't God today the same as the God in the Bible?" In other words, why doesn't God *talk* to people, perform miracles, and really prove to us that God is out there?

I don't believe God ever talked to people, even Moses, like you and I talk. But God does talk to our hearts. We can hear an inner voice telling us what we must do; that is God talking to us.

And the miracle part? Miracles are all around us, but we just get so used to them. Babies are born, people get well from disease, inventions are created, beautiful sunsets are enjoyed. These are all miracles, but we don't always see them that way because they are everyday miracles.

Let's take another example. I can explain *how* you got to this earth and how you got to be so terrific but not *why*. To me, each human being is a miracle. You are proof that God exists and is an important part of our lives.

But if you still don't absolutely know there is a God, don't worry. It is very tough to believe in someone you cannot see with your own eyes. I'm sure God understands that. But what should you do with your doubt? Maybe this quick story will be of some help.

The late Dr. Abraham Joshua Heschel once wrote about a little town full of clocks that no longer worked. No one in that town knew how to fix them. But some of the people kept winding the clocks every day anyway, while other people simply stopped, thinking there was no point in winding clocks that didn't work.

One day a wandering clock maker came into town. Everyone was excited and rushed to show him all the work they had for him. You know what? It turns out he could repair the clocks the people had continued to wind, but he couldn't fix the ones they had neglected.

Sometimes, the story teaches us, you have to keep winding the clock inside of you; sometimes you have to keep working at something, even if the results of that work are not yet clear.

If you don't feel the presence of God in your life or in your world, keep thinking, keep feeling, keep trying to find God. God may be looking for you, too, so keep an open mind and an open heart. And don't get frustrated. Believe me, God knows how hard a relationship with God is.

One last thing: The Bible tells us we are created in the image of God. That doesn't mean we look like God. I think it means that we, among all the species of the world, can act somewhat like God does. Even if we're not sure what we believe or even if there is a God in this world, we should act the best way we know how; we should be as helpful and sensitive to others as we can be.

You know what? Maybe when you show kindness, others will return kindness to you. By seeing more and more people act godlike, you may come to understand that there is a God who inspires goodness in people. So maybe the best way to believe in God is not to sit around and try to believe or even try to see or hear God, but to act as God would want you to act. Your actions very well might lead to believing, which could lead to a relationship with God, who cares about us and wants us to care about others.

I'm sure you will understand what the elderly rabbi was trying to teach his student in the following story. The student was bragging that he was able to make a beggar pray: "This man wanted bread," the student beamed, "but I told him he had to pray to God first. Only then would he get the bread he asked for."

Hearing the story, the rabbi was sad. "My son, you meant well, but you did not act well. There are times when you must act as if there is no God in the world."

"No God in the world?" the student sputtered. "What do you mean, dear rabbi? Your whole life is based upon serving God and doing God's will."

"You heard me—no God! When a person comes to you in need, you must act as if there is no one in the world, neither God nor human being, who can help him except you yourself."

"But what of his soul, dear rabbi?"

"Take care of your own soul," the rabbi replied, "but first take care of his body."

So maybe belief in God is not the most important thing. Rather, we must be as caring toward others as we can be, as God would want us to be.

When you act as if there is no God around and no one else able to help that person in need except you yourself, I think God will be very pleased. And God just might find some way to let you know it, too.

CHAPTER 12

Leaning on God Makes You Strong

he story is told of a little girl who said to her mother, "Mommy, the minister's talk confused me."

"Oh," the mother replied, "why is that?"

"Well, he said that God is bigger than we are. Is that true, Mommy?"

"Yes, that's true, honey."

"And he also said that God lives in us. Is that true?"

Again the mother replied yes.

"Well," said the little girl, "if God is bigger than us and lives in us, wouldn't God show through?"

God *does* show through. God shows through you and me. When we help other people, God shines through. When we are strong even though it hurts, God shows through. By all that we do, we can help God show through.

What makes God unique is the ability to be everywhere at the same time, including inside of us. There's a spark of God in each one of us, a little part of the sh'chinah, which inspires us toward goodness, which makes us feel better when we are in pain, which makes us feel stronger even when we need to lean on someone.

The story is told of the father who asks his daughter to use all her strength to move a big rock one inch. The child huffs and puffs and pushes really hard, but the rock doesn't budge. She tries again, but nothing happens.

"You aren't using all the strength you have," the father scolds.

"What other strength do I have?" the frustrated child asks.

"You have my strength," the father answers. "All you have to do is ask for it."

That's how we should feel about God. When we use God's strength, we feel stronger. We will still miss a loved one who dies or leaves us, but we will understand that our lives still can go on. We will feel better sensing that God, too, will feel some of our pain. God, in turn, will help us get stronger by letting us know we have God's strength as well.

In the words of Rabbi Harold Kushner, "God's promise is not that everything will be all right. God's promise is that when things are not all right, you will be all right, because God will be there with you."

Then there's the story of the man who dies, goes up to heaven, and looks down to see footprints in the desert sand, symbolic of his journey through life.

Emotionally distraught, he turns to God and complains, "When things were good I invariably saw four footprints together. During those times we walked through life together, side by side. But when things got rough, you obviously deserted me, because then there were only two footprints in the sand."

"No, my son," God responds gently. "I never abandoned you. Just the opposite. During the tough times, I carried you."

God can carry us. And when we stand up again, we very well may be stronger, knowing that we are not alone with our troubles. When we stand up again, we will be better able to carry someone else's burdens for a while.

I think God would be pleased if the next footprints found in the sand were yours.

CHAPTER 13

Meeting God

 was driving on a busy highway when suddenly the cars in front of me came to a complete halt. I hit the brakes and stopped my car. But in back of me I heard a frightening squeal and felt the impact of a big mail truck smacking me in the rear. My car jolted forward and hit a truck right in front of me.

Shocked and scared, I managed to move my car over to the shoulder of the road. Grateful to be alive, I said a little prayer as I unfastened my seat belt and shoulder harness. I stepped out of the car to see how other people had fared in the accident and was relieved to find that though they were banged up, nobody looked too seriously hurt.

Sirens wailed in the distance, then closer, and suddenly a man and a woman in white coats placed me on a hard stretcher, taped my head and neck down, and loaded me into an ambulance headed for the hospital.

My neck and back did hurt, I was still dazed by the accident, but what bothered me most was not being able to move a muscle. The ambulance crew rushed me into a busy emergency room and left me all alone, lying on a stretcher like a mummy.

But then a strange, beautiful thing happened. A nurse with soft, twinkling eyes and a kind smile appeared, touched me on the hand, and told me not to worry, that I would be all right. At that moment I felt that she was sent by God, a kind of angel on earth placed here to help people in pain.

In that emergency room I realized something I had always known: God works mostly through people, giving us the ability to be kind and caring and inspiring us to help God on behalf of others. You don't have to look for God on top of a mountain or through a telescope. You can find God everywhere, even in a hospital, maybe especially in a hospital.

When doctors perform delicate operations, for example, they are using human hands to help do God's work. God assists our healing, then, mostly by giving doctors and nurses the skill to help make us better. God also helps us heal by giving each of us important tools to help ourselves get better. Our immune systems, for instance, work with doctors and with us to fight disease. Our minds can contribute to our well-being also, because when we really want to get better, when we have a positive attitude, when we pray to God, these feelings and actions contribute more to our recovery than we might realize.

Thank God I am now feeling better. But the accident reminded me that our ability to meet God often depends on the outlook we bring to our lives. If, in fact, you don't appreciate everything you have and think that you and only you should get credit for what you are able to do, you probably will never make room for God in your life. On the other hand, if you feel grateful for what you have—like the ability to recover from illness or injury and the ability to feel and show love—and don't take everything for granted, chances are you will feel God's presence in your life.

You will sense God because you will see the miracles in everyday life and know that miracles probably do not happen by themselves. And you know what? Sometimes you can't fully appreciate all you have until something is taken away from you. Perhaps only those who have experienced pain will take the time to count their blessings.

A few years ago I met a remarkable man in the hospital who had lost both legs when a car hit him while he was on a ski trip. This is what he said to me:

"I don't blame God for the accident. That was caused by a guy who decided to drink alcohol and drive a car. God just couldn't stop the car from hitting me.

"No, I found God in here," he continued, pointing to his heart. "I prayed to God for the strength to want to live. God answered my prayer. I'm back to work, my family loves me, I lift weights every day. Life is a blessing," he said with tears in his eyes. "I just wish more people would know how much God loves us and does for us every day."

So do I. We should be grateful to God every day, but it's not always easy to feel so blessed. While there is so much to be thankful for, every one of us experiences the intrusion of pain into our lives at some point. So sometimes you will know God is there by all the miracles you see around you. But sometimes you will feel that it will take a miracle to sense God in your life again.

When I sat on that swing in my backyard thirty-five years ago, I didn't feel so confident in my beliefs all the time. Yes, I often felt the "tug of God," the sense that God was there and was listening to me. But I still had a lot of questions, such as whether God is present and involved in our world.

You probably still have many questions as well. Perhaps you even change your mind about God from time to time. That's very normal. I'll bet God understands how hard it is to understand God. Even so, God doesn't want you to stop thinking about

God, arguing with God, and feeling thankful when you can.

But whether you know it or not, God is always there—not always making the tough times all right, but helping to make *you* all right, making you stronger so that one day, somehow, things in your life will be all right, too.

During a time in history when things were really difficult—when the people of Israel were slaves, and God tried to convince Moses to go to Egypt and get them freed—Moses asked God a challenging question: "Behold, I shall come to the children of Israel and shall tell them the God of your ancestors has sent me to you. If they ask, 'What is God's name?' what shall I say to them?'"

God's answer was helpful to Moses and perhaps is helpful also to us: "My name is 'Ehyeh Asher Ehyeh': I will be what I will be." This amazing answer tells us that God will be what God has to be to help keep the world going according to plan. Perhaps the Bible also is saying that God will be what *we* need God to be, which will be different at different times.

Sometimes we will need a strong, powerful force to get us out of slavery or some other trouble. At other times we will need a gentle voice inside, reminding us that we must work together with God to make this world all God and we want it to be. And sometimes we will just need someone to listen to us as we pour out our hearts while we sit on an old swing—someone we can say anything to, ask anything of, argue or cry with, someone whose existence we can question one minute and praise the next.

The only one we can do that with is God, who finds a way to be distant and close at the same time, who is larger than life but always inside you and me.

God finds a way to be there even when we don't always know it. God is there—for you, for me, for everyone—even when life hurts.

Like a good friend. Like an Eternal Friend.

Questions for Family Discussion

1. How is God like our friends here on earth? How is God different from them?

2. What are some of the ways we feel God's presence in the world?

3. What are some of God's miracles we see in our world today?

4. How can we help God make this a better world?

5. What are some questions you still would like to ask God?

Before It's Too Late

Alzheimer's: Return of Childhood Emotions

Jane A. McAllister

authorHOUSE®

AuthorHouse™
1663 Liberty Drive
Bloomington, IN 47403
www.authorhouse.com
Phone: 1-800-839-8640

First published by AuthorHouse 10/20/2009

ISBN: 978-1-4490-2647-9 (e)
ISBN: 978-1-4490-2645-5 (sc)
ISBN: 978-1-4490-2646-2 (hc)

Library of Congress Control Number: 2009910201

Printed in the United States of America
Bloomington, Indiana

This book is printed on acid-free paper.

For My Three Daughters

Kathie, Bonnie, and Laura

Acknowledgments:

My gratitude to our long time friend and our Venezuela connection, Joseph Heim, of the Maryknoll Fathers, for being a reader of the manuscript and for his valuable insights.

I am indebted to Sara Rubloff, LCSW-C, our good friend and colleague of my husband, for her meticulous review of each chapter, her excellent suggestions, and her enthusiasm for the project.

My special thanks to my granddaughter, Casey McConville, for giving me permission to use her inspiring essay "My Hero" for the epilogue.

Finally, it is never "too late" to tell Robbie once more how much I am indebted to him for his loving assistance in this venture, for the life-changing gift of being my partner, and especially for his gentle, loving care during these difficult days.

Table of Contents

Before It's Too Late
Alzheimer's: Return of Childhood Emotions

Introduction

THE IDEA OF WRITING a book has been with me for a long time. Like so many other things I think about but never get to do, I decided a book would never really materialize. But suddenly at age seventy-eight, time is growing short, and I feel it pressing against my procrastinating nature. In the last few months the idea has weighed more heavily on my mind. During hospitalization for surgery two years ago, I had some additional "thinking time." The title came to me as I contemplated a recent dire event in my life, an event which sharply confronted my tendency to delay.

Now, there are two purposes for writing. The first is to tell in a simple manner the story of my life. The second is to record, as well as I am able, what happens in my mind as a person with Alzheimer's disease.

Why the story of my life? Why tell it? Is it worth putting on paper? I have never, except for brief periods, thought that I was worth while. It seems grandiose then to want to write about such an insignificant life. But there is some small voice within that nags me with "tell it, tell it, tell it." To tell it implies that I want someone to hear it. But that's not the way it is. I want to write it, to give it words, a voice, to give it existence, to grasp more clearly the substance of a life that has never felt completely real because so rarely has it been verified by anyone else. As years passed and family history faded with the passing and forgetting of others, my life became even more evanescent. And I became more desperate to give the memories the flesh of written words.

Much of what appears in the following chapters will include bits and pieces of things I have written through the years. I have never really been faithful to journaling, but I have often found comfort in writing about my thoughts, my feelings, my dreams, and many of the experiences that continue to live all too vividly for me. Notes from other times will be inserted in various chapters where they contribute in some way to the subject matter. The use of italics will identify past writings and will often not be dated because it was not my common practice to date things I wrote. I began these writings in my early 30's, about the time I began to recognize my life as my own.

Among notes from the past, I find items like the several that follow.

For as long as I can remember I've wanted to write my story. It has no beginning and no end…yet I can't let that stop me from telling it to myself. I have lived it…a day at a time…sometimes minute by desperate minute, and for such a verbal person I have lived it very much to myself. It's the "self" story, where it all happened to only me, that I must tell in order to find sanity. Will I be different if I do become sane…perhaps not, I'll see.

Almost every day now I think about my book. I call it that, "My Book." Is it a story? There are these thoughts…It is a story. It is a life, full, different from other people's. I wonder now who cares…must anyone… anyone but me? For whom does one tell his story…must it be for anyone? Why do I feel I want so much to tell it…is writing it telling it? For myself it seems now necessary…to say it all will be to understand…to put it all together.

January 24, 1975. It's hard to write insightful things when lack of insight is the problem of the moment. On being 45 today, on having to live again the day of birth and wondering. I can say only that it is a sadness in itself, not related I think to the feelings of the past month or other sadnesses. As with all else about my living, it could be changed quickly into a joyful celebration by certain words and treatment…but that's so shallow I guess. The word "Nothing" comes again as it did when I heard that tape suggesting one write one's own epitaph. "Nothing" would say it.

Waiting in a doctor's office after major surgery. Life has long ago stopped being "poetry." Is it necessary that my return to the world demands flatness? Is it only in pictures between pages of a book that imagination runs young and free?

I intend not only to describe those pieces of my life that have significance in its course and in its outcome but also to trace the changes that are forced on me by the progress of this illness. As I contemplate the project, I know that it is even more vital to "get to it" before it really is too late.

My husband, Robbie, has encouraged me in this and will collaborate with me, acting as memory prompter, as scribe (with his computer ability), and as companion through the time to come. Some historical facts are fading rather quickly, but Robbie and I have discussed them so often that he is able to fill in many of the spaces that have been created by my memory loss. Some past figures continue to dominate my thinking with the same pain they have always thrust into my life. Some events still live quite clearly in my present awareness and repeatedly bring me the gamut of feelings that originally surrounded them. I often wonder how the selections are made by the illness that will gradually destroy much of my memory. Why can't I make the choices?

I need to decide whether I should just write the story of my life and then write the story of my present struggle with Alzheimer's, or should I begin with information about my illness and then let it enter the life narrative wherever it seems appropriate. This dilemma dissolves with my growing awareness that the end of the story is in reality a painful shadow of the beginning. In many ways Alzheimer's is a continuation of my life story. So I shall keep the time sequence intact and begin when I began.

Chapter I

The Cast Of Characters

Mother
It is difficult for me to describe my mother because when I think of
her I think primarily of her stories. Unfortunately it was through her
stories that she attained significance in my life, and those stories left
me without affection for her or genuine regard for myself. She was
one of those women who was ill-prepared for motherhood and gave no
indication that it was anything but an unfortunate mishap in her life.
"Grandmotherhood" she took more gracefully. She was 42 instead of 21
by then. My three children came to love her, perhaps more as a "buddy"
than as a grandmother.

So the stories must be told to introduce you to the mother of my
memories. These stories were repeated over and over to me and to others
in my presence. I often wonder "why?" For laughs? For sympathy? And
why to me? In the hospital the night of my birth, January 24, 1930, it
was so hot in the room she opened the window and got up on the sill to
jump into the snow but was stopped by the nurse. The story was always
related as evidence of suicidal intent and with regret that the nurse had
intervened. During the agonizing delivery, she described the doctor, in
his desperation, commenting, "I thought I'd pull the damn kid's head
off." What a lovely scene she painted of my introduction to a non-
welcoming world! Why did she need to tell that so many times? Why
did I need to hear it even once? I often heard that the money it cost for
the delivery could have bought her a new car.

1

Never in my life did I remember her saying anything positive about my birth, about holding me, bringing me home from the hospital or caring for me in any way. She took many opportunities to tell me how much pain I had caused her during her pregnancy and delivery. On a page written 24 years ago: *In 53 years I have learned very few things, some not very well, some I've forgotten. Now I get through each day of sameness, remembering and almost living in the past, which is so real. I don't know if I should have believed my mother when she told me that she had really wanted me, considering that she told me over and over how much pain I had caused her and that she would never have another child.*

From past writing: *I knew she never wanted me because she often told me about her idea of giving me away. In fact, that is what she* **did**. *She gave me to her mother the day I came home from the hospital. My grandmother raised me, cared for me, provided whatever nurturing I received. I was like a detachable appendage of my mother's. No, not an appendage, more of a trinket that she picked up and put down at will.*

While I was a young child, my "trinket" life involved going with my mother to funeral parlors in the evenings to view the deceased. I probably saw more dead people than live people in those days. I presume she went as part of her union activities. I have no idea why she dragged me along unless it was part of our "togetherness." From my notes: *All the dead bodies…always expecting, hoping to see my father at one of the viewings. I thought it would make a difference… My mother told me stories over and over and over---about my birthing and my father's feelings.*

It seems so strange now that these trips to funeral homes are the most vivid memories I have of time spent with my mother. Past notes chronicle our outings: *Lacking attachment to others, one does not encounter loss and consequent sadness. But I was surrounded by people who were experiencing these. I saw it, I heard it, I was even taught to say consoling things to them. Viewing of coffins with "plasticized pale bodies" … averaged about two per month through my childhood and on through my teens. My mother's preoccupation in which I was always included! It was the only bonding for her and me. Never once attended any church, any movie together. Never once any trip, any party, any show. Never once picked out or purchased any clothes. Never once any doctor visit, any school activity, any beach, any pool. Where was evidence of love, admiration, enthusiasm, consolation, pride, tenderness, celebration, accomplishment?*

I need to say that my mother had a charitable bent, but it did not begin at home. It was not unusual for her to give the man who delivered coal extra money to put some coal in the basement of someone she knew who was out of work. In those days, beggars (that was the usual name for them) went door to door for a hand-out of money or food. They were never turned away at our house. From time to time my mother would decide that some other child (not necessarily poorer) in the neighborhood needed one of my dolls. My only choice was to give away whatever doll she chose, irrespective of my attachment to it. I never recall expressing any anger as a child because I'm sure I knew it was unacceptable. So where did my anger go? I believe it is still with me and causes me untold grief in its contemporary inappropriate expression.

My mother was involved in union activities at the hosiery mill where she worked most of her life. I remember on one occasion she returned home one evening rather badly bruised, especially her face. Presumably she had gone to a union meeting and got into a fight. Typical of my taciturn family, the matter was never addressed in any way. I was only left to wonder, but much about my mother made me wonder.

When I was 14, she married my stepfather, Ed, in a Protestant Church around the corner. Marriage did not change my mother's independent life style. Notes from long ago: *My mother did not eat with the family. She always ate something different in bed at night. Off she went, always with a sandwich. It was something strange. I was mystified by the fact that she could always get the Lone Ranger on the radio any night while she was eating in bed.* Another of her oddities was that in the evening she would leave the house any time she might chose and return usually after everyone was in bed for the night. This pattern continued the same after she married Ed. Much of my mother's behavior was never acknowledged by the family.

When I was 18, the local priest called one day to talk to my mother. When I said she was not home, he told me he was checking to find out if her marriage to her first husband had been a Catholic ceremony. It was clear that he was not talking about her marriage to my father, Edward Fox. Notes I wrote expressed my feelings: *My mother sat down with me and told me many things which I believed. She explained that she had not told me of her first brief marriage because I had no need to know about it.*

3

Looking back I realize I had all my life believed everything she told me! I am a tree cut off at the ground---living.

My mother apparently thought I needed to know something about sex. When I was 13, she asked her cousin, Ethel, to take me to see the movie "Grapes of Wrath" for my sex education. The movie must have had some meaning for my mother that didn't get to me.

In 1989: *I was lost and didn't know it. I saw myself as spoiled, self-centered. Could not understand my frustration, made attempts at satisfactions… solutions that never worked. I was lost. I was living someone else's life… and it was overshadowing my own. My mother was my past, and I had successfully put that behind me with Alanon. She was always a SHELL for me…I discarded that and came forth not as me alone…but me as Jane, Wife, Mother. A light turned on…then living in that light, became mostly comfortable. When my eyes were opened more and I had to face the reality that I had denied, I had to adjust to the light.*

My mother was an alcoholic. Of course, it was never referred to by anyone in the family, as far as I know. Another problem which was also ignored by everyone including my stepfather was her involvement with various men. Her behaviors on both counts seemed not to dim her relationship with the rest of the family, but they embarrassed me and created a wall that neither of us seemed willing or wanting to scale.

At some point before her death, I wrote words which I am sure I never would have voiced to her directly or given to her to read. By the time I wrote these, I was convinced that she would be too ignorant to understand them and too uncaring to value them. *To a Mother---then sober. Is any of this ever a beginning without at the same time being an ending of something else? Yet is it not possible that our hearts, being too busy experiencing the new, do not remove the old, do not totally replace it, but store it in the haunted halls of memory? Because the memory does not change and is not a growing, living thing, it lies dormant, but to fill and occupy and not to grow and change causes it at times to be a deadly thing. There was no turning point…no one time more important than another, no beginning that I can recall and no end, as yet, to the fear and pain and sadness of my heart. But there was a cause. Why didn't you tell me you had been hurt… or were you? If you were, could you have told me? If you had, would it have helped? How can I tell you what I have learned so late? You have lived your life without knowledge of it. It is too late for you to see it and understand me. It is too late for forgiving.*

My reflections on my mother have continued throughout my life. They haunt me. They bring me no peace. Shortly after my mother's death I found the following: *I thought to count my successes rather than failures of the past 10 days, then better yet not to count at all. I have piled up beside me (near, so as to be warmed by them) the treasures of togetherness with those I love. The morning, still shadowed as if to continue quiet resting itself...as long as possible...it rests in the memory of its quiet sleep and silence, so it seems to me. I do not know of the things that broke its dreaming. I know only what is real to me and what I experience. God, how colored it becomes by what has been formed by the mold that spit me forth. That I cannot change...or mostly ignore...to live with it as a start from which auspiciously to step forward...that's a goal and must be a force behind all actions. I search for meaning...then cover the discovery with smallness and learned behavior. What might have grown and matured dies in the seed so buried.*

As I write, I reflect that I have not now and never had a sense of warmth in the presence of my mother. I have nothing of hers, none of her possessions, no keepsakes, not even memories of her holding me, caressing me, caring for me. Yes, I have some memories of her stories, tales that made me wish I had never been born (as she seemed to wish). I have memories of funeral parlors and dead bodies, memories of her erratic and unpredictable behavior.

Father

I used to fantasize writing a book entitled "I Never Sang for My Father." Throughout most of my life, I knew my father primarily through what my mother told me, and that was not a very savory portrait. I have a picture of him in suit, tie, and hat holding me as an infant. It is not a treasure, because it has always been a reminder of my mother's story about his leaving. "Your father was holding you, and when you spit up on his suit he handed you to someone and said, 'Take her.' He was angry at you. He left and never came back." As a child I bore the burden and guilt of "home wrecker." I grew up with the knowledge of what my bad behavior had caused. It had driven my father away, his anger justified by my action. And my mother never failed to keep the image of my "sin" and its punishment fresh in my mind. His was a living, interminable anger that cast a dark shadow over me, and in some manner left me with a life-long fear of abandonment!

I learned as a child that my father had my name tattooed on his arm, only spelled "Jayne," the way he wanted to spell it. When I was about 10, my father gave me a doll house he had made for me, a replica of the house where he grew up. It was a Christmas present. I have no idea how it got to me. I often wondered why he didn't come to see me at the time. Or did he come, and my mother sent him away? I also knew that he remarried and had children by his second wife.

Notes from years ago, written about my father fantasy and titled: *I never sang for my father. We would sit and talk about so many things, for every plan of mine, there would be one given to me. What other things would there be? Little stories, lots of rhyming, songs, things learned of, and things pretended, much laughing, many tears, mingled together in hugs and pressing of faces, encircling of arms. My arms would be filled again as they were that first day so long ago, with a fullness less perfect than that which I share with my true love, yet another.*

I never remember a kiss from my father, his mother, or his other children. I wonder if… at one time… did he cry… was he consoled? Did he go to church?

Choose your way guided by your heart and your reward will come too late. I too, Daddy, will know joy too late, too late! The warmth of final tears will bathe me as I seek final rest. They will hold my hand and say they forgive me and then "Goodnight," as was between us. Or will they come at all? How little of what I felt for you will survive in them. I've seen it pass from my son, with the sometimes silence of his age, he has closed out much of his compassion. They are not with me to see what I could have showed them of love and forgiving. There is before them none of that.

In the 90's I wrote the following: *I am angry a lot of the time. I have feared that all my life. Why? Who was angry? How did I feel then? Was I afraid of them? I remember their anger better than I do my own! Why is that? They said my father was a moody person and that he got very angry, that when he got angry he sulked and went quiet. To me that meant he separated himself from everyone, and I know he finally left. It was as if he*

6

disappeared. *In my mind I had a picture of him. I looked for him on my street so often. I thought that someday he would be there...just walking up from the corner, and I'd be standing there, and we would see each other. I don't think I ever pictured what would happen next. There was a man who lived on my street who I thought looked like my father, and I used to watch him and wonder if he really was my father and that nobody was admitting that. I don't think I ever told that to anyone...so it just stayed there...part belief, part pretend.*

Grandmother

Edith was her name. She had three children. Aunt Edith was the eldest, my mother was next, and Uncle Jim was the last. When my grandmother was eight, her mother died. Her father was unable to take care of her and placed her with relatives. These substitute parents were abusive to her. Punishments included locking her in a closet. This was very frightening because she always believed someone had been killed in the closet. There were some splotches of red (possibly paint) on the floor, and these together with the harsh attitude of her relatives caused her fears. At age 14, the couple put her out of their home. She then lived in a boarding house where she worked for her "keep." Her future husband, my grandfather, Patrick McQuade, lived in the boarding house. They were married when she was 16.

The grandmother I knew was a very anxious, controlling woman who was limited both emotionally and socially. I would not know if she was limited intellectually because there was minimal intellectual stimulation or challenge in her life. "Limited" would describe her background, her experiences, her views, and her goals. For all of that she was what I would consider a "good woman." And she was good to me in the sense that she cared for me, looked after me. But her presence seriously intruded into my world and left me without a sense of privacy, personal space, or intimacy. I include intimacy because I believe that genuine intimacy can only occur when one has achieved an awareness of separation from others.

It shocks me to acknowledge even to myself that I slept in my grandmother's bed from the time I came home from the hospital as an infant until the night before I was married at age 21. It is embarrassing to say so. It is hard for me to believe that this never struck me as strange, bizarre, ridiculous, unthinkable. I cannot imagine this happening with any young person I know or any grandmother I have ever known—except my grandmother and me.

One might wonder, if one had the audacity to ask, how could this have occurred? Of course, the real answer is buried with so many others. My mother seemed quite willing to give me the following explanation. My grandmother had given birth to three children and was unwilling to have any more. My mother assumed that my grandparents would not practice birth control because my grandfather was a Catholic, although not active.

According to my mother's view, I was my grandmother's substitute for an "in-dwelling uterine device," a sort of "in-bed device" to keep my grandfather away. My mother probably relished such an explanation. Such matters always seemed to be a preoccupation with her.

By the time I entered the family in 1930, my grandparents' youngest child must have been at least 16 years old. I assume they had devised some sort of contraceptive procedure or contact avoidance prior to my entering my grandmother's bed. I wonder if my mother's story was an attempt to assuage some of her guilt for rejecting me.

My grandfather died when I was 12, but my grandmother and I continued as bed partners. She was a fearful person and perhaps quite lonely. My grandfather did imbibe excessively at times. I doubt that he was a very reassuring mate for her or a comfort in her loneliness. I served her well as an obedient, pliable, and amiable companion. Although she was a very modest person and taught me in many ways to imitate that attitude, she always had me wash her back as she sat naked in the tub. It was an unpleasant experience. From past notes: *Washing grandmother's back and being repulsed! And why did she have me do that?!! She was so modest, so private and held these "virtues" up to me intending that I follow them exactly. Why then this behavior?*

Through the years, grandmother and I knelt down by the bed each night and said our prayers together. She was indeed the channel of my early religion and a major influence on whatever religion I hold onto today. She not only taught me my prayers; she also took me to Mass every Sunday at the parish church.

I had to go to the children's Mass in the basement of the church even though I did not go to the Catholic school. My grandmother could not

8

attend the children's Mass. Against the rules! She could have gone to Mass in the upstairs church, but of course, she was too timid to do so. She would have been a stranger in an alien land, because she was not a Catholic and not familiar with the ceremony. So she walked home after leaving me at the church and then returned dutifully to get me after the conclusion of the service or after the occasional mandatory religious education class.

As far back as I can remember my grandmother had spoken to me about wanting to be a Catholic. It may have been the issue of birth control that kept her from completing her desire earlier. A few years before her death, I asked her if she would like to make arrangements to become a Catholic. She said she would. The parish priest was "too busy" to come to see her because it was Holy Week. I called a priest friend I knew from another parish, and he came willingly. He asked me to go over the instructions with my grandmother, so I had the satisfaction of sitting with her and providing the information that enabled her to be baptized in the religion which she had nurtured in me.

Grandmother was also a major influence in other areas, especially in my rather prominent obsessive-compulsive traits. Years ago I wrote the following: *I can't let go...I can't keep it. Grandmother said over and over: "hold it...let go." It was her bathroom mantra, and we went through the exercise regularly. I will not explain further...you do not need to know.* "Be honest, clean, punctual, loyal" were ingrained into my brain. "Be sure you have clean underwear in case you are in an accident" was never a reassuring remark for an anxious little girl heading out to school.

It was my grandmother who controlled my life. She was the one who decided what I could and could not do. Her rules were communicated though often unspoken. I "knew" what she expected of me, and it was always my goal to be "a good girl." I never had the feeling she was disappointed in me or angry at me. I don't think I could have survived either one. I knew she cared about me, but there was never any physical indication of affection. As I write I must acknowledge that she was disappointed in me on one occasion. It was an occasion that caused me to be disappointed in myself for years afterwards. It was my marriage to my first husband.

I didn't see my grandmother often after my marriage. She seemed to fade from my life, and at the same time she faded from her own. She became senile in her later years. When I last saw her alive she was a far cry from the mild, cautious grandmother I had known. She was cantankerous and highly verbal with a vocabulary she must have heard from the men who stayed at the boarding house of her earlier years. She died in 1966. Her funeral was from the church of which she had for so long wanted to be a member.

Grandfather

The memory of my grandfather is the warmest recollection of my childhood. He was a sweet man, and I loved him. I probably had more real affection from him than from anyone. I loved to listen to his rhymes. "Patty O'Flynn had no pants for to wear, so he bought him a sheepskin to make him a pair. With the skinny side out and the wooly side in, they'll be damn fine britches said Patty O'Flynn. It'll do." "My sweetheart's a mule in the mine, and I leads her without any line. And all day I sits and tobaccee I spits, and I spits on my sweetheart's behind." That was my grandfather—gentle, warm, simple, quiet, real—maybe a bit of a leprechaun. He was the Barry Fitzgerald of my life. Other men respected him. He was a block captain during the scary days of World War II. He was a friendly person, not well educated, but something of a gentleman and certainly a non-threatening figure in our household. I often watched him sitting reading the western stories that came in booklet form.

I remember him taking me on occasion to the tavern with him when I was quite young. He would sit me on the stool beside him as he had his drink and I had my hard boiled egg. He was a dear, dear man. Fridays were pay days, and almost invariably he would come home late from work and usually a bit tipsy. My grandmother would worry and fret until he arrived, and then she would verbally excoriate him. I joined in her anxiety and imagined all kinds of dire happenings to him on the way home. I dreaded my grandmother's wrath not just for him but for myself, because her anger frightened me. Anger always frightens me whether I observe it in someone close to me, or in a play or a movie, or in a public setting. Robbie rarely gets angry, but when he does it terrifies me. However, it is probably my own anger that frightens me most of all.

My grandfather had never practiced his faith as long as I knew him, but when he was seriously ill, prior to his death, he asked to see a priest.

I made the arrangements. When the priest came, the two spent time together in what I can only assume was a time for his confession. After the priest left my grandfather made one of his memorable remarks, "If I had known how easy it was to get in under the fence, I'd have gone a long time ago."

He got under the fence for good soon after that. When I was 12, I came home from school one day and was shooed out of the house to go visit a neighbor girl a few streets away. At that time my grandfather had a bed in the parlor downstairs. As I went out, I knew I was not supposed to look in the room so I put my hand over my eyes as I went by. It was all so secretive! It was all so stupid! I had seen lots of dead bodies, making rounds with my mother. I wish I could have said goodbye to him or at least touched his hand. I loved him! When they had me come back home, his body was gone.

Sometime before his death, he asked me to get some war bonds for him at my school, and I failed to do it. I forget the details. Years later, when my mother was irritated with me, she told me that my grandfather was angry at me when he died because I didn't get the war bonds when I was supposed to. Strike two! First, my father left because he was angry at something I had done, and now my grandfather died angry at me. I must have wondered if his anger had somehow been part of his leaving in death. Is it any wonder that I become utterly terrified when Robbie is angry at me? Strike three! I immediately begin thinking he will leave me, and I'll be alone forever. It is intolerable. I want to die.

Stepfather

My mother married Ed Dunigan when I was 14. He was sort of a non-entity in the household. The thing I remember most is that he would eat a Tasty Cupcake with two bites, a pack of two—four bites. He was a passive individual who worked at the hosiery mill, who stayed out of my life quite thoroughly, and who permitted my mother to live life as she pleased.

My "togetherness" with Ed consisted of our working together to build and paint a ply board Santa Claus for my son, Phil. Fifty odd years later the figure still adorns Phil's yard every Christmas in Georgetown, Delaware.

I also remember that when I was in art school and feeling some independence, I "smart mouthed" Ed during an argument with him, and he slapped me. My mother knew it and talked about putting him out of the house. I told her it was not his fault, and I apologized to Ed for my behavior. Other than that one incident there was never any open hostility between the two of us.

Once when Ed was working on a tape recorder for my son, he was testing the recording by repeating the words, "Who cares, nobody cares." My son and I used to joke about his words, but they were in truth a sad characterization of Ed's lonely life in "the bosom of my family." Now that I think of it perhaps that could have been my motto too.

Uncle Jim

Jim was my mother's younger brother and my grandmother's baby. I didn't realize it at the time but in retrospect I think I must have taken his coveted position with my grandmother. I knew I was "tops" with her, and I paid a heavy price for the role.

Uncle Jim visited the house often, and I was always happy to see him. The house became lively when he was there, a sort of chubby cherub. He teased me mercilessly, often focusing on my grandmother's bathroom rituals with me. I had a "big mouth," and sooner or later I would say something he didn't like, and he would explode. I never got angry at him or anyone else. I was not allowed to. He would call on my grandmother to discipline me, "Can't you do something with her?" She would remain silent, and after his storm continued to darken the household for a time, he would leave in a thunderous black cloud. Another male who left because of my behavior! But whenever he returned it was always sunshine, at least for awhile.

Uncle Jim taught me games, little tricks, shadows he could make with his fingers. He would tell me make-believe stories. He entertained me. He was playful. He was excitement in a dreary world. Once he took me for a ride on his motorcycle much to my grandmother's displeasure.

Of course, there was another side to Uncle Jim, a side which my mother made no attempt to hide from me. It was that particular area which always seemed to attract her attention. She reported to me on his involvements with different women and on questions relating to who may have fathered certain children. A note on my mother's stories: *My mother always harped on stories that seemed to have some unspoken sexual component...and she always seemed to want to tell them to me at a time in my life when sexual matters were mystery built on ignorance. She often talked about Jim's family, and I went through my early years wondering which kids were really Jim's and which were not. Dora married Jim after her first husband came home from the service. I knew Dora's five children and I spent years trying to figure out which kids were Jim's. Every time they visited at our house I was uncertain as to which ones were truly my cousins. It was never clarified. They kept poking into my life. It seemed to be shrouded in intrigue and left me confused.*

In retrospect I wonder if it may have been the way my mother told stories with that sense of something hidden, perhaps underhanded. She often told me similar stories about various people at the mill where she worked and where I worked too. She seemed to relish the hint of secrecy and implied sexual wrongdoing. When I worked at the mill I would see my mother making up to different men. I would eat lunch with my stepfather, Ed, and she would eat with her current boyfriend.

I remember one of the kids in grade school telling me that my uncle was a jailbird. Apparently he had stolen a car or failed to return one he leased. I also remember a particular childhood scene. The family decided to go to Washington, which we often did on a moments notice. Everyone was ready. But when we came out of the house to get in Jim's car, it was being repossessed. I still remember my grandfather shouting and running down the street after the car with his shirt tail flying in the wind. We canceled that trip.

I lost contact with Uncle Jim after I married Tom, my first husband. I don't remember his death or events surrounding it.

The Washington Family

For completion of the family circle I should mention the Ellis family in Washington, D.C. Edith Ellis was my mother's sister married to Uncle Pete, certainly the "Godfather" figure in the family. They had three daughters from oldest to youngest, Edie, Patricia, and Cathy. I was probably five when Edie was born.

I often wrote about them: *Uncle Pete was "sancto" to everyone. I liked Pete. When he went away, he would always return with four gifts, one for each of his three girls and one for me. I played games with my cousins, played house. I never liked the way they treated the black woman who came to clean house for them. They all treated her as their servant. It gave me the feeling they weren't doing the right thing to treat her differently than other people. I liked her. One day I put her hat on, just playing around. My cousins were horrified that I would even touch it. Edith and Pete always had nice clothes. I was impressed by the whole family. We visited his mother and sister in Philadelphia. They had a huge house, and I remember a life size portrait of Pete's nephew all decked out in a fancy uniform as a member of the Pope's guard.*

We visited the Ellis family frequently, and it often seemed with little notice. Somehow there was always room and always plenty of food. The three Ellis girls had a bedtime hour which was always enforced, but my grandmother kept me up with the adults until later. The privilege separated me from my cousins both physically and psychologically. I could say that the three of them hated our common grandmother. I got along well with the three girls and was closest to Edie.

Aunt Edith, their mother, was my godmother. She was always special to me, and I missed her greatly when she died, which was after Robbie and I moved back to Maryland in the 1990's. I found a note written shortly before her death: *So many stories will be buried with her, then with me. All those years of family will be gone with her...nobody will know it or keep it alive...lives and family will be dead with her.* A note after her death: *This was our first Christmas without her! Her house was home for me...always pens...tablets...water in colored glasses...salad...napkin committee...long, long talking at the table...discoveries.* I always wanted to be her kid.

Going to Washington was always a pleasure for me. I had different experiences there. Aunt Edith would drive us down to the big department stores and use valet parking. It seemed so opulent. And Uncle Pete would take us all for a drive and get us ice cream cones. He was generous and pleasant to be with—most of the time. When he got angry, it was a different story. In past writings: *I seemed to bond with the adults...like an illegal bond. We spent more time at the table together at Aunt Edith's house than we did at our own. My three cousins would be sent off to bed and I could stay up because of my grandmother. I thought I was the favorite and part of the adult group. I never acknowledged the anger of my cousins. I was always afraid when Uncle Pete would get angry. I would run and hide.*

Summary of Family

Comments written many years later still ring true. *The negative experiences I have continued to act out...to return to the scene...I went there and saw myself in doing that. I've lost the joy...the celebration of my life...the celebration of me, of Jane. To let them go would be to not have lived them. What parts of me are they now...were they? All sad...that can't be.*

I think if I begin to recall my life in a different medium, it must have had some importance to me...thinking and believing I didn't matter to anyone, how can I care? Did I care? I never believed in my whole life that I mattered to anyone.

What of my playing, my learning, discovering my humanity, my responses? Did I speak, cry, question? Was I cuddled and tucked into bed? Was I sad or happy? Did I learn to do things? Did I learn to sing, ask questions, love my family? Was I a joy to anyone?

The shared room when I came home from the hospital until I was married. I want to remember the years when I was alone...to remember the feelings I have forgotten, before I forget everything. I want to celebrate me...as I never learned to do...never...never. It must be possible.

Was there a long period of loneliness and isolation that I do remember but have never identified as such? Or accepted the resulting ongoing craving... from feelings of craziness.

More reflections on family life: *Is it time to begin forgiving people? Should I make a list or just take one at a time and pay the outstanding bill? Remember when "Letting go" came into style? I hated that and of course could never do that. Did I come home from school and talk at length about who said what, etc.? I don't feel that, if I did, a conversation followed.*

I did hate my mother. I was ungrateful for all my grandmother did for me. I did break her heart. How far back does it go? What about those things they told me I was guilty of...what about those? I ruined my mother's life. My father left because of me. I took my grandfather's place in my grandmother's

15

life. How I loved my Uncle Jim…how you always turned on me…why must I remember?

I've thought about loss lately…what comes to mind…something ripped out of me…taken away from me…having to give something away…something I really loved…something important to me…being made to do that…doing that because I was told to do that…being part of the doing and not resisting doing it…not saying, "No, this is mine. It's important to me. I want to keep it."

They didn't know me. My father obviously didn't. My mother rejected all that I cared about and said she couldn't understand where I got such ideas. My grandmother wanted so badly to control my whole life. With her there was a lot of talking, but I don't know how it fit in with the control and the power. I'm so like her in some ways, so different in other ways. She hated what I became. I think it was sad when we parted long before she died. When was that?

There were the fights. Some things came out that she could no longer keep hidden. I can't remember how she handled that. Then when I married she was broken hearted. Then my son, Phil, hated her, and she knew it, and I pushed her to take care of him sometimes. She watched my mother take him from me, and he became my mother's child. I wonder how my grandmother felt about that.

None of these words really summarize my relationship with my family. But because these comments are somewhat chaotic, sometimes contradictory, often uncertain, and definitely confusing, perhaps they portray well my legacy from these several people whose involvement or lack of involvement had a marked impact on my life.

Chapter II

The Journey Begins
(1930-1947)

ONE OF THE HAPPIEST memories of childhood was to be "under the fireplug" on a summer day. Everyone thought it was to escape the heat of summer in Philadelphia. It was much more than that. It was to elude the watchful eye of my grandmother and to slip away to the giggling, splashing, joy-filled moments of playing with other children. It was the best of times, and it often seems like the rest of childhood was the worst of times.

Many people talk about, laugh about, write about, and sing about their happy childhoods. Some of us either remain silent or pick out stories that gloss over the hard surface of those years or highlight bright spots that belie reality. I have been both silent and a teller of stories. On the one hand, I have been silent about the feelings that surrounded me during those years, feelings that continue even now to force their way into my daily life and distort my view of myself and the world around me. On the other hand, I have a repertoire of stories that I tell, perhaps too freely, to others. They will appear from time to time in this writing. They support the common belief that the experiences of childhood are the source of our self concept as adults.

Why do I tell disparaging tales about myself not only to people who know me well but also to those who are relative strangers? Is this story telling of mine a general confession of my ineptitude with supportive data? It does seem to be associated with some discomfort I feel when others appear to regard me in any sort of positive manner. I know that I doubt the genuineness of their affirming remarks, and I am aware of an inner thought process, "Sooner or later you will realize that you are mistaken, and then you will see me in a negative light. So let me give you a peak at the real me. Then I will not have to suffer your abandonment and criticism later on."

In the previous chapter, you met the family I lived with until I married at age 21. Your opinion of them is probably not an unfavorable one, and you might think, "They were not a bad lot. They lived peacefully with one another and accepted the advantages and the limitations of such an arrangement. Each did the task assigned by nature or by choice. The basic needs of each member of the household including the little one, Jane, were adequately provided for within the family unit."

I cannot disagree with such a summation, and yet, I do not feel my needs were met! Oh, I was clothed and fed, and I knew that I was part of the family. Is it because I wanted too much that I have felt cheated all my life when I hear others talk about the happiness they knew as children? Why do I find notes like this in my writings? *Home is not the place where you're born. It's where you're happy. Happiness comes only from the fulfillment of a childhood wish. I sat the other morning and read two issues of Reflections...and wished I could belong. To belong...my life-long desire... never did...never would. I wondered about the lives of all these writers and decided they were all somebody I was not and never would be. The draft coming in the cracks around the window chilled me. My arms were cold and began to feel stiff and uncomfortable. I didn't want to move...or leave the room...I didn't want to begin another day of being nobody and alone. To what use can I put this talent...not understood by anyone.*

I was a solitary figure in a household of individuals isolated from one another. My mother had her independent life and world. My grandfather was a non-intrusive backdrop for the rest of them. My grandmother did the cooking and ran the household and caught me in the iron cobweb of her ritualistic behaviors. I had no one who kissed me or hugged me or tucked me in at night when I was a small child. I had no one who asked about my school day, about my friends, about my lessons, or about my interests when I was in grade school. I had no one who cared about what I read, what I thought, or what I dreamed when I was a teenager.

The emotional limitations of my childhood were captured in the following: *We were poor in many ways and ignorant in others. I was conceived, born, raised, and grown in it. Nothing changed...I stayed there. I grew in body...not in soul or mind. What I saw touched my heart...but did not stay to touch me so that I might understand or learn.*

I feel this as I write...a line of life passing... but I neither felt nor saw it... through the box where I had been placed to live. Empty arms not knowing how to reach out to touch or hold...her name is Jane.

Emotions in my family seemed so weak and insignificant. No one paid attention to the emotions of others.

Everyone had a slot. My mother's was to do exactly what she wanted...the actress, comic...never a bad person...act like a fool. She was never feminine. She would smoke and drink with the guys...a prankster...never knew what she was going to do, but always something.

My imagination came to rescue me from the isolation of my emotional Siberia. I established a place to play in the basement of our house. It was more properly a cellar with a dirt floor and two small windows in the front (one used as a coal chute in the winter) and one dim light bulb. It became my private world. There were a few boards to protect my treasurers from the damp floor. I gathered boxes of all sizes and shapes and stacked them in various formations to hold my precious dolls and toys. From my pages: *Dolls... I acted out their lives as babies, not mine as a mothering person. They demanded all blankets perfect...all done up. I agreed. Coloring books: Perfectly inside all lines...to fill completely... not to create a finished work as the goal. Paper dolls: Perfectly cut, sorted, arranged, preserved...made to come alive as outside of myself. Doll houses: Apple boxes, great wooden bungalow of Maple Shade, N.J., red linoleum, covered roof.*

I often got my dress-up clothes in the neighborhood trash before it was collected. Trash cans were like gold mines...like Christmas. One could tell what houses were like from what they threw away. I still see trash cans as a source of treasure. The things were mine, my own; no one ever took them away. I remember two blankets I had, a pink one and a blue one, both with fine stitching around the edges. It is strange that these 70 plus years later, I should remember the detail of the blankets

19

so well that I can almost see them in front of me. At some point in my childhood the family moved to another house. I had the same private world in the "up-scale basement." It had a cement floor.

The stairs from my netherworld led to the kitchen above. Memories of that lower world often return as a sort of peaceful escape. Notes from the 60's: *There it is…the hours of paper dolls and houses…and dolls and being all of them myself…playing all their parts…needing nobody. I did not need any one. I had no one. How can I change that feeling? Where did the solace of childhood aloneness go?*

A section in my writings dated in 1991: *I ran through these pages hoping to add on to what I last wrote. Without caring about order, I felt the ink of need climb to the well top of my mind, and I again began to touch this familiar friend with the need to write. When I write I am truly alone, and there I find, in that flowing openness, my only peace. If only I could carry it with me as if, no_what if_…from that little child I was with paper dolls… what if it could continue? There are things that fill up the space of self-peace so that I cannot even remember it. Fear has to be listed first… then uncertainty, just as familiar, follows and at times pushes through and mingles. I've not thought of that before. Uncertainty …the letters flow and truly name what fills my lungs and mind and heart…yet turns me back, hungry and longing… wanting to hold on to…what?… everything?…to grasp and cling and seek and conquer. It says so many things not in answers but in the correctness of discovery, quickly now followed by "what now?"*

Uncertainty…UNCERTAINTY! I as a living being…with heart and soul nourished, conceived and nourished I know not how (only suspect from what followed)…in sickness of mind and souls…wrenched untimely from the nest that would have destroyed it as it slept…into whose arms, under whose eyes… into a being of conspiracy with uncertainty and fear. They have changed places these two partners, and now fear sees its reason for being…a first look at its creator…Uncertainty.

And so to make a certainty, I move a "me" of threads… bound together to make a fabric… called life. All began there, the pattern set…once learned so well…and unnamed and perfected and familiar from which "me" comes forth…feelings try to take words as their partners…and fail me.

So to breathe deeply doesn't solve anything. To be good and clean and honest, all this put on behavior, accomplishes nothing. All activity must follow…

20

turning...changing...knowing...remembering whatever discovery sits right with saving myself from drowning in that thread tight pattern.

Today is the place I am...now is where I stand. It is hard to name to myself what swells within me...or know even where it resides. I will touch the feeling that I have come to... a place of comfort for now, this moment. It is not called happiness. I will not name it except for here and now.

This book is so good in my hands. It has been a home for my thoughts... follows the feeling. I should have another since this will soon be filled. Where can I get one...I will try...and so it starts. I think there was never a time when one of something was enough, because holding on to it did not produce happiness that lasted.

Some things I heard today were good. That alone will not keep me from this well worn path to dark spaces where no warm lit clouds comfort me.

I will not justify or defend this holding on that sometimes takes the gentle form of collecting, which does not at all call it rightly.

Although I had a need to collect things as a child, there was another hand that was stronger than mine and separated me from my treasures. My mother's "charitable heart" did not beat for me. When I was still a pre-adolescent, my mother decided that the doll house my father made for me, a replica of his family home in Maple Shade, N.J., should be given away. At her insistence I gave one my favorite dolls to another girl because my mother said she was dying. She didn't die, and she didn't return the doll.

The "collecting" that I mention does not rule my life, but it does clutter it at times. I have recently concluded that when I do move forward and get rid of a few things, they usually turn out to be items which I wish I still had. My mother always seemed to be the one who basked in the generosity of giving. It is not surprising that I never felt any spiritual or emotional benefit from my "generosity," since it did not come from my heart or by my wishes. It would have been nice to believe I was gaining some good marks in my book of life because I always felt that I had accumulated a lot of black marks about which to feel extremely guilty. A note from many years ago: *Then I'm unforgiven and that's the worst feeling I can have. It increases all the other feelings. When I was little, people said I was often "sorry." I'd go off to myself. The family situation was so strange. I'd pout, cry, or be sad. The cat was my listener. I'd tell him not to tell anyone—he never said he wouldn't tell. I cried a lot; I didn't have the words.*

My collecting is surely reminiscent of compulsions sewn with the threads of childhood isolation. Sometimes Robbie teases me (carefully) saying he never saw a box I didn't love. He is basically right. I see boxes in grocery stores, in alley ways, in windows, in pictures, and I admire and yearn to have them. Sometimes I take them and bring them home. Sometimes I buy them, not because they contain truffles or small jars of jam, but because they are such pretty boxes.

Shopping bags take up more than a reasonable amount of space in my bathroom. Each one has a meaning far beyond the color of the paper or the shape of the handle. They represent the world outside my walls, and they connect me with people and places and things that have been part of this life which I hold onto so dearly. When we lived in the city and took walks, I used to persuade Robbie to go down alleys so I could "eye" the "treasures" that might be sticking out of someone's trash. More than once I have stopped to investigate a house that was being demolished or remodeled and brought home a discarded board or a small window. Everyone's trash is full of life stories and objects that were meaningful to someone else. I struggle with giving clothes, dishes, household objects away, because I want to know who will have them and what they will do with them.

When I was made to give the "treasures" of my childhood to others, those objects were lost forever to me. The thought of those losses is still with me and finds access to my mind and my mood when I lose an object, give something away, or have something stolen. It always seems like a violation, an intrusion into my world, an attack on my integrity. And no matter how much I tell myself, "It is ridiculous to be so upset about what just happened, and it has nothing to do with your childhood," it doesn't help.

I started kindergarten at age four with my fifth birthday the following January. My most common memory of school was being frightened. I was without my grandmother and that was reason enough to be afraid. In many ways school life was even less comfortable than home life. I was put in the "fat girls" class in gym because I couldn't keep up with the girls in the regular gym class. I couldn't climb the rope, and I couldn't run and jump like the others could. My grandmother refused to let me take a shower at school when I was in junior high and high school, so I became the brunt of various comments from my peers.

I was never a popular youngster and generally felt ill at ease with peers. I was a "steady ender" in jump rope. The other end was tied to a tree. My "rope duty" made me about as capable of jumping rope as the tree was. Not much of an "ego builder!" And I never learned to ride a bike! If I had ever written a resume that would probably have been the first sentence. The fat class, the shower edict, the steady ender, and the bike failure all belong to those self-deprecating stories that spill out on any occasion that provides the time and the audience. After all, I learned to tell negative stories about myself from my mother, who taught me how humiliating stories could be. From notes: *The school stories...I've held up as a description of who I was...who I am. Their telling and retelling may have been the most damaging part of the event. I wish I could remember happy times when I was in school. The first moment of wishing...that I could go back to some moment of innocence...that is long gone...I can hardly remember it. Childhood innocence...feels made up. Inside crying...after all these years of speaking out.*

I think I must have always been fearful as a child. I suppose it would now be called "having high anxiety," but to me it felt like unadulterated fear. School was not only intimidating because of the other children; it was intimidating because of the teachers and the classes. I never knew what I was supposed to do. I never knew what would happen. In short, there was nothing about it that was not a cause of fear. I would look out the window thinking that the teacher would not call on me. (The magical: if I don't see you, you don't see me.) Of course, she did. No matter how many times the ruse failed, I kept doing it and would get in trouble for looking out the window. That was so like me. I never raised my hand in class. I never thought I knew an answer. I was in a class play in seventh grade, some small insignificant part, but it required that I go up the usual couple of steps to reach the stage. As I went up, I tripped and fell onto the stage. These events stifled any self-confidence that might have emerged during those years.

Notes from years later: *There was no potential, no thought of growth or change, no process. There we were, had been and would forever be...as we were...cast.*

23

Whatever we did...how we acted...was what we were...who we were. And it was never considered that we might change or grow.

Certain things were right---certain things were wrong. One did this, and any other behavior meant that person was a certain kind of person---cruel, unkind. All the while...the stories of misbehavior...the tales told...the secrets told about things I had no need to know...and many secrets kept that I should have been told and wasn't.

I was created...carved out...made as someone wanted me to be.

My childhood years...I had no dreams. I've believed that and not understood... but it explains a lot...built on dreams vs. built on stone?

What choices would I have made if I had had a dream? Would my talent, creativity, my imagination been able to blossom in freedom?

Things in the neighborhood were not so terrifying. My grandmother was near at hand, and she saw to it that I never wandered far. I could play with peers on some occasions such as under the fire plug. At other times, we pretended to be "shop keepers" in the narrow alleys behind the houses and came up with creative ideas. Kids played kick ball in the street in front. I am sure I would have thought I was too awkward to participate even if my grandmother had allowed it. Before I started school and perhaps two or three years into school, the other kids would come on my porch and persuade me to bring my toys out to play together. Then they would take my toys across the street. But I was not allowed to cross the street. Then I'd have to get my grandmother to come out and recover my toys. This was a recurring scene in my early life. It may account in part for some of my severe possessiveness about "my things."

When I started school I didn't know any of the other children, because everyone from my neighborhood went to the local parochial school. My mother chose not to send me there and told me it was because the nuns "hit the students with a ruler." In later years, I came to believe that it was probably because my mother was twice married by then, neither time in the Catholic Church, and that she probably wanted to stay as far away from the Church as possible. In spite of all this, my grades were A's and B's in grade and high school. Of course, my conduct was always perfect. No one in my family ever came to the school for anything until I graduated from high school. My mother came that day.

I recently had a neurological evaluation. I am usually very cooperative and patient with doctors and hospital personnel no matter how much they need to stick and push and probe. But when the neurologist asked me to subtract 3 from 100 and continue subtracting 3's from the remainder, my patience went out the window. I was angry and simply refused to do it. Then he suggested I try it by 2's. I got 98 and that was as far as I could go. He then explained that he wanted to increase my anxiety so that he could evaluate involuntary movements. Well, there is nothing that could do more to increase my anxiety than to ask me to do something with numbers. My addition and subtraction faculties are probably average or above, until someone asks me to do it or observes me in any way. Sometime ago Robbie took over the math of my check book, simply because I don't need the swell of anxiety that engulfs me when I try to subtract 1 from 2. The fear of making a mistake that someone else may see is like sitting in the classroom once more.

My written comments: *I accepted the belief that I was stupid...like a drone...I so deserved it...others laughed at me. My mother's act included telling stories about me and about people at work. I used to tell my cat, Tom, what everyone did to me...acted mean to me...laughed at me. I would go to my room to do homework...get in bed...Tom curled up with me. It was the only place where no one bothered me...my privacy. No one seemed to care. I never talked to anyone about any of my feelings.*

Although I do not recall being angry as a child I apparently found a way of expressing some hostile feelings. On occasion, I would line up several of my dolls and then say to the first one, "What's that? Did you say 'Christ Almighty?'" Then I would slap her for her angry outburst. I would take each doll to task in the same way. The ritual may have seemingly relieved my unspoken and unrecognized anger and left the dolls with the guilt. But the relief was short lived. All the anger and guilt rests on **my** head these days.

About 20 years ago I wrote: *It is not what I am that I despise. It is, rather, how I feel about it...always dissatisfied...always wishes. Is this what it's like to have dreams...must one believe they might come true? What I see when, without any effort, I remember the past...the girl, the family, the actions. I was a minus...always frightened...always less than anyone else...*

25

handicapped...retarded. What do people see and feel when they look back? Can I change the memory?

About my street: *Nothing felt so black as the lamp post on the corner of Madison Street. The narrow slice of dark was all I thought there was in the whole world. I never thought of the sky or the world beyond that narrow band above my head, above Madison Street.*

When I was 14 I began working in the hosiery mill where my mother, and later my stepfather, worked. It was war time, and the age limit was lowered. I liked working at the mill. People treated me well. My mother would occasionally tell me that someone at the mill said I was pretty. Any such comment had to be out of the hearing of my grandmother. She would get very angry if anyone said I was pretty. She let me know that being pretty was not important and that the only things that were important were that I was a good girl and behaved well. Being a "good girl" was behaving as grandmother expected.

With my grandmother there were never specifics. I was left to discover them and found them in the behaviors I saw in her. Did I also find behaviors of my mother for my imitation, consciously or unconsciously? From my notes: *I had two standards in my life: my strict, compulsive, controlling grandmother's "Good Girl" and my mother's image of "No one really toes the line. Do as you please."* To this day it startles me when someone we meet makes the comment that I am beautiful. I feel embarrassed and almost guilty when it happens. My grandmother would not approve!

All the years I spent with my family were years of uncertainty. They say that children derive a sense of security from repetition and sameness. That was my grandmother's stock in trade. But uncertainty filled the air I breathed, days were unpredictable, and decisions were capricious. We moved five times before I began school. Each move was a surprise and came to me without warning or preparation. Money and rent were involved, but I only determined that in later years. Moving just seemed to be something that happened.

We frequently left for Washington to visit the Ellis family with as little as 10 or 15 minutes notice. There never seemed to be a particular reason for going. We just went. I have no idea how it was decided. They got me out of a matinee one Saturday afternoon because "we are going to Washington." My trips with my mother to the undertaker were never known prior to her saying, "Get your coat, we're going out." Uncle Jim showed up at the house unannounced and erratically. Beyond the exigencies of work and school, life seemed to have no structure, no order, no plan, no rhythm. It was pure happenstance!

My life was probably as mysterious to the family as theirs was to me. I never seemed to know or understand what was going on in the family, and they certainly didn't know or understand what was happening to me. They never asked me about school, about friends, about children I knew, about what I did when I was in or out of the house.

I suppose my grandmother and grandfather presented some picture of stability for my imitation. But they were quite a contrast to my mother and my Uncle Jim. He had a reputation in the family for being irresolute and unreliable. And he always met those expectations. My mother's unstable comings and goings are captured in a note I wrote some time ago: *Mother...where did she go at night...why didn't she come home? I saw her as a homely, ignorant person. At my cousin's wedding...everyone was there...my mother started dancing with another woman and became vulgar in her gestures and behavior. She embarrassed several of our relatives. But her behavior was never a concern for her. It often was for me.*

I have tried to understand my mother even now years after her death. I can only tell stories about her as she told stories about me. And I can describe my negative feelings about her. I truly wonder if there was much else. People always say, "You must have loved your mother." Why do they take for granted that children necessarily love their mother? What a ridiculous generality! Somehow the presence of my mother in my life had a powerful influence on me and still does. I hate myself whenever I have a sense of that presence.

My mother insisted I tell her every month when my period started. She provided me with no real sex education. Her insinuating stories about the behaviors of Uncle Jim and numerous people she knew at work were certainly far from instructive. On one occasion my menses was late. The event was later marked by this: *Even now I stand frozen as I speak the words I plan to write. I knew only one reason this would happen...she had told me, "That's what happens when you're going to have a baby!" I am at this moment in that same room looking down at her, smoking and reading her paperback book. The relief of being told, "It will come" I cannot now feel... the pain has to go away first.*

27

Totally alone speaking aloud to God...begging...asking, telling Him all my thoughts...16 years old...and I cry as I write.

That life...those years will remain in my heart as my brain shrinks to nothingness. I see the tears pass down from my eyes and feel them on my cheeks as I did almost 60 years ago. Now I give it up and just sit and cry and I am afraid again.

Crying is what one does at the end of something. Also it is sometimes what one holds back, if possible, until a private time.

Comments from past writings: *What do I do with all this hate and fear from the past? I can't keep smoothing over it with all these bitter sweet tales of the only child. The only child...is at once alone...separate...an individual... simple...a part of everyone...a piece of every plan...the center...the star...the needy...perhaps a necessary piece...is certainly many things to many people. She plays all the parts...the good girl, the bad girl...the beloved, the failure... the object of those who need to attack...the product...the project.*
I came first in all decisions is what I thought, because I was told that. How often I heard, "You get the first shoes, the best food, clothes. You were always provided for...and cared for...even brought back from the edge of death by all those who loved you."

I am not sure about the "edge of death" reference. I don't remember as a child being on the edge of death except for the impact of my own negative thoughts. As an adult I have been well aware that the edge of death sometimes borders my moods in an unholy manner.

Quite often I recall the suicide of Clare, a woman whom I regarded as a good friend. She lived next door to us in my pre-teen years. She was eight or ten years older than I. She talked to me, and I used to like to talk to her. I tried to be at her house around dinner time because her mother would sometimes ask me to stay for dinner, and my grandmother would usually consent.

Clare got married and moved into her own house with her husband. One year her house was flooded. She and her husband and two small children moved back into our neighborhood to stay with her mother while her new house was built. When the new house was ready for occupancy they were preparing to move in. But Clare shot herself back of the furnace in her mother's home. It was a tremendous loss for me and another of those many things about adults and the world of which I had no comprehension. I often think about Clare and wonder "Why?" At other times, suicide seems so sensible, so right!

I find another note: *I truly want to do something...accomplish something...stand apart from this child and be grown up...responsible, imaginative. I have not yet found what I want to be and do.*

I wish I could be 17 again and live all those years in a different way. I want to have some time in which I am free, free of myself. I sit here empty of all the things I need to be another.

My contact with religion and with the spiritual has been a strange, unpredictable, and often unfathomable influence in my life. I am Roman Catholic by the baptism which occurred 30 days after my birth. Aunt Edith was my Godmother and Uncle Jim my Godfather. I am quite certain Aunt Edith was there, since she was probably the person who made the arrangements. She was a devout Catholic. She had no children of her own at that time. Uncle Jim was probably a Catholic by name without doing much about it.

My first memories of religion are associated with my grandmother and our nightly prayers. Being at Sunday Mass without my grandmother's presence was another frightening experience. I never understood much of what was going on at Mass, and I felt out of place, a feeling which has often occurred throughout my adult life. Memories of being at Aunt Edith's house always included some religious overtones, whether a prayer before meals, attendance at Sunday Mass, or holy pictures here and there in the house.

In Philadelphia the children who did not attend Catholic school had to sit in the back of the church behind the Catholic school students. The nuns from the Catholic school monitored the entire group with some focus on the second class citizens in the back. All the children made their First Communion at the same time. We did not get one of the shiny white prayer books each of the Catholic school children had, nor did we get the same veils the other girls wore. Much was done to make us aware that we belonged in "the back of the bus," if they ever decided to take a load to heaven.

The children who did not attend Catholic school were expected to attend religious education classes after the Sunday Mass. That was quite an experience. The sisters appeared to resent the extra duty they had on Sunday and apparently concluded that if all the children went to Catholic school, as they were supposed to do, this Sunday duty would not be necessary. One could not say they were abusive, but they were, to say the least, unfriendly and harsh. It was the kind of atmosphere in which no one learns readily, and one in which I didn't learn much of anything. Which is exactly what I learned about my faith—not much of anything. But it caught me emotionally. Mary and the baby Jesus captured my feelings and my imagination. I liked stories from the Bible that are still familiar to most young Christian children.

My faith is built on my emotions. It is a "feeling faith," not an intellectual belief system. Most priests don't understand that. Perhaps many theologians would not find it "authentic." Is it because they are men? As I spoke with a priest-friend I tried to describe what I was talking about in regard to this "religion" of mine. He just "didn't get it." On another occasion, I spoke with another friend, a gay clergyman, and he understood exactly what I was talking about.

I continue not to know much about the Catholic faith. I know how I feel about homilies and religious services, and I know which ones touch my "sacred need" and satisfy the longing I have to be a good person, to do the right thing, and to be aware of God's presence in my life. And I know that I am ready to walk out the door when one homilist talks endlessly about the sweater he got for Christmas when he was a boy and another talks about his recent vacation of rock climbing, noting that it is not a sport for "girlie-men." The seed of my faith may be sewn on rocky ground where it has a difficult time maintaining roots, but it is frequently watered by my tears.

I understand that faith makes some kind of leap from what is known by reason to a place where reason cannot suffice. Priests talk about faith being a gift of the Holy Spirit so that one can go beyond where reason cannot go. I do wonder about those who want to get somewhere through a reasoning process when I'm already there sometimes because I "felt" it.

I want to go back to the Sunday school classes for a moment. That is an unlikely sentence because I don't ever want to go back to those classes. The atmosphere was hard and punitive. Through the winter months the heat was apparently turned off in the school from Friday evening until Monday morning. By Sunday the school building was freezing. Sometimes we were encouraged to walk around during the class so that we could keep warm. The nuns seemed to be well insulated from the cold.

One story from my early years suggests that I may have had some ability to fend for myself. In those days, women were obliged to wear hats in church. On one occasion I forgot and took my hat off. One of the girls reminded me that I needed to have my hat on. She was too unsure of herself to challenge my response, "You only have to have a hat on when you come through the door."

Graduation from high school was relatively uneventful. My mother and her cousin Ethel were there. It was the first school function my mother ever attended. My grades were all A's during my senior year. I was awarded a four year full scholarship to the Moore Institute of Art in Philadelphia. Another girl had been eligible for the award but she was unable to accept it because she had to go to work and would be unable to attend the full time classes. I felt unworthy of the award and suggested to the other girl that we could share it, each of us working half time and attending school the other half. Gracious but unrealistic!

I have never really admitted to myself that I deserved the scholarship because I had the intelligence, the grades, and the talent it required. A later note: *June. Graduations past… long ago…dead…dried…but not forgotten. Bobby pins on caps…smiles, paced marching, anticipation…never a thought to the after, yet always full of it and not of the reality of the event. No mellow embracing of all it meant…now won and earned.*

Completing high school represents a transition in the lives of graduates. The night of graduation was more than a simple transition for me. It plunged me into a world that I was poorly prepared to enter, a world in which my first major decisions were ill-conceived, poorly managed, wasteful of my life—decisions which to this day I cannot understand or explain to myself or to anyone else.

Chapter III

*The Path to Nowhere
(1947-1965)*

THE DAY OF MY graduation from high school I was ill prepared to confront any part of the rest of my life. Not only was I unprepared, I must have harbored doubts as to my readiness. Although I finished high school with excellent grades, I never saw myself as very intelligent. I had developed no social skills because I had few meaningful associations with peers. I was without even an inkling of self-confidence because no one had ever given me the gift of their confidence in me. I was unable to make reliable choices because my family had made all the choices in my life. I was overwhelmed by anything, fearful of everything, unhappy with life.

I was 17 when I graduated. On that fateful day two things happened that made the next 18 years of my life unsatisfying and unproductive. The first event plunged me into the first four years of this period, and the second event dragged me through the entire 18 years.

With the four year scholarship award I entered the Moore Institute of Art in Philadelphia in the fall of 1947. To someone else this would have been a grand prize, a challenging opportunity, an avenue to a future in the art world. The Institute was an excellent school at the time and in later years has become even more prestigious. Unfortunately it was a place of failure for me, a failure that I still look back on with remorse and self-disdain. What a waste! What a waste! I had natural talent, keen observational abilities, an innate sense of color, shading, and line---none of which I would have recognized or acknowledged then, but of which I am now aware and have come to appreciate in these later years. Even as I experience the deterioration from Alzheimer's disease, I remain aware of those assets which I failed to notice and respect when I was in art school.

There was little self-determination in my life at that time. I went to art school because I won the scholarship, not because I had any keen aspirations for my future. I don't recall giving much thought to the future. At the school I expressed a desire to focus on fashion design. I had designed and sewed most of my clothes by that time, and it was an area that interested me. (I had always dressed my dolls in the best cutout clothes I could find.) The director of the program encouraged me to take fashion illustration because the class I wanted was crowded. In my characteristic manner, I easily acquiesced.

In some ways I enjoyed the time in art school. I made some superficial friendships with other students and heard more about the world outside my narrow boundaries than I had ever imagined existed. A few of the students were quite familiar with the "free living" of the times. I was more than just interested; I was curious about their lives. Art school could have been a successful time in my life. I was accepted by my peers and got along well with them. The peer acceptance could have boosted my self-confidence enough to encourage an interest in my abilities and enhance my dedication to the educational offerings.

Reflections on art school have been in my mind and my notes. *The family conversations about my future, the future education, were hollow and meaningless. I had no opinions, no goals, no special or even any interest in anything. And so the die was cast...the scholarship...it was to be awarded to my close friend. She was unable to continue education because of a family restriction. Off I went...pencil in hand...small talent which would have been greatly enhanced with virtuous attention, work, and exclusion of distractions. It was completely wasted...even what I had when starting...even practice, hard work, concentration...necessary diligence could not be there...even loyalty to my talent.*

Why did I not benefit from art school, learn something that would provide a direction in my life, gain some sense of my own abilities? My notes indicate difficulties which were deeply embedded in my past. A *truth seemed to come to me today. It has been there since my birth ... now and only now I could speak because I understood why I am what I am. I do observe ... but I do not reason ... I do not conclude as others do. I often am not aware of conclusions that are obvious to others. Sometimes I lose sight of my own goal ... my attention and observation of the details along the way betray my journey ... hold me in their web of minutia ... unnecessary and irrelevant details ... but nevertheless captivating.*

Robbie often comments about my observational powers. I can observe and remember what each of fifteen people were wearing at a party two weeks ago; the bric-a-brac we saw in an antique store last week; the floor plan and details of an apartment or house we visited three months ago. I have been aware of this mental note taking for sometime. I attribute it to my interest in fashion, furnishings, decorations, and houses. I never realized before today that this observational bent comes into play in other areas and possibly serves as a handicap. I get waylaid on the road to somewhere or something by almost anything.

Rob sometimes jokingly says that I am far more likely to analyze something that a person says or does than he is. (Perhaps I haven't mentioned that Robbie is a psychiatrist.) Unfortunately while I get lost in the analysis of A and B, everyone else has skipped all the analysis and arrived at the goal of C. I am not only left behind ...I am left out ... feeling lost. I never learned how to use my perceptive abilities...or appreciate them ... or control them. My perceptions of life provide me with images...and often strong accompanying feelings ... but not always useful information.

I get caught up in preliminary details all the time. I always have. It's much worse now with the Alzheimer's. I attend to what someone in the group is wearing, how she holds her hands, how he talks, how she stands; and in the process I lose track of the conversation or of where I am or of why I'm there. Or I pick up on one comment someone makes or one particular act I notice and that becomes the content of the whole experience. All the rest escapes me. The terrible thing now is that my mind seems to fill in parts of conversations because, when Robbie and I talk about it later, I can end up with a distorted view of what was said or of what happened.

This is not just distractibility! I focus well but I focus on the unimportant, the incidental, something that others might not even notice.

Why do I focus on them? I believe that when I was a child I watched adults all the time, trying to understand what was going on, trying to recognize whether or not I was pleasing them, trying to find out how I fit into their world. (They never really talked to me about any of it.) It was the watching, the studying... and always the uncertainty... so...more observation, more wondering...and always the fear. I tried to resolve the uncertainty, control the fear by observing, observing, observing. The answer had to be in the details...but it never came...so more details.

I couldn't learn in school because I was focused not on the lengths of triangle sides or the steps in pollination but on the details of how to avoid being called on, how stupid I would look if the teacher did call on me, why my books had the edging they had, how they were glued together, why the blackboard didn't have better decorations, and on and on. While I was struggling with the details of the classroom and my reactions to the teacher, the day passed, and it was time to go home to another setting in which I again seemed not to be able to learn because I was caught up in observing.

I can compare my life to that of a baby who is learning to walk. Each step is tentative, expectant, individual... each has its own uncertainty... each has its own satisfaction or its own failure. But when the child learns to walk, she or he crosses the room to some goal without any thought to the process of walking. I never get beyond the learning phase, never get over concentrating on each step, hoping for a reassuring feeling and dreading a sense of another failure, watching the reactions of others, wondering if "now I have it right." Now my lack of self-confidence becomes more acute with Alzheimer's on the scene.

How many opportunities did I miss in life because I could not keep my mind on the desired but distant outcome? That's what happened in art school. There was no vision, no sense of my own talent, no goal that was beyond the focus of the moment. I never faced the uncertainties of the future because I concentrated on the insecurities of the present.

I know it could have been otherwise in my life had I had encouragement, guidance, and support. Years ago I wrote: *My sewing is one stellar example of "the might have been" ... because it not only was...it was good ... no, great. I made clothes for my children and for myself and as gifts for others. They were creative, imaginative, fine garments of which I was proud. I enjoyed making them. I could lose myself in the making. It was invigorating, stimulating. There was confidence, pure and simple ... and so sweet. How did that happen? It came to be because my grandmother took an interest in my sewing and worked with me and showed me how to do things and encouraged me and praised my work and filled me with a desire to do it and a tremendous satisfaction in the doing. How rich it was for me! What a valuable experience! It filled my head with confidence and my heart with courage ...but only in my sewing. The roots of the small gift she gave me were not strong... the branches were tender and weak ... no shoots or growth or vitality to spread to other areas of my life ... maybe some hints of growth in my modeling, in my decorating, and in my loving Rob. But sewing was the one area where I could take charge, set my goals, and achieve them in a timely manner with a satisfying product. What if my grandmother or my mother or my aunt Edith or some teacher had taken the kind of interest I am speaking of and helped me pursue my innate gifts with their interest, their encouragement, their support, and their occasional praise? Oh, the opportunities that might have been!*

The night of my high school graduation there was a companion event which not only burdened the next 18 years but pulled me down into a sense of hopelessness and helplessness that could have ended my life. After the graduation ceremony, my mother took me to celebrate at a little ice cream shop in our neighborhood. While we were in the shop, she told the owner that I had just won a four year scholarship to art school. Was this really my mother sounding proud about something I had accomplished? Or was she just trying to impress the owner with how important she must be to have such a daughter? In any case, my life might have been much better had she kept silent.

There was a young man in the shop at the time, a young man whom I did not even notice. But Tom noticed me, and the following evening he came to my house as the first person ever to ask me for a date. The only "date" I ever had was before I graduated from high school. My mother paid a guy from work to take me to my senior dance. He lived in some sort of boy's facility. My mother and stepfather drove us and another couple to the dance, waited for us, then took us for sodas after the prom, and then home.

Tom did nothing for my self-confidence or for me. He told me later that when he had heard my mother talking about the four year scholarship, he thought I must be intelligent and consequently wanted to date me. The clear implication was that he had been wrong in that assessment. The first night he came to my door he asked me to go on the river cruise with him the following night. My grandmother gave her consent, and my mother agreed. The night we went out we took a different route leaving the house. Later he told me that he went that way to avoid his friends who loitered around the ice cream store because he was "ashamed of me."

Dating him I took a step, and it never occurred to me that I could step back. I never questioned why he wanted to be with me. I had never been around any young men when I was young. I had no close friends and never stayed overnight with girl friends. Kensington High was for girls as was Moore Institute. I had no exposure. I was a drone. I began going steady with Tom, but I later realized he was not going steady with me.

Looking back I cannot understand why I continued to see him through those four years of art school. Our dating severely interfered with my education. Do I blame him? Yes! But I let it happen. So people wonder why I sometimes call myself "stupid!" Our school day was from 9 a.m. to 3 p.m., but if I had taken additional college classes from 3 p.m. to 5 p.m., I would have graduated with a degree instead of just receiving a diploma. I began taking the additional classes, but he soon persuaded me that I should meet him at 3 p.m. when he was available. He would show up at the school unannounced and hang around talking to the other girls until I came out. He often encouraged me to skip classes to be with him. I was foolishly at his beck and call.

I did consider him to be very handsome in those days, and my friends in art school seemed to agree. He typically turned on the charm when any of them were around. I found it irritating and disgusting. I don't think I was actually jealous, because I don't think I was really in love with him. He had no manners, no money, and no real esteem for me. But I did put up with it!

I had saved money from working in the mill since age 14. I also worked there during the summers when I went to Moore. He expected me to use that money to pay for some of our activities. I did. On occasion, with his encouragement, I even stole a few dollars from the jar in my family kitchen to finance things we did. Later I wrote: *"I was always the fool. Others would see me as having something wrong in my head."*

One night after we attended an Irish party, he took me home to meet his mother long after midnight. I think his mother was embarrassed due to the late hour and the unannounced visit. I doubt if Tom was ever embarrassed in his life. Both of his parents were from Ireland. There were three children in the family. John was the oldest, not very bright. Tom was smarter than John. Theresa was the youngest; I got along well with her.

I took his father to Sodality (an evening Catholic service) for years. I got along well with him and with the mother too. It was a strange, secretive family. His mother told me that she cleaned offices in downtown Philadelphia five nights a week, and no one in the family ever knew it. Tom would come home so drunk he couldn't make it up the stairs. His mother would drag him up and put him in bed, but she never believed he drank. Here is an example of the deceit they practiced with each other. Several months after my divorce from Tom was final, he asked me if I would go to the beach with him because his mother was going to be there, and he didn't want her to know we were no longer married.

It would, of course, be asking too much to suggest that Tom should have filled the gap left in my life by the lack of encouragement from my family members. But I surely did not need someone to treat me with such a contemptuous attitude. During the four years I dated him, he was often critical of me personally. He spoke to me and of me as if I were rather stupid. He never commented on my appearance or my clothes, although pictures indicate that I was an attractive woman. He never took me when he got together with his "buddies" even though they brought their wives or girl friends. I always "knew" that he was seeing other women. Did I somehow believe that was the way the world worked? I did have the example of my mother, my uncle Jim, and a few other close relatives.

My family certainly gave me mixed signals about our dating. On the one hand, I could not go out with Tom in a car. On the other hand, I could go to the beach with him and even stay overnight. There was no consistency. Tom would pick me up, and we would walk around the corner where his brother and his brother's girl friend would be waiting in their car. I probably enjoyed deceiving my family. I always felt they all hated Tom, but no one ever suggested I not marry him.

Perhaps my behavior with him was some sort of delayed adolescent rebellion that therapists talk about. I have heard it said that adolescent rebellion is a necessary step in developing into an adult. The danger is that adolescents may rebel in some way that destroys their lives or themselves in this period of transition. I almost did that.

Tom went to LaSalle College in Philadelphia. He told me where to meet him at a game, and when I went to the wrong place, he was furious when he found me and became verbally abusive. That's how he always treated me. I sat on the wrong side of the church at his college graduation, and he reacted in the same way. Everything seemed to get spoiled when we went any where. I made my dress for a college dance at the country club. When someone accidentally spilled a glass of beer in my lap, Tom laughed like it was the funniest thing he ever saw. There was never an apology, never a supportive or understanding remark. I stayed mad at him throughout most of our relationship.

I married him in June 1951. Years later I must have remembered the date, for I wrote: *Forty-one years ago right now, we – myself, my family of origin and those strange ones I had chosen to take into my future – gathered, sat, ate and drank. Hours before, we had at Mass literally been co-actors in various degrees of willingness in the ceremony of my downfall into an era of misfortune…I had myself decreed it should come about.*

I always knew and did what I was told, what I was supposed to do… Jane was a good little girl. Then years later I found my place. I had wasted the scholarship, the opportunity. I threw that away and jumped into a hell I was aware of. I lost my chance and my mind. However bent and shaped it was, it's gone.

There was another indication of my subservience to him. Tom insisted that we get married in his parish rather than in mine. My pastor was not pleased with the decision but did come to the reception. He was also not pleased with my marrying Tom. Would that I had listened to his wisdom!

The morning after our wedding we left on our honeymoon to Canada. The first night of our trip we stayed in a cabin motel that did not have running water. We had to use an outhouse along with other travelers. We stayed in the cheapest motels Tom could find during our entire trip, and he never made reservations in advance. We had received money from various people for wedding presents, but I never knew how much or where it went. Nor was I given the opportunity to send thank you notes.

All the travel plans were his and were never discussed with me. He said it was to provide an element of surprise. In reality it was done that way because my preferences or interests were never considered. Tom was determined to go to the Shrine of Sainte Anne de Beaupre in Quebec. He wanted to go up the steps on his knees. He never told me why, and I'm sure I never asked.

He had a number of weird attitudes about religion coupled with his weird attitudes about sex. I think they were joined in many ways that were never clear to me but which made both subjects unpleasant and somehow tainted. Neither provided a sense of worth, virtue, or integrity. I came to have disdain for his childish and somewhat perverted attitude and behavior in both areas. We never spoke about religious beliefs or attitudes, and the same thing happened with regard to sex. Both areas seemed to be something we needed to do but never to acknowledge with one another. We went to church together, but we never shared our religion. We had sex, but we never shared our love.

Friday night was always his "night out" come hell or high water or any needs of mine. I never knew where he was when he went out in the evening and rarely knew what time he came home because I would usually be asleep. It was his night to go drinking with his buddies, although I always believed it involved more than drinking.

One Friday evening when I was near term with my first child, I was in terrible pain. He left me alone in the house that night but was considerate enough to leave a tray of ice cubes that I could reach and put on my stomach. The pain was so bad I thought I would die. I called my mother, and she came. I was taken to the hospital, and my mother went from bar to bar to find Tom. I had my son that night. A few nights later when I came home from the hospital with my son, Tom went to bed. He never helped me with that baby or any of our others. But then he never helped me with anything.

A story about my father-in-law provides an insight into Tom's character. Not long after we were married, we planned to go to Wildwood beach for a few days. Tom decided at the last minute to take his father, so we dropped by the house and asked him to go with us. When we got to the beach we dropped him outside a motel in some town north of

Wildwood, and we went on. Tom didn't even go in with him to get him settled. His father was old; he had trouble walking; he was quite deaf; and he was unfamiliar with the area.

A day or two later, one of Tom's relatives called and told us that his father had been taken to the local hospital because he had fallen. From there he was taken by ambulance to Northeast Hospital in Philadelphia. His father was in that hospital for some time before he died. He had lost the ability to speak. I walked six blocks to and from the hospital every day to feed him his dinner because no one else in the family would do it. I was pregnant at the time and working at the mill. Later, Tom's mother thanked me for all I had done for him.

After several years, Tom got a job in Washington, D.C. with the Internal Revenue Service. He lived with Uncle Pete and Aunt Edith for several months before I was able to join him with the two children we had then. My son, Philip, was born in 1952 and my daughter, Kathie, was born in 1959.

We had an occasion to take our son to a pediatrician. It provided my first realization that Tom might use his IRS position to get even with those who crossed him. When we left the doctor's office, Tom paid him in cash. He saw the doctor put the money in his desk drawer. On the way out, he told me that he was going to report the doctor to the Internal Revenue Service. Later when I was in court over custody of my children, some of my family members were afraid to testify because they thought he would have their tax returns pulled. They had reason for their fears. He threatened one of my cousins with an IRS audit. After Rob and I married, we had our returns pulled two or three times without the discovery of any problems. A random audit or an act of retribution?

Stories about our life together could continue for many pages, but they would all be basically the same. My third child, Bonnie, was born in 1961. I also had one ectopic pregnancy and three miscarriages. Tom was one of those Catholics who believed in having as many children as possible. The children were and still are the only bright events in my life with Tom. There is nothing I can think of other than them which has any positive meaning for me from all those years. Living with him took its toll – on a daily basis.

Once again, I wonder why I married Tom. Why didn't I see it was all wrong? I knew it. I was never surprised by things he did or didn't do.

I never assumed anything was going to be nice. I continue to puzzle over much of my early adult behavior.

Life with Tom cost me emotionally. There is no doubt in my mind that I was just an object to him. I was attractive, personable, an energetic home-maker, and socially adept. In retrospect, I believe I provided window dressing for his life, nothing more. Through the years, life with Tom became more disagreeable for us both and more destructive for me. I became increasingly depressed with the unhappiness of the situation, and I was led by him and by my own poor self esteem to believe it must be due to my inadequacy.

I had the grace to decide on psychiatric care and first went to a doctor in Philadelphia. I saw him for several months and was gaining some better understanding of the complexity of my situation, and then in 1961 we moved to Adelphi, Maryland. Soon after the birth of my third child, I began to feel overwhelmed with my emotional struggles and again sought psychiatric care.

I saw a psychiatrist in Maryland for about two years and during that time continued to gain perspective on my life with greater appreciation of the emotional limits created by my childhood experiences and the effect of my current marriage. For the first time in my life, I began to appreciate some of my strengths, and I developed a more positive regard for myself. Because a personal relationship developed between the psychiatrist and me, I was referred to another psychiatrist whom I saw for a short time.

In this same time period, I received word from my mother that my father was very ill and wanted to see me. I went to visit him in the hospital. A later writing describes the reunion:

They called and said he was dying and wanted to see me. I was so anxious to get there, and it was such a good and non-scary visit. We were close, and it was right. Another visit and he died. I was very sad at his funeral. But we had healed the pain and the loss and spanned the years and the differences. There were no feelings of pain or the unfamiliar. It was so simple. I wrote about it and read what he had written those years, and I believed it and I believed him. It was good. I wasn't angry at anyone. I knew that and I told them and they knew that. Some wanted me to blame him and not to go. Some were angry because I went. But for the first time I did what I felt and wanted to do, and I never did feel angry at anyone nor did I place any blame.

43

It was as if we finally were honest and simple, just the two of us. I accepted all that he said. There wasn't much, but it was right and enough, and then, he was gone. Looking back I think it was the necessary simple acceptance and the gratitude for the opportunity and for being able to just love each other there and then. I always was aware that some other time or place or way, we may not have had all that.

I know I had changed in those years. I had started separating and freeing myself from the person I had married. Finally, I had found someone who told me I was a good person and worthy of being loved. I stood my ground and then headed out to freedom from that person, but I haven't yet been able to stand alone.

I knew after such a short time with my father I had much to write. *As my father was dying of cancer: I finished my letter to you, folded it and put it inside the card with the smiling daisy face that said "I miss you" and then inside the envelope and sealed it behind your name. There they were—your name and mine staring back at me from the white square as I wrote Air Mail in the corner and put the stamp in place. To you from me! I was sending the answer you had asked for in your card...saying what I thought was "right," not too much, most of all not too much. After the letter was gone, I knew that all I wanted to say to you was still with me...here inside where it had been for so long. Would I have the chance to tell you ever? Would you understand? By then, that someday in the distant future, if I had the chance, there would be too much to say, to one so loved for all a lifetime.*

One day in January my father died. So much had happened before that...so much has happened to me since that day. Another day in January, 33 years before, I was born. I'm not sure where he was. It depends on whose story I believe.

It took few words for me to understand what my father felt the day he sent for me. How lucky I felt to have known the meaning of a look, tears, out-stretched arms, an embrace and then a smile-filled "Jane, oh my Jane!" I thought at the time that all was forgiven. He needed me and I was there. It was only later reflecting on it during my trial of decision making that I knew there had been nothing to forgive.

Years before he had left me and my mother. I had been told and believed that he didn't want me. There were stories of another woman whom he later married, of his children and his adjustment to a family---a family which didn't include me.

But somehow all those years I must have believed differently, and then as we sat together my first adult day with him, I listened to his words not of explanation but of joy to see me, and little things, so many little things, I was assured.

I saw him again several weeks later. I kissed him goodbye and he died in the night. I have never been more sure of anything than I am that my father loved me, and he had a good reason for leaving me so long ago.

(On Cancer)Dear Dad: They fall like soldiers on a battlefield...having lost the fight to live. So many since you....Today their loss becomes part of my view of the ugliness of life. I need to remember how sweet it can be and how necessary it is to fight on and to win.

The period of psychiatric care and the reunion with my father seemed to provide me with a more positive view of myself and my inherent worth. I began to think seriously about the disastrous effect my marriage was having on my own health and the future stability of our family. Gradually I came to a realization that my emotional and spiritual well-being were in jeopardy in this degrading relationship to which I had been trying somehow to adjust. The decision came slowly, the deed came rapidly, the resolution of it all took years. I left Tom.

Chapter IV

New Directions
(Feb 65 – Sept 66)

I DON'T RECALL EXACTLY WHEN I decided to leave Tom, but I know it was not an easy decision. Not easy because of the children. I knew I could not take them with me, because I had no place to go with them. At the same time I knew I could not continue to live with their father. I had become afraid of Tom. Although he had never been physically violent toward me, he had become more verbally abusive, and he made repeated veiled threats about what he might do. The sensation that someone was sitting on my chest kept growing within me. I couldn't breathe emotionally.

At one point, I went to talk to one of the parish priests about the situation, looking for some support and some advice. While he would not support my thought of leaving Tom and the children, he did suggest I "get a gun," which didn't seem like very wise counsel to me. When that same priest was asked to testify at my custody hearing two years later, he claimed that our conversation had occurred during confession, and thus he was unable to divulge any of it. Since he was never on the stand, his lie could not be challenged by my attorney, so he was allowed to just walk away from the responsibility. It brought me no great sense of justice when I read in the local papers 30 years later that he was found guilty of sexually molesting children. Lying did not save him on that one.

Three things were critical in my decision as to where to go when I left Tom. My fears dictated that I needed to be in a place where Tom could not find me. I wanted to be in a state where I could get a divorce as soon as possible and then get custody of my children. I also did not want to go so far away that I would not be available to the children if needed. I decided Richmond, Virginia, was the place to go. When I moved there, on the advice of my attorney, I took a new name, Barbara Collins, and obtained a new social security number.

At this time in my life, Robbie, whom I had known for several years, was a godsend. He was very supportive in a number of ways. We went together to Richmond and found a small basement apartment for me. In February 1965 he helped me move the few things I took with me. It was the most painful day of my life. I said goodbye to my three children one by one as I did any other school day, uncertain as to when I would see them again. And I left. From old notes: *It had required a lot of thinking after the decision had been made. I think definitely I oversimplified the whole thing. I sat in my car by the curb and watched Kathie walk into the school – she turned and waved goodbye. It would be forever before I would see her again, let alone hold her and kiss her. I went forward.*

My tears have never washed away the sadness that surrounds that time. How could I have left them? I shudder at the casual comments of people who glibly discuss the marital issues of others and invariably conclude, "I don't see how a mother could leave her children." At the time I felt I had no alternative. Tom was destroying what little was left of me emotionally. I was gradually being stripped of any sense of self, any semblance of sanity. That sounds overly dramatic. It is not "overly" anything. It was so real! And even now after all these years, when I go back in my mind to my life with Tom, the answer to "how could I leave my children?" is perfectly obvious to me. And whether or not it is obvious to anyone else, including my children, does not undo my conviction that it needed to be done. Deep within my heart at that time I knew that I needed to get rid of Tom one way or another, or else I would have had to get rid of myself!

Some years ago I wrote: *Tues. 6/16/92. Thirty-three years ago today...I know where I was. It was the day before Kathie was born...I was 29 years old. I even remember what I wore...a black skirt...a colorful print waffle weave piqué top. I had seen myself in a mirror…and had stood there looking at "the me" …reflected. I felt attractive … feminine…alive.*

I didn't know then that I was going to, the next day, give birth to my first daughter. For the time being I had stopped hating, while at the same time I think I had taken on an attitude of independence. The years that followed were different from those before … never to return to what they had been.

My being pregnant with Kathie was a positive…it brought a deep happiness. I had spoken to her deep inside me and had said "hold on baby…don't let go…be all right in spite of the blows from outside…and I will be all right too." I held on.

I could not have believed at that time that in order to save myself I would leave her. I have never written those words anywhere.

Desert…run away…abandon…by these words you will know what I did. I alone did this…reasons have always mattered, to me at least, and only I have voiced reasons… but not said aloud these words describing what I did…why but not what.

Wed. 6/17/92 in Baltimore: The bagel tastes like the sea. This ½ hour is mine…I paid 25 cents for it. Some other Wednesday I will sit and write and remember today. The shop speaker is above my head…the unfamiliar instrumental is comforting…I don't know why.

I invite you into… at once… reality and the past…the security of the moment… the game I play alone…hide and hide. It's all feelings…all feelings…all words and lies…and make believe. Those who walk around me see me not. I cannot see myself…crumbs fall into the book…I smile.

Begin again…   I hold inside the measure of myself. Will it matter when I get old and ugly? Nobody will notice. I woke up this morning being afraid of leaving here…all that is family. The beginning will be easy…it always has been. I will be asking for understanding, acceptance and I feel that it will be there.

I called Kathie to wish her happy birthday. I didn't want her to call back. I left…I can never tell her how it was.

Let me alone…let me struggle…silence the words in my head…the thoughts and fears…the guilt. I find a space here and I will make this somewhere else….

I do not love myself. I give it all over to YOU.

When the dark street was my alone place…I cried and pleaded. I set the stage…the mold had been formed how I poured into it…and carried it on high…actually only I saw it and worshipped its God…Pride, Arrogance, Willfulness, Lack of Trust, Self-centeredness.

The fact that I left my children has brought me sadness throughout the years. Any loss is magnified by the ache in my heart from the loss of their childhood years. The sadness has been a recurring theme for my notes. *Don't come looking for me. I'm not there…I'm here. And you can't get from there to here. Only I can and did.*

I suppose all the times I thought I knew where you were, I didn't. Did you try to tell me? I wasn't listening.

It takes such tremendous effort to not cry. I'm not sure it will help to write, but if I seal this pain, this familiar feeling from the past inside my self, it will join the others. How can I look at those other times and handle them as I know I must with this fresh new one hurting so badly. Is it wanting to control? Could it be that?

My life is good as I live each day, one at a time. It's the storing it and taking it out and looking at it that's painful. If I could let go of that, I could let go of everything.

Crying will come…it always has. I've never peacefully lived with loss…or my inadequacies … so I've lived my life, feeling a failure. I've constantly reached back and highly colored the mistakes, the "sadnesses" in my heart…always being less…nothing to be proud of lives there.

Whose fault, whose fault, must quickly follow reading of past actions. "Who was responsible?" comes after "Yes, I did that." That was the me I was, the decision I made, the way I acted…that's not the way it's supposed to be.

Life in Richmond was not easy, but it was mine—mine for the first time. I had never lived alone. I had never been alone. I had never gone from one day to the next deciding for myself what I was going to do that day or the next. I had my own bedroom for the first time in my life. I could decorate as I wanted, cook as I pleased, eat what I liked, come and go without answering to anyone. The joy seemed better than it was. I missed my children. I had told my mother where I was, and she would keep in touch with the children.

Rob came to see me every week. Tuesday became our day. He would come from Washington early in the morning and stay until late afternoon, and we would spend the day together.

I went to the local Catholic parish and spoke to the pastor about becoming a member of the parish. He asked me about my circumstances. I told him that I had come to Richmond with the intent of getting a divorce. I also told him of my relationship with Robbie. He made it very clear that he did not approve of my situation and that unless I gave up my relationship with Rob I would not be welcome in the parish.

After the harsh treatment of the nuns in Sunday school and the feelings of rejection in my childhood church, I was well prepared once more to claim my church in spite of those who seemed to want to shut me out. I faithfully walked to Mass every Sunday. On the way home I would buy the Sunday paper and stop for coffee at a little neighborhood deli. Sunday was a lonely day because I rarely would get a call from Rob. He was at home with his family and calls were difficult for him to make.

Robbie and I were very much in love and committed ourselves to one another at sometime during this period of time. Rob had sought spiritual direction in his inner conflict and growing perception that his marriage was not a viable marriage. He had consulted a priest (Father John) in the area who was considered a rather conservative theologian. I met Father John while I was still living in Richmond. He maintained contact with us and visited us several times during the next 25 years.

During one of Robbie's Tuesday visits we went to the local Catholic Church that I attended every Sunday, and we exchanged private vows of love and fidelity to each other. By this time, Rob's counsel from Father John enabled him to take such a step. In view of my history with the ministry of the church, I found it easy to continue to live by my rather simplistic religious beliefs which were based more on my own inner experience than on any impact from religion professionals or church teachings.

After I became better acquainted with the area I began looking for a job. I had the good fortune to be hired at Thalhimer's Department Store in downtown Richmond. After a few weeks I became an assistant buyer and worked there until I left Virginia. It was an interesting job, and I met some very nice people. I kept in touch with two or three of them for many years and saw two of them again later in life.

The basement apartment where I lived was broken into a few months after I moved there. I got home late in the evening and found the door open. A television and a bottle of wine were all that had been taken. I was suspicious that Tom may have been there, although I had no idea how he might have found me. On the other hand, he used his Internal Revenue credentials to open a lot of doors in life. In any case, the robbery was a good incentive to look for another place. Rob encouraged me to get an efficiency apartment in a high rise a little closer to my job, and then I walked back and forth to work.

Robbie and I were not yet certain when we were going to be together or where, but we bought our first furniture in Richmond. We bought a lovely Ethan Allen dining room set, table and four chairs. We expanded with two more chairs in later years. Since our present apartment in Columbia, Maryland is rather small, we gave the dining room set to Kathie. We still have a fine credenza from Richmond which graces our living room.

My divorce went through smoothly. To my knowledge Tom never even responded to the papers. I didn't ask for alimony and decisions about the children were not addressed because they were not under the jurisdiction of the Virginia court. Divorce was granted based on "constructive desertion and abandonment" on the part of the defendant, my former husband. Legal language can be so deceptive and so oblique. Tom did not desert me. He had never really been with me. I deserted him, and my desertion of him was the most constructive thing I ever did in my life. My real desertion was of the children, and I felt that as keenly as any mother could. There was no abandonment of spouse on either his part or mine. There must be some connection, some significant relationship before one can be accused of abandonment. We were never connected in any meaningful way. We went through a ceremony, and we lived together, and we had children, but we were never joined as partners in anything. I detested the implication that we had somehow been united with one another.

Within a short time I had a court hearing in Maryland over custody of my children. Uncle Pete found an attorney for me. The hearing is an unbelievable story. The result left a stigma on my life.

It was the judge's first day back in court after having been out for brain tumor surgery. The judge brought his early teenage son to court because his wife had recently left him. The priest I had called to testify backed out with a lie. It was decided that my Aunt Edith would be "too upset" to testify as to my character and stability. My cousin refused to testify because Tom had threatened her with an IRS audit. My mother testified and sounded about as coarse and tangential as if she were talking at a union meeting. My Uncle Pete testified that my children and I could have come to live with them at any time (a completely ridiculous proposition). I think he wanted to impress the judge and our attorney with his magnanimity. He was something of a pompous ass! As I reflect on all of this now, another thought comes to me. Uncle Pete had his own business. I wonder if Tom may have threatened him with an audit, or since Pete probably knew about the threat to his daughter, he may have decided it was safer not to be too helpful to me. And he surely wasn't!

The judge took my 14 year old son in chambers with his own son in tow. He settled everything very quickly. He gave sole custody of the girls to their father and sole custody of my son to me. My son told him in chambers that he did not want to return to live with his father. I later found out that the judge and Tom were members of the same Parents without Partners group. How cozy! The bastards!

It was all over so quickly. But it has never been over for me. "Mother's always get their children in divorces" is the comment almost universally heard. Such remarks don't cause me pain because the pain is always there. Such remarks don't cause a feeling of shame, because I have never doubted that there was ample justification for my decision to leave. But such comments still make be angry because I find these people to be ignorant regarding the complexity of divorce and the arbitrary decisions of erratic judges.

References to this time: *4/9/90. Spring has no color for me. It is the same as every other time. Why am I only now remembering that?*

I wouldn't change how I handled it. It was best for me...only today "I did it for me—not for somebody else." It was unjust...because I was misjudged, and they cheated. I was being punished for other things. So I have told part of the story!

I was guilty all my life...a two sided person. Never sure of what I wanted to show to whom. Compliments don't fit. Criticisms don't fit.

I didn't do the best I could have done in court. I am only just now seeing some of that. I had a lifelong handicap, which is only now 25 years later beginning to be dealt with. His lawyer asked, "Were you afraid of him?" "Yes." "Are you still afraid of him?" I said, "Yes." They all laughed... and I was undone. Everything he did to me was made of the same fabric, and my responses were made of me and my training, and I was undone. Without anyone except Robbie ever understanding it.

I've spent 43 years trying to explain what happened...what Tom did...how I responded...to everyone and only now seeing that I walked through those years as a handicapped person...but a person, an individual, not part of somebody else...not a responder...but a separate person.

I'm able now, briefly, not very clearly, able to see her...there then...as she was... separate...and not like I am today. Sometimes it's like having to let it flow, sometimes it's like having to dig away everything around it and uncover her. It's awesome...it's good to do it.

About my last visit with the girls before Rob and I left for Nevada: *Mostly I flashed back, while touching that door, to the summer evening in 1966 ... when I slammed it behind me... after Tom ripped Kathie away from me...greater pain...maybe the worst...certainly up until then -- greater than any other loss of a child I had learned to love. Loss -- something ripped out of me! Away from me!*

With my divorce I was free to marry again. Robbie tried to begin separation proceedings in early 1966. He saw an attorney in Washington and discussed his desire to separate. The attorney advised him to ask his wife to get an attorney, and the two of them would work things out together. Rob did exactly that in early March of 1966. Through subsequent months his wife continued to deny that she had contacted an attorney and gave little assurance that she intended to do so.

In the meantime, Rob continued to move forward with his plan to make a change. He had hoped to remain in the Washington area, but since his wife was completely uncooperative, he thought it necessary to make other plans. In July he accepted a position as the Superintendent of the Nevada State Hospital, starting in September 1966. He wrote a letter to referring doctors informing them that he would be leaving the area. One of the referring doctors gave Rob's wife a copy of the letter.

One evening in late August, when Robbie was packing some of his things to move them to his office, two policemen came to the house and took him to jail. Rob's wife had retained an attorney several months earlier. Her attorney had obtained a Ne Exeat (thou shalt not leave) order from a judge dated July 4th of that same year. The order was based on the claim that Rob was leaving the jurisdiction of the court without making any provision for his wife or children. At that time, the couple jointly owned three furnished houses, two of which were income producing and which were under the sole discretion of his wife. The order simply put Rob in jail until the matter could be presented in court, which turned out to be 21 days later. Rob spent the night in "the tank" along with seven or eight other "dangerous criminals."

Rob's attorney could not get a bondsman to put up bail because the letter to the doctors had stated that he was leaving the state. The choices were for him to stay in jail until the court date or sign whatever papers the wife's attorney had prepared in advance. Staying in jail was not palatable and would jeopardize his Nevada job. He signed the papers presented by the wife's attorney, and then signed a check for the man's fee before his release was processed. The three houses became his wife's as well as any current assets, all furniture, two cars----and custody of the five children.

At the time, Robbie's three sons were in Montana at his brother's ranch. They were often there during the summer months to spare them the time with and the influence of their mother. He did not see any of his five children prior to our departure for Nevada a few days later. His wife's deception and trickery made any gracious departure impossible. He left with his clothing, his books, and his automobile. Payments to his wife based on the "jailhouse documents" left us with about $200 a month from his Nevada salary.

Before Robbie was taken out of his house by the police, he had a chance to call me and tell me quickly what was happening. I was staying at my Aunt Edith's house, anticipating our imminent departure for Reno. I called our friend, Father John, who came down from Philadelphia and went to see Rob in jail the following morning before the attorneys arrived.

The night after Rob was released from jail, he and I went to dinner with two of his long time psychiatrist friends. It was the first time I met Ed and Tony. We have maintained contact and seen them occasionally through the years. Both of them were later divorced. I think that was a night we all still remember. It was Robbie's and my farewell to Maryland.

Chapter V

The Road to Reno
(1966-1971)

SUDDENLY WE WERE POOR but free and happy. The mover picked up my furniture and belongings in Richmond and then stopped at Robbie's office to get his books and personal items that he had transferred there from his former home. Our drive to Reno took five days. We had much to see, much to think about, much to talk about as we drove across the country. When we went through Winnemucca, Nevada, we stopped to watch my first rodeo! Winnemucca is a small town, and I remember wondering if this place was anything like Reno would be. I began to have some apprehension that a Philadelphia girl might not do well in this country.

Rob's college friend, Jack Arant, and his wife, Mable, lived in Reno and were very gracious to us on our arrival. I had met them in Washington, so I already had become part of the bond they had with Rob. They were very welcoming and helped us get acquainted with the area.

A house was provided for us, because Nevada law required that the Superintendent live at the Hospital. Here was our first house, our first home, on the grounds of a mental hospital. We quickly made it our own as I, for the first time, had a place in which I could feel free and content and "at home." I have always been a decorator at heart, and this was my first opportunity to apply my gifts generously and gratefully.

Rob filed for divorce practically on arrival and received the decree on November 14, 1966. We were married that same afternoon in Truckee, California, with Jack and Mable as our witnesses. We then went to dinner at the Christmas Tree Restaurant on Mount Rose between Reno and Lake Tahoe, a restaurant we continued to frequent during our Nevada years. Jack and Mable remained our close friends until their deaths years later.

Robbie took over the State Hospital and brought new life to it. The hospital had never been accredited. Rob obtained the necessary documents and brought about the changes required to meet accreditation standards. This provided a new source of revenue for the hospital which was now eligible for Medicare payments for patients.

Robbie obtained an educational grant from the National Institute of Mental Health. Instead of selecting staff to go to out-of-state education programs, he brought a number of prominent psychiatrists to Reno to provide workshops for the entire hospital staff. Many of these lecturers were Rob's personal friends. We spent a good bit of time with each of them, and we enjoyed the benefit of our personal exchanges. I remember Dana Farnsworth from Harvard, Howard Rome from the Mayo Clinic, Chet Pierce from Harvard, Frank Braceland from the Institute of Living in Hartford, Judd Marmor from Los Angeles, and David Byrne from Los Angeles. It was a stimulating and exciting time for me, a mill worker from Northeast Philadelphia, entertaining and socializing with these prominent psychiatrists.

To close each workshop we invited the visiting professor, local psychiatrists, hospital staff, and the governor to an afternoon party at the superintendent's house. I was hostess for these and enjoyed them immensely. Robbie was always pleased with my participation, and I did receive frequent compliments from our guests. Governor Paul Laxalt was a great supporter of my husband and often attended these gatherings. We both had a warm relationship with him.

I have a personal story about a meeting with Governor Laxalt. When I had some surgery in Saint Mary's Hospital in Reno, the governor stopped in to see me. I was still groggy from the anesthetic and kept trying to say something. He decided I was trying to say, "It tingles." He tried to respond in a reassuring manner and said, "Yes, it tingles after you've had surgery." With some increasing clarity I set the record straight as to my problem. "No, I have to tinkle."

The years seemed to go by rather quickly. Many of the State Hospital staff became our friends. The maintenance crew took care of any items needing repairs at our residence. I enjoyed a pleasant, friendly relationship with the crew as well as the professional staff. It was always a pleasure to talk with them and get to know them. They all seemed to admire Robbie so much. On the Sunday before Christmas, Rob and I would have an open house at our residence and invite all the employees to drop in for a visit during the afternoon and evening. We would serve light snacks and beverages. We had lots of visitors on those occasions.

Our life in Reno was active and stimulating. I became very involved as a member of the Women's Auxiliary at the hospital. At one point, I bought a beautiful trunk doll and made doll clothes for her. The Women's Auxiliary raffled the doll and did well financially from it. I was also making clothes for Laura, our daughter, as well as for myself during our Reno years. I was full of energy and enthusiasm. Although my energy has waned, Robbie still says I am full of enthusiasm. Rob and I were socially involved with some of the auxiliary women and their husbands.

We often got together with our friends, Bob and Peg Ball, who were both employed at the hospital. One year Robbie and I were invited to Governor Laxalt's New Years Eve party. Out first elegant affair! Rob bought me a mink stole, and I bought an evening gown. Rob bought his first tuxedo. When we were telling Bob and Peg about our invitation, they suggested we stop by their house on the way to the party, have a drink, and show them my new dress. I commented that I couldn't afford to get out of the car unnecessarily because it would wrinkle my dress. Bob suggested that we get a horse trailer so I could stand up, not wrinkle the dress, and stop by their house on the way. Horse trailers were quite common in the area, but we decided against it.

Bob and Peg came to see us one Fourth of July, after they had spent most of the day with one of their children. As we sat talking in the back yard, Bob complained that he had a headache and went into the bathroom. After a few minutes Robbie found him on the floor of the bathroom. Bob lost consciousness very quickly and never spoke again. He had a cerebral hemorrhage. Rob visited him every day in the hospital until he died about one month later. We continued to visit with his wife for many years in various areas of the country. They were dear friends.

Several months after Bob died, a priest friend from Montana came to visit us. To celebrate his visit we took him to the Christmas Tree Restaurant on Mount Rose. Bob's stroke and death were still very much on my mind. During dinner I became aware that my right leg was starting to feel cold and was getting numb. My mind raced to my storehouse of fears, which never seems far away. Desperate thoughts came tumbling into my head. "It must be a stroke. This is the beginning. This is how it happens. My leg is getting colder. It's getting numb! How much longer will I be able to speak? Well, at least there is a priest here. What will Robbie do if I tell him? Do I have time to tell him how much I love him? How will the restaurant staff handle it? How soon will it take before I lose consciousness?" Then suddenly the waiter was beside me with some napkins. My glass that held ice water had spontaneously cracked near the bottom and the cold water was soaking through the table to my leg. The waiter apologized profusely but I could hardly hear him because I was so caught up in my "near death experience."

The State Hospital was not all roses and light. Robbie spent the first two or three months getting "the lay of the land." It became evident that there were staff members who were more dedicated to serving themselves than serving the patients. The hospital internist resigned after his duties and his working hours were made specific. He had been negligent in both areas. His wife left her nursing position when he left. One of the staff psychiatrists lived in the San Francisco area and drove over each week to work three days and draw a salary for five. He left because he did not wish to accommodate to a five day schedule. Another psychiatrist who had been on the staff for years was terminated for being intoxicated while on duty. A few other staff members left simply because they found accountability difficult.

It soon became clear that Rob had made some enemies during the first six months of his administration. Rob and I went to the Cathedral for Mass on Easter Sunday, the year following our arrival in Reno. When we came out of Mass, we found that a flier had been placed on the windshields of all the cars in the church parking lot and on the surrounding streets. With large, bold print it was headed: "**NEVADA'S ESTEEMED ADULTERER.**" It called my Robbie a neo-Nazi, a fascist, a communist, a liar, a traitor. The page attacked his religion and the Catholic Church, totally condemning him and the Pope in the same breath. It questioned his credentials and his character.

We felt quite certain it was produced by disgruntled former staff. They had done their home work. They knew the date of Rob's Nevada divorce and probably the date of our California marriage. We had been living together from the time we arrived in Reno in September. Hardly an event to shock the good people of Nevada!

The letter was very disturbing. Rob served at the pleasure of the governor, and we wondered if he might be asked to resign. As we drove home from Mass, our minds were filled with the thoughts people are bound to have in such a situation. Each time you see someone you know, you think, "Does this person know about the letter? If they know, what do they think? If they don't know, how soon will they find out? And then what will they think?"

That afternoon Robbie called his boss, Dr. Otto Ravenholt, who lived in Las Vegas. After Rob read the letter to him over the phone, Otto's reply was, "I'll fly up there tonight". He came to the house and had dinner with us -- not the first or the last time he sort of "dropped in" near dinner time. But he was always welcome. The three of us talked for a long time. Otto always included me in his conversations with Rob. He respected me and my opinions. He often said that before he would hire a person on his staff he wanted to "meet the wife." He and Rob had a good relationship. We kept in touch for years.

Otto decided that Rob should meet him in Carson City at 11a.m. the next morning. The state legislature was in session. Of course, they had all received copies of the "Easter document." One of the Senators escorted Rob to the floor of a joint session of the legislature and introduced him to the members, stating that no one in Nevada is seen as perfect and no one can get away with maligning someone in such a public manner. They gave Rob a standing ovation! He felt like he was one of their own. Through our years in Nevada the members of the legislature came to respect the work that Robbie did at the hospital and in the state.

Before Rob left for Carson City that Monday morning, he went to the staff meeting he held at 9a.m. each weekday morning. Prior to the meeting, he gave Ted Reynolds, his business manager, a copy of the letter. At the end of the morning meeting, he asked the staff to stay to listen to the letter Ted would read. Then he left. No one on the staff ever addressed it with Rob, and it appeared that there was very little discussion of it in the hospital. Staff members proved themselves very loyal to Rob.

That Easter afternoon, we had a call from Monsignor Reginne, the rector at the Reno Cathedral. He said he had seen a copy of the letter, and without further comment he asked Robbie if we could attend Mass at the Cathedral the following Sunday. We did. During the sermon Father Reginne spoke about the letter, castigating those who had written it and supporting our privacy. It was a "who will cast the first stone" homily.

Things settled down well at the hospital after this incident. The attempted "Easter morning massacre" had failed and seemed to have been forgotten. Then one Sunday morning months later, Rob looked out our front window which faced the entrance to the hospital and the public road that passed by. He saw one of the staff going around picking up papers that had been scattered around the area. They were "leftover" copies of the "Easter letter." That was the last assault by the hate mongers.

Our only child, Laura, was born at the Catholic hospital in Reno. Her birth weight was less than 5lb.8oz, placing her officially in the premature group. When I knew I was pregnant we were fearful of another miscarriage. A gynecologist I consulted recommended that my cervix be sutured, and we agreed to it. We were blessed with a lovely, healthy daughter whom we have gratefully shared these many years.

I still remember standing at the nursery window a day or two after her birth to look once more at my baby. One of the nuns came by and stopped to talk to another woman standing at the window. I heard the nun say to her, "That's Doctor McAllister's baby." Her comment stirred some feelings in me. I was so happy I had **his** baby, but it was **my** baby too.

I have not yet mentioned my other children in our Reno years. They were never forgotten. I cried almost every day, no matter how good other things were at the time. I wrote to the girls, who were with their father as the court had ordered. He apparently never gave them the letters.

Then one day in the summer of 1968 I had a call from Tom. They were traveling through Reno, and he would let me see the girls for a short time. He would bring them to the house, and they could visit me in his presence. Robbie was not to be there. When they arrived, he let them come in but he would not let them come to me. He sat on the sofa with the girls, and I sat across the room. I was not allowed to hug them, kiss them, or hold them. It was a painful visit for me, and it unleashed new torrents of tears over their loss. Why did he bring them to visit? Surely not for my sake! Was it to torment me? Or was it to torment them?

Later I went back to court in Maryland and was successful in getting mandatory visitation rights with my daughters. I believe he treated them as pawns for his vengefulness rather than as cherished children. Tom had remarried before I did. He and his wife had her son from a prior marriage, my two daughters, and then three daughters of their own. During the course of the years they also took in welfare children to provide temporary shelter. All of this in a three bedroom house. My girls were relegated to a make-shift room in the attic. I believe that my leaving the girls was a very hurtful thing for them. I also am confident that had I stayed it would have been more destructive to us all. I am reluctant to try to assess what impact the years they spent with their father had on their lives.

During the last two or three years in Reno, the two girls visited us for a short time each summer. Rob's three younger children were sometimes there at the same time. It was a major expense for us to fly all of them out, but we always felt that it was money well spent. The time the two sets of children spent together helped some of them build relationships with one another that remain strong to the present day.

My son, Phil, who was in my custody, initially stayed with my mother. During the five years we lived in Reno he must have changed locations between our house and my mother's house four or five times. He graduated from high school in Sparks, Nevada, while living with us. As was true of many teenagers then and now, Phil courted a different life style. He was picked up three or four times by the police for curfew violations. After Phil left Reno and was on his own, he became heavily involved in the drug culture of the 70's.

During our years in Reno we began visiting Robbie's brother and sister-in-law, Don and Helen, on the ranch in Montana where Rob grew up. They visited us in Reno several times, and during later years they came to visit us each time we moved. They remained an integral part of our lives until their deaths in recent years. Helen and I became closely attached to each other. We had common interests such as sewing, art, religion, and two McAllister men.

During Rob's second year as Superintendent, the State Director of Mental Health and Mental Retardation resigned. Otto Ravenholt and Governor Laxalt asked Robbie to take on those duties in addition to those of Superintendent. This job greatly expanded his work and gave him responsibility for programs throughout the state, which primarily meant Las Vegas. This necessitated frequent trips to Las Vegas, and on most occasions I had the opportunity to go along. Although neither of us ever caught the "gambling bug," we both enjoyed the excellent entertainment by celebrity stars at the casinos in Vegas as well as in Reno and at Lake Tahoe.

During our initial time at the hospital about 50% of the hospitalized patients came from Las Vegas. There was no facility for mental health patients there and no treatment capability except for three or four private psychiatrists. Anyone who needed hospitalization and was committed for care was placed in the local jail waiting for the state van to take them to the State Hospital once a week. The trip from Las Vegas took about eight hours across Nevada desert. Patients arrived in handcuffs and shackles transported by the sheriff. It seemed quite primitive and punitive.

With Robbie's new responsibility for state wide service he decided to do something to change the most obvious problem. He wrote and submitted to the National Institute of Mental Health a funding grant for a Comprehensive Community Mental Health Center in Las Vegas. It was the first grant ever approved in any of the western states. I remember all of this well because I became involved when the plans for the center were discussed and developed with the architect. It was a thrill for me to be asked to participate in the design of the building as well as the surrounding landscaping.

Rob tells me that I should have been an architect. Everywhere we go, I am fascinated by the buildings and call his attention to them. I was also involved in choosing the furniture and the fixtures for the facility. We remained in Nevada long enough to visit the new center when it was operating with a full staff. The weekly transportation of patients from Las Vegas to Reno was no longer necessary.

The Reno area was a great place for picnicking, camping, and sight seeing. During our third summer, we had nothing to do one Sunday so we decided to go to a car show. We bought a new Chevrolet pick-up with a Sierra over-the-cab camper on it. We still talk about the fantastic price ($5,000), and each year makes the price more and more fantastic. We called the camper Tolivar. (When I lived in Richmond we went to see Roger Miller, and I won a door prize of his record with the song, "They called our love Tolivar.") On weekends we often camped at Mt. Rose, Pyramid Lake, or other nearby camp grounds.

One of our favorite places in the area was Virginia City. We often went to Mass there on Sundays. Before long we discovered that there were buried bricks in the area, left by the disintegration of the much larger town that existed there during the gold rush days. We decided to make a patio in our yard at the hospital. We used our pickup and brought down several hundred bricks we dug from the ground in Virginia City. Laura has on her piano a small statue of the Madonna and Child which we bought at the church in Virginia City.

I treasure that beginning of our family, but I also struggled with my own doubts and fears. Something I wrote during our stay there: *It is April 24th. On this day in 1966 if I had journaled, I would have written: "Tomorrow I will see Robbie. He will be here with me." I would not have known that on the next day, Tues April 25th, 1966, I would have my freedom after years of torture…it was the day my divorce was granted. Those things did happen, and I am glad still and grateful. My life since then has been good. It has not always been peaceful…certainly not always been serene…or without mistakes and losses…hard lessons…and pain. I am glad to be here where I am today and I will be glad to rest before another 38 years have passed.*

They didn't teach me how to be a family. Tom kept me from learning how to be a family. And lastly I defended my "no family" position and substituted a perfect, close, supportive, and rewarding relationship for family.

Now what? Here it is… family. I don't even feel left out. Now there are new beginnings for me. Without my being "family" yet needing to interact with those who are. I try to be clear. I try to let go. I try to be at peace, but today is different. What should I do?

It has little to do with blame and guilt. I want more than forgiveness.

I want to understand. I want to make amends without explaining. I don't understand everything yet. I am afraid still...why? I am having to let go of some things... I didn't expect to need to. I am sad...partly. It is hard. It takes work.

Mostly I look at my progress and I am pleased. But what is happening around me stirs things inside me.

Another reference to Reno: 3/21/90 *I wanted at once to close out life and to embrace the world outside my nest. The music from the doll maker brings back the sounds of the dulcimer...and Reno. How simple life was then. What made it so, especially since they were such hard times? Is it too easy now? Have I taken things for granted? Have I forgotten...God, have I changed? If only I could return to something of what it was then. Is that possible?*

The hospital was often in the news, more frequently good than bad. Nevada was an interesting state. Everyone felt they should have direct access to the governor, so individuals were not likely to approach the person directly in charge of a program. Rob was often in the news related to the mental health and mental retardation programs of the state. He made the news on one occasion which was rather unexpected.

Rob's oldest son, Bob, had married a girl in Maryland and decided to move to Reno with his wife and baby. Sometime after they arrived things were not going well in the marriage, and Bob moved in with us for awhile. His wife had kept the only set of keys to the car as well as the car and was unwilling to return them to him.

Rob and his son decided they would go over one evening and retrieve the car, which Bob needed to travel to work. They were waiting by the house when the wife drove up to park. Within no time a police car drove up behind her. An officer got out of the car and approached them. Rob explained the situation. Then he reached in the driver's window and tried to take the keys out of the dash. The officer pulled him away. Bob became angry and verbally defended his father. The officer and his partner arrested them both and took them to the Sparks jail.

Robbie had previously participated in several projects with the Sparks sheriff, Bob Galli, and had brought Galli to the hospital to be part of a public program on Adolescent Substance Abuse. Galli decided that the two "convicts" could be released on their own recognizance, if they each posted $100 bail. The police allowed Rob to leave the jail and come home for his check book so he could cash checks at the local Casino to raise the bail money. Obviously I was a bit shocked when Rob came home to get his check book and told me the story. If I had been in a more humorous mood, I should have asked him, "Is going to jail getting to be a habit for you?"

They were both released and returned home. Later that night, Bob walked to Sparks, hotwired his car, and brought it to our house. The next day the newspaper had an account of the arrest of the State Hospital Superintendent and his son. Charges were dropped, and that was the end of the matter. Bob went back to his wife, and divorce was postponed until years later.

Thinking about jail and the courts reminds me of Tom Craven, one of the four district judges in Reno. Early in our Nevada days, Rob testified in Judge Craven's court about some matter, and later the judge asked Rob to come down to the court to talk with him. Soon we became personal friends with both Tom and his wife, Margaret. We often visited them at their house and had long talks together. Rob became something of a confidante to Tom.

In the course of our friendship, Robbie told Tom about the circumstances of his departure from Maryland and his loss of everything in signing the "jailhouse documents." Tom was concerned about what he saw as a grave injustice. He suggested to Rob that he continue paying child support but stop paying alimony with the expectation that the former wife would get an attorney in Nevada and thus come under the jurisdiction of the Nevada court. Then the whole matter could be brought up for review. Robbie and I decided to take the recommended route. Anything was better than facing lifetime alimony with every check that was written reminding Rob of darker times. It took almost another ten years before the matter was fully resolved.

Paul Laxalt served as Governor for four years from 1967 to 1971. Governor Callahan was elected to serve in 1971. Rob's job was "at the pleasure of the governor." We had not been concerned, because Rob was there to do a job, did it well, and that was that. The new governor appointed a Director of Health and Welfare to fill the position that Otto Ravenholt had once held. The new director, Roger Trounday, was a man we both knew. He had been a member of a discussion group we attended in our parish. We had been friendly with him and his wife prior to his appointment to the governor's cabinet. After he began working in Carson City with the governor, we sensed a coldness in our contacts with him.

A few years prior to all of this, we had vacationed on the Oregon coast in our camper. I have always been fascinated by and in love with the ocean. This trip only increased my attachment. We camped for several days on a beach south of Tillamook.   I talked a lot about a house on the ocean; so on the way home we checked real estate signs for coastal property.

In Gold Beach we asked a realtor to show us a property in Nesika Beach, a few miles to the north. The property consisted of two lots sitting on a cliff above the ocean. There was a small house on the land side lot. A kitchen, a living room, two bedrooms, a bath and an attached garage. What more could we have wished for? The cost was $20,000. We did not have our check book, and we were low on cash. The realtor took a $20 deposit, and we signed the contract. When we got back to Reno two days later, we mailed a check as additional deposit money. The trip from our house to this "vacation home" took about nine hours, but we returned there two or three times each year.

I mention our house on the Oregon coast because that ocean property took on new importance in our minds, as we sensed a chill from the governor's office. Was this politics? Laxalt was a prominent Republican. (He later became a U.S. Senator and then Chairman of the Republican National Committee.) Callahan was a Democrat. Rob had been pretty chummy with Laxalt. I suppose it is not too unusual for a newly elected Governor to clean out the "spies" and "non-loyalists" from the camp, although Rob was not in either category.

Rob's service with the state was certainly beyond reproach. In fact, he had taken the hospital and the state program through a number of very positive steps. There was certainly nothing personal between Callahan and Rob or between Trounday and Rob. At least, nothing we knew about. All three were Catholic. Did that mean anything? It was over four years since the "Esteemed Adulterer" letter. Were they the kind of Catholics who would purge a "sinner" from the state rolls in order to enhance their own standing in the state polls? Not really too far fetched a consideration. Who knows what an Irish Catholic politician might do? Something seemed amiss but we didn't know what or why.

The front door of our house was about 50 yards from the front door of the hospital. One morning in September 1971, Rob walked over to his office at 8 a.m. as usual. As he entered the building, he greeted the switchboard operator. She mentioned that Roger Trounday from the governor's office came in at 5 a.m. that day and had asked her to get someone who was on duty to escort him around the hospital. He visited all the units, talked to staff, and left. Both he and Callahan said nothing to Rob about the visit, before or after.

Robbie and I discussed the situation frequently over the next few days. Rob did not want to work for a man he could not trust and who apparently did not trust him. We agreed that we should leave the hospital. Where to go? We thought Reno was a great place to live, great climate, close enough that San Francisco was a nice weekend trip, and most of all a wealth of wonderful friends. Based on his reputation, Rob surely could have had a successful private practice in Reno. But he had given his heart to the hospital, and he thought it would be better to move away.

Our vacation home beckoned. We decided to move to Oregon. Rob began at once to begin the process of getting a license there. We told only a few close friends of our plans. The annual dinner celebration for the staff, which Rob had inaugurated a few years earlier, was scheduled for mid-October. Paul Laxalt had graced us with his presence on prior occasions. Callahan was not invited.

At the end of that wonderful evening, Rob spoke to the staff, thanked them for their service and their friendship, and announced our leaving in one month. A great surge of denial went through the audience. Robbie wept, I wept, most of the people there wept. We spent hours talking privately with staff afterwards. It was terribly, terribly sad. Staff members sent us cards or brought over small gifts before we left. One couple made a beautiful quilted coverlet for Laura which she still treasures.

We did all the things that needed to be done. Rob sent a curt letter of resignation to the governor. There was never a reply from either him or his henchman. Rob never discussed our reasons for leaving with anyone except his business manager, Otto Ravenholt, and Tom Craven.

Our mover, Tony, came on schedule from Fortuna, California. He moved us a second time some years later. We kept in touch with Tony for many years. He even visited us in Maryland just a few years ago. We got to meet his wife and have breakfast with them during that visit. Our camper took us back to Oregon. As time passed Robbie often said, "If Laxalt had remained governor of Nevada, we'd probably still be in Reno."

In completing this chapter, it occurs to me that much of it is about Robbie. That is true because I was very much part of his work in Nevada, more so than in subsequent years when he returned to private practice. I look back at those years with a great deal of satisfaction. Reno was **our** life, **our** work, **our** story.

Chapter VI

The Oregon Trail
(1971-1976)

ROBBIE BEGAN TO TALK about leaving Reno not long after Governor Callahan took office. Although he hadn't met Callahan, Rob had some misgivings about the man and whether or not he would be content to work for him. In July 1971 on one of our trips to Nesika Beach, we talked about the possibility of moving to Grants Pass, a town in Oregon where we branched off Interstate 5 to head for the Oregon coast.

We decided to drive around Grants Pass a bit to look at houses. On one of the streets not far from the center of town, we saw a nice looking three story Victorian style house with a turret on the front corner. It was a good distance back from the sidewalk on a lovely street. I commented to Robbie that, if we ever decided to move there, I would like to have that house, which of course was not for sale at the time.

Later on Robbie contacted the Mental Health Clinic in Grants Pass and eventually agreed to work there 12 hours a week, beginning January 1, 1972. In September we took a quick trip to Grants Pass to find a house to buy. You might guess what happened. The house, Victorian style built in the early 1900's, that I had seen in July was now on the market, and we bought it.

We moved in just a few days before Thanksgiving. There was much to be done after Tony arrived with our furniture and belongings. We settled in as quickly as we could because Don and Helen came for Thanksgiving

71

in response to our invitation. They were always very supportive of us, and we enjoyed their visits. By Thanksgiving the kitchen was going full blast, and we had the holiday dinner with "all the trimmings." The only thing missing was some flour to thicken my turkey gravy, and Laura went to a neighbor to obtain that.

Our plan was for Rob to open a private practice. He had previously applied for and obtained his medical license in the state. We spent considerable time looking at available office space. The two of us began to discuss the pros and cons of buying a small house to use as an office. The realtor from whom we bought the Fourth Street house showed us a small four room house for sale on Seventh Street. It was zoned commercial and had two parking spaces off the street plus street parking. It was ideal. We agreed to buy it and wanted to get it as soon as possible so we could fix it up for an office. We signed the contract for the asking price.

There was one difficulty in completing a quick sale. The owners were living in Wyoming and could not get to the post office in their small town because of heavy winter snows. It might be three or four weeks before they could pick up the contract and get it back to us. The realtor assured us of their honesty and dependability. They agreed by telephone that they would sign the contract upon its arrival. In the meantime, we started working on the house, now to be an "office." We would soon have three mortgages to pay in the state of Oregon.

We spent much of our time over the next three or four weeks re-doing this house, which we did not yet officially own. We put in a new sink and toilet. There was a very small room which we used for supplies. The entrance room was fairly large and became the waiting room. The room that had been the kitchen became Rob's office. Appliances were removed and stored in an adjoining closet. Since we worked together on the project and Laura was too young to be home alone, she spent many hours sitting on the floor with coloring books as we repaired and scraped and cleaned and puttied and painted. We bought rugs and furniture and fixtures to complete our work. The office was ready to use by early January.

As the office preparation was going on, I spent as much time as I could spare making our home more comfortable and more attractive. Although I felt quite free in decorating our house in Reno and had enjoyed compliments from many of our visitors regarding the charm and warmth of that house, this was the first house that was really ours. I was thrilled! At last a home with Robbie and Laura! A home where I would be appreciated, where I could apply my decorating abilities and know that I would be supported, where I need not be afraid of someone's disdain or disapproval, where I did not have to give an accounting for every dime I spent. I had waited 42 years for this!

Robbie grew up on a ranch in Montana where the care of animals was always a priority and buildings were respected for their utilitarian benefit. In spite of this background and rustic heritage, he was always supportive of my decorator inclinations and artistic interests. As the years went on in our life together, he became not just an advocate but an enthusiastic participant in searching for antiques, discussing plans for house modifications, helping with picture framing and hanging, changing furniture, building shelves and book cases and cabinets, painting, and countless other things we did together to make our houses into warm, comfortable, attractive homes that others greatly admired.

Robbie was quite adept at house projects that required major changes. He installed or rerouted electric lines to accommodate our decisions to rearrange rooms. He did the same for plumbing access as we modified, moved, or installed new kitchen or bathroom fixtures. He tiled floors, counters, and walls. Together we took out walls and installed walls. We built decks and patios. We must have painted over 100 rooms in our years together. We have remodeled every house in which we ever lived, doing 90 percent of the work ourselves.

So the house in Grants Pass was the first of our grand house projects. In addition to some major remodeling, we bought a seven foot tall Gothic style church window from a local antique dealer, and we installed it in the kitchen area, replacing two stationary French doors. It was something of a show piece for the house. We also bought a number of antiques that became especially significant for us and have become part of our life story.

The elevated section of the roof was a flat area about seven feet square. Robbie built four sections of balustrade six feet long and two feet high. The two of us carried them up through the house into the attic and then through the opening that led to the roof. Rob put them together and then fastened them to the roof, so we had a widow's walk on our house.

I do go on about our houses and how much we worked on them and changed them. Sometimes I feel I can hardly help myself. Houses were always important to me. As a child I built houses for my dolls with boxes I collected from the trash. And then there was the doll house my father made for me and which my mother made me give away. Houses are more than buildings; they are treasures; they are part of my life, of our lives. They took on a life of their own, and as Rob and I restored them, repaired them, renewed them they seemed to become part of our very existence. It was never their monetary value that interested me. It was their windows and their doors and their stairs and all the little corners and built-ins that brought them distinction and special meaning. And when Rob and I modified them in response to my structural interests, his handyman talents, and our imagination and creativity, their value exceeded monetary worth.

Our houses enabled me to unleash my best creative talents in designing and decorating. They became a home for pictures and pieces of furniture and ornamental objects that I collected with the same enthusiasm I had exhibited as a child going through a neighbor's trash. I would often walk from room to room to look, to touch, to soak in the warmth, the love that was there. There was a story behind every picture, every mirror, every piece of furniture.

I think the houses and the changes we made in them gave Robbie an outlet for the manual skills he learned as a youngster growing up on the Montana ranch. Working on the houses became something of a hobby for him and brought him a great deal of personal satisfaction. He found his work as a psychiatrist very rewarding, but he often said that patient improvement was a slow and uncertain process. The work on houses gave tangible and timed results which he could both see and enjoy.

Rob's brother, Don, was occasionally present during some of our renovations and helped us with several projects. There was some reciprocity however. One Thanksgiving we drove from Grants Pass to visit Don and Helen in Montana. Robbie and Laura and I were sitting in their living room one afternoon talking with Don. Helen was in the kitchen preparing food for dinner. She could hear us but could not see us because of a partial wall separating the two rooms. I started talking about the possibility of taking a section of the wall out so the kitchen would be visible from the living room. Everyone joined in, and before long, all had agreed that it was the thing to do.

After dinner that evening, I got a small wrecking bar from Don's tools and asked again if they were firmly agreed that they wanted the wall out. After affirmative answers all around, I began knocking holes in the wall to seal the bargain we had made.

The following morning Don and Robbie went to the nearest lumber yard to buy material to begin the project. By the time we left to return to Grants Pass, a six foot section of wall had been removed. On a later visit, Robbie tiled the new kitchen counter Don built to accommodate the changes. We visited the ranch often through the years prior to Don's death in 2006. Helen died in 2002. Every time we visited, we would all agree that the project had been a wonderful improvement in the house.

We enjoyed living in Grants Pass. It was a quiet little town on the Rogue River in Southern Oregon about a two hour drive to our ocean property at Nesika Beach. Robbie eventually began consulting once a month at the Mental Health Clinic in Gold Beach, a few miles south of Nesika Beach. We enjoyed the beautiful Oregon coast from the 40 foot cliff above the ocean where our house sat. It was certainly a more relaxed life than we had experienced at the media sensitive, newly politicized State Hospital in Reno.

But all was not as perfect as perhaps I pretended it to be. Writings regarding that time: *In my mind there is an uncertainty that is affecting almost all or perhaps all of my actions, my reactions, my behavior, relationships, and most certainly my thinking.*

Such uncertainty makes me realize what I now struggle to put on paper and what seems to be hazily filling my thoughts these days….. Should I make a list of certainties, absolutes, things I know I am content with and wish to remain the same?

Rob---always first, always closest, all good, all loving . Laura---child of true love and hope of today and the future.

The "list" seems to end there. Why is that? All else drops off into that hazy area of………. I am happy with, because………. I could change if I have to………maybe 10 years from now.

January---these were the days when I was preparing to depart to Richmond, so many years ago. Sometimes, not often, I recall those first months in Richmond and remember the clear feeling of determination, the simple tasks and simple goals of each day and wish I could apply myself now in that same way. But I'm sure that there was a reason for that, and I thank God the rest of it is gone and I will not allow myself to recall it.

It isn't sadness, this state of mind, because I can truly say I am happy and have a good life. I'm hardly ever sad. If ever, it is because of my separation from my children, and of the separation and injustice that my dear Robbie has had to live with for so long.

At this moment I really wonder if our living for so long with the "not knowing," the unsettling "what will happen" feeling hasn't also dulled some of my feelings about life in general.

I miss a very strong, deep religious feeling. That is gone. My faith is a small candle which I light, with the whisper that I still believe, that I know I can still ask with the childlike belief that I am heard and will be answered.

I accept what I know to have been injustice. It stirs no deep, long smoldering hate in me. Thoughts of it come, are handled appropriately, and put away. Perhaps the closeness I have lately felt to my children disturbs me because I am cut off from it and will always be. But that's that and I can deal with it. That sadness, I accept and will live with.

I am deeply happy with Robbie. I want to hold my happiness and sureness up to him and to myself and enjoy it more than I have lately. I have no doubts about what I am—all—to him, and he the same to me. Perhaps with all our rooms and places we somehow don't have the right setting for it. I am more content than I ever was in Reno—secure, stable. Yet I feel uninspired by our lifestyle. Can that be? If so, I have to find it where we are, now, today and not waste another minute. So to work…where to start?

Just the answers don't tell the story that took years to evolve. Not just these people, but so many more were part of it, each with his own life full of cares and needs, directed by goals and standards, by learned feelings and behaviors. Yet there in the middle of it all I stood.

Robbie's practice did well. He was the only psychiatrist in Josephine County. There were four psychiatrists practicing in Medford, Oregon, about 30 miles to the south. We did get together with them and their wives on occasion. And "occasionally" was plenty. I've always thought that psychiatrists are an odd lot for the most part, and Rob agrees with me.

Robbie's practice included some legal work. He attended court hearings for patients who were scheduled to be admitted involuntarily to the State Hospital. Cave Junction, Oregon, had become a haven for persons of the 60's counter-culture leaving the Haitt-Ashbury district of California. Related to this influx, there were several gruesome murders in the area, and Rob was called to evaluate and testify in the trials. When he testified I would try to be present in the courtroom. I remember sitting at our kitchen table with Rob, a young woman accused of murdering her husband, and the woman's attorney. We came to our house to have coffee while we waited for the jury deliberation. We returned to the court house together and heard the verdict of "guilty."

We developed some strong friendships in Grants Pass which lasted for years. Some of these grew out of contacts through Laura who was attending the local grade school. We also visited with friends we knew from the clinic where Robbie consulted, with members of the medical profession, and with friends from church. I considered it a friendly small town where there were ready opportunities to meet people. One of the local antique dealers and his wife became friends and visited us at our beach house.

I joined the volunteer group at one of the two hospitals in town. I also went to meetings of the doctor's wives, although I must say that I never felt at ease with this group. They seemed very prone to gossip, to compete with one another, and to be rather snobby.

We became acquainted with some of the people in Gold Beach where we went to Sunday Mass when we were at the Nesika Beach house on weekends. Our house projects frequently brought us to the local Ace Hardware store where we met the owner. One Sunday when we saw him at church, he mentioned that he had a friend who was building a big house in town and moving in from a house a few miles up the coast. I've always been interested in seeing houses, and our friend offered to take us over to see the house that was being built.

The owner was there and told us that he and his wife were moving from a 15 acre costal property that had a house overlooking the ocean.

He arranged to show it to us. His father-in-law had given his daughter the acreage when she married. Access to the home site was on a private road across the father-in-law's land. The price was very reasonable. The down payment was small. We bought it. Now we had four mortgages in the state of Oregon.

This one story house at Ophir was a dream home built of Port Orford cedar, with radiant heating, two large fireplaces, five bedrooms and two baths extending down a corridor at right angle to the front of the house. There were picture windows across the south side and western front, so that the kitchen, the dining area, the living room, and two bedrooms looked out over the ocean.

The house sat on a hill with a sharp slope about 90 feet down to the water. The land had 540 feet of ocean frontage. Ophir Creek emptied into the ocean in that area. I say in that area because the tides would do amazing things to the mouth of the creek. As the sands shifted, the creek might at one time exit 100 yards to the south of where the direct outlet would normally be. At other times the shifting sands would carry the creek northward beyond our property line before it found its way to join Pacific waters.

We took a couple of walls out; we built cabinets; we painted all the rooms; we put in new appliances and fixtures; we made a brick patio by the carport overlooking the ocean and Ophir Creek. We called it our "Ranch House." Until we made the house habitable, we would stay at our Nesika Beach house when we came on weekends to work on it. It was such an ideal setting, so serene and peaceful, so removed from the stress of life that we began to think about eventually retiring there. In fact, we talked to Don and Helen about building another house on the property and retiring there with us. We went so far as to present a request to the necessary local agency and obtain a permit to build a second house.

At some point I remember seeing a boy in very "rural clothing," lunch bucket in hand, waiting along the road for a school bus. It suddenly dawned on me, "This place is not for my daughter." I decided that perhaps I had fallen under the spell of the Pacific waves, and the moving sands beneath me had shifted me too easily from east to west.

I must say that our Oregon ocean was the most beautiful ocean I have ever seen. The waves would crash against the rocks and throw water "sky-high." At Nesika the giant waves would throw big logs half way up the cliff by our house. The three of us would have fires on the beach and cook hotdogs and then marshmallows by the glowing embers. We would run and play and sing and dance like we were all children.

Several of our children visited us in Grants Pass. It was always good to take them to enjoy our ocean house and beach. My two girls came three or four summers. Phil visited us, bringing various girl friends. Two of Rob's sons visited us there.

It seemed to be an idyllic life. But life has it downturns and ours was in process. I mentioned that Robbie had discontinued alimony payments quite some time before we left Reno. It was done to try to force his ex-wife to come into the Nevada court with the intent to challenge the initial settlement agreement signed in a jail cell in Montgomery County, Maryland. Two or three years after we moved to Oregon, we got word from our Reno attorney that a court date for a hearing was scheduled.

We went to Reno for the hearing. The ex-wife came to court looking like she just got off the boat from some backwater country. If her garb was coached by her attorney, she almost overdid it. She was accompanied by Robbie's oldest daughter with whom our touchy relationship had grown less than warm.

The ex-wife's initial position in Maryland was that she was a distraught war bride, hardly able to speak English, with no training or education that would enable her to find employment in the United States, and about to be abandoned without funds by the man whom she had put through medical school. She had some difficulty maintaining the same stance in the Reno court except that she was able to look the part.

Robbie had put himself through medical school working at a number of different part time jobs. Her English was very good. She was working at a bank and had been for several years. When Rob left Maryland, they had three houses jointly owned, one the family home and two which were rented and managed by his wife. The three houses now belonged to her. The attorney who handled Robbie's Reno divorce testified that Robbie had agreed to have the Maryland agreement incorporated in the Reno divorce.

After the hearing, Robbie visited with his judge friend, Tom Craven. When Tom knew which district judge had heard the case, he told Rob that the judgment would be slow in coming and might take several months. The hearing judge was well known for his inability to make up

79

his mind and render a verdict. Actually it took almost two years before the judge rendered a judgment in favor of the ex-wife.

Alimony had not been paid for five or six years with accumulated interest and with the clock still running. The alimony originally set in Maryland would only terminate on her death or her highly unlikely remarriage. The current debt was, as I remember, close to $150,000. The court essentially had ignored the details of the jailhouse settlement and only examined whether or not that settlement was made a part of the Nevada divorce. The divorce papers Rob has from the Reno court show no mention of incorporating the Maryland settlement.

The decision was certainly a blow to both of us since we were still bitter over the treatment Robbie had received at the time he was leaving Maryland. It rekindled all the feelings that we initially had. We felt very strongly that the coercion he had experienced during his jail time required a fairer review. We went to see an attorney in Grants Pass. His assessment was not encouraging. He told us that it was possible that some day a truck could pull up at our residence and at Rob's office and with a court order begin loading our furniture. Needless to say, this was very disconcerting news, and it cast a shadow on the sense of freedom and security which we had been enjoying.

The verdict changed our thinking and our planning. We had four houses in Oregon and were deeply planted there. As the months went by, we became increasingly apprehensive. Robbie believed very strongly that his ex-wife would do whatever was necessary to "bring him to **her** justice" and would delight in the process. We began thinking about the possibility of leaving Oregon. Where to go? We considered Canada as well as other states. Robbie preferred to go to a state that had reciprocity with the National Board of Medical Examiners.

Going back east was not an option at this time because that would expose us to the ex-wife's claims, and there was still a contempt of court citation in Maryland based on unpaid alimony. We went to Montana during the Christmas holidays in 1975. On the return trip we delayed in Spokane to look at houses for sale. Before we left, we had put a down payment on a house on Spokane's South Hill.

This decision was undoubtedly driven by a growing apprehension that the ex-wife would sooner or later come for her "pound of flesh." We felt very vulnerable with the four houses in Oregon. It seemed reasonable to convert the property into cash which could be made less accessible. It is also possible that we had outgrown the small town atmosphere of Grant's Pass, and I'm sure the fog-bound winter months contributed to our readiness to leave. The clouds could settle in Grants Pass in the winter and stay for months. One winter we did not see the sun for over four months unless we drove up on one of the surrounding hills, and there it was.

On return to Grants Pass there was much to do. We planned to move to Spokane in June. We had houses to sell, an office to close, and other preparations to make. Fortunately all worked out well. Robbie gave notice of terminating his practice to his patients and the clinics where he was consulting.

Our best friends, Ken and Lola Dougherty, bought the house at Nesika Beach. Ken later sold the land side lot where the house was. Then he put a mobile home on the lot overlooking the ocean. This became their vacation home until a few years later when the bank gave way due to erosion from heavy rains, and the mobile home fell over the edge.

The office property was sold to the realtor who had been the agent when we purchased it. Her office was on adjoining property, and it provided a very workable arrangement for her. She was also the realtor for the Fourth Street house, which was only on the market a few weeks before selling at our asking price.

The large house at Ophir was a bit more problematic. There weren't many people looking for that expensive a house on the coast. One of the psychiatrists we knew in Medford, Oregon, had recently moved to Grants Pass and was beginning a practice there. His wife became interested in the Ophir property. They went to see the house two or three times. On one occasion, she insisted on lying down on the bed in our bedroom for a half hour or so to "get a better feel for the place." Her attachment to the property became a sort of love-hate relationship. She wanted it. She didn't want it.

When Robbie went to work one morning, he found a note on the windshield of his pick-up. The woman who wanted to buy the house, also wanted to buy our pick-up. Of course, the pick-up was not for sale. Next, she wanted to buy the house furnished just as it was. With some increase in price to compensate for the furnishings, we agreed. The papers were finally signed, but until the last minute we had been uncertain as to what would happen. It's probably the only house we wish we still had. But of course, it would have to be on the Maryland shore with the same amount of acreage.

We went to Spokane during spring vacation. While there, Robbie contacted the manager of an office building near Holy Family Hospital on the north side of town. He arranged with them to prepare an office space for him beginning in July of that year.

We got in touch with our mover, Tony, in California. He was not available for mid June, but he recommended a friend. Then we took up the final stages of packing all our belongings. We were becoming increasingly adept at this phase. We did our own packing in Richmond and at Rob's office in Maryland. That was lesson one. Then we packed for ourselves when we left Reno. Lesson number two. Now we had moved up to lesson number three, not even thinking at the time that there would be four more moves before we finished. We had over 200 boxes for this move. Robbie now says that the next move for each of us will require only one box.

We enjoyed our life in Oregon, especially the beach. We had some good solid friendships in Grants Pass and kept in touch with people there for many years. Some of them visited us in Spokane and later when we moved to Baltimore.

Laura was happy in the small grade school which seemed to have high standards. She had a wonderful teacher in kindergarten with whom she still maintains contact. Perhaps that teacher was an early inspiration for Laura choosing teaching as a profession. Before we left the area, I made a patch work skirt out of pieces from Laura's dresses and gave it to the teacher. Years later when Laura was married and had her first child, that teacher made a baby blanket out of the skirt and sent it to Laura. What goes around comes around!

Chapter VII

Frontier Justice
(1976-1985)

WE MOVED TO SPOKANE in the spring of 1976. We settled into our new home on South Hill rather quickly. It was a beautiful house with myrtle woodwork in the entrance hall, in the large living room with fireplace to the left and in the sizeable dinning room to the right. There was a myrtle wood staircase parallel to the entrance with a landing half way up and from the landing back stairs to the kitchen. I always wanted back stairs! What a joy! The living room and dinning room had myrtle beams across their ceilings. They were truly graceful. Robbie had a small office between the living room and the kitchen with a half-bath in the hallway.

As with all our houses we made several improvements and modifications during our stay. In the back of the house off the kitchen there was a small eating area and an exit along the side of it going out to the unattached garage. Rob and his brother, Don, enclosed that exit, making the eating area almost twice as large. They opened the wall on the other side and installed a three panel Pella French door, taking up nearly the entire wall. They built a deck with steps down to the yard.

Where the former exit had been, we put a Franklin stove which gave a warm and comforting touch to many of the evening meals that Laura and Robbie and I ate there over a nine year period. Later we installed a hot tub in the deck from where we could watch the snow fall in Spokane winters.

The second floor had a large master bedroom with adjoining sitting room, two other bedrooms and two bathrooms. Off one bedroom there was an enclosed porch with windows on three sides. It was a lovely room, and it became my sewing room and a focus for much of my creative work. Rob shared the room with me as he wrote his second book, "Living the Vows," published by Harper and Row in 1986.

The house had a finished basement with a large recreation room with fireplace, a laundry room, a full bathroom and a large shop with additional storage and closet space in the basement.

Soon after we arrived in Spokane, our realtor took us to meet the pastor at Sacred Heart Parish on South Hill. While we were visiting with him, he looked closely at Robbie and then asked him if he had attended St. Edward's seminary in Kenmore, Washington. Rob went there in 1941 but left in 1943 and joined the army. He would have been ordained as a priest had he stayed another year. The pastor, although several years younger than Rob, had been there at that same time.

Spokane was probably our most social time. We made a number of friends in the neighborhood and also in our parish. Laura went to Cataldo Grade School through eighth grade and then to Gonzaga High School. It is interesting that Rob's five older brothers had traveled from Montana to attend that same high school. At that time it had a residence on campus for out-of-state students, and it was for boys only.

Not long after our arrival, one of our neighbors, Trish, invited us to a dinner and auction at the local parish. It was an annual affair and an opportunity to meet new people. At some point during the evening festivities, Trish approached me and asked me if I had ever thought of modeling. Of course, I had not, and I was astonished that she would ask me. At the time, she was the fashion coordinator for the Nordstrom store in Spokane. I felt uncertain of my ability but said I would think about it. Robbie was very encouraging when we talked about it after we got home. I contacted Trish and said, "Yes."

Modeling was a challenge. Every time I faced the runway my heart was in my mouth, and I was sure I was going to turn into stone or maybe a pillar of salt. Most of the models were professionals, but they were friendly and helpful. I believe I was a quick study and soon was involved in all the "Nordy" fashion shows. I loved the clothes and the shoes.

Fashion had always been a keen interest of mine. If the reader recalls, I had wanted to go into fashion design in art school. I had made my own clothes for years and was keenly interested in what was happening in the fashion industry. Modeling was an exciting experience. Rob rarely was able to attend any of the shows because he was busy in the office, but he did get to some of the evening shows, especially the fur show before the Christmas holidays, which was a sumptuous and festive affair.

I enjoyed modeling in the window, although it was particularly tedious. Two or three of us would strike a pose like a mannequin and maintain it motionless for about 15 minutes. People would stop and we could see them wondering, "Is she real or is that a mannequin?" Then I would wink or move a finger slightly and watch their reaction.

Trish asked me if I would be a "Sally Brown" (a personal shopper) for the store during the holiday season. Helping customers find what they were looking for and helping them with their choices gave me personal contact and interaction with people which I enjoyed. And I certainly knew the store well since I shopped there regularly. I loved the Nordstrom store and have always felt a kinship and loyalty to the store since those days working for them.

Robbie and I became close friends with Pat Kennedy, the manager at Nordstrom, and his wife, Judy. I took long morning walks with Judy in the South Hill area where we both lived. At the time, Rob was teaching a course on the Psychology of Leadership at Gonzaga University in Spokane. He asked Pat Kennedy to give a lecture to the class each semester.

We had an interesting social life in Spokane. Our friends enjoyed our great Christmas parties, specializing in Rob's Southern Comfort punch. We invited a variety of people whom we liked and admired from our contact with them. And the Dougherty's with their two daughters would always come from Grants Pass and would stay with us for a few days. I miss those times, and they are fond memories for Rob and me.

We visited our banker and his wife at our house and at theirs. Their daughter was a classmate and good friend of Laura's. They had observed some of the structural modifications we had made at our home. The wife began talking about changes she wanted to make on the first floor of their house, changes which would involve taking a section of wall out adjoining their kitchen. She regularly mentioned it and had won her husband over to the idea. During a visit to their house we looked at the area that needed removal.

During our conversation, Robbie volunteered that the two of us would be willing to take the wall out for them so they could get the project underway. They were quite agreeable, so we decided on a Saturday when they would be away for the day, and we could go about our "demolition" project. On the appointed day, we arrived about eight a.m. with hammers, nail pullers, and wrecking bars. They left lunch for us. We worked throughout the day, and when they arrived home at about five in the afternoon, the wall was out, and we had even tidied up our mess. Of course, the electric cables and attached switches were hanging in mid-air, and there were rough studs and lathe exposed where our work ended. They seemed genuinely pleased with what we had done. The only problem, which we had no way of anticipating, was that the wife was apparently either a procrastinator or a very indecisive woman. When we moved from Spokane three years later, the wall was as we had left it.

We lived on Rockwood Boulevard, an attractive street with magnificent trees and beautiful homes. We had a half-circle driveway installed which made entrance and exit from our house much easier in the traffic. Rob and I built a wall of lava rock along the side walk extending from the entrance of the driveway to the exit. It was a major undertaking and rather hard work. Then we hauled excess dirt by wheelbarrow from our back yard to fill in the front yard back of the rock wall. In the end it was not only serviceable but it made the yard and house look much more attractive.

We often visited local antique stores. We never bought a lot of antiques, but I was always interested in them, and Robbie came more and more to share my interest as the years went by. We found an excellent store in Spokane, and on one visit, we had the opportunity to meet the parents of the young man who owned it. We "hit it off well" as they say, and the couple became two of our closest friends. We became favored customers in the store, not because of our spending but because of the personal bonds that developed.

Before long the owner would let us know when a "shipment" was coming in, and we could go down in the evening after it was unloaded and rummage through everything. The owner bought from sources in England and France. When his containers were unloaded it was a thrill for me to be the first to see things with the opportunity to buy, if desired. Since I've always felt that I was just a "steady ender" in life, waiting for my turn that never seemed to come, it was especially gratifying. We did find some unusual and very attractive pieces which we still cherish.

I volunteered to work with Hospice and went through the full training course. After working with two patients, I found that it was too overwhelming for me emotionally. I identified too closely with them, and my lifelong need to make things right for others plunged me into their private world. I met two women in the program and became close friends with them both. One was the wife of a Presbyterian minister who taught at one of the local colleges. Rob and I maintained contact with the latter couple for many years.

I had some rather extensive abdominal surgery while we lived in Spokane. Even the fact of the surgery is almost lost in my memory now. And the pain is long gone. It seems that we can remember having had pain, but it is rare that we can remember the pain itself. Even my written comments from the time only note the pain as an historical event. *Spokane March 79-----after surgery. I have before awakened to pain... which was not there as sleep swept over me and removed me. To discover myself... unbound from the boards which had held me, yet still unable to move my body. I was cold and alone, yet surrounded by people talking, making strange sounds, asking questions of me and those who with me inhabited this world of neither sleep nor wakefulness. The pain came slowly... but was held up in hands of fear to a place where it was all I could see. It was the loneliness, the knowledge that no one else knew what I felt, which was the real agony...as if I had been in and passed through another world, the memory of which clung to me and held me a prisoner... unable to return to the familiar and safe place which I had been in before sleep had been forced upon me.*

Several weeks later I was apparently still caught up in the experience of the previous surgery. *As I knelt in the yard digging up the plants, which grew as if destined to take over the entire world, my thoughts fled inside my own brain... now seeming sharper and more keen than usual. What if this was the "other" life... and where we were yet to go was what we thought we* lived today. *The ugliness of this world, the pain, the mental torture… surely this was death, and to live was just beyond us, and we would hopefully, upon being removed from this existence, know it and live it… perhaps for eternity. What then had I done to be punished so strongly here and now, and would I perhaps be denied traveling into the "hereafter" which I now concluded must be fulfillment and peace.*

Robbie and I traveled quite often from Spokane. He was a member of the summer faculty at St. John's University in Collegeville, Minnesota. He also gave lectures and workshops to a variety of religious groups in various parts of the country. We took Laura on some of these trips when she was not in school. The three of us went several times to a community of Benedictine nuns in southern California when Rob was doing workshops there. It was a wonderful opportunity for all of us to be touched by their warmth, their hospitality, and their love. Later on they contracted with Rob to come on a monthly basis to work with an internal evaluation committee. Rob would fly down Friday evening and come back home Sunday evening. I missed him each time, but it did provide some special times that Laura and I could be together.

The three of us also went to the Benedictine Convent in Atchison, Kansas, for several summer workshops that Robbie gave there. One evening, quite unexpectedly, Mother Theresa from Calcutta came to visit the Sisters. It was such a privilege for the three of us to hear her speak to the community. The following morning Rob was away, giving a lecture to a group of Benedictine monks at a neighboring college. As Laura and I were walking to our room, the Prioress called us over and introduced us to Mother Theresa. What a memorable moment! Mother Theresa asked Laura if she wanted to come to India someday. Laura's reply, "I don't think so."

Writing after one of our trips to Atchison: *The Sisters of Kansas: They are there in the grassy knolls below the porch, those virtuous nuns of Kansas— for all to remember. Why now does their vision come to me? I shall not join their number or their rest. Do they whisper to each other through their moss covered pine boxes? Are they aware of their sisters carried so young from the common attic room to the grassy field below? Are they bound together in their gift to Him… whom they have served and answered, their white coiffed heads, laid gently on pillows homespun covered, have long since lost their pale and become part of the verdant mound. I walk above them and ponder.*

On another occasion, Rob was scheduled to give a workshop for a community of Benedictine Sisters near Collegeville followed by a workshop for another community of Benedictines in St. Cloud, Minnesota. We decided to make a real trip out of it, so we took our camper and visited the Black Hills on the way. We traveled back through Canada on the transcontinental highway taking in Waterton Lakes National Park and Glacier National Park.

Robbie and I traveled to Miami on two or three occasions when he took some courses there to prepare for the Board of Neurology and Psychiatry examinations. Laura stayed in Spokane with friends. I recently found a note I had written on one of those trips. *(Miami Beach) First, I write postcards, nothing to tell, but I write.*

The water is so pale, blue, salty—familiar. The coffee shop is dark, so is the Danish.

Would I want to live here? I rolled the top of the white paper bag and stuffed it under the chaise lounge next to my shoes. Those miniature Danish would make a nice little snack later in the morning. The taste left in my mouth was familiar—cheese, pale, sweet—cheese pockets. That's what I should buy at home. I think that's my favorite—like lovers and friends...when you find a flavor you like why not always get the same...shopping around is a disappointment and one gets used up without reward.

Day after tomorrow we go home. Will I feel the same as when I left? Or has this really helped?

The bright brass trim around the booth reflects a band of my eyes...as I turn to look at people in the restaurant. See yourself...look outside, but see your self! I want to see the children. I miss them—a new feeling to deal with. Something is stirred—brought to the surface—recovered—a truth—a joy so long hidden... as if to be nonexistent. There is a swell of warmth.

Nothing has fallen apart ...no one has turned away or refused to be counted. Rather they stand—actors, now playing the roles they have accepted or been given. Their lines are said, or they just stand in silence like planted trees. Sometimes their shadows shade another, sometimes they touch. They have their own work to do on all that has happened. It is all right this way.

Soon after we arrived in Spokane, Rob contacted an attorney, Bob Crotty, who had been recommended to us. We were immediately impressed and had two or three sessions with him regarding Rob's legal situation. Crotty had some bad news at our last meeting. The firm he belonged to recently held a major meeting including attorneys from the firm's branch in Portland, Oregon. As they reviewed cases, they discovered that Rob's former wife had contacted their attorneys in Portland when we were still living in Oregon. It seems she was preparing for the move we had feared.

Because of a possible conflict of interest, Bob Crotty referred us to another lawyer in Spokane. Once more we went through the details of our story. It was an excellent referral because we again felt heard and understood. He was obviously knowledgeable, intensely interested in our situation, and determined to do his best to get a resolution of the matter. We were heartened by the relationship, lessening our disappointment in not being able to continue with Crotty. A few weeks after our last appointment with the new attorney, Rob picked up the morning newspaper one day and on the front page was an article reporting our attorney's sudden death from a heart attack. We mourned his loss in a very personal way.

Although we did not talk about it a great deal, I think Robbie and I both felt the threat that was constantly out there. After a few months, we contacted the office of the deceased attorney and went to see the associate who had taken over his cases. The appointment was a disappointment. He seemed poorly focused on the information we were giving him as he kept shuffling papers around on his desk. After we left we decided that he was not someone with whom we could feel comfortable or confident.

By then it was well over a year since we last spoke to Bob Crotty. We called and brought him up to date and asked for another referral. Since considerable time had elapsed, he checked with the senior partners about the possibility of taking our case back. They found that there had been no further activity in the Portland office from Rob's former wife. We were back in business with Crotty, who proved to be a very able advocate.

While on a visit to the District of Columbia for his firm, Crotty contacted Rob's former wife. He apparently encouraged the ex-wife to get an attorney in the State of Washington which she eventually did. Negotiations took months, and the case finally was taken to court. Crotty's took the position that the agreement reached under the duress of disingenuous imprisonment was "unconscionable." Rob agreed to pay the ex-wife something in the area of $5,000. On April 27, 1982 "the above-incaptioned case has been fully settled and compromised, and said action is dismissed with prejudice and without cost to either party."

Another area that could be considered to relate to justice came to a conclusion during our time in Spokane. This involved our relationship with the Catholic Church. We both had received spiritual counsel from a fairly conservative priest theologian prior to the time we left the East to go to Reno. After considerable thought and prayer, we both believed that our first marriages had not truly met the Church's criteria for a valid marriage. We took the position that if each of us in conscience believed this, then we could continue to receive the sacraments without a dispensation. It seemed that a dispensation would only confirm what we already knew to be true. We were living in a different environment in the West where we were not widely known and where no one knew the prior details of our lives. This avoided what some theologians might consider "scandal" to others.

We had a beloved pastor in Spokane to whom we confided our ecclesiastical situation. We let him know that we were not at odds with our present state. One day at his office, Robbie received a call from a Monsignor at the chancery office whom we knew casually. He asked if the two of us would like to request dispensations. We both agreed that we would. We filled out the necessary papers and gave the names of those who might be witnesses. Rob's brother, Don, and his wife were asked for information. I believe that persons from the Church contacted my former husband and Rob's former wife. I do not know what other information was gathered. Each of us received a letter from the Marriage Tribunal of the Spokane Diocese dated December 12, 1983 decreeing that each was "free to enter a new marriage in spite of the marriage previously contracted…"

Then we arranged our third wedding to each other! We had taken private vows in Richmond in April 1965. We had been married in Truckee, California on November 14, 1966 with our friends Jack and Mable in attendance. Now we were to be married in an equally quiet ceremony in St. Aloysius Church in Spokane, Washington on December

91

17, 1983. They say, "Three is a charm," but in this case each of the three was a charm.

The pastor had been transferred to Seattle prior to our annulments. He came to Spokane, and in the chapel at St. Al's on a Saturday evening he said a private Mass, and we said our wedding vows for a third time. Laura was our witness.

When we lived in Grants Pass several of our children visited at various times. I became very conscious of people learning that my children had not been growing up in our household. Of course, people knew we had been divorced, but they invariable made the assumption that the children always remain with the mother **unless she is an unfit mother.** I heard people say it in idle conversation. I saw people "thinking" it. It was a constant grief for me not to have my children with me, but to realize the attitude of the people we knew just seemed too much to bear. The true story was too long to be told and would only be considered "defensive." The people of Reno didn't have the same preconceived ideas as the people of Oregon. Renoites were more in touch with the realities and inequities of divorce proceedings.

When we decided to move to Spokane, Rob brought up the possibility of just not telling others about our past history. He wanted to shield me from the comments, looks, thoughts of others in regard to divorced mothers and their children. The plan seemed worth it at the time. So Laura became, in our new town, an only child. I wonder now if that was fair to her. I think perhaps not. Other children talked about their brothers and sisters, their families. It must have been difficult for her. It eventually became increasingly difficult for me.

My older daughter visited us a couple of days, and I tried to avoid introducing her to friends we met in town. Now I deeply regret the decision we made. My decision to leave the children goes on and on in my mind, and while I know it was the only choice I could have made to preserve my sanity and perhaps my life, it is a decision I live with every day of my life. We told some of our close friends before we left Spokane. By then they knew me well and would judge me for myself and not by some false standard based on a court decree. They were surprised but sympathetic to what our reasoning had been in not telling them sooner.

Robbie and I often talk about the events of our life, and we are of the belief that nothing in life occurs by chance. There were certain incidents which clearly shaped our future. The resolution of Rob's legal situation seemed monumental to us, and it was a tremendous relief to have it behind us.

By the time the legalities were disposed of, we had lived in Spokane nearly seven years. It was a nice sized town, a pleasant place to live. We had a lovely house with multiple improvements we had made through our own labor and money outlay. Robbie had a full practice, was teaching at Gonzaga, and was well respected by his colleagues. I was still working at Nordstrom, doing things I liked to do. We had good neighbors and lots of friends. We visited regularly with Don and Helen either at their house or ours. Life in the West had been good to me. I had been comfortable each place we lived. I adapted well. I enjoyed our friends. My life with Laura and Robbie had been fulfilling all those years.

I especially enjoyed the outdoors, the scenery of the West. Our camper provided us with great opportunities to explore and enjoy most of the western states. But we sold our camper before we moved to Spokane and limited our camping excursions. We did purchase a tent in Spokane and often went camping overnight on weekends. Rob used to tease me because when we went camping I would take some pictures to put on the walls of the tent, a small rug for the floor, one or two small statues, and other minor items to make it seem more homelike.

One day during a walk, Robbie said to me, "Do you ever think you would like to move back East?" I can't recall what my thoughts were nor can I even imagine the kinds of things that must have gone through my mind. The children must have been my first thought, to be near them, to see them more frequently. And Laura was thinking of college in the East, and she would be graduating in less than two years.

Suddenly Rob was presenting me with an alternative to the life style which had been familiar to us for the past 18 years. Whatever went through my mind initially became secondary to the lengthy and frequent conversations the two of us had about the prospect of such a major change. Certainly the legal settlement contributed to the possibility of returning to the East Coast, but I don't think it was the primary factor when Robbie raised the question with me. I think he knew that deep inside I yearned for closer ties with my children, my cousins, and with

Aunt Edith and Uncle Pete. We had visited all of them the summer of 1984 when we went east to look at colleges with Laura. I'm sure that trip stimulated our interest in returning.

Did I visit my mother during that summer trip? Yes, I did when we stayed overnight in a motel in Philadelphia on our way to visit Yale University. Phil was living with my mother at the time and brought her to see us at the motel. After the visit, even Laura commented on how little attention my mother paid to me. She focused her attention on Rob, who certainly did not encourage it in any way. It only served to renew my unpleasant memories of my past with her. I also was surprised at how little attention she gave to Laura. She must have known that this was a grandchild far beyond her grasp.

Another note written later: *I remember very clearly the last time my mother and I were in a restaurant together—Philadelphia---1984---the coffee shop of that hotel. Robbie and Laura and I were staying there overnight; and Phil brought her to our room. She behaved strangely but not unusually. She was engaging toward Robbie and for the most part ignored Laura, the grandchild she had not had a chance to beguile. Laura was 17 at the time. She noted, as did I, that my mother only spoke to me in a very superficial way. Today I wish for the first time that she were not dead. I wish that she could be "all right" again. I can't remember what she was like when she wasn't crazy.*

In early spring of 1985 we decided to move to the Baltimore-Washington area. By then we knew that Laura would be attending Georgetown University in Washington. She had been offered early acceptance on the basis of her grades and SAT scores, and this college was her first choice. Rob and I went east for a week to explore housing arrangements and to look at employment prospects. Rob accepted a position on the staff at Taylor Manor Hospital in Ellicott City. We bought a house in the Homeland area of Northern Baltimore.

When we returned to Spokane we began preparations for our departure. Our friends responded to our decision with affection and good wishes for our future. Telling the Kennedy's made my notification at Nordstrom a simple matter. Rob notified Gonzaga University and then informed each of his patients. Our beloved house was sold just a few days before we left town. Those last weeks were a very busy time for all of us. Some notes I wrote: *Goodbyes begin... and have been so many...mostly inside, unspoken. The sounds of old crying wash me to a level familiar. Loss again and again, but if not separate from the rest, then constant...a life time fixer...a life time placebo dream...unsolved, unsaved. Goodbye Spokane...I may never stand again in your hallowed place...this truly was and is a womb like surround...give it up echoes in my mind...give it up for always...put it in its place. All these places for putting things!*

In addition to all our preparations for departure, Laura was graduating from high school. I wonder if we were keenly aware of how painful this must have been for her to leave familiar surroundings, friends, the successes of her high school years. We had developed a natural response to her which may or may not have filled her needs. Whenever she came home at night, we were usually watching television, but we would turn off the TV and talk about her day and her evening. Did we get so busy at this time that we overlooked what was happening in her life and within her mind and her heart?

I often doubt myself when it comes to interactions with my children. I think this is a reflection of doubts I have about my own personal journey through childhood and my inability to bridge the gap that existed between me and my mother. In my immature thinking I possibly blamed myself for that chasm.

Within three weeks of Laura's graduation we were at last prepared to go. Tony once more became our mover. I felt relieved that "my things" were safe with him. Don and Helen came before we left. Don brought his pickup to take some of the things we were leaving behind. Our snow blower found a new home in the Montana winters.

We said our goodbyes to Don and Helen in front of our vacated house, and they left for Montana. With our three cars we formed a caravan heading east. Rob was in the lead, then Laura in the Volvo, and I followed. We had prepared our lunch with the plan to stop at a rest stop high in the mountains of the Continental Divide. When we arrived, Don and Helen were just about to leave the spot. They had stopped to have coffee and a cookie. As we said our goodbyes again, we felt the meeting was a positive omen for our long trek to Baltimore.

It was a generally good trip without any serious mishaps. We stopped four nights and arrived at our new home in Baltimore on the 4th of July, 1985. We had our personal reasons for celebration!

Chapter VIII

Eastward Ho!
(1985—1992)

I **LOVED OUR YEARS IN** the West and had been thrilled by the beauty of the western states. Reno introduced me to a whole new world of professional men and women whom I came to know personally and often with great mutual affection and respect. Our houses by the ocean in Oregon had only made me more attached to the sea. Spokane had become a comfortable living situation that invited permanence. But in spite of all this I had a deep yearning to return to the area where my children lived. It felt like each of them was attached in some way to my heart. I had never stopped praying to be more involved in their lives.

I certainly had no attachment to childhood memories, to Philadelphia, or to my mother. She was still alive at this time, but there was no pressing reason to see her. We had maintained minimal contact through the years—notes or cards or occasional phone calls when some relative died. She was still living in the house where I lived before I married my first husband. My son, Phil, and his girl friend were living with her, supposedly taking care of her. They may have made some effort to control her alcoholism, but they all had similar backgrounds. I don't remember going to see her after our return, nor was there any request on her part to see me.

The house we bought in Baltimore was "on the lakes" in the Homeland area. We moved in on the 4ᵗʰ of July and the heat of that summer convinced us that air conditioning was a necessity. It is rather surprising that it had never been done before. Through the years we made some other dramatic changes. We completely redid the kitchen; we repainted most of the house including the wood work; Rob created a wonderful sewing room for me on the third floor.

After we were there several years, my scavenger instincts paid off handsomely. One day I drove by a group of apartment houses where the wooden windows were being replaced with new double panes. I stopped and asked a worker if we could have some of the discarded windows. His reply, "How many do you want? Let me know and I'll deliver them." We enclosed a large screened back porch with about twenty of the windows, one above the other, each with six panes. We bought a French door at Home Depot and Rob installed that. It was now a lovely sun room with multiple window panes. I love windows!

We were in the house only two months before it was time for Laura to move into a dorm at Georgetown University. Although my memories for things are fading rapidly, I remember that day and the deep sadness I felt as we drove away from the college. It was a separation that has never been completely bridged during the many years that have followed. From past notes: *When I am left at home alone I can't stay long. I like it there... why can't I stay? Loss...I can't face losing her. I lost the three and all the years with Laura have been the process of losing her. Then I will leave her.*

Rob and I both looked forward to having increased contact with our children after our move to Baltimore. My three lived in the general area, and four of his were there. All the contacts were not as we might have wished them to be. My son, Philip, was still going through some very late "growing up pains," which led to some sharp conflicts. He divorced his first wife with whom he had a son. As years passed he gained some greater maturity, and after resolving some severely conflicted relationships of his own, he married the mother of his second child, a daughter.

My older daughter, Kathie, had married when we were still in Spokane, and I had not attended her wedding. My second daughter, Bonnie, married after we were living in Baltimore. Her father said he would not pay for her wedding if she invited both of us to the reception. I could go, but Rob could not. We went to the church only.

When my son married, his father again took the position that he would not help out with the wedding if we attended. My son's maturity came to the fore when he told his father that we would be invited whether he participated or not. At the reception, his father and I spoke, and I even danced with him once.

A note prior to the wedding: *Wednesday, 2/90. I could, after feeling upset for a while this afternoon, begin to separate and identify my feelings. I knew that I felt OK with what I had said to Philip, and I thought I had listened well to him and had reflected that to him. I told Phil my stipulations and also that if he couldn't ask us both to the wedding I would not be happy about that. I would be disappointed, but he should know now that it would not change things between him and me, that I would not do anything to hurt him.*

After we talked, I felt anxious, sad and quiet inside...not able to focus well. Then I was very angry at Tom...really angry. I expect the worst, and it is so familiar when dealing with him. As I continued to recognize the anger I began to realize that it was joined by old anger...a specific anger...of being kept from doing something by another person...another person causing me not to be able to go where I had been invited. I remember it well. I was so angry I cried, and I went to my room and stayed and hated my mother. It felt the same today. I cried then while driving. I felt soft and sad and helpless. At the same time I wanted to think it out. I have continued thinking now for hours.

Two years later I wrote: *Today a peace much made of joy came over me...even if I can't describe it, I will keep it where I can remember it. It's not happiness or even contentment which may possibly be carved above my ancient ashes...The world looked different. Is it possible that I don't fear what people decide to feel about me? Is this the place to stand and not be uncontrollably sad or afraid? I don't know. Maybe the glass in my "mind windows" needs to be changed...to what I don't know...How to do it? I'm not sure. I can pray and reason things out...I can talk, but only with a loving open mind...I can walk the steps.*

Fear comes first...now appearing...I pick it up...my drug of choice or one of them...worry, anxiety, fear. "Is it worth this to have a soul?"

We continued contact with Rob's oldest daughter and her family and also with his second son who was not yet married. Contact with his youngest daughter was problematic and eventually through the years was completely lost. She was married soon after we came to Baltimore. We were not invited to the wedding. I'm sure her mother would not have allowed it even if she considered asking us.

I always felt that neither of his daughters had any particular affection for me, and they seemed not to accept the reality that we had a daughter of our own. Perhaps Laura was the critical negative in their view. Rob's youngest son was a dentist in Maryland. We had no contact during our Baltimore years. We became alienated from him when we lived in Reno over an incident that involved my relationship with him. The separation remained a heart ache for both Rob and me, and as yet was not ready for healing.

Kathie had her first baby during our Baltimore time. After the birth: *"At moments I can barely center on the quiet of Kathie's baby…of the wholeness of Kathie now. I must decide to leave the heights of excitement and joy for the contact with the gift, the development, the continuation of life…the positive…and above all the miracle she is part of. My child with whom I talked while I was pregnant…who caused me such silent joy so many times, with whom I had the instinctive response of mother and child… is now beginning…now experiencing what she and I had…now for these months for the first time she knows and feels what I did. But for her it is hers, alone with her child.*

Sometime it will be Laura feeling these things…I pray I will be there… if it is to be and best that I am…I will be."

A few days later: *"Yesterday was real, I'm not sure I knew it then, but I do now. There we were… all together…the warming of the shirt…a message…the lesson of worry and fear and feeling that the end will always be death and all that surrounds it…a message. The first heals me…the second was learned to be the only response.*

I hate them. I wish I could remember happy times when I was in school. The first moment of wishing I could go back to some moment of innocence…that is long gone…I can hardly remember it. Childhood innocence…feels made up. Inside crying…after all these years of speaking out. I am not crying now for who I had or that they are gone…lost from me…for the first time it's for what

100

I was, for remembering that…for feeling it for the first time. I can feel her…I can see her in flashes of sweet contentment…mostly alone…mostly alone."

About eighteen months after we arrived in Baltimore, I was home alone one day and responded to our door bell with no thought of concern or gloom. A man handed me a paper and told me that it had to do with a lawsuit in the State of Washington. Prior to leaving Spokane, Rob had treated a Catholic priest who allegedly molested a number of young men after we left the area. Nineteen of them joined in a lawsuit naming Robbie and me as defendants along with sundry other individuals and institutions with which this priest had had some relationship. Fortunately Rob's malpractice insurance was intact, but the anxiety this created for both of us was considerable. The judge found in favor of Rob's petition for us to be dismissed from the case.

Soon after his arrival at Taylor Manor Hospital, Rob's second book was published: "Living the Vows, Emotional Conflicts of Celibate Religious," Harper & Row, 1986. The administration at the hospital decided to begin a special program for the psychiatric care of religion professionals. Rob was appointed the Director of the newly established Isaac Taylor Institute of Psychiatry and Religion.

In order to promote the Institute, major symposia were arranged over a period of several years. For me these were somewhat reminiscent of the many workshops we had hosted at the Nevada State Hospital 20 years earlier. Although in this case I was not involved in the arrangements, I participated in minor ways by attending the lectures and all of the social functions and sharing the role of host with Rob and other staff.

The most noteworthy participants in these symposia were Harriet Lerner, Ph.D. and M. Scott Peck, M.D. Harriet Lerner was a gracious, warm, brilliant woman with whom I seemed to form a personal bond at our first meeting. She was invited to participate in two of the symposia because of her national reputation and her excellent presentations. We have maintained some contact through the years. She sent us two of her children's books for our grandchildren, and she wrote an endorsement for Rob's last book: "Emotions, Mystery or Madness," Authorhouse, 2007.

My mother was dying in December 1988. Robbie and I were on our way to New York where he was attending a two day psychiatric conference. In my writings: *I wonder if this is one of those times when it* would be good to stop and look at where I am, where I have been, and what I have done. Some constants, not necessarily all, needing to be changed. Philip called again and said my mother was dying. I packed and closed my mind to any possibility of going to Philadelphia. I rode on the train to New York with Rob, searching the glass square in which the pictures of my childhood flew by.

After we arrived in New York, Robbie and I talked about my mother's impending death. I was thinking about the possibility of going to Philadelphia after all, and Rob encouraged me to do so. The next morning he went to Penn Station with me as I left to see my mother. On the train it seemed natural to write. *The only thing I can do this minute is write. It's like a cave in here. I hate the way it feels. The train will begin to move soon and I will feel a little differently. I don't want to cry. Sometimes when I write I do cry. I'll try to tell a story. The train is moving now. This is a new notebook. When I bought it I had no idea I would start it on the way to Philadelphia. Last night it was brisk and clear in the streets of New York. I wanted to fill myself with the Christmas windows and the lights. I slept quickly and soundly and dreamed unremembered dreams about my mother. When I get to Philadelphia I'll take a cab to the hospital and face what I need to face.*

I saw my mother before she died. She was unresponsive at the time. She died when I was in the room alone with her. Strange that the three grandchildren she was devoted to were all out of the room at that moment, and the only child she could never emotionally connect with was with her. *I have seen death. He stood beside me, telling me what to do. He did not reach down and stop her heart until I had done his bidding. I had gone there. He hadn't. I cleared my mind so that I thought she would reach out, that she would speak, although before I had thought she wouldn't. He took her heart in his hand and stilled it and took her with him. I had told her to let go, to sleep the sleep of peace. I know not of that peace or if she really let go, as I thought then she had. Maybe he just took her. He was ready. She sealed a bargain with him so long ago. He was to be the last of them--of her lovers. I felt then that we were all free. I walked in a cold trance as soon as she had left with him. The trance is over and so is the freedom. It would have been better for me if she had left altogether when my father did. It was the living through, the pacing, the doing good for the poor souls that was confusing—the coming home after each night of "leaving" time after time. She won't come home this time.*

On the way back to meet Robbie in New York: *I can't run this train. I decided to get on and now I've turned the rest over. I can sit with my face against the window—searching, remembering, digging with my eyes the spots in the ground where the weeds take life, the piles of leftovers from living. I can remember other trains...other lookings. While I wrote before, my mother continued her journey to her final letting go. She had no more experience with letting go than with dying. She breathed deeply...then lightly. Suddenly after hours of stillness she appeared to come awake, reach upward, and begin to speak...then stopped the shallow breathing altogether and let go. She let go and was gone and peaceful and still...still staring, only now nothing unpeaceful about her...anywhere.*

She had heard Philip say he was going to pray in the Chapel and leave the room. I'm sure of that. She let go and let go of him for the first time in his life. With one last triumphant victory she did finally give him life. It's what she had claimed to have done 35 years ago. He was finally born...a man free and very grown. I felt today as if only now I will be able to tell these three children of mine deeply heartfelt things. Why only now? What claim has she held on me? Strange that today the memory of those recent meetings comes pushing back. I know what I said and I know I meant it. I never thought today of saying, "I'm sorry." Why didn't I? I'm OK with that. If in fact she had to hear and understand it, that was not possible...nor would it have been for the past many years. Gratitude list: for deciding to go to Philadelphia, for the safe speedy trip, for being there for a few hours, for those three kids, for their honesty with me, for their not saying too much, for their reassurance, for their saying, "I'm glad we are together," Kathie; "I'm glad you decided yourself to come," Bonnie, "Don't question motives. I'm glad you're here." The sound of Phil's voice and words when I said I was at the 30th Street Station. For the love we gave each other and her.

*   *   *   *   *   *

We traveled a good deal during those years in Baltimore. We went to several annual meetings of the American Psychiatric Association in a variety of cities including San Francisco, Chicago, New Orleans, Miami,

Quebec, and Montreal. We also went to several summer workshops that Rob attended in Cape Cod.

Being in Cape Cod and waiting for Robbie at his meetings, I had lots of time to write. *7/16/90 Cape Cod. Yesterday was a joy. How I loved being in Chatham again! I would go there and stay for a month if I could. I could walk and write and read. How I wish I could have the Sea Ranch (in Oregon) now...right now in my life!*

Funny how we discover too late to do some things...then the chance has passed. We've wasted it or spoiled it. Oregon Beach was at the wrong time. Now I could live what it was of itself and what it could have been to me.

Yesterday lying by the pool, I thought, "I'll make my house just what I want... what I need it to be...just for myself...I should have the freedom to do that." Grants Pass was in a way a little what I wanted...but parts of it were so tight, so static.

Is it a waste to keep looking back? How old am I? And how long will I live? Will I write the book?

Tues. 7/17/90 Has this journal been a soft collection of worthlessness (so far)?

My emotional life is about me, no one else. I didn't know that before. Rob is the most important person in that life...but the life is about me...how I became what I am...what I am...what I do...how I feel...how I deal with others...with the world... and now what I will do next. He is part of all I do. I am the whole of it and he is my friend...my love, the source of my greatest joy of sharing and living with...

Pondering previous surgery: *March poem: I run up to death and allow myself to be saved, to return again to the awesome edge. Am I invited or is he...and by whose invitation do we meet? I am at once the dancer and the tune.*

Alone before the yellow numbered wall, fear joins our pair—and lengthens the moments of waiting. Now we are three, as though unnoticed.

The eyelet topped green towering sheets now called to the yellow band of wall...

As though to make comrades of those of us who lay between them waiting for our fate to beat again.

I reach up and choose a number from its yellow ground and hear it called above my ears.

They come to me and ask and tell...they leave for that hole beyond color...

They hear not my music nor know my dance or partner. Why have I stepped to this edge again? The return seems so unsure, and finally—I am afraid.

To follow March: I shall never have peace until I die. It wasn't meant to be that I ride the flow presented by the Author of Torture. Sometimes it comes to me clearly that there is a method and a way that I am unable to discover, to traverse this path to finality—and it is being just outside my reach or comprehension. I will wear myself to nothingness and therefore not be counted in the number of those who understood. This thought provides not an excuse that will in any way comfort me.

I take nothing with me but the self that came here...to walk through these days. I found neither an answer nor even a question that I can carry away with me.

Many things have harbored with me and I call to them to stay in thought and prayer. I had nothing in the start and have been pressed upon by many self-made artists.

After we had lived in Baltimore for several years I began to feel restless at times, uncertain of what I wanted to do or to be. I began at some point attending Alanon meetings. I think I was entitled to membership as a result of an alcoholic mother, first husband, son, and daughter. I developed several good friendships there and felt that I benefited from the exchanges. The meetings prompted me to do more journaling, and I would often find myself at some little coffee shop writing my notes which now seem rather random and uncertain.

11/15/90. I always think how will I look...get ready...do I hide the ugliness I feel behind this face I create. When I saw the bump in the center of the scar I couldn't hide, I felt devastated. It's my fault I know.

What has happened, what has changed, why now? I don't think I could ever survive being alone. I've always thought that. Why now do I run for help? I want to fix it. Maybe though it's a kind of honesty. I'm old. I'm not beautiful any more. Before I could and did attract people. I had some friends. It wasn't different because I still couldn't be alone and I certainly didn't love myself. The difference is now I am aware that I have nothing that people find attractive, and I have no friends.

To feel that I need to so something, to find something, when I don't know what it is or how to do it, is scary and I feel alone, but I'm not stuck. I'm just used to finding something to "fix it until I feel better" and I don't want to do that now. I can't really get up...I'm not down...I just can't get up.

I find that I wrote a good deal more than usual during the 1989-90 period. Some of this may have resulted from medical issues and surgeries that Rob and I both had. I needed a bladder suspension, so a second tummy tuck was included. *(1989) I can't remember where or when I bought this book with its world of little spaces. The page looks like I see my life. I've spent years trying to fit everything into such perfect spots. I've had the book a long time. Only now am I able to write in it. Now my world has for eight days been spun of drugs and sleep of half awareness, of acute observations, of loss, sadness, and of fear.*

All this I brought with my decision to again have surgery...to turn every part of myself over to another... to give up totally any control.

To write this much has tired me physically...but at last I am at ease with the process...As usual I wish I had started sooner.

I will put down things as they come to my mind and not care about the form or plan. Perhaps it will continue then to be easy. I will hope so.

This week there has been some time between an event and my thinking of it, as if playing it back with sound. The sound has been a story I have heard in my mind, not always in sequence but with a discovery and an acceptance of what I feel at the time. For the latter I am grateful.

Only now I notice these pages can be thrown away. What is written is not necessarily for all time. I am encouraged!

One day since surgery I saw myself as a child, in some situation that I felt I had never recalled before. I remember feeling the joy of discovering "why" about something. Now all that remains is what I have just written.

More hospital writings: *It was such a surprise to look up and see that red sign "Patients only beyond this point." Is that what it said? It was so clear that day when I passed under it and Robbie stayed ... with me beyond it. He didn't want to let go of me, I know that was it. No poetry about this day. It is a different fear I feel...and instead of being still and quiet like that other time...I talk and laugh...as my heart breaks. The thing that is the same...I am alone. That brings the tears...so close. The wall I lean against here while I wait...in this tiny benched cell...the wall I lean against is cold... My God this wall is yellow.*

As I waited to be admitted through the locked door of this unit I could see the doctors scrubbing and I knew that was where they were talking that other day when I lay waiting against the curtained wall for the number to be called. I thought I would never see these striped curtains again, and here they are making the fourth wall of this little cubicle...again I wait. Why do I wish it was then and not now? Do I again want to choose my fear? Or did I feel a possible escape or rescue from that and not from this? I know the sea and the light and the rough, hot sand wait for me, but I will never find peace in it again, until I resolve at least my feelings and my helplessness. I'm tired. I couldn't touch that wall last March. Now I can lean on it and feel it cool and supporting my back. I don't have a place I want to be and for now I am content to wait here hidden from the world.

The seal that gets the treats---after performing the trick. Return to hopelessness. I'm terribly afraid you won't be able to keep me---that I'm too sick or too late.........Which face do you see? It must be that one I prepare for you. I will not let you see the real me. My hands hurt. I'm glad. I will not forget. My head is wrapped in cheese cloth made of pain.

A note from 1990: *Am I at this moment God's child who made a decision using the right input? How will this change my life? Our lives?*

The helplessness of the past returns...the gestures... disgust of the nurse as I had my baby on the stretcher on the way to the delivery room. I was angry for a long time.

Kathie came to visit last evening and sat with us while we ate. We talked, she talked at great length. She is at once wise and gentle, funny, outrageous, and determined. At times I feel she was so damaged... my fear that she will not step clearly out of the past is great. Over and over I've said the same things to her. Should I stop doing that or find new words and continue?

The baseboard around this windowed room, which has been my week long home, fails under its many layers of sealing paint. It is not adequate and erect, as my cousin, Edie, would say. With time and renewed strength and agility I could relieve its symptoms, and, if not return it to its original state, at least retrieve it and give it pride again. Is the joy therein in my confidence in myself or in the "unlost" character of the baseboard?

As I turn and see in the mirror my yellowed face, my narrow, sunken, unlined eyes, head projecting from mountained shoulders, I celebrate the confidence and am grateful for the thought of it.

Several months after my medical problems were resolved, there came more threatening news. Rob's internist discovered a lump on rectal examination. There were appointments, tests, repeated examinations. Then the two of us met with the urologist, Dr. Busky, one Friday evening to get the final conclusions. Rob had Grade IV cancer of the prostate! Radiation, surgery, possibly both or just "live it out?"

For weeks I seemed to pour my heart out to my pages: *6/1/90. Another hospital, another carpeted and chaired square room...grim faces, only now do I hear piped music...the long wait.*

In the cafeteria I wonder how many of these same spaces I have shared over the years with fellow travelers. I should write all the time. Holy Family hundreds of times...Sacred Heart with Laura...last week I was at Holy Cross... next week it will be at GBMC.

12:20p.m. Again the waiting room...Rob's been gone with the nurse 45 minutes now. I keep wondering what he is feeling...is he sick to his stomach?

The mothers in this room are typical of the people of the world in which I live...I hate it...my stomach churns. What if I lost him? Wednesday it was all I could think of. Could this be the end I dreaded all these years? I am beginning recently to see clearly... us, we, me, him...the spaces...the bridge.

Thursday. I do not aspire to one great creation...discovery...accomplishment. I do not feel that I have inside me something that will someday burst out as in birth. This thought could relieve me of the frustration that it has not happened and may not, and all will be wasted... .

Friday. At 5p.m. we met with Dr. Busky. Later I hold Robbie, crying in my arms, and I slept.

Saturday. I cannot relate to anything as I usually do...I am strong and unafraid now, but stoic, still. Love is strong and brave...again I am under the sky light...the mottled gray table becomes my desk...my altar...my altar indeed...to pray...to protest.

Why must the beginning and the end be so painful? We paid in advance for our joy, and now another bill? No guarantee. The tears well up and return to the hot, lonely place inside me. The questions Robbie asked me were astounding...should we hold some ten years of happiness and affection tightly and forget this growing death...put it aside...and live for what we are sure of now...or should he go ahead and do the job and take the security of having acted rightly and take what follows?

I will not be angry at myself or regret anything I failed to do...or did stupidly or half way. I am here at this moment in the leather seated, armed waiting room chair again and will return to it many times. Today, I will cut the vow into paper...and try...try to keep the promise to self.

After a visit with Kathie: *Thurs. 6/26/90. Holding this precious new child close to me is so simple, such a joy. I feel love and tenderness pour between us. When I am with Kathie and her baby, Grace, I only think of*

109

the three of us mostly, yet I can talk about other things. It just seems to warm me and I feel relaxed.

Thurs. 7/12/90. I dream about the surgery now. Yesterday was the most anxious day so far...maybe not the saddest. But I was beside myself...almost truly...I didn't have a sense of direction... or time...or appropriateness. I have to find a way to calm myself.

Wed. 8/1/90. Still another waiting room. The color of the day is dark... from Rob's mood. And it covers me. I won't let it fill me. It does though make me wonder what my surface feelings cover. I feel that our life will never be the same. That is real. I can't know how it will be. Where will I stand now? Maybe that's why I cover all this over and refuse (or am I not able) to let go and let my reactions come to the surface.

I can't affect his feelings, and I can't wish to change them. I have to stay put where I am and live today and then tomorrow.

It is painful to me to be held... as in other times...as an observer of his low and dark self. I heard all that he heard at five o'clock that Friday. Am I hiding something from myself?

Tues. 8/7/90. 7:30 p.m. Another need to compromise... to let go of what I had planned and decided to do. Dr. Busky asked me to stay home tomorrow and I agreed, because he said it was better for him. So I'll be here at 6:30 a.m. and see Robbie, then go home to wait. It is as though I've turned onto a different path. It's a familiar feeling. It is here... and I am unaware of it.

I am tired. I deny it but I am. I hate the odor in the halls. It reminds me of my mother's bathroom, especially in the basement...like a nursing home... pungent...junky stuff. I've never smelled it in a hospital before. I'd like to go home now, but I can't.

Wed. 8/8/90. 3:30 in the gray afternoon. It's over. It's over.

This time it's over. I felt so strongly that he would be all right, and then at noon I got dressed to come here and then I was nervous. After Dr. Busky called, I was here in 10 minutes. I could no longer wait. Rob is asleep downstairs... down the hall we walked for all those tests. I forgot that. I walked to those doors...only this morning... that they took him through... and kept me there in that very hall.

Now the breathing, that is second only to my own, fills the room...the pace beats its rhythm and lulls me as I assume the rest of having lived through and past the fear of losing him.

Today I do not know for sure what I believed would happen. It was a working, living job of being full of sadness and fear. Those things are suddenly behind me and I am empty without them...strange to be empty after such fullness. Relief does not express it.

Thursday. Cafeteria... I got up at six...don't know why. It's as if the rules of the game...the pattern of life...the tide...the players are all off...or tilted... not in a bad way...just mildly disconcerting. I almost went into the gift shop and bought a coloring book for myself. I am busy in my mind. Usually I see things that inspire me, interest me, make me want to create. Right now it's as if the power is turned on low. I see and react but do not move into the usual process.

He sleeps...at first I stared a lot...now I am tired...I don't rest well these days.

Time is here, a mass, a shape to be lived---we say "spent."

The pain of friendlessness enters again unexpectedly...I haven't needed or wanted a "someone"...I will stand against that old need...the cultivation.

Maybe it's not being called upon to give, to rise to the expectations of myself that is necessary when standing hand in hand with a friend. "When the best in me touches the best in you."

To be called friend by one whose face I look forward to seeing ...to go to the trouble...to say yes...yes I will...yes I can...come with me my friend... and at the same sound to hear the call, the invitation to togetherness...a land of finding...an association...a loyal faithfulness.

It would be too difficult to try again. I may settle for not listing the failures, the losses.

Just think, I will be alone, totally without anyone. I will sit like this, my feet planted squarely on the hard floor. If I'm lucky I'll look out of a nearby window then as I do now...and I'll write...what will be left...I'll probably still make lists...and put little slips between magazine pages. I am tired now.

Be careful when you reach out to touch me...How will your prints affect my path?

We come into and leave this world alone...the hardest acts for which we are first time actors and for all acts in between, there are those who would have us "do it their way."

Rob remained in the hospital over what became a very long weekend for me. During the hours at home I kept myself company by writing. *Saturday: Aloneness is something I think about a lot...and must write about when it comes into my mind...although it is not in my mind that I have knowledge of it.*

Besides my own aloneness I feel someone else's deeply. I never thought of that in such simple terms. I almost cannot abide another's aloneness...their loss... lack of recognition...I truly ache from that.

Our life together is different from anyone else's I know. He was all I didn't know existed...he gave me love and contentment and security and warmth... He was my hero. I finally began overcoming the behaviors I was responsible for...the "problem causingness," and, in my sickness, I continued to be a foil for some of his...the circle turned and was always complete.

It is true that there is no complete happiness...the spoiler is myself more often than someone else...I know so well the perfect plan.

The outcome of Rob's surgery was positive, and he was eventually restored to full activity and health. He continues to see Dr. Busky on a yearly basis without evidence of recurrence.

Rob taught in the Pastoral Counseling Department of Loyola College from 1985 until 2007. Father Joseph Heim of the Maryknoll Fathers was in Rob's class in 1985-86. A few years later when Joe returned to his life long work in the Venezuela missions, he asked Rob if he would come to Venezuela as a consultant to his work. We had the wonderful opportunity to visit Joe there on four or five occasions. On one trip, we stayed with Joe in his very humble and primitive quarters in the barrio in Barinas. These were truly life-altering trips for both of us, and we remain indebted to Joe for giving us a view of life in "the third world."

Looking back in my mind and in my notes, I find that Laura was very much in my thoughts during the years in Baltimore. She was so much the product of our love, and she had been an integral part of our life as a threesome. She graduated from Georgetown in 1989. She remained in the D.C. area, and her life continued to be her own as she had claimed it during those college years. She decided to study primary education and obtained her M.A. from George Washington University. Not long after completing college she became engaged to one of her Georgetown classmates.

Notes for Laura: *Wed. 2/19/92. It's just a coincidence that my last entry is about Laura moving to New Jersey. She and I just talked...it's 10a.m. This morning she acts out her decision to go to the rehab and sign herself in.*

This space I am suspended in is guarded by an unfamiliar air. At once I want to stay and not too strongly want to reach back...out of it...to reality...not sure where I want to be. In this book I am safe and more than that am "with myself"...no poetry now...life is real...even here... suspended by my need to hold tight until I can see where to stand.

Where is that...that place for standing? I have yelled God's name this morning when I knew that it was all I could say and needed to say.

Is it possible I can be feeling a sense of freedom? I think I should have to earn that...see...it is a thing "I have to earn"...and have found myself unworthy of.

There is a place beyond tears...I'm not sure I've ever been before.

For a moment I stepped there and said out loud...she got me where I wanted to be...now the other words I said are back there where I am not...I know the feeling of having said them. "She was the one always." No one can relieve me of the remaining knowledge. I left the others for what I needed to do...

so we were a team. "I'm not to blame" may be unreachable from here...I don't know.

I am not separated in any way from what Laura has become. I was there in the beginning...set the path...taught the beat...sang the song of marching... led...criticized the carrying out. I stood tall above her and said...this is the right way...my way...the only way....

Notes about Laura keep showing up in my journal during those seven years in Baltimore. These are separated by unknown bits of time in the writing.

No writing of Laura can tell of her...I am again full of her, only now she is separate and complete. What I see in her face is food for my very soul. She said she was proud of me and that she was glad I had the surgery and that I had done such a good job of all this. For the first time I was really comfortable with her, as if I didn't have to wonder if she was comfortable with me. There is a deep contentment inside me. I am grateful for that.

Laura is a dear, strong, honest, loving person, daughter, mother, friend. Laura is my daughter...our daughter of LOVE. That love existed...was present in our relationship with her father and me long before we gave birth to her. Strong words, yes...true, from our hearts, part of our life and loving... inspiration for both of us? Yes! Yes!

Laura: I cannot give you the doll house my father made for me or the doll he got me in Atlantic City. Here are the white gloves I wore the day your father and I were married, and the white beaded bag he bought me for the Governor's Ball in Carson City.

Dear Laura: If anything that I have given you or that was once mine gets lost or something like "lost," I know you will be sad. I do want you to remember that I know how that feels. I do want to tell you though that I think part of letting go, so not to torture ourselves, is to remember how lovely our "being with each other is."

"Being with" is wide and deep and many faceted and more, much more, than being together, as wonderful as that is.

At times I have been tempted to write some kind of a freedom or letting you go letter—as if I could or should do that for you. Now I have come to believe that one person can't do that for another, that you have already done much of that, and that we have gone beyond needing to do that.

Change for us, I think at least for me, includes the things of the past as it was, because I have worked at that and continue to look at it in as honest a way as I can. And then it is today and how grateful I am for where we are with each other.

Perhaps there are no endings, because nothing is ever really over but carries on in some small or great way through another time---influencing all and every thing—the nature of its way.

She has not lived in our home for 6 years. She has all that time lived in my mind and my heart. I stay at the kitchen table wishing she would come through the door and sit beside me. Wishes take the space of prayers. Holding on fills the space of letting go and takes as much energy and negative strength.

Laura called. She has been responsible. She has grown grand. My heart is truly sad...amid my children's celebration comes the crooked devil's finger from the past...pointing...then joining others to form a clasp upon my heart. I am held still, now calm but sullen and somewhat resigned. She said she knew about broken things. I wanted to hold her and tell her it was all right. I couldn't and knew I shouldn't.

When did the true important talking end, and was I so anxious for the bad parts to stop that I did the talking of things unimportant.

Sad is sad, not death. Angry is angry, not death. They are feelings.

I will not be deserted for feeling them...sadness, anger. I do not need to feel guilty for being sad or angry. It is acceptable when I am sad... to acknowledge that, especially to myself. Going to meet Laura and spend another day with her. It's to help her sort and pack. It's to be with her. It's to be with each other, I know. Tears are just behind my painted eyes. I am not sad because she is moving. I am touched because we are so close and I will miss her more than I can tell anybody.

*   *   *   *   *   *

Sometime in late 1991, Rob first brought up the possibility of moving to Maine. We had been there on a brief vacation the year before. Why did he suggest moving? Why did he suggest Maine? He talked of retiring or at least partially retiring. I don't think he was tired of working or disenchanted with his job at Taylor Manor. I don't think he knows why he got started on the idea. Whatever his reasoning was or might have been, as usual I bought into the idea quite readily and hid my lack of enthusiasm from him and everyone else.

We traveled to Maine in the early spring of 1992 and bought a house on the St.George River across from Friendship. Rob also contacted the Midcoast Mental Health Clinic in Rockland and signed up to work half time there. On return Rob gave notice of his plans to Taylor Manor Hospital and to Loyola College.

Several of my writings suggest the secret struggle I was having with the pending move. *Mon. 6/29/92 Only now the recollection of June dates...41 years...longer than my children's lives...when I get still and quiet and allow the seeping of energy...the escape of gratitude and excitement... then today for the first time...I am worried...guilt accompanies fear. Perhaps I should have been the "warner"... to say "not now...let's not do this." I don't know today if it will work...at once I want to be gone and for one brief minute I wanted not to be going...the latter thought passed...and I accepted.*

Thurs. 7/9/92 Rob will leave his office soon...fly to Maine. As I knelt in my closet...large skirt box before me...panic struck...where will I keep this next? I can't FAKE that. The magazines can go...the picture frames...the furniture, the pots and scarves...but the jewelry...how will I handle that?

There is no poetry in this...no words.

In the bagel shop: *Fri. 7/25/92 This is a habit...twice this week... something else to miss but for now, something to hold on to. I have followed this very pattern through every move...attach now...hold tight...the entire time I am looking at my life and all that has filled it and shaped it. The framers reappear…speak their lines…hold forth on the policies and what is to them the unconditional truth.*

They visit me less frequently these days…more likely…I have called them up less often. I am more whole…alone…. Music sounds outside my head and matters little.

An ambulance passing. The hordes of flashing lights atop the wagons of doom evoke my familiar prayer whispered for strangers, but inspire a rerouting, not a frantic escape.

I like to be here and regret having to leave this place._

We gave several precious pieces of furniture to a consignment shop along with countless "smalls," as our antique dealer friend used to call them. We packed, we said our goodbyes, and we left for Maine. Rob talked about it as if it were to be part time retirement. Thank God it did not become that.

Chapter IX

Retirement Route

Phase 1—MAINE
(1992—1993)

Although we had talked like Maine would be the beginning of the road to retirement, I had no idea that the road would stretch as far as it did. Rob was to continue working another 13 years before he finally ended his medical career and thus completed what was started when we made this move.

Sometimes I think of our move to Maine as a romantic but foolhardy venture. Rob seemed compelled to make this move. I was the "good wife." I played the role because it was my role. I think his enthusiasm for things has always carried me along in difficult times. I see him as thoughtful and wise. Written before our move: *Moving is much on my mind...it fills a space...no it "takes me away"...I need that. I hate these houses...this tight common development...where will we be next?*

I won't see my kids for a long time. There is a sadness in that...but also excitement. There has always been that. To start again begins with a feeling of "another chance"...always ends up the same. It's very hard ...looking back it was always the right thing for us. This time I haven't come to believe that totally, or that it will join the other moves and be the same.

Adjusting to Maine certainly had its difficulties. There is a story about a family moving from Connecticut to Friendship, Maine, just across the St. George River from our new home. When they made the move, they had a three year old son. The boy grew to manhood in Friendship, became quite successful in his profession, was prominent in the community, and donated a good portion of his accumulated wealth to local charitable causes. When he died at age 90, the local newspaper printed the headline, "Connecticut Man Dies in Maine." I had the distinct feeling an outsider remains an outsider.

Our new home was an extremely attractive post and beam house, something we had never seen before. We both fell in love with the house when we first saw it. My delight in the house was, I believe, a major moving force for Rob in the purchase of it.

True to form we did make a number of improvements in the house. We installed a large wood burning stove in the basement to supplement the propane furnace and later a smaller stove for the upstairs master bedroom. Rob finished off a small second floor room and made it into a walk-in closet. We decorated, hung pictures and mirrors throughout the house, and found suitable spots for all the furniture we brought with us.

We moved to Maine in August of 1992. A major event in our life took place in late November of that same year when Laura married Brian McConville in Baltimore. All the preparations had been made prior to our move so there was no unusual involvement for us. We drove back to Baltimore and stayed with our good friends, Morris and Priscilla Scherr, who were guests at the wedding. The event was all that any of us could have dreamed of, "a beautiful wedding." One should remember that beautiful weddings don't always become beautiful marriages.

Robbie worked half time at the local Mental Health Clinic. When he was at the clinic I attended some AA meetings in Rockland. There were no Alanon meetings in the area. I would browse in some of the local shops, but since I was no longer a tourist, the greeting and service no longer seemed as cordial. I would often sit in one of the small coffee houses and write. Looking back at a number of pages from those days I am struck by their somber tone. I certainly grieved for what we had left behind in Baltimore. *Our final summer in that house! We had made it a dream house as we did with all of them, and then we moved away. Our only bad decision in our life together!*

As I sit and wait for him I feel the pain, the ache of leaving the house we had created into home. The things we left behind...but mostly our family...our dear children. We turned away from them and closed all the doors...cut the ties...and moved alone into the wilderness on the edge of the world.

We took long walks in the woods and along the river or the ocean. We went to the state park overlooking Camden where Edna St. Vincent Millay found inspiration for much of her poetry. When winter came we invested in equipment for cross country skiing, and we made the most of the winter snows. We never seemed to acquire the rhythm in our life that has always been so natural for us.

For me, all was not well. I wasn't happy there. I felt a deep sadness for the children. Maine seemed so inhospitable. We had no close neighbors. The AA meetings only made me miss more desperately my friends from the Alanon meetings in Baltimore. Rob was very attentive, and I was aware that he was putting a great deal of effort into helping me accommodate.

In a note to a friend in Baltimore: *Lately I have been beset by the deepening awareness that my spirit has gotten lower and lower. All the world has been continuing to learn and grow and stand and be counted while I've been working on living, just pretty much living. Here I am—alone with Jane. I've changed, grown, learned. I have to get on with it. Living is all right. I am me, wholly, not anybody else at all. Are you by yourself? Yes, I certainly am!*

If only I could be where I began to grow old. That's what all these folks look like they've done!

In December I wrote to my friend again: *The sermon this morning was about acceptance and well said, ending with the serenity prayer. The pastor said things as if he knew my heart, and I will hold those things and be grateful.*

Tears have not come. I have acknowledged only to myself that I am terribly lonely.

Rob seemed content. He kept busy with the house and work at the clinic. He always adjusts better than I do. I sank lower into the pit of loneliness through the fall and winter months. My writings began to show the current of my thinking, which I did not reveal to Robbie.

Feb 3ʳᵈ,1993 For over an hour now I've watched the river as if it weren't there and I wasn't here. I can let myself disappear into space which becomes empty while seeing. The view is doubled. The candle holder rattles as I write. It distracts me—a rush of hate swells and recalls an old feeling—"matter less"—"matter less." What difference does it make? Moved onto the place mat it becomes silent. I have only myself now. I will not care if what I write is trite and unimportant. I can tear out this page.

If only I could tear out pages from my head—actions of 40 years ago would be among the first to go—without confidence I would be frozen.

3/11 It won't be easy to put four years on the shelf, but I now believe that's what I have to do—the pages finished—my comfortable companion—leave it—then take it to a safe place where you can find it. So seldom has my thought-voice been with me for anything but to torment me—isolated, passing torture—not poetry, not joyous prayers. The past, ever present, has been for me to reach to and hold near myself and at times relate with pride for remembering—perhaps a safe shelf must be found for its harbor. God, a water theme! How can I? Stranger-water stay away! Still I want not to be here. I wake as someone else—the litanies of fears grow more.

4/17 I have endured disaster by the hands of others and of my own. I should have broken into a melted heap. I cried and stood weakened by my reaction—fear turned into myself over and over.

I've done it all before—left behind all dear and familiar—lived in fear and hate—not in love with love or with myself—loving hard and feeling unworthy.

Oh God, how much a part ugliness has played in all this.

Don't sound like that! Care, care, feel and care and cry—all that is all right.

What was right and what wrong. I miss the innocence without having ever felt it.

Words will not serve my need nor will the flowing water or the view.

(At the coffee shop) here, take my place…sit here beside the man who spills his words into my space…here, I will sit isolated and in the black and white blocked space…a little apart from the word polluted air he continues to spew at me.

Again and again I have walked and talked, sometimes teared and saddened but never broken, never broken.

The wish, the prayer is that it will not change before I get to a safe place. Then it will be all right—a place to stand—a plot of standing place. If I believe it has been and continues to be a pattern and that I have lived it before and survived, then don't let the brokenness come now. Maybe I can keep on doing it until I don't need to do it any more. Help is not the answer—it can be no more available than that which I have.

I sat alone at home not caring about anything. The phone broke through and I had missed my hair appointment. The days are not what I think. The brushed gray—part ocean, part sky.

My dark mood continued through the spring. *4/28/93 Wednesday swells over Tuesday and all but erases it from my mind. Things done mark the space of what is punctuated by darkness and sleep…always the passage of a portion of one's life measured and scored by things done. I lose and waste and grade myself on what is past.*

This moment would be well spent in quiet emptiness. I would run to that if I knew the way. The very thought of it and the notion that it could be possible brings a peace to me.

"Is it worth this to have a soul?" I wrote that many answers long ago. Let me ask that question again…and again.

Thursday: I will get a tape recorder of my very own...and read this book of blue words on gray blocks...no question why... I want to hear it because it is what I am made of...what and where I've been.

The sea is there. I will join it soon and take my book and maybe my recorder with me.

That's where I want to rest...take me there...and leave me...present me without words...though untamed with thoughts and sadness.

Whatever you feel...know that this is what I want...do this for me...keep this book...read it with kindness and charity...then do what you wish with it. Perhaps much will happen between now and then, and if for any reason you cannot do what I ask, know that it's all right and that I am already at rest and peace...and the place doesn't matter at all!!

Fri. These days seem like anniversaries of something...I don't now remember. Each day is an anniversary of another and yet goes unrecognized.

Driving over the bridge there seemed to be nothing to keep me from taking off into the cloudless sky. I almost wanted to do that. It would not be the wrong time for me I thought. I am ready. There's nothing more I can do. I've done my best...quickly followed by "maybe." I've just done what I've done...and that's it.

It would be a hard time for everyone near me, but not for me. It would be a relief. I've done what I can. I remember another thought...maybe...maybe... there will be something else...something else I will do.

I think I'm beginning to be afraid...the "what if" ... "what will we do if----?"

I will finish my coffee and go buy a card with a lady standing on a purple elephant and go home.

Wed. At the top of the cellar steps where I have voiced to many helpers...my plea for sanity. I have confided and pleaded, heard with gratitude the calls to sanity and rules for living. Here I sit and write in the shadow of my hand. There are few pages left in this journal. I must face its transformation into a

124

test--- from it being the refuge it has been. But for today it remains my inner self. I am again empty...standing "sole alone" as Uncle Jim used to say...only then, it was a breakfast cake and he was justifying eating it.

My memories...I have lived in them and have not grown up.

The realization of my mistakes is like lead in my chest. No one can hear my truth or see my pictures—only God. He has been holding the empty canvas waiting for me to draw the truth, knowing as He does the finished memory that will appear.

I thought of death often. Did I think of suicide? Probably, because that has been a recurring thought. *Who would come to pick up the pieces of my life---the sweet, the odd, the ugly...fragments dismantled? What would they tell the children? Would there be guilt? A wish to return to some past time? I know there would be hate...and the question: "Why did she do this to us" ---before "Why did she do this?"*

Another indicator of my thinking: *What else? I would like to lie rotting before myself. To comment on every piece of flesh and bone, silent but able to know all the feelings of my past...needing not to be aware of the pain except of my life. That I would want in full, and only when that was over, would I be gone from this world...hopefully not to know any other. I have been there. I have already suffered that here to which my mother brought me.*

Hidden papers to be found by anyone but my love! Perhaps he will be already gone to fulfill the wish ... "rest in peace—good and gentle servant. Here is your reward."

Can there be a beginning after a beginning? I think not. I thought otherwise in the time of meetings and slogans...that being over...truth fills me with disbelief.

Several of the children came to Maine to visit. Bob and his wife had visited after Laura's wedding. Laura and Brian were there during the Christmas holidays. John flew up two or three times. Rob's son, Paul, made contact with his father while we were in Maine. We had been out of touch since the events of Reno that brought about long standing alienation. Paul had separated from his first wife, and Sharlene was his companion. It was she who strongly encouraged Paul to contact his father, and we shall be eternally grateful for that. Paul and Sharlene came to visit during the winter. He has become one of our dearest children over the subsequent years.

Speaking of Paul, I remember that he and I had a special affinity even when he visited Reno. After Rob went to his office in the morning, Paul and I would sit at the breakfast table and talk. He has always reminded me of his father. That's another reason why he is so dear to me.

My Bonnie and her husband, Craig, visited us for a day. Craig was a pilot, and they flew up in his small plane. Don and Helen visited shortly after we arrived. So we were not at a loss for out-of-state company. But rather than heal my aching heart, I think they only made me more aware that we were too far from everyone we loved.

In the spring we drove to Baltimore again and stayed a few days with Morris and Priscilla as we had in the fall. We were sitting in their living room one evening enjoying a drink and their wonderful companionship, and suddenly Morris asked a question completely out of the context of our conversation. Morris was a master of the "home run" question. He turned to me and said, "Janie, you've been in Maine several months now. Are you happy there?" My answer was quick and clear, "No." My answer made a deep and motivating impression on Robbie. He truly had not realized how depressed I was, which is rather surprising considering how close we are. I don't know how deliberate my deception had been, but it certainly had been successful.

On the trip back to Maine, Rob opened up the possibility of returning to the Baltimore area. I could hardly believe it! I was going to be released from the prison that had been developing in my mind! I had never even considered that we could leave. It was like we had to serve out our sentence until death. What a relief!

In our usual productive fashion we began to make plans for the return. Rob contacted Bruce Taylor at the hospital to see if he might return there. We drove down sometime in June and stayed with my cousin, Edie, for a few days to look for a house to buy. After several days we found a suitable house in our price range in Ellicott City.

While we were in the Baltimore area, Rob contacted the mover who had moved us to Maine and asked if we could have the same couple move us back to Ellicott City. We later arranged our move date to coordinate with a trip the mover-couple would be making to the New England area.

Summer notes show a brighter mood. *6/24 The border on which I live is peaceful and turns a smile quickly—without crying. Will I feel loss and pain? Is it possible to cry in this cocoon of partial numbness? I am glad to be here though, in this edged part of the cloth of life. Expressing myself is easy with Rob as always, but at times I feel dull, blocked, contrived.*

7/10 Painted in the squares of my studio windows the river...icy blue behind the lacey trees... all absolutely still...summer still...heavy damp without message.

Notes from August through October: *8/24/93 I begin to describe in my mind the scene around me ...that red maple ... the birdbath a little farther away. The warm, smiling fall is gone—replaced by lengthened lower lip brought up to join the narrow line above it. A cue for reviving guilt—there, it is familiar—especially when a goal has been reached—a job has been done—perfect timing, best opportunity in a long time.*

So now what? The swell begins, only now I remember to acknowledge that it won't last forever. That's the thing that keeps me alive.

Never did I accept the anger inside me that closed me off. It was not of my construction.

9/1 I'll call Kathie tonight and remind her that a year ago we had dinner in Columbia. She looked so beautiful, and now she has had another child. She is so dear—so close. I miss her. August has faded—ups and downs have flowed and passed and left me weary. What secrets could this brick wall tell? Of people and their lives, of times long ago and yesterday. Adrift by the river. The leaves call to me, played by the breeze.

Laura and Brian moved to London soon after they were married. We went to visit them in September, 1993. *9/12 Surely not just another day—in the air—landing in 15 minutes in London. Now my heart beats hard, and I breathe more deeply. For the first time since we planned this trip I am excited. Another world—a mystery! Early in the darkness, I thought of leaving Laura again and that it will be hard, as always. Now our lives meet, touch, pass, go on, come together again and repeat the dance. It is gray—gray—I have become tired of gray.*

I live now in the past and the future. What of today? What will this be—what—how will these days play out? I want to move on to be there. Let me look with honest eyes and speak purely—let me continue what I have begun—and not be afraid. "Here I am Lord, it is I Lord."

I wrote a letter (never sent) to Laura on the trip home from London. *Dear Laura, Flying home from London I want so much to write my thoughts and then mail them to you. We're taxiing for miles…almost noon. The clouds and the sky are vast, as if they are coming down to meet us before we ascend.*

I don't remember if I told you that I don't cry any more. I try not to remember the last time I did, because then I might figure that it was about something so enormous that I could never cry again.

If I were crying these days I surely would have last night when you did. I guess I wanted you to know all the feelings were shared. I've not gotten to be a "tough old bird!"

My head could explode with all that I feel now. I actually would like to write it all down, but know I can't. It helps to try.

We could have spent hours last night, you and I, looking at clippings and talking about ideas. I regret the time was short, but celebrate having done it.

A flash into my mind, be patient. At my age, and your father being his, thoughts of the future are different than when I was 50. I think we, you and I, have been so close always that I will take the risk of sharing—how would it be? I remember a long time ago Dad's son, Bob, said, "You will always have a home with us." I dismissed that, and still do. I will have a place of my own for always. Remember, I lived alone for the first time when I was 35, and I did well. In my file of memories that is a success and a positive.

To be with the past (with history) as we were on this trip gives me strength. I have no fears. I am strong really.

One thing I thought of and did not do is to reassure Brian and you that I will always be OK. I bet you wonder what brought all this on. I have a strong faith in myself which I show to no one, and that's OK.

There is a peace and a determination that is part of me. On to other things!

We are over the sea. As far as my view takes me, there are blankets of white clouds. I have seen the sea below them and am not afraid!

Forgive me for being so frank, Laura. If whatever keeps me from crying were to disappear, I would now wish to be there with you. Is it a burden to be a child of dreams, of love unexpected, not imagined? (The love was unexpected—not you. From the time I came to love your Dad, my greatest dream was to have YOU!!!)

Here, I say, you are a child of love, joy, new found freedom, discovery, faith.

I must begin again if this is to really be a letter.

You told me we would look at the boxes—things I sent you. Laura, how tender you are. The joy of giving love is, I think, expanded by the open arms of those to whom we give.

I have eaten, slept and seen 50 little green and blue video squares in front of me. Now I am at last tired. Acceptance takes me home, joy repeats in my thoughts and keeps me with you.

Love, Mom

When we returned to Maine we put our house on the market, and we were set to go. We did have one last memorable event. The driver drove the moving van down the narrow gravel road to the house, which sat near the river bank. After loading all of our precious items, he closed up and prepared to leave. Backing up the steep road was a difficult maneuver. The rear wheels on the trailer went off the road into a deep ditch.

Eventually they called for a crane to hoist the rear of the trailer back on the road. I didn't see any of this, because once Robbie told me what had happened I decided to stay in the house and keep busy. I didn't want to see it. I kept busy dusting and cleaning the same places over and over again so I wouldn't go crazy. It was a great relief to see the load on its way in the dark of eight o'clock.

129

I was surprised that I was not more seriously disturbed by this episode. Perhaps the fact that we were escaping from Maine outweighed all else.

Phase 2—ELLICOTT CITY
(1993—2003)

THE MOVERS ARRIVED IN Ellicott City on Halloween. As always, it was a great relief for me to see our things safely unloaded and in our new home.

Unfortunately the house in Maine did not sell for over a year. That is the only house that turned out to be a financial loss for us. That fact probably added to my strong feelings that the move to Maine had been an enormous mistake. Robbie tried to console me by saying that indeed it was a mistake, but we made it in time to turn it around, and perhaps we learned something about how not to retire. We soon became very content with the situation to which we returned. Rob points out rather often that if we are happy now we have to accept the path that got us here. When I think of that I can readily accept it all.

Our new home was a two story brick house with attached garage and an in-ground pool with fenced yard, and located in a very pleasant residential neighborhood. Actually we did not want a house with a pool because Rob didn't swim and I swam poorly. But we liked the house too much to let the pool deter us.

Most of our children were in the general area, my three, Kathie, Bonnie, and Phil, and four of Rob's, Paul, Fran, John, and Patricia. My Aunt Edith was still alive at the time, and I visited her regularly in the D.C. area. I was in contact with my three cousins as well and for a time the four of us would go out to lunch together. And of course, we saw Morris and Priscilla on a fairly regular basis. Indeed it was good to be back!

Don and Helen came from Montana for Thanksgiving. Paul and his two children were also there for the holiday. Don and Helen were always welcome guests whatever the circumstances. They visited us another time in Ellicott City before Helen's death, and then Don visited once after Helen died.

One of the special benefits in returning to Maryland was the closeness I reestablished with Aunt Edith during the time before her death. After she became ill and confined to her house I visited her on a weekly basis. Several notes indicate our attachment to each other.

4/8/94 Today I got a gift. With it comes responsibility…but what a joy. Aunt Edith and I together again, really together. That I can give her something after all she has given to me. She is my role model. I want to write about it now…no danger I will forget it.

4/29/94 Yesterday was one of the best days of my life. When I tucked Aunt Edith into bed and knelt beside her to tell her goodbye, she held my face in her hands, pressed my cheek against hers and said, "I love you so much. Imagine, you taking care of me." All day as I moved from small job to job, as I sat beside her bed and listened and talked and laughed…heard familiar stories and strung together words, I gazed attentively at her face. It had a peaceful, content, glowing look. I brushed her hair and could feel her tiny head beneath her glorious, only partly graying, thick hair. When I finished, we were both pleased, and I brought her a hand mirror from the hall bath.

There was a pile of newspaper clippings on her bed when I followed her with her walker into her room. She looked at the pile and said, "Throw those away, I won't read them. I can't any more." Acceptance was below her words. I knew then I would gather them up and gently take them home to my own room and go through them. I knew too that I would not keep them. She had accepted…I was learning to let go. I gently put the snips of current news, Ms. Manners, ads, biographies, and shiny Sunday sections in a plastic bag in the recycles. I had decided at a good time I had to let them go…small steps to another time…I know not when. I wish I were there again today. Only God knows how I will miss her.

6/3/94 She was growing up and I was being born in 1930…both happening a little late, painful experiences. She was escaping her mother for the last time. I for the first. Actually I became her replacement…my turn to spend 21 years with HER mother—if belonging to, being dominated by, tied to can create a sisterhood, then she and I are surely sisters. As if she is giving me back 21 years in dying, leaving me here to again follow her.

Life drops away—falls away—melts a person—not really changing—evolving—disappearing.

6/8/94 To know where the quiet of the soul stands waiting for my return to rest, breathe deeply of the bouquet of being loved for myself—not above all, but of inclusion. If I were to play the day's tape, what would I learn about myself?

Robbie had a month before he resumed his employment at Taylor Manor Hospital. During that time we began to make changes in the house which took several years to complete. We redid the entire kitchen, and Rob built a small pantry in one corner. On the second floor, we had new tubs installed in both bathrooms, one a Jacuzzi. Rob tiled the floors in both baths. The basement was finished with a nice family room, a full bath, a laundry room, a large shop area, and eventually a large cedar closet Rob built.

I took swimming lessons, and as a reward, Rob had a heater installed in the pool. Rob built a large deck off the back screened porch. We did a lot of landscape work and ended with a very attractive yard front and back, including a new shed we built, hidden in the trees of the back yard.

I adjusted rather quickly to our new setting partly because the area was familiar to us and also because we were near family again. My notes suggest the same old struggles:

2/24/94 What I feel is up to me. I have made a step toward peace. If I begin asking the questions and living a whole life, i.e., in one direction, not scattered all over the place, it will be a start. To be honest, kind, thoughtful, ambitious…to put down the old guilt…to be grateful. I am a good person. I am faithful and loving. Why do I carry old, old guilt?

3/1/94 To write the story I would have to be honest…about the beginning, not where it all started to be a plan, but what had happened before that… I suddenly realize was part of it. If I wrote about that it would need to be just my feelings, not a factual account. I couldn't do that. But then what we decided, Rob and I… every time we chose to do something, it was all because of FEELINGS. Is it always like that for everyone? Lately I've been recalling clearly my enormous burning desire in the beginning to be with him. Nothing could stop me! As it turns out, nothing did stop me. Now after more than

30 years I love him as much, different only by security and certainty of being together forever…and so we will be…forever.

I am trying now not to be afraid and guilt ridden. This is a higher priority than being productive. Creativity will come out of it. I guess that I am what I am. It's like learning about me…again…again. I always thought I'd learn… and no…I'd keep trying to figure it out…keep hacking away without knowing what that statue was inside. I had a goal…but…

3/10/94 My days are not "good" or "bad"…they are divided during the day. Very much depends on what I do. As I began my usual Mall walk, I saw clearly that this is important to me. I need to come here. It satisfies something. I look. I love to go and look. Again I can let myself have no friends. They are here, so I can put the real thing off. The job of making friends is so hard… too dangerous. I must call and meet my neighbor soon.

3/11/94 Every day is NEW. I can't be new or go back…or even go forward any differently than as I am doing…but each day is new. God will not desert me. I desert him at times. Keep it simple!

Honesty is important. There's no security in pretending. Real is best. Real is good. I have done nothing to regret. I am faithful and loyal. My life is full of love. I am not ever alone…gratitude…gratitude. To smile at myself would be good.

3/18/94 I miss Laura…even her name…the letters put together…begin… start the missing her…give name to the feeling…her life with me and apart from me and after me. What will she remember when I am gone? How will the negatives play in her memory? Will she have learned from them as she holds her life…her children? Will she feel what I have felt? I miss Laura… Laura.

As we slowly moved toward retirement, I'm sure we were both convinced that this would be our final home. We talked about someday installing an electric chair to the second floor and a ramp in from the garage. We were thinking in terms of life's end stages, appropriately so since Rob was in his late 70's and I was in my late 60's.

Rob returned to work at Taylor Manor Hospital and was quite happy there. He became the Director of the Adolescent Program and was soon working full time. Later he cut back to half-time and then worked in the Out Patient Department. When Taylor Manor sold out in 2002 to Shepperd Pratt Hospital, he refused to consider the possibility of continuing with the new management. So at that time he rented an office in Ellicott City and once more began a private practice.

Robbie celebrated his 80th birthday in August of '99. He suggested that we have a reunion and invite the children and their families. It was a grand celebration. They came to our house for lunch on Saturday and then stayed for the afternoon and enjoyed the pool. We reserved rooms for them at the local Sheraton and gathered there for dinner that evening. The following morning we invited them to go to our parish Mass and then to join us for brunch afterwards. This became an annual affair for the next five years and ended as we began Phase III of our retirement.

A few weeks after the first reunion we had some frightening news. My routine mammogram showed a suspicious mass in my left breast. I find no notes on this period of my life. I wonder why? I went through the full course of care. Biopsy, lumpectomy with axillary nodes removed, chemotherapy, radiation, breast reconstruction, and continuing medication for five years. Rob took me to all my appointments and treatments and stayed with me whenever it was possible. It cast a shadow over our lives for several years, a shadow that changed to threatening black clouds as Alzheimer's came into view. The shadow has become almost imperceptible with the reassurance of annual mammograms and examinations. But the black clouds become ever more ominous.

During this period of time we continued to be active and took a number of trips in the United States as well as to Europe. We visited London and Paris on two occasions and on both trips took the Chunnel Train to Paris. We extended our second trip to include Lucerne, Venice, Florence and Milan. We also went to Venezuela one more time.

In the fall of 2003 we took a short trip to New Hope, PA. When we came home we discovered that we were without electricity as a result of a hurricane that struck the area the day before our return. That hurricane had a major influence on our future. We were without electricity for about ten days. In church on Sunday morning, a woman we knew heard about out predicament and asked us if we would come to their place for dinner that evening. We agreed.

She and her husband lived in a Life Care Community in Columbia. We knew nothing about such retirement facilities and had generally regarded them as places where "old fogeys go to live." We accompanied the couple to dinner and two other residents joined us. We were served a delicious dinner in a large, attractive dinning room. We heard about the facility in considerable detail, and it all sounded good.

On our short drive home, Rob said, "What do you think?" And I said, "Let's do it." Rob called the marketing department on Monday; we had an appointment on Tuesday and signed up. It seemed like a precipitous decision. We had not talked about such a move before. But for the first time, Rob had hired someone that summer to cut the grass and to mulch the yard. I was certainly more than content with our house and with our life, but somehow the retirement home did have its appeal.

This occurred in mid-September. We tentatively set a date to move before Thanksgiving. Obviously there was a great deal to do during those eight or nine remaining weeks. It was hectic. We had a house and yard full of things to pare down to fit into a five room apartment. We measured space in the apartment and picked out furniture, pictures, and mirrors that would fit. We contacted an antique dealer in Ellicott City who bought a number of our things. She was very charming and I enjoyed working with her. It made the sacrifices a bit less painful. The Salvation Army filled the biggest truck they had with house and yard items.

I had a difficult time during this period. Making decisions was not easy, and I felt like I was being pressured all the time. I don't think Robbie realized how perplexing it was for me. He was busy trimming trees at the request of our realtor, getting things ready for the Salvation Army, and making decisions about all his tools and his books. Parting with my belongings has always been traumatic for me. This was undoubtedly the worst time of "leaving behind." Many of the clothes I had made were given away, together with patterns, sewing material, and yards and yards of fabric.

Robbie praised me a great deal and always told everyone that I did a great job in completing the move. It has never seemed that way to me. The day the movers came, I was sorting buttons in my sewing room, and Rob had to remind me that indeed this was our moving day. In retrospect, I wonder if I may have had some initial symptoms of Alzheimer's which neither of us recognized.

Phase 3—VANTAGE HOUSE
(2003—present)

WE MOVED INTO VANTAGE House in Columbia, Maryland, a few days before Thanksgiving 2003. Laura came down from New Jersey and spent Thanksgiving with us and helped with some initial unpacking.

My notes have the following: *We moved to a high-rise, stone channeled into the clouds where we look ahead to dying. A choice quick and certain. We gave away years of treasures and memories: our art, our tools, our works of love...our independence, our two-some way of life. I watched the only remaining clothes of my creation hauled away and took just what would fit into our miniature final home of five rooms.*

We are pleased with the location of our apartment in the 13 story building. We are on the fourth floor with windows on three sides and a balcony off the bedroom on one side and off the living room on the other side. We are close to the tops of the surrounding evergreens, and farther away are deciduous trees as far as we can see. Some of the evergreens had branches that almost touched our balconies.

The location of Vantage House was only a few miles from where we had previously lived in Ellicott City. We continued going to the same church, the same grocery store, and the same restaurants. We continued shopping at the Columbia Mall. Rob's practice continued in the same office which was equidistant from our new residence as from our old one.

The transition to the new dwelling was challenging. It was reminiscent of the short time I lived in a high rise in Richmond, Virginia. Initially it felt more like we were living in a rather elaborate hotel. Our monthly fee includes one meal each day, and for us this is usually the evening meal. There is one dining room which accommodates 150 people. During the first few weeks we met a number of other residents. Some of these early contacts have become established friendships for us. Living here it became rather simple to invite family members or friends to lunch or dinner as guests in the dining room.

As the years passed, we used our own tastes and skills to make the apartment unique. And we do believe it is unique in this building of 230 apartments. We expanded our art collection, and now we have 125 pictures hanging on our walls. When I say "our art collection" I mean pictures we collected through the years in antique stores and various shops we visited. It also includes numerous pictures I have gathered from magazines and art books. We spent many hours matting and framing them on our dining room table. You might think that our walls are full of pictures. But not entirely pictures, because we have also hung 17 decorative mirrors of various sizes. When our children and friends visit, they often comment on how much our apartment looks like our previous home.

There weren't many things we could do to make changes in the apartment. But we did alter the appearance when Rob put up chandeliers in our bedroom, the living room, and the dining room, running the electricity in wire mold to outlets.

This was the first time Don and Helen were unable to visit our new home. Helen died in 2002. We attended the funeral. We visited Montana three times to see Don after her death. When he died in 2006 we did not go to the funeral because I was unable to make the trip, and Rob did not want to go without me.

A note after Helen's death: *Leave me alone and let me be…and let me see who I can be without holding on! Alone, the crying inside comes and the remembering of the past—back to 40 years ago. Laura and our threesome life—and Helen and Don. We were bound together the five of us for so many years. Helen was my best friend, my only truly best friend…so alike in many ways……so different in our life style, our personalities. I never saw or heard of her angering. The huge painting… I cannot longer see its scene…but clearing its colors it will remain in my heart as a gift she promised me, to live between us…. We were so alike in our seeing and caring…she the far better than I. Her path follows her family of origin to heaven. I shall never see her again. Her painting was the only physical connection.*

I sometimes feel pressured to begin to dispose of some of our belongings. I want to know and be in control of what happens to them. I don't want others to make those decisions after I am gone. When I talk about this, Rob always responds by telling me that he thinks we should maintain the apartment just as it is so that I will continue to experience its familiarity and its comforting presence in my life. The apartment speaks to me of many things, many places, many times. I enjoy our furnishings, the mirrors, the pictures, and all the jars and jugs and statues that I have placed just where I want them. I often find myself just looking and sometimes touching. I'm not sure whether I caress them or they caress me.

My life was seriously and directly affected by the move to Vantage House. Although I had not been employed for many years, I had always kept quite busy with various homemaker tasks. Decorating the house and keeping it clean and attractive had always been a priority for me. We liked to entertain. I loved to sew and continued to make many of my own clothes. I particularly enjoyed washing and ironing clothes. Rob always joked with me about how those chores seemed to cheer me up.

Our move took on greater significance for me as I began to realize that I was essentially out of a job. Housekeeping service came with fresh laundry every week, changed the linens, cleaned the bathrooms and kitchen, and vacuumed the apartment. Initially I did our personal laundry in the washer and dryer provided in the laundry room on our floor. Later on it became more difficult for me to remember how to adjust the controls on the machines, and Rob began to help me with the task. I am left with little to do.

After our arrival it was some time before I reached a point where I felt like sewing again. Then I could not find patterns that were suitable for what I wanted. As the months and years passed, my sewing machine sat idle in our studio. More recently I have begun to face the likelihood that I will not be sewing again. I think about it; I talk about it; but I don't get to it. That seems to be how it is with a number of things I would like to do. Is this also Alzheimer's?

In this new setting we quickly got to know many of the other residents. We had dinner regularly with a variety of our new friends and neighbors. We attended most of the scheduled evening activities. On Saturday afternoons we attended the community "sing-a-long" which was associated with a "wine and cheese" gathering before dinner. With some encouragement from Rachael, the woman in charge of the "sing-a-long," I joined the chorus, which met every Wednesday. I continued in the chorus for several years and on one occasion, with much encouragement from Rachael, sang a solo for the Christmas program given by the residents. It occurs to me that the only other time I ever sang a solo was in a program the staff at the State Hospital in Nevada did for the patients. I sang in a church choir years ago.

About two years ago I dropped out of the chorus. There were really two reasons. I began to sleep later in the mornings, sometimes until ten o'clock, and rehearsals were at eleven. It was also becoming more difficult for me to keep my music in order. I became increasingly "nervous" during the rehearsals and found them somewhat overwhelming, as I lost the ability to "keep up." It felt a bit like not being able to keep up in gym class in grade school.

Rob and I joined the square dance group. After two years, square dancing was discontinued because the room was taken for a game room. We joined the line dancing group and continued that for over a year, but then I had the same conflicts I had with the chorus. I was having increasing difficulty meeting the morning schedule and "keeping up" with the new steps we were learning.

There had been a time when I looked forward to going to the dining room to spend the time with friends and sometimes newcomers. But gradually the dining room seemed to become too noisy, too active, too demanding for me. It was becoming more difficult for me to understand what was going on. The many residents with walkers or in wheel chairs made it seem more crowded and confining. And deep inside me, every person in a wheel chair raised the specter of myself ... next month ... next year ... sometime soon. I don't need reminders!

At Vantage House we have the option of having our evening meal in our apartment. We began doing this with increasing frequency although we continued going to the dining room twice a week for several months. Then the number of people, the noise, the wheel chairs and walkers, the frequent and unexpected exchanges with various other residents became more than I could deal with comfortably. The stress seemed to result in a need for more sleep and in greater irritability. We talked about the gain as opposed to the "pain" of having dinner in the dining room. We canceled the two dinner evenings with others and started having dinner in our apartment regularly.

This arrangement fits our current life style much better. When we were eating dinner with others, there was, of course, a scheduled time. If we were out somewhere, we felt an obligation to be home at the appointed time. Now that we have dinner in our apartment we are not bound by any time schedule. This gives us a freedom that seems to me more in accord with retirement.

This freedom has contributed greatly to the daily patterns we began to develop in the past year. We began going to the Mall more often, and after window shopping for a while we would end up in the eatery. Turkey Subs became our staple for meals at the Mall. The people who work at the Subway became so familiar with Rob and his repetitive order for two turkey Subs that they routinely did the complete order without any prompting.

Trips to the Mall have become a priority for us over the past year. As a result of art school, my sewing, my modeling, and my work as an assistant buyer, I have always been interested in fashion. Robbie is generous with his time, his patience, and his energy as we walk hand in hand through the Mall and I comment on shoes and purses and window displays and almost every piece of clothing I see. I observe them all, and, of course, I express my opinions quite freely. We walk the length of the Mall at least twice, providing a modicum of exercise.

There is an interesting story about the Subway Shop. We initially had turkey wraps each time we ate there. The manager was very apologetic the day Subway stopped selling wraps. But she told Rob that she had already called other Subway Shops and asked them to save what wraps they had and she would pick them up later in the day. They kept them in the back area and continued to serve us two wraps each time we came for the next six or seven weeks. When the wraps were gone they were all concerned if we were pleased with the nine grain honey oat bread. We assured them with "YES!"

I believe that regular exercise, mental stimulation, and social contacts are encouraged for persons with Alzheimer's. Going to the Mall provides all of that for me. We have lunch or dinner there four or five times each week now. Subway shops have health oriented food and are quite inexpensive. We have a favorite spot where we sit in the eatery. From there we view a slice of our multi-racial, multi-cultured, multi-garbed country pass before our eyes. It is the best side-walk café in the world. We sometimes sit for over two hours talking about all sorts of topics, many stimulated by our surroundings.

There is another feature at the Mall that always takes some of our time. In front of one of the main department stores, there is a play area for small children, a large oval area enclosed by a wall about three feet high. There are a variety of objects for children to play on and a padded floor. The area is provided by Howard County General Hospital. It is a delight to stop and watch the little children, some just beginning to walk, play and interact with each other.

I often think of how fortunate Robbie and I are that we can get out and do this. It provides such a contrast to the facility where we live. If we were not going to the Mall, we would rarely see any children, rarely see young adults (except for staff members here), and rarely see a variety of ethnic groups or a variety of clothing styles. I believe that the great majority of residents at Vantage House must truly feel cut off from the world they used to know. And I continue to have the good fortune to feel quite attached to all that goes on in real life—and not just through the newspapers and television.

Vantage House with its 300 residents provides a neighborhood for us. For some others it provides a community. We come and go quite independently at the present time, because Robbie still drives. We rarely attend any of the programs or activities. Consequently, we see most of our fellow residents only in passing through the common areas. We still have a large number whom we consider friends. It is always a pleasure to see them and to stop and chat for a while.

Two or three times a week we have our lunch in the informal Skipjack Café. The three women who prepare the orders in the café are absolutely wonderful. They are warm and caring, and we have developed a close relationship with them. Other staff and residents often stop to talk and occasionally sit down for a visit. This setting is much easier for me to handle emotionally and socially. There are no extended conversations; there is no time schedule; people move about freely in the room. In short, I don't feel trapped like I did in the dining room.

Shortly after we moved here I found that the streets we knew no longer seemed familiar to me. I have been unable to remember our new telephone number and our new address (even though they are now six years old). I began to have some difficulty in finding my way when I was driving locally. About five years ago Rob and I decided that it was fairly certain that I was developing symptoms of early dementia, later confirmed as Alzheimer's by our physician. I accepted the need to quit driving but certainly mourned the fact.

Rob closed his psychiatric practice in December 2005. He said that he thought he was old enough to retire and that he was getting tired of dealing with managed care companies. He never clearly admitted it, but I think he felt that he should be more available to me. After twenty years at Loyola College, he discontinued teaching there the summer of 2007.

Robbie's retirement was good news for me. It is wonderful to spend all of our time together. That was something I had looked forward to for a long time. But I grieve the fact that we are curtailing some of our activities because they create too much anxiety and confusion for me. We have not gone to the beach in over a year, and we no longer go to the Bavarian Inn in Shepherdstown or to local plays as we used to do.

In the fall of 2004 we took a trip to Russia with a delegation from the American Psychiatric Association. It was a rather unpleasant trip and our last trip abroad. Robbie and I had always agreed that we would not travel anywhere on a group tour. For me, it was regrettable that we changed that decision. I had difficulty coping with the competitive atmosphere within the group. There was no warmth shown by our hosts except for our guide, Tatania. I was also having difficulty getting ready for the tours and keeping up with a less than leisurely pace.

We have in the past year discontinued going out to dinner with friends as we formerly did quite regularly. The dinner situation became too stressful for me. I had difficulty keeping up with the conversation and often felt quite exhausted after such an evening.

I did participate in a "peace making" event. My daughter, Kathie, reported that her father was interested in meeting with me for a talk. I thought it was a good thing to do. Tom and I met in the Mall just outside the Nordstrom store. It was worthwhile and probably brought some closure for both of us. He did concede that "we were both too young when we got married."

Our good friend, Morris Scherr, died about two years ago. We had met him for lunch a few months before his death. His wife, Priscilla, has had Alzheimer's for years and has been in a care facility for the past two or three years. I accompanied Rob when he went to visit Morris in the hospital a day or two before he died. I wrote: *Rob said I was in this hospital once. I asked for no reason. When I find a place inside, I want to sit and come to peace within myself and with what Morris's future is. I don't want to see him. I want to be inside some quiet place and open a part of my brain where there are no tears or sadness. I'll just be still and wish that to happen. On the way here, it's been pages, huge and sickening in my head...*

roads…trees…houses familiar from years ago…now some overgrown after all these years. Before we parked, I told Rob I would sit in the lobby or go into the gift shop. He was fine with that. I knew at that moment I didn't want to see Morris like that.

Sometime in the past few years I wrote the following letter but never sent it.

Dearest Priscilla,

Your face is with me as are my prayers, dear friend of old times and first, and so often we wrapped in each others arms. We grew and bloomed in different gardens, having lessons and experiences so far from one another.

Our loved ones brought us into each others lives and together we warmed and learned and grew and shone on one another.

I always wanted to be more like you were … you knew so much … looked and behaved in a special way, kind of like my Aunt Edith whom I adored.

I must write because I am so full of feelings. I've known for long that I would never see you again. Then suddenly it seems…but really slowly…not admitting…I too developed (strange word for a disease which tears one's brain apart and leaves it useless), I joined the quiet, sullen ones. At least I will be a full member of that group soon.

For whom do I cry? I've cried for the losing of my life as it was and the dread of what it will become, never losing knowledge that you were farther on that path.

I know that all these years you have not wanted my company, and I assumed properly I am sure. How long will this new road hold you to this earth…not long…I hope that will be the same for me.

Some place inside, how would it be if we could SHARE as we did our lives? If I could tell you what I still can tell… … ….

I'm sorry that you have this incurable disease, sorry that you suffer and there is no hope of a cure. I'm sorry for the hard times that you suffer, for the fear in your heart, for the feeling that people avoid talking to you, that they won't acknowledge your fear and your pain, that they close their hearts and their minds, and don't ask you anything about or even acknowledge when they discover you are a victim. No marchers for a cure, no explanation of the cause, no letting them talk about what they feel and fear.

Robbie is very helpful as we continue to evaluate which situations are unduly stressful for me. On occasion, stress is associated with an individual rather than a situation. I develop anxiety rather easily with physicians. We found a new internist after we moved here. I was generally satisfied with him. He probably had a good text book familiarity with Alzheimer's but he never seemed to have much understanding of what I was experiencing. That may have been because he talked more than he listened. He eventually joined the M.D.,V.I.P. program, which Rob calls corporate medicine. He wanted to "have more time to spend with his patients." We were reluctant to pay $3,000 a year out of pocket to have him spend time talking about politics, religion, social issues, art, etc.

Again we changed internists, and I hope that the new doctor will be a good match for me. I am not so much interested in how much my internist knows about Alzheimer's. What is important is how much interest they have in what I tell them and how much they know about my situation.

About twice each week we attend noon Mass at our church. It is comforting for me, and I think it enhances my courage and helps me maintain a more accepting attitude. The small group that attends the Mass is warm, welcoming, and very supportive. I hope and pray that I may achieve greater inward calm and simplicity of life than I have had in the past few years.

When we are at home Robbie and I play gin rummy, do cross word puzzles, putter around, sit and talk, or watch television. I continue to have difficulty keeping my things neat. I gather too much, and discard too little. That's a battle I don't ever expect to win, but I can't give up the fight.

Rob reads articles to me from the daily newspaper while I do my hair and my cosmetics. This helps me keep my focus on the present, because I tend to daydream when I am in my bathroom alone, and when I daydream I am very likely to wander back to the dark times in my life. His reading is stimulating to my mind. I am quite able to attend to and understand what he reads, better than when I hear the same news on television.

Rob gets up every morning shortly after six. He exercises for 30 minutes and then reads or works on the computer until he wakes me about 9:30 a.m. He checks the morning paper for articles that might interest me. His intention is to do all he can to maintain his good health so that he will be around to care for me in the years ahead.

I am often surprised by similarities between my current reactions and the experiences of my childhood. So many times it seems like the strong feelings I have, feelings that far exceed propriety in the immediate situation, are associated with things that happened to me long ago. Whatever is happening to my memory these days, feelings linked to childhood scenes periodically run rampant in my mind.

No matter where we go, no matter what we do, no matter how good the evening may have been, no matter how well I sleep, no matter how sweet and loving Rob is when he wakes me in the morning, each day begins with Alzheimer's staring me in the face.

Chapter 8

Jigsaw Puzzle Mind

IN ONE OF THE lounges here at Vantage House, I frequently see a seated gentleman working on a jigsaw puzzle. Years ago, a stroke confined him to a wheel chair and severely limited his speech. When he has some parts of the picture filled in and he is looking for the pieces to complete the area he is working on, his puzzle seems to fit what's going on in my head. I remember conversations, but I can't make a meaning from them. I remember pieces of the day but I can't make the pieces fit together to make a whole day. I remember faces but I don't know where they belong. Rob mentions something from the past and I have no idea what part of our life he is talking about.

Many people appear to be uncomfortable with the mention of Alzheimer's. Even after Robbie and I accepted the illness in my life and were using the word "Alzheimer's" regularly, our primary care doctor at the time would only refer to "memory loss." We changed internists about five years ago. When we discussed my symptoms with him, his astute comment was, "I don't think tests would tell us anything we don't already know." We concur, although sometimes I do think I'd like to see one of those colored pictures they show of the brains of people with Alzheimer's. Some days I don't find much color in the world outside my head; maybe there's color inside.

A few months ago I had an evaluation at Copper Ridge, an Alzheimer facility affiliated with Johns Hopkins Medical Institutions. The doctor there expressed the opinion that the progress of my illness has been relatively slow, which, he said, suggests that the future course may be protracted. I don't really know if that is good news or bad news.

I am aware that most members of the medical community recognize the impossibility of stating with certainty that a person has Alzheimer's. Dementia, the often used and more generalized term, is unpleasant for me. "Alzheimer's" has meaning, even if I don't quite know what the meaning is. It is an entity in my mind and, I believe, in the minds of most people. "Dementia" has an unpleasant ring to it. In my childhood, people talked about someone being "demented" when they were terribly stupid, unwittingly foolish, or mentally deranged. I see it as being associated with any of the above, but essentially referring to someone who is "out of his mind" or behaving as if he were. I'm not out of my mind, and I pray, God, I will not become so.

I mention having Alzheimer's quite readily to others. When I do, they seem not to know how to respond. Most people apparently picture Alzheimer's patients sitting mute in a corner, not recognizing their family, and not communicating with anyone. So they seek verification that I have it by asking, "How does your doctor know? Have you seen a specialist? Have you had testing done?"

How do I prove the presence of Alzheimer's to these "doubters?" I'm well aware that I look the same (unless I forgot to finish putting on my lipstick or make-up on both eyes) and sound the same (unless the conversation stretches beyond the shallow depths of my current information). They would not see me as the same if they caught me on a day when emotions run rampant and take me to thoughts I don't understand, responses I hate myself for, and behaviors I describe as "crazy." Why do people only envision the end stages of Alzheimer's? Are they not aware that the early stages may last for years? But then, I often find myself caught up in my own picture of "the end stage."

By nature I'm a sociable person and rather talkative so I quite readily converse with people. These interactions probably have not changed noticeably to others because my words are appropriate to the situation, my demeanor is correct, my emotional reactions are suitable to the content of our conversation. I "perform" as needed even though I do not know what day it is, what name this person has, what relationship we may have, or why I'm here, or where I'm going. Rob observes these

150

interactions and marvels at my ability to respond so appropriately. We are getting used to the comment, "You don't have Alzheimer's." It used to irritate me; now it amuses me.

I've been reluctant to read material about Alzheimer's that Rob gave me months ago. I don't look forward to reading about my brain disintegrating. I picked it up one day and read about memory loss and loss of objects. I soon learned that, "Nothing can be done to cure it." Why read on? They can't give me a time table, and I'll learn the details as I go along. I don't want to read about it. They're not going to fix it. I don't want to hear about research. Sometimes I feel like I want to know everything about Alzheimer's, and then suddenly I don't want to know anything more. I already know too much; I live it.

Sometimes I think, "Why don't I tell myself I don't have it and just go on with my life?" But my life does not just "go on." I feel so unlike myself at times that I can't pass it off as just insignificant change. There is a tremendous difference between good times and other times. There is a lack of emotional propriety in relation to people and things. Everything is flat but at the same time it tears me apart. Sometimes I feel like I have no control over my responses. At other times it takes great effort to respond at all. The average person has no idea how I feel. Oftentimes I don't either.

A recent note: *I sometimes have the thought that people may reach a point where they won't know who I am. Of course, it's more likely I will reach a point where I won't know who they are. But still the first fear stays with me. I dread not being known by others because I dread being alone. I'll try not to stop being who I am.*

We talked about the possibility of joining a support group. I had experience with Alanon and found it helpful. But those groups have survivors or even cures. While there may be some benefit in talking about some of the feelings I have, I'm not sure I could tolerate listening to other people talk about their experience. When Rob and I sit and talk, it is very helpful and better than any group we could attend.

I have always talked a good deal, and I believe Robbie truly loves that I do. He, by nature and probably by nurture, is quiet. We have great talks together, sometimes for hours, and there always seems to be something new to talk about. But when I get angry and depressed and frightened, all of which Rob calls being "upset" or "having a bad day," he seems to shut down, and I interpret it as his being angry at me or shutting me out. I get furious and unreasonable. Then I feel not just like a leper but like a "crazy leper" and that he is avoiding me when I need him the most.

Changes occur so gradually that I don't remember when they started. How does anyone know when Alzheimer's begins? There are no "events of presentation." It's like someone sneaks into my head when I'm not looking and steals pieces of my brain. I became aware of some marked changes when we moved here in November 2003.

Although the move was only about five miles from where we had lived, I began to have marked difficulty knowing the roads we had traveled and keeping directions straight. When I drove, it was easy for me to get lost even in familiar areas. When Rob was driving, I seemed not to recognize places that had been well known. Our new phone number and our address still elude me. It is so embarrassing when a store clerk asks me for my phone number, and I have to look it up in my wallet.

I have always had some difficulty losing things, maybe because I keep so many things around. Now it is much worse. I put things in strange places and can't find them. Rob must be part blood hound. He usually does the finding. Once I put my wallet under the sink in my bathroom. It was days before we found it. When I put something in an unusual place I tell myself, "You'll remember this." Rob says I should change my mantra to, "You won't remember this." Recently we have adopted a plan that I keep my wallet and some of my jewelry in his desk drawer. That seems to work well. But I can't keep all my scarves and shoes and skirts and blouses in his desk drawer.

Here is a page that gives some idea of how Alzheimer's is affecting my daily life. *12/01/06: I discovered something the other day, but I'm not sure I can explain it. Rob's last remaining sibling, Don, died a few weeks ago. His wife, Helen, and I were very close. Helen was an excellent painter and I admired her seascapes and mountain pictures. One that I particularly liked, she had done from our beach house in Oregon when they were visiting us there. She said it would be mine after her death. She put my name on the back of it to indicate her gift. It became increasingly dear to me after her death in 2002.*

Don died last month. His only daughter, Donna, inherited the belongings of the home. Rob called her about three weeks after the funeral and asked her about the picture. She promised to contact one of her children and ask that it be sent to us. I strongly doubted that she would follow through or that the picture would ever get to me.

I became very angry over the entire matter, and over the next week or two my anger grew and grew. I was angry at Donna for being so highhanded, giving things away right and left to her children who seemed unworthy of getting anything of Helen's. I recalled any irritating interactions we had had with Donna through the years and added those sticks to the fire. I recalled a previous conflict with Don and how justly angry I felt I had been at that time. During our last visit to Montana in March 06, Don's son, Jim, was part of a conversation we had about the picture being marked for me. I became angry at Jim for not remembering that the picture was to be mine.

I focused on all of this for several weeks, mentioning it repeatedly to Rob and becoming angrier with each repetition. It finally became a major issue that I spent a great deal of time mulling over and feeling increasingly wounded as a result of it.

Then a day or two ago something happened in my mind. As Rob and I spoke about it today, I described it as "thinking clearly and rationally." It was as if my previous thoughts were not thoughts at all but feelings that made connections with one another in my mind and carried me to conclusions that had been in my head waiting to be justified. Now I could see everything in a new light. The circumstances were understandable.

Jim's father had just died; he could hardly be expected to be thinking about my picture. Donna's father had just died. We knew she was extremely distraught over his death and that she has typically reacted to most things in a rather intense manner. My picture would hardly have been a #1 item for her and her children. It's likely that no one even thought of looking for "bequeaths" on the back of pictures. It became so clear, so reasonable, and so different.

I wonder how often I do this same thing. My emotions seem to carry me to places that are so familiar from the past, and so angry and unforgiving. It was a striking event in my thought process. Rob pointed out that when one of these "episodes" is happening he feels that he cannot make any "corrective comments" because it would only anger me more. And he's right. He said that he wishes I could find peace with my early life. I yearn for that. It would be a strange twist if Alzheimer's brought me a tranquility that I have never known, while I can still remember the people and the events that have tainted my view of life for so long. I do need to give much thought to forgiveness. It almost seems that a serene soul would be worth this present journey that appears so frightening to me.

About six weeks after I wrote the above note, my picture arrived carefully wrapped and sent by one of Donna's daughters.

A page in December 2006 gives another description of what happens in my head and in my life. *12/14/06: This morning was not good. I could not find anything when I was getting ready to go for a walk. Everything I put down seemed to disappear. On days like this, I can feel a difference in the impairment, and it frightens me and makes me think the time may be short. I told Rob that I don't think I will be here next Christmas, because the Alzheimer's seems to be moving so quickly. He didn't say much, but then there probably wasn't much he could say. He reminded me that the illness varies a lot from person to person and is unpredictable. Later I worried that I had upset Robbie by what I had said about Christmas, but he assured me that it is better to get those thoughts out in the open, and that it is better for him when I do because then he can better understand what I'm going through.*

I was still concerned about this morning when everything was so disorganized, and I felt confused. I said that we should probably be doing more to prepare for how things are going to be. I am always thinking of "how things are going to be." And it's frightening because I have no idea how they are going to be. We talked about how hard it is even to think about the limitations that have entered my life, seemingly so rapidly these last few years. Last evening I could not find a sleeveless black pullover I wore a day or two ago. It's so difficult because I am never sure when I last wore something or when I last saw it. Sometimes I don't know whether something may have been missing for weeks and I just now remembered I had it, or if I wore it this morning and it's now gone. As we searched for the pullover, I said it was the sweater I loved the best of all my sweaters. The one that's missing always turns out to be the one I loved the most. I'm sure that's just the way it seems. There's that evasive, uncertain, insecure, make-believe word again, "seems."

Some notes I wrote about a year ago: *I can get so mixed up dealing with time segments; sometimes it seems like there are no divisions of time, no portions of life. It just flows by without identifying markers or labeling events. I feel as if I'm on the bank of a stream watching time float by, not recognizing minutes or hours or even days. I have difficulty keeping the day straight, even when Rob has reminded me several times. I forget what we did yesterday, but usually remember doing it when I'm reminded. But then I don't know if it was yesterday or last week that it happened.*

If a person is lost, they try to get their bearings by looking for familiar scenes. I get lost in time and can't find familiar event-memories to provide clues. I told Rob it's like walking down a road without a map and knowing that the end is oblivion, to disappear, to know no more, and eventually to be no more. It is a pathway of mystery, and I expect, of some misery. Rob assures me that we will walk the road together, and he will be my constant companion.

I think of all the things I used to do and at times find myself planning some new project. New projects never seem to materialize. There seems to be a very long distance between the thought of sewing or drawing or painting and getting to it. I'm not sure I know how to get from the idea to the act in several areas of life. It's bad enough that my head doesn't work right, but then when it does work but I can't follow through from the idea to some action, therein lays a lot of frustration.

The times we talk are wonderful. I tell Rob some of the things that go on in my head, but some thoughts seem not to have words that match them. Talking brings Alzheimer's out in the open, and even though it is frightening to look at it, it helps to look at it together. Rob tells me I am doing a great job dealing with it. I often promise him I'll be a good sport and take what comes, but of course, that doesn't always happen quite the way I want it to. Sometimes it just overwhelms me with its constant presence in my waking moments. I think it follows me into sleep and causes some of the terrifying dreams I have.

I believe that others must experience Alzheimer's differently than I do, because I assume the symptoms and to some extent the course of their illness must bear the imprint of their early life, their emotional make-up, and their developed coping mechanisms. It is so clear to me at times that my erratic and powerful emotional reactions relate to an earlier time, to absent persons, to painfully remembered situations of

155

long ago. And the distorted coping devices I use in the "bad times" are the same as those I used when I was a child. But now only one other person is here to be on the receiving end of these reactions and these attempts to cope. Rob becomes the substitute, the proxy for my rejecting mother, for my controlling grandmother, for my irritating Uncle Jim, for my abandoning father, for nasty Olga (a particularly spiteful neighbor child), for my demeaning first husband, for my faithful but unresponsive cat.

I want to mention that during one of our recent talks Rob spoke to me about my thought that people equate "crazy" and Alzheimer's. He took some time to explain to me the difference between mental illness and the dementias. I appreciated hearing that because I have always had a fear of "going crazy."

To discontinue driving was very difficult for me. It still represents a loss of freedom. When I am in the car with Rob, it becomes quite obvious to me that driving is not something I could even consider doing, and I am grateful I stopped when I did. Rob tells me that I stopped driving in May 2006. I am now dependent on Rob for where I go and when I go and how long I stay. He is very willing to oblige my requests to go any where and stay as long as I want, but I resent that it is so. I can no longer get in the car and go where I please when I please. On a more realistic note, I must acknowledge that I would be afraid to be out somewhere without Rob beside me.

A note written several months ago: *I know that I have lost the life I had before Alzheimer's took it over. I should say "tried to take it over" because I have not yet capitulated nor will I capitulate as long I can talk and laugh and cry with Rob, as long as I can love Rob and the kids, as long as I can remember that God still loves me.*

In early 2007: *At Christmas time I spent a lot of time wondering if I will be alive next Christmas, and if I am, what will my condition be? What will I recognize, how will I react? I see the various pictures and art objects in our apartment and wonder who will get them and when. Sometimes I want to give them all to the kids now while I can still make decisions and know where they are going. I guess I fear the loss of control over my things. They are mine and I want to decide about them.*

We went to Laura's the following Christmas. Another missive never sent: *Dear Laura, I'm afraid I won't be able to tell you what I want to—before it's too late. We look back and think of things we wish we had said and didn't, and sometimes we think, "We'll have another time, another chance, another visit, or letter." I can't believe that any more.*

Today while it was busy and happy celebrating Christmas with you and your girls, it came to me. I won't have another chance. What can I do, say, "Laura, sit here, just you and me, and let me pour out my mind to you. If we cry, it's OK. I need to tell you what I think and feel, how it is when I'm afraid, how it has been. I have no planned words. I need to know you understand."

Last night you put your arms around me and said, "I love you so much Mom! I'm sorry about the last visit here. I love you. I'm OK. It is different now!" I was glad to hear it.

My words are frozen in my disintegrating brain. I keep feeling them, words melting before I speak them—and then I can't remember.

I see you as a child, as a little girl, as the child of my love, and I'm not sure if I can talk about it. I don't know. I'm sad and sometimes so alone, Laura.

Your life has been so very difficult. Your dreams blew away. You've had years of worry and sadness. You are a wonderful mother, a good friend, and I know you'll be a grand teacher. It doesn't mean it's at all simple, but if I said these things to you, would it matter? I don't really know. You are in my mind daily. I had years of different pain than yours. I don't compare our lives. But how can I talk to you about mine? I don't know. Maybe I shouldn't want to.

Here is another example of how a minor incident can reach major proportions. *02/06/07 We went to the 60th birthday party of Frances, Rob's oldest daughter. I felt relaxed. Everything went well through dinner. I had an opportunity to give Fran the ceramic shard we had found in the ruins of the Chinese settlement in Virginia City, Nevada, back in the late 60's. It has always been an important keepsake for me. Fran noticed it when she visited a while ago, asked about it, and seemed interested in it. I thought I would give it to her as a special thing between us, not as a birthday gift. Rob and I told her its history when I gave it to her. She seemed pleased.*

After dessert was served, they brought in Fran's first gift, a photo album of Fran's life through the years. There were photos with her mother and Rob together with the kids, and one picture of Rob in his mortarboard and gown for his graduation. I was numb. I didn't know what to do. I didn't know what to think. I got up and went in the kitchen, becoming increasingly angry and ill at ease. I began cleaning up and working at the sink with my back to the dining room.

Rob came out before the album was finished. He knew I was disturbed by the whole thing. After a while he suggested we go and I agreed. He got our coats and left after obligatory goodbyes. I wish we could have just disappeared. I became increasingly angry on the way home, but I was proud of the fact that I had not let loose on everyone there, which certainly entered my mind. I have to say that Rob's son, Bob, was very thoughtful and loving as we departed.

Now it is the third day since the party. I continue to feel devastated. The scene continues to replay in my mind. I sleep poorly, I dream about it over and over. It feels like I will never get over it. I am angry at them all and I repeatedly go through all of it. I feel like I hate them all, no exceptions. I want to do something to hurt them in return for what they did to me, to us. What were Michael and Becky (Fran's son and daughter-in-law who gave the party) thinking? They said they thought about calling to let us know about the album. Why didn't they? Are they stupid? Do they not care about me? Did they intend to hurt me? And the rest of them, did they not know how disturbing it would be for me and for Rob? Why didn't someone stop it? Why didn't someone just say, "Let's look at this later and get to the other presents now?" Why didn't Fran think of it? Why didn't Paul say it?

I'm angry at Rob for giving Fran a check for her birthday. I want the shard back that I gave Fran, and I intend to ask her for it. I never want to see any of them again, and I have no intention of going to any "family" gatherings. They are no longer my family. I thought I was part of them all these years. It's like losing a whole family overnight. I told Rob I want to change our Wills.

Needless to say this has all caused some difficulty between the two of us. I do take all my anger out on Robbie. I don't mean to hurt him, but I have talked about this repeatedly over the past days. I get so angry that I sound angry at him. And I do get angry at him easily these days over little things that otherwise would not bother me. He bears up pretty well but Sunday night he was angry at me and said some mean things. I became frantic as I always do when he is irritated with me. Then I have no one, and I feel lost. I am all alone, and I want to die. I know it frightens him when I talk of killing myself, but at times like that it is what I want to do. We made up, but I slept poorly as I had the night before.

I wonder where things will go from here. Rob is supportive of me and beside me in my decisions. I know that if I reject any future invitations it will be acceptable to him, and he would chose not to go if I don't go. But I'm hurt and I'm sad and I think it has all been very unfair. It reminds me of all the times in my life I felt left out, overlooked. At the party they behaved as if I wasn't there, as if I had no feelings. I grew up with no one recognizing any of my feelings. And I never expressed them much. I guess I didn't dare. Maybe that's why they are so strong now when they come. And they are strong! They tear at me. They flood my being. I feel like I'm drowning in my own hate. Even though they frighten me I feed them with my thoughts and my words, and I watch them grow uglier and more wicked. My feelings become my thoughts and I cannot separate myself from them. I cannot look at them because I am in them, and they are me.

It was months before I stopped talking about all of this with the same strong feelings coming to the fore each time. These issues never were resolved. We have not attended any family gatherings since that time, although we have had invitations. Rob has minimal contact with Fran and no contact with Michael and Becky as a result of the incident.

The last lengthy writing that I find: *9/11/07 I am quite aware that my memory is getting worse these days. Rob and I talk about it quite freely. I often start to say something, and if I get interrupted, I may forget what I wanted to say.*

In addition to loss of memory, I have noted an alteration in memory function that seems to be new or at least is newly noticeable. Rob and I have talked about it several times in the last couple of weeks. Things I observe or remember are like a series of separate pictures rather than like a running film. Rob mentioned how he recognizes it when we play gin rummy. I have difficulty seeing the relationship between two cards because each card seems to be its own snapshot, and I have to study and compare the snapshots.

I think this snapshot view covers a lot of what I do. When I lose something and then look for it, I can easily miss it, even if it is in front of me. For example, if I lose a bottle of hair spray, I look for it among the various cans and bottles I have on my shelves, but I can't remember what it looks like. I could just as well say, "I don't know what I'm looking for." When I write this I think it all sounds pretty crazy, and I hardly understand it myself. I get more and more frustrated as it goes on and increasingly angry with my own "stupidity" and the disabling effect of this illness.

From my observations I only have snapshots of this or that person, this or that verbal exchange. It is rare that an experience comes back to me as "a whole cloth," because I do not take it in as a whole. Afterwards as I try to put the snapshots together, it is frustrating to discover that they often do not make a complete picture. Pieces do not fit or seem to be missing. I never know whether the missing pieces are incidental or critical to my understanding. Then there is always the question, "Have I filled in a piece that doesn't belong here? A piece that comes from some other time, some other incident? (And that does happen.) If so, how trustworthy can I be?" It is frustrating! It is frightening!

This snapshot memory often makes it difficult to watch television. I'm registering "pieces," and there are too many pieces to keep up with, hold onto, and put together. Robbie often tries to "catch me up" during commercial time.

Sometimes I wonder why it feels so good, so helpful, and so reassuring to talk with Robbie about these things. It doesn't change them. It doesn't clearly tell me why they happen or how they happen, just that they happen. It does give me some better knowledge of what is happening, so perhaps it becomes a little less frightening. Robbie assures me regularly that I'm not going crazy. Sometimes I see myself on the back ward of some psychiatric hospital because these things are so weird. Robbie gives me a sense of not being so horribly alone. I think that is what I fear the most!

Before closing this chapter I want to bring things up to date in this June 2009. First and most important, Robbie and I grow closer as the days go on. He is ever my companion, my true love, my "other" memory, the one who does all he can to fill in the pieces that are missing in the puzzles of each day. While my memory loss broadens and hastens, my moods have improved somewhat in the past two or three months. The emotional storms have been less devastating and less destructive to my own sense of personal worth. They are less violent; they have been briefer. For that I am most grateful. Although the fear, the anger, the sadness, the sense of isolation associated with my Alzheimer's come less frequently, I accept now that it is "my Alzheimer's," and I must and will live with it as long as I have life and my Robbie.

A note from 2009: *I will ask Rob to make what he can of these things I have been writing these past few years and comment accordingly. I assume that he will arrange them in a manner to expose and perhaps explain some of the changes that are occurring in my thinking, in my mood, and in my behavior. And I will leave it to him to tell, finally, the end...because by then it will be too late!*

Chapter XI

Bits And Pieces

This note is from the scribe, Robbie. Jane no longer writes lengthy pieces. It seems that her concentration cannot hold long enough, and she finds it difficult to find words, to spell them, and to write legibly.

This chapter will consist of short writings Jane has done over the past year or two. They are gathered from several books in which she wrote brief notes or from scraps of paper she found in the café or at Laura's or in the apartment or in her pocket at church or anywhere else. I have placed these under different arbitrary headings which identify areas of focus in her life and her illness. Each paragraph represents a separately written item. Although some have dates, they have been chosen at random and have no special sequence. Connections to Jane's childhood are frequent and obvious.

Writing

I have to hurry…write before the thought is gone. It does that in a second. I lose the thought. At this time in my life my mind is still full of feelings, yes, feelings unwritten, and soon to be forgotten.

There is no way for anyone to know so many things about me. It's all right. There's no need for most. But there are a few people I want to tell. There are lots of things about me you do not know...things I care about...things I think, want to do, have done.

So much has happened. I've become 78 for one thing. I am so much closer to insanity. Will I be able to continue to write? Not for my life!

How, all my life I wanted to journal—with my head always full of thoughts which were never to be heard by anyone, and now forgotten by me.

What is "book worthy" and what is not? In my head forever so long—to write on a page, especially in a mostly new, blank book—ahh. Not so now. It is mine to write in...and the thoughts come to me...only now I am aware of how quickly they are gone...not remembered.

The unsentenced words reach out...touch my heart...not my mind. The page being read by another ---the pain I must consume...alone...in the space where my brain fails and again the child returns.

My feelings flow...I can feel them going from me to the page! Yes, I love to write. So I go on...there is never a Jane's day in my mind—never. This is today though I never know the name of it! I need to write, forgive me if it seems strange to do so!

The change in my handwriting disturbs me somewhat when I come across notes written so long ago in some ring book—each letter clear, each word as if there had been lines on the page, holding the names I now cannot remember. I feel flushed and not relaxed as the letters grow crooked making misspelled words.

Alzheimer's

4/16/06 I love my life the way it is and being forgetful is an opportunity to be philosophical. When we talk about each period in our life, one of our great joys is to remember things we've done, places we've been, people we've known. I will eventually forget those things. They will be gone from my mind. That is frightening to me when I think about it, and I wish it would not happen. But as I thought about it now, I realized that I can have a philosophical attitude. We have experienced the world together, life together in the broadest sense. That's how I seek to look at it, how I plan to look at it.

You said something you had told me, and I said I don't remember. Then I thought-- that's the way it will always be. You'll tell me what you said. Then my realizing will still be there, and what I always knew to be true will be there. This is a better thing. It will help me to think of that as I go along on the path of forgetting. This is a good thing to think about. I can do it. I didn't want to look ahead. I was frightened of it. This helps me not to feel that, gives me courage. I don't allow myself to be depressed, but sometimes it comes…just like a wave. It has the control, the power. The reassurance you'll stick with me is important, but for a moment the wave is strong, too strong.

It's like being some place you've never been before. When I wake up after 12 hours of sleep I don't feel any better. What went wrong? What happens when someone doesn't understand any more? I guess they still feel lots of things.

Still so much to do—after years of wasting time, thinking incorrectly. The pain burns my heart. I want this monster disease to end—and let me rest in peace, or begin the price for all those years that were supposed to be happy, good, and clear and instead are an opening to this hell on earth and forever.

I'd be happy if I was crazy at night. Do what I have to do in the day and then happy hour at night. It takes a while to get revved up in the morning.

Remembering something that I loved and lived with…there was always a picture in my mind…I lived with pictures…pictures that I could describe… because I saw them from memory of them. Now it becomes a feeling. I think to acknowledge that will help. There are so many things I remember loving, but because I can't see them in my mind doesn't mean I don't remember them.

My notes have been strange I know. My mind is failing continually. I feel it in so many ways. Yes, I am sad because it is such a huge loss. Expecting it was of no help, nor is it a help to pretend it isn't happening when I feel it constantly.

*Alzheimer's is like traveling a road that one has never traveled before…
without a map…without directions. I know that others have traveled it, but
I also know that no one ever comes back to tell about it. I wonder what it's
like up ahead. It feels like I get off in different places. They seem real…like
I'm familiar with them. But then before I know it I'm back on the road which
seems to move under me, rather than me moving ahead on it. I don't want
to move ahead because I'm afraid of what's out there……but the road keeps
going by me anyway.*

*Finally, why me? Punishment that ends all potential? I never understood
this "punishment disease," this that is happening and increasing all those
years with my not knowing. Today it hurts my heart to know, my eyes to
look at where I am…my home…all the other homes run through my head,
each corner sometimes…all the while not being able to recall which house
sometimes.*

*I do believe this is a punishment…this dread disease that destroys a bit of my
brain every day. When did it start? How will it end? Will my breathing,
seeing, speaking, living continue even after my brain is dead? I say all day, "I
can't remember." Will I stop when there is no brain to know, to understand,
to think? I know it is happening…this daily changing…the wafting between
contentment and uncontrollable anger…mostly that. I grasp at a thought
and can't let go…if it passes it's only for a little and it's back…it returns. I
do remember details of the hurting things…the losses…the mistakes. There
is some part of my thinking that dreads, fears, mourns…and of course the
"why me?"*

*The day dawned and every thing was painted the same inside my head, even
though the blossoms and the leaves had grown and changed. I am not afraid.
I accept the disease I have.*

*I clearly noted how differently I often feel between the morning and the
evening. It feels like I'm running out of fuel later in the day…particularly
when the day has been full…not full of our talking or our being together…but
full of…I don't know what…maybe the unfamiliar. Yes, it is the unfamiliar
that seems to take more fuel…or whatever keeps me going.*

It is so hard to lose control of one's life…as if we ever had control! I have been frightened all my life…of making mistakes, of people not liking me, of sudden changes, of all things unknown. So when I feel I have some control of a situation, it reduces my anxiety. With wanting to control such a high priority, I am devastated when I lose control of myself in some fit of rage. I am totally humiliated, scornful of myself, deeply embarrassed…coming away feeling that I should be punished.

I sometimes tell Rob that my head feels like crossed fingers, and I cross my fingers to show him how it is inside my head. The experts talk about "tangles" in the brain of Alzheimer's patients. I celebrate when my head is working…it feels so wonderful. But when it gets "crossed" and little things start to go wrong: I can't get the top off a bottle, I spill something, I can't find something…I see it all changing…going. And very quickly I discover myself sitting in a wheel chair, slumped over, unaware of my surroundings…or maybe acutely aware of my surroundings, but unable to communicate with those nearby. I'm old and wrinkled and ugly, and I don't want anyone to see me, and I don't want to see anyone.

It all goes through my head, and I don't want to be here. I plunge into the abyss…dark, frightening, cut off from the world…from life…living. All of this brings fear…no terror, anger…no rage, loneliness…no abandonment. It is a punishment from God for my life. I keep saying, "I'm a good person." But how can I be, and be under this curse.

It is almost like the pieces in my mind are not discrete thoughts but rather separate feelings that act like they are chained to one another and force me along into the words and actions that come out. It is terrifying to watch my feelings take over and put ideas in my head that I don't want to be there and cause me to say hurtful things that I don't want to say. When it's over (and I'm not really sure why it is over, how it is over, or when it is over) I am remorseful, apologetic, and embarrassed. Then with the return of clarity, I wonder how Rob can put up with all of this. But he does, and I know he always will because in the core of myself I know he loves me deeply and everlastingly.

Last evening I talked to Robbie about Alzheimer's. I sounded angry. I was angry. I want to know what is going to happen to me and I want to know when it is going to happen. I want someone to tell me, to explain it to me, to let me know. Sometimes I think I want it to go quickly so it will be over. And other times I don't dare hope that it might progress slowly. I had a hard time getting it out of my head last night. No wonder, my head is where it is.

This morning I woke up feeling depressed, tired, uninterested in anything. After breakfast I wanted to go back to bed. I didn't want to think any more today. I couldn't stop the constant negative thoughts and the noose of worry that strangles me.

Now I am "injected" every waking morning with the word "Alzheimer's." It has been five years since I was first told. I criticize myself for slowing down or completely stopping doing so much that I loved all my life...while at the same time I've given up trying in a deliberate manner...and it doesn't hurt.

Memory

3/05/07 I began to tell someone about an incident...... I said the first sentence, then emptiness in my mind. My mind was as if I had not another word to say. It is not just forgetting. It is disconnecting. I knew the first sentence...then disconnected and nothing is there...but I remember the first sentence.

One of our favorite songs: "What now my love?" The time has truly come. I can't remember where I lived, worked, my last name, the care I needed! What now?

I've been to some of those spots ...but now, the story told with clear and loving memories...each with a picture. I was able to visualize...I saw it...I felt it. Rob told of living it and I was taken there with him and by him. My heart is full.

I told a poem in my head. It went on and on .... I saw a tablet but by the time I got a pencil... the poem was gone—forever. The thought, feeling, love in which it was held in my heart...all gone! It was to Laura, and I would write it and send it to her. But it was forever gone!

8/11/08 *ABC's no longer come easily to me...notes...letters ...jottings...the distance from my hand to my brain has lengthened to the point where they hardly make connection.*

Under the sink, that's where the iron is. I fill a measuring cup with water. The ironing board is in the closet. Move the table in front of the doors. Precariously take out the board to the living room. I stand the board up, fill the iron, and put it on the board. That's what the scene is in the living room until later when I reverse the behaviors and have not ironed at all.

Your words remain in my heart although I know that I will not remember them in my damaged brain. You spoke to me and to my life.

The table I use as a desk was positioned and used as a piece of furniture in every house we had. I must not mourn the absence of memory. Not in one home can I recall where it was!

To go back, to try to remember -- my childhood memories are frozen in my mind – the bad and the good – as if I read in silence the story printed there. Never does it vary, even now when I can see it.

Moods

Life has always been full of color, and I've been especially aware of colors. I used to show Rob the colors in the clouds when all he could see were shades of grey. I'm big on color. Now it is becoming a black and white world and shades of dark grey. It's hard to deal with these days. My feelings, my moods respond to colors. Now there seem to be no painted clouds, vibrant skies, soothing horizons in nature or in my contact with others.

Things have changed markedly. Moods fill my head with wordless "bulk." I am more of the time unhappy, confused, sad, angry—afraid. The latter makes me cry and want not to be alive. Like most things all these feelings pass – except the crying. I cry now as I write.

When upset, thoughts are readily available without words. How can I make them understand it's a physical thing? I get very angry at you—long before you—I get so not logical—no hope—if I keep talking, you should understand what I'm feeling. It's pathetic because I can't get across to you. I'm generally a nice person; I could understand it better if I were a mean bitch. Then I feel unforgiven, and that's the worst feeling I can have—it enlarges all the other feelings. Sometimes I'm sure I am so kind of "strange" and wish I could reach out and hold you as I want to......I'll keep trying.

I had never known love, admiration, contentment, sharing, peace of heart and soul, caring, to be full of mind and body, to enjoy the thrill of life together, to walk hand in hand always. No one said, "Welcome home. I'm so happy to be here with you." No together, no face telling without words that I was grand, good or worthwhile. No pride. No small moments full of warmth and feeling. Is it possible that is what comes back when I face the anger, the stark face, the almost practiced consistent words? My fear of the above turns me to fury, fear, aggressive comments, shouting, crying. I am demolished as of long ago, but then I just stood and wished it to be over!

Only today I realize the result in my head is the same. The quiet inflicts the same pain, and I turn to myself for the peace and forgiveness that will not come, as it did not years ago. I believe I am the VICTIM as I always had been without knowing it. So the beat goes on. After a while I cry and say "I'm sorry," but my heart tells me now "that's not my line." It can only get worse!!

7/08 In the beginning when counting the "best" part of our life, we count the obvious. Later we reach more deeply and find the best part is many times the things we either took for granted or just did not notice. Now there is a warm glow which lights up my every day, and I am so thankful and cherish these times.

5/1/07 We saw clips from the old movie "What's New Pussycat" a couple of nights ago. Rob reminded me that he had seen it with several other psychiatrists when he was on the faculty of a summer workshop at St. John's in Minnesota. I had a typical internal reaction that is very familiar to me and which I seem unable to control. I felt like he had been out drinking with friends, like he was cheating on me. Feelings like that don't melt away. They just hang out somewhere inside me. I don't think that is healthy. It makes me always vulnerable. Things like that upset me, and I entertain them. I *know that's an extreme. I know a sane person wouldn't do that. So then I'm left with being insane too.*

I had decided I had done something to offend Robbie and that he was mad at me. "What did I do to make you angry?" He denied being angry, held me in his arms, and tried to comfort me. It is like this so often these days. Some little thing happens: Rob is quiet; I can't find something; I can't remember something; Rob doesn't tell me I look nice when we are ready to go out; I have a difficult time getting things together to go somewhere. I get impatient with myself and with others rather easily, and it seems to turn to some kind of anger which I don't understand. I don't want to be angry, and I think I know that there really isn't a reason to be angry, but it just seems to happen. When it happens I'm feeling so lonely, so desolate, so completely isolated. It's like no one knows I'm there. I'm invisible to everyone. It happened that way when I was a child, over and over and over again.

I live in fear of loneliness. You are there holding me and making me secure and unafraid. I love you, darling. But the pain returns, and it cannot be shared, only looked upon as something I could change if I tried. We stand apart, and my anger and my habitual fear of being alone with it push me to angry behavior and self hatred.

Your closed arms and your listening to what is happening have you searching for peace. I'm not there, and I am separated from you. I fall into my own hell. I am a frequent visitor, and no one can visit me there.

Today comes. It is fine and good, yet something stands in the way of feeling the fullness of it......it's always "today is fine" and tonight will be. It's always—what about this next night and its sleep—and, Oh God, the morning and the next day??!! Might it be what I fear? Surely it's time, or when will it be time??

Where, if at all, will I find peace—surely not as this disease increases? It has to increase, doesn't it? The beginning years of pain are so much more in my head. I cry inside. Is the truth available? Somewhere there is a place of peace for me. I believe now surely it is not here in this world. This dark, grim place—how would it be to live here? I don't want to go home. Take me somewhere else where I can be at peace—maybe I will find that only in death.

Today, for the first time, I felt it, saw it, mourned it—with no word to tell of it—to even be able to write it. The depth was the farthest, the emotion the saddest, the reality complete—no words—completely alone. What next? No anticipation, yet a compelling force to explain it to myself. Is it a start, a view of what is to be? No idea of it's being true. A feeling. To be open to it, if it continues. It will fade, I know as I write. Yet perhaps it will linger in other ways. The fear of not being able to speak of it overtakes me. It is not like other "aloneness." It's brand new. A "taste" perhaps of the future, of my future life. At that the tears are heard in my head, waiting to appear on my face—quiet now, but not at peace.

Negative feelings...hostile reactions...fear...inner hatred...though unspoken or expressed to the "victim" rots the relationship as much as though they had been spoken...a wall, though even one sided, is definitely built over which the old love cannot climb. How can a wall be one sided?

It's so very difficult to have just what I want and to feel the beating of the pain in my chest—that is unreal though still really there—throwing me off the path to peace—which I have never found other than for the moment! Is it possible this is a return of early times in other places? It must be. Oh, the pain is so familiar—with no relief, no hope of it stopping—the foretelling of the forever!!

I thought Saturday was the most horrible day of my life. Little did I know what was to follow on Sunday!! I know there is in each of our hearts a place for forgiving and why not for letting go? We've all had to do that at times with someone. When it can be, as it has to be soon...no left over, held hate, or anger.

When I get angry I am ugly. I become terribly sad. Soon I am alone and defenseless. I get furious. I feel as if I want to destroy the object of my anger. I have had fits of rage. I cry and lash out. I don't know how to be angry. I just do it. But there are certain situations in which I do not acknowledge my anger or even know that's what I'm feeling. I feel and know I feel the other parts...sad...ugly...tense...ridged...and begin to feel deserted...and misunderstood, and I definitely do not say, "I am angry, and it's OK to be angry." My heart is full of hate, again, yes again----Do I sound proud? I'm not. I'm broken and have no reason to believe I will mend.

Moods...they come to me...in the dark and quiet times, insisting to be heard. A list of things over, gone, lived so long ago—is of no use when it still hurts and causes anger.

You know what's left? The uncertainty and the fear! I literally forget the words said ... when at the time of them happening, I think they are carved in my mind ... time passes and the closeness and the resuming warmth and faith in one another soothes—and helps recovery tonight.

Confusion

I stood for what seemed like forever trying to figure a sale price at a store. Today was my most difficult with change...impossible to figure out the coins. The lady helped me.

It is the fear of being somewhere I don't want to be! It covered me...nothing soothing in it. I looked but didn't see. It stayed through dinner in a milder way...then gone. I felt it leave. It was not freedom I missed...it was reality... then it returned.

I feel helpless—without a way to go back. There can be no answer, only the continued lost love. That has been my life, my reason for living. What can I do? Is there a way to kill this monster I have become? Must I follow the path of illness to my death?

May 08. Thursday at the Mall. I truly wonder if this will be my last trip here. After lunch until now I've been in another world—one step into the death trap—but somehow a big step—confusion, crying, anger, the pain of needing to be alone!

My fears, uncertainty, having to stand alone, feelings of the past mistreatment come out like swarms of bugs!

I don't want it to be over. I've never wanted it to be over. "It"—so many things, times, places, being something, being somewhere. The days disappear with my not recognizing them. Today is one for a big exclamation mark, if I were doing that. I'll never forget it—no, I'll never remember it.

Must we go there again? To the place of mystery. I don't know why we would. I don't know why we did before. God, I thought that was over. Will goodbyes be sad—unresolved—misunderstood? Now, what is this NOW PLACE—why don't I know? Come back! I need you here!

4/6/07 Good Friday Service at the Monastery. A woman approached us with a book in her hand. She held it out and said something to me. I did not understand what she was saying. Suddenly I was back in Sunday school with the nuns. It was all so vivid, so deeply disturbing. It came so quickly…parts, one at a time, adding up to a life experience. The feeling was there before I could have put it into thought…no, not thought…pure feeling, returning wholly and truly to the past. I was there without words. Not understanding what was said makes answers impossible, and whatever the beast is, it fills the well of my heart and mind. I was there…where I thought, yet had buried… but they were not.

As though there was nothing inside my head, I came to you this morning and I cried……Now my head begins to print out words feverishly, words that cannot reach my mind and help me to think!

As we entered the Mall, I looked at the book store to my left. I can scan these places (all but the price tags) very quickly. Continuing into the building, it was pictured as always. We slowed down and Rob said, "We'll sit here." I had seen the shops across the way and read the names. I knew what they were. But this table? Why here? Why this table? Rob said, "We always sit here." Oh, God, the biggest…what should I call them…now that they are here…clearly, odd word "clearly"…total blank…total empty…total. Where are we? Total first time!

Reflections

I have thought I had to do it all. I've lived always thinking that. I have been overloaded and not known how to deal with it. Mistakes had to be my fault. Who did that to me and how? I thought I was lacking something, something I've always searched for. Joy and delight came, but didn't stay.

Crying will come...it always has. I've never peacefully lived with loss...or my inadequacies, so I've lived my life feeling a failure. I've constantly reached back and highly colored the mistakes, the sadness in my heart...always being less...nothing to be proud of lives there.

The attainment of peace, the resolution of conflict, the forgiveness of others sometimes requires a solitary solution, a private accomplishment, a personal surrender.

One makes no sharp narrow line with an old brush but strokes and accepts the marks!

And then it comes like love forgotten—there is no swell or washing over consciousness. It is ever present...and, as breathing, is necessary and supports life. Acceptance...not surging...it was laid as dew. It is a spirit...composed of peace.

I am free from everyone except myself. All the talking didn't change anything. What burdens do I impose on those who love me? The other women—those before me—always did that—always. There was payment due. To be loved was to pay the price. Would I want to control as they did? I am not able to handle the control I have!! Don't go back and read. Go on. The lessons are learned in the writing, not the reading.

There is no place of happiness for me. It does not exist. No peace, now knowing that perhaps I can stop wishing for it. What then are other needs? No one to ask. Nowhere to look. Be glad to be alive? Look at the world in a new way? I have little hope, but I could try.

This is your time, Jane, use it—not to make up for something you did or didn't do. You don't have to have a goal or a plan. Have faith, believe you have something you can still do, and that is a good thing. God will help you. Don't get mad at Him for your condition. Don't try too hard! So much I don't know. Don't keep score! Try to forgive yourself a little piece at a time. Really, just be the you you want to be. It's never too late, no matter what you feel sometimes.

This is my only chance, and if it turns out to be a waste of a life, I suppose I won't know it, in the sense that I know things now. I am deeply saddened by the thought that I will have spent all these years...used all this being...this personhood...for nothing.

I feel a tremendous loss! How can I strive and change into becoming what I have never known? It feels like such a waste. I want another chance to be something...I don't know what.

I don't want to change the people in my life. I don't even want to understand them. I just want not to care what they do and what they are. I want to be untied from them. I don't want it to matter to me. I want to start over again with me...with making something out of this mess of a person.

I have poured it all out until there is nothing left. For years, for always, I have poured out. I have not been giving, really. I've watched and looked and busied myself with seeing and keeping score, and I am drained. What if I were to say: I'm tired of all this...just let me be...and I got quiet ...and stopped pouring? That would be the end of them loving me...ever again... and what would I be?

You know there were times long ago when I didn't understand and should have, or when I should have at least been more aware of what I was living and learning. I never understood about "growing up." I did it until now at 78, but I did not "know" it. At times now I still face being there—with the mystery of being surrounded by adults, and I remember how they were and how I felt and how I have never really grown up. Oh God, now I return to being unable to do the few things I finally taught myself through the struggle. And soon that will be gone.

In college I had no goals. I doubted my art abilities...didn't know what was expected of me...I showed up...did what I had to do...had no passion for the craft…no appreciation for what I was exposed to. I never stood and loved a piece as I do now. I had no thirst…sought out nothing. I did not esteem, appreciate, celebrate, value myself. Everyone has a place where he stands…where was mine? I continued looking for that standing place and substituted other things for it. It worked out OK. I'm not really sure why. Finally someone else saw and showed me my value. What else can I call it… something I was without and now am empowered by?

Someday it will be different from today. Today will be okay soon, and we will be happy I know. The time will come when that will not happen. That will be the last day. If I walk as far as I can, it will be over.

Recently I have been able to tell Robbie when he does something that irritates me. A few days ago it was a tone of voice he used when he said something. The tone made me feel "put down," not respected, not important. That is such a familiar, long ago feeling and now becomes monumentally offensive. But when he responds in touch, with that it evaporates. We need to continue to work together this way.

I am not a different person … on this emotional ride. It is Jane and who she partly is and always was, once she found a voice for all the hell she felt inside. The voice inside becomes clear as I wade back into the years ago and continue obviously the reaction, the behavior, the violent self-hatred. Once I blamed it on someone and couldn't let go or change my thinking. I was in that place…it's where I've been before. I know it well…described as hell…and still I respond to what someone else cannot change.

Who to be? No one ever helped me to plan, to learn to understand, to even think of being a grown up. I'm 79 now…all those years……no goals, no hopes, no plans, no expectations…just moving along. Or was it even that? I can't even remember what it was that gave me the peace of mind I must have had…at times.

My stepfather threw away my dolls. I saw my Dolly Dimple spread wide across the bottom of the trash can---she was looking up at me with her pale blue eyes seeming to dislike the newer less friendly dolls piled upon her. I stared but didn't reach for her. That was our last farewell. For years I have seen her under the other dolls… piled… making her invisible to me.

You always cry for those things you have given away and cry when you see the things you haven't given......you cry for what you said...for what you couldn't tell.

I'm sure it is from the giving and receiving of years ago and from being forced to give the dearly precious things you have not yet held tightly and given your love to. I wasn't finished loving them so the guilt was mine to last forever.

We walked to the beach, the sand met the ocean, and the ocean touched the sky. We turned and saw how far we had come. The joy of love fills my soul.

The remembering stays alive and relives in our lives. There are small moments when I wonder --- how can this living be life? In my heart where I live, I know the answer.

Friends and Family

You see me blindly. You make pictures of me behind your closed eyes. Pictures sit, confirmed forever what you have made of me. When I am not what you see, you close your eyes and either run your own pictures or shut me off entirely and see something else. Either way, I am here performing...trying to be what you have envisioned or trying to love you back to "looking."

9/12/08 The line I need drawn is there, but where? Where? Bring me to it for recognition. It will not hold still for me...but goes on long after I have died of hate. They are, if not understood, at least to be forgiven. Those who speak and push forward their ignorance...what of those? What understanding to be brought to that?

The people I love best can and do hurt me the most. They seem to be so satisfied with their picture, their truth...for them their door closes and it's gone because they are so sure. And I am left...cut and bleeding.

I had finally learned to live and be loved. How can I truly love like I am? Yes, I want my family to understand and help me live with this, my beloved through now and on...but the ashes...the door was never really open to me to be part of their lives.

Love is not something to be given only in return for love. It must be given sometimes to those whom one does not understand and maybe to those whom one finds difficult to understand and to love.

After Xmas visit—2008. I had a chance to see you in many ways...in lights and shades, mother, daughter, friend, home maker, peace maker, creator of all beautiful...your home, your kitchen...cooking, baking...the tables, the food... how grand! Playing your violin, speaking creatively to your children...I watched them see you and watched their love and yours for them circle. I saw it! Thank God!

Oh Laura...a new, another, a familiar love for you...that has always been and will always be in my heart, and I wrap myself around it so gratefully.

01/31/08 Yesterday was not a good day. I was sad and spent a lot of time worrying about all sorts of things. It would be difficult to enumerate or even to put into words all the things I worry about. All the contacts with family bring up questions. Will I ever get to see them again? Will I know them when I do see them? Will I remember when I last saw them? Even if I do know them, will I remember anything about past times we were together?

I think I had no idea—yes, I did, that I am so consistently a pain in the ass. Can't I keep still and not blather? Why? Why? I have to trip again—again. I will always be Jane. Will anyone ever know who and what I really am, so they could remember that with love, find thoughts knowing they had missed it during my life with them?

The strength of my childhood belief remains. No, it wasn't innocent then. It filled me with the only strength I had ---not to be expressed but to hold me. I'm certain I didn't know how or why to ask for my family's love?

Death

This is the "it" it always was, all of the tiles lined together, one after one to tell the story of life. And still you're left alone with yourself—the self you grew up with and always were and will be, until by the hand of God it will be ended. Is it a wonder that somewhere inside of me I wish for that day to be soon? No change—no hope for that. I awaken to a day of being ME, believing it to be a punishment for something still unknown.

Lord have mercy on this soul which fights and wonders how to die. How was it born, the product of ignorance and disbelief?

So many words about the past, of loneliness unfelt during its happening. I feel my soul at times and hold it in my hands, knowing my separation from it. The lifelong guilt is gone, and as if the space must be filled—sadness by some other name—pours in. Ugliness pains my being.

The past hour... I died again...the feeling still remains. All day I've thought of death...that we will not return home. It didn't matter how...I kept it. I sometimes wish it would happen...what a relief. There!

As the little girl next door used to say "how if," how if it ended now? O.K. Jane, how? Today? Tomorrow? A clear message to start to work on the plan now? Yes!!

To whom do I write when I am angry and sad? When I am so close, I can touch the end of my life...I stand and find reasons for not wanting to die this moment, but in my head and my mind that truly is what I want to do now.

"The return to real life"...I wrote those words so long ago! How could my life today be more real? I am on a measured path to dying! Be found then or rather this very day...I hold not hope in my heart...it's a little like being constantly in a daze.

I look down at my own hands and they are dead...blue in places and some jaundice... the skin is dry...they might even be hard...my ring pressing against an almost transparent flesh...a part of me wishes for the release of death. "I am making my last effort to return that which is divine in me to that which is divine in the universe." Possibly I have not yet made my first effort to that end, and it is the desire to do so that haunts me. I have been unaware of anyone's effort to do so, living well has been the thing...yet that not too successfully done.

Somewhere there is a place of peace for me. I believe now surely it is not here in this world. This dark, grim place—how would it be to live here? I don't want to go "home." Take me somewhere else where I can be at peace—maybe I will find that only in death.

Robbie

I will not be there when Christmas comes…as I have been for all the years of our life. Knowing that to be true…what…what now can I touch, reach and touch…tell you of my undying love for you?

As I waited I watched you as long as I could see you… then there were people here and there blocking my complete view…yet a piece of blue shirt…the back of your head…you did not disappear…you continued on in my head and heart. You are my world. I began to live when we met, all those years ago!

I have tried for months to tell Rob details of how I feel—of what fills my mind—of my fears—one hears so much and wonders as one's brain sinks into "mush." I don't want answers. I do need to know someone hears what I say and listens to how I think and feel and portray the unknown future. Questions cannot be answered—future is not known—listen to what I say—know what I feel while I can still tell you—while I can talk—speak—and realize that I am a live being. Listen to me—hear me—who can understand? I expect that of no one—but hear me, will you? Pay attention to what I am saying. Do you notice when it stops before the thought is finished?

A new fear…just recently discovered. What if I should lose Robbie? What if "something happens to him?"—a euphemism for death. What would I do? I couldn't take care of myself…or could I? I don't really know. But the thought brings panic. I know his prayer is that he will be able to care for me until my death. But he is ten years older than I, and longevity in women is greater than in men. His health is good, and he takes good care of it. But there are accidents; there are unexpected, unpredictable events. When Rob and I quarrel I sometimes think I could lose him by his leaving. What an intolerable feeling! I know it isn't possible…but I think…no feel the worst when I am isolated.

Who really knows me? Robbie...yes, he is the only person on earth who does! How does he rebuild himself after so much pain and loss of faith that I can direct my own life? If I could change, how would I feel? I wish I really could do that...even for these last few years (if I have that).

After all this togetherness at the Mall, Rob cleared the table and went to put it in the trash. He left our coffee cups on the table and pulled his chair out when he got up. He was away about 15 seconds. I engaged in one of my automatic thought processes that have been happening all my life. "When he comes back he'll push the chair in and say, 'It's time to go.' It would be so nice if he would just sit down and talk for a while longer." He did! It made my day or at least a span of time. Nothing seems to last long these days.

Dear Robbie: Now the shadows grow along the path of endings. How can I tell you how much I love you, and how that love washes over me and fills my soul? I am happier than I know how to tell you...something has come to be settled in my soul...it has no name...it comes upon me...quickly I recognize it...and I rest in it. It is what our togetherness is and will always be. I welcome it, cannot bring it to happen, but it is full and lovely! It bodes me well to bring the rest of my life to "it."

On reading old books: Now when I rediscover these bound expressions of our love that we once exchanged with joy, I cannot recall the day or the occasion for their giving. I read the words that made the text appropriate and meaningful and "re-feel" the quickening of my breathing even as then, those long years ago.

Not the same tears well within me, for those have been long since shed one hundred times, often in the purple, red, and blue of stained glass lighted afternoons, and later in the shadowed payment for that light...without regret and willingly.

The words take hold of me as they have before and lift me from this place I am, holding me as if they exist in a place I only know with them and you. I return as if awakening.

When I think of all the words I wrote of you or came to read which told you how I felt, I wish I had them still to know again. I have learned well to cry inside and do so now at the thought of them. More would be too sad to hide from you here beside me, and my secret sadness would be unfolded upon you. They are, after all, only words of love, and you are here as I only then wished you to be.

You inspire me, Rob, my hero, my guiding light, my shinning star, my partner, holding my hand tightly on our way to heaven! Stay by me until then, beloved!

Where are my peace and the everlasting love and warmth and security of my beloved's arms? He created a place of peace and security that was never there before I found him. I stand alone and devastated without him, because of my behavior. I hold my empty head in my hands and ask God why?

No place is secure and safe from hatred and loss of fullness and security. Again I am reminded of the loss of being.

When I looked at Rob's face, I saw clearly my love of the first days and all the years that have followed. It is I who am changing, not he. I have at times another voice. When I speak I don't understand it. I know what I hear myself saying. It is to an enemy---and at the moment I feel justified.

How, with such limited and bent things in my heart, can I write more than I can tell you or than you can ever know?

I begin to think I have no love left to give to others. But I suppose that can't be true.

The anger...the overwhelming sadness I feel---bewilders me. There can be no way to understand that. I have not one regret about us---you and me! Start there! I say that because either you will never read this or I won't be able to answer or explain. I become full of a tearful, tearful sadness now as I write. I don't know why.

So tired I went back to bed...Robbie coming in the bedroom behind...lowering the blind...pulling the black leather desk chair to the side of the bed and softly rubbing my feet...closed eyes. I knew, thinking I was asleep, he would quietly leave and partly close the door. Then I heard the oh so soft sound of *the chair...as he stood up. I will hear that same sound another day. Will I recognize it...without being able to see or speak?*

I am secure--truly loved. My heart is covered and kept alive and warm with my love for Rob. I am privileged, after all the pain I endured, to be free for the first time to give and to be part of a loving, deep relationship. We are one. We are the same person. I stand not alone ever.

When the partnership is ended and I am no longer one of a pair...there will be nothing for me but that one which will no longer be a one of anything else... just...only one. What will I do? Where will I go or be or stand?

In the beginning, from the first that I knew I had Alzheimer's, I was startled, afraid, sad, very angry at God for this punishment, especially when I thought of all my life of punishment thus far. I was not easy to get along with at various times...hard to deal with...more angry than afraid. Between that time and now there have been many variations, much despair, more acceptances. I have a love unending, beyond imagination. I have failed again and again in attitude...in behaviors...along with the stronger fullness of the deep love he and I have for each other. His love fills my soul...our happiness overflows me.

Religion

Writing to God seems easy for me, although clearing my head is sometimes very difficult.

This is not a complaint, although I am so often MAD at God, and I can feel the emptiness so powerfully. I never talk about it. One just stands by and keeps silent.

God, let me not be proud, help me with the words, the thoughts, the gifts you have given me! You do not make living appear to be easy. You make life appear to be worth living. Do not follow my path...walk beside me for a little while. In seeking perfection we miss the joy of the journey.

My prayer: not to learn to be wise—but rather to seek the truth. Have no regrets for me.

Each day: accept the "bad" days...live bravely...remember this is God's plan. He knows you are here...and holds you in his hands, even though I forget he does!

Pray...support Rob by helping in these things...pray for him...and our togetherness!

And "now" the prayer I had forgotten. "Please, God stay with us and help me to be the person I know I can be! Connect me with thoughts, feelings, observations that will hold my heart and mind in your hand. It is what will save me. It is the only way I can renew my sense of 'giving,' of going on to be the person I've all my life prayed to be."

Could it be the answer to the "Why?" This gift—pure, full, inspiring, confirming education. My God, I believe it is, after 70 years of praying, not knowing for what. It is the answer. I have found the peace, the gift...so long awaited...not knowing what I asked for...fighting to keep close to God... failing...time after time in all things.

I have folded my hands and prayed and asked: open my hands so I can hold what you give me...so I can lift what you put before me...so I can reach out and touch and love...empty hands, full heart. Let me be myself, maybe I don't want to be quiet, silent—maybe I need to shout and cry and sing and rejoice and tell you and ask you. Today let me be with you in Paradise, a little girl still dressing up with clothes from under the cellar steps.

The desire to be alone and to commune with God is now joined with a sense of giving over my desires to what in His judgment is best for me. The belief in God is an ever present, rich, full part of my life, my being. He is real... childhood visions...manhood not removed but developed and increased by an overwhelming spirit...three in one...truly existing for me.

If you change too much, at the end of your life God may not know you. I will try to be quiet and perhaps all I discovered today will become part of me.

185

Quiet does not happen without my making it happen. In the stillness waits the self—at times of confusion rarely.

I might have been mad at God at another time, but not mad at God now. Part of my life to come, I wish some good could come out of it. I always wanted it to be that way. If you and I get through it----I know we will.

Rob and I went to the Monastery yesterday for a "Day of Quiet and Solitude." I was absorbed with the overwhelming beauty of the towers of little white candles beside every statue. I talked to them and to God as I did for all those growing up years, reminding them that I knew I wasn't part of all this but I longed to be.

I signed up to talk to the priest not so much because I had something I wanted to talk about but because it made me feel that I was really part of what was going on. I wasn't on the outside looking in.

I am 77 years old, and as this disease continues to worsen will I forget all those alone years, or will they be enlarged in my mind and keep the guilt filling the empty space that is now growing larger. I cry now alone. This "growing up"… terrified… by all those purported to protect and save me---smothered me. Mass darkness and fear, shame and unworthiness were built into the high wall behind which I exist…and nobody knows more than what they see me to be. The protective hand I hold up high is not what they see it to be…I'm reaching up to God to remind Him that I am here…asking His forgiveness.

Forgiveness, as so often is the case, was the center star in the homily. Make peace with those from whom you have separated yourself, those with whom you have exchanged ugly words, those who need to know now that you have and still do love them. For some it is not possible…it's too late…all the more reason to seek out the living.

I talk to God constantly as I have always done. I have stopped asking "why?" Shame, guilt, anger, and "why didn't I do what I had the talent to do" fill my head!!! I no longer create. I have trouble being relaxed with anyone but Rob.

I carry old memories and am highly critical, mainly of myself, but judgmental of others.

God has been my companion forever, but guilt was always huge. I have confessed; I have been forgiven...haven't I?

I can't seem to be as creative as I was. I need only touch something and I am pleased, but the rest is gone.

Give up what's gone. Can I be poor in spirit? I kept taking. God and going to him. I have been told stories of my life, all bad, and I hung on; but I have retold them until they are engraved. God was the only one!!! I carry the two equally, the memories of injustice I can repeat over and over and I do. When did I fall in love with God?

If this is alone with God, as I have often believed and felt, then I miss this... and had forgotten that feeling. It was so important to me. I need to remember what is important to me. I need to find those things and touch them again.

Perhaps God does not expect so much of me now. I'm not Jane, not myself. I am someone so much less ... I never thought I could ever be less ... but I am helpless to be more and like I was.

I call to you in the darkness, knowing you are the light—and if for some failure of mine I do not recognize my visitor, forgive me and take me to your heart. Do I pray as loudly as I sing and beg?

Please, God, no more dazes. No more even thinking of death. I am alive. I am here---my heart beats. Something lately has boggled my thinking. I am angry---blow-ups so often...I fought it. I cried...Why? Why? Blow-ups often. That has passed---long time ago now. How good God has been to me. Safe in his arms. Yes. Yes. And Rob! God is good---grow, walk, Jane, look at whatever you want to look at. Breathe deeply, pray and be happy!

When my mind takes me to revisit a trip of long ago, do you go with me, God? Do you hear me? Do you hear me when I rebel? When I am indescribably angry? What are you thinking? Do you know my pain?

A fresh page…a very similar feeling…I want to see Mary…I want to be here for that…so it will be right. God hold my face in your hands!

(Robbie: Life has changed. There are increasing restrictions in our exchanges and our activities. Jane's memory of the day is gone by nightfall. But she remains my best companion, my love, the source of my strength and my happiness.)

Epilogue

My Hero

IN 2008 MY ELEVEN year old granddaughter, Laura's child, had a class assignment to write a short essay about someone in their lives whom they saw as a hero. I have received Laura's and Casey's permission to close this book with her essay.

My Hero

Sickness. Forgetfulness. Brain Damage. Frustration. Not understanding. Dying. All these define one thing: Alzheimer's. I learned just one or two years ago that my grandmother had gotten this sickness. At first I had no clue what it was. I just thought my mother meant a bad cold or a fever maybe, something she could get over. I had no clue it would be a sickness that slowly made you forget more and more, get frustrated and bothered by every little thing, or say something over and over again without knowing you said it. I had absolutely no clue that slowly, you don't know how much time it would take, you would die from it. I was so scared when I heard all of this from my mother thinking that she would forget us and who we were. But really the time I saw her after my mom told me about her disease she seemed perfectly fine, like nothing had happened. But since then it has gotten worse. She has forgotten more, has said things again and again, and even gotten lost sometimes.

But though this sickness has disabled her in numerous ways, she has fought through it no matter how hard it gets. Whenever we go to see her she tells stories. Stories, stories, stories. Stories about her childhood, like how she went to art school and how she always played with her dolls. And she is always telling us about how she used to work in a mall and pretend to be a manikin. But no matter what they are or how recently they happened, she will always have a story to tell. Another major trait she hung on to is that she has always had style. You will always see her walking around with her hair nicely put up and a stylin' blouse and slacks. Nothing will ever stop her style from showing. But most importantly, it doesn't matter what kind of mood she's in that day, she will always come up to us when we visit and embrace like there's no tomorrow. She will listen caringly to whatever we have to say and support us in whatever we do. She questions us about our year and never even coming close to forgetting who we are. I couldn't have asked for a better grandmother: one who fights her sickness and who keeps strong through everything. One who still cares and loves us with all her heart even though Alzheimer's threatens to erase all her memories more and more each day.

So lastly, my grandmother is my hero because of her strength, not physically but inside her heart. She fights the disease for not just herself and her memory, but for me and my mom and sister and for everyone else who cares and loves her. She fights to keep our memories of her wonderful and cheerful. And even though she knows that someday she will pass on from this sickness, she makes the times that we spend with her seem like they will never end. She is still the amazing person she has always been, even after Alzheimer's took hold of her and her memories. Stay strong Gram!!

Casey McConville

10111468R0

www.wadsworth.com

wadsworth.com is the World Wide Web site for Wadsworth and is your direct source to dozens of online resources.

At *wadsworth.com* you can find out about supplements, demonstration software, and student resources. You can also send email to many of our authors and preview new publications and exciting new technologies.

wadsworth.com
Changing the way the world learns®

Essentials of
WESTERN
CIVILIZATION

A HISTORY OF EUROPEAN SOCIETY

Steven Hause
University of Missouri–St. Louis

William Maltby
University of Missouri–St. Louis

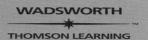

WADSWORTH

THOMSON LEARNING

Australia • Canada • Mexico • Singapore • Spain • United Kingdom • United States

WADSWORTH
THOMSON LEARNING

History Publisher: Clark Baxter
Senior Development Editor: Sharon Adams Poore
Assistant Editor: Cherie Hackelberg
Editorial Assistant: Jennifer Ellis
Marketing Manager: Diane McOscar
Marketing Assistant: Kristin Anderson
Print Buyer: Barbara Britton
Production Management: Lori Dalberg, Carlisle Publishers Services
Text Designer: Harry Voigt
Copy Editor: Pat Eichhorst
Maps: MapQuest.com
Cover Designer: Harry Voigt
Cover Image: Erich Lessing/Art Resource, NY. Angrand, Charles (1854–1926). Couple in the Street. 1887, Musee d'Orsay, Paris, France.
Compositor: Carlisle Communications
Text and Cover Printer: R.R. Donnelley & Sons, Willard

Wadsworth/Thomson Learning
10 Davis Drive
Belmont, CA 94002-3098
USA

For more information about our products, contact us:
Thomson Learning Academic Resource Center
1-800-423-0563
http://www.wadsworth.com

International Headquarters
Thomson Learning
International Division
290 Harbor Drive, 2nd Floor
Stamford, CT 06902-7477
USA

UK/Europe/Middle East/South Africa
Thomson Learning
Berkshire House
168-173 High Holborn
London WC1V 7AA
United Kingdom

Asia
Thomson Learning
60 Albert Street, #15-01
Albert Complex
Singapore 189969

Canada
Nelson Thomson Learning
1120 Birchmount Road
Toronto, Ontario M1K 5G4
Canada

ISBN: 0-534-57870-5

ABOUT THE AUTHORS

◆◆◆◆◆◆◆◆◆◆◆◆◆◆◆◆◆◆◆◆◆◆◆◆

Steven C. Hause is Professor of History and Fellow in International Studies at the University of Missouri–St. Louis, where he has won the Chancellor's Award for Excellence in Teaching (1996) and the Pierre Laclede Honors College Teacher of the Year Award (1989). He is the author and co-author of three previous books on the history of the women's rights movement in modern France, which have won four research prizes: *Women's Suffrage and Social Politics in the French Third Republic*, with Anne R. Kenney (Princeton University Press, 1984); *Hubertine Auclert, the French Suffragette* (Yale University Press, 1987); and *Feminisms of the Belle Epoque*, with Jennifer Waelti-Walters (University of Nebraska Press, 1994). His essays have appeared in several journals, including *American Historical Review* and *French Historical Studies.*

William S. Maltby is Professor of History Emeritus at the University of Missouri–St. Louis, where he continues to teach on a regular basis. Among his publications are: *The Black Legend in England: The Development of Anti-Spanish Sentiment, 1558–1660.* (Duke University Press, 1971), *Alba: A Biography of Fernando Alvarez de Toledo, Third Duke of Alba, 1507–1582.* (University of California Press, 1983), and articles on various aspects of Early Modern European history. From 1977 to 1997 he also served as Executive Director of the Center for Reformation Research and as editor of several volumes and series of volumes on the history of the Reformation.

CONTENTS IN BRIEF

◆◆◆◆◆◆◆◆◆◆◆◆◆◆◆◆◆◆◆

▨ CHAPTER ▨

CONTENTS IN DETAIL
◆◆◆◆◆◆◆◆◆◆◆◆◆◆◆◆◆◆◆◆

Chapter 22   Industrialization and the Social and Economic Structure of Europe   414

Chapter 23   Daily Life in the Nineteenth Century   435

Chapter 24   The Defense of the Old Regime, 1815–48   458

DOCUMENTS
◆◆◆◆◆◆◆◆◆◆◆◆◆◆◆◆◆◆◆◆◆

TABLES

◆◆◆◆◆◆◆◆◆◆◆◆◆◆◆◆◆◆◆◆◆◆◆

MAPS

❖❖❖❖❖❖❖❖❖❖❖❖❖❖❖❖❖❖❖❖❖❖

PREFACE

◆◆◆◆◆◆◆◆◆◆◆◆◆◆◆◆◆◆◆◆◆◆◆

*E*ssentials of Western Civilization: A History of European Society is a compact introduction to a large subject. Like other Western civilization texts, we have written a text that interweaves into a coherent narrative the development of political institutions; the cultural, religious, and intellectual contributions of the European elite; the military history that shaped the lives of everyone; and the everyday life experiences of ordinary men, women, and children. We have sought to locate that social history in its economic and political context and in relation to other historical issues. Similarly, we have treated war and technology as phenomena that influenced, and were influenced by, social and economic structures, and we have given popular culture its due without sacrificing the special interests of the elites.

A Brief Text

In the words of Jonson's Volpone, we think the many virtues of this book are too numerous not to mention. But we will emphasize only a few in this preface. First, the book is intentionally briefer than many standard survey texts, including our own recent *Western Civilization: A History of European Society*. We think a briefer text is more useful for those instructors who use a textbook chiefly as the core of a course that includes numerous outside readings or use of other supplementary material. We hope that by omitting a degree of detail that is not central to an understanding of the subject that we have made it easier for students to absorb and understand the broad currents of Western civilization. This less expensive text also makes the purchase of outside readings more affordable. A brief examination of the text itself will reveal that we have not skimped on full-color maps illustrations, which help bring this material to life.

Learning History Through Primary Source Documents

The second thing we want to bring to the attention of the first-time reader is the boxed inserts we have included. These are of two types. In every chapter we have included written primary source documents similar to the material that most instructors use to supplement their courses. We have chosen a broad range of letters, treaties, poems, broadsides, declarations, and other things that bring to the attention of students the kinds of material that historians have traditionally used in doing their own research. We have enjoyed watching our own students wrestle with these excerpts from primary documents, and we hope other students will find them as stimulating as our students do.

Learning History Through Tables and Charts

In addition, the book is filled with numerous tables and charts of historical data, involving trade balances, the relative size of various European cities over time, and military expenditures. But the majority of these tables involve the details of everyday life. Until very recently, of course, the great majority of Europeans was illiterate and unable to leave behind a written record of their lives. But the story of these people is, to say the least, an important part of the overall account of Western civilization. This statistical information appears most frequently in those chapters that cover modern times when such records are more reliable and available. They provide us with our best information on life outside the court or castle, and we are delighted to include many of them in this text. These are especially helpful in teaching students about the lives of the millions of ordinary men and women who left behind no written accounts of their lives. By examining parish, municipal, and other records, we are able to piece together such information as wages and prices in ancient Rome, life expectancy in the middle ages, the incidence of abandoned children in major cities, and other telling details of everyday life over time.

Studying the Past Through Maps, Tables, Charts, and Art

Most historians are more accustomed to explaining the past through prose than with numbers. We are pleased, therefore, that John Soares, a gifted historian and teacher, has written a brief booklet, entitled Studying the Past through Maps, Tables, Charts, and Art, that helps students see the human faces hidden just behind each column of numbers. For example, table 18.3 in chapter 18 shows that 45 percent of a worker's family income in late 18th-century Berlin was spent on bread, 12 percent was spent on other vegetable products, and 15 percent on meat and dairy products. The booklet helps students see that for many centuries bread was the major source of nutrition among peasants and workers, rather than the side dish it has become today. The booklet goes on to help students realize that the recurring bread riots discussed in the text arose out of real deprivation: when the price of bread rose, ordinary people starved. The numbers make these things starkly plain, and this wonderful manual make them easy for the first-time reader to decipher. This manual is free with every student copy of the text.

In Addition to an explication and directed questions about each of the book's tables, the booklet also helps students see the cultural information imbedded in one of the pieces of art in every chapter. For example, an illustration in chapter 18 shows a coach stop in a small 18th-century town. Students will enjoy the picture on their own. But many may need to be prodded to speculate on the time it will take to fix the broken wheel on one of the stage coaches, and to think further about the pace of transportation in 18th-century Europe. This invaluable booklet brings these historically important considerations to the attention of the first-time reader.

Maps

All of the book's many maps appear in full color, and may include such topographic features as mountains and rivers. Like most historians, we use maps extensively in our teaching. And we know that color can convey more information than can hash marks or degrees of shading. Likewise, we think it essential that a

map of archaic Greece, for example, reinforce the text by showing students the mountainous terrain that led to development of independent city-states. The map of archaic Greece in chapter two does this.

Illustrations

The book includes some 200 illustrations, most of them in color. Each is identified in the text and bears directly on the discussion in the adjoining pages on which they appear. And each includes a caption that adds some additional information that complements the text.

Ancillaries

The package that accompanies this book is full of print and electronic ancillaries that cost a fortune to produce and sucked the life blood out of the people who prepared and produced them. Among them are the following:

Instructor's Manual with Test Bank   Prepared by John Soares. Each chapter contains Chapter Outlines, Learning Objectives, Suggested Lecture Topics, Suggested Student Activities, Test Questions (Multiple Choice, True/False, Essay, and Identification), Table, Figure, and Art analysis, Internet resources, and Video Resources.
One volume for all three versions of the text.

ExamView   Create, deliver, and customize tests and study guides (both print and online) in minutes with this easy-to-use assessment and tutorial system. ExamView offers both a Quick Test Wizard and an Online Test Wizard that guide you step-by-step through the process of creating tests, while its unique "WYSIWYG" capability allows you to see the test you are creating on the screen exactly as it will print or display online. You can build tests of up to 250 questions using up to 12 question types. Using ExamView's complete word processing capabilities, you can enter an unlimited number of new questions or edit existing questions.

Study Guides   Volume I, Volume II
Prepared by John Soares. Contains Chapter Outlines, Learning Objectives, Identifications, Matching, Multiple Choice questions, Fill-in-the Blank questions, Chronologies, Questions for Critical Thought, Analysis of Primary Source Documents, Geography and Map Analysis, and Table, Figure, and Art analysis. Two volumes to correspond with volumes I and II of the main text.

Map Acetates and Commentary for Western Civilization, 2000 Edition   This extensive four-color acetate package includes maps from the text and from other sources and includes map commentary prepared by James Harrison, Siena College. The acetates and commentary are 3-hole punched and shrink-wrapped.

Western Civilization PowerPoint   Windows and Macintosh Contains all the four-color maps from the map acetate package, described above.

Document Exercises Workbooks   Volume I, Volume II Prepared by Donna Van Raaphorst, Cuyahoga Community College is a two-volume collection of exercises based around primary sources, teaching students how to use documents and historiographic methods.

Map Workbooks   Volume I, Volume II Prepared by Cynthia Kosso, Northern Arizona University, this two-volume workbook features over 20 map exercises. The exercises are designed to help students understand the relationship between places and people through time. All map exercises incorporate three parts; an introduction, a locations section where students are asked to correctly place a city, site, or boundary, and a question section.

Sights and Sounds of History   VHS video Short, focused video clips, photos, artwork, animation's, music, and dramatic readings are used to bring life to historical topics and events which are most difficult for students to appreciate from a textbook alone. For example, students will experience the grandeur of Versailles and the defeat felt by a German soldier at Stalingrad. The video segments, each averaging 4 minutes long, make excellent lecture launchers.

CNN Today Videos: Western Civilization   Volume I, Volume II These 3-4 minute introductions to various topics make great lecture launchers.

History Video Library   Many new videos for this edition. Available to qualified adoptions.

Journey of Civilization CD-ROM   This CD-ROM takes the student on 18 interactive journeys through history. Enhanced with QuickTime movies, animations, sound clips, maps, and more, the journeys allow students to engage in history as active participants rather than as readers of past events.

Internet Guide for History, Third Edition   Prepared by John Soares. Provides newly revised and up-to-date internet exercises by topic. Can be found at http://history.wadsworth.com.

Archer, Documents of Western Civilization, Volume I: To 1715

Archer, Documents of Western Civilization, Volume II: Since 1550   A broad selection of carefully selected documents.

Magellan World History Atlas   Available to bundle with any History text contains 44 historical four-color maps.

Webtutor   Volume I, Volume II Two volumes to correspond with Volumes I and II of the main text. This content-rich, Web-based teaching and learning tool helps students succeed by taking the course beyond classroom boundaries to an anywhere, anytime environment. *Web Tutor* offers real-time access to a full array of study tools, including flashcards (with audio), practice quizzes, online tutorials, and Web links.

Acknowledgments

We owe our gratitude to all those who helped us in the preparation of *Essentials of Western Civilization: A History of European Society*:

We would also like to thank all those at Wadsworth Publishing who have assisted us in producing this book: Clark Baxter, our editor who suggested the book and carried it into production; Sharon Adams Poore, our developmental editor; Cherie Hackelberg, assistant editor, who put the supplement package together; Hal Humphrey, project editor; Diane McOscar, marketing manager; Jennifer Ellis, editorial assistant, and Lori Dalberg at Carlisle Publishers Services.

Reviewers

Gerald D. Anderson, North Dakota State University; Roz L. Ashby, Yavapai College; David Bartley, Indiana Wesleyan University; Anthony Bedford. Modesto Junior College; Rodney E. Bell, South Dakota University; Richard Camp, California State University–Northridge; Elizabeth Carney, Clemson University; Sherri Cole, Arizona Western College; Jeffrey Cox, University of Iowa; Philip B. Crow; Leslie Derfler, Florida Atlantic University; Marsha L. Frey, University of

Montana; Sarah Gravelle, University of Detroit; Stephen Haliczer, Northern Illinois University; Barry Hankins, Baylor University; William Hartel, Marietta College; Mack Holt, George Mason University; Frank Josserand, Southwest Texas State University; Gary Kates, Trinity University; Paul Leuschen, University of Arkansas; Eleanor Long, Hinds Community College; Olivia H. McIntyre, Eckerd College; David L. Longfellow, Baylor University; Bill Mackey, University of Alaska–Anchorage; Tom McMullen, Georgia Southern University; Paul L. Maier, Western Michigan University; Larry Marvin, St. Louis University; Carol Bresnahan Menning, University of Toledo; Jeffrey Merrick, University of Wisconsin–Milwaukee; Dennis Mihelich, Creighton University; Charles G. Nauert, Jr., University of Missouri–Columbia; Thomas C. Owen, Louisiana State University; William E. Painter, University of North Texas;

Kathleen Paul, University of Southern Florida; Nancy Rachels, Hillsborough Community College; Elsa Rapp, Montgomery County Community College; Miriam Raub Vivian, California State University–Bakersfield; Richard R. Rivers, Macomb Community College; Kenneth W. Rock, Colorado State University; Karl A. Roider, Louisiana State University; Leonard Rosenband, Utah State University; Joyce E. Salisbury, University of Wisconsin–Green Bay; Jerry Sandvick, North Hennepin Community College; Thomas P. Schlunz, University of New Orleans; Donna Simpson, Wheeling Jesuit University; Elisabeth Sommer, Grand Valley State University; Ira Spar, Ramapo College of New Jersey; Jake W. Spidle, University of New Mexico; Roger D. Tate, Somerset Community College; Jackson Taylor, Jr., University of Mississippi; Timothy M. Teeter, Georgia Southern University; Lee Shai Weissbach, University of Louisville

Essentials of
WESTERN CIVILIZATION

CHAPTER **1**

THE ANCIENT NEAR EAST: MESOPOTAMIA, EGYPT, PHOENICIA, ISRAEL

CHAPTER OUTLINE

◆◆◆◆◆◆◆◆◆◆◆◆◆◆◆◆◆◆◆◆

Western civlization rests upon the achievements of far more ancient societies. Long before the Greeks or Romans, the peoples of the ancient Near East had learned to domesticate animals, grow crops, and produce useful articles of pottery and metal. The ancient Mesoptamians and Egyptians developed writing, mathematics, and sophisticated methods of engineering while contributing a rich variety of legal, scientific, and religious ideas to those who would come after them. The Phoenicians invented the alphabet and facilitated cultural borrowing by trading throughout the known world, and ancient Israel gave birth to religious concepts that form the basis of modern Judaism, Christianity, and Islam. Chapter 1 will look briefly at life in the Paleolithic or Old Stone Age before examining the Neolithic revolution and its material consequences, including its impact on diet, demography, and the advent of warfare. It will then describe the development and structure of two great ancient socieities, the Mesopotamian and the Egyptian, before concluding with descriptions of the Phoenicians and of the life and religion of ancient Israel.

◆

The First Europeans: The Paleolithic Era

Few subjects are more controversial than the origins of the human species. During the long series of ice ages, the fringes of the European ice pack were inhabited by a race of tool-making bipeds known conventionally as Neanderthals. Heavier, stronger, and hairier than modern *Homo sapiens*, they hunted the great herding animals of the day: mammoth, bison, wooly rhinoceros, and reindeer. They lived in caves, knew how to make flint tools and weapons, and buried their dead in ways that suggest some form of religious belief.

About thirty thousand years ago the Neanderthals were abruptly superseded by people who were physically identical to modern men and women. Where they came from or whether they somehow evolved within a few generations from a basically Neanderthal stock is unclear, but within a short time the Neanderthals were no more. This development remains a mystery because the first true humans did not have a more advanced culture or technology than their more established neighbors and were by comparison weak and puny. Some have suggested that the Neanderthals fell victim to an epidemic disease or that they could not adapt to warmer weather after the retreat of the glaciers. They may also have found hunting the faster, more solitary animals of modern times difficult after the extinction of their traditional prey, but no one knows.

The new people, like their predecessors, were hunter-gatherers who lived in caves and buried their dead. They, too, used stone tools and weapons that became steadily more sophisticated over time, which is why the period up to about 9000 B.C. is known as the Paleolithic or Old Stone Age. Paleolithic people lived on a healthy diet of game and fish supplemented by fruit, berries, nuts, and wild plants, but little is known about their social structure. If the hunter-gatherer societies of modern times are an indication, they probably lived in extended families that, if they survived and prospered, eventually became tribes. Extended families may contain older surviving relatives—siblings, aunts, uncles, nieces, nephews, and cousins—as opposed to nuclear families of only parents and children. Tribes are composed of several nuclear or extended families that claim common descent. The division of responsibilities probably was straightforward. Men hunted and perhaps made tools; women cared for the children, preserved the fire, and did most of the gathering.

Among the most extraordinary achievements of these paleographic cultures was their art. Caves from Spain to southern Russia are decorated with magnificent wall paintings, usually of animals. Many groups also produced small clay figurines with exaggerated female features. This suggests the widespread worship of a fertility goddess, but Paleolithic religious beliefs remain unclear. Were the cave paintings a form of magic designed to bring game animals under the hunter's power, or were they art for art's sake? The question may sound silly, but articles of personal adornment in caves and grave sites indicate, as do the paintings themselves, that these people had a well-developed sense of aesthetics (see illustration 1.1).

Illustration 1.1

▨ Paleolithic Cave Paintings of Bison, at Altamira, Spain. The cave paintings at Altamira in Spain and at Lascaux in France were evidently produced by the same Paleolithic culture and date from c. 15,000 B.C. to 10,000 B.C. The purpose of the paintings is unclear, but the technical skill of the artists was anything but primitive.

The Neolithic Revolution

Hunting and gathering remained the chief economic activity for a long time, and even today they provide supplementary food for many westerners. The bow and arrow as well as the basic tools still used to hook or net fish or to trap game were developed long before the advent of agriculture, pottery, or writing. The domestication of animals probably began at an early date with the use of dogs in hunting, but was later extended to sheep, goats, and cattle that could be herded to provide a reliable source of protein when game was scarce. Shortly thereafter, about ten thousand years ago, the first efforts were made to cultivate edible plants. The domestication of animals and the invention of agriculture marked one of the great turning points in human history.

Several species of edible grasses are native to the upper reaches of the Tigris and Euphrates valleys in Asia Minor, including wild barley and two varieties of wheat. Of the latter, einkorn (one-corn), with its single row of seeds per stalk, produces only modest yields, but emmer, with multiple rows on each stem, is the ancestor of modern wheat. When people learned to convert these seeds into gruel or bread is unknown, but once they did so the value of systematic cultivation became apparent. By 7000 B.C. farming was well established from Iran to Palestine. It spread into the Nile valley and the Aegean by 5000 B.C. and from the Balkans up the Danube and into central Europe in the years that followed. Radiocarbon dating has established the existence of farming settlements in the Netherlands by 4000 B.C. and in Britain by 3200 B.C.

The diffusion of agricultural techniques came about through borrowing and cultural contact as well as through migration. Farming, in other words, developed in response to local conditions. As the last ice age ended and hunting and fishing techniques improved, a general increase in population upset the Paleolithic ecology. Game became scarcer and more elusive while the human competition for dwindling resources grew more intense. Herding and the cultivation of row crops were soon essential to survival. In time, as the human population continued to grow, herding diminished. It provides fewer calories per unit of land than farming and was increasingly restricted to tracts otherwise unsuitable for cultivation. Though crop raising would always be supplemented to some extent by other sources of food, it gradually emerged as the primary activity wherever land could be tilled.

The invention of agriculture marked the beginning of the Neolithic or New Stone Age. The cultivation of plants, beginning with grains and expanding to include beans, peas, olives, and eventually grapes, made food supplies far more predictable than in a hunting or herding economy. At the same time, it greatly increased the number of calories that could be produced from a given area of land. Efficiency was further enhanced by the invention of the wheel and the wooden plow, both of which came into common use around 3000 B.C. Farming therefore promoted demographic growth both absolutely and in the density of population that a given area could support.

On the negative side, the transition to a farming economy often resulted in diets that were deficient in protein and other important elements. Bread became the staff of life, largely because land supports more people if planted with grain. The nuts, animal proteins, and wild fruits typical of the Paleolithic diet became luxuries to be eaten only on special occasions. As a result, the skeletal remains of Neolithic farmers indicate that they were shorter and less healthy than their Paleolithic ancestors. Though beans, peas, lentils, and other pulses became a valuable source of protein, ordinary people consumed as much as 80 percent of their calories in the form of carbohydrates.

Caloric intake varied widely. An adult male engaged in heavy labor requires a minimum of thirty-seven hundred calories per day. No way exists to measure a normal diet in Neolithic or ancient times, but the average peasant or laborer probably made do on far less, perhaps only twenty-five hundred to twenty-seven hundred calories per day. Grain yields on unfertilized land are relatively inelastic, typically ranging from three to twelve bushels per acre with a probable average of five. Populations expand to meet the availability of resources, and Neolithic communities soon reached their ecological limits. If they could not expand the area under cultivation, they reached a balance that barely sustained life. Moreover, because grain harvests depend upon good weather and are susceptible to destruction by pests, shortfalls were common. In years of famine, caloric intake dropped below the level of sustenance.

The establishment of permanent farming settlements also encouraged the spread of disease. The hunter-gatherers of Paleolithic times had lived in small groups and moved frequently in pursuit of game, a way of life that virtually precluded epidemics. Farming, however, is by definition sedentary. Fields and orchards require constant attention, and the old way of moving about while camping in caves or temporary shelters had to be abandoned. Early farmers built houses of sun-dried brick or of reeds and wood in close proximity to one another for security and to facilitate cooperation. The establishment of such villages encouraged the accumulation of refuse and human waste. Water supplies became contaminated while disease-bearing rats, flies, lice, and cockroaches became the village or town dweller's constant companions.

Inadequate nutrition and susceptibility to epidemic disease created the so-called biological old regime, a demographic pattern that prevailed in Europe until the middle of the nineteenth century. Though few people starved, disease kept death rates high while poor nutrition kept birth rates low. Malnutrition raises the age of first menstruation and can prevent ovulation in mature women, thereby reducing the rate of conception. After conception, poor maternal diet led to a high rate of stillbirths and of complications during pregnancy. If a child were brought to term and survived the primitive obstetrics of the age, it faced the possibility that its mother would be too malnourished to nurse. Statistics are unavailable, but infant mortality probably ranged from 30 to 70 percent in the first two years of life.

The distribution of Neolithic and ancient populations therefore bore little resemblance to that of a modern industrial society. Ancient people were younger and had far shorter working lives than their modern counterparts. Their reproductive lifetimes were also shorter, and in people of mature years (aged thirty to fifty), men may have outnumbered women, primarily because so many women died in childbirth. The life expectancy for either gender may not have been much more than thirty years at birth, but those who survived their fifties had as good a chance as their modern counterparts of reaching an advanced age. This pattern, like the conditions that produced it, would persist until the industrial revolution of modern times.

The invention of agriculture expanded the idea of property to include land and domesticated animals, which were not only personal possessions but also the means of survival. In Paleolithic times the primary measure of individual worth was probably a person's ability as a hunter or gatherer, skills from which the entire tribe presumably benefited. The Neolithic world measured status in terms of flocks, herds, and fields. This change affected the structure of human societies in three important ways. First, because luck and management skills vary widely, certain individuals amassed greater wealth than others. To gain the maximum advantage from their wealth, they found it necessary to utilize, and often to exploit, the labor of their poorer neighbors. Neolithic society was therefore characterized by social stratification, though a measure of cooperation could be found at the village level in the performance of agricultural and construction tasks.

Second, the emergence of property seems to have affected the status of women. Little is known about the lives of women in Paleolithic times, but most theorists agree that, with the development of herds and landed property, controlling female sexuality became necessary in ways that would have been unnecessary in a community of hunter-gatherers. The issue was inheritance. The survival of the family depended upon the preservation and augmentation of its wealth. Women were expected to provide heirs who were the biological children of their partners. The result was the development of a double standard by which women had to be pure and seen to be pure by the entire community. If anthropologists are correct, the subjugation of women and the evolution of characteristically feminine behaviors were an outgrowth of the Neolithic revolution.

Third, the Neolithic age marked the beginning of warfare, the systematic use of force by one community against another. Though Paleolithic hunters may have fought one another on occasion, the development of settled communities provided new incentives for violence because homes, livestock, and cultivated land are property that must be defended against the predatory behavior of neighboring peoples. Dealing with the problems of population growth by annexing the land of others was all too easy. War, in turn, made possible the development of slavery. To a hunter-gatherer, slaves are unnecessary, but to herders and agriculturalists their labor makes possible the expansion of herds and the cultivation of more land because under normal circumstances slaves produce more than they consume.

At first, Neolithic communities seem to have been organized along tribal lines, a structure inherited from their hunting and gathering ancestors when they settled down to till the land. Most inhabitants shared a common ancestor, and chieftainship was probably the dominant form of social organization. The function of the chief in agricultural societies was far more complex than in the days of hunting and gathering, involving not only military leadership but also a primary role in the allocation of goods and labor. Efficiency in operations such as harvesting and sheep shearing requires cooperation and direction. In return, the chief demanded a share of an individual's agricultural surplus, which he then stored against hard times or allocated in other ways.

This function of the chief helps to explain the storehouses that were often constructed by early rulers. As agriculture developed, crops became more varied. Wheat, wine, and olives became the basic triad of products on which society depended in the Mediterranean basin. One farmer might have a grove of olive trees but no land capable of growing wheat, while another would be blessed with well-drained, south-facing hillsides that produce the best grapes. In such cases the chief encouraged a measure of agricultural specialization. He could collect a tribute of oil from one and grapes from another and barter both to a third farmer in return for his surplus wheat. In the north, different commodities were involved, but the principle was the same. Specialization in Neolithic times was rarely complete because prudent farmers knew that diversification offered a measure of security that monoculture, or the growing of only one crop, can never provide. If the major crop fails, something else must be available to fall back upon, but even a modest degree of specialization can increase efficiency and raise a community's standard of living.

Effective systems of distribution can also encourage the development of technology. Pottery was invented soon after the Neolithic revolution, primarily as a means of storing liquids. The first pots were probably made by women working at home and firing their pots in a communal oven, but the invention of the potter's wheel allowed for throwing pots with unprecedented speed and efficiency. Because the new method required great skill, those who mastered it tended to become specialists who were paid for their work in food or other commodities.

Illustration 1.2

Stonehenge. The greatest of all stone circles, shown here from the north, stands on England's Salisbury Plain. Some believe that Stonehenge served as an astronomical calculator, but the real purpose is as obscure as the culture of its builders. The huge stones were quarried, and perhaps shaped elsewhere, and transported many miles to their present site. The lintels are pegged and fitted into prepared holes in the standing stones or fitted with mortise-and-tenon joints. The stonemasonry as well as the size of the project is remarkable.

The advent of metallurgy provides a more dramatic example of occupational specialization. Pure copper, which is sometimes found in nature, was used for jewelry and personal items before 6000 B.C., but by 4500 B.C. it was being smelted from ores and forged into tools and weapons. These complex processes appear to have evolved separately in the Middle East and in the Balkans, where copper deposits were common. They were based on the development of ovens that could achieve both a controlled air flow and temperatures of more than two thousand degrees Fahrenheit. An analysis of pottery from these areas reveals that such ovens had already been developed to facilitate glazing. By 3500 B.C., bronze—a mixture of copper and tin—was in general use throughout the West for the manufacture of tools and weapons. The Neolithic Age was over, and the Bronze Age had begun. Because the skills involved in working bronze were highly specialized, smiths probably forged their wares almost exclusively for sale or barter. A sophisticated system of trade and governance must have been established. Furthermore, the large-scale production of metal weapons further enhanced the power of chiefs.

Chieftainship might also involve religious duties, though organized priesthoods evolved in some soci-eties at an early date. Chiefs almost certainly organized the building of communal burying places in the Aegean and along the Atlantic and North Sea coasts from Iberia to Scandinavia. Originally simple dolmens formed of a giant stone or megalith laid upon other stones, these tombs gradually evolved into domed chambers that were entered through long masonry passages.

Graves of this kind are often found in the vicinity of stone circles. Stonehenge, constructed around 3500 B.C. on England's Salisbury Plain, is the largest and best known of these structures (see illustration 1.2). Because the circles are oriented astronomically, many have as-sumed that they served as giant calendars, but their pre-cise function and the beliefs that mandated their construction are unknown.

The prevalence of these large-scale construction projects, whatever their purpose, indicates that Neo-lithic societies could achieve high levels of organization and technological sophistication. When survival—as opposed to the demands of ritual—required a major co-operative effort, some societies evolved into civiliza-tions. *Civilization* is a term loaded with subjective meanings. In this case, it refers to the establishment of political and cultural unity over a wide geographic area and the development of elaborate social, commercial,

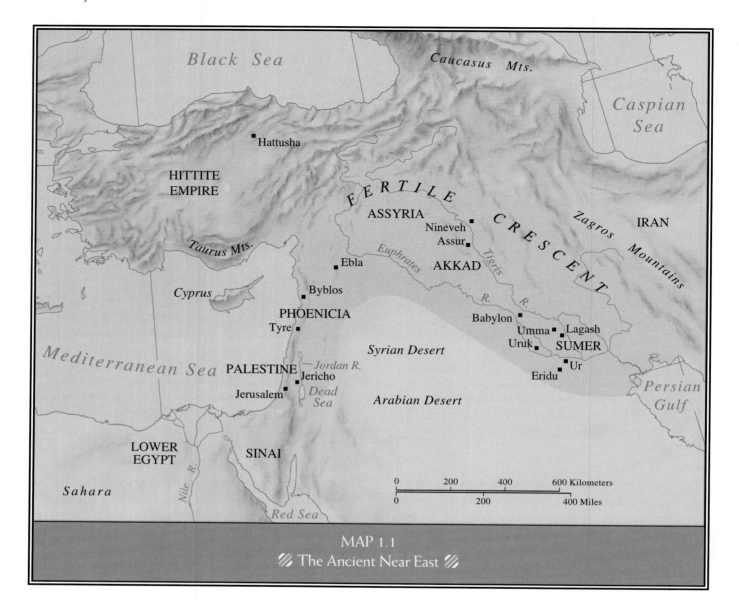

MAP 1.1

⚡ The Ancient Near East ⚡

and administrative structures based upon high population densities and the production of substantial wealth.

In most cases, civilization also meant the development of mathematics and written languages. Both were needed for surveying, administration, and the distribution of goods and services in a complex society. As chiefs became kings, the record of taxes and tributes paid, of lands annexed, and of the provisions consumed by their ever-larger armies acquired great significance. The desire to record the ruler's glorious deeds for posterity came slightly later but was nevertheless important. Writing gives names to individuals and permits the dead to speak in their own words. Without it there is no history.

The emergence of societies at this level of complexity affected even those areas that they did not directly control. Great civilizations are magnets that draw other cultures into their orbits. As peoples on the periphery become involved with the larger market through trade or tribute, cultural borrowing accelerates. Then, as civilizations expand, they come into conflict with one another, a process that brings neighboring peoples into their systems of war and diplomacy as well. By 3000 B.C., at least two such civilizations had begun to emerge, one in the valley of Tigris and Euphrates rivers, the other in the valley of the Nile.

◆

Mesopotamia: The Social and Economic Structures of Mesopotamian Life

Mesopotamia, in Greek, means the land between the rivers, in this case the Tigris and the Euphrates (see map 1.1). It is a hot, fertile flood plain, most of which falls within the borders of modern Iraq. Summer high temperatures reach 110 to 120 degrees Fahrenheit, and no rain falls from May to late October. Winters are more moderate, but only Assyria in the north receives enough rainfall to support agriculture without irrigation. In the lower valley, everything depends upon water supplied by the two rivers.

Of the two, the Tigris carries by far the larger volume of water. The Euphrates on the east has fewer tributaries and loses more of its flow to evaporation as it passes through the dry plains of Syria. In April and May the melting of snow in the Zagros Mountains causes massive flooding throughout the region. This provides needed water and deposits a rich layer of alluvial silt, but the inundation presents enormous problems of management. The floods must not only be controlled to protect human settlement, but water also must somehow be preserved to provide irrigation during the rainless summer. To make matters worse, both rivers create natural embankments or levees that inhibit the flow of tributaries and over time have raised the water level above that of the surrounding countryside. If spring floods wash the embankments away, the river changes its course, often with disasterous results. The biblical story of Noah and the Flood originated in Mesopotamia, though there was probably not one flood but many (see document 1.1).

The first known settlements in the region were village cultures possibly speaking a Semitic language distantly related to the more modern Hebrew or Arabic. They grew wheat and barley and were established as far south as Akkad, near modern Baghdad, by 4500 B.C. Other Semitic peoples continued to migrate into the region from the west and southwest until the Arab invasions of the ninth century A.D., but by 3000 B.C. the Sumerians, a non-Semitic people who may have come originally from India, had achieved dominance in the lower valley. They introduced large-scale irrigation and built the first true cities.

Sumerian cities were usually built on a tributary and dominated a territory of perhaps a hundred square miles. Their inhabitants cultivated cereals, especially barley, and had learned the secret of making beer. Sumerian homes, made of sun-baked brick, originally were small and circular like a peasant's hut but gradually expanded to become large one-story structures with square or rectangular rooms built around a central courtyard. Governance seems to have been by elected city councils. Each city also had a king who ruled with the assistance of a palace bureaucracy. The precise division of powers is unknown, but the later Babylonian council had judicial as well as legislative authority.

◈ DOCUMENT 1.1 ◈

The Flood

The great Mesopotamian epic about Gilgamesh contains an account of the Flood that strongly resembles the biblical account in Genesis, although divine caprice, not human wickedness, brings on the disaster. Here, Utnapashtim, the Mesopotamian equivalent of Noah, tells his story to the hero Gilgamesh.

In those days the world teemed, the people multiplied, the world bellowed like a wild bull, and the great god was aroused by the clamor. Enlil heard the clamor and said to the gods in council, "the uproar of mankind is intolerable and sleep is no longer possible by reason of the babel." So the gods agreed to exterminate mankind. Enlil did this, but Ea [the god of the waters] because of his oath warned me in a dream . . . "tear down your house and build a boat, abandon possessions and look for life, despise worldly goods and save your soul alive . . . then take up into the boat the seed of all living creatures . . ."

[After Utnapashtim did this] for six days and six nights the winds blew, torrent and tempest and flood overwhelmed the world, tempest and flood raged together like warring hosts. When the seventh day dawned the storm from the south subsided, the sea grew calm, the flood was stilled; I looked at the face of the world and there was silence, all mankind was turned to clay. The surface of the sea stretched as flat as a rooftop; I opened a hatch and the light fell on my face. . . . I looked for land in vain, but fourteen leagues distant there appeared a mountain, and there the boat grounded; on the mountain of Nisir the boat held fast. . . . When the seventh day dawned I loosed a dove and let her go. She flew away, but finding no resting place she returned. Then I loosed a swallow, and she flew away but finding no resting place she returned. I loosed a raven, she saw that the waters had retreated, she ate, she flew around, she cawed, and she did not come back. Then I threw everything open to the four winds, I made a sacrifice and poured out a libation on the mountain top.

The Epic of Gilgamesh, trans. N.K. Sandars. Rev. ed. Harmondsworth, England. Penguin Classics, 1964.

An organized priesthood served in the great raised temple or ziggurat that dominated the town. The ziggurat was a stepped pyramidal tower dedicated to the god or goddess who was the patron of the city. The earliest examples were built of packed earth. After about 2000 B.C. most were constructed on a foundation of imported stone and decorated with glazed tiles. The temple and its priests were supported by extensive landholdings. Other large tracts were owned by the royal family and its retainers. Sumerian kings were likely at first war chiefs whose powers became hereditary as their responsibilities for the distribution of goods and labor grew. Like chiefs in other societies, they stood at the center of a system of clientage that involved their families and their servants as well as officials, commoners, and probably priests.

Clientage is best defined as a system of mutual dependency in which a powerful individual protects the interests of others in return for their political or economic support. With or without legal sanction, clientage is the basic form of social organization in many cultures and was destined to become a powerful force in the history of the West. In Sumer, clients formed a separate class of free individuals who were given the use of small parcels of land in return for labor and a share of their produce. Their patrons—kings, noble officials, or temple priests—retained title to the land and a compelling hold on their client's political loyalties. The cities were therefore ruled by a relatively small group. Clients had full rights as citizens, but they could not be expected to vote against those who controlled their economic lives.

The rest of the land was owned by private families that were apparently extended, multigenerational, and organized on patriarchal lines. Though rarely rich, these freeholders enjoyed full civil rights and participated in the city's representative assembly. The greatest threat to their independence was debt, which could lead to enslavement. Other slaves were sometimes acquired for the temple or palace through war, but Sumer was not a slave-based economy. The organization of trade, like that of agriculture, reflected this social structure. For centuries Sumerian business was based on the extended family or what would today be called family corporations. Some firms ran caravans to every part of the Middle East or shipped goods by sea via the Persian Gulf. They exported textiles, copper implements, and other products of Mesopotamian craftsmanship and imported wood, stone, copper ingots, and precious metals. Iron and steel were as yet unknown. Later, in the time of Hammurabi, Babylonian rulers attempted to

Illustration 1.3

A Cuneiform Tablet. This fragment of the eleventh tablet of the *Epic of Gilgamesh* from Ashurbanipal's great library at Nineveh is a superb example of cuneiform text.

bring some of these trading concerns under government regulation.

The organization of Sumerian society was probably much like that of earlier Neolithic communities, and its political institutions reflect the ancient idea of chieftainship. More is known about it only because the Sumerians were the first Western people to create a written language. Their political and economic relationships had reached a level of complexity that required something more than the use of movable clay tokens to record transactions, a practice characteristic of many earlier cultures. Though the Sumerian language was apparently unrelated to any other and was used only for ritual purposes after the second millennium B.C., all later Mesopotamian cultures adopted its cuneiform system of writing.

Cuneiform refers to the wedge-shaped marks left by a stylus when it is pressed into a wet clay tablet. Sumeria was rich in mud, and slabs of clay were perfect for recording taxes, land transfers, and legal agreements. When the document was ready, the tablet could be baked hard and stored for future reference (see illustration 1.3).

The Sumerians, Akkad, Babylonia, and Assyria

Even with written records, political relations between the Sumerian city-states are difficult to reconstruct. As populations increased, struggles over boundaries and trading rights grew more violent, and by 2300 B.C. inter-city conflicts engulfed all of Mesopotamia. At times, a king would claim to rule over more than one city or over Sumer as a whole. There may therefore have been no Sumerian Empire, or if there was, its existence could have been brief. According to his inscriptions, Lugalzaggeszi of Umma (c. 2375 B.C.) achieved control over the entire region only to have it taken from him by a non-Sumerian, Sargon of Akkad (reigned c. 2350–2300 B.C.).

The Akkadian triumph marked the beginning of a new imperial age. The unification of southern and central Mesopotamia provided Sargon with the means to conquer the north together with Syria. Though Akkadian rule was brief, it transmitted elements of Mesopotamian culture throughout the Middle East, and Akkadian, a Semitic language, became standard throughout the Tigris and Euphrates valleys. But the brevity of Sargon's triumph set a pattern for the political future. For a millennium and a half, the rulers of different regions in succession achieved hegemony over all or part of Mesopotamia. This was normally achieved by force combined with the careful manipulation of alliances and ended when the ruling dynasty fell prey either to the divisive forces that had created it or to invasions by people from the surrounding highlands. Throughout its history, Mesopotamia's wealth and lack of natural defenses made it a tempting prize for conquerors.

After the overthrow of Sargon's descendents by a desert people known as the Guti and a brief revival of Sumerian power under the Third Dynasty of Ur, Babylon became the chief political and cultural center of the region. Under Hammurabi (ruled c. 1792–1750 B.C.) the Babylonians achieved hegemony over all of Mesopotamia, but a series of invasions after 1600 B.C. led to a long period of political disorder. The invaders, the most important of whom were Hittites, an Indo-European people from central Asia Minor. Their influence was otherwise impermanent, but a rivalry soon developed between Babylon and Assyria, a kingdom in the northern part of the valley centered first on the city of Ashur and later on Nineveh.

The Assyrians, a fierce people who spoke a dialect of Akkadian, may have been the first people to coordinate the use of cavalry, infantry, and missile weapons. Not only were their armies well organized, but their grasp of logistics also appears to have surpassed that of other ancient empires. Though in other respects a highly civilized people whose literary and artistic achievements continued the traditions of Sumer and Babylon, they waged psychological warfare by cultivating a reputation for horrific cruelty. They eventually defeated the Babylonians and after 933 restored the achievements of Sargon by establishing an empire that stretched from Egypt to Persia. In spite of these violent political alterations, Mesopotamia remained culturally homogeneous for nearly three thousand years.

Mesopotamian Culture, Law, and Religion

Though capitals and dynasties rose and fell, the land between the rivers remained captive to the annual floods and to the consequent need for cooperation, superlative engineering, and frequent redistribution of land. The Mesopotamians' highest intellectual achievements were therefore practical rather than speculative. The development of writing is a prime example of their talents. The Mesopotamians were also the first great mathematicians. Using a numerical system based on sixty instead of the modern ten, they produced reference tables for multiplication, division, square roots, cube roots, and other functions. Their greatest achievement, however, was the place-value system of notation in which the value of each digit is determined by its position after the base instead of by a separate name. This makes describing large numbers possible and is the basis of all modern numeral systems.

The Babylonians also created one of the first comprehensive legal codes. Named after Hammurabi, it is almost certainly a compendium of existing laws rather than new legislation and reflects a legal tradition that had been developing for centuries. Its basic principles were retribution in kind and the sanctity of contracts. In criminal cases this meant literally "an eye for an eye, a tooth for a tooth," if the social status of the parties was equal. If not, a defendant of higher status could usually escape by paying a fine. Blood feuds, private retribution, and other features of tribal law were, however, forbidden. This same sense of retributive justice extended to the punishment of fraud and negligence. A builder whose house collapsed and killed its occupants could be executed; tavern keepers who watered their drinks were drowned. Craftsmen were required to replace poor workmanship at their own expense, and farmers who failed to keep their ditches and levees in good repair were sold into slavery if they could not compensate the victims of their

Illustration 1.4

⫸ **Sumerians Worshipping Abu, God of Vegetation.** This group of marble votive statues (the largest is thirty inches high and probably represents the local king) was carved at Eshnunna in southern Mesopotamia between 2700 and 2500 B.C. The figures were placed around the altar and were expected to serve as perpetual stand-ins for their donors. The huge, staring eyes reflect the rapt attention expected by the god.

carelessness. Contracts governed everything from marriage to interest rates and could not be broken without paying a heavy fine.

Hammurabi's Code was driven by an almost oppressive sense of social responsibility. The ecology of Mesopotamia was both fragile and highly artificial. Only elaborate regulation could prevent disaster, and the law is explicit on many aspects of trade, agriculture, and manufacturing. Courts and town councils took an interest in matters that other cultures have regarded as private. Furthermore, because there were no lawyers, the parties to a dispute were expected to plead their own cases.

Marriage, as in most ancient cultures, was arranged by parents. The bride received a dowry, which she was entitled to keep in the event of widowhood or divorce. Husbands could demand a divorce at any time but had to pay maintenance and child support unless they could demonstrate that the wife had failed in her duties. These duties, like all other aspects of the marriage arrangement, were spelled out in a detailed contract that in effect made the couple a single person, responsible before the law for their actions and their debts. The latter was an important point, for husbands had the right to sell wives and children into servitude, usually for no more than two or three years, to satisfy their creditors.

The system was patriarchal, but wives could sue for divorce on grounds of cruelty or neglect, or if their husband falsely accused them of adultery. If adultery were proved, the guilty couple would be tied together and drowned; if the aggrieved husband forgave his wife, her lover would be pardoned as well. All of these family issues were heard before the city councils, which demonstrates the continuing importance of local government even after the establishment of an empire. Women, like men, were expected to plead their own cases—a right often denied them in more modern legal systems—but recourse to the law had its perils. To reduce litigation, Hammurabi's Code decreed the death penalty for those who brought false accusations or frivolous suits.

Hammurabi, like most lawgivers, claimed divine sanction for his code, but Mesopotamian religion was not legalistic. The Sumerians had worshipped more than three thousand deities, most of whom represented natural forces or the spirit of a particular locality. In time many of them acquired human form, and a rich mythology developed around their adventures. Babylon made its city god, Marduk, its chief, while the Assyrians accorded similar honors to Ashur. Both were thought of as creators who had brought the universe out of primal chaos. Other gods and goddesses were still worshipped, but in an apparent step toward monotheism, they were increasingly described as agents of Marduk or Ashur and eventually as manifestations of a single god.

The power of the gods was absolute. Humans were dependent on their whims and could hope only to propitiate them through the ceremonies of the priests (see illustration 1.4). The problem of the righteous sufferer

A Mesopotamian Prayer

This fragment from a longer prayer displays the characteristic Mesopotamian attitude toward the gods, who are seen as hostile, demanding, and inscrutable.

The sin, which I have committed, I know not.
The iniquity, which I have done, I know not.
The offence, which I committed, I know not.
The transgression I have done, I know not.
The lord, in the anger of his heart, hath looked
    upon me.
The god, in the wrath of his heart, hath visited me.
The goddess hath become angry with me, and
    hath grievously stricken me.
The known or unknown god hath straightened
    me.
The known or unknown goddess hath brought af-
    fliction upon me.
I sought for help, but no one taketh my hand.
I wept, but no one came to my side.
May the known and unknown god be pacified!
May the known and unknown goddess be pacified!

"Penitential Psalms." In *Assyrian and Babylonian Literature*, trans. R. F. Harper. New York: D. Appleton, 1901.

was therefore a recurring theme in Babylonian literature. Even death offered no hope of relief. In the greatest of all Babylonian epics, the hero Gilgamesh is inspired by the death of his friend Enkidu to wrestle with the problem of the hereafter. His discoveries are not reassuring. The nether world is portrayed as a grim place, and neither the mythical Gilgamesh nor any other Mesopotamian could apparently imagine the idea of personal salvation. If their extensive literature is an indication, the peoples of ancient Mesopotamia knew how to enjoy life, but their enjoyment was tempered by a grim fatalism (see document 1.2). In the land between the rivers, with its terrible inundations and vulnerability to invaders, it could hardly have been otherwise.

◈

Ancient Egypt

While the Sumerians were establishing themselves in Mesopotamia, another great civilization was developing in the valley of the Nile. In central Africa, more than three thousand miles from the shores of the Mediterranean, streams running from a cluster of great lakes merge their waters to form the White Nile. The lakes serve as a reservoir, and the river's volume remains constant with the seasons as it flows north to meet the Blue Nile at Khartoum. The Blue Nile is smaller than the White, but its sources are in the Ethiopian highlands where the monsoon rains of June and the melting mountain snow become a torrent. This annual flood, which reaches the lower Nile valley in July or August, provides both the moisture and the rich layer of black silt that support Egyptian life.

From the confluence of the two rivers, the Nile makes a wide sweep to the west before flowing northward through a valley more than 350 miles long but rarely more than ten miles wide. The historic land of Egypt is a narrow well-watered passageway between the Mediterranean and the heart of Africa. To the west lies the vast emptiness of the Libyan desert; to the east, a line of parched and rugged hills mark the shores of the Red Sea. Open country is found only near the river's mouth, a vast alluvial delta through which, in antiquity at least, seven main channels provided access to the Mediterranean. Summer temperatures in the valley are not as hot as those of Mesopotamia, but little or no rain falls and, without the river, life would be insupportable.

As in Mesopotamia, the key to Egyptian agriculture was the proper management of the annual flood. The Nile is more predictable and less violent than the Tigris or Euphrates, but the construction of levees, catchments, and an extensive network of ditches, was essential both to protect settlements and to preserve water after the flood subsided in the fall. The high level of organization needed for such tasks and for the preservation and distribution of grain during the dry months may have been responsible for the centralized, hierarchical character of ancient Egyptian society, but the point is arguable. Little is known of politics before the advent of the First Dynasty around 3100 B.C. At that time, the kings of the First Dynasty or their immediate predecessors united the two lands of Upper (southern) and Lower (northern) Egypt and laid the foundations of a political culture that would endure for nearly three millennia. The essential characteristics of Egyptian society were in place when the Third Dynasty assumed power in 2686 B.C. and began the Old Kingdom.

The history of ancient Egypt is conventionally divided into three kingdoms and no fewer than twenty-six dynasties: the Old Kingdom (2686–2181 B.C.), the Middle Kingdom (2133–1786 B.C.), and the New

Kingdom (1567–525 B.C.). The terms *old, middle,* and *new* do not necessarily reflect progress. Some of Egypt's greatest achievements came during the predynastic period and the Old Kingdom. The Intermediate Periods between these kingdoms were troubled times during which provincial governors, known to the Greeks as nomarchs, increased their power at the expense of the central government. Eventually one would gain ascendancy over the others and establish a dynasty that served as the cornerstone of a new kingdom.

The Old Kingdom ended when massive crop failures coincided with the political collapse of the Sixth Dynasty. After an anarchic Intermediate Period of more than one-hundred years, Amenemhet I, the ruler of Thebes in Upper Egypt, reunited the country and established the Middle Kingdom. During the Twelfth Dynasty (c. 1991–1786 B.C.), Egypt found itself under military pressure in both the north and south and, for the first time in its history, created a standing army. Expeditions into Palestine, Syria, and Libya helped to stabilize the north, while massive fortresses were built in Upper Egypt as protection against the growing power of Kerma, an expansionist state in what is now Sudan. The Middle Kingdom dissolved when a series of foreign dynasties known as the Hyksos supplanted the native Egyptian rulers. From the late eighteenth century B.C., Egypt's wealth attracted an influx of immigrants from Palestine and other parts of the Middle East. They came to power by infiltrating high office instead of by invasion, but their success was deeply resented.

The restoration of a native dynasty in 1567 B.C. marked the beginning of the New Kingdom. A series of warlike pharaohs destroyed the capital of Kerma and briefly extended their authority to the banks of the Euphrates. Ramses II (1279–1213 B.C.), the ruler associated with the Hebrew exodus, fought the Hittite empire to a truce. Ramses III remained strong enough to protect Egypt against the great population movements of the early twelfth century B.C. Thereafter, the power of the monarchy declined, perhaps because the imports of gold and silver that sustained its armies began to shrink. After 525 B.C. Egypt fell first to the Persians and then to the Macedonians of Alexander the Great.

The society that survived these changes bore little resemblance to that of Mesopotamia. Its most unusual feature was the absolute power it accorded to the king, or pharaoh, a Middle Kingdom title meaning "great house." His authority in life was absolute, though in practice he presumably would always act according to *ma'at*, a concept of justice or social order based on the balance or reconciliation of conflicting principles. The

king could not therefore appear arbitrary or irresponsible, and his actions were further limited by precedent, for Egyptian society was conservative. If *ma'at* were not preserved, dynasties could fall, but the historical circumstances in which this took place are generally unknown.

When the king died, his spirit or *ka* would take its place in the divine pantheon and become one with Osiris, god of the dead. This was the purpose of the pyramids, the largest of which were built at Giza by the Fourth Dynasty (2613–2494 B.C.) monarchs—Khufu (Cheops), Khafre, and Menkaure. Constructed of between eighty million and one hundred million cubic feet of cut and fitted stone, these vast funeral monuments held the deceased ruler's mortal remains and served as the center of a temple complex dedicated to his worship.

Projects on this scale were a measure of the king's wealth and power. Scholars believe that the taming of the Nile was achieved by workers conscripted and directed by early rulers in the common interest. This right to labor services was retained by later kings, and conscript labor rather than slaves probably built the pyramids as well as the massive fortifications constructed in Upper Egypt to protect the kingdom from Nubian invasions. Similar works in the delta have been obliterated by shifts in the course of the river.

Bureaucrats, with multiple titles and responsibilities, supervised the construction of pyramids and other public projects. Many of these people combined priestly, secular, and military offices, which suggests that managerial competence was valued above specialized skills. The establishment of a standing army during the Middle Kingdom encouraged the emergence of professional soldiers, but no military aristocracy existed. Some high officials were royal relatives, while others were drawn from what may have been a hereditary caste of scribes and civil servants. All, like the laborers, were paid in food, drink, and various commodities including gold, for the Egyptians did not coin money until long after the end of the New Kingdom.

Pyramids after the Fourth Dynasty grew smaller and less expensive, but the Egyptian penchant for public works, temples, and funerary monuments continued until the Hellenistic era. The Egyptians were superior craftsmen in stone and could convert even the hardest granites into works of art. As architects they seem to have invented post-and-lintel construction in masonry. Their temples, whether cut into the limestone cliffs of the Nile valley or freestanding, are graced with magnificent galleries and porticoes supported by stone columns, many of which were decorated or inscribed with writing. The Egyptians also built spacious palaces for the kings and their officials, but few palaces survived the centuries intact.

These projects could be seen as an appalling waste of resources, but they may have served a vital economic and social purpose. They certainly provided sustenance for thousands of workers, especially during the months of flood from July to November when the fields could not be worked. As such, they were an important mechanism for the distribution and redistribution of wealth. Furthermore, by centralizing the direction of arts and crafts under royal patronage, the projects improved the quality of both and led to technological advances that might not otherwise have occurred.

The Social and Economic Structures of Ancient Egypt

The character of Egyptian society is difficult to reconstruct, in part because no legal code comparable to that of Hammurabi has been found. Little is known about land tenure, though vast tracts were held by the king and by pious foundations set up to support temples and those who served them. As many temples were small and as the priests and accolytes supported by their foundations were also farmers, it appears that the tax exemptions enjoyed by the trusts were a primary reason for their establishment. The owners of land held privately, which was abundant, had to pay an annual tribute in kind to the ruler. The king may also have been able to confiscate private property on the theory that, as a god, he owned the entire country. The remaining records of assessment are detailed and reveal a competent and often ruthless bureaucracy at work in even the humblest of villages.

Slaves, most of whom had been captured in war, were found in the fields and households of the rich. They belonged by law to the pharaoh who granted them in turn to private individuals or to the great trusts that managed the temples. They could hold property in their own right and were frequently manumitted, or freed, through a simple declaration by their owners. They were neither numerous nor central to the workings of the economy except perhaps in the expansionist period when the New Kingdom pharaohs conquered much of Phoenicia and Syria (c. 1560–1299 B.C.). The vast majority of Egyptians were humble farmers whose life probably resembled that of today's *fellahin*. They lived in small villages built of mud bricks and spent their days working in the fields and drawing precious

water by means of the *shaduf*, a bucket swung from a counterbalanced beam. They were subject to the payment of taxes as well as to labor services and perhaps to conscripted service in the army. The idea of conscription was so pervasive that people expected to labor in the fields of Osiris after death and placed small clay figurines of slaves in their tombs to help them with the work.

Crops were remarkably varied. Barley and wheat were the staples, and the average person's diet included large quantities of bread and beer with broad or fava beans for protein and the tender stalks of the young papyrus plant for an occasional salad. Papyrus was primarily valued because its fibers could be formed into a kind of paper, an Egyptian invention that takes its name from the plant, though modern paper is derived from a process developed originally in China. Wines for consumption by the upper classes were produced in the delta and painstakingly classified according to source and quality. Beef, too, was a delta product and formed an important part of a wealthy person's diet along with game birds, mutton, and pork. Poultry was common, as were many different kinds of fruit and, above all, onions. Cotton, so closely associated with the Egyptian economy in modern times, was not introduced until about 500 B.C., and most Egyptians wore simple linen garments made from locally grown flax.

Famines and epidemics were rare, but the life expectancy of ancient Egyptians was no more than thirty-five or thirty-six years, a figure comparable to that for most other societies before the industrial revolution. In spite of their belief in an afterlife, the Egyptians seemed unwilling to accept these harsh demographic realities. An extensive medical literature reflects their reputation as the greatest doctors of antiquity. Rules for diagnosis and treatment, lists of remedies, and careful instructions for surgical operations on every part of the body have been preserved. The Egyptian practice of embalming the dead and removing their organs contributed to a knowledge of anatomy unequaled by any other ancient culture.

Egypt was not a heavily urbanized society like Mesopotamia. The major cities, including Thebes, the capital of Upper Egypt, and Memphis, near the present site of Cairo, were centers of government and ceremony. Commerce, though important, was conducted mainly by royal officials. Traders operating at the village level served the modest needs of the countryside. Official expeditions collected the gold and copper that were among Egypt's most important exports. Copper was also used domestically for tools and weapons, but the Egyptians did not adopt the use of bronze until about 1500 B.C., long after it was common elsewhere.

Wood was the chief import. Egypt was self-sufficient in most other commodities, but the Nile valley contained few trees and those that existed were of species unsuitable for boat building or for the exquisite cabinetry favored by the royal court. Long before the First Dynasty, ships were sailing to Byblos on the coast of Lebanon and returning with cargos of rare timber. This trade probably was the primary vehicle for cultural and demographic contacts with Asia.

The role of Egypt as a connecting link between Asia and Africa was reflected in the appearance of its people. In Upper Egypt, the predominant physical type was slender with dark skin and African features. The people of the delta were heavier, with broad skulls and lighter complexions that betrayed Asian or European origins. But representatives of both types were found everywhere, and the Egyptians as a whole seem to have been indifferent to racial or ethnic classifications. No apparent connection was made between rank and skin color. Immigrants from Palestine to the north and Nubia in the south were found in the army as well as in civilian society and often achieved high office. The Egyptian language, too, contained a mixture of African and Semitic elements.

Women enjoyed considerable status. In art they were often, though not always, portrayed as equal to their husbands (see illustration 1.5). They could hold property, initiate divorce, and undertake contractual obligations in their own right. The women of the royal family owned vast estates and seem to have exerted an influence on politics. At least one queen ruled Old Kingdom Egypt in her own name, and two women ruled in the New Kingdom—Hatshepsut (c. 1503–1482 B.C.), who devoted her reign to the development of commerce and commissioned some of the finest monuments of Egyptian architecture, and Tawosre. But no evidence exists that women served as scribes or as officials in the royal administration.

The absence of a legal code and the shortage of court records makes evaluating the true status of women in Egyptian society difficult, but several factors seem to have operated in their behalf. The identity of a child's mother, not its father, established heredity, and the matrilineal inheritance of private property, a practice dating from predynastic times, was far more common in Egypt than in other parts of the ancient Near East. Attitudes may also have been affected by the respect accorded to women of the royal family.

Illustration 1.5

The Pharaoh Menkaure and His Queen. This statue from the Old Kingdom (Fourth Dynasty) is remarkable, not only for its artistic skill, but also for its intimacy. The couple is portrayed as affectionate equals, something that would have been virtually unthinkable in other ancient societies where the place of women was openly inferior.

Egyptian Culture, Science, and Religion

Writing evolved in Egypt and in Mesopotamia at about the same time, but the two systems were different. Egyptian writing is known as hieroglyphics and in its earliest form consisted of lifelike pictures representing specific objects or actions. By a process similar to word association certain hieroglyphs acquired additional meanings, and by about 2700 B.C., seventy-eight of them were being used phonetically to represent consonants or groups of consonants. As in the Semitic languages, Egyptian writing had no vowels. Symbols representing both the object or idea and its pronunciation were often used simultaneously to avoid confusion, and spelling was not standardized. Though Egyptian can be read vertically or horizontally in any direction, the hieroglyphic figures always face the beginning of the line.

Hieroglyphics were used primarily for inscriptions and were typically inscribed on stone. Correspondence, contracts, and other everyday documents were produced by professional scribes writing with reed pens on a paper made from papyrus fiber. The written script, known as hieratic, was based on hieroglyphics but became more cursive over time. Most of Egyptian literature, including poems and popular romances as well as learned treatises, was circulated in this form.

Egyptian mathematics were in general less sophisticated than those of Mesopotamia. The need for land surveys after each annual flood forced the Egyptians to become skilled measurers and the construction of the pyramids reveals an impressive grasp of geometry. The Egyptians never developed a place-value system of notation, so a bewildering combination of symbols was needed to express numbers that were not multiples of ten. Ancient Egyptians could multiply and divide only by doubling, but this appears to have been sufficient for their needs. They understood squares and square roots, and they knew, at an early date, the approximate value of π. The Greeks adopted, and passed on to other European peoples, the Egyptians' use of ten as the numerical base.

Though few cultures have devoted more attention to religion and philosophy or produced a larger body of speculative literature, the ancient Egyptians maintained ideas that are difficult to describe. This is in part because they saw no need to demonstrate the logical connection between different statements. Asserting principles or retelling illustrative myths was enough; analysis was left to the wit or imagination of the reader. If an oral tradition supplemented these utterances or provided a methodological guide to their interpretation, it has been lost. The surviving literature is therefore rich, complex, and allusive, but to literal-minded moderns, full of contradictions.

The earliest Egyptian gods and goddesses were nature spirits peculiar to a village or region. They were usually portrayed as animals, such as the vulture goddess Nekhbet who became the patroness of Upper Egypt and her Lower Egyptian counterpart, the cobra goddess Buto. The effigies of both adorned the

pharaoh's crown as a symbol of imperial unity. This animal imagery may reflect totemic beliefs of great antiquity, but in time the deities acquired human bodies while retaining their animal heads.

Eventually, new deities emerged who personified abstract qualities. *Ma'at*, the principle of justice and equilibrium, became the goddess of good order; Sia was the god of intelligence. None of this involved the displacement of other gods; the Egyptians, like other societies with polytheistic religions, sought to include and revere every conceivable aspect of the divine.

The Egyptians long resisted monotheism. Perhaps they felt that it was too simple a concept to account for the complexity of the universe. When the New Kingdom pharaoh Akhenaton (reigned c. 1379–1362 B.C.) banned all cults save that of Aton, the Sun disk (formerly an aspect of Re-Horus), his ideas were rejected as heretical and abandoned soon after his death. Akhenaton has been seen by some writers as an early pioneer of monotheism, but little reason can be found to believe that his views had much influence either in Egypt or elsewhere. Akhenaton's greatest legacy was probably artistic, for he and his queen, Nefertiti, were great patrons, and the art of the Amarna Age, named after the new capital he constructed at Tell el-Amarna, was magnificent.

Of the many facets of Egyptian religion, the one that most intrigued outsiders was its concern with eternal life. The funerary cults of the pharaohs, the practice of embalming, and the adoption of similar practices by men and women of lesser status have been noted, but a full description of Egyptian lore about the hereafter would require volumes. Broadly speaking, the Egyptians thought of eternal life as a continuation of life on Earth, spent somewhere beyond the "roads of the west" (see document 1.3). They also believed that, like the pharaoh, the virtuous dead would merge their identities with Osiris. This was possible because the human soul had many aspects or manifestations, including the *akh*, which emerged only after death. The fate of the wicked was not reassuring. Their sins were weighed in a scale against the feather of *ma'at*, and if the scale tipped, their souls were thrown to the monstrous, crocodile-like "devourer of hearts" (see illustration 1.6).

The richness and complexity of Egyptian belief extended beyond religion to astronomy, astrology, and natural magic. The works attributed by Greek scholars to Hermes Trismegistus (Hermes the Thrice-Great, or Thoth) may be a compilation of ancient Egyptian sources on these subjects, though their origins remain the subject of controversy. Indisputable, however, is

❖ DOCUMENT 1.3 ❖

An Egyptian Mortuary Text

This prayer or incantation was found on coffins during the Middle Kingdom. It provides not only a vision of the here-after, but also a sample of Egyptian religious imagery. The Eastern Doors mark the entry into paradise. Re is the Sun god, and Shu is the god of air who raised Heaven above the Earth and planted trees to support it. A cubit measures between seventeen and twenty-one inches.

Going in and Out of the Eastern Doors of Heaven among the Followers of Re. I know the Eastern Souls.

I know the central door from which Re issues in the east. Its south is the pool of *kha*-birds, in the place where Re sails with the breeze; its north is the waters of *ro*-fowl, in the place where Re sails with rowing. I am the keeper of the halyard of the boat of the god; I am the oarsman who does not weary in the barque of Re.

I know those two sycamores of turquoise between which Re comes forth, the two which came from the sowing of Shu at every eastern door at which Re rises.

I know the Field of Reeds of Re. The wall which is around it is of metal. The height of its barley is four cubits; its beard is one cubit; and its stalk is three cubits. Its emmer is seven cubits; its beard is two cubits, and its stalk is five cubits. It is the horizon dwellers, nine cubits in height, who reap it by the side of the Eastern Souls.

I know the Eastern Souls. They are Har-akhti, The *Khurrer*-Calf, and the Morning Star.

Pritchard, James B. *Ancient Near Eastern Texts Related to the Old Testament*, vol. 1, 2d ed. Princeton, NJ: Princeton University Press, 1955.

most unimaginably distant past. Growing involvement with the outside world after about 900 B.C. was in some ways a tragedy for the Egyptians. The country fell to a succession of foreign rulers, but most of them, whether Persian, Greek, or Roman, were content to preserve Egyptian institutions. Only the triumph of Islam in the the seventh century A.D. brought fundamental change. By this time much of the Egyptian achievement had been incorporated, often unconsciously, into the development of the West.

❖
Canaan, Phoenicia, and Philistia

The eastern shore of the Mediterranean has been inhabited since earliest times. Neanderthal and Cro-Magnon remains are found in close proximity to one another in the caves of Mt. Carmel, and agriculture was established on the eastern shore before it was introduced to Egypt or Mesopotamia. The climate is benign, with mild winters and enough rainfall to support the Mediterranean triad of crops—wheat, olives, and grapes. The Bible calls it "the land of milk and honey," but it was also a corridor and at times a disputed frontier between the civilizations of Mesopotamia and Egypt. Its inhabitants never enjoyed the political stability of the great river empires. The eastern shore of the Mediterranean was from the beginning a world of small, aggressive city-states whose wealth and strategic position attracted the unwelcome attention of stronger powers.

The first Canaanites or Phoenicians, as they were known to the Greeks, spoke a variety of Semitic dialects and moved into the region during the fourth millennium, superseding or blending with an earlier Neolithic population (see map 1.2). Their first urban foundations, at Sidon, Byblos, and Ras Shamra (Ugarit), date from around 3000 B.C. From the beginning, these and a host of other cities traded actively with both Egypt and Sumer. Their inhabitants were sailors, shipbuilders, and merchants who played a vital role in the process of cultural exchange.

They were also skilled craftsmen. Carved furniture of wood and ivory was an obvious speciality, but metalworking was equally important. The Phoenicians exported fine gold and copper jewelry, bronze tools, and weapons over a wide area. Around 1500 B.C. they seem to have invented the process of casting glass around a core of sand. Decorative glassware remained an important export throughout antiquity, and glassblowing likely was invented by their descendants in Roman

that the Greeks admired the Egyptians for their wisdom and would borrow heavily from them, especially after the establishment of a Greco-Egyptian dynasty by Ptolemy in 323 B.C.

Yet Egyptian culture, for all its concern with the unseen world, was at another level deeply practical. Its institutions, like its engineering, held up well. Conservative, inward-looking, and less aggressive than many empires, it served as a bridge not only between Africa and Europe, but also between historic times and an al-

Illustration 1.6

%% **Egyptian Beliefs about the Afterlife.** In this papyrus from the Theban *Book of the Dead*, the dead man and his wife watch as the god Anubis weighs his heart against a feather and Thoth records the results. The Devourer of Hearts waits at the far right. The writing in the background provides a good example of New Kingdom hieroglyphics.

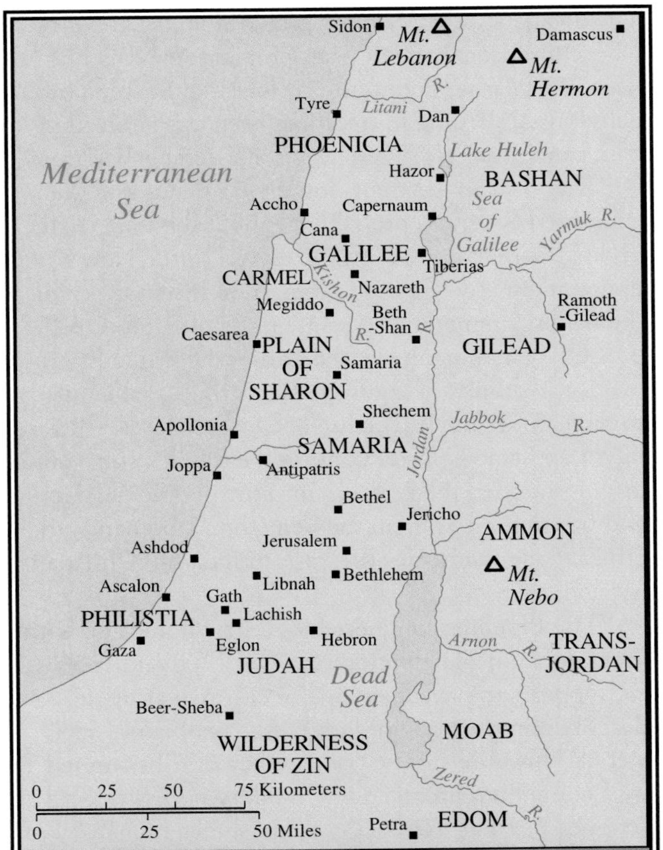

MAP 1.2
%% Ancient Palestine %%

times. The women of Sidon were known for their remarkable textiles, and Sidon and Tyre were the primary source of the purple dye that symbolized royalty throughout the ancient world. It was extracted with great difficulty from the shell of the *murex* snail, a creature abundant in the harbors of Lebanon.

Politically, Phoenician towns were governed by a hereditary king assisted by a council of elders. In practice, they were probably oligarchies in which policy was decided by the wealthy merchants who served on the council. Little is known of their civic life or even of their religious practices. The Phoenicians are credited with inventing the first true alphabet, a phonetic script with twenty-two abstract symbols representing the consonants. Vowels, as in the other Semitic languages, were omitted. Their system is regarded as the greatest of all Phoenician contributions to Western culture because it could be mastered without the kind of extensive education given to professional scribes in Egypt or Mesopotamia. Literacy was now available to nearly everyone, but because the Phoenicians normally wrote with ink on papyrus, most of their records have perished.

Political crises were common. Phoenicia was invaded and at times ruled by both Egypt and the Hittites of Asia Minor. In 1190 B.C. a mysterious group known as the Sea Peoples attacked the Egyptian delta. They were driven out but eventually established themselves along the coast south of Jaffa. They appear to have come from somewhere in the Aegean or western Asia Minor and to have brought with them the use of iron weapons. Little of their language has survived. Their gods appear to have been Canaanite deities adopted on arrival. The Sea People were great fighters and iron-smiths who dominated the iron trade in the Middle East for many years. Politically, their towns of Gaza, Ashkelon, Ashdod, Gath, and Eglon formed a powerful league known as Philistia or the Philistine confederacy. The Bible calls these people Philistines, and the Romans used Palestine, a term derived from that name, to describe the entire region.

While the Philistines annexed the southern coast, the Hebrews, recently escaped from Egypt, invaded the Canaanite highlands. They fought bitterly with the Philistines, but after establishing a united kingdom of Israel that stretched from the Negev to Galilee, they formed an alliance of sorts with the Phoenicians of Tyre. Both of these incursions were related to broader population movements in the eastern Mediterranean. They coincide roughly with the displacement of the Ionians in Greece and a successful assault on the western portion of the Hittite empire by the Phrygians, a people who may have come from the same region as the Philistines. In Canaan proper, both Philistines and Hebrews were forced to contend with other peoples pushing in from the Arabian desert and the country beyond the Jordan.

Canaan was becoming crowded. The newcomers encountered a land that may already have been reaching its ecological limits after several millennia of human settlement. The Phoenician cities, already closely spaced, now saw their hinterlands greatly reduced, and with that their ability to feed their people. Led by Tyre, the Phoenicians began planting colonies from one end of the Mediterranean to the other. The first was at Utica in North Africa, supposedly founded by 1101 B.C. In the next three centuries, dozens of others were established in Cyprus, Sicily, Sardinia, and Spain. At least twenty-six such communities were in North Africa, the most important of which was Carthage, founded about 800 B.C. near the present site of Tunis.

Like the colonies later established by the Greeks, those of the Phoenicians retained commercial and perhaps sentimental ties to their founding city but were for all practical purposes independent city-states. They did not normally try to establish control over large territories. They served as commercial stations that extracted wealth from the interior in return for goods from the civilizations of the eastern Mediterranean. They were also useful as safe harbors for Phoenician traders.

By the seventh century B.C., Phoenician ships had reached Britain in search of precious tin, and Phoenician caravan routes based on the African colonies had penetrated the regions south of the Sahara. The Carthaginians later claimed to have circumnavigated Africa, and, at the very beginnings of the age of colonization, Hiram I of Tyre and his ally Solomon of Israel sent triennial expeditions to Ophir, a place now thought to have been on the coast of India. Wherever they went, the Phoenicians carried their system of writing together with the ideas and products of a dozen other cultures. Though their history was all too often neglected or written by their enemies, they played a vital role in the establishment of Mediterranean civilization.

The Historical Development of Ancient Israel

The *Hapiru* who entered Canaan around 1200 B.C. came from Egypt. The name is thought to mean outsider or marauder and is the probable root of the term *Hebrew*. The invaders were a Semitic group of mixed ancestry whose forebears had left Mesopotamia some six hundred years earlier during the conquest of Sumeria by Babylon. According to tradition, their patriarch Abraham came from Ur. They lived for several generations as pastoralists in the trans–Jordan highlands and then emigrated to Egypt, probably at about the time of the Hyksos domination. With the revival of the New Kingdom under native Egyptian dynasties, the situation of the Semitic immigrants became more difficult. Oppressed by a pharaoh (or pharaohs) whose identity remains the subject of controversy, a group of them fled to Sinai under the leadership of Moses. Moses, whose Egyptian name helps to confirm the biblical story of his origins, molded the refugees into the people of Israel and transmitted to them the Ten Commandments, the ethical code that forms the basis of Judaism, Christianity, and Islam.

The Israelites conquered their new homeland with great difficulty. The period between 1200 and 1020 B.C. appears to have been one of constant struggle. As described in the Book of Judges, the people of Israel were at this time a loose confederacy of tribes united by a common religion and by military necessity. Saul (reigned c. 1020–1000 B.C.) established a monarchy of sorts in response to the Philistine threat, but it was not until after his death that David (ruled 1000–961 B.C.)

consolidated the territories between Beersheba and the Galilee into the kingdom of Israel.

Under David's son Solomon (reigned 961–922 B.C.), Israel became a major regional power. Commerce flourished, and the king used his wealth to construct a lavish palace as well as the First Temple at Jerusalem, a structure heavily influenced by Phoenician models. But Solomon's glory came at a price. Heavy taxation and religious disputes led to rebellion after his death, and Israel divided into two kingdoms: Israel in the north and Judah in the south. Israel was a loosely knit, aristocratic monarchy occupying the land later known as Samaria. Judah, with its walled capital of Jerusalem, was poorer but more cohesive. Both, in the end, would fall prey to more powerful neighbors.

The danger came from the north. In what is now Syria, remnants of the Hittite empire had survived as petty states. Many of them were annexed in the twelfth century by the Aramaeans, a Semitic people whose most important center was Damascus. The Aramaic language would become the vernacular of the Middle East—it was the language, for example, in which Jesus preached. However, Syria remained politically unstable. Assyria, once more in an expansionist phase and enriched by the conquest of Mesopotamia, filled the vacuum. The ministates of the region could not long expect to resist such a juggernaut. For a time, an alliance between Israel and Damascus held the Assyrians at bay, but by 722 B.C., both had fallen to the armies of the Assyrian conquerors Tiglath-pileser and Sargon II. Sennacherib (ruled 705–682 B.C.) annexed Philistia and Phoenicia, after which Esarhaddon (ruled 680–689 B.C.) and Assurbanipal (reigned 669–c.627 B.C.), the greatest and most cultivated of the Assyrian emperors, conquered Egypt. The tiny kingdom of Judah survived only by allying itself with the conquerors.

The end came in 587 B.C. A resurgent Babylonia had destroyed Assyria by allying itself with the Medes and adopting Assyrian military tactics. In a general settling of scores the Babylonian king Nebuchadrezzar II then sacked Jerusalem, destroyed the temple, and carried the Judaean leadership off to captivity in Babylon. Many of these people returned after Babylon was conquered by the Persians in 539 B.C., but the Israelites or Jews, a name derived from the kingdom of Judah, did not establish another independent state until 142 B.C. Judaea and Samaria would be ruled for four hundred years by Persians and by Hellenistic Greeks, while thousands of Jews, faced with the desolation of their homeland, dispersed to the corners of the known world.

The Origins of Judaism

Ancient Israel was not, in other words, a material success. Its people were never numerous or rich, and it was only briefly a regional power. Its contributions to art and technology were negligible, yet few societies have had a greater influence on those that followed. The reason for this paradox is that the Jews developed a religion that was unlike anything else in the ancient world. It was not wholly without precedent, for ideas were borrowed from Mesopotamian and perhaps from Egyptian sources. Moreover, though inspired by revelations that can be dated with some accuracy, its basic practices evolved over time. But if the history of the beliefs themselves can be traced like those of any other religion, the Jewish concept of the divine was nevertheless revolutionary.

Its central feature was a vision of one God who was indivisible and who could not be represented or understood in visual terms. Yahweh, the God of the Jews, could not be described. The name is formed from the Hebrew word *YHWH* and appears to be a derivative of the verb "to be," indicating that the deity is eternal and changeless. Creator of the universe and absolute in power, the God of Israel was at the same time a personal god who acted in history and who took an interest in the lives of individual Jews.

Above all, the worship of Yahweh demanded ethical behavior on the part of the worshipper. This was extraordinary, because though the Mesopotamians had emphasized the helplessness of humans and Akhenaton had thought of a single, all-powerful god, the idea that a god might be served by good deeds as well as by ritual and sacrifice was new. The concept was founded on the idea of a covenant or agreement made first between God and Abraham and reaffirmed at the time of the exodus from Egypt (see document 1.4).

The people of Israel formally reaffirmed the covenant on several occasions, but failure to observe it could bring terrible punishment. The fall of Jerusalem to Nebuchedrezzar was thought to be an example of what could happen if the Jews lapsed in their devotion, and a rich prophetic tradition developed that called upon the people of Israel to avoid God's wrath by behaving in an ethical manner. The Jews thus became the first people to write long narratives of human events as opposed to mere chronologies and king lists. Much of the Jewish Bible is devoted to the interaction between God and the children of Israel and is intended to provide a record of God's judgments on Earth to discern the divine will. Therefore, while not history as the

❖ DOCUMENT 1.4 ❖

The Covenant

This passage (Exod. 19:1–9) describes the making of the covenant between the Hebrews and their God that forms the basis of the Jewish religion and the concept of the Jews as a chosen people.

On the third new moon after the Israelites had gone out of the land of Egypt, on that very day, they came into the wilderness of Sinai. . . . Israel camped there in front of the mountain. Then Moses went up to God, the LORD called to him from the mountain, saying, "Thus you shall say to the house of Jacob, and tell the Israelites: You have seen what I did to the Egyptians, and how I bore you on eagle's wings and brought you to myself. Now, therefore, if you obey my voice and keep my covenant, you shall be my treasured possession out of all the peoples. Indeed, the whole earth is mine, but you shall be for me a priestly kingdom and a holy nation. These are the words that you shall speak to the Israelites." So Moses came, summoned the elders of the people, and set before them all these words that the LORD had commanded him. The people all answered as one: "Everything that the LORD has spoken we will do." Moses reported the words of the people to the LORD. Then the LORD said to Moses, "I am going to come to you in a dense cloud, in order that the people may hear when I speak to you and so trust you ever after.

❖ DOCUMENT 1.5 ❖

The Prophet Isaiah: Social Justice

This passage (Isa. 1:11–17), attributed to Isaiah of Jerusalem in the mid-eighth century B.C., demonstrates the increasing emphasis on social justice in Hebrew religious thought.

What to me is the multitude of your sacrifices? says the LORD. I have had enough of burnt offerings of rams and the fat of fed beasts; I do not delight in the blood of bulls, or of lambs, or of he-goats. When you come to appear before me, who requires of you this trampling of my courts? Bring no more vain offerings; incense is an abomination to me. New moon and sabbath and the calling of assemblies—I cannot endure iniquity and solemn assembly. Your new moons and your appointed feasts my soul hates; they have become a burden to me, I am weary of bearing them. When you spread forth your hands I will hide my eyes from you; even though you make many prayers, I will not listen; your hands are full of blood. Wash yourselves; make yourselves clean; remove the evil of your doings from before my eyes; cease to do evil, learn to do good; seek justice, correct oppression; defend the fatherless, plead for the widow.

Greeks would write it, it remains the first attempt to provide a coherent account of past events.

The primary expression of Yahweh's will is found, however, in the Ten Commandments and in the subsequent elaboration of the Mosaic Law. The Ten Commandments, brought down by Moses from Mt. Sinai and delivered to the people of Israel before their entry into Canaan, formed the basis of an elaborate legal and moral code that governed virtually every aspect of life and conduct. Like the concept of God, the law evolved over time. Refined and amplified by generations of priests, prophets, and teachers, it remains to this day the foundation of Jewish life.

Certain features of Mosaic Law—such as the principle of an eye for an eye, a tooth for a tooth—recall Babylonian precedents, but it went much further by seeking to govern private as well as public behavior. Dietary regulations were set forth in great detail along with rules for sexual conduct and the proper form of religious observances. Though legalistic in form, the Mosaic Law offered a comprehensive guide to ethical behavior whose force transcended social or political sanctions (see document 1.5). It was intended not only as legislation but also as a prescription for the godly life. God could mete out terrible punishment; but the commandments were to be kept, not in brute fear or from a sense of grudging duty, but in awe of God's majesty and holiness, and in gratitude for God's blessings. This concept of righteousness as an essential duty, together with many of the specific ethical principles enshrined in the Torah, or first five books of the Jewish Bible, would later be adopted by both Christianity and Islam. The influence of Mosaic Law on Western thought and society has therefore been incalculable.

The Social and Economic Structures of Ancient Israel

The society that produced these revolutionary concepts was not in other respects much different from its neighbors. From a federation of nomadic herdsmen initially organized into twelve tribes, the earliest Jews evolved into settled agriculturalists after their arrival in Canaan. Tribal survivals such as the communal ownership of resources gave way to a system of private property in which land and water were generally owned by families. Inevitably, some families were more successful than others, and many became substantial landholders with tenants and perhaps a few slaves. As in Mesopotamia, these families were often extended and always patriarchal in organization. A gradual process of urbanization increased the importance of crafts and trade, but the basic family structure remained.

In earliest times, fathers held absolute authority over wives and children. As ethical standards evolved, patriarchy was increasingly tempered by a sense of responsibility and mercy. However, the status of women was lower in ancient Israel than among the Hittites, the Egyptians, or the Mesopotamians. Under the Judges who ruled Israel from the invasion of Canaan to the emergence of the monarchy, women presided as priestesses over certain festivals. As interpretation of the Mosaic Law evolved, their participation in religious life was restricted (see document 1.6). The worship of Yahweh demanded purity as well as holiness, and women were regarded as ritually impure during menstruation and after childbirth. They were also exempted from regular prayer and other rituals on the theory that they should not be distracted from child care. In effect, they were excluded from direct participation in all public rites and were segregated from men even as observers because their presence was thought to be distracting. The proper role of women was in the home.

The home, however, was central to religious life. Marriages were arranged between families and sealed by contract as in Babylon, but only men could initiate

◆ DOCUMENT 1.6 ◆

Leviticus: The Impurity of Women

These passages of the Mosaic Law are part of a much longer section concerned with impurity; that is, those conditions under which performing religious rituals is not permissible. Note that, although men, too, could be impure, the purification of women took longer and the amount of time required for purification after the birth of a girl was twice as long as that for a boy.

12:2–5. If a woman conceives and bears a male child, she shall be ceremonially unclean seven days; as at the time of her menstruation she shall be unclean. On the eighth day the flesh of his foreskin shall be circumcised. Her time of blood purification shall be thirty-three days; she shall not touch any holy thing, or come into the sanctuary, until the days of her purification are completed. If she bears a female child, she shall be unclean two weeks, as in her menstruation; her time of blood purification shall be sixty-six days.

15:12–22. If a man has an emission of semen, he shall bathe his whole body in water, and be unclean until the evening. Everything made of cloth or skin on which the semen falls shall be washed with water and be unclean until the evening. If a man lies with a woman and has an emission of semen, both of them shall bathe in water and be unclean until the evening. When a woman has a discharge of blood that is her regular discharge from her body, she shall be in her impurity for seven days, and whoever touches her shall be unclean until the evening. Everything on which she lies during her impurity shall be unclean; everything also on which she sits shall be unclean. Whoever touches her bed shall wash his clothes, and bathe in water, and be unclean until the evening. Whoever touches anything on which she sits shall wash his clothes and bathe in water, and be unclean until the evening.

divorce and no provision was made for a dowry, which usually meant that a man could divorce his wife without financial loss. Divorces were nevertheless uncommon because Mosaic Law and Jewish custom placed a premium on the family. Polygyny and concubinage, though permitted, were rare for economic reasons, and adultery was punishable by death.

Within the home, women were more respected than their legal position might indicate. They had the right to name the children and were responsible for their early instruction in moral and practical matters. Theory aside, they often controlled the everyday life of the household. Furthermore, Jewish literature reveals none of the contempt for women and their capacities sometimes found in the writings of ancient Greece. The Bible abounds in heroic women such as Esther, Rachel, and Deborah, and the Book of Proverbs holds the value of a good woman as "beyond rubies." But the patriarchal nature of Jewish society coupled with the divine origin of the Mosaic Law would have a profound impact on subsequent history. Christianity, Islam, and modern Judaism absorbed from the Bible the idea that women's exclusion from many aspects of public and religious life was ordained by God.

The Mosaic emphasis on family placed a high value on children. Infanticide, a practice common in other ancient cultures, was forbidden, and child-raising practices, like every other aspect of life, were prescribed by law. On the eighth day after birth, male children were circumcised as a sign of their covenant with God. They received religious instruction from their fathers and at age thirteen assumed the full religious responsibilities of an adult. Eldest sons, who were especially honored, had extra responsibilities. Both boys and girls were expected to help in the fields and in the home, but gender roles were carefully preserved. Boys learned their father's trade or cared for the livestock. Girls were responsible for gleaning the fields after harvest and for keeping the house supplied with water from wells that, in town at least, were usually communal. What remained in the fields after gleaning was left for the poor.

The obligation to assist the poor and helpless—symbolized by this minor, yet divinely established, injunction—was central to the Jewish conception of righteousness. A comprehensive ideal of charity and communal responsibility gradually evolved from such precepts and, like monotheism itself, spread to Western society as a whole long after Israel as a political entity had ceased to exist.

The central features of the Jewish faith were well established at the time of the Babylonian exile. The subsequent history of the Jewish people and the transmission of their religious and ethical concepts to other cultures are important to consider, for the interaction of the Jewish, Christian, and Islamic faiths continues to this day.

CHAPTER 2

ANCIENT GREECE TO THE END OF THE PELOPONNESIAN WARS

Ancient Greece was part of the larger Mediterranean world. The eastern Mediterranean in particular may be likened to a great lake that facilitated trade, communication, and cultural borrowing. Phoenicians, Egyptians, Greeks, and many others shared a similar diet as well as some ideas and institutions, but each synthesized their borrowings in different ways. The Greeks, for example, took their alphabet from the Phoenicians and some of their scientific and philosophical ideas from Egypt, while their social organization resembled that of the Phoenician city-states. Greek civilization nevertheless remained unique. Its aesthetic ideals and its commitment to human self-development, competition, and linear thought transformed everything it touched and laid the foundations of a characteristically Western culture.

◆

Geography, the Aegean, and Crete

Mainland Greece is an extension of the Balkan Peninsula. It is, as it was in antiquity, a rugged land—mountainous, rocky, and dry, with much of the rainfall coming in the autumn and winter months. Large areas suitable for cultivation are rare, and deforestation, largely the result of overgrazing, was well advanced by the fifth century B.C. The Aegean Sea, with its innumerable islands, separates European Greece from Asia Minor. It has been a crossroads of trade and communication since the first sailors ventured forth in boats. At its northern end stood Troy, the earliest of whose nine cities, each one built upon the ruins of its predecessors, dates from before 3000 B.C. The town was built upon a ridge overlooking the southern entry to the Dardanelles, the long narrow strait through which ships must pass to enter the Sea of Marmara, the Bosporus, and the Black Sea. The current in the strait runs southward at about three knots and the prevailing winds are from the north, making it passable to early ships only under the most favorable of conditions. Fortunately, a small harbor just inside its mouth allowed goods to be transshipped from the Aegean and ships to lie at anchor while awaiting a favorable wind. That harbor was held by Troy, as was the best crossing point on the land route from Europe and Asia a few miles to the north. The city had great strategic importance, and its wealth was founded on tolls.

Far to the south is Crete, in ancient times the navigational center of the eastern Mediterranean. Approximately 150 miles long and no more than 35 miles wide, it lies across the southern end of the Aegean Sea, about 60 miles from the southernmost extremity of the Greek mainland and not more than 120 miles from the coast of Asia Minor. Africa is only 200 miles to the south. The importance of Crete was determined less by raw distances than by wind and current. Ships westbound from Egypt had to follow the currents north along the Phoenician coast and then west to Crete before proceeding to the ports of Italy or North Africa. Phoenicians on the way to Carthage or the Strait of Gibraltar did the same. They could pass either to the north or to the south of the island. Most preferred the northern shore because it offered more sandy inlets where their ships could be anchored for the night or hauled ashore for repairs and cleaning. Crete was therefore a natural waystation as well as a convenient point for the transshipment of Egyptian and Phoenician goods. The same harbors offered easy access to the Greek mainland, the Ionian islands, and Troy.

The Society of Minoan Crete (3000–1400 B.C.)

The first inhabitants of Crete arrived before 4000 B.C. They found not only a strategic location, but also land that was well suited for Neolithic agriculture. Crete's mountains rise to more than eight thousand feet, but the island has rich valleys and coastal plains that provide abundant grain. The climate is generally mild. Perfection is marred only by summer droughts, winter gales, and devastating earthquakes that are perhaps the most conspicuous feature of the island's history.

The civilization that had developed on Crete by 3000 B.C. is usually called Minoan, after Minos, a legendary ruler who became part of later Greek mythology. Its chief characteristics were the early manufacture of bronze and the construction of enormous palaces that combined political, religious, and economic functions. Four main complexes were constructed—at Knossos (see illustration 2.1), Phaistos, Zakros, and

Mallia—though the ruins of other large houses are found throughout the island. All are built around large rectangular courts that were apparently used for religious and public ceremonies. The upper levels of the palaces had decorative staircases and colonnades that resemble those of Egyptian temples. The walls were covered with thin layers of shiny gypsum or decorated with naturalistic wall paintings. Below were innumerable storerooms and a system of drains for the removal of wastes and rainwater. So elaborate was the floor plan that the Greek name for the palace at Knossos (the Labyrinth, after the heraldic labrys or two-headed axe of the Minoan royal house) became the common word for a maze.

The presence of such vast storage facilities indicates that Minoan rulers played an important part in the distribution of goods, but little is known of Minoan social or political life. The early language of Crete has not yet been deciphered. It was written at first in hieroglyphic characters derived from Egyptian models. A later linear script is equally unreadable, and only Linear B, dating from the last period of Minoan history, has been translated. The language revealed is an early form of Greek, probably introduced by a new ruling dynasty from the mainland around 1400 B.C.

Minoan religious beliefs are equally obscure. Wall paintings portray women in priestly roles, and the dominant cult was almost certainly that of the Earth Mother, the fertility goddess whose worship in the Mediterranean basin dates from Paleolithic times. Other paintings show young women and men vaulting over the heads of bulls and doing gymnastic routines on their backs (see illustration 2.2). This dangerous sport probably had religious significance and was performed in the palace courtyards, but its exact purpose is unknown. In any case, the prominence of women in Minoan art and the range of activities in which they were portrayed indicate a measure of equality rare in the ancient world.

The Mycenean Greeks

The people who seem to have conquered Crete around 1450 B.C. are known as Myceneans, though Mycenae was only one of their many cities. They spoke an early form of Greek and may have occupied Macedonia or Thessaly before establishing themselves along the western shores of the Aegean. Their chief centers—apart from Mycenae and its companion fortress, Tiryns—were Athens on its rich peninsula and Thebes in the Boetian plain. All were flourishing by 2000 B.C.

Illustration 2.1

Plan of the Palace at Knossos. This partial plan of the great palace at Knossos shows the central courtyard, private apartments, and what are probably storerooms.

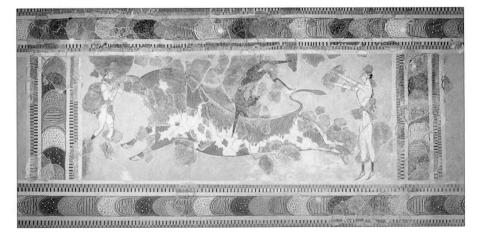

Illustration 2.2

Bull Leaping at Knossos. This fresco from the east wing of the palace at Knossos portrays a man and two women somersaulting over the back of a charging bull. Whether this was a sport, a religious ritual, or both is not known.

Kings or chieftains ruled each of the Mycenean communities and apparently distributed commodities in the traditional way. They built vast palaces and tombs using cut stones of as much as one hundred tons apiece and carried on an extensive trade with Crete and Egypt. The palaces, though similar in function to those on Crete, were more symmetrical in design, with spacious apartments and colonnaded porches on the upper levels and storerooms below. Olive oil was a major export, and some of the storage spaces were heated to keep it from congealing in the winter cold.

The earliest tombs were shaft graves of the sort found throughout Europe; later, vast corbeled vaults became common. The dead were buried with magnificent treasures, for the Myceneans collected art and luxury goods from other cultures as well as from their own. They were also skilled metalworkers. Their bronze armor and weapons, like their gold jewelry and face masks, were among the finest ever produced in the ancient world.

But aside from their material culture, these precursors of the ancient Greeks remain something of a mystery. Homer, the semimythical poet who stands at the beginnings of Greek culture, made them the heroes of his The Iliad (see document 2.1). This great epic describes their successful siege of Troy, an event partially supported by archaeological evidence, but the society he describes is unlike that revealed by the ruins of Mycenean cities. Homer's Myceneans cremate their dead and fight as individual champions. No mention is made of the tombs, the vast storerooms, the voluminous accounts, and the careful, hardheaded organization of vast enterprises that created them. Homer likely was describing a much later world—perhaps the one in which he lived—and attributing its values to its predecessors. Only the violence and the lack of political unity are the same.

Early Greek Society

Homer, or whoever created The Iliad and its companion piece The Odyssey, from an existing body of oral traditions, probably lived in the ninth century B.C. By this time the Aegean world had changed almost beyond recognition. The population movements of the thirteenth century B.C. inaugurated a kind of dark age about which little is known. The Homeric poems probably refer to this era but provide only fragmentary information about actual events. Greeks of the classical age believed that the Dorians, a Greek-speaking people from the north, swept into the peninsula and estab-

---

◈ DOCUMENT 2.1 ◈

The Iliad

Homer's great epic of the Trojan War—The Iliad—in many ways defined Greek values and ideals for later generations. Those values are humanistic in the sense that its heroes strive for excellence in human instead of religious terms, but underlying everything is a sense that even the greatest of mortals live within a universal order. This passage, in which the aging Priam of Troy comes to ask Achilles for the body of his son, Hector, who has been killed by Achilles, reflects the tragic side of Greek consciousness.

Priam had set Achilles thinking about his own father and brought him to the verge of tears. Taking the old man's hand, he gently put him from him; and overcome by their memories, they both broke down. Priam, crouching at Achilles's feet, wept bitterly for man-slaying Hector, and Achilles wept for his father, and then again for Patroclus. The house was filled with the sounds of their lamentation. But presently when he had had enough of tears and recovered his composure, the excellent Achilles leapt from his chair, and in compassion for the man's grey head and grey beard, took him by the arm and raised him. Then he spoke to him from his heart: "You are indeed a man of sorrows and have suffered much. How could you dare to come by yourself to the Achaean ships into the presence of a man who has killed so many of your gallant sons? You have a heart of iron. But pray be seated now, here on this chair, and let us leave our sorrows, bitter though they are, locked up in our own hearts, for weeping is cold comfort and does little good. We men are wretched things, and the gods, who have no cares themselves, have woven sorrow into the very pattern of our lives."

Homer. *The Iliad,* trans. E. V. Rieu. Harmondsworth, England: Penguin books, 1950.

---

lished themselves in the Peloponnese and other Mycenean centers. Mycenae was destroyed, but the lore is that the invaders bypassed Athens, which became the conduit for a vast eastward migration. Thousands of refugees, their lands taken by newcomers, fled to Attica. From there they colonized the islands of the Aegean and the western coast of Asia Minor. The migration of these Ionian Greeks displaced others who flowed eastward into Asia Minor. The Phrygians who toppled the weakened fragments of the Hittite Empire and the Philistines who descended on the Canaanite coast were almost certainly among them, for all of these events occurred at about the same time.

Recent scholarship casts doubt on the theory of a Dorian invasion, but by the ninth century B.C. the Greek world was divided into two major subgroups, the Dorians, who dominated most of the peninsula, and the Ionians, who inhabited Attica, Euboia, and the east. They spoke different dialects but shared many aspects of a common culture. Both groups thought of the Greek-speaking world as Hellas and referred to themselves as Hellenes.

The religion of the Greeks was based on an extended family of twelve gods who were supposed to inhabit Mt. Olympus in northeastern Greece. The greatest were Zeus, the father of the Gods; his consort, Hera; and his brother Poseidon, the god of the sea and of earthquakes. Hestia, the goddess of hearths, and Demeter, often associated with the earlier Earth Mother, were his sisters. His children were Aphrodite, goddess of love; Apollo, god of the Sun, music, and poetry; Ares, god of war; Athena, goddess of wisdom and the fine arts; Hephaestus, god of fire and metallurgy; and Hermes, their messenger, who was also god of commerce and other matters that involved cleverness or trickery. Perhaps the most popular was Artemis, the virgin nature goddess who symbolized chastity and to whom women prayed for help in childbirth.

The Greeks conceived of these deities in human terms, though the gods were immortal and possessed superhuman powers. Because Olympian behavior was often capricious and immoral, Greek ethical principles in the Archaic Period were derived not from divine precepts but from commonsense notions of how to get along with one's neighbors. Worship meant offering prayers and sacrifices in return for divine protection or to secure the goodwill of the spirits who ruled over particular localities. Little or no hope of personal immortality seemed to exist. By the eighth century B.C., centers of worship open to all Greeks had been established at several locations. Olympia, dedicated to Zeus, and the shrine of Poseidon at Corinth were famous for athletic contests held annually in the god's honor. The shrine of Apollo at Delphi was home to the Delphic oracle, whose cryptic predictions were widely sought until Roman times.

Common shrines, and above all the Olympic games, provided unifying elements in a culture that would for centuries remain politically fragmented. The

---

◆ DOCUMENT 2.2 ◆

Pindar: Ode to an Athlete

Pindar (c. 518–c. 438 b.c.) was a native of Thebes and one of the greatest lyric poets of ancient Greece. He is best known for odes composed in honor of successful athletes. Many—such as Isthmian V: For Phylakidas of Aegina, Winner in the Trial of Strength, presented here—were commissioned by the athlete's native cities. Pindar often included a brief warning against hubris, the fatal pride that leads men to challenge the gods.

In the struggle of the games he has won
The glory of his desire,
Whose hair is tied with thick garlands
For victory with his hands
Or swiftness of foot.
Men's valor is judged by their fates,
But two things alone
Look after the sweetest grace of life
Among the fine flowers of wealth.

If a man fares well and hears his good name
   spoken,
Seek not to become a Zeus!
You have everything, if a share
Of those beautiful things come to you.

Mortal ends befit mortal men.
For you Phylakidas, at the Isthmus
A double success is planted and thrives,
And at Nemea for you and your brother Pytheas
In the Trial of Strength. My heart tastes song.

Pindar. *The Odes of Pindar,* p. 47, trans. C. M. Bowra. Harmondsworth, England: Penguin Books, 1969. Copyright © The Estate of C. M. Bowra, 1969. Reproduced by permission of Penguin Books Ltd.

---

games drew men (women were not permitted to compete) from every part of the Greek world and provided a peaceful arena for the competitive spirit that was a great part of ancient Greek life. Winners were praised by poets (see document 2.2) and showered with gifts by their grateful communities. All Greek men participated in sports, for they saw athletics as an essential component of the good life. Physical fitness prepared them for war, but competition lay at the heart of their concept of personal worth, and athletic success was seen as almost godlike.

The Development of the Polis

The Dorians tended to settle in fortified high places that could be defended against their enemies, expelling some of the existing population and subjugating others. Each one of these communities—and there were scores of them—claimed full sovereign rights and vigorously defended its independence against all comers. On the rugged Greek peninsula, most of the arable land is found in valleys isolated from one another by mountains, but three or four of these ministates might be found in the same area with no geographical barriers between them. Many did not possess enough land to support their populations. The men organized themselves into war bands that, like those of Homer's heroes, might ally with the warriors of another community in the pursuit of a major objective, but cooperation was always fragile and warfare endemic.

Ionic settlements in the Aegean were similar. Some of the islands had been Cretan colonies, and most were inhabited when the Ionian refugees arrived. Like their Doric enemies, the Ionians established themselves in fortifiable places and sometimes imposed their rule on existing populations. Although a few smaller islands formed political units, others were divided into many settlements. These early communities were the precursors of the *polis*, the basis of Greek political and social life. Each, whether Doric or Ionic, claimed the primary loyalties of its inhabitants. To Greeks of the classical period, the polis was far more than a city-state; it was the only form of social organization in which the individual's full potential could be achieved. Composed in theory at least of those who shared common ancestors and worshiped the same gods, it molded the character of its inhabitants and provided a focus for their lives. To live apart from the polis was to live as a beast.

Security from outside threats made this political decentralization possible. The Greek city-states developed after the Hittites had fallen and when Egypt was in decline. The great Asian empires were not yet a threat. Conflict, and there was much of it, involved other cities whose population and resources were often minuscule. Many were little more than villages whose armies might number no more than eighty or one hundred men. Even the largest, including Athens and Corinth, were small by modern standards, but military resources could be augmented through the formation of temporary alliances.

In the beginning, the government of these communities was aristocractic. Kings might be hereditary or elected, but they ruled with the assistance of a council composed of warriors from the more distinguished families. Warfare, aimed largely at seizing or destroying a neighbor's crops, reflected the organization of society. Individual champions fought one another with sword, lance, and shield, while tactics in the larger sense were unknown.

This period of aristocratic dominance came to an end with the adoption of the hoplite phalanx, a formation of trained spearmen who fought shoulder to shoulder in a rectangle that was normally eight ranks deep (see illustration 2.3). As long as no one broke ranks, the phalanx was almost invincible against a frontal attack by horse or foot and could clear the field of traditional infantry at will. Only another band of hoplites could stand against them. Flanking attacks by cavalry were prevented by grounding the sides of the formation against natural or man-made obstacles, an easy task in the rugged Greek countryside. Missile weapons were only a minor threat because the hoplite's bronze armor was heavy and enemy archers usually had to fight in the open. After the first volley, the phalanx could cover the distance of a bowshot in the time it took to fire a second or third arrow, and the archers would be forced to flee in disorder. The major weakness of the formation was its immobility. Maneuvering was difficult and pursuit impossible without breaking ranks. This tended to reduce the number of casualties but made achieving decisive results difficult.

The hoplite phalanx gave birth to the polis in its classical form. The new tactics required the participation of every able-bodied freeman who could afford arms and armor, and men who fought for the city could not be denied a say in its governance. Those too poor to equip themselves as hoplites were expected to serve as support troops or to row in the city's galleys, for most Greek cities maintained a navy as well. Though wealth and heredity still counted, the eventual effect of the new warfare was to increase the number of those who participated in government. Slaves, women, and foreigners—meaning those who had been born in another polis—were excluded from public life, but all male citizens were expected to participate in matters of justice and public policy.

The growth of democracy, however, was slow, for the aristocrats resisted change. Efforts to maintain their traditional privileges caused disorder in every polis, and the late eighth and early seventh centuries B.C. were times of conflict. Tyrants or dictators who promised to resolve these struggles found achieving power easy. Though their rule was condemned by later theorists, they developed administrative structures and tried to

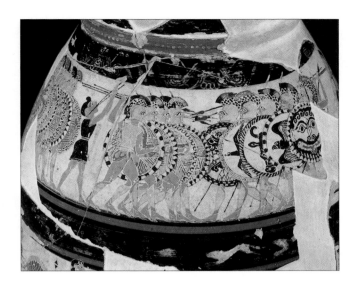

Illustration 2.3

Hoplite Warfare. This vase painting from the seventh century B.C. is one of the few surviving portrayals of hoplites at war. The piper on the left is leading another phalanx into the battle.

establish a broader patriotism by weakening the old loyalties based on tribe or district. Most of the tyrants were also great builders whose temples and public works gave form to the cities of the classical age.

Greek towns were usually built around an *acropolis*, the high point selected as a place of refuge by the original inhabitants. Here the first rude temples were established in honor of the city's gods. Under the tyrants, new and more magnificent structures replaced them, and private buildings were banished to the area around the base of the hill. With rare exceptions, Greek homes were simple, and much of daily life was lived in the streets or in the *agora*, an open space that served as the economic and social center of the town. This, perhaps as much as any other factor, accounts for the vitality of Greek politics and intellectual life; the life of the citizen was one of constant interaction with his fellows.

The more ambitious tyrants not only built temples, but also remodeled such public spaces as the agora. They strengthened the defensive walls that surrounded their cities and worked to improve the quality and quantity of the water supply. Some went even further. Corinth, one of the wealthiest Greek cities, bestrides the narrow isthmus that separates the Saronic Gulf from the Gulf of Corinth. The Corinthian tyrant Periander built a stone trackway across the isthmus, allowing entire ships to be hauled from the Aegean to the Adriatic. Merchants willing to pay a substantial toll could thereby save a voyage of several hundred miles.

The troubled years that gave birth to the tyrants were also the great age of Greek colonization. Greece was by any standards a poor country with little room for internal growth, but it had an extensive coastline with good harbors and it was inhabited by a seafaring

people. The limits of agricultural expansion were reached by the beginning of the eighth century B.C., and like the Phoenicians of a century before, Greek cities were forced to establish colonies in other parts of the Mediterranean world as an outlet for surplus population. Though some of the colonists were merchants or political exiles, most sought only enough land to feed their families.

The process seems to have begun around 750 B.C. with the establishment of a trading community in the Bay of Naples. It was intended to provide access to the copper of Etruria, but the colonies established during the next fifty years in eastern Sicily were almost purely agrarian. Settlements then spread throughout southern Italy and westward into France, where Massalia, the future Marseilles, was founded around 600 B.C. by the Ionic town of Phocaea. Others were founded around the shores of the Black Sea, and those in what is now the southern Ukraine would one day play an important role by supplying the Greek peninsula with grain.

Some Italian colonies, such as Sybaris on the Gulf of Taranto, became wealthy through trade. Though originally founded to exploit a rich agricultural plain, Sybaris became a point of transshipment for goods from the Adriatic to the Tyrrhenian Sea, thereby avoiding the treacherous Strait of Messina. Others, such as Syracuse in Sicily, owed their wealth to agriculture, but Syracuse grew as large as its parent Corinth and became a major regional power in the fifth century B.C. Virtually all of these towns came into conflict with the Phoenicians and Carthaginians who had settled in Spain, Africa, and western Sicily. By the beginning of the sixth century B.C. at least five hundred Greek *poleis* were in existence from Spain to the Crimea.

The use of the term *polis* is technically correct in this case, for these were not colonies but fully independent states. They venerated the divine patron of their founding city and sometimes extended special privileges to its citizens. "Mother" cities competed with their "colonies" for trade and on occasion fought them. All, however, were regarded as part of Hellas. Governing institutions paralleled those in the older Greek cities, and the colonies, too, were forced to confront the problem of tyranny. Some failed to eject their tyrants; others were able to achieve a measure of democracy in the course of the sixth century B.C.

Tyrants had been accepted for the most part out of necessity, but the Greeks had regarded their rule as an aberration, a temporary suspension of the laws instead of a permanent institution. Most were eventually overthrown and replaced by some form of representative government. This might be a narrowly based oligarchy, as at Corinth, or a true democracy of the kind that gradually evolved at Athens.

Life in the Polis: The Early History of Athens

Though Athens, on the Attic Peninsula north of the Saronic Gulf, would become the cultural center of classical Greece, its initial development was slow. Until 594 B.C. it was governed by an aristocratic council known as the Areopagus, which elected nine magistrates or archons on an annual basis. Membership in the Areopagus was hereditary, and there was no written law. The archons, who were always aristocrats, interpreted legal issues to suit themselves.

Aristocratic dominance and the gradual depletion of the soil eventually produced an agrarian crisis. Most Athenians—and most Greeks—were small farmers who grew wheat and barley and tried to maintain a few vines and olive trees (see document 2.3). Wheat yields probably averaged about five bushels per acre; barley, ten. Such yields are normal for unfertilized, unirrigated soils in almost any region. This was generally enough to guarantee subsistence but little more. When yields began declining in the early seventh century B.C., Attic farmers were forced to borrow from the aristocrats to survive. Inevitably, harvests failed to improve, and citizens who defaulted were enslaved and sometimes sold abroad.

Dissatisfaction with this state of affairs and with the endless blood feuds among aristocratic clans led to an abortive tyranny in 632 B.C. Eleven years later, a semi-legendary figure named Draco passed laws against aristocratic violence so harsh that *draconian* has become a byword for severity. However, the agrarian problem remained. Political tensions remained high until the election of Solon as the only archon in 594 B.C.

Solon was in effect a tyrant, though he had no intention of serving for life and retired when he had completed his reforms. He canceled outstanding debts, freed many slaves, and forbade the use of a citizen's person as collateral. Solon also broadened the social base of the Athenian government by creating a popularly elected Council of 400 as a check on the powers of the Areopagus. His economic ideas were less successful. Though he tried to encourage commerce and industry, Solon prohibited the export of wheat and encouraged that of olive oil. The larger landholders, seeing profit in olives and other cash crops, took wheat land out of production and Athens became permanently dependent upon imported food. Most of its grain would eventually come from the rich plains north of the Black Sea. This meant that, in later years, Athenian survival required control of the Hellespont, the narrow strait that separates Europe from Asia and provided access to the Greek ports of the Crimea.

These measures, though popular, failed to prevent the emergence of Pisistratus as tyrant, briefly in 560 B.C. and then from 546 B.C. to his death in 527 B.C. The constitution was unchanged, and Pisistratus ruled through his mastery of electoral politics, but like the tyrants of other cities, he worked tirelessly to break the remaining power of the aristocratic families. Taxation and subscriptions for more and more public festivals weakened them financially while magistrates were sent into the countryside to interfere in their legal disputes. Public works flourished, and such projects as temple construction and the remodeling of the agora provided work for thousands.

Pisistratus was succeeded by his son Hippias, but Hippias became a tyrant in the more conventional sense of the word. He was overthrown with Spartan assistance in 510 B.C. and replaced by Cleisthenes, who laid the foundations of the democratic system that lasted throughout the classical age.

Cleisthenes expanded the number of demes, or wards, which served as the primary units of local government, and divided them into ten tribes instead of four. A Council of 500 was elected with fifty members from each tribe. This body prepared legislation and supervised finances and foreign affairs. Final authority in all matters now rested with an assembly of all citizens that met at least forty times a year. Dangerous or unpopular politicians could be ostracized, a process by which the citizens voted to exile an individual from the

◈ DOCUMENT 2.3 ◈

The Life of a Greek Landowner

Hesiod (fl. late eighth century B.C.) was one of the first Greek poets and a landowner from Boeotia. His Works and Days *is a long didactic poem addressed to his ne'er-do-well brother, Perses. It provides an unforgettable description of rural life in an age when farmers still went to sea to sell their goods abroad.*

When the thistle blooms and the chirping cicada
sits on trees and pours down shrill song
from frenziedly quivering wings in the toilsome summer
then goats are fatter than ever and wine is at its best
women's lust knows no bounds and men are all dried up,
because the dog star parches their heads and knees
and the heat sears their skin. Then, ah then,
I wish you a shady ledge and your choice wine,
bread baked in the dusk and mid-August goat milk
and meat from a free-roving heifer that has never calved—
and from firstling kids. Drink sparkling wine,
sitting in the shade with your appetite sated,
and face Zephyr's breeze as it blows from mountain peaks.
Pour three measures of water fetched from a clear spring,
One that flows unchecked, and a fourth of wine.
As soon as mighty Orion rises above the horizon
exhort your slaves to thresh Demeter's holy grain
in a windy, well-rounded threshing floor.
Measure it first and then store it in bins.
But when your grain is tightly stored inside the house
then hire an unmarried worker and look for a female
servant with no children—nursing women are a burden.
Keep a dog with sharp teeth and feed it well,
wary of the day-sleepers who might rob you.

Bring in a lasting supply of hay and fodder
for your oxen and your mules. Once this is done let your
slaves rest their weary knees and unyoke the oxen.
When Orion and the dog star rise to the middle of the
sky and rosy-fingered dawn looks upon Arcturus,
then Perses, gather your grapes and bring them home
and leave them in the sun for ten days and nights,
in the shade for five, and on the sixth day
draw the gift of joyous Dionysos into your vats.
When the Pleiades, the Hyades, and mighty Orion set,
remember the time has come to plow again—
and may the earth nurse for you a full year's supply,
And if longing seizes you for sailing the stormy seas,
when the Pleiades flee mighty Orion
and plunge into the misty deep
and all the gusty winds are raging,
then do not take your ship on the wine-dark sea
but, as I bid you, remember to work the land.
Haul your ship onto land and secure it to the ground
with stones on all sides to stay the blast of rain and wind,
and pull the plug to avoid rotting caused by rain water.
Store up the tackle compactly inside your house
and neatly fold the sails, the wings of a seafaring ship.
Hang your rudder above the fireplace
and wait until the time to sail comes again.

city for ten years without a formal trial. Magistrates were chosen by lot, though the city's military commander or *strategos* continued to be elected, presumably on the basis of merit. Plato and others who sympathized with aristocracy found this system, which was liberalized even further after 461 B.C., absurd, but competence was at least partially ensured because candidates had to volunteer and were subjected to a stringent review of their actions at the end of the year.

Athens represented an extreme of democratic government, but its level of public participation was not unique. The system worked remarkably well for almost two hundred years and provided the basis for local gov-

ernment even after the city lost its freedom to the Macedonians. At the very least, it guaranteed intense involvement by the entire population of male citizens in the life of the polis, any one of whom could be part of its political, military, and judicial processes. Democratic theorists have held that this level of participation helps to account for the extraordinary intellectual and artistic achievements of the Athenians. Furthermore, Athens, its institutions, and its way of life became an inspiration to many throughout the later history of the West. While it fostered slavery and excluded women from public life, Athens was the first and perhaps the greatest of the early democracies.

The Social and Economic Structures of Athenian Society

In material terms, the Athenian way of life was remarkably simple. Athenians, like other Greeks, lived on bread, wine, and oil, often garnished with onions or garlic. Beans and various fruits supplemented this otherwise meager diet. Meat was expensive and normally consumed in small quantities. Even the largest houses were small by Egyptian or Mesopotamian standards, though their arrangement was similar. Square or rectangular rooms were grouped around a central courtyard, which might contain a private well. Some houses had second stories. Merchants and artisans often conducted their business from rooms on the street side of their dwellings. Housing for the poor, being more cheaply built, has not been well preserved.

The poor were numerous. Population estimates vary, but classical Athens probably had between forty thousand and fifty thousand male citizens in both town and country and at least an equal number of slaves. Most of the latter were either domestic servants and laborers of both sexes or artisans. A large number worked in the mines. As in the rest of the ancient world, slavery among the Greeks had begun with the taking of captives in war, but by the classical age most slaves were barbarians (that is, non-Greeks) purchased from itinerant traders. No great slave-worked estates existed, and even the richest citizens seem to have owned only a few. Slave artisans who toiled outside their master's home were normally paid wages, a fixed portion of which was returned to their owner. This practice tended to depress the pay rates of free workers and ensured that many citizens lived no better than the slaves. As in Mesopotamia, killing a slave was a crime, and slaves were guaranteed their freedom (manumission) if they could raise their price of purchase.

In addition to slaves and free citizens, Athens boasted a large population of foreigners. The city was a commercial center that, though located a few miles from the coast, had a bustling port at Piraeus. Unlike some Greeks, the Athenians welcomed foreign ideas— and capital. Though they could not participate in public life or own real estate, foreign residents were well treated and many became wealthy. They controlled many aspects of the city's commerce.

The situation of Athenian women, however, is a matter of some controversy. Even women who were citizens had no political rights, and their judicial rights had to be exercised for them by others, because their status was that of permanent legal minors. They did

have dowries, which protected them to some extent if they were divorced or widowed. But divorce seems to have been rare. As in other Mediterranean societies, wives usually controlled the management of their husband's household and avoided public life. The Athenians, like most ancient Greeks, made extraordinary efforts to segregate the sexes. Respectable women of the citizen class stayed at home except for occasional attendance at festivals, sacrifices, or the theater. Even then they were accompanied by male relatives, and it is thought that men also did the shopping to keep their wives and daughters from coming into contact with strangers. Furthermore, women were expected to avoid certain areas within the home. The *andron*, a room where men received their male guests, was strictly off-limits to women, and in many Greek houses it had a separate entrance to the street (see illustration 2.4).

Underlying these practices was the conviction, voiced frequently by Greek writers, that women were incapable of controlling their sexuality. A woman suspected of having a child by someone other than her lawful husband endangered the status of her other children, who might lose their citizenship if challenged in court by an enemy. For this reason, the head of a family had the right to kill any man who seduced his wife, daughter, or any other female relative under his protection. Being nonconsensual, rape was considered less serious. As one offended husband said in a famous case: "The lawgiver prescribed death for adultery because he who achieves his ends by persuasion thereby corrupts the mind as well as the body of the woman . . . gains access to all a man's possessions, and casts doubt on his children's parentage." The adulterous woman could not be killed because she was legally and morally irresponsible. If married, she could be divorced; if single, she ruined her prospects for finding a husband and spent the rest of her life as a virtual prisoner in the house of her father or guardian. In spite of these sanctions, adultery may not have been as uncommon as scholars once believed.

By modern standards, the women of middle-and upper-class families were virtual prisoners in any case (see document 2.4). They married early, often at fourteen or fifteen, to men chosen by their families who were usually far older than themselves, and they almost never received a formal education. Much of their time was spent in spinning and sewing because Greek clothing was simple and could easily be manufactured at home. There were, however, exceptions. As in other societies, a propertied widow might enjoy considerable influence and a few upper-class women, such as the sis-

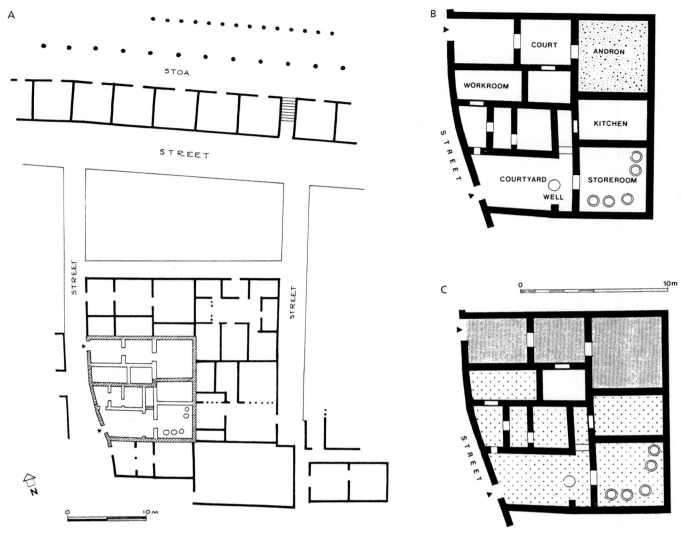

Illustration 2.4

▨ **Plan of a Typical Greek House.** This house was part of a residential block on the south slope of the Areopagus in Athens. Drawing A shows its location; drawing B, the probable function of the rooms. In drawing C the shaded area was used by men only. Note that the men's and women's areas of the house had separate street entrances (arrows) and that no interior access appears between them.

ter of the statesman Cimon, were well educated. From a modern perspective, poor and alien women had more interesting lives. Many worked or sold goods in the marketplace, activities essential to the survival of their families that guaranteed them a freedom of movement unknown to their wealthier sisters. The price of that freedom was extreme economic and physical vulnerability.

Segregation of the sexes led to an acceptance of male extramarital relations with slave and alien women. Prostitution was common, and at the higher levels of society, courtesans or *hetairai* were highly valued as companions at banquets and other social occasions from which respectable women were excluded. Courtesans were often highly educated. Some—such as Aspasia, the mistress of the fifth-century statesman Pericles—achieved considerable fame and could hold their own in intellectual discourse, but they were still regarded as prostitutes. Aspasia ended her days as the madam of an Athens brothel.

Homosexuality, too, was regarded by many Greeks as normal, and in some cases praiseworthy

◈ DOCUMENT 2.4 ◈

The Role of the Athenian Wife

In this excerpt from Xenophon's Oeconomicus (Household Management), Ischomachus tells Socrates how he began to train his fifteen-year-old bride. His views reflect conventional Athenian wisdom.

Well Socrates, as soon as I had tamed her and she was relaxed enough to talk, I asked her the following question: "Tell me, my dear," said I, "do you understand why I married you and why your parents gave you to me? You know as well as I do that neither of us would have had trouble finding someone else to share our beds. But after thinking about it carefully, it was you I chose and me your parents chose as the best partners we could find for our home and children. Now if God sends us children, we shall think about how best to raise them, for we share an interest in securing the best allies and support for our old age."

My wife answered, "But how can I help? What am I capable of doing? It is on you that everything depends. My duty, my mother said, is to be well-behaved."

"Oh, by Zeus," said I, "my father said the same to me. But the best behavior in a man and woman is that which will keep up their property and increase it as far as may be done by honest and legal means. . . ."

"It seems to me that God adapted women's nature to indoor and man's to outdoor work. . . . As Nature has entrusted woman with guarding the household supplies, and a timid nature is no disadvantage in such a job, it has endowed women with more fear than man. It is more proper for a woman to stay in the house than out of doors and less so for a man to be indoors instead of out. . . . You must stay indoors and send out the servants whose work is outside and supervise those who work indoors, receive what is brought in, give out what is to be spent, plan ahead for what is to be stored and ensure that provisions for a year are not used up in a month. . . . Many of your duties will give you pleasure: for instance, if you teach spinning and weaving to a slave who did not know how to do this when you got her, you double your usefulness to yourself."

Xenophon. "*Oeconomicus*." In Julia O'Faolain and Lauro Martines, *Not in God's Image: Women in History from the Greeks to the Victorians*. London: Temple Smith, 1973.

(see document 2.5). Soldiers, for example, were thought to fight more bravely when accompanied by their male lovers. Many of these relationships were formed in the gymnasia where men of the citizen class trained for war or athletics. It was not uncommon for a youth to become sexually involved with an older man who then served as his mentor in intellectual as well as athletic matters. Such arrangements were widely accepted. The Greeks, however, did not view homosexuality as an orientation that precluded sexual relations with women or a conventional family life. Furthermore, homosexual promiscuity could ruin a man's reputation or lead to exile, and many regarded it as inferior to married love.

As in many other cultures, Greek men and women may have belonged in effect to separate societies that met only in bed. If true, this would also account for the widespread acceptance of lesbianism. Greek men may not have cared about sex between women because it did not raise the issue of inheritance. The term *lesbian* is derived from the Ionic island of Lesbos, home of Sappho (c. 610–c. 580 B.C.), a woman and the greatest of Greek lyric poets. Europeans of a later age found her erotic poems to other women scandalous, and their renown has perhaps unfairly eclipsed the much wider range of her work in the minds of all but the most determined classicists.

Though Athenians, like other Greeks, were remarkably open about sexual matters, the assumption should not be made that they abandoned themselves to debauchery. Self-control remained the essence of the ideal citizen, and sexual restraint was admired along with physical fitness and moderation in the consumption of food and drink. A man who wasted his wealth and corrupted his body was of no value to the polis, for the polis was always at risk and demanded nothing less than excellence in those who would defend it.

Sparta: A Conservative Garrison State

To moderns, Athens represents the model Greek polis—free, cultivated, and inquiring—but to the ancients, and to many Athenians, an alternative existed. Far away to the south, in a remote valley of the Peloponnese, lay Sparta. Sparta produced few poets and no philosophers. Its unwalled capital, built on a raised mound to keep it from the floodwaters of the river Eurotas, was said to resemble an overgrown village. There was no commerce to speak of, and long after other Greeks had adopted money, Spartans continued to use iron bars as their only currency. Because the Spartans

❖ DOCUMENT 2.5 ❖

Plutarch: Dialogue on Love

Debates over the relative merits of homosexual and heterosexual love were commonplace. Plutarch, the author of this one, lived in the first century A.D. He was an avid propagandist for Hellenic values, and his works are thought to reflect the attitudes of an age long past. Here Protogenes, who believes that women are incapable of true feeling or intellect, argues that love is almost by definition homosexual. His friend Daphnaeus, who seems to represent Plutarch, vehemently disagrees.

"Do you call marriage and the union of man and wife shameful?" interposed Daphnaeus, "there can be no bond more sacred."

"Such unions are necessary for the propagation of the race," said Protogenes, "and so our lawgivers have been careful to endow them with sanctity and exalt them before the populace. But of true Love the women's apartment has no shred. For my part I deny that the word "love" can be applied to the sentiment you feel for women and girls, no more than flies can be said to 'love' milk, or bees honey, or victualers and cooks can be said to have amorous feelings for the beeves and fowl they fatten in the dark. . . ." A noble love which attaches to a youthful [male] spirit issues in excellence upon the path of friendship. From these desires for women, even if they turn out well, one may enjoy only physical pleasure and the satisfaction of a ripe body."

[After much argument, Daphnaeus responds:] "If we examine the truth of the matter, Protogenes, the passion for boys and for women derives from one and the same Love, but if you insist on distinguishing between them for argument's sake, you will find that the Love of boys does not comport himself decently; he is like a late issue, born unseasonably, illegitimate, and shady, who drives out the elder and legitimate love. It was only yesterday, my friend, or the day before, after lads began to strip and bare themselves for exercise that it crept surreptitiously into the gymnasia with its allurements and embraces, and then, little by little, when it had fledged its wings full in the palaestras, it could no longer be held in check; now it abuses and befouls that noble conjugal Love which assures immortality to our mortal kind, for by procreation it rekindles our nature when it is extinguished.

"Protogenes denies there is pleasure in the Love of boys: he does so out of shame and fear. He must have some decent pretext for attachment to his young beauties, and so he speaks of friendship and excellence. He covers himself with athlete's dust, takes cold baths, raises his eyebrows, and declares he is chastely philosophizing—to outward view and because of the law. But when night falls and all is quiet then 'sweet is the fruit when the keeper is gone.' "

Plutarch. "Dialogue on Love," trans. Moses Hadas. In Moses Hadas, ed., *On Love, the Family, and the Good Life: Selected Essays of Plutarch*, pp. 307–308. Mentor books, 1957.

wrote little, they are chiefly known through the writings of foreign political theorists. By all accounts, Sparta was a grim place: poor, rigidly conservative, and distinguished only by its magnificent army and by the single-minded discipline of its citizens.

Sparta was an aristocratic garrison state. The first Spartans were probably a band of Doric invaders who established their polis on the ruins of an earlier society. They displaced an earlier ruling class that was probably Dorian as well, allowing these *perioikoi* to retain property and personal freedom within their own communities. The original pre-Dorian inhabitants became serfs, or in Spartan terms, helots. This was not unusual, but around 725 B.C. Sparta conquered the neighboring polis of Messenia and reduced its inhabitants to serfdom as well. Helots outnumbered Spartans by a probable ra-

tio of ten-to-one. In the Second Messenian War (c. 650 B.C.) the helots of both communities rose against their masters and, with the help of some neighboring cities, came close to destroying the Spartan state. Unless the Spartans were prepared to give up Messenia, survival would require complete social reorganization.

The Spartans attributed their reorganization to the legendary figure of Lycurgus, but the new practices almost certainly evolved over time. The Spartan government had long been a dual monarchy in which two hereditary kings exerted equal powers in war and in religious matters. Their influence, however, was severely limited. A Council of Elders, composed of twenty-eight men over the age of sixty, advised them and served as a kind of appellate court in reviewing their legal decisions. The ephors, a committee of five, ran the

◈ DOCUMENT 2.6 ◈

A Spartan Childhood

This is one of several descriptions of Spartan values as perceived by other Greeks, many of whom were both attracted and repelled by them. It is taken from Xenophon's The Constitution of the Lacedaemonians.

In other Greek cities, parents who profess to give their sons the best education place their boys under the care and control of a moral tutor as soon as they can understand what is said to them, and send them to a school to learn letters, music, and the exercises of the wrestling ground. Moreover, they soften the children's feet by giving them sandals, and pamper their bodies with changes of clothing; and it is customary to allow them as much food as they can eat.

Lycurgus, on the contrary, instead of leaving each father to appoint a slave to act as tutor, gave the duty of controlling the boys to a member of the class from which the highest offices are filled, in fact to the "Warden" as he is called. He gave this person authority to punish them severely in case of misconduct. He also assigned to him a staff of youths provided with whips to chastise them when necessary. . . . [I]nstead of softening their feet with sandals he required them to harden their feet by going without shoes. He believed that if this habit were cultivated it would enable them to climb hills more easily and descend steep slopes with less danger. [A]nd instead of letting them be pampered in the matter of clothing, he introduced the custom of wearing one garment throughout the year, believing that they would thus be better prepared to face changes of heat and cold. As to the food, he required the prefect to bring with him such a moderate amount of it that the boys would never suffer from repletion and would know what it was to go with their hunger unsatisfied; for he believed that those who underwent this training would be better able to continue working on an empty stomach if necessary, and would be capable of carrying on longer without extra food. . . .

[H]e allowed them to alleviate their hunger by stealing something. It was not on account of a difficulty in providing for them that he encouraged them to get their food by cunning. . . . [O]bviously, a man who intends to take to thieving must spend sleepless nights and play the deceiver and lie in ambush by day, and moreover, if he means to make a capture, he must have spies ready. There can be no doubt then, that all this education was planned by him in order to make the boys more resourceful in getting supplies and be better fighting men.

Xenophon. "The Constitution of the Lacedemonians." in *Scripta Minora*. Loeb Classical Library. Cambridge, MA: Harvard University Press, 1925.

government. They conducted foreign policy, watched over the helots, and could, if necessary, override the military decisions of the kings. Both groups were elected by an assembly composed of all Spartan males over the age of thirty, the ephors for one-year terms, the councillors for life. Though the assembly voted by acclamation on all important matters, decisions were usually negotiated in advance and presented at meetings by the ephors.

The system struck other Greeks as old-fashioned, but they admired its effectiveness and stability. The social system over which it presided was far stranger. From the sixth century B.C. onward, everything in the Spartan's life was subordinated to the security of the polis (see document 2.6). Infants who appeared physically unfit were killed. At seven, males were taken from their mothers and trained to fight, endure pain, and survive without supplies in a hostile countryside. At

twenty, they entered a *phiditia,* a kind of barracks where they would live for most of their lives, taking their meals in common. Though allowed to marry, younger Spartans could visit their wives only in secret, and family life in the ordinary sense was discouraged. Their military obligation ended only at the age of sixty. To the Spartan, eternal vigilance was the price of survival. Foreigners were periodically expelled. Trade and agricultural work were forbidden; fitness, discipline, and courage were prized.

The Spartan warrior paid dues to his *phiditia* from the proceeds of land worked by the helots. That work was supervised to some extent by the Spartan women, who were renowned throughout Greece for their independence and assertiveness. Though not expected to fight, they received extensive physical training on the theory that a strong mother produces strong children. Spartan women dressed simply and wore no jewelry.

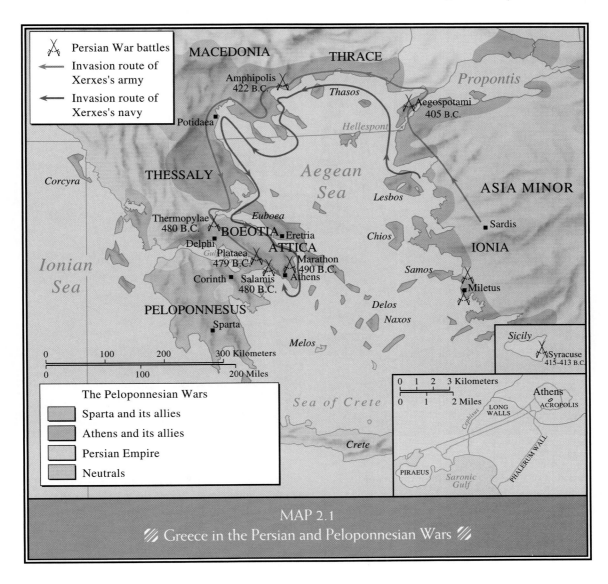

MAP 2.1

≈≈ Greece in the Persian and Peloponnesian Wars ≈≈

They could hold land in their own right and were capable of dealing with hostile and rebellious helots. Their courage, like that of the Spartan men, was legendary.

In spite of their military virtues, the Spartans were not an aggressive power until late in their history. The constant threat of helot insurrection made them wary of foreign entanglements, and Spartan policy was traditionally defensive and inward-looking. This changed in the course of the fifth century B.C. when the Persian invasion and the subsequent expansion of Athens forced them to take a more active role. They would eventually be drawn into a fatal rivalry with the Athenians, whose army was inferior but whose superior navy and greater wealth made them formidable antagonists. The story of those struggles forms the political background of the Greek classical age.

The Persian War

The Greeks developed their unique civilization in large part because for centuries they were isolated from the turbulent politics of the Asian land mass. That isolation came to an abrupt end in the Persian War of 499–479 B.C. (see map 2.1). The tiny states whose competition with one another had long since become traditional now faced the greatest military power the world had yet known.

The Persians were an Indo-European people from the Iranian highlands who emerged in the sixth century B.C. as the dominant power in the vast region between Mesopotamia and India. By the end of the sixth century B.C. the ruling elite had adopted Zoroastrianism, a religion preached by the prophet and reformer Zoroaster

Illustration 2.5

Reconstruction of a Greek Trireme from the Era of the Persian Wars. The *Olympias*, shown here coming into port, was constructed on the basis of ancient evidence and commissioned into the Greek navy in 1987. Like the triremes of Themistocle's day, it is propelled by 170 rowers arranged on three decks. Supplemental power is provided by square sails rigged on two masts. In this photo the stern where the triarch or commander sat is shown at left. The bow with its formidable ram is visible on the right.

(sometimes called Zarathustra). A dualistic system in which Ahura Mazda, the god of light, truth, and goodness contends eternally with Ahriman, the god of darkness and evil, Zoroastrianism condemned graven images and maintained the highest of ethical precepts. Its radical distinction between good and evil would influence early Christianity, and Ahriman has been seen by some as a prototype of the Christian Satan.

Under Cyrus I "the Great" (c. 585–c. 529 B.C.) the Persians conquered Babylon, together with Egypt, Syria, Palestine, and most of Asia Minor. Persian success was based largely upon imitating Assyrian military tactics while reversing the Assyrian policy toward conquered peoples. Like the Assyrians, the Persians used cavalry, many of them armed with bows, to pin down the enemy's infantry until their own infantry could destroy them. But Persian government was generally benign. It avoided atrocities, except in cases of outright

rebellion, and asked only that new subjects pay tribute and provide troops for the army. Because local institutions were typically preserved, many parts of the former Assyrian Empire welcomed the Persians as liberators.

Greek involvement with the Persian Empire began when Cyrus the Great conquered the kingdom of Lydia in 546 B.C. Located in western Asia Minor, Lydia was heavily influenced by Greek culture and famous for its wealth. The Lydians are credited with the invention of modern coinage. Under the fabulously wealthy king Croesus they established a loose dominance over the Ionic communities of the western Aegean. When Lydia fell, the Persians assumed control of its Greek dependencies. In 499 B.C. several Ionian states rebelled against local rulers backed by Persia and asked mainland Greeks to help. Sparta, worried about the internal threat of helot rebellion, refused, but Athens and the

Euboean city of Eretria sent twenty-five ships. Athenian rhetoric stressed the city's ancient and sentimental ties to Ionia, but the Athenians also feared that if the Persians gained control over the approaches to the Black Sea their vital supply of imported grain might be threatened.

In a short-lived triumph, the Ionians and their allies managed to burn Sardis, the Lydian capital. Persia soon reestablished control over western Asia Minor and in 490 B.C. dispatched a retaliatory expedition against Eretria and Athens. The Persians destroyed Eretria, but Athens fought and defeated them at Marathon. The marathon as a modern Olympic event commemorates the achievement of a courier who brought the news to Athens, twenty-two miles away. This victory, achieved in the absence of the feared Persian cavalry, was important because the Greeks gained confidence in their ability to defeat an enemy who until then had been regarded as invincible.

That confidence was tested in 480 B.C. when the new Persian emperor, Xerxes, launched a full-scale invasion of Greece by land and sea. It is a measure of Greek disunity that only thirty-one cities were prepared to resist. Sparta and Athens took the lead. Athenian politics were dominated by Themistocles, an advocate of seapower who used his influence to build a fleet of two hundred triremes in anticipation of a Persian attack. The trireme was a large, complex warship with three ranks of oarsmen and a metal prow for ramming (see illustration 2.5). Though far superior to earlier galleys, triremes were expensive, and only the discovery of new silver deposits at Laureion in Attica made their construction possible.

The ships were needed because Greek defensive strategy was essentially naval. The main Persian army was marching south along the European shore after crossing the Hellespont from Asia Minor. It was dependent for its supplies on a fleet of perhaps three hundred triremes manned by Persia's Phoenician and Ionian allies. Themistocles hoped to delay the Persian land forces at the narrow pass of Thermopylae while weather and a proposed naval action at nearby Artemisium depleted the Persian fleet (see document 2.7).

In spite of a heroic defense coordinated by the Spartans under their king Leonidas, Thermopylae fell when the invaders found a way to flank the Spartan position. Offshore, the Greeks fought an indecisive naval battle with a Persian force that, as Themistocles predicted, had been weakened by a series of earlier storms. These actions provided time for the evacuation of Athens and for the Greek fleet to take up a position

◈ DOCUMENT 2.7 ◈

The Spartans at Thermopylae

The doomed defense of the pass at Thermopylae by a handful of Spartans and their Thespian allies captured the imagination of the Greeks and has remained an archetypal story of heroism in the face of great odds. To the Greeks, it also showed, in dramatic terms, the difference between free Greeks fighting for their native soil and what they saw as servile Asians who had to be driven into battle with whips. This account is from Herodotus, the great historian of the Persian War.

As the Persian army advanced to the assault, the Greeks under Leonidas, knowing that the fight would be their last, pressed forward into the wider part of the pass. . . . Many of the invaders fell; behind them their company commanders plied their whips, driving the men remorselessly on. Many fell into the sea and were drowned, and still more were trampled to death by their friends. No one could count the number of the dead. The Greeks, who knew that the enemy were on their way round by the mountain track and that death was inevitable, fought with reckless desperation. . . . By this time most of their spears were broken, and they were killing Persians with their swords.

In the course of that fight Leonidas fell, having fought like a man indeed. Many distinguished Spartans were killed at his side. . . . There was a bitter struggle over the body of Leonidas; four times the Greeks drove the enemy off, and at last by their valor succeeded in dragging it away. So it went until the fresh troops with Ephialtes [the Greek who had revealed the secret track to the Persians] were close at hand; and then when the Greeks knew that they had come, the character of the fighting changed. They withdrew again into the narrow neck of the pass, behind the walls, and took up a position in a single compact body . . . on the little hill at the entrance to the pass, where the stone lion in memory of Leonidas stands today. Here they resisted to the last, with their swords if they had them, and if not, with their hands and teeth, until the Persians coming on in front over the ruins of the wall and closing in from behind, finally overwhelmed them.

Herodotus. *The Histories,* pp. 492–493, trans. Aubrey de Sélincourt. Baltimore: Penguin Books, 1954.

some miles to the east near the island of Salamis. The Athenians and their allies hoped that by forcing a sea battle in the narrow waters between the island and the mainland they could compensate for the greater speed and maneuverability of the Persian fleet.

Xerxes's army entered the deserted city and burned it. Shortly thereafter half of his fleet was destroyed by the Greek triremes in the battle of Salamis, one of the greatest naval engagements in history. As Themistocles had foreseen, the Persians crowded into the narrow strait and could not maneuver properly. The Greek ships, though slower, carried more fighting men and found it easy to ram and overwhelm their opponents as they came in. Salamis was the turning point of the war. Without the support of his fleet, Xerxes returned to Persia, leaving a portion of his army to winter in Greece. The garrison was defeated at Plataea in the summer of 479 B.C. and fled, never to return. At the same time, a fleet under Spartan command dislodged the enemy from the Ionian coast in the battle of Mycale.

The Peloponnesian Wars

The Persian threat had been repelled but not extinguished. Under the direction of Themistocles, the Athenians began to rebuild their city, fortifying its port at Piraeus, and constructing the Long Walls that protected the road connecting the two. After Themistocles was ostracized in 472 B.C. (the great enemy of the Persians ended his life as a Persian governor in Asia Minor), the work was continued by his successor, Cimon. Then, in the winter of 478–477 B.C. Athens, as the leading Greek naval power, joined with a number of its allies to form the Delian League, an association dedicated to protecting the cities of the Aegean from Persians and pirates. Sparta, though it had led the war on land, did not join, preferring instead to concentrate on the helot problem and on strengthening its own Peloponnesian League. By 467 B.C. the Athenian navy and its Delian allies had secured the coasts of Asia Minor and achieved unquestioned dominance at sea. Greece was now divided into two increasingly competitive alliance systems.

The size of its fleet made Athens the dominant partner in the Delian League, and though at first the Athenians maintained the rhetoric of friendship, they used the alliance to further their own purposes. Under Cimon's leadership, Athens sought to control grain supplies in the Aegean and to improve its access to ship's timber and precious metals by seizing new territory.

Heavy tributes swelled the Athenian treasury. Some of the conquered land was distributed to poor citizens, and wealthier Athenians acquired property in allied cities without regard for local law. The true nature of the league was revealed when the island of Thasos tried to withdraw from it in 465 B.C. Athens treated the matter as a rebellion and laid siege to the place for two years. Corinth, Athen's chief commercial rival and an ally of Sparta, had long argued against what it saw as Athenian imperialism. Now both Delians and Peloponnesians began to fear that Athens sought nothing less than political hegemony over the Greek world. As long as Cimon, an admirer of Sparta, controlled Athenian policy, every effort was made to avoid open conflict with the Peloponnesian League. But he, too, was ostracized in 461 B.C.

The removal of Cimon coincided with a further democratization of Athenian government under the leadership of Ephialtes and his younger colleague Pericles (c. 495–429 B.C.). The Persian War and its aftermath had for the first time involved large numbers of poor citizens in combat, especially in the navy. Their claims to full participation in civic life could no longer be ignored, and Pericles, who would play a dominant role in Athenian politics for more than thirty years, built his career on changes that further liberalized the constitution of Cleisthenes.

Realizing that most people could not afford to serve the polis, the reformers adopted the novel policy of paying men for public service, including jury duty, a measure paid for by the wealth accumulated in Cimon's day. Citizenship, which now became more valuable than ever, was restricted for the first time to men with two citizen parents, but by 450 B.C. Athens had become a participatory democracy in which every male citizen could play a role. Some have held that this democratization contributed to the tremendous flowering of high culture in the classical or Periclean age (see chapter 3); others that it fueled the increasingly aggressive and reckless character of Athenian policy. The two arguments are not incompatible, but war followed almost immediately upon the downfall of Cimon.

In the First Peloponnesian War (460–445 B.C.) the Delian league defeated both the Peloponnesians and the Persians, but when several allies rebelled against the arrogance of Athenian leadership Pericles agreed to a thirty years' peace. His skills as an orator and popular leader were balanced with prudence. The peace, which enabled Athens to recover its strength and reorganize its empire, lasted only fourteen years. In 435 B.C. war broke out between Corinth and Corcyra. Corcyra was a former

Corinthian colony in the Adriatic that had long been neutral. The Athenians feared that if its powerful fleet fell into Corinthian hands, their own naval dominance would be lost. When they allied themselves with the Corcyrans, Corinth protested to the Peloponnesian League, claiming again that the Athenians wanted total hegemony over all the Greeks. Attempts at negotiation failed, and in 431 B.C. the Spartans invaded Attica (see map 2.1).

Realizing that the Spartans could not be defeated on land, Pericles allowed them to occupy the Athenian countryside. People from the rural demes crowded into the city. Though the Athenians mounted cavalry raids against Spartan garrisons, the major thrust of their policy was to launch amphibious expeditions against Sparta's allies. Pericles reasoned that because Athens was wealthy and its fleet controlled the seas, the city could survive on imports for up to five years before further tribute had to be demanded from the empire. Sparta's Peloponnesian allies were more vulnerable and would, he thought, sue for peace within three years.

Unfortunately, a great plague struck Athens in the second year of the war and killed a third of its population. Pericles was driven from office. He was recalled briefly only to die of the pestilence, and his defensive policies were eventually abandoned. The more aggressive strategy advocated by Cleon, who followed Pericles as leader of the popular faction, at first succeeded. The Athenians fomented popular revolutions in a number of cities and supported democratic factions within them, while the Spartans predictably backed their opponents. The Athenians then fortified Pylos on the western coast of Messenia and defeated a Spartan fleet that had been sent to drive them out. More than four hundred Spartans were isolated on a nearby island. This was a significant portion of Sparta's fighting elite. Without a navy and facing yet another helot revolt, the Spartans were desperate to recover their men and sued for peace.

Once again, the Athenians were undone by overconfidence. Dreaming of total victory, they refused to negotiate, but their attempts to recapture Megara and Boeotia failed. The Spartan general Brasidas easily detached a number of cities from their allegiance and ended by capturing Amphipolis, the most important Athenian base in the northwestern Aegean. When relief efforts failed, it was the Athenian's turn to ask for a truce.

The peace of Nicias (421 B.C.) accomplished little, in part because several important cities on both sides of the dispute refused to accept it. Hostilities continued, though Athens and Sparta remained only indirectly involved. Both sides attempted through diplomacy to lure away each other's allies. Athens was hampered in its efforts by internal factions and instability. Cleon died in the attempted relief of Amphipolis. Alcibiades, an unscrupulous young aristocrat who had been a pupil of Socrates, succeeded him as the dominant voice in Athenian politics. Under his guidance, Athens supported a Persian governor and his son in their revolt against the king. Persia, which had remained neutral, now had reason to back Sparta if hostilities resumed. Then in 415 B.C., Alcibiades convinced the Athenians to mount a great expedition against Sicily. It was a brazen attempt to acquire new resources by broadening the scope of the war, and it failed. Syracuse alone proved to be the equal of Athens in wealth, population, and naval preparedness, and the rest of Sicily backed Syracuse. The Sicilians, with their superior cavalry, disrupted the Athenian siege and defeated their army on land. In 413 B.C. they destroyed the Athenian fleet in the city's harbor. All told, the Athenians lost two hundred ships, more than forty-five hundred of their own men, and perhaps twenty thousand of their allies.

Though Athens rebuilt its fleet and continued the struggle, its allies deserted one by one. The Spartans, under the command of Lysander and backed by Persian money, launched a series of naval campaigns against them. Most were unsuccessful, but in 405 B.C. the Athenian fleet was destroyed at Aegospotami and Lysander cut off his enemy's grain supplies by seizing the Hellespont. Faced with starvation, the Athenians surrendered unconditionally in 404 B.C.

The Peloponnesian Wars revealed the tragic flaw at the heart of Greek society, a flaw that had been obscured by the successful war against Persia. The independent, competitive psychology of the polis made it difficult, if not impossible, for the Greeks to unite or to live at peace with one another. They had driven off the Persians, but even then much of the Greek world had sided with the enemy out of rivalry with either Athens or Sparta or, in some cases, with one of their allies. The failure of Athens—or Sparta—to forge an effective Panhellenic alliance created a power vacuum that would eventually be filled by the Macedonians, a people who, though related to the Greeks, did not share in the culture of the polis. As a result, the independence of the polis would be gravely compromised. Athens fell under the control of the Thirty Tyrants, a group of collaborators who ruled with Spartan support. The city's empire disintegrated and its trade diminished, though it remained the cultural heart of the Greek world for centuries to come. The great struggles of the fifth century B.C. may be regarded as the high-water mark of classical Greek civilization.

GREEK CULTURE AND ITS HELLENISTIC DIFFUSION

For all its violence and insecurity, the age of the Persian and Peloponnesian wars was for the Greeks, and in particular for Athens, a time of unparalleled creativity. The intensity of life in the midst of almost perpetual crisis called forth their best efforts, not only in war and politics, but also in art, literature, and philosophy.

The conquests of Alexander spread Greek culture and values to the limits of the known world, but the process was one of diffusion rather than imposition. The peoples of the Middle East retained their own identities while adopting Greek ideas, and the Greeks changed through contacts with ancient civilizations whose cultural norms differed radically from their own. The result was a rich and cosmopolitan fusion that is usually referred to as the Hellenistic Age.

◆

Art and Literature in Classical Greece

Greek literary and artistic inspiration stemmed from two basic sources: the Homeric poems and the mythology that had grown up around the adventures of the gods. Together, these wellsprings of the Greek tradition provided a rich fund of themes and motifs that illustrated in graphic terms what it meant to be Greek. The influence of that tradition had little to do with religious teachings as they are now understood. The behavior of the gods—and of Homer's heroes—was often highly improper, and Greek religion offered few ethical prescriptions. The ancient tales did not preach, but even when they taught by bad example, they offered a precious guide to values, social attitudes, and conduct. For this reason, each polis sought to encourage the arts to the best of its financial ability. They were the means by which citizens were created and common values reaffirmed.

Nowhere was this concern more evident than in the drama. Plays, like athletic contests, accompanied many religious festivals. They were performed in open-air amphitheaters constructed at public expense, and the actors were usually paid by the state. In fifth-century Athens, as many as thirty thousand people might attend a single performance. The first plays were tragedies, a dramatic form probably invented by the Athenians. The themes of Attic tragedy came with rare exceptions from mythology and drew their dramatic power from irreconcilable conflicts. The hero, who might be a man or woman, is faced with a conflict, not always between right and wrong, but sometimes between right and right. He or she is undone either by an unsuspected personal flaw or by *hubris*, the pride born of overconfidence.

Among the greatest of the Greek dramatists were Aeschylus (c. 525–456 B.C.), who may have invented the tragedy as a dramatic form, and Sophocles (c. 495–406 B.C.), whose *Antigone, Oedipus Rex, Electra,* and other works continue to inspire modern authors. Euripides (c. 484–406 B.C.) was more popular in the fourth century B.C. than in his own time. His later plays diluted the original tragic formula and led the way to more personal and unheroic themes. A similar progression is seen in comedy. The plays of Aristophanes (c. 450–c. 388 B.C.) and his contemporaries, usually known as the Old Comedy, were political satire with a razor's edge. As the third century B.C. progressed, comedy lost its public focus and turned to love stories and domestic situations.

The Greeks may also be said to have created history. Earlier peoples preserved king lists and inscriptions that record the doings of royalty. The Hebrews had chronicled their history to illuminate God's purposes, but the Greeks made history a branch of literature. The first writer to do this was Herodotus, whose history of the Persian War was written specifically "to preserve the memory of the past by putting on record the astonishing achievements both of our own and of the Asiatic peoples; secondly, and more particularly, to show how the two races came into conflict." The result is both history and anthropology—an entertaining tour of the ancient world, its cultures, and its myths. The story of the war itself comes only toward the end of the book. However, his portraits of individual leaders are unforgettable, and he probably deserves his title, "the father of history."

The history of the Peloponnesian Wars by the Athenian Thucydides (c. 460–c. 404 B.C.) is different (see document 3.1). Exiled for his role as a naval commander in the ill-fated attempt to relieve Amphipolis, Thucydides was determined to understand the past be-

◈ DOCUMENT 3.1 ◈

Thucydides: The Practice of History

In this famous passage, from The Peloponnesian War, *Thucydides lays the foundation for history as a serious intellectual discipline. Few historians today believe that history repeats itself in any predictable way, but they appreciate Thucydides's critical approach to his sources.*

And with regard to my factual reporting of the events of the war I have made it a principle not to write down the first story that came my way, and not even to be guided by my own general impressions; either I was present myself at the events which I described or else I heard of them from eyewitnesses whose reports I have checked with as much thoroughness as possible. Not that even so the truth was easy to discover: different eyewitnesses have different accounts of the same events, speaking out of partiality for one side or the other or else from imperfect memories. And it may well be that my history will seem less easy to read because of the absence in it of romantic elements. It will be enough for me, however, if these words of mine are judged useful by those who want to understand clearly the events which happened in the past and which (human nature being what it is) will at some time or other and in much the same ways, be repeated in the future. My work is not a piece of writing designed to meet the taste of an immediate public, but was done to last forever.

Thucydides. The Peloponnesian War, trans. Rex Warner. Baltimore: Penguin Books, 1954. Copyright © Rex Warner, 1954. Reproduced by permission of Penguin Books Ltd.

cause he believed that human nature was constant and that history therefore repeats itself. If one knows the past, it should be possible to avoid similar mistakes in the future. Other cultures had believed that history moves in cycles and that, as the biblical author of Ecclesiastes said in a notable departure from Jewish tradition, "there is no new thing under the sun." But the Greeks, beginning with Thucydides, used this ancient notion to justify the systematic study of history. It was among the most original of their achievements. Many of the better Roman historians studied history to avoid the mistakes of the past,

Corinthian
capital

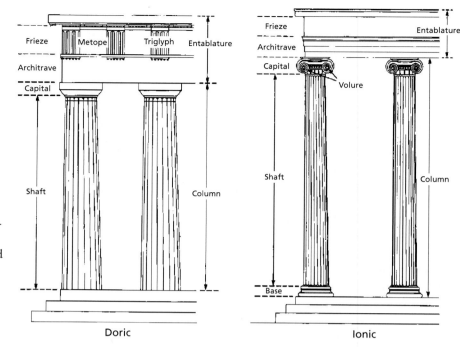

Illustration 3.1

Architectural Orders. The architectural orders were an important part of Greek temple architecture and were used by the Romans as well as by European architects from the Renaissance to the present day. The Corinthian order was similar to the Ionic but featured a leaf motif in its capitals.

and the idea, revived during the Renaissance, remained influential until well into the twentieth century.

Greek art, too, served public purposes. Though a fine aesthetic sense extended to everyday objects such as jewelry, armor, and decorated pottery, the greatest artistic achievement of ancient Greece was its monumental sculpture and architecture. The Greeks built temples to the gods who protected the polis or to house the oracles who were consulted on all important occasions. These structures, whose function was as much civic as religious, were subtle adaptations of earlier Egyptian or Minoan ideas.

Construction was basic post-and-lintel; the genius lay in the proportions and the details. The heart of the temple was an inner sanctuary that housed the statue of the deity. It was surrounded by a colonnade supporting a sloped roof with triangular pediments at each end. The columns, which might or might not have decorated capitals (see illustration 3.1), were wider at the middle and tapered gently toward the top to counteract the optical illusion known as parallax and make them appear straight. The frieze, the entablature, and the pediments were decorated with sculptured reliefs of gods, goddesses, and heroes.

Greek sculpture was concerned almost exclusively with the lifelike portrayal of the human figure (see illustration 3.2). Early statues had a formal, abstract quality, with power and dignity that reflected their subjects: gods, goddesses, heroes, and athletes. Male figures were almost invariably nude, a preference that reflected the Greek willingness to appear naked in games and on the battlefield and that non-Greeks found shocking. Female figures were invariably clothed. Gradually, during the sixth century B.C., sculptors began to work toward a more lifelike image. By the fifth century B.C. sculptors such as Phidias had achieved a level of skill that has never been surpassed, but realism was not their goal. Faces and figures reflect an idealized vision of human beauty rarely seen in nature. Female nudes, reflecting a sensuality hitherto seen only in the portrayal of men, became common. The aesthetic conventions developed by Phidias and the fourth-century B.C. master Praxiteles became the basis of later Hellenistic and Roman tastes. Like the conventions of Greek architecture, they have been restored to temporary dominance by classic revivals in more modern times and remain an underlying part of the Western visual tradition.

Unfortunately, that vision may be historically misleading. Most of Greek art was destroyed by the early Christians, who saw it as idolatrous if not obscene, and modern taste has been formed largely by Roman copies. Painting, which to many ancient Greeks was more important than sculpture, has been lost entirely. The Greeks loved color, and statues preserved only in

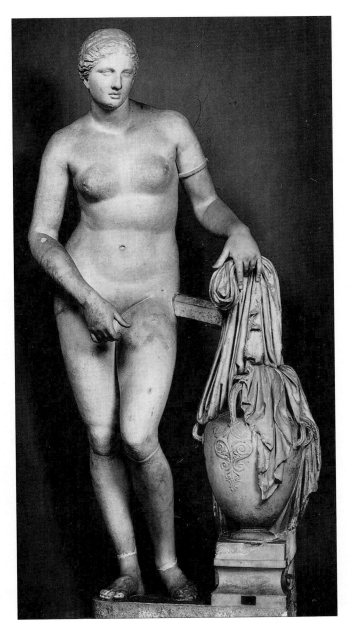

Illustration 3.2

 The Evolution of Greek Sculpture. The figure on the left is a *kore* (masc. *koros*) from the Athenian acropolis, c. 520 B.C. Figures of this kind were used as tomb markers or votive statues and are one of the most common forms of early Greek sculpture. Though more delicately modeled than most, this piece is still for-

mal, two-dimensional, and somewhat abstract. On the right is a Roman copy of the famous Aphrodite by Praxiteles. Though the statue reflects a certain classical serenity, the sensuality is, by earlier Greek standards, remarkable. In archaic times, only male figures were portrayed in the nude.

their undecorated state were once brilliantly painted. Some had precious stones for eyes. The overall impression must have been unlike the serene appearance that later generations associated with classicism, and the more refined modern critics of the eighteenth and nineteenth centuries would probably have found the statues tasteless.

Greek Thought from the Pre-Socratics to Aristotle

The earliest Greek thought concerned the nature of the physical universe and was formulated in terms that suggest Egyptian or Mesopotamian influence. According to tradition, the sixth-century B.C. philosopher Thales of Miletus introduced geometry and astronomy to Greece after visiting Egypt. He may also have encountered there the idea that the universe was based ultimately upon water. But Greek thought was unlike that of the Egyptians in several important respects. Perhaps because of the structure of their language, the Greeks sought from the beginning to demonstrate the logical connection between statements in the clearest possible way. This in turn forced them to confront the problem of epistemology, or how what is known is known. These two issues, epistemology and the nature of the physical universe, have remained among the central concerns of Western thought.

Most Greek thinkers believed that the impressions produced by the senses are deceptive. To be truly knowable, something must be both permanent and accessible to thought. Thales, like most early philosophers, assumed the essential unity and permanence of all matter. The view of Heraclitus (c. 500 B.C.) that the universe was in a state of perpetual movement at first found little support, and much effort was expended on determining the fundamental element or elements upon which the universe was based. Eventually, Empedocles of Acragas (c. 490–c. 430 B.C.) declared that four existed: earth, air, fire, and water. His theory was later accepted by Aristotle and formed the basis of most physical speculation until the scientific revolution of modern times. An alternative, proposed by Leucippus of Miletus and his pupil Democritus, seemed less persuasive. It held that everything was composed of atoms, invisible particles that combined and separated to produce the various forms of matter.

If these early philosophers speculated on ethical matters, their writings on the subject have been lost, but the proper conduct of life was vitally important to people who lacked a moral code based on divine revelation. Pythagoras, who founded a school at Croton in Italy around the year 500 B.C., taught ethics based in part on the cult of Orpheus. In the process he discovered the mathematical basis of musical harmony and decided that the fundamental organizing principle of the universe was number. This idea, like his theory that the Earth revolved around the Sun, would prove interesting to later thinkers.

By the fifth century B.C., however, most people learned their ethics and the practical arts of rhetoric and persuasion from the Sophists. These itinerant teachers charged high fees for their services but offered nothing less than a prescription for success in private and public life. Their teachings varied, but most were subjectivists. As Protagoras, the most famous of them,

said: "Man is the measure." He meant that the individual's experience, however imperfect in an absolute sense, is the only conceivable basis for knowledge or judgment. Everything is relative.

The implications of such a view were profoundly disturbing. Extreme Sophists held that truth was objectively unknowable. Law and even the polis were based on convention and mutual agreement, not fundamental principles. Some went so far as to claim that justice was merely the interest of the strong and that the gods had been invented by clever men as a means of social control. The teachings of Socrates and of his pupil Plato were intended in part to refute these ideas.

Socrates (c. 470–399 B.C.) wrote nothing. He wandered about the streets of Athens asking questions that revealed the underlying assumptions behind human values and institutions. Using logic and irony, he would then question the validity of those assumptions. His purpose, unlike that of the Sophists whom he otherwise resembled, was to find an objective basis for ethical and political behavior. He made no promises and took no fees, but his questions were rarely open-ended and made people feel foolish.

The patience of the Athenians was severely tried. In 399 B.C. they executed him for corrupting the youth of Athens and inventing new gods. The charges were largely specious, but they reflected something more than public irritation. Socrates, though himself of humble origins, favored aristocracy as the ideal form of government and mocked the democratic notions then in favor.

His views on other subjects are unknown, but Plato (428–347 B.C.) made him the leading character in his dialogues. As a young man from an aristocratic Athenian family, Plato toyed with the idea of a political career until the aftermath of the Sicilian expedition and the execution of Socrates convinced him that politics was incompatible with a good conscience. Around the year 387 B.C. he founded the Academy, a kind of institute for advanced studies in mathematics, the physical sciences, and philosophy.

Plato's dialogues present philosophical arguments in dramatic form. The Socrates character reflects the author's views. With the exception of the *Timaeus*, a later dialogue that deals with cosmology and mathematics, most explore questions of ethics, education, government, and religion. The *Republic* describes the ideal state, while the *Protagoras* argues against the Sophists.

Their underlying principle is the theory of forms. Plato argued that the form of a thing has an objective reality of its own. It is a "universal" or "idea" that can be understood only by the intellect and that exists apart from any object perceived by the senses. Because the senses are deceptive, understanding can be achieved only through the knowledge of forms. When extended to such universal qualities as justice or beauty, the theory of forms becomes the basis for absolute standards that can be applied to human conduct, both public and private. To Plato, the relativism of the Sophists was an illusion (see document 3.2).

Platonic Idealism (also known as Realism, because it affirms the reality of ideas) was one pole of the epistemological debate that would occupy Western philosophy for centuries. Subjectivism in its various forms was the other. Because the argument dealt with what was real and what was knowable, the position of philosophers on epistemology influenced and in some cases determined their view of everything else.

Aristotle (384–322 B.C.) was the most famous of Plato's pupils. After studying at Plato's Academy until Plato's death, Aristotle served as tutor to the future conqueror Alexander the Great. In 336 B.C. Aristotle established his own school at Athens called the Lyceum. His followers were known in later years as the Peripatetics after the covered walkway or *peripatos* under which they met. Most of the enormous body of work attributed to him appears to be derived from lecture notes and other materials collected by the Peripatetics in the course of their studies.

Though he accepted Plato's theory of forms, Aristotle rejected the notion that they were wholly separate from empirical reality. He relied heavily upon observation, especially in his scientific work. His basic viewpoint, however, remained, like Plato's, teleological. Both thinkers believed that things could be understood only in relation to their end or purpose. To Aristotle, for example, actions must be judged in terms of the result they produce, an ethical principle that in medieval times would form the basis of natural law. In politics, this led him to an impassioned defense of the polis as the best form of social organization. Although these contributions to ethics and politics were enormously important, Aristotle's greatest influence lay elsewhere.

Logic, or the process by which statements are formed and relate to one another, was central to Greek discourse. Aristotle was the first to analyze this process and, in so doing, codified a logical method that dominated formal thought until the twentieth century. Its basis is the syllogism, an argument that in its simplest form says that if all A is B and all C is A, then all C must be B. Aristotle went far beyond this, and his six treatises on logic, known collectively as the *Organon*, describe many types of syllogisms, the formation and

DOCUMENT 3.2

Plato: The Parable of the Cave

The parable of the cave appears in The Republic *by Plato. It describes in graphic terms the difference between sense perceptions and reality, which can only be perceived through thought. The cave is a metaphor for the world of sense impressions in which nothing is as it appears, and to Plato all people are prisoners within it. The author is speaking to his friend Glaucon.*

"Picture men dwelling in a sort of subterranean cavern with a long entrance open to the light on its entire width. Conceive of them as having their legs and necks fettered from childhood, so that they remain in the same spot, able to look forward only, and prevented by the fetters from turning their heads. Picture further the light from a fire burning higher up and at a distance behind them, and between the fire and the prisoners and above them a road along which a low wall has been built, as the exhibitors of puppet-shows have partitions before the men themselves above which they show the puppets." "All that I see," he said. "See also, then, men carrying past the wall implements of all kinds that rise above the wall, and human images and shapes of animals as well, wrought in stone and wood and every material, some of these bearers presumably speaking and others silent." "A strange image you speak of," he said, "and strange prisoners." "Like to us," I said: "for, to begin with, tell me do you think that these men would have seen anything of themselves or of one another except the shadows cast from the fire on the wall of the cave that fronted them?" "How could they," he said, "if they were compelled to hold their heads unmoved through life." "And again, would not the same be true of the objects carried past them?" . . . "Then in every way such prisoners would deem reality to be nothing else than the shadows of artificial objects."

Plato. *The Republic*, trans. Paul Shorey. Cambridge, MA: Harvard University Press, 1963.

categorization of statements, and the nature of language itself.

In the physical sciences, Aristotle's influence dominated thought until the scientific revolution of the sixteenth and seventeenth centuries. He wrote extensively on biology, physics, and human psychology and was responsible for collecting and transmitting much of what is known about the early Greek philosophers. His method was to observe natural phenomena and to understand them in terms of what he called the "four causes." These were not causes in the modern sense, but aspects of a problem that had to be considered in its solution. The four causes are the matter out of which a thing is made (material cause), its form or shape (formal cause), the purpose it is intended to fulfill (final cause), and the force that brings it into being (efficient cause).

These causes are discovered by logical inference from empirical observations. Aristotle made no effort to create predictive mathematical models based upon these inferences and did not attempt to verify them by experiment. His method was therefore unlike that of modern science and produced different results. Scientists no longer believe that the process by which a physical change occurs can be fully explained by its final cause or teleological purpose. Since the seventeenth century they have asked different questions and have rejected most of Aristotle's conclusions about the behavior of matter. But even if the scientific theories of this ancient philosopher are no longer accepted, his work is still of great importance. Aristotle's observations and hypotheses set the agenda for more than a thousand years of speculation, while his teleological bias and preoccupation with qualitative descriptions (the material and formal causes) was a compelling if not always productive influence on later thought. His insistence on careful observation and logically constructed argument remains a part of the scientific tradition today. No other thinker has had such a powerful impact on later generations.

The Macedonian Conquests

Aristotle lived in the twilight of classical Greek civilization. Though he probably did little to inspire them, the exploits of his pupil Alexander of Macedon changed the political structure of the Greek world and spread Greek values and ideas throughout the Middle East. Inevitably, those values were changed and diluted in the process, and the culture that emerged from the Macedonian con-

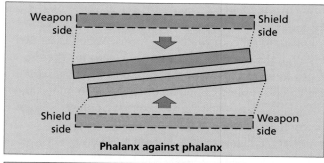

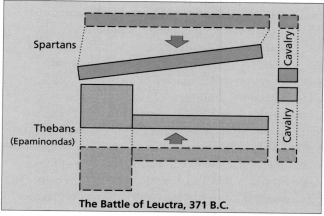

Illustration 3.3

The Theban Formation. The top drawing shows the traditional pattern of hoplite warfare with the shield side of each formation slowly giving way as the battle develops. The bottom drawing shows how Epaminondas weighted his formation at Leuctra to crush the Spartans at their strongest point (the "weapon side" or right).

quests was at the same time more cosmopolitan and less intense than that of the ancient polis.

The end of the Peloponnesian Wars had left the Greek states under the political influence of Sparta. The Spartans, like the Athenians before them, soon made themselves hated by interfering with the internal policies of their allies. Athens and Thebes combined against them, and in 371 B.C. the Spartans were defeated at Leuctra by a Theban army under the command of Epaminondas (c. 410–362 B.C.). Sparta's role as a major power ended, and a new era of military innovation began. Epaminondas had given careful thought to a peculiarity of hoplite warfare (see illustration 3.3). Hoplites carried their shields on the left. In combat they shifted toward the right, away from the point of impact. This threw the phalanx out of balance, but the consequent strengthening of its right side meant that the right frequently won the battle. Epaminondas took advantage of this oddity and weighted his phalanx heavily to the left and held back the right. This unbalanced formation, supported by cavalry on his right flank, enabled him to crush the Spartans at their strongest point and envelop them. The use of deep formations, effectively supported for the first time by cavalry, would be greatly expanded by the Macedonians.

Though supported by the relative wealth of Boeotia, Theban hegemony lasted no longer than that of the Spartans. The Athenians had revived their alliance system in the years immediately before Leuctra and, fearing Theban ambition, soon turned it against Epaminondas. By 362 B.C. the Peloponnesians had also reconstituted their confederacy, and though Epaminondas defeated the combined forces of Athens and Sparta at Mantinea, he died in the battle. Deprived of his leadership, Theban military power declined. Without the stimulus of threats from Thebes or Sparta, the "second" Athenian Empire collapsed, and Greece reverted to its traditional state of disorganization.

A century of warfare had brought economic decline and social tension to the Greek cities. The Carthaginians encroached upon their overseas markets while the Greek colonies in Italy became, of necessity, more self-sufficient. As exports diminished, thousands of Greeks sought employment as mercenaries. One such group found itself stranded in Mesopotamia when the schemes of their Persian employer miscarried. A leader of the expedition, the Athenian writer and military theorist Xenophon (c. 431–c. 350 B.C.) left a vivid account of their march to the Black Sea coast and safety. Xenophon and the career of Epaminondas show that Greek fighting men had lost nothing of their skill and valor. The artistic and intellectual achievements of the fourth century B.C. demonstrate that the culture was alive and well. But for all its evident vigor, Greece had become a political vacuum.

That vacuum was filled by the Macedonians. Ancient Macedonia occupied the broad plain at the head of the Thermaic Gulf in northeastern Greece. Its people spoke a dialect of Greek, but their social and political institutions were different from those of the *poleis*. The population was almost entirely rural and, by Greek standards, widely scattered. Rich pastures encouraged the raising of horses. Macedonian society was therefore dominated by a landholding aristocracy that fought on horseback, usually against the neighboring hill tribes whose raids posed a constant threat to the country's borders. Hereditary kings tried to rule, with or without cooperation from the aristocracy, and internal strife was common. To other Greeks, the Macedonians seemed primitive, but their homeland was rich in timber, miner-

als, and agricultural resources. Many believed that if Macedon could achieve stability it would one day become a major power.

That goal was achieved by Philip II (382–336 B.C.). Philip was a younger son of the Macedonian royal family who, while hostage at Thebes, had observed the military reforms of Epaminondas. His brother died in 359 B.C. and left Philip as regent for the youthful heir, Amyntas IV. Cunning and energetic, Philip used his position to remove political rivals and suppress the local hill tribes. In 357–356 B.C. he seized Amphipolis and then Mt. Pangaeus with its rich deposits of gold and silver. At about this time he also took control of his nephew's throne.

With his political base secure, and fortified by the wealth of Mt. Pangaeus, Philip moved to extend his power over Greece as a whole. Through warfare, bribery, and skilled diplomacy, Philip played upon the disunity of the Greeks until it was too late for them to mount an effective resistance. In 338 B.C. he defeated a poorly organized army of Thebans and Athenians at Chaeronea and became master of the Greek world. For the most part, Philip wore his new authority lightly. He secured a measure of acceptance by not interfering in local politics, but his plan to lead the united Greeks against Persia did not materialize in his lifetime.

Philip II left a formidable legacy. Not only did he unite the Greeks, but he also created the army with which his son Alexander III, "the Great," would conquer most of the known world (see illustration 3.4). The heart of the Macedonian army remained the companions of the king, some two thousand cavalry armed with sword and spear. They were supported by infantry drawn up in the Macedonian phalanx, a formation that differed substantially from that of the hoplites. The peasants of Macedonia could not afford hoplite equipment, and their geographic isolation made intensive training difficult. Philip solved these problems by arranging his men into deep formations and arming them with spears longer than those used by the hoplites. By fighting in tightly closed ranks, the Macedonians could thereby present an almost impenetrable front without the need for highly specialized combat skills.

Hoplites were added to the Macedonian ranks as Philip's system of alliances grew. He also recruited mercenary horsemen from Thessaly and supplemented his infantry with slingers, bowmen, and javelin throwers. The genius of Philip (and Alexander) lay in the ability to coordinate these varied elements and to make even the cavalry fight as a disciplined tactical unit instead of as individual champions. But the Macedonians were

Illustration 3.4

✏ **Alexander the Great.** This bust of Alexander the Great is a Roman copy of the lost original. It closely resembles literary descriptions of the conqueror's appearance by Plutarch and Appian.

equally attentive to the problems of siegecraft. Philip introduced to the Aegean world the techniques and siege engines developed by Dionysius, the Tyrant of Syracuse, and used them successfully against Perinthus and Byzantium. His son would employ them against the more distant cities of Tyre, Halicarnassus, and Gaza.

In ten years (334–324 B.C.) Alexander used this formidable army to conquer the Persian Empire and extend his authority from Greece to Egypt and from Egypt to India (see map 3.1). His exploits caught the imagination of his contemporaries and of historians ever since, but his character remains something of a mystery.

He was clearly an outstanding general. His great battles on the Granicus in Asia Minor, at Issus in Syria, at Gaugamela on the upper Tigris, and on the Hydaspes

in India were brilliant cavalry actions in which the infantry played only a secondary role. His sieges were consistently successful, and his ability to hold a multiethnic army together on hard campaigns in unfamiliar territory attest to an extraordinary capacity for leadership. In the end, the Macedonians mutinied and demanded to return home, but even then he preserved their loyalty by officially making them his kinsmen.

His purposes, however, are not entirely clear. Many of his contemporaries saw only personal ambition. Arrian, the chronicler of his campaigns, said that "if he had found no one else to strive with he would have striven with himself." Others, including Plutarch, detected more noble motives (see document 3.3). Alexander's publicists encouraged the notion of a vast state based upon universal brotherhood. He proclaimed the equality of all subjects regardless of religion or ethnicity and gave this policy tangible form by marrying Roxana, a princess from Bactria in central Asia.

He may also have hoped to spread the benefits of Hellenic culture, but he seems to have stressed this only in dealing with Greeks. Not all Greeks were convinced. They resented his acceptance of foreign customs and his tendency to claim divine attributes when dealing with easterners. His idealism, if such it was, was accompanied by utter ruthlessness and by a casual brutality aggravated by heavy drinking. When he died in 323 B.C. at the age of thirty-two, he left no successors and only the most general plan for the governance of his realms.

The Hellenistic Kingdoms

Alexander's death led to a prolonged struggle among the Macedonian generals. Though Roxana was pregnant when he died, there was no immediate successor. The commanders at first divided the empire into governorships with the intention of preserving it for the conqueror's unborn heir, but they soon fell to fighting among themselves. In the civil wars that followed, Roxana and her son, together with several of the generals, were murdered. Three main successor states emerged from the shambles. Macedon, much of Asia Minor, and a dominant position in the Greek alliance fell to Antigonus (382–301 B.C.). The descendants of Ptolemy (d. 283 B.C.) ruled Egypt as its thirty-third Dynasty until the death of Cleopatra in 30 B.C., while Seleucus (d. 281 B.C.) established an empire based on Syria and Mesopotamia (see map 3.1).

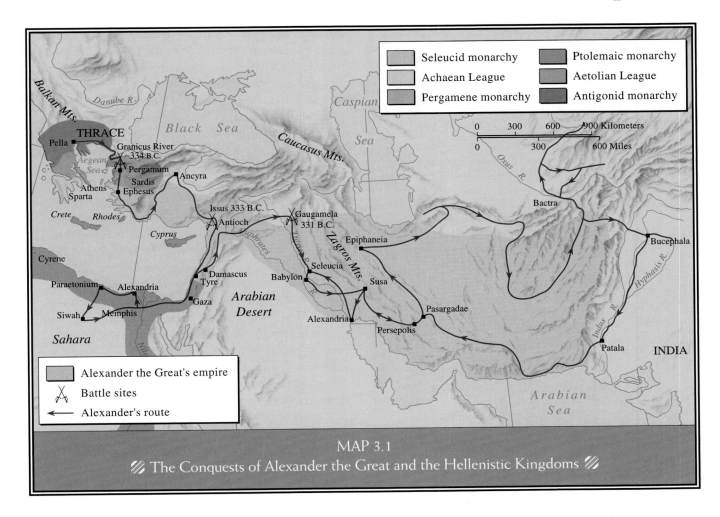

MAP 3.1

▓ The Conquests of Alexander the Great and the Hellenistic Kingdoms ▓

All three dynasties, the Antigonids, the Ptolemies, and the Seleucids are called Hellenistic, presumably because their Hellenism was less pure than that of the polis, but the term is unduly patronizing. The Hellenistic period was one of unprecedented cultural borrowing and transmission. Ideas, religions, and artistic motifs from Egypt and the Middle East fused with those of the Greeks and spread throughout the Mediterranean world. Science, philosophy, and the arts flourished. But the term is unfortunate for another reason. It implies a uniformity that did not exist. Politically and socially, the successor kingdoms differed widely from one another. If they shared a certain veneer of Greek culture, their problems were unique and for more than a century they maintained a rivalry that sometimes degenerated into open war.

The chief foreign policy goal of the Ptolemies was to protect the Nile delta from foreign invasion. This required the maintenance of a large navy and, from the Egyptian point of view, control over Phoenicia and the Syrian coast, which supplied the fleet with timber and

naval stores. The Seleucids resisted Ptolemaic claims to Syria because they needed the Mediterranean ports to maintain their trade with the west. After a series of wars, the Seleucids ultimately gained control of both Syria and Palestine, but not before the Antigonids, too, became entangled in the web of Ptolemaic diplomacy. Fearing an alliance between the Seleucids and the Antigonids, the Ptolemies supported the growth of Pergamum as a buffer state between the two kingdoms and, whenever possible, stirred up anti-Macedonian sentiment in Greece. This usually meant support for one of the two leagues of city-states that formed in third-century Greece: the Aetolian League in the west-central part of the peninsula and the Achaean League, headed by Corinth, in the northern Peloponnese. Egyptian policy collapsed when, in about 230 B.C., the Ptolemies also formed an alliance with Sparta. The frightened Achaeans turned to the Antigonids for help, and the Ptolemies, under attack by the Seleucid king, Antiochus III, "the Great," could do nothing to protect the Aetolians. In the end Antiochus conquered Syria,

◆ DOCUMENT 3.3 ◆

Plutarch: A Positive View of Alexander's Conquests

Plutarch, who wrote the important Life of Alexander, *believed in the conqueror's "civilizing" mission and dedication to the universal brotherhood of humankind. In this oration he makes the best possible case for his hero's motives.*

Alexander did not follow Aristotle's advice to treat the Greeks as a leader, the barbarians as a master, cultivating the former as friends and kinsmen, and treating the latter as animals or plants. Had he done so his kingdom would have been filled with warfare, banishments and secret plots, but he regarded himself as divinely sent to mediate and govern the world. And those whom he failed to win over by persuasion he overpowered in arms, bringing them together from every land, combining, as it were in a loving cup, their lives, customs, marriages, and manners of living. . . .

For he did not cross Asia like a robber, nor did he have it in mind to ravage and despoil it for the booty and loot presented by such an unheard-of stroke of fortune. . . . Instead he conducted himself as he did out of a desire to subject all the races in the world to one rule and one form of government, making all mankind a single people. Had not the divinity that sent Alexander recalled his soul so soon, there would have been a single law, as it were, watching over all mankind, and all men would have looked to one form of justice as their common source of light. But now, that portion of the world that never beheld Alexander has remained as if deprived of the sun.

Plutarch. "De Alexandri Magni Fortuna ast Virtute, Oratio I." In *Sources in Western Civilization: Ancient Greece,* pp. 199–200, ed. and trans. Truesdell S. Brown. New York: The Free Press (Simon & Schuster), 1965.

Phoenicia, and Palestine, and the Aetolians allied themselves with a new power then emerging in the west: Rome.

The struggles between the Hellenistic kingdoms, though occasionally dramatic, seem to have had little impact on everyday life. The most important social and economic effect was a periodic influx of slaves into the labor market as one side or the other succeeded in tak-ing large numbers of captives. As a result, slavery became increasingly important to the Hellenistic economy, forcing free laborers into marginal occupations or outright unemployment. By the end of the third century B.C., the cities of all three kingdoms were struggling with the social problems created by poverty.

Otherwise, in the Antigonid kingdom, life went on largely as before, though without the endless warfare of Greek against Greek that had characterized the classical period. Under Macedonian rule the states retained their separate identities, but loss of control over foreign and military affairs blunted the intensity of their political life. Not even the formation of the Achaean and Aetolian leagues could restore it. Economic decline continued. Poor yields as a result of erosion and soil exhaustion forced landowners to compensate by experimenting with fertilizers and new agricultural techniques. These methods were modestly successful, but for small farmers their cost was prohibitive. Large estates, many of them worked by slaves, became more common. For thousands of Greeks, service as mercenaries or as administrators in the other Hellenistic kingdoms remained the most promising route to success.

Most of these ambitious folk were absorbed by the Seleucid kingdom. Alexander had established almost seventy Greek cities in what had been the Persian Empire. He sought to provide homes for his veterans and for those fleeing overpopulation in their native land. He also hoped to establish trustworthy centers of administration in a vast region populated by dozens of different ethnic and religious groups. This policy was greatly expanded by the Seleucids. The new cities tried to duplicate as far as possible the life of the polis. In the years after Alexander's death, the wealth extracted from his conquests paid for the construction of temples, theaters, and other public buildings in the Greek style. Greek law and Greek political institutions were imposed, but these cities, for all their magnificence, remained cultural hybrids thronged with people of many cultures. Unlike the citizens of a polis, they had neither gods nor ancestors in common.

The Seleucids respected the cultural and religious sensibilities of their subjects but preferred to rely on Greek or Macedonian soldiers and administrators for the day-to-day business of governing. The Greek population of the cities, reinforced until the second century B.C. by emigration from Greece, formed a dominant though not especially cohesive elite. Their own origins were diverse and their perspective was essentially careerist. They formed few emotional ties to their new homes and were usually prepared to go elsewhere if opportunity knocked. The Syrians, Persians, and Babylonians who made up the bulk of the population adopted a few Greek ideas and customs while retaining their own cultural identities.

The result was a cosmopolitan society held together largely by military force. The cities were unstable amalgams of contending ethnic and religious groups. They had their own administrations and popular assemblies but were legally the possessions of the king and had to deal with him through emissaries to protect their interests. Riots were common. *Koine*, a universal Greek dialect, evolved as the language of trade and administration but never fully displaced Aramaic or the other tongues of the ancient Middle East. In the countryside Greek influence remained negligible. Village societies retained their traditional structure even when they were regarded as part of the royal domain and paid taxes directly to the crown. Some were allotted to the cities by royal grant, while others were legally subject to a variety of private landholders. The forms of land tenure, taxation, and provincial administration were diverse.

The Seleucid Empire survived for nearly three hundred years largely because its cities and provinces had no common basis for resistance to the crown and because—until the coming of the Romans—it faced no serious outside threats. The conflicts with the Ptolemies over Palestine and Syria and with the Antigonids over portions of Asia Minor were largely settled by the early second century B.C. Border provinces, especially in the east and in Asia Minor, sometimes broke away, but the royal administration was generally competent. If the empire failed to attract the loyalty of its subjects, its cosmopolitanism offered at least some of them increased opportunities for profit.

Until the disorders of the first century B.C., the eastern empire enjoyed a relative prosperity. No internal trade barriers were established, and the Seleucids guaranteed the safety of caravans as a matter of policy. Even when its leaders were fighting over Alexander's inheritance, the entire Hellenistic world had been open to commerce. A merchant in Damascus or Babylon could trade unimpeded with Greece or Egypt. The more adventurous sent their goods into India or traded with Carthaginians and Romans in the west. Perhaps the most enduring of Alexander's legacies was the creation of a great world market in goods and ideas. It was this, more than anything else, that led to what traditionalists called a dilution of Greek values. Under the influence of Syria and Egypt, Greek legal traditions and even the status of women began to change (see document 3.4).

◆ DOCUMENT 3.4 ◆

A Hellenistic Marriage Contract

This marriage contract, dated 311 b.c., between Heracleides and Demetria, a Greek couple from the island of Cos on the shores of Asia Minor, demonstrates how the status of women had improved since the days of classical Attic Law. It not only mentions Demetria's mother, but also takes the infidelities of the husband as seriously as those of his wife.

Heracleides takes Demetria of Cos as his lawful wife. He receives her from her father, Leptines of Cos, and from her mother, Philotis. He is a free man and she a free woman. She brings with her clothes and jewels worth 1000 drachmas. Heracleides will provide Demetria with all the requirements of a free woman. They shall live in whatever place seems best to Leptines and Heracleides.

If Demetria is found to have done something which disgraces her husband, she shall lose everything she brought with her. And Heracleides shall accuse her before three men chosen by the pair of them. Heracleides shall not be permitted to wrong Demetria by keeping another woman or having children by another woman, nor to harm Demetria in any way under any pretext. If Heracleides is found to have done such a thing, Demetria shall accuse him before three men whom they shall have selected together. Heracleides shall then pay Demetria back the 1000 drachmas she brought as dowry and a further 1000 drachmas in Alexandrian silver as recompense.

Préaux, Claire. "*Le Statut de la femme à l'époque hellénistique, principalment en Egypte.*" In Julia O'Faolain and Lauro Martines, *Not in God's Image: Women in History from the Greeks to the Victorians.* London: Temple Smith.

Egypt under the Ptolemies contrasted vividly with the decentralized empire of the Seleucids. Egypt was a far more homogeneous society than that of the old Persian Empire, and Ptolemy I (d. c. 282 B.C.) had little difficulty in substituting his own rule for that of the pharaohs. After reaching an accommodation with the country's religious leaders, he established a royal despotism that reached into every corner of Egyptian life. With the exception of three Greek cities, only one of which was established by the Ptolemies, all of the country's land was regarded as the property of the king.

A large and efficient bureaucracy managed royal monopolies in essential goods and collected more than two hundred different taxes. The most important of these monopolies was in grain. Royal officials distributed seed to the peasants in return for a substantial percentage of their yields. The grain was then stored and released to the export market when prices were high. Grain was Egypt's leading export, and the profits from this trade were immense. The crown also held a complete monopoly on the production of vegetable oils, which it protected with a 50 percent duty on imported olive oil, and partial monopolies on virtually every other commodity from meat to papyrus. Policy was based on extracting the maximum amount of wealth from the country. By the middle of the second century B.C. many peasants were desperate. But being in a narrow valley surrounded by desert, they had nowhere to flee. The Ptolemies continued to pile up a great treasury until the fall of the dynasty in 30 B.C.

Much of that wealth was lavished on their capital at Alexandria. The city had been founded on the shores of the Mediterranean by Alexander. The narrow offshore island of Pharos was connected to the mainland by a causeway forming two spacious harbors, one of which was linked to Lake Mareotis by a canal. A second canal connected the lake with the western branch of the Nile. This enormous port soon formed the nucleus of the Mediterranean's largest city. Under the first and second Ptolemies, the population of Alexandria grew to nearly 500,000 Greeks, Macedonians, Egyptians, and Jews. Its people drew their water supply from vast cisterns built beneath the city, and a lighthouse, said to have been more than four hundred feet in height, was constructed on Pharos.

The cosmopolitan nature of its population and the patronage of the Ptolemies made Alexandria the cultural and intellectual center of the Hellenistic world. Its center was the Museum, which was a kind of research institute, and a library that collected materials from every literate culture known to the Greeks. The crown used some of its vast revenues to subsidize these institutions as well as the scholars who attended them, and the learned flocked to Alexandria from all over the Mediterranean basin.

Hellenistic Science, Philosophy, and Religion

The encouragement of the Ptolemies and the intellectual foundations laid down by Aristotle made the third century B.C. a period of extraordinary achievement in science, mathematics, engineering, and navigation.

Nothing like it would be seen again until the scientific revolution of the sixteenth and seventeenth centuries.

Some of the work done at Alexandria was scholarship—the compilation and transmission of earlier ideas. Euclid's *Elements of Geometry*, composed early in the century, contained little that was completely new but became the basis of geometric instruction until the present day. Hellenistic speculations on cosmography and physics were more original. Aristarchus of Samos (c. 310–230 B.C.) disputed Aristotle's theory that the Earth was the center of the universe. He reasoned, without benefit of telescopes or other instruments, that the Sun was larger than the Earth and that the planets were far more distant from one another than Aristotle had imagined. The Sun was therefore the center around which the Earth and planets revolved. Eratosthenes of Cyrene (c. 276–c. 194 B.C.), a mathematician who spent most of his life as head of the Library at Alexandria, founded mathematical geography. Among other things, he calculated the circumference of the Earth to within fifty miles of modern estimates and devised a calendar that used leap years.

Like much of Hellenistic science, these theories bore little fruit until they were revived by scholars in the sixteenth century. The authority of Aristotle was too great to permit their acceptance without independent proof, and the telescopes and navigational instruments needed to support them were not yet invented.

In physics, the work of Archimedes of Syracuse (c. 287–c. 212 B.C.) encountered no such resistance. Archimedes, who studied at Alexandria and was a friend of Eratosthenes, spent most of his life in his native city. A close associate and perhaps a relative of the ruling dynasty, he was valued for his work on catapults; compound pulleys; and the screw of Archimedes, a helical device for lifting water out of wells, mineshafts, and the hulls of ships. Most of these devices had both military and civilian applications, but Archimedes regarded them as little better than toys. He is best known for his work *On Plane Equilibriums*, which describes the basic principle of levers, and for his discovery that solids can be weighed by measuring the amount of liquid they displace. These achievements stand at the beginning of modern physics. In physics, cosmology, and biology, where Theophrastus (d. c. 287 B.C.) used the methods of Aristotle to classify plants and animals discovered in the east, the inspiration of Hellenistic science was largely Greek. In medicine, however, two ancient traditions merged. The Greek Hippocratic tradition was based on the teachings of Hippocrates, a semimythical figure who is supposed to have lived on the island of Cos in the fifth century B.C. (see document 3.5). Its main feature was the theory of the humors. Until late in the eighteenth century, most doctors believed that the human body contained four humors: blood, black bile, yellow bile, and phlegm. Good health depended upon keeping these humors in perfect balance, and medication was typically prescribed if one or more of them was either deficient or present in excess. An excess of blood, for example, could be reduced by bleeding.

The Alexandrians added Egyptian surgery and anatomy to the Hippocratic tradition and passed their findings on to the Romans.

Greeks of the classical era derived much of their identity from the polis and assumed that the good life could be lived only within its social framework. In the great empires of Hellenistic times, that framework no longer existed. For the Greco-Macedonian elite, cut off from their homelands and living essentially as mercenaries, the gratifications of private life gradually replaced those of the organic community. For the non-Greek masses with their long history of subjection to alien empires, there was no issue: The individual and the family were all that mattered.

The arts reflected this new individualism. Hellenistic drama abandoned the great themes of tragic conflict in favor of domestic comedies and tragedies that dealt with pathetic events on the personal level. The works of Menander (c. 300 B.C.) are typical of this genre.

Painting and sculpture flourished as never before. Painting especially is said to have reached unprecedented levels of excellence. However, owing to the perishable nature of the colors, all of it has been lost. In sculpture, much of which has been preserved in Roman copies, many of the best artists abandoned the serene classicism of Phidias and Praxiteles and sought to express emotion through the dramatic arrangement of their figures, agonized facial expressions, and exaggerated muscular tension. The famous statue of Laocoön and his sons is an outstanding example (see illustration 3.5). Others chose humble figures from everyday life and portrayed them in sympathetic detail (see illustration 3.6). Whatever their subject, the artists of the Hellenistic age achieved new heights of technical virtuosity that would astonish and at times dismay the critics of a later age.

Hellenistic philosophy, too, reflected this shift in values, abandoning political theory in favor of individualistic prescriptions for the good life. The philosophic school known as the Cynics carried this tendency further than anyone else. They argued that the best life

◈ DOCUMENT 3.5 ◈

The Hippocratic Oath

The origins of the Hippocratic oath are unclear. Hippocrates was supposed to have imposed the oath upon his students, but it may have appeared at any time between the fifth century B.C. and the first century A.D. Latin and Arabic versions appear throughout the Middle Ages. The text more closely resembles an indenture between master and apprentice than a pure statement of medical ethics.

I swear by Apollo Physician, by Asclepius, by Health, by Panacea, and by all the gods and goddesses, making them by witnesses, that I will carry out, according to my ability and judgment, this oath and this indenture. To hold my teacher in this art equal to my own parents; to make him partner in my livelihood; when he is in need of money to share mine with him; to consider his family as my own brothers, and to teach them this art, if they want to learn it, without fee or indenture; to impart precept, oral instruction, and all other instruction to my own sons, the sons of my teacher, and to indentured pupils who have taken the physician's oath, but to nobody else. I will use treatment to help the sick according to my ability and judgment, but never with a view to injury and wrongdoing. Neither will I administer a poison to anybody when asked to do so, nor will I suggest such a course. Similarly I will not give a woman a pessary to cause abortion. But I will keep pure and holy both my life and my art. I will not use the knife, not even, verily, on sufferers from stone, but I will give place to such as are craftsmen therein. Into whatsoever houses I enter, I will enter to help the sick, and I will abstain from all intentional wrong-doing and harm, especially from abusing the bodies of man or woman, bond or free. And whatsoever I shall see or hear in the course of my profession, as well as outside my profession in my intercourse with men, if it be what should be published abroad, I will never divulge, holding such things to be holy secrets. Now if I carry out this oath, and break it not, may I gain for ever reputation among all men for my life and for my art; but if I forswear myself, may the opposite befall me.

"The Hippocratic Oath." In Logan Clendening, ed., *Source-Book of Medical History*. pp. 14–15. New York: Dover, 1960.

Illustration 3.5

Laocoön and His Sons. This monumental sculpture from Pergamon is an example of the way in which Hellenistic artists used formal arrangement, exaggerated musculature, and agonized facial expressions to portray emotion. The serene classicism of Praxiteles and his contemporaries has been abandoned. Even the theme, an episode from *The Iliad* in which the gods sent serpents to destroy the Trojan priest Laocoön and his children, is chosen for its emotional impact. The work as shown is probably a Roman copy.

was lived closest to nature and that wisdom lay in abandoning worldly goods and ambition. Diogenes (d. 320 B.C.), their most effective spokesman, delighted in exposing the folly and vanity of others. Popular legend has it that he lived in a tub and carried a lantern with which he hoped—unsuccessfully—to find an honest man.

Among those attracted to the teachings of the Cynics was Zeno (c. 335–c. 263 B.C.). A native of Phoenician Cyprus, he established a school at Athens named the Stoa after the portico in the Agora where his disciples met. The Stoics, as they were called, believed that living in harmony with nature was essential. They identified nature with the divine principle or *logos*. Each human being and each object had the *logos* within it and acted according to a divine, predetermined plan. This plan, though good in itself, might not always work in the best interests of a particular individual. Sickness,

death, and misfortune were all part of a providential order that could not be escaped but only endured.

The implications of this theory were liberating. Moral qualities such as prudence, courage, folly, and intemperance were good or bad. Wealth, pleasure, beauty, and health were morally indifferent because they were essentially states of mind—the products of feeling or passion. The wise person, regardless of condition, should realize that it is not what happens but how one reacts to it that determines the good life. The goal of wisdom is therefore *apatheia*, or indifference to that which is morally neutral, coupled with ethical behavior and the cultivation of personal qualities that are morally good. According to the Stoics, anyone could achieve this goal. Men and women, slaves and princes, all possessed the same divine spark. Though the conditions of their lives might differ, they were all inherently equal.

Illustration 3.6

⧉ **Hellenistic Realism.** This life-size statue of a poor shepherdess is part of an important Hellenistic genre that portrayed the life of the poor, and particularly of poor women, with a sympathetic but unflinching eye.

Unlike the teachings of the Cynics, Stoicism was rooted in physical and epistemological principles derived at some distance from Aristotle. It offered not only an ethical code but also a means of understanding and accepting an often hostile universe. Of all the philosophical schools of late antiquity, it was the most popular among educated people. It became the dominant belief among the Roman upper classes and would strongly influence the development of Christianity.

Stoicism's chief rival was Epicureanism. Epicurus (341–270 B.C.) was born to an Athenian family on the island of Samos and established a school at Athens that was notable among other things for being open to women. He argued, as Leucippus and Democritus had done, that the universe was composed of atoms that combined and recombined in an infinite variety of patterns. Growth and dissolution were inevitable, but no providential order existed of the sort claimed by the Stoics. In the absence of such an order, the greatest good from the human point of view was pleasure, and the search for pleasure should be the philosopher's primary goal. By pleasure, Epicurus meant peace of mind and the absence of pain, not the active pursuit of dissipation. He sought a quiet life, removed from the troubles of the world and governed by the principle of moderation in all things. Even the gods were not to be feared but emulated in their Olympian detachment from the things of this world. Epicureanism, too, had its followers, but detachment from the world did not always recommend itself to those with practical responsibilities.

Like all philosophical schools, Stoicism and Epicureanism appealed primarily to the educated. The mass of people in the Hellenistic world found solace in religion. This in itself was a relatively new development, at least among the Greeks, for the gods of Olympus had offered little to their worshipers beyond a conditional protection from their wrath. In the classical age, while the learned took refuge in philosophy, ordinary men and women had resorted to superstition and a helpless resignation to *tyche*, or fate.

Hellenistic religions were different. Many, though not all, had Eastern or Egyptian roots, and most were what are called mystery religions. That is, they claimed to guarantee personal immortality, often through the intervention of a god or goddess who came to Earth in human form and suffered for the sins of humankind. Among the more important were the cult of Serapis, encouraged by Ptolemy I, and the far more ancient veneration of Isis.

The Jews in the Hellenistic World

Hellenistic culture, for all its richness and sophistication, was not universally admired. Among those who resisted it most persistently were the Jews. The dispersions of the sixth century B.C. had created a vast Jewish exile population. The largest of these communities were in Egypt and Babylon, but virtually every city in the ancient world had Jewish residents. Most were artisans or small tradesmen. While some were eventually submerged in the local population, others gathered together in close-knit communities to preserve their religious and cultural identity.

In Palestine, a remnant of impoverished peasants held on, reinforced after the Persian conquest of Babylon by small numbers of the devout who sought to re-

◆ DOCUMENT 3.6 ◆

The Jewish Struggle Against Hellenism

The First and Second Book of Maccabees tells the story of the struggle against the hellenizing policies of Antiochus Epiphanes from the standpoint of observant Jews. Not all Jews opposed Greek tendencies, and the struggle waged by the Maccabees was not only against Antiochus, but also against his local supporters.

Jason obtained the high priesthood by corruption, promising the king in his petition 360 talents of silver and 80 talents from other revenues. When the king had consented and he had taken office, he immediately brought his countrymen over to the Greek way of living. He set aside the royal ordinances especially favoring the Jews . . . and abrogating the lawful ways of living he introduced new customs contrary to the Law. For he willingly estab-lished a gymnasium right under the citadel, and he made the finest of the young men wear the Greek hat. And to such a pitch did the cultivation of Greek fashions and the coming-in of foreign customs rise . . . that the priests were no longer earnest about the services of the altar, but disdaining the sacrifices, they hurried to take part in the unlawful exercises of the wrestling school, after the summons to the discus throwing, regarding as worthless the things their forefathers valued, and thinking Greek standards the finest. [2 Macc. 2:23–27]

The Apocrypha. First Maccabees 2:23–27, 42–48. trans. Edgar J. Goodspeed. New York: Random House, 1959.

---

turn to their homeland. In 516 B.C. they rebuilt the Temple at Jerusalem. Not so grand as the Temple of Solomon, it served as the center of Jewish faith and aspirations until its destruction by the Romans in A.D. 70.

The glue that held the many Jewish communities together was the teaching of prophets and devotion to the Law, as symbolized by the gradual evolution of the Talmud from the fifth century B.C. onward. The Prophets, many of whose writings have been preserved in the Bible, exhorted the Jews to remain faithful. The Talmud was the product of scribes who sought to uncover the full meaning of the Mosaic Law and apply it to every conceivable circumstance. This process of commentary, which continues today, was central to the development of mature Judaism, but certain aspects of it were not unopposed. The biblical books of Jonah and of Ruth are veiled protests against what many saw as an increasingly narrow and overly proscriptive faith.

This struggle between a Judaism based firmly upon the Law and a broader tolerance of the non-Jewish world reached its greatest intensity in the Hellenistic era (see document 3.6). The conflict between Hellenism and Hebraism was fundamental. A life lived according to divinely revealed law was incompatible with the Greek love of speculation and with aesthetic standards based upon the beauties of nature and the perfection of the human body. In spite of this, many Jews were clearly attracted to Greek thought and customs.

The excesses of the Seleucid monarch Antiochus IV Epiphanes (c. 215–164 B.C.) turned the tide decisively against them. When he introduced the worship of Zeus to the temple at Jerusalem, a revolt led by the Maccabees, the five sons of the priest Mattathias, resulted in the restoration of an independent Jewish state.

In later years the dynasty founded by the Maccabees embarked upon a policy of expansion and forced conversions to Judaism. This was opposed by the Pharisees, who sought a return to the Law and to traditional Jewish values. A bloody civil war between the Pharisees and the Sadducees, as the supporters of the dynasty were known, ended only with Roman intervention in 64 B.C. and the abolition of the monarchy in the following year. Though political independence was lost, the danger of Hellenism had been avoided. The Romans made no effort to interfere with the Jewish faith, and the Pharisees emerged as the dominant faction in religious life—both at home and in the scattered communities of the dispersion.

Unlike that of the Jews, the culture of ancient Greece was profoundly humanistic in the sense that Greek thinkers emphasized the cultivation of virtue and the good life within a social instead of a religious framework. Greek artists concentrated almost exclusively on the human form, while poets found inspiration in the heroic dignity of men and women in the face of tragedy. This intense concentration on the human experience was coupled with an extraordinary spirit of inquiry. Other ancient societies, notably the Egyptians and Mesopotamians, had rich speculative traditions, but the Greeks were unique in insisting upon a rigorous form of logic in which the connections between each part of a statement had to be made perfectly clear.

These habits of thought, together with a mass of learning and speculation drawn from the most diverse sources, were the Greek legacy to Western society. From the beginning the Greeks were borrowers. They had a rare ability to absorb the ideas and beliefs of others without threatening their own sense of what it meant to be Greek. When, in the Hellenistic age, they penetrated to the edges of the known world, this tendency accelerated. Elements from every ancient culture were adopted and transformed according to their own needs and preconceptions. In so doing they imposed a kind of intellectual unity that, if it distorted some things and neglected others, was passed on intact to the Romans and from the Romans to the modern Western world. For good or ill, the ancient world is viewed through Greek eyes.

THE RISE OF THE ROMAN REPUBLIC

CHAPTER OUTLINE

◆◆◆◆◆◆◆◆◆◆◆◆◆◆◆◆◆◆◆◆◆◆

Rome united the ancient Mediterranean and joined it to western Europe. In the process, the Romans created an amalgam of ideas and institutions that would become the basis of later European life. This achievement, while enormous, was not especially original. The Romans excelled in the practical arts of war, law, engineering, and administration. They possessed in Latin a language of great richness and flexibility that would become the mother of many other tongues, but they borrowed virtually everything else from the Greeks, the Etruscans, the Egyptians, and other ancient cultures of the Near East. This was not simple mimicry but creative assimilation, for Roman culture had a coherence and integrity of its own. The Romans borrowed selectively, taking only what they found useful and transforming it according to their own traditions and social norms.

In the years when Greek civilization was at its height, Rome was still a modest settlement in central Italy. Poor and surrounded by powerful enemies, it survived by developing a superb army and a political system that, though authoritarian enough to be effective in times of crisis, was based upon the active participation of its citizens and the rule of law. By the middle of the third century B.C. Rome controlled the Italian peninsula. By 133 B.C. it had defeated both Carthage and Macedon and acquired an empire that stretched from Spain to Greece.

The creation of this empire was, at least in the beginning, a response to adversity rather than the product of deliberate intent. Surrounded by more powerful enemies, it developed a culture that stressed the military values of courage, discipline, and endurance. The early history of Rome is therefore one of harsh adaptations followed by explosive growth—the tale of how a poor, often beleaguered community developed political and military institutions capable of ruling an empire.

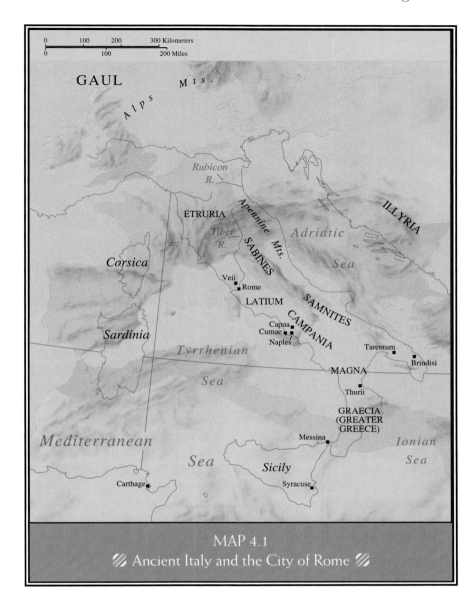

MAP 4.1
〽 Ancient Italy and the City of Rome 〽

Ancient Italy

The long, boot-shaped Italian peninsula bisects the Mediterranean (see map 4.1). At first glance it seems especially favored by nature. Its central location lends it strategic and commercial importance while its climate is generally milder and wetter than that of Greece. Agricultural yields are higher, and some of the upland regions, which in Greece have become a moonscape of rocks and dry scrub, can support grazing. These advantages, however, are relative. The development of prehistoric Italy was at first hindered by natural obstacles of every kind. For most of its length the Italian peninsula is dominated by the Appenines, a mountain range that in its central portions reaches nearly ten thousand

feet in height. On the east, the mountains drop precipitously to the Adriatic Sea. Few good harbors can be found on the Italian shore of the Adriatic, and arable land is scarce except in Apulia, the region immediately southeast of Mt. Garganus, which protrudes like a spur into the Adriatic.

The western coast, also lacking in good harbors, is more hospitable. The valleys of the Arno and the Tiber are suitable for agriculture and open out onto an extensive coastal plain that, though potentially fertile, was in early times marshy and subject to floods. Further south, around the Bay of Naples, is the rich plain of Campania whose soil is the gift of volcanic deposits from Mt. Vesuvius. Another active volcano, Mt. Etna, dominates the eastern part of Sicily, the large, wedge-shaped is-

Illustration 4.1

An Etruscan Tomb. Wealthy Etruscans often buried the dead in replicas of their homes. In this example of a domestic interior from the third century B.C., the household goods are portrayed in stucco relief.

land immediately southwest of the mainland. As a consequence of climatic change, Sicily today is dry and relatively poor, but until the sixteenth century A.D. it supplied much of Italy with grain.

At the opposite end of the peninsula, between the westward curve of the Appenines and the great northern barrier of the Alps, is the valley of the Po. Flowing eastward into the Adriatic, it is now among the world's richest agricultural and industrial regions, but its wealth is largely the fruit of human effort. As recently as the fourth century B.C. it was a wild marshland, not yet tamed by two millennia of canalization and levee building.

Beginning in the eighth century B.C., Greek colonists had established themselves in the richest of the southern coastal lands. Eastern Sicily, Apulia, and Campania, as well as Calabria (the heel of the boot) and the shores of the Gulf of Taranto (its arch), were soon dominated by *poleis* of the Aegean type, rich and vigorous, but as combative and incapable of unified action as their models. At the same time, the Carthaginians colonized western Sicily and contended violently with their Greek neighbors for land and trade. Of the original inhabitants of these areas, some became slaves or tenants of the colonists, while others retreated to the interior and retained their tribal cultures.

A variety of tribes, Latins, Umbrians, and Samnites—each speaking its own Italic or other Indo-European language—inhabited Latium, the central part of the peninsula. The Etruscans dominated the region between the Tiber and the Arno. Their language can be only partially deciphered, but their alphabet was similar to that of the Greeks and their art seems also to have been derived from Greek models. Most of what is known about the Etruscans comes from archaeology, and little has survived from the days when Etruscan power was at its height (see illustration 4.1). Above all, the Etruscans were city dwellers. Their economy was based heavily on trade and manufacturing, and though they were also accomplished farmers, they preferred whenever possible to live in town. They constructed their twelve main cities according to engineering and religious principles that would profoundly influence the Romans. Where terrain permitted, the Etruscans favored a symmetrical and axial city plan that was unlike anything devised by the Greeks. Elaborate tunnels of dressed stone drained low-lying areas or brought fresh water for the consumption of the townspeople, while the buildings featured arches and vaulted ceilings, construction techniques that appear to have been invented by Etruscans.

This sophistication did not extend to political arrangements. Etruscan society was rigidly stratified. A handful of wealthy families dominated each of the twelve cities through legally enforceable clientage and the ownership of many slaves. In war, the rich fought on horseback under a king who may have been elective. By the fifth century B.C. the Etruscans had adopted the hoplite tactics of the Greeks and replaced their kings with aristocratic magistrates. No movement toward democracy is evident. But if the political evolution of the Etruscans differed from that of the Greeks, in another respect they closely resembled them: The twelve cities were almost incapable of united action. At an early date they formed a league, which was chiefly religious and athletic in purpose. The cities also celebrated certain religious festivals in common, but otherwise they fought incessantly and their merchants competed for each other's markets as well as for those of the Greek and Carthaginian colonies to the south.

The Origins of Rome

The Tiber is the largest river in central Italy. Its valley, running roughly from north to south, is strategically important because it provides the easiest land route for travelers—and armies—moving between the Po valley and southern Italy. The last point at which the river can be easily crossed lies about fifteen miles from its mouth, where the valley is broad and marshy. Seven low hills in the immediate area provide a refuge from floods and invaders alike. In the eighth century B.C. one hill, the Palatine, was occupied by a tribe of people who spoke an early version of Latin. Shortly afterward, a related group took up residence on the nearby Aventine hill. These two settlements formed the nucleus of ancient Rome. They were part of a larger group of Italic communities that formed themselves into the Latin League for political and religious purposes, but their common ties did not prevent them from fighting among themselves.

Blessed with rich land and abundant water, the early Romans were nevertheless too few to preserve full autonomy in the face of Etruscan influence. The nearest of the Etruscan cities was Veii, only twelve miles away, and almost from the first, the Romans found themselves under the influence of their more powerful neighbors. Some of the first kings of Rome bore Etruscan names, and reportedly the last of them was not deposed and replaced by a Roman republic ruled by two magistrates until 509 B.C. (although it could have been a generation later).

In any event, Etruscan influence contributed greatly to Roman civilization. The Romans adopted the Etruscan alphabet, though not the language itself, and learned most of what they knew about metalworking, civic planning, and architecture from their northern neighbors. Many religious customs described by Livy, together with a number of Roman political institutions, have Etruscan roots as well.

Under the kings, Rome used its dominant position in the Latin League to subdue the Sabines and other Italic communities along the lower Tiber, absorbing their populations and granting citizenship to the leading families. This enlightened policy, a marked contrast to the exclusiveness of the Greek *poleis*, was largely responsible for Rome's successful expansion. The prospect of fair treatment discouraged fanatic resistance among the city's enemies and made accepting Roman hegemony far easier for its neighbors.

The policy was continued after the formation of the republic. The Romans expelled the Etruscans as part of a larger movement that involved Rome's Greek and Latin neighbors. The Etruscan city of Veii was taken after an extensive siege in 396 B.C., almost doubling Roman territory. Nine years later, however, disaster struck. The Gauls, a Celtic people from central Europe, descended on the peninsula and burned Rome in 387 B.C. The action was a tremendous psychological blow, for the Gauls, with their vast numbers and sheer ferocity, appalled the Romans. They sometimes fought naked and seemed to live exclusively on meat and alcohol. Fortunately, they made no effort to consolidate their victory and retired to the sparsely inhabited valley of the Po. They settled down to a more-or-less ordered agricultural life and began the long process of clearing and draining the region, which in later times would be known as Cisalpine Gaul.

Among the more serious consequences of the Gallic invasion was that it undermined the loyalty of Rome's Latin allies. The Latin League rebelled against Roman hegemony, but the Romans recovered quickly. By 338 B.C. all of Latium was again subdued. Once more, the Romans showed a restraint and a grasp of political realities that were all too rare in the ancient world. The towns nearest Rome received full citizenship. Others, farther away, were granted municipal status, which meant that their citizens could marry or trade with Romans but had no voting rights outside their own communities. The specific provisions of these agreements were tailored to individual circumstances and were open-ended in the sense that Rome always held out the prospect of new privileges in return for good behavior. Some towns were merely enrolled as allies, but all save those that received citizenship retained self-government. The one universally enforced rule was that none of the federated communities could make similar agreements with each other.

To ensure communication and provide for the common defense, the first of a series of paved, all-weather roads were built linking Rome with her allies (see illustration 4.2). A policy that would be followed until the end of the empire was thus begun. Because all roads led to Rome, these highways had the effect of separating the allies from one another while allowing Rome to intervene militarily in case of rebellion or some other

Illustration 4.2

🔲 **A Section of the Appian Way.** Begun about 312 B.C., the Appian Way was the first of the great paved highways built to link Rome with its allies and eventually with the farthest reaches of its empire. As this modern photo demonstrates, Roman engineering was built to last.

threat. Surfaced in stone and often lined with trees, a few of the roads are still in use today.

These arrangements proved effective in the next great crisis. The consolidation of Latium threatened the Samnites, a warlike people who inhabited the uplands between Rome and the Greek settlements around the Bay of Naples. Joined by the Gauls and by the Etruscans, whose power was greatly reduced, they launched a series of bitter struggles that ended with the Roman victory at Sentinium in 295 B.C. Though a few of Rome's Latin allies deserted, the coalition as a whole held firm.

The Roman military system achieved maturity during the Samnite wars. Under the monarchy, the Romans had learned to use hoplites flanked by cavalry from the Etruscans. Their greater success resulted largely from a superior discipline rooted ultimately in cultural values. The Romans prized self-discipline, de-

termination, and a sense of duty to the community above all else, but they were not indifferent to practical concerns. After about 400 B.C. they paid their troops while on duty. The Samnites, who were as tough as the Romans and who enjoyed the defensive advantage of a rugged, mountainous terrain, forced them to change tactics. To achieve greater maneuverability, the Romans abandoned the phalanx in favor of smaller units known as maniples. A maniple contained 100 to 120 foot soldiers and was commanded by an officer known in later days as a centurion. Thirty maniples, plus five in reserve, made up a legion. In battle, the maniples were arranged in three lines, with a space between each unit large enough to permit the forward ranks to move back or the rear ranks to move forward as needed. Such a formation required discipline and control, while permitting an almost infinite number of tactical combinations regardless of the terrain. The new system, which in its basic outlines lasted until the end of the fourth century A.D., was badly needed in the years after it brought success in the battle of Sentinium. The Romans had to defend themselves against a series of powerful neighbors, but each victory made them new enemies (see document 4.1). The defeat of the Samnites and their allies awakened the Greek cities of the south. The Romans now controlled all of Italy from the borders of Campania to the Po, and the Greeks feared that such a concentration of power would lead to their downfall. Bickering and complaining to the last, they nevertheless united enough to hire the greatest mercenary of the age to defend their interests.

Pyrrhus of Epirus was ruler of a small state in what is now Albania. Backed by Greek wealth and supported by a contingent of war elephants, he twice defeated the Romans but suffered such heavy casualties that he retreated to Sicily in 278 B.C., saying that if he won another such victory he would be ruined. Nevertheless, he returned again in 275 B.C. only to be defeated. These wars gave rise to the term *Pyrrhic victory* and marked the end of Greek independence on the Italian mainland. The Greek cities, too, were incorporated into the Roman system, and the Roman republic thus ruled all Italy south of the Po.

◆

The Economic and Social Structures of Early Rome

The city that conquered Italy was similar in its social arrangements to the classical Greek polis. A majority of early Romans were small farmers. Though their plots

❖ DOCUMENT 4.1 ❖

Livy: Roman Tactics at the Time of the Samnite Wars

Titus Livius (59 B.C.–A.D. 17), known as Livy, was the greatest historian of ancient Rome. Writing with the patronage of the Emperor Augustus, Livy compiled a history of Rome from its origins to 9 B.C. This work, known as The Annals of the Roman People, *consisted of 142 books; only 35 of these (plus fragments) have survived. Livy was a conservative analyst who stressed the traditional strengths of Rome, such as the citizen army. The following excerpt from Livy's history explains the organization of the army during the Samnite Wars (343–341 B.C.) of the early republic.*

The foremost line consisted of the *hastati*, forming 15 maniples [companies] stationed a short distance from each other. This front line . . . consisted of the flower of the young men who were growing ripe for service. Behind them were stationed an equal number of maniples, called *principes*, made up of men of a more stalwart age. . . . This body of 30 maniples was called the *antepilani* because behind the standards there were stationed 15 other companies, each of which was divided into three sections, the first section being called the *pilus*. The company consisted of three *vexilla* [banners]. A single *vexillum* had 60 soldiers, two centurions, and one *vexillarius*, or color-bearer; the company numbered 186 men. The first *vexillum* led the *triarii*, veterans of proven courage; the second, the *rorarii*, or skirmishers, younger and less distinguished men; the third, the *accensi*, who were least to be depended upon and were therefore assigned to the rearmost line.

When an army had been drawn up in these ranks, the *hastati* were the first of all to engage. If the *hastati* failed to repulse the enemy, they slowly retired through the intervals between the companies of the *principes*, who then took up the fight, the *hastati* following in their rear. The *triarii*, meanwhile, were kneeling under their standards with left leg advanced, their shields leaning against their shoulders, and their spears planted in the ground with points obliquely upward, as if their battle line were fortified by a bristling palisade. If the *principes* were also unsuccessful, they slowly retired from the battle line to the *triarii* (which has given rise to the proverbial saying, when people are in great trouble, "matters have come down to the *triarii*"). When the *triarii* had admitted the *hastati* and *principes* through the intervals between their companies, they rose up and, instantly closing their companies up, blocked the lanes, as it were, and in one compact mass fell on the enemy, there being no more reserves left behind them. The enemy, who had pursued the others as though they had defeated them, saw with the greatest dread a new line suddenly rising up with increased numbers.

Livy. "History of Rome," book 8, from *Roman Civilization: Third Edition: 2. Vol. Set.* Naphtali and Meyer Rheinhold, eds. Copyright © 1990, Columbia University Press. Reprinted with permission of the publisher.

probably averaged no more than two or three acres—twenty acres was regarded as a substantial estate—the intensive cultivation of many different crops provided them with a measure of self-sufficiency (see illustration 4.3). Wherever possible, grain was planted between rows of vines or olive trees and replaced with beans or other legumes in alternate years, for the Romans practiced crop rotation and were careful to enrich the soil through composting and animal fertilizers. Because grazing land was scarce, there was never enough manure. Sheep were raised for their wool and for milk, while cattle were used mainly as draft animals. Everyone tried to maintain a miniature orchard of apples, pears, or figs.

This kind of farming required skill and a great deal of effort in virtually every month of the year. Fields had to be plowed at least three times, then hoed frequently during the growing season to reduce soil temperature and preserve moisture. Water was always a problem in the hot, dry Italian summer and often had to be carried from some distance to irrigate the garden vegetables. Compost piles, which used every bit of organic matter available, needed water as well as frequent turning with the pitchfork. The successful cultivation of vineyards and fruit trees demanded clever techniques for grafting and pruning.

Heroic efforts produced a balanced but simple diet: wheat or barley gruel supplemented by olives, cabbage, and beans. Milk, cheese, fruit, and baked bread provided variety, but meat—usually pork—was reserved for special occasions. Sheep, goats, and cattle were too valuable to be slaughtered for their meat but sometimes found their way to the table after serving as burnt offerings to the gods. Hogs, which could root in the oak forests or in other waste spaces, provided not only

Illustration 4.3

✏️ **Roman Agriculture.** These mosaics from Saint Roman-en-Gal, France, show Roman farmers engaged in gathering grapes, picking apples, and bundling straw.

hams and sausages but also that greatest of all Roman delicacies: roast suckling pig.

Roman farms were usually worked by the owner and his *familia*—the legal definition of which, though precise, was remarkably inclusive. It meant the nuclear family as well as the entire household including dependent relatives and slaves. Most plots could support only the owner, his wife, and his children, but the labor-intensive character of Italian agriculture favored the growth of extended families whenever sufficient land was available. It also encouraged slavery, even on properties that seem small by modern standards. No great slave-worked estates existed of the kind that be-

came common in the second century B.C., but many families found that owning a few extra workers was a good investment.

Some slaves were war captives, but most were Romans subjugated for debt. As in Mesopotamia or early Greece, those unable to satisfy their creditors were forced to sell themselves or their children to discharge their obligation. Under the early republic, slavery was not as harsh as it would later become. The term of debt servitude was usually limited, with freedom guaranteed after a fixed period of years. Dehumanization was further reduced by the fact that most slaves lived under their master's roof and shared his table. Marcus Porcius

Cato (234–149 B.C.), the author, general, and statesman from whom much information is derived about rural society under the republic (see document 4.2), reported that his wife sometimes nursed the children of slaves. But slaves were still property and could be sold, beaten, or killed without recourse to law.

In this, slaves were little different from the other members of the *familia*. Theoretically and legally, the father, or *paterfamilias*, had absolute power of life and death over his children and slaves. His wife, too, was subject to his will, but he could neither kill nor sell her. In practice, affection and the need for domestic tranquility diluted the brutality of the law. By the second century B.C. women had, through court decisions and senatorial decrees, gained a much larger measure of control over their persons and dowries than they had enjoyed in the early years of the republic.

In much the same way, the sale or execution of a child rarely took place without the approval of the entire family, and public opinion had to be considered as well. Rome, like ancient Greece, was a "shame" society that exercised social control primarily through community pressure. Reputation was vitally important, and the mistreatment of women and children was regarded as shameful.

Women guarded their reputations and were generally respected. Like their Greek counterparts, they managed the day-to-day life of the household. Women, no less than men, were expected to conform to the ideals of *dignitas*, *fides*, and *pietas* (dignity, faithfulness, and piety) and to exhibit physical and moral courage of the highest order. They were also expected to remind their menfolk when they failed to honor those ancient virtues. In many ways, the Roman model of feminine behavior was more Spartan than Athenian.

Roman families were part of larger social groupings that influenced their conduct. The importance of clans, tribes, and other survivals from an earlier time has been much debated, but clientage, the system of mutual dependency in which a powerful individual protects the interests of others in return for their political or economic support, was legally enforceable and even more highly developed than in Mesopotamia.

All of these arrangements were sanctioned by religion. The Roman pantheon of gods was superficially like that of the Greeks, with Jupiter corresponding to Zeus, Juno to Hera, Venus to Aphrodite, and so on. However, in the early days at least, the gods do not seem to have had clearly defined human forms. No myths sprung up about them, and no suggestion was made that they engaged in the kind of sexual antics

---

◆ DOCUMENT 4.2 ◆

Cato: Farm Management

Marcus Porcius Cato (234–149 B.C.) was the first Latin writer of prose. Though he wrote in the second century B.C., his fervent traditionalism led him to value the social ideals of a far earlier time, and much of his political career was devoted to a vigorous attack on luxury and the importation of foreign ideas. His De agri cultura, the first of many Roman tracts on farming, was directed to men like himself who had farmed modest acreage with the help of an overseer and a few slaves, not toward the owners of opulent estates. It includes a wealth of technical information on every aspect of farming as well as advice on management. The following passages reflect a hard-bitten attitude that must have been common among Romans in the earliest days of the republic.

Sell worn-out oxen, blemished cattle, blemished sheep, wool, hides, an old slave, a sickly slave, and whatever else is superfluous. The master should be in the selling habit, not the buying habit. . . .

[O]n feast days, old ditches might have been cleaned, road work done, brambles cut, the garden spaded, a meadow cleared, faggots bundled, thorns rooted out, spelt ground, and general cleaning done. When the slaves were sick, such large rations should not have been issued.

When the weather is bad and no other work can be done, clear out manure for the compost heap; clean thoroughly the ox stalls, sheep pens, barnyard, and farmstead; and mend wine-jars with lead, or hoop them with thoroughly dried oak wood. . . . In rainy weather try to find something to do indoors. Clean up rather than be idle. Remember that even though work stops, expenses run on none the less.

Cato. *De agricultura*, trans. W. D. Hooper and H. D. Ash. Loeb Classical Library. Cambridge, MA: Harvard University Press, 1934.

---

common among the Olympians. When Greek culture became fashionable in the second half of the third century B.C., such distinctions tended to vanish. Greek myths were adapted to the Roman pantheon, and the Roman gods and goddesses were portrayed according to the conventions of Greek art. The Romans also believed in a host of spirits that governed places and natural processes (see document 4.3). They consulted the

◈ DOCUMENT 4.3 ◈

St. Augustine: Animistic Spirits in Roman Religion

St. Augustine (A.D. 354–430) was born Aurelius Augustinus in the Roman province of Numidia in north Africa, the son of a Christian mother and pagan father. Augustine moved to Rome, where he taught rhetoric and continued to accept traditional Roman religious practice. He converted to Christianity in his thirties and became a priest, returning to Africa, where he served as bishop of Hippo. His writings, especially his autobiographical Confessions *and* The City of God, *were extremely influential in shaping early Christianity. The following excerpt from* The City of God *describes the polytheistic Roman religion of his youth.*

But how is it possible to mention in one part of this book all the names of gods or goddesses, which the Romans scarcely could comprise in great volumes, distributing among these divine powers their peculiar functions concerning separate things? They did not even think that the care of their lands should be entrusted to any one god; but they entrusted their farms to the goddess Rumina, and the ridges of the mountains to the god Jugatinus; over the hills they placed the goddess Collatina, over the valleys, Vallonia. Nor could they even find one Segetia so potent that they could commend their cereal crops entirely to her care; but so long as their seed grain was still under the ground, they desired to have the goddess Seia watch over it; then, when it was already above ground and formed standing grain, they set over it the goddess Segetia; and when the grain was collected and stored, they entrusted it to the goddess Tutilina, that it might be kept safe. Who would not have thought the goddess Segetia sufficient to protect the standing grain until it had passed from the first green blades to the dry ears? Yet she was not enough for men who loved a multitude of gods. . . . Therefore they set Proserpina over the germinating seeds; over the joints and knobs of the stems, the god Nodutus; over the sheaths enfolding the ears, the goddess Volutina; when the sheaths opened and the spikes emerged, it was ascribed to the goddess Patelana; when the stems were of the same height as new ears, because the ancients described this equalizing by the term *hostire*, it was ascribed to the goddess Hostilina; when the grain was in flower, it was dedicated to the goddess Flora; when full of milk, to the god Lacturnus; when maturing, to the goddess Matuta; when the crop was "runcated"—that is, removed from the soil—to the goddess Runcina.

St. Augustine. *The City of God,* books 4, 8, from *Roman Civilization: Third Edition: 2 Vol. Set,* Naphtali Lewis and Meyer Rheinhold, eds. Copyright © 1990, Columbia University Press. Reprinted with permission of the publisher.

omens before virtually every act, public or private, and performed sacrifices to assure its success. The sacrifices might involve the burnt offering of an animal, which was usually then eaten, or a libation of wine or oil. Gods and spirits alike had to be appeased. The Romans were not, however, a priest-ridden people. Priests of both sexes specialized in the care of temples or in foretelling the future. They were never a separate caste. At home, the father presided over religious rites and was responsible for making sure that the family did not offend the gods. No concept of personal salvation is evident, and ethical concepts were largely unrelated to divine will.

Some Romans were richer than others. The source or extent of their greater wealth is hard to determine, but at an early date the Etruscan kings identified one hundred men of substance and appointed them to an advisory body known as the Senate. The senators represented families that owned land, held slaves, and could afford to fight on horseback instead of on foot. Like their Etruscan counterparts, they presided over elaborate networks of clientage in which mutual obligation was enforced by religious and legal sanctions. When the monarchy fell, the Senate remained to advise the two governing magistrates, who would eventually be known as *consuls,* and the senatorial families became the core of the patrician order.

The patricians were the hereditary aristocracy of the Roman republic. While other citizens could vote, only the patricians could hold office as magistrates or serve in the Senate. The plebeians, who were free citizens even though many of them were bound by ties of clientage, resisted this situation from the start. Some of them had grown rich during the years of expansion under the monarchy and resented being excluded from public life.

The majority of plebeians had grown poorer. Their farms, which had never been large, were divided and divided again by inheritance until many citizens were virtually landless. Roman law insisted on partible inheritance, the more-or-less equal division of property among heirs. The practice persists today wherever the Roman legal tradition remains. It is a major obstacle to the preservation of a family's wealth. The only solution to the problems it created, apart from demographic catastrophe, was territorial growth. New lands acquired through conquest were distributed to Roman citizens, with those who commanded the legions taking the lion's share. Poor plebeians, faced with imminent bankruptcy, wanted a fairer division of this public land and an end to debt slavery.

These aims were not incompatible. Rich and poor knew that both could be achieved by combining forces against the patriciate. As a result, plebeian efforts to develop institutions and win for themselves a place in government were the dominant theme of Roman politics from the beginnings of the republic until the third century B.C. This Struggle of the Orders forged the basic institutions of the Roman state.

The Evolution of Roman Government

The power of the patricians was deeply rooted in law and custom, but even before the fall of the monarchy it was in one sense an anachronism. The heart of the Roman army was infantry, and Roman survival depended upon the swords and spears of plebeians, not horse-mounted aristocrats. In Rome, as in the Greek polis, political rights would grow from military service.

The plebeians began their struggle in 494 B.C. when they answered a senatorial call to arms by leaving the city and refusing to fight against the Volscians, a neighboring people who threatened to invade Roman territory. This dramatic gesture won them the right to elect *tribunes*, who could represent their interests and defend them against unjust decrees by the magistrates. In the following year they erected a temple on the Aventine to Ceres, the Roman variant of the Earth Mother. Ceres, unlike the sky-gods favored by the patricians, had long been associated with peasants and artisans. The temple, along with its *aediles*, or wardens, gave sacred status to the plebeian cause and placed its tribunes under divine protection. It also provided the basis for a political organization. The meetings of the cult, which were open only to plebeians, issued decrees or *plebiscites* in opposition to the public assembly. This body soon evolved into an assembly that was regarded by plebeians as a kind of alternative government.

Pressure from the plebeian assembly bore fruit more than a generation later in the publication of the Twelve Tables (c. 451–450 B.C.). They were the first body of written law in Roman history, and Livy called them, with some exaggeration, "the fountainhead of all public and private laws." The codified laws reinforced the privileges of the patricians, recognized the plebeians as a distinct order, and indirectly offered them a measure of legal protection. Laws that were written down could not be altered at will by patrician judges who often acted out of self-interest or class prejudice. The tables also introduced the principle of equality before the law (*aequatio iuris*) because these laws applied to patricians and plebeians alike. The Twelve Tables themselves were destroyed during the Gallic sack of Rome in 387 B.C., and their provisions are known today primarily through the commentaries of later jurists (see document 4.4). Seen through the eyes of these commentators, the tables seem harsh and regressive. The principle of *patria potestas*, for example, gave the husband the powers of "head of the family" and instructed him to kill a deformed baby. Another table stated that women were perpetual minors under the guardianship of their fathers or husbands, a legal principle that persisted in European law for more than two thousand years. But if the Twelve Tables seem conservative in many respects, they were also an important step in the establishment of plebeian rights and the rule of law.

Among the more revolutionary features of the Twelve Tables was their recognition of wealth, in addition to birth, as a measure of social stratification. This may not seem like an advance, but it reflected an important part of the plebeian agenda. By 443 B.C. all citizens were ranked by property qualifications, which determined not only their military role but also their right to participate in the public or centuriate assembly that elected the magistrates. A new official, the *censor*, was elected to determine the rankings on an ongoing basis, and the census became an important civic and religious ritual (see illustration 4.4).

The entire body of male citizens was divided into centuries, roughly corresponding to the size of a maniple, the military unit that, in its original form, had probably contained about one hundred troops (see table 4.1). The centuries were in turn divided into classes ranging from the first class of heavily armed hoplites to a fifth class armed only with slings. The patrician *equites*, or cavalry, and the *proletarii*, who owned only their children and could afford no weapons, were technically outside the class system, but this was little more than a convenient social fiction. The important point

◈ DOCUMENT 4.4 ◈

Ulpian: Roman Law

The Roman jurist Ulpian was born at Tyre in Phoenicia and died in A.D. 225. His writings on the law comprise almost a third of Justinian's Digest of the Laws. *(see chapter 6). In this selection he describes the moral and intellectual basis of Roman law and, in so doing, demonstrates its importance in Roman thought and practice. Note in particular Ulpian's understanding of natural law, which was to have a great influence on Western jurisprudence down to the present day.*

When a man means to give his attention to law, he ought first to know whence the term law (*ius*) is derived. Now it is so called from justice (*iustitia*). In fact, as Celsus neatly defines it, *ius* is the art of the good and fair. Of this art we may deservedly be called the priests; we cherish justice and profess the knowledge of the good and the fair, separating the fair from the unfair, discriminating between the permitted and the forbidden, desiring to make men good, not only by the feat of penalties, but also by the incentives of rewards, affecting, if I mistake not, a true and not a simulated philosophy.

This subject comprises two categories, public law and private law. Public law is that which regards the constitution of the Roman state, private law that which looks to the interest of individuals; for some things are beneficial from the point of view of the state, and some with reference to private persons. Public law is concerned with sacred rites, with priests, with public officers. Private law is tripartite, being derived from the rules of natural law, or of the law of nations, or of civil law. Natural law is that which all animals are taught by nature; this law is not peculiar to the human race, but is common to animals which are produced on land or sea, and to the birds as well. From it comes the union of male and female, which we call matrimony, and the procreation and bearing of children; we find in fact that animals in general, even the wild beasts, are marked by acquaintance with this law. The law of nations is that which the various people of mankind observe. It is easy to see that it falls short of natural law, because the latter is common to all living creatures, whereas the former is common only to human beings in their mutual relations.

Justinian. *Digest of the Laws* I: 3–4, from *Roman Civilization: Third Edition: 2 Vol. Set,* Naphtali Lewis and Meyer Rheinhold, eds. Copyright © 1990, Columbia University Press. Reprinted with permission of the publisher.

was that the *equites* and the hoplite class had enough votes between them to outnumber everyone else. This protected the wealthy of both orders and, on property issues at least, made them allies. Wealth rather than birth was becoming the chief source of political power.

Property issues came to a head after the Gallic invasion of 387 B.C. Many poor Romans lost their property and were forced into debt slavery. Popular rebellions in 385 B.C. and 375 B.C., though unsuccessful, led to a series of reforms. Under the Licinian-Sextian Laws of 367 B.C., plebeians were admitted to the highest offices of the state, and the popular assembly was allowed to pass laws, subject to senatorial approval. The result was a century of reforms. New laws abolished debt slavery and expanded the distribution of public land to poor citizens. Implementation was made easier by rapid territorial expansion during the second half of the fourth century B.C. The rich were prevented from seizing all of the gains. Finally, in 312 B.C., the Senate admitted plebeians to membership for the first time, and in 287 B.C. it lost its veto power over the popular assembly. The Struggle of the Orders had ended.

The government that emerged from this prolonged controversy was, in theory at least, carefully balanced to represent the interests of all Roman citizens and was for this reason of great interest to the theorists who, two thousand years later, framed the U.S. Constitution. Legislative authority rested in the centuriate and plebeian assemblies, though the decrees of the latter may not have been binding upon all citizens and the most important function of the centuriate assembly was to elect the consuls and other magistrates. Leadership of the state, including command of the army, was vested in two consuls who served one-year terms and could succeed themselves only after a ten-year interval. In theory, the consuls inherited the full *imperium* or authority of the old monarchy, and their edicts had the force of law. In practice, they consulted closely with the Senate and could veto each other's measures if necessary. In war, one consul normally commanded the legions while the other remained at home to govern, but it was not uncommon for both consuls to take the field and command the army on alternate days. In moments of extreme crisis, the consuls could also appoint a *dictator,* subject to senatorial approval. The dictator, who was always an experienced general, held absolute power for six months and could mobilize the resources of the state without legal interference.

These arrangements met the defensive needs of a small community, but as Rome expanded, campaigns grew longer. Armies had to be maintained in distant ar-

Illustration 4.4

A Census. A census was taken every five years by the consuls of the republic to ensure that citizens were properly assigned to their classes and to facilitate recruitment into the army. On the right, citizens make their declarations to a scribe and an assessor in the presence of soldiers. On the left, a bull, a sheep, and a pig are offered in sacrifice. Like most civic rituals in the Republic, the census had a religious dimension as well. The reliefs probably date from 115 B.C. to 97 B.C.

TABLE 4.1
The 'Servian' Classification of Male Citizens

The classification of troops by the first census after the Servian reforms of 444 B.C. provides a measure of Roman wealth and population in the early republic. The classifications of wealth in terms of *asses*, a coin introduced in the third century B.C. when about thirty-three of them were needed to purchase a bushel of wheat, are therefore approximate, but scholars believe that they provide a fair estimate of the citizen population and its relative poverty.

Class	Number of centuries	Number of men	Property qualification (in *asses*)
Cavalry	18	1,800	
I	80	8,000	100,000
II	20	2,000	75,000
III	20	2,000	50,000
IV	20	2,000	25,000
V	30	3,000	12,500
Engineers	2	200	Ranked with class I
Musicians, proletarians, and others	3	300	None
Total	193	19,300	

Source: Adapted from T. Frank, ed., *An Economic Survey of Ancient Rome*, vol. 1 (Paterson, N.J.: Pageant Books, 1959), p. 20.

Other magistrates called *praetors* administered justice, though they, too, might serve as generals in time of war. Upon taking office they made a public declaration of the principles by which they would interpret the law, and these statements became landmarks in the development of Roman jurisprudence. The most respected office in the Roman state was that of *censor*. There were two of them, and they registered citizens as well as supervised morals and guaranteed public contracts. They could also remove senators from office on financial or ethical grounds. Other offices included the *quaestors* who assisted the consuls, especially on financial matters, and four *aediles*, who supervised markets and other public services. All were subject to interference from the tribunes, whose persons were still sacrosanct and who served as spokesmen for those who felt oppressed by the magistrates.

But the Senate, in theory no more than an advisory body, remained the most powerful institution of the Roman state (see document 4.5). Its members were originally appointed by the consuls; after 312 B.C. that right was given to the censors. Most senators were former consuls, which meant that they were men of great wealth and experience—the leading citizens of Rome. Few consuls dared to ignore their advice, and the quaestors, who were mostly young men ambitious for higher office, followed them without hesitation. Because the quaestors administered public expenditures, this gave the Senate *de facto* control over finance.

The Senate was also responsible for provincial affairs, including the distribution of newly acquired public lands and of income derived from provincial sources. This enormous source of patronage supplemented the vast resources already available to the rich and powerful. Whether patrician or plebeian, the senators were all *nobiles* and patrons who could count on the support of clients in the assemblies and at every level of the administration. They could therefore influence legislation

eas for years at a time. In 325 B.C., the office of *proconsul* was created by extending a consul's field command for the duration of the campaign even though his term as consul had expired. This institution, even more than the dictatorship, became a threat to the survival of the republic in later years, for it allowed the proconsul to develop an independent geographic and military base.

◈ DOCUMENT 4.5 ◈

The Roman Constitution

Polybius (c. 200–c. 118 B.C.) was a Greek who wrote the history of Rome's wars with Carthage and Macedon. He was also fascinated by the Roman system of government. The following is an excerpt from The Historics *describing it as a mixed constitution with monarchic, aristocratic, and democratic elements.*

The consuls, before leading out the legions, remain in Rome and are supreme masters of the administration. All other magistrates, except the Tribunes, are under them and take their orders. They introduce foreign ambassadors to the Senate; bring matters requiring deliberation before it; and see to the execution of its decrees. If, again, there are any matters of state which require the authorization of the people, it is their business to see to them, to summon the popular meetings, to bring the proposals before them, and to carry out the decrees of the majority. . . .

The Senate has control of the treasury and regulates receipts and disbursements alike. . . . Similarly, all crimes committed in Italy requiring a public investigation such as treason, conspiracy, poisoning, or willful murder, are in the hands of the Senate. Besides, if any individual or state among the Italian allies requires a controversy to be settled, a penalty to be assessed, help or protection to be afforded,—all this is the province of the Senate. Or again, outside Italy, if it is necessary to send an embassy to reconcile warring communities, or to remind them of their duty, or sometimes to impose requisitions upon them, or to receive their submission, or finally to proclaim war upon them, this too is the business of the Senate.

After this, one would naturally be inclined to ask what part is left for the people. . . . Again, it is the people who bestow offices upon the deserving, which are the most honorable rewards of virtue. It also has the absolute power of passing laws; and, most important of all, it is the people who deliberate on the question of peace and war.

Polybius. "The Histories." In *The Histories of Polybius,* vol. 1, trans. Evelyn S. Shuckburgh. London: Macmillan, 1889.

in a dozen ways and affect its implementation by the magistrates when it passed.

The power of such networks was augmented by their tendency to combine within the Senate. There were no political parties as such, but the senators grouped themselves into factions or cliques associated with five great historic clans—the Fabii, Claudii, Cornelii, Aemelii, and the Valerii. At this level, cohesion was maintained in large part through friendship or agreement on policy. Able men of relatively humble parentage might also attach themselves to a senatorial clan and be carried by this informal sort of clientage to the highest levels of the state. In many ways, the organization of senatorial cliques mirrored that of society as a whole.

Factions of this sort could wield enormous power at every level of society. When they could agree on a policy, which was not unusual because they all came from the same social and economic group, their combined influence was overwhelming. The Senate's constitutional role as a mere advisory body was therefore an illusion. By controlling the informal mechanisms through which business was done, the Senate remained the heart of the Roman state.

◈

The Wars with Carthage

The new constitutional order was put to the test in less than a generation. In 264 B.C. Rome embarked upon a mortal struggle with Carthage that threatened its existence and ended only after more than a century of bitter conflict (see document 4.6). The former Phoenician colony had become the dominant naval power in the western Mediterranean. Like their ancestors, the Carthaginians were great merchants and colonizers, but unlike them, they gradually assumed direct control of the colonies they had planted in western Sicily, Spain, Sardinia, Corsica, and the Balearic islands. Theirs was a true empire, financed by trade with three continents and defended by a magnificent fleet. Because Rome was still an agrarian state with few commercial interests, the Carthaginians did not regard it as a threat. For centuries the two powers had enjoyed a cordial if somewhat distant relationship.

The conflict known as the First Punic War (*punic* is the adjectival form of the Roman word for Phoenician) started in Sicily. A nest of pirates and mercenaries, the Mamertines, had established themselves at Messana

❖ DOCUMENT 4.6 ❖

Polybius: Rome Compared with Carthage

This comparison of the rivals Rome and Carthage is conditioned by the author's suspicion of democracy, but it remains a useful measure of their strengths and weaknesses.

The constitution of Carthage seems to me to have been originally well contrived as regards its most distinctive points. For there were kings [sic] [the chief officials were annually elected *shofetim*, or judges] and the house of elders was an aristocratic force, and the people were supreme in matters appropriate to them, the entire frame of the state much resembling that of Rome or Sparta. But at the time when they entered on the Hannabalic War, the Carthaginian constitution had degenerated, and that of Rome was better. . . . [T]he multitude of Carthage had already acquired the chief voice in deliberations; while at Rome the senate still retained this, as in the one case the masses deliberated and in the other the most eminent men, the Roman decisions on public affairs were superior. . . .

But to pass to differences of detail . . . the Carthaginians are naturally superior at sea, both in efficiency and equipment, because seamanship has long been their natural craft, and they busy themselves with the sea more than any other people; but as regards infantry services, the Romans are much more efficient. They indeed devote their whole energies to this matter, whereas the Carthaginians wholly neglect their infantry, though they do pay some slight attention to their cavalry. The reason for this is that the troops they employ are foreign and mercenary, whereas those of the Romans are natives of the soil and citizens. So that in this respect also we must pronounce the political system of Rome to be superior to that of Carthage, the Carthaginians continuing to depend for the maintenance of their freedom on the courage of a mercenary force but the Romans on their own valor and that of their allies.

Adapted from Polybius, Histories, books 4: 2–3, trans. W. R. Paton. Loeb Classical Library. Cambridge, MA: Harvard University Press, 1960–1968.

(Messina), which controls the strait between Sicily and the Italian mainland. The Syracusans sent an army to root them out, whereupon one faction among the Mamertines appealed to Carthage, the traditional enemy of the Sicilian Greeks. When the Carthaginians gained control of the city, the other faction appealed to Rome. After long debate, the Senate agreed to help. The majority apparently felt that, if Carthage conquered Sicily, it could threaten the basis of Roman power in the south. No real evidence existed of Carthaginian interest in the mainland, however.

The resulting war was a long, drawn-out affair in which the Romans tried to besiege the Carthaginian towns in western Sicily. Though the Roman army won consistently in the field, it could do nothing to prevent the Carthaginians from bringing in supplies by sea. The Romans soon realized that only seapower could defeat Carthage and, for the first time in their history, constructed a navy (see illustration 4.5). After some remarkable victories and one catastrophic defeat, they destroyed the main Carthaginian fleet in an epic battle off Drepanum (Trapani) in March 241 B.C. Knowing that it could no longer hold Sicily, Carthage sued for peace.

Rome was now a major naval power and the ruler of Sicily, but peace did not last, for the attitude of Rome's political elite was changing. After the First Punic War, Rome's intentions became more openly aggressive and expansionist when the possibility of achieving vast wealth through conquest began to dawn on even the most honorable of men.

Sicily became the first Roman province. Its people were granted neither citizenship nor allied status. Roman governors exercised full powers unlimited by local custom—or by interference from the capital. They raised taxes to ruinous levels and distributed large tracts of land to wealthy Romans who worked them with slaves captured in the war. When Carthage's army, composed largely of mercenaries, rebelled in 238 B.C., the Romans took advantage of the situation and annexed the islands of Corsica and Sardinia. The Carthaginians saw that Roman imperialism had to be stopped.

Fortunately for Carthage, Rome was distracted for some years by a new war with the Gauls. Hamilcar Barca, a prominent Carthaginian who had waged guerrilla warfare against the Roman army in Sicily, used this respite to consolidate the Carthaginian hold on Spain. The Spanish interior was inhabited by a variety of Celtiberian tribes whose common characteristics included an aptitude for war. Hamilcar and his son-in-law

Ilustration 4.5

 A Roman Warship of the Late Republic. The wars with Carthage forced the Romans to become a maritime power for the first time in their history. This segment of a frieze in the Vatican Museum shows troops disembarking from a galley of the type used during the Punic Wars.

and successor, Hasdrubal, bound them to Carthage by force or negotiation, creating in the process the nucleus of a formidable army. The Second Punic War (218–202 B.C.) grew out of Roman attempts to interfere with this process and nearly ended in the destruction of Rome. Rome demanded a treaty limiting Carthaginian expansion to the region south of the river Ebro but then formed an alliance with Saguntum, a city within the Carthaginian sphere of influence. The new Carthaginian commander, Hamilcar's son Hannibal (247–c. 183 B.C.), had long dreamed of avenging his country's defeat in the First Punic War. Knowing that the Romans would retaliate, he took Saguntum by siege. Then, while the Romans raised an army to invade Spain, he took the war to Italy, threatening Rome and forcing the Romans to divide their forces.

With his Spanish army, his African mercenaries, and a famous contingent of war elephants, Hannibal crossed the Alps and allied himself with the Gauls, whose hatred for Rome had in no way diminished. He knew that Rome was too large and well fortified to be conquered, but he hoped by a show of force to disengage the Italian allies from their allegiance. In spite of tireless diplomacy and exquisite care for the lives and property of the Italians, this effort was largely a failure.

Success in battle was easier to achieve. Hannibal defeated the Romans on the banks of the river Trebbia and then crossed the Appenines to defeat them again at Lake Trasimeno. The Romans adopted a mobile defense under the leadership of the dictator Quintus Fabius Maximus (known as Cunctator, or the delayer). Realizing that he could not defeat the Carthaginians in the

field, Fabius drew them into southern Italy, maintaining contact with the enemy but avoiding a battle. Many Romans felt that this strategy was for cowards, but when the successors of Fabius reversed his policies and sought a battle at Cannae in 216 B.C., the Roman legions were virtually annihilated. Hannibal had uncovered the tactical weakness of the Roman legions: They were trained only to move forward and were therefore vulnerable to cavalry attacks from the sides and rear. His Spanish and African infantry fell back before the Roman assault but did not break; his Carthaginian cavalry enveloped the Romans, leaving them surrounded. As many as forty-eight thousand were slain on the spot.

Cannae was the worst defeat in the history of the Roman republic and one of the great military disasters of all time. It led to the defection of Capua, the largest city in Campania, and indirectly to a revolt in Syracuse that threatened Roman control over Sicily. The Romans were forced to besiege both cities while reverting to Fabian tactics in Apulia where Hannibal remained at large. Rome was approaching the end of its agricultural and financial resources. Nearly 200,000 men were under arms in Spain, Italy, and Sicily. Italian agriculture had been devastated by the campaigns, and Rome was increasingly dependent upon imports of grain from Sicily and Sardinia. The Carthaginians, who understood the economic dimensions of war better than most, attacked the latter in 215 B.C. while forming an alliance with Philip V of Macedon, who harassed Rome's allies on the eastern shore of the Adriatic. Rome was engaged on no fewer than five fronts.

The turning point came in 207 B.C. when Hannibal's younger brother, who was in command of the Carthaginian garrisons in Spain, decided to reinforce him. A second Carthaginian army crossed the Alps, but the Romans, who had remedied the tactical deficiencies that had plagued them at Cannae, destroyed it before it could join forces with Hannibal. Hannibal's brother was killed, leaving Spain helpless in the face of a new Roman offensive. The Roman commander Publius Cornelius Scipio (236–c. 183 B.C.) was not yet twenty-five years old when he assumed the proconsulship, but he proved to be Hannibal's equal and the greatest Roman general of the age. By the end of 206 B.C. he had driven the Carthaginians from Spain (see illustration 4.6).

The loss of Spain meant that Carthage was deprived of its chief source of wealth and manpower. In 204 B.C. Scipio landed in Africa with a powerful army. Hannibal was recalled from Italy, and in 202 B.C. he fought his last battle against the Romans at Zama. Hannibal's North African allies deserted him, and Scipio won the title Africanus by defeating Hannibal with tactics similar to those used by Hannibal at Cannae. With their army destroyed, the Carthaginians agreed to peace terms that included the surrender of Spain and the islands and the dismantling of their war fleet. Rome was the undisputed master of the western Mediterranean.

The Establishment of Roman Hegemony

Rome's victory over Carthage had been in doubt almost until the end. It was purchased with enormous expenditures of wealth and manpower. The ink on the treaty had scarcely dried when the Senate called for yet another war, this time in Greece. The motives for Roman intervention in that troubled region are unclear. The power of Macedon had waned during the third century B.C., and Greek politics was dominated by two loose and turbulent federations: the more aggressive Aetolian League in central Greece, and the Achaean League in the south. The result was constant warfare. This suited the purposes of three neighboring states with vested interests in the area. Rhodes, a commercial center with a fine navy, and Pergamum, a growing kingdom in western Asia Minor, feared the revival of Macedonian power and saw Rome as a potential ally. The third state, Ptolemaic Egypt, had since its founding attempted to undermine both Macedon and the Seleucid kingdom in Syria (see chapter 3). By 202 B.C. the balance of power among the three Hellenistic monarchies had been upset

Illustration 4.6

Scipio Africanus. The Roman commander who defeated the Carthaginians was also the head of the aristocratic Scipio clan and a leading advocate of Greek culture. This bust from Herculaneum was carved after his death and is thought to be an accurate likeness.

by the accession of a child to the throne of the Ptolemies. Freed from the restraining influence of Egypt, Philip V of Macedon (238–179 B.C.) hoped to regain control over Greece and made common cause with the Seleucid monarch Antiochus III. Antiochus was not interested in Europe, seeking only to annex Palestine and those parts of Asia Minor that were under Egyptian rule. Though the situation was unstable, it did not appear to endanger Rome.

Many senators pretended to feel otherwise. On the eve of the Second Punic War, Rome had sent a naval expedition to suppress piracy along the eastern shore of the Adriatic. Philip V felt threatened by the navy's presence and, in the dark days after the battle of Cannae, declared war against Rome in alliance with Carthage. His action had little effect on the outcome of the war, but it was remembered. Many prominent Romans had grown enamored of Greek culture. Rome was still in many ways a crude place. It had yet to develop a literature of its own, and wealthy families relied upon Greek tutors to educate their sons. Some of these boys, including Scipio Africanus and most of his extended family, grew up to become ardent Grecophiles. Even hard-bitten traditionalists such as Cato spoke Greek and were familiar with Greek literature. The appeals of Rhodes and other Greek communities for protection against Philip therefore fell upon sympathetic ears.

In the war that followed, seapower gave Rome a decisive advantage, while the Roman maniples outmaneuvered the Macedonian phalanx at the battle of Cynoscephalae (197 B.C.). Philip was forced to retreat within his borders. He became a staunch ally of Rome and for the remainder of his reign concentrated on rebuilding the shattered Macedonian economy. The Greek leagues were left intact.

The Romans then turned their attention to Antiochus III. The Seleucid monarch had by this time achieved his goals in Palestine and Asia Minor. Egged on by Hannibal, who had taken refuge at his court, and by the Aetolian League, which had turned against Rome as soon as it was delivered from Philip, he took advantage of Macedonian weakness to cross the Hellespont and annex Thrace. This time, the Senate was less eager for war. Efforts to remove Antiochus from Europe by negotiation failed. He was routed in 191 B.C. at the historic site of Thermopylae by a Roman force under Cato. In the winter of 190–189 B.C. a second Roman army marched into Asia to defeat him again near Sardis. Antiochus abandoned all thought of Europe and surrendered most of his lands in Asia Minor to Rome's ally, Pergamon. The Romans kept nothing, but in 133 B.C. the childless Attalus III of Pergamum bequeathed the entire kingdom to Rome in his will.

The defeat of the two Hellenistic kingdoms proved that Rome was the dominant power in the Mediterranean world. Greece, meanwhile, remained unstable. Rome was forced to intervene repeatedly in Greek affairs, and with each new intervention, the Senate's impatience grew. Two main factions emerged. The Grecophile Scipios and their allies still hoped to achieve a settlement based on friendship with the Greek leagues. Their views have been preserved by Polybius (c. 200–c. 118 B.C.), an Achaean Greek who wrote the history of Rome's wars in Greece and with

Illustration 4.7

Marcus Porcius Cato. This bust, like that of Scipio Africanus, was carved after its subject's death. It captures the power of the great orator's personality and agrees with literary descriptions of his appearance. As a defender of traditional Roman values, Cato was the mortal enemy of the hellenizing Scipios and ultimately triumphed over them in the Senate. He failed, however, in his efforts to restrict the spread of Greek ideas.

Carthage and who was an important example of Greek influence on Roman thinking. The opposing faction was headed by Cato (see illustration 4.7), who was immune to any form of sentimentality and wanted an end to adventures in the east. He thought that contact with Greeks was corroding the traditional Roman values that he had extolled in his writings and, though he had no desire to annex Greek territory, was prepared to end their mischief-making by any means possible.

Cato's views gradually prevailed. Philip V's son, Perseus, allowed Pergamum to maneuver him into another disastrous war with Rome. The Romans defeated him at Pydna in 168 B.C. and divided Macedon into four parts, but their patience was wearing thin. They destroyed seventy towns in Epirus, which had supported Macedon, and sold 150,000 of its inhabitants into slavery. Troops were then sent to bolster the pro-Roman party in the Aetolian League, while one thousand hostages were taken from Achaea even though the Achaeans had supported Rome. One of them was Polybius, who used his exile to form a connection with the Scipios. The others were not so fortunate. Most were dispersed among the Italian provincial towns. Those who survived were returned in 151 B.C. after seventeen years in exile.

Meanwhile, a revolt had broken out in Macedonia under the leadership of a man who claimed to be Perseus's son. The Romans easily suppressed it and annexed Macedon as a Roman province, but the Achaeans, still angry over the hostage issue, decided to challenge Roman authority on several fronts. The response was devastating. In 146 B.C. the Achaean League suffered its last defeat on the battlefield. The Romans, thoroughly exasperated, destroyed the ancient city of Corinth in reprisal. They killed the men, enslaved the women and children, and carried away the city's priceless art treasures. They then abolished the Greek leagues and replaced democratic governments in several cities with oligarchies responsive to Rome. Years later the terms of settlement were loosened, but Greece remained a Roman protectorate with no independent policy of its own.

It is a measure of Rome's enormous power that, while annexing Macedon, defeating Antiochus, and reordering the affairs of Greece, the republic abandoned none of its ambitions in the west. Between 201 B.C. and 183 B.C. the Romans annexed Liguria, the area around modern Genoa, and settled their old score with the Gauls. The Gallic tribes south of the Po were defeated, and many fled beyond the Alps to be replaced by Italian colonists.

At the same time, the Romans embarked upon a bitter struggle for the Iberian Peninsula. After Carthage surrendered, Roman magistrates seized its Spanish colonies and extracted a fortune in tribute that came ultimately from mines in the interior. The towns, supported by a number of Celtiberian tribes, rebelled in 197 B.C., and Cato was sent to suppress them. Cato believed that "war supports itself." He insisted that his troops live off the country, and though modestly successful in military terms, his campaign of atrocity and confiscation ensured that the war would continue.

The Celtiberians resorted to guerrilla warfare. Other communities became involved, and it was not until 133 B.C. that Numantia, the last center of Span-

ish resistance, fell to the Romans after a lengthy siege. Scipio Aemilianus, the Roman commander and adopted grandson of Africanus, ordered it burned to the ground without waiting to consult the Senate. The siege of Numantia, like the war itself, had been conducted with unparalleled savagery on both sides. Whole tribes had been massacred even when they surrendered to the Romans on terms, but Spain, too, was now Roman territory.

Meanwhile, Carthage had been observing the terms of the peace treaty. Its military power and much of its wealth were gone, but the Roman faction headed by Cato wanted nothing less than the total destruction of its old rival. For years Cato had ended every speech in the Senate, regardless of the subject, by saying *"Ceterum censeo delendam esse Carthaginem"* ("Moreover, I think Carthage must be destroyed"). In 151 B.C. he and his followers saw their chance.

Since joining the Romans at the battle of Zama, the able and ambitious Masinissa, king of Numidia, had built a powerful North African state at Carthage's expense. When the Carthaginians tried to stop him, his Roman allies saw their action as a breach of the treaty. In a series of cunning diplomatic moves, the Romans demanded ever greater concessions, ending with a demand for the destruction of the city and the removal of its population. Surprisingly, the Carthaginians, who had been deprived of most of their weapons, refused. After a long and bitter siege, the city fell in 146 B.C. Carthage was destroyed as promised, and a furrow plowed through it that was then sown to salt to indicate that the land would never be occupied again.

By 133 B.C. Rome had acquired seven overseas provinces. Carthaginian territory was incorporated into the province of Africa and protected by an alliance with the Numidians. Spain, though technically a single province, had been divided in two by Scipio Africanus: Nearer Spain (*Hispania Citerior*), comprising the east coast from the Ebro valley to Cartagena, and Further Spain (*Hispania Ulterior*) to the south and west in what is now Andalusia. Macedon was protected by alliances with the Illyrians and by the utter dependency of the Greeks, while Sicily, Corsica, and Sardinia were islands in a sea commanded by the Roman fleet. Pergamum became the Roman province of Asia Minor.

The Romans had not planned to create a world empire and were at first unprepared to govern it. Their political institutions, though sophisticated, were those of a city-state. Financial structures remained primitive. The Senate would not extend ally status to the newly conquered regions and was at first reluctant to organize them into provinces or to maintain armies

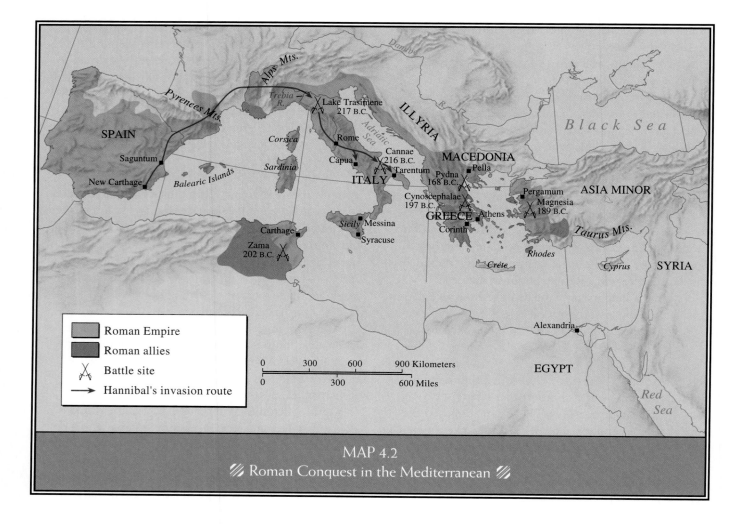

MAP 4.2
〰 Roman Conquest in the Mediterranean 〰

for their defense. Among other things, the senators feared that the creation of new magistrates and proconsuls might dilute their own membership and weaken their power as individuals.

Provincial charters varied widely. Different provinces were taxed at different rates and certain towns paid no taxes at all. In some places overtaxation caused widespread poverty, but whatever the rates, collection was almost always inefficient. Private contractors extracted cash, bullion, or agricultural commodities from taxpayers and kept a portion of the yield for themselves, a system that bred corruption and led to interminable complaints. The governors were at first admired for their honesty, but Roman virtue soon crumbled in the face of older, more cynical traditions. Bribes and extortion could make a magistrate rich beyond imagining. No imperial bureaucracy provided effective oversight and, for many, the temptation proved irresistible. Provincial government under the republic was not, in other words, as efficient or capable as it

would eventually become. It could be brutal and even extortionate, but for most of those who found themselves under Roman rule, it was probably no worse than the governments to which they had long been accustomed. The majority offered no resistance to the new order and in time accepted it as preferable to any conceivable alternative.

From humble beginnings, Rome had first conquered Italy and then an empire. In the mid-second century B.C. the Mediterranean world was politically united for the first time. Roman provinces stretched from the Atlantic to Asia Minor (see map 4.2), and those peoples who were not under Roman rule were Roman allies or dependents.

The Romans had not set out, like Alexander, to conquer new worlds, but neither had they acquired their empire in a fit of absentmindedness. They understood from the beginning that security depended upon controlling the activities of their neighbors. Gradually, "fear of the enemy," as Polybius put it, gave way to larger ambitions. Though hard evidence could come only from a transcript of Senate debates, Rome's elite seems to have adopted the goal of imposing order upon the world as they knew it. The Second Punic War was the turning point. After that narrow brush with catastrophe, a combination of greed and impatience led the Romans onward. But if the Senate was willing to shoulder new massive responsibilities, it refused to follow that willingness to its logical conclusion. Many years would pass before Rome learned to govern its new possessions effectively, and in the meantime, Rome had itself changed almost beyond recognition.

CHAPTER 5

SOCIAL, POLITICAL, AND ECONOMIC STRUCTURES OF IMPERIAL ROME

CHAPTER OUTLINE

The acquisition of an empire changed the basic fabric of Roman society and created tensions that could not be resolved by the existing political system. Civil strife produced by these tensions, and by the emergence of a professional army whose members had no stake in the preservation of traditional society, led in turn to the breakdown of republican institutions. Rival commanders struggled for control of the state until, in 31 B.C., Octavian, known as Augustus, emerged supreme and imposed a new system of government. Though he retained the outward forms of republicanism, Augustus was an autocrat. During the first century A.D. his successors gradually abandoned republican pretense and adopted the ceremonial trappings of the Hellenistic monarchies. The Roman world, governed by a quasi-divine emperor, was far larger than it had been under the republic and increasingly less "Roman."

The Transformation of Roman Society

Ordinary Romans gained little from the acquisition of an empire. Thousands found only an unmarked grave in some remote corner of Spain or the Balkans. Those who returned often discovered that their ancestral farms had been devastated by neglect or—after the Second Punic War—by the passage of armies. All faced a burden of wartime taxation that would have made economic survival difficult in any circumstances. The great senatorial families, meanwhile, profited enormously. Roman military commanders came almost exclusively from this class, and they took most of the loot from captured provinces. This included not only gold, silver, and commodities of every sort, but also tens of thousands of slaves. In addition, the Senate granted vast provincial estates to those whose leadership it regarded as outstanding.

The recipients of this new wealth invested much of it in Italy. Small farmers, impoverished by war and taxes, sold their plots to former officers who incorporated them into large, slave-worked plantations. Whenever possible, investors purchased land in different parts of the peninsula so that each property could be devoted to a specialized crop. This allowed owners to take maximum advantage of soil and climate while minimizing the risks of a bad harvest, for it was unlikely that every part of Italy would be hit simultaneously by drought or other catastrophes. Specialization also permitted economies of scale. Owners devoted careful thought to the optimum size for a vineyard, an olive plantation, or a ranch. Slaves may have been cheap in the aftermath of the wars, but feeding more of them than necessary was pointless.

Ideally, in addition to its cash crop, an estate produced just enough to support its labor force. Self-sufficiency reduced costs and was relatively easy to achieve, in part because slaves were no longer regarded as part of the family. In the past, most slaves had been Italian. Now they were foreign captives and therefore harder to fit into the fabric of Roman life. Conditions on some of the estates were appalling. In the Sicilian grain lands, slaves worked on chain gangs and were locked up at night. To be sold to the Spanish mines was a death sentence. Elsewhere, conditions were better, but even the most enlightened owners viewed slaves as an investment, and slave revolts were common (see document 5.1).

In this way wealthy families developed networks of specialized properties that brought in huge profits and insured them against risk through diversification (see illustration 5.1). Ordinary farmers could not compete. Their small plots were inherently inefficient, and they lacked the capital either to expand or to make improvements. If they tried to do so, they had to borrow from their wealthier neighbors, and though debt slavery had long been abolished, many lost their land through foreclosures. Others were forced out of business by unfair competition. Someone with a half-dozen great estates could easily sell below cost if by so doing he or she could drive out a competitor and pick up his land at distress-sale prices.

Citizens by the thousands gave up their land and migrated to the cities, but opportunities were limited. Imperialism had concentrated wealth in the hands of a few while doing little to increase the overall rate of economic activity. The rich developed habits of conspicuous consumption that horrified traditionalists such as Cato, but their most extravagant wants could be met by a handful of artisans, many of whom were skilled slaves

---

◈ DOCUMENT 5.1 ◈

A Slave Revolt in Sicily

The habitual mistreatment of slaves under the late republic provoked a series of terrifying slave revolts. The one described below by Diodorus of Sicily lasted from 134 to 131 B.C. and involved an army of more than seventy thousand slaves. Another great uprising occurred in Sicily in 104–100 B.C., and yet another in Italy under the gladiator Spartacus (73–71 B.C.) in which 100,000 slaves were said to have been killed.

The Servile War broke out from the following cause. The Sicilians, being grown very rich and elegant in their manner of living, bought up large numbers of slaves . . . and immediately branded them with marks on their bodies. Oppressed by the grinding toil and beatings, maltreated for the most part beyond all reason, the slaves could endure it no longer.

The whole revolt began in the following manner. There was a man in Enna named Damophilus, magnanimous in his wealth but arrogant in disposition. This man was exceedingly cruel to his slaves, and his wife Megallis strove to outdo her husband in torture and general inhumanity toward them. As a result, those who were thus cruelly abused were enraged like wild beasts and plotted together to rise in arms and kill their masters. They applied to Eunus [a slave from Syria who was also a well-known magician] and asked whether the gods would speed them in their design. Performing some of his usual mumbo-jumbo, he concluded that the gods granted it, and urged them to begin at once. Thereupon they forthwith collected 400 of their fellow slaves and, when the opportunity presented itself, they burst fully armed into the city of Enna with Eunus leading them and performing tricks with flames of fire for them. They stole into the houses and wrought great slaughter. They spared not even the suckling babes, but tore them from the breast and dashed them to the ground. It cannot be expressed with what wanton outrage they treated wives before the very eyes of their husbands. They were joined by a large throng of the slaves in the city, who first visited the extreme penalty upon their masters and then turned to murdering others.

Illustration 5.1

Plan of a Typical Villa. This villa at Boscoreale near Pompeii was the headquarters of a typical working estate. Wealthy Romans spread their financial risks by investing in several such properties during the later republic. Worked by slaves, this one produced wine. The existence of a threshing floor (*T*) indicates that it was more diversified in its products than some other farms. Though comfortable enough by the standards of the time, the primary emphasis is on efficiency and practicality.

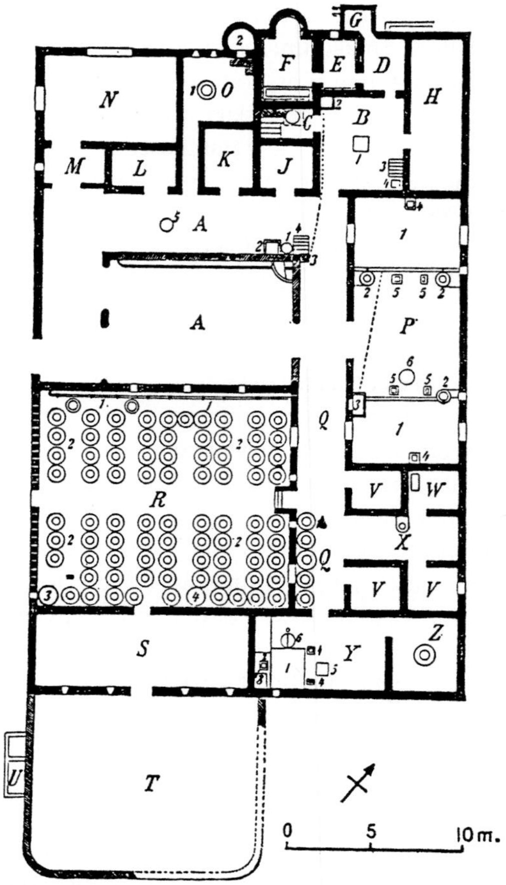

Villa no. 13 at Boscoreale. A, court: 1, 5, cistern curbs; 2, wash basin; 3, lead reservoir; 4, steps. B, kitchen: 1, hearth; 2, reservoir; 3, stairway; 4, entrance to cellar. C–G, bath complex. H, stable. J, tool room. K, L, sleeping rooms. M, anteroom. N, dining room. O, bakery: 1, mill; 2, oven. P, two wine presses: 1, foundations of the presses; 2, receptacles for the grape juice; 3, receptacle for the product of the second pressing; 4, holes for the standards of the press beams; 5, holes for the posts of the windlasses for raising and lowering the beams; 6, access pit to the windlass framework. Q, corridor: 1, wine vats. R, court for fermentation of wine: 1, channel; 2, fermentation vats; 3, lead kettle; 4, cistern curb. S, use unknown. T, threshing floor. U, cistern for water falling on the threshing floor. V, sleeping rooms. W, entrance to cellar. X, hand mill. Y, oil press: 1, foundations of the press; 2, hole for the standard of the press beam; 3, entrance to cellar; 4, holes for windlass posts; 5, access to windlass framework; 6, receptacle for oil. Z, olive-crusher

from the east. Slaves, whether in town or country, consumed little, and citizens who had been driven from the land consumed less. Most of the latter were destitute. After 213 B.C., senatorial factions began to distribute charity among them in return for votes.

Aside from the senatorial elite, only one other group appears to have benefited from the wars—the merchants, purveyors, and military contractors who organized the logisitics of imperial expansion. Most were men of humble origin, often manumitted slaves who used knowledge and connections gained from their former masters to win contracts. They amassed great wealth in shipbuilding, arms manufacture, and commodity speculation and made an effort to acquire estates because land remained the most secure and prestigious source of income. Others followed the lead of certain senators and invested their surplus capital in urban real estate—ramshackle five-story tenements built to house the growing masses of urban poor. In later years these people would be known as equestrians, a separate class with a political agenda of its own.

Roman society had changed beyond recognition in little more than a century. Though pockets of traditional life remained, most small independent farmers who were the backbone of the republic had been reduced to dependency. Production was largely in the hands of slaves, while a few families lived in luxury that seemed more oriental than Roman. The situation could lead only to civil strife.

Social Conflict: The Reforms of the Gracchi

In 133 B.C., the same year in which Numantia fell and Pergamum was ceded to Rome, a newly elected tribune, Tiberius Sempronius Gracchus, initiated reform legislation. A member of the aristocracy and a descendant of Scipio Africanus, he hoped to improve the condition of landless Romans by redistributing public lands acquired through conquest. Such properties were to have been allocated among the citizens as a whole, but families like his own often had seized them illegally through the use of political influence. His motives included both moral outrage and personal ambition; his most persuasive argument was practical. From the beginning of the republic, land ownership was a prerequisite for military service. An absolute decline in the number of free citizens caused by the wars, coupled with a loss of property by thousands of others, threatened the security of the state by shrinking its base of recruitment. Only by restoring land to Roman citizens could the legions be preserved.

A number of powerful senators agreed. The dislocations of the past century threatened to undermine recruitment as well as the moral fiber of society. Moreover, Tiberius tried to couch the proposal in terms acceptable to the landowners. Up to one thousand *iugera* (about six hundred acres) of land per family could be excluded from the distribution even if it had been taken illegally, and only Romans would receive the proceeds of the confiscations. This was not enough. Some senators balked at giving up land held by their families for three or four generations. They were backed by a tremendous outcry from the Italian allies. Wealthy Italians, too, had received public lands. They would be forced to surrender them, not to other Italians, but to Romans. To them, the reform was clearly discriminatory.

Faced with an uncertain outcome in the Senate, Tiberius decided to bypass it altogether. He went to the plebeian assembly, which rapidly authorized the necessary legislation. When another tribune vetoed the bill, he convinced the plebeians to vote the man out of office. Ignoring the Senate was bad politics, but deposing a tribune was unconstitutional. Then, to make matters worse, Tiberius left himself open to charges of corruption by entrusting the redistribution of lands to a committee composed of himself, his brother Gaius, and his father-in-law.

The Senate began to close ranks against Tiberius. While allowing the committee to proceed with its work, the senators refused to appropriate money for its support. This was critical, because land reform proved more difficult than Tiberius had expected. Establishing clear title to many public lands was nearly impossible, and virtually every decision aroused protest. Desperate for funds, he asked that revenues from the newly acquired kingdom of Pergamum be devoted to the task. The Senate saw this as an assault on its traditional dominance in the areas of finance and provincial policy. In its view, Tiberius and his reforms had become a threat to the constitution.

Knowing that, if he left the tribuneship, he would lose judicial immunity and be charged with treason by his enemies, Tiberius decided to run for a second term.

This, too, was unprecedented, if not unconstitutional. A group of senators claimed that he was trying to establish himself as a tyrant and instigated riots in which they and their clients killed Tiberius and three hundred of his followers. It was the first outbreak of civil violence in the history of the Roman republic, but it would not be the last. The divisions in Roman society were too great to be resolved without constitutional change, and ambitious politicians had learned from Tiberius Gracchus that they could ride to power on the shoulders of the multitude. Such people were called *populares*. Their opponents, who supported the traditional role of the Senate, were known as *optimates*.

Among the *populares* was Gaius Gracchus, the younger brother of Tiberius. When elected tribune in 123 B.C. he prepared to implement reforms more far-reaching than those favored by his brother (see document 5.2). Gaius realized that the agrarian problem was only one of many created by the transformation of Roman society. First he reenacted his brother's agrarian law, which had been repealed in 129 B.C. Then, knowing that not everyone could receive land in Italy, he guaranteed annual grain rations to every poor Roman at a fixed price and tried to set up overseas colonies for those willing to emigrate in return for land. The first of the new settlements was to be established on the site of Carthage.

To prevent the reversal of these policies by the Senate, he allied himself with the equestrians to weaken its power. The assemblies were given the sole right to establish capital courts, and he replaced senators with equestrians as jurors in cases of extortion. A more important attack on senatorial prerogatives came in the area of provincial administration. The Senate had for years influenced the behavior of consuls by waiting until after their election to designate which provinces they would control. By forcing them to make their appointments before the election, Gaius deprived the senators of an important source of political leverage. From the senatorial point of view this was even worse than another new policy by which he allowed syndicates of rich equestrians or *publicani* (the biblical publicans) to bid at auction for the right to collect provincial taxes. In later years this practice became a fertile source of corruption.

The issue of whether a tribune could succeed himself had apparently been resolved since Tiberius Gracchus's death, and Gaius was reelected tribune in 122 B.C. Having addressed the grievances of the poor and satisfied the equestrians in his first term, he turned to the problem of the Italian allies, who remained angry over agrarian reform and a host of other slights. His

◆ DOCUMENT 5.2 ◆

The Reform Program of Gaius Gracchus

Here Plutarch summarizes Gaius Gracchus's plan for reforming Roman society as presented in 123–121 B.C. It is easy to see why the senators felt that he must be destroyed.

Of the laws which he now proposed with the object of gratifying the people and destroying the power of the senate, the first concerned public lands, which were to be divided among the poor citizens; another provided that the common soldiers should be clothed at public expense without any reduction in pay, and that no one under seventeen years of age should be conscripted for military service; another concerned the allies, giving the Italians equal suffrage rights with the citizens of Rome; a fourth related to grain, lowering the market price for the poor; a fifth, dealing with the courts of justice, was the greatest blow to the power of the senators, for hitherto they alone could sit on the juries, and they were therefore much dreaded by the plebs and *equites*. But Gaius joined 300 citizens of equestrian rank with the senators, who were also 300 in number, and made jury service the common prerogative of the 600. . . . When the people not only ratified this law but gave him power to select those of the *equites* who were to serve as jurors, he was invested with almost kingly power, and even the senate submitted to receiving his counsel. . . .

He also proposed measures for sending out colonies, for constructing roads, and for building public granaries. He himself undertook the management and superintendence of these works and was never too busy to attend to the execution of all these different and great undertakings.

for reelection in 121 B.C. When the assembly began to repeal its earlier reforms, rioting began. Gaius and a band of followers fortified themselves on the Aventine hill. The Senate declared martial law for the first time in its history, and the reformers were slaughtered. The violence was committed by Roman troops, not by members of the senatorial opposition and their clients.

The Fall of the Republic

The Gracchi had tried to address Rome's fundamental problems and failed. Though the Senate's view of the constitution triumphed, at least for the moment, that failure led ultimately to the collapse of the republic. Equestrians and Italian allies felt excluded from their rightful place in the political system, and far too many citizens remained landless and dependent upon what amounted to welfare. The army, deprived of an adequate number of recruits, grew steadily weaker. Although not the time for foreign adventures, in 111 B.C. the Senate reluctantly declared war on Numidia. The African kingdom had been engulfed by a succession struggle during which the Romans backed the losing candidate. The winner, Jugurtha, celebrated his victory by murdering a number of Roman businessmen. Because most of the victims were equestrians, a tremendous outcry arose in the plebeian assembly, and the Senate was forced to give way.

For nearly four years the war went badly. The plebeian assembly and its equestrian allies knew that the senators disliked the war and began to suspect that some of them were taking Numidian bribes. In 107 B.C. they elected Gaius Marius consul. Like Cato before him, Marius (c. 157–86 B.C.) was a "new man" who came to politics with the support of an old senatorial family. To gain the votes of the assembly, he turned against his patrons. If his ethics were questionable, his military abilities were not. He defeated Jugurtha without capturing him and then turned his attention to the north where two Germanic tribes, the Cimbri and the Teutones, threatened the Roman settlements in Gaul. His lieutenant, the quaestor Lucius Cornelius Sulla (138–78 B.C.), was left to track down the Numidian and destroy him in a hard-fought guerrilla campaign that made his reputation and infuriated Marius, who thought that the younger man had taken too much credit for the victory.

War on two fronts when social dislocation had reduced the pool of eligible recruits made keeping the legions up to strength virtually impossible. Marius felt that he had no choice but to reform the army by admit-

proposal, though not original, was straightforward: Admit them to Roman citizenship. Had this been done, Rome might have been spared a bloody war, but the plebeian assembly had no desire to share its privileges. A conservative reaction set in, and Gaius was defeated ting volunteers even if they owned no land. Recruits were to be paid in cash as they had always been. Marius also promised them a plot of land in Gaul or Africa when they retired.

To thousands of slum dwellers and landless peasants, the Marian reforms offered an escape from grinding poverty, but the recruitment of proletarians created a new danger for the state. Lacking property of their own, the men became wholly dependent upon their commander for pay and, more important, for the security of their old age. Though land and money came ultimately from the Senate, neither could be obtained without the influence of the consul or proconsul who requested them. The troops, in short, became the clients of their general who could use military force to threaten the government. Rome was at the mercy of its own armies.

The implications of this change became evident after the Italian wars of 90–88 B.C. For decades the Italian allies had sought Roman citizenship to no avail (see table 5.1). Their patience exhausted, they abandoned Rome and decided to form an independent confederation. Belatedly, the Romans extended citizenship to all who returned to their allegiance, but two years of fighting were required to reach a final settlement.

Sulla, whose reputation as a soldier had grown greater during the Italian wars, was elected consul in 88 B.C. with the support of the Senate. His services were needed in the east, where Mithradates, King of Pontus, had annexed parts of Asia Minor and invaded Greece. The aged Marius came out of retirement and convinced the plebeian assembly to appoint him commander instead. His action, based in part on personal resentment of Sulla, provoked a lengthy crisis. Sulla, ostensibly to defend the Senate, marched on Rome and drove out Marius. When Sulla left for Asia, Marius returned with his own army and conducted a bloody purge of his opponent's senatorial friends. Finally, in 83 B.C. Sulla returned and established a dictatorship. To do so he had to conclude a compromise peace with Mithradates and fight a civil war on Italian soil against the followers of Marius, who had died of a stroke three years before.

Sulla's dictatorship was unlike any that had yet been declared. It lasted four years and was intended to reform the state from within, not to protect the state from outside enemies. To do this, Sulla launched a reign of terror by proscribing or outlawing his opponents, his personal enemies, and the rich, whose only crime was that their property was needed to pay his troops. He then passed a series of laws intended to strengthen senatorial power and improve the criminal justice system. Some of these changes survived his re-

❈ TABLE 5.1 ❈

Citizenship in the Roman Republic, 264–70 B.C.

These census estimates refer only to adult male citizens and are taken primarily from Livy. The lower figure for 208 B.C. seems to reflect the defection of Capua and other allies after the defeat at Cannae as well as war losses. The major increases after 204 B.C. and 115 B.C. reflect the expansion of citizenship rather than a change in underlying demographics.

Year	Census total	Year	Census total
264 B.C.	292,234	147 B.C.	322,000
251 B.C.	297,797	142 B.C.	328,442
246 B.C.	241,212	136 B.C.	317,933
240 B.C.	260,000	131 B.C.	318,823
233 B.C.	270,713	125 B.C.	394,736
208 B.C.	137,108	115 B.C.	394,436
204 B.C.	214,000	86 B.C.	463,000
154 B.C.	324,000	70 B.C.	910,000

Source: Data from Tenney Frank, ed., *An Economic Survey of Ancient Rome,* vol. 1 (New York, N.Y.: Pageant Books, 1959), pp. 56, 216–17.

tirement in 79 B.C. Although Sulla was in theory a conservative who sought only to preserve the traditional system, his career marked the end of constitutional government. For almost a decade Roman soldiers had been used repeatedly against Roman citizens and against each other. Power now rested with the legions and those who commmanded them, not with the Senate or the assemblies.

Sulla's departure created a political vacuum. Generals, including his former lieutenants Pompey and Crassus, vied for preeminence using the wealth and power generated by proconsular commands. Such commands proliferated mainly because the perception of disorder encouraged Rome's enemies. Roman politicians welcomed the commands because they wanted armies of their own as protection against their domestic rivals. Spain rebelled under a former ally of Marius and had to be suppressed by Pompey. At the same time, Italy was threatened by a massive slave rebellion led by Spartacus, a Thracian gladiator. A direct result of the brutality and greed of the slaveowners, it was put down with great difficulty by Crassus, who crucified six thousand of the rebels along the Appian Way between Rome and

Capua. To the east, Mithradates of Pontus resumed his aggression, while in the Mediterranean as a whole, widespread piracy threatened trade and communications throughout the empire.

The Senate responded to each crisis by granting extraordinary appointments, often in violation of the constitution, and then refusing full honors to the victors when they returned. The Senate was especially stingy in denying them the great ceremonial processions known as triumphs. Grants to veterans were also delayed. The senators thought that in this way they could weaken the authority of successful commanders, but their policy served only to irritate them. Although Pompey and Crassus feared and disliked each other, in 60 B.C. they made common cause with another popular politician, Gaius Julius Caesar (100–44 B.C.), to dominate the elections and create a kind of governing committee known as the First Triumvirate.

Pompey and Crassus had disbanded their legions when they returned to Rome. They either were loyal to republican institutions or failed to understand that Marius and Sulla had changed the political rules. Caesar's vision was clearer. He knew that talent alone was useless without an army, and he used the power of the triumvirate to grant him proconsular authority over Cisalpine Gaul. From 58 to 50 B.C. he conquered Gaul, an area roughly equivalent to modern France, and raided Britain. A master of public relations, he offered a selective account of these exploits in the *Commentaries,* a classic that remains the first book read by most students of Latin.

The Gallic campaign brought Caesar enormous wealth, an army of hardened veterans, and a reputation. The other triumvirs were less fortunate. Crassus died in 53 B.C. while fighting in Asia. At Rome, an inactive Pompey grew fearful of Caesar's ambitions, and the Senate, sharing his distrust, ordered Caesar to return home as a private citizen. Knowing that to do so would end his career and perhaps his life, Caesar crossed the Rubicon, the small river that divided Cisalpine Gaul from Italy, and marched on Rome in 49 B.C.

The civil war that followed lasted three years. Because legions loyal to either Pompey or Caesar could be found from Spain to Syria, it involved almost every part of the empire. Pompey was murdered at Alexandria in 48 B.C., but his friends continued the struggle until 46 B.C. when Caesar returned to Rome in triumph as sole consul. Caesar's power, like Sulla's before him, was based on control of a professional army whose ties to the political order had been broken by the Marian reforms. Unlike Sulla, Caesar did not in-

tend to retire. Though Caesar's rule was destined to be brief, the Roman republic had fallen, never to be revived.

The Rise of Augustus and the Augustan Principate

Caesar's rule was generally benign and devoted to reform, including the proclamation of a new calendar that remained standard in Europe until the sixteenth century, but it was autocratic and clearly unconstitutional. On the ides of March (March 15) in 44 B.C. he was assassinated as he entered the Senate house. The conspiracy involved sixty senators under the leadership of G. Cassius Longinus and Marcus Junius Brutus, who believed that his death would restore the powers of the senatorial class. The murder led to thirteen more years of war and the establishment of what amounted to an autocratic state. The violent and dramatic events of this period have fired the imagination of writers and artists down to the present day and have been analyzed by a host of political theorists.

Caesar's heirs were his close associate Marcus Antonius (Mark Antony) and his grandnephew Gaius Octavius (63 B.C.–A.D. 14), then a boy of eighteen. Antony, in a famous funeral oration, turned the mob against Caesar's assassins and forced them to flee the city. Those senators who were not assassins but who favored the restoration of the republic feared that Antony, or Antony in combination with Octavius, would seize control of the state. Their leader was Marcus Tullius Cicero (106–43 B.C.), the brilliant lawyer, writer, and philosopher whose works are among the finest monuments of Latin literature. Cicero's political career had been blocked only by his failure to achieve military command. He was the finest orator of the age. He easily persuaded the Senate that Antony was unprincipled and a potential tyrant and that a consular army should be sent against him. He then tried to drive a wedge between Octavius and Antony, who resented that most of Caesar's enormous wealth had been left to the younger man.

Caesar's heirs disliked one another, but the policy misfired. When the consuls of 43 B.C. died fighting against Antony in Cisalpine Gaul, the Senate, on Cicero's advice, gave Octavius command of the armies but refused him the consulship because he was still only nineteen years old. The future Augustus, who now called himself Julius Caesar Octavianus, went to Rome with his legions and took the office by force.

Octavian, though young, understood the need for overwhelming military power. He made peace with those who commanded the remaining legions—Antony and a former Caesarian governor named Lepidus—and together they formed the Second Triumvirate. To consolidate their position and, above all to pay their legions, they launched a proscription that led to the death of more than three hundred senators, including Cicero, and two thousand equestrians who had, by definition, no part in politics. Octavian then turned his army against Brutus, who had taken refuge in Macedon, while Antony defeated Cassius in Syria. In the course of these actions, both of Caesar's assassins were killed in battle.

Octavian and Antony were the dominant figures of the triumvirate. With the removal of Lepidus in 36 B.C., they divided the empire between them. Octavian took the west; Antony, the east. Realizing that conflict with Octavian was inevitable, Antony turned for assistance to the Egyptian queen Cleopatra VII (69–30 B.C.). A woman of great charm and intelligence, Cleopatra was determined not only to revive the power of the Ptolemies, but also to play a part in Roman affairs (see illustration 5.2). To that end she had become Julius Caesar's mistress and traveled to Rome where she bore him a son. When Caesar died, she returned to Alexandria and arranged for the murder of her brother, who was also her husband and coruler according to the Egyptian custom. Now sole ruler of Egypt, she hoped that through Antony she could preserve the empire of the Ptolemies for herself and her children.

For his part, Antony needed the immense wealth of the Ptolemies to defeat Octavian. The alliance of Antony and Cleopatra resulted in the birth of twins as well as in a formidable conjunction of military and financial power. Octavian, in a skillful propaganda campaign, portrayed himself as the champion of Rome and the west against the decadent east as symbolized by the Egyptian queen. In 31 B.C. he defeated Antony and Cleopatra at the naval battle of Actium and followed them to Alexandria where, in the summer of A.D. 30, they both committed suicide.

Octavian became the undisputed ruler of the western world. With characteristic subtlety, he asked only that he be called *princeps*, or first citizen, and moved over the next seven years to consolidate his influence in ways that would not offend the Senate or other traditionalists. He treated the senators with courtesy, expanding their numbers and increasing their legislative power, but his much vaunted partnership with the Senate was a sham. The real basis of his power was proconsular authority over Spain, Gaul, and Syria, the border provinces that contained a majority of the legions. After 23 B.C. his proconsular authority was extended to Rome, and he was awarded the powers of a tribune, to

Illustration 5.2

⫸ **Portrait Bust of Cleopatra.** Cleopatra, the last of the Ptolemaic dynasty, failed to preserve Egypt's independence from Rome. Her defeat at Actium in 31 B.C. and subsequent suicide paved the way for Octavian's triumph.

be renewed annually for the remainder of his life. This enabled him to participate in the assemblies and gave him veto power over their legislation. As tribune, his person was also sacrosanct, though the Senate, in 27 B.C., had already granted him the semidivine title Augustus (see illustration 5.3). After 23 B.C. he left consular authority to others, accepting the office only on occasion.

In person, the new Augustus tried to appear modest and unassuming (see document 5.3). As an administrator, he was without equal. By controlling the electoral apparatus, Augustus made certain that magistracies went to men of ability with little regard for their origins. Provincial administration, a disgrace under the later republic, was greatly improved. Wherever possi-

Illustration 5.3

Augustus as Princeps. An idealized but recognizable statue of Augustus from Prima Porta.

◈ DOCUMENT 5.3 ◈

Suetonius Describes the Political Style of Augustus

The following passage from Lives of the Caesars *by Suetonius (c. 69–after 122) describes what might be called the political style of Augustus. It helps to explain how he could rule the empire without arousing significant opposition.*

He always shrank from the title *dominus* ["master," a title that became obligatory under Caligula and his successors]. . . He did not if he could help it leave or enter the city or town except in the evening or at night, to avoid disturbing anyone by the obligations of ceremony. In his consulship he commonly went through the streets on foot, and when he was not consul, generally in a closed litter. His morning receptions were open to all, including even the commons, and he met the requests of those who approached him with great affability, jocosely reproving one man because he presented a petition to him with as much hesitation "as he would a penny to an elephant." On the day of a meeting in the Senate he always greeted the members in the House and in their seats, calling each man by name without a prompter; and when he left the House, he used to take leave of them in the same manner, while they remained seated. He exchanged social calls with many, and did not cease to attend all their anniversaries until he was well on in years.

Suetonius, vol. 1, trans. R. C. Rolfe. Loeb Classical Library. Cambridge, MA: Harvard University Press, 1913.

ble, Augustus and his successors encouraged provincial cities to adopt Roman institutions and granted Roman citizenship to their leaders. Where this was impossible, they encouraged similar developments on a tribal level, often with considerable success.

The improvement of provincial government was essential in part because the empire continued to expand. The defeat of Antony and Cleopatra resulted in the annexation of Egypt. Augustus added several provinces in Asia, including Judaea, and extended the northern borders of the empire to the Danube and the Rhine. His successors would add Britain and Mauretania (Morocco), Armenia, Assyria, Dacia (Romania), and Mesopotamia (see map 5.1).

In Rome, Augustus embarked upon an ambitious program that replaced many of the city's old wooden tenements, established rudimentary fire and police ser-

vices, and improved the city's water supply. Much of this was accomplished by using the vast resources of Egypt, which he had appropriated, not by taxing the Romans. When Augustus died in A.D. 14, he had established a legacy of sound administration and what has been called the *pax romana*, an era of peace and prosperity that later ages would look upon with envy (see document 5.4).

The First Emperors

Augustus's successors, the Julio-Claudian emperors, continued his administrative policies, though none of them was his equal as statesmen. His adopted son,

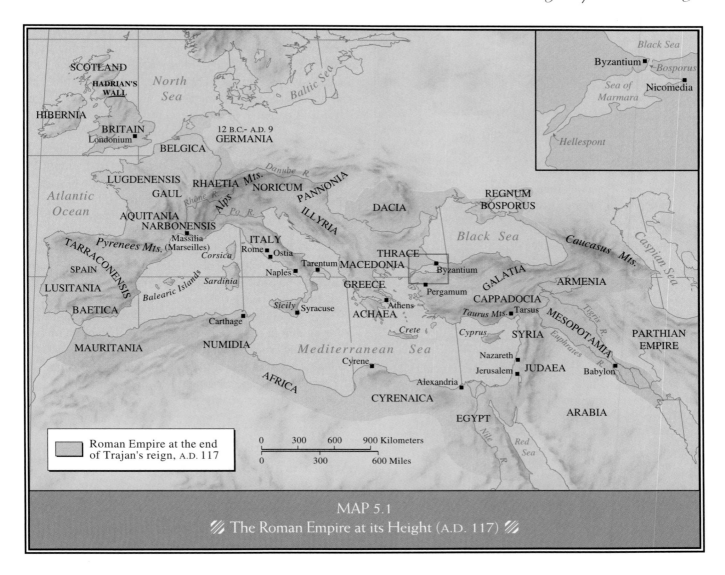

MAP 5.1
✺ The Roman Empire at its Height (A.D. 117) ✺

Tiberius, succeeded him by inheritance; Tiberius ruled A.D. 14–37. Caligula, Claudius, and Nero abandoned republican formalities, expanded the imperial bureaucracy, and sometimes treated the Senate with open contempt. Caligula so scorned the republican tradition that he designated his horse, Incitatus, as his coconsul. Augustus's successors institutionalized the powers that had been granted personally to Augustus and gradually appropriated semidivine status (see illustration 5.4). The Roman Empire became a hereditary monarchy, though as always, real power rested with the army. Claudius, thought wrongly by the Senate to be an incompetent figurehead, was placed on the throne by the Praetorian guard, an elite unit established by Augustus for the protection of the *princeps*. In spite of a speech defect and physical disabilities, Claudius astonished everyone by ruling capably and conscientiously. He took the first steps toward

establishing a regular imperial civil service staffed by members of the equestrian order.

Nero, whose tutor and chief adviser at the beginning of his reign was the Stoic philosopher Seneca, showed early promise. He neither was responsible for the great fire that consumed much of Rome in A.D. 64, nor did he fiddle while it burned, but his behavior grew increasingly more erratic with the passage of time. In A.D. 68, the legions began a series of revolts that ended with the emperor's suicide. The next year saw no fewer than four separate emperors, each a commander supported by his troops in the hope of securing their retirements by seizing the *imperium*. The last of them, Vespasian (ruled A.D. 69–79), established the Flavian dynasty, which lasted until A.D. 96, and formally adopted the title *imperator* or emperor. When his descendant, Domitian, left no successor, the Senate revived sufficiently to appoint another general in his

◆ DOCUMENT 5.4 ◆

Plutarch: The *Pax Romana*

The pax romana *referred to the peace within the empire that had been established by Augustus. Though it did not preclude a number of regional revolts, it was a remarkable achievement and, as this sensible if unheroic passage from* Precepts of Statecraft *makes clear, the primary justification for Roman rule.*

The greatest blessings that cities can enjoy are peace, prosperity, populousness, and concord. As far as peace is concerned, the people have no need of political activity, for all war, both Greek and foreign, has been banished and has disappeared from among us. Of liberty the people enjoy as much as our rulers allot them, and perhaps more would not be better. A bounteous productiveness of soil; a mild, temperate climate; wives bearing "children like their sires" [a quotation from Hesiod] and security for their offspring—these are the things that a wise man will ask for his fellow citizens in his prayers to the gods.

Plutarch. "Precepts of Statecraft," 32, from *Roman Civilization: Third Edition, 2 Vol. Set,* Naphtali Lewis and Meyer Rheinhold, eds. Copyright © 1990, Columbia University Press. Reprinted with permission of the publisher.

place named Nerva, who ushered in the age of the five good emperors. Neither Nerva nor the three emperors who followed him (Trajan, Hadrian, and Antoninus Pius) had sons, and each appointed a successor who was acceptable to both the Senate and the legions. (The fifth emperor of the period was Marcus Aurelius.)

The age of the five good emperors (A.D. 96–180) was later remembered as one of exceptional happiness. The *pax romana* or Roman Peace described by Plutarch seemed to be a permanent condition, and trade flourished. Trajan and Hadrian sponsored lavish building programs, and Trajan introduced the *alimenta*, a subsidy to help poor parents in raising their children. All five emperors refined and strengthened imperial administration, but the possibility of military intervention remained. The Stoic philosopher Marcus Aurelius (ruled A.D. 161–180) broke the tradition of appointment by merit, not only by having a son, but also by having the poor judgment to leave him the throne. The reign of Commodus, from A.D. 180 to 192, was a disaster that ended in yet another military revolt. But by this time the empire was experiencing difficulties that had little to do with the personality of its rulers.

Art, Literature, and Thought in Imperial Rome

Throughout the late republic and early empire, the culture of Rome's elite remained heavily dependent upon Greek models. Painting and sculpture were an integral

Illlustration 5.4

▨ **Base of the Column of Antoninus Pius.** This scene shows the apotheosis of the emperor Antoninus (reigned A.D. 138–161) and his wife, Faustina; that is, the imperial pair are in the process of becoming gods after their death. Based on the symbolism of the eagles, they are about to become the new Jupiter and Juno, an indication of how the imperial office had become deified.

Ilustration 5.5

🖎 **A Roman Family.** This relief probably came from a tomb on the outskirts of Rome. It shows L. Vibius, his wife, and what appears to be the death mask of a son who died in childhood. Based on the woman's hairdo, the work has been attributed to the time of Augustus.

◆ DOCUMENT 5.5 ◆

Seneca: The Stoic Ideal

Seneca was tutor to the emperor Nero and the dominant political figure of the early part of his reign. Though Seneca enriched himself in dubious ways and was involved in the judicial murder of Nero's mother, his writings on Stoic themes reflect a different, more attractive side of his character. He committed suicide on Nero's orders in A.D. 65. Here he describes the Stoic equanimity that comes from an understanding of divine providence.

What is the principal thing in human life? . . . To raise the soul above threats and promises of fortune; to consider nothing as worth hoping for. For what does fortune possess worth setting your heart upon? What is the principle thing? To be able to enjoy adversity with a joyful heart; to bear whatever betide just as if it were the very thing you desired . . . For you would have felt it your duty to desire it, had you known that all things happened by divine decree. Tears, complaints, lamentations are rebellion.

Seneca. *Natural Questions*, trans. J. Clarke. London: 1910.

part of most public places and adorned the luxurious palaces of the rich. Reliefs on public buildings featured mythological subjects or idealized versions of historic events. Private collectors bought reproductions of famous Greek statues from Roman workshops, and a thriving trade existed in bronzes from Greece. In some cases these skillful copies provide the only access to lost originals. Only in portrait statuary did the Romans break with established tradition. Ignoring the Greek tendency to idealize the human form, they produced busts whose photographic realism is a monument to individual men and women (see illustration 5.5).

Architecture, too, abandoned Greek precedent. Temples and theaters recalled Hellenistic models, while other public buildings used the arch and vault construction favored by the Etruscans. Augustus and his successors built baths, aqueducts, warehouses, and stadia for games and chariot races whose scale virtually precluded the post-and-lintel construction of the Greeks. Some structures, such as the Mausoleum built by Augustus for his family and the Pantheon constructed by Hadrian, featured domes that spanned enormous spaces. Increasingly, columns, friezes, and pediments evolved into decorative elements without structural purpose. Engineering and an imperial taste for grandeur triumphed over the aesthetics of simplicity.

In philosophy as in art, the Romans tended to borrow Greek conventions and adapt them to their own

purposes. The dominant current in Roman thought was Stoicism. Cicero, Seneca (4 B.C.?–A.D. 65), and the emperor Marcus Aurelius wrote extensively on Stoic themes, in part because, as men of affairs, they appreciated the philosophy's moral activism and the comfort it offered a politician in difficult times (see document 5.5). Their emphasis, however, was on the practical application of Stoic principles, and their writings added little or nothing to the speculative tradition.

The same might be said of Roman writings on science. Alexandria remained the center of scientific and philosophical inquiry, and Greek the primary language of scientific publication. The most important scientific work in Latin, the *Natural History* of Pliny the Elder (A.D. 23–79), was little more than a vast compendium of information, much of it false, gleaned by the author from nearly 500 sources—327 of them Greek. The work is important primarily because it summarized ancient knowledge and transmitted it to a later age.

Roman literature was more original than Roman thought. By ancient standards, literacy was widespread in the late republic and early empire (perhaps 15 percent of the population), and books were produced in large numbers. As many as thirty copies at a time could be produced by having a reader dictate to slaves who wrote the words on papyrus scrolls. A more modern form of the book, the codex, made its appearance in the first century B.C. Written on vellum or parchment and bound in leather, it was preferred by lawyers and, later, by Christian scholars who needed to compare several texts at a time and found codices more convenient to handle than scrolls.

The Romans favored practical treatises on agriculture, the mechanical arts, law, and rhetoric. Cicero, as the most successful litigator of his day, was especially valued for his attempt to reconcile traditional jurisprudence with the Stoic idea of natural law and for his writings on oratory. His work, together with that of Quintilian (c. A.D. 35–c. 100), elevated rhetoric to a science and had a profound impact on educational theory. Another literary form unique to Rome was the publication of personal correspondence, with Cicero and Pliny the Younger providing the best and most interesting examples. History, too, was popular, though it was rarely studied in a spirit of objective inquiry. Caesar wrote to advance his political career, while Livy (see chapter 3) sought to revive republican virtue. Tacitus (c. A.D. 56–c. 120) produced a history of the early emperors from a similar point of view, while his younger contemporary, Suetonius, provided a background of scandalous personal gossip in his *Lives of the Caesars.* The vices he attributes to the Julio-Claudian emperors transcend normal human capacities. Plutarch (c. A.D. 46–after 119), a Greek whose popular *Lives* included famous Romans as well as Greeks, pursued a less sensational approach to biography and wrote extensively on ethics.

These contributions, however great, pale by comparison with the poetry that made the Augustan age synonymous with Rome's highest literary achievement. The greatest of the Augustan poets, Virgil (70–19 B.C.), was responsible for the *Eclogues,* a series of pastoral poems based loosely on Hesiod, and for his masterpiece, *The Aeneid,* the national epic about the founding of Rome. Both were gratefully received by Augustus as expressions of the civic virtue he was trying to encourage. The *Odes* and *Satires* of Horace (65–8 B.C.) were equally acceptable, but the works of Ovid (43 B.C.–A.D. 17) were not. Augustus was sufficiently offended by his *Ars Amatoria,* a poetic manual of seduction, to exile the poet to a remote town on the Black Sea.

Surprisingly, drama, the most public and political of all art forms, never achieved greater importance in Rome. Greek tragedies aroused enthusiasm among Roman intellectuals, but the public preferred comedy. Plautus, in the late third century B.C., and Terence in the second century B.C., produced works that, though based heavily upon the Greek New Comedy, had a ribald vigor. In later years, public taste turned toward mime and simpleminded farce, while theater attendance declined as gladiatorial combats and similar entertainments became more popular. The nine tragedies of Seneca, so inspiring to the great dramatists of the late Renaissance, were apparently written to be read, not performed.

The Social and Economic Structures of the Early Empire

The age of Augustus and the century that followed were a time of relative prosperity. Italy and the regions affected by the civil wars recovered quickly, and neither Augustus nor his successors afflicted their subjects with excessive taxation. Their policies were conducive to economic growth, because the *pax romana,* by uniting the western world under a single government, limited warfare to the periphery of the empire and created a market of unprecedented size. Tariffs on the transfer of goods between provinces generated revenue but were too low to inhibit trade. For the first and last time in its history, the west had uniform coinage and systems of banking and credit that transcended national boundaries.

The policy of settling veterans on land of their own, though it sometimes dispossessed existing farmers, may also have temporarily improved the well-being of the peasant class. The initial effect of these resettlements was to reduce the number of *latifundia,* or great slave-worked estates. Many regions saw a resurgence of the small independent farm, while middling properties of the kind described by Cato prospered. The number of slaves declined, in part because the annexations of Augustus did not involve the large-scale enslavement of new subjects, and in part because manumission was common. On the estates that remained, the treatment of slaves appears to have improved. Slaves grew more valuable as the supply dwindled, and owners found that they could best be replaced by encouraging them to reproduce. The Augustan age did not see a resumption of the three Servile Wars, such as the slave rebellion led by the gladiator Spartacus, fought during the last century of the republic.

In time, however, the economies of scale that had doomed the small farmers of the republic reasserted themselves. Not every veteran understood agriculture; those who did could not always compete with their larger neighbors. Eventually, these men or their descendants sold their farms and returned to the city, or they became tenants (*coloni*) of the great estates. In the early empire, *coloni* remained technically free, leasing their land and returning a portion of the yield to the estate owner. This was thought to be less efficient than slavery, but it became increasingly common as slaves grew scarcer. Once again the average size of properties began to grow and peasant income resumed its decline. By the end of the first century A.D. half of the land in the province of Africa was owned by six men.

Changes in the distribution of wealth were therefore both temporary and relative. If veterans benefited from the distribution of land and from cash payments derived from booty, the wealthy gained even more from imperial gifts. Townspeople, too, received payments from the emperors as a kind of bribe for good behavior and sometimes found work on the construction projects funded by Augustus from the spoils of Egypt. Another burst of prosperity seems to have followed the great fire of A.D. 67, which destroyed much of Rome; Nero financed a massive reconstruction that gave work to thousands. Temporary benefits of this kind may have improved the lives of ordinary people, especially in Italy, but the amounts involved were too small to expand significantly their role as consumers or to change the basic distribution of wealth.

The economic polarization that had characterized Roman society since the second century B.C. continued to influence the development of trade (see table 5.2). Though Julius Caesar had attempted to limit the number of Romans eligible for the grain dole, it remained available to all Roman citizens under Augustus. This, together with the policy of urbanization in the provinces, ensured the continuation of a massive trade in bulk agricultural commodities (see map 5.2). Spain, Africa, Sicily, and, above all, Egypt exported vast quantities of grain to the growing cities of the empire. Italy produced wine and oil, but it had many competitors and probably lost in relative economic importance as the first century B.C. progressed.

Meanwhile, the lack of an adequate consumer base limited manufacturing. Something like a mass market existed for metal tools and weapons, and several Italian towns produced red-glazed pottery for export to every corner of the empire. Some potteries may have employed more than fifty workers, most of them slaves.

❧ TABLE 5.2 ❧
Roman Wages and Prices in the Late Republic

These figures regarding wages and prices are estimates for central Italy c. 150 B.C. Prices of wheat in particular fluctuated wildly during the civil wars, but the numbers listed below are a fair estimate of those in the early years of Augustus. Prices were lower in the Po valley and in other areas remote from Rome. There were sixteen copper asses or four sesterces in a silver denarius. The difference in wages between a slave hired for the day and a free laborer demonstrates why so many of the latter were unemployed.

Service or product	Average cost
Unskilled slave laborer	2 sesterces per diem
Free laborer	3 sesterces per diem
Soldier	120 denarius per annum
Wheat (enough for 20 lbs. of bread)	3 sesterces per *modius*
Barley	2 sesterces per *modius*
Wine (average grade Italian)	3–4 *asses* per liter
Wine (best imported)	1–4 denarius per liter
Olive oil	6–8 *asses* per liter
Beef	4–5 *asses* per lb.
Pork	2–3 *asses* per lb.
Clothing (Cato's toga, tunic, and shoes)	100 denarius
A farm slave	500 denarius
An ox for plowing	60–80 denarius
A sheep	6–8 denarius
A cavalry horse	500 denarius

Source: Data from Tenney Frank, ed., *An Economic Survey of Ancient Rome*, vol. 1 (New York, N.Y.: Pageant Books, 1959), p. 200.

Woolen cloth, once processed in the home, was more commonly manufactured for sale. The size of this trade is difficult to estimate, and it, too, probably employed mostly slaves. Generally speaking, the availability of slave labor, though declining, continued to hold down the wages of free workers and to restrict the development of technology. Perhaps the greatest innovation of the period was the development of glassblowing at Sidon.

Most commodities were more limited in their distribution. Egypt retained its monopoly on papyrus, and the cities of what had once been Phoenicia produced glass and the expensive dyes and textiles for which they

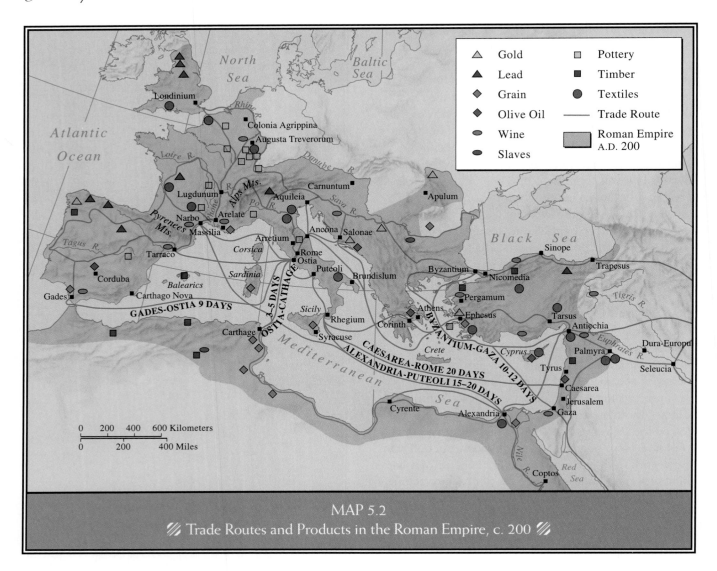

MAP 5.2

Trade Routes and Products in the Roman Empire, c. 200

had long been famous. Linens, drugs, perfumes, precious stones, and such delicacies as dried fruit and pickled fish came from various sources within the empire. Other luxuries came from far away. The Silk Road across central Asia connected Syria with China. More than a hundred ships sailed annually from the Red Sea ports to India for cargoes of spice, and Africa continued as it had for centuries to provide the Mediterranean world with gold, ivory, palm oil, and those hardy perennials, frankincense and rhinoceros horn.

Almost without exception, these were low-volume, high-profit trades that entailed a substantial element of risk. They made a few people, mostly equestrians or freedmen who eventually merged with the equestrian class, enormously rich, but the prosperity they generated was not widely shared. Aristocrats, too, sometimes invested in such ventures or speculated on the com-

modities market. They usually did so through agents because the old prejudice against trade died hard. Overall, the economy of the empire remained agrarian, and mercantile activities were restricted to a few.

In the first century A.D. a million people may have lived in the city of Rome, a nearly incredible total given the limits of ancient technology and systems of distribution. As in any community, their lives were constrained by an elaborate social structure. While most were desperately poor, few would have chosen to live anywhere else. Rome was, to the Romans, the center of the world.

About one-third of the city's land area was occupied by the palaces of the rich, the most spectacular of which were clustered on the Palatine Hill. Some of these structures, with their courtyards, galleries, baths, and gardens, covered several acres and employed hun-

Illlustration 5.6

⬚ **Central Courtyard of a Roman Villa (First Century** A.D.**)**
The homes of wealthy Romans were normally one story in
height and built around a series of courtyards. This one, from
the House of the Vettii in Pompeii, is unusually graceful. It was
preserved in 79 A.D. when the volcano Mt. Vesuvius buried Pompeii in volcanic ash, killing most of the city's twenty thousand
inhabitants.

dreds of domestic slaves. Because Romans believed, or
pretended to believe, that the pursuit of wealth and luxury for their own sake was dishonorable, such homes
were meant to fulfill a public function. The atrium, or
courtyard, and the rooms that surrounded it were devoted to entertaining and conducting business (see illustration 5.6). The rear of the house with its garden or
gardens provided a retreat for the family.

The senatorial or equestrian families that lived
within derived their wealth primarily from land, though
virtually all engaged in some form of trade or speculation as well. Most therefore owned country villas in addition to their city property. Cicero, who was not
particularly wealthy, owned eight such residences in
various parts of Italy and visited them according to the
season.

The life of such a man began at dawn, when he was
visited by his clients who came to show their respect,
request favors, or receive his instructions. Most of the
day was devoted to politics, business, or the law courts,
but like Romans of every class, the rich found time for
physical exercise and an elaborate bath before the main
meal of the day. In imperial times, this was usually
taken in the evening and might involve a banquet of
epic proportions. Women sat upright, while the male
guests reclined on couches around a central table and

consumed delicacies brought from specialized farms in
the area around the city. Songbirds, exotic fruits, and
fish grown in special ponds were extremely popular, as
were vintage wines such as the famous Falernian. Excess
was common. Afterward, the guests would return
home, sometimes in coaches or litters, but always accompanied by a small army of bodyguards. After dark,
the Roman streets were dangerous.

Moralists seeking a return to the more restrained
attitudes of an earlier time objected to this behavior.
Their complaints had little effect until Augustus began
to support reform as a matter of official policy. Romans
of the late republic and early empire believed in physical fitness, but they had long since lost Cato's taste for
simplicity and their attitude toward sex had become remarkably casual. Homosexuality and bisexuality,
though perhaps not as common as among the Greeks,
were mocked but tolerated even in public figures such
as Julius Caesar. Casual sex of every kind was encouraged by the institution of slavery.

Roman women, too, had achieved a level of sexual
and personal freedom that has rarely been equaled before or since. In the first century B.C. they acquired the
legal right to own and manage their property apart
from that of their husbands. The women of the upper
classes therefore owned slaves and managed estates of
their own. Many were successful businesswomen, and
not a few involved themselves in politics.

Economic independence freed such women from
marital tyranny, and in some cases encouraged both
sexes to seek divorce for political or financial advantage. Among the more prominent families, four or five
marriages in succession were not uncommon, and extramarital affairs were frequent. No real penalty was
meted out for such behavior, because divorce was regarded as a private matter under the laws of the republic and could be concluded by simple agreement.
Wives in such cases retained their dowries. Tradition
held that adultery was punishable by death, but the
law in question was confusing and had not been enforced for generations.

Augustus believed that this situation undermined
traditional Roman virtues and deterred men from marrying, at least in part because they could not control
their wives. Other reasons existed for a precipitous decline in marriage rates among the Roman upper class.
An increasing number of both sexes regarded children
as an expensive nuisance and preferred to remain single,
believing that they could guarantee a far more pleasant
life by surrounding themselves with legacy hunters who
hoped to be included in their wills. Beginning in 18 B.C.

Augustus tried to legislate against these abuses by demanding seven witnesses to a divorce and making it possible for a man—though not a woman—to sue for adultery thereafter. Legacy hunters were restrained by limiting the bequests that could be received by widowed or unmarried persons. Augustus's efforts aroused intense opposition and seem to have had little immediate effect beyond enriching the treasury with the estates of those whose heirs had been disqualified, but they mark a turning point of sorts in the history of Roman morals. Others shared his distaste for sexual license and their attitudes, later reflected in those of Christianity, gained ground with the passage of time.

Augustus may have been right in thinking that divorce and sexual misconduct led to social instability, but their prevalence did not imply that all of the men and women of the Roman upper class were irresponsible pleasure seekers. A high level of education, secured largely by private tutors, was common to both sexes, and magnificent private libraries were a status symbol. Moreover, a measure of debauchery did not seem to interfere with the effective management of complex enterprises. In the Roman system of values, the ability when necessary to control the passions, not the vice, mattered.

Slaves were the constant companions of the rich, and even poor households might own one or two. They may at various times have numbered as much as a third of the city's population, but their role in Roman society defies easy categorization. The lot of the urban slave was in some ways preferable to that of the poor citizen.

Domestic slaves lived as part of their master's household and were sometimes friends or lovers. Others were highly skilled professionals: teachers, physicians, librarians, or entertainers who might have homes of their own in the city and earn additional fees by offering their services to the general public. Craftsmen and industrial workers generally lived apart and returned a portion of their earnings to their owners, keeping the rest for themselves. Though slaves, their daily lives were similar to those of ordinary citizens.

Roman slavery was a legal and personal relationship that had little to do with lifestyle. Simply put, slaves were not persons under the law. The only virtue required of them was loyalty to their master, and they could neither serve in the army nor participate in public life. Though slaves could testify in court, it was customary to torture them first on the theory that this released them from their obligation of loyalty. Corporal punishment was sometimes inflicted by owners as well, but the emperors introduced legislation against the worst

excesses. Claudius forbade the exposure of slaves who were old or sick. Domitian prohibited castration, and Hadrian abolished private executions, even for criminal behavior.

As is often the case with legislation, these acts lagged far behind practice. Most owners knew that the system worked only if the loyalty of the slaves were genuine. No one would want to be shaved by a malcontent or protected by untrustworthy bodyguards. Slaves who rebelled might expect the fate of Spartacus. Those who were merely difficult might be threatened with being sent to the farm, a fate that for most of them must have seemed worse than death.

Though kindness was important, the prospect of manumission was a better guarantor of personal and public safety. Urban slaves of either sex could look forward to being freed, usually by the time they reached age thirty. This was about the average life expectancy in ancient Rome, but many lived far longer, and, as in all preindustrial societies, the percentage of very old people in the population was probably not much less than it is today. To know with reasonable certainty that one would be freed mitigated despair, but it also made economic sense for the owners.

The Roman system allowed slaves to purchase their freedom as soon as they could accumulate their purchase price. Those who worked outside the household could do this easily. Domestics, too, were often encouraged to develop private sources of income. The owner could then use the most productive years of a slave's life and recover his or her purchase price before sickness and old age diminished the total profit. As an added incentive to manumission, the freed slave became the owner's client, a relationship that might work to the advantage of both.

After the third century B.C. nearly all slaves were foreigners, with Gauls, Syrians, and Africans being perhaps the most numerous. Rome was therefore a multihued city of immigrants in which people from every corner of the known world mingled without apparent racial tension. Consciously or not, slavery was the means by which they were turned into Romans. The owner purchased them, introduced them to Roman ways, and in many cases provided them with the training and education needed to survive. Once free, their lives were often more prosperous than those of citizens who had nothing but a monthly allotment of grain.

Most of Rome's free citizens were officially categorized as poor. Some found work, often in jobs so hazardous or unhealthy that they could not be given to valuable slaves. Those who ran small shops faced intense competition from slaves and freedmen who were

Illustration 5.7

Reconstruction of a Typical *Insula* or Apartment House, Ostia. These strikingly modern-looking apartment blocks were based on design codes established during Nero's reconstruction of Rome. By the second century A.D., when the one depicted here was built at Rome's port of Ostia, they had become the standard form of urban housing in Italy.

better connected than themselves, while a few managed, for a time at least, to hang on to whatever money they had realized from the sale of their country farms. The majority lived in near destitution, kept alive only by occasional labor, the grain dole, and contributions from the rich. Nearly everyone, however, belonged to mutual aid societies that helped their members in time of need and guaranteed them a decent burial.

Like most of the urban slaves and freedmen, the poor inhabited a room or two in one of the innumerable *insulae* or tenements that packed the lower regions of the city (see illustration 5.7). After the rebuilding projects of Augustus and the fire of A.D. 64, these structures were usually of brick with concrete grills instead of windows. Though an improvement over the makeshift buildings of the republic, the new *insulae* were not safe. Wooden floors, stairs, and roofs kept the fire companies busy, while excessive height and cheap construction sometimes caused them to collapse and kill their inhabitants (see document 5.6). Individual apartments must have been dark and smoky with poor ventilation and no heat beyond that provided by a charcoal brazier for cooking.

Fortunately, the Romans spent little time at home. They met their friends in the street or in the Forum, where they would gather to pick up gossip and make their views known by rowdy demonstrations. Wealthy Romans affected to despise the mob, but no politician, not even the emperor, could afford to ignore it. Great efforts were made to distract and amuse the citizenry, for the stability of the state depended upon "bread and circuses." Those with political ambitions funded theatrical presentations, circuses, gladiatorial combats, chariot races, and huge public feasts in which the en-

tire body of Roman citizens ate and drank itself into oblivion. Only the enormous cost of such entertainments could justify the wealth amassed by the Roman aristocracy.

Whatever their political function, such spectacles did little to elevate public taste. Circuses involved the slaughter of exotic animals by men, or of men by animals. The Romans enjoyed seeing convicted criminals mauled by bears or lions almost as much as the gladiatorial contests in which specially trained slaves fought to the death. Chariot racing, too, was a blood sport in which fatal accidents were common. Various teams represented political factions and betting was heavy.

After the games—or a hard day's work—Romans headed for the public baths. These massive facilities, which could be enjoyed by anyone, provided exercise rooms, steambaths, and hot and cold pools for bathing. Separate areas were reserved for men and women, though the women were given no place to exercise. Because the Romans had no soap, the bathing ritual began with a steambath. They then scraped their bodies with an instrument called a *strigel* and immersed themselves successively in hot and cold water. The whole process was lengthy enough to provide further opportunity for socializing.

Amenities provided at little or no cost made life in the city tolerable, even for the poor. The streets were noisy—even at night—and the crime rate was relatively high, but those who had neither jobs nor possessions could ignore such problems. The city was clean by all but twentieth-century standards. Massive aqueducts brought pure water into every neighborhood where it bubbled up in innumerable fountains, and even the meanest apartment had a terrace garden or a few potted

◆ DOCUMENT 5.6 ◆

City Life in the Roman Empire

In his Third Satire, *the poet Juvenal (c. A.D. 60–after 128) congratulates a friend on his decision to leave Rome for a small country town by cataloging the hazards of urban life.*

Who, on Tivoli's heights, or a small town like
Gabii, say,
Fears the collapse of his house? But Rome is sup-
ported on pipestems,
Matchsticks; it's cheaper, so, for the landlord to
shore up his ruins,
Patch up the old cracked walls, and notify all the
tenants
They can sleep secure, though the beams are in ru-
ins above them.
No, the place to live is out there, where no cry of
Fire!
Sounds the alarm of the night, with a neighbor
yelling for water,
Moving his chattels and goods, and the whole
third story is smoking.
This you'll never know: for if the ground floor is
scared first,
You are the first to burn, up where the eaves of the
attic
Keep off the rain, and the doves are brooding over
their nest eggs.

Look at the other things, the various dangers of
nighttime. . . .
You are a thoughtless fool, unmindful of sudden
disaster,
If you don't make your will before you go out to
have dinner.
There are as many deaths in the night as there are
open windows
Where you pass by; if you're wise, you will pray in
your wretched devotions,
People may be content with no more than emptying slop jars.

The Satires of Juvenal, pp. 40, 43, trans. Rolfe Humphries. Bloomington: Indiana University Press, 1958. Used by permission.

plants, for the Romans, though thoroughly urbanized, never lost their taste for growing things.

Yet by modern standards, the lives of ordinary Romans must have been largely without root or purpose. Marriage was rare, and people tended to contract casual relationships with little regard for the social standing of their partners. The birthrate remained correspondingly low, and children born to these unions were sometimes left to be found by slave traders. The population of the city would have declined had it not been for the steady influx of slaves and of refugees fleeing from the hard life of the countryside.

The Romans made little effort to impose their culture on the peoples of the empire, asking only that taxes be paid and peace maintained. Areas such as Egypt or Judea whose cultures were long established and fundamentally alien to Greco-Roman values therefore remained unassimilated. Tribal societies, or those in which the ideal of civic life had native roots, were more likely to imitate Roman models. By the end of the principate, Italy, Spain, Africa, and much of Gaul had been thoroughly Romanized, while Greece, Syria, and the Greek-speaking communities of Asia Minor, though they retained their native cultures, were drawing closer to the Roman orbit.

In general, the social structure and daily life of western cities resembled that of Rome. Eastern towns were different. Slavery was much less widespread, and the bulk of the artisans and laborers were citizens. Most of the latter, though poor, appear to have been self-supporting. In general, craft production in the eastern cities was far more important than in the more agrarian west, and their average size was probably greater. Alexandria, still more Greek than Egyptian, was almost as large as Rome, while places such as Pergamum and Antioch probably had close to a half million inhabitants.

Country life also differed. In the west, large farms and latifundia, worked either by slaves or *coloni*, were common. In the east, wealthy townsmen and city governments owned tracts that they rented to tenant farmers in return for cash payments or a portion of the yield. In both regions, independent farmers worked freehold plots with varying degrees of success. Egypt remained as it had been under the Ptolemies—a world of impoverished peasants laboring for the state under an appalling burden of taxation.

The age of Augustus and the early emperors has been called the peak of Roman civilization and its achievements were great, but beneath the surface, social polarization continued to limit economic growth and lay the foundation for future crises. The *pax romana* was something of an illusion. Roman rule masked, but did not resolve, underlying political and economic tensions in many parts of the empire. Riots and revolts were common and became more so with the passage of time. The empire, in short, was barely sustainable even in the absence of external threats, and it had become obvious even in the reign of Augustus that a threat of monumental proportions was developing in the north. Masses of Germanic tribesmen had begun to press against the Rhine and Danube frontiers. Unprecedented efforts were needed to contain them, and, as time would tell, the social and economic structures of the empire proved unequal to the task.

CHAPTER **6**

THE ORIGINS OF CHRISTIANITY AND THE DECLINE OF THE ROMAN EMPIRE

CHAPTER OUTLINE

The triumphal expansion of the early Roman Empire brought with it the seeds of change. Judaea, one of the poorer, more remote places annexed by the Romans, gave birth to Christianity, a religion that, after three centuries of sporadic persecution and relative obscurity, became the empire's dominant faith. Meanwhile, as Christianity grew, the empire fell into decline. The cause of that decline was not Christianity but a generalized crisis whose basic outlines had become apparent by the end of the second century. Put simply, the empire had expanded beyond the limits imposed by its economic resources. The emperors of the third and fourth centuries tried in various ways to reverse the process of economic and social decay, but gradually, the western and eastern halves of the empire grew further apart. The west, pressured by Germanic invaders and weakened by a stagnant economy, disintegrated. The Greek-speaking east, richer and untroubled by Germans, survived until 1453.

◆

The Origins of Christianity: Rome and the Jews

The breakup of the Hasmonaean dynasty, as the descendants of the Maccabees were known, resulted in a protracted, messy civil war in which the various contenders were supported by outside forces. Rome, in the person of Pompey, became involved in 66–64 B.C. as part of the effort to defeat Mithridates and capitalize on the collapse of the Seleucid Empire. The consequent spread of Roman influence in the Middle East alarmed Parthia, the successor of the Persian Empire, and aroused the interest of Cleopatra, who opposed Roman policy in the region even as she seduced Caesar and Antony. The situation was further complicated by the religious struggle between Jewish Sadducees and Pharisees (see chapter 3).

Eventually, a Roman client, Herod "the Great" (73–4 B.C.), emerged supreme and imposed an interval of much-needed peace. Though an Arab by birth,

Illustration 6.1

Relief from the Arch of Titus, Rome. The relief shows the spoils taken from the capture of Jerusalem. The arch was erected after Titus's death, probably about A.D. 81, and commemorates the dual triumph celebrated by Vespasian and Titus in A.D. 71 after their victory over the Jews and the destruction of the Temple. Note the menorah at center left. The seven-branched candelabra first became a symbol of the Jewish people during this era.

Herod practiced Judaism and generally favored the more numerous Pharisees over their opponents. His realms extended north to the borders of Syria and east into Transjordan and provided the revenues for an extensive building campaign, the jewel of which was the reconstruction of the Temple at Jerusalem. Some of its huge stones are still visible at the base of the Western Wall. None of this endeared him to the more observant Jews, but they accepted his rule.

When Herod died, he divided his kingdom into three tetrarchies, each ruled by a son. Archelaus, the Tetrarch of Judaea, so offended his Jewish subjects that they asked Augustus to replace him with a Roman procurator. Augustus agreed to do so, but the experiment was a failure. In theory, the procurators were supposed to look out for Roman interests while leaving internal matters to the Jewish court known as the Sanhedrin, but, if the Jewish historian Josephus (c. 37–c. 100) may be believed, each procurator found new ways of insulting Jewish religious and political sensibilities. By A.D. 7 a group known as the Zealots had dedicated themselves to the overthrow of Roman rule.

After this, the turmoil in Jerusalem was broken only by the short reign of Herod Agrippa, a Jewish prince who governed Judaea from A.D. 41 to 44 under Roman protection. Riots and protests accompanied a growing belief in the coming of the Messiah, who would deliver the Jews from their enemies and restore the world. False messiahs appeared with predictable regularity and caused great concern among the Romans who feared that one of them might organize a general revolt. Finally, in A.D. 66 the emperor Nero dispatched an army under Vespasian to restore order. The Zealots and most of the population resisted, and Jerusalem fell to the Romans only after a long and terrible siege (see illustration 6.1).

Exasperated by his inability to come to terms with the Jews even after their defeat, Vespasian, who had by this time succeeded Nero as emperor, ordered the Temple destroyed and the Jews scattered to the far corners of the empire in A.D. 70. They retained their freedom to worship and the exemption from sacrificing to the state cult that had been granted them by Julius Caesar, but the new exile or diaspora changed the character of Judaism. The destruction of the Temple forced the abandonment of sacrifices and other temple rites, for it was thought that the Temple could be restored only by the coming of the Messiah. The role of the priesthood diminished. Religious guidance was provided by rabbis, or teachers, who interpreted the law to the far-flung congregations. The more distinguished of their opinions helped form the Talmud, the vast collection of scriptural commentaries that is the basis of Jewish learning and of modern Judaism. Only a handful of Jews remained in Judaea. A band of perhaps nine hundred Zealots held out in the great desert fortress of Masada until A.D. 73 when they committed mass suicide instead of surrendering to the Romans. Sixty years later, another small group of Jews launched a futile rebellion under Bar Kochva, but nearly two thousand years would pass before the establishment of another Jewish state.

Jesus of Nazareth

Jesus lived in the midst of this chronic turbulence. He was probably born at Bethlehem in Judaea, between 7 and 4 B.C. Both the year and date of his birth are now regarded as the products of later calculation and tradition. A precise chronology is impossible because the Gospels provide no dates. The four Gospels are the most important sources dealing with his life and ministry. Though written by different authors more than a generation after his death (Mark, the earliest, was written about A.D. 70; John, the latest, shortly before 100), their accounts, though different in important ways, are in broad general agreement.

They describe the circumstances of Jesus's birth and of an appearance at the Temple when he was about twelve but remain silent about his activities until the age of thirty, the point at which he began to attract a following as an itinerant rabbi. Accompanied by twelve close associates or disciples, he preached throughout the Judaean countryside to ever-increasing crowds. His message was directed primarily against the Pharisees. Jesus felt that their rigid observance of the Law was an obstacle to faith and that it could largely be superseded by the simple commandment to "love thy neighbor as thyself." At the same time, his preaching left no doubt that he regarded himself as the Messiah (the Greek word for which is *christos*, or Christ). By this he did not mean the traditional Messiah who would lead the Jews to earthly glory, but the Son of God who brought them eternal salvation. His kingdom, he said, was "not of this world," and those who believed in him "would not perish but have eternal life."

This message enraged the Pharisees but attracted many, especially among the poor. When he entered Jerusalem at Passover accompanied by symbols attributed to the Messiah by prophetic tradition, Jesus provoked a crisis. The Sanhedrin demanded his arrest. The Roman procurator, Pontius Pilate, agreed, fearing that his presence would provoke further disorders when virtually the entire country had come to town for the festival. Jesus was tried by the Sanhedrin for blasphemy

and by Pilate for treason, though both trials as described by the Gospels were of dubious legality. Everyone responsible seems to have been motivated by political expediency, and Jesus was crucified with uncommon haste to avoid the possibility of demonstrations. After his execution, his followers reported that he had returned from the dead and ascended into Heaven after promising to return on the Day of Judgment.

The Spread of Christianity

The story of Jesus's death and resurrection solidified his followers into a new Jewish sect, but someone who had never heard him preach spread his teachings throughout the Roman world. Saul of Tarsus was a Pharisee who had originally persecuted the followers of Jesus. After a dramatic conversion to the faith of his opponents, he began to use his Roman name, Paul, and devoted the rest of his life to the task of converting Jews and non-Jews alike. Though a Pharisee, Paul's early education had been cosmopolitan and strongly influenced by Hellenism. To him, the teachings of Jesus were universal. With some difficulty, he persuaded the more conservative disciples to accept converts without forcing them to observe the Jewish dietary laws or be circumcised. Had he not done so, Christianity probably would never have become a universal church. By emphasizing faith over the minute observance of the law, Paul influenced the theology of the growing church as well.

In his letters, Paul portrayed himself as small of stature and physically weak, but his efforts on behalf of the faith were heroic. While Jesus was still alive, his teachings had begun to spread through the Jewish communities of the Roman Empire. Opposition from the Jewish leadership could not prevent the formation of small, usually secret, congregations that became the organizational basis of Paul's efforts. Traveling incessantly, he moved from one to the other, prevailing upon them to accept non-Jews as converts, preaching to the gentiles, and helping individual churches with matters of belief and practice. By so doing, he not only gained converts but also provided stability and a vital link between isolated communities that might otherwise have lost contact with one another and drifted into confusion.

When he could not visit the churches in person, Paul communicated with them by letters that he seems to have composed in answer to specific questions. These Epistles, written in Greek, form an important part of the New Testament. In some, he deals with theological questions; in others, with morality, ethics, and church organization. For issues not addressed by Jesus, Paul's Epistles—logical, fervent, and rooted solidly in

Illustration 6.2

The Catacomb of San Callisto, Rome. Unlike pagans, who generally cremated their dead, Christians insisted on burial, often in underground vaults known as catacombs. In times of persecution, they held religious services in these tombs to avoid detection. This one, the so-called Chapel of the Popes, is unusually elaborate and dates from c. 250.

Scripture—became the basis of later church doctrine. Through his efforts and those of the other disciples, the Christian church grew rapidly.

In the beginning, Christianity appealed largely to women, slaves, and other people of modest social standing, for it was universal in the sense that it accepted converts regardless of gender or background. Salvation was open to all, though Paul objected strongly to women preaching and church offices were apparently restricted to men. Its high ethical standards appealed to a generation that seems to have been increasingly repelled by pagan vice, and its ceremonies were neither as terrifying nor expensive as those of the mystery cults. The most important were baptism with water—not bull's blood, as in the rites of Mithra—and a love feast or *agape* in which the entire congregation joined. After a common meal, the Christians celebrated communion in bread and wine. By 153 the love feast had been abandoned in favor of communion alone, which was preceded by a service that included preaching and the singing of hymns.

Though humble, the early church was remarkably well organized. Each congregation was governed by a committee of presbyters or elders, who were assisted by deacons, readers, and exorcists. Bishops were elected by their congregations to lead worship services and administer the community's finances. The extent of their power in earliest times has been the subject of much debate, but its expansion was clearly assisted by the doctrine of apostolic succession. This teaching, which holds that episcopal authority derives from powers given by Jesus to the disciple Peter, was generally accepted by the end of the second century.

Organization helped the young church to survive persecution, for the Christians were hated. Persecution came from two sources. Many Jews felt that Christianity divided and weakened their communities and were quick to denounce Christians to the authorities. The authorities, whether Roman or provincial, had other motives. Like the Jews, Christians refused to sacrifice to the Roman gods. The Jews were exempt from this requirement by their status as a separate nation whose customs were honored by Roman law, but Christianity was not. Many Romans feared that Christian exclusiveness masked a certain hostility to the state. Their suspicions were fed by the low social status of the Christians and, ironically, by the secrecy they had adopted for their protection. To avoid detection, Christians met in private houses or in the underground burial places known as catacombs (see illustration 6.2). Rumors of cannibalism, based upon a misunderstanding of communion, only made matters worse.

Christians, in short, were unpopular and lacked the protection of powerful individuals who might otherwise have intervened on their behalf. They made ideal scapegoats. Nero, for example, blamed them for the great fire at Rome and launched the first wave of executions that claimed the life of Paul in A.D. 64 (see document 6.1). Persecutions by later emperors caused great loss of life until well into the third century. They were chronicled in horrific detail by Eusebius of Caesarea (c. 260–c. 340) in his *History of the Church*, but to the annoyance of the pagans, "the blood of martyrs" was, as Tertullian had put it, "the seed of the church." Too many Christians died bravely. Their cheerful heroism, even as they were torn

❖ DOCUMENT 6.1 ❖

Tacitus: Nero's Persecution of Christians

Tacitus (c. A.D. 56–120) is the best known of the ancient Roman historians. He was born to a patrician family in Gaul, educated at Rome, and rose to the Senate and then to become consul under Nerva in A.D. 97. Tacitus produced two long histories, The Annals *(covering A.D. 14–68) and* The Histories *(covering A.D. 68–96). Together they provide the best record of the early Principate. The Annals, from which the following excerpt is taken, is one of the few contemporary sources to mention Jesus of Nazareth.*

A disaster followed, whether accidental or treacherously contrived by the Emperor is uncertain, as authors have given both accounts; a fire—worse, and more dreadful than any which have ever happened to this city—broke out amid the shops containing inflammable wares, and instantly became fierce and rapid from the wind. . . . It devastated everyplace below the hills, outstripping all preventive measures; the city, with the narrow winding passages and irregular streets that characterized old Rome, was at its mercy. . . .

All human efforts, all the lavish gifts of the Emperor, all attempts to placate the Gods, did not dispel the infamous suspicion the fire had been started at someone's command. To quiet the rumor, Nero blamed and ingeniously tortured a people popularly called Christians, hated for their abominations [including their prediction

that the world would soon end in a conflagration marking the second coming]. Christus, from whom the cult had its origin, suffered the extreme penalty during the reign of Tiberius, at the hands of one of our procurators, Pontius Pilate, but this noxious superstition [Christianity], suppressed for a moment, broke out again not only in Judea, where it began, but in Rome itself, where all things hideous and shameful from every part of the world become popular.

Nero first arrested all who confessed [to being Christians]; then, upon their testimony, a vast multitude was convicted not so much of arson as of hatred of the human race. Mockery of every sort was added to their deaths. They were sewn in the skins of beasts and torn to pieces by dogs. Many died nailed on crosses or burned at the stake to illuminate the night. Nero gave his gardens for the spectacle and put on a circus, mingling with the crowd in the costume of a charioteer. . . . Thus, even though the victims deserved the severest penalty, a feeling of compassion arose on the ground that they suffered not for the public good but to glut the cruelty of one man.

Tacitus. *The Annals,* book 15, chaps. 38, 44, trans. A. J. Church and W. J. Brodribb. New York: Macmillan, 1906.

apart by wild beasts, impressed spectators and powerfully endorsed the concept of eternal life. Many pagans converted in spite of the obvious danger. Admittedly, had the persecutions been consistent they might have succeeded, but not all emperors were anti-Christian. Each persecution was followed by a generation or more in which the numbers of the faithful could be replaced and even grow.

Though persecution backfired, Christianity needed to explain itself to the educated elite to gain general acceptance. Moreover, as the movement spread, differences of opinion began to develop within it. During the second and third centuries, a growing number of writers addressed themselves both to the task of defining Christian doctrine and explaining it in terms acceptable to those who had received a Greco-Roman philosophical education. These men, who eventually became known as the Fathers of the Church, included the apologist Justin Martyr and theologians such as Tertullian, Origen, and Clement of Alexandria. Together, they be-

gan the process of forging a new intellectual tradition based upon faith as well as reason.

By the end of the third century, perhaps 10 percent of the empire was Christian. Most of the followers were concentrated in the east or in Africa. More significant, the Fathers had done their work: Converts were coming increasingly from the upper classes. In cities in Syria and Asia Minor, Christians had become a majority and even the leading families had accepted the faith. The last, and one of the most terrible, of the persecutions occurred under Diocletian in 303, but by then the church was too strong to be destroyed (see chronology 6.1).

❖

The Crisis of the Later Roman Empire

In 1776, Edward Gibbon described the fall of Rome as "the triumph of Christianity and barbarism." Though his *The Decline and Fall of the Roman Empire* is one of the

◆ CHRONOLOGY 6.1 ◆

The Important Roman Emperors

27 B.C.–A.D.14	Augustus
A.D. 14–37	Tiberius
37–41	Caligula
41–54	Claudius
54–68	Nero*
68–69	The year of the four emperors
69–79	Vespasian
79–81	Titus
81–96	Domitian*
96–98	Nerva
98–117	Trajan
117–138	Hadrian
138–161	Antoninus Pius
161–180	Marcus Aurelius*
180–192	Commodus
193–211	Septimius Severus
211–217	Caracalla
218–222	Elagabalus
222–235	Severus Alexander
249–251	Decius*
253–260	Valerian*
253–268	Gallienus
268–270	Claudius II Gothicus
270–275	Aurelian
284–305	Diocletian*
306–337	Constantine
337–361	Constantius II
361–363	Julian the Apostate
364–375	Valentinian
364–378	Valens
379–395	Theodosius

*Launched major persecutions of the Christians.

The true cause of imperial decline was instead a generalized crisis whose basic outlines had become apparent as early as the second century. When Marcus Aurelius died in A.D. 180, an army of more than a half million men patrolled a border of several thousand miles. Within that border the *pax romana* was broken only by occasional riots, but beyond it, powerful forces were gathering. Germanic tribes—Franks, Alemanni, Burgundians, and others in the west; Visigoths and Ostrogoths to the east—pressed against the Rhine and Danube frontiers. For reasons that remain unclear, their populations had grown beyond the available food supply in central Europe. Behind them, on the eastern steppes, other peoples with similar problems pushed westward into the German tribal lands. Population movements on this scale created intolerable pressure when they came up against settled borders. The Germans did not hate Rome. They sought only to settle within it. They were hard, determined fighters whose grasp of strategy was anything but primitive. In fighting them, Marcus Aurelius faced unpredictable attacks in force delivered along a perimeter too extensive to be manned completely by the legions. His bitter struggle with the tribes was an inkling of things to come.

To the east, the Romans faced a more conventional foe. The Parthian Empire was a sophisticated territorial state based, like Rome, on taxes and tribute. It fought until it exhausted its resources and then made peace until its economy could recover. The pressure it exerted on the eastern borders was therefore sporadic rather than constant, but it was nevertheless severe. Rome defeated the Parthians in A.D. 198 and briefly annexed Mesopotamia. This success was followed by a change of dynasty in the eastern kingdom. An Iranian prince, Ardashir I, overthrew the Parthians and established the Sassanid dynasty, which lasted until the Arab conquests of the seventh century. Determined to recapture Mesopotamia, he and his successors launched a series of wars that further depleted the Roman treasury, weakened the eastern provinces, and ended in 260 with the capture of the emperor Valerian.

The Roman economy could not sustain this level of military commitment, and the third century was one of almost unrelieved crisis. The prosperity of Augustan times had been in some respects artificial. Much of it was based on the exploitation of new wealth derived from imperial expansion. When the expansion stopped, that wealth was not replaced. Beneath the glittering surface of the early empire, the economy remained stagnant. The mass of slaves, tenant farmers, and unemployed citizens consumed little. Their productivity was

great masterworks of history, he was at best only half right. Neither Christianity nor pagan immorality contributed to the catastrophe that befell the western empire in the fifth century A.D. While the "barbarians" clearly played a major role, they were little more barbaric than some of the emperors they replaced.

low, and they had no incentive to improve efficiency to encourage growth. Without growth, the number of rich could not increase, and it was only they who, in the Roman system, could provide a market for luxuries and craft goods.

Arguably, had the Roman economy been able to expand, the empire might have been able to meet its military obligations. Instead, the imperial government was forced to extract more and more resources from an economy that may already have been shrinking. Taxes and forced requisitions to support the army consumed capital, reduced the expenditures of the rich, and drove ordinary people to destitution. Basic industries such as the trade in earthenware vanished, and food shortages became common as harvests were diverted to feed the troops. Trade languished.

Economic decline, though general, did not affect all regions of the empire equally. Those provinces closest to the front suffered the most because they were subject to requisitions of food, draft animals, and equipment and because governors could extract forced loans from citizens who found themselves in harm's way. Both east and west suffered, but the strain was greater in the west because the Germans exerted a steady, unrelenting pressure while the cyclical nature of the struggle with Persia allowed time for the eastern provinces to recover between wars. Africa and Egypt, far from the battlefields, were troubled only by the same ruinous taxes that afflicted everyone.

The crisis fed upon itself in an unending spiral of decline. The imperial government became more brutal and authoritarian in its efforts to extract resources from an ever-narrowing economic base, and with each exaction, poverty increased. The social consequences were appalling. A steady decline in population is evident from the mid-second century onward, which inhibited recruitment for the army and reduced the tax base even further (see table 6.1). Growing poverty and political helplessness blurred social distinctions and encouraged resistance that, in turn, forced the government to adopt even sterner measures.

Much of this new authoritarianism was the legacy of Septimius Severus, emperor from 193 to 211. Having commanded legions on the Danube, he believed that the full human and economic resources of the state had to be mobilized to meet the German threat. He introduced laws that imposed forced labor on the poor and trapped the decurions (officials who served as an urban elite) in an inescapable web of obligations. The army, meanwhile, was showered with favors. Severus doubled the soldier's pay—the first increase in more than two hundred years—and allowed officers to wear the gold

TABLE 6.1
The Population of the Roman Empire, A.D. 1–600

These estimates (in millions) of the population of the Roman Empire are necessarily imprecise, but they show dramatic population declines in every region of the empire after about A.D. 200. The Balkan figures include Illyria, Pannonia, Dacia, Macedonia, and Thrace. The dramatic decline around 400 marks the loss of Dacia. Note that, even at its peak, the population of the empire remained small relative to the size of the army it was forced to maintain.

Region	A.D. 1	200	400	600
Africa	3.75	4.0	3.5	2.75
Asia Minor	6.0	7.0	6.0	5.0
Balkans	2.8	3.25	1.75	1.25
Britain	a	1.75	a	a
Egypt	4.75	4.75	4.0	3.25
Gaul	5.75	7.5	5.75	4.75
Greece	2.0	2.0	1.5	.8
Italy	7.0	7.0	5.0	3.5
Spain	4.5	5.0	4.5	3.5
Syria and Palestine	2.25	2.25	1.75	1.5
Total	38.8	44.5	33.75	26.3

Source: Figures derived from C. McEvedy and R. Jones, *Atlas of World Population History* (Harmondsworth: Penguin Books, 1978).
aBritain was not part of the empire.

ring that signified membership in the equestrian order. Such measures improved morale, but they were not enough. Hard terms of service and the declining population of the interior provinces continued to make recruitment difficult. To compensate, Severus opened even the highest ranks to men from the border provinces and, for the first time since the days of Marius, allowed soldiers to marry.

These reforms, though rational and probably necessary, widened the gap between soldiers and civilians. The post-Severan army, composed largely of men with only the slightest exposure to Roman culture, was privileged as well as self-perpetuating. Children raised in the camps usually followed their father's profession. When they did not, they remained part of a garrison community whose political and economic interests were in conflict with those of the society it protected.

Because the soldiers, now half-barbarian themselves, continued to make emperors, the implications of this change were potentially disastrous. Severus was an African, whose family members had long been senators and were thoroughly romanized. His wife, Julia Domna, was a gifted administrator and a patron of Greek and Latin intellectuals who worked tirelessly for cultural unity. The emperors who followed were of a different sort. The tyrannical son of Severus and Julia, Caracalla, was followed by men whose only common characteristic was the support of a faction within the army. Most were poorly educated provincials who seemed like foreigners to a majority of their subjects. A few were eccentrics or even children, and their average tenure in office was short. All, however, tried to follow the deathbed advice of Severus: "Stay on good terms, enrich the soldiers, and don't take much notice of anything else." He had been nothing if not a realist.

Imperial Efforts at Reform from Septimius Severus to Diocletian

As the third century progressed, "enriching the soldiers" grew more difficult. Both the economy and the population continued to decline. The rate of conception slowed, in part because people felt that they could no longer afford to raise families. Furthermore, malnutrition and disease contributed to the population loss. The first great epidemic struck in the reign of Marcus Aurelius. It was followed by others, whose exact nature is unknown.

Defense costs could not be reduced. The middle years of the third century saw a renewal of the Persian wars and the invasion of the Goths, a Germanic people who forced the Romans to abandon their provinces north of the Danube (the area now known as Romania) and threatened the interior as well. Imperial politics alone demanded enormous expenditures as regional commanders struggled against one another for the throne. Of the twenty-six emperors who ruled between A.D. 235 and 283, only one died of natural causes. All were forced to bribe the legions for their support; some even bribed the enemy. Large sums were expended to buy peace from both the Sassanids and the Goths. Such efforts predictably failed.

Emperors beginning with Caracalla tried to deal with these problems by reducing the precious metal content of their coinage, a practice that did little more than add inflation to the empire's list of economic woes. Taxation and forced requisitions had long since reached the limits of productivity. Decurions and tenant farmers, impoverished by an insatiable bureaucracy, abandoned their properties in favor of begging, banditry, and piracy. The emperors, distracted by war and by the

Illustration 6.3

The Tetrarchs, St. Mark's Venice. The sculpture shows Diocletian and his colleagues as an inseparable unit for purposes of propaganda.

requirements of personal survival, could do little about it. Whole regions fell under the control of men who were, in effect, warlords. In the east, Zenobia, queen of the caravan city of Palmyra, managed briefly to gain control of Syria, Egypt, and much of Asia Minor.

The emperors Claudius II Gothicus and Aurelian brought the military situation under control between 268 and 275. However, major reforms were necessary. Diocletian, who came to the throne in 284, embarked upon a reorganization of the entire empire. To enlarge the army without increasing its potential for anarchy, he divided the empire into two halves, each ruled by an augustus. Each augustus then adopted a caesar to serve as his subordinate and successor.

Diocletian created four emperors, for each caesar had primary responsibility for a region of his own (see illustration 6.3). His colleague Maximian was

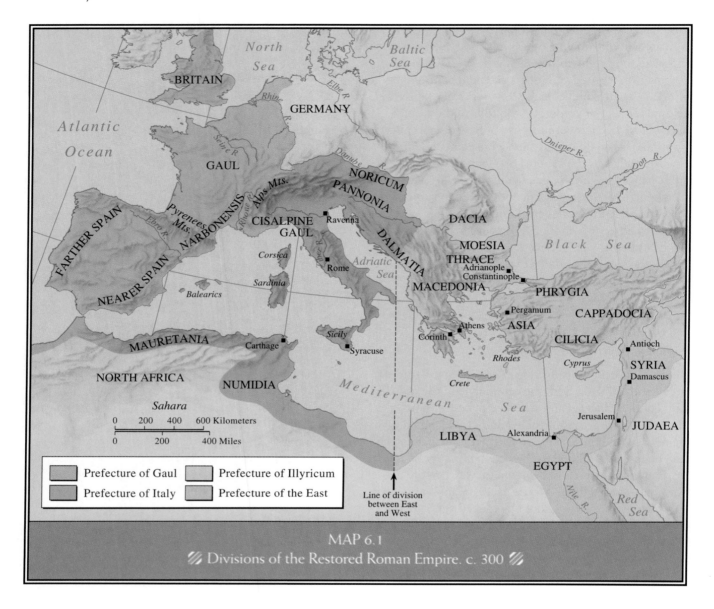

MAP 6.1

🟊 Divisions of the Restored Roman Empire. c. 300 🟊

Prefecture of Gaul **Prefecture of Illyricum**
Prefecture of Italy **Prefecture of the East**

Line of division
between East
and West

given responsibility for the west, with another, Constantius, serving as caesar in Gaul and Britain. In recognition of its greater wealth and importance, Diocletian took the east for himself and established his headquarters at Nicomedia in Asia Minor. His trusted lieutenant Galerius was made caesar with special responsibility for Syria and Egypt.

Decentralization worked well as long as the authority of Diocletian remained intact (see map 6.1). He was probably right in assuming that no one man could effectively govern so vast and beleaguered an empire. If Maximian and the two caesars remained loyal, they could respond more quickly to crises without losing control of an army that numbered more than 650,000 men. To ensure even quicker response, the army was divided into

permanent garrisons and mobile expeditionary forces. The latter, reinforced with heavily armored cavalry (*cataphracti*) on an unprecedented scale, were capable of moving rapidly to threatened sectors of the frontier.

To separate military from civilian authority, Diocletian assigned each augustus and caesar a praetorian prefect with broad judicial and administrative powers. He then subdivided the existing provinces, increased the civil powers of their governors, and grouped the new, smaller units into *dioceses* supervised by imperial vicars. The vicars reported to the praetorian prefects.

The new administrative system would be the model for the later empire—and for the Christian church when it eventually achieved official status. Diocletian used it primarily to implement economic reforms. To him, and to his successors, only a command economy in which the government regulated nearly every aspect of economic life could provide the resources needed to maintain both the army and a newly expanded bureaucracy. All pretense of a free market was abandoned. Diocletian attempted to solve the labor shortage by forbidding workers to leave their trades and by binding tenants to the great estates for life. In later years, these provisions were made hereditary, but they did nothing to retard economic stagnation. In the long run, restricting the free movement of labor probably made matters worse, as did continued tax increases and a new, more efficient system of forced requisitions that he introduced early in his reign.

The long-term effect of these changes was obscured by peace, which enabled the economy to recover somewhat in spite of them, but Diocletian's effort to control inflation failed quickly and visibly (see table 6.2). He restored the metal content of silver and gold coins, devalued under his predecessors, but could not issue enough of them to meet demand. Silver-washed copper coins known as *nummi* remained the most common money in circulation and depreciated even faster in relation to the new coinage. Prices continued to rise. In 301, Diocletian responded by placing a ceiling on wages and prices. Like all such measures, the edict proved impossible to enforce. Riots and black marketeering greeted its introduction in the more commercial east, while the agricultural west seems to have ignored it altogether. The program was abandoned after a year.

Whatever their shortcomings, the reforms of Diocletian were perhaps the best answer that administrative genius alone could apply to the problems of the later empire. Little else could have been done within the constraints imposed by Rome's defensive needs. To preserve his achievements, Diocletian abdicated in 305 and retired to the magnificent fortified palace he constructed on the shores of the Adriatic (see illustration 6.4). Though many of his reforms endured, all plans for an orderly succession collapsed long before he died in 313.

The Age of Constantine

Even had Diocletian's colleagues been fully willing to accept his settlement, their sons were not. Maximian, the western augustus, abdicated in favor of his caesar, Constantius, but when the latter died in 306, his son Constantine was proclaimed augustus by the troops and Maximian's son, Maxentius, rebelled against him. In

TABLE 6.2

Diocletian: Edict of Maximum Prices, A.D. 301

The emperor Diocletian's reforms included an important effort to control the inflation of prices. His edict stated the maximum permissible price of wages in many jobs, of many commodities, and of transportation. Although the edict was often circumvented, it provides a remarkable portrait of daily life in the Roman Empire.

For one *modius* (c. 2 gallons):		For 1 *sextarius* (approx. 16 ounces):			
Wheat	100 *denarii*	Wine	30 *denarii*	Honey	40
Rye	60	Ordinary		1 pheasant	250 *denarii*
Millet	50	wine	8	2 chickens	60
Beans	60	Beer	4	10 sparrows	16
Rice	200	Egyptian		100 oysters	100
Salt	100	beer	2	12 oz. pork	12
		Olive oil	40	12 oz. fish	24

For daily labor:		For skilled wages:	
Farm laborer	25 *denarii*	Scribe, per 100 lines	25
Carpenter	50	Notary, per document	10
Painter	75	Tailor, cutting one cloak	60
Baker	50	Tailor, for breeches	20
Shipwright	60		
Camel driver	25	Monthly scale for teachers, per pupil	
Shepherd	20		
Sewer cleaner	25	Elementary teacher	50
		Arithmetic teacher	75
For lawyer, simple		Teacher of Greek	200
case	1,000	Rhetoric teacher	250

Transactions of the American Philological Association, 71 (1940), 157.

312 Constantine defeated Maxentius at the battle of the Milvian bridge and became undisputed augustus of the west. In the east, Licinius, who governed the dioceses on the Danube frontier, eventually succeeded Galerius and made an uneasy alliance with Constantine that ended, after much maneuvering, with the defeat and execution of Licinius in 324. Constantine, known thereafter as "the Great," had reunited the empire under his personal rule.

Constantine, like Diocletian and the rest of his imperial colleagues, came from the provinces along the lower Danube and had only an approximate acquaintance with traditional Roman culture. In administrative

Illustration 6.4

Model of Diocletian's Palace at Split. The emperor built this palace on the Dalmatian Coast after A.D. 293 for his retirement. The concern for security indicates the limited success of his reforms and a certain distrust of his fellow tetrarchs.

matters, he continued the policies of his predecessor and surpassed him in ritualizing the imperial office. All trace of republican values were abandoned. Under Constantine, the emperor became a godlike figure surrounded by eastern rituals who spoke to all but the most privileged of his subjects from behind a screen (see illustration 6.5).

Eastern ritual was appropriate because the empire's center of gravity had long since shifted to the east. The constant military pressure exerted by the Germans had drained the west of much of its wealth. What little remained tended to flow eastward, as westerners continued to purchase craft and luxury items from the more advanced cities of Syria and Asia Minor. More than ever, the west had become a land of vast, self-sufficient latifundia, worked by tenants and isolated from the shrinking towns whose chief remaining function was to house a bloated imperial administration. Constantine, who had spent most of his adult life in the west, knew this all too well. That was why, in 324, he established a new capital at Byzantium on the shores of the Bosporus. Rome, the city, had declined in importance. Most of the emperors since Marcus Aurelius had passed their reigns

closer to the military frontiers, and some had never visited the ancient capital. Constantine's move was therefore an acknowledgment of existing realities. Byzantium, renamed Constantinople in honor of himself, was at the strategic and economic center of the empire. Rome, though still a great city, was becoming a museum.

Moving the imperial capital from Rome to Constantinople hastened the decline of the west, but it was only one of several steps taken by Constantine that revealed the shape of the future. The most important was his personal acceptance of the Christian religion. His reasons for doing so are not entirely clear. Constantine's mother, Helen, was a Christian, but he grew up a virtual hostage at the pagan court of Diocletian. It was not until the battle of the Milvian Bridge in 312 that he had his troops paint Christian symbols on their shields. Afterward, he claimed that a flaming cross in the sky had led them to victory. Constantine's grasp of Christian principles remained weak to the end, and he may have converted simply because he thought that the magic of the Christians was stronger. An element of political calculation probably also entered into his decision.

Illustration 6.5

/// **Monumental Head of the Emperor Constantine.** Originally part of a much larger seated statue, the head alone is more than eight feet tall and is meant to convey a godlike impression.

In the course of the third century, the Christians had become a political force in the eastern half of the empire. No longer a church of the weak and helpless, it included people of great influence in Diocletian's administration, some of whom were thought capable of fraud and violence. In 303 Diocletian became convinced that they were plotting against him and launched the last and most savage of the persecutions. He was encouraged in this by Galerius, whose tenure in the east had convinced him that the Christians were a menace to imperial government as a whole. When Diocletian abdicated, Galerius continued to pursue anti-Christian policies until his own death in 311 and bequeathed them to his successor, Maximin Daia. Constantine perhaps adopted Christianity because he and

his then-ally Licinius needed Christian support in their successful struggle with Maximin Daia. However, no direct evidence of this is available, and little reason exists to suppose that Christian support affected the final outcome of these imperial struggles.

In any case, Constantine's adoption of Christianity changed the basic character of the church. Though paganism continued to be tolerated, Christianity now had many of the characteristics of an official religion. Homes and catacombs were abandoned as centers of worship in favor of the basilica, an oblong structure of the sort used for Roman public assemblies (see illustration 6.6). The new construction—and the clergy itself—was funded in part with imperial monies, and membership was both a mark of status and essential for those who wished to reach the highest levels of the imperial service.

Converts poured in, and Christian principles became the basis for a mass of legislation. Even before his final victory in 324, Constantine moved to limit the brutality of official punishments and to expand poor relief. To provide poor women with an alternative to infanticide, the most common and effective method of birth control in ancient times, arrangements were made for the care of foundlings. Most measures were benign, but the sterner side of Christian morality was reflected in new and savage penalties for adultery, prostitution, and premarital sex.

Constantine might not have understood the intricacies of Christian theology. As a practical ruler, however, he knew that doctrinal disputes could lead to political disorder. He sought from the beginning of his reign to end the heresies that disturbed the church.

The most important of these involved the Trinity. By 260 a majority of Christians believed that there was one God, but that God had three persons—the Father, the Son (Christ), and the Holy Spirit. In the reign of Constantine, an Alexandrian priest named Arius advanced the view that Christ was a created being, neither fully God nor fully man. This called the nature of Christ's sacrifice into question, for, if he were not both fully man and fully God, how could his suffering on the cross have atoned for the sins of humankind?

The popular interest aroused by this argument is hard to imagine today, but trinitarian disputes became a fruitful source of riots and other violence in the cities of the empire. Arianism may have masked political and regional grievances that owed little to religion. In any case, Constantine was forced to call another general meeting of the church. In 325 the Council of Nicaea decreed that Christ was both fully man and fully God,

Illustration 6.6

The Basilica of Santa Maria Maggiore, Rome. The basilica, with its columned side isles and flat roof, was adapted from earlier Roman architectural practice and became the standard for Christian church construction in the west after Constantine's conversion. This example was built between 432 and 440.

and this formula was defined even more carefully by the Council of Chalcedon in 451 (see document 6.2). It eventually became the orthodox position in both the eastern and the western churches, but, for many, the question remained unsettled.

The Final Division of the Empire and the Decline of the West

In retrospect, the reign of Constantine seemed to many a golden age. People saw the reunification of the empire, the establishment of a new capital, and the acceptance of Christianity as extraordinary achievements whose luster was enhanced by the godlike ritual that surrounded the emperor and by the overall competence of his administration. Yet for all his apparent brilliance, Constantine failed to solve the basic problems that were tearing apart the empire. He did nothing to limit the political influence of the army or to develop an orderly process of imperial succession. Though he was lucky enough to escape a major crisis along his northern and western borders, the underlying military and economic weakness of the west remained (see map 6.2). By shifting the center of government from west to east, he may have accelerated the west's decline.

Constantine's death in 337 was followed by a bitter struggle between his sons that ended with the victory

of the Arian Constantius II (d. 361). Constantius's successor, Julian, known as the Apostate, rejected Christianity altogether. His effort to restore paganism died with him in 363 on a remote Mesopotamian battlefield. Imperial unity died as well. To western Germans such as the Franks and Alemanni, Julian's ill-fated attempt to destroy the Sassanid Empire provided them with an opportunity for renewed attacks along the Rhine and upper Danube. Realizing that the German threat would require all of his attention, the new emperor, Valentinian (reigned 364–375), established himself at Milan in northern Italy and left the eastern half of the empire to his brother Valens (reigned 364–378). The brothers maintained separate courts and administrations—the one Latin-speaking, the other Greek. The division between east and west, which had slowed at least outwardly under Constantine, accelerated.

Valentinian neutralized the Germans on the Rhine. Upon his death in 375, he left the western half of the empire to his son, Gratian. The next year a more serious crisis developed in the Balkans. The Huns, an Asiatic people of uncertain origin, conquered the Ostrogothic kingdom north of the Black Sea and pressed westward against the Visigoths who inhabited the lower Danube. The Visigoths asked and received permission to seek refuge within the empire. They repaid Valen's generosity by looting the Balkan provinces. The emperor was forced to break off yet another war with the Persians to confront them. The result was dis-

DOCUMENT 6.2

The Council of Chalcedon: The Nature of Christ

The formula devised by the Council of Chalcedon in 451 defines the nature of Christ in such a way as to leave no room for Arian, Monophysite, or other interpretations of the Trinity. That is the reason for its precise, legalistic, and inelegant language.

Following the holy fathers we teach with one voice that the Son [of God] and our Lord Jesus Christ is to be confessed as one and the same [Person], that he is perfect in manhood, very God and very man, of a reasonable soul and [human] body consisting consubstantial with the Father as touching his Godhead, and with us as touching his manhood; made in all things like unto us, sin only excepted; begotten of his Father before the worlds according to his Godhead; but in these last days for us men and for our salvation born of the Virgin Mary, the Mother of God according to his manhood. This one and the same Jesus Christ, the only begotten Son [of God] must be confessed to be in two natures, unconfusedly, immutably, indivisibly, inseparably, and that without the distinction of natures being taken away by such union, but rather the peculiar property of each nature being preserved and being united in one Person and subsistence, not separated or divided into two persons, but one and the same Son and only-begotten, God the Word, our Lord Jesus Christ.

Chalcedon, in P. Schaff and H. Wace, eds. *A Select Library of Nicene and Post-Nicene Fathers of the Christian Church*, vol. 14, 2d series. New York: 1899–1900.

aster. In 378 the Visigothic cavalry destroyed Valens and his army at Adrianople (now Edirne in European Turkey), a strategic site that controls the land approaches to Constantinople. Gratian, as the surviving augustus, appointed the Spanish general Theodosius (347–395) to succeed his uncle as emperor in the east.

Theodosius was in many respects a remarkable character. He restored order in the Balkans by allowing the Visigoths to set up an independent, though allied, Germanic state on imperial soil. Believing that the battle of Adrianople had demonstrated the superiority of

cavalry, he reduced the role of the legions and made heavily armored *cataphracti* the dominant element in a reorganized Roman army. It was a major step in the development of medieval warfare. The importance of cavalry had been growing steadily since the military reforms of Diocletian.

His religious policies were equally important. Theodosius made Christianity the official religion of the empire and actively suppressed not only the pagans but also Arianism. Paganism remained more firmly entrenched in the west than in the east, especially among the educated upper classes. When Gratian's successor, Valentinian II, died in 392, Theodosius became sole emperor after suppressing a revolt in the west that had been inspired at least partially by paganism. Nicaean Christianity was imposed upon the west, and for two brief years the empire was once again united.

The final division came in 395, when the dying Theodosius left the empire to his two sons. The eastern half went on as before, an empire in its own right that, though Greek in language, continued to evolve according to Roman legal and administrative precedents. The west, as a political entity, ceased to exist within two generations. Long before the reign of Theodosius it had begun to exhibit the economic, political, and religious decentralization that is thought of today as medieval. As trade and the circulation of money decreased, the great estates grew larger and more self-sufficient. Their powerful owners, anxious to protect their workforce, prevented their tenants from joining the army. This, together with a slow but persistent decline in population, forced the emperors to recruit barbarians by offering them land within the empire. Barbarian chiefs or commanders sometimes acquired latifundia as a reward for their services, and by the end of the fourth century, the line between Roman and barbarian had become blurred, especially in Gaul.

Few of these men understood, or accepted, Roman ideas of law and culture. The persistence of old tribal or personal allegiances, in addition to conflict between Romans and barbarians, led to internal violence that the imperial government could rarely control. Faced with increasing disorder in the countryside, the latifundia developed small armies of their own, while peasants—both Roman and barbarian—were forced to seek protection by becoming their tenants. Those whose situation was truly desperate were accepted only under the harshest of terms and became little more than serfs.

Even the church did little to promote unity. It remained essentially an urban institution. The term *pagani*, or pagans, was originally Latin slang for rustics,

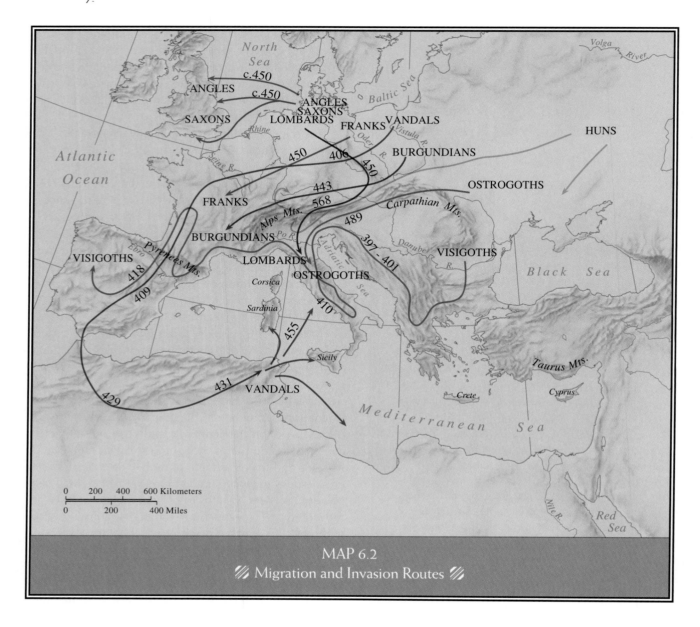

MAP 6.2

Migration and Invasion Routes

and Christianity had long found penetrating the rural world difficult. That world was dominated by the estate owners, some of whom were still attached to the values of ancient Rome. Others, especially those of German origin, were Christian but remained Arians until well into the seventh century.

The church was more powerful in the western towns. It maintained a degree of independence that contrasted sharply with attitudes prevalent in the east. There, the imperial office retained some of the religious character it had inherited from paganism. The emperor normally controlled the appointment of eastern bishops and, in later years, would acquire the right to define dogma. Western bishops, meanwhile, were elected, sometimes by public acclamation. They often controlled their city governments and were beginning to formulate the idea of separation between church and state. St. Ambrose (c. 339–397), as bishop of Milan, once imposed a public penance on Theodosius for ordering the massacre of rebels and told him on another occasion: "[D]o not burden your conscience with the thought that you have any right as Emperor over sacred things."

A society so burdened by poverty and decentralization could not defend itself against the renewed onslaughts of the barbarians (see documents 6.3 and 6.4). After 406 a Germanic people known as the Vandals marched through Gaul and Spain to establish themselves in Africa. In 410 an army of Visigoths sacked Rome. Attila the Hun invaded Italy between

◆ DOCUMENT 6.3 ◆

St. Jerome: Conditions in the Early Fifth Century

St. Jerome (c. 347–c. 420) is best known as the translator of the Bible into Latin. He was also deeply attached to Roman culture. This fragment from his letters is dramatic evidence of his dismay as well as of his skill as a rhetorician.

Nations innumerable and most savage have invaded all Gaul. The whole region between the Alps and the Pyrenees, the Ocean and the Rhine, has been devastated by the Quadi, the Vandals, the Sarmati, the Alani, the Gepidae, the hostile Heruli, the Saxons, the Burgundians, the Alemanni, and the Pannonians. O wretched Empire. Mayence, formerly so noble a city, has been taken and ruined, and in the church many thousands of men have been massacred. Worms has been destroyed after a long siege. Rheims, that powerful city, Amiens, Arras, Speyer, Strasbourg—all have seen their citizens led away captive into Germany. Aquitaine and the provinces of Lyon and Narbonne, all save a few towns, have been depopulated; and these the sword threatens from without, while hunger ravages within. I cannot speak without tears of Toulouse, which the merits of the holy Bishop Exuperius have prevailed so far to preserve from destruction. Spain, even, is in daily terror lest it perish, remembering the invasion of the Cimbri; and whatsoever the other provinces have suffered once, they continue to suffer in their fear.

I will keep silence concerning the rest, lest I seem to despair of the mercy of God. For a long time, from the Black Sea to the Julian Alps, those things which are ours have not been ours; and for thirty years, since the Danube boundary was broken, war has been waged in the very midst of the Roman Empire. Our tears are dried by old age. Except for a few old men, all were born in captivity and siege, and do not desire the liberty they never knew. Who could believe this? How could the whole tale be worthily told?

Robinson, James Harvey, eds. *Readings in European History*, vol. 1. Boston: Ginn, 1904.

◆ DOCUMENT 6.4 ◆

Roman Acceptance of Barbarian Rule

Salvianus (c. 400–480) saw the fall of Rome as God's judgment on those who had oppressed the poor. His view is a valuable correction to that of St. Jerome and explains clearly why most Romans accepted barbarian rule without serious protest.

But what else can these wretched people wish for, they who suffer the incessant and even continuous destruction of public tax levies. To them there is always imminent a heavy and relentless proscription. They desert their homes, lest they be tortured in their very homes. They seek exile, lest they suffer torture. The enemy is more lenient to them than the tax collectors. This is proved by this very fact, that they flee to the enemy in order to avoid the full force of the heavy tax levy. This very tax levying, although hard and inhuman, would nevertheless be less heavy and harsh if all would bear it equally and in common. Taxation is made more shameful and burdensome because all do not bear the burden of all. They extort tribute from the poor man for the taxes of the rich, and the weaker carry the load for the stronger. There is no other reason that they cannot bear all the taxation except that the burden imposed on the wretched is greater than their resources.

The Writing of Salvian the Presbyter, trans. J. F. O'Sullivan. Washington, DC: Catholic University of America Press, 1947.

451 and his death in 453. In 455 Rome was sacked again, this time by Vandals. Lacking an effective army of their own, the emperors were forced to rely upon barbarian chieftains for protection. As the barbarians soon realized, the emperor had become largely irrelevant.

The wars of the fifth century were struggles between various barbarian armies for control over the remains of the western empire. In 476 the Ostrogothic general Odoacer (c. 433–493) deposed the emperor Romulus Augustulus and was recognized by the eastern emperor as his viceroy. This event is known conventionally as "the fall of Rome," but the western empire had long since ceased to exist. Vandals ruled Africa, Visigoths governed Spain, and Gaul was now divided into a variety of jurisdictions ruled by Franks, Burgundians, and other tribes. Italy was given over to the Ostrogoths, but their rule was not destined to last.

In one final effort to reunite the empire, the eastern emperor Justinian "the Great" (reigned 527–565) conquered North Africa from the Vandals and mounted a campaign for the recovery of Italy. Assisted by his wife, Theodora (c. 497–548), a former actress and prostitute who was his equal in political skill and his superior in courage, Justinian sought to rebuild the empire of Constantine. He accomplished much, including the building of the great church of St. Sophia at Constantinople and the long overdue codification of Roman law, but his attempts at reunification failed. He was the first of the Byzantine emperors.

In 552, after seventeen years of warfare, an army under his eunuch general Narses defeated the Ostrogoths. The resources of the peninsula were by now depleted. Byzantine war taxes, together with forced requisitions and looting by both sides, destroyed the basis of subsistence while terrible plagues, spread by the passage of armies, killed tens of thousands who had survived the war. Some parts of Italy were reduced to a mere seventh of their former population.

Devastated by war and by years of economic decline, the country became easy prey for yet another wave of Germanic invaders, the Lombards. These fierce people quickly seized most of northern Italy. Unlike the Ostrogoths, they preferred to kill the remaining Roman landholders and confiscate their estates. The successors of Justinian, impoverished by his ambitious policies, could do little to stop them. By the end of the seventh century, Byzantine control was limited to the coastal regions along the Adriatic. The exarch or military governor who ruled this territory did so from Ravenna, a city built on a sandbar and protected from the armies of the mainland by a broad lagoon.

The Evolution of the Western Church (A.D. 306–529)

In the midst of political turmoil, the church in the west continued to expand. As St. Augustine (354–430) pointed out in his book *The City of God,* no essential connection existed between the kingdom of Heaven and any earthly power, and Christians should leave politics alone if they valued their souls. Augustine was bishop of Hippo, near Carthage, and his view grew naturally from the suspicion of political authority that had been characteristic of the African church. He was also

the friend and convert of St. Ambrose. *The City of God,* completed in 426, was written in response to the first sack of Rome. In it, Augustine argued that "two cities have been formed by two loves: the earthly by love of self, even to the contempt of God; the heavenly by the love of God, even to the contempt of self." The earthly city must inevitably pass away as the city of God grows. In practical terms, this implied that the authority of the church must eventually supersede that of the state, though ideally church and state should cooperate for the greater protection of the faithful.

Augustine's work lies at the root of medieval political thought and reflects the growing gap between western and eastern concepts of the church's role. That gap was further widened by the evolution of the papacy. The early church recognized four patriarchs—bishops whose authority exceeded that of the others. They ruled the dioceses (ecclesiastical districts) of Rome, Constantinople, Alexandria, and Antioch. Of these, the bishop of Rome was most venerated, though veneration did not necessarily imply obedience. The erosion of political authority in the west and the removal of the capital to Constantinople caused the popes, notably Innocent I (served 402–417) and Leo I (served 440–461), to claim universal jurisdiction over the church and to base their claims more firmly upon the doctrine of apostolic succession (see document 6.5).

Such claims were contested, and the Council of Chalcedon greatly annoyed Leo by granting the patriarch of Constantinople primacy in the east, but papal claims were based to some extent on political reality. Throughout the dark years of the fifth century, the popes often provided leadership when the imperial office failed.

Intellectually, too, the western church continued to flourish. In addition to *The City of God,* St. Augustine elaborated on a concept of sin and grace that was to have a long-lasting impact on Western thought. He was moved to write on this subject by the teachings of Pelagius, a Briton who believed in unlimited free will. Pelagius argued that a Christian could achieve salvation simply by choosing to live a godly life. Augustine, whose early struggles with sin are chronicled in his *Confessions,* claimed that human nature was so corrupted by its Fall from the Garden of Eden that salvation was impossible without God's grace and that grace is given selectively. God, in other words, predestines some to salvation and some to punishment. In 529, long after both men were dead, the Synod of Orange rejected Pelagianism but did not officially endorse the Augustinian view, which remained an undercurrent in medieval theology, only to surface again with renewed vigor in

DOCUMENT 6.5

The Petrine Theory

One of the clearest expositions of the Petrine theory or doctrine of the apostolic succession was by Pope Leo I "the Great" who claimed universal authority over the Christian church because as bishop of Rome he was the successor to St. Peter and in Matthew 16:18 Jesus had said: "Thou art Peter, and upon this rock I will build my church; and the gates of hell shall not prevail against it."

Our Lord Jesus Christ, the Saviour of the world, caused his truth to be promulgated through the apostles. And while this duty was placed on all of the apostles, the Lord made St. Peter the head of them all, that from him as from their head his gifts should flow out into all the body. So that if anyone separates himself from St. Peter he should know that he has no share in the Divine blessing. . . . Constantinople has its own glory and by the mercy of God has become the seat of the empire. But secular matters are based on one thing, ecclesiastical matters on another. For nothing will stand which is not built on the rock [Peter] which the Lord laid in the foundation [Matt. 16:18]. . . . Your city is royal, but you cannot make it apostolic.

Thatcher, O. J., and McNeal, E. H., eds. *A Source Book of Medieval History.* New York: Scribner's, 1905.

the Protestant Reformation of the sixteenth century. The rest of Augustine's thought was less controversial. His concept of the church, its sacraments, and even his view of history were widely accepted in the Middle Ages and remain influential among Christians today.

Though not an original theologian, Augustine's older contemporary St. Jerome (c. 347–c. 420) was an outstanding scholar and Latin stylist who supported Augustine in the Pelagian controversy and continued the history of the church begun by Eusebius. His most important contribution, however, was the Latin translation of the Bible known as the Vulgate, which remained the standard for western Christendom until the sixteenth century.

Perhaps the most striking feature of Christian life in the later Roman Empire was the spread of monasticism. Most of the world's great religions have produced, at one time or another, men and women who dedicate

themselves to a life of religious devotion away from the distractions of the secular world. In Christianity, this impulse first surfaced when the church began to change from a persecuted congregation of believers to a universal faith. In 291 a young Egyptian named Anthony took to heart the words of Jesus: "If you will be perfect, go sell all thou hast and give to the poor, and come, follow me." He retired to a cave in the desert and became the first of many hermits who followed his example.

Within only a few years, another Egyptian, Pachomius (c. 290–346), realized that the isolated life of the hermit placed demands upon the mind and body that only the strongest could survive. Ordinary mortals, however devout, needed the support and discipline of a community that shared their goals. He therefore organized the first formal congregations of hermits and gave them a rule that became the basis of all subsequent monastic institutions in the west. The monks were to live in common and divide their time between work and prayer. Poverty and chastity were assumed as essential to a life lived in imitation of Christ, and obedience was regarded as a natural part of communal living.

During the age of Constantine, monasteries, some of them with congregations numbering in the thousands, sprang up throughout Egypt, Palestine, and Syria. Women were as attracted to the movement as men. Athanasius (c. 293–373), bishop of Alexandria and energetic opponent of the Arians, spread the gospel of monasticism during his travels in the west, and by the end of the fourth century, the institution was solidly established in every part of Europe. Augustine practiced communal living as a matter of course, and Jerome established a convent of saintly women at Jerusalem.

The chaos of the fifth century may have enhanced the attractions of monastic life, but monasteries were not as isolated from the world as their inmates might have wished. Many, if not most, houses were established in rural areas whose populations were imperfectly Christianized. Monks surrounded by pagans were obligated to attempt their conversion, and the monasteries became centers for the spreading of the faith. Each community, moreover, had to be supported economically. Peasants attached themselves to nearby convents and monasteries in much the same way that they became tenants of the great secular estates—and for many of the same reasons. The larger foundations became latifundia in their own right. Abbots and abbesses mastered the art of administration and exerted a substantial influence on regional politics. But monasticism made its greatest contributions in the intellectual realm. In a world of declining literacy, monasteries remained the chief purveyors of education and the heart of whatever intellectual life remained. Their libraries preserved the Latin classics for a later, more appreciative age.

The heart of monastic life was the rule that governed the lives of monks or nuns. In the west, the rule of St. Benedict of Nursia (c. 480–c. 547) was universally accepted for nearly six centuries and remains the basis of daily life in many religious orders today (see document 6.6). Benedict was abbott of the great monastery at Monte Cassino, north of Naples. His rule, though not wholly original, was brief, moderate, and wise in its understanding of human nature. He based it on the ideal of *mens sano en corpore sano,* a healthy mind in a healthy body. Work, prayer, and study were stressed equally in an atmosphere governed by loving discipline. The Benedictine rule prescribes an ordered, pious life well suited to the development of one of medieval Europe's most powerful institutions.

The growing importance of monasticism was only one of the ways in which late Roman society began to foreshadow that of the Middle Ages. It was above all increasingly Christian, though the western church had long since begun to diverge in organization and practice from its eastern counterpart. It was also agrarian and generally poor. Though small freeholds continued to exist in Italy, Frankish Gaul, and elsewhere, much of the countryside was dominated by self-sufficient estates worked by tenants and defended by bands of armed retainers. An increasing number of these estates supported monasteries. For reasons that are as yet poorly understood, crop yields rarely rose above the subsistence level. Western cities, reduced to a fraction of their former size, were often little more than large agricultural villages whose inhabitants tilled their fields by day and retreated within the walls at night. Ruled in many cases by their bishops, they retained something of their Roman character, but lack of specie and the violence endemic in the countryside limited trade and communications. Contacts with the eastern empire, though never entirely abandoned, became rare. By the end of the fifth century, the Mediterranean unity forged by Rome had ceased to exist. A distinctively European society, formed of Roman, Celtic, and Germanic elements, was beginning to emerge.

❖ DOCUMENT 6.6 ❖

The Rule of St. Benedict

The following sections capture St. Benedict's view that monks should live a disciplined but balanced life dedicated to apostolic poverty.

Chapter 33—The sin of owning private property should be entirely eradicated from the monastery. No one shall presume to give or receive anything except by order of the abbot; no one shall possess anything of his own, books, paper, pens, or anything else, for monks are not to own even their own bodies and wills to be used at their own desire, but are to look to the father of the monastery for everything.

Chapter 48—Idleness is the great enemy of the soul, therefore monks should always be occupied, either in manual labor or in holy reading. The hours for these occupations should be arranged according to the seasons, as follows: From Easter to the first of October, the monks shall go to work at the first hour and labor until the fourth hour, and the time from the fourth to the sixth hour shall be spent in reading. After dinner, which comes at the sixth hour, they shall lie down and rest in silence; but anyone who wishes may read, if he does it so as not to disturb anyone else. Nones shall be observed a little earlier, about the middle of the eighth hour, and the monks shall go back to work, laboring until vespers. But if the conditions of the locality or the needs of the monastery, such as may occur at harvest time, should make it necessary to labor longer hours, they shall not feel themselves ill-used, for true monks should live by the labor of their own hands, as did the apostles and the holy fathers.

"Regula Monchorum." in O. J. Thatcher and E. H. McNeal, eds., *A Source Book of Medieval History.* New York: Scribner's, 1905.

CHAPTER 7

ROME'S SUCCESSORS: BYZANTIUM, ISLAM, AND THE GERMANIC WEST

CHAPTER OUTLINE

The fall of Rome conventionally marks the beginning of European history, but Europe did not develop wholly in isolation. It was one of three great societies that emerged after the breakup of Mediterranean civilization. Byzantium and the world of Islam, were, like medieval Europe, heirs to the broader culture that had been consolidated and refined by centuries of Roman rule. They developed along radically different lines, but each exerted a powerful influence on Western civilization.

The Byzantine Empire and Its Government

The reforms of Diocletian and Constantine established the institutional framework of the Byzantine Empire long before the separation of east and west. The system they created evolved without interruption until 1453, though the empire had been reduced in size by the conquests of Islam in the seventh century and weakened after 1100 by the impact of the Crusades.

The heart of that system remained the person of the emperor. Though he was usually the designated heir of his predecessor, he had to be acclaimed by the Senate, the army, and the people of Constantinople before he could be crowned. The empress, who might be the emperor's wife, sister, mother, or aunt, often exerted substantial power of her own and could rule independently if the emperor were incapacitated or a minor. Once in office, the emperor's power was theoretically absolute. As the vicar of God on Earth, he held the lives and property of every subject in his hands and could punish or confiscate without appeal. In practice, law and common sense limited the exercise of this arbitrary power. Any of the electoral groups—usually the army—could proclaim a successor if an emperor proved unsatisfactory. The choice then had to be confirmed by the Senate and the people before the usurpation was

◆ DOCUMENT 7.1 ◆

Justinian: Institutes on Justice and the Law

The Institutes *is the shortest of the four parts of the* Corpus Iuris Civilis, *and it provides a framework for the entire* Corpus. *The first section of the first book of the* Institutes *opens with a preamble on the nature of justice and law, and the best means of teaching it to students. The discussion then moves to general categories in the law ranging from the law of persons to penalties for overeager litigants. The section on disinheriting children reflects partibility as the basis of inheritance in Roman law; that is, children must normally inherit equally.*

1.1   JUSTICE AND LAW. Justice is an unswerving and perpetual determination to acknowledge all men's rights. 1. Learning in the law entails knowledge of God and man, and mastery of the difference between justice and injustice. 2. As we embark on the exposition of Roman law after these general statements, the best plan will be to give brief, straightforward accounts of each topics. The denser detail must be kept till later. Any other approach would mean making students take in a huge number of distinctions right at the start while their minds were still untrained and short of stamina. Half of them would give up. Or else they would lose their self-confidence—a frequent source of discouragement for the young—and at the cost of toil and tears would in the end reach the very standard they could have attained earlier and without overwork or self-doubt if they had been taken along an easier road. 3. The commandments of the law are these: live honorably; harm nobody; give everyone his due.

1.3   THE LAW OF PERSONS. The main classification in the law of persons is this: all men are either free or slaves. 1. Liberty—the Latin *libertas* give us *liberi*, free men—denotes a man's natural ability to do what he wants as long as the law or some other force does not prevent him. 2. Slavery, on the other hand, is an institution of the law of all peoples; it makes a man the property of another, contrary to the law of nature.

2.13   DISINHERITING CHILDREN. Someone with a son within his authority must be sure to appoint him heir or to disinherit him specifically. If he passes over him in silence, his will becomes a nullity. . . . However, the old rules did not apply with the same rigour to daughters or to other male or female members of the family descended through the male line. If they were neither appointed heirs nor disinherited the will was not wholly invalidated. Instead they had a right to come in for their proper shares. The head of the family was also not obliged to disinherit them by name but could do it by a general clause.

4.16   PENALTIES FOR OVER-EAGER LITIGANTS. We should notice what pains the guardians of the law have taken to see that people do not turn lightly to litigation. This is our concern as well. The main checks on the eagerness of plaintiffs and defendants are money penalties, oaths to bind the conscience, and the fear of disgrace.

Justinian's Institutes, pp. 37–39, ed. and trans. Peter Birks and Grant MacLeod. Ithaca, NY: Cornell University Press, 1987.

complete. The voice of the people was normally expressed by the crowd at the Hippodrome, the great racetrack that lay next to the imperial palace at the heart of the city. Chariot racing remained a dominant passion in Byzantine life, and as many as 100,000 spectators would gather to cheer on the Blues or the Greens, racing teams that were also political factions. The possibility of being deposed and blinded by rival generals, or perhaps dismembered by the mob, preserved a measure of imperial accountability. Only about half of the Byzantine emperors died a natural death in office.

The Roman legal tradition acted as a further restraint on arbitrary behavior. The emperor Justinian, who came to the throne in A.D. 527 and reigned for nearly forty years before dying at age eighty-three,

saved the body of Roman law that has reached modern times. The distillation of Roman law and commentaries on it, compiled by Justinian and his advisers and collectively known as the *Corpus Iuris Civilis* (Body of the Civil Law) were published at Constantinople in A.D. 533. (see document 7.1). They filled three large volumes that became one of the most influential law books ever written. Ironically, the *Codex, Digest,* and *Institutes* produced under Justinian may have been more important in the west than in the east. In the west, Roman law was largely replaced by Germanic traditions and had to be revived in the twelfth century, a process that would have been impossible without accessible texts. In contrast, eastern courts maintained Roman law without interruption, modifying it on occasion to reflect Christian values. Respect for the tradition was universal, and though the emperor had the power to appoint and remove judges, he rarely if ever ignored their opinions.

A massive bureaucracy, established originally by Diocletian and greatly expanded in the centuries after his death, carried out the imperial commands. It regulated every aspect of economic, political, and religious life. Prices and wages were fixed by law, and movement within the empire was controlled by a system of internal passports designed to prevent people from leaving their homes or hereditary occupations. An effective police system unlike anything in the medieval west maintained order in town and countryside, while a fleet of galleys patrolled the seas to keep them free of pirates. Other officials managed state-owned factories, the mines, and the distribution of water.

Many of these people, especially at the higher levels of the bureaucracy, were eunuchs—men who had been castrated in youth. Eunuchs were excluded from the imperial office by law, and their inability to produce heirs prevented the establishment of administrative dynasties, much less the kind of hereditary aristocracy that encouraged political decentralization in the medieval west. Emperors thus trusted them, and their employment made a substantial contribution to Byzantine stability. Ambitious parents sometimes had their sons castrated to advance their careers, not only in the church or civil service, but also in the army.

The Byzantine military, like the civil service, evolved from Roman precedents modified by experience in the east. The army was composed of heavy armored cavalry (*cataphracti*) supported by archers and by a heavy infantry armed with shields and swords or axes. "Greek fire," a kind of napalm whose composition remains secret to this day, was used on both land and sea, and siegecraft was a highly developed art. Though the Byzantines prided themselves on their superior grasp of strategy, they preferred whenever possible to rely upon negotiation. Their diplomacy was known for its subtlety as well as for its lavishness. They believed that even massive subsidies were cheaper than a war. Magnificent gifts were given to prospective enemies, and if such people chose to call it tribute, what else could one expect from barbarians?

The Byzantines paid heavily for all of this security and regulation. A land tax fell upon every property in the empire, including monasteries and the imperial estates. Reassessment took place every fifteen years. If a farmer could not pay, his obligation had to be assumed by his neighbors under a system known as *epiboli*. A head tax also was imposed. Levies on farm animals, business inventories, imports, and exports were supplemented by surtaxes in times of special need.

Few governments have been more efficient in their extraction of surplus wealth, but some of the proceeds were spent on alleviating poverty. Though regular distributions of grain to the poor stopped at the beginning of the seventh century, officials were expected to provide food in times of scarcity and to administer a host of orphanages and other charities. The heavy taxes may have permitted only a few to rise above the poverty level, but fewer still were destitute.

The Economic and Social Structures of Byzantine Society

In time, the autocratic and intrusive character of the Byzantine state produced a social structure that had few parallels in the medieval world. Asia Minor and the Balkan Peninsula formed the heartland of the Byzantine Empire even before the Muslims took Syria, Egypt, and North Africa in the seventh century. Both are rugged lands whose narrow valleys and small plateaus are cut off from one another because of geography and because their inhabitants come from different ethnic groups with long histories of mutual conflict. It would be hard to imagine a site less likely to encourage social equality and weak kinship ties, but that is what happened.

In the face of overwhelming imperial power, social distinctions receded. Below the throne, everyone was equal. Variations were seen in wealth, but Byzantine society had absorbed Christian teachings so that it did not regard money as a measure of virtue. Prestige depended primarily upon bureaucratic rank, and rank depended upon merit or on the bureaucrat's usefulness to the emperor. The widespread employment of eunuchs and the principle that all wealth could be appropriated to the service of the state inhibited the growth of those elaborate social hierarchies characteristic of the medieval west. As a result, social distinctions were fluid and relatively minor. The empress Theodora was not the only great personage to come from the lowest levels of society (see illustration 7.1).

Even ethnic distinctions became largely irrelevant. The Byzantines were remarkably free of prejudice, though they sometimes persecuted Jews on religious grounds and may, in the early years, have looked down upon the Germans who were found in disproportionate numbers among their slaves and household servants. The imperial court embraced Greeks, Serbs, Bulgars, Armenians, Cappadocians, and a score of other ethnic groups without distinction; the ordinary citizen could do no less.

Illustration 7.1

Empress Theodora and Her Attendants. This mosaic from the church of San Vitale, Ravenna, Italy, is one of a pair; the other shows Theodora's husband, Justinian, with his own entourage in a similar pose.

The same conditions that promoted social equality may have discouraged the growth of extended families. A few great clans attached themselves to the imperial court, often for several generations, but the western development of lineages—extended families who took their names and social identities from their estates— had no parallel in the east until the tenth or eleventh century. Instead, the Byzantines lived overwhelmingly in tight-knit nuclear families, often maintaining a certain distance in their dealings with others. Some writers warned against friendship because it might arouse the suspicions of the state. Most people, encouraged perhaps by the *epiboli*, acknowledged the obligation to help one's neighbors. However, Byzantine society, for all its outward regimentation, remained on the personal level individualistic, self-seeking, and often cynical in its relationships.

Roman law reinforced these tendencies to some extent by ensuring the equal division of property among heirs and by favoring the preservation of freehold tenures. Most Byzantines were small farmers who owned their own land. Some were serfs or tenants on the estates of the emperor or his more important servants, and some were slaves, though the incidence of slavery declined throughout the Byzantine era and by the eleventh century had attracted the opposition of the church on moral grounds. Commerce centered in the great city of Constantinople, which, until the Crusades, dominated the trade between Asia and the west. With its population of more than 400,000 it dwarfed the other towns of the empire. Provincial cities declined steadily in importance throughout the Byzantine centuries as bureaucracy and centralization strangled the ancient Greek municipal tradition.

Christianity, not civic ideals, formed the moral and intellectual center of Byzantine life. Even the Byzantines sometimes complained that buying a piece of fruit in the market was impossible without becoming immersed in a discussion of the Trinity, but religion to them was more than a mental exercise; it was the conceptual framework of their lives. Religious disputes thus played an important role in Byzantine politics. The struggle between the orthodox and the Monophysites, who held that Christ's nature was fully human but that

Illustration 7.2

🕮 **Mosaic of Christ Pancrator, Daphni, Greece.** In Byzantine art, Jesus is normally portrayed as Christ Almighty, who mediates between God and humankind, and images such as this one are placed in the central dome or the main apse of eastern churches. In contrast, western church art tends to emphasize the crucifixion.

it had been transformed by the divine, convulsed the empire for nearly four centuries. The Iconoclastic Controversy over the use of religious images or icons generated revolts and persecutions from 726 to 843.

Though the Greek and Latin churches did not divide formally until 1054, they followed different lines of development almost from the first. In the east, church organization continued to parallel that of the imperial bureaucracy. Its higher officials—patriarchs, bishops, and metropolitans—were monks appointed by the emperor. They were expected to be celibate, if not eunuchs. Village priests, however, were normally married, in part because popular wisdom held that this would protect them from sexual temptation.

Like Byzantine society as a whole, eastern Christianity maintained a high degree of individualism within its rigidly hierarchical framework. It emphasized the inner transformation of the believer rather than sin and redemption. Its icons, or religious paintings, portray God as *Pantocrator* or ruler of the universe and virtually ignore Christ the crucified redeemer until late in

the empire's history (see illustration 7.2). The saints are abstract figures whose holiness is indicated by the golden aura of sanctity that surrounds them, not by individual features. Western legalism—the tendency to enumerate sins and prescribe penances—was almost wholly absent, and even monasteries encouraged individual development at the expense of communal living. Saintly hermits remained the most revered figures in Byzantium, advising emperors from their caves or from the top of pillars where they lived exposed to the elements, often for decades.

Before the death of Constantine, this faith had transformed the Greek way of life beyond recognition. The preoccupation with personal salvation, as well as the vast weight of the imperial bureaucracy, rendered the old idea of community meaningless. The ancient preoccupation with the human body vanished. The Byzantines wore long brocaded robes and heavy makeup that disguised the body's natural outlines and, like westerners, gradually abandoned the practice of bathing because the church thought of it as self-indulgent. For medieval Christians, the "odor of sanctity" was no mere figure of speech. In deportment, solemnity became the ideal even for children, who, like their elders, were supposed to mimic the icons that gazed down serenely from the domes of churches.

Byzantium and the Slavs

At the height of its power, the Byzantine Empire exerted only a minor influence on the development of western Europe. It maintained contact with the west through the irregular correspondence of churchmen and through the remaining Byzantine possessions in southern Italy. Western poverty imposed severe limitations on trade as a medium of cultural exchange. The greatest impact of Byzantium on the west came later, through the Crusades and through the cultural borrowings transmitted by Slavs and Muslims. Byzantine influence on eastern Europe was, however, profound.

The Slavs came originally from central Asia and, by 2000 B.C., had settled a broad arc of territory from the shores of the Black Sea northwestward into what is now Poland. They appear to have weathered the passage of Celts and Germans, but the collapse of the Hunnish Empire after A.D. 455 started another cycle of population movements in eastern Europe. Slavic peoples from the valley of the Dnieper moved northward into Russia, while those from the Vistula and Oder valleys moved westward as far as the river Elbe in eastern Germany and south into Bohemia, Moravia, and what is now Hungary. By the middle of the sixth century, they had penetrated deep into the Balkan Peninsula. The Serbs, Bulgars, and Vlachs then became involved in a long and fruitful interaction with the Byzantine Empire. The northern shores of the Black Sea, long the granary of Greece and Asia Minor, remained a vital focus of Byzantine diplomacy as well, and here, too, relations were quickly established.

Contacts were not always peaceful, but the ties between Slavs and Byzantines were ultimately those of economic self-interest. War, trade, and diplomacy brought the Slavs within the larger orbit of Byzantium. With their usual indifference to ethnicity, the Byzantines accepted many of these people into the empire. By the ninth century a number of emperors had been of slavic origin, and Slavs of many sorts were firmly entrenched in the bureaucracy.

The churches, both eastern and western, made every effort to convert those Slavs who lived outside imperial territory. A bitter competition broke out between the Greeks and the Germans over whether the Greek or Latin rites should triumph. In the end, the Serbs and Bulgars were converted to the Greek rite by Sts. Cyril and Methodius in the middle of the ninth century. The Croats, Slovenes, Poles, and Czechs, among others, accepted the Latin church. In each case, the acceptance of Christianity appears to have been part of a movement toward political consolidation. During the ninth and tenth centuries Bohemia, Serbia, and Croatia emerged as independent states, and Bulgaria, which had existed in rudimentary form since the seventh century, evolved into an empire that became a serious threat to Byzantine power until the Byzantines destroyed it in 1014.

Finally, at the end of the tenth century, Byzantine missionaries converted Vladimir "the Saint," ruler of Kiev. Located on the Dnieper river, Kiev was the center of a trading network that connected the Baltic and Black seas and drew furs, amber, and wood from the forests of central Russia. Scandinavian adventurers had gained control of the city a century before. By Vladimir's time, Kiev was again thoroughly Slavic in language and culture and the center of the first great Russian state. The conversion of Kievan Rus ensured that the eastern Slavs would adopt not only Greek Christianity, but also the Greek alphabet and many elements of Byzantine culture. The connections forged in these centuries between the Byzantine Greeks and the Serbs, Bulgars, and Russians remain a powerful cultural bond to this day.

Muhammad the Prophet and the Origins of Islam

Islam is the other great society whose interaction with Byzantium was to have profound consequences (see, map 7.1). Islam is a religion, a civilization, and a way of life. The word means submission, in this case to the will of Allah, and the followers of Islam are known as Muslims. Both the religion and the civilization based upon it grew from the revelation granted to one man.

Muhammad, the founder of Islam, was born about 570 in the Arabian caravan town of Mecca. He married a wealthy widow named Khadija and became a merchant. As he entered middle age he formed the habit of going into the mountains to meditate and pray. There, in about the year 610, the first of the teachings that make up the Koran were revealed to him by the angel Gabriel. Three years later, with his wife's encouragement, he began to preach, but Mecca was the center of an important pagan cult, and the townspeople saw his activities as a threat to their livelihood. In 622 he and his followers fled to the nearby city of Medina. This *hejira*, or immigration, marks the beginning date of the Muslim calendar. After a series of battles and negotiations, the Prophet and his followers returned and Mecca became once again the spiritual center of the movement.

The Koran is the scriptural basis of Islam, which, to Muslims, supersedes the earlier revelations found in the Jewish and Christian Bibles. It is supplemented by the *sunna*, or tradition of the prophet, a collection of sayings attributed to Muhammad that are not thought to be divinely revealed. The distinction is important because Islam is uncompromisingly monotheistic. As the *shahada* or profession of faith says: "There is no God but God, and Mohammed is his prophet." That is to say, Muhammad is not regarded as divine but only as the man through whom God's will was revealed. That revelation, embodied in the Koran, provides the Muslim with a comprehensive guide to life and thought that has the force of divine law.

Islam, like every other great world religion, eventually developed elaborate theologies, heresies, and schisms, but its essence is simple. Its creed demands belief in the one God, the angels, the revealed books, the prophets, and the Day of Judgment. The Five Pillars, or obligatory duties, are to recite the profession of faith; pray five times daily; pay the *zakat* or purification tax for the benefit of the poor; fast during the month of Ramadan, which commemorates the time in which the Koran was "sent down"; and make a pilgrimage to Mecca if wealth and family duties permit.

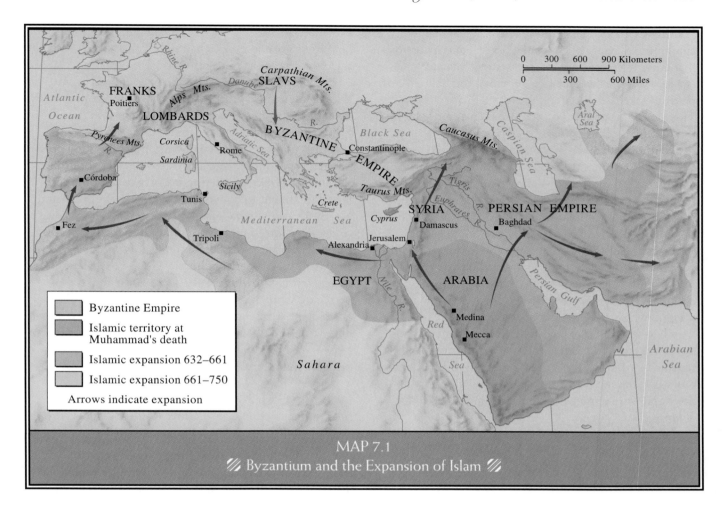

MAP 7.1

Byzantium and the Expansion of Islam

These are the basic requirements of Islam, but the goal of pious Muslims is to live according to *shari`a*, a way of life totally commanded by God. The guides to that life are the Koran, the tradition, and reason; no mysteries are required. Islam, like Judaism, is essentially a religion of the law. Based firmly on the Arabic of the Koran, which in theory cannot be translated, Islam has always been committed to the conversion of all peoples. This universality, together with the clarity of its ethical and theological demands, made the Muslim faith attractive to millions. By the time Muhammad died in 632, Islam had conquered most of the Arabian peninsula. Within the space of another generation, it had spread throughout the Middle East.

The Expansion of Islam

From the beginning, Islam spread largely through military conquest. Muhammad had been a capable commander, and his caliphs or successors followed in his footsteps. The first Muslim attack on the Byzantine

Empire occurred in 629, while Muhammad was still alive. In 635 Arab armies seized Damascus for the first time. Recently converted Syrians took Mesopotamia in 638–639, and Egypt fell to an Arab army in 640. The motives behind this expansion were not entirely religious. Some Muslims regarded the conquests as a *jihad*, or holy war, and believed that they could attain paradise through death on the battlefield. Not all of the conquerors were religious, however, and some were not even Muslim. For such men, the Arabic tradition of raiding and the hope of booty would have been reason enough. Because Islam prohibits war against fellow Muslims, the raiding impulse tended to be directed outward, at least in the early years when the memory of the Prophet was still fresh.

The terrifying speed of the Arab conquests was in part a measure of Byzantine weakness. The emperor Heraclius (c. 575–641) had been engaged from 603 to 628 in a bitter struggle with the Persian Empire during which parts of Syria and Palestine had been ruined or occupied. At the same time he was forced to deal with

Lombard attacks on Byzantine Italy, increased activity among the Slavs on the Danube border, and incursions by Berber tribesmen against the settlements in North Africa. Heraclius was an able general—the first emperor to take the field in person since the days of Theodosius—but a war on four fronts was more than the resources of his empire could bear.

Without adequate manpower in Syria and Palestine, the Byzantines resorted to a mobile defense-in-depth conducted in part by Arab mercenaries. That is, they tried to draw the enemy into the interior, disrupting his communications and defeating his smaller contingents in detail. The size and speed of the Muslim attack coupled with an almost complete lack of intelligence about Arab intentions rendered this strategy futile. The Muslims overwhelmed their Byzantine opponents and then consolidated their victory with mass conversions in the conquered territories. By 640 they had seized Syria, Palestine, Mesopotamia, and Egypt, often without encountering significant local resistance. Many of the empire's subjects disliked both its taxes and its insistence upon religious orthodoxy and were unprepared to exert themselves in its defense.

The Sassanid Empire of Persia proved a more difficult target, but it, too, had been weakened by its long war with Byzantium. Attacked by several Arab contingents from Mesopotamia, the Persians maintained a heroic struggle until their last armies were overwhelmed in 651. In only twenty years, Islam had conquered everything from the Nile to Afghanistan.

But the death of the Caliph Omar in 644 marked the beginning of disputes over who should succeed him, and for another twenty years the newborn world of Islam was convulsed by civil wars. The eventual triumph of Mu'awia (ruled 661–680), founder of the Ommayad dynasty, led to Islam's first and greatest schism. His rival, Muhammad's son-in-law Ali, was murdered in 661, but his supporters refused to recognize Mu'awia and became the first Shi'ites. Most of these people were Persians who may have resented Arab dominance even after their conversion to Islam. In the centuries to come they would develop their own system of law; their own version of the *Hadith*, or tradition; and a number of ideas borrowed from Zoroastrian and other sources. Though a minority among Muslims as a whole, Shi'ites became the dominant Islamic sect in Iran and what is now Pakistan. The majority of western Muslims remained loyal to the *sunna* and are called Sunni Muslims to this day. In 681 a Sunni army marched from Egypt to the Atlantic Ocean and added North Africa to the house of Islam. From there, a mixed army of Berbers and Arabs crossed

the Strait of Gibraltar in 711, defeated the Visigothic king Rodrigo, and by 713 had seized all of Spain with the exception of its northern coast.

Islam may have been spread by conquest, but it does not sanction forced conversions. The attractive qualities of the faith aside, Islamic triumphs in the Middle East appear to have resulted in part from anti-Byzantine sentiment among populations long persecuted for Monophysite and other heresies and from the shrewd policy of offering tax breaks and other preferred treatment to converts. In such areas as Spain and North Africa the invaders may have seemed less alien to the Romanized population than their Germanic rulers. Their faith was different, but the Muslims generally shared the broader cultural values of the Mediterranean world. Nowhere was an attempt made to persecute Christians or Jews, the other "peoples of the book." Christian and Jewish communities lived peacefully within the Islamic world until Muslim intolerance arose in the twentieth century as a response to European colonialism.

Social and Economic Structures in the Islamic World

The Arab warriors who conquered the world from the Indus to the Pyrenees came from a society that was still largely tribal in its organization. Lacking governmental institutions, they retained those of the Byzantines or Persians, modifying them when necessary to conform with Islamic law. Roman law was abandoned.

In theory, the caliphs, or successors to the Prophet, ruled the entire Islamic world as the executors of God's law, which they interpreted with the assistance of a body of religious scholars known as the *ulama*. The Abbasid dynasty, which claimed descent from the Prophet's uncle Abbas, displaced the Omayyads in 749 after a bitter struggle and occupied the office with declining effectiveness until 1538. After the reign of al-Mansūr from 754 to 775, they made their capital in the magnificent, newly founded city of Baghdad and administered their decrees through bureaucratic departments or *diwans* supervised by a *vizier* or prime minister. In practice, local governors enjoyed the independent powers conferred by distance. By the middle of the ninth century political decentralization was far advanced, and by 1200 the power of the Abbasids had become largely honorific. The Muslim world was ruled by local dynasties, which pursued their own policies while nominally acknowledging the authority of the caliph. Spain, which had never accepted the Abbasids, retained an Omayyad caliphate of its own. Though the caliph at Baghdad might call himself "the shadow of God on Earth," the dream of a politically united Islam proved as elusive as that of reviving the Roman Empire in the west.

The world of Islam was immense. Its geographic extent and its many different ethnic and religious groups ensured that it would be no more monolithic, politically or socially, than Catholic Europe. What unity it possessed derived from the fact that, though Jews and Christians continued to make valuable contributions to its culture, a majority of its peoples accepted the teachings of the Koran.

Generalizing about social structure in the Muslim world is difficult because of this diversity. In theory, Islam is wholly indifferent to race or class. However, the first Arab conquerors inevitably became a kind of urban aristocracy that superimposed itself on the older societies of the countryside without changing their economic structures. Systems of land tenure varied widely. Slavery was common in all parts of the Muslim world but was rarely the basis of anything except narrowly defined regional economies. It provided domestic servants and, in a development almost unique to Islam, soldiers. In the days of the great conquests, every male had the duty to defend the faith in battle. The Abbasid caliphs soon introduced the practice of purchasing slaves on the central Asian frontier, converting them to Islam, and training them in the martial arts. These *Mamluks* were mainly of Turkic origin and became the backbone of Islamic armies until well into the nineteenth century. When they enjoyed a local monopoly of military force, they sometimes usurped political power and established regional governments of their own.

Muslim clerics never became a privileged class like their Christian counterparts in the west. The scholars of the *ulama* were revered on the basis of their piety and wisdom, and some engaged in preaching, but no Muslim equivalent existed of the Christian sacraments, and any male Muslim can participate equally in prayers. The mosque, or Muslim place of worship, admits no hierarchies, and monasticism was unknown. Consequently, institutionalized religion based on the Christian model did not develop, though pious Muslims often established *waqfs* or religious endowments for charitable and other purposes.

Another unusual feature of Islamic society, at least by Western standards, was its treatment of women. The Koran permits Muslims to have as many as four wives, provided they are treated justly. In the Muslim past, practical considerations restricted polygamy largely to the rich; in modern times it has vanished almost entirely. Though shocking to Western sensibilities, this limited form of polygyny was a major improvement

over the customs of pagan Arabia, which seems to have permitted unlimited numbers of wives and unlimited freedom in divorcing them. Under Islamic law, divorce remained far easier than in contemporary Christian codes. The Prophet's clear distaste for what he called "repudiation" has influenced subsequent legislation and made divorce more difficult in modern times. Another improvement was the Koranic injunction that permitted daughters to inherit property, albeit at half of the amount allotted to their brothers.

As in all such matters, the intent of the Koran was to protect women and encourage domestic morality, but the ultimate responsibility for their welfare was placed firmly in the hands of men (see document 7.2). Moreover, a number of customs that are regarded as typically Muslim have no Koranic basis.

For example, the common practice of having women wear a veil in public was not based directly on the Koran, which says only that "women should not make an exhibition of their beauty." The custom seems to have arisen in the eighth century when Muslim conquerors found themselves among people whose behaviour seemed dangerously immoral. They covered the faces of their wives to protect their virtue in what was perceived as an alien and dangerous environment.

Islamic Culture, Science, and the Arts

Intellectually, the first few centuries after the Muslim conquests were a kind of golden age. Drawing from Greek, Persian, and Indian sources, Muslim thinkers made broad advances in mathematics, astronomy, and medicine that would eventually be adopted by the west (see document 7.3). The use of Arabic numerals and the Arabic names of the stars are examples of this influence. Western medicine, too, was based largely on the translation of Arabic texts until the "anatomical" revolution of the sixteenth century.

Philosophy reached its highest development later, between the ninth and the twelfth centuries. Muslim thinkers had better access to Greek sources than their western counterparts, and the works of such men as al-Kindi or Ibn Sina (Avicenna) were rooted firmly in the Aristotelian tradition. When they were translated into Latin in the twelfth century, their impact forced a major transformation in western thought (see chapter 9).

The arts also flourished. The Arab elite cultivated an image of sophisticated refinement that is reflected in their poetry and in the elegant calligraphy that dominated the visual arts. The Koran forbids the

❖ DOCUMENT 7.2 ❖

The Koran on Wives and Orphans

Sûrah 4, An-Nisâ (Women), is one of the longest sections in the Koran and is thought to have been revealed shortly after the battle of Uhud, in which many Muslims were killed. This brief extract is the basis of the Islamic toleration of polygyny and reveals the underlying concern for widows and orphans that was its inspiration.

In the Name of Allah, the Compassionate, the Merciful

Men, have fear of your Lord, who created you from a single soul. From that soul He created its mate, and through them He bestrewed the earth with countless men and women.

Fear Allah, in whose name you plead with one another, and honour the mothers who bore you. Allah is ever watching over you.

Give orphans the property which belongs to them. Do not exchange their valuables for worthless things or cheat them of their possession; for this would surely be a great sin. If you fear that you cannot treat orphans [girls] with fairness, then you may marry other women who seem good to you: two, three, or four of them. But if you fear that you cannot maintain equality among them, marry one only or any slave-girls you may own. This will make it easier for you to avoid injustice.

Give women their dowry as a free gift; but if they choose to make over to you a part of it, you may regard it as lawfully yours.

Do not give the feeble-minded the property with which Allah has entrusted you for their support; but maintain and clothe them with its proceeds, and give them good advice.

Take care of orphans until they reach a marriageable age. If you find them capable of sound judgement, hand over to them their property, and do not deprive them of it by squandering it before they come of age.

Let the rich guardian not touch the property of his orphan ward; and let him who is poor use no more than a fair portion of it for his own advantage.

When you hand over to them their property; Allah takes sufficient account of all your actions.

The Koran, trans. N. J. Dawood. Penguin Books, 1956. Copyright © N. J. Dawood, 1956, 1959, 1966, 1968, 1974. Reproduced by permission of Penguin Books, Ltd.

representation of human or animal figures. Muslim artists excelled in calligraphic, geometrical, and floral decorations that were an integral part of both architecture and illuminated manuscripts (see illustration 7.3). Muslim architecture, based ultimately on late Roman and Byzantine technology but with a character all its own, was a great achievement that influenced builders in Spain, Italy, the Balkans, and Central Europe. The pointed arch favored by Muslim builders became a standard feature of gothic architecture in places as far away as England.

Throughout most of the Middle Ages, the Islamic world was richer and more sophisticated than the Christian west. Its technology, military and otherwise, was generally superior. While not escaping the limitations imposed by epidemic disease, marginal food supplies, and the other miseries of life before the industrial revolution, it probably offered a more comfortable standard of living as well. Yet westerners perceived that world as implacably hostile and tended to define themselves in opposition to its religious and cultural values.

They knew little or nothing about either, while Muslims, if they thought about westerners at all, regarded them as ignorant barbarians useful primarily as slaves.

From the eleventh century onward, the economic and military balance between the two cultures began to shift slowly in favor of the west. The advent of the Crusades and the revival of western trade increased contact between the two civilizations at every level, but the hostility remained. Europeans borrowed Muslim ideas, Muslim technologies, and Muslim tastes while waging war against Islam on land and sea. These borrowings were rarely acknowledged even though they became an important component of western culture.

❖

Social and Economic Structures in the Post-Roman West

After the fifth century, Europe was dominated by the Germanic peoples whose migrations had brought about

◆ DOCUMENT 7.3 ◆

Al-Ghazzali: Science and Religion

Al-Ghazzali (1058–1111) was a leading defender of Islamic orthodoxy, but he understood clearly the difference between religion and science. In this passage he demonstrates the attitudes that encouraged mathematical and scientific studies in the Islamic world.

Mathematics comprises the knowledge of calculation, geometry, and cosmography; it has no connection with the religious sciences, and proves nothing for or against religion; it rests on a foundation of proofs which, once known and understood, cannot be refuted. . . .

It is therefore a great injury to religion to suppose that the defense of Islam involves the condemnation of the exact sciences. The religious law contains nothing which approves them or condemns them, and in their turn they make no attack on religion. The words of the Prophet: "The sun and the moon are two signs of the power of God; they are not eclipsed for the birth or death of any one; when you see these signs take refuge in prayer and invoke the name of God"—these words, I say, do not in any way condemn the astronomical calculations which define the orbits of these two bodies, their conjunction and opposition according to particular laws.

The Confession of Al-Ghazzali, pp. 33–34, trans. Claud Field, London: John Murray, 1908.

the fall of Rome. Visigoths (West Goths) ruled Spain, and Vandals controlled the ancient province of Africa until they were supplanted in the eighth century by the Muslims. In Italy, Lombards superseded the Ostrogoths (East Goths) and maintained a violent and precarious frontier with the Byzantine Greeks. Gaul was divided among Visigoths in the southwest, Burgundians in the east, and Franks in the north. Most of these groups were themselves divided into subtribes with chieftains of their own.

Beyond the Rhine were the Alamanni, the Bavarians, and the Saxons. Slower to accept Christianity than their western cousins, they served as a barrier between the lands of what had once been the empire and the non-Germanic peoples to the east. Of these, the most important were the Slavs and the Avars, an Asiatic tribe related to the Huns who had seized control of the middle Danube valley.

Most of Britain fell to Germanic conquerors in the course of the sixth century. Small bands of Angles, Saxons, Jutes, and Frisians obtained a foothold on the eastern coast before the year 500. They seem to have made few efforts to preserve their tribal identities, and the large-scale migration that followed resulted in the establishment of seven small kingdoms that covered virtually the entire island from the English Channel to the Firth of Forth. Wales and West Wales (Cornwall) remained Celtic strongholds as did western Scotland and the Highlands, but England proper had become Anglo-Saxon. A society of Germanic warriors had once again superimposed itself on a larger body of partially romanized Celts. Anglo-Saxon cultural values are portrayed in

Illustration 7.3

⫻ **The Dome of the Rock, Jerusalem.** This superb example of early Islamic architecture was built on the site of Solomon's temple in 687–691. Though Byzantine influence is clear, the structure is a new departure. It encloses the rock formation from which Muhammad, led by the angel Gabriel, ascended into Heaven. The site remains a fertile source of controversy between Muslims and Israelis to this day. Note the Arabic calligraphy that encircles the entire cornice.

◈ DOCUMENT 7.4 ◈

Rape and Murder in Frankish Law

These excerpts from the law of the Salian Franks show how the assessment of fines was based not only upon the presumed seriousness of the crime but also upon the status of the victim. Note that while rape was taken more lightly than murder, the murder of a pregnant woman was regarded as far more serious than that of a free man. The value of a woman was related almost solely to her fertility. The higher fines for concealment may reflect a presumption of premeditation.

Title XIII. Concerning Rape Committed by Freemen

1. If three men carry off a free born girl, they shall be compelled to pay 30 shillings.
2. If there are more than three, each shall pay 5 shillings.
4. But those who commit rape shall be compelled to pay 2500 denars, which makes 63 shillings.

Title XXIV. Concerning the Killing of Little Children and Women

1. If any have slain a boy under 10 years . . . and it shall have been proved on him, he shall be sentenced to 24,000 denars, which is 600 shillings.
3. If any one have hit a free woman who is pregnant, and she dies, he shall be sentenced to 28,000 denars, which make 700 shillings.
6. If any one shall have killed a free woman after she has begun bearing children, he shall be sentenced to 24,000 denars, which make 600 shillings.

7. After she can have no more children, he who kills her shall be sentenced to 8000 denars, which make 200 shillings.

Title XLI. Concerning the Murder of Freemen

1. If any one shall have killed a free Frank, or a barbarian living under the Salic Law, and it have been proved on him, he shall be sentenced to 8000 denars.
2. But if he shall have thrown him into a well or into the water, or shall have covered him with branches or anything else to conceal him, he shall be sentenced to 24,000 denars, which make 600 shillings.
3. But if any one has slain a man who is in the service of the king, he shall be sentenced to 24,000 denars, which make 600 shillings.
4. But if he have put him in the water or in a well, and covered him with anything to conceal him, he shall be sentenced to 72,000 denars, which make 1800 shillings.
5. If any one have slain a Roman who eats at the king's palace, and it be proved on him, he shall be sentenced to 12000 denars, which make 300 shillings.
6. But if the Roman shall not have been a landed proprietor and table companion of the king, he who killed him shall be sentenced to 4000 denars, which make 100 shillings.

Henderson, E. F. *Select Historical Documents of the Middle Ages*, pp. 176–189. London: G. Bell & Sons, 1892.

the great epic *Beowulf* (first written down about the year 1000), while Anglo-Saxon conversion to Christianity was ably chronicled in the *Ecclesiastical History of the English People* by Bede (d. 735).

Though politically fragmented, the Germanic world was unified by its social and cultural similarities. War chiefs provided leadership in battle and divided the spoils among the *comites,* or warriors sworn to their support. The more prominent leaders acquired landed estates through conquest or through intermarriage with older, non-Germanic families. In time they formed the nucleus of an ethnically mixed aristocracy. The estates continued to be farmed by *coloni* or tenants, almost all of whom were drawn from the original, preinvasion, populations.

Poorer tribesmen held small *allods* or freehold properties, which they worked with their nuclear families and perhaps a slave or two. During the summer fighting season, the women typically managed the farms. This gave them a measure of independence unknown to their Byzantine or Muslim sisters, but marriage laws were loose and concubinage common. Kings and tribal chieftains often remained openly polygamous even while claiming to be Christian. The church devoted some of its best efforts to modifying these customs but had only modest success until the great religious revivals of the eleventh and twelfth centuries.

Clerical attempts to restrain violence were even less successful. Endemic warfare among the tribes and sub-tribes reflected a society based firmly on the vendetta or feud. As a result, Germanic legal codes developed an elaborate system of fines as punishment for acts of violence. Their purpose had nothing to do with justice but was intended to prevent feuds by compensating the families of those who were killed or injured (see document 7.4). Though this worked often enough within the framework of the tribe, it was almost useless when applied to outsiders. Each of the Germanic peoples "lived its own law," even when on foreign territory. That is, a crime committed by a Frank against a Burgundian on Burgundian land could be resolved only by a duel—if the parties could agree upon terms—or by war. The only common feature of these Germanic codes, apart from their reliance upon fines, was that they were customary: Judges based their decisions upon the resolution of similar cases in the past. Precedent was supposed to reflect the accumulated wisdom of the people, or "folk," and formed the basis of "common" as opposed to Roman law.

Taking their cue from the Romans, historians have characterized these people as barbarians and the period from the fifth to the eighth century as the Dark Ages. It is, like most such characterizations, exaggerated, but material life in these years reached a level far lower than it had been or than it was later to become. Intellectually and artistically, the glories of antiquity dimmed and for a time almost vanished, while those of the Middle Ages were as yet only beginning to emerge.

Learning flourished primarily in far-off Ireland, a Celtic society that had been spared the turbulence of the continent. Though not unlike the Germanic lands in its social and political organization, the Christianization of the island in the early fifth century had released extraordinary energies. St. Patrick, who is generally credited with converting the Irish, had little interest in monasticism, but by the seventh century a rich monastic culture had evolved that stressed knowledge of the Latin classics—religious and secular—as well as a strict personal discipline. Irish monks transmitted Christianity to many parts of northern Europe, often at great personal risk. They also preserved much of Latin learning, ornamenting it with manuscript illuminations based on a rich artistic heritage. The eighth-century Book of Kells is a superb example of their work (see illustration 7.4).

Frankish Society and Politics

The development of a Frankish kingdom that would by the eighth century impose political unity on much of continental Europe began with the reign of Clovis (c. 466–511), a chief of the Salian or "salty" Franks whose center was at Tournai in what is now Belgium. With skill and ferocity he consolidated his power over other branches of the Franks and seized all of Gaul north of the Loire River. He then routed an invasion by the Alamanni, conquered the Burgundians, and drove the Visigoths out of Aquitaine. When he died at what

Illustration 7.4

Page from the Book of Kells. The Book of Kells is perhaps the greatest monument to the art and scholarship of the Irish golden age. This illumination forms the first word of the Gospel of St. Luke.

was, for a Frank, the ripe old age of forty-five, Clovis was master of everything from the North Sea coast to the borders of Septimania, the province that extended along the Mediterranean coast from Provence to the Pyrenees. To his biographer, the Gallo-Roman bishop Gregory of Tours (c. 539–c. 595), he was a new Constantine because he converted to Catholic Christianity under the influence of his wife, Clotilda, probably in the year 506. His subjects therefore became Catholics, unlike the Arian Burgundians and Visigoths. To traditional historians, Clovis was the first king of France and founder of the Merovingian dynasty.

The Frankish kings regarded the monarchy as their private possession. They divided its lands and privileges equally among their sons when they died and seemed to have no sense of obligation toward their subjects. Personal interest dictated policy. Their subjects in turn felt no special loyalty to the king and served him only in return for benefices or gifts. These might take the form of land, grants of revenue, or other valuables. Unlike the benefices of later—feudal—times, such gifts implied no long-term obligation or relationship. Each new service demanded a new favor.

All of this was typical Germanic practice. The major difference between the Frankish idea of kingship and that of the other Germanic peoples was that Frankish kings from the time of Clovis onward were invested by the church with a sacred quality that other chieftains lacked. A bishop anointed the king with oil at his coronation to indicate that he ruled by God's grace. Such an endorsement could not always save the life of an individual, but it helped to stabilize the position of the dynasty.

Economically, Francia or Frankish Gaul had changed little since the days of the Roman Empire. Most of its people were non-Frankish tenants on estates owned either by members of the old Gallo-Roman aristocracy or by Frankish warriors. The poorer Franks and a few Gallo-Romans owned smaller farms, but life even for the freeholder remained a struggle. Yields were far lower than in Roman times—one-and-a-half grains for each grain planted seems to have been the rule. Coins were rarely seen by any but the rich, who tended to hoard them or convert them into jewelry, which became one of the dominant art forms of the day (see illustration 7.5).

In any case, little was available to buy. Every landowner, great or small, tried to be self-sufficient. When necessary, bartering for necessities was possible at a town fair, but towns were few and poor and often far away. A handful of Jews and Syrians managed the remnants of the long-distance trade in which metalwork was the chief Frankish export. The superbly crafted iron tools and weapons of the Franks found a market in nearly every part of Europe.

Better weapons may have given the Franks a small advantage over their neighbors, for their military organization remained no better than that of any other Germanic tribe. Every male Frank, as opposed to the Gallo-Romans and other non-Frankish inhabitants of the realm, was expected to answer the king's call to arms and to support himself for the duration of the campaign. Most Franks fought on foot, armed with a short sword and the small throwing axe that served as an emblem of their tribe. Unlike their ancestors who fought the legions of Rome, they seem to have been wholly innocent of strategy or of tactics that went much beyond the straightforward brawl, but this impression may reflect only the inadequacy of historical sources. Literacy had declined during the years of

Illustration 7.5

Jewelled Cover of the Lindau Gospels. This book cover, from the ninth century, is an example of Carolingian jewel work.

imperial collapse, and written records in this period are few and incomplete.

The Merovingian dynasty began to decline almost immediately after the death of its founder. The Frankish custom of dividing even a kingdom equally among heirs ensured that each generation would be involved in bitter feuds that often ended in murder if not civil war. Many of the kings appeared to suffer from physical or mental problems and left the political direction of their realms to their queens. Fredegund (d. 597) and Brunhilda (d. 613) were especially notable for their cunning and forcefulness.

After the death of Dagobert I in 639 the dynasty sank into utter incompetence. War leadership as well as the administration of the royal properties fell into the hands of the mayor of the palace. This official was usually one of the Arnulfings, a powerful clan whose wealth derived from estates in the same region from which Clovis had sprung. Originally no more than the majordomo of the royal household, the mayor had, by the end of the seventh century, become the de facto ruler of Francia. Only the sacred character of Merovingian kingship, derived ultimately from the sanctions of the church, prevented the Arnulfings from claiming the throne for themselves.

Eventually, they were able to do just that. The Arnulfing mayors of the palace were capable men whose military exploits brought them respect. One of them, Charles Martel (Charles the Hammer), united the Frankish realms that had long been divided among various Merovingian heirs and won special glory in 732 by defeating a Muslim raiding party near Poitiers in central France. Though not perhaps as decisive an encounter as was sometimes claimed, this battle marked the furthest penetration of Islam in Europe and caught the imagination of the Franks. Finally, Charles's son, Pepin the Short, used the growing prestige of his family and his close relations with the church to depose the last Merovingian. With the full support of Rome he had himself crowned king of the Franks in the winter of 751–752.

The Empire of Charlemagne

The dynasty founded by Pepin is called Carolingian after its greatest member: Charles the Great, or Charlemagne (c. 742–814). In forty-seven years he brought most of what is now France, Germany, and northern Italy under his rule, had himself crowned Roman emperor, and either reformed or created a host of institutions both secular and religious. To the historians of a generation ago he stood at the beginning of European history. To Einhard, his biographer and a contemporary (see document 7.5), Charlemagne held out the promise of a new Roman empire. But few of the emperor's achievements survived his death, and even fewer were the product of a grand and systematic historical vision.

The great king was above all a warlord who, like his father, allied himself with the church to further his interests. Pepin had left him western and northern France and the Frankish territories along the lower Rhine. A brother, Carloman, took the rest of France and parts of southwest Germany including the western Alps. When Carloman died in 771, Charlemagne annexed his brother's kingdom, forcing his wife and children to take refuge among the Lombards of northern Italy who had for some time been hostile to Charlemagne. Realizing that the Lombards were a threat to the papal territories, and perhaps to Rome itself, Pope Adrian I allied himself with Charlemagne. After two years of hard fighting, Charlemagne defeated the Lombards in 774 and annexed their kingdom. North Germany, too, required attention. The region

---

◈ DOCUMENT 7.5 ◈

Einhard: Description of Charlemagne

This brief passage from Einhard's biography of Charlemagne is both vivid and unusual in that it provides personal details often omitted by the authors of the day.

Charles had a big and powerful body and was tall but well-proportioned. That his height was seven times the length of his own feet is well known. [He seems to have been about 6'3" or more than a foot taller than the average man of his day.] He had a round head, his eyes were unusually large and lively, his nose a little longer than average, his gray hair attractive, and his face cheerful and friendly. Whether he was standing or sitting his appearance was always impressive and dignified. His neck was somewhat short and thick and his stomach protruded a little, but this was rendered inconspicuous by the good proportions of the rest of his body. He walked firmly and his carriage was manly, yet his voice, though clear, was not as strong as one might have expected from someone his size. His health was always excellent, except during the last four years of his life, when he frequently suffered from attacks of fever. And at the end he also limped with one foot. All the same, he continued to rely on his own judgment more than on that of his physicians, whom he almost hated because they ordered him to give up his customary roast meat and eat only boiled meat instead.

Einhard. *The Life of Charlemagne*, p. 87, trans. Evelyn Scherabon Firchow and Edwin H. Zeydel. Coral Gables: University of Miami Press, 1972.

---

between the Rhine and the Elbe was inhabited mainly by pagan Saxons who raided Frankish settlements in the Rhineland and murdered the missionaries sent to convert them. Treaties and agreements were useless because the Saxons acknowledged no political authority beyond that of the individual war band, and each chieftain felt free to act on his own.

Characteristically, Charlemagne's strategy focused on religion. In 772 he raided deep into Saxon territory and destroyed the Irminsul, the great tree that formed the heart of one of their most sacred shrines. He apparently thought that by doing so he would demonstrate the stronger magic of the Christian God, but the

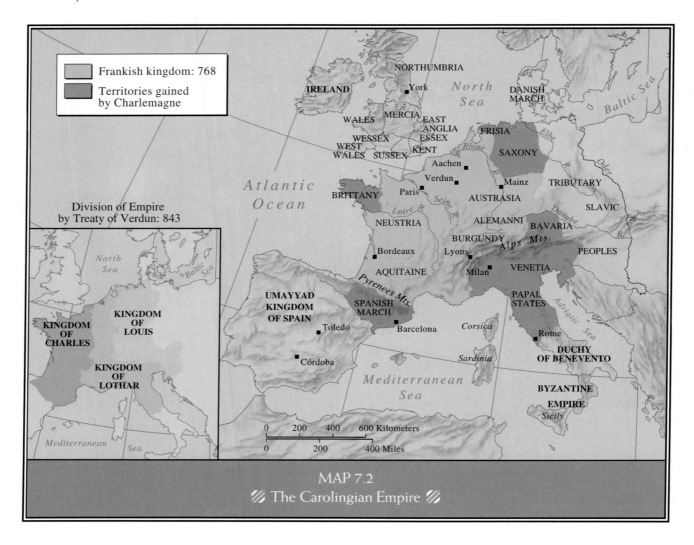

Frankish kingdom: 768

Territories gained by Charlemagne

Division of Empire by Treaty of Verdun: 843

NORTHUMBRIA

IRELAND   York   *North Sea*   DANISH MARCH   *Baltic Sea*

WALES   MERCIA   EAST ANGLIA   FRISIA   *Elbe*   SAXONY   *Oder*

WESSEX   ESSEX   *Rhine*

WEST WALES   SUSSEX   KENT   Aachen   Mainz   TRIBUTARY

Atlantic Ocean   BRITTANY   Paris   Verdun   AUSTRASIA   SLAVIC

Seine R.   *Loire R.*

NEUSTRIA   ALEMANNI   BAVARIA   *Danube R.*

BURGUNDY   *Alps Mts.*   PEOPLES

North Sea   *Baltic Sea*   Bordeaux   Lyons   VENETIA

KINGDOM OF CHARLES   KINGDOM OF LOUIS   AQUITAINE   Milan

Pyrenees Mts.   PAPAL STATES   *Adriatic Sea*

KINGDOM OF LOTHAR   UMAYYAD KINGDOM OF SPAIN   SPANISH MARCH   *Corsica*   Rome

Toledo   Barcelona   DUCHY OF BENEVENTO

Mediterranean Sea   Córdoba   *Sardinia*

Mediterranean Sea   *Mediterranean Sea*   BYZANTINE EMPIRE   *Sicily*

0   200   400   600 Kilometers

0   200   400 Miles

MAP 7.2

The Carolingian Empire

outrage marked the beginning of a long and bloody struggle. The Saxons destroyed Christian settlements and monasteries. The Franks resorted to wholesale massacre and deportations and the Saxons were at last converted and incorporated into the empire in 797. Charlemagne did not shrink from converting people at swordspoint.

The rest of Germany fell into his hands when he deposed the ruler of Bavaria, who was not only a Christian but also a nominal tributary of the Franks. Then, to secure his borders, he defeated the Avars in 791 and 803, pressing into Croatia, which was partially resettled with Slavic and German immigrants. In the west, he repelled a Muslim raid on Narbonne and seized Catalonia, which after 811 became a Christian enclave in Muslim Spain. When he died three years later Charlemagne ruled everything from Catalonia to the Baltic and from the Netherlands to the middle Danube (see map 7.2).

To govern this vast territory, he relied upon counts, dukes, and bishops who supposedly acted on his behalf

in their own regions and who transmitted his decrees to their subjects. These men were bound to him by personal allegiance fortified with powerful oaths, but distance, poverty, and primitive communications left them with a great deal of independence. Though imperial administration remained fragmentary, communication was maintained through *missi dominici*, officials who traveled constantly from place to place on the ruler's business (see document 7.6). Charlemagne did, however, establish the principle that law was to be administered on a territorial instead of a tribal basis. That is, if a Frank committed a crime in Burgundian territory he was to be tried under Burgundian, not Frankish, law. This change represented a greater advance than it seems, for law was no longer paralyzed by jurisdictional disputes.

Everywhere, Charlemagne relied heavily upon the church to support his policies. In return, he strengthened its financial and institutional base. Monasteries established by royal grants on the fringes of the empire converted, and in some cases civilized, new subjects.

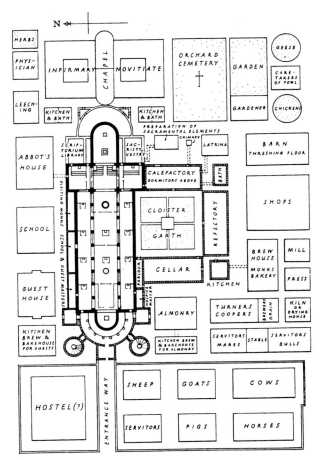

Illustration 7.6

Plan for the Monastery of St. Gall. This is a modernized and redrawn version of a plan devised late in the reign of Charlemagne. The original, which still exists, was apparently a monk-architect's vision of an ideal monastic facility. Though the great Swiss monastery of St. Gall was not rebuilt precisely along these lines, the drawing reflects, on a grand scale, the basic layout favored by the Benedictine monks. It also indicates something of the size and scope of monastic ambitions in the Carolingian age.

Many of these foundations were unparalleled in their size and magnificence (see illustration 7.6). The parish system, long established among the Franks to provide spiritual care in rural areas, was extended throughout Europe, and parish priests were firmly subordinated to their bishops. Bishops, in turn, were forced to obey the pope. To further secure the work of conversion he established new dioceses, reformed old ones, and introduced a compulsory tithe for their support. His efforts, though not always popular, became the model for the medieval church.

None of these measures could have been imposed by religious authority alone. They required the threat of military force wielded by a ruthless and dedicated monarch. Charlemagne had become the chief supporter of the papacy and the mainstay of its efforts to convert the Slavs and Germans. His assumption of the imperial title at the hands of Pope Leo III on Christmas Day in 800 reflected only what had become obvious to many: He, not the pope, was the true leader of western Christendom. In spite of this, the motives and conduct of everyone involved in the coronation have been the subject of controversy, and even its practical consequences remain unclear. It seems to have meant little to the governing of Charlemagne's empire or to his relations with other princes. Even the Byzantine emperor, after initial protests, acknowledged the title in 811.

Regardless of its impressive achievements, the empire of Charlemagne rested in the last analysis on the personal authority of its ruler. The Frankish custom of divided or partible inheritance ensured that his

Illustration 7.7

Carolingian Minuscule. Carolingian minuscule is the basis of modern writing. This example is from Bede's *Expositio in Lucam,* copied at Tours c. 820.

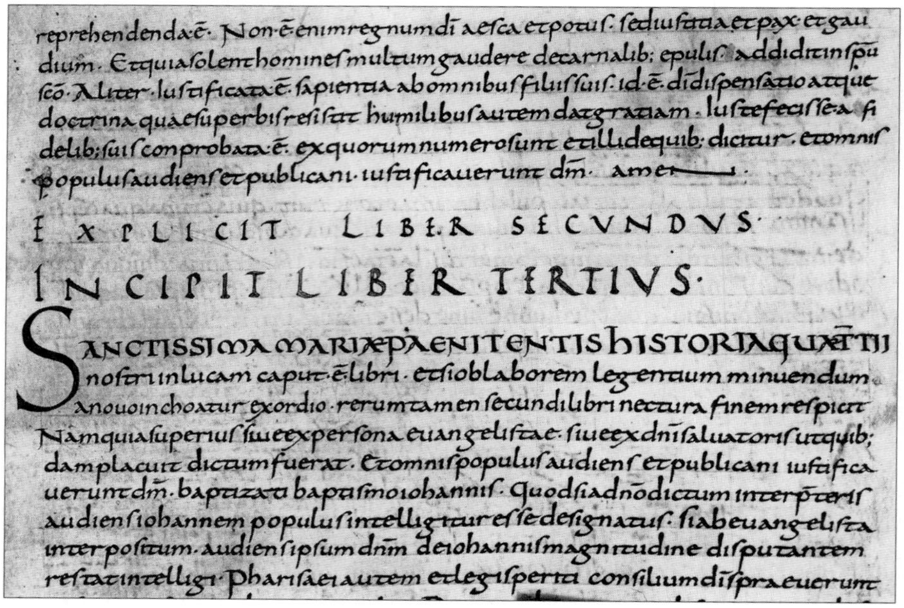
reprehendenda ē. Non ē enim regnum dī aesca et potus. sed iustitia et pax et gau
dium. Et quia solent homines multum gaudere de carnalib; epulis addidit in spu
scō. Aliter. Iustificata ē sapientia ab omnibus filiis suis. id ē. di dispensatio atque
doctrina quae superbis resistit humilibus autem dat gratiam. Iuste fecisse a fi
delib; suis conprobata ē. ex quorum numero sunt et illi de quib; dicitur. Et omnis
populus audiens et publicani iustificauerunt dm̄. amen
EXPLICIT LIBER SECUNDUS
INCIPIT LIBER TERTIUS
SANCTISSIMA MARIAE PAENITENTIS HISTORIA QUAE TII
nostri in lucam caput ē libri. et si ob laborem legentium minuendum
a nouo inchoatur exordio. rerumtamen secundi libri nectura finem respicit
Nam quia superius siue ex persona euangelistae. siue ex dnī saluatoris ut quib;
dam placuit dictum fuerat. Et omnis populus audiens et publicani iustifica
uerunt dm̄. baptizati baptismo iohannis. Quod si ad nōdictum interpraeteris
audiens iohannem populus intelligitur esse designatus. si ab euangelista
interpositum. audiens ipsum dnm de iohannis magnitudine disputantem
restat intelligi. Pharisaei autem et legis periti consilium di spraeuerunt

arrangements would not long survive him. Even had his son and grandsons been willing to ignore the ancient Salic law, the difficulties they faced would have been insurmountable. The empire's weak subsistence economy and poor communications could not sustain the development of institutions that might have saved it. For all its Roman and ecclesiastical trappings, the Carolingian Empire remained a Germanic chieftainship, different from its predecessors primarily in scale.

Charlemagne's interest in the church went beyond mere political calculation. Though he used the church—and the papacy—to further his interests, his personal piety and dedication to the conversion of pagans cannot be questioned. In addition to the essentially administrative reforms instituted, he took a lively interest in matters that might in other circumstances have been left to the pope. He also tried, with some success, to reintroduce the Gregorian chant and to encourage the practice of auricular confession in which the laity confess their sins, not to one another, but to a priest.

A major obstacle to the adoption of these reforms was the ignorance of the clergy. To correct their deficiencies, he established a school at his palace in Aachen and staffed it largely with Irish and English scholars, the most famous of whom was Alcuin of York (c. 732–804). Charlemagne intended these men to raise the intellectual level of his court and to educate his sons. Under the king's patronage, his scholars began the task of recovering the classics, especially the religious ones, and copying them accurately in the beautiful, standardized hand known today as carolingian minuscule (see illustration 7.7). It is the basis of all modern systems of handwriting.

The major purpose of this activity was to provide a body of texts that could serve the needs of clerical education. Gathering the best minds of Europe together in a common enterprise paid other dividends as well. The courts of Charlemagne and his son, Louis the Pious, would serve as an intellectual beacon in the dark days to come. To be sure, the achievements of the Carolingian Renaissance were in some cases forgotten if not obliterated in the chaos of the ninth century. At no time did their volume or importance equal that of later classical revivals, but Charlemagne's scholars laid the foundations of medieval learning.

CHAPTER **8**

THE BEGINNINGS OF THE FEUDAL AGE

CHAPTER OUTLINE

◆◆◆◆◆◆◆◆◆◆◆◆◆◆◆◆◆◆◆◆◆

The empire of Charlemagne did not long survive his death. As his grandsons divided their vast inheritance, Europe was attacked from all sides by ferocious warriors. Political decentralization aggravated by devastating raids threatened to destroy the fabric of society. New forms of military and social organization arose to combat the threat and gradually hardened into the system known as feudalism. Feudalism rested upon the far older social and economic system known as manorialism, which, though it had existed in Roman times, adapted to feudal circumstances and expanded enormously during the dark years of the ninth and tenth centuries. Together, feudalism and manorialism became the dominant institutions of medieval Europe and profoundly influenced the development of politics and social attitudes until well into modern times. Although feudalism pervaded most of what had been the Carolingian Empire and spread eventually to England and southern Italy, many parts of the subcontinent escaped its grasp.

◇

The Great Raids of the Ninth and Tenth Centuries

Even before the death of Charlemagne, reports reached him that trouble was brewing along the borders of his empire. Muslim raiders, sailing out of their North African ports in search of slaves and booty, had begun to harry the Mediterranean coasts. In the north the dragon prows of Viking longships made an unwelcome appearance in seacoast villages. The northmen came to trade if a village were well defended and to loot if it were not. By the middle of the ninth century these first tentative incursions had become massive raiding expeditions that threatened the survival of European life. Some years later the Magyars, a nation of horsemen whose origins lay in the steppes of central Asia, pastured their herds on the rich grasses of the

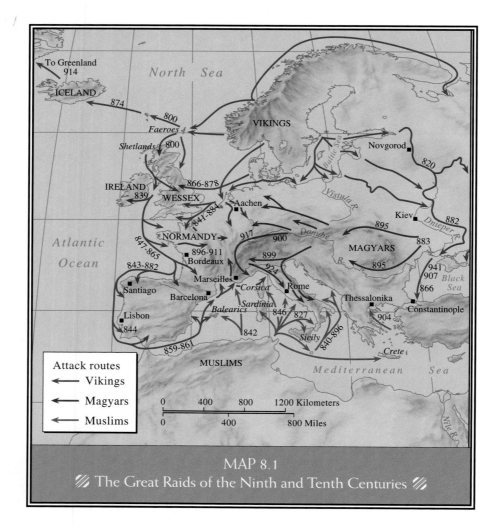

MAP 8.1

%% The Great Raids of the Ninth and Tenth Centuries %%

Danube Valley and began to plunder their neighbors to the west (see map 8.1).

The motives behind this activity varied. For many Muslims, the Christian west represented a backward society that could be pillaged at will. A wealthier, more technologically advanced society usually attempts to exploit a poorer one in close proximity. In fast sailing vessels using the triangular lateen rig of the Arab dhows, the North Africans raided extensively along the coasts, primarily to acquire slaves. An advanced base was established in the Balearic Islands. By 842 they had infested the Camargue, a marshy region on the European mainland, and were raiding in the valley of the Rhone as far as Arles. A half-century later they established themselves in an impregnable position at Freinet near the present site of Saint-Tropez. From these European bases they could devastate the countryside in a systematic way. By the middle of the tenth century detachments of Muslims had raided villages and monasteries as far afield as St. Gall in the Swiss Alps. In Italy, the raider's task was simplified by the Muslim conquest

of Sicily. Palermo fell to the North Africans in 831, but more than seventy years of warfare, enlivened by native revolts against both Greeks and Muslims, were required to gain control of the island. The last Byzantine garrison was not expelled until 965. Long before this, western Sicily had become a staging point for raids on the Italian mainland. Muslim slavers were still encountered as far north as the environs of Rome at the beginning of the eleventh century.

The Magyars had been driven westward across the Carpathians by another of those population movements characteristic of the central Asian heartland. Organized into seven hordes, they probably numbered no more than twenty-five thousand people, but they were formidable warriors and had little trouble in moving into the power vacuum created by Charlemagne's defeat of the Avars. Their raids, which extended as far west as the Meuse, were an extension of their nomadic tradition. The Magyars moved rapidly in fairly large numbers and were at first willing to meet western armies on equal terms. Later, they became more cautious and relied upon speed and evasion to make good their escapes.

The Vikings were perhaps the most formidable raiders of all. The name is generic and refers to all of those Scandinavians—Danish, Norwegian, and Swedish—who terrorized the coasts of Europe between 800 and 1050. Their society bore a marked resemblance to that of the early Germanic tribes. Scandinavia was a world of small farmers and fishermen who lived in widely scattered communities connected primarily by the sea. The heart of such communities was their market and their Thing, the assembly of free men that met, usually on market days, to discuss matters of public concern. These gatherings also ratified the selection of kings, who were in the beginning little more than regional warlords. Drawn mostly from the ranks of a hereditary aristocracy, these chieftains relied upon personal loyalties, the fellowship of the chief's great hall where warriors drank and celebrated, and the distribution of loot to organize war parties of free farmers and craftsmen. The leisure for such pursuits was provided by a large population of slaves, or thralls. Even the smallest farms might have at least three, and the need to replenish their numbers was an important incentive for the raids. In the summers while the men raided, the women managed the farms, the slaves, and the continued production of craft goods and services. Following the pattern of other maritime communities before and since, Scandinavian women tended to be far more independent and economically active than their inland sisters.

Warfare and raiding was endemic in the region long before the dawn of the Viking age, as was an extensive trading network that helps to explain the cultural similarities of the Scandinavian peoples. Danes, Swedes, and Norwegians spoke related languages, shared the system of formal writing known as runes, and enjoyed a common tradition of oral literature that was finally committed to writing in the thirteenth century. Its characteristic form was the saga, a mixture of historical fact and legend that reached its highest development in Iceland. Scandinavian religion was polytheistic and bore a close resemblance to that of other Germanic peoples.

Viking burial customs reveal much about Scandinavian art and technology. Dead chiefs were sometimes surrounded by their possessions and buried in their boats, a practice that left behind rich hordes of artifacts including exquisite carvings and jewelry. The boats were an extraordinary technical achievement. The typical Viking longship was about sixty-five feet in length, open-decked, and double ended (see illustration 8.1). It could be propelled by oars at speeds up to ten knots or by a single square sail and was strongly built of overlapping planks that carried the structural load of the hull. Such vessels could cross oceans. Because their draft was rarely more than three feet they could also be beached without damage or rowed far into the interior on the shallowest of rivers. With a crew of forty to sixty men and no decks for shelter they cannot have been comfortable, but they provided the ultimate in operational flexibility.

The reasons for the Viking incursions are unclear. The Scandinavian population presumably had begun to exceed the available supply of food, perhaps because the cold, wet weather that troubled the rest of Europe in this period reduced northern harvests to an untenable level. Charlemagne's conquest of the Saxons may also have roused the suspicions of their Danish neighbors. In any case, the Northmen grew more aggressive with the passage of time. In the early years of the ninth century they contented themselves with lightning raids on coastal settlements, stealing what they could and putting out to sea before the inhabitants could call for reinforcements. Within a generation they had adopted the Muslim tactic of establishing bases from which they could loot the surrounding countryside. By midcentury they were establishing permanent colonies on the European mainland.

Their range was enormous. In 844 Vikings raided the Atlantic ports of Spain. In the following year they sacked Paris, and in 859–860 they reached Italy, penetrating the Val d'Arno almost to the outskirts of Florence. Fortunately for the Italians they did not return. In the north the Vikings soon learned how to extend their range by traveling on stolen horses when their ships reached the limits of navigation. Nothing seemed beyond their reach.

The establishment of permanent settlements grew from the habit of wintering in England or on the Continent in preparation for the next raiding season. Given that the dangers of this practice were minimal, Vikings brought their wives and families. In the decades after 851 they occupied all of northeastern England from Essex to the further limits of Yorkshire. The region came to be known as the Danelaw because the legal autonomy granted to the Danes by Saxon kings survived until the thirteenth century. From 1014 to 1042 England was ruled by a Danish dynasty. In 1066 it was conquered by the Normans, who as their name indicates, were also of Viking origin. They were the inhabitants of the great Norse state established around the mouth of the Seine at the beginning of the tenth century.

At the opposite end of Europe, Viking traders penetrated the Russian heartland by following the great

Illustration 8.1

⁄⁄ **Viking Longship.** This Viking longship has elegant, and sea-worthy, lines. The general impression is one of both beauty and menace.

rivers. From the western branch of the Dvina, which flows into the Baltic at Riga, they were able to reach the headwaters of both the Dnieper and the Volga and to float from there to the gates of Constantinople. In the process they founded Novgorod and established themselves as the ruling aristocracy at Kiev, but they had little impact upon what was to remain a thoroughly slavic culture. Somewhat ironically, they gave Russia its name: "Rus" or "Rhos" was the slavic word for Viking.

The establishment of these Viking enclaves, like the contemporary colonization of Iceland and Green-land and the exploration of the North American coast by Bjarni Herjolfsson (c. 986) and Leif Ericsson (c. 1000), indicates that hunger for arable land was an important reason for the great raids. In the two cen-turies between 850 and 1050 the North Sea became the center of a cosmopolitan society in which interaction between Scandinavian and non-Scandinavian cultures grew increasingly complex. The Norsemen were even-

tually assimilated as the medieval kingdoms of France and England evolved, but their incursions had helped to provoke a reorganization of European society.

The Emergence of Feudal Institutions

The great raids, whether Muslim, Magyar, or Viking, brought something like anarchy to most of Europe. The normal bonds of social interaction were submerged in an orgy of violence. No one's person or property was safe. Agricultural production fell, and the tenuous lines of trade and communication that held the empire to-gether were virtually severed (see document 8.1).

The raids were inflicted on a political order that was in the process of disintegration. The empire of Charlemagne had been doomed from the start by poverty and by the problem of distance. Little surplus wealth was available to support either war or gover-nance. Harvests, never abundant in the Carolingian age, may have declined even before the destructive ef-fects of the raids were felt. The European climate had entered one of its cold, damp cycles, and yields of one-

❖ DOCUMENT 8.1 ❖

The Great Raids

The following is extracted from the Annals of Xanten, a chronicle thought to have been written in the archdiocese of Cologne at about the time of the events it describes. The year is 846, with the final sentence coming from the entry for 847. Frisia includes most of the northern Netherlands and the coastal region of northwest Germany. Lothaire was the grandson of Charlemagne who ruled the middle part of his empire known as Lotharingia. The passage reveals the sense of helplessness and isolation induced by disasters on every front.

According to their custom the Northmen plundered Eastern and Western Frisia and burned the town of Dordrecht with two other villages, before the eyes of Lothaire, who was then in the castle of Nimwegen, but could not punish the crime. The Northmen, with their boats filled with immense booty, including both men and goods, returned to their own country.

At the same time, as no one can mention or hear without great sadness, the mother of all churches, the basilica of the apostle Peter, was taken and plundered by the Moors or Saracens, who had already occupied the region of Beneventum. The Saracens, moreover, slaughtered all the Christians whom they found outside the walls of Rome, either within or without this church. They also carried men and women away prisoners. They tore down, among many others, the altar of the blessed Peter, and their crimes from day to day bring sorrow to Christians. Pope Sergius departed life this year.

After the death of Sergius no mention of the apostolic see has come in any way to our ears.

Robinson, James Harvey, ed. *Readings in European History,* vol. 1. Boston: Ginn, 1904.

Charlemagne's son Louis the Pious (reigned 814–840) had hoped to pass on the empire intact, though the Salic law required that it be split equally among his heirs. He had three sons by his first marriage: Lothair, Pepin, and Louis "the German." A fourth son, Charles "the Bald," was born to his second wife, Judith of Bavaria, in 823. Lothair was the intended heir, but Judith instigated a civil war among the brothers in the hope of securing a kingdom for her son. After the emperor's death in 840, the surviving heirs divided his lands by the Treaty of Verdun (843). Lothair took the central portion including Italy, the Rhineland, and the Low Countries. Charles (d. 877) held most of what is now France, and Louis (d. 875) was given Bavaria, Austria, and the eastern part of Germany. Pepin had died in 838. When Lothair died in 855 the middle kingdom was divided again among his three sons and quickly ceased to be a major factor in European politics. By 870 transalpine Europe was divided into a West Frankish kingdom (France) under Charles, and an East Frankish kingdom (Germany) under Louis, while Italy became the playground of regional factions and Byzantine generals.

None of these states possessed the resources to mount a credible defense against the raiders. Cash remained scarce, and the kings that followed Charles the Bald and Louis the German were not always inspiring leaders. Militarily, the problem was not unlike that faced by the Roman emperors in the second and third centuries, but its scale was far greater and complicated by the decentralization of political power within the empire. Each of the successor kingdoms faced attacks along borders that extended for thousands of miles. The attacks might come by land or by sea. Their objective was unknown, and the size of the forces involved could not be anticipated. Post-Carolingian Europe was poor and sparsely settled. Peasant communities could not defend themselves against such formidable enemies as the Vikings, and the old Frankish system of levies was slow and cumbersome. By the time infantry was mobilized and marched to the point of contact, the enemy would be gone. Fortunately for the Europeans, Scandinavians and North Africans tended to fight on foot without benefit of the massed infantry tactics known to antiquity. The Magyars were a typical nomadic light cavalry. If they could be intercepted, all of these foes were vulnerable to attack by heavily armed and armored horsemen, the prototypes of the medieval knight.

From the technological point of view, the knight and his way of fighting was enhanced by

and-a-half grains for every seed planted were probably normal. Distances were huge and major population centers were connected, as they would be for centuries to come, by primitive tracks. Local magnates and local loyalties began to assert themselves while Charlemagne was still alive. Neither his lines of communication nor his military resources were able to hold them fully in check. After his death the division of the empire among his three grandsons only made matters worse.

Illustration 8.2

🖋 **A Knight and His Equipment.** This manuscript illumination shows a knight wearing the conical helmet and long coat of chain mail or birney typical of the feudal period. He is shown at the charge with lance in hand. The high saddle made him difficult to unhorse, while the stirrups allowed him to stand up for greater impact.

two innovations: the iron horseshoe and the stirrup. Neither were in common use before the ninth century. The iron shoe permitted a horse to carry heavy weights over bad ground without splitting its hooves. The stirrup allowed an armored man to brace himself and even to stand in the saddle, which made it easier to wield a heavy lance, shield, and double-edged sword on horseback. The new system produced an increase in offensive power over that available to ancient or nomadic cavalry, while a heavy chain mail coat offered an effective defense against most edged weapons (see illustration 8.2). The Franks, with their skill in ironwork, could easily fashion the necessary equipment.

A defensive system evolved that was based on mobile detachments of heavy cavalry garrisoned in scattered strongholds or castles and supported directly by the people they were intended to protect. In theory, a band of horsemen could reach the site of a raid within hours or, at worst, a day or two. As hundreds of smoking villages continued to attest, this solution was not perfect, but it forced the marauders to pay a higher cost in blood than they might otherwise have done. With time and practice the knights became a reasonably effective deterrent.

The new system was also used in disputes that had nothing to do with the raids. The division of the em-

pire encouraged territorial disputes that continued even in the face of external threats. Armored knights could be used to harry the lands of a hostile neighbor. Other knights could be sent out to oppose them, but castles provided the more effective defense. The presence of a castle filled with armed men posed a serious threat to any invading force, and operations had to be suspended until that threat could be eliminated. For this reason sieges were perhaps more common in medieval warfare than pitched battles between mounted knights. Knights directed the sieges and played a prominent role in the fighting. The hard work of digging, undermining the walls, and manning the rams or catapults fell to peasants levied for the occasion.

A major defect of this kind of warfare was its expense. The cost of a horse and armor was roughly equivalent to that of two dozen cattle, and few could afford it. Charlemagne had begun to encourage the development of heavy cavalry, but the tiny elite that served him had to be supplemented under his successors by the enlistment of nearly everyone who was rich enough and strong enough to fight on horseback. Moreover, the kind of warfare in which they were engaged demanded constant readiness and a level of skill that was difficult to acquire and could be maintained only through constant practice. The construction and maintenance of castles required vast reserves of labor and materials. Even those who were able to afford the initial outlay could not be expected to support themselves indefinitely. In an age chronically short of cash, the most practical, and perhaps the only, solution was to provide these men with grants of land that could be set aside for their use in return for military service.

The term *feudalism* refers to the social institutions that arose from this exchange of land for military service. In its simplest form, a feudal bond was created when a fighting man placed his hands between those of his lord or liege and vowed to support him on the battlefield in return for a grant of land known as a benefice or fief. By so doing he became the lord's man, or vassal. The terms of such contracts varied widely and were the subject of much negotiation, but the basic principle of mutual obligation remained constant. A vassal was to support his lord and do nothing contrary to his interest; the lord was obligated to provide his vassal with personal and legal protection as well as material support. "Money fiefs," in which cash was provided in return for military service, existed, but in a virtually cashless society they were rare.

The precedents for such arrangements were ancient. In principle, feudalism is a form of clientage that has been given sanction in law. In practice, the idea probably dates back to the oaths taken by members of a Germanic *comitatus* or war band (see document 8.2). The great men of Visigothic Spain and Merovingian Gaul had maintained bodies of armed companions who were pledged to them by oath. Some of them were free, but others were *vassi* who had entered into contractual relationships of dependency. Under the early Carolingians, the term began to lose its humble connotations. Charles Martel and his successors sometimes granted land to their retainers, who often became great lords in their own right. Charlemagne tried to make such arrangements legally binding, but the legal union of vassalage and benefice was achieved only in the reign of his son, Louis the Pious. By this time, the term *vassal* had lost all taint of servility.

In the dark years after Louis's death, feudalism spread throughout the Frankish kingdoms. Vassal homage was extended not only to household companions but also to regional magnates whose military assistance was valued. Bishops and abbots, though they were not supposed to shed blood, became vassals as well because for most purposes little difference existed between secular and ecclesiastical lordships. Monasteries and episcopal sees had long been endowed with "temporalities" or grants of land that in difficult times required the protection of armed men. A prominent churchman might therefore command a substantial force. In some cases, including most of those that involved the church, land was surrendered to the liege in return for his protection and then returned to the vassal after the oath of fealty had been taken. In most cases, the vassal received a new estate ranging in size from a few acres to an entire county, which might or might not contain a castle. The vassal was expected to make some provision for the security of his fief. When a fief was very large, this could be done only through subinfeudation. The vassal would recruit his own contingent of fighting men by offering them portions of his fief in return for their oaths of fealty. In this way the number of feudal jurisdictions increased rapidly within a few short years.

This decentralization of military force worked as well as could be expected. Its chief virtue was flexibility. Units of heavy cavalry based upon fortified strongholds were usually able to break up minor raids or at least to impose unacceptable casualties on the raiders. The building of castles, many of which were little more than halls surrounded by wooden palisades, was often a deterrent. Greater threats could be met by a general levy, which gathered the war bands of many vassals into a

---

◆ DOCUMENT 8.2 ◆

The Act of Homage

Galbert of Bruges described this act of homage in 1127. The form is thought to have changed little since the beginning of the feudal age.

On Thursday, the seventh of the ides of April [April 7, 1127], acts of homage were again made before the count, which were brought to a conclusion through this method of giving faith and assurance. First, they performed the homage in this fashion: the count inquired if [the prospective vassal] wished completely to become his man. He replied, "I do wish it," and with his hands joined and covered by the hands of the count, the two were united by a kiss. Second, he who had done the homage gave faith to the representative of the count in these words: "I promise in my faith that I shall henceforth be faithful to count William, and I shall fully observe the homage owed him against all men, in good faith and without deceit." Third, he took an oath on the relics of the saints. Then the count, with the rod which he had in his hand, gave investiture to all those who by this promise had given assurance and due homage to the count, and had taken the oath.

Galbert of Bruges. "*Histoire du meurtre de Charles Bon comte de Flandre,*" trans. David Herlihy. In David Herlihy, ed., *The History of Feudalism*, p. 98. New York: Walker, 1970.

---

great host. Such an army, organized by Otto the Great (912–973), met and defeated the Magyars at the battle of the Lechfeld in 955.

Otto's victory ended the last major incursion from the east. His reign as king of the East Franks—he was crowned Holy Roman emperor in 962—marked the turning of the tide. The Muslims were driven from Freinet in 972, and the number of Viking raids began to decline even in the west. They ceased entirely after about 1030.

How much of this resulted from the new military organization and how much from other factors is hard to determine. The Magyars were clearly discouraged by Otto the Great, but they had already begun to turn away from raiding as they discovered the rich agricultural possibilities of the Hungarian plain. After 950 the

Muslims were increasingly distracted by a series of civil wars. The hard work of dislodging them from their bases in Spain and the Balearics was for the most part undertaken by naval forces based on the Italian towns, not by feudal levies. Relative security was achieved in the western Mediterranean only by the end of the eleventh century.

The Vikings, too, may have returned home for reasons of their own. Even as they raided, the Scandinavian chiefs fought for hegemony among themselves. Much of the treasure they seized was used to buy influence and hire mercenaries for their dynastic quarrels. By the beginning of the eleventh century, this process had created the kingdoms of Denmark, Norway, and Sweden. The new rulers sought divine sanction by adopting Christianity and did everything in their power to monopolize the use of military force. Freebooting was actively discouraged because it led to the creation of alternative centers of power. The church condemned freebooting because it was directed against Christians. In the meantime, agricultural productivity seems to have improved, allowing reformed Vikings to accept the new policy without too much hardship.

The Consolidation of Feudalism: Subinfeudation and the Heritability of Fiefs

Feudalism did not guarantee the salvation of Europe, but in much of the subcontinent it altered the structure of society beyond recognition. An expedient adopted in a time of poverty and dire peril evolved into a complex of social and economic relationships that survived for half a millennium.

The process began with subinfeudation, which increased political decentralization and weakened the power of kings (see document 8.3). The bonds of homage and fealty were entirely personal. A vassal who held his benefice from a count owed nothing to the king. If a tenant-in-chief (a lord who held land directly from the sovereign) chose not to honor his obligations under the feudal contract, all of his subtenants could be expected to follow suit. Moreover, fiefs commonly were accumulated from more than one lord. Conflicts of loyalty were therefore inevitable, and some of the greater vassals used them to build a power base of their own. The counts of Flanders, for example, held lands from the kings of both East Francia and West Francia. They easily played one against the other to create what amounted to an independent state by the end of the ninth century.

Because feudal tenures were theoretically based on service and good only for the lifetime of the vassal, de-

---

◆ DOCUMENT 8.3 ◆

Subinfeudation

This declaration of homage indicates some of the problems caused by subinfeudation as well as the kind of compromise that might, in theory, alleviate them.

I, John of Toul, make known that I am the liege man of the lady Beatrice, countess of Troyes, and of her son, Theobald, count of Champagne, against every creature, living or dead, saving my allegiance to Enjourand of Coucy, lord John of Arcis, and the count of Grandpré. If it should happen that the count of Grandpré should be at war with the countess and count of Champagne on his own quarrel, I will aid the count of Grandpré in my own person, and will send to the count and countess of Champagne the knights whose service I owe to them for the fief which I hold of them. But if the count of Grandpré shall make war on the countess and the count of Champagne on behalf of his friends and not by his own quarrel, I will aid in my own person the countess and count of Champagne, and will send one knight to the count of Grandpré for the service which I owe him for the fief which I hold of him, but I will not go myself into the territory of the count of Grandpré to make war on him.

Thatcher, O. J., and McNeal, E. H., eds. *A Source Book of Medieval History.* New York: Scribner's, 1905.

---

priving a disloyal tenant of his benefice should have been easy, but this was not the case. By granting their lands in fief, kings reduced their military force to a household guard that might be no more numerous than the companions of any major tenant-in-chief. Deprivation of one important vassal therefore required the assistance of others, and most were reluctant to participate in an action that could one day be applied to them.

Political pressures were moving strongly in the opposite direction. As the decentralization of military force increased, kings were forced to offer better terms in return for support. Fiefs inevitably became heritable. Vassals wished to provide for the security of their families, and the right to pass lands on to their children was demanded with increasing frequency in negotiating feudal contracts. Rulers were reluctant to impoverish the widows and orphans of loyal vassals. The inheritance of fiefs was already common in France and Italy by the end of the ninth century and became universal in the eleventh. In Germany, heritability was at first applied only to the more important benefices. By the end of the twelfth century fiefs for life had become a rarity even there.

Heirs were supposed to renew their father's oaths and be capable of fulfilling them. In the early days, women were therefore denied the right of succession because they could not provide military service. Neither of these rules survived the first feudal age. Heirs frequently failed to appear before their liege but retained possession of their benefices. Women were inheriting fiefs in southern France before the end of the tenth century, and the practice spread quickly throughout the feudal world. Lords tried to ensure that the service aspects of the contract were fulfilled in these cases by a representative, usually the woman's husband, and used this as an excuse to intervene in the marriage plans of their female vassals. Such claims were frequently ignored. Matilda of Tuscany (c. 1046–1115) did not remarry after the death of her husband and became a dominant figure in Italian politics for almost forty years.

Alienation of fiefs for cash or other considerations was far more difficult to achieve than heritability, but it had become common by the twelfth century. Permission of the lord was still necessary if a fief changed hands, but the increasing frequency of such transactions indicates that the long process of transition to private property and a cash-based economy had already begun.

Private jurisdiction, or the establishment by vassals of feudal and manorial courts, was another matter. The practice of allowing great men to maintain their own law courts dates back to the latter days of the Roman Empire. Feudalism extended this benefit to nearly every vassal with subjects of his or her own. The right to preside over one's own court was commonly demanded by prospective vassals, and princes and tenants-in-chief were willing to accept it because their own courts could not cope with the proliferation of local disputes. Feudal society was contentious. A distinction was maintained between minor and major causes, the latter being reserved for royal or county jurisdictions. The proliferation of feudal and manorial courts inevitably weakened what threads of central authority remained.

Within a few short generations, feudalism had created a political system based upon decentralization and hereditary privilege. Though at first confined within the limits of the old Carolingian Empire, feudal institutions were extended to England in 1066 and after 1072 to Sicily and southern Italy by the Norman expansion. In all of these regions, the permanence of the system was ensured by a tangled web of legal contracts and by the diffusion of military power among what had become a warrior caste.

The values and attitudes of that caste were increasingly defined by adherence to the ideals of chivalry. The term is derived from the French word for horse and reflects the self-conscious superiority of the mounted warrior. In the centuries to come the chivalric code would grow increasingly elaborate and its rituals would be fixed by a vast literature. Ceremonial initiations, designed to set the warrior apart from society as a whole, marked the creation of knights from the beginning of feudalism. They are not to be confused with the ceremony of vassalage but were the culmination of a long period of training and preparation. Boys of ten or twelve were usually sent by their fathers to serve as pages in the household of another lord. There they were trained in the art of war, including horsemanship and the use of lance, shield, and sword. Physical training was intense and consumed much of their time. The pages also learned fortification and enough physics to construct siege engines and other military devices.

Their first exposure to warfare was as squires who attended a knight on the battlefield, tended his horses and weapons, and protected him if he fell. When and if this apprenticeship was successfully completed the squire was dubbed a knight. In the early days the ceremony could be performed by any other knight and was usually concluded with a blow to the head or shoulders. Touching with the flat of a sword came later. In the Germanic world, the new knight was girded with his sword, a practice that probably dates from the knighting of Louis the Pious by his father, Charlemagne. Religious elements began to creep into these initiations by the middle of the tenth century and symbolized the growing sense that knights, like priests, had a divinely established vocation.

Feudalism and the Manor

A fief could support a fighting man only if someone were available to work it. As a general rule, knights did not till the soil even in the days before their status became too great to permit physical labor. They were on call whenever danger threatened, and their training normally required several hours of practice and exercise each day. Even hunting, which was their primary recreation and which they always pursued on horseback, was a form of military exercise. The provision of labor was therefore a problem from the start, and the manorial system that was adapted to provide it grew hand in hand with the feudal institutions of the new aristocracy.

Manorialism as a means of securing scarce labor had existed since ancient times and would survive in eastern Europe until the nineteenth century. The basis of the medieval system was the manorial tenure, which in some respects paralleled the feudal tenures of the knights. In its simplest form, a peasant would surrender his allod or freehold to a lord in return for the lord's protection. The lord would then grant it back to him as a tenement with stipulations that made the tenant the legal subject of the lord. Those who possessed little or no land could also request protection, but their poverty placed them at a disadvantage in negotiating the terms.

The nature of manorial tenures varied widely. Although a tenant could remain technically free, in most cases tenancy involved a descent into serfdom. Serfs were unlike slaves in that they could not be sold and were entitled to hold property. They could also, within certain limits, negotiate contracts, undertake obligations, and testify in court. Both their land and their personal rights were contractually encumbered. Once they had placed themselves under a lord's protection, they were bound to their tenement for life and were often forbidden to marry anyone other than a subject of the same lord. Because they were legally subject to another person, they lost all political rights including the right to sue a free man in court.

Economically, the tenant was further obligated to return a portion of his annual crop to the lord or provide labor on the lord's lands for a fixed number of days per year or both (see document 8.4). Labor services might also involve maintenance work on the lord's castle or on the infrastructure of the manor, including roads, ditches, and other facilities. In some cases, military service was required, usually for a maximum of forty days per year between planting and harvest. Peasant troops were ineffective in a military environment dominated by heavy cavalry, but they could provide logistical support, dig trenches, and guard the baggage.

Another feature of these agreements involved services that could be provided only by the lord. The tenant accepted the jurisdiction of the lord's court and agreed to use only the lord's mill or the lord's animals at stud in return for payments in kind. Sometimes stipulations were made about access to orchards, woodlands, or streams. The right of tenants to hunt, fish, or gather fallen wood for fuel was strictly regulated. In return, the lord agreed to protect the tenant and his property both physically and in law. Though manorial tenures were usually heritable, an investiture fee was commonly required from the heirs when a tenement changed hands.

Women rarely had the right to make such agreements in the first instance. If they were married, their legal rights were largely subsumed under those of their husbands and even their testimony in a peasant court was acceptable only in limited circumstances. They could, however, inherit tenements. In such cases military and labor obligations were fulfilled by substitutes who were usually paid in goods or services instead of in cash.

The sum of these burdens could be great or relatively small and might be compounded by tithes or other obligations owed to the parish church. Rents calculated as a portion of the total harvest were better from the peasant's point of view than those expressed in fixed amounts. Miller's fees and similar charges would have to have been paid in any case and involved only a theoretical loss of freedom because transporting grain or livestock to distant villages for milling or stud services was impractical. Labor services, meanwhile, could be onerous and were often deeply resented. In a society that was still largely illiterate, these contracts were not written down, and the precise terms of each tenure were submerged in the "custom of the manor." In later years the margin of survival for a peasant family often depended upon the negotiating skills of their ancestors.

The bargains struck between lords and peasants were unequal, but the harshness of the system was modified to some extent by the ideal of mutual obligation. In feudal Europe, land—the basis of nearly all wealth—was no longer regarded as private property. Peasants held their tenements from lords, who held their fiefs from the king, who held his kingdom ultimately from God. The terms by which land was occupied were spelled out in law and custom, and they could rarely be changed or abrogated without difficulty. Fiefs could not be sold at will, and tenants could not be dispossessed without cause. Moreover, lords were obligated to protect their subjects' property as well as their persons. Some were wise enough to take a paternalistic interest in the well-being of those who inhabited their estates. Whether a lord was good or bad, tenants enjoyed a measure of security that the wage laborers of a later day would never know. If the lot of a medieval peasant was hard, it was in part because the margin of subsistence was small and the contribution of any of it was more than most people could afford.

Generally, manorial tenures were accepted voluntarily. A peasant without protection was at the mercy of

◈ DOCUMENT 8.4 ◈

Manorial Obligations

John Cayworth was one of the larger tenants on the English manor of Bernholme in 1307. His obligations were correspondingly great and may be compared with the data in tables 11.1 and 11.2. This excerpt from the Custumals of Battle Abbey *provides a good example of how manorial tenures worked. Such agreements were almost never written down before the end of the thirteenth century, and it is doubtful if the monetary value of the obligations would have been calculated in this way before the widespread commutation of services for cash.*

They say, moreover, that John Cayworth holds a house and 30 acres of land, and owes yearly 2s. at Easter and Michaelmas; and he owes a cock and two hens at Christmas, of the value of 4d.

And he ought to harrow for two days at the Lenten sowing with one man and his own horse and his own harrow, the value of the work being 4d.; and he is to receive from the lord on each day 3 meals, of the value of 5d.; and then the lord will be at a loss of 1d. . . .

And he ought to carry the manure of the lord for 2 days with 1 cart, with his own 2 oxen, the value of the work being 8d.; and he is to receive from the lord each day 3 meals of the price as above, and thus the service is worth 3d. clear.

And he shall find 1 man for two days for mowing on the meadow of the lord, who can mow, by estimation 1 acre and a half, the value of the mowing of an acre being 6d.; the sum is therefore 9d.; and he is to receive each day 3 meals of the value given above; and thus the mowing is worth 4d. clear. And he ought to gather and carry that same hay which he has cut, the price of the work being 3d. . . .

And he ought to carry wood from the woods of the lord as far as the manor [house] for two days in summer with a cart and 3 animals of his own, the value of the work being 9d. And he shall receive from the lord each day 3 meals of the price given above; and thus the work is worth 4d. clear.

And he ought to find a man for 2 days to cut heath, the value of the work being 4d., and he shall have 3 meals each day of the value given above; and thus the lord will lose, if he receives the service, 3d.

And he ought to carry the heath which he has cut, the value of the work being 5d., and he shall receive from the lord 3 meals at the price of 2 1/2d., and thus the work will be worth 2 1/2d. clear.

And he ought to carry to Battle twice in the summer season, each time half a load of grain, the value of the service being 4d. And he shall receive in the manor each time 1 meal of the value of 2d. And thus the work is worth 2d. clear.

The total of the rents with the value of the hens is 2s. 4d.

The total of the value of the works is 2s., 3 1/2d., owed from the said John yearly.

"Custumals of Battle Abbey." In Edward P. Cheyney, ed., *Pennsylvania Translations and Reprints,* vol. 3, no. 5, p. 30. Philadelphia: University of Pennsylvania Press, 1902.

---

all sorts of armed marauders, including neighboring lords whose behavior was often no better than the Vikings'. Faced with the prospect of unending, uncontrolled violence, most people accepted their loss of freedom as a necessity. Instances of coercion by prospective lords were apparently rare and sometimes subtle. The manorial system was, like its feudal counterpart, a necessary adaptation to a world gone mad.

In physical terms, no two manors were exactly alike. Their character differed widely according to topography, agricultural practices, and local custom (see illustration 8.3). Some constituted entire villages of peasant huts with their household gardens and perhaps a church. Not every manor boasted a lord in residence, and the church sometimes served as a fortified refuge in case of attack. Paths radiating out from the village provided access to fields, which might be divided from one another by narrow balks of turf. Where the iron plow (see chapter 10) was in use, the fields were laid out in long strips to facilitate plowing with draft animals. They were often worked in common because not everyone could afford a plow or a team. In lands cultivated by the old Roman plow, fields might be irregular in shape and worked only by the peasant family or its servants.

The lands of an individual tenement were not necessarily contiguous. The equivalent of between thirty and forty acres was the maximum that could be cultivated by a peasant family. Many plots were far smaller. With the passage of time and the vagaries of inheritance, farmers might find themselves holding

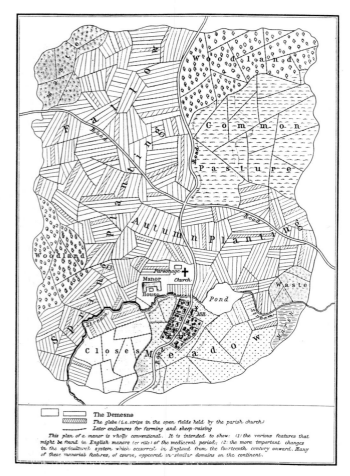

Illustration 8.3

▨ **Plan of a Medieval Manor.** The drawing shows how a typical English manor might have been laid out. Not all manors were single villages of this kind in which all the inhabitants were subjects of the same lord.

fragments of land scattered over several square miles. Parcels of arable land might also be set aside for the lord and for the priest if there was one. Most communities also possessed common land that was available for allocation by the village elders.

Collection of the lord's dues and the maintenance of his property was typically in the hands of an appointed steward. The steward (reeve, *maire*, or *Bauermeister*) was originally a capable peasant who received lands, exemptions, or special privileges for his work on the lord's behalf. Such men almost invariably became wealthy, and in the later Middle Ages some of them were able to transcend the limitations of peasant status and acquire a coat of arms. Together with the *ministeriales*, the household officials who served the immediate needs of the lord and his castle, the stewards constituted an intermediate social class of some importance.

Few, however, were popular. Some were petty tyrants who extorted goods and favors from the peasants while embezzling from their lord. Even the best of them were powerful figures who had to be placated at every turn. In some regions they not only collected rents and dues, but also served as judges in peasant courts and determined the boundaries of tenements in case of dispute. In other, happier, places, these latter functions were assumed by the villagers.

Manors that contained one or more entire villages were the ideal because they were easier to administer and defend. In practice a manor was often spread through several villages with each village containing the subjects of more than one lord. This situation arose in Germany and parts of France because, in the beginning at least, peasants could sometimes commend themselves to the lord of their choice. In Italy and southern France the situation was further complicated by the survival of allodial holdings amidst the feudal and manorial tenures. A villager might own some of his land outright and hold the rest as a tenement from his lord. Only in England was the village manor almost universal.

Manorialism, defined as any system in which the tenants of an estate are the legal subjects of their lord, could exist without feudalism. Where manorialism and feudalism were combined, they produced a social and political system that was highly resistant to change. The knights had achieved a monopoly of both economic and military power and thus could impose the values of their class upon society as a whole.

Social and Economic Structures in Nonfeudal Europe

By the middle of the tenth century feudal institutions were dominant in what had been the Carolingian Empire. Another, nonfeudal Europe successfully resisted the new social order. Scandinavia, untroubled by raids or invasions, preserved the main features of its social structure and system of land tenure until well into the early modern period. Individual farmsteads, often located at a distance from the nearest village and worked by the owner's family and its servants, continued to be common. Slavery declined and eventually disappeared under the influence of Christianity. The houses, built of logs and connected to their outbuildings for protection against the winter, retained the sturdy simplicity of Viking days.

Until the Norman invasion of 1066 (see illustration 8.4) the Anglo-Saxons, too, were able to function

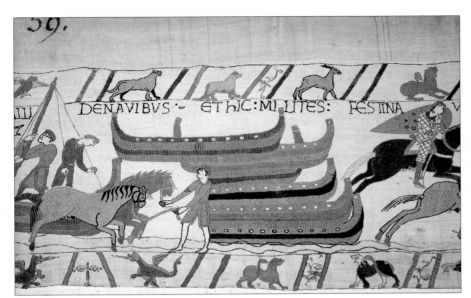

Illustration 8.4

Detail from the Bayeux Tapestry. The Bayeux Tapestry commemorates the Norman invasion of England in narrative form. It was designed to run clockwise around the entire nave of the Cathedral of Bayeux (consecrated 1077) and was originally 230 feet long and twenty inches high. It is an embroidery, not a true, woven tapestry. The work was probably done by the women of the court, who seem to have known a great deal about war and seafaring. In this segment, the Normans are beaching their Viking-style longboats and disembarking horses on the English coast for the invasion.

within the limits of their traditional social order, though the basis of land tenure changed dramatically. The Anglo-Saxon *ceorl* (churl), or peasant, was typically a freeholder who paid taxes for the support of his king's household and served in the *fyrd*, a kind of militia whose tactics resembled those of the Frankish hosts. As in other Germanic cultures, the kings were further served by a *comitatus* of fighting men, known as *gesiths*. *Gesiths* sometimes received land as a reward when they retired. They were usually supported during their fighting careers by the bounty of the king's hall and by the sharing of treasure.

On the eve of the Viking invasions, England was divided into seven kingdoms: East Anglia, Essex, Kent, Mercia, Northumberland, Sussex, and Wessex. Their small size made a decentralized mobile defense unnecessary, and feudal institutions did not develop, but the chaos of the mid-ninth century forced large numbers of hitherto independent *ceorls* to seek the protection of manorial relationships. Manorialism was firmly established and may have been the dominant form of English economic organization when Alfred the Great of Wessex (reigned 871–899) began the process of uniting the country into a single kingdom.

In Alfred's view, the achievement of political unity depended in part upon the revival of learning and of a sense of common cultural identity. He arranged for the translation of religious classics into Old English and commissioned the *Anglo-Saxon Chronicle*, one version of which was updated continuously until 1154. His policies bore fruit in the reign of Edgar, from 959 to 974, when political unity was achieved and the rich body of Anglo-Saxon poetry was compiled into four great

books, the most important of which was the epic *Beowulf*. The political failure of the succeeding years should not obscure the vibrant, functional society that fell to the Normans in 1066.

The Celtic world, though also subject to the full fury of the Norsemen, resisted the temptation to exchange land for military service until forced to do so in the twelfth and thirteenth centuries. Even then, the penetration of feudalism was far from complete. Ireland was ravaged from end to end by the Vikings, and Viking enclaves were established in the vicinity of Dublin and elsewhere. However, the old system of clans and kings survived. Feudalism was introduced only to those portions of the island that were conquered by Henry II of England in 1171–72, and even some of this territory was lost in the Irish revival of the fourteenth century.

The fate of Wales was similar. A kind of manorialism had been established in the more exposed coastal areas at the height of the raids. It was dominated by traditional chieftains instead of by feudal lords. The upland areas, rugged and inaccessible, remained free. After 1093 Norman adventurers tried to impose feudal tenures on certain parts of South Wales and Pembrokeshire. These efforts were partial and usually contested. Even in the areas of greatest Norman penetration, traditional institutions stood side by side with the new until well into the modern age.

The Welsh owed much of their independence to the ruggedness of their native land. In general, upland areas even in the heart of continental Europe stood a good chance of escaping feudal domination. Peasant communities in the Alps and the Pyrenees were remote as well as poor. Their inhabitants lived by herding and subsistence agriculture supplemented by hunting and gathering. Because they produced no surplus and were prohibited by geography from engaging in large-scale monoculture, they tempted neither the raiders nor the lords. They were also easily defended. Mounted knights were at a disadvantage in a largely vertical landscape, and narrow gorges were ideal sites for an ambush. Peasants of the high valleys found retaining their ancient freedoms relatively easy.

A rugged landscape also protected the remnants of Christian Spain. The situation in Cantabria and on the southern slopes of the Pyrenees was unique. The tiny states that survived the Muslim advance found themselves on a turbulent military frontier. Frankish influence brought feudalism to Cataluña, but the system that evolved in the northwest reflects a society that had begun, however tentatively, to take the offensive against *al Islam*. In the ninth and tenth centuries the kingdoms of Asturias, León, and Castile began to expand slowly at the expense of their Muslim neighbors, drawing back if the opposition became too intense, moving forward when a target of opportunity arose. Virtually the entire male population was militarized because warfare against the Muslims involved infantry and light cavalry as well as armored knights.

Advances were often achieved by individual nobles who were then free to keep the territory they conquered and rule it as they saw fit. Kings, however, reserved the right to grant and revoke titles at will. Feudal tenures were unknown, and private jurisdiction was strictly limited. Nobles placed themselves in *encomienda*, or commendation, to the crown, a term that was to have a different meaning in later centuries. Small landholders, who in this frontier society were usually free men and fighters, placed themselves in a similar relationship to the nobles. It was an exchange of military service for protection that might or might not involve a grant of land. More commonly it involved dues and services that created a *de facto* manor without the surrender of allodial property or of personal freedom. The *señorios* or lordships created by these arrangements were often vast. They were based upon a legal and political system unlike that of feudal Europe.

Spanish towns also played an important role in territorial expansion. Urban militias were established in the early ninth century and had become an important component of the Christian military effort by the tenth century. Whether they fought on their own behalf or under the direct orders of the king, towns were rewarded with booty and with royal grants whose provisions resembled those of the *señorios*. Large tracts of land

and many villages came under their control as peasants commended themselves to towns instead of to secular or ecclesiastical lords.

In northern Italy, towns were more effective as a barrier to feudal institutions, but for different reasons. Larger and richer than their Spanish counterparts, they could offer credible protection to their neighbors from the beginning of the feudal age. A patchwork of tenures developed in which allods, feudal manors, and urban jurisdictions might exist side by side in a relatively restricted space. The situation in some ways resembled that of southern France. The feudal component remained smaller, in part because the region was generally immune to large-scale raids. The south had been a region of large estates since Roman times. When Norman rulers imposed feudalism at the end of the eleventh century they substituted one set of lords for another while changing the legal basis of their holdings.

The Feudal Monarchies

This rapid survey of nonfeudal Europe reveals that, though feudalism was not universal, the disorders of the ninth and tenth centuries led to the growth of manorialism or other systems of collective security in all but the most isolated sections of Europe. A majority of Europeans were forced to renounce personal and economic freedom as the price of survival. Peasants who had formerly been free, slave, or *coloni* shared a common servility.

The impact of this change on everyday life should not be exaggerated. The correlation between personal freedom and political or social influence has always been inexact. The free Anglo-Saxon or Frankish peasant had often been subordinated as effectively by debt and by the threat of personal force as his descendants were by the custom of the manor, and he was subjected to taxes and demands for military service that could be as onerous as the feudal dues of a later period. Women had never been free in the sense that they remained the legal subjects of their fathers or husbands.

Moreover, the world that emerged from the aftermath of the great raids retained many distinctions of wealth and status, even among peasants. Servility was not incompatible with a secure and even comfortable life, while freedom could mean a hardscrabble existence on marginal lands. Those who remained free often did so because they inhabited malarial swamps or mountain crags unwanted by either knights or Vikings.

The conversion to feudal and manorial tenures seems more dramatic when seen in relation to its effect on social institutions and attitudes—the ties that bound society together. After the great raids, the gap between the vast majority of the population and the aristocracy that ruled them widened perceptibly. Social mobility was not only difficult to achieve but also generally condemned. Chivalric and ecclesiastical writers maintained that people should not attempt to rise above their class. Permanence and stability were valued by a society that had just emerged from two centuries of near-anarchy, but the longevity of feudal institutions was based only in part on the conservatism of those who had suffered much.

The apparent success of heavy cavalry in dealing with the crises of the ninth and tenth centuries had created a powerful myth of class superiority. The medieval knight believed in it and made it the basis of an entire way of life. His education, leisure activities, and ultimately the moral and aesthetic values of his class were grounded in the perception of himself as the armed and mounted protector of society—a perception that also gave him his chief claim to social privilege. By the end of the tenth century the conditions that created the knights had largely disappeared, but the knights were now in possession of the bulk of society's resources and could be neither displaced nor effectively controlled. Class divisions would henceforth widen and acquire a more elaborate ideological basis than they had formerly possessed. A system of military tactics that was not suitable for all occasions would be preserved until long after it had outlived its usefulness. Above all, the creation of a dominant social class whose power was based upon widely scattered estates would perpetuate the decentralization of political authority for centuries to come.

An immediate consequence of this decentralization was feudal warfare, disruptive and endemic, though not as devastating as the great raids. The warrior's sense of vocation, the development of a code of conduct based upon the ideals of honor and courage, and the emphasis on individual and corporate rights characteristic of feudal law all encouraged the lords to fight one another in defense of what they considered their honor and their right. The church sought to restrain these tendencies by encouraging the "Peace of God" movement. Councils or bishops issued decrees against wanton violence and tried to limit the fighting to certain days of the week. Such measures could achieve little. The political history of the age became in large measure an attempt to control the centrifugal tendencies of feudalism in the interests of public order.

France and Norman England

In northwestern Europe a protracted struggle between the kings of France and England was the legacy of Norman expansion. England fell to the Normans when Edward the Confessor died without heirs. There were three claimants to the throne: Edward's first cousin, William, duke of Normandy (c. 1028–87); Harald Hardrada, king of Norway; and the Saxon Harold Godwinsson. When the English Witan, or council, chose Harold Godwinsson, the new king found himself under attack on two fronts. He defeated the Norwegians at Stamford Bridge on September 23, 1066, and rushed south to meet William, who had landed near Hastings on the same day. Exhausted by the battle and by a march of almost three hundred miles, the Saxon army was crushed on October 14.

William was no friend of feudal decentralization. The fiefs he established in England were composed of manors in different parts of the country to prevent a concentration of power. He retained the Saxon office of sheriff or shire reeve, who collected taxes, administered the royal domains, and presided over the shire courts. In 1086 his officials produced a comprehensive survey of all English properties known as the Domesday Book (see document 8.5). Norman England was perhaps the most tightly administered monarchy of the central Middle Ages, but William's conquest gave birth to a political anomaly: The king of England was still duke of Normandy and vassal to the king of France for one of the richest provinces on the Continent.

The situation became critical in the reign of Henry II from 1154 to 1189. The development of the French monarchy had been slow and painful. In 987 the great French feudatories had elected Hugh Capet king, primarily because his small holdings in the region of Paris made it unlikely that he would ever pose a threat to their interests. The area was a hotbed of feudal anarchy, and the Capetian kings took more than a century to establish control. When Louis VI "the Fat" died in 1137, he left a small but powerful state in the Ile de France to his son Louis VII. Guided by his chief adviser, Suger, abbot of St. Denis, Louis VII tried to double his holdings by marrying Eleanor of Aquitaine (c. 1122–1204), the heir to vast estates in southwestern France (see illustration 8.5). The marriage was a disaster. Louis was pious and ascetic; Eleanor was attractive, witty, and a patron of troubadours. She apparently took the adulterous conventions of chivalric love too seriously, and the marriage was annulled in 1152 amid charges of infidelity with one of her cousins. The couple had two

◈ DOCUMENT 8.5 ◈

The Domesday Book: Description of a Manor

This description of the manor of Hecham, Essex, in 1086 il-
lustrates the care with which William the Conqueror's admin-
istrators catalogued the wealth of England. It also provides a
sense of what a medium-sized manor was like and of the dra-
matic changes brought by the conquest. A hide is a measure
of land that varied between eighty and one hundred modern
acres. A bordar was the lowest rank of villein, who per-
formed menial service in return for a cottage.

Peter de Valence holds in domain Hecham, which
Haldane a freeman held in the time of King Edward, as a manor, and as 5 hides. There have always
been 2 ploughs in the demesne, 4 ploughs of the
men. At that time there were 8 villeins, now 10;
then there were 2 bordars, now 3; at both times 4
servi, woods for 300 swine, 18 acres of meadow.
Then there were 2 fish ponds and a half, now there
are none. At that time there was 1 ox, now there
are 15 cattle and 1 small horse and 18 swine and 2
hives of bees. At that time it was worth 69s., now
4£10s. When he received this manor he found only
1 ox and 1 acre planted. Of those 5 hides spoken of
above, one was held in the time of King Edward by
2 freemen, and it was added to the manor in the
time of King William. It was worth in the time of
King Edward 10s., now 22s., and William holds
this from Peter de Valence.

"Domesday Book," II, 78b. In *Translations and Reprints from*
the Original Sources of European History, vol. 3, no. 5,
pp. 3–4. Philadelphia: University of Pennsylvania, 1896.

Illustration 8.5

〰 **Funeral Effigy of Eleanor of Aquitaine.** Eleanor, who had
been both queen of France and queen of England, was a major
political figure of the twelfth century as well as a great patron of
troubadours and chivalric literature. This carving is from her
tomb at the abbey of Fontrevault in France.

daughters but no son. Eleanor soon married Henry II of
England, her junior by ten years.

Henry was a man of boundless energy and ambition. He was responsible, among other things, for the
establishment of itinerant courts (the "justices in eyre")
that offered sworn inquests and juries as an alternative
to the duels and ordeals of the baronial courts and
whose decisions became the basis of English common
law. He also strengthened the Exchequer, or treasury,
so called because calculations were made by moving
counters on a checkered tabletop. Though Henry made
mistakes—the worst being the murder of St. Thomas à

Becket, archbishop of Canterbury, who was killed by
his henchmen in a dispute over the independence of
ecclesiastical courts—he left the country far stronger
than he had found it.

Unfortunately, his marriage to Eleanor of Aquitaine
left Henry in possession of half of France. To Louis VII
it was a personal affront as well as a threat to his sovereignty. For the next three hundred years the primary
goal of French policy was to secure either the obedience or the expulsion of the English (see map 8.2). It
was not at first an ethnic issue, for the English court
was culturally and linguistically French. But the situation raised questions that went to the heart of feudal relationships: Could a sovereign prince be the vassal of
another? What happened to ties of dependence when
the vassal was richer and more powerful than his lord?
The issue had been brought up in a somewhat different
form by the powerful counts of Flanders and would be
revived in later years by the growth of Burgundy. The
dispute between France and England remained the

an unsuccessful rebellion against their father. Two of these sons, Richard I Lion-Heart (reigned 1189–99) and John (reigned 1199–1216), would, as kings of England, bring ruin to Henry's cause.

Richard spent most of his reign crusading in the Holy Land at ruinous expense. On his return he was captured by the emperor Henry VI and forced to pay an enormous ransom that pushed the English to the brink of revolt. His brother John compounded the folly with a series of catastrophic mistakes. In 1200 he married a woman who was already engaged to a vassal of Philip Augustus. The vassal appealed to his lord, and Philip called upon John, as duke of Normandy, to present himself so that the case could be judged. It was the normal way of dealing with disputes between vassals of the same lord, but John, acting in his capacity as king of England, refused to submit to the justice of another sovereign. Philip responded by confiscating Normandy in 1204.

John's attempts to recover his lost duchy forced him to extreme financial measures that further alienated his subjects and brought him into conflict with the church. He was excommunicated in 1209, and England was placed under an interdict, a papal decree that forbade the administration of the sacraments. To lift it, John had to declare England a papal fief and renounce the royal appointment of bishops. The final blow occurred at Bouvines in 1214 when Philip Augustus defeated John's Anglo-Flemish-Imperial coalition in battle. Disgusted, a coalition of English barons rebelled and forced John to accept the Magna Carta (Great Charter). Though the Magna Carta (see document 8.6) is widely regarded as a landmark in the development of Anglo-Saxon constitutional thought, it was primarily an affirmation of feudal privileges. It did nothing for ordinary men and women and was largely ignored by John's successors. A later age would see it as a bulwark of individual rights against the claims of the state.

The failures of King John left Philip Augustus the most powerful figure in western Europe. By 1204 he had already added Artois and the Vermandois to his realms. The struggle with John brought him Normandy, Maine, Anjou, and Touraine. Bouvines brought him Flanders. To govern his new estates he appointed royal officials known as *baillis* or *seneschals*. Their function was like that of an English sheriff, but they were usually lawyers with no prior connection to the territories in which they served. They were therefore dependent upon the king and had no opportunity to build a power base of their own. This would be the pattern of French administration until 1789: Provinces retained

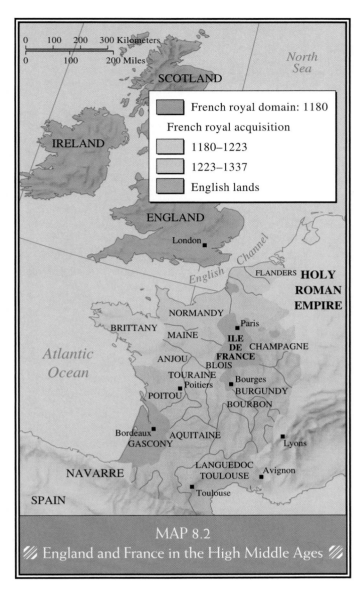

MAP 8.2
England and France in the High Middle Ages

central issue of west European politics until the fifteenth century.

The establishment of Henry II's Angevin Empire inspired a reorganization of the French monarchy. Begun by Louis VII, the work was completed by his son, Philip II Augustus (reigned 1179–1223). Louis created an effective royal army and, on the diplomatic front, concluded an improbable alliance with his ex-wife, Eleanor of Aquitaine. After sixteen years of marriage and eight children, Eleanor decided that she would no longer tolerate Henry's infidelity or his increasingly abusive behavior. She retired to Poitiers with her daughter, Mary, countess of Champagne, and established a court that was to become a veritable school of chivalry. In 1173 she and Louis encouraged her sons in

❖ DOCUMENT 8.6 ❖

Magna Carta

The following sections from the Magna Carta show that it was primarily intended to confirm and extend the privileges of the barons, but some of the provisions, such as number thirty-nine, had broader implications. Taken as a whole, the Great Charter set clear limits on the authority of the crown, and it is easy to understand why English revolutionaries of the seventeenth century regarded the document as one of the foundations of English liberty. Sections two and three restrict the crown's ability to extort fees from its vassals when a fief is inherited. Scutage in number twelve was a fee paid by a tenant in lieu of military service. John and some of his predecessors had begun to levy it for other purposes.

1. In the first place we have granted to God, and by this our present charter confirmed, for us and our heirs forever, that the English church shall be free, and shall hold its rights entire and its liberties uninjured.

2. If any of our earls or barons, or others holding from us in chief by military service shall have died, and when he had died his heir shall be of full age and owe relief, he shall have his inheritance by the ancient relief; that is to say, the heir or heirs of an earl for the whole barony of an earl a hundred pounds; the heir or heirs of a baron for a whole barony a hundred pounds; the heir or heirs of a knight, for a whole knight's fee, a hundred shillings at most; and who owes less let him give less according to the ancient custom of fiefs.

3. If, moreover, the heir of any one of such shall be under age, and shall be in wardship, when he comes of age he shall have his inheritance without relief and without a fine. . . .

12. No scutage or aid shall be imposed in our kingdom except by the common council of our kingdom, except for the ransoming of our own body, for the making of our oldest son a knight, and for the once marrying of our oldest daughter, and for these purposes it shall be only a reasonable aid.

13. And the city of London shall have all its ancient liberties and free customs, as well by land as by water. Moreover, we will and grant that all other cities and boroughs and villages and ports shall have all their liberties and free customs.

39. No free man shall be taken or imprisoned or dispossessed, or outlawed, or banished, or in any way destroyed, nor will we go upon him, nor send upon him, except by the legal judgments of his peers or by the law of the land.

"Magna Carta." *Pennsylvania Translations and Reprints*, pp. 6–16, trans. Edward P. Cheyney. Philadelphia: University of Pennsylvania Press, 1897.

---

their institutions, which were controlled by officers of the crown. By the end of the thirteenth century, Philip's successors had acquired Languedoc, Toulouse, Poitou, and Champagne. Only English Aquitaine and Gascony remained outside their grasp.

The Ottonian Empire

France and England would remain the archetypical feudal monarchies. In the German-speaking lands to the east, an effort to revive the empire along feudal lines was begun by Otto I the Great (reigned 936–973), the victor at the Lechfeld (see map 8.3). Otto was a self-conscious imitator of Charlemagne, though he never sought to extend his rule over West Francia. Like Charlemagne, he enlisted the church in his behalf, drawing both his administrators and many of his feudal

levies from the great ecclesiastical estates. In 962 Pope John XII crowned him emperor at Aachen in return for his help against an Italian enemy, Berengar of Friuli, and Otto agreed to protect the territorial integrity of the papal states. The price for all this was imperial control over ecclesiastical appointments. When John objected, he was deposed and his successor was forced to take an oath of allegiance to Otto.

These events were recorded in detail because Otto, like Charlemagne, knew the value of a good biographer. Hroswitha of Gandersheim (c. 935–1000) was one of the great literary figures of the age. In addition to the *Deeds of Otto* she wrote a history of her convent, some religious poems, and six comedies based on the works of Terence. They are thought to be the first dramas written in medieval times. Hroswitha did not write in isolation but was part of a broader flowering of literary culture and manuscript illumination among

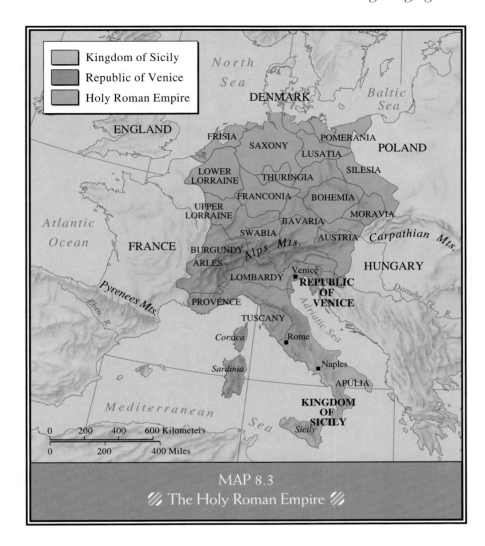

MAP 8.3

/// The Holy Roman Empire ///

women in religious orders in the Ottonian Empire (see illustration 8.6). Abbesses of great convents such as Uta of Niedermünster seem to have been even more powerful in Germany than elsewhere, and they took the responsibilities of patronage seriously. One of the extraordinary figures to emerge from this tradition was Hildegard of Bingen (1098–1179). The *Scivias*, a powerful record of her mystical visions, remains a classic of devotional and apocalyptic literature. She also wrote a treatise on medicine, at least one play, and the *Physica*, a categorical description of the natural world.

Otto's involvement with the papacy drew him and his successors more deeply into the quagmire of Italian politics. Their efforts to limit the growing power of the north Italian towns and their bitter struggle with the papacy over the issue of lay investiture (the imperial appointment of bishops) were among the most important political conflicts of the Middle Ages (see chapter 9).

The issues were intertwined, and both required massive investments of political and military capital. Emperors could easily neglect German affairs or subordinate them to the needs of their Italian policy. German nobles and ultimately the German towns found it equally easy to preserve their autonomy and to resist the development of a feudal monarchy on the French or English model. Germany, with its hundreds of small states, remained a stronghold of feudal particularism until the beginning of the modern age.

At their strongest, feudal monarchies such as England and France could command impressive resources. Their power was nevertheless limited. As long as fighting men were supported with land or by payments in kind, feudal lords could raise private armies and threaten the integrity of the realm. Kings had prestige and the legal advantages of sovereignty—their courts took theoretical precedence over all others, they could declare

Illustration 8.6

Illumination from the Uta Codex. This magnificent example of Romanesque manuscript illumination was commissioned by Uta, abbess of the convent at Niedermünster, and completed between 1002 and 1025, probably by the nuns in her own scriptorium. Uta, who appears in the upper right-hand corner, was one of many powerful abbesses in the Ottonian Empire. Women frequently served as manuscript illuminators. The subject here is "Saint Erhard Celebrating Mass."

war, and they could coin money—but feudal kingdoms were inherently unstable because the crown held no monopoly on the use of force. Such a monopoly could be achieved only by eroding the foundations of feudalism itself. Until then, good governance would be largely a matter of personal character and good luck. For most of the Middle Ages, Europe would remain politically fragmented while retaining a social structure that conserved feudal privilege long after its original justification had passed.

CHAPTER 9

MEDIEVAL RELIGION AND THOUGHT

The Latin church survived the fall of the Roman Empire in the west to become the major unifying element in European society. Though it suffered from episodes of fragmentation and disorder throughout the early Middle Ages, it provided western Europeans with a common set of values and, through its universality and the preservation of the Latin language, with a measure of diplomatic and intellectual communication. With the passing of the great raids, the church gradually evolved into something more: a vast, institutionalized bureaucracy headed by popes who claimed full authority over a subordinate clergy as well as secular rulers. That authority was vehemently contested by the emperor and other princes, but all agreed that Europe, for all its divisions, was a Christian commonwealth ruled in theory by divine law.

The church of the High Middle Ages possessed vast wealth, political influence, and a virtual monopoly of thought and education, but its importance cannot be understood in purely institutional terms. Its values, sacraments, and holidays defined the lives of ordinary people in ways that are almost inconceivable today. While medieval people were neither excessively good nor moral, their personal identities and habits of thought were formed by near total emersion in Christian practices and categories of thought. The sacraments, from baptism to extreme unction, defined the stages of people's lives. They measured time by reference to the canonical hours and holidays of the church. They bound themselves by religious oaths that, to their minds, carried with them the real threat of eternal damnation, and they explained everything from politics to natural phenomena as an expression of God's will. In more concrete terms the church building was both the physical and social center of their communities and the most visible expression of communal or civic pride. Priests, monks, and nuns organized the distribution of charity, cared for the sick, and provided lodging for travelers in the great monasteries that dotted the countryside. Chapter 9 describes how the church evolved from the dark days of the tenth century to the glories of the twelfth and thirteenth centuries—the great age of cathedrals and crusades, of the founding of universities, and of scholasticism, a system of thought that retains its influence today.

Monastic Revival and Papal Reform

The disorder created by the great raids profoundly weakened the western church. Cut off from contact with each other and from Rome, bishoprics and monasteries fell under the control of secular rulers who could protect them. These lords then appointed political henchmen or their own younger sons to episcopal rank with little regard for spiritual qualities. Monasteries suffered the same fate. Even when a monastery retained its independence, isolation and the absence of supervision often led to relaxations of the rule. Lay people, who in this age tended to believe that their chances of salvation depended on the prayers of those holier than themselves, were scandalized and frightened.

The papacy shared in the general decline. As bishop of Rome, the pope was both spiritual and secular ruler of the city. From the deposition of Pope Nicholas the Great in 867 to the appointment of Clement II in 1046, a generalized state of anarchy permitted the great Roman families to vie for control of the office with only an occasional nod to religious priorities or to the wishes of the emperors. To the laity and to pious churchmen alike, the situation was intolerable.

A reform movement that would transform both the papacy and the medieval church began in the Burgundian monastery of Cluny. Founded in 910 by William the Pious, duke of Aquitaine, its community followed a strict version of the Benedictine rule that emphasized liturgy and vocal prayer. In the decades that followed its establishment the Cluniac ideal attracted those who sought a more spiritual and disciplined religious life. The original foundation became the mother house to nearly fifteen hundred affiliated monasteries.

The agenda of the Cluniac monks included more than prayer. They saw themselves as the vanguard of a broader reform that would enhance the spirituality of the church and free it forever from secular control. To achieve this, they sought to create an independent, reformed papacy and to restore episcopal subordination as a first step to rooting out corruption among parish priests and monks.

The reformer's first step was to gain the support of the emperor Henry III (1017–56), who agreed with many of their ideas and saw in them an opportunity to expand his own political influence. Henry entered Italy in 1046, deposed the three existing popes, and suppressed the Roman political factions that had supported them. He then used his authority to appoint a series of popes, the most important of whom was the Cluniac reformer Leo IX (served 1049–54). Leo condemned simony, or the sale of church offices, called for the enforcement of clerical celibacy, and brought with him to Rome a number of young men who shared his convictions.

Henry's actions brought improvement, but to the monks, a papacy under imperial control was only slightly better than one controlled by Roman politicians. In the confusion that followed Henry's death, the reformers achieved something like full independence for the papacy. Taking advantage of the minority of Henry's young son, Henry IV (1050–1106), Pope Nicholas II placed the election of all future popes in the hands of the College of Cardinals, an advisory body composed of the most important, or cardinal, priests of the Roman diocese. The first such election took place in 1061, and the basic procedure used on that occasion has remained more or less intact to this day.

The Investiture Controversy and Its Aftermath

The next step was to achieve papal control over the appointment of bishops. With the establishment of feudalism, bishops came to hold fiefs over which they exercised civil as well as ecclesiastical authority. The secular rulers whose vassals they became usurped the right to invest, or formally install, them as bishops. When Hildebrand of Soana, one of the men who had come to Rome with Leo IX, was elected Pope Gregory VII in 1073 he made the abolition of lay investiture his chief priority. The emperor, like all other secular authorities, was forbidden to invest bishops with ring and crozier, the symbols of their office, on pain of excommunication. To Henry IV, this edict was a serious threat, not only because it seemed to question the religious basis of imperial power but also because bishops were the temporal as well as spiritual lords over much of Germany. All hope of imperial consolidation, to say nothing of good governance, would be thwarted if such men were appointed by an outsider. To the pope, lay investiture prevented him from exercising full control over the church and seemed to guarantee that its highest offices would be occupied by political hacks incapable of furthering the work of reform. At a more fundamental level, the quarrel was about the nature of political power itself (see document 9.1). Pope and emperor agreed that all authority derived from God's grace, but was that grace transmitted directly to the ruler or through the agency of the church?

The political crisis that resulted was known as the Investiture Controversy, and it set the stage for generations of conflict between the emperors and the popes. Henry called upon his bishops to reject Gregory VII (see document 9.2). Gregory responded by excommunicating him and absolving his subjects of their allegiance. The entire empire chose sides. Because most of the imperial princes and many of the growing towns felt that they would profit from a weakening of imperial authority, a revolt led by the dukes of Saxony placed the emperor in dire peril. In a clever move, Henry decided to ask absolution of the pope. Gregory could not deny absolution to a legitimate penitent. At the castle of Canossa in the Italian Alps he supposedly forced the emperor to stand barefoot in the snow for three days before readmitting him to the fellowship of the church. Whatever satisfaction Gregory may have found in humiliating his rival did not compensate for being outmaneuvered. The revolt, deprived of its legitimacy, was over. Henry quickly reestablished his authority over the princes and in 1084 drove Gregory into exile.

The dispute over investiture was finally resolved in 1122 by the Concordat of Worms. Henry V (1086–1125) and Calixtus II (served 1119–24) reached a compromise by which Henry renounced his right to appoint bishops but retained the power to grant them fiefs and other temporal benefits. In theory, the freedom of the church from secular interference was securely established. In practice, episcopal appointments were still heavily influenced by the emperor who could withhold the income of a bishop who displeased him.

Whatever its importance for the evolution of church-state relationships, the investiture struggle marked the birth of a more assertive papacy that would one day claim *dominium* over the secular state. Gregory VII thought of the church as a body capable of giving law to all of Christendom and carefully fostered a growing interest in the study of canon or church law. This movement, which sparked a parallel revival of Roman civil law, reached its peak with the publication of Gratian's *Decretals* (c. 1140), an authoritative collection of papal and conciliar rulings supplemented by thirty-six *causae* or sample cases. Subsequent popes and

---

◆ DOCUMENT 9.1 ◆

Dictatus Papae

The Dictatus Papae *appears to be an internal memorandum produced by the circle of churchmen around Gregory VII. Though he did not in all probability write it himself, it sets forth his concept of papal rights and prerogatives under twenty-seven headings, the most important of which are listed below.*

1. That the Roman church was established by God alone.
2. That the Roman pontiff alone is rightly called universal.
3. That he alone has the power to depose and reinstate bishops.
8. That he alone may use the imperial insignia.
9. That all princes shall kiss the foot of the pope alone.
10. That his name alone is to be recited in the churches.
12. That he has the power to depose emperors.
16. That no general synod may be called without his order.
17. That no action of a synod and no book shall be regarded as canonical without his authority.
18. That his decree can be annulled by no one, and that he can annul the decrees of anyone.
19. That he can be judged by no one.
20. That no one shall dare to condemn a person who has appealed to the apostolic seat.
22. That the Roman church has never erred and will never err to all eternity, according to the testimony of the holy scriptures.
24. That by his command or permission subjects may accuse their rulers.
25. That he can depose and reinstate bishops without calling a synod.
26. That no one can be regarded as catholic who does not agree with the Roman church.
27. That he has the power to absolve subjects from their oath of fidelity to wicked rulers.

"Ordericus Vitalis" (1119), trans. T. Forester. In *Ecclesiastical History.* London: Bohn, 1853–1856. Reprinted in James Bruce Ross and Mary Martin McLaughlin, eds., *The Portable Medieval Reader.* New York: Viking, 1949.

◆ DOCUMENT 9.2 ◆

Henry IV to Gregory VII

This excerpt is from a letter sent by the emperor Henry IV to Pope Gregory VII in 1076. It sets out the basis of Henry's case and, in its mastery of invective, shows something of the heat generated by the argument over papal authority.

Henry, king not through usurpation but through the holy ordination of God, to Hildebrand, at present not pope but false monk. Such greeting as this hast though merited through thy disturbances, inasmuch as there is no grade in the church which thou hast omitted to make a partaker not of honor but of confusion, not of benediction, but of malediction. For, to mention few and special cases out of many, not only hast thou not feared to lay hands upon the rulers of the holy church, the anointed of the Lord—the archbishops, namely bishops and priests—but thou hast trodden them underfoot like slaves ignorant of what their master is doing. . . . As if we had received our kingdom from thee! As if the kingdom and the empire were in thine and not in God's hands! And this although our Lord Jesus Christ did call us to this kingdom, did not, however, call thee to the priesthood. For thou has ascended by the following steps. By wiles, namely, which the profession of monk abhors, thou hast achieved money; by money, favor; by the sword, the throne of peace. And from the throne of peace thou hast disturbed peace. . . . Let another ascend the throne of St. Peter, who shall not practice violence under the cloak of religion, but shall teach the sound doctrine of St. Peter. I Henry, king by the grace of God, do say unto thee, together with all our bishops: Descend, descend, to be damned throughout all the ages.

"Dictatus Papae." In O. J. Thatcher, and E. H. McNeal, eds. *A Source Book of Medieval History*, pp. 136–137. New York: Scribner's, 1905.

councils legislated so profusely that five new compilations were added in less than a century.

By the pontificate of Innocent III (served 1198–1216) the papacy had established itself as the legal arbiter of all matters, a *speculator* or overseer working in the best interests of the entire Christian common-

wealth. The church had developed a legal bureaucracy that was the envy of secular princes. Appeals from both secular and ecclesiastical authorities were referred to the Papal Tribunal, which included the Penitentiary (for matters of faith and morals) and the Court of the Sacred Palace. Cases were prepared by a corps of Auditors who in 1322 were organized into the *Rota Romana* with appellate jurisdiction of its own. Difficult or important issues were referred to the pope, who might choose to decide them in consultation with the cardinals. Their role was purely advisory, for no earthly power exceeded his own. Papal decisions were then handed down as decretals that formed the evolving basis of canon law. In theory, popes could overrule legal precedent, though they rarely did so.

The claims of the papacy had reached their peak. Innocent, like his predecessors, believed that all earthly power was based upon God's grace and that grace was administered by the church. When he argued that a pope could dethrone those who were ruling improperly, he did no more than carry the ideas of Gregory VII to their logical conclusion. Such theories were often difficult to implement, but the case of King John of England showed that he was fully prepared to intervene in the affairs of a sovereign kingdom.

The New Monastic Orders and the Building of the Great Cathedrals

Though dramatic and politically controversial, the exalted notion of papal authority did not define the Cluniac program or the Hildebrandine or Gregorian reformation that arose from it. At the heart of the movement was a profound attachment to the monastic ideal and the belief that celibacy was essential to a truly Christian life. For this reason the reformers were suspicious of priests who lived in the world without monastic vows. The distinction between the "secular" clergy who serve bishops and parishes and the "regular" or monastic clergy dates from this period, with the regulars quickly gaining an advantage in the pursuit of high ecclesiastical office. This inevitably caused resentment among the seculars, but the monastic ideal continued to spread. Several new orders of both men and women were created, including the Carthusians in 1084 and the Premonstratensians in 1134. The Cistercians, founded in 1119, expanded under the leadership of St. Bernard of Clairvaux (1090–1153) to include 338 monasteries at the time of his death. Secular priests were also forced for the first time to take a vow of

❖ DOCUMENT 9.3 ❖

The Cluniac Reformers and Clerical Celibacy

The reforms of Pope Leo IX spread slowly in Western Christendom, and fifty years later, archbishops were still trying to impose a celibate life on priests. The following document is an account by Ordericus Vitalis in 1119 of how one French archbishop tried to enforce Leo's reforms.

Geoffrey, the archbishop, having returned to Rouen from attending the church council at Reims, held a synod of priests in the third week in November. Stirred up by the late papal decrees, he dealt sharply and rigorously with the priests of his diocese. Among other canons of the council which he promulgated was that which interdicted them from commerce with females of any description, and against such transgressors he launched the terrible sentence of excommunication. As the priests shrunk from submitting to this grievous burden, and in loud mutterings among themselves vented their complaints of the struggle between the flesh and the spirit to which they were subjected, the archbishop ordered one Albert, a man of free speech, who had used some offensive words, I know not what, to be arrested on the spot, and he was presently thrust into the common prison.

This prelate was a Breton and guilty of many indiscretions, warm and obstinate in temper, and severe in his aspect and manner, harsh in his censures, and withal, indiscreet and a great talker. The other priests, witnessing this extraordinary proceeding, were utterly confounded; and when they saw that, without being charged with any crime or undergoing any legal examination, a priest was dragged, like a thief, from a church to a dungeon, they became so exceedingly terrified that they knew not how to act, doubting whether they had best defend themselves or take flight.

William of Malmesbury. *Chronicle*, trans. J. A. Giles. London: Bohn, 1847. Reprinted in James Bruce Ross and Mary Martin McLaughlin, eds. *The Portable Medieval Reader*, pp. 57–58. New York: Viking, 1949.

Illustration 9.1

The Romanesque Church of the Abbey of St. Léger at Merbach, Alsace. A typical Romanesque exterior has square towers and round arches. The structure was built between 1134 and 1155.

celibacy. The policy was first adopted by Leo IX, but implementation was gradual because it left concubines without support and because the laity was often suspicious of priests who lacked a woman of their own (see document 9.3).

The reformers were, in other words, triumphalists who believed that their monastic ideals should dominate the church and that the church should be the dominant institution in a Christian society. The visible symbols of that dominance were the great churches constructed during the eleventh and twelfth centuries in what has become known as the Romanesque style (see illustration 9.1). Abandoning the basilica with its

Illustration 9.2

✍ **A Romanesque Interior.** The nave and choir of St.-Sernin at Toulouse, France, shows the round arches, simple barrel vaulting, and massive piers typical of Romanesque churches.

wooden roof, the builders covered the nave, or central isle of the church, with a massive barrel vault that rested upon a clerestory. The clerestory, with its arched windows, rested upon round arches reinforced by side aisles that served as buttresses (see illustration 9.2). The new style consumed vast quantities of cut stone, producing an overwhelming impression of power and serenity.

In the course of the twelfth century, a new style evolved based upon ribbed groin vaults and pointed arches. Flying buttresses were developed to support the weight of the vaulting, and the size of windows was increased until, in the High Gothic style of the thirteenth and fourteenth centuries, interiors were illuminated by vast sheets of stained glass that portrayed

episodes from the Scriptures so that even the illiterate might absorb the teachings of the church (see illustration 9.3 and 9.4).

The construction of cathedrals required enormous commitments of time and money. Some required centuries to build, and most were embellished with painting, sculpture, and stained glass on a grand scale. Such aesthetic achievements were made possible by the improved collection of tithes and the more efficient management of church estates. Medieval society was prepared to invest much of its meager economic surplus in religious buildings. However, not everyone viewed this development with enthusiasm. The glories of Durham or Palermo, Chartres or Amiens, were ultimately paid for by the labor of peasants. Some complained that such magnificence was inappropriate for the worship of a simple carpenter from Galilee, but the reformers were inspired by a vision of divine grandeur that demanded tangible expression on Earth.

Unfortunately, this vision could not comprehend dissent. The faith born originally of the Cluniac revival would inspire intellectual and artistic achievement for years to come. It would also provoke the Crusades and the virtual expulsion of the Jews from western Europe.

The Crusades: The Reconquest of Muslim Europe

The Crusades were both an expression of religious militancy and the first of several European attempts to expand geographically at the expense of non-Christians. For the inhabitants of northern Europe, the Crusades provided their first sustained encounter with Islam, a society that was still in many ways more advanced than their own.

The model for Christian expansionism was provided by the beginnings of the Spanish *reconquista*, or reconquest. In 1031 the caliph of Córdoba was deposed during a prolonged civil war and Muslim Spain disintegrated into petty principalities based on the major towns. Their number reached as high as twenty-three. These small states, wealthy but militarily weak, offered a tempting opportunity to the Christian kingdoms. Taking advantage of Muslim disunity, the kings of León and Castile began extending their realms southward and received special privileges and plenary indulgences (remissions of the punishment for sins

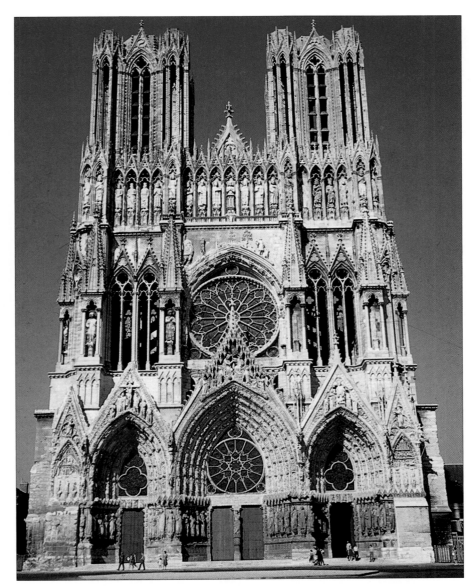

Illustration 9.3

Reims Cathedral. Begun about 1200, Reims is a superb example of High Gothic cathedral building.

committed on behalf of the faith) from the papacy as an encouragement.

The reconquest was not, however, a unified movement. Muslim Spain was reunited in 1086 under the Almoravides, a religious reform movement originating in North Africa, and again in 1172 by an even more puritanical group, the Almohades. Christian gains were made in the intervals between periods of Muslim strength. In the meantime, the Christian princes continued to fight among themselves, which led to the creation of the kingdom of Portugal in 1143. The age is best symbolized by the career of Rodrigo Díaz de Vivar, known as "El Cid" (c. 1043–99). El Cid fought for both Christian and Muslim potentates, changing

sides as his interest required, until he acquired the kingdom of Valencia in 1092. His ruthless cynicism did not prevent him from becoming the hero of chivalric romances.

Medieval Spain was a multicultural society in which Muslims, Christians, and Jews lived in uneasy balance. Religious tolerance was for the most part maintained out of necessity and gave birth to a rich philosophical and scientific tradition that flourished in spite of war and occasional outbreaks of religious violence. The balance was tipped in 1212 when Alfonso VIII of Castile defeated the Almohades at the battle of Las Navas de Tolosa. The Muslim towns fell one by one until in 1248 Sevilla surrendered to the Christians,

Illustration 9.4

The Cathedral of Saint-Pierre, Beauvais. Beauvais is in some ways an extreme example of Gothic architectural ambition. The choir was the tallest in Europe until it collapsed in 1284.

leaving the kingdom of Granada as the only Muslim enclave in Christian Europe (see map 9.1).

Christendom was also on the advance in Sicily. One problem with feudalism was that increases in the population of the knightly class rapidly produced more men trained in the profession of arms than could be supported by existing fiefs. An expansion of their opportunities, like the Norman invasion of England, could be seen as essential to social peace. Another group of Norman adventurers, including the twelve sons of the minor feudatory Tancred of Hauteville, had established themselves in Italy by 1050. Pope Leo IX regarded

them as a threat. Later popes, realizing that the Normans could be useful allies in the investiture crisis, supported one of Tancred's sons, Robert Guiscard (d. 1085), in his attempt to seize control of the Italian south. Robert drove the Byzantine Greeks from Calabria but left the conquest of Muslim Sicily to his brother Roger (d. 1101). The process was completed in 1092. Roger's son, Roger II, used his inheritance to create a powerful feudal kingdom on the Anglo-Norman model. Its superior resources and his qualities as a general enabled Roger to conquer all of southern Italy before his death in 1154.

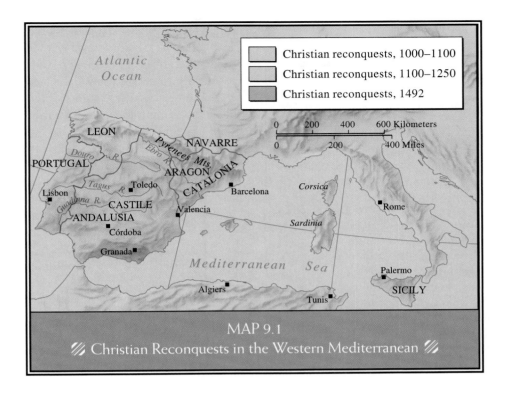

MAP 9.1
Christian Reconquests in the Western Mediterranean

The Struggle for the Holy Land

Christian successes in Spain and Sicily were greeted with enthusiasm throughout Europe. When added to the great wave of piety unleashed by the Cluniac reforms, they raised the prospect of a general offensive against the Muslim infidel. In 1095 Pope Urban II proclaimed a crusade to free Jerusalem and the Holy Land from Muslim control. The privileges and indulgences were similar to those granted earlier in Spain (see document 9.4), but Urban's decision was rooted in the complexities of Middle Eastern politics.

Turkish tribes, most of them converts to Islam, were beginning their long migration from the steppes of central Asia into the lands of the Greek empire. One such group, called the Seljuks after the name of their ruling family, defeated the armies of Byzantium and seized control of eastern Anatolia at the battle of Manzikert in 1071. Alarmed, the Byzantine emperors hinted delicately at the reunification of the eastern and western churches if only the west would come to their aid.

Twenty years later, the death of the Abbasid sultan of Baghdad, Malek Shah, inaugurated a civil war among his emirs in Syria and Palestine. The disorder was such that Christian pilgrims could no longer visit the Holy Land in safety. This was intolerable, especially when Islam seemed elsewhere in retreat. The disintegration of the Caliphate of Córdoba, the expulsion of the Mus-

lims from the Balearic Islands in 1087, and the chaos in Syria could only encourage the dream of liberating Jerusalem and perhaps of uniting all Christendom under papal rule.

The proclamation of the First Crusade was met with more enthusiasm than the pope had anticipated. Thousands of European men and women were prepared to leave their homes and travel to fight in an unknown and hostile land. Their motives were in large part pious, but they had other reasons as well. The social pressures that had produced the Norman expansion were still at work throughout the feudal world. Younger sons hoped to claim Middle Eastern lands as their own, and an increasing number of landless peasants were happy to accompany them. Princes in turn were happy to see them go. The martial enthusiasm of the feudal classes had produced an alarming number of local wars. The church tried unsuccessfully to restrain them by proclaiming the Truce of God, which attempted to restrict fighting to certain days of the week. The Crusades provided an acceptable outlet for these energies. In a broader sense they justified the continuing privileges of a feudal class that no longer had an external threat to combat.

Though the Christian command was deeply divided, Jerusalem fell to the Christians on July 15, 1099. The Muslim and Jewish population of the city was

◆ DOCUMENT 9.4 ◆

The Privileges of the Crusaders

These privileges, granted to prospective crusaders by Pope Eugenius III in 1146, demonstrate some of the spiritual and material advantages that induced men to go to the Holy Land.

Moreover, by the authority vested by God in us, we who with paternal care provide for your safety and the needs of the church, have promised and granted to those who from a spirit of devotion have decided to enter upon and accomplish such a holy and necessary undertaking and task, that remission of sins which our predecessor Pope Urban instituted. We have also commanded that their wives and children, their property and possessions, shall be under the protection of the holy church, of ourselves, of the archbishops, bishops and other prelates of the church of God. Moreover, we ordain by our apostolic authority that until their return or death is full proven, no law suit shall be instituted hereafter in regard to any property of which they were in peaceful possession when they took the cross.

Those who with pure hearts enter upon such a sacred journey and who are in debt shall pay no interest. And if they or others for them are bound by oath or promise to pay interest, we free them by our apostolic authority. And after they have sought aid of their relatives or lords of whom they hold their fiefs, and the latter are unable or unwilling to advance them money, we allow them freely to mortgage their lands and other possessions to churches, ecclesiastics, or other Christians, and their lords shall have no redress.

Otto of Freising. *Gesta Federici*, I, 35. *Pennsylvania Translations and Reprints*, p. 13, trans. Edward P. Cheyney. Philadelphia: University of Pennsylvania Press, 1897.

military orders were established—the Knights of the Hospital of St. John of Jerusalem (1113) and the Knights Templars (1119). Religious orders of fighting men, sworn to celibacy and dedicated to the protection of the holy places, the Knights were a model for later orders that sought to expand the frontiers of Christendom in Spain and Germany.

In spite of these efforts, Edessa fell in 1144, and a Second Crusade was launched in retaliation. It accomplished little. In 1187 Jerusalem was taken by the Kurdish general Saladin (c. 1137–93). The Third Crusade (1189–92) was a fiasco. The emperor Frederick Barbarossa (c. 1123–90) drowned in a stream, weighed down by his body armor. Richard I Lion-Heart, king of England, quarreled with Philip Augustus, who abandoned the siege of Jerusalem and returned to confiscate Richard's fiefs in France. Richard, trying to return home, was captured and held for ransom by the emperor Henry VI.

Subsequent crusades were even less edifying. The Fourth Crusade (1202–1204) foundered when the crusaders failed to provide for the cost of their passage in Venetian ships. The Venetians demanded that they seize Zara in payment and then inveigled them into attacking Constantinople. Constantinople fell in July 1203. The Venetians eventually abandoned their conquest after extorting more favorable trade privileges from the Greeks in return for the city. In 1228 the emperor Frederick II was excommunicated for abandoning the Sixth Crusade, ostensibly because of seasickness. He acquired Jerusalem by negotiation in the following year. The pope, who thought that he should have taken the city by force, was not pleased. The Muslims recovered it in 1244. Two more crusades by St. Louis IX of France accomplished nothing, and by 1291 the last Christian strongholds in the Levant had fallen to the Muslims (see map 9.2).

The Impact of the Crusades upon Europe

The first attempt at European expansion had mixed results. Only in Spain and Portugal was new territory added to Christendom, but a precedent was set for the more sustained efforts of the fifteenth and sixteenth centuries. In the meantime, the effort to convert non-Christian populations by the sword—a notion hardly envisioned by the fathers of the church—poisoned relations with the Islamic world and probably strengthened the forces of intolerance and rigidity within Islam. European Jews suffered as well. The militant attitude deliberately fostered by a reformed papacy led to perse-

massacred, and the region as a whole was divided into the County of Tripoli and three kingdoms organized on the feudal model: Jerusalem, Edessa, and Antioch. All four were papal fiefs that provided new lands for ambitious knights and churchmen. In reality they were fragile enclaves surrounded by a population that despised the Christians as barbarians. To protect them, fortifications based upon the more sophisticated engineering techniques of the Muslims were constructed and two

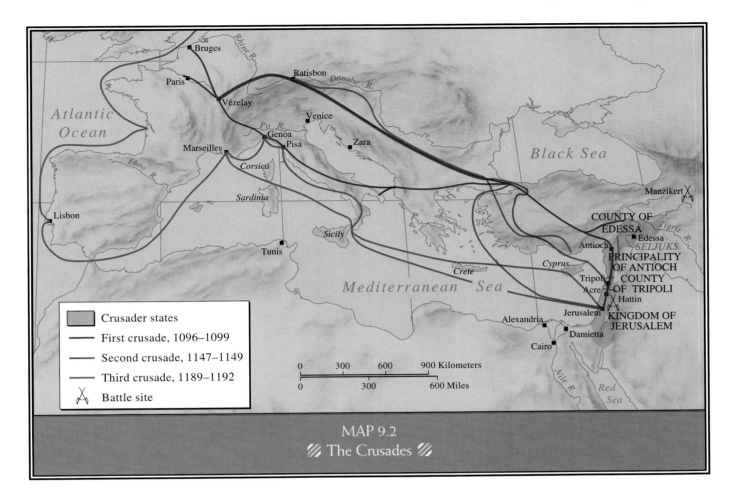

MAP 9.2
/// The Crusades ///

cutions, most of which were based on the blood libel that Jews sacrificed Christian children as part of their rituals (see document 9.5). It was no accident that such crusading princes as Richard Lion-Heart and St. Louis IX supported the expulsion of Jews from their lands.

The general climate of intolerance may also have affected the treatment of homosexuals. Though formally condemned by church doctrine, homosexuality appears to have been tolerated until the mid-thirteenth century. A substantial literature on homosexual love had been created by clerical writers in the great days of the Hildebrandine reform. After 1250, for reasons that are not clear, virtually every region of Europe passed laws making homosexual activity a capital crime. These laws, and the sentiments they reflected, remained in effect until well into modern times.

In personal terms, few of the crusaders gained the wealth and status they sought, but for western women of the upper classes the Crusades were probably beneficial. Many accompanied their husbands to the Middle East where they astonished the Muslims with their freespo-

ken manners. Those who stayed home often assumed the role of managers and defenders of the family's estates. In either case their independence and economic value were often enhanced. At the level of international politics the Crusades were the beginning of the end for the Byzantine Empire. Fatally weakened by the Fourth Crusade, the Greeks continued to lose ground until they were at last overwhelmed by Turkish expansion in 1453. The Venetians, as the architect of Greek misfortunes, benefited for a time by establishing a series of colonies on Greek soil. In the end these, too, were lost to the Turks.

Of more permanent value was the increase of trade in Eastern luxury goods. The Crusades, by bringing western Europeans into contact with a more technologically advanced civilization, fueled their growing taste for spices, silks, damascus cutlery, and similar items. The Eastern trade not only broadened cultural perspectives, at least in a material sense, but also encouraged capital accumulation, especially in the Italian towns. A related benefit was the improved knowledge of engineering, stonemasonry, and fortification that was

◈ DOCUMENT 9.5 ◈

Pope Gregory X Denounces the Blood Libel

A succession of popes inveighed against the blood libel with varying degrees of success. This letter by Gregory X (served 1271–76) is similar in tone to earlier letters by Innocent III and Innocent IV. The expulsions reveal that papal good sense had little impact on some of Europe's monarchs and their subjects.

Since it happens occasionally that some Christians lose their Christian children, the Jews are accused by their enemies of secretly carrying off and killing these same Christian children and of making sacrifices of the heart and blood of these very children. It happens, too, that parents of these children or some other Christian enemies of these Jews, secretly hide these very children in order that they may be able to injure these Jews, and in order that they may be able to extort from them a certain amount of money by redeeming them from their straits.

And most falsely do these Christians claim that the Jews have secretly and furtively carried away these children and killed them, and that the Jews offer sacrifice from the heart and blood of these children, since their law in this matter precisely and expressly forbids Jews to sacrifice, eat, or drink, the blood, or to eat the flesh of animals having claws. This has been demonstrated many times at our court by Jews converted to the Christian faith; nevertheless very many Jews are often seized and detained unjustly because of this.

We decree, therefore, that Christians need not be obeyed against Jews in a case or situation of this type, and we order that Jews seized under such a silly pretext be freed from imprisonment, and that they shall not be arrested henceforth on such a miserable pretext, unless—which we do not believe—they be caught in the commission of the crime. We decree that no Christian shall stir up anything new against them, but that they should be maintained in that status and position in which they were in the time of our predecessors, from antiquity till now.

Marcus, Jacob R. *The Jew in the Medieval World,* p. 154. New York: Atheneum, 1972.

Illustration 9.5

//// **The Mausoleum of Bohemond, Prince of Taranto.** This mausoleum at Canossa di Puglia illustrates the powerful influence of Islamic culture on the crusaders. Bohemond eventually became king of Antioch in Syria but was buried on his ancestral estates in Italy. His tomb combines Romanesque and Muslim styles and is meant to resemble a *turbeh,* the shrine of a Muslim holy man. It was probably built by Muslim craftsmen.

acquired through the observation of Arab models (see illustration 9.5).

Unfortunately, the nature of the crusading enterprise severely limited exchanges at the intellectual level. The glories of Arab philosophy, mathematics, astronomy, and medicine were viewed with deep suspicion by the average crusader. When they were eventually introduced—not by crusaders but by scholars working in the free atmosphere of multicultural Spain—the church reacted defensively. Arab poetry, mysticism, and religious thought were ignored.

The Intellectual Crisis of the Twelfth Century

By the beginning of the twelfth century the Latin church was the dominant institution and chief unifying force of western and central Europe. Though feudal monarchies did not always acknowledge its political pretensions, they were usually prepared to accept its spiritual direction and to heed its calls for crusades or other actions on behalf of the faith. Religiously and intellectually it had no rivals.

As a result neither theology nor speculative philosophy was highly developed. Creative thought rarely evolves in an atmosphere of unanimity, and the teachings of the church had not been seriously challenged since the patristic era. The monastic and cathedral schools, which educated the priesthood, were able to avoid major controversies until the middle of the eleventh century. After that, whatever intellectual complacency Christians may have felt began to erode, and by 1200 it was entirely shattered.

Around 1050 a heated controversy developed over the ideas of Berengar of Tours (d. 1080). Arguing from logic, he rejected the doctrine of transubstantiation, which explained how, in the miracle of the mass, the bread and wine were transformed into the body and blood of Jesus Christ. Transubstantiation was not yet a dogma of the church, but his writings created a furor.

The dispute opened up two issues that were to perplex the church for centuries. The first was over the use of reason itself. St. Peter Damian espoused Tertullian's argument that faith required no support from logic; revelation was enough. Others, including St. Anselm of Canterbury (1033–1109), argued that reason could only illuminate faith and improve understanding.

Though the advocates of formal logic would triumph, at least in the schools, a third group distrusted them for other reasons. Led by John of Salisbury (d. 1180) and centered at the cathedral school of Chartres, these scholars feared that an excessive concentration on reason might narrow the scope of learned inquiry. They developed an interest in the secular literature of ancient Rome. Their efforts have been called the "Renaissance of the Twelfth Century" because modern historians thought that they foreshadowed the Renaissance of the fourteenth and fifteenth centuries.

The second issue was that of universals, which had first been raised by the sixth-century Christian philosopher Boethius and was implicit in the arguments of Berengar of Tours. The question, central to virtually all medieval thought, is: Are ideas or qualities objectively real? Does such a thing as "redness," for example, exist apart from any physical object that is "red"? "Realists" held that such universals were real and that they constituted the "substance" of things. The physical manifestation of a substance was its "accident." "Nominalists" believed that universals are merely *nomina,* or names that reflect little more than arbitrary linguistic convention. No distinction could be made between substance and accident.

Christian doctrines such as the Trinity and transubstantiation were usually explained in language that implied the reality of universals. In the miracle of the mass, the substance of the bread and wine in communion is changed or transubstantiated into the substance of the body and blood of Christ; the accidents remain unchanged. If, like Berengar, one did not believe in the distinction between substance and accident, this was difficult to accept. A partial solution to the problem was proposed by Pierre Abelard (1079–1142), who argued that a universal was a logical term related to both things and concepts. The controversy, however, was only beginning.

While Abelard avoided the extremes of either realism or nominalism, his career as a whole intensified the growing spirit of contention. He is best known outside theological circles for his affair with Heloise, the brilliant niece of Canon Fulbert of Chartres. Their relationship produced a child and some memorable letters before her relatives had him castrated. He thereupon became a monk and she a nun, but his penchant for making enemies was not yet satisfied. Abelard was determined to provide a rational basis for Christian doctrine, and his provocative writings—including *Sic et Non,* a list of apparently contradictory passages from the Fathers—set the agenda for much of what would one day be called Scholasticism .

To Abelard, Anselm, and the other philosophers of the cathedral schools, reason meant the logic of Aristotle as embodied in those parts of the *Organon* that had been translated into Latin by Boethius. They had no direct access to Aristotle's works and their knowledge of his thought was largely derived from the commentaries of his translator, but they were convinced that God's world must necessarily operate on logical principles. They also believed that Aristotle and other virtuous pagans would have accepted Christianity had they not been born before the time of Christ. It was in many ways an age of innocence.

That innocence was shattered after the mid-twelfth century by the discovery that Aristotle was far better known in Baghdad and Cairo than he was in the west and that his logic had been employed for centuries by thinkers who were not Christian, but Muslim or Jewish. A group of scholars, established themselves in the Spanish frontier city of Toledo and began to translate the works of Aristotle, Galen, Ptolemy, and other Greeks from Arabic into Latin. They then produced Latin editions of Arabic writers. Many of these works were on science or medicine. The medical treatises revolutionized the thinking of western physicians, but works on logic and speculative philosophy were received with greater caution.

A new world of philosophical sophistication was revealed, and it was not a reassuring place. Al-Kindi (d. circa 870) and Ibn-Sina (Avicenna, 980–1037) were more or less orthodox Muslims. Abu Bakr al-Razi (c. 865–c. 923) was an enemy of all religion, and Maimonides (1135–1204) was a pious Jew. Ibn-Rushd (Averroës, 1126–98) was perhaps the most influential. The greatest of the commentators on Aristotle, he believed as firmly as Anselm or Abelard that the logic of the Philosopher could be used to uphold revelation, but in his case, the revelation was that of the Koran. For the first time since antiquity, the church was faced with an intellectual challenge of threatening proportions.

Before a counterattack could be fully mounted, an even more serious challenge to orthodoxy appeared. Formal heresies attracting thousands of adherents surfaced, not in the newly converted regions of the north and west, but in the earliest established centers of Western Christendom: northern Italy and the south of France. To some extent these movements were a reaction against what was perceived as the greed and arrogance of a triumphant clergy. The newly exalted claims of the papacy, the cost of church buildings, and the more rigorous collection of the tithe led to demands for a return to apostolic poverty. This was the primary concern of the Waldensians, named after their apparent founder Waldes of Lyon, later known as Peter Waldo (fl. 1170–79). Their condemnation by the orthodox eventually led them to reject papal authority. Like the Protestants of the sixteenth century, the Waldensians regarded Scripture as the sole source of religious truth and translated the Bible into the vernacular. They also rejected several of the church's sacraments.

A far larger movement, the Cathars (sometimes known as Albigensians after the southern French town of Albi that served as one of their centers), went further. They embraced a dualistic system reminiscent of Zoroastrianism or the ancient Manichees. The physical world and the God of the Old Testament who had created it were evil. Spirit, as exemplified in Christ, whose own physical body was an illusion, was good. They had no clergy. *Parfaits* or perfects of both sexes administered the rite of *consolamentum* that guaranteed passage into Heaven. After consolation, one became a *parfait.* It was then forbidden to own property, to have sex, or to eat anything that was the product of a sexual union: meat, fish, eggs, or cheese. The meager necessities that remained were provided by begging. Some new converts deliberately starved themselves to death, but for the ordinary believer, Albigensianism held few terrors. Those who died without receiving the *consolamentum* would merely be reincarnated into a new life on Earth. The church, its hierarchy, its sacraments, and its monetary levies were categorically rejected. By the year 1200 the Cathar faith had attracted tens of thousands of adherents in southern France. It enjoyed the support of powerful political figures and even of priests, who retained their ecclesiastical rank while openly assisting the heretics. Once again, the church was on the defensive.

Repression and Renewal (1215–92)

The official response to these challenges was crafted largely by Innocent III, who was not the man to shrink from repressive measures. The church's first reaction to the heretics had been gentle. Preachers, including Bernard of Clairvaux, were sent to reconvert the Albigensians, but their eloquence had little effect. In 1209 Innocent, infuriated by the murder of a papal legate, proclaimed a crusade. Under the leadership of Simon de Montfort, an army composed largely of knights from northern France embarked on a campaign of massacre and atrocity. The worst slaughter of the Albigensian Crusade happened near the Pyrenees Mountains in the town of Béziers. The people of Béziers refused to surrender some two hundred Cathars living there, so the crusaders stormed the town and killed twenty thousand of its inhabitants indiscriminately, following the exhortation of the abbot of Cîteau: "Kill them all; God will know his own." Like their compatriots who went to the Holy Land, the crusaders were inspired by the hope of acquiring new lands as well as salvation.

By 1212 most of Languedoc was in their hands, but the Cathars and the southern lords who supported them took refuge in remote castles and waged guerrilla warfare until 1226. A decisive campaign then was launched by Louis VIII of France. He saw the crusade as an opportunity to expand his royal domain and forced the southerners to surrender in 1229. The last great Cathar stronghold, a mountain-top castle known as Montségur, finally fell in 1244. More than two hundred Cathars refused to abjure their faith and were burned together on a huge pyre. Great cathedrals were built at Albi and Narbonne to proclaim the triumph of the faith, but Cathar communities flourished in secret until after 1300.

The papal Inquisition was established to ferret them out. An inquisition is basically a court established to investigate and root out heresy. Bishops had begun organizing inquisitions at the diocesan level in the mid-twelfth century. These episcopal inquisitions proved ineffective in the Albigensian heartland where heresy permeated entire communities. Even bishops who were themselves untainted by error might be reluctant to proceed against prominent individuals or members of their own families. By placing the Inquisition under papal control, Innocent III was able to secure a measure of impartiality. Legates responsible only to him were dispatched as needed, making it more difficult for heretics to take refuge behind local privilege. To believers, heresy was a terrible crime because it brought about the eternal damnation of those who accepted it. Inquisitors therefore felt justified in using every means available, including torture, to secure a confession. If none were forthcoming, or if the heretic confessed but would not repent, he or she would be turned over to the secular authorities and burned alive, the standard penalty for heresy in both canon and civil law.

After 1233 Gregory IX introduced the tribunal to the south of France on a systematic basis. As many as five thousand heretics were burned there by the end of the century. The Inquisition had other interests as well. Anyone, including academic theorists who overstepped the bounds of theological propriety, was subject to its jurisdiction. If the church of the early Middle Ages had been absorbed in its missionary role and relatively indifferent to the definition of orthodoxy, those days were gone.

The new order was solidified by the Fourth Lateran Council. Called by Innocent III in 1215, it was designed to resemble the great councils of the early church. Not only bishops, abbots, and the heads of religious and military orders, but also princes and municipal authorities from all over the Latin west were invited to consider a carefully prepared agenda. In only three days of formal meetings, the delegates adopted a confession of faith that specifically rejected Albigensian beliefs, defined the seven sacraments, and enshrined

transubstantiation as dogma. All Christians were ordered to confess and receive communion at least once a year, and a wide variety of reforms aimed at the purification of ecclesiastical life were adopted. In terms of its influence on both doctrine and practice, it was the most important council of the Middle Ages.

The organization of mendicant orders, the Dominicans and the Franciscans, must also be seen as a response to the crisis of the twelfth century. Among those who had hoped to convert the Albigensians by peaceful means was the Castilian preacher Domingo de Guzmán, or St. Dominic (c. 1170–1221). After several years among the heretics, he came to believe that, if the teachings of the church were presented by competent preachers who lived a life of apostolic poverty, heresy could not survive. In 1207 he organized a convent of women who had recently converted. In 1216 he secured papal confirmation of an order of men dedicated to preaching and living a life of austerity equal to that of the *parfaits*. Popularly known as the Dominicans, they stressed the intellectual formation of their members and lived by begging. Within a generation they had taken their place among the intellectual leaders of the church.

A second order, founded by Dominic's contemporary St. Francis of Assisi (c. 1181–1226), was not directly concerned with the problem of heresy but embraced the idea of evangelical poverty with even greater fervor (see illustration 9.6). The son of a wealthy merchant, Francis was inspired by a series of visions to abandon his family and retire to the town of Assisi where he began to preach, though still a layman. He had no intention of forming a religious order in the conventional sense, but his preaching and the holiness of his life attracted disciples. In 1209 he went to Rome with eleven others and secured Innocent III's approval of a new rule dedicated to the imitation of Christ.

The Franciscans, as they were called, met a contemporary need. Their dedication to absolute poverty and the attractive spirit of their founder endeared them to the laity, and they soon became the largest of the mendicant orders. The Second Order of St. Francis, sometimes known as the Poor Clares, was created for women.

Two smaller mendicant orders, the Carmelites and the Augustinians, were created in the same period. The friars, as the mendicants were called, emerged as the leaders of the great intellectual revival already under way in response to the challenges of the twelfth century.

Illustration 9.6

/// **St. Francis.** In this fresco by Italian master Giotto (1266?–1337), St. Francis renounces his patrimony. The decision to abandon all worldly goods to live in poverty marked the beginning of his ministry to the poor.

The Founding of the Universities

The locus of that revival was a new institution: the university. The first universities emerged from the same regularizing impulses that inspired the consolidation of feudal states and the reforms of Innocent III. The twelfth century revival of learning had led to a proliferation of competing schools in such centers as Paris and Bologna. Church and municipal authorities became alarmed at the potential for disorder, and the masters soon recognized the need for an organization that could both protect their interests and ensure that new masters were properly trained. By the mid-twelfth century, a rudimentary guild system was beginning to evolve.

At Paris, the scholars soon found themselves in conflict with the cathedral chapter of Notre Dame, which tried to control them, and the townspeople, who were trying to protect their lives and property against the students (see document 9.6). The students were for the most part adolescent males who lived without supervision and were capable of rape, theft, and murder. They in turn complained of gouging by landlords and tavern keepers. Such grievances were ignored, while at-

❖ DOCUMENT 9.6 ❖

Privileges of the Students at Paris

The following privilege was granted to the students at Paris by King Philip Augustus in 1200. It seeks to protect academic freedom by ensuring that students accused of crimes are tried only by ecclesiastical courts.

Neither our provost nor our judges shall lay hands on a student for any offense whatever; nor shall they place him in our prison, unless such a crime has been committed by the student that he ought to be arrested. And in that case, our judge shall arrest him on the spot, without striking him at all, unless he resists, and shall hand him over to the ecclesiastical judge, who ought to guard him in order to satisfy us and the one suffering the injury. . . . But if the students are arrested by our count at such an hour that the ecclesiastical judge cannot be found and be present at once, our provost shall cause the culprits to be guarded in some student's house without any ill-treatment as is said above, until they are delivered to the ecclesiastical judge. . . . In order, moreover, that these decrees may be kept more carefully and be established by a fixed law, we have decided that our present provost and the people of Paris shall affirm by an oath, in the presence of the scholars, that they will carry out in good faith all the above-mentioned points.

Philip Augustus. "Privileges of the Students at Paris." *Pennsylvania Translations and Reprints*, vol. 2, pp. 5–7, trans. Edward P. Cheyney. Philadelphia: University of Pennsylvania Press, 1897.

tempts to arrest student criminals often led to bloody riots. Each new outrage brought a flood of appeals to the pope or the king. Between 1215 and 1231 a series of statutes and charters were issued that established the privileges of the university in both civil and canon law.

The situation at Oxford was not much different. The English masters had gathered in a market town that had no cathedral or other ecclesiastical organization against which to rebel, but their relations with the townsfolk were as envenomed as those at Paris. In 1209, after a violent riot, teaching was suspended and many of the scholars departed for Cambridge to found a separate university. Oxford's privileges were guaranteed only by the papal humiliation of King John in 1214. John had supported the town against what he perceived as clerical privilege, and Innocent III not only sided with the masters but also forced the municipality to provide an annual subsidy for impoverished students.

If the origins of Bologna were less violent, it was because its faculty emphasized the study of law instead of theology or the liberal arts. The students tended to be older men of considerable influence who were adept at securing imperial and papal privileges without knife-play. They were also unwilling to be ruled by their teachers. Bologna and the Italian universities based upon its model were dominated by the students, who hired the faculty and determined the curriculum.

As the idea of universities grew popular, a number were founded by royal or papal edict. By 1500, Spain and every region of Germany, including Switzerland and the Low Countries, had its own university. Most of them were princely foundations, while some, including Erfurt and Cologne, were established by clerics with the help of city governments.

Medical schools were at first unrelated to the universities and, in at least two cases, predated them. Salerno, in the kingdom of Sicily, was a center of medical studies in the eleventh century, well before the introduction of Arabic learning. The interference of the state in the person of Frederick II reduced its vitality, and it was largely superseded by Montpellier after 1231. Montpellier, in southern France, had been founded before 1140 and was a center of Arabic learning from the start. It gradually evolved during the thirteenth century into the major university that it is today. Other medical faculties were incorporated into universities at an early date, with Bologna and Paris achieving particular renown.

Organizationally, the heart of Paris, Oxford, and Cambridge was the faculty of liberal arts. The masters of arts had secured the independence of the universities. The theologians, though important, had been compromised by their obedience to ecclesiastical authority. The arts curriculum included the *trivium* (grammar, dialectic, and rhetoric) and the *quadrivium* (geometry, arithmetic, astronomy, and music). Dialectic meant the logic of Aristotle; rhetoric was largely the science by which one could unravel figures of speech. Those who received the master of arts were licensed to teach these subjects.

A course of the liberal arts had to be completed before being admitted to the schools of theology, which by midcentury were dominated by the mendicant friars. Their curriculum was based heavily on the *Sentences* of Peter Lombard (c. 1100–60), a collection of theological

Illustration 9.7

A University Lecture. In this illumination from fourteenth-century Germany, a master lectures to his class by reading from a text and explaining its meaning. The students are of different ages and a few are sound asleep.

arguments and propositions that was first published about 1150. Legal education was based on Gratian's *Decretals*. Because books were handwritten and expensive, teaching methods were the essence of simplicity: The master read the text and explained its meaning (see illustration 9.7). Formal disputations between masters were a welcome alternative to the lectures and often drew large crowds.

The students were under the control of the masters, at least in their academic lives. Both enjoyed full clerical immunity as part of their university charters. They could be tried only in ecclesiastical courts, even if they committed civil crimes. The university as a whole was governed by its rector who was elected for a term of no more than three months. The only administrator in the modern sense was the beadle, or "common servant of the scholars," who collected funds and tried to enforce the regulations.

By the end of the thirteenth century, universities had become powerful corporations whose independence guaranteed them a certain freedom of thought. This freedom, though not unconditional, brought a great breadth and vigor to Western culture.

Scholastic Thought

The term *scholasticism* is generally used to describe the thought of the medieval universities. It was not an "ism" in the modern sense—that is, an ideology or system of belief—but a method for dealing with a wide range of questions in theology, philosophy, ethics, and the natural sciences. It relied almost exclusively on the system of linguistic logic adopted from Aristotle and, by the mid-thirteenth century, had evolved a standard form of argumentation. A question was posed, an answer was suggested, and all possible objections to the answers were analyzed before a final resolution was achieved. Authorities were cited in support of theses and objections alike. The final appeal was to reason unless a clear statement on the issue could be drawn from Scripture or the authority of the church. Even then, some of the more radical thinkers were prepared to venture forward on the basis of logic alone. It was a method of extraordinary power, and in the universities of thirteenth-century Europe it created an unparalleled flowering of creative thought.

Much of this effort was initially based on the need to confute the followers of Averroes. Some of them, such as Siger of Brabant (d.c. 1281), held that faith could not be supported by reason and adopted a view that was essentially skeptical. Others developed ideas that could be described as pantheistic.

Early attempts to suppress the Arabic commentators failed, though the teachings of the Averroists were finally condemned by the University of Paris in 1269–70. In the meantime, an effective synthesis of Aristotelianism and Christian doctrine was developed by two Dominicans, Albertus Magnus (c. 1200–1280) and his pupil St. Thomas Aquinas (c. 1225–74). Aquinas is generally regarded as one of the world's greatest thinkers. His approach to philosophy and theology, known as Thomism, has had a profound influence on Western thought and underlies much of Roman Catholic theology to this day. At the same time, he was a man of his times. His condemnation of Jews and homosexuals and his belief in the natural inferiority of women, though commonplace in the thirteenth century, had a disproportionate effect on Western attitudes as well.

Born to a noble family in the marches between Naples and Rome, Thomas spent most of his life at the University of Paris and at Rome, where he was theological adviser to the papal curia. In his student days his massive physique and natural reticence caused him to be nicknamed "the dumb ox," but his gentleness and courtesy, unique among the cantankerous academics of his day, endeared him even to opponents. His best known works, the *Summa contra Gentiles* and the unfinished *Summa Theologica*, reveal his purpose. They are comprehensive summations on practically every subject of contemporary theological and philosophical interest, and for all his insistence that learning is done even from errors, their intent is polemical.

An Aristotelian to his fingertips, Aquinas believed that God's universe was both rational and intelligible. On the question of universals he was a moderate realist whose views were reminiscent of Abelard's. Knowledge must be based on the experience of the senses; thought enables the universal to be isolated in the particular. Both substance and accident are real, but substance provides the limits within which accidents may exist. This position was the basis of equally moderate conclusions on subjects ranging from the nature of the soul to the origins of evil and the problem of time, and it sets Aquinas firmly in the tradition of Aristotelian humanism. The intellect, though sustained by God, is a part of every human being. The soul is the form or essence of the body, of sensation, and of thought. In thinking, the soul transcends this form and becomes independent of matter.

These ideas were eventually adopted by a majority of Aquinas's fellow Dominicans. They were disputed by the Franciscans, including his friend St. Bonaventura (c. 1217–74). Franciscan thought generally followed the tradition of St. Augustine and emphasized the importance of love and will as opposed to intellect. The gulf that separates human beings from God cannot be minimized or forgotten, and the intellect should not be identified too closely with the soul.

Several aspects of this Franciscan approach crystallized in the work of John Duns Scotus (1265–1308). A Scot who studied and taught at Paris, Oxford, Cambridge, and Cologne, he sought to preserve the concerns of St. Bonaventura without doing violence to Aristotle. To Scotus, everything had a reality of its own that existed independently of any universal. Universals existed only in the mind. This view enabled him to emphasize the uniqueness both of God and of individuals, but by denying the connection between human and divine intellect, he opened a gulf so vast that it could be bridged only by extraordinary means. To Scotus and many of his contemporaries, the majesty and isolation of God were so great that special intercession was required. It could be provided only by the Virgin Mary, whose veneration became a central feature of their piety. The Marian cult that emerged around the beginning of the fourteenth century would have a profound influence on Catholic spirituality. Scotus was its early advocate and one of the first to formulate the doctrine of the Immaculate Conception, which holds that Mary was preserved from all taint of original sin when she was conceived.

Scotus never saw himself as an opponent of Aquinas. He did not question the usefulness of reason in illuminating faith. That task was left to another Franciscan, William of Ockham (c. 1285–c. 1349). Ockham carried the ideas of Scotus a step further and declared that only individuals are real and that the object of the senses and of the intellect are the same. Universals are no more than mental patterns created by recurring similarities of experience. Although a subtle difference, it meant that God was unknowable, at least to the intellect.

Ockham was a Spiritual Franciscan who opposed the papacy after the condemnation of 1322. He was not a heretic. When his conclusions were questioned, he insisted that the doctrines of the church must be ac-cepted in their entirety as revealed truth. His followers, known as nominalists because they supposedly believed that universals were only *nomina*, or names, became one of the three dominant philosophical schools of the later Middle Ages and by the fifteenth century were a majority on most university faculties. Some, such as Nicholas of Autrecourt (fl. 1340), went further than their master and declared that not even the existence of the material world could be demonstrated by rational means. Each person knows only his or her own soul. Though Thomism and Scotism continued to attract adherents, the Ockhamist critique of reason was highly corrosive. It presumed a dichotomy with faith that made formal thought virtually irrelevant. When such views became widespread, the creative age of scholasticism was over.

CHAPTER 10

ECONOMIC DEVELOPMENT AND URBAN GROWTH IN THE HIGH MIDDLE AGES

CHAPTER OUTLINE

Two centuries of relative peace and prosperity after the end of the great raids permitted a general increase in agricultural production. This growth in productivity increased real wealth and allowed the population of Europe to double during the same period. It also encouraged agricultural specialization, which led to the development of a widespread trade in bulk agricultural commodities. Eventually, new wealth and the influence of the Crusades created a long-distance trade in luxury goods as well.

The chief beneficiaries of this new commercial activity were the towns. From about 1000 to 1250 they experienced rapid growth—in size, wealth, and power. As popes and princes grew more dependent upon their resources, the towns used their wealth to free themselves from feudal or ecclesiastical rule and to negotiate new privileges that made them bastions of civic freedom in the midst of feudal Europe. Some became sovereign states. Rich, free, and self-confident, the towns of medieval Europe began the great tradition of urban culture that would eventually leaven the whole of Western society.

Medieval Technology: Energy, Tools, and Transport

Medieval technology, like that of the Romans, was based on wood and iron. Its primary energy source remained the muscle power of humans or animals, though by the eleventh century water mills were universally employed for the grinding of grain. The water wheel had been used in Anatolia as early as the first century, but it was apparently unknown in the west until the brewers of Picardy adopted it around 820. By the mid-thirteenth century water power was also used in the fulling of cloth and to drive the hammers and bellows of forges. Wind provided assistance for ships at sea, but windmills, a Persian invention introduced to Europe at the end of the twelfth century, did not become common until the fifteenth century.

Fuel was limited almost entirely to wood and charcoal and was rarely used to generate power. Wood was burned for cooking and to supply heat. In western Europe, interior heating was usually accomplished, if at all, with residual heat from cooking. Charcoal, an expensive commodity, was used primarily in the smelting and forging of metals, while coal, first mentioned in European sources around the year 1200, did not come into general use for another four hundred years. This was largely because mining techniques remained primitive. In the absence of effective pumps the pits could not be kept dry, and the development of effective pumps depended upon metallurgical techniques that were as yet unknown. Mine pumps also require a cheap, reliable source of power because they must be worked continuously. Windmills, used from the fifteenth century onward to drain the tidal wetlands of Holland, were a possible solution, but they proved ineffective in hilly country or in regions where wind strength was inconstant. None of these problems was fully solved until the age of steam. In the meantime, coal and ores could be mined only from shallow pits, and transportation costs ensured that coal would be used only in the immediate vicinity of the mines. The scarcity of metals made ore worth transporting, but it was always best if deposits were located near abundant sources of charcoal so that smelting might occur on the spot.

Tools tended to be made of wood or of wood tipped with iron. Alloy steel was unknown, and the handwrought carbon steel used in knives and edged weapons was expensive. The process required great skill and enormous quantities of fuel. Even implements made from lower grades of iron represented a major capital outlay for farmers and artisans.

The high cost of iron resulted in part from the limitations of mining technology, but skilled iron workers were few in number, and the making of charcoal for use in the forges consumed large quantities of wood. Wood had long been scarce in the Mediterranean basin. By the end of the Middle Ages its availability was limited in northwest Europe as well. Only in the Baltic regions and in eastern Europe was timber plentiful, and even there prices increased steadily throughout the Middle Ages in response to increased demand from other regions. Given that wood was a primary building material as well as the major source of fuel, this is hardly surprising.

Ships were built almost entirely of wood and consumed vast quantities of the best timber. Their keels and frames demanded rare, naturally curved compass timbers, and their masts required tall, straight trees with few branches. Planking was almost invariably of the best available oak. However high the quality of planking, constant immersion in water and the ravages of marine organisms ensured a maximum life of seven or eight years before a ship's timbers had to be replaced. Given the hazards of navigation, many ships went to the bottom long before such repairs could be made, with even higher replacement costs as a result.

On land, most buildings were at least framed in wood. Fully wooden structures had once been common in northern Europe. By the twelfth century they were already becoming rare outside of Scandinavia and the Baltic. The growing cost of lumber was forcing builders to construct walls out of cob, wattle and daub, or some other combination of earth mixed with straw. Roofs were usually thatched and floors were of earth or clay. Only public buildings and the homes of the very rich were built of stone and roofed with slate or tile. Masonry construction was more common in the Mediterranean basin, although precious wood was used for joists and roof beams.

The high cost of iron and wood was symptomatic not only of scarcity but also of the problem of distance. They were heavy and expensive to ship. Owing to political fragmentation and the decay of the Roman highway system, transportation was more arduous and expensive than in antiquity. Besides raising shipping costs in general, this made compensating for local shortages or crop failures by importing goods from other regions difficult. Shipping grain overland for two hundred miles might raise its price by a factor of seven, making it unaffordable to the poor even if they were starving.

Land transport was generally conducted over roads that were little more than tracks, choked with dust in dry weather and mired axle-deep in mud when it rained. If the mud froze, ruts made the highways impassable for wheeled vehicles. For this reason, people traveled on foot or on horseback, and pack animals were generally preferred to ox-driven carts except in optimum conditions.

Water transport, if available, was more efficient (see illustration 10.1). Many European rivers are navigable for much of their length. Boats, rafts, and barges became increasingly important with the passage of time. The sea remained the greatest highway of all, uniting the peoples who lived along its shores. The Baltic, the North Sea, and the Atlantic coasts were served by a wide variety of ship types whose chief common feature was the use of a square sail set amidships. This rig was easy to handle and provided excellent performance

Illustration 10.1

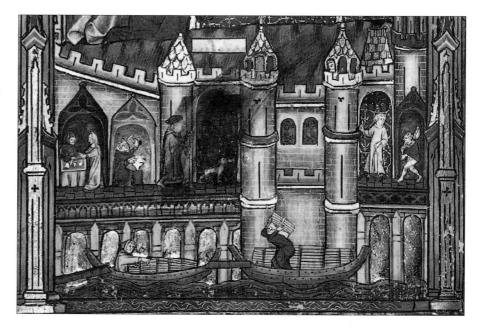

🖊 **Unloading Wine at Paris.** The commercial revolution began with the bulk trade in such agricultural commodities as wine. Wine was always shipped in barrels, as bottling was unknown. Given the condition of the roads, shipping by river boat was almost always cheaper and faster. Here boatmen are delivering their casks at the port of Paris on the river Seine.

downwind. It was virtually useless in other conditions. Many of the smaller craft were therefore assisted by oars or sweeps and could penetrate coastal estuaries as had the Viking longships on which they were often modeled.

In the Mediterranean, many ships carried the triangular lateen sail, invented by Arab sailors in the Indian Ocean and introduced to Europe by the Byzantine Greeks. It permitted a ship to sail close to the wind and was used on both galleys and the larger round ships that were propelled by sails alone. The round ship, broad-beamed and steered by long oars slung from the stern quarters, was sturdy, capacious, and very slow. It was the bulk carrier of the Middle Ages. Galleys were still used for warfare and for cargos that were either perishable or whose value-to-weight ratio was high. Fast and maneuverable, they were as dependent on the land as their ancient counterparts and too fragile for extensive use in the open Atlantic.

These generalizations, referring as they do to a period of more than a thousand years, imply that little technological change was evident in the Middle Ages. This is not true, but by modern standards the rate of change was relatively slow. The medieval economy remained basically agricultural, with more than 90 percent of the population directly engaged in the production of food. Cash remained scarce, and the surplus of goods and services beyond those needed for mere subsistence was small. The accumulation of capital for investment in new technologies was therefore difficult, and the demand for innovations was slight because most people had little or no discretionary income.

The Agricultural Revolution of the Eleventh and Twelfth Centuries

The rate of technological change, though slow by modern standards, did not prevent Europe from doubling its agricultural productivity between the years 1000 and 1250. Population doubled as well (see table 10.1). Climatological evidence suggests that a general warming trend extended the growing season and permitted the extension of cultivation to more northern regions and to higher elevations. No major famines occurred during this period, and crises of subsistence tended to be local and of short duration. However, changes in the climate alone cannot account for such an unprecedented expansion.

The return of more-or-less settled conditions after the great raids of the ninth and tenth centuries was certainly a factor. The annual loss of food, tools, livestock, and seed grain to the marauders had been substantial. When augmented by forced requisitions and by the depredations of local feudatories its impact on subsistence must have been great. A number of technical innovations increased productivity, though some were dependent upon a preexistent improvement in conditions for their success. The extension of the three-field system through much of northwest Europe is an example. By leaving only one-third of the land fallow in any given year, as opposed to half under the earlier system, peasants were able to increase their yields without seriously diminishing the fertility of their land. They typically planted a winter crop in one

TABLE 10.1

Population Changes in Medieval Europe

The chart shows the dramatic reductions in population from A.D. 500 to 1450 that followed the collapse of the Roman Empire, the equally dramatic increase during the so-called agricultural revolution, and the precipitous drop after 1340 in the wake of the Black Death. Estimates are in millions.

Region	500	600	1000	1340	1450
British Isles	0.5	0.5	2	5	3
France-Low Countries	5	3	6	19	12
Germany-Scandinavia	3.5	2	4	11.5	7.5
Greece and the Balkans	5	3	5	6	4.5
Hungary	0.5	0.5	1.5	2	1.5
Iberia	4	3.5	7	9	7
Italy	4	2.5	5	10	7.5
Slavic lands	5	3			
Poland-Lithuania			2	3	2
Russia			6	8	6
Total	27.5	18	38.5	73.5	51

Source: Adapted from: Carlo Cipolla, *The Middle Ages*, Fontana Economic History of Europe (London: Colliers, 1973) p. 36. Used with permission of HarperCollins Publishers Ltd.

Illustration 10.2

The Mediterranean "Scratch" Plow. The Mediterranean scratch plow preceded the heavy wheeled plow and had been used throughout the Roman Empire. It remained popular in dry regions until modern times because it did not turn over the furrows and therefore helped to preserve moisture in the soil.

field and a summer crop in another while leaving the third free to regenerate itself.

The success of this scheme depended upon the quality of the soil and the availability of adequate rainfall. Northwestern Europe, though at the same latitude as Newfoundland or Labrador, is mild and moist. Its weather is moderated by the Atlantic Ocean and, in particular, by the Gulf Stream, a warm water current that rises in the Caribbean and washes the shores of England and France. Pleasant summers with temperatures that usually do not exceed 80 degrees Fahrenheit follow long, wet winters in which prolonged freezes are rare. The prevailing winds are westerly, bringing abundant rainfall even in the summer months as Atlantic squalls, forced northward by high pressure over the Iberian Peninsula, drop their moisture on the land. In much of the Mediterranean basin, where little or no rain falls to support summer crops, the two-field system remained dominant; in the harsh, dry tablelands of Castile, seven-field systems in which only one-seventh of the land was cultivated at a time was common.

Production was further increased by the introduction of the heavy iron plow, or *carruca*, and the complex technology that surrounded it. This device was apparently of Slavic origin. Mounted on wheels, it consisted of a horizontal plowshare and an angled mould-board that turned the sliced earth aside. Cutting a deeper furrow than its Roman predecessor (see illustration 10.2), the iron plow made the seed less vulnerable to late frosts and to the depredations of birds and rodents. This increased yields and extended the limits of cultivation by allowing the seed to survive in colder climates. Heavy clay soils that were impervious to the scratchings of ancient plowmen could now be utilized for the first time, and the clearing of virgin land was greatly simplified (see illustration 10.3).

Iron plows were expensive. They also required the increased use of draft animals if their full potential was to be realized. The old Roman plow required, at the most, a single team of oxen and in light soils could often be pulled by a pair of human beings. The heavy plow might require as many as eight beasts. The increasing use of three- and four-yoke teams from the ninth century onward was responsible for a reorganization of labor on more cooperative lines. It was also an indication of greater prosperity, as was the innovation of plowing with horses. Horses are not as strong in absolute terms as draft oxen, but they are much faster. Horse plowing increases the amount of land that can be cultivated in a day by more than 30 percent. This represented a great increase in efficiency. However, horses are more inclined to sickness and injury than oxen, and their diet must be supplemented by feed grains. Oxen, for the most part, need only to graze. The introduction of horse plowing was therefore limited to those regions

Illustration 10.3

🖏 **The Heavy Wheeled Plow.** This illustration from an early sixteenth-century prayer book shows a typical wheeled plow in operation. It is not much different from those introduced in the ninth and tenth centuries. Note the arrangement of the harnesses on the team of horses.

ter 1100, livestock production for meat remained modest until the second half of the fourteenth century.

Perhaps the most important advance in this area was the Frankish invention of the scythe, which largely replaced the sickle and permitted large-scale haying and the stall feeding of cattle. The cattle were kept for meat and dairy products, and their manure was carefully collected and spread on the fields. However, stockraising is a fundamentally inefficient use of land. Vegetable crops suited for direct human consumption fed more people from the same acreage. In marginal economies where even intensive cultivation provides modest yields, animal protein is a luxury. Supplies of manure, though improved, were therefore limited and were probably applied most frequently to household gardens and other small plots. The use of human waste as fertilizer, though common in Asia, was apparently rare in the West.

Larger fields could retain their productivity only by being left fallow or through crop rotation. Yields by modern standards remained poor, but they were a great improvement over those of Charlemagne's time. Whereas harvesting one-and-a-half grains for every grain planted was once common, harvesting four or five became possible. Theoretically, the maximum yield of wheat from an unfertilized field is about twelve bushels per acre. Peasants in the thirteenth century probably averaged about half this amount from fields that today produce sixty bushels per acre or more, but five to seven bushels per acre was a substantial improvement over times past (see table 10.2).

The improvement of yields, the extension of cultivation into new areas, and the reduction in the amount of labor required to produce a given quantity of food produced consistent surpluses of crops in those areas where they grew best. This in turn led to agricultural specialization. The Beauvaisis or the Ile de France, for example, were ideal for the cultivation of wheat but produced only small quantities of inferior wine. Parts of Burgundy produced excellent wine but relatively meager stands of wheat. Landholders found that they could improve their revenues as well as their standard of living by selling off surpluses and using the profits to purchase commodities that grew poorly, if at all, on their own manors. In time, whole regions were devoted to the cultivation of grains, while others specialized in wine, olives, or other commodities. The great wine-growing areas were planted for the most part in the twelfth century, usually along navigable rivers such as the Loire, the Rhone, or the Rhine. Corking and bottling had not yet been invented, so wine was shipped in casks that were too heavy to transport easily on land.

that already enjoyed a considerable surplus of grain. It also required the development of a new type of harness. Horses cannot be yoked like oxen without constricting their windpipes, and attaching the plow to their withers or tail is not only cruel but also woefully ineffective. The modern harness, without which a draft horse is virtually useless, appears to have been developed in Asia and introduced to Europe around the year 800.

A fringe benefit associated with the increased use of draft animals was the greater availability of manure. Medieval peasants knew that manure greatly increased the fertility of soils, just as they knew that marl could be used to reduce soil acidity and that soils could be mixed to improve workability or drainage. All of these techniques were labor-intensive. Substantial quantities of manure were required to fertilize even a moderately sized field, and though draft animals were numerous af-

TABLE 10.2

Medieval Grain Yields

The following range of grain yields is taken from harvest records on the estates of the bishops of Winchester (England) between 1209 and 1349, a relatively fertile area that enjoyed good management. The figures are therefore probably higher than those for medieval Europe as a whole, but far below what can be achieved with modern technology. Yields of wheat on similar lands today have been known to reach seventy to eighty bushels per acre. The difference goes far to explain the insufficiency of medieval diets.

Grain	Yield in grains per grain planted		Yield in bushels per acre	
	Maximum	Minimum	Maximum	Minimum
Barley	5.6	2.8	27.6	11.0
Oats	3.4	1.8	16.0	7.5
Wheat	5.3	2.6	13.6	5.8

Source: J. Z. Titow, *Winchester Yields* (Cambridge: Cambridge University Press, 1972), p. 14.

For peasants, specialization was a mixed blessing. Monoculture left them more vulnerable to crop failures than were the subsistence farmers who grew a little bit of everything. Some evidence is available that diets deteriorated as more and more land was devoted to the cash crop. But from the standpoint of the European economy as a whole, specialization improved efficiency. It increased the overall production of commodities because land was not wasted on unsuitable crops, and it probably improved their quality as well. It also, by definition, created the basis for a trade in bulk agricultural commodities that grew into a full-blown commercial revolution.

The Commercial Revolution

In the early Middle Ages most trading was local and conducted through barter. With the growth of agricultural specialization, this form of commerce expanded without changing its essential principles. Villagers brought their surplus goods to weekly markets held in a nearby town and exchanged them for clothing, tools, or agricultural products that they could not produce efficiently themselves. Larger transactions were conducted at great annual fairs, such as the one at Champagne that attracted merchants from all over Europe until well into modern times.

At first, long-distance commerce was largely in the hands of Jews. Though Jews were not invariably barred from holding land, Christian hostility kept them socially peripheral and reinforced the natural cosmopolitanism of a people in exile. Their wide-ranging contacts, reinforced by strong kinship ties, gave them a powerful advantage when virtually everyone else was bound by interest and circumstance to the locality of their birth. This situation began to change in the eleventh century. The increased volume, safety, and profitability of trade began to make it more attractive to Christian entrepreneurs who were able to squeeze out their Jewish competitors by securing favored treatment from Christian authorities. The anti-Semitic persecutions that began in the twelfth century arose primarily from the crusading impulse, but they coincided with a perceived decline in the economic usefulness of the Jews.

The most aggressive of the new traders were the inhabitants of the Italian coastal towns. By the beginning of the eleventh century, a number of Italian cities had outgrown their local food supplies and emerged as net importers of agricultural commodities. Grain, oil, and other commodities had to be purchased abroad, usually in Spain or Sicily. Ports such as Pisa, Amalfi, and Genoa possessed the maritime skills necessary for this trade and were often forced to engage in it for their own survival. Only the threat of Muslim piracy stood in their way. By combining their fleets and taking advantage of political disorder in North Africa, the three cities were able to drive the Muslims from their bases in Sardinia, Corsica, and the Balearic Islands by 1088.

Venice, the greatest trading city of them all, had no *contado* or agricultural land of its own. It produced little more than glass and sea salt, but being located at the head of the Adriatic, it was the perfect center for trade between the eastern Mediterranean and central Europe. Dependent upon commerce almost from its beginnings, Venice, like other Italian ports, owed its eventual success to sheer necessity, maritime skill, and location. By the beginning of the twelfth century, the Italians were dominant in the Mediterranean carrying trade and were beginning to extend their routes northward.

The Crusades expanded Italian trade and greatly increased its value. Those crusaders who wished to go to the Holy Land by sea went for the most part in Italian ships and paid dearly for the privilege. When they arrived, they found a civilization that was in many ways more sophisticated than their own. They quickly developed a taste for silks, for spices from India, and for the superior cutlery of Damascus, to name a few of the items that by 1250 had become the components of an immense commerce. Those who returned to Europe brought their new tastes with them and created a fashion for Eastern luxuries that the Italians were well positioned to fill. Each shipload of crusaders offered its master the opportunity to make commercial contacts along the route, and elaborate trading networks soon developed between the Italians and their merchant counterparts in Greece, the Aegean, Anatolia, and the Levant.

The demand for Eastern luxuries was possible only because the real wealth of the west had increased since Carolingian times. The agricultural revolution was primarily responsible for this phenomenon. The return of settled conditions also permitted gold and silver that had been hoarded during the bad old days to be released into circulation. This, together with the slow but steady increase in European mining during the eleventh and twelfth centuries, increased the amount of specie available for trade. Copper coinage remained the standard in everyday transactions. Silver became more common, and in the mid-thirteenth century gold was introduced for the first time on a large scale.

From the Italian point of view, the Eastern trade was ideal. Luxuries from the East possessed a far higher ratio of value to weight than did agricultural products and could generate greater profits. The risks were correspondingly high. But, as in the case of the spice trade, a single voyage could make a trader's fortune. Spices, the most important of which were black pepper, nutmeg, and cinnamon, originated in India or in what is now Indonesia and were transported across the Indian Ocean in the dhows of Arab merchants. They were then transhipped by caravan to the Mediterranean ports where they were purchased by Italian traders who carried them home by ship. Other merchants carried them overland to consumers beyond the Alps. At each stage of this journey except the last, profits might amount to several hundred percent on invested capital. However, ships were frequently lost to pirates, bad weather, or the unpredictable fortunes of war and politics.

Risky ventures of this kind were often supported by a *commenda* contract (see document 10.1). An investor, usually an older man or a woman, would finance the voyage of a younger merchant in return for half of the total profits. After two or three such voyages, the younger man could then retire and become an investor in his own right. The Eastern trade never equaled bulk commodities either in volume or in total value, but as a means of capital accumulation it was

◆ DOCUMENT 10.1 ◆

A Commenda from Venice, 1073

This is a fairly standard example of a commenda contract from the early period of the commercial revolution.

In the name of the Lord God and of our Savior, Jesus Christ. In the year of the Incarnation of the same Redeemer 1073, in the month of August, eleventh indiction, at Rialto, I, Giovanni Lissado of Luprio, together with my heirs, have received in partnership from you, Sevasto Orefice, son of Ser Trudimondo, and from your heirs, this amount: £200 Venetian. And I myself have invested £100 in it. And with this capital we have aquired two shares of the ship in which Gosmiro da Molina is captain. And I am under obligation to bring all of this with me on a commercial voyage to Thebes in the ship which the aforesaid Gosmiro da Molino sails as captain. Indeed, by this agreement and understanding of ours I promise to put to work this entire capital and to strive the best way I can. Then if the capital is saved, we are to divide whatever profit the Lord may grant us from it by exact halves, without fraud and evil device. And whatever I can gain with these goods from any source, I am under obligation to invest all of it in the partnership. And if all these goods are lost because of the sea or of hostile people, and this is proved— may this be averted—neither party ought to ask any of them from the other; if, however, some of them remain, in proportion as we invested, so shall we share. Let this partnership exist between us so long as our wills are fully agreed.

But if I do not observe everything just as is stated above, I, together with my heirs, then promise to give and to return to you and your heirs everything in the double, both capital and profit, out of my land and my house or out of anything that I am known to have in this world.

Lopez, Robert S., and Raymond, Irving W. *Medieval Trade in the Mediterrean World.* New York: Columbia University Press, 1955.

not surpassed. Many Italians became enormously rich. Much of this wealth was then reinvested in banking, which soon became international in scope. Banking began when traders sought to deposit their cash with goldsmiths or moneychangers who had the facilities for storing it safely. A fee was normally charged for this service. As the number of customers grew, the likelihood that they would try to redeem their deposits at the same time decreased. As long as the banker maintained an adequate reserve, a portion of his deposits could be loaned out to other businessmen at a profit.

Aware that a stable coinage was essential to a trading community, Venice and Florence established the ducat and the florin, respectively, at fixed values that made them the currency of choice throughout Europe and much of the Middle East. The rulers of other countries often reduced the precious metal content of their coins so that they might pay off their debts in depreciated money. Investors preferred currencies that protected them from this inflationary practice and, wherever possible, deposited their money with the Italians. To facilitate this, and to take advantage of the need for capital in other, less developed parts of Europe, Florentine, Venetian, and Milanese bankers established branches in leading centers of trade throughout the subcontinent.

By the thirteenth century, Italian bankers were the dominant force in international moneylending. Though in theory Christians could not loan money at interest, the Italians used their branch banks and the natural variations in exchange rates at different locations to avoid the church's ban. Bills of exchange would be issued at the Venetian rate, for example, and redeemed after a fixed period or usance at the higher London rate (see document 10.2). The difference between the two exchange rates would reflect the cost of the loan. Many churchmen probably were not fooled by this, but the technical requirements of theology were satisfied.

Additional Italian wealth was invested in manufacturing. A major problem with the eastern trade was that at first the East had little or no interest in Western merchandise and tended to demand payment for its goods in cash. A real chance existed that the trade would be destroyed by balance of payment problems similar to those that had beset the later Roman Empire. Many of the wiser merchants began to invest in the creation of products that would attract Eastern consumers. Among them were fine finished cloths based on merino wool from Spain, which were dyed and woven according to specialized techniques in Italy. Florence took an early lead in this trade, as it did in the production of fine leather goods. Silk, too, became an important Italian export when it was discovered that the mulberry trees on which silk worms grew could survive in southern Italy. The technique of spinning and weaving silk was

---

◈ DOCUMENT 10.2 ◈

A Bill of Exchange

This sample bill of exchange demonstrates how the system worked. Barna, in Avignon, orders his correspondents, the Bartoli of Pisa, to pay off a loan of 4.5 percent from Tancredi Bonagiunta and partners. Landuccio Busdraghi and compagni (partners) were Bonagiunta's correspondents in Lucca, which is only a few miles from Pisa. Several copies of such documents were usually sent to avoid accidental loss in transit. This one is marked "First" as the original.

Avignon, October 5, 1339

In the name of God, amen. To Bartolo and partners [*compagni*], Barna of Lucca and partners [send] greetings from Avignon.

You shall pay by this letter on November 20 [1]339, to Landuccio Busdraghi and partners of Lucca, gold florins three hundred twelve and three fourths for the exchange [*per cambio*] of gold florins three hundred, because I have received such money today from Tancredi Bonagiunta and partners at the rate [*raxione*] of 4 1/2 per 100 to their advantage. And charge [it] to our account. Done on October 5 [1]339.

Francesco Falconetti has ordered us to pay in your behalf 230 gold *scudi* to the Acciajuoli *compagnia*.

[Address on outside:]

To Bartolo Casini and Partners, in Pisa   First.

Lopez, Robert S., and Raymond, Irving W. *Medieval Trade in the Mediterranean World*. New York: Columbia University Press, 1955.

---

mastered, and though the primary market for this commodity remained European, imports from the east were reduced and a highly profitable sideline was developed (see map 10.1).

As a result of these activities, Italy was perhaps fifty years ahead of the rest of Europe in economic development, but other areas enjoyed remarkable growth as well. The Catalans were formidable competitors in the Mediterranean trade. In the Baltic, German traders achieved a commanding position after the decline of their Scandinavian rivals in the tenth and eleventh centuries. The north German towns, of which Lübeck was the most important, dealt in salt herring, furs, amber,

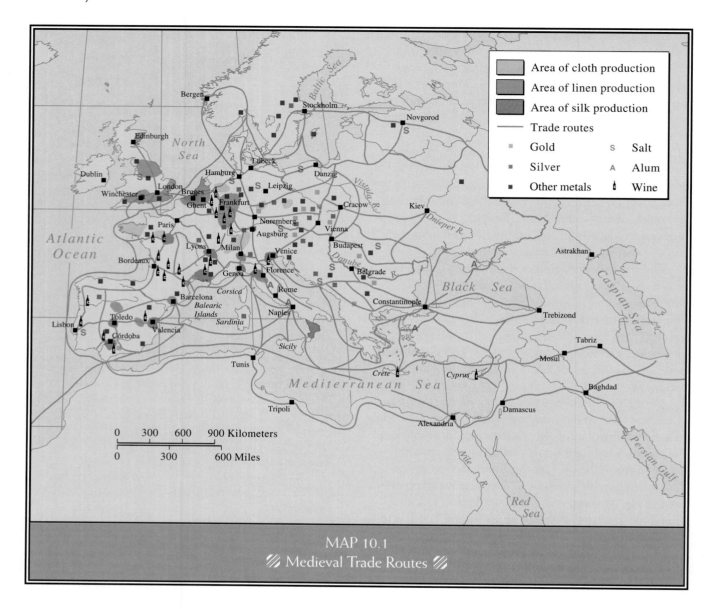

MAP 10.1

Medieval Trade Routes

wax, timber, pitch, tar, iron, and all the other products of the northern world. Organized into *hansas,* or merchant leagues, they prospered greatly throughout the High Middle Ages.

Ghent, Bruges, Ypres, and the other Flemish cities concentrated primarily on the manufacture of cloth. Their position near the mouths of the Meuse and Rhine made them natural ports that connected the European interior with England, Scandinavia, and northern Spain. Some of them also rivaled the Hanse in the salt trade, which was vital because salt was the primary means of preserving food. By the end of the thirteenth century, the Low Countries had become a highly urbanized center of wealth that rivaled Italy in commercial importance. Other, smaller, centers of trade and

manufacturing developed along the main trade routes or wherever a local product achieved some level of renown.

Manufacturing in the Middle Ages did not normally employ elaborate machinery or the techniques of mass production and cannot, therefore, be described as truly industrial, though some of the larger wool shops in Italy or Flanders employed as many as 150 workers. Goods were produced by artisans who, after the tenth century, were typically organized into guilds or associations that attempted to regulate price and quality in a particular trade. Because they included not only journeymen but also the masters who owned the shops and the apprentices who would one day be admitted to full membership, guilds combined a variety of functions.

◆ DOCUMENT 10.3 ◆

The Guilds and Social Welfare

This excerpt is from the "customs" of the Guild of the Holy Trinity at Lynn, England, dating from the late fourteenth century. Customs illustrate the degree to which guilds provided for the security and social welfare of member families.

If any of the aforesaid brethren shall die in the said town or elsewhere, as soon as the knowledge thereof shall come to the alderman, the said alderman shall order solemn mass to be celebrated for him, at which every brother of the said guild that is in town shall make his offering; and further, the alderman shall cause every chaplain of the said guild, immediately on the death of any brother, to say thirty masses for the deceased.

The aldermen and skevins [from the French *echevin*—essentially the same as an alderman; in this case both terms refer to the guild's governing board] of the said guild are by duty obliged to visit four times a year all the infirm, all that are in want, need, or poverty, and to minister to and relieve all such out of the alms of the said guild.

If any brother shall become poor and needy, he shall be supported in food and clothing, according to his exigency, out of the profits of the lands and tenements, goods and chattels of the said guild.

The Guilds and Social Welfare. From *Pennsylvania Translations and Reprints*, vol. 2. trans. Edward P. Cheyney. Philadelphia: University of Pennsylvania Press, 1897.

They set wages and prices as far as market forces would permit. They supervised the training of apprentices and tried to guarantee a quality product through inspections and the use of such devices as the masterpiece, a work whose acknowledged excellence permitted its creator to be enrolled as a master in the guild. Because mechanisms for social support were few, guilds often attempted to provide for the welfare of widows, orphans, and those members who could no longer work (see document 10.3). They sponsored banquets and drinking parties, and they inevitably became the vehicle through which their members exerted political influence in the community. For the town-dwelling artisan family, the guild was the center of social, political, and economic life.

◆

The Growth of Towns

The commercial revolution brought a revival of the urban life that had been largely dormant since the fall of Rome. Trade inevitably centered on the towns. As trade increased, towns grew into cities and some of those cities became sovereign states. Many of the more important medieval towns, including Paris, London, Florence, Milan, and Naples, had existed in Roman times, but others were relatively new or had grown from humble beginnings. Venice was founded by refugees fleeing from the Lombard invasion. Other communities grew up around the castles of bishops or secular lords. Still others grew up at river crossings or heads of navigation, or near natural harbors.

The pattern of urban growth in frontier areas was different. Dozens of Spanish towns in New Castile and Extremadura were built on lands captured from the Muslims during the twelfth and thirteenth centuries. Laid out geometrically around a central plaza, they were apparently modeled on the Roman *colonia* whose function had been much the same. Along the Baltic coasts, in Silesia, and eastward into Poland and the Ukraine, German towns were founded throughout this period, often by princely fiat, to secure newly acquired regions or to protect existing borders. Because Germany remained politically decentralized and because territories changed hands frequently owing to the vagaries of partible inheritance, princely foundations of this kind were common there as well. Though most were intended to be garrisons, market towns, or princely residences, a few were located with an eye to commercial development.

Whatever their origins, towns soon became a magnet for the unemployed, the ambitious, and the malcontent. The rapid increase in population after the tenth century coupled with more efficient agricultural methods tended to displace villagers whose labor was redundant and for whom no new land was available. These workers were "freed from the soil," an economist's euphemism for becoming unemployed, and moved to the towns in the hope of finding work as laborers. Some succeeded. If they survived, their descendants eventually became citizens and, in a few cases, grew rich. The Medici, arguably the greatest of Renaissance families, were descended from humble immigrants who came down from the Mugello during the thirteenth century to work as laborers in the wool shops of Florence.

Most immigrants, however, simply died. The rapid growth of medieval and early modern towns was almost

TABLE 10.3	
Urban Populations Before the Black Death	

Estimated populations of various European cities are given below for the period 1250–1300. This was, for most of them, a peak not reached again until the later sixteenth century, but none of them probably had more than 100,000 people. As the numbers indicate, Italy was by far the most urbanized region of medieval Europe. Most German cities had fewer than 20,000 people. All figures are approximate.

Population	City
100,000	Milan, Italy
	Venice, Italy
	Florence, Italy
80,000	Paris, France
50,000	Barcelona, Cataluña
	Bologna, Italy
	Cologne, Germany
	Córdoba, Spain
	Ghent, Low Countries
	London, England
	Palermo, Sicily
30,000–40,000	Bruges, Low Countries
	Hamburg, Germany
	Lübeck, Germany
	Montpellier, France
	Padua, Italy
	Pisa, Italy
	Naples, Italy
	Rome, Italy
	Sevilla, Spain
	Toledo, Spain
20,000	Nuremburg, Germany
	Strasburg, Germany

Source: Estimates compiled by the authors from various sources.

Illustration 10.4

Medieval Italian Tower Houses. This view of San Gimignano, Tuscany, shows a cluster of typical medieval tower houses. Their survival is a tribute to San Gimignano's relative isolation from the troubles of the thirteenth century.

purely a function of inward migration, for urban death rates greatly exceeded live births until the eighteenth century. Yet for some cities, including Venice, Florence, and Milan, populations reached 100,000 or more by the mid-thirteenth century, and several others topped 50,000 (see table 10.3).

Rapid increases in population and commercial activity mandated sweeping changes in town government. The old system of rule by a bishop or secular lord assisted only by a handful of administrators was no longer effective. Town life was not just becoming more complex. An increasingly wealthy and educated class of merchants, rentiers, and artisans was growing more assertive and less willing to have its affairs controlled by traditional authorities whose knowledge of commerce was deficient and whose interests were not always those of the business community. From an early date, these people began organizing themselves into what became communes or representative town governments.

The basis of the communes varied widely. The more substantial townspeople had long been members of occupational organizations such as the guilds or of neighborhood organizations that dealt with problems too minor to concern the bishop or lord. These neighborhood organizations might be based on the parish, the gate company (a volunteer organization created to maintain and defend one of the city's gates or a portion of its walls), or, as in Italy, the tower association, a group of citizens whose tower homes (see illustration 10.4) stood in close proximity to one another, usually around a single piazza, and whose members were usually related to one another by blood or clientage.

In times of crisis, such as an attack on the city, representatives of these groups would gather together to concert a common policy. As the meetings of these ad hoc committees became more frequent they gradually evolved into town councils or permanent *signorie*, which increasingly challenged the political and judicial authority of their nominal lords. They succeeded in this primarily because the nascent communes represented wealth and manpower that the lords desperately

◆ DOCUMENT 10.4 ◆

The Liberties of Toulouse, 1147

The following is a typical, if somewhat abbreviated, example of the liberties granted by princes and noblemen to towns in the High Middle Ages.

Let it be known to all men living and to be born that I, Alphonse, Count of Toulouse, proclaim, recognize, and grant that in no way do I have tallage or tolls in the city of Toulouse, nor in the suburb of St. Sernin, nor against the men and women living there or who will live there, nor shall I have in the city the right to summon the militia to campaign unless war be waged against me in Toulouse, nor shall I make any loan there unless it should be the lender's wish. Wherefore I confirm and commend to all citizens of Toulouse and its suburb, present and future, all their good customs and privileges, those they now enjoy and which I may give and allow to them. All this, as it is written above, Raymond of St. Gilles, son of the said count, approves and grants.

Mundy, John H., and Riesenberg, Peter, eds. *The Medieval Town.* Princeton, NJ: Van Nostrand, 1958.

needed. Negotiations were rarely high-minded. A lord or bishop would request money to meet a crisis, and the commune would grant it on condition that he surrender a coveted right (see document 10.4). In time, a substantial measure of self-government was achieved even by cities such as London that were located in powerful kingdoms. In regions such as Italy or north Germany where conflicting ecclesiastical or feudal authorities created a power vacuum, cities might easily evolve into sovereign states.

Italy and the Emergence of the City-States

In Italy, this process was set in motion by the Investiture Controversy. Communes apparently arose as a reponse to military threats posed by the struggle between pope and emperor. Once established, they were courted by both parties in the hope of securing their material support. The townsmen were happy to oblige in return for privileges that escalated as the crisis became more dire, and something like a bidding war de-

veloped between political authorities who supported the pope and those who supported the emperor. By the time the investiture issue was settled by the Concordat of Worms (1122), most Italian cities had achieved full sovereignty as a result of charters granted by one side or the other. They now had the right to coin money, declare war, and govern their own affairs without limitations of any kind. They immediately used these powers to secure control over the surrounding countryside or *contado* and to pursue policies of aggression against neighboring towns. Control over the *contado* was essential to stabilizing food supplies that were inadequate. Landholders were given the opportunity to become citizens of the commune. If they refused, the city militia would annex their estates and drive them into exile, whereupon they typically complained to their liege lord, the emperor, who was obliged by feudal agreement to support them.

The whole process was attended by bloodshed and disorder. The violent conflicts between cities were worse. Localism in Italy was intensified by trade rivalries and by disputes over the control of scarce agricultural land. This had been evident even in the throes of the investiture crisis. Because Florence supported the pope and had received its charter from his ally Matilda of Tuscany, neighboring towns such as Siena or Pisa were inevitably pro-imperial and received their charters from Henry IV. Once free of political constraints, they pursued their vendettas with enthusiasm. The resulting wars were unnecessarily bloody and accompanied by the wholesale destruction of vines, crops, and olive groves. Pressured by dispossessed vassals and hoping to profit from Italian disunity, the emperor Frederick Barbarossa (c. 1123–90) decided to intervene.

Pope Alexander III responded by organizing the Lombard League, which defeated Frederick at the battle of Legnano in 1176. At the Peace of Constance in 1183, Frederick confirmed the sovereign rights of the Lombard towns. The Tuscans had refused to join the league out of hatred for their northern neighbors and were specifically excluded from the settlement. An imperial *podestà* or governor was installed at San Miniato, a town on the road between Florence and Pisa that was known thereafter as San Miniato del Tedesco (San Miniato of the German). The Tuscans destroyed the place when they regained their freedom in 1197, after the premature death of Henry VII.

Internally, the Italian cities were beset from the start by factionalism. Clientage and kinship ties often proved stronger than allegiance to the commune, and by the beginning of the thirteenth century, civil strife was universal. Constitutional remedies such as elections

Illustration 10.5

▨ **The Condottiere.** The mercenary lived apart from the communal values of the Italian city-state. In this painting from 1328, Simone Martini shows the Sienese commander Guidoriccio da Fogliano riding in splendid isolation across a war-torn landscape.

by lot or the institution of the *podestà*, an administrative judge who was by law a foreigner, proved relatively ineffective. The emperor Frederick II (1194–1250) tried to use this situation to restore imperial authority in northern Italy, but the papacy proved as effective an obstacle to his designs as it had to those of his grandfather. The son of Henry VI and Constance, daughter of Roger II of Sicily, Frederick inherited a powerful, well-organized kingdom in southern Italy that, together with his imperial election in Izzo, made him a genuine threat both to the freedom of the Italian towns and to papal autonomy. When a political faction, hard-pressed by its rivals, sought his support, its enemies invariably turned to the pope. In this way two great "parties," the Guelfs and the Ghibellines, were born. In theory, Guelfs supported the pope and Ghibellines the emperor, but ideological and even class differences were minimal. The real issue was which faction among the richer citizens would control the city.

The Guelf-Ghibelline struggles led to the breakdown of civil government in many Italian cities. Fearful of their own citizens, governments began the practice of hiring *condottiere* or mercenaries to defend them against their neighbors (see illustration 10.5). In so doing they created another mortal danger to their independence. Victorious captains proved capable of

seizing the town when the danger had passed. By the end of the thirteenth century, an exhausted citizenry was prepared to accept almost any remedy, and nearly all of the towns fell under the rule of despots. In some cases, as in Milan, the despot was the leader of a faction that finally triumphed over its rivals. In others, desperate citizens sought or accepted the rule of a prominent local family, a mercenary captain, or a popular *podestà*. They abandoned their cherished republican constitutions in return for the right to pursue business and personal interests in relative peace. It was not always a good bargain. Whatever their titles, despots were absolute rulers whose survival demanded a certain ruthlessness. Some were competent and relatively benign; a few were bloodthirsty psychopaths; but none was prepared to encourage the rich culture of civic participation that would one day produce the Renaissance.

That task was left to Florence and Venice, two cities that escaped the soft trap of despotism. In Florence, the Guelf triumph of 1266 paved the way for a guild-based democracy that survived, in theory at least, until the end of the fifteenth century. Social and economic tensions were expressed in the long struggle over whether or not the major guilds, which were dominated by the great bankers, should control the electoral process and therefore the *signoria*. The issue was revolved in favor of the major guilds in 1382, but in 1434 a clientage group headed by the banker-statesman Cosimo de' Medici gained control of the machinery of government. Though republican institutions were ostensibly maintained, the Medici and their friends were able to manipulate the constitution for their own purposes until 1494.

Venice, settled only in 568 and located among the desolate islands at the head of the Adriatic, had never been part of the Holy Roman Empire. Its development was therefore unlike that of any other Italian town. Several small refugee settlements coalesced during the ninth century into a single city ruled by an elective doge, or duke. Isolated from the imperial struggles on the mainland and interested primarily in the development of trade and an overseas empire, the Venetians evolved a system of government that has been called both a model republic and a class despotism.

Like other cities, Venice was troubled by clientage groups headed by prominent merchant families. To prevent any one family from gaining control of the state, the monarchical powers of the doge were eliminated between 1140 and 1160, and legislative power was vested in an elected Great Council with forty-five members. A Minor Council was established to assist the doge in his new role as administrator. The system was given its final form between 1290 and 1310 when a series of mishaps and scandals raised the specter of social revolution. The Great Council was expanded and then closed to anyone who did not have an ancestor sitting on it in 1297. A geneological registry was kept to establish pedigrees, and the membership hovered thereafter between twelve hundred and fourteen hundred certifiable members of the Venetian aristocracy. The Great Council elected the doge, whose role became largely ceremonial; his counsellors; and the Senate, a 160-man body that controlled the state. The Great Council was thus both the electorate and the pool from which officeholders were drawn. Only a direct appeal to the people could alter this closed system, and the chances of such an appeal succeeding were greatly diminished by the Council of Ten. This was a committee on state security, elected by the Great Council for one-year, nonrenewable terms, and granted almost unlimited power to deal with threats to the Venetian state at home or abroad. The constitution remained in effect until 1798.

Broad-based participation in public affairs, at least among the upper classes, is thought to have produced a civic culture of unusual vitality in both Florence and Venice. Though the government of the Medici has been called a family despotism, Cosimo made every effort to draw everyone of importance into his web of clientage. In Venice, a fairly numerous aristocracy had no alternative to participation in civic life, whereas in a true depotism, participation was restricted to the ruler and his immediate entourage. This level of civic activity contributed to the cultural and intellectual movement known as the Renaissance, but from the standpoint of social history, the Renaissance as a historical period has little meaning. The underlying realities of daily life in the Italian towns changed little between 1200 and 1500, and most generalizations that can be made about urban society, whether in Italy or elsewhere, are good for the Middle Ages as well as much of the early modern period.

The Cities of Northern Europe

Beyond the Alps only a relative handful of cities achieved anything like full sovereignty. Most were in Germany. In the period of imperial disintegration that followed the death of Frederick II, free cities and those that owed their allegiance to the emperor were generally able to expand their privileges. The larger, richer communities, such as Nürnberg or Lübeck, were virtually city-states on the Italian model, though they retained their allegiance to the empire. Others were less secure, as emperors had been known to pledge them to neighboring princes in return for support or in the settlement of disputes.

Though almost all German towns, including those that had been founded by princes, enjoyed a wide measure of freedom guaranteed by charter, the threat of noble encroachment and the uncertainties of imperial politics favored the formation of leagues. The various Hansas of north Germany had political and economic purposes. The Rhenish League (1254) and the Swabian League (1376) provide further examples, while the Swiss Confederation, founded in 1291, evolved with relatively minor changes into the Switzerland of today. The original nucleus of three small forest cantons—Uri, Schwyz, and Unterwalden—was joined by larger communities when it demonstrated its ability to defend itself against the Habsburgs at Morgarten (1315). The process of confederation culminated only with the admission of Basel in 1501 and Geneva in 1536. Each canton governed itself as an independent unit and sent representatives to the Swiss Diet when presenting a united front became necessary. Though in many ways typical of late medieval leagues, the Swiss survived through sheer military prowess and the democratic character of their cantonal governments, which tended to limit social strife.

In those areas that possessed a strong monarchy, urban development took a somewhat different form. In Spain, France, and England, the king retained a large measure of control over the towns. London achieved substantial autonomy in the chaotic reigns of Richard I and John. Urban privileges, when they were granted, were usually the fruit of royal weakness.

In the Low Countries, cities enjoyed more independence than their French or English counterparts because the counts of Flanders and Holland and the dukes of Brabant were rarely able to bring them to full obedience. With the consolidation of a powerful Burgundian state in the fifteenth century, some of their freedoms were curtailed. However, they retained more independence than royal towns whose government was influenced at every stage by the presence of a royal bailiff.

Even in France or England the towns enjoyed a freedom unknown in the countryside. In matters of taxation, public works, social policy, sanitation, and the regulation of trades, the elected town councils were remarkably autonomous. The decisions of city courts were honored except when they came into conflict with the king's justice. In France the towns were represented both in the provincial estates and the Estates General. Royal taxes were normally collected by city officials who compounded with the crown for a specified amount and then made the assessments themselves. Citizens had the opportunity to participate in their own governance and were exempt from feudal dues and obligations. Though royal authority might be strong, the German saying held true: *Stadtluft macht frei* (city air makes one free). Personal freedom and the demands of civic responsibility made medieval cities, though they held less than 10 percent of Europe's population, its primary agents of cultural and intellectual change.

Town Life in the Middle Ages

The freedom of a medieval town was a matter of personal status; the life lived within it was by most modern standards highly regulated and even claustrophobic (see illustration 10.6). The town walls defined a world of perpetual shade—a constricted maze of narrow, winding streets broken only occasionally by the open spaces of a churchyard or market. Because space within the walls was scarce and expensive, houses tended to be narrow, deep, and high, with upper stories that often overhung the street below until they nearly touched their neighbors. Light and ventilation were usually

poor, and privacy nonexistent. Much of the intensity of town life came from everyone knowing everyone else's business.

Crowding, together with the virtual absence of sanitary facilities, account for the extreme susceptibility of urban populations to epidemic disease. Regulations were established against dumping human waste into the streets, but piling it in courtyards, sometimes in close proximity to wells, was common. Travelers could smell a town long before it came into view. Town councils made valiant, if usually futile, efforts to keep the streets clean and to ensure the purity of the water supply. In the absence of a germ theory, this usually meant prohibitions on washing wool in the public fountains or orders restricting tanneries to locations downstream if not necessarily downwind. Death rates predictably exceeded birth rates in almost every European city.

Other regulations tried to preserve order as well as public health. Virtually every occupation had to be licensed. Business hours and practices were narrowly defined in the hope of protecting the consumer and reducing conflict between trades. Market women were the object of special scrutiny because their activities often threatened the prerogatives of the guilds. Standards of quality, enforced by official inspections, were laid down for the cloth industry and the victualing trades. The age and condition of meat or fish, the often dubious contents of sausages, and the conditions under which perishables of all kinds were prepared and sold were concerns, as was the integrity of weights and measures. Efforts were made to prevent the adulteration of grain or flour by adding sand or other substances to increase its weight. Every aspect of the operation of taverns, inns, wineshops, and bathhouses was minutely regulated. City ordinances and court records are a rich catalog of ingenious frauds and entrepreneurial excess.

After disease, the other great curse of medieval towns was fire. Fire companies were organized and regulations were proposed to prevent the most hazardous practices, but the combination of wood or wood frame construction and gross overcrowding could still turn ordinary kitchen mishaps into holocausts that threatened the entire community.

The city's walls not only defined the space in which townspeople lived, but also symbolized their attitude toward the outside world. For all their far-flung interests, medieval towns were intensely parochial. Carnival plays and masks are a useful key to a people's deepest fears. In cities such as late medieval Nürnberg, the citizens' nightmares seem to have revolved around nobles, Jews, peasants, and Turks. The fear of Jews and Turks

Illustration 10.6

An Urban Street Scene in Fourteenth-Century Siena. The mules are carrying wool and wood. On the left, a teacher conducts a class.

was the fear of infidels, and the nobles were everywhere a threat to the freedoms of the town. Peasants were seen as deceitful, sexually promiscuous, and vio-

lent. In even the largest cities, the countryside was never more than a few minutes' walk away, and the urban economy could not have existed without its rural suppliers. However, mutual distrust was universal. The city's gates were locked every evening, and all visitors had to secure permission to enter even in broad daylight. Jews and foreigners were commonly restricted to ghettos, often for their own protection. The word *ghetto* is of Venetian origin and refers to the section of the city reserved for Jews, but London had its Steelyard, where the Hansa merchants locked themselves up at night, and a Lombard Street where Italians were supposed to reside and operate their businesses. The outside world was perceived as threatening and only the citizen could be fully trusted.

Citizenship was a coveted honor and often difficult to achieve. With the exception of certain Swiss towns where the franchise was unusually broad, only a minority of the male residents in most cities enjoyed the right to participate in public affairs. For the most part that right was hereditary. Citizenship could be earned by those who performed extraordinary services for the commune or who had achieved substantial wealth in a respectable trade. Town councils tended to be stingy in granting citizenship, which carried with it status and responsibility. The citizen was relied upon to vote, hold office, perform public service without pay, and contribute to special assessments in time of need. Full participation in the life of the commune could be expensive and required a certain stability and firmness of character.

The distinction between citizen and noncitizen was the primary social division in the medieval town, but there were others. In most cities economic and political power rested in the hands of the richest citizens: bankers, long-distance traders, or their descendants who lived from rents and investments. Their wealth and leisure enabled them to dominate political life. They were also jealous of their prerogatives and resistant to the claims of other social groups. Serving the patricians, and sometimes related to them by blood, was a professional class composed of lawyers, notaries, and the higher ranks of the local clergy.

The men of this class frequently enjoyed close relations with princes and nobles and served as representatives of their cities to the outside world. In the later Middle Ages their contribution to the world of literature and scholarship would be disproportionate to their numbers. The women of the urban patriciate, however, were probably more isolated from society and more economically dependent than the women of any other social class. As wives, their economic role was negligible. Even housework and the care of children were usually entrusted to servants. As widows, however, they could inherit property, enter into contracts, and in some cities, sue on their own behalf in court. These rights allowed patrician widows to become investors, though, unlike the women of the artisan class, their direct involvement in management was rare.

Compared with the patricians and rentiers, artisans were a large and varied group not all of whom were cre-

ated equal. The social gap between a goldsmith and a tanner was vast, but their lives bore certain similarities. Artisans were skilled workers who processed or manufactured goods and who belonged to the guild appropriate to their trade. Patricians were rarely guild members except in such towns as Florence where guild membership was a prerequisite for public office. The masters of a given trade owned their own workshops, which doubled as retail salesrooms and typically occupied the ground floor of their homes. They sometimes worked alone but more often employed journeymen to assist them. These skilled workers had served their apprenticeships but did not own their own shops and usually lived in rented quarters elsewhere. Because the master had demonstrated his competence with a masterpiece that had been accepted by the other masters of his guild, he was also expected to train apprentices. These young men, often the sons of other guild members, learned the trade by working in the master's shop and living in his household. Apprenticeships typically began around the age of twelve and continued for seven years in northern Europe and three or four in Italy.

Artisan households were often large, complex units. Their management and the management of the family business were usually entrusted to the artisan's wife. While her husband concentrated on production and training, she dealt with marketing, purchasing, and finance. If the artisan died, she often continued the enterprise, using hired journeymen in his place or doing the work herself, for many women had learned their father's trade as children. In some cities, widows were admitted to guilds, though not without restrictions.

Women's work was therefore crucial to the medieval town economy. According to the *Livre des Métiers*, written by Etienne Boileau in the thirteenth century, women were active in eighty-six of the one hundred occupations listed for contemporary Paris. Six *métiers* or trades, all of which would today be called part of the fashion industry, were exclusively female (see document 10.5). In addition, women everywhere played an important part in the victualing trades (brewing, butchering, fishmongering, and so on) and in the manufacture of small metal objects including needles, pins, buckles, knives, and jewelry.

Women also played an important role as street peddlars. Operating from makeshift booths or simply spreading their goods on the ground, the market women sold everything from trinkets to used clothing, household implements, and food. After the expulsion of the Jews, many women became pawnbrokers. Their central role in retail distribution, their aggressive sales techniques, and their propensity to engage (like their

❖ DOCUMENT 10.5 ❖

Women in the Paris Silk Industry

Silk spinning in thirteenth-century Paris was a woman's trade. The women owned their own spindles and could take apprentices. Paris, however, lacked the freedom of the Italian and German towns. Like other métiers in this era, the spinsters had no true guild organization. Craft ordinances were proclaimed and enforced in the king's name by the provost of Paris, and the spun silk was purchased by merchants operating on the "putting-out" system. Those ordinances listed below were compiled between 1254 and 1271 and offer a glimpse of the conditions under which medieval tradeswomen worked.

Any woman who wishes to be a silk spinster on large spindles in the city of Paris—i.e. reeling, spinning, doubling, and retwisting—may freely do so, provided she observe the following usages and customs of the craft:

No spinster on large spindles may have more than three apprentices, unless they be her own or her husband's children born in true wedlock; nor may she contract with them for an apprenticeship of less than seven years or for a fee of less than 20 Parisian sols to be paid to her, their mistress. The apprenticeship shall be for eight years if there is no fee, but she may accept more years and money if she can get them. . . .

No woman of the said craft may hire an apprentice or work-girl who has not completed her years of service with the mistress to whom she was apprenticed. If a spinster has assumed an apprentice, she may not take on another before the first has completed her seven years unless the apprentice die or foreswear the craft forever. If an apprentice spinster buy her freedom before serving the said seven years, she may not herself take an apprentice until she has practiced the craft seven years. . . .

If a working woman comes from outside Paris and wishes to practice the said craft in the city, she must swear before two guardians of the craft that she will practice it well and loyally and conform to its customs and usages.

If anyone give a woman of the said craft silk to be spun and the woman pawn it, and the owner complains, the fine shall be 5 sols.

No workwoman shall farm out another's silk to be worked upon outside her own house.

The said craft has as guardians two men of integrity sworn in the king's name but appointed and charged at the will of the provost of Paris. Taking an oath in the provost's presence, they shall swear to guard the craft truly, loyally, and to their utmost, and to inform him or his agents of all malpractices discovered therein.

Boileau, Etienne. *"Livres de Métiers."* In Julia O'Faolain and Lauro Martines, *Not in God's Image: Women in History from the Greeks to the Victorians.* New York: HarperCollins, 1973.

male counterparts) in monopolies and restrictive trading practices brought them into frequent conflict with the guilds and with the authorities who tried, often in vain, to regulate their activities.

Many market women were the wives or daughters of journeymen; most probably came from a lower echelon of urban society—the semiskilled or unskilled laborers who served as porters, construction helpers, wool carders, or any one of a hundred menial occupations. Such people were rarely guild members or citizens, and their existence was often precarious.

Employment tended to be sporadic. A laborer's wage was sometimes capable of supporting a bachelor but rarely a family, and everyone had to work to survive. In cloth towns, women often worked in the wool shops along with the men. For the aggressive and quick-witted, the street market was a viable alternative. Domestic service was another and provided employment for a substantial number of both men and women.

These respectable, if disenfranchised, workers were probably the most numerous group in any city. An underclass also was present of beggars, prostitutes, criminals, and people who for one reason or another were dependent on charity for their survival. In theory, the poor were the responsibility of the church or of pious individuals who contributed to their welfare. Town governments tended to see poverty, like criminality, as a question of social control, though by the later Middle Ages, some communities had begun to follow the lead of Venice in establishing hospitals and regular distributions of food to the needy. Even when they were established with government funds, these institutions were staffed mainly by the religious orders. Begging in many places was licensed, as was prostitution. The latter could be an important source of revenue, and most towns, such as Nürnberg, preferred to localize the trade in official brothels whose profits could be taxed.

Crime was more difficult to control. The intimacy of town life encouraged theft, and the labyrinth of streets and alleys provided robbers with multiple escape routes. No police force existed. Most towns had a watch for night patrols and a militia that could intervene in riots and other disturbances, but competent thieves were rarely caught and interpersonal violence, which was fairly common, aroused little concern. If an encounter stopped short of murder or serious disfigurement the authorities were inclined to look the other way. They were far more concerned with maintaining the social and economic order and with public health. Politically, even this was by no means easy. The close proximity between rich and poor and the exclusivity of most town governments made social tension inevitable. Laborers, the urban poor, and even some of the journeymen lived in grinding poverty. Entire families often occupied a single, unheated room and subsisted on inadequate diets while the urban rich lived with an ostentation that even the feudal aristocracy could rarely equal. The contrast was a fertile source of discontent. Though riots and revolts were not always led by the poor but by prosperous malcontents who had been excluded from leadership in the commune, such people found it easy to play upon the bitter resentments of those who had nothing to lose but their lives.

Civil disturbances would reach a peak in the years after the Black Death, but urban patriciates had long been fearful of popular revolts. Disgruntled weavers and other cloth workers in the towns of thirteenth-century Flanders launched revolts based openly on class warfare. Everywhere the apprentices, who shared the violent impulses of most adolescent males, were available on call to reinforce the social and economic demands of the artisans. Riots were common, and rebellion was suppressed with extreme brutality.

In southern Europe, social tensions were muted though not eliminated by clientage. The factions that dominated city politics had tentacles that reached down to the artisan and the laboring classes. Mutual obligation, though unequal in its benefits, tended to moderate class feeling and reduce the social isolation of the patriciate, which, in Flemish and German towns, was far more extreme. In spite of this, Venice faced the specter of revolution in the late thirteenth century, and the political life of fourteenth-century Florence was dominated by a struggle between the major and minor guilds that revealed deep social divisions. Where city governments were backed by the authority of a strong monarchy, as in France, England, and Castile, discontent was easier to control.

The commercial revolution of the Middle Ages marked a turning point in the history of the West. The years of relative isolation were over. By the mid-thirteenth century, even the most remote European villages were touched, at least peripherally, by an economy that spanned the known world. Trading connections gave Europeans access to the gold and ivory of Africa, the furs and amber of Russia, and the spices of the Far East. Even China, at the end of the long Silk Road across central Asia, was within reach, and a few Europeans, among whom the Venetian Marco Polo (1254–1324) is the most famous, traveled there. Few rural communities were in any sense dependent upon long distance trade and most were still largely self-sustaining, but their horizons had been broadened immeasureably.

The towns, themselves the products of trade, were the connecting links between the agrarian hinterland in which most Europeans lived, and the great world outside. They were also the cultural and intellectual catalysts for society as a whole. The requirements of business and of participation in government demanded literacy. The intensity of urban life encouraged vigorous debate. Some measure of intellectual life therefore flourished within the city walls. At the same time the tendency of surplus wealth to concentrate in cities permitted an investment in culture that was far beyond the capacity of even the greatest agricultural estates. Much of that investment was inspired by civic pride. If funds were available, city councils were prepared to support the building and decoration of churches or other public buildings and to lay out substantial sums for festivals and celebrations whose chief purpose was to demonstrate the superiority of their town over its neighbors. The absurd competition over the height of church towers may have been unproductive and at times hazardous, but it symbolized a spirit that produced much of medieval art and architecture.

Even the strife endemic to medieval towns had its positive side. Resistance to social injustice reflected the vitality of ancient ideals. Ordinary people continued to believe that the town was, or should be, a refuge for those seeking personal freedom and economic opportunity. They demonstrated by their actions that the Greco-Roman ideal of civic participation was far from dead. Medieval cities may often have been deficient and even brutal in their social arrangements, but they preserved important values that had no place in the feudal countryside. As the institutional matrix for creating, preserving, and disseminating the Western cultural tradition, the town had, by the thirteenth century, replaced the monastery.

CHAPTER 11

MATERIAL AND SOCIAL LIFE IN THE MIDDLE AGES

CHAPTER OUTLINE

Though towns had become important, more than 90 percent of all medieval Europeans still lived in the countryside. Because society was organized along rigidly hierarchical lines, family and behavioral norms varied greatly according to class (see tables 11.1 and 11.2). Peasants and their feudal overlords, in effect, inhabited different worlds. In some cases, they spoke different languages even though they lived on the same land. A useful comparison between these two styles of life must take into consideration not only their physical environments, but also the impact of chivalric values on the feudal class and the wide variety of social and economic strategies adopted by peasants to ensure an often precarious survival.

◈

The Ecology of Medieval Life: The Medieval Diet

The material life of medieval Europe was not unlike that of antiquity in several important respects and would remain substantially unchanged until the industrial revolution. The biological regime established by the Neolithic revolution remained in effect. Grain remained the basic food. Wheat was preferred, but millet, spelt, barley, oats, and rye were also staples, especially among the poor. Ground into flour and then baked as bread or served in the form of gruels and porridges, grains were the staff of life and provided most of the calories in the average person's diet.

Bread was commonly baked outside the home because medieval ovens were large brick affairs that consumed great quantities of fuel. Several hours were required to heat them to the proper temperature, and economies of scale demanded that many loaves be baked at the same time. Only the households of the very rich, with their dozens of servants and retainers, required ovens of their own or could afford to dispense

❧ TABLE 11.1 ❧
Wages and Earnings in Thirteenth-Century England

The relationship between earnings and prices is an important measure of living standards. This table provides estimated average earnings for several occupations in medieval England. Women, then as now, earned far less than men for the same work. The annual wage of a mason reflects the fact that bad weather shortened the number of days he could work. For the same reason, a carpenter doing outdoor work would make less than the amount noted below. There were twelve pennies (d.) in a shilling (s.) and twenty shillings in a pound (£). The wages for skilled laborers increased by 40 to 50 percent after the Black Death.

Occupation	Estimated earnings Per day	Per year
Agricultural laborer		
Boy	1/2d.	
Female	1d.	£1.7s. 3d.
Male	2d.	£2.14s.6d.
Carpenter	3d.–3 1/2d.	£4
Mason	5d.–6d.	£4. 8s.5d.
Peasant family with 20 acres		£4
Royal huntsman	7 1/2d.	
Rural priest		£5–£15
Sawyer	3 1/2d.–4d.	£5
Stonecutter	4d.	£5. 8s.
Thatcher's assistant (female)	1d.	£1.7s. 3d.
Town priest		£75–100
Unskilled laborer	2d.	£2.14s.6d.

Source: Figures abstracted from John Burnett, *A History of the Cost of Living* (Harmondsworth: Pelican Books, 1969), pp. 17–54.

❧ TABLE 11.2 ❧
Prices in Thirteenth-Century England

The prices listed below are averages only. In reality, the medieval family had to contend with wild fluctuations according to the harvests.

Product	Average price
Ale (per gallon)	1/4d.–3/4d.
Bread (per loaf, weight varied)	1/4d.–1/2d.
Candle wax (per pound)	4d.–5d.
Capons (each, fully fattened)	2d.–3d.
Eggs (per 100)	4d.
Hens (per 1)	1/2d.
Pears (per 100)	3 1/2d.
Pepper (per pound)	10d.2s.
Pike (per 1)	6s.8d.
Salt herrings (per 10)	1d.
Second-quality malt—2 quarters (1 year supply of ale for 4)	7s. 7d.
Sugar (per pound)	1s.–2d.
Wine (per quart)	£1.3s. 6d.
Wheat—4 quarters (sufficient for a family of 4 for 1 year)	1d.

Source: Figures taken from John Burnett, *A History of the Cost of Living* (Harmondsworth: Pelican Books), 1969, pp. 17–54.

with the services of the village baker. Many different kinds of bread existed, ranging from the fine white loaves and cakes prized by the nobles and high-ranking clergy to coarse breads made of rye or of oats and mixed grains. An important consideration in the grading of bread was the proportion of bran left in the flour. This created a strange paradox: The lower grades of bread consumed by the poor were often higher in nutritional quality than was the bread of the rich with its bleached, highly refined, wheaten flour. Another oddity of the baker's trade was that in many countries the price of a loaf of bread was fixed by law or custom but the size

was not. A ha'penny loaf in England always cost 1/2 d., but its weight might vary radically according to the price of grain. The shape and appearance of loaves was a matter of local preference and differed widely from region to region. Whatever its form or content, baked bread was often too expensive for the very poor, especially on a regular basis. Unbaked bread, or gruel, could be cooked at home and was commonly eaten by all classes for its economy and ease of preparation.

Baked or unbaked, bread accounted for at least 50 percent of a rich family's diet and for more than 80 percent of the calories consumed by poor people. The price and availability of grain was therefore a valid measure of living standards because few substitutes were available and a bad harvest brought widespread misery. Rice was expensive and little known outside parts of Spain and the Middle East until the fifteenth century. It seems to have been consumed largely by wealthy invalids. In some upland areas, chestnuts were ground and baked into a coarse but nutritious bread. In most areas the best insurance against hunger was to grow several kinds of grain at different seasons.

A diet of bread was monotonous and poor in virtually every nutritional element save carbohydrates. Whenever possible, people tried to supplement it with other foods, but their choices were limited. Protein was provided mainly by dried peas, beans, lentils, or chickpeas that were cooked into a wide variety of soups and stews. Meat was rare except on the tables of the feudal aristocracy. Their chief leisure pastime was hunting, and they tended to consume vast quantities of game, seasoned after the twelfth century with powerful spices from the East and washed down with great drafts of wine or beer. Many peasants could not afford to keep animals at all, though ducks and chickens were raised for their eggs and stewed or made into soup when they had passed their prime. Those with capital or excess land might have some hogs or a cow. Even for them, meat was likely to be a seasonal delicacy. The cost of feeding livestock over the winter was high, and even the wealthier peasants slaughtered their animals in the fall, eating some and preserving the rest by smoking or salting. By Lent, this had been consumed, which probably meant that the prohibition against eating flesh in the holy season caused little hardship.

Hunting and fishing provided other dietary supplements, though in many areas both fish and game belonged to the lord and poaching was discouraged by ferocious penalties. Even the gathering of nuts in the forest might be prohibited. Other sources of protein were milk and cheese, and salted herring became increasingly important as an item of commerce in the thirteenth century. Owing to the widespread use of salt as a preservative and to the general monotony of diets, scholars believe that medieval people consumed many times the quantity of salt that Westerners are accustomed to eating today.

Fresh fruits and vegetables were also rare. Those who possessed a kitchen garden might have a fruit tree or a cabbage patch, but many of today's most common vegetables were either unknown or raised, such as lettuce, for medicinal purposes. Onions and garlic, however, were common, as were indigenous spices such as thyme, rosemary, basil, and marjoram. Honey was the primary sweetener. Sugar was largely unknown and remained prohibitively expensive until the seventeenth century when it could be imported in quantity from the New World.

A wide variety of fermented beverages completed the medieval diet. Wine was rarely produced north of the forty-ninth parallel (roughly the latitude of Paris), though it was consumed everywhere, especially by the rich. North of the wine districts, the popularity of mead, a drink made from fermented honey, declined during the Middle Ages while that of cider appears to have increased. Beer, or "liquid bread," was an important food supplement throughout all of central and northern Europe. Properly speaking, medieval beer was a form of ale. It was brewed from malted grain, preferably barley, using the top fermentation process. Hops were sometimes used on the continent but never in the British Isles. The result was a dark, rather sweet concoction that resembled the stouts and Scotch ales of today. Bottom fermentation, which produces lager or pilsner beers, was invented by the Germans in the fifteenth century. Brewing was usually done in the home and, like other aspects of the beverage trade, was dominated by women. It was an important economic sideline for those families who could afford the vats and other equipment. A skilled woman who was otherwise housebound by small children could manage the process. Tea, coffee, and tobacco were as yet unknown in the West, while alcohol, distilled in alembics on a small scale, was used primarily for medicinal purposes. Water was regarded with suspicion because it was thought to cause an imbalance of humors, an impression no doubt created by the effects of drinking from polluted sources.

The nutritional value of medieval diets is difficult to determine. It varied widely according to region and social class and tended to fluctuate with the seasons. Autumn, when trees bore their fruit and animals were killed for the winter, was usually a time of relative abundance, while spring, for all its promise of harvests to come, was the leanest of seasons. Important as they were, even these variables were overridden by considerations of price and availability. Fluctuations based on the relative scarcity or abundance of different commodities were dramatic and often terrifying, especially for the poor who had limited opportunities to store food. The failure of a single harvest could lead to hunger for those who were economically marginal.

The best balance between protein, fats, and carbohydrates was probably found in pastoral villages and on the tables of rich townsfolk. Urban laborers and peasants on manors whose primary crop was grain suffered chronic deficiencies of everything except carbohydrates. Everyone else fell somewhere in between, though the feudal aristocracy may be suspected of eating too much animal protein. The concept of vitamins was unknown. The general scarcity of fresh fruits and vegetables ensured that minimum daily requirements would rarely have been met by anyone and deficiencies were probably common. The poor in particular were often deformed by rickets or goiter and likely were physically smaller than those with better access to protein in youth. The average height of an adult male was probably not much above five feet, though this differed widely by class and region.

Disease and Demography

Inadequate nutrition continued to affect population rates in several ways. The number of live births is determined in large part by the rate of conception and by maternal nutrition, both of which are directly related to diet. A third factor, obstetrical technique, is also important but changed little until the revolutionary developments of the nineteenth and twentieth centuries.

Rates of conception in a given population are determined in part by the total number of childbearing years available to a woman. Malnutrition, obstetrical accidents, and epidemic disease shortened life expectancy and reduced the childbearing years dramatically. They were also reduced by a far higher age of first menstruation than is now common. Though marriages were sometimes contracted at an early age, especially among the upper classes, medieval women are thought to have reached puberty at an average age of seventeen as opposed to today's average of 12.4. Nutrition is usually blamed for the difference. Inadequate nutrition can also prevent ovulation in mature women, which probably reduced conception rates even further.

After conception, poor maternal diet led to a high rate of stillbirths and complications during pregnancy. If a child were brought to term it then faced the hazards of childbirth. Babies were normally delivered at home in unsanitary conditions. The midwives who delivered babies were often experienced, but they knew nothing of sterilization and lacked the most elementary equipment (see illustration 11.1). Forceps, for example, were not invented until the middle of the eighteenth century. Though Trotula, a woman physician, taught at the University of Salerno in the thirteenth century and published a treatise on obstetrics, most medieval physicians were men and knew no more than a competent midwife. They were, in any case, available only to the rich.

Infants who survived the obstetrical techniques of the day then faced the possibility that their mothers would be unable to nurse. Malnutrition interferes with lactation as does the stress of poverty, exposure to war, and other forms of physical and mental insecurity. The problem could be solved by turning the child over to a wet nurse, but this was not always a satisfactory solution. The wet nurse was normally another woman in the village who had milk to spare because she had recently lost

Illustration 11.1

Midwives at Work. Midwives, or perhaps a midwife assisted by relatives, are trying to hasten a birth by shaking the mother up and down. Such obstetric techniques ensured a high rate of mortality for infants and mothers alike.

her own baby. She had to be paid—a serious problem for a poor woman—and did not always care for the child as she might have cared for her own. Babies put out for nursing had a higher mortality rate than those who remained at home. Either way, the children of poorly nourished mothers were often weak and susceptible to disease. The birthrate was therefore by modern standards low and the rate of infant mortality high. Valid statistics are unavailable for medieval times, but deaths presumably ranged from 30 to 70 percent in the first two years of life, depending upon such variables as current food supply and the presence or absence of epidemics.

In hard times, personal decisions hindered population growth as well. Those whose own survival was in doubt abstained from sex, used the primitive means of contraception then available (notably *coitus interruptus*), or, when all else failed, resorted to infanticide. Abortion, though not unknown, was extremely dangerous, and most women preferred to carry a child to term even if they could not afford to keep it. Infanticide may

❧ TABLE 11.3 ❧

Life Expectancy in the Middle Ages

The figures below represent the estimated life expectancy of male landholders in medieval England. They are arranged by dates of birth and demonstrate the substantial changes in mortality that occurred over time. Life expectancy for women was probably somewhat shorter owing to the dangers of childbirth.

Age	1200–76	1276–1301	1301–26	1326–48	1348–76	1376–1401	1401–25	1425–50
0	35.3	31.3	29.8	27.2	17.3	20.5	23.8	32.8
10	36.3	32.2	31.0	28.1	25.1	24.5	29.7	34.5
20	28.7	25.2	23.8	22.1	23.9	21.4	29.4	27.7
30	22.8	21.8	20.0	21.1	22.0	22.3	25.0	24.1
40	17.8	16.6	15.7	17.7	18.1	19.2	19.3	20.4
60	9.4	8.3	9.3	10.8	10.9	10.0	10.5	13.7
80	5.2	3.8	4.5	6.0	4.7	3.1	4.8	7.9

Source: Carlo Cipolla, *The Middle Ages*, Fontana Economic History of Europe (London: Colliers, 1973), p. 47. Used by permission of HarperCollins Publishers Ltd.

have been emotionally devastating to the mother and murder in the eyes of the law, but it was easy to conceal in a world where infant mortality was common and doctors scarce. Its incidence in the Middle Ages is therefore a matter of controversy. Contemporary religious and civil authorities thought it was common, and many an old folk tale recalls its horrors.

Abandonment, the most common alternative to infanticide, appears to have declined sharply in the prosperous years of the eleventh and twelfth centuries. It became more frequent as population pressures increased during the thirteenth century and revived between the famines of 1315–17 and the Black Death. As in ancient times, estimating how many of these abandoned children survived is impossible. If hard times persisted, less dramatic forms of birth control came into play. People simply refused to marry and remained celibate, sometimes for life. The marriage rate almost invariably declined during periods of economic stress.

Those who survived infancy still faced heavy odds. Medieval life expectancy was probably in the low thirties at birth (see table 11.3). Averages, however, can be deceiving. Many people lived into their fifties, and the proportionate number of individuals over the age of eighty-five was probably not much smaller than it is today. The primary causes of early death remained disease, often complicated by malnutrition, and the inadequate treatment of wounds and injuries.

The spread of disease was encouraged by crowding and by a widespread indifference to personal hygiene. In the absence of a germ theory, personal cleanliness was a matter of aesthetics, and bathing was regarded with suspicion by Christian thinkers who associated it with pagan luxury or with Jewish and Muslim rituals. Its alternative was difficult and expensive to achieve. By the twelfth century, firewood, like timber, had become scarce and expensive everywhere in western and central Europe. Bathing in cold water in an unheated room was unattractive. Most people had better uses for their limited supplies of precious firewood. Rashes and skin infections were therefore common. Crowding, often for warmth, and the custom of keeping livestock and pets in the home added to the problem by ensuring that many Europeans would play host to a variety of insect pests. This encouraged the spread of epidemics because lice and fleas carried infectious diseases including typhus and, later, plague.

Contaminated drinking water accounted for another group of deadly ailments, while airborne viruses and bacteria were as numerous as they are today. Here, too, the absence of a germ theory rendered public health measures ineffective. Water that looked clean was thought to be safe, and indoor air was purified by scenting it with perfumes and herbs. Malaria, endemic in southern Europe, was thought to be caused by breathing miasmas, or foul air. It is actually spread by mosquitoes. The offending parasite remains in the bloodstream for life, causing recurring attacks of chills and fever even if it fails to kill its victim outright. Those weakened by malnutrition or other ailments were the most likely to succumb.

◈ DOCUMENT 11.1 ◈

The Treatment of Disease

The following remedies are taken from a standard medical text, Rosa Anglica practica medicine a capite ad pedes *(The Rose of England, the Practice of Medicine from the Head to the Feet), by John of Gaddesden (1280–1361), a graduate of Oxford and of the medical school at Montpellier. The treatments he prescribes are a typical mixture of common sense and natural magic.*

For smallpox: [I]n the case of the noble son of the English king, when he was infected with this disease . . . I made everything around the bed to be red.

For tuberculosis: 1). Keep in check the catarrh and the rheumata; 2). cleanse the body; 3). divert and draw away the matter [of the disease] to a different part; 4). strengthen the chest and head so that they do not take up the matter, and that it there multiply; 5). cleanse and dry up the ulcers and expel the matter from them; 6). consolidate them; 7). restrain and cure the cough by using demulcent drinks with ointments and stupes; 8). assist the patient to sleep; 9). strengthen and bring back the appetite; 10). keep in check the spitting of blood; 11). do what can be done to make the breathing more easy and to remove the asthma and the hoarseness; 12). regulate the

way of life so far as the six non-naturals; 13). cure the putrid or hectic fever which goes with the disease. As to food, the best is the milk of a young brunette with her first child, which should be a boy; the young woman should be well-favored and should eat and drink in moderation.

For toothache: Again, write these words on the jaw of the patient: In the name of the Father, the Son, and the Holy Ghost, Amen. +Rex+Pax+Nax+ in Christo Filio, and the pain will cease at once as I have often seen. . . . Again, some say that the beak of a magpie hung from the neck cures pain in the teeth and the uvula and the quinsy. Again, when the gospel for Sunday is read in the mass, let the man hearing mass sign his tooth and head with the sign of the holy Cross and say a pater noster and an ave for the souls of the father and mother of St. Philip, and this without stopping; it will keep them from pain in the future and will cure that which may be present, so say trustworthy authorities.

Clendening, L., ed. *A Source Book of Medical History,* pp. 83–85. New York: Dover, 1960.

Some medieval diseases appear to have no modern counterparts, a tribute to the rapidity with which viruses and bacteria can evolve. Others, such as measles and chicken pox, the great killers of late antiquity, were now restricted largely to children. The population had acquired an hereditary immunity. But even childhood diseases were capable of carrying off the weak or poorly nourished. In general, malnutrition weakened resistance to every ailment and, like crowding, was a silent partner in the high rate of mortality. Towns may have been more dangerous than the countryside, but poverty, whatever its location, was likely to prove fatal.

Death by injury or misadventure was also common. Upper-class males were likely to destroy themselves in battle or in hunting accidents. Villagers were exposed to the inevitable hazards of agricultural life. Infants fell into fires, crawled into the path of carts, or were mauled by hogs. Adults fell out of trees while picking fruit or gathering firewood or toppled into wells while drawing water. They severed limbs and arteries with

their scythes or accidentally brained each other with their flails. Drink and the absence of illumination by night also took its toll. Happy harvesters fell off their carts and were run over while people returning from late-night drinking bouts drowned in ditches or passed out and froze to death in the road.

Against this formidable array of human ills, doctors were as helpless as they had been in antiquity. Their theories and the remedies available to them had changed little. By the thirteenth century many physicians were university-trained, but they tended to concentrate on diagnosis and the prescription of drugs, most of which were of dubious value (see document 11.1). The surgeons who, unlike physicians, performed medical procedures were educated by apprenticeship. They operated without sterilization and without anesthetics. Broken bones could sometimes be set, but wounds were likely to become infected with fatal results. In any case, most people had no access to either physicians or surgeons and relied upon folk remedies about which little is known. They were probably as effective as the nostrums advocated by learned doctors. Survival still depended upon good luck, heredity, and the recuperative powers of the patient.

All of these things affected the distribution of population. Medieval people were younger and had far shorter working lives than their modern counterparts. Their reproductive lifetimes were also shorter. For people of mature years (aged thirty to fifty), men may have outnumbered women, primarily because so many women died in childbirth. At the same time, population levels were more closely related to epidemics and to fluctuations in the food supply than they have been since the industrial revolution. The doubling of the European population between the eleventh and the thirteenth centuries was a direct consequence of increased agricultural production, but because that increase was proportionate, nutrition did not improve. Instead, population densities, though still low by modern standards, had begun by the end of the thirteenth century to push against the limits of available land. Events would prove that when production and population were so closely balanced, epidemic disease or a series of failed harvests could serve as a corrective to demographic growth.

The Rural Upper Classes

Knightly families made up only a small part of Europe's population. Most villages had no lord in residence, but such was the legal and economic power of the feudal class that the castle or manor house cast a figurative shadow over the entire countryside.

The symbol of feudal authority, the castle underwent an architectural metamorphosis during the eleventh and twelfth centuries. Kings and the greater vassals had always tried to build in stone. As society's wealth increased, the practice was extended to relatively modest structures. Wooden palisades gave way to stone curtains with towers spaced at regular intervals on the Roman model. The keep, or central stronghold, became more liveable, if not luxurious. Windows, side aisles, and even fireplaces were added to the hall. Separate kitchens and chapels became commonplace, while private chambers were built for the use of the lord and his immediate family. This tended to remove them from the life of the hall and introduced the revolutionary idea of personal privacy. In politically secure areas, stone manor houses were built on the same model with-

Illustration 11.2

The Moat and Gatehouse of the Bishop's Palace, Wells, England. The fortifications were built in 1340 to protect the bishop from his tenants.

out troubling about walls. Setting the hall above a raised ground floor and entering it by a staircase was protection enough.

These developments reflected a basic change, not only in the function of the castle, but also in the feudal class as a whole. With the passing of the great raids, society no longer needed the protection of the knights and the purely military function of the castles was minimized. Castle building declined at the end of the twelfth century. Its revival, at the beginning of the thirteenth century, was primarily a response to growing social unrest (see illustration 11.2). Some structures, such as the great Welsh castles of Edward I, were intended to hold territory newly annexed by an expanding monarchy. Both purposes involved an element of political theater. The castles built to protect country gentlemen against their tenants, like those built to overawe the Welsh, were stronger and more sophisticated than any attack that was likely to be made against them (see illustration 11.3).

Illustration 11.3

Harlech Castle, Wales. Built by Edward I of England between 1283 and 1289, Harlech Castle's chief purpose was to serve as a visible symbol of English power. The Welsh were not rich, numerous, or threatening to a far weaker structure.

The Evolution of the Chivalric Ideal

The knights, too, became more decorative and theatrical with the passage of time. As the importance of their original function began to diminish, the concept of nobility began to evolve in its place. The qualities of courage, loyalty, strength, and courtesy came to be regarded as hereditary attributes. The process began with the introduction of dubbing to knighthood in the late eleventh century. Knights were then regarded, in the language of the church, as an *ordo* or order in their own right, a social institution instead of a mere body of fighting men. Before long a priest customarily blessed the knight's arms and invested him with them in a rite reminiscent of ordination. This was perhaps inevitable when crusades were becoming the last legitimate outlet for military virtues. Finally, in the century after 1130, knighthood was transformed into a hereditary privilege. In 1140, Roger II of Sicily declared that only the descendants of knights would be admitted to knighthood. By 1187, it had become illegal to knight a peasant in the empire, and peasants were prohibited from carrying a sword or lance. Similar provisions were found in almost every European kingdom by the second half of the twelfth century.

Such prohibitions were not airtight. Members of the urban patriciate were sometimes able to achieve knightly rank, but their elevation was neither cheap nor easy. In a reversal of earlier practice, peasants were ex-cluded from knighthood almost by definition. To forestall the proliferation of titles, kings achieved a statutory monopoly over the granting of knighthoods and forbade the ancient custom whereby any knight could make another. At the same time, they created a profusion of counts and barons to distinguish between their greater and lesser vassals. This process reached a peak in the empire, where the status of noble families was eventually graded in exquisite detail. When the military revolution of the fourteenth century brought commoners back to the battlefield in great numbers, such policies had to be reversed. Kings retained the sole right to grant titles but bestowed them once again on people of humble origin. The feudal nobility, whose importance in war was by this time greatly diminished, regarded such creations as an outrageous betrayal of chivalry.

Legal developments went hand in hand with an expansion of the chivalric ideal. What had once been little more than a prescription for courage and loyalty evolved into an all-encompassing moral and esthetic code. The church, in its drive to influence all European institutions, bore partial responsibility for the change. Courtesy, clemency to a fallen enemy, and the respectful treatment of women became hallmarks of the knight, though such behavior was extended only to members of the noble class. Peasants could still be raped and murdered with impunity under the laws of war.

Along with these presumed virtues went a style of speech and personal carriage that clearly set the knight

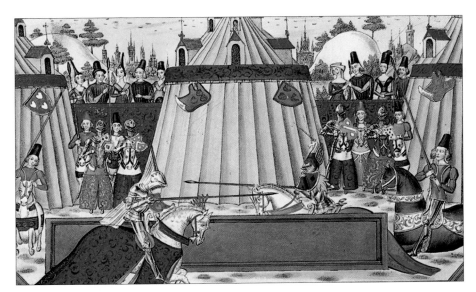

Illustration 11.4

⁂ **A Tournament.** The tournament provided knights with training, entertainment, and, in some cases, wealth. This illumination captures the pageantry and spectacle that fascinated onlookers and participants alike.

and his lady apart from the rest of society. It could not be easily imitated because peasants no longer associated with the nobility on a regular basis and had few opportunities to observe them. The speech, movements, and gestures of ordinary men and women were eventually stigmatized as uncouth and boorish.

Chivalric values were disseminated by the troubadours and by the kings of arms who presided over the conventions of heraldry and acted to some extent as arbiters of taste. As literacy spread, the oral tradition of the troubadours was written down and circulated in manuscript form as the romance. Five works based upon the legendary court of King Arthur were composed by Chrétien de Troyes sometime after 1164 and formed the basis of an entire literary genre. Many others of similar importance also existed. A body of lyric poetry that exalted chivalric love served as further reinforcement for the new values. The language of this literature was French, and French, which had spread from England to Sicily by the Normans, became the language of the chivalric class. Social separation was now virtually complete. In some regions, knights could no longer speak the language of their tenants.

Theoretically, war remained the center of noble life and the justification for its privileges. Males were still expected to master the profession of arms in youth and practice it until age, wounds, or ill health permitted a dignified retirement. In practice, this ideal was gravely weakened by the development of hereditary knighthood. In the first feudal age, men who lacked the requisite ability commonly remained squires for life. In the twelfth and thirteenth centuries they could expect to be knighted regardless of their achievements.

Relative peace was an even greater threat to the knightly ethos. In the absence of Vikings or Magyars, the Crusades became a useful outlet for martial talents. As the interval between crusades grew longer, tournaments gradually took the place of war as the central preoccupation of the feudal class. Tournaments were a stylized form of combat in which two mounted knights, generally separated by a barrier, attempted to unhorse one another with their lances (see illustration 11.4). They might then attempt to fight on foot with swords or other weapons. The rules were elaborate and varied widely according to the occasion. It was, in other words, a sport. The bouts were refereed; murder was not the primary object but serious injuries and fatal mishaps were unavoidable. Women, who participated only as spectators, were a powerful symbolic presence. A knight entered the lists as champion of a particular lady and wore her scarf or some more intimate garment as a token of her favor. Because the conventions of chivalric love encouraged adulterous flirtations, the lady was not ordinarily expected to be his wife.

For all its frivolity, the importance of the tournament as a social ritual should not be underestimated. Those who were good at it could expect great rewards. A penniless younger son and knight errant such as William the Marshall (d. 1219) could parlay his athletic talent into an advantageous marriage, an estate, and a remarkable political career that ended with his appointment as regent for the King of England.

This was the point of the whole system. Beneath the veneer of chivalry, the advancement of personal and family interests through the accumulation of estates was a compelling goal. A sense of lineage developed early in feudal families and was strengthened immeasurably by the concept of nobility. Kinship ties were therefore stronger among the feudal classes than in other segments of society. The possession of landed estates ensured that the extended family would be a relatively common form of household organization.

For the same reason, weddings were almost invariably arranged, often at an early age. The disposition of great properties could not be entrusted to the vagaries of youthful lust. This may help to account for the fascination with adultery that characterized chivalric literature. However, a surprising number of noble marriages appear to have been happy and mutually supportive. The women of the feudal class were often formidable personages, capable of managing an estate or defending their castle against a siege in the absence of their husbands. Some, such as Matilda of Tuscany or Eleanor of Aquitaine, were major political figures in their own right. Virtually all were at home in the world of political intrigue. Their survival and that of their children often depended upon it.

Clientage, of which feudalism was in some respects a formalized expression, was also highly developed at this level of society. Almost everyone sought the favor and protection of those more powerful than themselves and tried wherever possible to develop clients and retainers of their own. The importance of the castle and even of the manor house was measured less by the grandeur of the masonry than by the hospitality of its hall. The greater households often included not only the lord and his nuclear family but also a respectable number of collateral relatives, stewards, servants, knights, and other retainers who owed him their allegiance and lived at least partially from his bounty. This much, at least, had changed little, and as always, the cost was born by the peasant.

Ironically, these developments took place as the economic fortunes of the feudal class began to decline. The greater availability of specie in the twelfth century led to the widespread commutation of feudal obligations for cash. Landholders greeted this development with enthusiasm because it increased their liquidity, but they made the mistake of commuting payments hitherto made in labor or in kind for fixed sums of money. These sums, not the proportional values that had determined them, quickly became enshrined in law and precedent while their value was slowly consumed by inflation (see table 11.4). A consequent decline in the real value of rents was masked during the thirteenth century by a strong demand for

land created by population growth. When harvest failures were followed by the demographic collapse of 1347–50, property values fell as well and social tensions became insupportable.

TABLE 11.4

The Expenses of the Rich

An earl's income in thirteenth-century England might range from £1000 per year to more than £5000. From this a nobleman or noblewoman was expected to maintain a large household of servants and spend huge sums on food, building, travel, and recreation. A single household, for example, might require forty horses and more than one hundred servants, and spices were consumed in large quantities. Some of the costs, few of which would ever have been incurred by a peasant, are given below.

Household item	Cost
Bonnet	16d.
Candlewax	5d. per pound
Cloth cloak	3s. 4d.
Fowler	3s. 4d. per week
Fur coverlet	£20
Hunting bow	2s. 4d.
Hunting falcon	£5–10
Huntsman	7 1/2d. per day
Lady's gold girdle	£37. 12s.
Minstrel	12d. per day
Pack of hounds	£100 per year
Saddle horse	£5–27
Stockings	4s. the pair
War horse	£40–80
Spices and delicacies (per pound)	
Almonds (5 pounds)	1s.
Anise	3d.
Black pepper	10d.–2s.
Cloves	3d.
Cumin	2d.–10d.
Ginger	10d.–2s.6d.
Horseradish	3d.
Nutmeg	3d.
Pomegranates	6d. each
Rice	1 1/2d.
Saffron	10s.–14s.
Sugar	1s.–2s.

Source: Figures abstracted from John Burnett, *A History of the Cost of Living* (Harmondsworth: Pelican Books, 1969), pp. 31, 34–35, 37.

Medieval Society: The Village

In the High Middle Ages, 90 percent of all Europeans lived in villages and engaged directly in agriculture. They were not exclusively occupied with farming; many people had special skills that brought in supplementary income. Most communities could boast millers, carpenters, brewers, seamstresses, harness makers, blacksmiths, midwives, and other specialists, but these people also worked in the fields as needed and frequently held land in their own right. The wealthier peasants were more likely to have a trade than were their poorer neighbors, for a trade required skills as well as a substantial investment in tools or equipment.

The physical environment of medieval villages varied widely. The heart of a larger village was the parish church, which by the twelfth century was almost always of masonry construction. Timber churches continued to survive in northwest England, parts of Germany, and Scandinavia, but their numbers were declining. Lords frequently built or improved village churches as an act of piety and to increase their family's prestige. Some of them were, and are, architectural gems. Their cost was borne ultimately by the peasants in the form of dues and tithes, but the church was at least a form of expenditure that the villagers could enjoy. It was usually the only substantial building in the community unless the lord maintained a residence there.

The character of domestic architecture was determined by the availability of building materials and by the structure of families. In southern Europe, where timber had been scarce since biblical times, brick or stone construction was the rule. Peasant houses were sometimes large, having been expanded at various times to accommodate an increase in family size. If the family subsequently grew smaller, the permanence of the building materials often precluded the demolition of all or part of the house. This helps to explain why Mediterranean villages often appear larger today than their census figures indicate. It may also have encouraged the formation of extended families by making free space available to newly married couples.

Thanks to their sturdy construction, many communities in Spain, Italy, and southern France have changed little since the Middle Ages. Existing knowledge of northern villages is the product of painstaking archeological reconstruction. The use of wattle and daub (interwoven twigs or rushes covered by mud) or other impermanent materials meant that peasant housing in England, northern France, the Low Countries, and north Germany was often good only for a generation or two. Entire villages sometimes moved to a different location for reasons of health or economic advantage, leaving nothing behind but rubble and the outlines of their foundations.

In the days of Charlemagne, many houses were made of solid wood or logs, a practice that became prohibitively expensive with the passage of time (see document 11.2). By the end of the eleventh century, a house in a northern village was typically framed in wood and composed of bays or sections added together, usually in a linear pattern (see illustration 11.5). Bays could be built or torn down as needed because the walls were so flimsy that thieves sometimes broke through them rather than bothering with the door. Such homes were inexpensive. Newlyweds had little difficulty in setting up a place of their own, and people often had cottages built for them in their old age to separate them from their grown children. Though some houses had lofts or attics, true second stories were rare. Windows were few, small, and covered with wooden shutters, while chimneys were introduced only at the end of the Middle Ages. At the center of the house was a raised hearth, the smoke from which typically exited through a hole in the thatched roof. Most people went to bed at nightfall and rose at dawn. Interior lighting was available in the form of candles if a family could afford them. As the floors were of swept earth covered with straw or rushes, the danger of fire was ever present.

In these circumstances, cleanliness was as hard to achieve as safety. The interior of a peasant home was inevitably dark and smoky. Though the marks of vigorously wielded medieval brooms are still visible in archaeological digs, housekeeping inevitably fell below modern standards. This was in part because people lived in close proximity with their livestock. Most peasant homes, north or south, possessed a yard or garden and even outbuildings. Animals were often housed in a separate bay or in an unused room of the house. In one-room cottages, livestock might share the living space with humans.

The yard, croft, or close was an integral part of the family's living space. It was basically a walled or fenced-in working area in which children and animals wandered at will, and great efforts were made to prevent its disorder from invading the sleeping quarters. Drainage ditches and thresholds were the best defense, but muddy feet and wandering livestock were an inevitable part of the farmer's world. Dusting, however, was not. Most homes contained no furniture beyond the pallets on which people slept; their blankets, which were sometimes used as wraps in winter; and their cooking

The Timber Problem in Medieval Europe

In 1140 Suger, abbot of Saint-Denis (near Paris), decided to construct a new church that would require twelve thirty-five-foot beams. His experience in a landscape virtually denuded of large trees indicates how serious the problem of adequate timber supplies had become.

On a certain night, when I had returned from Matins, I began to think in bed that I myself should go through all the forests of these parts. . . . Quickly disposing of all duties and hurrying up in the early morning, we hastened with our carpenters, and with the measurements of the beams, to the forest called Ivelines. When we traversed our possession in the Valley of Chevreuse we summoned . . . the keepers of our own forests as well as men who know about the other woods, and questioned them under oath whether we would find there, no matter with how much trouble, any timbers of that measure. At this they smiled, or rather would have laughed at us if they had dared; they wondered whether we were quite ignorant of the fact that nothing of the kind could be found in the entire region, especially since Milon, the Castellan of Chevreuse . . . had left nothing unimpaired or untouched that could be used for palisades and bulwarks while he was long subjected to wars both by our Lord the King and Amaury de Montfort. We however—scorning what they might say—began with the courage of our faith as it were, to search the woods; and toward the first hour we found one timber adequate to our measure. Why say more? By the ninth hour or sooner, we had, through the thickets, the depths of the forest and the dense, thorny tangles, marked down twelve timbers (for so many were necessary) to the astonishment of all.

Panovsky, Erwin, trans. and ed. *Abbot Suger, on the Abbey Church of St. Denis*. Princeton, NJ: Princeton University Press, 1973.

Illustration 11.5

▨ **A Peasant Cottage in Winter.** This depiction of a peasant cottage is from the *Tres riches heures* of the Duc de Berry by Paul, Herman, and Jean Limbourg (1413–16). The beehives, the number of animals in the close, and even the dresses of the women indicate that this was a wealthy household. The magnificent prayer book from which this illustration comes was intended to provide an idealized view of rural life.

This material simplicity extended to purely personal possessions as well. Like the lord in his hall, the peasant ate with his fingers and a knife. Stews and gruels were served from a wooden bowl or straight from the pot and eaten with wooden spoons. Soups were often drunk. Among the rich, a piece of coarse bread served as a plate for meat and was ideally given to the poor after it had absorbed the juices of the meal. On special occasions, the wealthy might eat from wooden trenchers. Even at formal banquets, two people might be expected to share a plate, a custom that sometimes contributed violence to the day's entertainment.

Clothing, for the peasant, consisted of little more than a homespun smock, leggings, and perhaps a hat for men, and a simple smock or dress for women. Shoes were normally reserved for bad weather. Until the late fourteenth century, peasants who could afford to do otherwise appear to have ignored the dictates of fashion. Most people seem to have owned only one set of working clothes and another outfit of better quality for

utensils. Castles and manor houses might contain a bedstead for the lord and cupboards for the storage of leftovers. Chairs were rare enough to be considered symbols of royalty. Much of medieval life was lived on the floor.

◈ DOCUMENT 11.3 ◈

A Peasant Family in the Fields

The following excerpt from Peres the Plowman's Crede, *a long English poem by William Langland (c. 1330–c. 1400), provides a heartbreaking glimpse of peasant life.*

And as I went by the way, weeping for sorrow
I saw a poor man o'er the plow bending,
His coat was of a cloth that cary was called
His hood was full of holes and his hair seen
through it.
With his shoes so worn and patched very thick
His toes pushed through as the fields he trod.
His hose o'erhung his gaiters all about
And he dragged in the mud as the plow he
followed.
Two mittens had he, skimpy, made of rags,
The fingers uncovered and coated with mud.
This poor creature, beslimed in the mud almost to
the ankle,
Four oxen before him, that feeble had become,
One might count the ribs, so pitiful they were.
Beside him his wife, with a long goad.
In a cutted skirt, cutted full high;
Wrapped in a winnowing sheet, to guard her from
weather,
Barefoot on bare ice, so that the blood flowed.
And at the field's end lay a little basket
And therein a little child, covered in rags,
And twins of two years old upon another side.
And they all sang a song that was sorrow to hear,
They all cried a cry, a note full of woe—
The poor man sighed sore, and said "Children
be still!"

Langland, William. *Peres the Ploughman's Crede,* trans.
D. Resnick. In L. F. Schaefer et al., eds., *The Shaping of Western Civilization.* New York: Holt, Rinehart, and Winston, 1970.

or hired laborers as needed. They were more likely than poorer peasants to own draft animals and to graze livestock on the village common. If they were careful in planning their marriages or were able to form a business relationship with the lord or his steward they could become as wealthy as minor nobles. Their families tended to be larger than those of the poor and their houses were often substantial.

Perhaps the largest group in any community were smallholders whose land was insufficient to support their families, but who supplemented their earnings by leasing additional fields, practicing a trade, or engaging in occasional labor in return for food or wages. They usually had their own house and garden, and they might keep poultry or a hog. Below them on the economic scale were landless laborers whose situation was often precarious. Numbering perhaps a quarter of the community, they were dependent upon charity in hard times and sometimes resorted to petty theft. Small-scale pilfering was a common income supplement for other classes as well. Slavery, though still common in the cities of southern Europe, disappeared in the north and in rural areas during the twelfth century.

Social movement was extremely limited. The evolution of nobility as a social ideal opened an unbridgeable gap between the peasantry and those who bore arms. Wealthier peasants were sometimes able to place one of their children in the church, but even in this, the most egalitarian of medieval institutions, humble birth was a grave barrier to advancement. Within the narrow world of the village, wealth and social status could be increased through careful management, good marriage strategies, and luck. Over time, many families and a few individuals did so, but the pinnacle of ambition remained a place on the manorial court, control of a mill, or an appointment as one of the lord's stewards. Generally, the medieval villager had no choice other than to accept the status into which he or she had been born. To do otherwise would not only have been fruitless, it also would have run counter to the most cherished prejudices of an age in which stability was a paramount social goal.

Though stratified by wealth, the medieval village was a powerful, tightly knit social organism whose survival into modern times testifies to its adaptability. In size, it typically numbered between 250 and 500 inhabitants, with smaller villages being the more common. Many of its inhabitants were interrelated. However, the ecclesiastical prohibition against marrying one's relatives worked steadily against the pressures of isolation and an endemic distrust of strangers. People identified strongly with their village and tended to see it for what

church or festive occasions (see document 11.3). Both were washed when possible. Workday garments were worn until they fell apart. Children, once they were out of swaddling clothes, dressed like their parents.

Village society was stratified by wealth instead of by social class. The wealthier peasants held tenements or other lands on secure contracts. Such properties were often larger than they could work themselves, and they either sublet portions of their property to others it was: a community made up exclusively of peasants, which, after the family, was their chief protection against a hostile world.

Cooperation was therefore an essential feature of village life, though the relative wealth of individual peasants varied immensely. At the very least, villagers had to maintain a united front in negotiating with outside forces that might pose a threat to their prosperity—their lord, the church, a city, or a neighboring village whose inhabitants tried to encroach on their lands or rights. If peasants seemed wily, grasping, and suspicious to outsiders it was because the outsiders were often trying to detach the peasants from their wealth.

Internally, some measure of cooperation was essential to the peasants' daily pursuits. In villages where the open field system was practiced, agricultural operations from plowing to harvesting were usually undertaken in common for efficiency's sake. In grazing areas, the rounding up and shearing of sheep was, and for the most part still is, a cooperative effort involving the entire population of the village. If the village possessed common lands, their use had to be regulated to prevent overexploitation, either by individuals or by the community as a whole. Peasants tended to be keenly aware of the limits of their local ecology and took great care to limit the number of animals that could be grazed on a particular parcel or the quantity of wood, nuts, and other products that could be harvested from woodlots. If the commons were planted to row crops, the land had to be allocated fairly. This was sometimes done on a customary basis. In Spain and in many other places allocation was often by lot.

The maintenance of what today would be called the village's infrastructure was also a community affair. The construction and repair of roads, bridges, and ditches may have been mandated by feudal obligation and was typically discharged by teams of peasants working in common. Villages were also capable of undertaking public improvements on their own. Private projects such as the construction or modification of a house or the digging of a drainage ditch around the close were usually undertaken with the help of friends or relatives. Such help was intended to be reciprocal. Labor exchanges were central to the peasant economy and are in themselves an extension of communal bonds.

Peasant communities also tried to control the social behavior of their inhabitants. The more prosperous villagers often sat on manorial courts that judged minor disputes within the village. Where the influence of the lord was weak, such matters might be dealt with by a council of village elders. The selection of village leaders, including those who supervised communal labor and the allocation of common lands, remains something of a mystery. Some may have been elected. In most places they seem to have been chosen through an informal process of consensus building that avoided the confrontation of a vote.

Criminals were apprehended by what the English called a hue and cry, in which every able-bodied man was supposed to give chase if a crime were committed. This could be dangerous and was uncommon. Most villages were relatively peaceful, in part because everyone knew everyone else's business. Privacy, as in the towns, was unknown and probably would have been impossible to achieve. If an individual's behavior ran counter to prevailing local standards, he or she would be subjected to ridicule and abuse that in extreme cases might make life insupportable. In general, public opinion was a more powerful instrument of social control than courts or the bailiff.

The Peasant Family

The structure of medieval family life varied immensely according to location, social class, and individual preference. It also varied over time as individual households adjusted to economic change and to the life cycles of their members. As a general rule, wealthier households were larger than those of the poor.

In northern Europe, the nuclear family predominated, at least among peasants. A married couple and their children lived together, rarely sharing their space with other relatives. When children married, they left the home and established a household of their own. Old people tried to maintain their independence as long as they could. The wasting diseases of old age were not prolonged as they are today by the miracles of modern medicine. If someone grew feeble or senile, they sometimes moved in with one of their grown children. That the elderly often preferred to board with another villager is a tribute to the relative weakness of kinship ties. Such an arrangement usually involved the transfer of land or other payments.

The nuclear family was also the most common form of household organization in Mediterranean Europe, but extended families in which adult siblings and grandparents lived under the same roof were not unusual. Many others lived as nuclear units in close proximity to their relatives and acted in common with them when necessary. Such behavior indicates that kinship obligations were more broadly defined than they were in the north. The phenomenon is probably related to the concept of the *domus*, or house, as a basic component of family identity.

In the north, the idea of family as a lineage group associated with a particular estate was largely restricted to the feudal aristocracy. The continuing presence of allodial land and the relative weakness of feudal ties in Mediterranean society extended the concept to relatively humble folk, though rarely to the very poor. In its extreme forms—the Catalan *masia*, for example—the name of the family, the stone house in which it lived, and the property upon which it was located were the same. The prevalence of family names among the more prosperous peasants reveals the degree to which *domus* was associated with family in a given region. In Italy, family names were well established in the twelfth century, while in England they did not become common among ordinary folk until after the Black Death. Those who did not own their own land could have adopted the custom in imitation of their social superiors, and with it the concept of familial obligation that it implies.

To southern Europeans with modest property and a name, the extended family was likely to be seen as a source of economic and social support. This created a sense of mutual obligation that many chose to ignore but that could be of great value in difficult times for those who did not. For them, the family was both a refuge and a protection against a hostile world. Some no doubt went further and agreed with Peter Lombard that those outside the family were *inimici*, or enemies. This, however, was a notion that disturbed jurists and helps to explain why the villages of Spain and Italy were as troubled by faction and vendetta as their cities.

The organization of all European families was typically patriarchal. Households dominated by widows have been recorded, as have phratries in which two or more brothers with their own nuclear families inhabited the same house. Such variants probably were family strategies adopted to meet specific conditions. Otherwise, the authority of the husband or father was universally recognized in law and custom. It was not an absolute authority over life and death and was typically modified by familial love, an emotion fully recognized by medieval writers from Augustine to Albertus Magnus. In extended families, the problem of authority was more complex. Decisions might sometimes require consensus, but one individual, usually a mature male characterized by greater wealth or force of character than the others, was generally acknowledged as the family's leader. This pattern was also found in the clientage groups that developed, as they had done in antiquity, from the economic or political success of prominent families.

The laws of inheritance had less to do with family organization than might be supposed. They, too, exhibit wide regional variations, but two main types emerged—partible and impartible. Partible inheritance provides equally for all heirs. It was a fundamental principle in Roman law and was far more common than its alternative, especially in continental Europe. Its chief disadvantage is that a multiplicity of holdings eventually results that are too small to support a family. Impartible inheritance leaves everything to a single heir. This preserves a family's estate while reducing most of its members to penury. Primogeniture, or exclusive inheritance by the eldest son, is the best known form of impartible inheritance, but in some peasant societies leaving everything to the youngest was the rule.

Everyone knew that partibility could impoverish and eventually destroy a family, while impartibility was grossly unfair and tended to destroy the family's bonds of affection. Many people therefore adopted strategies to circumvent the law or regional custom. Much of England, Scandinavia, and northern France had adopted primogeniture by the twelfth century. Bequeathing the bulk of a family's land to a single heir and making other provisions for noninheriting children while the parents were still alive became customary. A couple could also make special legacies in their wills that partially subverted the law's intent.

Where partibility was preferred, strategies varied widely. In Italy and southern France, siblings entered into a variety of arrangements (*consorterie* in Italian) that helped to preserve the integrity of the estate. Some sold or leased their portion to an elder brother in return for monetary or other considerations. Others agreed not to marry and remained on the family property. Such arrangements worked best when there was an extended family structure or, at the very least, a strong sense of family identity. In Castile, the practice of entailing parts of an estate on behalf of a single heir began as early as the thirteenth century. The grim alternatives were illustrated in places such as Galicia and parts of southwest Germany where partibility was strictly enforced. The inexorable subdivision of the land caused widespread misery among the peasants, while among the princely families of the empire it led to a bewildering proliferation of petty states.

Marriage

The proportion of married people in the medieval population was undoubtedly lower than it is today, but most people eventually married. In the peasant societies of

❧ TABLE 11.5 ❧

Average Age of Women at First Marriage

Most of the statistics in the following table are taken from sixteenth- and seventeenth-century sources because data were not compiled outside of Italy in the Middle Ages. They are probably a reasonable approximation of medieval figures because the age at which women married does not seem to have changed substantially in the preindustrial period. It did, however, fluctuate according to economic conditions, as the figures from Colyton, Elversele, and Amsterdam demonstrate. Note the disparity between the Florentine data and that from northern Europe.

Place	Time	Age
Amiens (France)	1674–78	25
Amsterdam	1626–27	25
	1676–77	27
Elversele (Flanders)	1608–49	25
	1650–59	27
England	1575–1624	21
Titled nobility	1625–75	22
Village of Colyton	1560–1646	27
	1647–1719	30
Florence	1351–1400	18
	1401–50	17
	1451–75	19

Source: Adapted from Carlo Cipolla, *Before the Industrial Revolution*, 2d. ed. (New York, N.Y.: W. W. Norton, 1980), p. 154.

northern Europe, this normally happened in the early or mid-twenties for both men and women, a pattern now regarded as the Western norm (see table 11.5). In southern Europe and among the upper classes, the custom was different. In Italy, husbands were on average seven to ten years older than their wives, and women were often married in their teens to men already in their thirties or older. The most extreme disparities were found in royal and princely families where marriages were used to cement political alliances and might be arranged when the bride was a mere child. Thankfully, such unions were not immediately consummated.

Freedom to choose one's mate was greatest at the lower end of the social scale. Arranged marriages were almost unknown among the landless poor, slightly more common among established peasants, and virtually obligatory among the rich. However, the wishes of the couple were not invariably ignored and even peasants did not marry as a general rule without seeking

their parents' blessing. Like almost everything else connected with the institution of marriage, a wedding was usually the product of delicate and informal negotiations involving the couple, both families, and the village opinion makers. The degree to which the couple controlled the process was determined by local custom and family attitudes and varied enormously within the same village or social class.

When a couple publicly announced their intention to marry, village opinion generally permitted them to begin living together immediately. This practice was officially confirmed by the church at the beginning of the thirteenth century. In villages without a resident priest, or when the costs of a wedding could not immediately be met, this was often essential. If a child was born before the sacrament of marriage could be officially celebrated, that child was legitimate. The assumption was that the couple would marry as soon as the opportunity arose. Townspeople, wealthy peasants, and the aristocracy could afford to be less relaxed about such matters and tended to celebrate their family weddings with as much ostentation as possible. Wedding feasts were as central to medieval social life and folklore as they are today.

When a medieval woman married, she was expected to present her husband with a dowry. The early medieval custom of giving the bride a husband's gift had largely disappeared by the end of the twelfth century. The dowry was normally returnable if the husband died first. While he lived, he controlled it and all of the other resources owned by the couple. In some regions, the return of the dowry was all that a widow could legally expect from her husband's estate. In others, she was entitled to at least a portion of his property. As in all other aspects of inheritance law, many husbands found ways to subvert the system and provide other legacies for her support.

The choice, though, was his. Married women had few legal rights. They could not hold property in their own name. Though they were not to be killed or permanently maimed they could be beaten with impunity, and domestic violence appears to have been even more frequent than it is today. In some jurisdictions, women could not testify in court. Where they could, their testimony was not equal to that of a man. However, legal status did not always reflect the balance of power in everyday life. No two relationships were, or are, the same, and medieval marriages ranged from the abusive to the happily companionate. Medieval people presumably did not enter into marriage with modern expectations. The idea of romantic love was not yet fully developed and, to the degree that it existed at all, was associated with the adulterous conventions of chivalry.

Practical considerations were more important in the selection of a mate. Property, strength, temperance, and, in the case of wives, the ability to bear children, were essential. The hope was that, given these virtues, *caritas* would find a place in the household and a genuine affection would develop with time.

Many of these ideas and practices were a departure from those of the early Middle Ages. The church had adopted marriage as its own in the days of the Cluniac and Hildebrandine reforms and, in spite of its own mysogynistic traditions, had greatly improved the condition of women as a result. Concubinage was condemned if not eradicated, as was feudal interference in the marriage of vassals and tenants. Divorce, a catastrophe for women who had no means of support, was virtually eliminated for all but the very rich. Canon law, confirmed by the Fourth Lateran Council of 1215, defined the terms under which a wedding might take place and spelled out the impediments that might prevent it. Most of them involved prohibited degrees of relationship or consanguinity, including godparenthood. As the regulations were strictly enforced by parish priests, they posed a considerable hardship for the inhabitants of remote villages.

These efforts can be seen as a positive step toward the development of patrilineal descent and companionate marriages, but they did not assure domestic bliss. Hostility between the sexes remained a common theme in medieval writings. Evidence is available that many women deeply resented their subordinate status. Beginning in the early thirteenth century, increasing numbers sought refuge in the convent, and widows frequently chose not to remarry. A woman who was past the age of childbearing and who could claim property of her own experienced an immediate change of status upon the death of her husband. With her legal and personal rights restored, she could become a powerful figure in the village community. Some, such as Chaucer's Wife of Bath, remarried, but they did so usually to a younger, poorer man who posed little threat to their independence. Companionship aside, only the poor suffered from widowhood. Without property, a woman might have to depend upon the kindness of her surviving children or become a semioutcast living on the charity of her neighbors.

Childhood, Old Age, and Death

In the natural law theories favored by the scholastic philosophers, the birth of children was the justification for marriage. A medieval child was brought into the world by the village midwife and baptized as quickly as possible, lest the terrible infant mortality of the day carry it into Limbo before its salvation was assured. So deep was this concern that the sacrament could be administered by a layman if no priest were available. Godparents, usually family friends, were designated to support the child if its parents should die. In southern Europe this role was sometimes given to a powerful friend or patron of the father. The baby was typically named for one of the godparents, a favored relative, or a patron saint. This practice, together with the limited number of names in contemporary use, sometimes resulted in more than one sibling having the same name. In everyday life, such children were differentiated by the appellations major or minor or by nicknames.

If possible, most women preferred to nurse their own babies. Infants were typically swaddled during the day. At night they sometimes slept with their mothers, though this practice was frowned upon because the mother might roll over in her sleep and smother the child. By the end of the first year children were permitted to crawl about on their own.

Medieval parents did not sentimentalize childhood as a world of innocence, but they loved their children and were emotionally affected by their loss. This would seem self-evident, but it has been the subject of a scholarly controversy. Parents also permitted their children to develop in stages that were not unlike those of today. Young children spent most of their time playing. As they grew older and stronger they took on responsibility for various tasks until, in their mid-to-late teens, they began to do the work of adults. For most children, this kind of informal apprenticeship was the only education that they would receive. Few villages had a school, and lords often claimed a fee from the parents for sending their children away. Fearing that workers would be lost to the manor, they also sought agreements that forbade children to enter the church.

The little that is known about child rearing practices comes from the end of the Middle Ages and seems to indicate that discipline was very harsh. This may not be applicable to earlier times. The fourteenth and fifteenth centuries were characterized by a deep fear of social disintegration and the perceived decline of parental authority. Criminals were punished more savagely than they had been before. Children, too, may have been increasingly victimized by the frustrations of society as a whole.

As efforts to circumvent the laws of inheritance indicate, every attempt was made to provide for a child's future. This included the possibility of orphanhood, which was not uncommon in a world of high mortality. Godparents were nominally responsible for the care of children whose parents had died. The task was more often undertaken by aunts, uncles, or other relatives. Stepparenting was also common because men, at least, tended to remarry upon the death of their wives. This created a form of extended family that has once again become common as a result of divorce. Legends about wicked stepmothers indicate that the new relationships were often difficult for all concerned. However, stepparents who loved their spouse's children as their own were common enough to be accepted as the ideal.

Wardship in any form created problems because children were sometimes financially or sexually exploited by their guardians. A substantial body of case law developed around these issues. Orphanages as such were unknown until the fourteenth century when foundling hospitals were opened in several Italian towns. The work of these institutions is not to be confused with oblation, in which children were given to the church by placing them in monastic houses at an early age. Such placements required a substantial donation. For the rich it was an effective means of providing a living for children without encumbering the family estate. The practice fell into disfavor during the twelfth and thirteenth centuries when churchmen began to realize that those consigned to a monastery or convent at the age of seven did not necessarily have a secure vocation.

The available evidence seems to indicate that medieval attitudes toward children were not radically different from those of today. Noble families sent their sons to learn courtesy and the profession of arms in the household of a powerful friend or patron. Townsmen sent their children to be apprenticed, and those who could afford to do so offered them to the church at an early age. None of these practices implied indifference. They were in some ways analogous to sending a child to boarding school, and the normal expectation was that contact with the family would be maintained or, at least, resumed at some point in the future.

Medieval attitudes toward death are less familiar. They were conditioned by the realization that life was likely to be short and by the universal belief in a hereafter. Death was seen in Christian terms as a transition. The preservation of life, though an important value, was not the all-consuming passion that it was later to become, in part because the soul was meant to live eternally. This was why heresy was thought by most jurists to be worse than murder. It killed the soul, whereas murder killed only that which was destined in any case to perish.

People tried to live as long as possible, but they also hoped to make a "good death." They knew that the means of preserving life indefinitely in the face of disease or injury were severely limited, and they were deeply concerned for the future of their souls. When the end drew near, they prepared themselves with prayer, pious reflections, and the last rites of the church. Suffering was regarded as a trial sent by God, to be born with patience and Christian fortitude. Above all, they hoped to die with dignity, because death, like so many other aspects of medieval life, was a public affair. Medieval people wanted to die in their own beds, surrounded by family, friends, and neighbors who could ease their passage to a better world. Most of them appear to have succeeded. Hospitals were few and were intended for travelers, the homeless, and other unfortunates. The injured, if possible, were carried to their homes, and a priest was called if one were available. Not everyone died well, but edifying deathbed scenes were by no means uncommon and few people reached adulthood without having been present at a number of them. In a sense, death was a part of everyday experience.

Burial was in the churchyard. It, too, was a communal experience because space was limited and an understandable reluctance existed to use good agricultural land as cemeteries. Archaeological digs reveal that bodies were often buried several layers deep. The dead slept as they had lived, in close proximity to their friends and relatives with no monument to mark their passing. The wealthy, as in so many other things, were the exception. Their graves were marked, increasingly decorated by their effigies, and located indoors, either within the parish church or in a separate crypt. Husband and wife were typically portrayed together; he in his armor, she in court attire. In the later Middle Ages, humility of a sort set in and tombs were sometimes adorned with effigies of corpses or skeletons (see illustration 11.6), but the idea of the grave as a memorial to the deceased remained.

Medieval society differed in almost every respect from that of the modern industrial world. The basic conditions of material life had changed little since the Neolithic revolution and would remain relatively constant until the industrial revolution. Social behavior, however, was influenced by feudal and Christian values that had been unknown to the ancients. Those values achieved gradual acceptance in the early Middle Ages but would, at least among the privileged, undergo substantial modification in the centuries after the Black Death. The breakdown of the feudal system and the intellectual upheavals of the sixteenth and seventeenth

Illustration 11.6

A Cadaver Effigy of Sir John Golafre (d. 1442) at Fyfield Church, England. Another fully clad effigy of Sir John appears on the bier immediately above the cadaver effigy pictured here.

centuries profoundly altered the behavior and self-image of the upper classes. The lives of peasants changed more slowly. Without mass communication to inform them of changes in learning or fashion, they remained immersed in the demands of an agricultural routine that was much the same in the eighteenth century as it had been five hundred years earlier. The castle, in other words, was eventually transformed, but the village remained largely intact until industrialization altered the material conditions on which it was based.

For some, conditions may have grown worse with the passage of time. The lives of most Europeans in the twelfth and thirteenth centuries were simple and, by modern standards, hard, but society was more secure than it had been for many centuries. Wars were either limited or far away, and famines were rare. The activities of ordinary men and women, like the great intellectual and architectural triumphs of the age, reveal a certain confidence in the world's predictability and a willingness to build for the future. Yet society in the later thirteenth century was beginning to show signs of stress. There seemed to be too many people. They still ate, but poverty and landlessness were increasing. Wealthy people began to build moats around their houses to protect them from their neighbors, while moralists lamented the passing of a golden age. The following century would show that the moralists were in a sense correct: The relative balance of social and economic forces that characterized the High Middle Ages was giving way to conditions that people of all classes would find profoundly troubling.

CHAPTER 12

PLAGUE, WAR, AND SOCIAL CHANGE IN THE "LONG" FOURTEENTH CENTURY

CHAPTER OUTLINE

The transition from medieval to early modern times is generally thought to have begun in the fourteenth century when economic decline, plague, and endemic warfare weakened the bonds of feudal society and undermined its values. Great historical transformations rarely limit themselves to the confines of a single century, and this one was no exception. Thinking, therefore, in terms of a "long" fourteenth century is helpful; that is, of an extended period of demographic, social, and political stress that in some of its manifestations lasted until well into the fifteenth century and beyond.

Famine, Economic Decline, and the Black Death (1315–50)

The fourteenth century was marked by a series of economic and demographic crises that had a profound effect on the social structure of Europe. Local crises of subsistence became common and, for the first time in two centuries, a large-scale famine struck northern Europe in 1315–17 (see document 12.1). Southern Europe suffered a similar catastrophe in 1339–40. Overpopulation was the underlying cause. By 1300 only the cultivation of marginal soils could feed the ever-growing populace. A succession of bad harvests brought on by unusually cold, wet weather made these lands virtually unusable and destroyed the ecological balance between the people and their food supply. The result was widespread misery and an end to population growth. Scarcity pushed the price of bread to levels that only the rich could afford. Desperate peasants ate their seed grain, thereby destroying all hope for a harvest in the year to come. Others ate leaves, bark, and rats. Though adult deaths from malnutrition were probably rare, the demographic impact of the famine was seen in a declining rate of conception and increased infant mortality.

◈ DOCUMENT 12.1 ◈

The Famine of 1315 in England

This dramatic account of the famine is from the English chronicler Johannes de Trokelowe. The prices may be compared with those given for the preceding century in document 11.1.

Meat and eggs began to run out, capons and fowl could hardly be found, animals died of pest, swine could not be fed because of the excessive price of fodder. A quarter of wheat or beans or peas sold for twenty shillings, barley for a mark, oats for ten shillings. A quarter of salt was commonly sold for thirty-five shillings, which in former times was quite unheard of. The land was so oppressed with want that when the king came to St. Albans on the feast of St. Lawrence [August 10] it was hardly possible to find bread on sale to supply his immediate household. . . .

The dearth began in the month of May and lasted until the nativity of the Virgin [September 8]. The summer rains were so heavy that grain could not ripen. It could hardly be gathered and used to make bread down to the said feast day unless it was first put in vessels to dry. Around the end of autumn the dearth was mitigated in part, but toward Christmas it became as bad as before. Bread did not have its usual nourishing power and strength because the grain was not nourished by the warmth of summer sunshine. Hence those who had it, even in large quantities, were hungry again after a little while. There can be no doubt that the poor wasted away when even the rich were constantly hungry. . . .

Four pennies worth of coarse bread was not enough to feed a common man for one day. The usual kinds of meat, suitable for eating, were too scarce; horse meat was precious; plump dogs were stolen. And according to many reports, men and women in many places secretly ate their own children.

Trokelowe, Johannes. "*Annales*," trans. Brian Tierney. In Brian Tierney, ed., *Sources of Medieval History,* 4th ed. New York: Knopf, 1983.

branch failed it created a domino effect that might bring down the entire structure. This happened in 1343 when the two leading Florentine banks—the Bardi and the Peruzzi—failed, setting off a widespread financial panic. The immediate cause of their failure was the repudiation of war debts by a major borrower, Edward III of England, but both banks had been gravely weakened before the final blow.

The Black Death struck in 1347–51. Endemic in Asia since the eleventh century, the disease first entered Europe through the Mediterranean ports and spread with terrifying speed throughout the subcontinent. Following the trade routes it reached Paris in the summer of 1348, Denmark and Norway in 1349, and Russia in 1351. Estimates are that within four years a third of the population of Europe died. It was the greatest demographic catastrophe in European history, and its ravages did not end with the first virulent outbreak. Subsequent epidemics occurred regularly in every decade until the beginning of the eighteenth century. Given that immunity apparently cannot be transmitted from generation to generation, the plague served as a long-term check on population growth, and most countries required more than two centuries to recover the population levels they had in 1300 (see table 12.1).

The relationship, if any, between the plague and poverty or malnutrition is unclear. In its most common form, bubonic plague is spread by fleas, which are carried by rats and other small mammals. A pneumonic form of the plague is spread by coughing. The onset of either form is rapid, and death usually comes within three days (see illustration 12.1). The mortality rate seems to have been about the same for all who contracted the disease, so that lowered resistance as a result of malnutrition likely did not play an important part in its spread. At the same time, death came most frequently to those who lived in crowded conditions. Soldiers, ship's crews, and the urban poor were at greatest risk, followed by those country folk whose poverty forced them to huddle together in their one-room cottages for warmth. The rich often escaped, either because they lived in more sanitary conditions or because, like the characters in Giovanni Boccaccio's *Decameron,* they had the means to flee from the centers of population (see document 12.2).

No one knew what caused the plague. Most probably believed that it was a visitation from God and took refuge in prayer and religious ceremonies. Flagellants paraded from town to town, beating each other with metal-tipped scourges in the hope of averting God's wrath, while preachers demanded the reform of the

Predictably, trade declined. Defaults on loans increased, and the banking system came under stress. The great international banks still controlled their branches directly and had unlimited liability for their losses. If a

❧ TABLE 12.1 ❧

Indices of Population Increase in Europe, 1000–1950

The data presented in this table show the dramatic effects of the Black Death as well as the substantial increases in the European population between 1150 and 1250 and between 1400 and 1450. The indices are based on the figures for 100 (that is 1000 = 100). These figures are estimates only and have proved controversial.

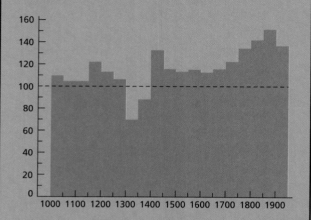

Indices per period of fifty years

Period	Index	Period	Index
1000–50	109.5	1500–50	113.0
1050–1100	104.3	1550–1600	114.1
1100–50	104.2	1600–50	112.4
1150–1200	122.0	1650–1700	115.0
1200–50	113.1	1700–50	121.7
1250–1300	105.8	1750–1800	134.3
1300–50	69.9	1800–50	141.5
1350–1400	88.2	1850–1900	150.8
1400–50	133.3	1900–50	136.7
1450–1500	115.0		

Source: B. H. Slicher van Bath, *The Agrarian History of Western Europe, A.D. 500–1800,* trans. Olive Ordish (London: Edward Arnold, 1963), p. 79.

◈ DOCUMENT 12.2 ◈

The Symptoms of the Plague

A description of the Black Death survives from one of the greatest of the late medieval writers. In 1348–53 Giovanni Boccaccio, who would later become a founder of Renaissance humanism (see chapter 13), wrote the Decameron, a series of stories told in a villa outside Florence where a group of fashionable young people take refuge from the plague. The book begins with a description of the epidemic.

In the year of our Lord 1348, there happened at Florence, the finest city in all Italy, a most terrible plague; which, whether owing to the influence of the planets, or that it was sent from God as a just punishment for our sins, had broken out some years before in the Levant, and after passing from place to place, and making incredible havoc all the way, had now reached the west. There, in spite of all the means that art and human foresight could suggest, such as keeping the city free from filth, the exclusion of all suspected persons, and the publication of copious instructions for the preservation of health; and not withstanding manifold humble supplications offered to God in processions and otherwise; it began to show itself in the aforesaid year, and in a sad and wonderful manner. Unlike what had been seen in the east, where bleeding from the nose is the fatal prognostic, here there appeared certain tumors in the groin or under the armpits, some as big as a small apple, others as an egg; and afterwards purple spots in most parts of the body; in some cases large and but few in number, in others smaller and more numerous—both sorts the usual messengers of death. To the cure of this malady, neither medical knowledge nor the power of drugs was of any effect; whether because the disease was in its own nature mortal, or that the physicians (the number of whom, taking quacks and women pretenders into the account, was grown very great) could form no just idea of the cause, nor consequently devise a true method of cure; whichever was the reason, few escaped; but nearly all died the third day from the first appearance of the symptoms, some sooner, some later, without any fever or accessory symptoms.

Boccaccio, Giovanni. "The Decameron." In Stories of *Boccaccio,* p. 1, trans. John Payne. London: The Bibliophilist Society, 1903.

Illustration 12.1

The Burial of Plague Victims at Tournai, 1349. Tournai is located in what is now Belgium. Similar scenes of mass burial were replayed throughout Europe during the plague years. As the death toll increased, attempts to provide coffins and individual funerals had to be abandoned. The overwhelmed survivors could only dump the bodies in mass graves.

church on the theory that its increasing interest in secular affairs had provoked divine retribution. Some have argued that the plague created a genuine and long-lasting demand for spiritual renewal. However, other, more sinister results were evident as well. In parts of Germany whole communities of Jews were burned alive because they were thought to have spread the disease by poisoning wells.

The Economic Consequences of the Black Death

The psychological effects of the Black Death would have a profound impact on religious belief, but its material consequences were equally dramatic (see table 12.2). Demographic collapse relieved pressure on the land. Food prices dropped immediately. Land values and rents followed close behind, declining by 30 to 40 percent in most parts of Europe between 1350 and 1400. For landholders, both lay and religious, this was a serious loss; for ordinary men and women, it was a windfall. Stunned by the horror they had experienced, the survivors found not only that food was cheaper and land more abundant, but also that most of them had inherited varying amounts of property from their dead relatives.

The delicate ecological balance of the thirteenth century no longer existed. Acreage could be diverted to pursuits that were less efficient in purely nutritional terms, but more profitable and less labor intensive. Fields were converted to pasture for grazing sheep and cattle. Marginal lands in Germany and elsewhere reverted to forest where hogs could root at will and where the next generation of peasants could presumably find

⬧ TABLE 12.2 ⬧

Population, Prices, and Wages in England, 1300–1500

The information presented in this graph shows the relationship of agricultural prices, industrial wages and prices, and population in the century and a half following the Black Death. After dramatic rises during the crises of 1315–17 and in the decade of the 1360s, agricultural prices remained fairly steady until the 1530s. The graph is much simplified, and the index numbers are based on prices, wages, and population in 1300.

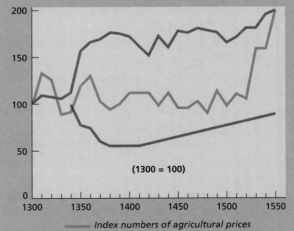

(1300 = 100)

— Index numbers of agricultural prices
— Index numbers of industrial prices and wages
— Index numbers of English population figures

Source: E. Perroy, "Les crises du XIVe siècle," *Annales*, vol. 4 (1949): pp. 167–82, as adapted in B. H. Slicher van Bath, *The Agrarian History of Western Europe, A.D. 500–1800*, trans. Olive Ordish (London: Edward Arnold, 1963), p. 139.

cheap firewood and building material. A larger percentage of the grain crop was devoted to the brewing of beer, and, in the south, vineyards spread over hillsides upon which in earlier times people had sought to grow food. If the prosperity of Europeans may be measured by their consumption of meat and alcohol, these were comfortable years. Some historians have referred to the period after the Black Death as the golden age of European peasantry. It did not last long.

For most people, calorie and protein consumption undoubtedly improved. Wages, too, increased, because the plague created a labor shortage of unprecedented severity. In Italy, employers tried to compensate by purchasing slaves from the Balkans or from dealers in the region of the Black Sea. This expedient was temporary and not successful. Before 1450 Turkish expansion brought an end to the trade, and although the Portuguese imported African slaves throughout the fifteenth century, they for the most part remained in Portugal. The handful of Africans who served the households of the very rich made no impact on the labor market. Wages remained high, and many people were able for the first time to leave their ancestral homes in search of better land or higher pay. Hundreds of communities were abandoned completely. Such movements cannot be accurately traced, but the century after 1350 appears to have been a time of extraordinary mobility in which the traditional isolation of village life diminished greatly.

These developments provoked a reaction from the propertied classes. Caught between rising wages and declining rents they faced a catastrophic reduction in their incomes. With the passage of time, some eased the situation by turning to such cash crops as wool or wine. Their initial response was to seek legislation that would freeze wages and restrict the movement of peasants. Between 1349 and 1351, virtually every European government tried to fix wages and prices (see document 12.3). For the most part, their efforts produced only resistance.

The failure of such measures led to strategies based upon the selective modification of feudal agreements. New restrictions were developed and long-forgotten obligations were revived. Southwest Germany provides some instructive examples. Peasants subject to one lord were often forbidden to marry the subject of another. If they did so, their tenures would revert to the husband's lord after the couple's death. As population movements had created a situation in which few subjects of the same lord inhabited the same village, this practically guaranteed the wholesale confiscation of peasant estates. At the same time, peasants were denied access to

◈ DOCUMENT 12.3 ◈

The Statute of Laborers

Issued by Edward III of England in 1351, this is a typical example of legislation designed to restrict the increase in labor costs created by the Black Death.

The King to the sheriff of Kent, greetings; Because a great part of the people, and especially of working men and servants, have lately died of the pestilence, many seeing the necessity of masters and great scarcity of servants, will not serve unless they may receive excessive wages, and others preferring to beg in idleness rather than by labor to get their living; we, considering the grievous incommodities which of the lack especially of ploughmen and such laborers may hereafter become, have upon deliberation and treaty with the prelates and the nobles and the learned men assisting us, with their unanimous counsel ordained:

That every man and woman of our realm of England, of what condition he be, free or bond, able in body, and within the age of sixty years, not living in merchandise, nor exercising any craft, nor having of his own whereof he may live, nor land of his own about whose tillage he may occupy himself, and not serving any other; if he be required to serve in suitable service, his estate considered, he shall be bound to serve him which shall so require him; and take only the wages, livery, meed, or salary which were accustomed to be given in the places where he oweth to serve, the twentieth year of our reign of England [that is, in 1347], or five or six other common years next before.

The Statute of Laborers. From *Pennsylvania Translations and Reprints*, vol. 2, no. 5, trans. Edward P. Cheyney. Philadelphia: University of Pennsylvania Press, 1897.

the forests, whose game, wood, nuts, and berries were reserved for the landholders. These forest laws created enormous hardships and were similar in their effects to the enclosure of common lands by the English gentry a century later. Peasants who depended upon these resources for firewood and for a supplement to their diet might be driven from the land.

When such measures failed to raise enough money, landholders were often forced to sell part of their holdings to investors. If the land in question was held in fief, the permission of the liege lord was usually required and could be secured by a cash payment or in return for political favors. Some of the buyers were merchants, lawyers, or servants of the crown who wanted the status provided by a country estate. Others were simply landholders who sought to consolidate their holdings at bargain rates. In either case the purchase of land tended to eliminate feudal obligations in fact and sometimes in law. The new owners had no personal ties to the peasants on their newly acquired estates and felt free to exploit their property as efficiently as possible. The net effect was to accelerate the shift toward private ownership of land that had begun with the commutation of feudal dues in the twelfth and thirteenth centuries.

Princes, too, were affected by the drop in land values. Medieval rulers drew the bulk of their ordinary revenues from exploiting their domains. Domain revenue came from a variety of dues, rights, and privileges, as well as from rents, which were an important part of the whole. Most princes were happy to make common cause with the other great landholders or to compensate for their losses by levying new taxes.

Social Disorder from the Jacqueries to the Bundschuh Revolts

Attempts to reverse the economic trends set in motion by the plague created widespread discontent. In 1358, much of northern France rose in a bloody revolt called the Jacquerie (Jacques Bonhomme being more-or-less the French equivalent of John Doe). Peasants attacked the castles of their lords in one of the worst outbreaks of social violence in centuries. There was no program, no plan—only violence born of sheer desperation. In this case peasant distress was greatly aggravated by that portion of the Hundred Years' War that had ended with the French defeat at Poitiers in 1356. The countryside was devastated, and the peasants were taxed to pay the ransoms of the king and his aristocratic followers who had been captured by the English on the battlefield.

Other revolts grew less from poverty than from the frustration of rising expectations. The English revolt of 1381, known as Wat Tyler's Rebellion in memory of one of its leaders, was triggered by the imposition of a poll or head tax on every individual. The rebels saw it as regressive, meaning it fell heavier on the poor than on the rich, and as a threat to the economic gains achieved since the plague. In Germany the exactions of princes and landholders, including the clergy, provoked a series of rebellions that flared periodically throughout the fifteenth century and culminated in the great Peas-

ant Revolt of 1524–25. These are generally referred to as the *bundschuh* revolts after the laced boots that served as a symbol of peasant unity.

Much urban unrest also was in evidence, but its relationship to the plague and its aftermath is unclear. The overall volume of European trade declined after 1350, which was offset to some extent by continuing strength in the market for manufactured and luxury items. A more equitable distribution of wealth broadened the demand for clothing, leather goods, and various furnishings, while the rich, in an apparent effort to maintain their status in the face of economic threats, indulged in luxuries on an unprecedented scale. The trade in manufactured articles, though smaller in total than it had been in the thirteenth century, was therefore larger in proportion to the trade in bulk agricultural commodities. It was also more profitable. Towns, now considerably smaller, seem to have enjoyed a certain measure of prosperity throughout the period.

Their political balance, however, was changed by the new importance of manufacturing. Craft guilds and the artisans they represented were generally strengthened at the expense of the urban patriciate, whose rents were greatly reduced in value. The process was not entirely new. The Flemish cloth towns of Ghent, Bruges, and Ypres had been the scene of periodic revolts for a century before 1350, and outbreaks continued for years thereafter. By 1345 the guilds had triumphed, at least in Flanders, but this in itself failed to create tranquility. The patriciate refused to accept exclusion from the government, and various factions among the guilds fought among themselves to achieve supremacy. Given the chronic discontent among the mass of laborers, most of whom were not guild members and therefore disenfranchised, riots were easy to incite almost regardless of the cause. The disturbances in the German towns of Braunschweig (1374) and Lübeck (1408) were apparently of similar origin. Political factions were able to mobilize popular discontent in the service of their own, decidedly nonpopular, interests.

The revolts of 1382 in Paris and Rouen appear to have been more spontaneous and closer in spirit to the rural uprisings of the same period, but the seizure of Rome by Cola di Rienzi in May 1347 was unique. Demanding a return to the ancient Roman form of government, he raised a great mob and held the city for seven months under the title of Tribune. The whole episode remains the subject of historical controversy. It was related to the absence of the pope at Avignon (see chapter 14). The departure of the papal court in 1305 had wrecked the Roman economy and placed the city's government in the hands of such old aristocratic families as the Orsini and the Colonna. Popular dissatisfaction kept the city in turmoil for several years even after Rienzi was forced into exile.

The revolt of the Florentine *Ciompi* in 1378 was the culmination of thirty years of civic strife. The depression of 1343 had led the *popolo grasso* (literally, fat people) to betray their city's republican traditions by introducing a despot who would, they hoped, control the population. The subsequent revolt led to a government dominated by the minor, craft-oriented guilds and to the incorporation of the semiskilled woolcarders (*ciompi*) into a guild of their own. In 1378 the Ciompi seized control of the city and introduced a popular and democratic form of government that lasted until the great merchants of the city hired a mercenary army to overthrow it in 1382.

Few of these rebellions, urban or rural, had clearly developed aims, and none of them resulted in permanent institutional changes beneficial to the rebels. For the most part, the privileged classes found them easy to suppress. The wealthy still possessed a near monopoly of military force and had little difficulty in presenting a united front. Their opponents, though numerous, were poor and usually disorganized. Communication among different groups of rebels was difficult, and outbreaks of violence tended to be as isolated as they were brief. These rebellions probably did not pose a fundamental threat to the existing social order, but they inspired fear. The chroniclers, who were by definition members of an educated elite, described appalling scenes of murder, rape, and cannibalism. They noted that women sometimes played a part in the agitation, and they regarded this as a monstrous perversion of nature. True or exaggerated, these accounts made it difficult for readers to sympathize with the rebels. The restoration of order was often followed by mass executions and sometimes by new burdens on the peasantry as a whole.

In general, the social disorders of the fourteenth century weakened whatever sense of mutual obligation had been retained from the age of feudalism and probably hastened the trend toward private ownership of land. Moreover they increased the fear and insecurity of the elite, who reacted by developing an attitude of increased social exclusivity. The division between popular and elite culture became dramatic at about this time. The tendency was to ridicule and suppress customs that had once belonged to rich and poor alike but were now regarded as loutish or wicked.

Meanwhile, an impulse that must have been largely unconscious led the upper classes into new extravagance and the elaboration of an extreme form of chivalric excess. The tournaments and banquets described in the *Chronicle* of Jean Froissart (c. 1333–c. 1400) surpassed anything that an earlier age could afford and were at least partially inspired by the flowering of chivalric romance as a literary form. Ironically, this "indian summer" of chivalry occurred not only amid social and economic insecurity but at a time when the feudal aristocracy was losing the remnants of its military function.

The Transformation of Warfare: The Emergence of the Soldier

Fourteenth-century Europe suffered not only from famine and plague, but also from war. While the age was probably not more violent than others before or since, the scale and complexity of warfare was beginning to increase in highly visible ways. By 1500 the evidence was clear that the preceeding two hundred years had witnessed a military revolution.

Long before the Black Death, the feudal system of warfare had begun to break down. The warrior was becoming a soldier. The term *soldier* is used here in its original meaning: a fighting man who receives a cash payment or *solde* for his efforts as opposed to one who serves in return for land or in the discharge of some nonmonetary obligation. This was an important development, not only because it changed the way in which wars were fought, but also because it altered the structure of western European society.

The increase in real wealth and in the circulation of money between 1000 and 1250 allowed princes to alter the basis of military service. Their own revenues, which were based in part on import-export duties and occasional levies on movable goods, were augmented by the revival of trade. Beyond that the commutation of military and other services for cash helped to create substantial war revenues exclusive of taxes. Scutage, the payment of knight's fees, and similar arrangements by which even the feudal class could escape military service in return for cash payments are first noted in the mid-twelfth century. By 1250 they had become commonplace. In 1227 the emperor Frederick II demanded eight ounces of gold from every fief in his realms, but only one knight from every eight fiefs. A quarter-century later, the pope declared his preference for money over personal service from his vassals. The money was used to hire mercenaries or to pay knights to extend their service, often for an indefinite period. The case of Edward I of England is typical. His attempts to subjugate the Welsh and Scots could not be abandoned every autumn when his feudal levies went home. He therefore contracted with certain knights on a long-term basis, paying their wages from the proceeds of knight's fees and from the nine great levies on moveable property that he collected between 1297 and 1302.

The need for long-service troops and the superior professionalism of those who fought year in and year out for their livelihood were decisive. By 1340 unpaid feudal service was becoming rare in western Europe, though the crown was not yet the sole paymaster of its armies. Men from the great estates were still paid by the lords who employed them. Townsmen were paid by the towns. This changed by the mid-fifteenth century in England and France and by 1480 in Spain, though towns and nobles could be called upon to provide equipment. In Italy, the mercenary was dominant by 1300.

The major exceptions to this state of affairs were found in eastern Europe. In Poland a numerous class of small and middling gentry continued to perform unpaid military service throughout the fifteenth century. Those who account for this by pointing to the frontier character of Polish society would be wrong. In Hungary, Europe's most exposed frontier, even the *banderia*, a heavy cavalry unit composed of noblemen, was paid in cash at an early date, and the armies of János Hunyadi (c. 1407–56) and his son, Matthias I, were composed largely of mercenaries. Aside from such quasitribal survivals as the *szechely* of eastern Transylvania, the decision to pay or not to pay seems everywhere to have been governed by the availability of cash.

The first soldiers were probably poor knights or younger sons whose only inheritance was a sword, a horse, and a sound training in the profession of arms. They were soon joined by paid infantry, most of whom came from different social worlds. The fourteenth century also saw the evolution of infantry tactics that required either specialized skills or exceptional discipline and cohesion in battle. As those who possessed such training were rarely part of traditional feudal society, they, too, had to be paid in cash.

The skills were largely associated with the development of new or improved missile weapons. Archery had always been a factor in medieval warfare, but its effectiveness was diminished by improvements in personal armor. The introduction of the crossbow therefore marked the beginning of a major change. This weapon offered great accuracy and powers of penetration, though at a relatively slow rate of fire. Originating in the Mediterranean, it was first used as a naval weapon and found special favor among the shipmasters of Genoa and Barcelona as a defense against pirates. Men selected and trained for this purpose had become numerous in the port cities of the western Mediterranean by 1300 and were willing to transfer their skills to land when the volume of maritime trade declined. The Genoese were especially noted for their service to France during the Hundred Years' War; natives of Barcelona and Marseilles were not far behind.

The advent of the crossbowmen marked an alien intrusion into the world of feudal warfare and was resented by many knights. Their world held little place for the urban poor. However, the involvement of marginal people with deviant forms of social organization was only beginning. The famous longbow was another case in point. Basically a poacher's weapon, it evolved beyond the edges of the feudal world in Wales and the English forests. Edward III introduced it in the Hundred Years' War with devastating effect. The longbow combined a high rate of fire with penetration and accuracy superior to that of early firearms. It required many years of training to be properly employed. As most of those who were expert in its use were marginal men in an economic and social sense they were usually happy to serve as mercenaries.

Handguns followed a similar pattern. First seen in Italy during the 1390s, they achieved importance in Bohemia during the Hussite wars. When peace returned, companies of handgun men found employment in Hungary and in the west.

All of these categories were overshadowed in the fifteenth century by the emergence of the pike as a primary battle weapon (see illustration 12.2). The pike was a spear, twelve to sixteen feet in length. It was used in a square formation similar to the Macedonian phalanx and could, if the pikemen stood their ground, stop a cavalry charge or clear the field of opposing infantry. Massed infantry formations of this kind had been neglected during most of the Middle Ages because such tactics were incompatible with feudalism as a social system. Infantry had to be highly motivated and carefully trained to meet a cavalry charge without flinching.

In medieval Europe, two main forms of social organization could meet this requirement: the city and the peasant league. Medieval towns were surrounded by enemies. In those areas where princely authority was weak (Italy, the Low Countries, and parts of Germany), they were forced to develop effective armies at a relatively early date. As most towns lacked either extensive territory or a large native nobility trained in the profession of arms, this meant that they had to rely on the creation of citizen militias supplemented on occasion

Illlustration 12.2

Pikes in Action. This illustration of the opening of a battle between formations of pikemen shows the "fall" of pikes as the units come into action. It is a detail of *The Terrible Swiss War* by Albrecht Altdorfer, c. 1515.

by mercenaries. Those townsmen who could afford to, bought horse and armor and tried to fight like knights. The majority served with pike or halberd (a long-handled battle axe) and drilled on Sundays and holidays until they achieved a level of effectiveness far superior to that of peasant levies. The victory of the Flemish town militias over the chivalry of France at Courtrai in 1302 was a promise of things to come.

By 1422 pike tactics had been adopted by the Swiss Confederation, one of several peasant leagues formed in the later thirteenth century to preserve their independence from feudal demands. The successful defense of their liberties earned them a formidable military reputation, and after 1444 the Swiss were regularly employed as mercenaries by the French and by the pope. Their example was taken up by other poor peasants in south Germany who emulated their system of training and hired themselves out to the emperor and other princes. Pike squares remained a feature of European armies for two hundred years, and mercenary contracting became an important element in the Swiss and south German economies.

The emergence of paid troops, new missile weapons, and massed infantry tactics changed the character of European warfare. By the end of the fourteenth century, armies were larger and cavalry was declining in importance. The social consequences of these changes

were profound because they tended, among other things, to monetarize the costs of war. In the simplest form of feudal warfare, cash outlays were few. Men served without pay and normally provided their own food and equipment in the field. Feudal levies consumed resources in kind, but these costs rarely involved the state. This changed dramatically with the advent of the soldier, because only a sovereign state could coin money or raise taxes. As feudal nobles could rarely do either, they gradually lost their preeminent role as the organizers of war while the eclipse of cavalry reduced their presence on the battlefield. During the fifteenth century, many great feudal families began to withdraw from the traditional function as protectors of society, leaving the field to men who served the sovereign for pay and privileges. In the process, the state, too, was transformed. Where the feudal world had demanded little more than justice and military leadership from its kings, the new warfare demanded the collection and distribution of resources on an unprecedented scale. The monarchies of Europe were at first unprepared for such a task, and the difficulties they faced were compounded by a contemporary revolution in military technology.

The development of Western technology is often seen as a sporadic affair in which periods of innovation were interspersed with longer intervals of slow, almost imperceptible change. This is an illusion that comes from thinking of the inventions themselves instead of the complex process that created them, but periods certainly existed during which breakthroughs occurred at an accelerated rate. One of these was the later Middle Ages. Few of the changes had an immediate impact on everyday life, but their effects on war, trade, and government were great.

The development of artillery and portable firearms is a case in point. Evolution began with the invention of gunpowder. In Europe, saltpeter was first identified in the twelfth century. How or why it was combined with charcoal and sulphur is unknown, but the mixture was mentioned by Roger Bacon in 1248. A number of years passed before it was used as a propellent, and its first application probably was in mining. This, however, is uncertain. Only the obstacles to its use are fully documented. Saltpeter was scarce and expensive. Years of experimentation were needed to arrive at the proper ratio of ingredients and even longer to develop grains of the proper consistency. Mistakes were often fatal, for black powder was not totally safe or dependable in use, and its chemistry has only recently been understood. Nevertheless it presented fewer problems than the construction of the guns. Metallurgy, not powder milling, controlled the pace of artillery development.

The first guns, which appeared around the middle of the fourteenth century, were hand forged from wrought-iron bars and bound with iron hoops. They were heavy, expensive, and prone to bursting when fired. In spite of these drawbacks, they remained dominant until the middle of the fifteenth century when they were superseded by guns cast from bronze. The bronze used was approximately 80 percent copper and 20 percent tin. Large quantities of both metals were therefore required, and gun production on a large scale was prevented during the fourteenth century by the exhaustion of existing mines. Copper in particular was in short supply. In 1450 a new process was introduced that extracted copper from ores in which copper and silver were found together. Large, previously unusable deposits in Saxony, Hungary, and Slovakia thus could be exploited, and copper production increased dramatically.

The introduction of bronze cannons was further delayed by the lack of adequate furnaces and by an inability to deal with a physical property characteristic of bronze. Copper and tin tend to segregate as they cool, causing variations in the strength of the metal that might cause the guns to burst when fired (see illustration 12.3). Generations of experience were needed to

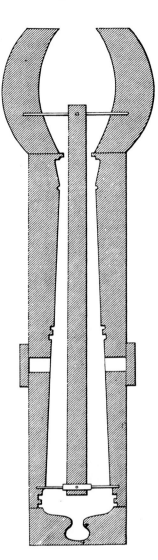

Illustration 12.3

Gun-Casting Technique (after c. 1450). The gun was cast around a core that was lowered into the mold and centered by an iron "cross" that was left in the casting. The pouring head at the top ensured that the mixture of tin and copper would not segregate during cooling and weaken the breach. The head was sawed off after the casting process was complete.

solve these problems. By the 1460s they were largely under control, and large numbers of bronze cannons were quickly added to European armories. Within a half-century, every existing fortress was obsolete, for the high, relatively thin walls of medieval fortifications could withstand no more than a few hours of battering by the big guns. Towns and strongholds in militarily exposed areas were forced to rebuild if they were to survive. Between 1500 and 1530, Italian engineers developed a system of fortifcation that set the pattern for defensive works until the nineteenth century. Walls were lowered and thickened to widths of forty feet or more. Bastions became wedge-shaped and were laid out geometrically so that every section of wall could be covered by the defender's guns. The works were then surrounded by a broad, steep-sided ditch that was usually faced with brick or stone.

The cost was enormous. The guns were expensive and required large numbers of skilled men and draft animals to maneuver. The new fortifications required less skill to construct than their medieval predecessors, but their scale was far larger and their expense proportionately high. The development of artillery had increased the already heavy burden of warfare on states and subjects alike.

The development of navies, though not taking place in earnest until the sixteenth century, was destined to have a similar effect. It rested upon changes in shipbuilding that by the fifteenth century had created vessels capable of crossing an ocean or using artillery in a ship-to-ship duel. The new ships were the result of a hybrid cross between two traditions of shipbuilding—the Mediterranean and the north European. The ships changed the world as few innovations have done before or since.

The dominant ship types in the medieval Mediterranean were the galley and the round ship. The galley was intended primarily for war. Long, narrow, and light, its chief virtues were speed and maneuverabilty independent of the wind. However, it was too fragile for use in the open Atlantic or for extended use in its home waters between October and May. It also lacked carrying capacity, and this, together with its high manpower requirements, limited its usefulness. Though galleys were sometimes used for commerce, especially by the Venetians, the preeminent Mediterranean cargo carrier was the round ship. As its name implies, it was double-ended and broad of beam with a high freeboard. Steered like a galley by side rudders located near the stern, it normally carried a two-masted rig with triangular lateen sails (see illustration 12.4). The round ship was not fast or graceful, but it was safe, roomy, and thanks to its high freeboard, relatively easy to defend against boarders. Its carvel type construction was typically Mediterranean. The hull planking was nailed or pegged edge on edge to a skeleton frame and then caulked to create a water-tight, non-load-bearing hull.

The ships of northern Europe were different. Most were clinker-built like the old Viking longships with overlapping planks fastened to each other by nails or rivets. Their variety was almost infinite. By the middle

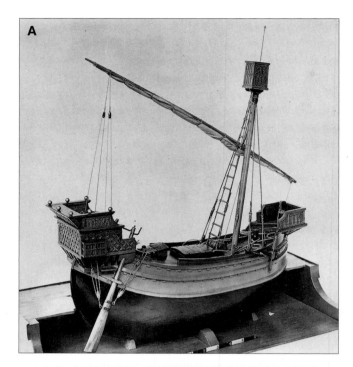

Ilustration 12.4

The Evolution of Medieval Ship Types. These two ship models represent the best current thinking on the appearance and construction of medieval ships. (A) is a medieval round ship with a lateen sail and steering oars of the type used to carry crusaders. (B) is a model of the *Mary Rose,* Henry VIII's "great ship" that capsized in 1545. It may be regarded as an early galleon. Note the gunports.

of the thirteenth century, the cog had emerged as the preferred choice for long voyages over open water. Of Baltic origin, the cog was as high and beamy as the roundship. A long, straight keel and sternpost rudder made it different from and more controllable than its Mediterranean counterpart. The Genoese, in ships designed for their Atlantic trade, adapted carvel construction to this design to create a lighter, cheaper hull with greater carrying capacity.

The final step was the addition of multiple masts. Shipbuilders soon discovered that a divided rig reduced manning requirements because smaller sails were easier to handle. It also made possible the use of different sails—combined according to need, thereby increasing speed and maneuverability under a wider variety of conditions. With Portuguese, Dutch, and Basque innovators leading the way, a recognizably modern ship had evolved by 1500.

Given the military rivalry among states, a marriage between the new shipbuilding techniques and the cast bronze cannon was inevitable. The full tactical implications of this were not immediately apparent, but by the last quarter of the fifteenth century the major states were acquiring ships capable of mounting heavy guns. The competition to control the seas was on, and no state with maritime interests could afford to ignore it.

◆

Centers of Conflict: The Eastern Frontiers

For much of the later Middle Ages, the great north European plain, where it made a borderless transition into Asia, was in turmoil. East of the Elbe, two great movements were under way. The first was the eastward expansion of the German-speaking peoples. Population growth in the twelfth and thirteenth centuries led to the establishment of German settlements in Poland, Lithuania, and the Baltic regions as well as in Transylvania and the Ukraine. The movement was not always peaceful, bringing the Germans into conflict with the Slavs who inhabited the region. Relations improved little with time, and the German "colonies" tended to remain isolated from their neighbors by linguistic barriers and mutual resentments. In its later phases, German expansion was led by the Teutonic Knights, a military order on the crusading model. From the mid-thirteenth century, the Knights attempted the large-scale conquest of Slavic as well as unclaimed land on which German peasants were then encouraged to settle (see map 12.1).

On its eastern fringes (see document 12.4) the Slavic world was under equal pressure from the Mongols, who conquered most of Russia and the Ukraine in 1240–42 and who raided as far west as Breslau in Silesia. The center of resistance to Mongol rule became the grand duchy of Moscow, founded by the son of the Russian hero, Alexander Nevsky. Nevsky had defeated

---

◆ DOCUMENT 12.4 ◆

The Novgorod Chronicle

Novgorod was an important trading city north of Moscow. This excerpt from its city chronicle provides a vivid picture of conditions on Europe's eastern frontier in the year 1224.

A.D. 1224. Prince Vsevolod Gyurgevits came to Novgorod. The same year the Germans killed Prince Vyachko in Gyurgev and took the town. The same year, for our sins, this was not [all] the evil that happened: *Posadnik* [an elected official somewhat resembling a burgomaster or mayor] Fedor rode out with the men of Russia and fought with the Lithuanians; and they drove the men of Russia from their horses and took many horses, and killed Domazhir Torlinits and his son and of the men of Russa Boghsa and many others, and the rest they drove asunder into the forest. The same year, for our sins, unknown tribes came, whom no one exactly knows, who they are, nor whence they came out, nor what their language is, nor of what race they are, nor what their faith is, but they call them Tartars. . . . God alone knows who they are and whence they came out. Very wise men know them exactly, who understand books, but we do not know who they are, but have written of them here for the sake of the memory of the Russian princes and of the misfortune which came to them from them.

The Chronicle of Novgorod, 1016–1471, trans. Robert Michell and Nevill Forbes. Camden Society, 3d series, vol. 25. London: Camden Society Publications, 1914.

---

a Swedish incursion in 1238 and the Teutonic Knights in 1240. His descendants were forced to concern themselves almost exclusively with Asia. Though continuing to pay tribute to the Mongol khans, the Musovites engaged in sporadic warfare with them until 1480 when Ivan III refused payment and became, in effect, the first tsar. An early sign of the grand duchy's preeminence was the transfer of the Russian Orthodox patriarchate from Kiev to Moscow in 1299.

During the fourteenth century, Russian preoccupation with the Mongols encouraged the Teutonic Knights to step up their activities in the Baltic. Resistance was provided by the Catholic kingdom of

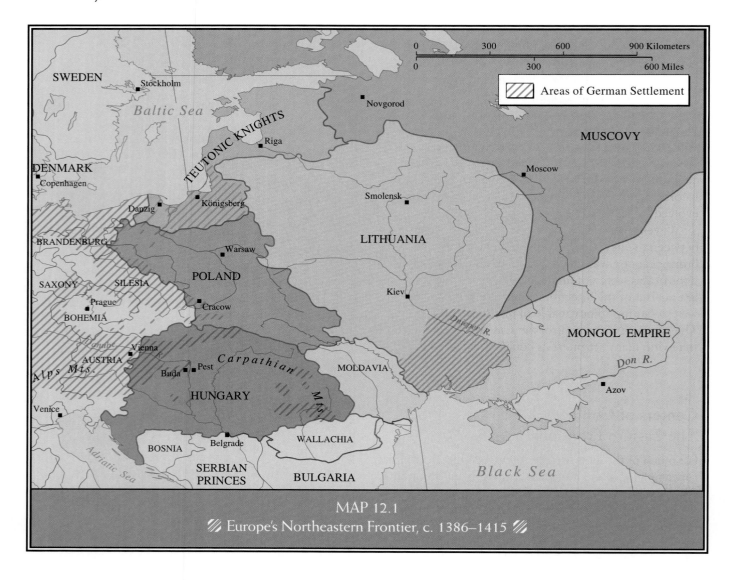

MAP 12.1
Europe's Northeastern Frontier, c. 1386–1415

Poland, established early in the eleventh century, and by a rapidly expanding Lithuanian state whose rulers were still pagan. In 1386 the two states merged for mutual defense. Under the leadership of the Lithuanian Jagiello, who converted to Catholicism and became king of Poland as well, the Knights were defeated at the battle of Tannenburg in 1410.

The Knights no longer existed as an aggressive force, but conflict did not end. Poland-Lithuania did not evolve into a centralized territorial state. It remained an aristocratic commonwealth with an elected king and few natural defenses. However, it was at this time a remarkably open society in which people of many faiths and languages could coexist. It even became the place of refuge for thousands of Jews. Driven from western Europe by the persecutions that followed the Black Death, they found that their capital and fi-

nancial skills were welcomed by the rulers of an underdeveloped frontier state. The parallels with the Iberian kingdoms are striking. By the mid-fifteenth century, Poland and Lithuania were the centers of a vigorous Jewish culture characterized by a powerful tradition of rabbinic learning and the use of Yiddish, a German dialect, as the language of everyday speech.

To the south, in the Balkan Peninsula, the fourteenth and fifteenth centuries marked the emergence of the Ottoman Empire as a threat to Christian Europe. By 1300 virtually all of the Byzantine lands in Anatolia had fallen under the control of *ghazi* principalities. The *ghazis*, of predominantly Turkish origin, were the Muslim equivalent of crusaders, pledged to the advancement of Islam. The last of their states to possess a common frontier with Byzantium was centered on the city of Bursa in northwest Anatolia. Under the aggressive leadership of Osman (1258–1324), it offered the opportunity for continued warfare to ambitious men from all over the Turkic world and a refuge to others who had fled from the Mongol advance in central Asia. With the population of the Ottoman state swelled by thousands of immigrants, the tiny emirate became the nucleus of the Ottoman Empire.

From the beginning, it was a serious threat to the Byzantine state revived by Michael Paleologus after the Fourth Crusade. Deprived of his Anatolian heartland and caught between the Ottomans on one side and the Serbian Empire of Stephen Dushan (d. 1355) on the other, the Greek emperor was only one of many regional princes striving for preeminence in the tangled world of Balkan politics. Taking advantage of divisions among the Christians, Osman's son, Orhan, ordered the first Turkish invasion of Europe in 1356. The best hope of expelling him lay in an alliance between the Serbians and the Bulgarians. A history of mutual distrust inhibited their cooperation, however, and the Serbian army was defeated in 1371. By 1389 the Turks had achieved military predominance in the peninsula.

The threat to Constantinople was now imminent, and the Greeks sent missions to Rome in the hope of enlisting western support against the Turks. Negotiations broke down over theological and other issues. The pope was reluctant to compromise, and some Greeks came to believe that the Latin church was a greater threat to the survival of their religion than Islam. From the standpoint of Western intellectual development, this contact between Greek and Latin scholar-diplomats would have far-reaching consequences, but politically it was a failure.

Meanwhile, southeastern Europe settled into a period of almost chronic warfare. The Serbs and Bulgarians were restless and unreliable tributaries of the Turks. The Byzantine emperor lacked a credible offensive force, but the Albanians remained a threat. In the northwest, the Hungarians were growing uneasy. Eventually a crusade was organized by János Hunyadi, the voivod of Transylvania who would one day become king of Hungary. His defeat at Varna in 1444 and again on the plain of Kossovo in 1448 left the Turks in control of virtually everything south of the Danube. Only the Albanian mountains and Constantinople remained free.

In 1453 the great city, now seriously depopulated, fell to Mehmet "the Conqueror" after a long siege. The Byzantine Empire had ceased to exist. The church of St. Sophia became a mosque, and the Greeks, together with the other Balkan peoples, became subjects of the Ottoman sultan. Their faith and much of their culture was preserved, for the Turks did not believe in forced conversions. They would not regain political independence until the nineteenth century.

The Hundred Years' War in the West

The Hundred Years' War, though centered on France and England, was a generalized west European conflict that also involved the Low Countries and the Iberian kingdoms of Castile, Aragon, and Portugal. Because its active phases were interspersed with periods of relative peace, regarding it not as one war but as several whose underlying causes were related is probably best. The most immediate of these causes was the ongoing struggle over the status of English fiefs in France. The situation was complicated by dynastic instability and by the weakening of feudal institutions as a whole.

Of all the problems created by feudalism, none was more exasperating than the ambivalent situation of the kings of England. For two centuries they had struggled with their dual role as French vassals and as sovereign princes whose interests were frequently in conflict with those of France (see chapter 8). Every reign since that of Henry II had produced disputes over Guienne and Gascony. Another French attempt to confiscate these fiefs led to the outbreak of the Hundred Years' War in spring 1337 (see map 12.2).

This action by Philip VI of France came at the end of a long diplomatic crisis. Nearly a decade earlier, Philip had been proclaimed king when his cousin, Charles IV, died without male heirs. The claim of England's Edward III, son of Charles's sister, had been denied on the controversial premise that the Salic law forbade royal inheritance through the female line. Edward, young and beset with internal enemies, chose not to press the point. Relations gradually deteriorated when Philip began to pursue more aggressive policies on several fronts. In the year of his coronation he recaptured the county of Flanders from the urban rebels who had achieved independence from France at Courtrai in 1302. This represented a threat to the primary market for English wool, as Philip was now in a position to forbid its importation. Worst of all, he began to support Edward's enemies in Scotland.

By 1336 Edward was secure on his throne and began preparing for war. Papal attempts at mediation failed, and in May 1337, Philip ordered the confiscation of English fiefs in France, citing Edward's support for the Flemish rebels and other sins against feudal obligation as a pretext.

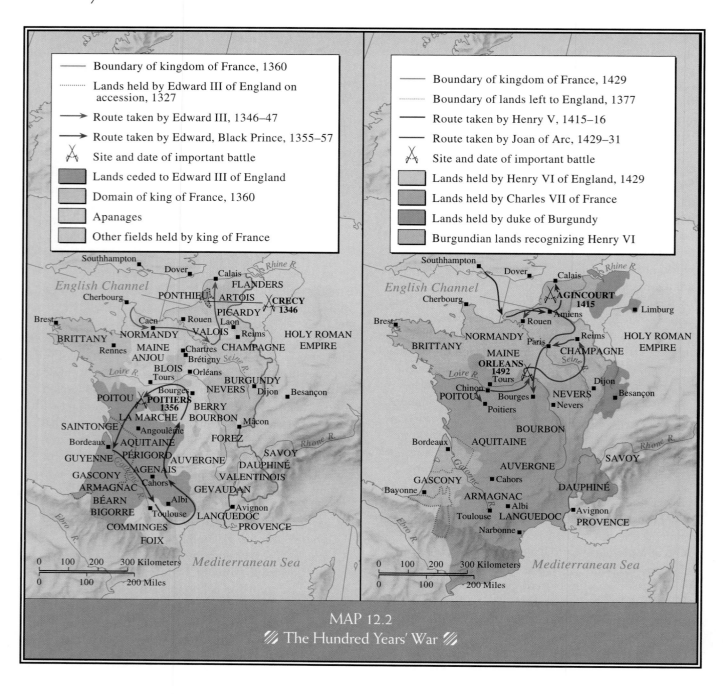

MAP 12.2
⁀ The Hundred Years' War ⁀

The first phase of the war went badly for France. This is at first sight surprising as England was by far the smaller and poorer of the two countries with a population only one-third that of her rival. The difference lay in superior leadership. Edward quickly proved to be not only an able commander, but also a master at extracting resources from Parliament. By defeating the French in a naval battle off Sluys in 1340, he secured control of the English Channel. Subsequent campaigns were fought on French soil, including the ones that culminated in the victories of Crécy (1346) and Poitiers (1356). In both cases, French cavalry employing traditional tactics were defeated by the imaginative use of longbows in massed formations.

The treaty of Bretigny (1360) secured a breathing space of seven years during which the locus of violence shifted to the Iberian Peninsula. Conflict there centered on the policies of Pedro of Castile, known to the Castilian aristocracy as "the Cruel" and to his other subjects as "the Just." Pedro's nicknames arose from his efforts to strengthen the crown against the landed nobility. When he became involved in a border war with Pedro "the Ceremonious" of Aragon, the latter encouraged an uprising of Castilian nobles under the leadership of Enrique of Trastámara, Pedro the Cruel's half-brother. Enrique and his Aragonese ally then sought assistance from France.

They received it in part because of a phenomenon that surfaced for the first time after the peace of Bretigny. The practice of paying troops had created a class of men whose only trade was war and who, after a generation of fighting, had no place in civilian society. For them peace was a catastrophe that forced them to become beggars or bandits. Most, understandably, chose the latter. Roaming the countryside, often in their original companies, they lived by systematic pillage and extortion reinforced by the threat of murder, arson, and rape.

The new French king, Charles V, was happy to dispatch a multinational contingent of these people to Spain under the command of Bertrand Duguesclin. Pedro of Castile responded by calling in the English under Edward of Woodstock, known as the Black Prince. The eldest son of Edward III and the winning commander at Poitiers, he repeated his triumph at Nájera in 1367. The Castilian war dragged on until 1398 when Enrique was able to kill Pedro with his own hands and gain the throne. Because Enrique had won with the aid of the Castilian aristocracy, he was forced to confirm and extend their privileges, thereby guaranteeing that his successors would be faced with internal disorder. His victory was a defeat, not only for Pedro, but also for the state-building ideals he represented.

An aftereffect of the Spanish war was the pretext for reviving Anglo-French hostilities. To pay for his Castilian adventure, the Black Prince so taxed his subjects in Guienne that they appealed to Charles V for help. The war that followed was far less dramatic than the first. Charles adopted a strategy of attrition, avoiding battle whenever possible and using the tactical skills of Duguesclin to harry and outmaneuver the English. By 1380 the English presence in France had been greatly reduced, but both kingdoms were at the limit of their resources. Fighting did not end completely. The next thirty-five years may be characterized as a period of military stalemate and internal disorder in both countries.

The last stage of the war began when Henry V of England invaded the continent in 1415. Ambitious and new to the throne, he sought to take advantage of the civil war then raging in France. The French king, Charles VI, had gone mad. His brother, the duke of Orleáns, was named regent, thereby arousing the envy of John the Fearless, duke of Burgundy. Burgundy was perhaps the most powerful of the king's relatives. His appanage—estates granted to members of the ruling family—included the rich duchy of Burgundy and most of what is now Belgium and the Netherlands. He was probably wealthier than the king. John arranged the assassination of Orleáns in 1407 only to see another rival, Count Bertrand VII of Armagnac, installed in his place. In the struggle that followed, Burgundy tried to ally himself with England, drawing back when he perceived the extent of Henry's ambitions. The English king saw that John would do nothing to defend Charles VI or his Armagnac supporters.

The English invasion was an immediate success. Using a variant of the tactics developed at Crécy and Poitiers, Henry crushed the French at Agincourt on October 25, 1415. Alarmed by the magnitude of the French defeat, Burgundy began to rethink his position, but he, too, was assassinated in 1419 by soldiers in the pay of the Armagnacs. His son, Philip, whose nickname "the Good" belied a ferocious temper, sought revenge by allying Burgundy once again with England.

The French king was virtually isolated. In 1420 he was forced to ratify the treaty of Troyes, which disinherited his son, the future Charles VII, in favor of Henry V. When Charles VI and Henry both died in 1422, Henry's infant son, Henry VI of England, was proclaimed king of France with the English duke of Bedford as regent. The proclamation aroused great indignation in much of France where Charles of Valois was accepted as the rightful king. Charles, unfortunately, was not an inspiring figure. Inarticulate, physically unimpressive, and only nineteen years old, he retired with his supporters to Bourges where he quickly developed a reputation for lethargy and indecision. The task of galvanizing public opinion fell to an extraordinary woman, Joan of Arc.

Joan was an illiterate peasant from the remote border village of Domrémy. When she came to Charles in March 1429 she was probably no older than twenty but had already achieved local fame for her religious visions. She told him that "voices" had instructed her to raise the English siege of Orleáns, and Charles, who probably thought that he had little to lose, allowed her to go. The result was electrifying. By the time she arrived, the English had decided to give up, but the French did not know this. The apparently miraculous appearance of a young woman, dressed in armor and with her hair cut like a man's, was thought to have been the reason for the subsequent English retreat, and it created a sensation. The relief of Orleáns, which preserved the south of France for Charles, was followed by a string of victories that led to the repudiation of the treaty of Troyes and his coronation at Rheims in July. All of this was popularly attributed to Joan who was present throughout. She never commanded troops, but her inspiration gave them confidence, and even civilians, oppressed by a century of apparently pointless warfare, were roused to enthusiasm.

Unfortunately for Joan, Charles was not quite the fool he sometimes appeared to be. When she was captured by the English in 1430, he did nothing to secure her release or to prevent her from being tried at Rouen on charges of witchcraft and heresy. He no doubt preferred to take credit for his own victories and may have regarded her popularity as an embarrassment. The verdict was a foregone conclusion. Bedford was determined to discredit her as an agent of the devil, and she was burned at the stake on May 30, 1431. Her habit of dressing as a man was taken as evidence of diabolical intent. Twenty-five years later, in a gesture of belated gratitude, Charles VII reopened the case and had her declared innocent. The church made her a saint in 1920.

Joan's brief career offers a disquieting vision of fifteenth-century attitudes toward women, but it was a turning point for France. In 1435 Charles was reconciled with Philip the Good of Burgundy, and by 1453 the English had been driven out of France in a series of successful campaigns that left them with only the port of Calais as a continental base.

Political Turbulence and Dynastic Collapse: France, Castile, and England

Dynastic failures played a major role in continuing and intensifying the Hundred Years' War. In a system based on heredity, the failure of a ruling dynasty to produce competent heirs in a timely manner meant either a disputed succession or a regency. The effect of a disputed succession may be seen in the origins of the war itself, in which the failure of all three of Philip IV's sons to produce heirs gave Edward III of England a pretext for his quarrel with Philip of Valois, or in Castile, where a similar failure by Pedro the Cruel encouraged the pretensions of his half-brother Enrique.

Regencies occurred when the legitimate heir could not govern by reason of youth or mental incapacity. An individual regent or a regency council might be designated in the will of a dying monarch or by agreement within the royal family, but these appointments were almost always contested. The reason lay in the struc-

ture of European elites. Each branch of the royal family and each of the great landholding clans were a center of wealth, power, and patronage to which other elements of society were drawn by interest or by hereditary obligation. Rivalries were inevitable, and the king's duty was to serve as a kind of referee, using his superior rank to ensure that no one became an "overmighty subject." Failure to perform this role in an adequate manner was often equated with bad governance.

By these standards, no regency could be good. Regents were usually either princes of the blood or connected with a particular faction of the royal family. They were partial almost by definition. Once installed, they were in a position to use the wealth and power of the crown to advance their factional interests while threatening the estates and the lives of their rivals. Those excluded from a regency often felt that they had no alternative but to rebel, though their rebellions were usually directed not at the semisacred person of the king, but at his "evil counselors." This happened in the struggle between John the Fearless and the Armagnacs. The result was a civil war and renewed English intervention in France.

Other forms of dynastic failure had similar effects. In some cases, adult, presumably functional, rulers behaved so foolishly that their subjects rebelled. Castile in particular suffered from this ailment throughout much of the fifteenth century. Juan II (1405–54) left the government in the hands of Alvaro de Luna, a powerful noble whose de facto regency factionalized the grandees, the highest rank of Spanish nobles who were not princes of the blood. Juan's son, Enrique IV "the Impotent" was generally despised for his homosexuality, his tendency to promote low-born lovers over the hereditary nobility, and his failure to maintain order. Faced with a monarchy they could neither support nor respect, the great landholding families raised private armies and kept the country in a state of near-anarchy until 1479.

In England, the regency appointed during the minority of Richard II was accepted largely because the social unrest that culminated in the revolt of 1381 forced the aristocracy to close ranks. When he came of age, the favoritism and ineptitude of the young king aroused such opposition that he was deposed and murdered in 1399. Reflecting contemporary attitudes, Richard, like Enrique IV of Castile, was accused of homosexuality. The reign of Henry VI—from 1422 to 1461 and 1470 to 1471—was even more chaotic than that of Richard II. Coming to the throne as an infant, Henry remained under the control of others throughout his life. Though respected for his piety, he was wholly incapable of governing and suffered a complete mental breakdown in 1453. His incapacity led to the War of the Roses, a nine-year struggle between the Lancastrian and Yorkist branches of the royal family that ended with a Yorkist victory at Tewksbury in 1471 and the murder of yet another English king (see chapter 13).

Whether the result of royal inbreeding or sheer bad luck, these dynastic failures retarded the development of western European states. The increasing cost of and sophistication of war were a powerful impetus to the growth of royal power, but these anarchic interludes tended to interfere with bureaucratic development and to strengthen local privilege, at least temporarily. Feudal nobles whose position was threatened by economic and military change often saw them as an opportunity to recover lost ground. Above all, they added to the sense of dislocation created by plague, war, and social change.

Art and Literature: The Measure of Discontent

By the end of the fourteenth century, the accumulation of disasters was having an impact on the art and literature of Europe. The bonds of society seemed to be unraveling. Lords abandoned their ostensible function as the military protectors of society and compensated for declining rents by preying upon their tenants. Peasants responded when they could by abandoning their tenures. The idea of mutual obligation that lay at the heart of feudalism could no longer be sustained, and many, including the fourteenth-century author of the English poem *Piers Plowman*, came to believe that greed and self-interest were everywhere triumphant. Moralists complained that the simpler manners of an earlier day had given way to extravagance and debauchery. War was endemic and all the more intolerable because it did not end for the common people when a truce was signed. They still had to pay for it through taxes while trying to defend themselves against unemployed soldiers who often did more damage than the war itself. Plague, the conquests by the Turk, and the rule of imbecile kings were seen by many as signs of God's wrath.

The expression of these concerns varied. At one extreme was the upper-class tendency to take refuge in nostalgia for a largely fictional past. This took the form not only of chivalric fantasies, but also of the idyllic visions offered in the *Tres riches heures du Duc du Berry*, a

Illustration 12.5

Nostalgia for a Past That Had Never Been. Happy peasants toil beneath the walls of a fairy tale castle in this fifteenth-century illumination, which is from the *Très riches heures du Duc du Berry.*

magnificently illustrated prayer book in which happy peasants toil near palaces that seem to float on air (see illustration 12.5). At the other extreme was a fascination with the physical aspects of death (see document 12.5). The art of the period abounds with representations of skeletons and putrifying corpses. The Dance of Death in which corpses lead the living in a frenzied round that ends with the grave became a common motif in art and literature and was performed in costume on festive occasions. Popular sermons emphasized the brevity of life and the art of dying well, while series of popular woodcuts illustrated in horrifying detail how death would come to the knight, the scholar, the

Ilustration 12.6

🏵 **Detail from the Ghent Alterpiece.** This panel, "The Knights of Christ," with its lovingly rendered costumes and harness is an example of fifteenth-century Flemish painter Jan van Eyck's preoccupation with the world of the senses.

beauty, and a whole host of other human stereotypes. Not surprisingly, the word *macabre* seems to have entered the French language at about this time.

Despair became fashionable, but it was not universal. In Brabant and Flanders artists such as Roger van der Weyden and the van Eycks developed techniques for portraying the beauties of the world with unprecedented mastery (see illustration 12.6). Their paintings, intended for display in churches and hospitals, dwelled lovingly on fine costumes, the brilliance of jewels, and the richness of everyday objects while portraying the hard, worldly faces of their owners with unflinching honesty. Regarding their work as an affirmative answer to the emphasis on death is tempting. Some certainly felt that because life was grim and short its pleasures should be enjoyed to the fullest. However, more exists to these paintings than meets the eye. Many of the beautifully rendered objects they portray are also symbols of a moral or spiritual value whose meaning would have been clear to all who saw them. The medieval fondness for allegory survived the fourteenth century and may even have grown stronger with time.

The people of the later Middle Ages still used religious language and religious imagery to express themselves. They still thought in religious, traditional, and hierarchic terms, but their faith in traditional assumptions and values had been shaken badly by events they barely understood. They looked with dismay upon what had happened, but the transformation of their world had just begun.

CHAPTER 13

THE RENAISSANCE: POLITICAL RENEWAL AND INTELLECTUAL CHANGE

CHAPTER OUTLINE

◆◆◆◆◆◆◆◆◆◆◆◆◆◆◆◆◆◆◆◆◆

Changes in the conduct of warfare and the erosion of feudal institutions after 1300 created a new kind of state, administered by salaried bureaucrats and defended by paid soldiers. Though the policies of these states were governed by dynastic instead of national considerations and regional differences were accepted to a degree unimaginable today, the monarchies that emerged from this process in the later fifteenth century are the recognizable ancestors of the modern state.

At approximately the same time, a new intellectual movement began in the Italian city-states and, by the end of the fifteenth century, had spread throughout Europe. Under the influence of such writers as Petrarch and Boccaccio, Italians began to reinterpret the ancient Greco-Roman past and apply the lessons of that reimagined period to their own times. In the process, they transformed virtually all of the arts and sciences, gave birth to the modern study of politics and history, and created a model for liberal arts education that persisted, with some modifications, into the early twentieth century. They changed the way in which Westerners thought, not only about human affairs, but also about the physical sciences. This movement is known as the Renaissance, and the term has been used conventionally to describe the entire age in which Western learning moved away from medieval precedents and began to lay the foundations of the modern world.

◈

The Consolidation of the State (c.1350–1500)

Medieval princes had worked, with varying degrees of success, to improve administration and strengthen royal authority. Most royal governments remained modest in size and centered firmly on the royal household until the later years of the thirteenth century. Under Henry

III of England (reigned 1234–72), for example, the royal budget hovered consistently in the range of £12,500 per annum. His son, Edward I, managed to spend more than £750,000 on war alone from 1297 to 1302, in part because he paid most of his fighting men in cash. Such figures indicate why the military revolution of the fourteenth and fifteenth centuries intensified the process of state building begun by such monarchs as Edward I and Philip the Fair. Faced with a massive increase in the cost of war, sovereign states had to maximize their incomes from every conceivable source to survive.

One way of achieving this was to expand the ruler's personal domain and to exploit it more efficiently. Domain revenues fell into two main categories. First, rents, fees, and other income were taken from lands held directly by the prince. The size of the domain could be increased by keeping property that reverted to the sovereign through confiscation or in default of heirs. In the feudal past such lands had often been given to other subjects almost as soon as they were received. By 1450 most states were trying to reverse this practice, and some were actively seeking new pretexts for confiscation. Second, other domain revenues came from the exercise of traditional rights that might include anything from the collection of customs duties to monopolies on such vital commodities as salt. The yield from these sources was regarded as the personal property of the crown and, like profits from the land, could be increased primarily through better administration.

Bureaucracies composed of "servants of the crown," paid in cash and serving at the pleasure of their ruler, were a legacy of the thirteenth century. They grew larger and more assertive with the passage of time. As the careers of the bureaucrats depended upon producing new revenue, they sought not only to improve efficiency but also to discover new rights for which few precedents often existed. Their efforts brought the state into conflict with privileges that had long been claimed by towns, guilds, private individuals, and the church. As such conflicts usually ended in the law courts, the state found strengthening its control over the legal system desirable. Manorial courts and other forms of private jurisdiction were therefore attacked for their independence as well as for the fines and court costs they levied that might otherwise go to the state. From the ruler's point of view, establishing courts by his or her own prerogative was far better, because a court in which the judge was a servant of the crown might deliver more favorable verdicts and bring in money that might otherwise be lost.

The expansion of prerogative courts, though controversial, was eased by the growing acceptance of Roman or civil law. The extensive development of canon law by the church during the eleventh and twelfth centuries had sparked a revival of interest in Justinian's code among laymen. By the thirteenth century, Roman legal principles had almost supplanted customary law in the empire and in Castile, where they formed the basis of the *Siete Partidas*, the great legal code adopted by Alfonso X (reigned 1252–84). In France and England, the principles of civil law tended instead to modify common law practice, but Roman law gained ground steadily through the fifteenth century. Everywhere, rulers—and the prerogative courts they established—preferred Roman procedures because the customary law, with its reliance on precedent and the use of juries, provided a stronger basis for resisting the claims of sovereignty. But these same virtues ensured that court proceedings would be long and therefore costly. People often asked that their cases be transferred to prerogative or civil law courts in the hope of a speedier judgment.

Though individuals might sometimes benefit from the state's activities, as a general rule, all attempts to increase domain revenue carried a high political cost. Only a strong, popular prince could overcome the entrenched resistance of powerful interests, which is why the dynastic failures of the late fourteenth and early fifteenth centuries delayed the extension of sovereignty even if they could not stop it completely.

The character of princes also affected their ability to impose taxes, the second route by which the power of the state might be increased. Taxes, unlike domain revenues, could be raised only with the consent of representative bodies. Late medieval assemblies generally voted taxes for a specified period of time, thereby forcing the princes to come back each year, hat in hand, to hear the complaints of their subjects. If the prince was popular, or if the taxes were needed to meet a genuine crisis, the sums involved might vastly exceed those generated from domain revenues, yet parliamentary bodies that held "the power of the purse" restricted the exercise of sovereignty. Most rulers no doubt preferred to "live of their own," but this was rarely possible in time of war.

The only solution to this dilemma was to convince hard-headed representatives of the landholding and merchant classes to grant at least some taxes on a perpetual basis on the theory that threats to the kingdom's integrity would never end. This was not easy, even in the interminable chaos of the Hundred Years' War, but the states that succeeded, notably France and Castile, became the great powers of the succeeding age. Not only did perpetual taxes make the revenues of these countries greater in real terms than those of their neighbors, but they also made them predictable. Budgeting for the long term became possible without the interference of elected bodies whose interests were not necessarily those of the prince. Above all, perpetual taxes made borrowing money easier because lenders could be guaranteed a return based on projected revenues.

Whether perpetual or temporary, late medieval and early modern taxes were usually levied on some form of moveable property. The governments of the day lacked the administrative technology to monitor personal incomes, and land, though it was the principle form of wealth, was usually tax exempt for a variety of political and historical reasons. The goods of merchants and artisans were fair game, as were the commodities offered for sale by peasants. Taxes on moveable property were regressive in the sense that wealthy landholders and rentiers could usually avoid them, but their impact on other social groups is hard to measure. Collection was never uniform and was rarely undertaken directly by the state. The most common practice was to negotiate the proposed yield from a tax with local authorities who would then be responsible for its collection. The rates collected were usually not those set by the legislation. Whatever their amount, late medieval taxes fell predominantly on the most economically active, if not the richest, segments of the population.

Governments knew this and attempted to encourage the transfer of resources from tax-exempt to taxable activities. This is one reason for their almost universal efforts to foster trade, mining, and manufacturing. It also helps to explain the policy, common to both England and Castile, of favoring sheepherders at the expense of those who cultivated the soil. Wool could be taxed; subsistence agriculture could not. Such policies clearly influenced economic development, but their overall impact on growth or on public well-being may have been negative. Taxes were ultimately paid by the consumer and were therefore a burden to be added to those already imposed by landholders in their efforts to compensate for falling rents.

Moreover, the maximization of tax yields often required changes in land use. Governments, through the decisions of their prerogative courts, tended to favor the extension of personal property rights over the claims of feudal privilege. An example was the English policy of encouraging landholders to enclose common lands for grazing. This practice, which reached a peak at the beginning of the sixteenth century, broke feudal precedent and sometimes forced the expulsion of peasants who needed the marginal income provided by the commons for survival. As Sir Thomas More put it, "[I]n England, sheep eat men." This was perhaps an extreme case, and enclosures may not have been as common as More thought, but everywhere the extension of personal property rights to land had the immediate effect of favoring governments and landholders at the expense of peasants. Thus, the most insistent demand of German peasant revolutionaries was for a return to the "old law" that protected their feudal status.

If one part of state building was finding new revenues, the other was developing more efficient mechanisms by which they could be spent. Most late medieval states found this more difficult than locating the money in the first place. Bureaucracies whose purpose was to supply the needs of war grew like mushrooms but remained inefficient by modern standards until after the industrial revolution. They were inhibited in part by the same sense of corporate and personal privilege that resisted other aspects of state growth, but the underlying problem was structural. Communications were poor, and no precedent had been set for many basic administrative procedures. Archives, the basic tool of record keeping, were rare before the mid-sixteenth century. Censuses were unknown outside the Italian city-states, and how they might have been conducted in such kingdoms as France with their immense distances and isolated populations is hard to imagine. To make matters worse, the costs of war continued to grow more rapidly than the sources of revenue. Neither taxation nor the development of public credit kept pace, and money was often in desperately short supply. Because soldiers and officials were often paid poorly and at irregular intervals, governments were forced to tolerate high levels of what would today be called corruption. Bribery, the sale of offices, and the misappropriation of funds were common even in those states that prided themselves on their high administrative standards. The situation would improve under the "absolutist" regimes of the eighteenth century, but the improvements were relative.

No two states were alike. Though all were confronted with the need for consolidation and new revenues, they achieved their objectives in different ways according to their circumstances and traditions. The city-states of Italy evolved along lines of their own and have been considered separately in Chapter 10. The sovereign kingdoms and principalities must be examined individually or in regional groups if their development is to be understood.

The Iberian Kingdoms: Ferdinand and Isabella

The Iberian Peninsula was in some ways an unlikely birthplace for two of the most successful early modern states. Difficult terrain and an average annual rainfall of twenty inches or less produced little surplus wealth. Ethnic, political, and religious differences were great. In 1400 no fewer than five kingdoms shared this rugged land. Portugal was probably the most homogeneous, though it possessed significant Muslim and Jewish minorities. Castile, comprising the two ancient kingdoms of León and Castile, contained not only Jews and Muslims, but also Basques and Galicians who, though devoutly Christian, possessed their own languages and cultures. The kingdom of Aragon had three separate regions: Aragon, Cataluña, and Valencia. Each of them had its own language and traditions, though the Aragonese spoke Castilian and some linguists regard Valencian as a dialect of Catalan. Finally, there was the kingdom of Granada, the last but still vigorous remnant of the Islamic Empire on European soil, and the tiny mountain kingdom of Navarre straddling the Pyrenees between Castile and France.

Portugal was the first European state to achieve consolidation, just as it would be the first to acquire an overseas empire. During most of the fourteenth century, it suffered like other monarchies from intrigue, dynastic failures, and ill-advised forays into the Hundred Years' War. In 1385 the Portuguese Cortes solved a succession crisis by crowning the late king's illegitimate son as John I. In the same year, John defeated the Castilians in a decisive battle at Aljubarrotta and suppressed most of the old feudal nobility, many of whom had supported the enemy. Under his descendants, the house of Avis, Portugal avoided the revolts and dynastic failures that troubled other states and evolved virtually without interruption until 1580.

Spain was another matter. Aragon and Castile had long been troubled by civil wars. Castile established a precedent for perpetual taxes in 1367, but the usurpation of Enrique of Trastámara left the crown dependent upon the nobles who had supported him. His successors, especially Juan II and Enrique IV "the Impotent," were incapable of maintaining order, in part because their favorites aroused the jealousy of the grandees. The accession of Enrique's half-sister Isabella and her marriage to Ferdinand of Aragon brought an end to the period of anarchy and led to the eventual union of the two kingdoms. Isabella and Ferdinand inherited their respective thrones in 1479, a decade after their marriage. Each ruled independently, but they cooperated on the broad outlines of policy, and an agreement was reached that their heirs would rule a united Spain by hereditary right.

The program of the Catholic kings, as they were called, was greatly assisted by the weariness brought on by decades of civil strife. The nobles of Castile were pacified by confirming their titles to all lands acquired by them, legally or illegally, before 1466 and by the judicious granting of *mayorazgos* or entails permitting them to exclude younger children from their inheritances. This was important because, under Spanish law, property was normally divided equally among the heirs, a practice that tended to deplete a family's wealth and influence over time. In return, the grandees agreed to give up all the land they had taken illegally after 1466 and to disband their private armies.

The towns, too, had suffered in the civil wars. Clientage and kinship ties were powerful in Castilian society, and many cities had fallen under the control of factions that persecuted their rivals mercilessly. At the Cortes of Toledo in 1480 the royal towns of Castile agreed to the appointment of *corregidores*, royal officials who would reside in the city, protect the interests of the crown, and supervise elections. This ensured a high degree of royal authority over city governments and over those who were elected to represent them in the Cortes. The consequent willingness of this body to support new taxes and other royal initiatives was to become an important cornerstone of Spanish power.

None of these measures applied to Aragon. To ensure domestic peace, Ferdinand was forced to confirm a series of rights and privileges granted by his father in 1472 at the height of the civil wars. These concessions, however, were less important than they might appear. The kingdom of Aragon was far smaller than Castile, and its most vital region, Cataluña, had been declining economically for more than a century. Castile was destined to be the dominant partner in this union of the crowns, and its dominance was only enhanced by its centralized institutions and higher level of taxation. In both kingdoms, administration was reformed and the crown's already extensive control over church appointments was strengthened.

With their realms at peace, the monarchs turned their attention to the kingdom of Granada. After ten years of bitter warfare, the Muslim state was conquered in 1492, the same year in which Columbus sailed for the New World. It was also the year in which the Jews were expelled from Spain, for the Catholic kings were committed to a policy of religious uniformity. Fanned by popular preachers, anti-Jewish sentiment had led to

MAP 13.1
Europe in the Renaissance

pogroms and a wave of forced conversions between 1390 and 1450. Many of these conversions were thought to be false, and the Spanish Inquisition, an organization wholly unrelated to the Papal Inquisition, was founded early in Ferdinand and Isabella's reign to root out *conversos* who had presumably returned to the faith of their ancestors. Large numbers of converts were executed or forced to do penance during the 1480s, and their property was confiscated to help finance the Granadan war. The Inquisition, as a church court, had jurisdiction over only those who had been baptized. The Jews who had escaped forced conversion were comparatively few and usually poor, but even a small minority was seen as a threat to the faith of the *conversos*. Those who still refused conversion were at last expelled. Some fled to Portugal, only to be expelled by the Portuguese as well in 1496. Others went to North

Africa or found refuge within the Turkish Empire, while a few eventually settled in the growing commercial cities of the Low Countries.

The war for Granada and the supplies of money guaranteed by the perpetual taxes and cooperative legislature of Castile enabled Ferdinand to create a formidable army that was put to almost constant use in the last years of the reign. Through bluff, diplomacy, and hard fighting, he restored Cerdanya and Rosseló to Cataluña and conquered the ancient kingdom of Navarre. When Charles VIII of France invaded Italy in 1495, Ferdinand used his actions as a pretext to intervene. This first phase of the Italian wars lasted until 1513. Under the command of Gonsalvo de Córdoba, "the Great Captain," Spanish armies devised a new method of combining pikes with shot that defeated the French and their Swiss mercenaries and drove them

❖ DOCUMENT 13.1 ❖

Complaints of the French Estates General, 1484

When the French Estates General brought together representatives of the clergy, the nobility, and the commons (or third estate), these representatives produced pamphlets known as cahiers, *describing their grievances. The following excerpt from a* cahier *of 1484 gives a vivid complaint of the third estate against royal taxation.*

One cannot imagine the persecution, poverty, and misery that the little people have suffered, and still suffer in many ways.

First of all, no region has been safe from the continual coming and going of armies, living off the poor. . . . One should note with pity the injustice, the iniquity, suffered by the poor: the armies are hired to defend them, yet these armies oppress them the most. The poor laborer must hire the soldiers who beat him, evict him from his house, make him sleep on the ground, and consume his substance. . . . When the poor laborer has worked long, weary, sweaty days, when he has harvested those fruits of his labor from which he expects to live, they come to take a share of it from him, to pay the armed men who may come to beat him soon. . . . If God did not speak to the poor and give them patience, they would succumb in despair.

For the intolerable burden of the *taille,* and the taxes—which the poor people of this kingdom have not carried alone, to be sure, because that is impossible—the burden under which they have died from hunger and poverty, the mere description of these taxes would cause infinite sadness and woe, tears of woe and pity, great sighs and groans from sorrowful hearts. And that is not mentioning the enormous evils that followed, the injustice, the violence, and the extortion whereby these taxes were imposed and seized.

Bernier, A., ed. *Journal des états généraux de France tenus à Tours en 1484,* Paris: 1835. trans. Steven C. Hause.

---

from the peninsula. Spain added the kingdoms of Sicily and Naples to its growing empire and became the dominant power in Italian affairs at the expense of Italy's independence.

Isabella died in 1504; Ferdinand in 1516. So firm were the foundations they had built that the two crowns were able to survive the unpopular regency of Cardinal Francisco Jiménez (or Ximénez) de Cisneros in Castile. The cardinal not only preserved the authority of the crown, but also made substantial progress in reforming abuses in the Spanish church and in improving the education of the clergy. When the grandson of the Catholic kings, the emperor Charles V, ascended the two thrones and unified them in 1522, he inherited a realm that stretched from Italy to Mexico, the finest army in Europe, and a regular income from taxes that rested firmly on the shoulders of Castilian taxpayers.

France: Charles VII and Louis XI

France, too, emerged from the Hundred Years' War with perpetual taxes that freed its monarchs from their dependence on representative institutions. The most important of these was the *taille,* a direct tax of feudal origin that was assigned exclusively to the crown in 1439. In a series of ordinances passed between 1445 and 1459, Charles VII made it perpetual and extended it throughout his realm. The *taille* became the largest and most predictable source of crown revenue and virtually eliminated the need for the Estates General, which met only once between 1484 and 1789. The meetings of the Estates General at Tours in 1484 redoubled the royal desire to avoid future meetings by producing loud complaints about the impoverishment of the people by royal taxes (see document 13.1). Charles also laid the goundwork for a professional army, a national administration, and a diplomatic corps.

His son, Louis XI (ruled 1461–83), went further. Most of Louis's reign was consumed by a bitter feud with the dukes of Burgundy, who had established a formidable, multilingual state along his eastern borders. Including Burgundy, the Franche-Comté, Artois, Picardy, the Boulonnais, and most of what is now Belgium and the Netherlands, it was almost certainly the wealthiest principality in Europe. Under Duke Philip "the Good" (d. 1467), it surpassed most kingdoms in courtly magnificence and in the richness of its musical and artistic life, but it was not a kingdom. Most of its territories were held in fief either from the Holy Roman

Empire or from France. To enhance his independence, Philip had supported the English and some discontented elements of the French nobility against Louis in the League of the Common Weal, which Louis defeated in 1465. Philip's son, Charles (known to some as "the Bold" and to others as "the Rash"), hoped to weld his holdings into a single territorial state stretching from the Alps to the North Sea. His ambitions brought him into conflict with the duke of Lorraine and with the Swiss, whose independence he seemed to threaten. These formidable opponents, richly subsidized by Louis, defeated and killed Charles at the battle of Nancy in 1477.

Charles died without male heirs. His daughter Mary was the wife of the Hapsburg archduke, Maximilian, who would become emperor in 1486. Under Louis's interpretation of the Salic law, she could not, as a woman, inherit her father's French fiefs. Maximilian was unable to defend his wife's claims, and in 1482 Burgundy, Picardy, and the Boulonnais reverted to the French crown.

The dismemberment of the Burgundian state was the capstone of Louis's career. It was accompanied by acquisitions of equal value. Louis may have been clever and ruthless, but he was also lucky. In 1480 René of Anjou died without heirs, leaving Anjou and the French segment of Bar to the crown. Maine and the kingdom of Provence were incorporated in the following year after the death of Duke Charles II, and the rights of succession to Brittany were purchased when it became apparent that its duke, too, would die without producing male heirs. When Louis died in 1483, he left a France whose borders were recognizably similar to those of today. Luck and a consistently antifemale interpretation of the laws of inheritance played their part, but he could not have done it without a superior army, fiscal independence, and great diplomatic skill. His immense resources permitted him to take advantage of the dynastic misfortunes of others.

England: The Yorkists and Tudors

England was far smaller in land area and in population than either France or Spain. Its population was also more homogeneous, though regional differences were still important until well into the sixteenth century. Perhaps because it dominated an island whose integrity was rarely threatened by foreign enemies, it failed to develop perpetual taxes and its Parliament never lost "the power of the purse." England's development was therefore unlike that of the great continental powers,

and it remained a relatively minor player in international politics until late in the early modern period.

Henry VI (reigned 1422–61, 1470–71) came to the throne as an infant and suffered from protracted bouts of mental illness as an adult. He was never competent to rule in his own right. For the first thirty years of the reign, his regency council fought bitterly among themselves, brought the kingdom to the edge of bankruptcy, and lost the remaining English possessions in France with the exception of Calais. Eventually, Richard, duke of York claimed the throne with the support of a powerful segment of the nobility. Richard was descended from Edmund of Langley, the fourth surviving son of Edward III, while the king was the great grandson of Edward's third son, John of Gaunt, duke of Lancaster. The civil war that followed is called the War of the Roses because the heraldic symbol of the Yorkists was a white rose; that of the Lancastrians, a red.

In the first phase of the war (1455–61), the Lancastrians were led by Henry's formidable queen, Margaret of Anjou. She defeated the Yorkists at Wakefield and at St. Albans but failed to take London. Richard was killed at Wakefield. His son, an able commander, took advantage of her hesitation. He entered London and had himself proclaimed king as Edward IV. The struggle continued, but Edward retained the throne with one brief interruption until 1483. The last half of his reign was characterized by imaginative and energetic reforms in the administration of the royal domain. As customs duties were an important part of crown revenues, Edward used his extensive personal contacts in the London merchant community to encourage the growth of trade. He eventually became a major investor himself. The proceeds from these efforts, together with a pension extorted from Louis XI to prevent Edward from invading France, left him largely independent of Parliament. Some thought his methods unkingly, but when he died in 1483, he left behind an improved administration and an immense fortune.

He also left two young sons under the guardianship of his brother. The brother quickly had himself proclaimed king as Richard III, and the two little princes disappeared from the Tower of London, never to be seen again. This usurpation caused several of the leading Yorkists to make common cause with the Lancastrians, and in 1485, Henry Tudor, the last remaining Lancastrian claimant to the throne, defeated and killed Richard at the battle of Bosworth.

As Henry VII (reigned 1485–1509), Tudor followed the policies of Edward IV (see illustration 13.1). A subtle diplomat, he avoided war, intensified the

Illustration 13.1

🕮 **Henry VII of England.** This portrait by an unknown Flemish artist was painted c. 1505. Shrewd, cynical, and devoid of chivalric illusions, Henry was typical of a generation of monarchs who transformed their kingdoms into something resembling the modern state.

exploitation of his domain, and encouraged the development of trade. His Welsh connections—he had been born in Pembrokeshire and was partially of Welsh descent—secured him the cooperation of the principality and laid the groundwork for its eventual union with England in 1536.

The greatest threat to Henry's regime was the belligerence of the great nobles, many of whom continued to maintain private armies. He dealt with this menace through prerogative courts, including the Court of King's Bench and the Star Chamber, so called because it met in a room decorated with painted stars. Staffed by royal appointees, these bodies levied heavy fines for a variety of offenses against the crown that eventually destroyed the military power of the great families. Para-

doxically, Henry may have been aided by several pretenders to the throne who claimed to be one or another of the missing princes and who enjoyed the support of disgruntled Yorkists or other "over-mighty" subjects. The fines, confiscations, and executions imposed after each of these episodes added to the royal domain and further reduced the number of his enemies.

When Henry died in 1509, the treasury was full and the kingdom at peace. Many of the old feudal families were either impoverished or extinct, and a new elite composed largely of servants of the crown was beginning to develop. The authority of the crown, in other words, was great, but the state as a whole remained dependent upon domain revenues. The later Tudors would find this dependence limiting. The Stuarts would be destroyed by it.

The Holy Roman Empire

The Holy Roman Empire of the later Middle Ages should be regarded as a confederation of cities and principalities instead of as a territorial state that failed. German parallels to the growth of Spain, France, or England may be found in states such as Brandenburg, Saxony, and Bavaria, not at the imperial level. Their rulers sought, with varying degrees of success, to enhance domain revenues, control representative bodies, and impose new taxes. The imperial office was an unlikely vehicle for this type of development because it was elective and because it lacked several of the more important attributes of sovereignty.

The century before the Black Death had been one of imperial paralysis and decentralization, caused in part by papal interference. The turning point came in 1355 when Charles IV renounced his Italian claims and turned his attention to reorganizing what would soon be called the Holy Roman Empire of the German Nation. The Golden Bull of 1356 regularized imperial elections by placing them in the hands of seven permanent electors: the archbishops of Trier, Mainz, and Cologne, the duke of Saxony, the margrave of Brandenburg, the count of Palatine, and the king of Bohemia. It further declared that the territory of these princes would be indivisible and that inheritance in the secular electorates would be by primogeniture.

These measures strengthened the electors and made consolidation of their territories easier, but they did little to create a more viable imperial government. No incentive existed to increase the power of the emperor, and the lesser states feared the growing influence of the electors. Efforts to create an electoral union or

◆ DOCUMENT 13.2 ◆

The Twelve Articles of the German Peasants

The Great Peasant War of 1524–25 was the last in a long series of revolts against the claims of lords, princes, and the church. Some of the Twelve Articles reflect the peasants' understanding of the Protestant Reformation. Most of them expressed grievances that had been accumulating for centuries. Those abridged below would have been as valid in 1424 as in 1524.

The Third Article. It has been the custom hitherto for men to hold us as their own property, which is pitiable enough considering that Christ has redeemed and purchased us without exception, by the shedding of His precious blood, the lowly as well as the great. Accordingly, it is consistent with Scripture that we should be free and wish to be so. . . .

The Fourth Article. [I]t has been the custom heretofore that no poor man was allowed to catch venison or wild fowl, or fish in flowing water, which seems to us quite unseemly and unbrotherly. . . . Accordingly, it is our desire if a man holds possession of waters that he should prove from satisfactory documents that his right has been wittingly acquired by purchase.

The Fifth Article. [W]e are aggrieved in the matter of woodcutting, for our noble folk have appropriated all the woods to themselves alone. . . . It should be free to every member of the community to help himself to such firewood as he needs in his home.

The Eighth Article. [W]e are greatly burdened by holdings that cannot support the rent exacted from them. We ask that the lords may appoint persons of honor to inspect these holdings and fix a rent in accordance with justice.

The Ninth Article. [W]e are burdened with the great evil in the constant making of new laws. In our opinion we should be judged according to the old written law, so that the case shall be decided according to its merits and not with favors.

The Eleventh Article. [W]e will entirely abolish the custom called *Todfall* [death dues], and will no longer allow it, nor allow widows and orphans to be thus shamefully robbed against God's will.

"The Twelve Articles of the German Peasants." In Hans Hillerbrand, ed., *The Protestant Reformation*, pp. 65–66. New York: Harper Torchbooks, 1967.

Kurfürstverein with many of the powers of a central government were defeated in 1424, 1453, and 1500. The Common Penny, an imperial tax, was rejected by a majority of German states after it had been approved by their representatives in the Imperial Diet or *Reichstag*. The empire would remain an unstable grouping of eighty-nine free Imperial Cities together with more than two hundred independent principalities, most of which continued to divide and re-form according to the vagaries of partible inheritance. A few, such as Bavaria, achieved near-equality with the electoral states by introducing primogeniture. However, all sought to maximize their own power and to resist imperial and electoral encroachments.

In the process, German states—and cities—imitated the western monarchies by trying to increase revenues at the expense of traditional rights and privileges. The peasants, already squeezed by landholders trying to reverse the economic effects of a declining population, added the actions of the princes to their list of grievances and rebelled. The last and most serious of the *bundschuh* revolts was the Great Peasant War of

1524–25 that ended with the defeat of the peasant armies and the imposition of serfdom in many parts of the empire (see document 13.2). Serfs had no personal or legal rights and were usually transferred from one owner to another whenever the property on which they lived changed hands. Their status differed from that of slaves only in that they could not be sold as individuals. Serfdom was the final step in the destruction of peasant freedom.

Central and Eastern Europe

Serfdom as an institution was also established in eastern Europe. In Bohemia, Hungary, and Poland-Lithuania, the growing power of aristocratic landholders deprived peasants of their traditional freedoms and blocked the development of western-style states. If western kings may be said to have tamed their nobles, in the east the nobles tamed their kings.

Bohemia and Hungary were in some ways politically similar, though Bohemia was part of the Holy

Roman Empire and Hungary was not. Both were elective monarchies whose powerful Diets or representative assemblies were dominated by the landed aristocracy. Rich mineral deposits provided a source of revenues for both crowns. Once elected, a capable monarch could use this wealth as the basis for administrative and military reforms, but his achievements were unlikely to survive him. By the late fifteenth century Diets customarily demanded concessions as the price of election, and as Diets were dominated by the great magnates, their demands invariably tended to weaken the authority of the crown and threaten the rights of common people.

Bohemia, though wealthy and cultured, was convulsed throughout the fifteenth century by the Hussite wars and their aftermath. The Czechs, deeply resentful of a powerful German minority, launched what was probably the first national movement in European history. It was anti-German, anti-empire, and under the leadership of Jan Hus, increasingly associated with demands for religious reform. Hus was burned as a heretic in 1415. After many years of civil war, the Czechs succeeded in placing the Hussite noble George of Podebrady (ruled 1458–71) on the throne. The king's ability and popularity were eventually seen as a threat to the great Bohemian landholders. When he died, the Diet elected Vladislav II (ruled 1471–1516), a member of the Polish Jagiello dynasty, on the promise that he would support their interests. Under Vladislav, the Bohemian nobles gained virtual control over the state, expelled the towns from the Diet, and introduced serfdom. The towns eventually achieved readmission, but the Bohemian peasantry did not recover its freedom until the eighteenth century.

The policies of Vladislav could only recommend him to the Hungarian nobility. During the long and brilliant reign of Matthias Corvinus (ruled 1458–90), the crown acquired unprecedented authority and supported a court that was admired even in Renaissance Italy. When Matthias died, the Hungarian Diet elected the more controllable Vladislav to succeed him. Vladislav and his son, Louis II, who was in turn elected king of both Hungary and Bohemia, reversed the achievements of Matthias and left the Diet free to promote repressive legislation. Driven to desperation, the peasants rebelled in 1514 only to be soundly defeated. After bloody reprisals, the Diet imposed "real and perpetual servitude" on the entire Hungarian peasant class.

By this time Hungary was on the edge of an abyss. The Turkish Empire, under the formidable Süleyman the Magnificent (reigned 1520–66), was preparing an invasion, and Louis was crippled by the aristocratic independence he had done so much to encourage. Though king of Bohemia as well as Hungary, he was unable to gain the support of the Bohemians. The Hungarians were divided not only by rivalries among the leading clans, but also by an increasingly bitter feud between the magnates and the lesser nobility. Süleyman had little difficulty in annihilating a weak, divided, and badly led Hungarian army at Mohács in 1526. Louis, along with many great nobles and churchmen, was killed, and Hungary was partitioned into three sections. The center of the country would thereafter be ruled directly by the Turks. In the east, Transylvania became a Turkish client and tributary, while a narrow strip of territory in the west fell under Hapsburg rule.

After their union in 1386, Poland and Lithuania occupied an immense territory stretching from the borders of Baltic Prussia to the Black Sea. In spite of its ethnic and religious diversity and a substantial number of prosperous towns, it was primarily a land of great estates whose titled owners profited during this period from a rapidly expanding grain trade with the west. At the same time, the vast spaces of the north European plain and the Ukrainian steppe preserved the importance of cavalry and with it the military dominance of the knightly class.

The great magnates of both Poland and Lithuania negotiated their union after the death of Casimir the Great, and they continued to increase their power throughout the fifteenth century. The Jagiello dynasty survived mainly through capitulations. By 1500 Poland-Lithuania could be described as two aristocratic commonwealths joined by a largely ceremonial monarchy, not as a dynastic state. Serfdom was imposed in a series of edicts passed by the Polish *Sejm* or parliament between 1492 and 1501, and the crown, already elective in practice, became so in theory by 1572.

As in the case of Hungary, these aristocratic triumphs unfolded in the growing shadow of a menace to the east. Autocratic Russia, not the Polish-Lithuanian commonwealth, was destined to become the dominant power in eastern Europe, and by 1505 the borders of Lithuania were already shrinking. The process of transforming the grand duchy of Moscow into the Russian Empire began in earnest during the reign of Ivan III from 1462 to 1505. In the first thirteen years of his reign, Ivan was able to annex most of the independent Russian principalities and the city-states of Vyatka and Novgorod. In 1480 he refused to pay tribute to the Mongol khans and began to style himself "tsar of all Russia." Finally, in 1492, he invaded Lithuania and, in two successive campaigns, was able to annex much of Beloruss and the Ukraine.

Ivan was not a great field general. His son-in-law claimed rather sourly that "he increased his dominions while sitting at home and sleeping." But Ivan built an effective army and introduced the first usable artillery to eastern Europe. As most of his troops were cavalry, and therefore expensive to maintain, either he or his state secretary introduced the "service land" or *pomest'e* system, which granted land directly to cavalrymen instead of paying them in cash. It was an ideal way of supporting troops in a land that was still underpopulated and cash-poor. *Pomest'e* offered other dividends as well. It created an armed class that owed its prosperity directly to the tsar and permitted him to destroy local allegiances through the massive resettlement of populations. The annexation of Novgorod, for example, was followed by the removal of more than seven thousand citizens who were located elsewhere in Russia and replaced by Muscovites, many of whom were members of this service class.

The new service class cavalry were drawn primarily from the middle ranks of society and depended for their economic survival on peasant cultivators who worked their land. To ensure the stability of the labor force, they secured an edict in 1497 that restricted peasant movement. Thereafter, peasants were allowed to change employers only during a brief period centered on the feast of St. George (April 23). It was the first step toward serfdom. True serfdom on the Hungarian or Polish model did not become general until the end of the sixteenth century.

The Russia of Ivan III had little in common with western states or with its immediate neighbors. The tsar was an autocrat who ruled with little regard for representative institutions. The Orthodox church was implacably hostile to Latin christendom. The *pomest'e* system, like many other Russian institutions, derived from Turkish, Persian, and Byzantine precedents, and even daily life had an oriental flavor. Men wore beards and skirtlike garments that touched the ground while women were secluded and often veiled.

In the reign of Ivan's grandson, Ivan IV "the Terrible" (1530–84), the Russian state expanded eastward, adding Kazan and Astrakhan to its dominions. An effort to annex the areas now known as Latvia and Estonia was unsuccessful. Ivan attributed this failure to dissatisfaction among the *boyars*, or great nobles, and pretended to abdicate, returning only on the condition that he be allowed to establish an *oprichnina*. A bizarre

state within a state, the *oprichnina* was regarded as the tsar's private property. Land and even certain streets in Moscow were assigned to it, and the original owners were settled elsewhere. The purpose was to dismantle *boyar* estates as well as to provide income for Ivan's court and for a praetorian guard of six thousand men. Dressed in black and mounted upon black horses, these *oprichniki* carried a broom and the severed head of a dog as symbols of their primary mission: to root out "treason" and terrorize the enemies of the tsar. They succeeded admirably. Though disbanded in 1572, the *oprichniki* represented an institutionalization of autocracy and state terror that was unique in Europe.

Russia's size and military strength made it a great power, but its autocratic system of government ensured that political effectiveness would inevitably depend upon the personal qualities of the tsar. After Ivan IV, ability was conspicuously lacking. Russia turned inward for more than a hundred years, to emerge once again under the not-too-gentle guidance of Peter the Great at the beginning of the eighteenth century.

The New Learning: Learned Culture in the Late Medieval Italian City-State

The social and political transformations of the late Middle Ages were accompanied, as great changes often are, by the development of new intellectual interests. The most important of these was the Renaissance, or, as it was sometimes called, the New Learning. The word *renaissance* means rebirth in French. It is often applied to the entire age that marked the end of the Middle Ages and the beginning of modern times, but its original meaning was more restricted. Beginning in the fourteenth century, a number of scholars became interested in the Greco-Roman past. They sought to recover the glories of classical literature because the learning of their own day seemed to them stagnant and largely irrelevant to their needs. A later generation saw the "renaissance" of classical antiquity that they created as the birth of modern times; more recent scholarship has emphasized its continuity with the medieval past. In its original form, the Renaissance was a direct outgrowth of life in the medieval Italian city-state, and its first proponents were Italian.

The status of medieval town dwellers was unclear. Even the richest were, by feudal standards, of humble origin, yet their wealth and literacy set them apart from the peasants. Chivalric literature affected to despise them, and ecclesiastical theorists found their activities dubious if not wicked. Trade, the lifeblood of any city, was often regarded as parasitic. The merchant bought low and sold high, profiting from the honest toil of the peasant and raising prices for everyone. The need for mechanisms of distribution was not always fully understood. Worse yet, the townsman was frequently a citizen (women, though they engaged in trade, had neither civic rights nor obligations). Under law he was compelled to vote and to hold public office if elected. Even before St. Augustine, western Christianity had been deeply suspicious of public life, regarding it as incompatible with concern for one's soul. In short, two of the most significant features of town life were either ignored by medieval writers or condemned by them outright.

A certain alienation from the norms of medieval culture was therefore to be expected among townsfolk even if it was not always fully conscious or easily articulated. This alienation was most intense in Italy. Italian town life had developed early. The acquisition of full sovereignty, rare in other parts of Europe, gave a peculiar intensity to political life in the Italian city-states while imposing heavy moral and intellectual responsibilities on their citizens. Extensive contact with the Muslim and Byzantine worlds may also have left the Italians more open to influences that came from outside the orbit of chivalric or scholastic ideas.

By the end of the thirteenth century, the intellectual life of the Italian towns was beginning to acquire a distinct flavor of its own. This was evident to some extent in the works of Dante Alighieri (1265–1321). His masterwork, *The Divine Comedy*, a brilliant evocation of hell, purgatory, and paradise written in the Tuscan vernacular (the basis of modern Italian), is arguably the greatest poem ever written by a European. It is filled with classical allusions and references to Florentine politics but remains essentially medieval in inspiration. The widening gap between Italian culture and that of the scholastic, chivalric north is far more striking in the city chronicles that were becoming popular with the urban elite. Unlike northern chronicles, which were often little more than a simple record of events, they increasingly sought to analyze the causes of political and economic phenomena to provide guidance for policy makers. On a less practical level, the *Decameron*, by the Florentine Giovanni Boccaccio (1313–75), was a collection of stories that portrayed the lives of city people with little reference to the conventions of chivalry.

That Boccaccio and another Florentine, Francesco Petrarca (or Petrarch, 1304–74), were among the first to develop a serious interest in the Roman past is no accident. Petrarch grew up in exile and spent most of his life at the papal court in Avignon, an existence that no doubt sharpened his personal sense of distance from chivalric and scholastic values. Believing, like other Italians, that he was descended from the ancient Romans, he began to seek out classical manuscripts and to compose works in Latin that demonstrated his affinity with the antique past. Among them were letters addressed to such ancient figures as Cicero and Livy and an epic poem, *Africa*, inspired by his reading of Virgil's *Aeniad*. His friend Boccaccio followed his lead in collecting manuscripts and compiled an encyclopedia of Greco-Roman mythology.

Petrarch is probably best known today for his sonnets written in the Tuscan vernacular, but classical studies consumed most of his working life. His efforts made an undeniably vital point. To Petrarch and to many of his readers, the society of ancient Rome had more in common with that of the Italian states than did the chivalric, scholastic world of transalpine Europe. The ancients had lived in cities and had believed that good citizenship was the highest of virtues. Accordingly, they had produced a vast body of literature on rhetoric, politics, history, and the other arts needed to produce effective citizens. Many Italians would eventually find these works to be of great practical value in the conduct of their lives.

Those who did so, and who made the study of antiquity their primary task, became known as humanists. The term was coined by Leonardo Bruni (c. 1370–1444) to describe those engaged in *studia humanitatis*, the study of secular letters as opposed to theology or divine letters. The movement became popular in Florence during the political crisis of 1392–1402 when Bruni and other publicists used classical examples of civic virtue to stir up the public against Giangaleazzo Visconti, despot of Milan, and his expansionist schemes. Even more important was the enthusiasm aroused by the arrival in Italy of Greek scholars who were seeking western aid against the Turks. Petrarch had known that Roman culture had Greek roots but could find no one to teach him classical Greek. Manuel Chrysaloras, Cardinal Bessarion, and other members of the Greek delegation were able to do this for Bruni's generation and, by so doing, opened up a great literary tradition that had been lost to the west for centuries. Spurred by these developments, humanism spread from Florence and

Rome to Venice and the other Italian states. By the mid-fifteenth century, it was attracting followers beyond the Alps.

Humanism: Its Methods and Its Goals

Associating the early humanists with any fixed ideological or philosophical system is difficult. Most of them were either teachers of rhetoric or the editors of classical texts whose chief purpose was to study the classics and to apply ancient ideas and values to life in their own time. As such they might be found on almost any side of a given issue. But for all their variety, they shared certain presuppositions that defined them as a movement. Humanists by definition believed in the superiority of ancient culture. Errors, they said, were modern. Where medieval writers had seen their world as a historical extension of antiquity, the humanists saw a radical disjuncture between ancient and modern times, and they regarded the interval between the fall of Rome and their revival of antique ideals as a "middle age" of barbarity, ignorance, and above all, bad style. Immersed in the elegance of classical Latin, they were deeply concerned with form, sometimes, according to their critics, at the expense of substance.

Because they revered the classical past, they shared a preference for argument based on the authority of ancient sources and a suspicion of formal reason that bordered on contempt. The scholastics in particular were thought to be sterile and misguided, in part because of their bad Latin, but also because the nominalist rejection of reason as a support for faith had led the philosophers into pursuits that humanists regarded as trivial. Scholastics sometimes counterattacked by accusing them of irreligion. Though humanists were to be found among the critics of the church, few if any rejected conventional religious belief. The Renaissance moved Western society strongly toward secularism by reviving the ancient preoccupation with human beings and their social relationships. Writers such as Giovanni Pico della Mirandola asserted "the dignity of man" against preachers who saw humanity as wholly depraved (see document 13.3), but even Pico believed that human dignity derived largely from man's central place in a divinely established universe. Unbelief was not at issue. The humanists believed in perfecting their minds and bodies on Earth while preparing their souls for the hereafter.

Such a goal was fundamentally educational, and the humanists were predictably concerned with educational theory. Their purpose was to create *il uomo universale*, the universal man whose person combined intellectual and physical excellence and who was capable of functioning honorably in virtually any situation. It was the ancient Greco-Roman ideal, brought up-to-date and applied to life in the Italian city-state where the small size of the community forced citizens or courtiers to play many roles. Though most fully described in *The Courtier* by Baldassare Castiglione (published in 1528), it had long been present in the thinking of such educational theorists as Vittorino da Feltre (1386–1446) and Leon Battista Alberti (1404–72).

The heart of Renaissance education was ancient literature and history (see document 13.4). The classics were thought to provide both moral instruction and the deep understanding of human behavior without which correct action in the present is impossible. They were also a guide to style. The ability to communicate is essential to political life, and good writing comes largely from immersion in good literature. Humanists taught the art of persuasion through an exhaustive study of rhetoric based on the writings of Quintilian and Cicero.

Because citizens and courtiers would almost certainly participate in war, study was thought to be necessary in military history and theory, the art of fortification, and ballistics. Educators regarded proficiency with weapons and physical fitness as essential for war, furthermore, like the ancients, they regarded athletic skill as of value in its own right. The Renaissance man or woman was also expected to be good company. Sports were a social skill as was dancing, the ability to play musical instruments, and the possession of a trained singing voice. Art was useful, not merely for the sake of appreciation, but also as a tool of observation. Before the camera, only drawing or sketching could preserve a record of visual impressions—or accurately portray the fortifications of one's enemies. Other useful subjects included mathematics, accounting, medicine, and the natural sciences.

The preferred means of imparting this rather daunting quantity of knowledge was in small academies or by means of a tutor. The teacher was supposed to live with his students and be a moral example and friend as well as a purveyor of knowledge. Students were not to be beaten or threatened but induced to learn by arousing their interest in the subject at hand. These humanist theories, and the classical examples from which they came, remain the basis of today's liberal arts education. They have had an enormous impact on the formation of European youth and on the devel-

---

◈ DOCUMENT 13.4 ◈

The Value of the Liberal Arts

Peter Paul Vergerio (1370–1444) was a leading Renaissance educational theorist. The following is from a letter he wrote to another humanist, Ubertino of Carrara.

For no wealth, no possible security against the future, can be compared with the gift of education in grave and liberal studies. By them a man may win distinction for the most modest name, and bring honor to the city of his birth however obscure it may be. . . .

We come now to the consideration of the various subjects which may rightly be included under the name of "Liberal Studies." Among these I accord the first place to History, on grounds both of its attractiveness and its utility, qualities which appeal equally to the scholar and to the statesman. Next in importance is Moral Philosphy, which indeed is, in a peculiar sense, a "Liberal Art" in that its purpose is to teach men the secret of true freedom. History, then, gives us the concrete examples of the precepts inculcated by philosophy. The one shows what men should do, the other what men have said and done in the past, and what lessons we may draw therefrom for the present day. I would indicate as the third main branch of study, Eloquence, which indeed holds a place of distinction among the refined Arts. By philosophy we learn the essential truth of things, which by eloquence we so exhibit in orderly adornment as to bring conviction to differing minds. And history provides the light of experience.

Vergirio, Peter Paul. Letter to Ubertino of Carrara. In W.H. Woodward, ed., *Vittorino da Feltre and Other Humanist Educators*, pp. 106–107. New York: Bureau of Publications, Teachers College, Columbia University, 1963.

---

opment of Western culture. However, humanist education was intended only for a relatively narrow social elite: the select group that participated in public life and exercised some degree of control over its own destiny. Even women were largely excluded, though humanists such as Leonardo Bruni, Juan Luis Vives, and Thomas More argued that women should be educated in much the same way as men (see document 13.5).

◈ DOCUMENT 13.5 ◈

Louise Labé: The Education of Women

Though the Renaissance ideal of education extended only to a minority of women, many saw even this as a liberating step forward in the development of women as a whole. One of them was Louise Labé (c. 1524–66), an important French poet whose ideas in some ways foreshadow modern feminism. The following is from a dedicatory preface written to a friend.

Since a time has come, Mademoiselle, when the severe laws of men no longer prevent women from applying themselves to the sciences and other disciplines, it seems to me that those of us who can should use this long-craved freedom to study and to let men see how greatly they wronged us when depriving us of its honor and advantages. And if any woman becomes so proficient as to be able to write down her thoughts, let her do so and not despise the honor but rather flaunt it instead of fine clothes, necklaces, and rings. For these may be considered ours only by use, whereas the honor of being educated is ours entirely. . . . If the heavens had endowed me with sufficient wit to understand all I would have liked, I would serve in this as an example rather than an admonishment.

But having devoted part of my youth to musical exercises, and finding the time left too short for the crudeness of my understanding, I am unable in my own case, to achieve what I want for our sex, which is to see it outstrip men not only in beauty but in learning and virtue. All I can do is to beg our virtuous ladies to raise their minds somewhat above their distaffs and spindles and try to prove to the world that if we were not made to command, still we should not be disdained in domestic and public matters by those who govern and command obedience.

If there is anything to be recommended after honor and glory, anything to incite us to study, it is the pleasure which study affords. Study differs in this from all other recreations, of which all one can say, after enjoying them, is that one has passed the time. But study gives a more enduring sense of satisfaction. For the past delights us and serves more than the present.

Labé, Louise. Dedicatory preface. From J. Aynard, ed., *Les poétes lyonnais précurseurs de la Pléide*. In Julia O'Faolain and Lauro Martines, *Not in God's Image: Women in History from the Greeks to the Victorians*, pp. 184–185. London: Temple Smith, 1973.

Such women as Vitoria Colonna and More's daughter, Margaret Roper, developed a reputation for classical learning. But for the most part, the education of upper-class women continued to emphasize the domestic and social graces as it had done for centuries.

The usefulness of the Renaissance educational ideal was in part responsible for the spread of humanism beyond the Alps. The requirements of life as a courtier or servant of the crown in England, France, or Spain were not unlike those demanded of the upper-class Italian. Such people were among the first non-Italians to develop an interest in the classics, but they were quickly followed by their princes. Isabella of Castile, for example, imported Italian humanists to raise the educational standards of her court and administration. Lawyers, too, were intrigued by humanist methods. The development of philology and of the historical analysis of texts had been among the first achievements of humanist scholarship. The legal profession in France and Germany was soon divided between those who added the new tech-

niques to their arsenals and those who refused to do so. Above all, town councils were quick to recognize the usefulness of officials trained in the new learning. It became desirable, especially in the cities of the Holy Roman Empire, to have town clerks who could communicate with one another in classical Latin and who possessed the training to interpret and decipher old documents. Usefulness aside, the presence of learned humanists within a town or principality had become a matter of prestige.

The universities were in general more resistant to change. They remained the strongholds of Aristotelianism if for no other reason than that their traditional role had been the training of theologians. Some, however, such as John Colet at Oxford and Lefèvre d'Etaples at Paris, began to perceive the usefulness of humanism for the study of religious literature, which was another form of ancient text. Others, outside the universities, shared their concern. The most famous of those who turned humanist methods to the study of Scripture and

Illustration 13.2

Erasmus of Rotterdam. In this famous portrait by Hans Holbein, the greatest of the northern humanists is shown at his writing desk.

of the Fathers of the church was Erasmus of Rotterdam (1469–1536). Believing that corrupted texts had led to false interpretations, he devoted much of his extraordinarily busy and productive life to providing authoritative editions of religious texts. Best known today for his satirical attacks on ecclesiastical ignorance and for his bitter controversy with Martin Luther over the issue of free will, he was in many ways the epitome of the humanist whose chief interests were religious (see illustration 13.2). His English friend Sir Thomas More (1477–1535) combined religious with secular interests. A lawyer who ultimately became lord chancellor to Henry VIII, he is perhaps best known for *Utopia*, his vision of a perfect society that recalls Plato's *Republic*. More also applied humanist scholarship to the law and to religious questions before being martyred for his opposition to the Reformation. He was sainted by the Catholic Church in 1935. The value of humanist studies was recognized on occasion by even the most conservative of churchmen. Cardinal Francisco Jiménez de

Cisneros, archbishop of Toledo, grand inquisitor, and ultimately regent of Castile, established the University of Alcalá de Henares in 1508 to provide humanist training for the Spanish clergy. Among its first products was the Complutensian Polyglot Bible, printed in Greek, Hebrew, and Latin.

The Impact of Renaissance Humanism on the Arts and Sciences

By 1500 humanist methods and values had spread to virtually every part of Europe. Their impact on the arts and sciences was enormous, though not always what one might expect. The humanists developed classical studies as they are known today. They created the first standardized editions of classical works and distributed them widely after printing with moveable type was invented, probably by Johan Gutenberg, in the mid-fifteenth century. In the process, humanism gave birth to the disciplines of linguistics, philology (the study of words), and historical criticism.

In literature, however, humanist devotion to the classics retarded the development of vernacular writing for more than a century. Those with literary inclinations preferred to write in Latin, often in slavish imitation of the elaborate Roman style that had developed during the Augustan Age. When vernacular literature was revived in the sixteenth century by such figures as Tasso and Ariosto in Italy, Cervantes and Garcilaso de la Vega in Spain, Rabelais and Montaigne in France, and Marlowe and Shakespeare in England, it was transformed by classical themes and rules of composition. The fifteenth century, however, had been remarkably unproductive. Latin, in the meantime, was practically destroyed as a living language. Because the humanists insisted on weeding out all nonclassical usages, the language ceased to evolve as it had done throughout the Middle Ages when it was the day-to-day language of diplomacy and administration in both church and state. Ironically, by the middle of the sixteenth century, Latin had largely been supplanted by the various European vernaculars in every western government outside the papal states.

The contribution of humanism to the study of history and politics was far more positive. From the beginning, humanists had regarded history as essential to a political education. At the very least, it provided inspiring examples of civic virtue and cautionary tales that would help the citizen or courtier to avoid the mistakes of the past.

In the Middle Ages, the dominant form of history had been the chronicle. Outside the Italian cities, chroniclers tended to record events without troubling themselves greatly over causation or the objective accuracy of their sources. The cause of historical events was after all God's will. The Greeks and Romans had taken a different view. Beginning with Thucydides, the best of them had defined their topics as questions to be answered in causal terms because they believed that human nature was consistent and that history therefore repeated itself. If history was cyclical, it offered a priceless guide to action in the present, not so much because it was predictive in absolute terms, but because the process of historical causation could be understood and used by the educated to their own advantage.

The most effective exponent of this view during the Renaissance was the Florentine lawyer and sometime politician Niccolò Machiavelli (1469–1527). In works such as *The Prince* and *The Discourses on Livy* he attempted to establish rules for the conduct of political life based upon examples from the historical past. In the process, he freed political theory from the theological principles upon which it had long been based. While his name became a byword for cynicism and political manipulation, Machiavelli was in his own way an idealist. The Italian wars begun by Charles VIII of France in 1495 eventually destroyed the independence of the Italian cities with only Venice retaining full sovereignty. Machiavelli believed that this calamity could be understood and remedied only by looking with a clear eye at the way in which politics was conducted (see document 13.6).

His younger contemporary, Francesco Guicciardini (1483–1540), agreed but thought that governing oneself by the kind of rules proposed by Machiavelli was impossible. As he said in his *Ricordi*, a grim collection of musings on a variety of subjects, no two situations were the same; there were always exceptions. He seems to have believed that by studying history one absorbed what he called discretion: the ability to react intelligently to unforeseen contingencies. His *History of Italy*, which examines the loss of Italian freedom in the years after 1494, is probably the first modern historical work and remains a useful source for the political and military history of the age.

By comparison with its impact on politics and history, the humanist contribution to philosophy was indirect. The Renaissance was not a great age of formal speculation, but the course of modern philosophy would be hard to imagine without the recovery of classical works that had been lost during the Middle Ages.

◆ **DOCUMENT 13.6** ◆

The Political Philosophy of Machiavelli

Niccolò Machiavelli's most famous book was The Prince *in which he appears to favor despotic rule as a means of ridding Italy of its "barbarian" invaders. However, he was an ardent republican both in theory and in his own career as secretary to the second chancery of the Florentine republic. The following passage from* The Discourses *sets out what may be taken as his real view.*

And finally to sum up this matter, I say that both governments of princes and of the people have lasted a long time, but both require to be regulated by laws. For a prince who knows no other control but his own will is like a madman, and a people that can do as it pleases will hardly be wise. If now we compare a prince who is controlled by laws, and a people who is untrammeled by them, we shall find more virtue in the people than in the prince; and if we compare them when both are freed from such control, we shall see that the people are guilty of fewer excesses than the prince, and that the errors of the people are of less importance, and may therefore be more easily remedied. For a licentious and mutinous people can be brought back to good conduct by the influence and persuasion of a good man, but an evil-minded prince is not amenable to such influences, and there is therefore no other remedy against him but cold steel.

Macchiavelli, Nicoló, *The Discourses* I, 58, trans. Luigi Ricci, rev. E.R.P. Vincent. Modern Library Editions. New York: Random House, 1950.

Much of Aristotle, most of Plato and the Alexandrian Neoplatonists, the Pre-Socratics, and many of the Epicureans and Stoics were either unknown or had been studied with little regard to their historical and intellectual context. By recovering lost works and seeking a deeper understanding of the mental world that had produced them, the humanists immeasurably broadened philosophic discourse in the West. By attacking the scholastics, they opened the way for the acceptance of ideas that lay outside the Aristotelian tradition as it was then understood. They may have done little to exploit their own discoveries, but they made possible the great philosophical achievements of the seventeenth century. The impact of humanism on science was similar. Few humanists were scientists in the modern sense of the word. Many were devotees of what would now be called superstition, though the term is unhistorical. Believing that the wisdom of the ancients was superior, and aware that Greeks and Romans had believed in divination, sorcery, astrology, and natural magic, some humanists deliberately encouraged a revival of these practices. Notions that would have been regarded as absurd in the days of Aquinas were taken seriously. Nevertheless, in their zeal to recover every aspect of the ancient past, they found and edited works that would eventually revolutionize Western thought. Galen in medicine, Eratosthenes and Aristarchus of Samos in cosmology, Archimedes in physics, and a host of other writers were rediscovered, edited, and popularized.

The humanists also transmitted the idea, derived ultimately from Pythagoras, that the universe was based on number. This is the basic principle of numerology, now regarded as a pseudoscience, but it inspired such figures as Leonardo da Vinci (1452–1519) to explore the mathematization of physics. Leonardo is best known today as an artist and inventor whose ideas were far in advance of their time. Though Leonardo failed in his effort regarding physics, Galileo and others would eventually learn to express physical relationships in mathematical formulae, an important step in the development of modern science (see chapter 16).

Few of these achievements had an immediate impact on the life of ordinary Europeans. The recovery of classical antiquity was an intellectual movement created by and for a self-conscious elite, and many years would pass before it touched the consciousness of the general public. In one area, however, classical values intruded on material life, redefining the public spaces in which people moved and altering their visual perceptions of the world. Renaissance art, architecture, and city planning brought the aesthetic values of Greece and Rome down to street level. They eventually spread from the Italian towns to the farthest reaches of Europe and America.

Italian artists had turned to classical ruins for inspiration as early as the thirteenth century. With the emergence of humanism, ancient models became universal. The architect Filippo Brunelleschi (1377–1446) measured ancient ruins to determine their proportions. He then sketched their pediments, columns, and ornamentation with the intention of adapting Roman forms to

Illustration 13.3

Leon Battista Alberti's Tempio Malatesta. The unfinished church of San Francesco at Rimini was built about 1450. Rimini was a city in the papal states whose ruler, the infamous Sigismundo Malatesta, was a great admirer of all things Roman. At his request, Alberti transformed an existing church into a Roman temple whose facade resembles a triumphal arch. Sigismundo commissioned a statue of the Virgin Mary whose features were modeled on those of his mistress, Isotta degli Atti.

the purposes of his own day. Within a generation, churches were being built that resembled pagan temples (see illustration 13.3). New construction, private and public, sported columns, pilasters, and window treatments borrowed from the porticoes of Roman buildings. It was not mere antiquarianism because Brunelleschi and his successors—Alberti, Bramante, and the sixteenth-century master Palladio—knew that modern structures were different in function from those of the past. So successful were their adaptations that Roman forms and ornamentation remained a standard feature of Western architecture until the twentieth century.

The revival of classical taste in painting and sculpture was equally important. Medieval artists had illustrated classical themes, and some of them, such as Nicola Pisano (c. 1220–c. 1278), had successfully imitated classical forms, though only in portraying scenes from the Bible (see illustration 13.4). In medieval practice, tales from ancient history or mythology were normally portrayed in contemporary settings because they were intended as moral or religious allegories whose

Illustration 13.4

🌀 **The Anunciation, by Nicola Pisano.** This panel from the Baptistry at Pisa was completed in 1260. It demonstrates that classical models had come to influence Italian art long before the Renaissance took root as a literary movement.

Illustration 13.5

🌀 **St. James Led to Execution, by Andrea Mantegna.** Mantegna was one of the first Renaissance painters to use the laws of perspective discovered by the architect Filippo Brunelleschi. In this fresco from the Ovetari Chapel, Church of the Erimitani, Padua, painted c. 1454–57, the vanishing point is below the bottom of the picture. Note also the classicism of the triumphal arch.

message was often unlike that of their pagan originals. To the humanists, with their archaeological view of history, this was absurd. Classical forms were appropriate to classical subjects as well as to those derived from the Bible. The imitation of classical models and the use of classical settings therefore became almost universal. Ancient ideas of beauty and proportion were adopted, especially for the portrayal of the human body.

But Renaissance art was not an exercise in antiquarianism. The technique of painting with oils, developed in the Low Countries during the fifteenth century, was soon in general use. The effort to portray the world in three dimensions, begun with the use of *chiaroscuro* or shading by Giotto (c. 1266– c. 1337), was brought to a triumphal conclusion with Brunelleschi's discovery of the mathematical laws of perspective. Their application in the paintings of Andrea Mantegna (c. 1431–1506) inspired other artists, and the viewing public soon came to accept foreshortening and perspective as the norm (see illustration 13.5).

These techniques were new. Furthermore, Renaissance artists differed from the ancients in other ways. They were not pagans, and though they admired antiquity, they retained many of the ideas and symbols of the medieval past. Their art combined classical and Christian sensibilities in a new synthesis that shaped European aesthetic values until their vision was challenged by the rise of photography and nonrepresenta-

tional art in the nineteenth century. Eventually, artists such as Michelangelo Buonarroti (1475–1564) would transcend the rules of classical composition, distorting the proportions of the human body to express dramatic spiritual and emotional truths (see illustration 13.6). But even he and his Baroque followers in the seventeenth century remained well within the bounds of classical inspiration.

A century ago, most historians believed that the Renaissance marked the beginning of the modern world. As the full implications of the industrial revolution became clear, that conviction has dimmed and the distance between twentieth-century Westerners and the preoccupations of the humanists has widened. Few today believe that the Renaissance was a true rebirth of classical antiquity or as revolutionary as its more enthusiastic supporters claimed. There had been a Carolingian Renaissance and a Renaissance of the Twelfth

Century. Medieval scholars knew and quoted classical writers, but the Renaissance that began in Florence in the generation of the Black Death was far more than just another in a series of European infatuations with the antique past. By rediscovering the lost masterpieces of Greek and Roman literature, by reviving the ancient preoccupation with history, and by reexamining scientific theories ignored during the Middle Ages, the humanists redefined learning and transformed education. By the early fifteenth century, the new learning had become the dominant movement in European intellectual life. Directly or indirectly, it remade each of the arts and sciences in its own image and changed forever the way in which Westerners looked at their world.

Illustration 13.6

Tombs of Giuliano de' Medici, Duke of Nemours and Lorenzo de' Medici, Duke of Urbino, by Michelangelo. Michelangelo executed this magnificent group in the New Sacristy of San Lorenzo, Florence, between 1520 and 1534. The distorted poses of the heavily muscled reclining figures as well as the dramatic arrangement of the entire piece point away from classical balance and serenity while retaining a basically antique frame of reference.

CHAPTER 14

THE RELIGIOUS REFORMATIONS
OF THE SIXTEENTH CENTURY

CHAPTER OUTLINE

◆◆◆◆◆◆◆◆◆◆◆◆◆◆◆◆◆◆◆◆◆◆

Much of Europe's religious life was transformed in the course of the sixteenth century. Scholars have called this period the Age of the Reformation, but this is somewhat misleading. There was more than one religious reformation. Several forms of piety arose that may be called Protestant, though their competing religious visions sometimes had little in common beyond opposition to the old church. Lutherans, Calvinists, Anabaptists, and a host of other groups distrusted and at times persecuted each other with un-Christian vigor. Others, such as the Antitrinitarians, were perhaps radical enough to require a classification of their own. Roman Catholicism was changed, in part by forces that had long been stirring within and in part by the church's need to defend itself against Protestantism.

All of these reformations arose from conflicts within the church and from its broader struggle with the claims of the state. Some of the issues were institutional and political. Others grew from changes in lay attitudes or from the influence of movements such as humanism and nominalism. Chapter 14 will examine the demands for church reform that arose during the later Middle Ages and describe how they grew into a series of religious movements that split western Christendom and transformed the old church even as they created new forms of religious belief.

◈

Late Medieval Demands for Religious Reform

The new assertiveness of the secular states brought them almost immediately into conflict with the church over rights, privileges, and revenues. That this occurred when the laity and many clergy were demanding higher standards of spirituality than ever before was the church's misfortune. Plague, war, and the perception of social collapse had raised the overall level of spiritual anxiety. At the same time, higher literacy rates, already apparent in the fourteenth century, narrowed the intellectual gap between the clergy and their flocks and led to an increased sophistication in matters religious. When the church, beset with enemies and divided internally, failed to meet this revolution of rising spiritual expectations, the call for reform became strident and ultimately irresistible.

The role of the late medieval church was broader and more closely integrated with the secular world than it is today. The pope was responsible not only for the spiritual welfare of western Christians, but also for the administration and defense of the papal states, a territory that embraced much of central Italy. At the local level, bishops, parishes, monasteries, and other ecclesiastical foundations probably controlled 20 percent of the arable land in Europe. In less-settled areas such as the north of England the total may have approached 70 percent. Many Europeans therefore lived on estates held by the church or had regular business dealings with those who managed them. Such contacts often caused resentment and may at times have encouraged the appearance of corruption.

Social services, too, were the church's responsibility. Hospitals, the care of orphans, and the distribution of charity were commonly administered by clerics, as was formal education from the grammar school to the university. In an age when inns were few and wretched, monasteries often served as hotels, offering food and lodging to travelers in return for nominal donations.

Involvement with the world bred a certain worldliness. Because its practical responsibilities were great, the church was often forced to reward those in whom administrative skills were more developed than spirituality. Because the church offered one of the few available routes to upward social mobility, ambition or family interest caused many to become clerics without an adequate religious vocation. Some had little choice. Children were often destined for the priesthood at a tender age, while unmarriageable women or those who preferred a career other than that of wife and mother had only the convent as a refuge. For women of talent and ambition, the opportunity to govern an abbey or a charitable institution was a route to self-fulfillment and public service that was otherwise unavailable in medieval society.

Not all late medieval clerics were governed by worldly motives. Alongside spiritual indifference and corruption were extreme piety and asceticism. For many people the contrast may have been too painful in an era of great spiritual need. In any case the anticlericalism that had always been present in European life ran especially high in the fourteenth and fifteenth centuries. Though by no means universal—the ties between lay people and their parish priests often remained close—it was an underlying accompaniment to the events that convulsed the church throughout this period.

Anticlericalism and the Decline of Papal Authority

Papal authority was one of the first casualties of the conflict between church and state and of the growing confusion over the temporal and spiritual roles of the clergy. A series of scandals beginning around 1300 gravely weakened the ability of the popes either to govern the church or to institute effective reforms in the face of popular demand.

In 1294 the saintly Celestine V resigned from the papacy in part because he feared that the exercise of its duties imperiled his soul. His successor, Boniface VIII, had no such concerns. A vigorous advocate of papal authority, Boniface came into conflict with both Edward I of England and Philip IV of France over the issue of clerical taxation. The two kings were at war with one another, and each sought to tax the clergy of their respective realms to pay for it. When the pope forbade the practice in the bull *Clericis Laicos*, Philip blocked the transmission of money from France to Rome. Boniface backed down, but Philip was not content with partial victories. In 1301, he convicted the papal legate of treason and demanded that Boniface ratify the decision of the French courts. This he could not do without sacrificing papal jurisdiction over the French church. When Boniface issued the decree *Unam Sanctam*, a bold assertion of papal authority over the secular state, Philip had him kidnapped at Anagni in 1303. Physically mistreated by his captors and furious over this unprecedented assault on papal dignity, Boniface died shortly thereafter.

After the brief pontificate of Benedict IX, French influence in the College of Cardinals secured the election of the bishop of Bordeaux, who became pope as Clement V (served 1305–14). The Roman populace was outraged. Riot and disorder convinced Clement that Rome would be an unhealthy place for a Frenchman. He decided to establish himself at Avignon, a papal territory in the south of France. The papacy would remain there for seventy-three years.

The stay of the popes at Avignon was called the Babylonian Captivity because the church appeared to have been taken captive by the French as the biblical children of Israel had been held at Babylon. It was an

Illustration 14.1

The Papal Palace at Avignon. The luxury and massive size of the papal residence built during the so-called Babylonian Captiv- ity helps to explain why the Avignon popes developed a reputa- tion for greed and spiritual indifference.

international scandal for several reasons. The pope was living outside his diocese, and absenteeism had long been considered an abuse by reformers. Worse yet, the pope seemed to be a mere agent of the French monar- chy. This was not quite true. The Avignon popes were more independent than they appeared to be at the time, but their support of France against England in the later stages of the Hundred Years' War reinforced nega- tive impressions. Their best efforts were devoted to strengthening papal finances and to the construction of a magnificent palace complex at Avignon (see illustra- tion 14.1). Fiscal reforms backfired politically because most countries responded to it with legislation limiting papal jurisdiction and taxation within their borders. The palace was ostentatious and fostered the idea that the popes had no intention of returning to Rome. The overall impression was that the popes were subservient to France as well as greedy and luxurious.

Criticism mounted, and in 1377 Gregory XI re- turned the papacy to Rome. He died in the following year, and his Italian successor, Urban VI, was elected amid rioting by the Roman mob and dissension among the cardinals. Urban quickly alienated those who had elected him by his erratic behavior and by his demands for an immediate reform of the papal court. Thirteen cardinals, twelve of whom were French, left Rome. Claiming that the election had been held under duress, they elected an antipope, Clement VII. The Great Schism (1378–1417) had begun.

The church now had two popes. England, the Holy Roman Empire, Hungary, and Poland supported Urban VI. France, Castile, Aragon, Naples, and Scot- land supported Clement. International and dynastic is- sues were involved, and neither claimant would step down. For nearly forty years each side elected its own successors while papal administration deteriorated and the prestige of the office sank to levels not seen since before the Cluniac reforms.

The most promising solution was to convene a general council of the church. In 1409 the Council of

◈ DOCUMENT 14.1 ◈

The Decree *Sacrosancta*

By issuing the decree Sacrosancta, *the Council of Constance (1414–17) justified its deposition of three existing popes and the election of Martin V. Though repudiated by later popes, the decree helped to end the Great Schism and provided a concise statement of the conciliarist position for future generations.*

In the name of the Holy and indivisible Trinity, of the Father, Son, and Holy Ghost. Amen.

This holy synod of Constance, forming a general council for the extirpation of the present schism and the union and reformation, in head and members, of the church of God, legitimately assembled in the Holy Ghost, to the praise of Omnipotent God, in order that it may the more easily, safely, effectively, and freely bring about the union and reformation of the church of God, hereby determines, decrees, and declares what follows:

It first declares that this same council, legitimately assembled in the Holy Ghost, forming a general council and representing the Catholic Church militant, has its power immediately from Christ, and everyone, whatever his state or position, even if it be the Papal dignity itself, is bound to obey it in all those things which pertain to the faith and the healing of the said schism, and to the general reformation of the Church of God in head and members.

It further declares that anyone, whatever his condition, station or rank, even if it be the Papal, who shall contumaciously refuse to obey the mandates, decrees, ordinances or instructions which have been, or shall be issued by this holy council, or by any other general council, legitimately summoned, which concern, or in any way relate to the above mentioned subjects, shall, unless he repudiate his conduct, be subjected to condign penance and be suitably punished, having recourse, if necessary, to the other resources of the law.

Council of Constance. "*Sacrosancta.*" In Edward P. Cheyney, ed., *Pennsylvania Translations and Reprints*, vol. 3, no. 6 Philadelphia: University of Pennsylvania Press, 1898.

Pisa elected Alexander V, who was generally accepted throughout Europe. However, the two prior claimants, arguing that the council had been called illegally by the cardinals instead of by a pope, refused to quit. There were now three popes. Finally, in 1413 Alexander's successor, John XXIII, called the Council of Constance, which declared itself superior to any pope (see document 14.1). John, who had in the meantime been found guilty of heresy, and the Avignon claimant Benedict XIII were deposed and Gregory XIII resigned. Martin V was elected to succeed Gregory, thereby preserving the legitimacy of the Roman line, which has since been regarded as official.

The Schism was over, but the papacy had been gravely weakened in both fact and theory. The actions of the council were supported by the work of three generations of thinkers who had come to believe that councils representing the entire body of the faithful had ultimate authority over the church and that the pope was little more than a symbol of unity. Made plausible by more than a century of papal scandals, conciliarism became a formidable obstacle to the governance of the church. Fifteenth-century popes feared with some justification that they might be deposed for any controversial act, while councils, by their nature, found making everyday administrative decisions impossible. Legally, the issue was resolved in 1460 when Pius II forbade appeals to a council without papal authorization in the bull *Execrabilis*. The memory of conciliarism nevertheless would inhibit papal efforts at reform for years to come.

Conciliarism also served as a focus for criticisms of the papacy that had been simmering since the Babylonian Captivity. Other complaints against the papacy, some of which were adopted by the conciliarists, grew out of the possessionist controversy. By the end of the thirteenth century, the Franciscan order had split into two main factions: the Observant or Spiritual Franciscans, who insisted on a literal interpretation of the Rule of St. Francis, which prohibited the order from owning property; and the Conventuals, who believed that the work of the order could be done only if the brothers lived an orderly life in convents and possessed the material resources with which to perform their tasks. After much argument, the Observant position was condemned by John XXII. The Observant Franciscans responded with attacks on the validity of papal authority, many of which would be used by later critics of the church.

The Struggle for the Transformation of Piety

The issue of church governance became entangled in a growing dispute over the forms of piety. This conflict, which was about two different ways of living a Christian life, had been present implicitly in the reform movements of the twelfth century. The dominant form of piety that had emerged from the early Middle Ages was forged by the monastic tradition. It saw the clergy as heroic champions whose chief function was to serve as intermediaries between the laity and a God of judgment. They did this primarily through the sacrament of communion (the Eucharist), which was considered a sacrifice, and through oral prayers of intercession. This view, with its necessary emphasis on the public repetition of formulae, was challenged in the eleventh and twelfth centuries by Bernard of Clairvaux and other monastic theorists who sought a more personal experience of God through private devotions and mental prayer. Their views were adopted by the Franciscans and eventually popularized by them, though the process was lengthy and incomplete. Personal piety was especially attractive to the Observant Franciscans, whose interpretation of the Rule of St. Francis made corporate devotions difficult.

To those who sought a transformation of their inner life through personal contact with God, the older forms of piety were unacceptable. They came to believe that excessive emphasis on the sacraments and on oral prayer encouraged complacency as well as contractualism, the habit of making deals with God in return for special favors. The point is arguable, but in their critique of popular piety they were on firmer ground. Much late medieval piety was mechanistic and involved practices that would today be regarded as abuses. The sale of indulgences, the misuse of pilgrimages, and the proliferation of masses for the dead were all symptoms of the popular obsession with death and purgatory that followed in the wake of the bubonic plague. Salvation was assured by the sacraments of the church, but every sin committed in life carried with it a sentence to be served in purgatory. As the pains of purgatory were like those of hell, without the curse of eternal separation from God, much effort was spent in avoiding them. A mass said for the soul of the dead reduced the penalty by a specified number of years. Henry VII of England, who seems to have had a bad conscience, left money in his will for ten thousand masses. Many priests survived entirely on the proceeds from such bequests and had no other duties. An indulgence was a remission of the "temporal" or purgatorial punishment for sins that could be granted by the pope out of the church's "treasury of merits." Its price, too, was related to the number of years it subtracted from the buyer's term in purgatory, and an indulgence sometimes could be purchased in advance for sins not yet committed.

Such practices were deeply rooted in the rich and varied piety of the Middle Ages. If some religious were scandalized by them, other priests were unwilling to condemn genuine expressions of religious feeling, and still others no doubt accepted them out of ignorance. No systematic education had been established for parish priests, and thanks to absenteeism, many parishes were served by vicars or substitutes whose qualifications were minimal at best. However, the church's critics did not reject pilgrimages, indulgences, the proper use of relics, or masses for the dead. They merely wished to ground these "works" in the faith and good intentions that would make them spiritually valid. They opposed simpleminded contractualism and "arithmetical" piety, but their concerns intensified their conflict with a church that remained immobilized by political and organizational difficulties.

Of those forms of piety that sought personal contact with God, the most ambitious was mysticism. The enormous popularity of mysticism in the later Middle Ages was in some respects a measure of the growing influence of women on religious life. Many of the great mystics were women. Others were men who became involved with the movement as confessors to convents of nuns. Mysticism may be defined as the effort to achieve spiritual union with God through ecstatic contemplation. Because the experience is highly personal, it had many variants, but most of them fell into two broad categories. The first, and probably the most common, was to experience visions or infusions of the Holy Spirit in the manner of St. Catherine of Siena (1347–80) or Julian of Norwich (1342–c. 1416). The second, best typified by Meister Eckhardt (c. 1260–1328) and the Rhineland mystics, was influenced by the Neoplatonic concept of ideas and aimed at a real union of the soul with God (see document 14.2). They sought to penetrate the divine intelligence and perceive the universe as God perceives it. Both views were rooted firmly in the medieval tradition of interior piety, but Eckhardt and those like him were suspected of heresy because they seemed to deny the vital distinction between the Creator and the human soul.

Neither form of experience was easy to achieve. Both involved a long process of mental and spiritual preparation that was described in an ever-growing

◆ DOCUMENT 14.2 ◆

The Mystic Experience

In this passage Jan van Ruysbroeck (1293–1381) attempts to capture the sense of unity with God that was at least one of the late medieval mystic's primary goals. In the process he demonstrates both the late medieval desire to experience God without intermediaries and the mystic's postscholastic conviction that reason is an obstacle to faith.

And after this, there follows the third way of feeling; namely, that we feel ourselves to be one *with* God; for through the transformation in God, we feel ourselves to be swallowed up in the fathomless abyss of our eternal blessedness, wherein we can nevermore find any distinction between ourselves and God. And this is our highest feeling, which we cannot experience in any other way than in the immersion in love. And therefore, so soon as we are uplifted and drawn into our highest feeling, all our powers stand idle in an essential fruition; but our powers do not pass away into nothingness, for then we should lose our created being. And as long as we stand idle, with an inclined spirit, and with open eyes, but without reflection, so long can we contemplate and have fruition. But, at the very moment in which we seek to prove and to comprehend what it is that we feel, we fall back into reason, and there we find a distinction and an otherness between ourselves and God, and find God outside ourselves in incomprehensibility.

Ruysbroeck, Jan van. "The Sparkling Stone," trans. C.A. Wynschenck Dom. In E. Underhill, ed., *Jan van Ruysbroeck*. London: Dent, 1916.

literature. Manuals such as Walter Hilton's *Scale of Perfection* became extremely popular with lay people and were circulated in large numbers both before and after the invention of printing.

Though mysticism was essentially private, it influenced the development of a powerful corporate movement known as the *Devotio Moderna,* or modern devotion. Its founder was Gerhard Groote (1340–84) who organized a community of religious women at Deventer in the Netherlands. These Sisters of the Common Life were laywomen, not nuns. They pledged themselves to a communal life informed by contemplation but directed toward service in the world. A parallel group for men, the Brethren of the Common Life, was founded shortly thereafter by Groote's disciple Florens Radewijns. These two groups, together with the Augustinian Canons of the Windesheim Congregation, a fully monastic order also founded by Radewijns, formed the nucleus of a movement that spread rapidly through the Low Countries and western Germany. Catholic, but highly critical of the clergy, it emphasized charitable works, private devotion, and its own form of education. The goal of its adherents was the imitation of Christ. A book titled *The Imitation of Christ* by one of the Brethren, Thomas à Kempis, was a best-seller until well into the twentieth century and did much to popularize a style of piety that was the opposite of contractualism.

The Heretics: Wycliffe and Hus

Other religious movements were less innocent, at least from the perspective of the church. Full-scale heresies emerged in England and Bohemia in response to the teachings of John Wycliffe (1330–84) and Jan Hus (c. 1372–1415). Wycliffe was a successful teacher of theology at Oxford who became involved with politics during the 1370s. England was attempting to follow the French lead in restricting papal rights of appointment and taxation, and Wycliffe became the chief spokesman for the anticlerical views of Edward III's son, John of Gaunt. At first Wycliffe restricted himself to the traditional arguments in favor of clerical poverty, but as his views began to attract criticism and as he came to realize that his personal ambitions would not be fulfilled, he drifted further into radicalism. In his last years, he rejected papal authority and declared that the Bible was the sole source of religious truth. Strongly influenced by St. Augustine and committed to an extreme form of philosophical realism, he supported predestination and ended by rejecting transubstantiation because it involved what he saw as the annihilation of the substance of the bread and wine. In his view, substance was by definition unchangeable, and the miracle of the mass was therefore an impossibility. This was heresy, as was his revival of the ancient Donatist idea that the value of the sacraments depended upon the personal virtue of the priest who administered them.

Though John of Gaunt discretely withdrew his support, Wycliffe died before the church could bring him to trial. By this time his ideas and the extraordinary violence of his attacks on the clergy had begun to attract popular attention. His followers, the Lollards, produced an English translation of the Bible and organized a march on London in 1413. Fearing that the egalitarian tendencies of the Lollards encouraged social disorder, Henry V suppressed the movement, but scattered communities preserved their traditions until the outbreak of the Protestant Reformation.

Because England and Bohemia were diplomatically aligned on the Great Schism, a number of Czech students left the University of Paris for Oxford after 1378. There they came in contact with the teachings of Wycliffe, and by 1400 his works were being openly debated at Prague. Wycliffe's ideas were popular because they seemed to coincide with an already well-developed reform movement. Czech preachers had long attacked the morality of the clergy and were now demanding a Czech translation of the Bible. Great resentment also existed over denying the communion to the laity in both kinds. Reserving both bread and wine for the priest while giving only bread to the laity was common throughout Europe. In Bohemia the practice was seen as an expression of clerical arrogance.

Though basically religious, these issues were hopelessly intertwined with the ethnic rivalry between Czechs and Germans that had troubled Bohemia for centuries. The Kingdom of Bohemia had a large population of Germans who were often resented by their Slavic neighbors. Moreover, the church held nearly 40 percent of the land, and many of the leading churchmen were German. To many, anticlericalism was therefore an expression of Czech national feeling as well as of frustrated piety, and this association quickly drew the reform movement into the arena of imperial politics.

The University of Prague found itself at the center of these controversies. In 1409 King Vaclav expelled the German students and faculty and appointed Jan Hus, a Czech professor, as rector. Hus had been attracted to Wycliffe's writings by their anticlericalism, but he also saw their extreme philosophical realism as a weapon against the German theologians, most of whom were nominalists. He did not, however, reject transubstantiation and was in general more conservative than Wycliffe on every issue save that of papal authority. Hus did not think of himself as a heretic, and in 1415 he accepted an invitation to defend his views before the Council of Constance. The invitation had been orchestrated by Sigismund who offered him a safe-conduct, but the promised guarantee was little more than a passport, and Hus was burned at the stake on July 6.

The burning of Hus provoked a national outcry in Bohemia. Taking the communion chalice as their symbol, the Czechs broke with Rome and developed a liturgy in the Czech language. When their protector, Vaclav, died in 1419, he was succeeded by Sigismund. The Hussites, as they were now called, rose in armed revolt and resoundingly defeated the papal-imperial crusades against them in 1420, 1422, and 1431. Finally, in 1436 the Hussites secured a treaty that guaranteed them control over the Bohemian church and confirmed their earlier expropriation of church property.

The Religious Impact of Nominalism, Humanism, and the Printing Press

The religious tensions and controversies of the later Middle Ages were heightened by intellectual movements that threatened the church's authority in more subtle ways. Nominalism (see chapter 9), which grew in popularity during the fourteenth and fifteenth centuries, tended to undermine the foundations of dogma by denying that they were susceptible to rational proof. Though never the dominant school in late medieval thought, it influenced many theologians including Martin Luther.

Humanism exerted an even stronger influence on religious issues. Humanists such as Erasmus criticized the moral shortcomings of the clergy and used their mastery of rhetoric to attack the scholastic philosophers. Their belief in the superiority of ancient over modern texts contributed to the idea that scripture alone was the ultimate source of religious truth. Though many humanists, including Erasmus, remained within the old church, this concept of *sola scriptura* would be central to the teachings of the reformers. Many of them, including Zwingli, Calvin, and Melanchthon had been trained as humanists. They used humanist methodology in their analysis of sacred texts. Humanist respect for antiquity may also have influenced the growing belief that the practices of the early church most closely approximated the intentions of Christ and that subsequent developments, including the rise of the papacy, were modern corruptions.

The reform movements that destroyed the unity of western Christendom in the sixteenth century may therefore be seen as the products of a generalized dissatisfaction with the church. The development of printing, which made the writings of the reformers available to thousands of people, and the conjunction of religious reform with the political needs of certain states and cities transformed that dissatisfaction into what is usually called the Protestant Reformation.

Martin Luther and the Outbreak of the Protestant Reformation

The first and in many ways the most influential of these movements was the one created in Germany by Martin Luther (1483–1546). A monk of the Augustinian Observant order and professor of the New Testament at the University of Wittenberg in electoral Saxony, Luther experienced a profound spiritual crisis that eventually brought him into open conflict with the church (see illustration 14.2). Like many of his contemporaries, Luther was troubled by an overwhelming sense of sin and unworthiness for which the teachings of the church provided no relief. Neither the rigors of monastic life nor the sacrament of penance could provide him with assurance of salvation. In the course of his biblical studies, he gradually arrived at a solution. Based on his reading of Paul's Epistle to the Romans and on his growing admiration for the works of St. Augustine, he concluded that souls were not saved by religious ceremonies and good works but by faith alone. Human beings could never be righteous enough to merit God's forgiveness, but they could be saved if only they would believe and have faith in the righteousness of Christ.

Luther felt himself transformed by this insight. Even as he formulated it, he was confronted by the issue of indulgences. In 1517 a special indulgence was made available in the territories surrounding electoral Saxony. Its purpose was to raise money for the construction of St. Peter's basilica in Rome and to retire the debt incurred by Albrecht of Mainz in securing for himself through bribery the archbishoprics of Mainz and Magdeburg and the bishopric of Halberstadt. Albrecht had committed not only pluralism but also simony (the illegal purchase of church offices). To Luther, however, this was not the central issue. To him, as to many other clerics, the sale of indulgences was a symbol of the contractualism that beset medieval piety and blinded lay people to the true path of salvation. On October 31, 1517, he posted ninety-five theses condemning this practice to the door of Wittenberg's Castle Church.

His action was in no way unusual. It was the traditional means by which a professor offered to debate all comers on a particular issue, and the positions taken by Luther were not heretical. Furthermore, the sale of indulgences was later condemned by the Council of Trent. However, Luther's action unleashed a storm of controversy. Spread throughout Germany by the printing press, the theses were endorsed by advocates of reform and condemned by the pope, the Dominican

Illustration 14.2

Martin Luther. This portrait of Luther as a young monk was painted by Lucas Cranach the Elder about a year before the Diet of Worms and shows the reformer as he must have looked when he confronted the Imperial Diet.

order, the archbishop of Mainz, and the Fugger bank of Augsburg, which had loaned Albrecht the money for the elections.

In the debates that followed, Luther was forced to work out the broader implications of his teachings. At Leipzig in June 1519, he challenged the doctrinal authority of popes and councils and declared that Scripture took precedence over all other sources of religious truth. In 1520 he published three pamphlets that drew him at last into formal heresy. In his *Address to the Christian Nobility of the German Nation,* he encouraged the princes to demand reform (see document 14.3). *On the Babylonian Captivity of the Church* abolished five of the seven sacraments and declared that the efficacy of baptism and communion were dependent on the faith of the recipient, not the ordination of the priest. He also

◆ DOCUMENT 14.3 ◆

Luther: Address to the German Nobility

Martin Luther's primary concerns were always spiritual and theological, but he knew how to appeal to other emotions as well. These extracts from his Address to the Christian Nobility of the German Nation *are a relatively modest example of the rhetoric with which he attacked the authority of the Catholic Church.*

What is the use in Christendom of those who are called "cardinals"? I will tell you. In Italy and Germany there are many rich convents, endowments, holdings, and benefices; and as the best way of getting these into the hands of Rome they created cardinals, and gave to them the bishoprics, convents, and prelacies, and thus destroyed the service of God. That is why Italy is almost a desert now. . . . Why? Because the cardinals must have the wealth. The Turk himself could not have so desolated Italy and so overthrown the worship of God.

Now that Italy is sucked dry, they come to Germany. They begin in a quiet way, but we shall soon have Germany brought into the same state as Italy. We have a few cardinals already. What the Romanists really mean to do, the "drunken" Germans are not to see until they have lost everything . . . .

Now this devilish state of things is not only open robbery and deceit and the prevailing of the gates of hell, but it is destroying the very life and soul of Christianity; therefore we are bound to use all our diligence to ward off this misery and destruction. If we want to fight Turks, let us begin here—we cannot find worse ones. If we rightly hang thieves and robbers, why do we leave the greed of Rome unpunished? for Rome is the greatest thief and robber that has ever appeared on earth, or ever will.

Luther, Martin. "Address to the Nobility of the German Nation," (1520), trans. Wace and Buckheim. In B.J. Kidd, *Documents Illustrative of the Continental Reformation*, No. 35. Oxford, England: Oxford University Press, 1911.

Illustration 14.3

The Lutheran Sacraments. This altar painting from the Lutheran church at Thorslunde, Denmark, is intended as a graphic lesson in theology. Infant baptism is shown at the left. In the center, two communicants receive the sacrament in both kinds, while the preacher at the right emphasizes the importance of God's word.

rejected transubstantiation while arguing that Christ was nevertheless truly present in the Eucharist (see illustration 14.3). *The Freedom of a Christian* summarized Luther's doctrine of salvation by faith. Luther had not intended to break with the church, but his extraordinary skill as a writer and propagandist ignited anticlerical and antipapal feeling throughout Germany.

Compromise was now impossible, and he was excommunicated on January 31, 1521.

The affair might have ended with Luther's trial and execution, but political considerations intervened. His own prince, Frederick "the Wise" of Saxony, arranged for him to defend his position before the Imperial Diet at Worms in April. The new emperor Charles V was unimpressed. He placed Luther under the Imperial Ban, and Frederick was forced to protect his monk by hiding him in the Wartburg Castle for nearly a year. Luther used this enforced period of leisure to translate the New Testament into German.

Frederick's motives and those of the other princes and city magistrates who eventually supported Luther's reformation varied widely. Some were inspired by genuine religious feeling or, like Frederick, by a proprietary responsibility for "their" churches that transcended loyalty to a distant and non-German papacy. Others, especially in the towns, responded to the public enthusiasm generated by Luther's writings. Regardless of personal feelings, everyone understood the practical advantages of breaking with Rome. Revenues could be increased by confiscating church property and by ending ecclesiastical immunity to taxation, while the control of church courts and ecclesiastical patronage were valuable prizes to those engaged in state building.

The emperor objected on both political and religious grounds. Charles V was a devout Catholic. He was also committed to the ideal of imperial unity, which was clearly threatened by anything that increased the power and revenues of the princes. Only twenty-one at the Diet of Worms, he was heir to an enormous accumulation of states including Austria, Spain, the Netherlands, and much of Italy (see chapter 15). In theory, only the Ottoman Empire could stand against him. When he abdicated and retired to a Spanish monastery in 1556, the Reformation was still intact. His power, though great, had not been equal to his responsibilities. Pressed on the Danube and in the Mediterranean by the Turks, forced to fight seven wars with France, and beset simultaneously by Protestant princes, urban revolutionaries, and popes who feared the extension of his influence in Italy, Charles failed utterly in his attempts to impose orthodoxy. The empire remained open to religious turmoil.

Other Forms of Protestantism: The Radicals, Zwingli, and Calvin

Some of that turmoil began while Luther was still hidden in the Wartburg. The reformer had believed that, once the gospel was freely preached, congregations would follow it without the direction of an institutional church. He discovered that not all of the pope's enemies shared his interpretation of the Bible. Movements arose that rejected what he saw as the basic insight of the reformation: salvation by faith alone. To many ordinary men and women, this doctrine weakened the ethical imperatives that lay at the heart of Christianity. They wanted a restoration of the primitive, apostolic church—a "gathered" community of Christians who lived by the letter of Scripture. Luther had not gone far enough. Luther in turn thought that they were *schwärmer*, or enthusiasts who wanted to return to the works righteousness of the medieval church. Faced with what he saw as a fundamental threat to reform, Luther turned to the state. In 1527 a system of visitations was instituted throughout Saxony that for all practical purposes placed temporal control of the church in the hands of the prince. It was to be the model for Lutheran Church discipline throughout Germany and Scandinavia, but it did not at first halt the spread of radicalism.

Because these radical movements were often popular in origin or had coalesced around the teachings of an individual preacher, they varied widely in character. Perhaps the most radical were the Antitrinitarians, who rejected the doctrine of the Trinity and argued for a piety based wholly upon good works. Under the leadership of two Italian brothers, Laelio and Fausto Sozzini, they found converts among the Polish nobility but had little influence on western Europe. The most numerous were the Anabaptists, a loosely affiliated group who were the spiritual ancestors of the modern Mennonites and Amish. Their name derives from the practice of adult baptism, which they saw not only as a sacrament, but also as the heart of the redemptive process. Baptism was the deliberate decision to follow Christ and could therefore be made only by a responsible adult acting in complete freedom of will. It signified entrance into a visible church of the saints that must, by definition, be separate from the world around it. Most Anabaptists were therefore pacifists who would accept no civic responsibilities, refusing even to take an oath in court (see document 14.4).

This rejection of civic responsibility was seen as a threat to the political order. Hatred of the Anabaptists was one issue on which Lutherans and Catholics could agree, and in 1529 an imperial edict made belief in adult baptism a capital offense. Hatred became something like panic when an atypically violent group of Anabaptists gained control of the city of Münster and proclaimed it the New Jerusalem, complete with polygamy and communal sharing of property. They were eventually dislodged and their leaders executed, but the episode, though unparalleled elsewhere, convinced political and ecclesiastical leaders that their suspicions had been correct. They executed tens of thousands of Anabaptists throughout Germany and the

◆ DOCUMENT 14.4 ◆

The Anabaptists Reject Civic Life

In 1527 a group of Anabaptists met at Schleitheim on the Swiss-German border to clarify issues connected with their teachings. The result was the Schleitheim Confession, *a document widely accepted by later Anabaptists. In this excerpt, demands are made for separation from the world.*

Fourth. We are agreed as follows on separation: A separation shall be made from the evil and the wickedness which the devil planted in the world; in this manner, simply that we should not have fellowship with them, the wicked, and not run with them in the multitude of their abominations. This is the way it is: Since all who do not walk in the obedience of faith and have not united themselves with God so that they wish to do his will, are a great abomination before God, it is not possible for anything to grow or issue from them except abominable things. For truly all creatures are in but two classes, good and bad, believing and unbelieving, darkness and light, the world and those who have come out of the world, God's temple and idols, Christ and Belial; and none can have part with the other.

To us then the command of the Lord is clear when He calls us to separate from the evil and thus He will be our God and we shall be his sons and daughters.

He further admonishes us to withdraw from Babylon and the earthly Egypt that we may not be partakers of the pain and suffering which the Lord will bring upon them.

From all this we should learn that everything which is not united with our God and Christ cannot be other than an abomination which we should shun and flee from. By this is meant all popish and anti-popish works and church services, meetings and church attendance, drinking houses, civic affairs, the commitments made in unbelief [oaths] and other things of that kind, which are highly regarded by the world and yet carried on in flat contradiction to the command of God.

Therefore there will also unquestionably fall from us the un-Christian, devilish weapons of force—such as sword, armor and the like, and all their use for friends or against one's enemies.

"The Schleitheim Confession." In Hans Hillerbrand, ed., *The Protestant Reformation*, pp. 132–133. New York: Harper Torchbooks, 1967.

Low Countries, and by 1550 the movement had dwindled to a remnant. A group of survivors, afterwards known as Mennonites, were reorganized under the leadership of Menno Simons. Their moderation and emphasis on high ethical standards became a model for other dissenting groups.

Meanwhile, another kind of reform had emerged in Switzerland. Zürich, like other Swiss cantons, was a center of the mercenary industry. By 1518 a growing party of citizens had come to oppose what they called the exchange of blood for money. The innovations of Gonsalvo de Córdoba had cost the Swiss their tactical advantage on the battlefield, and their casualties during the latter part of the Italian wars had been very heavy. Moreover, the trade had enriched a few contractors who were now thought to exert undue influence on local politics while compromising the city's neutrality through their relations with France and the papacy. One of the leading spokesmen for the antimercenary forces was a priest, Huldrych Zwingli (1484–1531), who had been a chaplain to the troops in Italy. He had received a good humanist education and, like Luther,

was known for attacking indulgences and for sermons that relied heavily on the Scriptures. In 1519 the antimercenary party gained control of the Zürich city council and named Zwingli people's priest of the city's main church, a post from which he was able to guide the process of reform.

Zwingli's concept of reformation grew out of the democratic traditions of his native land. Believing that each congregation should determine its own policies under the guidance of the gospel, he saw no real distinction between the government of the church and that of the state. Both elected representatives to determine policy. Both should be guided by the law of God. He therefore proceeded to reform the city step by step, providing guidance and advice but leaving the implementation of reforms to the city council.

Like Luther, Zwingli was challenged at an early date by those who felt that his reforms were insufficiently thorough. In responding to such Anabaptist critics as Conrad Grebel and Georg Blaurock, Zwingli developed teachings that were at variance with Luther's as well. When the Anabaptists asked how a child could be baptized if the efficacy of the sacrament depended upon the faith of the recipient, Zwingli responded that the faith was that of the parent or guardian and that the sacrament was in effect a covenant to raise the child as a Christian. The rite was analogous to circumcision among the Jews. He also rejected Luther's doctrine of the Real Presence in communion and argued, after some hesitation, that for those with faith Christ was present in spirit though not in body.

Zwingli's ideas were theologically original and appealed strongly to other reformers, but Luther rejected them at the Marburg Colloquy in 1529. The failure of this meeting marked the beginning of a separation between the Lutheran and Reformed traditions that persists to this day. It also coincided with a vote by the Imperial Diet to enforce the Edict of Worms against all non-Catholics. Those who protested against this measure, Lutheran and Reformed, became known as Protestants. In the meantime, the efforts of Zürich to export its reformation to other parts of Switzerland led to conflict, and Zwingli was killed, sword in hand, at the battle of Kappel.

Among those influenced by Zwingli's teachings was John Calvin (1509–64). Calvin was born at Noyon in France, the son of a wealthy lawyer who for most of his career had been secretary to the local bishop. A brilliant student, Calvin was educated at Paris and at Orléans where he earned a law degree. His interests eventually turned to humanism and then to theology. In 1534 he adopted the reformed faith. His conversion bore immediate fruit in *The Institutes of the Christian Religion*, a more-or-less systematic explanation of reformed teachings. The first edition appeared in March 1536, and though Calvin continued to revise and expand it throughout his lifetime, this early effort contained the basic elements of his mature thought.

Calvin is best known for his uncompromising position on predestination, holding, like Zwingli, that God divides the elect from the reprobate by His own "dread decree" (see document 14.5). Luther, like St. Augustine, believed that God predestines certain individuals to salvation, but he had stopped short of declaring that some are predestined to hell. To Calvin, this seemed illogical. To select some is by definition to reject others. This doctrine of "double predestination," like many of his formulations on the sacraments and other issues, may be seen as refinements of ideas originally suggested by others, but Calvin was far more than a mere compiler. He made reformed doctrines more intelligible, educated a corps of pastors who spread his teachings to the farthest corners of Europe, and provided a model for

◈ DOCUMENT 14.5 ◈

John Calvin: Predestination

The importance of John Calvin's doctrine of predestination has probably been overstated. It was neither unique to him nor the center of his own theology, which emphasized what he called the knowledge of God. Nevertheless, the power of this summary statement from the Institutes of the Christian Religion *indicates why Calvin's teachings on predestination made an indelible impression.*

As Scripture, then, clearly shows, we say that God once established by his eternal and unchangeable plan those whom he long before determined once for all to receive into salvation and those whom, on the other hand, he would devote to destruction. We assert that, with respect to the elect, this plan was founded upon his freely given mercy, without regard to human worth; but by his just and irreprehensible judgment he has barred the door of life to those whom he has given over to damnation. Now among the elect we regard the call as a testimony of election. Then we hold justification [that is, acceptance by God] another sign of its manifestation, until they come into the glory in which the fulfillment of that election lies. But as the Lord seals his elect by call and justification, so, by shutting off the reprobate from knowledge of his name or from the sanctification of his Spirit, he, as it were, reveals by these marks what sort of judgment awaits them.

Calvin, John. *Institutes of the Christian Religion*, vol. 2, p. 931, ed. J.T. McNeill, trans. Ford Lewis Battles. Philadelphia: Westminster Press, 1960.

the governance of Christian communities that would be influential for generations to come.

The unlikely vehicle for these achievements was the small city of Geneva. When Calvin arrived there in July 1536, the city was emerging from a period of political and religious turmoil. It had long been governed by a bishop whose appointment was controlled by the neighboring dukes of Savoy. The belated development of civic institutions and dissatisfaction with Savoyard influence led to an alliance with the Swiss cantons of Bern and Fribourg and to the overthrow of the bishop. The Bernese, who had accepted the Reformation while remaining nominally Catholic for diplomatic reasons, then dispatched a French refugee, Guillaume Farel, to convert the French-speaking Genevans. Farel was a fine preacher, but he realized that he was not the man to organize a church. When Calvin stopped at Geneva on his way from Ferrara to Strasburg, he prevailed upon the young scholar to stay and assist him in the task of reformation.

Calvin's first years in Geneva were full of turmoil. Though they had no love for the pope, the Genevans resisted Calvin's attempts to reform their morals. He established the kind of godly commonwealth he sought only with great difficulty. His opponents finally discredited themselves by supporting Miguel Servetus, an antitrinitarian executed by the Genevan city council as a heretic in 1553. This act, now regarded as an example of gross intolerance, was universally applauded by Catholics and Protestants and secured Calvin's position in the city until his death.

Calvin's Geneva has been called a theocracy, but Calvin believed in the separation of church and state. Neither he nor any other Genevan pastor could hold public office, and the temporal affairs of the Genevan church were guided by an elected committee or presbytery of laymen. The city continued to be governed by its two elected councils. These bodies were empowered, as in Zürich, to enforce conformity in faith and morals. A Consistory, composed of church elders and certain municipal officials, was responsible for defining both. Geneva soon became known as a center of the Reformed movement and as a refuge for those who were persecuted elsewhere. An academy was established to train pastors who were then dispatched to create missionary congregations in other parts of Europe. They were most successful in France, the Netherlands, and in those countries such as Hungary, Bohemia, and Poland where resistance to German culture inhibited the spread of Lutheranism. When the reformer died in 1564, Calvinism was already a major international movement.

The English Reformation

England's revolt against the papacy was an example of reformation from the top. Henry VIII (reigned 1509–47; see illustration 14.4) and his chief minister, Cardinal Thomas Wolsey (c. 1475–1530), had little use for reformed doctrines. Henry had even earned the papal title "Defender of the Faith" for publishing an attack on Luther's view of the sacraments and would probably

Illustration 14.4

Henry VIII of England. This portrait by Hans Holbein shows the king as he looked at the time of the Reformation.

have been content to remain in the church had he not decided to divorce his queen, Catherine of Aragon.

Catherine had suffered a series of miscarriages and stillbirths. One child, Mary, survived, but Henry feared that without a male heir the succession would be endangered. He resolved to ask for a papal annulment and to marry Anne Boleyn, a court lady with whom he had fallen in love. His request posed serious difficulties for pope Clement VII. The emperor Charles V was Catherine's nephew. Charles vehemently opposed the divorce, and as his troops had recently sacked Rome (1527), albeit in the course of a mutiny, the pope was intimidated. Moreover, the basis of the request struck many canon lawyers as dubious. Catherine had originally been married to Henry's brother Arthur, who died before he could ascend the throne. To preserve the vital alliance with Catherine's father, Ferdinand of Aragon, Henry VII had quickly married her to his second son, but this had required a papal dispensation because marriage to the wife of one's brother is prohibited by Leviticus 18:16 and 20:21. Another biblical passage, Deuteronomy 25:5, specifically commands such marriages, but an annulment would involve repudiation of the earlier dispensation. Moreover, the fact that the marriage had endured for eighteen years raised what canon lawyers called "the impediment of public honesty."

Clement temporized. He appointed Cardinals Wolsey and Campeggio as legates to resolve the matter on the theory that their opinions would cancel each other out. Henry could not wait. In 1529 he deprived Wolsey of his secular offices and took Thomas Cromwell (1485–1540) and Thomas Cranmer (1489–1556) as his advisers. These two, a lawyer and a churchman, respectively, were sympathetic to reformed ideas and firm supporters of a strategy that would put pressure on the pope by attacking the privileges and immunities of the church in England.

This strategy was implemented primarily through the Reformation Parliament that sat from 1529 to 1536. Though its proceedings were managed to some extent by Cromwell, a consistent majority supported the crown throughout. Parliament passed a series of acts that restricted the dispatch of church revenues to Rome and placed the legal affairs of the clergy under royal jurisdiction. Finally, in 1532, Anne Boleyn became pregnant. To ensure the child's legitimacy, Cranmer married the couple in January 1533, and two months later he granted the king his divorce from Catherine. He was able to do so because William Warham, the archbishop of Canterbury and a wily opponent of the divorce, had died at last (he was at least ninety-eight), permitting Henry to appoint Cranmer in his place. In September Anne Boleyn gave birth to a daughter, Elizabeth, and in 1534 Parliament passed the Act of Supremacy, which declared that Henry was "the only supreme head of the Church in England."

Opposition was minimal. John Fisher, bishop of Rochester and Sir Thomas More, the great humanist who had been Henry's lord chancellor, were executed for their misgivings, but most of political England either supported the king or remained indifferent. The Lincolnshire rebellion and the northern revolt known as the Pilgrimage of Grace were localized reactions to Henry's proposed closing of the monasteries in 1536 and he suppressed them easily. The dissolution of the monasteries proceeded apace. Unfortunately for his successors, Henry chose to sell off the monastic properties at bargain basement prices. By doing so he enriched those who had supported him in the Reforma-

tion Parliament and satisfied his need for ready cash. His failure to incorporate these lands into the royal domain deprived the crown of renewable income.

Henry now ruled the English church. He closed the monasteries and convents and adopted Coverdale's English Bible, but other changes were minimal. The clergy remained celibate (with the exception of Cranmer, who had been secretly married before his appointment as archbishop of Canterbury), and the principles of Catholic theology were reaffirmed in the Six Articles of 1539. A visibly Protestant English church began to emerge only after Henry's death in 1547.

In 1536 Henry arranged the execution of Anne Boleyn on charges of adultery and had their marriage annulled. His third wife, Jane Seymour, gave him a male heir in 1537 but died in childbirth, and three subsequent wives failed to produce further children. Both Mary and Elizabeth were officially illegitimate. Jane Seymour's son, aged ten, ascended the throne as Edward VI under the regency of his uncle, Edward Seymour, duke of Somerset. Somerset was a convinced Protestant with close ties to Cranmer and to the continental reformers. He and the young king, "that right godly imp," lost little time in abolishing the Six Articles, encouraging clerical marriage, and imposing Cranmer's *Book of Common Prayer* as the standard liturgy for English churches. An Order in Council abolished images in an act of official iconoclasm that destroyed centuries of English art.

In 1550 Somerset was succeeded by the equally Protestant duke of Northumberland who imposed a revised edition of the new liturgy and adopted the Forty-Two Articles, also written by Cranmer, as an official confession of faith. The articles proclaimed salvation by faith, reduced the sacraments to two, and denied transubstantiation, though not the Real Presence. Though many lay people remained loyal to the old church, they found no effective way to express their views. Aside from a brief and unsuccessful rebellion in the west of England, little resistance emerged. In 1553 Edward died at the age of sixteen. His sister Mary assumed the crown and immediately restored Catholicism with the assent of Parliament, which demanded only that she not return the lands taken from the church.

Mary's reign was a failure. Her marriage to Philip II of Spain aroused fears of Spanish-papal domination even among those English who were still unfavorably disposed to Protestantism. Her persecution of the reformers, though hardly the bloodbath portrayed in John Foxe's *Acts and Monuments*, the great martyrology of the English reformation, deeply offended others and earned her the historical nickname "Bloody Mary." When her sister, Elizabeth, succeeded her in 1558 she was able to restore a moderate Protestantism leavened by virtual tolerance for all who would acknowledge the royal supremacy. The Elizabethan Settlement, as it is called, was the foundation on which modern Anglicanism would be built after years of effort and struggle.

The Catholic Reformation

Not all reformations of the sixteenth century were anti-Catholic. The church transformed itself as well in a movement that is sometimes called the Counter Reformation, but not all reforms undertaken by Catholics in the sixteenth century were a response to the challenge of the reformers. Cardinal Francisco Jiménez de Cisneros had begun to reform the church in Spain long before Luther nailed his Ninety-Five Theses to the church door, and similar changes were introduced in France by Cardinal Georges d'Amboise between 1501 and his death in 1510. Even Wolsey had attempted to reform the English monasteries during the 1520s. The impetus behind these reforms arguably came from the secular authorities and were largely directed toward the revival of monastic life. However, each of these cardinals received broad legatine authority from several popes, and monastic reform was a central issue in the late medieval church.

Moreover, the reform of existing orders and the creation of new ones was often undertaken without secular involvement. The Theatines, confirmed by the pope in 1524, were an outgrowth of the Oratory of Divine Love whose origins date to 1494. The Barnabites (1533–35), Somaschi (1540), and the Capuchins, an order of reformed Franciscans, were all voluntary associations of churchmen pledged to the ideal of monastic reform. The female counterpart of the Capuchins was founded by Maria Laurentia Longo (d. 1542), and in 1535 Angela Merici (c. 1473–1540) founded the Ursulines, an order that would play a decisive role in the education of Catholic women for centuries. None of these foundations was related in any way to the Protestant threat. Most popes regarded the proliferation of religious orders with suspicion. Their rivalries had long been a fruitful source of trouble, and most reform-minded clerics believed in consolidation rather than in new confirmations.

Of all the religious orders founded or reformed during the sixteenth century, the Society of Jesus, or Jesuits, played the largest part in the struggle against Protestantism, but they had been created for other purposes. Their founder, Ignatius of Loyola (1491–1556), was originally inspired by the idea of converting the Muslims. After a long period of educational and religious development that produced *The Spiritual Exercises*, a manual of meditation that remains the foundation of Jesuit discipline, he and nine companions formed their order in 1534. Their asceticism, vigor, and vow of unconditional obedience to the pope led to their confirmation in 1540.

Though the order did little to convert the Muslims, it achieved moderate success in Asia under the leadership of St. Francis Xavier (1506–52). In Europe, the Jesuits became the intellectual shock troops of the Counter Reformation. Their high standards in recruitment and education made them natural leaders to reconvert areas of Europe that had deserted to Protestantism. Jesuit missions helped to restore a Catholic majority in regions as diverse as Bavaria and Poland. An important means of achieving this was through education. Jesuit academies combining humanist educational principles with religious instruction spread through the subcontinent after 1555 and served much the same purpose for men that the Ursuline academies served for women.

Efforts of this sort were essentially spontaneous, arising from reform-minded elements within the church, but the papacy itself was not idle. Reform was difficult if not impossible until the ghost of conciliarism was laid to rest, and for this reason the popes proceeded with great caution. Clement VII, besieged by the mutinous troops of Charles V and the demands of Henry VIII, accomplished little. Paul III (reigned 1534–49) at first sought reconciliation by appointing a commission to investigate abuses within the church. Its report, a detailed analysis with recommendations for change, caused great embarrassment when the contents leaked to the public. Then an attempt to negotiate a settlement with the Lutherans broke down at the Regensburg Colloquy in 1541. These failures encouraged a policy of repression, and in 1542 the Roman Inquisition was revived under the direction of Gian Pietro Caraffa, an implacable conservative and one of the founders of the Theatine order. Later, as Pope Paul IV (served 1555–59), Caraffa would conduct a veritable reign of terror against those whom he regarded as corrupt or heretical. To protect the faithful from intellectual contamination, he also established the celebrated *Index Librorum Prohibitorum*, an ever-expanding list of books that Catholics were forbidden to read.

Repression alone could not solve the problems of the church. In spite of the obvious danger to papal

Illustration 14.5

The Final Session of the Council of Trent, 1563. Attributed to Titian, this painting shows the conclusion of the great council whose decrees inspired the Catholic Church until the 1960s.

authority, Paul III decided to convene a general council at Trent in 1542. Sessions were held from 1543 to 1549, in 1551–52, and in 1562–63 (see illustration 14.5). Much disagreement arose over goals and the meetings were often sparsely attended, but the Council of Trent was a conspicuous success.

Theologically, Trent marked the triumph of Thomism. Luther's ideas on justification, the sacraments, and the priesthood of all believers were specifically rejected. The medieval concept of the priestly office and the value of good works was reasserted, and at the organizational level efforts were made to correct most of the abuses that had been attacked by the reformers. These included not only the clerical sins of pluralism, absenteeism, nepotism, and simony, but also such distortions of popular piety as the sale of indulgences and the misuse of images. The strengthening of ecclesiastical discipline was one of the council's greatest achievements.

Knowing that many of the church's problems arose from ignorance, the delegates mandated the use of catechisms in instructing the laity and the establishment of diocesan seminaries for the education of priests. The Council of Trent, in short, marked the beginning of the modern Catholic Church. Its institutional principles and the forms of piety that it established were not substantially modified until Vatican II (1962–65).

The Political, Economic, and Social Consequences of Reform

The impact of the sixteenth-century reformations has been the subject of much scholarly debate. The religious unity of western Christendom was clearly shattered, but this had always been more an ideal than a practical reality. Politically, cities and territorial states were the chief beneficiaries of reform, for Protestantism tended to increase their control over church patronage and revenues. Even Catholic states exhibited more independence because the papacy became more cautious in its claims than it had been in the Middle Ages. Though hardly decisive, reform was therefore an important influence on the development of the modern state.

The economic consequences of the Reformation are far less clear. The idea that Protestantism somehow liberated acquisitive instincts and paved the way for the development of capitalism is highly suspect if for no other reason than that capitalism existed long before the Reformation and that the economic growth of such Protestant states as England and the Netherlands can be explained adequately in other ways. In some areas, notably England, the alienation of church property may have accelerated the capitalization of land that had be-

◆ DOCUMENT 14.6 ◆

A Protestant View of Marriage

The reformer of Strasbourg, Martin Bucer (1491–1551), was more generous than most in his attitude toward women. Here, he argues that under certain circumstances a woman may leave her adulterous or abusive spouse and be free to remarry.

For the Holy Spirit says that there is neither male nor female in Christ. In all things that pertain to salvation one should have as much regard for woman as for man. For though she is bound to keep her place, to put herself under the authority of her husband, just as the church does in relation to Christ, yet her subjection does not cancel the right of an honest woman, in accordance with the laws of God, to have recourse to and demand, by legitimate means, deliverance from a husband who hates her. For the Lord has certainly not made married woman subservient to have her polluted and tormented by the extortions and injuries of her husband, but rather so that she may receive discipline from him, as if from her master and savior, like the church from Christ. A wife is not so subject to her husband that she is bound to suffer anything he may impose upon her. Being free, she is joined to him in holy marriage that she may be loved, nourished, and maintained by him, as if she were his own flesh, just as the church is maintained by Christ. . . . Again, though a wife may be something less than her husband and subject to him, in order that they be rightly joined, the Holy Spirit has declared, through its apostle, that man and woman are equal before God in things pertaining to the alliance and mutual confederation of marriage. This is the meaning of the apostle's saying that a wife has power over the body of her husband, just as a husband has power over the body of his wife (1 Corinthians 7). . . . Hence, if wives feel that their association and cohabitation with their husbands is injurious to salvation as well of one as of the other, owing to the hardening and hatred on the part of their husbands, let them have recourse to the civil authority, which is enjoined by the Lord to help the afflicted.

Bucer, Martin. *"De Regno Christi,"* book 2, chap. 34. In Julia O'Faolain and Lauro Martines, *Not in God's Image: Women in History from the Greeks to the Victorians*, pp. 200–201. New York: HarperCollins, 1973.

---

gun in the years after the Black Death, but in others it served primarily to increase the domain revenues of the crown. In Denmark, for example, 40 percent of the arable land was under direct royal control by 1620, primarily because the crown retained church lands confiscated during the Reformation.

The reformers also sought to change the status of European women. Beginning with Luther and Zwingli, they rejected the ideal of clerical celibacy and declared that a Christian marriage was the ideal basis for a godly life. They specifically attacked medieval writings that either condemned women as temptresses or extolled virginity as the highest of female callings, and drew attractive and sentimental portraits of the virtuous wife. A chief virtue of that ideal woman was her willingness to submit to male authority, but the attachment of the reformers to traditional social hierarchies should not be misinterpreted. The companionate marriage in which wife and husband offered each other mutual support was the Reformation ideal (see document 14.6). If women were subordinate it was, as Calvin said, because women "by the very order of nature are bound to obey."

To him, other reformers, and Catholic theologians, the traditionally ordered family was both part and symbol of a divinely established hierarchy. To disrupt that hierarchy risked chaos.

The Reformation endorsement of women was qualified, but it increased the status of wife and mother and placed new demands upon men, who were encouraged to treat their wives with consideration. As early as the 1520s, some German towns permitted women to divorce husbands who were guilty of gross abuse. The reformers also encouraged female literacy, at least in the vernacular, because they wanted women to have access to the Scriptures. The impact of these prescriptions on the lives of real women may be questioned. On the negative side, the Protestant emphasis on marriage narrowed a woman's career choices to one. Catholic Europe continued to offer productive lives to women who chose not to marry, but Protestant women could rarely escape the dominance of men. If they did, it was through widowhood or divorce, and Protestant societies offered no institutional support for the unmarried. St. Teresa de Avila, Angelique Arnauld, Madame Acarie,

Illustration 14.6

A Village Wedding. In this painting, Pieter Bruegel the Younger illustrates the sort of peasant behavior that political and ecclesiastical authorities hoped to restrict in the later sixteenth century.

Jeanne de Chantal, and the other great female figures of post-Tridentine Catholicism had few Protestant counterparts.

From the standpoint of the reformers, whether Catholic or Protestant, such issues were of secondary importance. Their primary concern was the salvation of souls and the transformation of popular piety. Heroic efforts were made to catechize or otherwise educate the laity in most parts of Europe, and after about 1570 an increasing tendency was seen toward clerical interference in lay morals. Catholic church courts and Protestant consistories sought to eliminate such evils as brawling, public drunkenness, and sexual misbehavior. Inevitably the churchmen were forced to condemn the occasions on which such activity arose. The celebration of holidays and popular festivals came under scrutiny as did public performances of every kind from street jugglers to those of Shakespeare and his troop of actors. Dancing aroused special concern. No one worried about the stately measures trod by courtiers, but the rowdy and often sexually explicit dances of the peasants seemed, after years of familiarity, to induce shock (see illustration 14.6).

Civil authorities supported this attack on popular culture for practical reasons. The celebration of holidays and popular festivals encouraged disorder. When accompanied as they usually were by heavy drinking, public amusements could lead to violence and even riots. Moreover, like street theater, most celebrations contained seditious skits or pageants. They mocked the privileged classes, satirized the great, and delighted in the reversal of social and gender roles. The triumph of a Lord of Misrule, even for a day, made magistrates nervous, and prudence demanded that such activities be regulated or prohibited outright. Popular beliefs and practices were attacked with equal vigor. The authorities rarely took action against academic magic, astrology, or alchemy—sciences that, though dubious, were widely accepted by the wealthy and educated—but they no longer tolerated folk magic. In some cases, official suspicion extended even to the traditional remedies used by midwives and village "wise women."

The epidemic of witch hunting that convulsed Europe in the late sixteenth and early seventeenth centuries may have been related to these concerns. In the century after 1550, Protestant and Catholic governments in virtually every part of Europe executed more than sixty thousand people for being witches or satanists. Medieval thinkers such as Thomas Aquinas had denied the power of witches, but a later age thought differently. Magistrates and learned men built theories of a vast satanic plot around their imperfect knowledge of folk beliefs. Their ideas crystallized in manuals for witch hunters, the most famous of which, the *Malleus Maleficarum* (Hammer of Witches) went through twenty-nine editions between 1495 and 1669. Its authors, like most people in early modern Europe, believed that in a providential world there could be no accidents; evil required an explanation. Otherwise unexplained disasters were caused by witches who gained extraordinary powers through worshipping the devil and used those powers to injure their neighbors. The community could be protected only by burning witches alive.

In this case, ordinary people shared the concerns of the intellectual elite. Accusations of witchcraft tended to multiply in waves of hysteria that convulsed entire regions. Many of those denounced were no doubt guilty of trying to cast spells or some other unsavory act, but the victims fit a profile that suggests a generalized hostility toward women and perhaps that the persecutions were in part a means of exerting social control. The great majority of those burned were single women, old and poor, who lived at the margins of their communities. The rest, whether male or female, tended to be people whose assertive or uncooperative behavior had aroused hostility.

The trials subsided after 1650, but not before other traditional beliefs had been discredited by their association with witchcraft. Some of these involved "white" magic, the normally harmless spells and preparations used to ensure good harvests or to cure disease. Others were "errors," or what the Spanish Inquisition called "propositions." This was a broad category that included everything from the popular notion that premarital sex was no sin to alternative cosmologies devised by imaginative peasants. Post-Tridentine Catholicism, no less than its Protestant rivals, discouraged uncontrolled speculation and was deeply suspicious of those forms of piety that lacked ecclesiastical sanction. Popular beliefs about the Virgin Mary, the saints, and miracles were scrutinized, while lay people claiming to have religious visions were ridiculed and sometimes prosecuted.

The efforts of the reformers, in other words, bore modest fruit. Drunkenness proved ineradicable, but some evidence is available that interpersonal violence decreased and that behavior in general became somewhat more sedate. Though lay morals and religious knowledge improved slowly if at all, the forms of piety were transformed in some cases beyond recognition. Many ideas and practices vanished so completely that historians of popular culture can recover their memory only with great difficulty. Devotion based upon personal contact with God through mental prayer became common in virtually all communions. Catholics abandoned the sale of indulgences and consciously sought to limit such abuses as the misuse of pilgrimages and relics. Protestants abandoned all three, together with Latin, vigils, the cult of the saints, masses for the dead, and mandatory fasts. By 1600, the religious landscape of Europe was transformed, and much of the richness, vitality, and cohesion of peasant life had been lost beyond all hope of recovery.

CHAPTER 15

OVERSEAS CONQUEST AND RELIGIOUS WAR TO 1648

The age of the Renaissance and Reformation marked the beginning of European conquests overseas. Their purpose in the first instance was to expand the resources available to the emerging monarchies of western Europe. The conquests were therefore an extension of the state-building process, but a religious motive was evident, too, which at times recalled the Christian triumphalism of the Crusades. To say that European expansion overseas changed the world forever is an understatement. Though it laid the foundations of a world market and added much to Europe's store of wealth and knowledge, it did so at a terrible cost in human misery.

In Europe itself, the rivalries that encouraged overseas exploration fueled the imperial struggles of the early sixteenth century and the so-called Religious Wars of 1559–1648. The growing cost of warfare stretched the resources of princes to the breaking point. This led to massive unrest as subjects sought to recover rights and privileges lost to rulers who were desperate to pay for security. Both the subsequent revolts and the international conflict that helped to sustain them were complicated by religious issues that made them extremely difficult to resolve. In the end, the wars of what has been called the Iron Age brought much of Europe to the brink of political and economic disintegration.

The Portuguese Voyages to Africa, India, and Brazil

The process of overseas exploration began appropriately enough in Portugal, the first modern monarchy and the center of the fourteenth-century revolution in shipbuilding. The Portuguese state had been effectively consolidated by John I in 1385. Like other medieval rulers, he and his descendants hoped to maximize domain revenue by increasing taxable commerce. The gold and ivory of Africa were a tempting goal, but that

Illustration 15.1

 A Portuguese Caravel of the Fifteenth Century. Though
rarely more than seventy or eighty feet in length, these vessels
were extremely seaworthy and formed the mainstay of Portugal's
explorations along the coasts of Africa and in the Atlantic. This
one is lateen rigged for better performance to windward, but
some of them carried square sails as well, usually on the foremast.

trade was dominated by Moroccan intermediaries who
shipped products from the African heartland by camel
caravan and sold them to Europeans through such ports
as Ceuta and Tangier. The Portuguese knew that enormous profits could be realized by sailing directly to the
source of these commodities and bypassing the middlemen, who were in any case Muslims and their traditional enemies.

These considerations, and others of a more spiritual
nature, inspired Prince Henry "the Navigator"
(1394–1460) to establish a center for navigational development on the windswept bluffs of Sagres at the far
southwestern tip of Europe. While Henry's cosmogra-
phers and mathematicians worked steadily to improve
the quality of charts and navigational techniques, his
captains sailed ever further along the African coast, returning with growing quantities of gold, ivory, pepper,
and slaves, for the enslavement of Africans was part of
the expansionist enterprise from the start. Their ships
were fast, handy caravels that combined the best features of northern and Mediterranean construction (see
illustration 15.1). Their instruments were improved versions of the compass, the quadrant, and the astrolabe.
The compass had been introduced to the Mediterranean
in the twelfth or thirteenth century, probably by the

Arabs. The quadrant and the astrolabe permitted the
sailor to find his latitude based on the elevation of the
sun above the horizon.

Before the death of Prince Henry, the Portuguese
adopted the idea of sailing around the tip of Africa to
India as their primary goal. By so doing they hoped to
bypass the Italian-Arab monopoly and gain direct access to the spice trade. In May 1498, Vasco da Gama
reached Calicut on the coast of India after a voyage of
two years. His arrival disturbed political and commercial relationships that had endured for centuries. Indian
and Arab merchants found the newcomers rude and
barbaric and their trade goods of little interest. Though
the voyages of da Gama and Cabral made a profit, only
the judicious use of force could secure a major Portuguese share in the trade. After 1508 Afonso de Albuquerque (1453–1515) tried to gain control of the Indian
Ocean by seizing its major ports. Aden and Ormuz
eluded him, but Goa became the chief Portuguese base
in India and the capture of Malacca (1511) opened the
way to China. A Portuguese settlement was established
there at Macao in 1556. Trade with Japan was initiated
in 1543, and for seventy-five years thereafter ships from
Macao brought luxury goods to Nagasaki in return for
silver.

These achievements earned Portugal a modest
place in Asian commerce. The Portuguese may have
been the first people of any race to trade on a truly
worldwide basis, but the total volume of spices exported to Europe did not immediately increase as a result of their activities. Furthermore, the Arab and
Gujerati merchants of the Indian Ocean remained formidable competitors for more than a century.

Columbus and the Opening of America

Meanwhile, the Spanish, by sailing west, had reached
America. Isabella of Castile and Ferdinand of Aragon
regarded the expansion of their Portuguese rivals with
dismay and believed, as Prince Henry had done, that
they were obligated by morality and the requirements
of dynastic prestige to spread the Catholic faith. When
a Genoese mariner named Christopher Columbus proposed to reach Asia by sailing across the Atlantic, they
were prepared to listen.

In August 1492, Columbus set sail in the ship *Santa
Maria* accompanied by two small caravels, the *Pinta*
and the *Niña*. Their combined crews totaled about
ninety men. Columbus sailed southwest to the Canary
Islands and then westward across the Atlantic, taking

◆ DOCUMENT 15.1 ◆

The Hazards of a Long Voyage

This extract is taken from a firsthand account of Fernando Magellan's voyage around the world by Antonio Pigafetta, but similar conditions might be expected on any sea journey if it lasted long enough. The disease described is scurvy, which results from a deficiency of vitamin C. It was a serious problem even on transatlantic voyages. The cause was not understood until the eighteenth century, but captains could usually predict the first date of its appearance in a ship's company with some accuracy.

Wednesday, November 28, we debauched from that strait [since named after Magellan], engulfing ourselves in the Pacific Sea. We were three months and twenty days without getting any kind of fresh food. We ate biscuit, which was no longer biscuit, but powder of biscuits swarming with worms, for they had eaten the good. It stank strongly of the urine of rats. We drank yellow water that had been putrid for many days. We also ate some ox hides that covered the top of the mainyard to prevent the yard from chafing the shrouds, and which had become exceedingly hard because of the sun, rain, and wind. We left them in the sea for four or five days, and then placed them on top of the embers and so ate them; and we often ate sawdust from boards. Rats were sold for one-half ducat a piece, and even then we could not get them. But above all the other misfortunes the following was the worst. The gums of both the lower and upper teeth of some of our men swelled so that they could not eat under any circumstances and therefore died. Nineteen men died from that sickness. . . . Twenty-five or thirty men fell sick.

Pigafetta, Antonio. *Magellan's Voyage Around the World*, ed. and trans. J. A. Robertson. Cleveland: 1902.

by Europeans was left to others. One of them, a Florentine navigator named Amerigo Vespucci (1454–1512), gave it his name. The true dimensions of the "New World" became clearer in 1513 when Vasco Núñez de Balboa crossed the Isthmus of Panama on foot and became the first European to look upon the Pacific.

The achievement of Columbus has been somewhat diminished by his own failure to grasp its significance and by the fact that others had no doubt preceded him. The Vikings visited Newfoundland and may have explored the North American coast as far south as Cape Cod. Portuguese and Basque fishermen had almost certainly landed there in the course of their annual expeditions to the Grand Banks, but being fishermen, they kept their discoveries secret and these early contacts came to nothing.

The voyage of Columbus, however, set off a frenzy of exploration and conquest. By the Treaty of Tordesillas (1494), the Spanish and Portuguese agreed to a line of demarcation established in mid-Atlantic by the pope. Lands "discovered" to the east of that line belonged to Portugal; those to the west belonged to Spain. The inhabitants of those lands were not consulted. This left Brazil, Africa, and the route to India in Portuguese hands, but a line of demarcation in the Pacific was not defined. Much of Asia remained in dispute.

To establish a Spanish presence there, an expedition was dispatched in 1515 to reach the Moluccas by sailing west around the southern tip of South America. Its leader was Fernando Magellan, a Portuguese sailor in Spanish pay. Magellan crossed the Pacific only to be killed in the Moluccas by natives unimpressed with the benefits of Spanish sovereignty (see document 15.1). His navigator, Sebastian del Cano, became the first captain to circumnavigate the globe when he brought the expedition's only remaining ship back to Spain with fifteen survivors in 1522. The broad outlines of the world were now apparent (see map 15.1).

◆

The First Colonial Empires: Portugal and Spain

Conquest and the imposition of European government accompanied exploration from the beginning. The Portuguese made no effort to impose their direct rule on large native populations, in part because they lacked the manpower to do so and in part because the primary purpose of Portuguese expansion was trade. Instead they established a series of merchant colonies to collect

advantage of winds and currents that he could not fully have understood. In spite of the season he encountered no hurricanes and, on October 12, sighted what he believed to be an island off the coast of Japan. It was one of the Bahamas.

Columbus made three more voyages before his death in 1506, insisting until the end that he had found the western passage to Asia. The realization that it was a continent whose existence had only been suspected

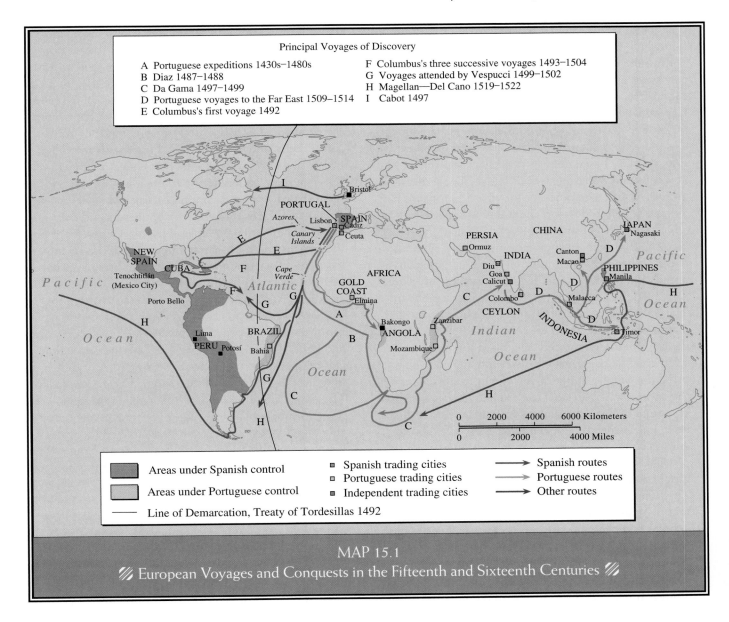

Principal Voyages of Discovery

A Portuguese expeditions 1430s–1480s
B Diaz 1487–1488
C Da Gama 1497–1499
D Portuguese voyages to the Far East 1509–1514
E Columbus's first voyage 1492
F Columbus's three successive voyages 1493–1504
G Voyages attended by Vespucci 1499–1502
H Magellan—Del Cano 1519–1522
I Cabot 1497

Areas under Spanish control
Areas under Portuguese control
—— Line of Demarcation, Treaty of Tordesillas 1492

▫ Spanish trading cities
▫ Portuguese trading cities
▪ Independent trading cities

⟶ Spanish routes
⟶ Portuguese routes
⟶ Other routes

MAP 15.1
European Voyages and Conquests in the Fifteenth and Sixteenth Centuries

goods from the African, Indian, or Asian interior for transshipment to Portugal in return for cash or European commodities. These colonies were rarely more than towns protected by a Portuguese garrison and governed by Portuguese law. They were not, for the most part, self-sustaining. To prosper, they had to maintain diplomatic and commercial relations with their neighbors while retaining the option of force, either for self-protection or to obtain a favorable market share in regional trade. Because Portugal's population was small, there was no question of large-scale immigration. Governors from Albuquerque onward sought to maintain colonial populations and to solidify Portuguese control by encouraging intermarriage with native peoples.

Communication between these far-flung stations and the mother country was maintained by the largest ships of the age, the thousand-ton carracks of the *Carreira da India*. The voyage around the tip of Africa took months and the mortality among crews was dreadful, but profit to the crown made it all seem worthwhile. To discourage smuggling, everything had to be shipped to and from a central point—the Guinea Mines House at Lagos, near Sagres—where royal officials could inspect the cargoes of spice and silks and assess the one-third share owed to the king. In return, the monarchy provided military and naval protection for the colonies and for the convoys that served them. Colonial governors, though appointed by the crown, enjoyed the freedom that comes from being far from home. Corruption flourished, but Portuguese rule was rarely harsh.

Where controlling large tracts of land became necessary, as in Brazil, the Portuguese established captaincies that were in fact proprietary colonies. Captains-general would be appointed in return for their promise to settle and develop their grants. The model was the settlement of Madeira. However, Brazil evolved into a society based upon African slavery. Its most valuable resources were dye woods and a climate ideal for growing sugar, a commodity for which Europeans had already begun to develop an insatiable craving.

The first Spanish attempts at colonization resembled the Portuguese experience in Brazil. Columbus had set a bad example by trying to enslave the native population of Hispaniola. Similar unsuccessful efforts were made at Cuba and elsewhere in the Caribbean. The Indians died of disease and overwork, fled to the mainland, or were killed while trying to resist. African slaves were then imported to work in the mines and sugar-cane fields. Royal efforts eventually were able to bring the situation under control, but in the meantime, the conquest of Mexico and Peru had changed the basic nature of Spanish colonial enterprise. For the first time, Europeans sought to impose their rule on societies as complex and populous as their own.

The various nations of central Mexico were grouped into political units that resembled city-states. Their combined population almost certainly exceeded that of Spain. By the fifteenth century, most of these peoples had become either subjects or tributaries of the warlike Aztecs whose capital, Tenochtitlán, was a vast city built in the midst of a lake where Mexico City now stands. With a force that originally numbered only six hundred men, Hernán Cortés seized control of this great empire in only two years (1519–21). He could not have done it without the assistance of the Aztecs' many native enemies, but his success left Spain with the problem of governing millions whose culture was wholly unlike that of Europeans.

The problem was compounded in Peru a decade later. In 1530 Francisco Pizarro landed at Tumbez on the Pacific coast with 180 men and set about the destruction of the Inca Empire. The Incas were the ruling dynasty of the Quechua people. From their capital at Cuzco they controlled a region nearly two thousand miles in length by means of an elaborate system of roads and military supply depots. More tightly organized than the Mexicans, Quechua society was based on communal landholding and a system of forced labor that supported both the rulers and a complex religious establishment that did not, unlike that of the Aztecs, demand human sacrifice. Pizarro had the good fortune to arrive in the midst of a dynastic dispute that divided the Indians and virtually paralyzed resistance. By 1533 the Spanish, numbering about six hundred, had seized the capital and a vast golden treasure, but they soon began to fight among themselves. Pizarro was murdered in one of a series of civil wars that ended only in 1548.

The rapid conquest of two great empires forced the Spanish crown to confront basic issues of morality and governance. Tension between conquerors and the crown had begun with Columbus. His enslavement of the Indians and high-handed treatment of his own men led to his replacement as governor of Hispaniola. Balboa was executed for his misbehavior in Darien by officials sent from Spain. To regularize the situation, the *encomienda* system, an institution with deep medieval roots, was introduced after the conquests of Mexico and Peru. Conquistadores were to provide protection and religious instruction for a fixed number of Indians in return for a portion of their labor. The system failed. The conquistadores were for the most part desperadoes, members of a large class of otherwise unemployable military adventurers that had survived the wars of Granada or of Italy. They had braved great dangers to win what they thought of as a New World and had no intention of allowing priests and bureaucrats to deprive them of their rewards.

In the meantime, the Indians of the mainland had begun to die in enormous numbers like those of the islands before them. Though many were killed while trying to defend themselves, most fell victim to European diseases for which they had developed no immunities. Smallpox was probably the worst. Estimates of mortality by the end of the sixteenth century range as high as 90 percent, and though all figures from this period are open to question, the conquest clearly was responsible for the greatest demographic catastrophe in historical times (see table 15.1).

Given the state of medical knowledge, little could be done to control the epidemics, but church and state alike were determined to do something about the conquistadores. The Dominican friar Bartolomé de Las Casas (1474–1566) launched a vigorous propaganda campaign on behalf of the Indians that ended in a series of debates at the University of Salamanca. Las Casas won his point. Between 1542 and 1543, the emperor Charles V (1500–58) issued the so-called New Laws, forbidding Indian slavery and abolishing the encomienda system.

◈ TABLE 15.1 ◈

Population Decline in Central Mexico

Little agreement exists on the size of Mexico's pre-Columbian population. These figures are more conservative than most but reflect a stunning rate of mortality.

Region	Population in 1530–35	Population in 1568
Basin of Mexico (excluding Mexico City)	589,070–743,337	294,535–297,335
Mexico City	218,546–273,183	109, 273
Morelos	460,797–614,396	153,599
Southern Hidalgo	257,442–321,802	128,721
Tlaxcala	140,000–165,000	140,000–165,000
West Puebla		
Above 2000 meters	160,664–200,830	80,332
Below 2000 meters	152,412–190,515	38,103
Total	1,978,931–2,509,063	944,563–972,363

Source: Adapted from William T. Sanders, "The Population of the Central Mexican Symbiotic Region, the Basin of Mexico, and the Teotihuacán Valley in the Sixteenth Century," in *The Native Population of the Americas in 1492*, 2d ed., William M. Denevan (Madison, Wis.: University of Wisconsin Press, 1992), p. 128.

The edicts for the protection of the Indians met with powerful resistance (see document 15.2), and not until the reign of Philip II from 1556 to 1598 did a system of governance become fully implemented that would last throughout the colonial era. The basis of that system was the establishment of Mexico and Peru as kingdoms to be ruled by viceroys who were the personal representatives of the king. Like the Portuguese, Spain tried to limit access to its colonial trade. Foreigners were excluded, and all goods were to be shipped and received through the Casa de Contratación, a vast government establishment in Sevilla. From the middle of the sixteenth century, French and English adventurers sought to break this monopoly and eventually became a threat to Spanish shipping in both Caribbean and European waters. By this time, massive silver deposits had been discovered at Potosí in what is now Bolivia (1545) and at Zacatecas in Mexico (1548). Bullion shipments from the New World soon accounted for more than 20 percent of the empire's revenues, and a system of convoys or *flotas* was established for their protection.

◈ DOCUMENT 15.2 ◈

Proclamation of the New Laws in Peru

In 1544 a new viceroy, Blasco Nuñez Vela, introduced the New Laws to Peru. The popular outrage recounted here by Francisco López de Gómara led to a serious but unsuccessful revolt under the leadership of Gonzalo Pizarro, the conqueror's brother.

Blasco Nuñez entered Trujillo amid great gloom on the part of the Spaniards; he publicly proclaimed the New Laws, regulating Indian tributes, freeing the Indians, and forbidding their use as carriers against their will and without pay. He told them, however, that if they had reason to complain of the ordinances they should take their case to the emperor; and that he would write to the king that he had been badly informed to order those laws.

When the citizens perceived the severity behind his soft words, they began to curse. [Some] said that they were ill-requited for their labor and services if in their declining years they were to have no one to serve them; these showed their teeth, decayed from eating roasted corn in the conquest of Peru; others displayed many wounds, bruises, and great lizard bites; the conquerors complained that after wasting their estates and shedding their blood in gaining Peru for the emperor, he was depriving them of the few vassals he had given them.

The priests and friars also declared that they could not support themselves nor serve their churches if they were deprived of their Indian towns; the one who spoke most shamelessly against the viceroy and even against the king was Fray Pedro Muñoz of the Mercedarian Order, saying . . . that the New Laws smelled of calculation rather than of saintliness, for the king was taking away the slaves that he had sold without returning the money received from them. . . . There was bad blood between this friar and the viceroy because the latter had stabbed the friar one evening in Málaga when the viceroy was *corregidor* there.

López de Gómara, Francisco. "*Historia de las Indias*," trans. B. Keen. In *Historiadores primitivos de las Indias*, vol. 1, p. 251. In *Latin American Civilization*, vol. 1, pp. 142–143. Boston: Houghton Mifflin, 1974.

A Clash of Empires: The Ottoman Challenge and the Emperor Charles V

The wars that plagued sixteenth- and early seventeenth-century Europe were for the most part a continuation of old dynastic rivalries, complicated after 1560 by rebellion and civil war in nearly all of the major states. These struggles were pursued with unparalleled vigor even though most Europeans believed, or claimed to believe, that the survival of Christendom was threatened by Ottoman expansion.

The Turks first became a serious threat to western Europe in the reign of Süleyman I (the Magnificent, reigned 1520–66). In 1522 his fleet drove the Knights of St. John from their stronghold at Rhodes, thereby permitting unimpeded communications between Constantinople and Egypt. After defeating the Hungarians at Mohács in 1526, Süleyman established control of the central Hungarian plain. The Austrian Hapsburgs were able to claim a narrow strip of northwestern Hungary, but Transylvania under the voivod János Zapolya (d. 1540) became a Turkish tributary, Calvinist in religion, and bitterly hostile to the Catholic west. Then, in 1529 and again in 1532, Süleyman besieged Vienna. He failed on both occasions, largely because Vienna was beyond the effective limits of Ottoman logistics. But the effort made a profound impression. The Turk was at the gates.

In retrospect, the attacks on Vienna probably were intended only to prevent a Hapsburg reconquest of Hungary. They were not repeated until 1689. In 1533 a new Turkish offensive was launched at sea. Fleets under the command of Khair-ed-Din, a Christian convert to Islam known as "Barbarossa" for his flaming red beard, ravaged the coasts of Italy, Sicily, and Spain and threatened Christian commerce throughout the Mediterranean.

The brunt of these struggles ultimately fell upon the Spanish Empire. In 1517 Charles of Hapsburg (1500–58) ascended the thrones of Castile and Aragon to become Charles I, first king of a united Spain. He was the son of Juana "la Loca" (the Crazy), daughter of Ferdinand and Isabella, and Philip "the Handsome" (d. 1506), son of the emperor Maximilian I and Mary of Burgundy. His mother lived until 1555, but she was thought to be insane and had been excluded from the succession. From her, Charles inherited Spain, its possessions in the New World, and much of Italy, including Naples, Sicily, and Sardinia. On the death of his grandfather Maximilian in 1519, he gained the Hapsburg lands in Austria and Germany and the remaining inheritance of the dukes of Burgundy including the seventeen provinces of the Netherlands. In 1521 he was elected Holy Roman emperor as Charles V (see illustration 15.2).

The massive accumulation of states and resources embroiled the young emperor in endless conflict. Though he had placed the Austrian lands under the rule of his brother Ferdinand, king of the Romans, Charles was forced to defend Vienna in person against the Turks. Because Turkish naval efforts were directed primarily against his possessions in Spain and Italy, he thought it necessary to invade Tunis in 1535 and Algiers in 1541. The Valois kings of France, seeing themselves surrounded by Charles's territories, fought seven wars with him in thirty years. This Hapsburg-Valois rivalry was in some ways a continuation of the Italian wars at the beginning of the century, but it was fought on three fronts: northern Italy, the Netherlands, and the Pyrenees. As a devout Catholic, the emperor also tried in 1546–47 and again in 1552–55 to bring the German Protestants to heel but received no help from the papacy. Paul III, fearing imperial domination of Italy, allied himself with the Most Christian King of France, who was in turn the ally of the major Protestant princes and of the Turks.

The empire of Charles V was multinational, but in time its center of gravity shifted toward Spain. Charles, born in the Low Countries and whose native tongue was French, became dependent upon the revenues of Castile, the only one of his realms in which permanent taxation had been established. Spanish soldiers, trained in the Italian wars, became the core of his army. Castilian administrators produced results, not endless complaints about the violation of traditional rights or procedures, and by 1545 his secretary, his chief military adviser, and his confessor were Spanish. Charles retired in 1556, sick and exhausted, to the remote monastery of Yuste in the heart of Spanish Extremadura. His son, Philip II (reigned 1556–98), was Spanish to his fingertips. His father's abdication left him Italy, the Netherlands, and the Spanish Empire, while the Hapsburg lands in central Europe were given to Charles's brother Ferdinand, who was elected emperor in 1558.

The war between France and Spain came to an end in 1559 with the treaty of Cateau-Cambrésis, but the underlying rivalry remained. Both sides were simply exhausted. Though Philip was forced to repudiate his father's debts, the predictability of Castilian revenues and a dramatic increase in wealth from the American mines

Illustration 15.2

🖎 **Charles V.** This portrait was painted by Titian after the battle of Mühlberg (1547) in which Charles defeated the Protestant princes of the Schmalkaldic League. It shows the emperor as he often was—on horseback and at war.

soon restored Spanish credit. The policies of the new king would be those of the late emperor: the containment of Islam and of Protestantism, and the neutralization of France.

The Crisis of the Early Modern State

The wars and rebellions of the later sixteenth century must be understood in this context. Moreover, the cost of war had continued to grow, forcing the state to increase its claims upon the resources of its subjects. By midcentury, nobles, cities, and their elected representatives had begun to resist those claims with unprecedented vigor. Reassertions of ancient privilege were brought forth to counter demands for more money or for greater royal authority. This heightened resistance was based in part upon economics. A series of bad harvests, partially attributed to the Little Ice Age that lasted from the 1550s to well after 1650, worked together with monetary inflation to keep trade and land revenues stagnant. Real wealth was not increasing in proportion to the demands made upon it, and though European elites continued to prosper by comparison with the poor, they grew ever more jealous of their prerogatives.

The controversies that arose in the wake of the Reformation made matters worse. Outside the Iberian Peninsula, the populations of most states were now bitterly divided along confessional as well as economic lines. Because nearly everyone believed that religious tolerance was incompatible with political order, each group sought to impose its views upon the others. This attitude was shared by many who were not fanatics. In a society that had always expressed political and economic grievances in religious language, the absence of a common faith made demonizing opponents easy, and reaching compromise difficult if not impossible.

In the light of these struggles, the evolution of dynastic states, for all its success, apparently had not resolved certain basic issues of sovereignty. The relationship of the crown to other elements of the governing elites was still open to question in France, England, and the Netherlands. In the Holy Roman Empire the role of the emperor was imperfectly defined, and many of the empire's constituent principalities were engaged in internal disputes. Underlying everything was the problem of dynastic continuity. The success of the early modern state still depended to an extraordinary degree upon the character and abilities of its ruler. Could its basic institutions continue to function if the prince were a child or an incompetent? Some even doubted that they could survive the accession of a woman.

The French Wars of Religion and the Revolt of the Netherlands

The peace of Cateau-Cambrésis was sealed by the marriage of Isabel of Valois, daughter of Henry II of France, to Philip II of Spain. The celebrations included a tournament in which the athletic, if middle-aged, Henry died when a splinter from his opponent's lance entered the eye socket of his helmet. The new king, Francis II, was a sickly child of fifteen. The establishment of a regency under the leadership of the Guise family marked the beginning of a series of conflicts known as the Wars of Religion that lasted until 1598. The Guise were from Lorraine and unrelated to the royal family. Their ascendancy threatened the Bourbons, a clan descended from Louis IX and headed by the brothers Antoine, king of Navarre, and Louis, prince of Condé. It was also a threat to Henry's widow, Catherine de Médicis (1519–89), who hoped to retain power on behalf of her son Francis and his three brothers. Yet another faction, headed by Anne de Montmorency, constable of France, sought, like Catherine, to play the Guise against the Bourbons for their own advantage.

At one level the Wars of Religion were an old-fashioned struggle between court factions for control of the crown, but the Guise were also devout Catholics who intensified Henry II's policy of persecuting Protestants. Most French Protestants, or Huguenots, were followers of John Calvin. In 1559 they numbered no more than 5 or 10 percent of the population, but their geographic and social distribution made them a formidable minority. Heavily concentrated in the south and west, Calvinism appealed most to rural nobles and to the artisans of the towns, two groups with a long history of political, regional, and economic grievances (see document 15.3). The nobles were for the most part trained in the profession of arms; unhappy artisans could easily disrupt trade and city governments.

Searching for allies, the Bourbons found the Huguenots and converted to Protestantism. The conflict was now both religious and to a degree regional, as the Catholics of Paris and the northeast rallied to the house of Guise, who were secretly allied with Philip II of Spain. Francis II died in 1560, shortly after Condé and

---

❖ DOCUMENT 15.3 ❖

The Defense of Liberty Against Tyrants

In both France and the Netherlands, the Protestants had to justify their revolt against the monarchy. One of the most important theorists to do so was Philippe du Plessis-Mornay, a councillor to Henry of Navarre, the leader of the Bourbon faction who later became Henry IV. Plessis-Mornay based his argument on an early version of the social contract theory, which argued that all rulers received their power from the people. His ideas would have a powerful impact on the political thinkers of the Enlightenment and on the framers of the United States Constitution. This is an exerpt from his treatise, Vindiciae contra tyrannos.

Thus, at the beginning all kings were elected. And even those who seem today to come to the throne by succession must first be inaugurated by the people. Furthermore, even if a people has customarily chosen its kings from a particular family because of its outstanding merits, that decision is not so unconditional that if the established line degenerates, the people may not select another.

We have shown . . . that kings receive their royal status from the people; that the whole people is greater than the king and is above him; that the king in his kingdom, the emperor in his empire, are supreme only as ministers and agents, while the people is the true proprietor. It follows, therefore, that a tyrant who commits felony against the people who is, as it were, the owner of his fief; that he commits *lèse majesté* [treason] against the kingdom or the empire; and that he is no better than any other rebel since he violates the same laws, although as king, he merits even graver punishment. And so . . . he may be either deposed by his superior or punished under the *lex Julia* [the Roman law on treason] for acts against the public majesty. But the superior here is the whole people or those who represent it. . . . And if things have gone so far that the tyrant cannot be expelled without resort to force, they may call the people to arms, recruit an army, and use force, strategy, and all the engines of war against him who is the declared enemy of the country and the commonwealth.

du Plessis-Mornay, Philippe. "*Vindiciae contra tyrannos.*" In *Constitutionalism and Resistance in the 16th Century,* trans. and ed. Julian H. Franklin. New York: Macmillan, 1969.

Illustration 15.3

The Massacre of the Innocents. In this work of art by Pieter Breughel the Younger, which is also a powerful propaganda piece, Spanish soldiers terrorize a Flemish village. The figure at the head of the troops bears a strong resemblence to the duke of Alba as he looked in 1567. To make a political point, Breughel the Younger may have repainted an earlier version of this work that had been done by his father.

the Huguenots tried unsuccessfully to kidnap him at Amboise. He was succeeded by his brother, Charles IX (reigned 1560–74), who was closely controlled by Catherine de Médicis, but the wars went on. Though the Huguenots were not at first successful on the battlefield, they gained limited religious toleration in 1570.

Meanwhile, the Netherlands had begun their long rebellion against the king of Spain. The seventeen provinces of the Low Countries were now the richest part of Europe, an urbanized region devoted to trade and intensive agriculture. Though divided by language (Dutch or Flemish was spoken in the north and west, French or Walloon in the south and east), they shared a common artistic and intellectual tradition and an easy-going tolerance for foreigners and heretics. Though a majority of the population remained Catholic, Lutherans and Calvinists flourished in the major cities. Government was decentralized and, from the Spanish point of view, woefully inefficient. Philip II was represented by a regent, his half-sister Margaret of Parma (1522–86), who presided over the privy council and the councils of finance and state. Seventeen provincial estates, all of which were represented in the States General, controlled taxes and legislation. A virulent localism based on the defense of historical privilege made agreement possible only on rare occasions. Taxes were usually defeated by squabbles over who should pay the largest share—nobles or townspeople. No common legal code existed, and a host of independent legal jurisdictions were controlled by nobles whose administration of justice was often corrupt.

None of this was acceptable to Philip II. He was determined to reorganize the government, reform the legal system, and root out heresy by reforming the church along the lines suggested by the Council of Trent. All of these proposals struck directly at the wealth and power of the Netherlandish nobles. Philip's plan to reorganize the governing councils weakened their authority, while legal reform would have eliminated the feudal courts from which many of the nobles drew large revenues. Though his reform of the church sought to increase the number of bishops, the king was determined to end the purchase of ecclesiastical offices and to appoint only clerics whose education and spirituality met the high standards imposed by the Council of Trent. The ancient custom by which nobles invested in church offices for the support of their younger sons was at an end.

Four years of accelerating protest by leading members of the aristocracy accomplished nothing. Finally, in 1566, a wave of iconoclasm brought matters to a head. The Protestants, acting in opposition to Philip's plan for ecclesiastical reform and encouraged by members of the higher nobility, removed the images from churches across the country. In some areas, iconoclasm was accompanied by rioting and violence. Though the regent's government was able to restore order, Philip responded in shock and anger. In 1567 he dispatched his leading general, the duke of Alba (1507–82), to put down what he saw as rebellion (see illustration 15.3). Though Alba was at first successful, the harshness of his government alienated virtually every segment of opinion. When he attempted to introduce a perpetual tax in 1572, most of the major cities declared their allegiance to William "the Silent," Prince of Orange (1533–84), the man who had emerged as leader of the revolt.

Though William was not yet a convert to Protestantism, he attempted to form an alliance with the French Huguenots, who, under the leadership of Gaspard de Coligny, had gained new influence with Charles IX. The situation was doubly perilous for Spain because Philip II, while maintaining Alba in the Netherlands, had renewed his father's struggles with the Turk. The Mediterranean war culminated in the great naval victory of Lepanto (October 7, 1571), but Philip's treasury was once again exhausted. French intervention in the Netherlands was averted only by the Massacre of St. Bartholomew (August 23–24, 1572) in which more than five thousand Protestants, Coligny included, were killed by Catholic mobs. The massacre revived the French civil wars and permitted Alba to retake many of the rebellious towns, but the duke was recalled in 1573 and his successors were unable to bring the revolt under control. Margaret's son, Alessandro Farnese, duke of Parma (1545–92), finally was able to reimpose Spanish rule on the ten southern provinces in 1585.

By this time, the seven northern provinces had organized into an independent state with William of Orange as stadtholder or chief executive. The United Netherlands was Dutch in language and culture. Enriched by trade, secure in its control of the sea, and defended by the heavily fortified "water line" of three broad rivers—the Rhine, the Maas, and the Waal—the new republic was almost invulnerable to Spanish attack. It was also Protestant. The government was dominated by Calvinists, and William converted to Protestantism before he was assassinated by a Spanish agent in 1584. Refugees from Spanish rule, most of them French-speaking Calvinists, poured into the north, while a number of Dutch Catholics headed south into what is now Belgium.

These developments critically altered the balance of power in northern Europe. Philip II was still determined to recover his lost provinces and to assist the Catholics of France in their battle against the Huguenots. The English, restored to Protestantism by Elizabeth I (ruled 1558–1603; see illustration 15.4), were equally determined to prevent a concentration of Spanish power on the coasts of the North Sea. When Parma took Antwerp, the largest and richest city in the Netherlands in 1584, they sent an expeditionary force to support the Dutch.

Illustration 15.4

Elizabeth I of England. This portrait from the workshop of Nicholas Hilliard dates from c. 1599, a time of great political difficulty for the queen. It is a propaganda piece intended to convey the wealth, majesty, and vigor of a ruler who was already in her sixty-sixth year.

Though a prosperous land of about three-and-a-half million people, Elizabethan England was no match for the Spanish Empire. It had the core of a fine navy but no army worthy of the name. Perpetual taxes were unknown, and the improvidence of Henry VIII had left his daughter with meager revenues from the royal domain. In the event of war, funds had to be sought from Parliament, and Parliament continually tried to interfere with the queen's policies. It was especially incensed at her refusal to marry, in part because it thought a woman incapable of governing on her own, and in part because it feared disorder if she died without an heir.

Parliament need not have worried about Elizabeth's ability, but this last concern, at least, was real. Catholics everywhere had rejected Henry VIII's divorce. To them, Elizabeth was illegitimate, and Mary Stuart, queen of Scots (1542–87), was the true queen of England. A devout Catholic, descended from Henry VII and connected on her mother's side to the house of Guise, Mary had been driven from Scotland in 1568 by a coalition of Protestants inspired by the

Illustration 15.5

⬛ **The Spanish Armada, 1588.** This painting by an unknown artist shows a critical moment in the defeat of the Spanish Armada. The Spanish fleet had anchored off Gravelines on the Flemish coast to support an invasion of England by the duke of Parma. The English sent fireships into the anchorage, forcing them to scatter and to abandon the invasion.

reformer John Knox and led by her kinsman the earl of Moray. Elizabeth offered her refuge but held her under house arrest for nineteen years before ordering her execution in 1587.

Mary was killed not only because she had plotted against Elizabeth, but also because the English queen was convinced that war with Spain was inevitable. Elizabeth wanted no rival to encourage the hopes of Philip II or of her own Catholic subjects. These fears, too, were realistic, because for more than twenty years Elizabeth had pursued a course of intermittent hostility toward Spain. She had encouraged her subjects, notably Sir John Hawkins and Sir Francis Drake, to raid Spanish colonies in the Caribbean and in 1586 sent an English force to assist the Dutch. From the Spanish point of view, the execution of Mary was the last straw. Philip responded by sending a fleet to invade England. The great Spanish Armada of 1588 failed (see illustration 15.5), but the disaster did not end the war. Philip rebuilt his navy and tried again without success in 1595, while Drake and the aged Hawkins made an-

other vain attempt on Havana and Cartagena de Indias in the same year.

By this time the Spanish were at war in France as well. In 1589 the Bourbon leader, Henry of Navarre, emerged from the "War of the Three Henrys" as the only surviving candidate for the throne. Henry of Guise and Henry III, the last surviving son of Catherine de Médicis, had been assassinated by each others' supporters. Philip thought that, if France were controlled by Huguenots, the Spanish Netherlands would be crushed between two Protestant enemies, and he sent Parma and his army into France. This expedition, too, was a costly failure, but Henry's interests turned out to be more political than religious. He converted to Catholicism in the interest of peace and ascended the throne as Henry IV (reigned 1589–1610). To protect the Huguenots he issued the Edict of Nantes (1598), which granted them freedom of worship and special judicial rights in a limited number of towns, most in the southwest. In some respects, a state within a state was created, but the ordeal of France was over.

The Thirty Years' War

The resolution of the French wars and the death of Philip II in 1598 marked the end of a political cycle. The Netherlands continued to struggle under the leadership of William's son, Maurice of Nassau (1567–1625), until a ten years' truce was concluded in 1608, but it was a truce, not a treaty. Though Spain was financially exhausted, it still refused to recognize the Dutch state. War was expected to break out again when the truce expired in 1618. The war, when it came, was much more than a resumption of the Dutch Revolt. It involved all of the European states and turned central Europe into a battleground from 1618 to 1648.

The first phase of the Thirty Years' War began with a struggle for the crown of Bohemia. In 1555 the Peace of Augsburg had established the principle *cuius regio, eius religio;* that is, princes within the empire had the right to determine the religious beliefs of their subjects. Calvinists, however, were excluded from its provisions, and issues regarding the disposition of church properties and the conversion of bishops were left in dispute. Since then, two electoral principalities, the Palatinate and Brandenburg, had turned Calvinist, and several bishops had converted to Protestantism while retaining possession of their endowed lands. Violent quarrels arose over these issues and by 1610 the empire was divided into two armed camps: the Protestant Union and the Catholic League.

The Bohemian controversy arose because Matthias, king of Bohemia in 1618, was also Holy Roman emperor, a Catholic Hapsburg, and uncle of the future emperor Ferdinand II of Austria (1578–1637). Matthias was determined to preserve Bohemia for the faith and for his family, and in 1617 he secured the election of Ferdinand as his successor to the throne of Bohemia. This election was opposed by many of the Bohemian gentry and lesser nobility. They were, for the most part, Calvinists or Hussites and feared persecution from the devout Ferdinand and his Jesuit advisers. On May 23, 1618, an assembly of Bohemians threw three of the Hapsburg's regents from a window of the Hradschin palace, appointed a provisional government, and began to raise an army.

The "Defenestration of Prague" was an act of war. Revolt spread to the hereditary lands, threatening not only Bohemia but also the basic integrity of the Hapsburg state. Worse yet, the king of Bohemia was an elector of the empire. If the Bohemians elected a Protestant, the Protestants would have a majority of electors just as a new imperial election appeared imminent. Matthias was in poor health and Ferdinand hoped to succeed

him as king of Bohemia as well as emperor. Ferdinand needed time to muster support, but in June 1619 he invaded Bohemia with the army of the Catholic League, drawn largely from his ally, Bavaria. The Bohemians responded by offering the crown to a Calvinist prince, Frederick V (1596–1632), elector palatine and son-in-law of James I of England.

Frederick accepted, after the death of Matthias and the election of Ferdinand as emperor on August 28. It was a tragic mistake. He was supported by only a part of the Protestant Union. James I refused to help, and a diversionary attack on Hungary by Bethlen Gabor (1580–1629), the Calvinist prince of Transylvania, was eventually contained by the Hapsburgs. Finally, on November 8, 1620, Frederick and his Protestant allies were soundly defeated at the White Mountain near Prague. Frederick's cause was now hopeless. The Spanish truce with the Netherlands had expired, and the palatinate lay squarely across the route by which Spanish troops and supplies were sent to the Low Countries. While Frederick's forces fought to preserve his claim to Bohemia, a Spanish army invaded his ancestral lands.

A second phase of the war began in 1625 when Christian IV of Denmark (1577–1648) emerged briefly as the champion of Protestantism. Christian's Lutheranism was reinforced by his territorial ambitions in north Germany, but he was no match for the imperial generals. By 1629 he was out of the war. His place was taken by the formidable Gustav Adolph of Sweden (1594–1632). Since the reign of Erik XIV, from 1560 to 1568, Swedish policy had aimed at control of the Baltic. Wars with Russia and Poland had taught Gustav the art of war and given him all of Livonia, a territory roughly equal to present-day Estonia, Latvia, and Lithuania. He now sought to defend his fellow Protestants and to establish Swedish control over Mecklenburg and Pomerania on the north German coast. His brilliant campaigns, financed in part by France, came to an end when he died victorious on the battlefield at Lützen on November 16, 1632.

The last phase of the war (1535–1648) continued the Franco-Swedish alliance, but with France acting openly as the leader of the anti-imperial forces. Henry IV had died at the hands of an assassin in 1610, leaving the queen, Marie de Médicis, as regent for the nine-year-old Louis XIII (1601–43). Her regency was unpopular, but the disasters of 1560 were not repeated. Louis seized power from his mother in 1617 and, after 1624, entrusted much of his government to Armand de Plessis, cardinal duke of Richelieu (1585–1642). One of the ablest statesmen of the age, Richelieu was alarmed by the Spanish-Imperial alliance and returned

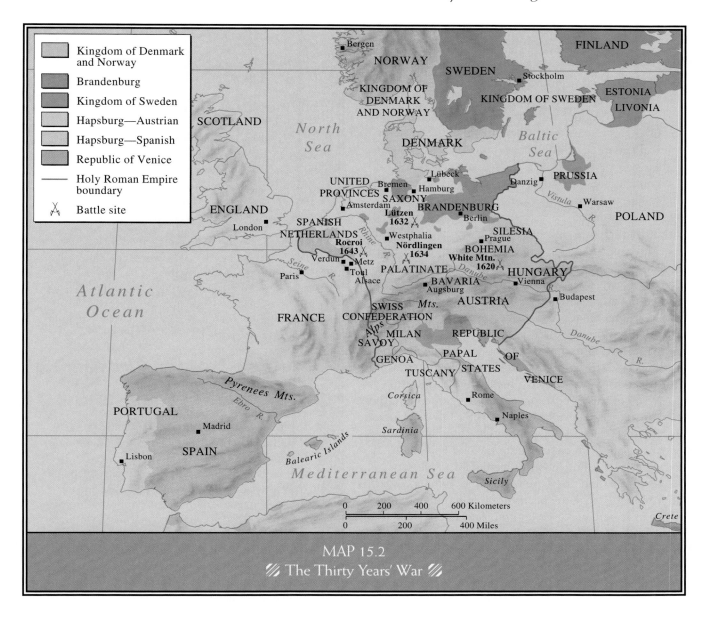

MAP 15.2
The Thirty Years' War

to the anti-Hapsburg policies of Francis I. He pursued the war through surrogates until the death of Gustav Adolph forced him into the open. The Spanish were by this time in irreversible decline, and their defeat by the French at Rocroi (1643) marked the end of their military power. Bavaria was ravaged by a Franco-Swedish force in 1648, and peace was at last concluded on October 24 of that year.

The Treaties of Westphalia brought the Thirty Years' War to an end, leaving France the dominant power in Europe (see map 15.2). The Netherlands, which had fought Spain in a series of bitter actions on land and sea, was at last recognized as an independent state, while the German principalities, many of which had been devastated, were restored to the boundaries of

1618. Bohemia reverted to the Hapsburgs, but imperial authority as a whole was weakened except in the Hapsburg lands of southeastern Europe. It was a meager return for three decades of unparalleled violence.

The English Civil War

England did not participate in the Thirty Years' War because the early Stuart monarchs, James I (reigned 1603–25) and Charles I (reigned 1625–49), were caught in a political dilemma from which they could not escape. Like Denmark and Sweden, England was a "domain" state: the regular revenues of the crown came not from taxes, which could be levied only by Parliament, but from the royal domain. This was not necessarily a disadvantage. The Danish monarch held more than 40 percent of the arable land in Denmark and derived vast revenues from the Sound Tolls levied on every ship passing from the North Sea into the Baltic. The Swedish royal estate derived great wealth from export duties on copper and iron, the country's major exports. Both countries were therefore able to exert a political and military influence wholly disproportionate to their size.

England had no comparable sources of revenue. The failure of Henry VIII to retain monastic lands taken at the time of the Reformation left the crown without sufficient property to "live of its own." Even import and export duties, though technically part of the domain, had to be authorized by Parliament. The resulting poverty, already evident under Elizabeth, restricted the crown's ability to reward its supporters. Worse, it forced her Stuart successors to seek wealth in ways that profoundly offended their subjects (see document 15.4). Knights' fines, ship money, *quo warranto* proceedings, and the abuse of wardships struck directly at property rights and aroused a firestorm of opposition.

Much of this opposition was at first centered in the legal profession where such jurists as Sir Edward Coke (1552–1634) revived the common law as a protection against royal prerogatives, but in the end Parliament proved to be the crown's most formidable adversary. Between 1540 and 1640 the wealth and numbers of the landholding gentry, the professions, and the merchant community had increased enormously. These elements of the English elite dominated the House of Commons, which took the lead in opposing royal policies. The Stuarts feared their disaffection and would have preferred to rule without calling Parliament. Except for relatively short periods, this was impossible. Even the smallest of crises forced the crown to seek relief through parliamentary taxation.

The growing resentment in Parliament might have been better managed had it not been for the personalities of the Stuart kings. Neither James nor Charles was capable of inspiring great loyalty. James was awkward, personally dirty, and a homosexual at a time when homosexuality was universally condemned. His son was arrogant and generally distrusted, while the court as a whole was thought to be morally and financially corrupt. Though James, who annoyed his subjects with treatises on everything from the evils of tobacco to witchcraft, wrote eloquently in support of the divine right of kings, the legitimacy of his family's rule was continually undermined by his own behavior and by the devious policies of his son.

❖ DOCUMENT 15.4 ❖

The English Petition of Right, 1628

The 1628 Petition of Right summarized Parliament's grievances against Charles I, who was trying to solve his financial problems through illegal and arbitrary means. The objections are based largely upon perceived violations of the Magna Carta, also known as the Great Charter. The following are excerpts from a much longer document.

And where also, by the statute called the Great Charter of the Liberties of England, it is declared and enacted that no freeman may be taken or imprisoned, or be disseised of his freehold or liberties or his free customs, or be outlawed or exiled or in any manner destroyed, but by the lawful judgment of his peers or by the law of the land. . . .

They do therefore humbly pray your most excellent majesty that no man hereafter be compelled to make or yield any gift, loan, benevolence, tax, or such like charge without common consent by act of parliament; and that none be called to make answer, or take such oath, or to give attendance, or be confined, or otherwise molested or disquieted concerning the same, or for refusal thereof; and that no freeman, in any such manner as is before mentioned, be imprisoned or detained; and that your majesty would be pleased to remove the said soldiers and mariners [who had been quartered in the counties to enforce the king's measures]; and that the foresaid commissions for proceeding by martial law may be revoked and annulled; and that hereafter no commissions of like nature may issue forth . . . lest by colour of them any of your majesty's subjects be destroyed or put to death, contrary to the laws and franchise of the land.

Journals of the House of Lords, vol. 3.

The religious question was more serious. Elizabeth, not wishing "to make windows into men's souls," had established a church that was Protestant but relatively tolerant. Some of her subjects had retained a fondness for the ideas and liturgical practices of the old church, while others, known as Puritans, followed Calvin with varying degrees of rigor. James was a Calvinist who commissioned the King James Bible in 1611 and established Protestant colonists in northern Ireland in the same year. He quarreled with the Puritans over church governance and other matters, but he managed to avoid an open breach as they grew more powerful over the course of his reign. Charles, however, supported the anti-Puritan reforms of Archbishop William Laud (1573–1645). Though Laud was no Catholic, Queen Henriette Marie (1609–1669) heard Mass regularly. She was the sister of Louis XIII and a strong personality who exerted great influence over her husband. The Puritans suspected that Charles meant to restore Catholicism. Faith, as well as liberty and property, was thought to be at risk.

Twenty years of increasingly bitter conflict between Parliament and the crown led to civil war in 1642. The Scots rebelled in 1638 when Charles tried to introduce the English *Book of Common Prayer* at Edinburgh. To pay for the Scottish war, he summoned what is called the Long Parliament because it met from 1640 to 1660. In response to his call for money, the Commons impeached Archbishop Laud and Charles's chief minister, Thomas Wentworth, earl of Strafford. They then abolished the prerogative courts of Star Chamber and High Commission. When Charles failed to impeach the parliamentary leaders he fled from London, and Parliament decided to raise an army in its own defense.

After three years of hard fighting, the royalists were defeated at Naseby (June 14, 1645), but serious divisions had appeared in the parliamentary ranks. The army was now dominated by Independents, who favored a congregational form of church government, while the Parliament they served was controlled by Presbyterians. The Independents refused to disband without guaranteed freedom of conscience and the removal of certain Presbyterians from Parliament. The Scots, fearing a threat to their own Presbyterian church order, were alarmed. Charles sought to capitalize on these strains by abolishing the Scottish episcopate in return for Presbyterian support, but the Scots and their English allies were defeated by the army at Preston (August 17–20, 1548). The victors now felt that compromise was impossible. In December the army captured Charles and purged the Commons of its Presbyterian members. A court appointed by the Rump, as the remnant of Parliament was now called, sentenced the king to death. He was beheaded at Whitehall on January 30, 1649.

For all practical purposes, England was governed by the army. A republican constitution had been established, but real power lay in the hands of Oliver Cromwell (1599–1658), the most successful of the parliamentary generals. In 1653 he was named lord protector of the Commonwealth of England, Scotland, and Ireland. A radical Protestant, Cromwell attempted to reform English society along Puritan lines while following a vigorous policy abroad. After subduing the Scots, he fought a naval war with the Dutch (1552–54) and started another with Spain in 1656. The Irish Catholics, who had massacred thousands of Protestants in 1641, were ruthlessly suppressed.

Cromwell had refused to accept the crown when it was offered to him in 1657, but when he died in the following year he left the Protectorate to his son Richard. Richard's rule was brief and troubled. He was forced to resign after only nine months, and a Convention Parliament restored Charles II (1630–85), son of Charles I, on May 8, 1660. The English had tired of Puritanism and military rule.

The Price of Conflict: Fiscal Crisis and Administrative Devolution

Surprisingly, this age of troubles was in many places a time of intellectual, literary, and artistic achievement. A distinction must be made between those regions that were combat zones, those that remained peaceful but were forced to assume heavy financial burdens, and those that were virtually untouched by the fighting. Even the most devastated regions experienced peace for at least a portion of the century between 1560 and 1660; their recovery was sometimes rapid.

In some cases the experience of war produced literary masterpieces. The age of the religious wars was not a golden one for France, but it produced the elegant and skeptical essays of Michel de Montaigne (1533–92), an antidote to sectarian madness. In Germany, the wreckage of the Thirty Years' War was nearly complete, but it was wryly chronicled in Grimmelshausen's *Simplicissimus. Don Quixote,* one of the greatest of all literary classics, was written by Miguel de Cervantes (1547–1616), who had lost an arm at Lepanto. It is, at least in part, a satire on his countrymen's fantastic dreams of glory.

Political turmoil gave birth to political theory. The English Civil War convinced Thomas Hobbes (1588–1679) that political salvation lay in *Leviathan,* an autocratic superstate, while *Oceana,* by James Harrington (1611–77) reflected the republican ideals of the Commonwealth. In *Paradise Lost,* Cromwell's Latin secretary, John Milton (1608–74), created a Puritan epic to rival the vision of Dante. Drama, too, flourished in the England of William Shakespeare (1564–1616) and in the Spain of Lope de Vega (1562–1635) and Calderón de la Barca (1600–81). The Netherlands, which after the 1590s enjoyed prosperity and internal peace in the midst of war, surpassed its own earlier achievements in the visual arts and became the center of a school of painting that influenced artists throughout northern Europe.

But if learning and the arts flourished, at least in some places, the struggles of the age were often highly destructive of political and economic life. This resulted primarily from the ways in which war was organized and fought. Armies had become vastly larger and more expensive in the course of the sixteenth century, and the wars were almost interminable. Given their political objectives, it could not have been otherwise. The French Wars of Religion were a struggle between two, and at times three, irreconcilable segments of the country's elite. Most of the battles were classic cavalry actions that resulted in a clear victory for one side or the other, but which could not end the war. Only the destruction of a major segment of the population could have prevented the losers from trying again.

In the Netherlands, the primary goal of both sides was to take and hold land or, conversely, to deny it to the enemy. After 1572 the war became a series of sieges that, thanks to the defensive value of the bastion trace, lasted months if not years. Both sides tended to avoid battles because their troops were, in the short term at least, irreplaceable. Sixteenth-century tactics demanded professional soldiers. The recruitment, training, and movement of replacements to the war zone took months, and positions under constant enemy pressure could not be left even partially defenseless.

If the war in the Netherlands was virtually static, the situation in Germany during the Thirty Years' War was too fluid. Central Europe had become a kind of power vacuum into which unpredictable forces were drawn. Bloody battles were fought only to see the victor confronted with yet another set of enemies. It is hard to imagine what, other than sheer exhaustion, might have ended the struggle. War, as Michael Roberts has said, "eternalized itself."

No early modern state could afford this. Even the wealthiest European monarchies lacked the ability to recruit and maintain full-scale standing armies. They relied instead on a core of subject troops (or, as in the French Wars of Religion, troops personally and ideologically committed to a cause), supplemented by a far larger number of mercenaries. The latter were usually recruited by contractors who commanded them in the field. If the mercenaries were not paid, they left; if they stayed, they had little incentive to risk their lives un-

necessarily. Their employers had little control over their actions, and even subject troops were capable of mutiny if they were left too long unpaid.

War, in other words, was a chaotic business. Rank in the modern sense meant little because officers sometimes refused to obey the orders of those who might have been their inferiors in civilian life. There were no uniforms, and weapons were not for the most part standardized. Logistics were a nightmare. An army might number anywhere from 30,000 to 100,000 combatants. The troops were housed either in makeshift field shelters or quartered on the civilian populations of the war zones, which meant that civilians might be forced to provide food and housing for months on end. The close contact between soldiers and civilians bred hostility and led to chronic breakdowns in military discipline. To complicate matters further, camp followers numbered at least three and often six for each combatant. These women and children were the support troops who made shelter, foraged for food, and nursed the sick and wounded. No army could function without them, but together with the men they made up a society that lived by its own rules with little concern for civilian norms.

The system reached a peak of absurdity during the Thirty Years' War when contractors such as the imperial general Albrecht von Wallenstein (1583–1634) offered recruits a month's pay—which they had to give back to pay for their arms and equipment—and then marched them so far from their homes that they could not easily return. From that point onward they were expected to live off the land. Such practices account for much of the dislocation caused by the German wars. It was safer to join an army with one's family than to remain at home to be robbed, raped, or killed by marauding soldiers (see document 15.5). Whole villages were depopulated only to reconstitute themselves wherever they found themselves when the war ended.

When a state tried to provide adequately for its troops, the costs were prohibitive and could lead to social breakdown. The fate of Spain is an example. In the 1570s Philip II was spending 140 percent of his annual revenues on warfare. The uncovered balance was provided by loans, often at high rates, from Italian or Dutch bankers. Not even American silver could long sustain this kind of expenditure, and in time the economy of Castile was badly damaged (see table 15.2). The other Spanish kingdoms were exempt from most forms of taxation, but in Castile taxes increased to the point that peasants were forced from the land and took refuge in the cities where the church periodically dis-

◆ DOCUMENT 15.5 ◆

Soldiers Loot a German Farm

The novel Simplicissimus *by Hans von Grimmelshausen (c.1622–74) was based in part on the author's own experiences in the Thirty Years' War. In these passages from the beginning of the book, the title character Simplicissimus, who is not as simple as he appears, describes the sack of his parent's farm. Like the hero, people took to the roads or joined the armies to avoid such horrors.*

The first thing these troopers did in the blackened room of my Dad was to stable their mounts. Thereafter, each fell to his appointed task, fraught in every case with ruin and destruction. For although some began to slaughter, cook, and roast, as if for a merry banquet, others stormed through the house from top to bottom, ransacking even the privy, as though they thought the Golden Fleece might be hidden there. Some packed great bundles of cloth, apparel, and household goods, as if to set up a stall for a jumble sale, but what they had no use for they smashed and destroyed. Some thrust their swords into the hay and straw as if they had not enough sheep and pigs to slaughter. Others emptied the feather-beds and pillows of their down, filling them instead with meat and other provender, as if that would make them more comfortable to sleep on. Others again smashed stoves and windows as if to herald an everlasting summer. They flattened copper and pewter utensils and packed up the bent and useless pieces; chests, tables, chairs, and benches they burnt, though in the yard they could have found many cords of firewood. Finally, they broke every dish and saucepan, either because they preferred their food roasted or because they intended to have no more than a single meal there.

And now they began to unscrew the flints from their pistols and to jam the peasant's thumbs into them, and to torture the poor lads as if they had been witches. Indeed, one of the captives had already been pushed into the bread oven and a fire lit under him, although he had confessed nothing. They put a sling around the head of another, twisting it tight with a piece of wood until the blood spurted from his mouth, nose, and ears. In short, each had his own device for torturing peasants, and each peasant received his individual torture. . . . Of the captured women, girls, and maidservants I have nothing in particular to tell, for the warriors would not let me see what they did with them. But this I do know: that from time to time one could hear pitiful screams coming from different parts of the house, and I don't suppose my Mum and Ursula fared any better than the others.

Grimmelshausen, H. J. C. von. *Adventures of a Simpleton*, pp. 8–9, trans. W. Wallich. New York: Ungar, 1963.

⬧ TABLE 15.2 ⬧

Crown Income and Debt in Castile

These figures (in millions of ducats) provide an idea of the financial burdens imposed on the Castilian economy by war. During most of this period, nonmilitary costs rarely rose above 10 percent of the annual budget.

Year	Revenue	Debt	Interest on debt
1515	1.5	12	0.8
1560	5.3	35	2.0
1575	6.0	50	3.8
1598	9.7	85	4.6
1623	15.0	112	5.6
1667	36.0	130	9.1

Source: C. Wilson and G. Parker, eds., *An Introduction to the Sources of European Economic History* (Ithaca, N.Y.: Cornell University Press, 1977), p. 49.

tributed grain and oil to the poor. Commerce and industry were virtually destroyed. Declining production increased the country's dependence on imports, which lowered the value of Spanish money and worsened an inflation that had been fueled for years by silver from the Indies. When Philip II died in 1598, the population of Castile had been shrinking for nearly a decade.

Economic decline provoked a chain reaction that raised the costs of war by increasing the interest on government loans, while unfavorable exchange rates raised the cost of goods and services that Spain had to purchase in Germany or the Netherlands. Troops were often poorly supplied or left without pay for as much as three years at a time. This caused mutinies, which prolonged the wars and raised costs even higher. Similar problems arose in other countries, but they were far more serious in Spain because the military effort lasted for more than a century and a half. From the wars of Granada to the Peace of Westphalia, little opportunity existed for recovery.

Philip III (ruled 1598–1621) and his minister, the shrewd but lethargic duke of Lerma, tried to provide Spain with a much-needed respite from war but were unable to restrain the aggressive tendencies of their viceroys. When Philip IV's chief minister, the energetic count-duke of Olivares (1587–1645), tried to spread the burdens of taxation and recruitment to other Spanish realms, he faced rebellion. Portugal, which had been annexed by Philip II in 1580 after its king died without heirs, declared independence in 1640. Cataluña, on the other side of the peninsula, rebelled in the same year. The government of Olivares lacked the resources to stop them, and Portugal remains free to this day. Cataluña returned to the fold in 1652 after France emerged as a greater threat to its liberties than Castile.

Spain was in some respects a special case, but the condition of Europe as a whole after a century of war and rebellion was grim. Most of the German states were a shambles, while the emperor's role was much di-minished outside his hereditary lands. Russia was still emerging from its "Time of Troubles," the period of anarchy that followed the death of Ivan the Terrible. The Romanov dynasty, established in 1613, had difficulty dealing with a series of Cossack rebellions and with the heresy of the Old Believers, a movement that rejected all innovation in the Russian church. Though Cromwellian England had briefly tapped the country's wealth in the service of the state, the restoration of Charles II revived many of the old conflicts between crown and Parliament and the king's wealth was once again severely limited. France with its enormous wealth was more resilient, but when the four-year-old Louis XIV ascended the throne under a regency, a series of aristocratic rebellions known as the Fronde (1648–52) revealed that the foundations of the monarchy were by no means fully secure. At midcentury only the Dutch Republic appeared strong and stable, and for Europe's monarchies the years of turmoil clearly had done little to resolve the problem of sovereignty.

CHAPTER 16

PREINDUSTRIAL EUROPE: SCIENCE, THE ECONOMY, AND POLITICAL REORGANIZATION

CHAPTER OUTLINE

◆◆◆◆◆◆◆◆◆◆◆◆◆◆◆◆◆◆◆◆◆◆◆◆

The political troubles of the late sixteenth and early seventeenth centuries did not preclude extraordinary developments in other areas. The scientific revolution changed the way Europeans thought about the physical universe. England, France, and above all the Netherlands challenged the Iberian powers and created substantial empires of their own. In the process they greatly expanded Europe's presence in world markets and accumulated capital in unprecedented amounts. The Netherlands emerged, however briefly, as a major power and a center of high culture. Eventually, states that had been nearly shattered by a century of war and revolution began to reconstruct themselves, reforming their governmental institutions, curbing the power of local elites, and gaining control over the armies and navies whose independence had threatened to engulf them. The model for many of these changes was the France of Louis XIV, but the rise of England as an economic and naval power would have an even greater influence on the age to come.

◈

Medieval Science and the Scientific Revolution

The scientific revolution of the late sixteenth and seventeenth centuries has no parallel among modern intellectual movements. Its impact was comparable to that made by the thinkers of ancient Greece because, like them, it changed not only ideas but also the process by which ideas are formulated. The Renaissance and the Reformation, for all their importance, were rooted in traditional patterns of thought. They could be understood without reordering the concepts that had permeated Western thinking for more than two thousand years. The development of modern science, though in some ways an outgrowth of these earlier movements, asked questions that were different from those that had been asked before and by so doing created a whole new way of looking at the universe. Modern science and the scientific method with which it is associated may be the one body of European ideas that has had a transforming effect on virtually every non-Western culture.

To appreciate the radicalism of the new views, examining what they replaced is useful. In 1500 the basic assumptions of science had changed little since the days of Pliny. The universe was thought to be organized according to rational principles. It was therefore open to human observation and deduction, but the principles of scientific inquiry were limited to those activities alone. As in other fields of thought, the logic of Aristotle, rooted firmly in language and in the meaning of words, was accepted as the most powerful tool of analysis. Scientific description therefore tended to be qualitative rather than quantitative. Accurate observation provided clues to the nature or essential quality of the object being observed. Reason could then determine the relationship of that object to other objects in the natural world.

This was important because ancient science believed that all parts of the universe were interrelated and that nothing could be studied in isolation. Today this idea is called holistic, or perhaps organic. It was stated expressly in Aristotle and, metaphorically, in the popular image of the individual human being as a microcosm of the universe as a whole. It formed the basis not only of academic science but also of the applied sciences of the day: medicine, natural magic, astrology, and alchemy. The last three were partially inspired by the Hermetic tradition, a body of occult literature that was supposedly derived from ancient Egypt. It was regarded with suspicion by the church because its practitioners were thought in various ways to interfere with Providence, but its theoretical assumptions did not conflict with those of the Aristotelians. Many, if not most, of the early scientists were as interested in astrology or alchemy as they were in physics and made no real distinction between the occult and what would today be regarded as more legitimate disciplines.

Whatever their interests, the learned agreed that the world was composed of the four elements—earth, air, fire, and water—and that the elements corresponded to the four humors that governed the body as well as the signs of the zodiac. Magic, "the chief power of all the sciences," sought to understand these and other relationships between natural objects and to manipulate them to achieve useful results. The causes of

natural phenomena were of academic but little practical interest and were generally explained teleologically. That is, they were understood in terms of the result they were intended to produce. Virtually everyone believed that the world had been created for a purpose and that the behavior of natural objects would necessarily be directed to that end. This preconception, together with the tendency to describe objects in qualitative terms, ensured that causation, too, would usually be explained in terms of the nature or qualities of the objects involved. It was a view that comported well with a providential understanding of the world.

Ideas of this kind are now found largely in the pages of supermarket tabloids, but they were once universally accepted by learned people. They provided a rational, comprehensive, and comforting vision of what might otherwise have been a terrifying universe. They have little in common with the principles of modern science, which substitutes measurement for qualitative description and attempts to express physical relationships in quantitative, mathematical terms. Because its vision of the world is mechanical instead of organic and providential, modern science concentrates heavily on the causes of physical and biological reactions and tries to reject teleological and qualitative explanations. It is more likely to ask "why?" than "what?" and has few compunctions about isolating a given problem to study it. Correspondences based upon qualitative or symbolic relationships are ignored.

The Origins of Modern Scientific Thought: Physics from Copernicus to Newton

Methodologically, modern science seeks to create a hypothesis by reasoning logically from accurate observations. If possible, the hypothesis is then tested by experiment and a mathematical model is constructed that will be both explanatory and predictive. The scientist can then formulate general laws of physical behavior without becoming entangled in the emotional overtones of language. The scientific model of the universe tends to be mechanistic rather than organic, mythological, or poetic. It is not necessarily godless, but its predictability does away with the need for divine intervention on a regular basis.

An intellectual shift of this magnitude did not occur quickly. Its roots are found in several traditions that coexisted uneasily in late medieval and Renaissance thought: the Aristotelian, the experimentalist, and the humanistic. During the sixteenth century a process of fusion began as thinkers adopted elements of each in their attempts to solve an ever-growing list of problems. The problems arose mainly from the perception that old, accepted answers, however logical and comforting they may have been, did not square with observed reality. The answers, and the accumulation of methods by which they were achieved, laid the groundwork of modern science.

The Aristotelian tradition contributed a rigorous concern for accurate observation and a logical method for the construction of hypotheses. In the wake of Ockhamist criticism, many Aristotelians, especially in the Italian universities, had turned their attention to the physical sciences, often with impressive results. Their tradition remained vital in some places until the eighteenth century. Experimentalism, once the province of medieval Franciscans and Joachimites, was revived and popularized by Sir Francis Bacon (1561–1626), the lord chancellor of England. Like his predecessors, he accomplished little because his hypotheses were faulty, but the elegance of his prose inspired a host of followers. His contemporary Galileo Galilei (1564–1642) used experiment to greater effect, though many of his best demonstrations were designed but never performed. The humanist tradition contributed classical texts that reintroduced half-forgotten ideas, including the physics of Archimedes and the heliocentric theories of Eratosthenes and Aristarchus of Samos. It also encouraged quantification by reviving the numerological theories of Pythagoras.

The thinkers of the sixteenth and seventeenth centuries were interested in nearly everything, but they achieved their greatest breakthroughs in astronomy and physics. The Copernican theory, though by no means universally accepted, became their starting point. Copernicus had brought the traditional cosmology into question, but his system with its epicycles and circular orbits remained mathematically complex and virtually incomprehensible as a description of physical reality (see illustration 16.1).

A more plausible model of the cosmos was devised by Johannes Kepler (1571–1630), court astrologer to the emperor Rudolph II. Kepler's views were a fusion of organic and mechanistic ideas. He believed that the Earth had a soul, but as a follower of Pythagoras he thought that the universe was organized on geometrical principles. The Copernican epicycles offended his notions of mathematical harmony. He wanted to believe in circular orbits, but when he posited eccentric circles that did not center on the Sun, he was left with a minute discrepancy in his formulae. It was a terrible dilemma: The circle may have been the perfect geometric figure,

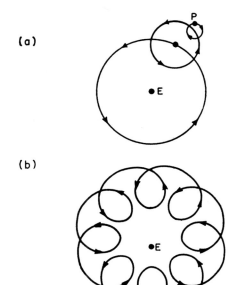

(a)

(b)

Illustration 16.1

The System of Epicycles as Used in Ptolemaic Cosmology. Epicycles were needed to predict the position of the planets, especially in the case of eccentrics and retrograde motions. These diagrams illustrate that the results were almost unimaginable. Drawing (a) shows an epicycle (P) on an epicycle, on a circular planetary orbit around the Earth (E). Drawing (b) shows the path a planet would have to take through space if this system of compound circles were taken literally. Copernicus and many of his contemporaries were dissatisfied with the Ptolemaic theory.

but he could not accept a universe founded on imperfect mathematics. In the end, he decided that planetary orbits had to be elliptical. This solution, which proved to be correct, was not generally accepted until long after his death, but Kepler did not mind. Like the number-mystic he was, he went on searching for other, more elusive cosmic harmonies that could be described in musical as well as mathematical terms.

Meanwhile, Galileo rejected the theory of elliptical orbits but provided important evidence that the planets rotated around the Sun. A professor at the University of Padua, Galileo was perhaps the first thinker to use something like the modern scientific method. He quarreled with the Aristotelians over their indifference to mathematical proofs and denounced their teleological obsession with final causes, but like them he was a careful observer. Unlike them, he tried to verify his hypotheses through experiment. From the Platonists and Pythagoreans, he adopted the view that the universe followed mathematical laws and expressed his theories

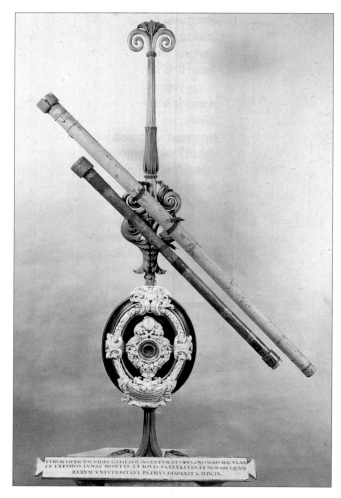

Illustration 16.2

Galileo's Telescopes (c. 1610) With instruments like these Galileo discovered the moons of Jupiter and launched a new era in observational astronomy. He also gained support for his work by donating them to wealthy patrons.

in mathematical formulae that were intended to be predictive. His vision, however, was mechanistic, not mystical or organic.

Galileo's exploration of the planets was inspired by the invention of the telescope. The basic principles of optics had been discovered by the Aristotelians, and eyeglasses were introduced early in the sixteenth century. By 1608 Dutch and Flemish lens grinders were combining two lenses at fixed distances from one another to create the first telescopes. Using a perfected version of the telescope that he had built himself, Galileo turned it upon the heavens (see illustration 16.2). The results created a sensation. His discovery of the moons of Jupiter and the phases of Venus seemed to support the Copernican theory, while his study of

sunspots raised the unsettling possibility that the Sun rotated on its axis like the planets.

Perhaps because he was not interested in astrology, Galileo ignored the problems of planetary motion that obsessed Kepler. Instead he concentrated on the mechanics of motion. Kepler had established the position of the planets with his *Rudolphine Tables* of 1627 but had been unable to explain either the causes of their motion or what kept them in their orbits. The issue had perplexed the ancients because they believed that rest was the normal state of any object. The Aristotelians had argued that an object remains at rest unless a force is applied against it and that the velocity of that object is proportionate to the force exerted in moving it. As a result, finding an explanation for why a projectile continued to move after the impetus behind it had ceased was difficult. Galileo turned the problem on its head by proving that a body in motion will move forever unless it is slowed or deflected by an external force and that the application of uniform force results in acceleration instead of motion at a constant rate. Movement is therefore as natural a state as rest. Once it had been set in motion by its Creator, the universe could in theory go on forever without further intervention.

It was a profoundly disturbing vision. To Galileo, God was the Great Craftsman who created the world as a self-sustaining and predictable machine. To those who saw the universe as an organic entity upon which God still imposed His will, such a view was not only frightening but also blasphemous. It brought Galileo before the Papal Inquisition. He was tried because he defended the Copernican system and because his ideas undermined a worldview that had prevailed for nearly two thousand years. Yet the importance of this celebrated trial should not be exaggerated. Galileo's condemnation forced him to retire to his country villa; it did not prevent him or any other Italian from proceeding with research along the lines he had suggested. Galileo was arrogant and bad-tempered with patrons and opponents alike. He was also a brilliant writer and publicist (see document 16.1). Had his ability to attract enemies not equaled his genius, the episode might never have occurred.

The mechanistic view of the universe was destined to triumph over its predecessor, and the church would not again mount a frontal attack against it. René Descartes (1596–1650), the most influential philosopher of his day, developed a mechanistic vision that attempted to integrate philosophy, mathematics, and the sciences into a coherent, unified theory. He failed, but his efforts inspired others such as Pierre Gassendi (1592–1655), who attempted to revive the atomic the-

◈ DOCUMENT 16.1 ◈

Galileo: Scientific Proof

In this excerpt from The Assayer, *Galileo attacks an opponent for arguing in the traditional manner by compiling lists of authorities who support his position. It shows not only the gulf that separated scientific thinking from that of the traditionalists, but also provides some indication of how Galileo made enemies with his pen.*

Sarsi goes on to say that since this experiment of Aristotle's has failed to convince us, many other great men have also written things of the same sort. But it is news to me that any man would actually put the testimony of writers ahead of what experience shows him. To adduce more witnesses serves no purposes, Sarsi, for we have never denied that such things have been written and believed. We did say they are false, but so far as authority is concerned yours alone is as effective as an army's in rendering the events true or false. You take your stand on the authority of many poets against our experiments. I reply that if those poets could be present at our experiments they would change their views, and without disgrace they could say they had been writing hyperbolically—or even admit they had been wrong. . . .

I cannot but be astonished that Sarsi would persist in trying to prove by means of witnesses something that I may see for myself at any time by means of experiment.

Galilei, Galileo. "The Assayer," trans. Stillman Drake. In Stillman Drake, *Discoveries and Opinions of Galileo*, pp. 270–271. New York: Doubleday, 1957.

ories of the Epicureans. To do so, he was forced to posit the existence of a vacuum. The possibility of nothingness had been denied by virtually everyone from Aristotle to Descartes, but the results of barometric experiments by Toricelli and by Blaise Pascal (1623–62) could be explained in no other way. In 1650 Otto von Guericke ended the debate by constructing an air pump with which a vacuum could be created. These efforts in turn inspired Robert Boyle (1627–91) to formulate his laws about the behavior of gases.

Interest in scientific inquiry was assuming the proportions of a fad. All over Europe, men of leisure and education were examining the physical world and developing theories about it. Many, including Boyle and Pascal, were also gifted writers whose work inspired others to emulate them. Science was becoming a movement, and it was only a matter of time until that movement was institutionalized. The English Royal Society and the French Academie des Sciences were founded in the 1660s, the latter under the patronage of Louis XIV's minister, Jean-Baptiste Colbert (1619–83). Colbert, like England's King Charles II, was quick to perceive the possible connection between the new science and improved technologies for war, agriculture, and manufacturing. Not all of the work performed was useful, and much of it remained tied to the earlier vision of an organic, providential universe, but mechanistic and mathematical views gained ground steadily throughout the century.

In physics, the movement culminated in the work of Isaac Newton (1642–1727). A professor at Cambridge and a member of the Royal Society, Newton was in some respects an odd character who spent at least as much time on alchemy and other occult speculations as he did on mathematics and physics. In spite of this, he formulated the laws of planetary motion and of gravity, thereby completing the work begun by Kepler and Galileo and establishing a cosmology that dominated Western thought until the publication of Einstein's theories in 1904.

In his *Principia,* or *Mathematical Principles of Natural Philosophy,* presented to the Royal Society in 1686, Newton formulated three laws of motion: (1) Every object remains either at rest or in motion along a straight line until it is deflected or resisted by another force (the law of inertia); (2) The rate of change in the motion of an object is proportionate to the force acting upon it; and (3) To every action there is an equal and opposite reaction. These formulations accounted not only for the behavior of moving objects on Earth, but also for the continuing movement of the planets. He then perfected Kepler's theories by demonstrating how the planets move through a vacuum in elliptical orbits under the influence of a force centered upon the Sun. That force was gravity, which he defined as the attractive force between two objects (see document 16.2). It is directly proportionate to the product of their masses and inversely proportionate to the square of the distances between them. To many, these theories explained the mysteries of a universe that acted like clockwork—smooth, mechanical, and eternal. Newton, who was a deeply religious man, would not have been pleased at the use to which his ideas would soon be put by the philosophers of the eighteenth-century Enlightenment.

◆ DOCUMENT 16.2 ◆

Newton: Gravity

In The Mathematical Principles of Natural Philosophy, *Sir Isaac Newton describes his revolutionary concept of gravity and, in the process, sets forth some of his thoughts on scientific method.*

Hitherto, we have explained the phenomena of the heavens and of our sea by the power of gravity, but have not yet assigned the cause of this power. This is certain, that it must proceed from a cause that penetrates to the very centers of the sun and planets, without suffering the least diminution of its force; that operates not according to the quantity of the surfaces of the particles upon which it acts (as mechanical causes used to do) but according to the quantity of solid matter which they contain, and propagates its virtue on all sides to immense distances, decreasing always in the duplicate portion of the distances. . . .

Hitherto I have not been able to discover the cause of those properties of gravity from the phenomena, and I frame no hypothesis; for whatever is not deduced from phenomena is to be called an hypothesis; and hypothesis, whether metaphysical or physical, whether of occult qualities or mechanical, have no place in experimental philosophy. In this philosophy particular propositions are inferred from the phenomena, and afterward rendered general by induction. Thus it was the impenetrability, the mobility, and the impulsive force of bodies, and the laws of motion and gravitation were discovered. And to us it is enough that gravity does really exist, and acts according to the laws that we have explained, and abundantly serves to account for all the motions of the celestial bodies, and of our sea.

Newton, Isaac. *The Mathematical Principles of Natural Philosophy,* book 3, vol. 2, p. 310, trans. Andrew Motte. London, 1803, II.

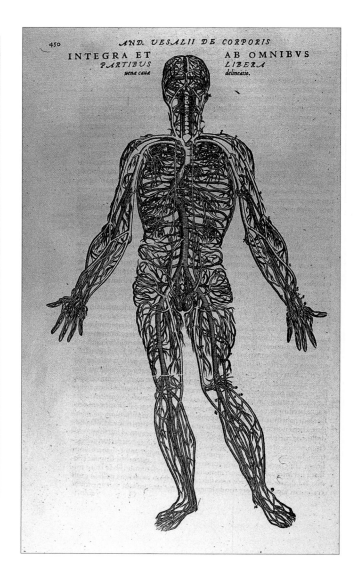

Illustration 16.3

〰️ **A Diagram of the Veins.** This diagram is from Andreas Vesalius (1514–64), *De humani corporis fabrica.* The venous system was especially important to physicians because drawing blood was the primary treatment for many ailments. As impressive as these drawings are, they contain anatomical errors. Vesalius did not understand the circulation of the blood and based some of his ideas on the dissection of animals (see the arrangement of veins at the base of the neck). However, his work, with its magnificent illustrations, is still a remarkable monument to the anatomical revolution.

Medicine: From Galen to Harvey

Mechanistic views would also triumph in medicine, but the process by which they did so was more convoluted than it had been in physics. Physicians moved from mechanism to magic and back again in the course of the sixteenth century. The works of the ancient Greek anatomist Galen had long been known through Arabic commentaries and translations. Galen's views were mechanistic in the sense that he was careful to relate the form of organs to their function and had little use for magic or for alchemical cures. The recovery and

❖ DOCUMENT 16.3 ❖

William Harvey: Conception

William Harvey (1578–1657) is best known as the physician who first described the circulation of the blood, but as this selection indicates, he was no more consistent in his application of scientific method than most of his contemporaries. Old modes of thinking had survived along with the new. In this description of conception he reverts to inadequate observation, metaphorical language, philosophical idealism, and sheer male vanity.

[As] the substance of the uterus, when ready to conceive, is very like the structure of the brain, why should we not suppose that the function of both is similar, and that there is excited by coitus within the uterus something identical with, or at least analogous to, an "imagination" or a "desire" in the brain, whence comes the generation or procreation of the ovum? For the functions of both are termed "conceptions" and both, although the primary sources of every action throughout the body, are immaterial, the one of natural or organic, the other of animal actions; the one (viz., the uterus) the first cause and beginning of every action which conduces to the generation of the animal, the other (viz., the brain) of every action done for its preservation. And just as a "desire" arises from a conception of the brain, and this conception springs from some external object of desire, so also from the male, as being the more perfect animal, and as it were, the most natural object of desire, does the natural (organic) conception arise in the uterus, even as the animal conception does in the brain.

From this desire, or conception, it results that the female produces an offspring like its father. For just saw we, from the conception of the "form" or "idea" in the brain, fashion in our works a form resembling it, so, in like manner, the "idea" or "form" of the father existing in the uterus generates an offspring like himself with the help of the formative faculty, impressing, however, on its work its own immaterial form.

Harvey, William. "On Conception." In *The Works of William Harvey,* trans. R. Willis. London: 1847.

---

translation of original Galenic texts by the humanists popularized his teachings, and by the early sixteenth century his influence dominated academic medicine.

In response, a Swiss physician and alchemist who called himself Paracelsus (1493–1541) launched a frontal attack on the entire medical establishment. Declaring that "wise women" and barbers cured more patients than all of the Galenists put together, he proposed a medical philosophy based upon natural magic and alchemy. All natural phenomena were chemical interactions between the four elements and what he called the three principles: sulphur, mercury, and salt—the combustible, gaseous, and solid components of matter. Because the human body was a microcosm of the universe and because diseases were produced by chemical forces acting upon particular organs of the body, sickness could be cured by chemical antidotes.

This chemical philosophy was widely accepted. Its hermetic and neoplatonic overtones recommended it to many scholars, while those who practiced it may have killed fewer patients than their Galenist opponents. Paracelsus believed in administering drugs in small, carefully measured doses. He rejected bleeding, purges, and the treatment of wounds with poultices whose vile ingredients almost guaranteed the onset of infection. As a result, the bodies of his patients had a fighting chance to heal themselves and he was credited with miraculous cures.

The war between the Galenists and the Paracelsians raged throughout the mid-sixteenth century. In the end, the Galenists won. Their theories, though virtually useless for the treatment of disease, produced new insights while those of Paracelsus did not. Andreas Vesalius (1514–64) was shocked to discover that Galen's dissections had been carried out primarily on animals. Using Galenic principles, he retraced the master's steps using human cadavers and in 1543 published his *De humani corporis fabrica* (On the Structure of the Human Body). Though not without error, it was a vast improvement over earlier anatomy texts and a work of art in its own right that inspired others to correct and improve his work (see illustration 16.3). The long debate over the circulation of the blood, culminating in William Harvey's explanation of 1628 (see document 16.3), was also a Galenist enterprise that owed little or nothing to the chemical tradition.

By the time microscopes were invented in Holland at the beginning of the seventeenth century, the anatomists had seized the initiative. The new device strengthened their position by allowing for the examination of small structures such as capillaries. Blood corpuscles were described for the first time and bacteria were identified, though a full-fledged germ theory would not be verified until the nineteenth century. These discoveries made sustaining the ancient metaphor of the human body as a microcosm of the universe even more difficult. The body was beginning to look more like a machine within a machine.

The Expansion of the Northern Powers: France, England, and the Netherlands

In the years when Galileo and others were transforming European thought, seafarers from France, England, and the Netherlands continued the work of mapping the globe and exploiting its economic resources. The centralized, closely controlled empires created by the Iberian powers had been resented from the first by northern Europeans who wished to engage in the American trade. French pirates and privateers were active in the Caribbean after the 1530s and sacked Havana in 1556. A colony of French Protestants was massacred by the Spanish near the present site of St. Augustine, Florida, in 1565. However, neither of these failures inhibited French, English, and Dutch captains from trying to enter the Caribbean market. The Englishman John Hawkins (1532–95) tried to break the Spanish-Portuguese monopoly by introducing cargoes of slaves in 1562 and again in 1567 but was caught by the incoming *flota* in 1567 and barely escaped with his life. One of his surviving captains, Francis Drake (c. 1543–96), raided Panama in 1572–73 and attacked Spanish shipping in the Pacific when he circumnavigated the globe in 1577–79.

To many in England these efforts, however inspiring, were no substitute for the establishment of permanent English colonies. Commercial interests and the growing political and religious rivalry with Spain demanded nothing less. The first English settlement in North America was planted on Roanoke Island, North Carolina, in 1585 but disappeared before it could be reinforced. Subsequent efforts at Jamestown (1603) and Plymouth (1620) were more successful. The Spanish claimed sovereignty over North America but lacked the resources to settle it or to protect it against interlopers. The native American population was, by comparison with that of Mexico or Peru, small, scattered, and politically disunited. The obstacles to settlement were there-

fore easy to overcome, and by 1650 the English were established at various locations along the entire Atlantic seaboard from Newfoundland to the Carolinas.

From the standpoint of global politics and immediate gain, these North American colonies were something of a disappointment. They produced no precious metals and offered England few strategic advantages. With the notable exception of tobacco from Virginia and Maryland, they had little of value to export and quickly became self-sufficient in everything but luxury items. In the meantime, the French had established themselves in the St. Lawrence valley and were developing an important trade in furs from the North American interior. English competition in the form of the Hudson's Bay Company did not emerge until 1670.

Expansion in the Caribbean remained a primary goal. An English colony was established on the uninhabited island of Barbados in 1624, and sugar was introduced in 1640. By 1660 its sugar exports made Barbados the most valuable of English colonies while its position to windward of the Spanish Main made it virtually invulnerable to Spanish attacks. Sugar colonies of equal wealth were established by the French on the nearby islands of Guadeloupe and Martinique. By this time, Spanish power was in decline. In 1656 an English fleet seized Jamaica. Eight years later the French West India Company took possession of some settlements that had been established years before by French buccaneers in the western part of Hispaniola and laid the foundations of St. Domingue, the rich slave colony that would one day become Haiti.

The French and English, like the Spanish and Portuguese, wanted their colonial systems to be self-contained and closed to outsiders, but in practice, this was as difficult to achieve as it had been for their rivals. Both France and England governed their possessions on the proprietary model, and neither developed anything like the elaborate colonial bureaucracy of Spain. Royal authority tended to be correspondingly weak. Distance, the limitations of sailing ship technology, and the perishability of certain cargos, notably slaves, encouraged smuggling and made it difficult to suppress. Planters and merchants had nothing to gain from dealing exclusively with their own countrymen when others might offer better prices or more rapid delivery. Cargos could always be landed secretly in remote coves, but much illegal activity was conducted in the open, for governors were under enormous pressure to look the other way.

Almost from the beginning, the chief beneficiaries of this illegal trade were the Dutch, whose maritime activities increased during their revolt against Spain. The Dutch had some ninety-eight thousand ships registered by 1598, but ships and skill were not enough. They needed bases from which to conduct their operations. Between 1621 and 1640 the newly formed Dutch West India Company seized Curaçao, St. Eustatius, St. Maarten, and Saba in the Caribbean and established a colony called New Amsterdam on the present site of New York. From 1624 to 1654 the Dutch controlled much of the Brazilian coast, and in 1637 they captured the African fortress and slave-trading station of Elmina from the Portuguese. Brazil and New Amsterdam were expensive ventures. The Dutch, like the Portuguese, lacked the manpower to impose their rule on large geographic areas, and when the English seized New Amsterdam in 1664 the West India Company settled down to a more modest, and in the end more profitable, career as a trading company based on Curaçao and St. Eustatius.

Only in the East did the Dutch manage to establish something like regional hegemony. Dutch traders first appeared in East Indian waters in 1595. Bypassing India, they sailed directly to the Spice Islands (Indonesia), rounding the Cape of Good Hope and running due east in the so-called roaring forties before turning north to Java or Sumatra. The fast but dangerous trip brought them directly to the sources of the Portuguese and Indian spice trade. To improve efficiency and minimize competition, the Dutch traders organized in 1602 into the East India Company.

Under the governor-generalship of Jan Pieterszoon Coen (1587–1629), the company's forces destroyed the Javan town of Djakarta and rebuilt it as Batavia, center of Dutch enterprise in the East. Local rulers were forced to restrict their trading activities to rice and other local necessities while European competition was violently discouraged. English traders especially had been active in Asian waters since 1591. They formed their own East India Company on Christmas Day in 1600 but lacked the ships and capital to match the Dutch. Coen expelled most of them from the region by 1620. His successors attacked the Portuguese colonies, seizing Malacca in 1641 and the Indian bases shortly thereafter, but Goa survived a Dutch blockade and remained in Portuguese hands until 1961. The Japanese trade fell into Dutch hands when the Portuguese were expelled in 1637, and for two centuries a Dutch trading station in Nagasaki harbor provided that country's only contact with the West.

By 1650 the Dutch had become the dominant force in Europe's Asian trade. More than one hundred Dutch ships sailed regularly to the East, exchanging German arms, armor, linens, and glass for spices and finished silks. Even the surviving Portuguese colonies were forced to deal largely through Dutch intermediaries. The major exception was Macao, which continued to export Chinese silks to Spain via Manila. This monopoly was successfully challenged in the eighteenth century by the revived British East India Company and to a lesser degree by the French, but the Dutch remained in control of Indonesia until the outbreak of World War II.

The Golden Age in the Netherlands

Long-distance trade made the Netherlands an island of wealth and culture amidst the turmoil of the early seventeenth century (see illustration 16.4). A century before, the economy of the region had been dominated by Antwerp. Its merchants traded in wool from Spain and England, finished cloth from the towns of Brabant and Flanders, wine from the Iberian Peninsula, and a variety of products exported from Germany to England and Scandinavia. The city's prosperity, however, did not survive the Revolt of the Netherlands. Antwerp is located at the head of navigation on the Scheldt, a broad estuary whose western approaches are controlled by the Zeeland towns of Vlissingen (Flushing) and Middelburg. When the Zeelanders joined the Dutch revolt, they cut off Antwerp from the sea and destroyed its prosperity.

Amsterdam took its place. Set in the marshes where the Amstel River meets the IJ, an inlet of the Zuider Zee, the city was virtually impregnable to attack by sea or land. Already the center of the Baltic trade, it grew enormously after 1585 when southern refugees poured in, bringing their capital with them. When Maurits of Nassau took the lands east of the Ijssel from Spain between 1591 and 1597, contact with Germany improved and Amsterdam replaced Antwerp as the conduit through which goods flowed from the German interior to the Atlantic and North Sea. The repeated failure of Spanish and Sicilian harvests in the same years made Amsterdam a dominant force in the Mediterranean trade as well. Dutch merchants had established themselves in the Baltic ports of Riga and Gdansk (Danzig) at an early date. The Amsterdam exchange determined the price of wheat, and vast quantities were shipped southward in Dutch ships, together with timber, Swedish iron, and other northern products.

Shipbuilding, always a major industry in the ports of Holland and Zeeland, expanded with the growth of the carrying trade. Economies of scale, better access to Baltic naval stores, and the presence of a skilled maritime population enabled the Dutch to charge

Illustration 16.4

The Amsterdam Bourse, or Stock Exchange. This painting by Job Berckheyde shows the Bourse as it was in the seventeenth century. Though not the first such exchange in Europe, it was by far the largest and most important of the early modern period. Small shareholders and great capitalists traded shares in the East India Company and many smaller enterprises.

lower shipping rates than their competitors. With the founding of the East and West India companies, this advantage became global. The axis of the spice trade shifted from Lisbon to Amsterdam while Dutch skippers took advantage of the delays occasioned by the *flota* system and by a general shortage of Iberian shipping to intrude upon the commerce of the Americas. The profits from these sources generated investment capital, and Amsterdam soon became Europe's banking center as well as its commercial hub.

In these years, the modern city with its canals and high, narrow townhouses took shape. For all its wealth and beauty, however, Amsterdam was never more than the largest of several towns that supported and at times competed with each other in a variety of markets. The

Dutch republic was overwhelmingly urban. A network of canals linked its cities and provided cheap, efficient transportation. Agriculturally, though a few large estates remained, most of the land was divided into relatively small plots and cultivated intensively to grow produce and dairy products for the nearby towns. Most peasants were independent farmers and relatively prosperous. Pockets of urban misery existed, but no real industrial proletariat was evident outside the cloth towns of Haarlem and Leiden. Dutch society was therefore resolutely bourgeois. Hard work, thrift, and cleanliness were valued; ostentation was suspect.

A series of extraordinary painters provide a vivid picture of Dutch life in the seventeenth century. Jan Vermeer (1632–75) portrayed bright, spotless interiors and virtuous housewives at work in an idealized vision of domesticity that was central to Dutch notions of the good life. Rembrandt van Rijn (1606–69), Frans Hals (c. 1581–1666), and a host of others left brilliant portraits of city magistrates, corporate directors, and everyday drunks as well as grand illustrations of historical events. The brooding skies and placid landscapes of the Netherlands were painted by such masters as Ruisdael and van Goyen, while dozens of still lifes dwell lovingly on food, flowers, and other everyday objects.

The political and the social structure of the republic rested on the values of the late medieval city, preserved tenaciously through the long struggle against Spanish regalism. Each town elected a council, which in turn elected representatives to the Provincial Estates. The States General was elected by the provinces. The stadtholder, when there was one, was not a king, but a kind of "first citizen" with special responsibilities for the conduct of war on land. Five admiralties, each of which was nominally independent and each of which supplemented its own warships with vessels leased from the chartered companies, conducted war at sea.

Local privilege was built into the system at every level, and conflict among the various components of the body politic was normally intense. Fortunately, the leadership of the councils, states, directorships, and committees formed a kind of interlocking directorship. A great merchant, banker, or rentier might hold several elected offices in the course of a lifetime, as well as directorships in one or more of the chartered companies. The Dutch republic was an oligarchy, not a democracy, but the existence of a well-defined group of prominent citizens facilitated communication, dampened local rivalries, and helped to ensure a measure of continuity in what might otherwise have been a fragmented and overly decentralized system.

National policies were remarkably consistent. Trade, even with the enemy, was encouraged and the states supported freedom of the seas long before Hugo Grotius (1583–1645), attorney general of Holland, publicized the modern concept of international law. Though aggressive in its pursuit of new markets and the protection of old ones, Dutch foreign policy was otherwise defensive.

Tension between the governing elite and the stadtholders of the House of Orange dominated internal politics. At times the struggle took the form of religious antagonism between extreme Calvinists, who tended to be Orangists supported by the artisan class, and the more relaxed Arminians, who rejected predestination and were supported by the great merchants. Class feeling played a major part in these struggles, but

by comparison with other countries, both sides remained committed to religious toleration. Jewish settlement was actively encouraged and Catholics were generally protected from harassment. Holland became a refuge for the persecuted, many of whom, such as Descartes and the philosopher Baruch Spinoza (1632–77), a Sephardic Jew, added luster to its intellectual life. The Dutch republic was an oasis of tolerance as well as prosperity.

The Reorganization of War and Government: France under Louis XIV

Most seventeenth-century states were not as fortunate as the Dutch. Between 1560 and 1648 France, Spain, England, and the German principalities all suffered in varying degrees from military stalemate and political disintegration. Public order, perhaps even dynastic survival, depended upon the reorganization of war and government. The restructuring of virtually every European state after 1660 has been called the triumph of absolutism (see document 16.4), but the term is in some ways misleading. No government before the industrial revolution could exert absolute control over the lives of its subjects. To do so even approximately requires modern transport and communications, but if by absolutism one means the theoretical subordination of all other elements of a country's power structure to the crown, the word is at least partially descriptive. The Spain of Philip II met this definition in the sixteenth century; after 1660 the model for all other states was the France of Louis XIV.

Louis XIV (ruled 1643–1715) came to the throne as a child of four. To the end of his life he harbored childhood memories of the Frondes and was determined to avoid further challenges from the French aristocracy at all costs. He knew that their influence derived from the networks of patronage that had long dominated rural life and used the fact that such networks are ultimately dependent upon favors to destroy them as independent bases of power. As king of a country in which perpetual taxation had long been established, Louis had more favors to hand out than anyone else. He developed the tactic of forcing aristocrats to remain at court as a condition of receiving the titles, grants, monopolies, offices, and commissions upon which their influence was based. By doing so he bound them to himself while cutting them off from their influence in the countryside.

This was the real purpose behind the construction of Versailles, a palace large enough to house the entire court while separating it from the mobs of Paris, twelve

◆ DOCUMENT 16.4 ◆

Absolutism in Theory

Jacques-Bénigne Bossuet, bishop of Meaux (1627–1704) was court preacher to Louis XIV and tutor to his son. In this passage, which reveals something of his power as a preacher, he describes the divine basis of royal absolutism in unmistakable terms.

The royal power is absolute. . . . The prince need render account of his acts to no one. . . . Without this absolute authority the king could neither do good nor repress evil. It is necessary that his power be such that no one can escape him, and finally, the only protection of individuals against the public authority should be their innocence. This confirms the teaching of St. Paul: "Wilt thou not be afraid of the power? Do that which is good" [Rom. 13:3].

God is infinite, God is all. The prince, as prince, is not regarded as a private person: he is a public personage, all the state is in him. As all perfection and all strength are united in God, so all power of individuals is united in the person of the prince. What grandeur that a single man should embody so much!

Behold an immense people united in a single person; behold this holy power, paternal and absolute; behold the secret cause which governs the whole body of the state, contained in a single head: you see the image of God in the king, and you have the idea of royal majesty. God is holiness itself, goodness itself, and power itself. In these things lies the majesty of God. In the image of these things lies the majesty of the prince.

Bossuet, Jacques-Bénigne. "Politics Drawn from the Very Words of Holy Scripture." In J. H. Robinson, ed. *Readings in European History*, vol. 2. Boston: Ginn, 1906.

miles away (see illustration 16.5). To occupy his new courtiers, Louis developed an elaborate ritual centered around his own person. Every royal action was accompanied by great ceremony, and proud aristocrats contended for the honor of emptying the king's chamberpot or handing him his shirt (see illustration 16.6). The world of Versailles was cramped, artificial, and riddled with intrigue, but it was a world controlled in every particular by a king who knew what was happening under his own roof (see document 16.5). To stay

was to sacrifice one's independence; to leave was to lose all hope of honor or profit. By 1670 the French nobility had been domesticated.

The centralization implied by Versailles was extended to the royal administration, though in this case Louis followed precedents established by Henry IV and Richelieu. Richelieu in particular had worked to replace the old system of governing through councils with ministries, in which one man was responsible to the crown for each of the major functions of government. He had also brought royal authority to the provinces by introducing intendants, commissioners who supervised the collection of taxes and served as a constant check on local authorities. Louis expanded and perfected this system. Intendancies transcended provincial borders, further weakening the ties of local privilege. The ministers of war, finance, foreign affairs, and even of roads and bridges reported directly to the king who, unlike his father, served as his own prime minister. Louis may have been the Sun King, surrounded by ritual and devoted to the pleasures of the bed, the table, and the hunt, but he was a hard worker. At least six hours a day, seven days a week, were devoted to public business. Significantly, he usually drew his ministers from the *nobles de la robe*, the great legal dynasties of the French towns, not from the old nobility.

Because war was the primary function of the early modern state and accounted for the vast majority of its expenditures, every effort was made to bring the military under control. Louis instituted a series of reforms under the guidance of the war ministers Michel Le Tellier (1603–85) and his son, the Marquis de Louvois (1639–91). A tableau of ranks, comparable to that used by most modern armies, established a hierarchy of command that in theory superseded civilian titles. The cost of quartering troops was allocated to entire provinces instead of to specific towns, and, like military justice, financial arrangements were placed under the control of the intendants.

On the battlefield, the French army abandoned the old combination of pike and shot in favor of volleys of musket fire from ranks that were rarely more than three deep. Based on the innovations of Gustav Adolph, this tactic required regular drill and marching in step, practices that had first been introduced by Maurice of Nassau but generally ignored by other armies. To improve discipline and unit cohesion, barracks, uniforms, and standardized muskets were all adopted by 1691. Combined with the scientific principles of siege warfare perfected by Sebastian le Prestre de Vauban (1633–1707), the reforms of Le Tellier and Louvois created what

Illustration 16.5

 Versailles. This view of the west front of Louis XIV's palace shows only a portion of the whole, but it provides a sense of the grandeur that Louis and his architects, Louis Le Vau and Jules Hardouin-Mansart, were attempting to convey as they created a magnificent stage set for the politics of the Sun King.

might be called the first modern army. It was given ample opportunity to prove itself.

In the early years of his reign, Louis's foreign policy was aggressive and, in the best French tradition, anti-Habsburg. His invasion of the Spanish Netherlands in 1667–68 brought him into conflict with the Dutch republic, which he tried to destroy in a bitter war that lasted from 1672 to 1679. Faced with almost certain destruction, the Dutch overthrew their government and made William III of Orange (1650–1702) stadtholder. Holland saved itself by flooding the countryside, and William's diplomacy brought Spain, Sweden, Brandenburg, and the Holy Roman Empire into the war. France fought them all to a standstill, but the alliance was a precursor of things to come.

Emboldened by the favorable terms he had negotiated at the Peace of Nijmegen (1679), Louis then tried to annex all territories that had ever belonged to France, whether in the Netherlands, Italy, the Pyrenees, or the Rhineland. Hostility to the Holy Roman Empire made him the only Christian prince to oppose the liberation of Hungary from the Turks (1682–99), though it was at last achieved with the assistance of Eugene of Savoy (1663–1736), a prince who had been raised at his court and who became one of his most formidable enemies. At the same time, Louis's revocation of the Edict of Nantes and expulsion of the Huguenots in 1685 alienated Europe's Protestants. Many believed that he aimed at nothing less than French hegemony, and by 1689 nearly all of Europe had turned against him. For the rest of his life he followed a basically defensive policy, but it was too late. In the War of the League of Augsburg (1689–97), Louis fought a powerful Anglo-Dutch coalition while France suffered through one of the worst economic depressions in its history. In the War of the Spanish Succession (1701–14), his armies were consistently defeated by an allied army commanded by John Churchill, duke of Marlborough (1650–1722). Not even France could sustain such burdens indefinitely, and when the Sun King died in 1715, the country was in a severe, if temporary, decline.

French Absolutism: A Model for Reform

The power of Louis XIV was not unlimited. Within France, his intentions were subject to modification by local privilege and by the rulings of the *parlements*, superior courts that could determine the validity of royal edicts under law. Moreover, neither he nor his successors were able to solve basic problems of credit and finance. Until the revolution of 1789, the kings of France were forced to borrow against tax revenues, which were then farmed out to the creditors. Tax farming by private individuals was not only inefficient but also woefully corrupt and left no room for the sophisticated financial practices being devised by Louis's Dutch and English rivals.

In spite of these shortcomings and of the uneven success of Louis's foreign policy, the France of Louis XIV became a model for other princes. From Spain to the Urals, they copied his court etiquette, his system of military and administrative organization, and even the architectural style of Versailles, which became the pattern for dozens of palaces and country estates. The last

Illustration 16.6

✍ **Louis XIV.** This 1701 painting by Hyacinthe Rigaud is an example of art as political propaganda. This vision of the king's magnificence was painted on the eve of the War of the Spanish Succession. Even at sixty-three, Louis was proud of his legs and sensitive about his height, hence the elevator shoes.

Hapsburg king of Spain, Charles II "the Bewitched" died childless in 1700, and the final war of Louis's reign was waged to place a Bourbon on the Spanish throne. The new ruler, Philip V (reigned 1700–46), began a process of reform that by 1788 had created a near replica of French administration. Austrian archduke Charles (1685–1740), though he failed to gain the allegiance of the Spanish in the War of the Spanish Succession, received the Spanish Netherlands as a consolation prize at the Peace of Utrecht in 1713. This territory, the present-day Belgium, was incorporated into the Austrian Empire as Hungary had been in 1699. After his election as Charles VI in 1711, he began to reform the far-flung Austrian administration on French lines.

Most of the German princes followed suit, though it could be argued that Frederick Wilhelm I of Prussia (1688–1740) had already carried reform beyond anything achieved by Louis XIV. Set without geographic defenses in the midst of the North German plain, Brandenburg-Prussia had been devastated in the

◆ DOCUMENT 16.5 ◆

Louis XIV at Versailles

The memoirs of Louis de Rouvroy, Duc de Saint-Simon (1675–1755) provide a detailed, if often venomous, picture of life at the court of Louis XIV. Here Saint-Simon, an aristocrat, describes the king's method of controlling the French aristocracy.

The frequent fêtes, the private promenades at Versailles, the journeys, were means on which the King seized in order to distinguish or mortify the courtiers, and thus render them more assiduous in pleasing him. He felt that of real favors he had not enough to bestow; in order to keep up the spirit of devotion, he therefore unceasingly invented all sorts of ideal ones, little preferences and petty distinctions, which answered his purpose as well.

He was exceedingly jealous of the attention paid him. Not only did he notice the presence of the most distinguished courtiers, but those of inferior degree also. He looked to the right and the left, not only upon rising but upon going to bed, at his meals, in passing through his apartments, or his gardens of Versailles, where alone the courtiers were allowed to follow him; he saw and noticed everybody; not one escaped him, not even those who hoped to remain unnoticed. He marked well all the absentees from the court, found out the reason of their absence, and never lost an opportunity of acting towards them as the occasion might seem to justify. With some of the courtiers (the most distinguished), it was a demerit not to make the court their ordinary abode; with others, 'twas a fault to come but rarely; for those who never or scarcely ever came it was certain disgrace. When their names were in any way mentioned, "I do not know them," the King would reply haughtily. Those who presented themselves but seldom were thus characterized: "They are people I never see;" these decrees were irrevocable.

Saint-Simon [Louis de Rouvroy, Duc de Saint-Simon]. *The Memoirs of the Duke of Saint-Simon*, trans. Bayle St. John, vol. 2, p. 364, 8th ed. London: 1913.

Illustration 16.7

Peter the Great. The tsar is shown by a Dutch painter during his visit to the Netherlands in 1697.

Thirty Years' War and remained vulnerable to the shifts of central European politics. A veteran of the war of the Spanish Succession, Frederick Wilhelm resolved to turn his kingdom into a military power of the first rank and ended by making its administration subservient to the army. After 1723 his government was little more than a branch of the *kriegskommisariat* or war ministry, but his reforms laid the groundwork for Prussia's emergence as a major power.

Perhaps the most spectacular efforts at reform were undertaken by Peter I "the Great" of Russia (1672–1725). Like Louis XIV he had survived a turbulent regency in his youth and came to the throne determined to place his monarchy on a firmer basis (see illustration 16.7). Peter realized that to do so he would have to copy Western models, and he spent 1697–98 traveling incognito to France, England, and the Netherlands as part of what he called the Grand Embassy. When he returned, he immediately began to institute reforms that, though Western in inspiration, were carefully adapted to Russian conditions.

Using knowledge acquired firsthand in the ship-yards of Holland and England, Peter supervised the building of a navy that could control the Baltic. The *streltsy*, or palace guard that formed the core of the Russian army and had long been a fruitful source of plots against the tsars, was destroyed and replaced by an army organized on the French model. Peter, however, raised his troops through conscription for life, a method suggested by Louvois that could not be implemented in the less autocratic atmosphere of France. The new forces served him well. In the Great Northern War (1700–20), he broke the power of Sweden and established Russian control over Estonia, Karelia, and Livonia. To consolidate his gains and to provide Russia with an all-weather port, he built the modern city of St. Petersburg near the mouth of the Neva River and made it his capital.

Internally, Peter established a series of colleges or boards to supervise the work of thirteen new governmental departments and divided the country into fifty provinces, each with its own governor appointed by himself. He created a table of ranks for civilian officials and opened state service for the first time to men of middle-class origin. To compensate the hereditary nobility for its loss of state positions, Peter abandoned the distinction between *pomest'e* and hereditary lands, and he introduced primogeniture. In some cases he resorted to large-scale distributions of land and serfs. The condition of the latter predictably worsened, and peasant rebellions were put down with memorable savagery.

The Emergence of England as a World Power

The system created by Peter the Great was more autocratic than its Western models—and more permanent. It lasted without major modifications into the nineteenth century. The situation in England was very different. Though Charles II reclaimed his father's throne in 1660, the fundamental issue of sovereignty had not been resolved. Like his predecessors, Charles was reluctant to call Parliament into session, and the taxpaying gentry were as unwilling as ever to provide adequate support for the crown. Shrewd, affable, and personally popular, the new king avoided open confrontations with his subjects, but his freedom of action was limited by poverty. For a time he even accepted a pension from Louis XIV, who hoped for English support against the Dutch. For this reason, England did not for some time develop the administrative structures that were being adopted on the continent.

Only in the creation of a modern navy could the English keep pace. Before 1660 England, like other countries, had possessed a handful of fighting ships that were supplemented in time of war by contracting with private owners who provided both ships and crews for the duration. No permanent officer corps existed, and fleets were typically commanded by men who owed their positions to civilian rank or to military experience on land. Administration was minimal, often temporary, and usually corrupt. The success of 1588 and the remarkable performance of the Commonwealth navies showed that such fleets could do well if they were properly motivated. But the system as a whole was analagous to military contracting on land: It was at best inefficient and at worst uncontrollable.

Both Charles II and his brother James, duke of York (1633–1701) were deeply interested in naval affairs, and their unswerving support of secretary of the Admiralty Samuel Pepys (1633–1703) enabled him to introduce reforms that, in effect, created the English navy. Pepys, who is probably best known today for his famous diary, created a permanent corps of naval officers who attained their rank by the passage of formal examinations. To ensure their availability when needed, they were kept on half-pay when not at sea. Provisioning and repair facilities were improved, and the number of royal ships increased under the command of a reformed Admiralty. By the end of the century, even tactics had been changed to permit better control of battle fleets.

But a reformed fleet was in itself no guarantor of world-power status. Colbert had introduced similar measures in France, only to have his plans abandoned during the fiscal crisis of the 1690s. Great ships, like great armies, need a consistent supply of money. Ironically, England achieved this only by overthrowing the men who had made the naval reforms possible. When Charles II died in 1685, his brother ascended the throne as James II. A convert to Roman Catholicism, James instituted policies that alienated virtually every segment of the English elite, and in the fall of 1688 he was deposed in favor of his daughter Mary and her husband, William of Orange. As stadtholder of the Netherlands and king of England, William III brought the island nation into the Grand Alliance against Louis XIV. The Glorious Revolution changed the basis of English politics. By overthrowing one king and effectively appointing another, Parliament and those it represented had at last resolved the issue of sovereignty. Parliament and not the king would rule England. Under William and again under his sister-in-law Anne

◆ DOCUMENT 16.6 ◆

Dutch Trade in Decline

The problem of maintaining Dutch trade reached a crisis during the War of the Spanish Succession (1702–13), when the conflict closed many traditional markets. The following memo was presented to the States General in 1706 by Adrianus Engelhard Helvetius, who points out that Holland's English allies were quick to take advantage of his countrymen's misfortunes.

The commerce of the United Provinces in Europe has never been in worse condition than it is today. During the course of earlier wars, although Dutch vessels were also open to the attacks of privateers, at least they could take refuge in the Atlantic and in the Mediterranean ports under Spanish rule, which are now closed to them. Furthermore, even when they were completely barred from the trade of France, they still continued to ply both the Baltic trades, which they continue to enjoy, and the trades of Spain, the kingdoms of Naples and Sicily, and Spanish Flanders, which now they have good reason to miss. Not only is the market greatly reduced for their cloth, both of their own manufacture as well as that made in India and the Baltic, and for their other wares, spices, salt fish, etc., but they are also deprived of the profitable return trade in wool, wine, and necessary commodities. . . .

As a result, there are frequent bankruptcies, word of which scares people and discourages them from entrusting money to the merchants, whose own funds are limited, as they are in the habit of doing in peacetime. This decline even affects the domestic commerce of the country, which is suffering badly, especially thanks to the cunning manipulations of the English, who take advantage of the opportunity to raise themselves upon the ruins of their allies.

The English, a people as fierce as they are capable, being convinced that the States General need their help so badly that they would not dare dispute anything with them, follow the maxim of making the Dutch pay their auxiliary troops, even when they are engaged in battle. They supply them with goods of every kind, sending cloth and Indian fabrics which are forbidden in England, butter, tallow, even manufactured candles, grain, etc., and in this they manage to make a profit on the support of troops for which they ought to be paying themselves.

Helvetius. *"Mémoire sur l'état présent du Government des Provinces Unis."* In M. van der Bijl, ed., *Bijdragen en Mededeldingen van het Historisch Genootshap 80* (1966), 226–227, trans. Herbert H. Rowen, *The Low Countries in Early Modern Times. A Documentary History.* New York: Harper & Row, 1972.

(reigned 1702–14), Parliament showed an unprecedented willingness to open its purse and support massive outlays for war, knowing that a weakened monarchy could not use the money to subvert the freedoms of its subjects.

The wealth that underwrote England's command of the sea and financed the campaigns of Marlborough on land came from nearly a century of unparalleled economic growth. England's growing commercial strength was based in part on geographic advantage. Faced with the implacable hostility of Louis XIV, the Dutch were forced to spend much of their wealth defending their borders on land. England, an island, was spared this expense. Moreover, with their deep water ports and location to windward of the continent, the English could disrupt Dutch trade by blocking access via the English Channel. The Anglo-Dutch wars of 1652–53, 1665–66, and 1672–73 were fought over this issue. As George

Monk, the English general-at-sea in the Second Dutch War said: "[W]hat we want is more of the trade the Dutch now have." Dutch seamen acquitted themselves well, but the cost of battles in which more than a hundred ships might be engaged on each side, together with the need to provide convoys for trading vessels even in peacetime, gradually eroded their competitive advantage (see document 16.6).

Even favorable geography probably could not have given England a decisive lead had it not been for a system of credit and finance that became the envy of Europe. The revolution of 1688 paved the way for the land tax of 1692 and the extension of excise taxes to a wide range of consumer goods. England acquired the benefits of permanent taxation for the first time in its history. The Bank of England, established in 1694, then stabilized English finances by underwriting government war loans. In the eighteenth century it became the first of Europe's central banks, allowing private bankers to draw upon its gold reserves in periods of financial crisis.

Credit, backed by reliable taxation, paid for the fleet, Marlborough's armies, and the large subsidies that England paid to its continental allies. England, which became Great Britain when it merged with Scotland in 1707, was therefore able to expand its empire and protect its markets more easily than the Dutch, whose war fleet declined after 1673 and whose decentralized institutions blocked the formation of more effective credit mechanisms. English trade, which had been expanding steadily throughout the seventeenth century, became a flood during the War of the Spanish Succession when the British navy swept the seas of all rivals (see table 16.1). In time the enormous wealth derived largely from overseas markets would provide the capital for the industrial revolution and further strengthen English claims to great power status.

⚮ TABLE 16.1 ⚮

English Trade Balances

The most active phase of the War of the Spanish Succession lasted from 1701 to 1711. During that period the English lost 1,061 merchant ships to enemy raiders, while the English balance of trade (surplus of exports over imports) increased enormously, owing primarily to increased exports of cloth and grain to Portugal, Holland, Germany, and Russia and to decreased imports from France and Spain. Because the increase in trade more than compensated for the subsidies sent to the continent for war, the British were, in mercantilist terms, net beneficiaries of the war.

Year	Extra-European trade balance	Overall trade balance
1699–1701	£ 489,000	£ 974,000
1702	233,000	971,000
1703	515,000	1,745,000
1704	968,000	1,519,000
1706	836,000	2,705,000
1707	672,000	2,024,000
1708	630,000	2,022,000
1709	271,000	2,111,000
1710	825,000	2,486,000
1711	969,000	2,731,000

Source: Adapted from D. W. Jones, *War and Economy in the Age of William III and Marlborough* (Oxford: Basil Blackwell, 1988), p. 220.

CHAPTER 17

THE SOCIAL AND ECONOMIC STRUCTURE
OF THE OLD REGIME

CHAPTER OUTLINE

◆◆◆◆◆◆◆◆◆◆◆◆◆◆◆◆◆◆◆◆

E uropean society before the political and industrial revolutions of the late eighteenth century is known as the Old Regime. For most people in the eighteenth century, life was little changed from the Middle Ages and closer in its essentials to that of ancient Rome than to the early twenty-first century. Though global commerce was growing and signs were seen of increased capital accumulation and preindustrial development, the vast majority of Europeans were still engaged in agriculture. Society reflected this by remaining hierarchical. A majority of the population worked the land but owned little or none of it, while most of the wealth continued to be held by a small landowning elite.

Chapter 17 examines the social and economic structure of the Old Regime. The chapter starts by looking at the population of Europe, then considers the social categories, called estates, into which people were divided. (The term *social class* is a product of nineteenth-century analysis.) The majority of Europeans lived in rural villages, so the chapter next surveys the rural economy, including preindustrial manufacturing. This leads to a detailed examination of three major social categories: the aristocracy, the peasantry, and town dwellers. The urban economy leads to a discussion of national economies, covering mercantilism, the dominant economic philosophy of the Old Regime, and the global economy.

◇

The Population of Europe in the Old Regime

Historians do not know with certainty how many people lived in Europe in 1680, or even in 1780. Governments did not yet record births and deaths (churches usually documented them), and they did not

TABLE 17.1

Estimated Population of Europe in 1700

Country	Population (in millions)
France	19.3
European Russia	17.0
German states	13.5
Prussia	1.6
Italian states	13.0
Austrian Empire	11.0
Poland	9.0
Spain	7.5
Great Britain	6.4
Turkish Empire	6.4
Ireland	2.5
Portugal	2.0
Holland	1.9
Sweden and Finland	1.5

Source: B. R. Mitchell, ed., *European Historical Statistics, 1750–1970* (London: Macmillan, 1975), pp. 17ff; and Jack Babuscio and Richard M. Dunn, eds., *European Political Facts, 1648–1789* (London: Macmillan, 1984), pp. 335ff.

conduct a regular census. The first modern census in England, for example, was held in 1801. Isolated census data exist for the eighteenth century, such as a Swedish census of 1750 and the Spanish census of 1768–69, but most population figures are estimates based on fragmentary records, local case studies, and demographic analysis.

The best estimate is that Europe at the start of the eighteenth century had a total population of 120 to 130 million people (see table 17.1)—less than one-seventh of the count at the end of the twentieth century. Spain, the richest world power of the sixteenth century, had a population of 9.2 million in 1769. A good estimate of the population of Great Britain (England, Scotland, and Wales) at the beginning of the eighteenth century is 6.4 million—less than the population of London in 1998. The strength of France during the Old Regime can be seen in its estimated population of 19.3 million in 1700. In all countries, most people lived in small villages and on isolated farms. Even in a city-state such as the republic of Venice, more than 80 percent of the population was rural. In France, one of the most developed countries of the Old Regime, the figure was more than 75 percent.

The Economic Structures of the Rural World

Most of Europe lived, as their ancestors had, in small villages surrounded by open fields. The land was parceled for farming in many ways, but the general pattern was consistent: Peasants and small farmers inhabited and worked land that belonged to aristocrats, the state, or the church. A typical village left some woodland standing (for gathering food and fuel), set aside some of the worst soil as wasteland (for grazing livestock), maintained some land as commonly owned, and left most of the land unfenced in open fields. Enclosed, or fenced in, fields were rare, but in some regions of western Europe—such as southwestern England, Brittany, and the Netherlands—the land was already subdivided by fences, stone walls, or hedgerows. Enclosure had occurred in some places to assist livestock farming and in others where peasants had been fortunate enough to acquire their own land. In most of Europe, however, the arable land was still farmed in the open field system. From the midlands of England to eastern Europe (especially the German states and Russia), open fields were divided into long rectangular strips of approximately one acre each, defined by grass pathways between them. A peasant family usually worked several strips scattered around the community, plus a kitchen garden near home. This was an inefficient system, but one that allowed the bad and good fields to be shared more equitably. In other regions of Europe (such as Spain, southern France, and Italy) the open fields were divided into small, irregular plots of land that peasant families farmed year after year.

Whatever system of land tenure was used, most plowland was planted with the grains on which the world lived—wheat, rye, barley, and oats. These crops were usually rotated annually, and each field laid fallow on a regular basis, normally every third year (see document 17.1). Leaving a field unplanted was needed for the replacement of nitrates in the soil because chemical fertilizers were unknown and animal manure was scarce. Fallow fields had the secondary advantage of providing additional pasture land for grazing.

Scientific agronomy—the study of field-crop production and soil management—was in its infancy in the Old Regime, but noteworthy changes were appearing. In Britain, the improvements suggested by the studies of Jethro Tull and the Viscount Charles Townshend significantly increased eighteenth-century harvests. Tull, a gentleman farmer and scientist introduced a new

◆ DOCUMENT 17.1 ◆

An Eighteenth-Century Sharecropping Contract

This list summarizes the chief points of a contract negotiated in southern France in 1779 on behalf of a great landowner. It was an agreement "at half fruits"—a 50/50 sharing of the crop between a marquis and the father and son who farmed his land. A study of this contract has estimated that this land would yield a harvest of 100 setiers of wheat. Thus, the peasant sharecroppers paid (1) 20 setiers off the top to the marquis; then (2) 10 setiers of wheat as the price of cutting and flailing the wheat, leaving a harvest of 70 setiers. They then paid (3) 35 setiers as "half fruits" and (4) 20 setiers for seed. The result was 55 setiers to the marquis, 15 setiers for the peasant family. A family of five ate 20 setiers of wheat per year.

1. The lease shall be for one year, at "half fruits" and under the following conditions.
2. The lessees will furnish the seed.
3. Before the division of the harvest, the marquis will receive twenty setiers of wheat off the top.
4. The lessees will deliver the wheat already cut and flailed, at no cost to the marquis.
5. The lessees must use the "three field" system of planting—1/3 of the land planted to wheat, 1/3 to some other grain, and 1/3 left unplanted.
6. If the lessees do not leave 1/3 of the land fallow, they forfeit the entire harvest.
7. All livestock will be held in common with profits and losses equally shared.
8. If there is a shortage of hay and straw for the livestock, the lessees must pay half of the cost of buying forage.
9. The lessees must maintain the land, including making drains for water, cutting brush, pruning vines. . . etc.
10. In addition to sharing the crop, the lessees must pay a rent of 72 chickens, 36 capons, and 600 eggs.
11. The lessees must raise pigs, geese, ducks, and turkeys, to be divided evenly; they must purchase the young animals to raise at their own expense.
12. The lessees must make their own ploughs and pay for the blacksmith work themselves.

Forster, Robert, and Forster, Elborg, eds. *European Society in the Eighteenth Century,* New York: Harper & Row, 1969.

system of plowing and hoeing to pulverize the soil, and invented a seed drill that increased yields and decreased labor. Townshend advocated a planting system that eliminated the need for summer fallowing of plowland. His Norfolk, or four-course, system rotated plantings of a root crop, barley, clover, and wheat. Townshend championed the choice of turnips as the root crop so vigorously (because they provided both nitrogen fixation and fodder for livestock) that he became known as "Turnip Townshend." Ideas such as these, circulated by a growing periodical press, raised crop yields to the extent that England fed an increasing population and still exported grain in the early eighteenth century.

Most European agriculture was not so successful, and peasant families faced a struggle to survive. Their primary concern was a harvest large enough to pay their obligations to the landowning aristocracy, to the royal tax collector, and to the church in the form of a compulsory tithe as well as to provide seed grain for the next year, with food left over to sustain life for another year (see document 17.1). The yield per acre was higher in western Europe than in eastern Europe, which explains much of the comparative prosperity and strength of the west. Each grain sown in Russia and Poland yielded an average harvest of four grains, while Spanish and Italian peasants harvested six grains, and English and Dutch farmers averaged more than ten grains. Peasants typically supplemented their meager stock of grains with the produce of a small garden and the luxury of some livestock such as a few pigs or chickens. Surplus grain would be sold or bartered—a money economy was not yet the rule throughout the rural world—at the nearest market town to acquire necessities that could not be produced at home. Even when livestock were slaughtered, peasants rarely ate the entire animal; they generally sold the choicer cuts of pork and kept the fatty remnants for soups, stews, or bacon.

Home production was an essential feature of this rural economy and meant more than churning butter or making cheese at home. Domestic manufacturing often included making all of a family's clothing, so many peasants learned to spin yarn, weave cloth, or sew clothing. This part-time textile production sometimes led to the sale of excess household products, and in some textile regions domestic manufacturing evolved into a system of production known as cottage industry (see illustration 17.1) in which a peasant family purposely made goods for sale instead of for use in the home. Cottage industry sometimes grew into a handcraft form of industrial manufacture (often called

Illustration 17.1

🪡 **Cottage Industry.** The textile industry began in rural cottages, not great factories. This scene depicts a family textile shop for making knitwear. Note the sexual division of labor: Women spin and wind yarn while a man operates a knitting frame, making stockings.

protoindustrialization), when entrepreneurs negotiated contracts with peasant spinners and weavers. An entrepreneur might provide raw materials and pay peasant spinners to produce homespun threads; the yarn could then be delivered to a peasant weaver who also worked at home. This "putting out" system of textile manufacture stimulated later industrialization by developing manufacturing skills, marketing networks, and a class of prosperous provincial entrepreneurs. By some estimates 10 percent of the rural population of Old Regime Europe was engaged in cottage industry.

Domestic manufacturing, like farming, depended upon a family economy; that is, everyone worked. Peasant society generally followed a sexual division of labor in which, for example, men did most of the plowing and women played an important role in the harvest. In the production of textiles, women did most of the spinning and men were more likely to be weavers. However, the labor of every family member, including children, was needed if the family were to survive. As an old poem recalls:

> Man, to the Plow
> Wife, to the Cow
> Girl, to the Yarn
> Boy, to the Barn
> And your Rent will be netted.

Working women were thus essential to the family economy long before industrialization and urbanization

transformed families and work. A study of peasant women in eighteenth-century Belgium, for example, has found that 45 percent of all married women were listed in government records as farmers and 27 percent were recorded as spinners; only 6 percent were listed without an occupation. Unmarried adults were at a disadvantage in this rural economy, and widows were often the poorest members of a rural community.

The rural community of peasant families was typically a village of fifty to a few hundred people. In parts of Europe, these villages had corporate structures with inherited rules and regulations. These might regulate weights and measures, or they might regulate morality and behavior such as the control of stray dogs or mandatory church attendance. Village assemblies, led by elders or by the heads of the households controlling most of the land, often held powers such as assigning land use (as they did in most German states and in Russia), dictating farming methods and crop rotation, settling disputes, collecting taxes, and even arranging marriages. Women were usually excluded from participation, though widows were sometimes accepted. Recent research has identified some exceptionally democratic villages in which women participated with full rights.

Corporative Society and the *Ständestaat*

Europeans of the Old Regime lived in highly stratified societies and generally accepted their fixed place in the hierarchy. In two-thirds of Europe (France, Savoy, part of Switzerland, Denmark, the German states, Austria, Bohemia, Hungary, the Danubian provinces, Poland, and Russia), law and custom divided people into estates. The division of the population into such bodies, with separate rights, duties, and laws, is known as corporative society, or by its German name, the *Ständestaat*.

Corporative society was a legacy of the Middle Ages. In much of western Europe, the legal basis for it had disappeared, whereas eastern Europe remained caste-ridden. Everywhere, hierarchical ideas provided the foundations of society. The structure of corporative society resembled a pyramid. Most of the population (peasants and laborers) formed the base of the pyramid while a few privileged people (aristocrats and wealthy town dwellers) sat at the top, with a monarch at the pinnacle. Everyone was born to a position in the hierarchy, a position that, according to most churches, was divinely ordained, and little social mobility was evident from one order to another.

❧ TABLE 17.2 ❧

The Social Structure of England in the Old Regime

The data in this table are based upon statistical calculations made by Gregory King in the last years of the seventeenth century, based upon a study of the tax rolls.

Social group	Individuals on tax rolls	Population (with families)	Percentage of England
Aristocracy	4,560	57,000	1.0
Landowning gentry	172,000	1,036,000	18.8
Small farmers	550,000	2,050,000	37.2
Rural total	726,560	3,143,000	57.0
Merchants	10,000	64,000	1.2
Educated professions	25,000	145,000	2.7
Clergy	10,020	52,520	0.9
Government service	10,000	70,000	1.3
Urban trades	110,000	465,000	8.5
Laborers	360,000	1,275,000	23.2
Urban total	525,020	2,101,520	38.3
Military officers	9,000	36,000	0.7
Soldiers and sailors	85,000	220,000	4.0
Military total	94,000	256,000	4.7

Historians have mostly studied corporative society in France, where the population was divided into three estates. The clergy, approximately 1 percent to 2 percent of the nation, comprised the first estate. The aristocracy, also less than 2 percent of the population, formed the second estate. The remaining 97 percent of France, from bankers to vagabonds, collectively made up the third estate. In central Europe, the *Ständestaat* often contained four orders (*Stände*) because Scandinavian and German law divided what the French called the third estate into two parts, an order of town dwellers and another of peasants. The constitutions of the Old Regime, such as the Swedish Constitution of 1720, retained the ideal of corporative society. German jurisprudence perpetuated this division of the population throughout the eighteenth century. A fifty-volume compendium published in the 1740s, reiterated the principles of the *Ständestaat,* and they were embodied in subsequent legal reforms, such as the Frederician Code in Prussia.

The society of the Old Regime was more complicated than simple legal categories suggest. In England, the legal distinctions among social groups were mostly abolished during the seventeenth century. The English aristocracy remained a privileged and dominant elite, but a new stratification based upon nonlanded wealth was also emerging (see table 17.2). In contrast, Russian fundamental laws perpetuated a rigid corporative society, and eighteenth-century reforms only tightened the system. In central Europe, yet another pattern developed where reformers known as cameralists refined the definitions of social categories. Austrian tax laws adopted in 1763, for example, divided the population into twenty-four distinct categories.

The composition and condition of each estate varied across Europe. The Polish aristocracy included 10 percent of the population compared with 1 percent in France; this meant that the Polish aristocracy included barefoot farmers who lived in simple homes with earthen floors. Only 1 percent of Poles lived in towns of ten thousand, compared with more than 15 percent of England and Wales. Sometimes, as in Spain, peasants lived in farming towns, but they were not part of an urban estate. But everywhere, peasants were the majority. In England, 65 percent of the population lived by farming; in France and Sweden, 75 percent of the population were peasants; in Poland, 85 percent.

The rights and duties of people in each estate also varied from country to country, with the most striking differences evident between eastern and western Europe. Historians frequently express this division of Europe by an imaginary line called the Elbe-Trieste line, running from the mouth of the Elbe River on the North Sea to the Adriatic Sea at the city of Trieste (see map 17.1). West of the Elbe-Trieste line (including Scandinavia), peasants could own farm land. French peasants, for example, owned between 30 percent and 40 percent of the arable land, although it was frequently of the poorest quality. East of the Elbe River, peasants lived in a form of legal servitude called serfdom. Millions of serfs were deprived of legal and civil rights, including the right to own land. Even those states that permitted peasant land ownership, however, saw little of it. Swedish peasants accounted for 75 percent of the population but owned only 31 percent of the land; the king and the aristocracy, less than 5 percent of the population, owned 69 percent of the land in 1700. Sweden, however, was far ahead of most of Europe in peasant land ownership. In Bohemia, one of the richest provinces of the Habsburg Empire, the monarch owned 5 percent of the land and the nobility owned 68.5 percent, while peasants owned less than 1 percent.

The Aristocracy: Varieties of the Privileged Elite

The pinnacle of the social structure in rural communities was the aristocracy, who enjoyed a life of comparative ease. In most countries, aristocrats formed a separate legal caste, bound by different laws and traditions that gave them special privileges, such as tax exemptions and the right to unpaid labor by the peasantry. Nobility was considered a hereditary condition, which originated when a monarch granted noble status to a family through a document called a patent of nobility. In each generation, the eldest son would bear the title of nobility (such as duke or count) and other males in the family might bear lesser titles. Lesser aris-

tocratic status was typically shown by the aristocratic particule within a family name; this was usually the word of (*de* in French, *di* in Italian, *von* in German). Pretenders sometimes tried to copy this habit, but the nobility zealously guarded its privileged status. In Venice, a Golden Book recorded the names of the nobility; in the German states, an annual publication (the *Almanac of Gotha*) kept watch on aristocratic pedigrees.

The aristocracy was a small class, but it was not homogeneous. Gradations of status depended upon the length of time that a family had been noble, the means by which it had acquired its title, and the wealth and political influence that the family held. One of the distinctions frequently made in western Europe separated a "nobility of the sword" composed of families ennobled for centuries as a result of military service to the monarch from a "nobility of the robe" composed of families more recently ennobled through service to the government. In central and eastern Europe, important distinctions rested upon the number of serfs an aristocrat owned. The aristocracy might include an elite of less land and wealth, known as the gentry, although in some countries, such as Britain, the landowning gentry did not possess aristocratic titles. While the gentry enjoyed a comfortable existence, it was far removed from the wealth of great nobles (see table 17.3).

The highest nobles often emphasized the length of time their family had been noble. British history provides a good example. The leading figure in early eighteenth-century English politics, Sir Robert Walpole, was not born to a noble title, but for his accomplishments, he was ennobled as the first earl of Orford in 1742. One of Walpole's leading opponents, however, was the fourth duke and eighth earl of Bedford, heir to a pedigree nearly three hundred years old and a title that originated with the third son of King Henry IV, born in 1389. Thus, the earl of Bedford was unlikely to consider the earl of Orford his equal. And both of them yielded precedence to the earl of Norfolk, whose title dated back to the year 1070, shortly after the Norman conquest of England.

Many of the fine distinctions within the aristocracy were simply matters of pride within a caste that paid excruciating attention to comparative status. The aristocratic competition for precedence, however, involved real issues of power and wealth. Only the top 5 percent (perhaps less) of the aristocracy could hope to be presented at court and meet the royal family; fewer still were invited to live at the royal court, hunting with King Louis XV of France in the royal forests, sharing the evening tabagerie (a smoking and drinking session) with King Frederick William I of Prussia, or enjoying

❧ TABLE 17.3 ❧

The Finances of a Great Noble in the Eighteenth Century

This table has excerpts from the financial records of a French noble family, the counts and countesses of Tavannes. The unit of measure is the livre, which had approximately the same value as an English shilling (one-twentieth of the pound sterling). Figures are given for mixed years because only partial records have survived.

Income or expenses	Amount
Income from land owned by the count	
Rent for lands in region #1 (annual average, 1696–1730)	5,000+
Rent for lands in region #2 (annual average, 1699–1726)	3,500+
Rent for lands in region #3 (annual average, 1698–1723)	8,700+
Income from sale of wood from forest in region #3 (1788)	40,000+
Gross revenue from all land (after paying upkeep and wages) in 1788	86,269
Income from pensions given by the king	
Total pensions for 1754	46,900
Pension as commander of royal forces in Burgundy	26,250
Income from seigneurial dues (obligations paid by peasants)	
Total dues paid in 1788	26,986
Income from the inheritance of the countess (1725)	
Income from four houses in Paris (value = 200,000)	10,000
Income from investments (value = 367,938)	8,698
Total capital inherited in 1725	803,924
Wages paid to the count's staff (1780–86)	
Annual wages for the count's agent in Paris	800
Annual wages for a forest warden in Burgundy	200
Annual wages for a gardener or a maid in Burgundy	70
Annual wages for a chef in Paris	945
Annual wages for a coachman in Paris	720
Personal expenses	
Total personal expenses in 1788	62,000
Expenses for clothing, jewelry, and gifts in 1788	20,000
Expenses for the theater in 1788	2,000
Monthly expenses for Roquefort cheese (January 1784)	32
Monthly expenses for cognac (January 1784)	30
Monthly expenses for cayenne coffee (January 1784)	30

Source: Data from Robert Forster, *The House of Saulx-Tavannes: Versailles and Burgundy, 1700–1830* (Baltimore, Md.: Johns Hopkins University Press, 1971), passim.

the life of lavish dinners and balls. Yet a position at court was often the route to political office, military command, or perhaps a pension providing a lifetime income. Most provincial nobles lacked the opportunities for such advancement.

The provincial aristocracy, living on inherited lands in the rural world, encompassed a great range of social and economic conditions. The Spanish, for example, distinguished between grandees (a term for the greatest nobles, such as the dukes of Alba) who possessed immense estates and national influence, locally important aristocrats (called *caballeros*) who owned enough land to live as a privileged elite, and a comparatively poor gentry (called *hidalgos*) who were said to have more titles than shirts. Such distinctions existed across Europe. In the east, a few families of grand seigneurs owned most of the land (and the serfs on it) while thousands of aristocrats owned little or nothing. The Polish aristocracy, known collectively as the *szlachta*, included 700,000 to one million people, but only thirty to forty magnate families possessed the wealth and power normally associated with the nobility. Part of the *szlachta* worked on the estates of great nobles as bailiffs, stewards, or tenant farmers; most of this caste lived as small farmers on rented land, and many were so poor that they were known as the *golota*, a barefoot aristocracy.

The Privileged Status of the Aristocracy

The wealth and power of the high nobility present one of the most vivid images of the corporative society of the Old Regime. Some aristocrats enjoyed dizzying wealth and a life of luxury. In the Austrian Netherlands (now Belgium), the duke of Arenberg had an annual income eighteen times the income of the richest merchant. In Poland, Prince Radziwill kept ten thousand retainers in his service. In England, the top four hundred noble families each owned estates of ten thousand to fifty thousand acres. In Russia, Empress Catherine the Great gave one of her discarded lovers a gift of thirty-seven thousand serfs, and Prince Menshikov owned 100,000 serfs. In Bohemia, one hundred noble families owned one-third of the entire province, and the poorer members of this group owned land encompassing thirty villages. In Spain, the count of Altamira owned the commercial city of Valencia.

Such wealth produced breathtaking inequality. The count of Tavannes in France paid a gardener or a maid on his provincial estates seventy livres per year, and the valued chef at his Paris residence earned 945 livres per year; yet the count lavished twenty thousand livres on clothing and jewelry. The count's monthly expenditure on coffee and cognac totaled nearly a year's wages for a servant, and his budget for theater tickets would have cost the total yearly earnings of twenty-eight servants. Sustaining a life of such extreme luxury led many lesser nobles into ruinous debt. Extravagance and debt became so typical of the nobility (including royalty) in the eighteenth century that some countries, such as Spain, made arresting aristocrats for their debts illegal.

In addition to enormous wealth, nobles held great power. They dominated offices of the state, both in the government and in the military. In some countries, notably Sweden, Prussia, and Russia, the concept of aristocratic service to the throne had led to an arrangement in which the aristocracy accepted compulsory state service and received in return a legal monopoly over certain positions. The eighteenth-century Russian Charter of the Nobility, for example, stated: "The title and privileges of the nobility . . . are acquired by service and work useful to the Empire." Therefore, it continued, whenever the emperor "needs the service of the nobility for the general well being, every nobleman is then obligated . . . to perform fully his duty." In return for this compulsory service, the Charter of the Nobility recognized the right of nobles to buy and sell villages, excluded nobles from some taxes that fell on commoners, gave nobles a monopoly of some positions, and spared nobles some of the punishments (such as flogging) specified in Russian law. In much of Europe, only aristocrats could become army officers. Nobles universally dominated the highest positions in government. At the beginning of the eighteenth century, the chief minister of the king of France was a marquis, the prime minister of the king of Prussia was a count, the head of the state council of the Habsburg Empire was a count, the chief minister of the tsar of Russia was a prince, and the chief adviser to the king of Spain was a cardinal. For the century before the French Revolution of 1789, the chief ministers of the kings of France were (in order): a marquis, a cardinal, a duke, a duke, a cardinal, a marquis, a count, a minor aristocrat, a duke, a duke, and a count.

In addition to personal wealth and powerful offices, aristocrats of the Old Regime usually held a privileged position in the law, exceptional rights on their landed estates, and great power over the people who lived on their land. In most countries, nobles were governed by substantially different laws than the rest of the population. Some countries had a separate legal code for aristocrats, some had legal charters detailing noble privileges, some simply adopted laws granting special treatment. Legal privileges took many forms. Exemption from the laws that applied to commoners was one of the most cherished. Aristocrats were exempted from most taxes that fell on peasants or town dwellers, and they tenaciously defended their exemptions even as the monarchy faced bankruptcy. In Hungary, the Magyar nobles were free from all direct taxes such as those on land or income; they guarded this privilege by giving regular contributions to the throne, but nobles controlled the process and the amount themselves. Aristocrats were exempt from the *corvée*, a labor tax by which peasants were obliged to maintain roads and bridges (see illustration 17.2). Penal codes usually exempted nobles from the corporal punishment common, such as flogging and branding.

Illustration 17.2

🏴 **The Corvée.** The highway system of eighteenth-century Europe required a great deal of labor to maintain it. In most of central and eastern Europe, where serfdom survived, monarchs expected great landowners to require roadwork as part of the *ro-* *bot* owed by serfs. In France, where serfdom had largely disappeared, peasants were required to pay a tax, called the *corvée*, by their labor, like the roadwork shown here.

Aristocratic privilege varied significantly from country to country. In Britain and the Netherlands, most exemptions were abolished by revolutions in the seventeenth century. Both countries made aristocrats and commoners equal before the law and allowed neither tax exemptions nor a monopoly on offices. Yet important privileges persisted there, too. English nobles held hereditary control of the upper house of Parliament, the House of Lords, and the right to be tried only by a jury of their peers.

The core of aristocratic privilege was found on their provincial estates. An aristocrat, as lord of the manor, held traditional manorial rights over the land and its inhabitants. These rights are also known as feudal rights, because many had survived from the feudal system of the Middle Ages, or seigneurial rights, because the lord of the manor was known as the seigneur. Manorial rights increased significantly as one passed from western Europe to eastern Europe, where peasants remained in the virtual slavery of serfdom. But even in regions where serfdom no longer existed, aristocratic landowners were often entitled to feudal dues (payments in money or in kind), to unpaid labor by peasants in the seigneurial fields, or to both. Thus, peasants might be expected to harvest an aristocrat's crops before they could harvest their own and then to pay a percentage of their own crops to the same aristocrat.

Seigneurial rights in many countries (particularly in central and eastern Europe) also included the powers of local governance. The seigneur provided, or oversaw, the functions of the police, the judiciary, and civil government on his lands; a noble might thereby preside over the arrest, trial, and punishment of a peasant. Many aristocrats thus governed their provincial estates as self-sufficient, miniature kingdoms. A study of the Old Regime manors of Bohemia shows this vividly. Only the noble landowner was legally a citizen of the larger state (the Austrian Empire). The residents of the noble's villages and farmlands were completely under his jurisdiction. Peasants farmed their fields for him. He conscripted them for the *corvée*, selected them for service in the Austrian army, and collected their taxes for the Habsburg government. The same lord arrested draft evaders or tax delinquents and punished them, and peasants could not appeal his justice.

Variations within the Peasantry: Serfdom

The majority of Europeans during the Old Regime were peasant farmers, but this peasantry, like the aristocracy, was not a homogeneous class. The foremost difference distinguished free peasants from those legally bound by virtual slavery. Outright slavery no longer existed in most of Europe by 1700, although European governments allowed slavery in their overseas colonies. Portugal (the only country to import African slaves into Europe), the Ottoman Empire, and the Danubian provinces (where 200,000 gypsies were enslaved) were exceptions.

Multitudes of European peasants still lived in the virtual slavery known as serfdom, a medieval institution that had survived into the Old Regime (and would last into the nineteenth century in parts of Europe). Serfdom was not slavery, but it resembled slavery in several ways. Serfs could not own land. They were bound to the soil, meaning that they could not choose to migrate from the land they farmed. In addition, serfs might be sold or given away, or gambled away. Entire villages could be abolished and relocated. Serfs might be subjected to corporal punishment such as flogging. One Russian count ordered the whipping of all serfs who did not attend church, and the penalty for missing Easter Communion was five thousand lashes. A Russian decree of 1767 summarized this situation simply: Serfs "owe their landlords proper submission and absolute obedience in all matters."

The distinction between serfdom and slavery was noteworthy. Unlike slaves, serfs were not chattel property (property other than real estate). Serfs were rarely sold without including the land that they farmed or without their families. Serfs enjoyed a few traditional legal rights. They could make a legal appeal to a village council or a seigneurial court. They could not press charges or give evidence against nobles or their bailiffs, so their legal rights protected them within the peasant community but not against their lords.

Serfdom survived in some portions of western Europe and became more common as one traveled east. East of the Elbe River, serfdom was the dominant social institution. In parts of France and the western German states, vestigial serfdom still restricted hundreds of thousands of people. In Prussia and Poland, approximately 20 percent of the peasants were free and 80 per-

cent serfs. In Hungary, only 2 percent of the peasants were free; in Denmark and in the Slavic provinces of the Austrian Empire (Bohemia and Silesia), perhaps 1 percent; in Russia, less than 1 percent.

Variations did exist within serfdom. In Russia, a peasant family typically belonged to a noble landowner, but 40 percent of the serfs were state serfs farming the imperial domains. These state serfs had been created by Peter the Great when he seized lands belonging to the Russian Orthodox Church. Those who labored for the nobility experienced conditions as diverse as did their seigneurs; more than 30 percent of landowners held small farms with fewer than ten serfs, while 16 percent of the Russian nobility owned estates large enough to encompass an entire village of one hundred or more serfs. The great nobility possessed so many souls that many served as house serfs, domestic servants whose life differed significantly from their counterparts who labored in the fields.

The basic legal obligation of serfs was compulsory, unpaid labor in the fields of landowners. This obligatory labor, called *robot* in much of central and eastern Europe, was defined by law but varied from region to region. In Prussia serfs owed the Junker aristocrats two or three days of unpaid labor every week and more during the harvest. Junkers, however, needed more labor than their serfs provided and therefore hired some free peasants. The feudal labor laws of Bohemia specified three days per week of *robot*, plus harvest labor "at the will" of a noble. A law of 1775 defined a day of labor as eight hours during the winter, twelve hours during the spring and summer, and fourteen hours during the harvest. Russian serfs commonly worked six days per week for a landowner (see document 17.2). In some regions, however, a different system applied: Serfs farmed an allotment of land and gave the landowners a large percentage of the harvest.

A study of the serfs in the Baltic provinces of Russia reveals how these obligations added up. A family of eight able-bodied peasants (including women) owed their master the following: two field workers for three days per week, every week of the year; ten to twelve days of miscellaneous labor such as livestock herding; four trips, totaling about fifty-six days of labor, carting goods for the seigneur; forty-two days of postal-relay services; and twenty-four days of spinning flax. In addition to such labor, European peasant families owed feudal payments in kind, such as grain, sheep, wool, chickens, and eggs. Even then they could not keep their remaining production. They had to guard 20 percent to 25 percent of a harvest as seed for the following year. Peasants also usually owed a compulsory tithe to

◆ DOCUMENT 17.2 ◆

A Traveler Observes the Life of Russian Serfs

One of the difficulties facing social historians is that the surviving records of the past were (by definition) written by literate, educated people. The illiterate masses could not record the conditions of their lives for posterity. Historians must therefore rely on the indirect evidence provided by observers (and their deductions from other sources). Alexander Radishchev (1749–1802) was a Russian writer who opposed serfdom and wrote about it, resulting in his exile to Siberia. The following excerpt is Radishchev's description of his meeting with a serf, as published in his A Voyage from St. Petersburg to Moscow *(1790).*

The corduroy road tortured my body; I climbed out of the carriage and (walked). A few steps from the road I saw a peasant ploughing a field. The weather was hot. . . . It was now Sunday. . . . The peasant was ploughing very carefully. The field, of course, was not part of his master's land. He turned the plow with astonishing ease.

"God help you," I said, walking up to the ploughman. . . .

"Thank you sir," the ploughman said to me, shaking the earth off the ploughshare. . . .

"You must be a Dissenter, since you plough on a Sunday."

"No, sir, I make the true sign of the cross," he said, showing me the three fingers together. "And God is merciful and does not bid us starve to death, so long as we have strength and a family."

"Have you no time to work during the week, then, and can you not have any rest on Sundays, in the hottest part of the day, at that?"

"In a week, sir, there are six days, and we go six times a week to work on the master's fields; in the evening, if the weather is good, we haul to the master's house the hay that is left in the woods. . . . God grant that it rains this evening. If you have peasants of your own, sir, they are praying to God for the same thing."

". . . But how do you manage to get food enough, if you have only the holidays free?"

"Not only the holidays: the nights are ours, too. If a fellow isn't lazy, he won't starve to death."

Radischev, Alexander. *A Journey from St. Petersburg to Moscow.* Cambridge, MA: Harvard University Press, 1958.

an established church—approximately 10 percent of a harvest—and taxes to the government, which frequently took between 30 percent and 40 percent of the crop. Studies have found that serfs owed 73 percent of their produce in Bohemia, 75 percent in eastern France, 83 percent in Silesia, and 86 percent in parts of Galicia. Such figures changed from year to year, but the burden remained crushing.

Variations within the Peasantry: Free Peasants

The free peasants of western and central Europe had been escaping from the burdens of serfdom since the fourteenth century. The evolution of a money economy reduced the importance of feudal services by enabling some peasants to commute *robot* or *corvée* with cash. To increase revenues from import and export tariffs, some governments had encouraged a shift to livestock production by allowing aristocrats to enclose their own, and sometimes their tenants', lands. As a result, the capitalization of land was far advanced in the west by

1700, though most families still owed at least some feudal obligations to the landowning aristocracy. Whereas eastern serfs were fortunate to keep 25 percent of their harvest, free peasants could expect to keep more than half. Two different studies of Old Regime France have found that peasants owed between 33 percent and 40 percent of their total production in feudal dues, taxes, and tithes.

The condition of free peasants varied according to the forms of land tenure. The most prosperous peasants were landowners themselves. Studies of the French free peasantry found that nearly four million peasants owned some land and their own home (see illustration 17.3) in the eighteenth century, though most families owned so little land that they could not afford to market any of their harvest. Although most free peasants were landless, one group of them found relatively comfortable lives. The most successful of the landless French peasants were usually tenant farmers, about 10 percent to 20 percent of the landless population. Tenant farmers rented land, typically for a long term—such as nine years—for a fixed money payment, and

Illustration 17.3

/// **The Home of a Successful Peasant Family.** Eighteenth-century peasant homes often had only one room, which was used for all purposes, including housing animals. This Breton family from a village near Morbihan possessed considerable wealth in its horses, cattle, and pigs. Note the limited furnishings and the absence of windows.

they then made the best profit that they could after paying the rent. Such long-term contracts protected peasant families from eviction after a single bad harvest, and many aristocrats discovered the advantages of short-term contracts, which were typical in Spain. Other tenant farmers managed the rented lands but did not labor in the fields themselves, or they became wealthy by trading in grain or other commodities.

The other 80 percent to 90 percent of landless peasants were not as fortunate as the tenant farmers. The most secure group were usually sharecroppers, often called *métayers*. They produced most of the grain marketed in France by farming the estates of great landowners under contracts negotiated as free peasants. The sharecropping contract (see document 17.1) typically provided leased land in return for a large share of its yield. Sharecropping contracts provided these peasant families with the means of survival, but little more. Below the sharecroppers was a lower class of agricultural laborers. Some worked for wages, others, called cotters in many countries, worked for the use of a cottage. Some found only seasonal employment (working to harvest grapes in the autumn, for example), in some cases living as migrant laborers, traveling with the changing harvests. Thus, the peasantry included a range of conditions that saw some peasants employed as laborers (or even domestic servants) by other peasants.

The Urban Population of the Old Regime

Urban Europe in the eighteenth century ranged from rural market towns of 2,000 people to great administra-

⋈ TABLE 17.4 ⋈	
The Great Cities of Europe in 1700	

Table shows all European cities with a population of 100,000 or more in 1700

City	Population
Constantinople	700,000
London	575,000
Paris	500,000
Naples	300,000
Amsterdam	200,000
Lisbon	180,000
Madrid	140,000
Venice	138,000
Rome	135,000
Moscow	130,000
Milan	125,000
Vienna	114,000
Palermo	100,000

tive and commercial capital cities of 500,000. Important regional towns—such as Heidelberg, Helsinki, and Liverpool—often had populations below ten thousand. A population of 100,000 constituted a great city, and only a few capital cities reached that level in the early eighteenth century (see table 17.4 and map 17.1). Berlin had fifty-five thousand people in 1700. St. Pe-

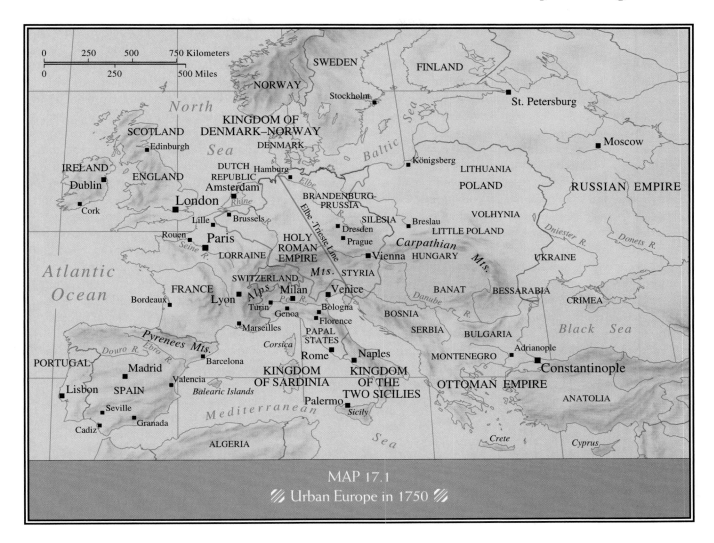

MAP 17.1

/// Urban Europe in 1750 ///

tersburg reached sixty-eight thousand in 1730. Buda and Pest were then separate towns with a combined total of seventeen thousand people. Many cities, such as Geneva, with a population of twenty-eight thousand in 1750, were so small that residents could easily walk their full width for an evening stroll.

The largest city in Europe sat on its southeastern edge: Constantinople had an estimated 700,000 persons. The two dominant cities in the development of modern European civilization, London and Paris, both exceeded 500,000 people, but no other cities rivaled them. Rome was smaller than it had been under the Caesars, with a population of 135,000 in 1700. Such large cities were the centers of western civilization, but they did not yet make it an urban civilization. If one defines *urban* as beginning at a population of ten thousand people, Europe was only 9.4 percent urban at the end of the eighteenth century; if the definition goes down to towns of five thousand people, Europe was

12.1 percent urban. Even if one counts small farming towns of two thousand people (which were different from manufacturing and commercial towns), Europe was still less than one-fourth urban, although some regions were one-third urban.

In legal terms, cities and towns of the Old Regime were corporate entities (hence the terms *incorporated* and *unincorporated* for towns). Towns held legal charters, often centuries old, from the government. Charters specified the rights of town dwellers—collectively called the bourgeoisie (from the French term *bourg*, for town) or burghers (from the similar German term)—rights that the rural population did not enjoy. As in the Middle Ages, the old German saying held true: "City air makes one free." The urban population thus formed a clearly defined estate, lacking many of the privileges of the aristocracy but freed from the obligations upon the peasantry. Hence, they came to be seen as a "middle" class. As a group, they possessed significant nonlanded wealth although they did not rival the wealth of landed nobles. Studies of wills probated during the Old Regime have shown that nobles possessed more than two-thirds of the wealth. A study of England in the 1740s has shown that the landowning aristocracy and upper gentry (a total of less than 3 percent of population) owned 95 percent of the national wealth.

Many countries, particularly those east of the Elbe-Trieste line, prohibited peasants from migrating to the towns and obtaining urban freedoms. Bavarian law, Austrian law, and the Prussian legal code, for example, all bound German peasants to stay on the soil. Even in western Europe, some town charters restricted residence and citizenship, usually to people who showed a means of support. Cities needed migration, however. Conditions were generally so unhealthy that the death rate exceeded the birthrate. Cities could only maintain their size or grow by attracting rural immigrants. Thus, restrictions on population mobility began to disappear during the Old Regime. London grew rapidly in the eighteenth century, yet recorded more deaths than births in every year of the century until 1790; in 1741, burials outnumbered baptisms by two to one.

The Social and Economic Structure of Urban Europe

The towns of the eighteenth century varied in their function as well as their size. Capital cities formed a special category of large cities where government and finance were centered, and the population was so huge that it was a challenge just to feed them. The next range of major cities were usually manufacturing centers (such as Lyons and Granada) or great port-cities (such as Marseilles, Hamburg, and Liverpool). Important regional towns similarly varied, as centers of administration (both governmental and religious) and manufacturing. European towns were not yet characterized by the heavy industry or mass production associated with modern urban life. Economic historians have estimated that in 1750 Britain had attained only 10 percent of the industrialization that it would reach by 1900; France, the Italian states, and the German states were only at 7 percent to 9 percent. Manufacturing in the eighteenth century chiefly meant textiles. Combined textile manufacturing (wool, cotton, linen, and silk) accounted for 28 percent of all British manufacturing, whereas combined heavy industries (mining, metalworking, and construction) accounted for only 22 percent. Textiles similarly provided the traditional basis

of urban prosperity in many regions of continental Europe, such as northeastern France, Flanders, and the city-states of northern Italy.

The occupational structure of towns varied with the town's function. A study of Bayeux, a provincial administrative town in Normandy, found a working adult male population of twelve hundred. Their employment shows how an administrative town was different from the image of towns as manufacturing centers. Slightly more than 10 percent of the men of Bayeux were in the educated professions, mostly lawyers and officials or people trained in medical arts—physicians, surgeons, and apothecaries. An additional 1 percent were tax collectors (an independent occupation) for the monarch or the regional nobility. The prosperous great merchants (not shopkeepers) who traded in regional agricultural or manufactured goods constituted nearly 3 percent of the male population. At the opposite end of Bayeux's social spectrum, 10 percent of the population were urban laborers—a low number that shows that this was not a manufacturing town. Between the two extremes, approximately 75 percent of the male population were engaged in trades. Most of them worked in the production or distribution of food (grocers, butchers, and bakers), clothing (tailors, cobblers, and wig makers), and housing (hoteliers and innkeepers or the building trades). The remainder of the population practiced other trades characteristic of urban life: coopers, goldsmiths, clock makers, saddlers, cabinetmakers, drapers, dozens of other crafts whose practitioners were called artisans.

At the pinnacle of the urban social structure sat the wealthy patrician class of the big cities and great manufacturing towns—a bourgeoisie of banking and finance, of manufacturing and commerce (see illustration 17.4). This urban oligarchy lacked the hereditary titles and privileges of the aristocracy. They were not yet as wealthy as nobles, and they held much less political power. But many families possessed enough wealth to live nobly and aspired to aristocratic status. A few members of this urban elite might enter the aristocracy through state service, and some families married into the aristocracy by providing lavish dowries to daughters who married nobles in debt. This wealthy class lived handsomely, but they represented only a small percentage of urban population, just as aristocrats did in the rural world.

The typical town dweller in the Old Regime was an artisan, and the dominant feature of an artisan's life was the guild—yet another corporation (see illustration 17.5). Guilds had developed in Europe in the late Middle Ages (between the twelfth and fifteenth centuries) for the purpose of organizing craft production. They received statutes or charters specifying their rights from the monarch, making them corporations like the towns themselves. Guild charters were still being reaffirmed

Illustration 17.4

//// **The Rising Middle Class.** The wealthy middle class of businessmen, merchants, manufacturers, and bankers became increasingly influential in the eighteenth century despite being largely excluded from aristocratic circles and institutions. In this painting, a prosperous British merchant flaunts his wealth: his docks and warehouses outside the window, his country estate in the painting, his gold on the table, and his richly dressed family.

by monarchs in the late eighteenth century, as the king of Saxony did in 1780. These corporate charters gave the guilds monopolistic control of manufacturing in their respective trades. Thus, only a member of the coopers' guild could make barrels. Such monopolies extended to all manufacturing for sale or for exchange, but not for home use, and this naturally caused some tension between urban guilds and rural domestic manufacturing. The men of an urban tailors' guild, for example, could fight against the sale of any goods produced by women who worked as seamstresses in the surrounding countryside. Guilds used their charters to regulate trade. They restricted access to, or training in, each occupation; defined the standards of quality; and regulated the right to sell goods.

Membership in a guild involved three stages of development: apprenticeship, when one learned the basic skills of a trade; journeyman, when one developed these skills as a paid employee; and master of a craft, when one obtained the full privilege of practicing it, including the right to train apprentices and hire journeymen. Children became apprentices, learning a trade from a master, at an early age. A study of the guilds of Venice, for example, shows that apprentice goldsmiths began at age seven, weavers at twelve; by age eighteen, one was too old to apprentice in most crafts. A child had to meet many requirements of the guild (such as proof of legitimate birth or practice of Christianity) and pay fees to both the guild and the master before becoming an apprentice. The children of masters had additional advantages. Guild regulations usually required masters to accept the children of other guild members as apprentices, to house them in their homes, and to provide them with adequate training and experience in a trade. Apprentices, in turn, were obliged to serve their masters for a fixed period of years (typically three or

Illustration 17.5

//// **Guild Labor in the Towns.** The larger towns of Europe were centers of skilled artisanal labor such as the German metalworkers depicted in this engraving. The master of such a shop would typically employ one or more journeymen; train children as apprentices in the trade; and entrust the business side of the shop to his wife, who oversaw sales and kept the records.

four, but often more) without pay. Upon the completion of their training, apprentices became journeymen and were expected to leave the town of their training and journey to work for wages with masters in other towns. The journeyman carried papers identifying him and his experience, signed by each of the masters for whom he had worked. Only after several years of such travels could a craftsman hope for acceptance as the master of a trade.

Master craftsmen were important figures in a town. They controlled the guilds and therefore most of the occupations. Masters were expected to marry and to lead respectable lives. They usually maintained their workroom, shop, and residence in the same building. Women were generally excluded from an independent role in a guild, but they were an integral part of the craftsman's family economy. The wife of a master usually handled sales in the shop, kept the accounts for her husband's business, and managed the household. If a master died, his widow had the right to keep their shop, to hire the journeymen to work in it, and to manage the business.

The lower rungs of the urban social structure were domestic servants and the laboring poor. At the beginning of the eighteenth century, domestic service was already becoming one of the largest sources of employment for the unskilled. Studies have found that 7 percent of the population of Ypres (Belgium), 15 percent of Münster (western Germany), and 20 percent of London were working as domestic servants. They lacked the independence and economic prospects of artisans, but they escaped from the poverty of unskilled labor while finding some comfort and security in the homes of their employers. For unmarried women, domestic service was often the only respectable employment available.

National Economies: The Doctrine of Mercantilism

Economics is an ancient word whose derivation goes back to Aristotle's *Oikonomia*, but economics as a field of study and theory is a recent development. In the eighteenth century economics in the modern sense formed a small part of the study called moral philosophy. The first university professorship in political economy was created at the University of Naples in 1754, and the field of political economy (the precursor of modern economics) chiefly prospered in Scotland under the

leadership of theorists such as Adam Smith, the most important founder of modern capitalism.

Despite the limited study of political economics in the Old Regime, governments followed a well-developed economic philosophy known as the mercantile system. The doctrine of mercantilism did not stress the predominant feature of the economy of the Old Regime (agriculture) or the greatest form of wealth of that world (land). Instead, the mercantile system chiefly concerned manufactures, trade, wealth in gold and silver, and the role of the state in encouraging these. The basic principle of mercantilism was a concept called autarky—the idea that a state should be self-sufficient in producing manufactured goods and should import as few foreign goods as possible. Simultaneously, the state sought export markets for its own goods. To achieve a favorable balance of trade and the consequent accumulation of wealth in gold required government regulation of the economy.

An important aspect of the mercantilist regulation of the economy was state support for manufactures and commerce. Many governments of the Old Regime chartered monopolies on the models of the British East India Company and the Dutch East India Company. During the 1720s alone, the Austrians chartered the Ostend Company to control trade with the Indies, the French merged several trading monopolies as the French Indies Company, and the Spanish gave the Chartered Company of Guipuzcoa (Caracas) a monopoly of the American trade. The shareholders in these mercantilist monopolies usually became rich. The Ostend Company, for example, paid its investors 137 percent interest in its first seven years (nearly 20 percent per annum) while serving the emperor's interests by reviving the port of Ostend, stimulating Belgian business, and bringing Austria closer to self-sufficiency.

The mercantilist practice of creating chartered companies with protected privileges applied to much manufacturing in Europe. The French monarchy, for example, held a state monopoly in tapestries and porcelain, high-quality manufactures that could be profitably traded abroad. Prussia created a state tobacco monopoly and Russia held a state salt monopoly. Many countries followed the Dutch example by chartering a national bank similar to the Bank of Amsterdam (1609). These banks served many important functions, such as supplying the mint with metals for coinage or providing the trading monopolies with credit. Parliament chartered the Bank of England in 1694 and gave it the privilege of printing paper money in 1718. The French created a Banque royale in 1717; the Prussians, a Bank of Prussia in 1765.

Mercantilism encouraged manufacturing through direct aid and state regulation of business. Direct aid might include subsidies, interest-free loans, or bonuses to manufacturers. Regulation took the form of explicit legislation. The French monarchy, for example, regulated mines, iron works, glass factories, and paper mills. French law specified what type and quality of raw materials could be used, which equipment and manufacturing processes must be employed, and standards of quality for the finished product. The French then sent factory inspectors to visit manufacturing sites and guarantee compliance with the law. A decree of 1740 explained that this procedure would maintain the quality of French manufactures and protect French trade from "the negligence and bad faith of the manufacturers and merchants."

The most common mercantilist laws were tariffs and Navigation Acts. Tariffs placed taxes on goods entering a country to discourage imports (which produced an unfavorable balance of trade and drained gold from a country) and to protect domestic manufactures from foreign competition. Peter the Great of Russia, for example, levied heavy taxes on imported goods in 1724, even though Russians relied upon European manufactures and luxury goods. In 1767 Charles Townshend, the British chancellor of the exchequer (minister of finance), drafted one of the most famous tariffs of the Old Regime: a high tax on glass, lead, paints, paper, and tea imported into Britain's American colonies, which led to the Boston Tea Party. While governments imposed such restrictions upon imports, they simultaneously controlled trade through Navigation Acts requiring that goods shipped into (or out of) a country be carried only on ships of that country, or that goods shipped into a country's colonies must depart from a port in the mother country.

Mercantilism was not unchallenged. Governments in the early eighteenth century remained generally pleased with the successes of mercantilism (Britain and France both had very favorable balances of trade), but by midcentury mercantilist policies were drawing increasing criticism. A group of theorists called the Physiocrats began to suggest major changes in economic policy, and their ideas supplanted the mercantile system with the basic doctrines of capitalism. The Physiocrats, led by French theorist François Quesnay, believed in limiting the powers of government, especially the power to intervene in economic activities. Quesnay and others proposed the abolition of monopolies and special privileges, the replacement of these policies by open competition in an unregulated marketplace, and the substitution of free trade for tariffs. The physiocratic school did not win great influence with the monarchical governments of the eighteenth century, but it opened the debate that ended mercantilism. Adam Smith employed many of the ideas of the physiocrats in writing his *Inquiry into the Nature and Causes of the Wealth of Nations* (1776), the cornerstone of the new political economy.

Global Economies: Slavery and the Triangular Trade

European world trade grew and changed significantly during the Old Regime. In the seventeenth century, global trade chiefly linked Europe to India and the Far East, as the chartering of the great east Indies companies indicates. This trade had originally concentrated upon the spice islands because great fortunes could be made by bringing pepper and other aromatic spices back to Europe, but the largest Asian trade evolved into competition for mainland markets such as India. During the seventeenth century, trade with the Indies might reward shareholders with more than 100 percent profits on their investment. By the eighteenth century, however, the focus of European global trade had turned to Africa and the Americas, where the profits had become larger.

The profits of eighteenth-century trade, and much of Europe's prosperity, depended upon slavery. The most profitable exploitation of slavery was a system called triangular trade, which began in the 1690s. The corners of this triangle were in Europe, Africa, and the Americas. British merchants were the most adept at the triangular trade, but it was practiced by slave traders from many countries. These slavers began their commerce by taking European manufactured goods (particularly textiles) to the western coast of Africa. These goods were sold or bartered for African slaves who were offered for sale by local African rulers, by rivals who had taken them prisoner, or by Moslem slave traders. In the second leg of the triangular trade, a ship filled with slaves made the Atlantic crossing to European colonies in the Americas. The British, for example, brought slaves to Caribbean colonies (where 85 percent of the population lived in slavery) such as Jamaica and Barbados or to the mainland colonies in North America (where 20 percent of the population

Illustration 17.6

Slave Labor on a Caribbean Sugar Plantation. The European craving for sugar created a growing slave economy in the West Indies. In this engraving, an armed white overseer (lower right) watches sugar making from harvesting sugarcane (center left edge) to milling it (upper right) and compressing it in molds.

lived in slavery). African slaves were then sold to plantation owners, and the revenue was used to buy the agricultural goods (chiefly tobacco in North America and sugar in the Caribbean), which slave labor had produced. On the third leg of the triangle, these goods were returned to England, where they were sold at huge profits.

All European states with American colonies (including Holland and Denmark), and a few states without colonies (notably Prussia), participated in the slave trade. The French triangular trade sent textiles, jewelry, and hardware to west Africa; then shipped slaves to Saint Domingue (Haiti), Guadeloupe, and Martinique in the Caribbean; and finally brought sugar and coffee back to France. The French amplified the British system by reexporting sugar to the rest of continental Europe. That sugar was the commodity upon which the Caribbean slave economy rested (see illustration 17.6). Sugarcane was not cultivated in Europe, and sugar was not yet extracted from beets. Slave-produced sugar from America sustained a growing European love of sweets. The European addiction to sugar cost humanity dearly: During the century 1690–1790, one African died for every ton of sugar shipped to Europe. When the consumption of Caribbean sugar reached its peak in 1801, the cost had become one dead slave to provide the sugar for every 250 consumers in Britain.

The scale of the slave trade was immense (see table 17.5). The British Board of Trade estimated in 1709 that British colonies needed twenty-five thousand additional slaves each year—four thousand for Barbados, five thousand for North America, and twelve thousand for Jamaica. When Britain obtained the *Asiento*, the contract for supplying slaves to Spanish America, in 1713, English slave traders brought an additional five thousand slaves for Spanish colonies. The French delivered only four thousand slaves per year in the early eighteenth century, but that figure rose to an average of thirty-seven thousand slaves per year by the 1780s. Britain and France alone sold approximately 3.5 million African slaves in the Americas during the eighteenth century. An average of 10 percent to 20 percent of the slaves died during an Atlantic crossing (50 percent to 75 percent on voyages when scurvy or amoebic dysentery broke out on the ship), so the number of African slaves initially taken was closer to four million. Adding the Portuguese, Dutch, Danish, and Prussian slave trade, the grand total probably surpasses five million Africans. The demand for slaves was so high because the average life expectancy of a Caribbean slave was seven years after arrival.

During the eighteenth century, signs were evident that this economy would also change. Moral revulsion with slavery began to create antislavery opinion, both in Europe and the Americas. An American, Samuel Sewall, published an antislavery tract, *The Selling of Joseph*, as early as 1700. Two Portuguese Jesuits who served in Brazil, Jorge Benci and Giovanni Andreoni, published works in Europe attacking slavery. By 1727 the Society of Friends (widely known as the Quakers) had begun an abolitionist crusade. The moral arguments against slavery made slow progress because they faced powerful economic arguments that slavery was essential for both the colonial and the home economies. The Portuguese example illustrates both the progress and its slowness.

❧ TABLE 17.5 ❧

Estimated Slave Population of European Colonies in the Americas, 1770

Region	Total population	Slave population	Percentage in slavery
Spanish colonies	12,144,000	290,000	2.4
Mainland	12,000,000	240,000	2.0
Caribbean	144,000	50,000	34.7
British colonies	2,600,000	878,000	33.8
Mainland	2,100,000	450,000	21.4
Caribbean	500,000	428,000	85.6
Portuguese Brazil	2,000,000	700,000	35.0
French Caribbean	430,000	379,000	88.1
Dutch Caribbean	90,000	75,000	83.3
Danish Caribbean	25,000	18,000	35.0
Total, Mainland colonies	16,100,000	1,390,000	8.6
Total, Caribbean islands	1,189,000	950,000	79.9

Source: Adapted from data in Robin Blackburn, *The Overthrow of Colonial Slavery, 1776–1848* (London: Verso, 1988), p. 5.

Royal decrees abolished the slavery of American Indians (1755) and Asians (1758), then freed any African slave brought into Portugal (1761), and finally emancipated all African slaves held in Portugal (1773). But these decrees permitted the continuance of the slave trade and the perpetuation of African slavery in the Portuguese colony of Brazil, where it continued until 1888.

DAILY LIFE IN THE OLD REGIME

For most Europeans, the basic conditions of life in the eighteenth century had changed little since the agricultural revolution of Neolithic times. Chapter 18 describes those conditions and shows in dramatic terms how life at the end of the Old Regime differed from that of the present day. It begins by exploring the basic relationships between people and their environment, including the density of population in Europe and the barriers to speedy travel and communication. The chapter then examines the life of ordinary people, beginning with its most striking feature: low life expectancy. The factors that help to explain that high level of mortality, especially inadequate diet and the prevalence of epidemic disease, are then discussed. Finally, the life cycle of those who survived infancy is considered, including such topics as the dangers of childbirth; the Old Regime's understanding of childhood; and its attitudes toward marriage, the family, sexuality, and reproduction.

◆◇◆

People and Space: Population Density, Travel, and Communication

The majority of the people who lived in Europe during the Old Regime never saw a great city or even a town of twenty-five thousand people. Most stayed within a few miles of their home village and the neighboring market town. Studies of birth and death records show that more than 90 percent of the population of the eighteenth century died in the same region where they were born, passing their lives amid relatively few people. Powerful countries and great cities of the eighteenth century were small by twentieth-century standards (see population tables in chapter 17). Great Britain numbered an estimated 6.4 million people in 1700 (less than the state of Georgia today) and Vienna held 114,000 (roughly the size of Fullerton, California, or Tallahassee, Florida). People at the start of the twenty-first century are also accustomed to life in densely concentrated populations. New York City has a population density of more than fifty-five thousand people per square mile, and Maryland has a population density of nearly five hundred people per square mile. The eighteenth century did not know such crowding: Great Britain had a population density of fifty-five people per square mile; Sweden, six (see table 18.1).

TABLE 18.1
European Population Density

Population density is measured by the number of people per square mile.

Country	Population density in 1700	Population density in the 1990s
Dutch republic (Netherlands)	119	959
Italian states (Italy)	112	499
German states (Germany)	98	588
France	92	275
Great Britain	55	616
Spain	38	201
Sweden	6	50

Source: Jack Babuscio and Richard M. Dunn, eds., *European Political Facts, 1648–1789* (London: Macmillian, 1984), pp. 335–53; and *The World Almanac and Book of Facts 1995* (Mahwah, N.J.: World Almanac Books, 1994), pp. 740–839.

Life in a rural world of sparse population was also shaped by the difficulty of travel and communication. The upper classes enjoyed a life of relative mobility that included such pleasures as owning homes in both town and country or taking a "grand tour" of historic cities in Europe. Journeymen who sought experience in their trade, agricultural laborers who were obliged to migrate with seasonal harvests, and peasants who were conscripted into the army were all exceptions in a world of limited mobility. Geographic obstacles, poor roads, weather, and bandits made travel slow and risky. For most people, the pace of travel was walking beside a mule or ox-drawn cart. Only well-to-do people traveled on horseback, fewer still in horse-drawn carriages (see illustration 18.1). In 1705 the twenty-year-old Johann Sebastian Bach wished to hear the greatest organist of that era perform; Bach left his work for two weeks and walked two hundred miles to hear good music.

Travelers were at the mercy of the weather, which often rendered roads impassable because of flooding, mud, or snow. The upkeep of roads and bridges varied greatly. Governments maintained a few post roads, but other roads depended upon the conscription of local labor. An English law of 1691, for example, simply required each parish to maintain the local roads and bridges; if upkeep were poor, the government fined the parish. Brigands also hindered travel. These bandits might become heroes to the peasants who protected them as rebels against authority and as benefactors of the poor, much as Robin Hood is regarded in English

Illustration 18.1

Coach Travel. Horse-drawn carriages and coaches remained the primary form of public transportation in Europe before the railroad age of the nineteenth century. Postal service, business, and government all relied upon a network of highways, stables, and coaching inns. In this illustration, travelers in the Pyrenees wait at a coaching station and hotel while a wheel is repaired.

folklore, but they made travel risky for the few who could afford it.

The fastest travel, for both people and goods, was often by water. Most cities had grown along rivers and coasts. Paris received the grain that sustained it by barges on the Seine; the timber that heated the city was floated down the river. The great transportation projects of the Old Regime were canals connecting these rivers. Travel on the open seas was normally fast, but it depended on fair weather. A voyager might be in England four hours after leaving France or trapped in port for days. If oceanic travel were involved, delays could reach remarkable lengths. In 1747 the electors of Portsmouth, England, selected Captain Edward Legge of the Royal Navy to represent them in Parliament; Legge, whose command had taken him to the Americas, had died eighty-seven days before his election but the news had not yet arrived in Portsmouth.

Travel and communication were agonizingly slow by twenty-first-century standards. In 1734 the coach trip between Edinburgh and London (372 miles) took twelve days; the royal mail along that route required forty-eight hours of constant travel by relay riders. The commercial leaders of Venice could send correspondence to Rome (more than 250 miles) in three to four days, if conditions were favorable; messages to Moscow (more than twelve hundred miles) required about four weeks. When King Louis XV of France died in 1774, this urgent news was rushed to the capitals of Europe via the fastest couriers: It arrived in Vienna and Rome three days later; Berlin, four days; and St. Petersburg, six days.

Life Expectancy in the Old Regime

The living conditions of the average person during the Old Regime holds little appeal for people accustomed to twenty-first-century conveniences. A famous writer of the mid-eighteenth century, Samuel Johnson, described the life of the masses as "little to be enjoyed and much to be endured." The most dramatic illustration of Johnson's point is life expectancy data. Although the figures vary by social class or region, their message is grim. For everyone born during the Old Regime, the average age at death was close to thirty. Demographic studies of northern France at the end of the seventeenth century found that the average age at death was twenty. Data for Sweden in 1755 give an average life of thirty-three. A comprehensive study of villages in southern

England found a range between thirty-five and forty-five. These numbers are misleading because of infant mortality, but they contain many truths about life in the past.

Short life expectancy meant that few people knew their grandparents. Research on a village in central England found that a population of four hundred included only one instance of three generations alive in the same family. A study of Russian demography found more shocking results: Between 20 and 30 percent of all serfs under age fifteen had already lost both parents. Similarly, when the French philosopher Denis Diderot in 1759 returned to the village of his birth at age forty-six, he found that not a single person whom he knew from childhood had survived. Life expectancy was significantly higher for the rich than for the poor. Those who could afford fuel for winter fires, warm clothing, a superior diet, or multiple residences reduced many risks. The rich lived an estimated ten years longer than the average in most regions and seventeen years longer than the poor.

Disease and the Biological Old Regime

Life expectancy averages were low because infant mortality was high, and death rates remained high throughout childhood. The study of northern France found that one-third of all children died each year and only 58 percent reached age fifteen. However, for those who survived infancy, life expectancy rose significantly. In a few healthier regions, especially where agriculture was strong, the people who lived through the terrors of childhood disease could expect to live nearly fifty more years.

The explanation for the shocking death rates and life expectancy figures of the Old Regime has been called the biological old regime, which suggests the natural restrictions created by chronic undernourishment, periodic famine, and unchecked disease. The first fact of existence in the eighteenth century was the probability of death from an infectious disease. Natural catastrophes (such as the Lisbon earthquake of 1755, which killed thirty thousand people) or the human violence of wartime (such as the battle of Blenheim in 1704, which took more than fifty thousand casualties in a single day) were terrible, but more people died from diseases. People who had the good fortune to survive natural and human catastrophe rarely died from heart disease or cancer, the great killers of the early twenty-

TABLE 18.2

The Causes of Death in the Eighteenth Century Compared with the Twentieth Century

	Deaths in Edinburgh in 1740		Deaths in the United States in the 1990s	
Rank	Cause	Percentage	Cause	Percentage
1	Consumption (tuberculosis)	22.4	Heart disease	32.6
2	Smallpox	22.1	Cancer	23.4
3	Fevers (including typhus and typhoid)	13.0	Stroke	6.6
4	Old age	8.2	Pulmonary condition	4.5
5	Measles	8.1	Accident	3.9

Source: Data for 1740 from John D. Post, *Food Shortage, Climatic Variability, and Epidemic Disease in Preindustrial Europe* (Ithaca, N.Y.: Cornell University Press, 1988), p. 241; data for the United States from *The World Almanac and Book of Facts 1995* (Mahwah, N.J.: World Almanac Books, 1994), p. 959.

first century. An examination of the 1740 death records for Edinburgh, for example, finds that the leading causes of death that year were tuberculosis and smallpox, which accounted for nearly half of all deaths (see table 18.2).

Some diseases were pandemic: The germs that spread them circulated throughout Europe at all times. The bacteria that attacked the lungs and caused tuberculosis (called consumption in the eighteenth century) were one such universal risk. Other diseases were endemic: They were a constant threat, but only in certain regions. Malaria, a febrile disease transmitted by mosquitoes, was endemic to warmer regions, especially where swamps or marshes were found. Rome and Venice were still in malarial regions in 1750; when Napoleon's army marched into Italy in 1796, his soldiers began to die from malaria before a single shot had been fired.

The most frightening diseases have always been epidemic diseases—waves of infection that periodically passed through a region. The worst epidemic disease of the Old Regime was smallpox. An epidemic of 1707 killed 36 percent of the population of Iceland. London lost three thousand people to smallpox in 1710, then experienced five more epidemics between 1719 and 1746. An epidemic decimated Berlin in 1740; another killed 6 percent of the population of Rome in 1746. Social historians have estimated that 95 percent of the population contracted smallpox, and 15 percent of all deaths in the eighteenth century can be attributed to it. Those who survived smallpox were immune thereafter, so it chiefly killed the young, accounting for one-third of all childhood deaths. In the eighty years between

1695 and 1775, smallpox killed a queen of England, a king of Austria, a king of Spain, a tsar of Russia, a queen of Sweden, and a king of France. Smallpox ravaged the Habsburgs, the royal family of Austria, and completely changed the history of their dynasty. Between 1654 and 1763, the disease killed nine immediate members of the royal family, causing the succession to the throne to shift four times. The death of Joseph I in 1711 cost the Habsburgs their claim to the throne of Spain, which would have gone to his younger brother Charles. When Charles accepted the Austrian throne, the Spanish crown (which he could not hold simultaneously) passed to a branch of the French royal family. The accession of Charles to the Austrian throne also meant that his daughter, Maria Theresa, would ultimately inherit it—an event that led to years of war.

Although smallpox was the greatest scourge of the eighteenth century, signs of a healthier future were evident. The Chinese and the Turks had already learned the benefits of intentionally infecting children with a mild case of smallpox to make them immune to the disease. A prominent English woman, Lady Mary Wortley Montagu, learned of the Turkish method of inoculating the young in 1717, and after it succeeded on her son, she became the first European champion of the procedure (see document 18.1). Inoculation (performed by opening a vein and introducing the disease) won acceptance slowly, often through royal patronage. Empress Maria Theresa had her family inoculated after she saw four of her children die of smallpox. Catherine the Great followed suit in 1768. But inoculation killed some people, and many feared it. The French outlawed the procedure in 1762, and the Vatican taught acceptance

◈ DOCUMENT 18.1 ◈

Mary Montagu: The Turkish Smallpox Inoculation

Lady Mary Wortley Montagu (1689–1762) was the wife of the British ambassador to the Ottoman Empire. While living in Constantinople, she observed the Turkish practice of inoculating children with small amounts of smallpox and was amazed at the Turkish ability to prevent the disease. The following excerpts are from a letter to a friend in which Montagu explains her discovery.

Mary Montagu to Sarah Chiswell, 1 April 1717:

I am going to tell you a thing that I am sure will make you wish yourself here. The smallpox, so fatal and so general amongst us, is here entirely harmless [because of] the invention of "engrafting" (which is the term they give it). There is a set of old women who make it their business to perform the operation. Every autumn in the month of September, when the great heat is abated, people send to one another to know if any of their family has a mind to have the smallpox. They make parties for this purpose, and when they are met (commonly 15 or 16 together), the old woman comes with a nutshell full of the matter of the best sort of smallpox [the fluid from a smallpox infection] and asks what veins you please to have opened. She immediately rips open that which you offer to her with a large needle (which gives no more pain than a common scratch) and puts into the vein as much venom as can lie upon the head of her needle, and after binds up the little wound with a hollow bit of shell, and in this manner opens four or five veins. . . .

The children, or young patients, play together all the rest of the day and are in perfect health till the eighth day. Then the fever begins to seize them and they keep to their beds for two days, very seldom three days. They have very rarely above 20 or 30 [smallpox sores] on their faces, which never leave marks, and in eight days time they are as well as before their illness. . . .

Every year thousands undergo this operation . . . [and] there is no example of any one that has died of it. You may believe I am very well satisfied of the safety of the experiment since I intend to try it on my dear little son. I am a patriot enough to take pains to bring this useful invention into fashion in England. . . .

Montagu, Mary Wortley. *The Complete Letters of Lady Mary Wortley Montagu,* ed. Robert Halsband. 3 vols. Oxford, England: Clarendon Press, 1965.

of the disease as a "visitation of divine will." Nonetheless, the death of Louis XV led to the inoculation of his three sons.

While smallpox devastated all levels of society, some epidemic diseases chiefly killed the poor. Typhus, spread by the bite of body lice, was common in squalid urban housing, jails, and army camps. Typhoid fever, transmitted by contaminated food or water, was equally at home in the unsanitary homes that peasants shared with their animals.

The most famous epidemic disease in European history was the bubonic plague, the Black Death that killed millions of people in the fourteenth century. The plague, introduced by fleas borne on rodents, no longer ravaged Europe, but it killed tens of thousands in the eighteenth century and evoked a special cultural terror. Between 1708 and 1713, the plague spread from Poland across central and northern Europe. Half the city of Danzig died, and the death rate was only slightly lower in Prague, Copenhagen, and Stockholm. Another epidemic spread from Russia in 1719. It reached the port of Marseilles in 1720, and forty thousand people perished. Russia experienced another epidemic in 1771, killing fifty-seven thousand people in Moscow alone.

Public Health before the Germ Theory

Ignorance and poverty compounded the dangers of the biological old regime. The germ theory of disease transmission—that invisible microorganisms such as bacteria and viruses spread diseases—had been suggested centuries earlier, but governments, scientists, and churches dismissed this theory until the late nineteenth century. Instead, the dominant theory was the miasma theory of contagion, holding that diseases spring from rotting matter in the earth. Acceptance of the miasma theory perpetuated dangerous conditions. Europeans did not understand the dangers of unsanitary housing, including royal palaces. Louis XIV's palace at Versailles was perhaps the greatest architectural ornament of an epoch, but human excrement accumulated in the corners and corridors of Versailles, just as it accumulated in dung-heaps alongside peasant cottages. One of the keenest observers of that age, the duke de Saint-Simon, noted that even the royal apartments at Versailles opened out "over the privies and other dark and evil smelling places."

The great cities of Europe were filthy. Few had more than rudimentary sewer systems. Gradually, enlightened monarchs realized that they must clean their capitals, as King Charles III (Don Carlos) ordered for Madrid in 1761. This Spanish decree required all households to install piping on their property to carry solid waste to a sewage pit, ordered the construction of tiled channels in the streets to carry liquid wastes, and committed the state to clean public places. Such public policies significantly improved urban sanitation, but they were partial steps, as the Spanish decree recognized, "until such time as it be possible to construct the underground sewage system." The worst sanitation was often found in public institutions. The standard French army barracks of the eighteenth century had rooms measuring sixteen feet by eighteen feet; each room accommodated thirteen to fifteen soldiers, sharing four or five beds and innumerable diseases. Prisons were worse yet.

Another dangerous characteristic of Old Regime housing was a lack of sufficient heat. During the eighteenth century the climatic condition known as the Little Ice Age persisted, with average temperatures a few degrees lower than the twentieth century experienced. Winters were longer and harder, summers and growing seasons were shorter. Glaciers advanced in the north, and timberlines receded on mountains. In European homes, the heat provided by open fires was so inadequate that even nobles saw their inkwells and wine freeze in severe weather. Among the urban poor, where many families occupied unheated rooms in the basement or attic, the chief source of warmth was body heat generated by the entire family sleeping together. Some town dwellers tried heating their garrets by burning coal, charcoal, or peat in open braziers, without chimneys or ventilation, creating a grim duel between freezing cold and poisonous air. Peasants found warmth by bringing their livestock indoors and sleeping with the animals, exacerbating the spread of disease.

In a world lacking a scientific explanation of epidemic disease, religious teaching exercised great influence over public health standards. Churches offered solace to the afflicted, but they also offered another explanation of disease: It was the scourge of God. This theory of disease, like the miasma theory, contributed to the inattention to public health. Many churches organized religious processions and ceremonies of expia-tion in hopes of divine cures. Unfortunately, such public assemblies often spread disease by bringing healthy people into contact with the infected. Processions and ceremonies also prevented effective measures because they persuaded churches to oppose quarantines. Churches were not alone; merchants in most towns joined them in fighting quarantines.

Medicine and the Biological Old Regime

Most Europeans during the Old Regime never received medical attention from trained physicians. Few doctors were found in rural areas. Peasants relied on folk medicine, consulted unlicensed healers, or allowed illness to run its course. Many town dwellers received their medical advice from apothecaries (druggists). The propertied classes could consult trained physicians, although this was often a mixed blessing. Many medical doctors were quacks, and even the educated often had minimal training. The best medical training in Europe was found at the University of Leiden in Holland, where Hermann Boerhaave pioneered clinical instruction at bedsides, and similar programs were created at the College of Physicians in Edinburgh in 1681 and in Vienna in 1745. Yet Jean-Paul Marat, one of the leaders of the French Revolution, received a medical degree at Edinburgh after staying there for a few weeks during the summer of 1774.

Medical science practiced curative medicine, following traditions that seem barbaric to later centuries. The pharmacopeia of medicinal preparations still favored ingredients such as unicorn's horn (ivory was usually used), crushed lice, incinerated toad, or ground shoe leather. One cherished medication, highly praised in the first edition of the *Encyclopaedia Britannica* (1771), was usnea, the moss scraped from the scalp of prisoners hung in irons. The medical profession also favored treatments such as bleeding (the intentional drawing of blood from a sick person) or purging the ill with emetics and enemas. The argument for bleeding was derived from the observation that if blood were drawn, the body temperature dropped. Because fevers accompanied most diseases, bleeding was employed to reduce the fever. This treatment often hastened death. King Louis XV of France was virtually bled to death by his physicians in 1774, although officially he succumbed to smallpox. As Baron von Leibnitz, a distinguished German philosopher and scientist, observed, "[A] great doctor kills more people than a great general."

The treatment given to King Charles II of England in 1685, as he died of an apparent embolism (a clot in

Illustration 18.2

An Eighteenth-Century Hospital. This scene of a German hospital ward in Hamburg depicts many aspects of pre-modern medicine. Note the mixture of patients with all afflictions, the nonsterile conditions, the amputation of a leg on a conscious patient, the arrival of a daily ration of bread, and the administration of the last rites to a patient.

an artery), shows the state of learned medicine. A team of a dozen physicians first drew a pint of blood from his right arm. They then cut open his right shoulder and cupped it with a vacuum jar to draw more blood. Charles then received an emetic to induce vomiting, followed by a purgative, then a second purgative. Next came an enema of antimony and herbs, followed by a second enema and a third purgative. Physicians then shaved the king's head, blistered it with heated glass, intentionally broke the blisters, and smeared a powder into the wounds (to "strengthen his brain"). Next came a plaster of pitch and pigeon excrement. Death was probably a relief to the tortured patient.

Hospitals were also scarce in the Old Regime. Nearly half of the counties of England contained no hospital in 1710; by 1800, there were still only four thousand hospital beds in the entire country, half of them in London. Avoiding hospitals was generally safer in any case (see illustration 18.2). These institutions had typically been founded by monastic orders as refuges for the destitute sick, and most of them were still operated by churches in the eighteenth century. There were a few specialized hospitals (the first children's clinic was founded at London in 1779), and most hospitals typically mixed together poor patients with a variety of diseases that spread inside the hospital. Patients received a minimal diet and rudimentary care but little medical treatment. The history of surgery is even more frightening. In many regions, surgeons were still members of the barbers' guild. Because eighteenth-century physicians did not believe in the germ theory

of disease transmission, surgeons often cut people in squalid surroundings with no thought for basic cleanliness of their hands or their instruments. Without antisepsis, gangrene (then called hospital putrefaction) was a common result of surgery. No general anesthetics were available, so surgeons operated upon a fully conscious patient.

In these circumstances, opium became a favorite medication of well-to-do patients. It was typically taken as a tincture with alcohol known as laudanum, and it was available from apothecaries without a prescription. Laudanum drugged the patient, and it often addicted survivors to opium, but it reduced suffering. Many famous figures of the eighteenth and nineteenth centuries died, as did the artist Sir Joshua Reynolds in 1792, "all but speechless from laudanum."

Subsistence Diet and the Biological Old Regime

The second critical feature of the biological old regime was a dangerously inadequate food supply. In all regions of Europe, much of the population lived with chronic undernourishment, dreading the possibility of famine. A subsistence diet (one that barely met the minimum needed to sustain life) weakened the immune system, making people more vulnerable to contracting diseases and less able to withstand their ravages. Diet was thus a major factor in the Old Regime's high mortality rates and short life expectancies.

Most of Europe lived chiefly on starches. The biblical description of bread as "the staff of life" was true, and most people obtained 50 percent to 75 percent of their total calories from bread. Interruptions of the grain supply meant suffering and death. In good times, a peasant family ate several pounds of bread a day, up to three pounds per capita; in lean times, they might share one pound of bread. A study of the food supply in Belgium has shown that the nation consumed a per capita average of one-and-a-quarter pounds of cereal grains per day. A study of eastern Prussia has shown that the adult population lived on nearly three pounds of grain per day. Peasant labors there received their entire annual wages in starches; the quantity ranged from thirty-two bushels of grain (1694) to twenty-five bushels of grain and one of peas (1760).

Bread made from wheat was costly because wheat yielded few grains harvested per grain sown. As a result, peasants lived on coarser, but bountiful, grains. Their heavy, dark bread normally came from rye and barley. In some poor areas, such as Scotland, oats were the staple grain. To save valuable fuel, many villages baked bread in large loaves once a month, or even once a season. This created a hard bread that had to be broken with a hammer and soaked in liquid before it could be eaten. For variety, cereals could be mixed with liquid (usually water) without baking to create a porridge or gruel.

Supplements to the monotonous diet of starches varied from region to region, but meat was a rarity. In a world without canning or refrigeration, meat was consumed only when livestock were slaughtered, in a salted or smoked form of preservation, or in a rancid condition. A study of the food supply in Rome in the 1750s has shown that the average daily consumption of meat amounted to slightly more than two ounces. For the lower classes, that meant a few ounces of sausage or dried meat per week. In that same decade, Romans consumed bread at an average varying between one and two pounds per day. Fruits and fresh vegetables were seasonal and typically limited to those regions where they were cultivated. A fresh orange was thus a luxury to most Europeans, and a fresh pineapple was rare and expensive. Occasional dairy products plus some cooking fats and oils (chiefly lard in northern Europe and olive oil in the south) brought urban diets close to twenty-five hundred calories per day in good times. A study of Parisian workers in 1780 found that adult males engaged in physical labor averaged two thousand calories per day, mostly from bread. (Figures of thirty-five hundred to four thousand are common today

among males doing physical labor.) Urban workers often spent more than half of their wages for food, even when they just ate bread. A study of Berlin at the end of the eighteenth century showed that a working-class family might spend more than 70 percent of its income on food (see table 18.3). Peasants ate only the few vegetables grown in kitchen gardens that they could afford to keep out of grain production.

Beverages varied regionally. In many places, the water was unhealthy to drink and peasants avoided it without knowing the scientific explanation of their fears. Southern Europe produced and consumed large quantities of wine, and beer could be made anywhere that grain was grown. In 1777 King Frederick the Great of Prussia urged his people to drink beer, stating that he had been raised on it and believed that a nation "nourished on beer" could be "depended on to endure hardships." Such beers were often dark, thick, and heavy. When Benjamin Franklin arrived in England, he called the beer "as black as bull's blood and as thick as mustard."

Wine and beer were consumed as staples of the diet, and peasants and urban workers alike derived

TABLE 18.3

Food in the Budget of a Berlin Worker's Family, c. 1800

Expense	Percentage
Food	
Bread	45
Other vegetable products	12
Animal products (meat and dairy)	15
Beverages	2
Total food	74
Nonfood	
Housing	14
Heating, lighting	7
Clothing, other expenses	6
Total Nonfood	27

Note: Figures exceed 100 percent because of rounding.

Source: From data in Fernand Braudel, *The Structures of Everyday Life* (New York, N.Y.: Harper and Row, 1981), p. 132.

Illustration 18.3

/// **Alcohol.** Alcohol consumption rates during the eighteenth century were higher than they are today. Drinking to excess was one behavior pattern that cut across social classes, from the taverns in poor districts advertising "dead drunk for a penny" to the falling down drunks of the upper class depicted in Hogarth's "A Midnight Modern Conversation" here. Note that smoking pipes is nearly universal and that women are excluded from this event. See also the chamber pot in the lower right corner.

much of their calories and carbohydrates from them, partly because few nonalcoholic choices were available. The consumption of milk depended upon the local economy. Beverages infused in water (coffee, tea, cocoa) became popular in European cities when global trading made them affordable. The Spanish introduced the drinking of chocolate (which was only a beverage until the nineteenth century) but it long remained a costly drink. Coffee drinking was brought to Europe from the Middle East, and it became a great vogue after 1650, producing numerous urban coffeehouses. But infused beverages never replaced wine and beer in the diet. Some governments feared that coffeehouses were centers of subversion and restricted them more than the taverns. Others worried about the mercantilist implications of coffee and tea imports. English coffee imports, for example, sextupled between 1700 and 1785, leading the government to tax tea and coffee. The king of Sweden issued an edict denouncing coffee in 1746, and when that failed to control the national addiction, he decreed total prohibition in 1756. Coffee smuggling produced such criminal problems, however, that the king legalized the drink again in 1766 and collected a heavy excise tax on it. Even with such popularity, infused beverages did not curtail the remarkable rate of alcohol consumption (see illustration 18.3). In addition to wines and beer, eighteenth-century England drank an enormous amount of gin. Only a steep gin tax in 1736 and vigorous enforcement of a Tippling Act of 1751 reduced consumption from 8.5 million gallons of gin per year to 2.1 million gallons during the 1750s.

The Columbian Exchange and the European Diet

The most important changes in the European diet of the Old Regime resulted from the gradual adoption of foods found in the Americas. In a reciprocal Columbian exchange of plants and animals unknown on the other continent, Europe and America both acquired new foods. No Italian tomato sauce or French fried potato existed before the Columbian exchange because the tomato and potato were plants native to the Americas and unknown in Europe. Similarly, the Columbian exchange introduced maize (American corn), peanuts, many peppers and beans, and cacao to Europe. The Americas had no wheat fields, grapevines, or melon patches; no horses, sheep, cattle, pigs, goats, or burros. In the second stage of this exchange, European plants established in the Americas began to flourish and yield exportation to Europe. The most historic example of this was the establishment of the sugarcane plantations in the Caribbean, where slave labor made sugar commonly available in Europe for the first time, but at a horrific human price (see map 18.1).

Europe's first benefit from the Columbian exchange came from the potato, which changed diets in the eighteenth century. The Spanish imported the potato in the sixteenth century after finding the Incas cultivating it in Peru, but Europeans initially refused to eat it because folk wisdom considered tubers dangerous. Churches opposed the potato because the Bible did not mention it. Potatoes, however, offer the tremendous advantage of yielding more calories per acre than grains do. In much of northern Europe, especially in western Ireland

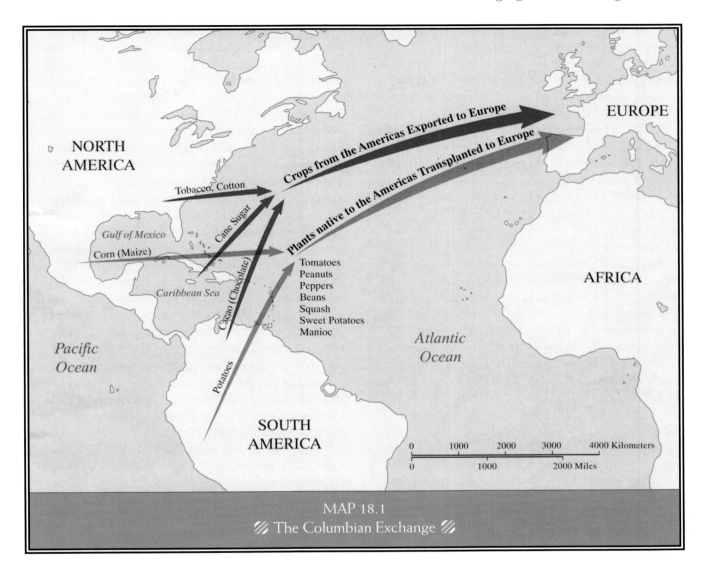

NORTH AMERICA

Tobacco, Cotton

Gulf of Mexico

Corn (Maize)

Caribbean Sea

Cane Sugar

Cacao (Chocolate)

Crops from the Americas Exported to Europe

Plants native to the Americas Transplanted to Europe

EUROPE

AFRICA

Tomatoes
Peanuts
Peppers
Beans
Squash
Sweet Potatoes
Manioc

Pacific Ocean

Potatoes

Atlantic Ocean

SOUTH AMERICA

| 0 | 1000 | 2000 | 3000 | 4000 Kilometers |

| 0 | 1000 | 2000 Miles |

MAP 18.1
The Columbian Exchange

and northern Germany, short and rainy summer seasons severely limited the crops that could be grown and the population that could be supported. Irish peasants discovered that just one acre of potatoes, planted in soil that was poor for grains, could support a full family. German peasants learned that they could grow potatoes in their fallow fields during crop rotation, then discovered an acre of potatoes could feed as many people as four acres of the rye that they traditionally planted. Peasants soon found another of the advantages of the potato: It could be left in the ground all winter without harvesting it. Ripe grain must be harvested and stored, becoming an easy target for civilian tax collectors or military requisitioners. Potatoes could be left in the ground until the day they were eaten, thereby providing peasants with much greater security. The steady growth of German population compared with France during the eighteenth and nineteenth centuries (with

tremendous historic implications) is partly the result of this peasant decision and the educational work of agronomists such as Antoine Parmentier, who showed its merits in his *Treatise on the Uses of the Potato*. Just as the potato changed the history of Germany and Ireland, the introduction of maize changed other regions. Historians of the Balkans credit the nutritional advantages of maize with the population increase and better health that facilitated the Serbian and Greek struggles for independence.

Famine in the Old Regime

Even after the introduction of the potato and maize, much of Europe lived on a subsistence diet. In bad times, the result was catastrophic. Famines, usually the result of two consecutive bad harvests, produced starvation. In such times, peasants ate their seed grain or harvested unripe grain and roasted it, prolonging both life and famine. They turned to making bread from ground chestnuts or acorns. They ate grass and weeds, cats and dogs, rodents, even human flesh. Such disasters were not rare. The records of Tuscany show that the three-hundred-year period between 1450 and 1750 included one hundred years of famine and sixteen years of bountiful harvests. Agriculture was more successful in England, but the period between 1660 and 1740 saw one bad harvest in every four years. France, an agriculturally fortunate country, experienced sixteen years of national famine during the eighteenth century, plus local famines.

The worst famine of the Old Regime, and one of the most deadly events in European history, occurred in Finland in 1696–97. The extreme cold weather of the Little Ice Age produced in Finland a summer too short for grain to ripen. Between one-fourth and one-third of the entire nation died before that famine passed—a death rate that equaled the horrors of the bubonic plague. The weather produced other famines in that decade. In northern Europe, excess rain caused crops to rot in the field before ripening. In Mediterranean Europe, especially in central Spain, a drought followed by an onslaught of grasshoppers produced a similar catastrophe. Hunger also followed seasonal fluctuations. In lean years, the previous year's grain might be consumed before July, when the new grain could be harvested. Late spring and early summer were consequently dangerous times when the food supply had political significance. Winter posed special threats for city dwellers. If the rivers and canals froze, the barges that supplied the cities could not move, and the water-powered mills could not grind flour.

Food supplies were such a concern in the Old Regime that marriage contracts and wills commonly provided food pensions. These pensions were intended to protect a wife or aged relatives by guaranteeing an annual supply of food. An examination of these pensions in southern France has shown that most of the food to be provided was in cereal grains. The typical form was a lifetime annuity intended to provide a supplement; the average grain given in wills provided fewer than fourteen hundred calories per day.

Diet, Disease, and Appearance

Malnutrition, famine, and disease were manifested in human appearance. A diet so reliant on starches meant that people were short compared with later standards. For example, the average adult male of the eighteenth

century stood slightly above five feet tall. Napoleon, ridiculed today for being so short, was as tall as most of his soldiers. Meticulous records kept for Napoleon's Army of Italy in the late 1790s (a victorious army) reveal that conscripts averaged 5'2" in height. Many famous figures of the era had similar heights: the notorious Marquis de Sade stood 5'3". Conversely, people known for their height were not tall by later standards. A French diplomat, Prince Talleyrand, appears in letters and memoirs to have had an advantage in negotiations because he "loomed over" other statesmen. Talleyrand stood 5'8". The kings of Prussia recruited peasants considered to be "giants" to serve in the royal guards at Potsdam; a height of 6'0" defined a giant. Extreme height did occur in some families. The Russian royal family, the Romanovs, produced some monarchs nearly seven feet tall. For the masses, diet limited their height. The superior diet of the aristocracy made them taller than peasants, just as it gave them a greater life expectancy; aristocrats explained such differences by their natural superiority as a caste.

Just as diet shaped appearance, so did disease. Vitamin and mineral deficiencies led to a variety of afflictions, such as rickets and scrofula. Rickets marked people with bone deformities; scrofula produced hard tumors on the body, especially under the chin. The most widespread effect of disease came from smallpox. As its name indicates, the disease often left pockmarks on its victims, the result of scratching the sores, which itched terribly. Because 95 percent of the population contracted smallpox, pockmarked faces were common. The noted Anglo-Irish dramatist Oliver Goldsmith described this in 1760:

> Lo, the smallpox with horrid glare
> Levelled its terrors at the fair;
> And, rifling every youthful grace,
> Left but the remnant of a face.

Smallpox and diseases that discolored the skin such as jaundice, which left a yellow complexion, explain the eighteenth-century popularity of heavy makeup and artificial "beauty marks" (which could cover a pockmark) in the fashions of the wealthy. Other fashion trends of the age originated in poor public health. The vogue for wigs and powdered hair for men and women alike derived in part from infestation by lice. Head lice could be controlled by shaving the head and wearing a wig.

Dental disease marked people with missing or dark, rotting teeth. The absence of sugar in the diet delayed tooth decay, but oral hygiene scarcely existed because

❧ TABLE 18.4 ❧

A Comparison of Life Cycles

Life cycle characteristic	Sweden, 1778–82	United States (1990 census)
Annual birthrate	34.5 per 1,000 population	15.6 per 1,000 population
Infant mortality (age 0–1)	211.6 deaths per 1,000 live births	9.2 deaths per 1,000 live births
Life expectancy at birth		
Male	36 years	71.8 years
Female	39 years	78.8 years
Life expectancy at age 1		
Male	44 years longer (45 total years)	72.3 years longer (73.3 total)
Female	46 years longer (47 total years)	78.9 years longer (79.9 total)
Life expectancy at age 50		
Male	19 years longer (69 total years)	26.7 years longer (76.7 total)
Female	20 years longer (70 total years)	31.6 years longer (81.6 total)
Population distribution	ages 0–14 = 31.9%	ages 0–19 = 28.9%
	ages 15–64 = 63.2%	ages 20–64 = 58.7%
	ages 65+ = 4.9%	ages 65+ = 12.5%
Annual death rate	25.9 deaths per 1,000 population	8.5 deaths per 1,000 population

Source: Swedish data from Carlo M. Cipolla, *Before the Industrial Revolution* (New York, N.Y.: Norton, 1976), pp. 286–87; U.S. data from *The World Almanac and Book of Fact, 1995* (Mahwah, N.J.: World Almanac Book, 1994), p. 957; and *Information Please Almanac, Atlas, and Yearbook 1994* (Boston, Mass.: Houghton Mifflin Co., 1993), pp. 829, 848, 850–52.

people did not know that bacteria caused their intense toothaches. Medical wisdom held that the pain came from a worm that bored into teeth. Anton van Leeuwenhoek, the Dutch naturalist who invented the microscope, had seen bacteria in dental tartar in the late seventeenth century, and Pierre Fauchard, a French physician considered the founder of modern dentistry, had denounced the worm theory, but their science did not persuade their colleagues. For brave urban dwellers, barber-surgeons offered the painful process of extraction. A simple, but excruciating, method involved inserting a whole peppercorn into a large cavity; the pepper expanded until the tooth shattered, facilitating extraction. More often, dental surgeons gripped the unanesthetized patient's head with their knees and used tongs to shake the tooth loose. Whether or not one faced such dreadful pain, dental disease left most people with only a partial set of teeth by their forties.

The Life Cycle: Birth

Consideration of the basic conditions of life provides a fundamental perspective on any period of the past. So-

cial historians also use another set of perspectives to examine the history of daily life: an examination of the life cycle from birth to old age (see table 18.4). Few experiences better illustrate the perils of the Old Regime than the process of entering it. Pregnancy and birth were extremely dangerous for mother and child. Malnutrition and poor prenatal care caused a high rate of miscarriages, stillbirths, and deformities. Childbirth was still an experience without anesthesia or antisepsis. The greatest menace to the mother was puerperal fever (child-bed fever), an acute infection of the genital tract resulting from the absence of aseptic methods. This disease swept Europe, particularly the few "laying-in" hospitals for women. An epidemic of puerperal fever in 1773 was so severe that folk memories in northern Italy recalled that not a single pregnant woman survived. Common diseases, such as rickets (from vitamin deficiency), made deliveries difficult and caused bone deformities in babies. No adequate treatment was available for hemorrhaging, which could cause death by bleeding or slower death by gangrene. Few ways existed to lower the risks of difficult deliveries. Surgical birth by a cesarean section gave the mother one chance in a thousand of surviving. Attempts to deliver a baby by using large forceps saved many lives but often produced horrifying injuries to the newborn or hemorrhaging in the mother. A delicate balance thus existed between the deep pride in bearing children and a deep fear of doing so. One of the most noted women of letters in early modern Europe, Madame de Sévigné, advised her daughter of two rules for survival: "Don't get pregnant and don't catch smallpox."

The established churches, backed by the medical profession, preached acceptance of the pain of childbirth by teaching that it represented the divine will. The explanation lay in the Bible. For "the sin of Eve" in succumbing to Satan and being "the devil's gateway" to Adam, God punished all women with the words: "I will greatly multiply thy sorrow and thy conception; in sorrow thou shalt bring forth children" (Gen. 3:16). Even when the means to diminish the pain of childbirth became available, this argument sustained opposition to it.

The Life Cycle: Infancy and Childhood

Statistics show that surviving the first year of infancy was more difficult than surviving birth. All across Europe, between 20 percent and 30 percent of the babies born died before their first birthday (see table 18.5). An additional one-fourth of all children did not live to be eight, meaning that approximately half of the population died in infancy or early childhood. A noted scientist of the 1760s, Michael Lomonosev, calculated that half of the infants born in Russia died before the age of three. So frightful was this toll that many families did not name a child until its first birthday; others gave a cherished family name to more than one child in the hope that one of them would carry it to adulthood. Johann Sebastian Bach fathered twenty children in two marriages and reckoned himself fortunate that ten lived into adulthood. The greatest historian of the century, Edward Gibbon, was the only child of seven in his family to survive infancy.

The newborn were acutely vulnerable to the biological old regime. Intestinal infections killed many in the first months. Unheated housing claimed more. Epidemic diseases killed more infants and young children than adults because some diseases, such as measles and smallpox, left surviving adults immune to them. The dangers touched all social classes. Madame de Montespan, the mistress of King Louis XIV of France, had seven children with him; three were born crippled or deformed, three others died in childhood, and one reached adulthood in good health.

TABLE 18.5

Infant Mortality in the Eighteenth Century

Percentages represent deaths before the first birthday; they do not include stillbirths.

Country	Period	Percentage of deaths before age 1
England	pre-1750	18.7
	1740–90	16.1
	1780–1820	12.2
France	pre-1750	25.2
	1740–90	21.3
	1780–1820	19.5
German states	pre-1750	15.4
	1740–90	38.8
	1780–1820	23.6
Spain	pre-1750	28.1
	1740–90	27.3
	1780–1820	22.0
Sweden	pre-1750	n.a.
	1740–90	22.5
	1780–1820	18.7
United States	1995	0.8

Source: European data from Michael W. Flinn, *The European Demographic System, 1500–1820* (Baltimore, Md.: Johns Hopkins University Press, 1971), p.92; U.S. data from *The World Almanac and Book of Facts, 1997* (Mahwah, N.J.: World Almanac Books, 1996), p. 962.
n.a. = Not available.

Eighteenth-century parents commonly killed unwanted infants (daughters more often than sons) before diseases did. Infanticide—frequently by smothering the baby, usually by abandoning an infant to the elements—has a long history in Western culture. The mythical founders of Rome depicted on many emblems of that city, Romulus and Remus, were abandoned infants who were raised by a wolf; the newborn Moses was abandoned to his fate on the Nile. Infanticide did not constitute murder in eighteenth-century British law (it was manslaughter) if done by the mother before the baby reached age one. In France, however, where infanticide was more common, Louis XIV ordered capital punishment for it, although few mothers were ever executed. The frequency of infanticide provoked instructions that all priests read the law in church in 1707 and again in 1731. A study of police records has found that more than 10 percent of all women arrested in Paris in the eighteenth century were nonetheless charged with infanticide. In central and eastern Europe, many midwives were also "killing nurses" who murdered babies for their parents.

A slightly more humane reaction to unwanted babies was to abandon them in public places in the hope that someone else would care for them. That happened so often that cities established hospitals for foundlings. The practice had begun at Rome in the late Middle Ages when Pope Innocent III found that he could seldom cross the Tiber River without seeing babies thrown into it. Paris established its foundling hospital in 1670. Thomas Coram opened the foundling hospital at London in 1739 because he could not endure the frequency with which he saw dying babies lying in the gutters and dead ones thrown onto dung-heaps. The London Foundling Hospital could scarcely handle all of the city's abandoned babies: In 1758, twenty-three hundred foundlings (under age one) were found abandoned in the streets of London. Abandonment increased in periods of famine and when the illegitimate birthrate rose (as it did during the eighteenth century). French data show that the famine of 1693–94 doubled the abandonment of children at Paris and tripled it at Lyon. Abandonments at Paris grew to an annual average of five thousand in the late eighteenth century, with a peak of 7,676 in 1772, which is a rate of twenty-one babies abandoned every day. Studies of foundlings in Italy have shown that 11 percent to 15 percent of all babies born at Milan between 1700 and 1729 were abandoned each year; at Venice, the figures ranged between 8 percent and 9 percent in 1756–87 (see illustration 18.4).

The abandonment of children at this rate overwhelmed the ability of church or state to help. With 390,000 abandonments at the Foundling Hospital of Paris between 1640 and 1789—with thirty abandonments on the single night of April 20, 1720—the prospects for these children were bleak. Finances were inadequate, partly because churches feared that fine facilities might encourage illicit sexuality, so the conditions in foundling homes stayed grim. Whereas 50 percent of the general population survived childhood, only 10 percent of abandoned children reached age ten. The infant (before age one) death rates for foundling homes in the late eighteenth century were 90 percent in Dublin, 80 percent in Paris, and only 52 percent in London (where infants were farmed out to wet nurses). Of 37,600 children admitted to the Foundling Hospital of Moscow between 1766 and 1786, more than thirty thousand died. The prospects of the survivors were poor, but one noteworthy exception was Jean d'Alembert, a mathematician and coeditor of the

Illustration 18.4

Abandoned Children. One of the most common forms of population control in the eighteenth century (and continuing through the nineteenth century) was the abandonment of newborn children. Because so many babies were left at churches and public buildings, and a shocking number were left to die outdoors, governments created foundling homes where babies could be abandoned. To encourage mothers to use foundling homes, many of them (such as this one in Italy) built revolving doors to the outside, allowing women to leave a baby without being seen or speaking to anyone.

Encyclopédie, who was discovered in a pine box at a Parisian church in 1717.

Young children were often separated from their parents for long periods of time. Immediately after birth, many were sent to wet nurses, foster mothers whose occupation was the breast feeding of infants. The studies of France show that more than 95 percent of the babies born in Paris in 1780 were nursed commercially, 75 percent going to wet nurses in the provinces. As breast feeding normally lasted twelve to eighteen months, only wealthy parents (who could hire a live-in wet nurse) or the poorest might see their infant children with any frequency. The great French novelist Honoré de Balzac was born in 1799 and immediately dispatched to a wet nurse; he bitterly remembered his infancy as being "neglected by my family for three years."

Infant care by rural wet nurses was not universal. It was most common in towns and cities, especially in social classes that could afford the service. The poor usually fed infants gruel—flour mixed in milk, or bread crumbs in water—by dipping a finger into it and letting the baby suck the finger. Upper-class families in England, France, and northern Italy chose wet-nursing; fewer did so in Central Europe. Every king of France, starting with Louis IX (Saint Louis), was nurtured by a succession of royal nurses; but mothers in the Habsburg royal family, including the empress Maria Theresa, were expected to nurse their own children.

Separation from parents remained a feature of life for young children after their weaning. Both Catholicism, which perceived early childhood as an age of innocence, and Protestantism, which held children to be marked by original sin, advocated the separation of the child from the corrupt world of adults. This meant the segregation of children from many parental activities as well as the segregation of boys and girls. Many extreme cases existed among the aristocracy. The Marquis de Lafayette, the hero of the American revolution, lost his father in infancy; his mother left the infant at the family's provincial estate while she resided in Paris and visited him during a brief vacation once a year. Balzac went straight from his wet nurse to a Catholic boarding school where the Oratorian Brothers allowed him no vacations and his mother visited him twice in six years.

Family structures were changing in early modern times, but most children grew up in patriarchal families. Modern parent-child relationships, with more emphasis upon affection than upon discipline, were beginning to appear. However, most children still lived with the emotional detachment of both parents and the stern discipline of a father whose authority had the sanction of law. The Russian novelist Sergei Aksakov recalled that, when his mother had rocked her infant daughter to sleep in the 1780s, relatives rebuked her for showing "such exaggerated love," which they considered contrary to good parenting and "a crime against God." Children in many countries heard the words of Martin Luther repeated: "I would rather have a dead son than a disobedient one."

Childhood had not yet become the distinct and separate phase of life that it later became. In many ways, children passed directly from a few years of infancy into treatment as virtual adults. Middle- and upper-class boys of the eighteenth century made a direct transition from wearing the gowns and frocks of infancy into wearing the pants and panoply (such as swords) of adulthood. This rite of passage, when boys went from the care of women to the care of men, normally happened at approximately age seven. European traditions and laws varied, but in most economic, legal, and religious ways, boys became adults between seven and fourteen. Peasant children became members of the household economy almost immediately, assuming such duties as tending to chickens or hoeing the kitchen garden. In the towns, a child seeking to learn a craft and enter a guild might begin with an apprenticeship (with another family) as early as age seven. Children of the elite were turned over to tutors or governesses, or they were sent away to receive their education at boarding schools. Children of all classes began to become adults by law at age seven. In English law seven was the adult age at which a child could be flogged or executed; the Spanish Inquisition withheld adult interrogation until age thirteen. Twelve was the most common adult age at which children could consent to marriage or to sexual relations.

Tradition and law treated girls differently from boys. In the Roman law tradition, prevalent across southern Europe and influential in most countries, girls never became adults in the legal sense of obtaining rights in their own name. Instead, a patriarchal social order expected fathers to exercise the rights of their daughters until they married; women's legal rights then passed to their husbands. Most legal systems contained other double standards for young men and women. The earliest age for sexual consent was typically younger for a girl than for a boy, although standards of respectable behavior were much stricter for young women than for young men. Economic considerations also created double standards: A family might send a daughter to the convent, for example, instead of providing her with a dowry.

The Life Cycle: Marriage and the Family

Despite the early ages at which children entered the adult world, marriage was normally postponed until later in life. Royal or noble children might sometimes be married in childhood for political or economic reasons, but most of the population married at significantly older ages than those common in the twentieth century.

A study of seventeenth-century marriages in southern England has found that the average age of men at a first marriage was nearly twenty-seven; their brides averaged 23.6 years of age. Research on England in the eighteenth century shows that the age at marriage rose further. In rural Europe, men married at twenty-seven to twenty-eight years, women at twenty-five to twenty-six. Many variations were hidden within such averages. The most notable is the unique situation of firstborn sons. They would inherit the property, which would make marriage economically feasible and earlier marriage to perpetuate the family line desirable.

Most people had to postpone marriage until they could afford it. This typically meant waiting until they could acquire the property or position that would support a family. Younger sons often could not marry before age thirty. The average age at first marriage of all males among the nobility of Milan was 33.4 years in the period 1700–49; their wives averaged 21.2 years. Daughters might not marry until they had accumulated a dowry—land or money for the well-to-do, household goods in the lower classes—which would favor the economic circumstances of a family. Given the constraints of a limited life expectancy and a meager income, many people experienced marriage for only a few years, and others never married. A study of marriage patterns in eighteenth-century England suggests that 25 percent of the younger sons in well-to-do families never married. Another historian has estimated that fully 10 percent of the population of Europe was comprised of unmarried adult women. For the middle class of Geneva in 1700, 26 percent of the women who died at over age fifty had never married; the study of the Milanese nobility found that 35 percent of the women never married.

The pattern of selecting a mate changed somewhat during the eighteenth century. Earlier habits in which parents arranged marriages for children (especially if property was involved) were changing, and a prospective couple frequently claimed the right to veto their parents' arrangement. Although propertied families often insisted upon arranged marriages (see document 18.2), it became more common during the eighteenth century for men and women to select their own partners, contingent upon parental vetoes. Marriages based upon the interests of the entire family line, and marriages based upon an economic alliance, yielded with increasing frequency to marriages based upon romantic attachment. However, marriage contracts remained common.

After a long scholarly debate, historians now agree that Western civilization had no single pattern of family structure, but a variety of arrangements. The most common pattern was not a large family, across more than two generations, living together; instead, the most frequent arrangement was the nuclear family in which parents and their children lived together (see illustration 18.5). Extended families, characterized by coresidence with grandparents or other kin—known by many names, such as the *Ganze Hauz* in German tradition or the zadruga in eastern Europe—were atypical. A study of British families has found that 70 percent were comprised of two generations, 24 percent were single-generation families, and only 6 percent fit the extended family pattern. Studies of southern and eastern Europe have found more complex, extended families. In Russia, 60 percent of peasant families fit this multigenerational pattern; in parts of Italy, 74 percent.

Family size also varied widely. Everywhere except France (where smaller families first became the norm), the average number of children born per family usually ranged between five and seven. Yet such averages hide many large families. For example, Brissot de Warville, a leader of the French Revolution, was born to a family of innkeepers who had seventeen children, seven of whom survived infancy; Mayer and Gutele Rothschild, whose sons created the House of Rothschild banks, had twenty children, ten of whom survived. The founder of Methodism, John Wesley, was the fifteenth of nineteen children. Households might also contain other people, such as servants, apprentices, and lodgers. Studies of eighteenth-century families in different regions have found a range between 13 percent and 50 percent of them containing servants. A survey of London in the 1690s estimated that 20 percent of the population lodged with nonrelatives.

One of the foremost characteristics of the early modern family was patriarchal authority. This trait was diminishing somewhat in western Europe in the eighteenth century, but it remained strong. A father exercised authority over the children; a husband exercised authority over his wife. A woman vowed to obey her husband in the wedding ceremony, following the Christian tradition based on the words of Saint Paul: "Wives, submit yourself unto your own husbands, as unto the Lord." The idea of masculine authority in marriage was deeply imbedded in popular culture. As a character in a play by Henry Fielding says to his wife, "Your person is mine. I bought it lawfully in church." The civil law in most countries enforced such patriarchy. In the greatest summary of English law, Sir William Blackstone's *Commentaries on the Law of England* (1765–69), this was stated

◈ DOCUMENT 18.2 ◈

Arranged Marriages in the Eighteenth Century

Richard Brinsley Sheridan (1751–1816) was an Irish dramatist who wrote comedies of manners for the London stage. One of his greatest plays, The Rivals *(1775), made fun of the tradition of arranged marriages. In it, a wealthy aristocratic father, Sir Anthony Absolute, arranges a suitable marriage for his son, Captain Jack Absolute (who is in love with a beautiful young woman), without consulting him. In the following scene, Captain Absolute tries to refuse the marriage and Sir Anthony tries first to bribe him and then to coerce him.*

Absolute: Now, Jack, I am sensible that the income of your commission, and what I have hitherto allowed you, is but a small pittance for a lad of your spirit.

Captain Jack: Sir, you are very good.

Absolute: And it is my wish, while yet I live, to have my boy make some figure in the world. I have resolved, therefore, to fix you at once in a noble independence.

Captain Jack: Sir, your kindness overpowers me—such generosity makes the gratitude of reason more lively than the sensations even of filial affection.

Absolute: I am glad you are so sensible of my attention—and you shall be master of a large estate in a few weeks.

Captain Jack: Let my future life, sir, speak my gratitude; I cannot express the sense I have of your munificence. — Yet, sir, I presume you would not wish me to quit the army?

Absolute: Oh, that shall be as your wife chooses.

Captain Jack: My wife, sir!

Absolute: Ay, ay, settle that between you—settle that between you.

Captain Jack: A wife, sir, did you say?

Absolute: Ay, a wife—why, did I not mention her before?

Captain Jack: Not a word of her sir.

Absolute: Odd, so! I mus'n't forget her though. —Yes, Jack, the independence I was talking of is by marriage—the fortune is saddled with a wife—but I suppose that makes no difference.

Captain Jack: Sir! Sir! You amaze me!

Absolute: Why, what the devil's the matter with you, fool? Just now you were all gratitude and duty.

Captain Jack: I was, sir—you talked of independence and a fortune, but not a word of a wife!

Absolute: Why—what difference does that make? Odds life, sir! If you had an estate, you must take it with the live stock on it, as it stands!

Captain Jack: If my happiness is to be the price, I must beg leave to decline the purchase. Pray, sir, who is the lady?

Absolute: What's that to you, sir? Come, give me your promise to love, and to marry her directly.

Captain Jack: Sure, sir, this is not very reasonable. . . . You must excuse me, sir, if I tell you, once for all, that in this point I cannot obey you. . . .

Absolute: Sir, I won't hear a word—not one word! . . .

Captain Jack: What, sir, promise to link myself to some mass of ugliness!

Absolute: Zounds! Sirrah! The lady shall be as ugly as I choose: she shall have a hump on each shoulder; she shall be as crooked as the crescent; her one eye shall roll like the bull's in Cox's Museum; she shall have a skin like a mummy, and the beard of a Jew—she shall be all this, sirrah! Yet I will make you ogle her all day, and sit up all night to write sonnets on her beauty.

Sheridan, Richard. *The Rivals.* London: 1775.

bluntly: "The husband and wife are one, and the husband is that one." A compilation of Prussian law under Frederick the Great, the Frederician Code of 1750, was similar: "The husband is master of his own household, and head of his family. And as the wife enters into it of her own accord, she is in some measure subject to his power" (see document 18.3).

Few ways of dissolving a marriage existed in the eighteenth century. In Catholic countries, the church considered marriage a sacrament and neither civil marriage by the state nor legal divorce existed. The church permitted a few annulments, exclusively for the upper classes. Protestant countries accepted the principle of divorce on the grounds of adultery or desertion, but divorces remained rare, even when legalized. Geneva, the home of Calvinism, recorded an average of one divorce per year during the eighteenth century. Divorce became possible in Britain in the late seventeenth century, but it required an individual act of parliament for each divorce. Between 1670 and 1750, a total of 17 parliamentary divorces were granted in Britain, although the number rose to 114 between 1750 and 1799. Almost all divorces were granted to men of prominent social position who wished to marry again, normally to produce heirs.

Illustration 18.5

The Family. Attitudes toward the family were beginning to change in the eighteenth century, as indicated by the increasing habit of the wealthy to commission paintings of the entire family. Note the subtle symbolism of this painting: The wife sits at the center of the family, with the husband somewhat in the background of family matters. The father relates to his eldest son and heir, but he is turned slightly away from his other children.

Where arranged marriages were still common, the alternative to divorce was separation. The civil laws in many countries provided for contracts of separation, by which the maintenance of both partners was guaranteed. Simpler alternatives to divorce evolved in the lower classes, such as desertion or bigamy. The most extraordinary method, practiced in parts of England well into the nineteenth century, was the custom of wife sale. Such sales were generally by mutual consent, but they nonetheless resembled cattle sales. Though the Old Regime was fundamentally an era of indissoluble, life-long marriage, this did not mean a couple lived together for long periods of time. Given an average age at marriage in the mid-twenties and an average age at death (for people who reached the mid-twenties) in the mid-forties, the typical marriage lasted for approximately twenty years.

The Life Cycle: Sexuality and Reproduction

Ignorance about human sexuality was widespread during the Old Regime, and remarkable theories still circulated about human reproduction, many of them restatements of sex manuals inherited from the ancient world. Medical science held that the loss of one ounce of semen debilitated a man's body the same way that the loss of forty ounces of blood would and that a woman's menstruation could turn meat rancid. Consequently, physicians advised people to avoid all sex during the summer because a man's body would become dried out. Similarly, people were taught to avoid sex during menstruation because a child conceived then would be born diseased.

There were other disincentives to sexual activity. The strongest came from Christian moral injunctions. A Christian tradition regarding sex as unclean and chastity as a spiritual ideal, dated from St. Paul and St. Jerome. Only marital intercourse was permissible, and then only for procreation; other sexual activity was understood to be a violation of the Seventh Commandment forbidding adultery. Good Christians were expected to practice chastity during pregnancy (when conception was impossible), on Sundays, and during the forty days of Lent.

In addition to the disincentives of medical advice and Christian teaching, poor health, uncleanliness, fears of pregnancy or venereal disease, and repressive laws also restricted behavior. Laws varied regionally, but most sexual practices were against the law. Ecclesiastical courts in Catholic countries tried priests and laity alike for sexual offenses; secular courts acted in a similar manner in Protestant countries. A study of the archdiocesan tribunal at Cambrai (France) has found that 38 percent of the moral offenses involved unmarried sex, 32 percent adultery, and 11 percent incest. Punishments ranged from death (for incest between father and daughter) to providing a dowry (for seducing a virgin). Bestiality merited burning to death, for both the human and the animal. Pornography (broadly defined) often led to imprisonment, as it did for Denis Diderot. Sentences to a public pillory, a flogging, or being paraded through the streets with a shaved head were also common.

Homosexuality was universally illegal before the French Revolution (which legalized consenting adult relationships in 1791). Assessing its frequency is diffi-

◆ DOCUMENT 18.3 ◆

The Husband in the Law: The Frederician Code of 1750

The Frederician Code, adopted in Prussia under Frederick the Great, was one of the greatest efforts to reorganize a legal system during the eighteenth century. It was chiefly the work of the minister of justice, Samuel von Cocceji. He relied on the principles of Roman law but also drew ideas from Germanic customary law and from the "enlightened" philosophy of the eighteenth century. The following excerpt states the legal rights of a husband; a similar section specified the rights and privileges of the wife, without curtailing the authority of husband.

1. As the domestic society, or family, is formed by the union of the husband and wife, we are to begin with enumerating the advantages and rights which result from this union.

2. The husband is by nature the head of his family. To be convinced of this, it is sufficient to consider, that the wife leaves her family to join herself to that of her husband; that she enters into his household, and into the habitation of which he is the master, with intention to have children by him to perpetuate the family.

3. Hence it follows, judging by the sole light of reason, that the husband is master of his own household, and head of his family. And as the wife enters into it of her own accord, she is in some measure subject to his power; whence flow several rights and privileges, which belong to the husband with regard to his wife.

For, (1) the husband has the liberty of prescribing laws and rules in his household, which the wife is to observe.

(2) If the wife be defective in her duty to her husband, and refuse to be subject, he is authorized to reduce her to her duty in a reasonable manner.

(3) The wife is bound, according to her quality, to assist her husband, to take upon her the care of the household affairs, according to his condition.

(4) The husband has the power over the wife's body, and she cannot refuse him the conjugal duty.

(5) As the husband and wife have promised not to leave each other during their lives, but to share the good and evil which may happen to them; the wife cannot, under pretext, for example, that her husband has lost his reason, leave him, without obtaining permission from the judge.

(6) For the same reason, the wife is obliged to follow her husband when he changes his habitation; unless, (a) it has been stipulated by the contract of marriage, or otherwise, that she shall not be bound to follow him if he should incline to settle elsewhere; or (b) unless it were for a crime that the husband changed his habitation, as if he had been banished from his country.

Bell, Susan G., and Offen, Karen M. eds. *Women, the Family, and Freedom: The Debate in Documents*, vol. 1. Stanford, Calif.: Stanford University Press, 1983.

---

cult. It had been a crime in England for centuries, normally punished by the pillory, and a public execution for homosexuality took place as late as 1772. Yet homosexuality was relatively open in England in the eighteenth century and gentlemen's clubs of homosexuals existed with impunity in London, though periodic arrests of sodomites (the term *homosexual* was not coined until the late nineteenth century) occurred, such as the police campaign of 1707. King Frederick William I of Prussia was horrified to discover that both of his sons—the future Frederick the Great and Prince Henry, whom the Continental Congress briefly considered as a constitutional king for the United States—were homosexuals. The double standard obscures the extent of lesbianism in the eighteenth century even more, but high society enjoyed widespread rumors about many prominent figures such as Queen Anne of England. Contemporary works such as Mary Wollstonecraft's

Mary: A Fiction, Diderot's *La Religieuse*, and Fielding's *The Female Husband* indicate that the subject was much discussed.

As the partial tolerance of homosexuality suggests, the eighteenth century was a period of comparatively relaxed sexual restrictions, especially compared with the more repressive sixteenth and seventeenth centuries. Some historians even describe the Old Regime as a period of sexual revolution. In Protestant countries, strict moral Puritanism weakened, and Catholicism repudiated its own version of Puritanism—Jansenism. In all countries, the ruling classes set an example of permissiveness. Most monarchs (who married for reasons of state, not for love) kept lovers, gently called favorites. Louis XV kept a small personal brothel and Catherine the Great had an equally long list of favorites. Augustus the Strong, king of Poland and elector of Saxony, fathered at least 365 children, only one of them legitimate.

The double standard remained a feature of the relaxed sexual standards. Tribunals assessing sex crimes typically gave harsher sentences to women, particularly for adultery. Women at the highest levels of society might act with some freedom if the legitimacy of heirs were certain. But European culture attached a value to female virginity and chastity and still associated a man's honor with the chastity of his female relations.

One of the foremost disincentives associated with eighteenth-century sexuality was the circulation of the venereal diseases (VD) syphilis and gonorrhea. These diseases, commonly called the pox, were rampant in the ruling classes and found in most of the royal families of Europe. Louis XIV, Louis XV, and Napoleon all had VD. Syphilis was not as fatal as when epidemics of it swept Europe in the fifteenth and sixteenth centuries, but it remained a debilitating disease. Gonorrhea was pandemic in urban Europe. The famous Venetian lover Giovanni Casanova contracted eleven cases of VD during his life although he survived until age seventy-three. James Boswell, the distinguished British writer, caught gonorrhea seventeen times. Physicians could provide only limited help; their favored cure was treatment with mercury, a dangerous poison.

Prostitution was one of the chief sources of the spread of venereal diseases. It was illegal but generally tolerated in public brothels. The open prostitution of the Middle Ages, with municipally operated (and even church-operated) brothels, no longer existed. Yet large numbers of prostitutes were found in all cities. King Frederick I of Prussia tried to end prostitution in Berlin by closing all brothels in 1690, causing an increase of prostitution practiced in taverns. When the Prussian government decided to tolerate brothels again, a survey of 1765 found that Berlin contained nearly nine thousand prostitutes in a population of approximately 120,000 people. The Parisian police estimated an even higher number of prostitutes there—between twenty thousand and thirty thousand, or one of every eight women of marriageable age. Even in the shadow of the Vatican, 2 percent of all adult women were officially registered prostitutes.

Draconian measures did not eliminate prostitution. The Austrian government sought to end it in Vienna in the 1720s with harsh treatment of prostitutes. After the failure of such punishments as the pillory or being made to sweep the streets with shaved heads, the government staged a public decapitation of a prostitute in 1723. Yet the empress Maria Theresa soon created a Chastity Commission to study the subject anew. Governments chose to control prostitution by limiting it to certain districts and keeping it off the streets or by registering prostitutes, thereby permitting some public health control and taxation. Governments were mostly concerned about the spread of disease (particularly to military garrisons) more than the condition of the women (frequently domestic servants who had been seduced or girls from the country who could not find employment) driven by economic necessity to prostitute themselves.

Another subject of social concern about eighteenth-century sexuality was the general increase in illegitimate births (see table 18.6). Illegitimacy had been relatively uncommon, particularly in rural areas, in the seventeenth century. The rate for rural France had been only 1 percent of all births. During the eighteenth century, and particularly after 1760, both illegitimate births and premarital conceptions increased significantly. The illegitimacy rate remained high because the practice of birth control was limited both by Christian moral injunctions and by slight knowledge of effective procedures. Tertullian had established the theological view of birth control in the third century, asserting that "to prevent a child being born is to commit homicide in advance." Religious opposition to birth control continued in the eighteenth century, even in Protestant Europe: It was the divine will that people "be fruitful and multiply." Despite Christian teaching, a significant percentage of the English upper classes and the general population of France practiced some forms of birth control in the eighteenth century, and both populations experienced a decline in their fertility rate compared with the rest of Europe. France had a birthrate of forty per one thousand population in the mid-eighteenth century, falling to thirty-three per one thousand at the end of the century, thirty per one thousand in some areas. Many people clearly had found economic advantages in smaller families and had chosen to put economic factors above religious ones.

Judging the extent to which knowledge about birth control circulated is difficult. Christianity offered one traditional method: abstinence. *Coitus interruptus* was practiced, but its extent is unknown. The French philosopher Jean-Jacques Rousseau discussed (with disapproval) that method of birth control ("cheating nature") in his *Discourse* of 1753 as well as many forms of nonreproductive sex, such as oral and manual sex. (Rousseau also fathered five illegitimate children and abandoned them to foundling homes.) Those who practiced birth control employed such methods. Condoms (made from animal membranes) had been virtually unknown in the seventeenth century but were available in late eighteenth-century London and Paris, although they were chiefly employed against VD, not

◈ TABLE 18.6 ◈

Premarital Conception and Illegitimate Birth in the Old Regime

Country	Period	Percentage of premarital conceptions	Percentage of illegitimate births
England	pre–1750	19.7	2.6
	1780–1820	34.5	5.9
France	pre–1750	6.2	2.9
	1780–1820	13.7	4.7
German states	pre–1750	13.8	2.5
	1780–1820	23.8	11.9
Spain	pre–1750	n.a.	5.4
	1780–1820	n.a.	6.5
United States	1940	n.a.	3.5
	1990	n.a.	28.0

Sources: Data for the Old Regime from Michael W. Flinn, *The European Demographic System, 1500–1820* (Baltimore, Md.: Johns Hopkins University Press, 1971), p. 82; data for the United States from *Information Please Almanac Atlas and Yearbook 1989* (Boston, Mass.: Houghton Mifflin Co., 1989), p. 788 and 1994, p. 844.

for family planning. Knowledge about female means of control, such as douching, also began to circulate in that period.

Abortion was also used to terminate unwanted pregnancies during the Old Regime. A Christian tradition received from Aristotle and passed onward by Roman law held that a soul was implanted in the fetus at the time of "animation" or "the quickening." Though all abortions were illegal, both moral law and criminal law distinguished between those before and after "ensoulment." The means of attempting abortions were crude and dangerous. Folk knowledge circulated about supposed abortifacient drugs and vegetal or mineral poisons, however, and the learned reference work of the century, the French *Encyclopédie*, discussed them in detail.

The Life Cycle: Old Age

Statistical averages showing the low life expectancies of the Old Regime should not produce the mistaken conclusion that older people were rare in the eighteenth century. Twenty percent of all newborns reached the age of fifty, and 10 percent lived until seventy. French demographic studies have found that, in the 1740s, 17 percent of men and 19 percent of women would reach age sixty; by the 1770s, this had risen to 24 percent for men and 25 percent for women. The aged clearly represented a significant group in society. Once someone had survived to the age of fifty, his life expectancy was not greatly different than it would be in the twentieth century.

Thus, a large proportion of the powerful and famous individuals who are remembered from the eighteenth century had life spans typical of twentieth-century leaders. King Louis XIV of France lived to be seventy-seven (1638–1715); his successor, Louis XV, died at sixty-four (1710–74). The three Hanoverian kings of eighteenth-century England (George I, George II, and George III) died at an average age of seventy-five (sixty-seven, seventy-seven, and eighty-two, respectively). Empress Catherine II of Russia and King Frederick II of Prussia earned their appellation, "the Great," partly because they lived long enough to achieve greatness—Catherine died at sixty-seven, Frederick at seventy-four. And the eight popes of the eighteenth century, who were typically elected at an advanced age, died at an average age of nearly seventy-eight; four lived into their eighties. Similar life spans characterized many of the famous cultural figures of the Old Regime. Christopher Wren and Anton van Leeuwenhoek both lived into their nineties; Goethe, Goya, Kant, and Newton all lived into their eighties.

CHAPTER **19**

THE POLITICAL EVOLUTION OF THE OLD REGIME, 1715–89

CHAPTER OUTLINE

◆◆◆◆◆◆◆◆◆◆◆◆◆◆◆◆◆◆◆◆◆

This chapter examines European politics during the last age of monarchical domination. Several varieties of monarchy emerged during the late seventeenth century—from limited monarchies, restricted by constitutions, parliaments, or aristocracies, to autocratic monarchies, with few restraints on despotic powers. In most of them, royal advisers slowly became cabinets of ministers led by a prime minister; in some, parliaments began to gain control over the cabinet system.

A prominent example of the latter was England under the Hanoverian kings, a monarchy severely limited by the strength of Parliament and the restrictions of the unwritten constitution. Under the first prime minister, Sir Robert Walpole, a cabinet system controlled by Parliament had emerged by the 1730s. In France, the Bourbon monarchy weakened after the death of Louis XIV, whose successor faced a resurgence of aristocratic power based upon control of the high courts or *parlements*. The costs of war and an inadequate system of taxation produced a financial crisis that helped precipitate the French Revolution.

Autocratic Prussia, meanwhile, emerged as a great power in the eighteenth century owing to the strength of its army. Frederick the Great tried to balance despotism and militarism with ideas of enlightened reform. Austria, however, is a better illustration of enlightened despotism, partly in the reign of Maria Theresa, but chiefly under Joseph II, the most advanced of eighteenth-century autocrats. Chapter 19 concludes with a discussion of Russia, where the monarch had despotic power and few restraints. Catherine II preserved autocracy in Russia by enlisting the support of powerful aristocrats.

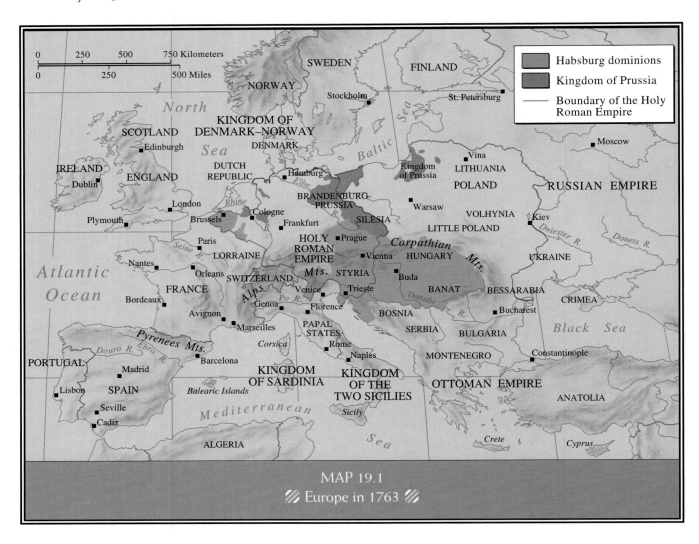

MAP 19.1

Europe in 1763

The Structures of Government: Monarchy

The basic political characteristic of the Old Regime was—as it had been for more than one thousand years—monarchical government. In the strictest sense, monarchy meant the rule of a single person who held sovereignty (supreme power) over a state. The power of monarchs was frequently challenged by the nobility, disputed by provinces, or attacked in open rebellions. But the concept of monarchy was almost universally accepted at the beginning of the eighteenth century. Even the skeptical intellectuals of that era still supported it, and only a few small states, such as the city-state of Genoa in northern Italy, sustained governments without monarchs, usually called republics.

The forms of monarchy varied significantly: from absolute monarchy (in which the monarch claimed unrestricted powers) to limited monarchy (in which clear legal limits were placed on royal sovereignty, to the benefit of the propertied classes). Absolutism remained the predominant form of European monarchy. Most monarchs wanted such power and aspired to emulate the absolute monarchs of the seventeenth century, King Gustavus Adolphus of Sweden and especially King Louis XIV of France, the exemplars of the era called the age of absolutism. The theory of absolute monarchy held that rulers received sovereignty directly from God. They governed by divine right, representing within their realm the sovereignty of God over all things. This idea rested on the exegesis of such biblical statements as "No authority exists unless it comes from God." Churches taught obedience to the monarch as a religious duty: God had given sovereignty, and "No one but God can judge the king." Resisting a monarch was to attack God's order. An anonymous poem of the eighteenth century entitled "The Vicar of Bray" summarized the alliance of throne and altar in a succinct rhyme:

Unto my flock I daily preached
Kings were by God appointed,
And damned was he that durst resist
Or touch the Lord's anointed.

Despite such ideas, true autocratic monarchy—most often called despotism—was rare, but parts of central and eastern Europe still lived under despotic rulers who were unrestrained by laws. A despot might strangle an opponent with his bare hands, have another torn apart by dogs, or have his own son and heir flogged to death, as Tsar Peter the Great of Russia did.

Most monarchs could not exercise such unrestrained powers. Their governments were limited monarchies, limited by privileges that earlier rulers had granted, a legal system enforced by independent courts, the nobility, the powers of an established state religion, rights delegated to an assembly, or financial dependency on others. The Braganza kings of Portugal were limited by the power of the Catholic Church; the Bourbon kings of the Two Sicilies, by having to ask an assembly for the money to rule. The Bourbon kings of France faced a resurgent aristocracy that used the law courts (*parlements*) to thwart the royal will.

The most formal restrictions upon royal sovereignty were constitutional laws. Few states possessed a constitution in the modern sense of a single written document. Sweden adopted the strictest constitution of the era in 1720. The Sweden nobility accepted the rule of a queen on the condition that she accept a document limiting her power. Most constitutions were less formal, usually a set of customary privileges claimed by the aristocracy as their national traditions. In Hungary, the Magyar aristocracy held virtual autonomy. When the Habsburgs incorporated Hungary into the Austrian Empire, the Hungarians insisted upon their ancient constitution and rebelled when they believed it to be violated. The English constitution is the most studied model of limiting monarchical power, but it, too, did not exist in a single document stating these limits. It was a body of constitutional law dating back to the Magna Carta of 1215 in which King John had acknowledged limits to his power. An unusual form of limited monarchy existed in Poland, where succession to the throne occurred by election. A representative body (the *Sejm*) of the Polish landowning gentry (the *szlachta*) chose each new king and claimed traditional rights, called "the five eternal principles," including the right to renounce allegiance to the king.

Republican governments held that sovereignty belonged to the citizens, usually to some privileged portion of them. Republicanism slowly evolved into the modern sense of republic—in which sovereignty is held by citizens who elect a government and delegate limited powers to it—but this form did not apply during the Old Regime. Most of the republics of 1715 were oligarchies—the rule of the few instead of the rule of one—typically small city-states in Italy. The only great power to attempt republican government during the eighteenth century was revolutionary France during the 1790s.

The Evolution of Government: Parliaments, Ministers, and Cabinets

Most countries of the Old Regime, except autocratic states such as Russia, possessed a representative assembly, typically called a parliament today but more often called a diet (from the Latin *diaeta*, a place of assembly). Diets had existed in Europe for centuries. The oldest was the Icelandic *Althing*, founded in A.D. 930. In some strong monarchies, such as France and Spain, assemblies existed in theory but not in practice. The French Estates General had once been a powerful body, elected by all classes of the population and able to limit taxation. However, it met only when convoked by the king, and between 1614 and 1789 French kings never called a meeting. In Württemberg, Duke Eberhard Ludwig ruled for forty years, from 1693 to 1733, and permitted only one meeting of the Diet during his entire reign. That meeting opposed a standing army and the levying of taxes, but the duke proceeded to raise an army, collect taxes, and prevent further meetings of the Diet. Only the British Parliament and the Swedish *Rikstag* had genuine legislative power.

The most powerful political figures of the eighteenth century were usually the advisers chosen by the monarch to manage the government. Another important trend in political history was the slow evolution of these royal advisers into a modern government. Advisers gradually became ministers of state, charged with the direction of a bureaucracy, such as the Ministry of Finance or the Ministry of War. In efficient governments, the advisers worked together as a cabinet of ministers, pursuing a common policy. During the eighteenth century this evolved into the cabinet system of government in Britain, culminating in the recognition of one minister as the head of the government, or the prime minister. Only the most energetic and able of monarchs, such as Frederick the Great of Prussia, served as their own prime minister, directing the bureaucracy. Instead, such strong leaders as Sir Robert Walpole in Britain (served 1721–42) or Cardinal Fleury in France (served 1726–43), laid the bases of modern ministerial government. The final stage of this evolution is known as ministerial responsibility, when the prime minister and the cabinet no longer served at the king's pleasure but were responsible to parliament and held office only as long as a majority supported them. Signs of ministerial responsibility were evident in eighteenth-century Britain, but the idea developed in the nineteenth century and was not widely accepted until the twentieth century.

Many ministers were selected by royal whim. The most powerful adviser might be the king's private secretary, as was Alexandrea de Gusmao, the strongest statesman in midcentury Portugal. Or power might be hidden behind a minor office. For example, the title of Adam Moltke, who dominated the government of Denmark for a generation, was master of the royal household. The two most influential advisers to King Louis XV of France were the man who had been his childhood tutor and one of the king's mistresses.

The Rise of Parliamentary Government in Hanoverian England

The strength of parliamentary government in England was the result of seventeenth-century revolutions that limited the royal power of the Stuart kings. When it became clear that the royal line was dying out, Parliament asserted its supremacy and selected a German princess from the House of Hanover (a relative of the Stuarts) as the heir to the throne. Thus, in 1714 the throne of England passed to a German, the elector of Hanover. He took the title of King George I, beginning the House of Hanover. His heirs took the names George II and George III, so eighteenth-century England is known as Georgian England as well as Hanoverian England.

King George I did not speak English, and he never bothered to learn the language of his new kingdom, although he had already learned Latin, French, and Italian. He preferred life in Germany and made long trips to Hanover, where he kept a series of plump mistresses whom the English press loved to satirize. The king married his own cousin, then accused her of adultery, divorced her, and imprisoned her for thirty years. This monarch did not win the affection of the English people who generally considered him indolent and ignorant. One of the sharpest tongued Englishmen, Samuel Johnson, summarized him simply: "George I knew nothing and desired to know nothing; did nothing and desired to do nothing."

The character of King George I contributed to the supremacy of Parliament. He showed little interest in government, and because of the language barrier, even his addresses to Parliament had to be read by someone else. Parliament asserted itself with a coronation oath, requiring each monarch to swear to obey parliamentary statutes. It established a mandatory term of office for itself and gained tighter control over the budget and the army. But the most important effect of George I's disinterest in governing was that it allowed the development of the cabinet system of government.

George I's adviser Sir Robert Walpole became the first prime minister in British history and the architect of the cabinet system. Walpole did not come from the titled nobility but was the son of large landowners with nearly a dozen manors. His marriage to a merchant's daughter brought him a dowry of £20,000 and the independence for a parliamentary career. He championed the Hanoverian succession and won the confidence of the royal family, who allowed him independence to shape the government. Walpole also had to win the confidence of parliament and he did so through remarkable managerial skills. He won the backing of the gentry by cutting the land tax from 20 percent to 5 percent. He gained the faith of others by restoring order to British finances after a crisis that was caused by stock speculation known as the South Seas Bubble. He got the support of manufacturing interests with a policy favorable to foreign trade. The key to Walpole's success, however, was probably his patronage system in which he tried to find a job or an income for everyone who would support him. "There is enough pasture for all the sheep," Walpole said. His opponents thought this scandalous. Jonathan Swift put it bluntly: "The whole system of his ministry was corruption; and he never gave bribe or pension without frankly telling the receivers what he expected from them." But in this way, Sir Robert Walpole held power for twenty-one years and laid the foundations of modern parliamentary government.

The British Parliament of the eighteenth century (see illustration 19.1) was far from a modern, democratic legislature. The upper house, the House of Lords, remained a bastion of the aristocracy where membership was inherited by the eldest son along with the family title. The lower house, the House of Commons, was elective, but voting was limited to adult males who paid forty shillings a year in property taxes, on the theory that men of property had a vested interest in or-

Illustration 19.1

/// **The House of Commons.** Parliamentary government was the institution that most distinguished the English monarchy from the other great powers. The lower house of Parliament, the elective House of Commons, effectively limited the power of the Hanoverian kings in contrast to the absolute monarchies of continental Europe. Note how the physical arrangement divides parliament into two sides (the government and the opposition), encouraging a two-party system.

derly government. This meant that fewer than 250,000 voted—approximately 3 percent of the nation. In addition to the poor, women, criminals, Catholics, Jews, some Protestants (notably Quakers), and nonbelievers were barred from voting. A Qualification Act required that to become a member of parliament (M.P.) a candidate must own land worth £300, leaving a tiny fraction of the nation eligible for office. Walpole, however, encouraged the dominance of the House of Commons and accepted that his cabinet stood collectively responsible to that body.

British voters typically deferred to the leadership of a small elite of great landowners. According to a study of British politics at the accession of King George III, this pattern of deference meant that a few prominent families controlled the House of Commons. The constituency of Wenlock in western England, for example, had a few hundred electors. Throughout the eighteenth century, they deferred to the leadership of the Forester family, choosing eight members of that family to represent them in the House of Commons. Some constituencies, called pocket boroughs, were owned by a single family, which had the seat in its pocket and chose the M.P.; others, called rotten boroughs, had so few votes that the seat could be bought. In 1761 the borough of Sudbury openly advertised that its seat in the House of Commons was for sale. The vast lands owned by the duke of Newcastle included seven boroughs for which he personally selected the M.P. In such ways, 111 wealthy landowners controlled more than two hundred seats in Parliament.

Eighteenth-century England also witnessed the origins of a political party system. Members of Parliament generally split into two large factions, not yet political parties in the modern sense, called the Tory and Whig parties. The Tories were somewhat more conservative (in the sense of supporting royal authority) than the Whigs (who were monarchists and defenders of the Hanoverian settlement, but who spoke for parliamentary supremacy). The leaders of both factions typically came from the aristocracy. Political parties did not yet dominate elections. A famous study of politics in the Georgian age concluded that party did not determine the outcome of a single election in the voting of 1761. Nonetheless, the Whigs—including Walpole—won a majority in the first elections under King George I and generally dominated British politics for the next two generations.

The strongest of Walpole's successors, William Pitt the Elder, strengthened the position of prime minister and the cabinet system of government. Like Walpole, Pitt was not born to the aristocracy, but he managed to die holding both the nickname "the great commoner" and the noble title the earl of Chatham. He was the grandson of a merchant who had made a fortune trading in India in illegal competition with the East India Company. That wealth had bought Pitt's marriage into high society and his seat in Parliament representing a famous rotten borough, Old Sarum. Pitt was polished and Oxford educated; his rise in Parliament was largely the result of exceptional oratorical skills. As prime minister during the Seven Years' War of 1756–63, Pitt's vigorous leadership helped to secure global victories over France and demonstrated the strength of cabinet government in times of crisis.

The evolution of parliamentary government in England was an important stage in the growth of European civilization, but it remained open to criticism. The most radical voice came from the son of a distiller, John Wilkes. Wilkes had an Oxford education and a helpful marriage to a wealthy older woman, whose dowry financed his campaign to abolish rotten boroughs and redistribute seats in a fairer representation of the population. Such reform won an important ally in 1783 when William Pitt the Younger (the son of Pitt the Elder) introduced a bill to disenfranchise thirty-six rotten boroughs and to give seventy-two more seats to London and other populous areas. Pitt's bill failed in 1785, however, and fairer electoral laws had to wait for half a century.

George III was the most complex and important of the Hanoverian kings. He was the first Hanoverian to be born and educated in England. Although some British historians have described him as "an unbalanced man of low intelligence," George began his long reign (1760–1820) as a popular, hard-working king, considered a decent man of domestic virtues (in contrast to his predecessors and many of his ministers) and high patriotism. George III was also the first Hanoverian to intervene deeply in politics, the first to try to rule. He was stubborn and arbitrary, and he fought with his ministers, dismissing them from office; he tried to abolish the emerging system of political parties; and for approximately a dozen years, he effectively ran the government through the choice of weak ministers and lavish application of Walpole's patronage system. George III is often best remembered for the mental imbalance that began to afflict him in 1765—now thought to have been caused by the metabolic disease porphyria—and led to his being stripped of royal powers in 1811. But for many years he was a formidable political figure, strong enough to order the arrest of Wilkes, who was expelled from parliament.

The political process did not stop with kings, parliaments, and radical reformers: The eighteenth century was an age of turbulent protest. One study has identified 275 urban disturbances in Britain between 1735 and 1800. The most common problem that drew crowds into the streets was hunger. Scarce or expensive bread caused food riots because many people lived on the margins of survival. Labor riots were also common during periods of high unemployment. Such protests in England frequently became anti-Irish demonstrations, such as the 1736 riots of London construction workers fearful

Illustration 19.2

The Gordon Riots. Urban riots were a recurring feature of eighteenth-century Europe, even in the prosperous states of the west. London suffered severe riots, of which the worst were the Gordon Riots of 1780. Crowds attacked Catholic churches and church property under the banner of "No Popery." The illustration here shows the rioters setting fire to Newgate Prison in London.

that Irish immigrants were taking their jobs and driving down the price of labor.

Religious hatred was a common cause of riots in the eighteenth century, and English crowds regularly expressed their anti-Catholicism with "pope-burnings." When the House of Commons in 1778 voted to abolish legal restrictions upon the seventy-eight thousand Catholics living in England, the public uproar grew into one of the largest riots of the century. A vehement defender of Protestant dominance, an M.P. named Lord George Gordon, in June 1780 led sixty thousand militant Protestants in a march on Parliament that precipitated three days of anti-Catholic riots, known as the Gordon Riots or the "No Popery Riots" (see illustration 19.2). Mobs assaulted Catholic chapels, major prisons, and the Bank of England. George III used the army to quell the

TABLE 19.1

British War Finances, 1702–83

War	War expenditure (in millions)	Government income (in millions)	Deficit in loans (in millions)	Percentage borrowed
War of the Spanish Succession, 1702–13	£93.6	£64.2	£29.4	31.4
War of the Austrian Succession, 1739–48	£95.6	£65.9	£29.7	31.1
Seven Years' War, 1756–63	£160.6	£100.6	£60.0	37.4
American Revolution, 1776–83	£236.5	£141.9	£94.6	39.9
Total	£586.3	£372.6	£213.7	36.4

Source: Adapted from data in Paul Kennedy, *The Rise and Fall of the Great Powers* (New York, N.Y.: Random House, 1987); p. 81.

riots, killing 285 members of the crowd. Gordon was tried for treason and acquitted; his campaign delayed Catholic emancipation for fifty years.

Britain and the Struggles of Empire

The eighteenth century was an age of nearly constant warfare for Britain; wars were fought in Europe, in North America, in India, and on the high seas. The British contested both French and Spanish power in Europe—fearing the hegemony of either Catholic power—and battled the French for global empire. And British military policy was successful in both objectives. The War of the Spanish Succession (1701–14) checked the French pursuit of continental hegemony, and a simultaneous war in North America (Queen Anne's War) resulted in a significant growth in English power. The War of the Quadruple Alliance (1718–20) seriously curtailed Spanish power.

War was one of the few political questions that deeply interested the Hanoverian kings. George I and George II gladly left English domestic politics in the hands of Walpole, but they resisted his policy of peace and international commerce. Both kings felt that the English army and navy represented the best defense of their Hanoverian homeland, and they accepted costly warfare to defend it. George II was the last king of England to take personal command of an army in the field, fighting in the War of the Austrian Succession in 1743. George III thus inherited a huge national debt (£138 million) along with the throne, the result of military profligacy. He, too, fought constant wars, however, and quintupled the English national debt to £800 million (see table 19.1).

The immense war debt that King George III inherited was the cost of participation in the first true world war—the Seven Years' War in Europe (1756–63), and its simultaneous theaters known as the French and Indian Wars in North America and the Bengal Wars in India. This global war produced a mixed blessing: The British Empire won but wound up deeper in debt; Britain became the dominant colonial power in the world, but she thereby acquired even greater administrative costs. The British nation—like many others during the Old Regime—was loathe to pay the taxes needed to repay war debts, support military expansion, and meet the expenses of empire. In 1764 the Tory government chose a compromise it thought safe: New taxes would be imposed in the colonies, which were the source of many imperial costs, but not in the British isles. The issue of this policy was the Stamp Act of 1765, a tax on the American colonies, requiring that a tax stamp be attached to official documents such as a will, a liquor license, or a college degree. The furious reaction in many colonies held that such taxes could not be imposed under British law without the consent of those being taxed. Representatives of nine American colonies (Britain possessed more than thirty colonies in the Americas) assembled in a Stamp Tax Congress and adopted an angry resolution challenging the decision of Parliament as subverting "the rights and liberties of the colonists."

The confrontation over taxation simmered for a decade and led to the American Revolution of 1776–83. Parliament initially backed down in the face of American protests and rescinded the Stamp Tax in 1766, but renewed protests led Parliament to adopt the punitive Coercive Acts of 1774 and to quarter troops in Boston. A few months later, in April 1775, the battles of

Lexington and Concord began the military phase of the revolution.

Although the British had won a global war in 1763, they were in a weaker position in 1775. They were deprived of the help that Americans had given them during the Seven Years' War. There was now no continental war to preoccupy and divide the European powers. One by one, the European powers exploited Britain's vulnerable position and declared war upon her. France entered the war in 1778, Spain in 1779, and Holland in 1780. The financial and military assistance of these states—especially the French—plus the division of British opinion over the war, helped to decide the war. France sent increasingly larger armies, such as the force of six thousand men that arrived with Count Jean de Rochambeau in 1780. By the later phases of the war, French forces were decisive. In the battle fought at Yorktown, Virginia, in 1781, the largest army was neither British nor American but French. Facing such growing forces, the British accepted the independence of thirteen of her American colonies in 1783.

The American Revolution obliged the British to reconsider the situation in other territories. Both nearby (in Ireland) and around the world (in India), Britain faced problems. The Anglo-Protestant domination of Ireland had grown steadily during English battles with Catholicism at home and abroad in the seventeenth and eighteenth centuries, especially after the Protestant victory in the battle of the Boyne in 1690. One striking consequence of these struggles could be seen in land tenure. In 1603 Catholics had owned 90 percent of the land in Ireland; in 1778, they owned 5 percent. Catholics protested their execution, which had left them at the mercy of absentee landlords who collected extortionate rents. When Parliament considered improving conditions in Ireland, such as the Relief Act of 1778, the result was a Protestant backlash. Protestants in the northern counties of Ulster founded the Protestant Volunteers, a paramilitary force of forty thousand armed men to defend their privileged position. The House of Commons capitulated to the Protestants by creating a Protestant-dominated parliament in Ireland known as Grattan's Parliament, which survived until Ireland was merged into the United Kingdom in 1801.

The Vulnerable Monarchy of Bourbon France

In contrast to the situation in England, the French monarchy carried the powers of absolutism into the eighteenth century: Louis XIV, *le Roi Soleil* (the Sun King), the most powerful of the seventeenth-century monarchs, died in 1715 after the longest reign in the history of European monarchy, nearly seventy-three years. Advocates of limiting absolutism had placed their hopes in the heirs of Louis XIV, but within a single year (1711–12), Louis's son, grandson, and eldest great-grandson all died. The death of Louis XIV consequently brought to the throne his five-year-old great-grandson, Louis XV, who would reign for most of the eighteenth century (from 1715 to 1774).

Louis XIV had practiced the distrustful but shrewd administrative principle of fragmenting power near to the throne, and he extended this policy after death by a will dividing the powers of the regency to rule France until Louis XV came of age. The regent of France during the childhood of Louis XV was his cousin, Philippe II, the duke d'Orléans, a liberal and tolerant man, although profligate enough to be considered dissipated even in the context of royal families. The duke skillfully obtained full power by making a deal with the chief judicial body in France, the *parlement* of Paris: The parlement invalidated the will of Louis XIV, and in return, Philippe d'Orléans allowed the fifteen parlements of France greater powers to review (and block) royal decrees. Thus, when Louis XV reached age thirteen and began to rule without a regent in 1723, he inherited a streamlined government, but he faced well-entrenched opposition from the aristocratic parlements.

Louis XV was an intelligent and capable young man, amiable enough to be called Louis "the Well-Beloved." He was not interested in controlling the government as his great-grandfather had; he liked the idea of absolutism but lacked enthusiasm for the daily chores of governing. Consequently, at age sixteen Louis XV entrusted the government of France to his tutor, Cardinal Fleury, who served as the virtual prime minister of France (without the title) between 1726 and 1743. Louis, who had been married at age fifteen for reasons of state, amused himself with a variety of women while Fleury used his long tenure, as Walpole did in Britain, to stabilize and organize the government.

When Fleury died, Louis XV tried to restore the system of Louis XIV—ruling personally instead of trusting a minister to govern. Like George II of England, he took command of his army and led it into battle in 1744. Ministers who wanted too much power were reduced to the shadows, as was a finance minister of 1759 who left behind his name for that condition: Etienne de Silhouette. Instead of trusting a prime minister and a cabinet, Louis chiefly took advice from his official mistress, the Marquise de Pompadour. She exerted a gener-

◆ TABLE 19.2 ◆

The Cost of Royal Extravagance, 1760

The following bill was presented by a Parisian jeweller in 1760 for a single piece of furniture, a jewelled, lacquered writing desk called an *escritoire*. To understand this level of royal spending, compare it with the annual incomes and prices in livres shown in Table 17.3.

Component of a lacquer desk with flower vase, powder box, and sponge case	Cost in livres
Gold	3,464
Lacquer	528
Labor (cabinet maker, joiner, and lock maker)	360
Labor (sublet jewellery work)	6,148
Miniature portrait of the empress	600
Packaging box with copper mounts	30
Labor (packaging)	28
Jewels	66,000
Total	77,158

Source: Condensed from data in Nancy Mitford, *Madame de Pompadour* (New York, N.Y.: E. P. Dutton, 1968); p. 276.

ally liberal and enlightened influence on French policy, but she was not able to master the king's greatest problem: Like George III of England, he found that he had inherited a government deep in debt, with disordered finances and no ready solutions.

The French Financial Crisis and the Resurgent Aristocracy

The foremost problem facing Louis XV was the disastrous state of French finances created by high military expenses and low taxation. The wars of Louis XIV left France in debt and near bankruptcy. The debt amounted to 36 percent of the government's budget in 1739. Royal opulence compounded the problem: The cost of maintaining the royal family, splendid palaces such as Versailles, and the life of the royal court exceeded 10 percent of the national budget, whereas all expenditures on social welfare, including royal pensions, got only 8 percent of the budget. The extravagant spending on luxuries could reach absurd levels. A single piece of furniture for a royal palace, gilded and bejewelled, cost more than the servant who dusted it could earn in two thousand years (see table 19.2).

Cardinal Fleury established financial order in France, but he could not resolve the underlying problems of inadequate taxation and therefore could not eliminate the debt. The principal direct tax, the *taille*, was collected on land and property, but it was inadequate because the aristocracy, the church, and some towns had exemptions from it. Attempts to create an income tax without exemptions, such as the *dixième* (10 percent) of 1710, had been blocked by the aristocracy, the church, and the parlements. The right to collect indirect taxes, such as tax stamps on documents, had been sold to "tax farmers" for a fixed sum, while they collected whatever excess they could. Many traditional taxes, such as the salt tax (*gabelle*), had been cut for some regions and could not be increased.

The Seven Years' War converted an intractable financial problem into a national crisis. France was populous, rich, and powerful, but the government was facing bankruptcy. The war cost most of the French colonial empire and 50 percent of French world trade. The national debt rose to 62 percent of the national budget in 1763, and it was growing because of huge interest obligations and a rigid tax structure; new loans to restructure the debt could reduce the percentage of the budget consumed but perpetuate the problem. So finances became the dominant issue in France during the twilight years of the Old Regime. Ultimately, neither side won. The financial crisis led France to one of the greatest revolutions of modern history.

King Louis XV, once beloved, was unable to handle these problems. His indebted and ineffective government plus his life of luxury and debauchery produced unpopularity and stately torpor. The death of Madame de Pompadour in 1764 left the king in despair. He slowly became an eighteenth-century stereotype, the aging voluptuary. After a few years of entertaining himself with a royal brothel at Versailles known as Deer Park, Louis selected another official mistress in 1769. Unfortunately, Madame du Barry lacked the insights and education of Madame de Pompadour.

The dominant figure in the French government after the Seven Years' War was Duke Etienne de Choiseul, a capable soldier-statesman who had been sponsored by Madame de Pompadour. Choiseul effectively rebuilt French military strength after 1763 but not French finances. To his credit, Louis XV attempted a solution. He ordered that a wartime tax, the *vingtième*—"the twentieth," a 5 percent income tax that fell on all classes—remain in force. This provoked a virtual rebellion of aristocrats who believed themselves exempt from such taxes. The aristocratic lawyers and magistrates of the *noblesse de robe*, who controlled the parlements of the higher

Illustration 19.3

The French *Parlements.* The French *parlements,* which were high courts of appeal, were a different institution from the English parliament, which was a legislative body. There was a parlement in each of thirteen provinces in eighteenth-century France, and the magistrates in each court were nobles (the nobility of the robe) who owned their office. The parlements resembled parliament in their mutual resistance to royal power. In this illustration, however, a parlement is seen deliberating an issue involving the church, as the proud princes of the church parade in the foreground.

court system, formed the center of the resistance (see illustration 19.3). The Parlement of Paris ruled that the king's decree was illegal. In the south of France, the Parlement of Toulouse even arrested the royal governor who tried to enforce the tax law.

Louis XV capitulated to the parlements in 1764, rescinding the *vingtième* and changing his government. This did not end his battles with the parlements. When he tried to introduce a road building program in Brittany, relying upon a royal *corvée* to provide labor, Breton nobles and the Parlement of Rennes protested. The frustrated king ordered the arrest of the president of the Parlement of Rennes, but this provoked a united protest from all fifteen parlements, claiming that they represented the nation whenever the Estates General (which had last met in 1614) was not in session. As the Parlement of Rouen stated, they considered themselves "the custodian and the depository" of the French constitution, and the king must bend before the law.

This time the king stood firm. In 1766 he sent royal troops to occupy the seat of the Parlement of Paris, then personally appeared before the parlement to express his anger. "I will not allow," Louis told the magistrates, this usurpation of power. "The magistrates are my officers, charged with the truly royal duty of rendering justice to my subjects." Louis insisted that the duties of the parlements did not restrict his sovereignty: "In my person only does the sovereign power rest. . . . To me alone belongs legislative power, unconditionally and indivisibly." To underscore his claim to absolute power, Louis XV named a new government, headed by René de Maupeou, to fight the parlements. In 1771

Maupeou abolished the parlements and created a simpler court system in which the magistrates were salaried state employees instead of owners of their office. He hoped to create a new tax system, both fairer and sufficient for the fiscal crisis, without facing an aristocratic veto. The aristocracy, backed by many philosophes who detested royal absolutism, naturally raised vociferous opposition. But much opinion also supported the king. Voltaire stood with Maupeou's dismissal of the parlements, saying that he would rather be governed by a fine lion than by two hundred rats.

The aristocracy won the day in 1774, when Louis XV died. His nineteen-year-old grandson, Louis XVI, possessed generally good intentions, but he was too timid and inexperienced to stand up to the nobility. His first acts were to dismiss Maupeou and to restore the parlements. Consequently, he faced a strengthened aristocracy throughout his reign. In 1777, when Joseph II of Austria visited his sister, Queen Marie Antoinette, in Paris, he concluded that the government of France was "an aristocratic despotism."

Louis XVI also inherited the desperate financial situation. In the year of his coronation, the state's revenues were 5 percent below its expenditures, increasing a debt that consumed a third of the budget just in interest payments. Those problems soon worsened. Beginning in 1778, France was again at war, supporting—and financing—the American Revolution. Other problems were beginning. The foremost source of French wealth was agriculture, and in 1774 an agricultural recession began. Farm profits, which translated into tax revenue, plummeted in 1775, and they never again during the

Old Regime reached the levels of 1772–74. The decade between 1777 and 1786 saw five harvests in which the average farmer lost money, plus two other poor harvests.

The reign of Louis XVI did show signs of hope, as a result of a reforming ministry led by the minister of finance, Robert Turgot, and the interior, Chrétien Malesherbes. Malesherbes was a liberal who had defended the publication of the *Encyclopédie*. Turgot was a minor aristocrat who had reached high office in a typical way for a venal society: He bought his position for 100,000 livres. He was also a free-thinker and a leader of the enlightened economic school of the Physiocrats, whose doctrines he explained in the *Encyclopédie*. In a series of decrees known as the Six Edicts (1776), Turgot and Malesherbes laid the basis for economic recovery. The edicts abolished the monopoly of the guilds to stimulate economic competition. They abolished the burden of the *corvée* on peasants and replaced it with a tax on all landowners. And they eliminated most internal tariffs on the grain trade to bring down the price of bread. At the same time, Turgot cut government spending, especially in the portion of the budget devoted to royal pensions and the royal court.

The reforms of 1774–76 made many enemies. The opposition of the parlements, pressure from powerful guilds, and intrigues at court brought down Turgot in 1776 and Malesherbes followed him. The Parlement of Paris, for example, claimed that the Six Edicts "imperil the constitution." The magistrates carried the day: Guild monopolies, the *corvée*, and internal tariffs were all restored. Another capable minister of finance, a Swiss-born, Protestant financier named Jacques Necker, succeeded Turgot. Necker had made a fortune as a banker during the Seven Years' War. His home was one of the most influential centers of the Enlightenment, where his wife, Suzanne (a prominent writer and the daughter of a Swiss pastor), and their daughter, Germaine (later famous as the Baroness de Staël, also a distinguished writer), directed a brilliant salon. Necker lived at the center of a network of financial, political, and intellectual leaders, and they shaped a series of enlightened reforms during his ministry from 1778 to 1781. He drafted a royal decree abolishing the limited form of serfdom that survived in France, although it applied only to royal lands. It condemned serfdom in principle and urged aristocrats to follow the king's lead; it did not force abolition in respect for the principle of private property. Few aristocrats followed the king, so serfdom lingered in France, especially in eastern France, where the parlement—most of whose members owned serfs—refused to register the royal decree.

The successors of Turgot and Necker as ministers of finance during the 1780s were utterly unable to break the logjam by which the aristocracy blocked meaningful tax reform. Charles de Calonne, a courtier and less able financier, skirted the edges of bankruptcy by continually increasing the debt. He, too, concluded that a new tax was essential and proposed a land tax, to be paid by aristocrats and the church as well as commoners. To win aristocratic support, an Assembly of Notables (a body of uncertain constitutional basis) was called in 1787; the assembly failed to agree upon anything except opposition to Calonne's tax. This led to Calonne's ouster and yet another minister of finance, who sought even bigger loans, asked the parlements to approve new taxes, and met yet another rejection.

The consequence of the aristocratic rejection of new taxes was that the French national debt reached 100 percent of the budget in 1789. A second consequence was that the aristocracy forced Louis XVI to call elections for the Estates General. The Parlement of Besançon had proposed that solution in 1783 and others had adopted the idea. Louis resisted, trying instead his grandfather's idea of abolishing the parlements in 1788. He finally conceded defeat, however, and agreed to a meeting of the Estates General in May 1789—which led directly to the French Revolution.

The Habsburg Empire in the Age of Maria Theresa

In contrast to Britain, where Parliament had broken the power of the king, or to France, where the resurgent aristocracy was restricting the power of the king, in Austria the Habsburg family still held nearly absolute power during the eighteenth century. The political evolution in Austria—known as enlightened despotism—showed how monarchy could respond to new problems.

The Habsburg Empire dominated Germanic central Europe at the start of the eighteenth century, dwarfing its rivals in size, population, and military might. Prussia numbered only 1.6 million persons and Bavaria 2.0 million; the Habsburg lands held 11.0 million. In the first decades of the century, Habsburg armies under the skillful command of Prince Eugene of Savoy had fought well in the War of the Spanish Succession, and the peace treaties of 1714 gave the Habsburgs the Austrian Netherlands (Belgium) and Lombardy. Wars with the Ottoman Empire at the end of the seventeenth century had acquired the Kingdom of Hungary, including vast territories in eastern Europe. Thus, in 1714 Vienna controlled lands from Brussels in the west to Milan in the south, Belgrade in the east, and Prague in the north—plus the crown of the Holy Roman Empire. This gave the Habsburg emperor Charles VI, who reigned from 1711 to 1740, daunting political problems. The heterogeneous, polyglot realm was united only by the person of the Habsburg monarch.

Hungary gave Charles the most difficulty. The magnate class had been largely autonomous under the Turkish sultan, and their diet expected no less from the Habsburgs. Some Hungarian nobles even claimed a remarkable right, the *jus resistandi*, which legalized resistance to central authority. Charles VI realized that "[I]t is very important that quiet should prevail in this country," and he made numerous concessions to the Hungarians, such as promises to continue their Diet, to tolerate religious minorities (many nobles were Protestants), and not to tax the magnates. Such concessions to regional rights, however, meant that Austria lagged behind rivals such as Prussia in the development of a centralized authority and bureaucracy.

The second formidable political problem confronting Charles VI was the issue of his heir. His only son died in infancy, and all Habsburg lands thus probably would pass to his daughter, Maria Theresa, who could not become Holy Roman Empress (because the Salic Law excluded women) but who could, under Austrian law, inherit the family dominions. Charles knew that powerful men might challenge his succession if the throne passed to a woman; he therefore devoted much of his reign to guaranteeing Maria Theresa's succession and preventing a war of Austrian succession. For Charles, the issue was not protecting his daughter or defending the rights of women, it was the perpetuation of the dynasty and the territorial integrity of the far-flung Habsburg lands. For his subject peoples, however, his death would open the prospect of independence or enhanced autonomy. For the European powers, it suggested the dismemberment of the Habsburg Empire.

The solution Charles VI proposed was a document called the Pragmatic Sanction. It proclaimed that the Habsburg lands were indivisible, and it outlined the Austrian succession through Maria Theresa. Charles obtained the agreement of his family and published the Pragmatic Sanction in 1719. For the next twenty years he bargained within the empire and abroad, buying acceptance of the Pragmatic Sanction. Negotiations with the Hungarian Diet produced its acceptance in 1723, at the price of further weakening Viennese central authority over Hungary. A lifetime of diplomatic bribery bought the consent (sometimes recanted and bought

again) of the European powers. Britain, for example, accepted the Pragmatic Sanction by a treaty of 1731; Charles paid Britain by closing the Austrian trading company (the Ostend Company) that competed with the British in global commerce. The king of Spain signed in return for the duchy of Parma.

Maria Theresa inherited the Habsburg dominions in 1740 at the age of twenty-three, and she stayed on the throne until her death in 1780. She possessed energy and determination but an empty treasury and a weakened army. She began to reorganize the government, but the Pragmatic Sanction failed almost immediately. Her realm accepted her, and the Hungarians were chivalrous in her defense, but the duke of Bavaria, the king of Spain, and the elector of Saxony each claimed the Habsburg crown for himself. The Holy Roman Empire sided with Bavaria, choosing the duke to be emperor. The king of Prussia demanded the province of Silesia as his price for honoring the Pragmatic Sanction. When Maria Theresa refused to surrender Silesia, the Prussians invaded it, beginning a series of wars known collectively as the War of the Austrian Succession (1740–48).

The war went poorly for Maria Theresa at first. The Prussians occupied Silesia. France, Spain, and Bavaria joined an alliance against her. The support of Britain and Holland, however, prevented the partitioning of the Habsburg Empire. When the duke of Bavaria died in 1745, the electors of the Holy Roman Empire acknowledged the stability of Maria Theresa's position by choosing her husband, the duke of Lorraine, as Emperor Francis I. The belligerents reached the same conclusion about Maria Theresa in 1748, ending the War of the Austrian Succession in a treaty that sustained the Pragmatic Sanction except for permitting Prussia to retain Silesia.

The Habsburg Empire had survived the coronation of a woman, but Maria Theresa's empire remained internally divided and less efficient than her rivals. Conditions improved when she entrusted the government to a strong chancellor, Count Kaunitz, but he could not block the rise of a hungry rival for leadership in central Europe, Prussia. Within a few years, Austrian armies again found themselves engaged with the Prussians. The Seven Years' War devastated both countries, leaving no true victors. When peace came again in 1763, the Austrian Empire remained firmly in the grip of Maria Theresa, but even larger financial and administrative problems plagued her. She faced the problems of recovery and reorganization, even establishing a national budget for the first time in her reign. The death of her husband in 1765, however, plunged her into

Illustration 19.4

 Enlightened Despotism in Austria. Joseph II, championed reform in Austria for twenty-five years. In this illustration (one of many versions of this theme) Joseph teaches modern agricultural techniques to peasants.

grief: In a world of arranged, loveless marriages Maria Theresa had been deeply attached to Francis. The young, exuberant empress who had loved theatricals and dances became a solemn, withdrawn, and increasingly religious figure who gave more and more of the government to trusted nobles such as Count Kaunitz.

The Habsburg Monarchy and the Enlightened Despotism of Joseph II

Solving the postwar financial problems of the 1760s led Maria Theresa into conflict with the aristocracy. In 1764 she tried to force the Hungarians to carry a fairer share of imperial taxes, but the Hungarian Diet blocked her plans. Resistance to tax reform led Maria Theresa in a surprising direction—toward the emancipation of the peasantry from the bondage of serfdom. Maria Theresa's most influential adviser in the emancipation of the serfs was her son, Joseph, whose reign in Austria would later provide the best illustration of enlightened despotism in eighteenth-century European monarchism (see illustration 19.4).

Joseph was Maria Theresa's first son, born most inconveniently in 1741 when his mother was confronted with the War of the Austrian Succession. His mother ordered that he not be given a rigorous, military education, and Joseph consequently acquired many of his ideas from reading the philosophes, not from strict tutors. Joseph came to see himself as the embodiment of the Enlightenment, the person who could link reason with absolute powers. When his father died in 1765, Joseph became the Holy Roman Emperor and coregent with his mother in Austria. Maria Theresa shared some of her son's reformist ideas but tried to keep tight control of him and his friends, whom she called the *Aufk-*

lärungs (Enlightenment) Party. After her death in 1780, Joseph could enthusiastically write, "I have made philosophy the legislator of my empire," but the same was not true of Maria Theresa. She had learned to rule in tough circumstances, and her policies often showed this. She believed in the use of torture, she was a brutal anti-Semite who launched a pogrom to drive all Jews out of Bohemia, and she often betrayed a startling insensitivity to the life of a peasant nation. But her stern, and sometimes cruel, policies created the stable, centralized government with a well-regulated army and well-balanced treasury that would make the enlightened policies of her son possible.

The mixed personalities of mother and son launched enlightened despotism in Austria with a compromise version of emancipation of the serfs. Years of famine and periodic peasant rebellion had shown that the serfs needed relief. Joseph urged his mother to act, and Maria Theresa accepted his arguments, writing, "The lords fleece the peasants dreadfully. . . . We know, and we have proof of the tyrannical oppression under which the poor people suffer." Maria Theresa hesitated to act against the interests of the great landowners, but the tax-resistance of the Hungarian nobles angered her enough to proceed. The emancipation of the peasantry in the Habsburg Empire began with an imperial decree of 1767 named the *Urbarium*. This gave Hungarian peasants a leasehold on the soil that they worked and the legal freedom to leave the land without the permission of the local lord. It did not, however, abolish the *robot*, the compulsory labor tax that peasants owed to lords. During the 1770s, mother and son slowly extended this emancipation. Peasant obligations were separately reduced in Austrian Silesia (1771), then in lower Austria (1772), Bohemia and Moravia (1775), and Styria

(1778). After a rebellion by Bohemian peasants in 1775, another imperial decree converted the detested *robot* into a money tax.

Joseph II carried this work to its logical conclusion—the complete emancipation of the serfs—after the death of his mother in 1780. His decree of 1781 (the *Untertanspatent*) gave peasants in Austria, Bohemia, and Galicia the right to appeal to the state in any disputes with their lords. That same year he abolished serfdom in Austria. Peasants obtained the right to marry, to move to the city, and to learn a trade without permission. Then, between 1781 and 1785, Joseph extended this emancipation to his other domains. Joseph II had practical reasons for his policy, such as asserting royal power against the aristocracy and creating a more efficient economy, but the ideas of the Enlightenment were an important factor. As the Patent to Abolish Serfdom of 1781 stated in its preface, "reason and humanity alike require this change." That did not mean, however, that Joseph was simply a gentle philosopher: He was both despot and enlightened. He had autocratic instincts, and those around him often commented on his domineering, uncompromising, irritable character.

Maria Theresa's financial needs and Joseph II's reforming zeal led to similar policies regarding the Catholic Church. The financial crisis of 1763 convinced the devout empress that she should challenge some of the tax exemptions and privileges of the church. She began by asking the church to make a greater "voluntary contribution" to the treasury and to limit future property donations to the church (which became tax-exempt land), but the Vatican refused. This led to imperial decrees restricting the church's acquisition of land, beginning with a patent that applied to the duchy of Milan in 1767. Thus, the financial crisis brought the monarchy into conflict with the church just as it had with the nobility, and this led to a variety of reforms. In 1768 the first tax on the clergy was created. In 1771 a decree established the maximum amount of property that an individual could bring to the church when joining a monastic order. In this struggle, Joseph pressed his mother even harder than he did against the aristocracy, and after her death, he acted vigorously. Between 1781 and 1789, Joseph closed more than seven hundred monasteries with thirty-six thousand members. He seized the lands of the dispersed orders, thereby raising revenues for the state and converting church properties into schools. In all matters, he tried to break the power of Rome over the Catholic Church in Austria, a national religious policy known as Josephinism.

◆ DOCUMENT 19.1 ◆

Joseph II on Religious Toleration

To an Austrian Noble, December 1787:

Till now the Protestant religion has been opposed in my states; its adherents have been treated like foreigners; civil rights, possession of estates, titles, and appointments, all were refused them.

I determined from the very commencement of my reign to adorn my diadem with the love of my people, to act in the administration of affairs according to just, impartial, and liberal principles; consequently, I granted toleration, and removed the yoke which had oppressed the Protestants for centuries.

Fanaticism shall in the future be known in my states only by the contempt I have for it; nobody shall any longer be exposed to hardships on account of his creed; no man shall be compelled in the future to profess the religion of the state. . . . [M]y Empire shall not be the scene of abominable intolerance.

"Letters of Joseph II." In Harry J. Carroll, Jr., et al., eds., *The Development of Civilization*, vol. 2. Chicago: Scott Foresman, 1969.

Joseph II also earned recognition for enlightenment by responding to two great concerns of the philosophes: the toleration of religious minorities (see document 19.1) and the Beccarian modernization of law codes. In 1781 he issued the Edict of Toleration that extended the rights of full citizenship to Protestants and Jews. Such minorities were allowed to enter businesses and professions or to hold previously closed offices. They obtained the right to hold religious services, although regulations still restricted such details as the right to have churches with steeples or bells. Joseph's policy was again a mixture of enlightened ideals and practical politics. Emancipating the minorities brought people of talent into state service and promoted economic growth. Joseph admitted this in the Edict of Toleration, saying that he granted it because he was "convinced on the one hand of the perniciousness of all restraints on conscience and, on the other, of the great benefits to religion and the state from true Christian tolerance."

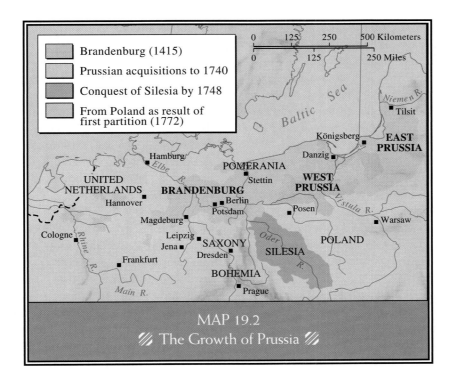

MAP 19.2
The Growth of Prussia

Brandenburg (1415)

Prussian acquisitions to 1740

Conquest of Silesia by 1748

From Poland as result of first partition (1772)

Joseph II's legal reforms came in a series of decrees in the 1780s, chiefly 1787–88. He introduced both a new Civil Code and a new Penal Code. Together they abolished torture and the death penalty (except in military courts martial), introduced civil marriage and burial, ended class distinctions in the law, permitted religious intermarriage, eliminated several categories of crime (such as witchcraft and religious apostasy), and even forbade the ancient aristocratic tradition of primogeniture, which concentrated inheritance in the hands of the eldest son.

These reforms did not make Joseph universally popular, nor the centralized powers of the state (such as strong police) welcome. He had infuriated the aristocracy and the Catholic church by attacking their traditional privileges. He was hated in many provinces, where he enforced the rule of Vienna over local customs, including the mandatory use of the German language in business and government.

The Army, the Bureaucracy, and the Rise of Hohenzollern Prussia

One of the most important political facts of the eighteenth century was the rise of Prussia (see map 19.2). The elector of Brandenburg had acquired the province of Prussia in the seventeenth century, making the combined state of Brandenburg-Prussia an important, but still secondary, German state. The Holy Roman Empire recognized this state as the Kingdom of Prussia in 1701. It was an absolute monarchy with an impotent Diet and obedient aristocracy, known as the Junker class. It was one of the most autocratic states in Europe, but strict, able administration by the House of Hohenzollern provided a solid basis for development.

The ruler at the beginning of the century, Frederick I, did little to advance Prussia into the ranks of the great powers. He admired the sophisticated life of the French royal court at Versailles and devoted his reign to making Berlin glitter with the same elegance. The generation gap between Frederick and his son, King Frederick William I, who reigned from 1713 to 1740, could not have been larger. Frederick William was a cruel, semiliterate man who detested his father's world as effeminate; he favored drunken nights with his advisers and soldiers. In the words of their successor Frederick II, Frederick I sought to turn Berlin into the Athens of Germany, then Frederick William I tried to make it Sparta.

Although contemporary observers found King Frederick William personally loathsome, they acknowledged that he was the person who converted Prussia into one of the great powers. His son, Frederick II—whose love of books, music, French, and men so horrified his father that he beat him violently, imprisoned him, and considered executing him—became Frederick "the Great" partly because he inherited the strong state that his father built. The rise of the Prussian state under Frederick William derived from several factors: the unchallenged authority of the monarchy, the subservience of the aristocracy to a duty called state service, an emphasis upon building a strong bureaucracy and the army officer corps, and the hoarding of resources through parsimony and the avoidance of war. Frederick William I, in short, neither admired nor copied western models of government. He took the concept of compulsory state service by the aristocracy from despotic Russia. Prussian nobles were expected to serve as army officers or as civil servants; in return they obtained a monopoly of many posts and great control over the peasants on their estates.

Frederick William's administration of Prussia rested on more than the domestication of the aristocracy and the conscription of bureaucrats. He made Prussia a center of the study of cameralism (state administration) and founded university positions in cameral studies. This set standards of professionalism for civil servants and bred a bureaucracy admired for its efficiency. What began as a duty for conscripted aristocrats grew into an honor that brought distinction. The best indication of Prussian administrative efficiency came in state finances. Monarchs in France, Spain, and Austria faced bankruptcy; Frederick William had inherited nearly empty coffers himself. But his Ministry of Finance, created in 1713, and its tax-collecting bureaucracy soon became the envy of Europe. A study of Frederick William's finances has shown that he doubled his revenue while reducing expenditures—chiefly by cutting the extravagant royal court that his father had maintained.

King Frederick William I became known as a miser, but he did not economize on military expenditures. European armies were changing in the early eighteenth century; larger armies, maintained in peacetime, were becoming common. Württemberg had a standing army of six thousand men in 1700; Poland, an army of twelve thousand. Saxony and Spain kept peacetime armies of approximately thirty thousand men. Frederick William inherited a standing army set at twenty-seven thousand men and tripled its size to eighty-three thousand. To do this, he divided Prussia into military districts, assigning a quota of new soldiers to each; when recruitment fell short, he added conscription. This meant that Prussia kept 4 percent of its population in uniform, a number previously unthinkable. An important element of this policy, however, was that soldiers be taken from the lowest levels of society, so that the large army not disrupt the productive classes of peasants and workers.

Criminals and debtors were released from prison to serve in the army. As Frederick II later explained this policy, "useful, hardworking people should be guarded as the apple of one's eye" because they paid the taxes that supported the army. The doctrine of state service gave sons of the aristocracy a monopoly of the ranks in the officer corps, and this meant that nearly 15 percent of the aristocracy was serving as army officers. Prussia, as Voltaire wryly commented, was not so much a country with an army to defend it, as it was an army with a country to support it.

Frederick William built the Prussian army upon such rigid discipline that he became known as "the sergeant-king" (see illustration 19.5). The Prussian ideal was an army that gave cadaver obedience—even the dead would still obey orders. Creating this obedience went far beyond the famous goose-step drilling of Prussian soldiers: Flogging and even mutilation were common punishments. The penalty for desertion was to have one's nose and an ear cut off, followed by a life sentence to slave labor. Nonetheless, desertion remained so common that Prussian army regulations required the cavalry to surround the infantry during any march through a wooded area. Capital punishment could be administered for merely raising a hand against an officer. This did not mean that Frederick William I frequently risked the lives of his soldiers. Prussia remained neutral in three major wars during his reign. When he did choose to fight, against troubled Sweden, he continued the expansion of Prussia with the acquisition of West Pomerania.

The Prussian Monarchy of Frederick the Great

Frederick William I's kingdom was inherited by his third son, the twenty-eight-year-old Frederick II, in 1740. The new king got absolute power, an enlarged kingdom, an efficient administration, a full treasury, and a feared army—the material opportunity to become Frederick the Great. His life did not begin that way. As a third son, he had not been expected to reach the throne. As a son of Frederick William, he had been expected to accept a rigid education and rigorous military training. Instead, Frederick had rebelled against his father at eighteen; formed an intimate relationship with his tutor, Lt. Katte; and tried to run off with him. Frederick William sentenced both men to death for desertion, forced Frederick to witness the beheading of his lover, and then imprisoned him with a suspended death sentence. Frederick accepted military training and learned his lessons well but infuriated his father by deciding that

Illustration 19.5

Two Views of Enlightened Despotism in Prussia. The rise of the Prussian state rested on an unusually large army for a small state, a thoroughly trained army that was maintained with brutal discipline. Frederick the Great, who spent more time in warfare than music, approved of the flogging of his soldiers because he expected cadaver obedience from them—the will to follow his orders even after death. Nonetheless, Frederick presented a cultivated and intellectual side to his monarchy. He was a fine musician and spent many hours composing his own music. In this illustration he plays the flute at his palace, Sans Souci.

French literature and music were more interesting (see illustration 19.5). Frederick became an excellent flute player and wrote flute compositions throughout his life. When he came to power and built Sans Souci ("Care-free")—an ornate palace with French gardens—in Potsdam, outside Berlin, he delighted in the visits of Johann Sebastian Bach, with whom he played duets, and Voltaire, with whom he debated philosophy. Frederick became such a voluminous writer that his collected works run for thirty volumes.

Frederick II did not become known as Frederick the Great for writing poetry and incidental pieces for the flute. He turned to the task of government with enthusiasm and extended his father's accomplishments. To the bureaucracy he added a system of competitive examinations for promotions and his own tireless labor as "the first servant of the state." He insisted upon daily written reports from his ministries and poured over them in a bureaucratic toil that would have been unthinkable for most monarchs. And when Frederick II decided upon ways to improve his kingdom, he did not hesitate to act. When he learned of the benefits of the potato, for example, he forced the nation to adopt it. He distributed free seed potatoes to the peasants in 1744, then issued an edict demanding that they grow potatoes or have their ears and nose cut off, and sent the army to check on crops being grown.

The rebellious and artistic Frederick became Frederick the Great as a soldier. Unlike his father, he was not reluctant to use the Prussian army. He came to the throne of Prussia in May 1740, five months before Maria Theresa inherited the Austrian throne; by December 1740 they were at war. Of his first twenty-three years on the throne of Prussia, Frederick was at war with Austria for fifteen years. He began by ignoring the Prussian promise of 1726 to honor the Pragmatic Sanction and invading Silesia in the first of three wars he would fight with Maria Theresa, sometimes called the Silesian Wars. Frederick II was neither a brilliant innovator nor a great battlefield strategist, but he was a superb tactician who found ways to defeat larger, or better placed, armies by concentrating his forces against a portion of his enemies. His success as a general was linked to a strategy of exhaustion in which he fought in indirect ways (such as occupying territory and destroying crops or commerce) rather than engaging in grand battles until one side or the other was annihilated. This won Silesia, Frederick's reputation as a genius, and international recognition of Prussia as a great power.

Another part of Frederick II's reputation rests on his claim to enlightened despotism alongside Joseph II of Austria. At the beginning of his reign, Frederick showed promise of becoming one of the most enlightened statesmen of the century. Within a few months, he abolished torture in criminal procedures, established freedom of religion, granted limited freedom of the press, and founded the Berlin Academy of Science. That early promise was poorly fulfilled, however. Frederick remained attached to the ideals of the Enlightenment, in theory, but his later years saw few reforms and they were chiefly to improve Prussian finances, curing the problems he had created himself with long wars.

Frederick II did continue to build the army. Frederick William's army of eighty-three thousand approached two hundred thousand near the end of Frederick II's reign. He did this by subordinating all government activity to the military. During a peacetime buildup in 1752, Frederick gave the army 90 percent of the Prussian budget. His arms factory at Potsdam manufactured fifteen thousand muskets per year, and the military warehouses at Berlin and Breslau stored enough grain to feed sixty thousand soldiers for two years. Frederick also expanded the army by implementing the plan of a Prussian civil servant, Justus Moser, for army reserves. Moser conceived the idea of universal military training with most citizens remaining active in a militia in case they were needed.

Frederick's militarism nearly destroyed Prussia. During the 1750s, Count Kaunitz engineered a diplomatic revolution that allied the Habsburgs with Russia and England and included promises of the return of Silesia to Austria. Frederick chose war and kept Silesia, but following the Seven Years' War, Prussia was, in the words of one historian, "a bleeding stump, drained of vitality." The war killed more than 10 percent of the population (500,000 of 4.5 million), and by 1763 boys of fourteen were being conscripted to fight. More than one hundred towns and villages had been burnt to the ground, and thirteen thousand families had lost their homes. The devastated towns of Prussia included Berlin, which the Russian army put to the torch in 1760. The overflowing treasury that Frederick II had inherited had been squandered on war, forcing Frederick to face the critical question of eighteenth-century government: taxation. "No government can exist without taxation," he wrote. "This money must necessarily be levied on the people; the grand art consists of levying so as not to oppress." He, like his peers, failed at the "grand art." Taxes were levied in inverse proportion to the ability to pay them: The rich and powerful had exemptions from taxation, so the poor and the middling were expected to carry the burden. That system worked in comfortable times, but the Seven Years' War broke it. Far from paying taxes, much of the population was near starvation in 1763. The monarch himself, although only fifty-one years old, seemed broken by age: His back was stooped, his face gaunt, his teeth missing, and he was plagued with both diarrhea and hemorrhoids. He returned to Berlin in military triumph known as *der alte Fritz* (Old Fritz)—partly an affectionate compliment, partly a sad comment. "It is a poor man who is coming home," the king acknowledged in 1763.

Little room existed for enlightenment in the despotism of Frederick the Great's later years. He was still remembered as the king who had insisted that "[A]ll religions must be tolerated," but he extended few freedoms. When the German dramatist Gotthold Lessing followed Voltaire's footsteps to Berlin with high hopes, he left protesting against a stifling environment: "Don't talk to me about your Berlinese freedom of thought and writing. It only consists of the freedom to make as much fun as you like of religion. . . . Let someone in Berlin stand up for the rights of the peasants, or protest against despotism and exploitation as they do now even in France and Denmark, and you will soon know by experience which country is to this day the most slavish in Europe." Some modern scholars, however, have concluded that Frederick was the greatest of the enlightened despots. One French historian, impressed by a king of intellect and culture, concluded that he possessed "the most complete character of the eighteenth century, being the only one to unite idea with power."

Catherine the Great and Despotism in Romanov Russia

The eighteenth century began in Russia, as it did in France, with one of the most powerful autocrats of the seventeenth century still holding the throne. When Peter the Great of Russia died in 1725, he left behind a royal succession even more troubled than Louis XIV's legacy to France. The French got a five-year-old king and a resurgent aristocracy; the Russians got a generation of chaotic government in which one heir to the throne was tortured to death, one former serf was crowned, and a council of nobles exercised central power in Russia until 1762 when a strong monarch, Catherine II, arrived on the throne.

Catherine was the daughter of an impoverished German duke who had married her off at age sixteen to a feeble-minded grandson of Peter the Great, the grand-duke Peter. After childhood worries that a spinal deformity would make Catherine an ugly, unmarriageable drain on her family, she grew into an attractive woman with deep black hair contrasting with a pale complexion. Before she had matured into such physical attractiveness, however, the future empress had built her identity around her education and her strong, probing mind. Her intelligence won the attention of the Russian royal family when hunting for a wife for the uneducated heir to the throne, Grand-Duke Peter. When Peter was unable to consummate the marriage, members of the royal family who were desperate to perpetuate the dynasty advised Catherine to find a lover who could produce children. She cheerfully complied and began a series of affairs that were among the most no-

torious features of her reign—although they hardly distinguished her from the behavior of male monarchs such as George I of England or Louis XV of France.

Catherine's lovers have historical importance because one of them, Grigori Orlov, an officer in the royal guards, helped her to usurp the throne. When her husband was crowned Czar Peter III in 1762, the army began to conspire against him because he favored an alliance with a recent Russian enemy, Frederick the Great of Prussia. Orlov became a leader of this conspiracy. When Peter threatened the arrest of his estranged wife, a military coup overthrew him and named Catherine empress. Her husband soon died in prison, apparently killed by one of Orlov's brothers and possibly with the connivance of Catherine, who ascended the throne at age thirty-two.

Catherine II of Russia reigned from 1762 until 1796. She initially faced significant opposition because she was a foreigner, Lutheran-born in an Orthodox land, and sexually scandalous. She obtained (and used) great power largely because she was able to strike a bargain with the aristocracy—the *dvorianstvo* class. Like Frederick II of Prussia, the basis of her reign became this compromise: She would enhance the position of the aristocracy and make no reforms at their expense. Catherine settled the deal by seducing the foremost leader of the old nobility, Nikita Panin, who then endorsed her claim. Thereafter, she exercised autocratic powers with a skill that rivaled Peter the Great, earning a reputation for enlightened despotism, although the evidence is greater for her despotism than for her enlightenment. She initially accepted, but later opposed, an imperial *ukase* drafted by Panin that would have delegated legislative power to a council of nobles. She did restore to the nobility freedoms it had lost under Peter the Great. She abolished compulsory state service by all aristocrats but kept nobles in high diplomatic and military posts, winning the gratitude of many. She granted a monopoly on vodka production to nobles, winning others.

Catherine II best placated the aristocracy by her policy on serfdom. She had read enough of the philosophes to be an enlightened enemy of serfdom in principle, and one of her first decrees upon coming to the throne had been to alleviate the conditions of serfs on the royal estates. As European Russia contained fifty million peasants—55 percent of them serfs on the royal estates—this was no small matter. And Catherine talked of abolishing serfdom. Her actions, however, were different: She consistently extended the power of aristocrats over their serfs. A decree of 1765, for example,

---

❖ DOCUMENT 19.2 ❖

Catherine the Great's Instructions for a New Law Code, 1768

Of the situation of the people in general

33. The laws ought to be so framed as to secure the safety of every citizen as much as possible.

34. The equality of the citizens consists in this: that they should all be subject to the same laws.

35. This equality requires institutions so well adapted as to prevent the rich from oppressing those who are not so wealthy as themselves. . . .

36. General or political liberty does not consist in that licentious notion, that man may do whatever he pleases.

37. In a state or assemblage of people that live together in a community where there are laws, liberty can only consist in doing that which every one ought to do, and not to be constrained to do that which one ought not to do.

38. A man ought to form in his own mind an exact and clear idea of what liberty is. Liberty is the right of doing whatsoever the laws allow: And if any one citizen could do what the laws forbid, there would be no more liberty, because others would have an equal power of doing the same.

39. The political liberty of a citizen is the peace of mind arising from the consciousness that every individual enjoys his peculiar safety; and in order that the people might attain this liberty, the laws ought to be so framed that no one citizen should stand in fear of another; but that all of them should stand in fear of the same laws.

Catherine the Great. *The Grand Instructions to the Commissioners Appointed to Frame a New Code of Laws.* London: 1768.

---

gave them the right to send troublesome peasants to Siberia.

Catherine's shrewd politics solidified her despotic authority by raising the Russian aristocracy to a level of power that they had not previously known. The culmination of this trend occurred in 1785 when Catherine issued the Charter of the Nobility, which codified the collective rights of the *dvorianstvo*, such as freedom from state service. It gave aristocrats the sole right to acquire serfs, which town dwellers and even free peasants had sought. It excluded the aristocracy from taxation and from corporal punishment.

Partly for consolidating imperial power for thirty years, and partly for her enlightened reforms, Catherine II became known as Catherine the Great. The enlightened side of her record, however, is ambiguous. She read many of the philosophes before ascending to the throne, and she was apparently much influenced by Blackstone, Beccaria, and Montesquieu. She corresponded with Voltaire and hosted Diderot on a visit to Russia. Her devotion to the ideals of the Enlightenment, however, remained stronger in theory than in action. She found it difficult to enact the ideas she liked. Diderot was dazzled to find "the soul of Brutus in the body of Cleopatra," but Catherine thought the philosopher's schemes were "sheer prattle." She wrote to him in 1770, rejecting many reforms for Russia, "All your work

is done on paper, which does not mind how you treat it. . . . But I, poor empress, must work upon human skin, which is much more ticklish and irritable."

Catherine's greatest effort at enlightened government produced almost no result. In 1767 she summoned a Legislative Commission of 564 delegates, representing all classes except the serfs. Only twenty-eight members were named to the commission, and the rest were elected. Catherine charged the commission with the task of considering the complete reform of the laws of Russia. To guide the commission, Catherine prepared one of the most famous documents of her reign, the Grand Instructions (*Nakaz*) of 1767 (see document 19.2). These instructions contained both halves of enlightened despotism. They opened by asserting that "[T]he sovereign is absolute, for there is no other authority but that which centers in his single person." That statement of despotic power was followed by many enlightened principles: Catherine opposed torture and capital punishment, called for a government based on the division of powers, and indicated her hostility to serfdom. The potential for change was enormous. As Panin reacted to the *Nakaz*, "[T]hese principles are strong enough to shatter walls!"

Despite the great promise of its beginning, the Legislative Commission of 1767–68 did not reform Russia. It received more than fourteen hundred petitions (more than one thousand of them from free peasants), held more than two hundred meetings, and quibbled over details. The commission agreed to vote Catherine a new title ("the Great and All-Wise Mother of the Fatherland"), but it could not agree upon a legal code. At best, it gave Catherine ideas for later years.

The need for reform in Russia was dramatized by a rebellion of serfs and the Cossacks of southern Russia in 1773–75, known as Pugachev's Rebellion. Emilian Pugachev was a Cossack—a people who had lost their autonomy in 1772—and a deserter from the Russian army. He organized discontented serfs, Cossacks, and religious minorities into a rebel army in 1773. Pugachev announced that he was Czar Peter III, claiming he had been dethroned by Catherine and the great nobles. He formed a "royal court" among the rebels and proclaimed the emancipation of the serfs, giving them the incentive to fight for his victory. Pugachev's rebels withstood the Imperial army for nearly two years, capturing the town of Kazan, and stimulating serf rebellions throughout the region. The government took Pugachev so seriously that new defenses were built around Moscow to prepare for his attack. The rebellion collapsed in 1775 when Pugachev's own forces betrayed him. He was taken to St. Petersburg, exhibited in an iron cage, and then beheaded. Catherine ordered that Pugachev not be tortured but agreed that his questioning could include the artful extraction of his teeth. Her principles against torture did not protect Pugachev's followers.

Special troops scoured the countryside, tracking down rebellious serfs. Most were executed "according to Christian canon"—cutting off their hands and feet before beheading them, then leaving the bodies to rot at roadside while heads were displayed on pikes in town.

Catherine II achieved her most important reforms in the aftermath of Pugachev's rebellion, but they did little to improve the conditions of serfdom. First, she reorganized the government of Russian provinces in 1775 by dividing Russia into fifty administrative provinces, each subdivided into districts. Local nobles were named to head district governments. Councils, elected by town dwellers as well as nobles, shared in the government. Separate courts were established for nobles, burghers, and free peasants. Catherine carried this administrative reform further in 1785 when she issued the Charter of Towns. Following the strict hierarchy of corporative society, the charter divided the urban population into six legal categories, ranging from the great merchants and leaders of the wealthiest guilds down to manual laborers. It allowed all six categories of town dwellers, including the unskilled working class, to participate in elections for the town council. Catherine the Great thus gave signs of enlightened aspiration, and she achieved a few noteworthy changes. But the foremost characteristic of her reign was still despotism, and the condition of the serfs worsened significantly under her rule.

CHAPTER 20

THE CULTURE OF OLD REGIME EUROPE

CHAPTER OUTLINE

◆◆◆◆◆◆◆◆◆◆◆◆◆◆◆◆◆◆◆◆◆◆

This chapter looks at the culture of eighteenth-century Europe from several perspectives. It begins by looking at traditional "high culture"—the art and architecture, the music and drama of the educated classes. A transition occurred from the baroque style to a revival of classicism, which became the dominant style in the arts of the eighteenth century. The discussion then focuses on "popular culture" in the lives of ordinary people. It compares a basic institution of high culture, the salon, with the equivalent institution of popular culture, the coffeehouse.

Although other themes seemed to dominate the culture of the eighteenth century, Christianity remained central to European civilization. Chapter 20 explains the religious division of Europe into Protestant, Catholic, and Orthodox regions and examines the position of Jewish, Islamic, and dissenting Christian minorities. Most of the chapter is devoted to the dominant intellectual phenomenon of the eighteenth century, the Enlightenment. Described are the origins of the Enlightenment in seventeenth-century skepticism, the rationalism of the scientific revolution, and the cultural revival of classicism. The basic concepts that connected enlightened thought—natural law, reason, and progress—are then explained. This leads to a discussion of the French Enlightenment, French philosophes, and the most typical work of the Enlightenment, the *Encyclopédie.* After describing the Enlightenment in other parts of Europe, the chapter ends with an examination of its impact on religion and government.

◇

High Culture: From the Baroque to the Classical

The predominant cultural style of the seventeenth century, known as the baroque, still dominated many of the arts in the early eighteenth century. The baroque appealed to the emotions and spirituality through the

Ilustration 20.1

⧅ **Secular Rococo Architecture.** As the monarchs of Europe emulated the French Bourbons in building lavish new palaces, they did not make precise copies of Versailles. Instead they built luxurious homes in the newest architectural style. The Wittelsbach family, who ruled the south German state of Bavaria, were among the most active builders, and their palaces included Schloss Nymphenburg at Munich, whose gilded rococo "Hall of Mirrors" is shown here.

ornately decorated, the extravagantly expressed. Whether looking at the energetic statues of Bernini, paintings of suffering martyrs by Caravaggio, or the voluptuous pastel nudes of Rubens, the viewer was overwhelmed by the lavish baroque style. Architects brought baroque emotions to palaces and churches, composers brought them to oratorios and fugues, artisans even sought the baroque style in gilded chairs and writing tables. This style culminated in an extravagant artistic style, characterized by fanciful curved forms and elaborate ornamentation, known as rococo (see illustration 20.1). Frederick the Great's Sans Souci Palace was rococo—there a warrior king could write French poetry, compose flute music, and dispute philosophers in a home he helped to design, with the gaudy yellow walls and the plump cherubs a soldier wanted.

Historians chiefly remember the high culture of the eighteenth century for the reaction against the baroque style. A revival of the styles and aesthetics of the classical Graeco-Roman world rapidly supplanted the baroque during the middle decades of the century. The elegant simplicity of classical architecture—characterized by symmetry, mathematical proportions, the harmony of forms, and severe rules—became a vogue in the 1740s after archaeologists began to excavate the Roman cities of Pompeii and Herculaneum, which had been buried (and preserved) by volcanic ash in A.D. 79. A classical revival swept European architecture, producing such masterpieces as the Romanov Winter Palace in St. Petersburg (now the Hermitage Museum), La Scala opera house in Milan, and the Royal Crescent in Bath, England. In some cases, neoclassical buildings closely resembled classical structures built eighteen hundred years earlier (see illustration 20.2).

Classicism soon came to dominate the arts of the eighteenth century. Histories of the ancient world, such as Edward Gibbon's *The Decline and Fall of the Roman Empire*, became popular reading together with the ancients themselves. Universities required Latin and Greek of their students, and in some countries an honors degree in classics became the best route to a high-paying job or a government post. Painters, sculptors, dramatists, poets, and composers all mined classical literature for inspiration. The French painter Jacques-Louis David, for example, inspired a generation of politicians with his dramatic canvases depicting stirring moments in Roman history. Music was perhaps most shaped by eighteenth-century classicism. The strict attention to form, the mathematical precision, the symmetry learned from architecture became the basis of a new

Illlustration 20.2

The Parisian church of St. Mary Magdalen, known as la Madeleine, was begun in 1764 and redesigned several times. The final version, a neoclassical temple with imposing Corinthian columns, bears a striking resemblance to temples built two thousand years earlier.

music: The development of the sonata, the symphony, the string quartet, and the concerto so changed musical composition that the name *classical music* remained long after the classical era.

Popular Culture in the Eighteenth Century

In recent decades, cultural historians have paid closer attention to the culture of the lower classes, as distinct from the high culture of the elite. The distinction is not absolute, because high culture and popular culture are often remarkably similar. In the eighteenth century, the plays of Shakespeare were popular with the agricultural classes of rural England, who welcomed the touring troops of actors who brought drama to the countryside. In London, David Garrick's famous theater on Drury Lane was as popular with the artisans and laborers who flocked to the cheap seats as it was with the wealthy who bought the boxes. In the capitals of opera such as Milan and Vienna, few shopkeepers could afford to attend the lavish productions. But Mozart had a popular following, too, and versions of his operas were produced in lower-class music halls.

Popular culture and high culture also intersected for the converse reason: The well-bred, well-educated, and well-off also frequented the robust entertainments of ordinary folk. The world of popular culture—a world of rope-walkers, jugglers, and acrobats of village bands and workers' music halls; of folktales and folksong; of races, fights, animal sports, and gambling; of marionettes, pantomimes, and magic lantern shows projected on smoke; of inns, taverns, public houses ("pubs"), cafes, and coffeehouses; of broadsheets and limericks; of carnivals and fairs; of entertainment in public parks and on the village commons—was not the exclusive province of the laboring classes who gave these their meanings and values. High culture honored this intersection by regularly borrowing from popular culture, from the folk theme that reappeared as a leitmotif in a symphony or the tales of oral culture that reappeared in learned anthologies.

A good illustration of the parallels in high culture and popular culture can be seen in two of their centers: the salon (high culture) and the coffeehouse (popular culture). The salon, a social gathering held in a private home where notable literary, artistic, and political figures discussed the issues of the day, characterized the educated world of high culture in the eighteenth century. Salons were typically organized and directed by women of grace and style who shaped European culture by sponsoring rising young talents, protecting unpopular opinions, finding financial support for impoverished writers, and sometimes fostering political intrigues (see illustration 20.3). The salons glorified conversation—about the republic of letters, the arts, politics and policies, scandal and gossip, and wit and flirtation. Salon hostesses were sometimes the wives, daughters, or mistresses of powerful men, such as the duchess de Maine, the mistress of Philippe d'Orleans, the regent of France; some were prominent intellectuals in their own right. Their ranks included women such as Madame de Lambert, the author of *Advice of a Mother to Her Daughter* (1734), which advocated university education for women. Another salon hostess, Louise d'Epinay, won the French academy's prize for 1774 for her *Conversations with Emile.*

The habit of organizing salons originated in the French aristocracy, but it was adopted by other elements of the educated classes and spread across Europe. By the middle of the century, salons were flourishing in London, Berlin, Vienna, Rome, and Copenhagen, usually assuming a national character somewhat different from Parisian salons. In England, they ranged from the formal salon of Elizabeth Montagu, the granddaughter of Lady Mary Wortley Montagu, who forbade such frivolity as playing cards, to the less formal salon of Mary Monckton, the countess of Cork, which included such prominent figures as Samuel Johnson. Salons in the German states provided an opportunity for Jewish families to win social acceptance previously denied them. Moses Mendelssohn began the habit of holding

Illustration 20.3

 The Salon of Madame Geoffrin. Marie-Thérèse Geoffrin (1699–1777) was the hostess of one of the most influential salons of eighteenth-century France. In presiding over such private meetings of writers, philosophers, artists, and politicians, women played a central role in the shaping and transmission of the ideas of the Enlightenment.

open houses for intellectuals, and his daughter, Dorothea von Schlegel, built on this habit to emulate the French salons. Most German salons, however, insisted upon a stricter sexual respectability than characterized Parisian salons.

The coffeehouse served a similar cultural role for other social strata. Coffeehouses—and sometimes taverns, which were less expensive and less formal—served as meeting houses, reading rooms, and debating halls. The daily newspaper was at the center of this phenomenon. Dailies were born and began to flourish in the eighteenth century, starting with the *Daily Courant* in London in 1702. Moscow had a newspaper later that same year, Berlin a daily paper from 1704, and Rome from 1716. Paris even had a women's newspaper, advocating the equality of the sexes—*Le Journal des dames,* founded in 1759—before it had a daily newspaper. Larger Sunday newspapers appeared in London in 1780. Until the technological innovations of the mid-nineteenth century, however, these newspapers remained expensive and their circulation low. Subscription libraries and "reading societies" appeared in the German states as early as 1704. But the coffeehouse provided the most popular solution by subscribing to multiple newspapers, holding public readings of newspaper stories for the benefit of the illiterate majority, and providing the sociable setting. The towns and cities of eighteenth-century Europe were filled with coffeehouses. The first coffeehouse opened in Paris in 1672 and soon failed; in 1754, however, fifty-six were flourishing. There were none in London in 1650, but more than two thousand had opened by 1725. The first coffeehouse in central Europe opened in Vienna in 1683, after a few sacks of coffee were taken from a retreating Turkish army. After the eighteenth-century boom, the Viennese all but lived in fifteen thousand coffeehouses. Coffeehouses became so popular in Berlin that Frederick the Great blocked the importation of coffee as a drain on the national wealth—a hint at how expensive coffee was initially.

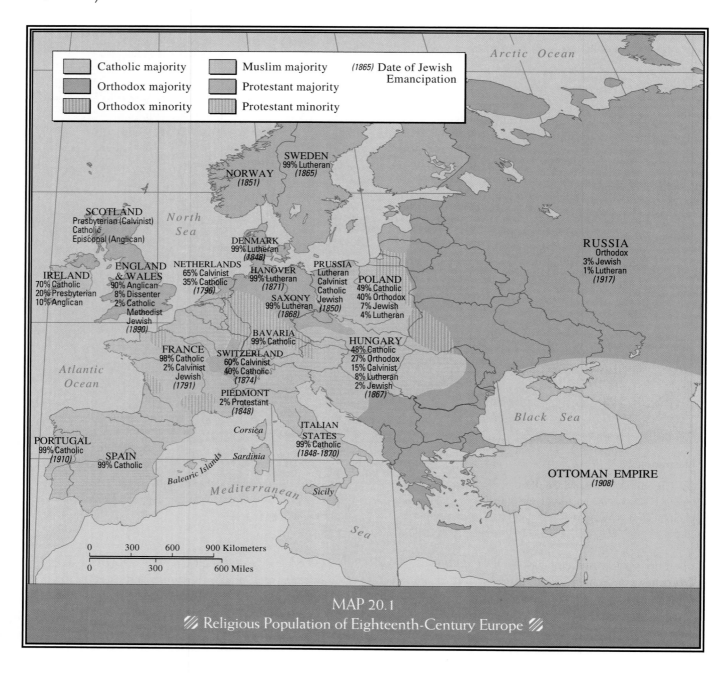

Catholic majority   Muslim majority   (1865) Date of Jewish Emancipation

Orthodox majority   Protestant majority

Orthodox minority   Protestant minority

Arctic Ocean

SWEDEN
99% Lutheran
(1865)

NORWAY
(1851)

North Sea

RUSSIA
Orthodox
3% Jewish
1% Lutheran
(1917)

SCOTLAND
Presbyterian (Calvinist)
Catholic
Episcopal (Anglican)

DENMARK
99% Lutheran
(1848)

IRELAND
70% Catholic
20% Presbyterian
10% Anglican

NETHERLANDS
65% Calvinist
35% Catholic
(1796)

HANOVER
99% Lutheran
(1871)

PRUSSIA
Lutheran
Calvinist
Catholic
Jewish
(1850)

POLAND
49% Catholic
40% Orthodox
7% Jewish
4% Lutheran

ENGLAND
& WALES
90% Anglican
8% Dissenter
2% Catholic
Methodist
Jewish
(1890)

SAXONY
99% Lutheran
(1868)

BAVARIA
99% Catholic

HUNGARY
48% Catholic
27% Orthodox
15% Calvinist
8% Lutheran
2% Jewish
(1867)

FRANCE
98% Catholic
2% Calvinist
Jewish
(1791)

SWITZERLAND
60% Calvinist
40% Catholic
(1874)

Atlantic Ocean

PIEDMONT
2% Protestant
(1848)

Corsica

ITALIAN
STATES
99% Catholic
(1848-1870)

Black Sea

PORTUGAL
99% Catholic
(1910)

SPAIN
99% Catholic

Sardinia

Balearic Islands

Mediterranean

Sicily

Sea

OTTOMAN EMPIRE
(1908)

0   300   600   900 Kilometers

0   300   600 Miles

MAP 20.1

Religious Population of Eighteenth-Century Europe

Religion and Eighteenth-Century Culture

Christianity stood at the center of European culture in the eighteenth century, as it had for more than a thousand years. Although European civilization was almost exclusively a Christian civilization, it was split into many conflicting sects. The religious map of the Old Regime followed lines drawn by the Peace of Westphalia in 1648, which had ended a period of ferocious religious warfare (see map 20.1). At the simplest level, most of northern Europe was Protestant, most of southern Europe was Roman Catholic, and much of eastern Europe was Orthodox. Protestant Europe included Great Britain, the Dutch republic, the northern German states (notably Hanover, Saxony, and Prussia), all of Scandinavia, part of divided Switzerland, and pockets in eastern Europe (notably in Hungary). Catholic Europe included Portugal, Spain, France, all of the Italian states, the southern German states (notably Bavaria), and the Austrian Empire, plus most of the population in religiously divided Ireland and Poland. Orthodox Europe included Russia plus large portions of Poland and the Ottoman Empire (such as Greece and Serbia).

This religious division of Europe left many minority populations inside hostile countries. Important Catholic minorities existed in Britain (only 2 percent of the population, but including many powerful families), Holland (35 percent), Switzerland (40 percent), and Prussia (especially after the annexation of Silesia). Similar Protestant minorities were found in Ireland (30 percent), France (2 percent, but disproportionately important, like Catholics in Britain), Piedmont (2 percent), Poland (4 percent), and Hungary (23 percent). In addition to Christian minorities, Europe contained small Jewish and Moslem populations. Jews were forbidden to live in some countries (notably Spain) but formed a small minority (less than 1 percent) in many states, especially Britain, France, Holland, and Prussia; they constituted larger minorities in eastern Europe, chiefly in Poland (7 percent), Hungary (2 percent), Russia, and the Ottoman territories. Moslems were almost entirely confined to the Ottoman Empire, in the provinces of modern Bosnia and Albania.

Protestant Europe included three predominant faiths: Anglicanism, Calvinism, and Lutheranism. Virtually all of the membership of the Anglican Church (the Church of England) was found in England, Wales, Scotland, and Ireland. Lutheranism was the dominant form of Protestantism in the German states and Scandinavia, and Lutheran minorities were scattered in many east European states. A variety of Calvinist churches—usually called the Reformed Church—existed in western Europe. Their traditional center was Geneva, where Calvin had established his church. Calvinist churches were predominant in Switzerland, Holland (the Dutch Reformed Church), and Scotland (the Presbyterian Church); Calvinist minorities existed in many states, notably France—where the Reformed Church was illegal though 500,000 followed it in secret—Prussia, and Hungary.

In addition to these primary Protestant churches, many smaller Christian sects existed in 1700, and more were founded during the eighteenth century. Small populations of diverse Protestants—such as Quakers (the Society of Friends) in England and the Baptists in central Europe—lived even within Protestant states. In England, approximately 8 percent of the population, collectively called Dissenters or Nonconformists, belonged to Protestant sects outside of the Church of England.

The Roman Catholic Church was more unified and centralized than Protestantism, but it, too, encom-

passed diversity. Catholicism remained united by the authority of the pope and by the hierarchical administrative structure directed by the Vatican. However, the eighteenth-century papacy was too weak to resist the absolute monarchs of Catholic lands. Louis XIV of France had created a virtually autonomous French Catholic Church, often called the Gallican Church. (Gallicanism meant that the king named French cardinals and bishops himself and decided whether papal decrees would apply in France.) Other Catholic monarchs copied the French administrative independence from Rome, as the kings of Piedmont did in the early eighteenth century and Joseph II of Austria did later. Variations of Catholicism also depended upon the local strength of individual orders (such as the Jesuits) or doctrines (such as Jansenism). The Jesuits began the eighteenth century as the most important of all Catholic orders. They were rigorously trained men who had acquired global influence through their educational and missionary efforts, and they had increasingly turned their attention to politics. Their role in statecraft made the Jesuits controversial, however, and they were expelled from Portugal in 1759, from France in 1762, from Spain and many Italian states in 1767, and finally dissolved by Pope Clement XIV in 1773. Jansenism, named for a Dutch theologian, was equally controversial for teaching an austere, puritanical—almost Calvinistic—form of Catholicism, particularly in Belgium and France, and the doctrine was condemned by a papal bull.

Important differences existed between Catholicism and Protestantism, shaping cultural differences in Europe. These extended far beyond matters of faith—beyond the fine points of theological doctrines, such as the nature of Christian sacraments or the route to salvation. Protestant pastors, unlike Catholic priests, married and raised families, frequently producing dynasties of preachers when their sons also entered the church and their wives and daughters took leading roles in Protestant organizations. Protestant states abolished the monastic orders that existed in Catholic countries and seized church lands; thus, the church had a greater physical presence in Catholic countries through land ownership and especially the far greater size of the clerical population. The Catholic Church owned 10 percent of the land in France (30 percent in some regions), 15 percent of Castile and central Spain, and 40 percent of Naples and southern Italy. The ecclesiastical population of Portugal has been estimated at 80,000 to 300,000—at least 4 percent of the population, and perhaps as much as 15 percent. A study of the island of

Corsica has found that a population of 220,000 people sustained sixty-five monasteries. The situation was dramatically different in England, where a population of 5.8 million people, 90 percent of whom were nominally Anglican, sustained eleven thousand clergymen in the Church of England—less than 0.2 percent of the population.

Within these variations, all of Europe lived in a deeply Christian culture. Churches provided most of the social services that existed for the poor, crippled, aged, orphaned, released prisoners, and reformed prostitutes. Hospitals and schools were run by the church, not by the state. Schools provide perhaps the best illustration of the Christian character of European civilization. Few people received a formal education in the eighteenth century—most of the population in all countries remained illiterate—but the majority of the schools that existed were run by churches. The Presbyterian Church ran most of the schools in Scotland, the Anglican Church the majority of the schools in England, the Lutheran Church dominated Scandinavian education, and the Orthodox Church conducted most of the schools in Russia. In many Catholic countries—including Spain, Portugal, Poland, and most of the Italian states—the church totally controlled teaching. Religion formed a large part of the educational curriculum. The need to be literate to read the Bible was frequently the decisive reason in creating new schools, especially in Protestant faiths that stressed Bible reading.

Religion remained central to both high culture and popular culture, but Christian themes no longer dominated painting and sculpture, and literature had entered a thoroughly secular age; European culture reflected an "age of reason" more than an "age of faith." Still, the arts of the eighteenth century relied heavily upon religion. Goethe's *Faust* (1773), one of the masterpieces of German literature, is a Christian tragedy of lost faith and damnation. The dominant buildings of the age were royal palaces and stately homes, yet many of the structures that characterized baroque and rococo architecture were churches, such as the lavish Karlskirche in Vienna (see illustration 20.4). Composers may have favored secular subjects for the flourishing opera of the eighteenth century, but many of the masterpieces of baroque music originated in Christianity, such as Marc-Antoine Charpentier's powerful *Te Deum*. Johann Sebastian Bach long earned his living as cantor and organist at the Thomaskirche in Leipzig, where he composed a huge array of music on Christian themes, such as his *Mass in B minor*. And perhaps no music composed in the eighteenth century is more famous than Handel's *Messiah*.

Christianity similarly remained central to popular culture and the rhythms of daily life. The sound of church bells marked the time of day for most Europeans, and a church clock was often the only timekeeping that the poor knew until late in the eighteenth century. Sunday remained the day of rest—often the only day of rest—for shopkeepers, laborers, and peasants alike. The only vacation most people knew came from religious holidays and festivals, and the calendar of the Old Regime was filled with such days. In addition to the universal holidays of the Christian calendar, such as Christmas and Easter, every region, village, and occupation added the celebration of patron saints.

Most governments maintained a state religion, rewarding its members and limiting the rights of non-members. In Denmark and Sweden, non-Lutherans could not teach, hold public office, or conduct religious services. In Britain, a series of laws called the Test Acts excluded non-Anglicans from military command, sitting in parliament, or attending Oxford or Cambridge universities. Catholics could not live in London, nor Protestants in Paris, in 1750. Restrictions were stricter in regions where the Inquisition retained power. More than seven hundred Spaniards condemned by the Inquisition were burnt at the stake between 1700 and 1746; the last burning for heresy in Spain came in 1781. The Inquisition exerted a greater force on European culture by regulating behavior. A trial before the Inquisition in 1777 listed some of the behavior that true Christians must cease: (1) eating meat on Friday; (2) crossing one's legs during a church service; (3) believing that the Earth revolved around the Sun; (4) not believing in acts of the faith, such as ringing church bells during a storm to beg God to stop it; (5) owning prohibited books, listed on the church's Index of forbidden books; (6) corresponding with non-Catholics; and (7) disputing the idea that only Catholics could go to Heaven. No Protestant equivalent of the Inquisition existed, but that did not make Protestant lands models of toleration. Denmark forbade Catholic priests from entering the country under threat of the death penalty.

The Enlightenment and Its Origins

The eighteenth century is one of the most famous periods in the history of European thought. Historians often call that century the Age of Enlightenment (or the Age of Reason) because eighteenth-century writers smugly considered their epoch more enlightened than earlier eras. It was an age that cherished universities,

Illustration 20.4

🖉 **Ecclesiastical Rococo Architechure.** Much of the finest rococo architecture is found in the eighteenth-century churches of Germanic central Europe. The Abbey Church at Ottobeuren, shown here, uses colored stucco, marble, frescoes, and gilded frames to achieve a spectacular image.

learned academies, scientific laboratories and observatories, libraries, philosophic journals, books (especially great reference works), and talking about all of them (see map 20.2). Although the term *the Enlightenment* was not used during the eighteenth century, synonymous terms—particularly the German term, *Aufklärung*—were used.

The history of the Enlightenment focuses on the influential thinkers and writers of the age. They are usually identified by a French name, the *philosophes,* which is a broader term than *philosophers* in English. The importance of the Enlightenment rests in the circulation of the ideas of the philosophes among a small

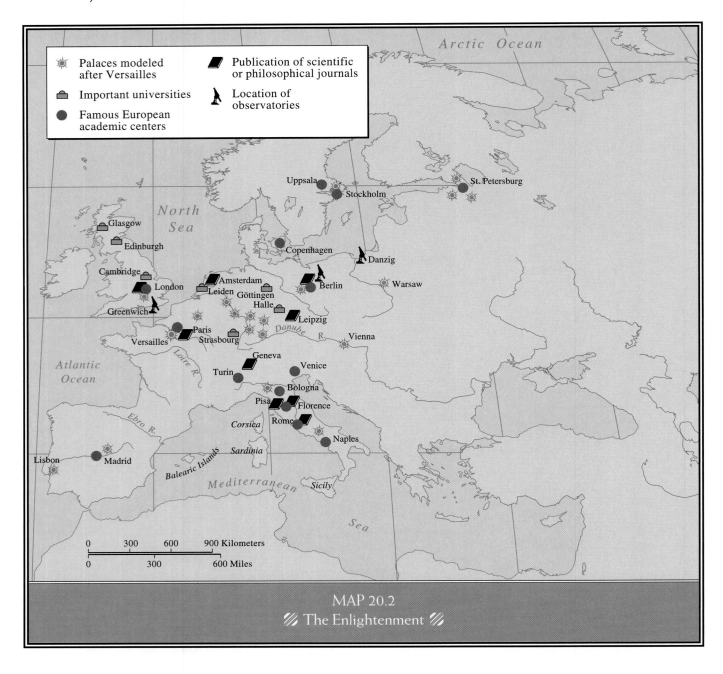

MAP 20.2

The Enlightenment

literate population and the influence of these ideas in changing the Old Regime. The central ideas of the Enlightenment are frequently simplified to a few basic concepts. The philosophes often differed, but a few concepts were nearly universal: (1) *skepticism*—questioning the validity of assumptions about society and the physical world without regard for traditional authority; (2) belief in the existence of *natural laws*—such as the law of gravity—that govern both the social and physical worlds; (3) confidence that *human reason*, rigorously applied, can discover these natural laws and establish them as the basis of human activity; and

(4) optimism that the application of reason and obedience to natural laws will produce *progress*, leading to the perfection of human institutions.

One of the most eminent German philosophes, Immanuel Kant, summarized many of these attitudes in an essay of 1784 entitled "What Is Enlightenment?" His definition of Enlightenment was the liberation of individuals from direction by others (see document 20.1). Kant held that people achieved this liberation when they resolved to use their reason and to follow its dictates. Thus, he suggested a Latin motto for the Enlightenment: *Sapere aude!* (literally, "Dare to know!"), which

◆ DOCUMENT 20.1 ◆

Immanuel Kant: Enlightenment

*Immanuel Kant (1724–1804) was a distinguished German philosopher and a professor of logic and metaphysics at the University of Königsberg in eastern Prussia. He was already famous for his greatest work—*The Critique of Pure Reason *(1781)—when he published the essay "What Is Enlightenment?" (1784), from which the following excerpt is taken.*

Enlightenment is man's leaving his self-caused immaturity. Immaturity is the incapacity to use one's intelligence without the guidance of another. Such immaturity is self-caused if it is not caused by lack of intelligence, but by lack of determination and courage to use one's intelligence without being guided by another. *Sapere Aude!* Have the courage to use your own reason! is therefore the motto of the enlightenment.

Through laziness and cowardice, a large part of mankind, even after nature has freed them from alien guidance, gladly remain immature. It is because of laziness and cowardice that it is so easy to usurp the role of guardians. It is so comfortable to be a minor! If I have a book which provides meaning for me, a pastor who has conscience for me, a doctor who will judge my diet for me, and so on, then I do not need to exert myself. I do not have any need to think; if I can pay, others will take over the tedious job for me. . . .

But it is more nearly possible for a public to enlighten itself: this is even inescapable if only the public is given its freedom. . . . All that is required for this enlightenment is *freedom*, and particularly the least harmful of all that may be called freedom, namely the freedom for man to make public use of his reason in all matters.

Kant, Immanuel. "What Is Enlightenment?" In Carl J. Friedrich, ed., *The Philosophy of Kant.* New York: Modern Library, 1949.

he translated as "Have the courage to use your own reason!"

The Enlightenment developed from several trends in European thought. Skepticism had been one of the dominant themes of seventeenth-century philosophy, chiefly associated with the French philosopher René Descartes. In works such as the *Discourse on Method* (1637), he had advocated universal doubt; that is, the doubting of everything until it can be proven.

Pierre Bayle had even taken the dramatic step of applying skeptical philosophy to the Bible. Bayle, a Frenchman whose advanced ideas forced him to live in the greater freedom of Holland, proposed "a detailed refutation of the unreasonable deference given to tradition," and he included Christianity within that tradition. All religious questions, including the reading of the Bible, "require the use of reason."

A second fundamental source of the Enlightenment thought was the scientific revolution of the seventeenth century, especially Sir Isaac Newton's synthesis of the accomplishments of many scientists. Newton had built upon a scientific revolution that had destroyed the geocentric theory of the universe, instead placing the Sun at the center in a heliocentric theory. This required sweeping, counterintuitive adjustments in European thought. For the heliocentric theory to be true, the Earth must move, at tremendously high speeds, around the Sun and the Sun did not rise or set, it merely appeared to do so because the rotation of the Earth turned a viewer toward or away from the Sun. Christian theologians fought such conclusions. The Catholic Church placed the writings of astronomers on the Index of prohibited books, arguing that "it is the Holy Spirit's intention to teach us how to go to heaven, not how the heavens go."

The Enlightenment canonized Newton because he convinced the intelligentsia that the new astronomy was correct and the churches were wrong. His greatest fame resulted from stating the Principle of Universal Gravitation (the law of gravity) in his masterwork, *Principia mathematica* (1687). The "universal" element of the law of gravity fascinated the philosophes of the eighteenth century. Newton proved to them that human reason could discover "the universal qualities of all bodies whatsoever." Voltaire, who popularized Newton's work in *Elements of the Philosophy of Newton* (1738), proclaimed him "the greatest and rarest genius that ever rose for the ornamentation and instruction of the species." The English poet Alexander Pope was equally lavish in praising the Newtonian synthesis in his *Essay on Man* (1734): "Nature and nature's law lay hid in night/God said, 'Let Newton be,' and all was light." And around the Western world, philosophes placed a bust of Newton in their study—as Thomas Jefferson did at Monticello—as a reminder that human reason could find universal natural laws.

A third source of Enlightenment thought, alongside philosophic skepticism and scientific rationalism, was the revival of classicism Like the humanists of the Renaissance, the philosophes revered the Graeco-Roman past, but with a different emphasis. To them, antiquity represented the historical model of a society that had revered scientific observation and reasoned objectively from these observations. This admiration of antiquity implied the rejection of knowledge supported only by authority, dogma, or superstition—the traits that the philosophes often associated with the history of Europe after the fall of Rome.

Natural Law, Reason, and Progress

When the scientific revolution convinced the European intelligentsia that natural laws existed, the philosophes concluded that laws governing human activity—the organization of governments, economic relations, the efficient operation of prisons, and the writing of history—similarly "lay hid in night." Such laws merely awaited the Newton of economics or penology. The belief in natural law was not new; ancient authors had asserted its existence, too. The scientific revolution merely allowed thinkers to embrace this old idea with a new self-confidence.

One of the leading figures of the French Enlightenment, the Baron Charles-Louis de Montesquieu, illustrates this interest in natural law in his writings on political theory. Montesquieu was a wealthy provincial noble, educated in law, who inherited a position in the Parlement of Bordeaux. Although he was elected the chief justice of the parlement, he was more interested in theories of government than in the day-to-day drudgery of his highly political job. He sold his office—such positions were often the property of nobles in the eighteenth century—and turned to writing. His *The Spirit of the Laws* (1748) became one of the most widely influential books of the century, joining the seventeenth-century works of John Locke, who had attacked the divine right of royalty and asserted the divine royalty of right, in laying the foundations of modern political theory.

Montesquieu began *The Spirit of the Laws* by asserting that people, like the physical world, are "governed by invariable laws." This did not mean laws promulgated by the government and enforced by the courts; Montesquieu called that type of law "positive laws." Instead, Montesquieu meant laws in a scientific sense—laws that exist in nature, laws that state "fixed and invariable relationships" just as much as the law of gravity did. For example, Montesquieu believed that natural law proclaimed the need for food and the attraction of the sexes. Other natural laws governing human relations were less certain. Montesquieu, for example, asserted that people were, by nature, peaceful rather than warlike. One consequence of asserting the existence of natural laws and trying to define them was that they might be different from the positive laws enforced by the government or the moral laws of the established church. Philosophes such as Montesquieu insisted that positive law must therefore be changed to agree with natural law. "The intelligent world," he wrote, "is far from being so well governed as the physical."

References to "nature" and "nature's law" are found in a great variety of eighteenth-century works in addition to Newton's physics, Pope's poetry, and Montesquieu's political theory. The most typical work of the Enlightenment, the French *Encyclopedia of the Arts and Sciences* (the *Encyclopédie*), devoted three full articles to natural law. Jean-Jacques Rousseau wrote one of the famous books in the history of education, *Emile, or Concerning Education* (1762), stressing natural education. "Nature," he wrote, "never deceives us; it is always we who deceive ourselves." The first draft of the American Declaration of Independence proclaimed that people were entitled to independence and self-government by "the Laws of Nature." Not all philosophes used the theory of natural law, however. But even those who rejected it—as did the Scottish philosopher David Hume, who called it a "fallacious and sophistical" theory—discussed the idea at length.

To discover natural laws, the philosophes relied on skepticism and rationalism. Skepticism meant questioning and criticizing everything. "A thing is not proved when no one has ever questioned it," wrote one of the editors of the *Encyclopédie*. "Skepticism is the first step toward the truth." Kant insisted upon the skeptical evaluation of everything, including church and state, in *The Critique of Pure Reason* (1781):

> Our age is the age of criticism, to which everything must be subjected. The sacredness of religion, and the authority of legislation, are by many regarded as grounds for exemption from the examination by this tribunal. But, if they are exempted, they become the subjects of just suspicion, and cannot lay claim to sincere respect, which reason accords only to that which has stood the test of a free and public examination.

Most philosophes shared this glorification of reason. Montesquieu stressed that reason must be the basis of law. An American philosophe, Thomas Jefferson, advised: "Fix reason firmly in her seat, and call on her tribunal for every fact, every opinion." Denis Diderot, the coeditor of the *Encyclopédie*, wrote that the philosophe must be "actuated in everything by reason."

◆ CHRONOLOGY 20.1 ◆

Landmark Works of the Enlightenment

1702 Daniel Defoe's *The Shortest Way with Dissenters* satirizes intolerance

1721 Baron Montesquieu's *Persian Letters* derides French institutions

1725 Madame de Sévigné's posthumous *Letters* reveal life of the aristocracy

1729 Sir Isaac Newton's *Principia mathematica* translated into English from Latin

1733 Voltaire's *Letters Concerning the English* popularizes Newtonian science and representative government

1734 Madame de Lambert's *Advice of a Mother* advocates university education for women

1739 David Hume's *A Treatise of Human Nature* states utilitarian principles

1739 Sophia's *Woman Not Inferior to Man* asserts the equality of women

1741 Johann Süssmilch's *The Divine Order* pioneers the field of statistics

1748 David Hume's *Essays Concerning Human Understanding* states case for complete skepticism

1749 Baron de Montesquieu's *The Spirit of the Laws* establishes study of comparative government

1751 Denis Diderot and Jean d'Alembert publish the first volume of the *Encyclopédie*

1755 Jean-Jacques Rousseau's *Discourse on the Origin of Inequality* attacks the social order of Europe

1755 Samuel Johnson publishes first comprehensive dictionary of the English language

1758 Claude Helvétius's *De l'esprit* asserts the principle of enlightened self-interest

1759 Voltaire's *Candide* satirizes ideas and institutions of the eighteenth century

1762 Jean-Jacques Rousseau's *The Social Contract* propounds radical ideas about rights and liberties

1762 Jean-Jacques Rousseau's *Emile* urges "natural" education

1763 Voltaire's *Essay on Toleration* denounces religious intolerance

1764 Cesare Beccaria's *Treatise on Crimes and Punishments* urges penal reforms

1764 Voltaire's *Philosophical Dictionary* criticizes both church and state

1768 Joseph Priestley's *Essay on the First Principles of Government* stresses the happiness of citizens

1770 Baron d'Holbach's *The System of Nature* attacks organized religion

1771 First edition of the *Encyclopedia Britannica* appears

1776 Adam Smith's *The Wealth of Nations* outlines principles of capitalist economics

1777 John Howard's *The State of the Prisons* exposes horrible prison conditions

1779 Gotthold Lessing's *Nathan the Wise*, a dramatic poem on toleration published

1781 Immanuel Kant's *Critique of Pure Reason* published

1781 Moses Mendelssohn's *On the Civil Amelioration of the Condition of the Jews* published

1781 Johann Pestalozzi's *Leonard and Gertrude* advocates the reform of education

1782 Joseph Priestley's *A History of the Corruptions of Christianity* criticizes the church

1784 Immanuel Kant's "What Is Enlightenment?" urges people to dare to use their reason

1788 Immanuel Kant's *Critique of Practical Reason* states "the categorical imperative" for behavior

1792 Mary Wollstonecraft's *A Vindication of the Rights of Woman* calls for equal education

1795 Marquis de Condorcet's *Progress of the Human Spirit* proclaims the doctrine of progress

1798 Thomas Malthus's *Essay on the Principle of Population* foresees world overpopulation

---

The insistence upon rationalism caused collisions between the philosophes and the established authorities. This was especially true of the Christian churches, which insisted upon the primacy of faith as a standard of knowledge rather than, or in addition to, reason.

One of the first popes directly rejected reason as the standard of the church, arguing that "[i]f the word of God could be comprehended by reason, it would no longer be wonderful." The conflict between reason and faith had interested many thinkers across the centuries, but faith had remained the Christian standard even after the Protestant Reformation, when Martin Luther had condemned reason as "the Devil's Harlot."

Despite such conflicts, the philosophes were generally confident that the use of human reason to discover natural laws would produce a better world. Thus, the glorification of reason led to an optimistic cult of progress. The French mathematician Jean d'Alembert, Diderot's coeditor of the *Encyclopédie*, thought "it is impossible to deny that philosophy has shown progress among us. Day by day natural science accumulates new riches." The greatest champion of the doctrine of progress was another French mathematician, the marquis Antoine de Condorcet, whose *Progress of the Human Spirit* (1795) foresaw nothing less than "the indefinite perfectibility of the human race"—a passage written shortly before Condorcet died in a prison of the French Revolution.

The French Enlightenment and the Encyclopédie

Although skepticism and rationalism attracted the educated classes of many regions, the home of the Enlightenment was in France, where the authority of church and throne were already weakened and the political duel between the aristocracy and the monarchy created an environment more favorable to radical thought than existed in most of Europe. The most famous and internationally read philosophes were French, as the universal use of a French word for them suggests. Voltaire's famous satiric novel *Candide* (1759), filled with witty criticism of the Old Regime, went through eight editions in the year of its publication alone. Rousseau's radical political tract *The Social Contract* (1762) had thirteen French editions in 1762–63. Montesquieu's *The Spirit of the Laws* (1748) saw twenty-two French editions by 1751 and ten editions in its English translation by 1773; it had appeared in Dutch, Polish, Italian, and German editions by the 1780s and was so widely read that it was translated into Latin for the benefit of well-educated people in regions with less common languages, such as Hungary.

Nothing characterizes the French leadership of the Enlightenment better than the publication of the twenty-eight volumes of the *Encyclopédie* by Diderot and d'Alembert between 1751 and 1772. Many of the most famous writers of the eighteenth century contributed to what was perhaps the greatest intellectual accomplishment of the Enlightenment. The idea of compiling an encyclopedia was not new. The word itself came from the classical Greek *encyclios*—meaning instruction in the whole circle of learning—in both the arts and the sciences. Many famous efforts had been made to encompass the entire circle of learning, from Pliny's *Natural History* in the first century A.D. through a number of encyclopedic works in the seventeenth century.

Denis Diderot was an unlikely figure to produce the *Encyclopédie*. He was the son of a lower-middle class family—his father was a cutlery maker—in provincial France. Diderot received his formal education from the Jesuits, then prepared for a career in the church so devoutly that he fasted, slept on straw, and wore a hair shirt. Further study in Paris, however, changed Diderot into a Bohemian writer who broke with church and family alike, angering the former with his writing and the latter with his behavior. Like many philosophes, Diderot's writings earned him poverty and time in a royal prison. Thus, he eagerly accepted the opportunity to edit an encyclopedia, which was originally intended to be merely a translation of an English work.

The resultant *Encyclopédie* was a work of uneven quality and numerous inaccuracies, but it nonetheless became *the* encyclopedia. It owed its fame and influence to two characteristics. First, it was a collaborative enterprise, not simply the work of its editors. The contributors included many of the most influential writers of the Enlightenment; Condorcet, Montesquieu, Rousseau, and Voltaire all wrote for the *Encyclopédie*, with Voltaire alone contributing more than forty articles. Baron Paul d'Holbach wrote on the history of religion, including daring essays on priests and theocracy that made him one of the most controversial philosophes. Two leading Physiocrats, François Quesnay and Jacques Turgot, summarized the economic ideas that dominated contemporary thought and would be adopted by many governments. Such contributors guaranteed the *Encyclopédie* a large readership and extended the influence of the French Enlightenment across Europe.

The second reason for the importance of the *Encyclopédie* was that the ideas and opinions that it contained made it notorious. The *Encyclopédie* did not merely record information, it became a forum for the philosophes. They began in the first volumes by criticizing despotic government and the established church; subsequent volumes contained direct attacks. As early as 1752, with only two volumes in print, King Louis XV of France ordered the *Encyclopédie* "to be and to remain suppressed." The support of friends in high places—especially the king's mistress, Madame de Pompadour—allowed publication to proceed, but it did so amidst controversy. In 1759 French courts turned the work over to a panel of churchmen and scholars to censor. The government again denounced it, this time for

❖ DOCUMENT 20.2 ❖

Excerpts from the *Encyclopédie*

Each of the subjects in bold type are entries in the Encyclopédie, *from which brief excerpts are taken.*

Censors of Books: Name given to men of learning who are in charge of the examination of books to be printed. . . . These censors have been created in various states in order to examine literary works and pass judgment on books which are to be printed, so that nothing would become public that could seduce minds with false doctrines or corrupt morals with dangerous maxims.

Intolerance: The word intolerance is generally understood to designate the savage passion that prompts us to hate and persecute those who are in error. . . . Ecclesiastic intolerance consists in considering as false all religions other than one's own. Teaching, persuasion, and prayer—these are the only legitimate means of spreading the faith. Whatever means provoke hate, indignation, and scorn are blasphemous. . . . Whatever means would tend to incite men to rebellion, bring the nations under arms, and drench the earth with blood are blasphemous.

Natural Law: The term is taken to designate certain principles which nature alone inspires and which all animals as well as men have in common. On this law are based the union of male and female, the begetting of children as well as their education, love of liberty, self-preservation, concern for self-defense. . . .

We understand by natural law certain laws of justice and equity which only natural reason has established among men, or better, God has engraved in our hearts. The fundamental principles of law and all justice are: to live honestly, not to give offense to anyone, and to render unto each whatever is his. . . . Since this natural law is based on such fundamental principles, it is perpetual and unchangeable: no agreement can debase it, no law can alter it or exempt anyone from the obligation it imposes.

Negroes: For the last few centuries the Europeans have carried on a trade in Negroes whom they obtain from Guinea and other coasts of Africa and whom they use to maintain the colonies established in various parts of America and in the West Indies. To justify this loathsome commerce, which is contrary to natural law, it is argued that ordinarily these slaves find the salvation of their souls in the loss of their liberty, and that the Christian teaching they receive, together with their indispensable role in the cultivation of sugar cane, tobacco, indigo, etc., softens the apparent inhumanity of a commerce where men buy and sell their fellow men as they would animals used in the cultivation of the land.

Diderot, Denis, D'Alembert, Jean le Rond, et al. *The Encyclopédie; Selections,* trans. Nelly S. Hoyt and Thomas Cassirer. Indianapolis: Bobbs-Merrill, 1965. Reprinted by permission of Prentice-Hall.

causing "irreparable damage to morality and religion." Pope Clement XIII condemned it for "false, pernicious, and scandalous doctrines and propositions, inducing unbelief and scorn for religion." None of these threats, including excommunication for mere possession of it, stopped the publication (see document 20.2).

The Enlightenment beyond France

French leadership may have been unquestioned, but the Enlightenment was a widespread experience. The German Enlightenment (the *Aufklärung*) drew on the excellence of German education, from compulsory education laws to superior universities. Rulers even encouraged the process in some regions. Frederick the Great of Prussia

considered himself a philosophe and corresponded with Voltaire. He wrote dozens of books and composed more than one hundred symphonies, sonatas, and concertos. And he typically bought five copies of each book by the philosophes, to have one at each of his palaces. Frederick kept Prussian intellectuals on a short leash, however, and once said that the way to punish a region was to have it governed by philosophers. But he allowed sufficient tolerance that letters flourished, as they had begun to do under his grandfather (Frederick I), whose Berlin had boasted the first subscription library (1702), one of the first newspapers (the *Vossische Zeitung,* 1704), and an Academy of Sciences (1711). Habsburg Austria, in contrast, was largely closed to the Enlightenment by strict censorship, intolerance of minorities, and the hostility to science of the Austrian Catholic Church. Alchemists outnumbered chemists in Vienna in the early eighteenth century.

The German Enlightenment produced a number of notable figures. The century began with Gottfried von Leibnitz, Newton's equal as a mathematician and superior as a philosopher, presiding over the Berlin Academy. Leibnitz's reputation suffered somewhat when Voltaire's *Candide* ridiculed a sentence taken out of context from his *Théodicée* (1710): "God created the best of all possible worlds." His philosophy, however, did much to establish the scientific concept of natural law in eighteenth-century thought. And Leibnitz came closer than Voltaire to being the intellectual who mastered all fields of thought, from the scientific to the philosophic.

At the end of the century, the *Aufklärung* produced Germany's greatest poet, Wolfgang von Goethe. Goethe was at the center of a remarkable intellectual circle in Weimar that marks the beginnings of modern German literature; it included the poet and dramatist Friedrich von Schiller and the philosopher Gottfried von Herder. The dramatist Gotthold Lessing in Leipzig and Berlin, the philosopher Moses Mendelssohn in Dessau and Berlin, Immanuel Kant in Königsberg, Johann Süssmilch (one of the founders of the science of statistics) at Berlin, and the Bavarian Academy of Sciences in Munich show that the German Enlightenment spread widely across central Europe.

Other parts of Europe were centers of the Enlightenment. A Swedish Enlightenment, evident in northern Europe, was known as the Gustavian Enlightenment because it was encouraged by King Gustavus III of Sweden. It centered upon the Swedish Royal Academy of Sciences (1741), Linnaeus's Botanical Gardens at Uppsala (1741), and the Swedish Academy at Stockholm (1786). There was also a noteworthy Neapolitan Enlightenment and a Scottish Enlightenment, which included Adam Smith (one of the founders of capitalist economics), David Hume (one of the greatest skeptics of the age), and James Hutton (one of the founders of modern geology). The prestige of the Enlightenment was so great that historians in every country have labored to show their national role in it, but for some regions—such as Spain, Portugal, and eastern Europe—the local Enlightenment was limited. In Spain, the hostility of the church limited the movement to a minority of the governing class. The largest periodical in Spain had a circulation of 630 copies, and a daring aristocrat who spoke publicly of the importance of reason was brought before the Inquisition on charges of heresy.

The Enlightenment and Christianity

Wherever the Enlightenment stirred the educated classes, it had important implications for European civilization. This becomes especially clear when one views the relationship between the Enlightenment and Christianity. Many of the philosophes bluntly attacked Christian beliefs and institutions, challenging the churches in ways that might have led them to the stake in other eras. Hume, for example, applied skepticism to Christianity: "[T]he Christian religion not only was at first attended by miracles, but even at this day cannot be believed by any reasonable person without one." Diderot called Christianity "the most prejudicial of all the superstitions of the earth" (see document 20.3). Privately, he denounced the Judeo-Christian deity as "a partial God who chooses or rejects, who loves or hates, according to his caprice; in short, a tyrant who plays with his creatures."

Such ideas were not limited to one or two radical, dechristianized writers. Tom Paine attacked the concept of the Trinity ("The notion of a Trinity of Gods has enfeebled the belief in one God.") and the Bible ("Whenever we read the obscene stories, the voluptuous debaucheries, the cruel and tortuous executions, the unrelenting vindictiveness with which more than half the Bible is filled, it would be more consistent that we call it the word of a demon than the word of God. It is a history of wickedness that has served to corrupt and brutalize mankind."). Voltaire's *Candide* ridiculed churchmen by depicting a friar who seduces women, monks who consort with prostitutes, and priests who spread venereal disease; other churchmen committed robbery, torture, and murder. Edward Gibbon ended his monumental, six-volume *The Decline and Fall of the Roman Empire* with the conclusion that Christianity was one of the primary causes of the fall of Rome. He portrayed a church filled with "the inevitable mixture of error and corruption" contained in all human institutions.

The most famous critic of Christianity during the Enlightenment was Voltaire, the pen name of a Frenchman named François-Marie Arouet. Voltaire, the frail child of a Parisian legal official, received the finest classical education from the church, at the Jesuit *collège* Louis-le-Grand. A priest who admired Voltaire's intelligence led him into a freethinking group whose members did not hesitate to criticize or deride any institution. Voltaire threw himself into this sport and wrote a poem satirizing the regent, the duke of Orleans. Under the arbitrary legal system of the Old

◆ DOCUMENT 20.3 ◆

Diderot: The Church

Denis Diderot studied to become a priest but instead became one of the church's sharpest critics. The following excerpt is taken from a short work that he published in 1775, "Discourse of a Philosopher to a King."

Sire, if you want priests you do not need philosophers, and if you want philosophers you do not need priests; for the ones being by their calling the friends of reason and the promoters of science, the others the enemies of reason and the favorers of ignorance, if the first do good, the others do evil.

You have both philosophers and priests; philosophers who are poor and not very formidable, priests who are rich and very dangerous. You should not much concern yourself with enriching your philosophers, because riches are harmful to philosophy, but your design should be to keep them; and you should strongly desire to impoverish your priests and to rid yourself of them. . . .

But, you will say to me, I shall no longer have any religion.

You are deceived, Sire, you will always have one; for religion is a climbing and lively plant which never perishes; it only changes form. That religion which will result from the poverty and degradation of its members will be the least troublesome. . . .

And if you deign to listen to me, I shall be the most dangerous of all philosophers for the priests. For the most dangerous is he who brings to the monarch's attention the immense sums which these arrogant and useless loafers cost his state; he who tells him, as I tell you, that you have a hundred and fifty thousand men to whom you and your subjects pay about a hundred and fifty thousand crowns a day to bawl in a building and deafen us with their bells. . . .

Since you have the secret of making a philosopher hold his tongue, why not employ it to silence the priest?

Diederot, Dennis. "Disclosure of a Philosopher to a King." In Denis Diderot, *Interpreter of Nature*, trans. Jean Stewart and Jonathan Kemp. New York: International Publishers, 1943.

Regime, this poem was sufficient grounds for Voltaire's imprisonment without a trial. Thus, at age twenty-three, Voltaire was thrown into the Bastille for eleven months. Shortly after his release, Voltaire insulted another powerful noble who arranged to have the young poet beaten by a gang of thugs and imprisoned in the Bastille a second time. Voltaire wisely chose exile in England after his second release.

Voltaire's principal criticism of Christianity was the intolerance that he found among Christians. He was not the first philosophe to adopt this theme. Daniel Defoe had already written a stinging satire in 1702 entitled *The Shortest Way with Dissenters,* a book that persuaded too few people because Defoe was pilloried in public stocks and sent to prison. Voltaire returned to the theme so often that he made tolerance one of the highest principles of the Enlightenment. In a *Treatise on Tolerance* (1763), he denounced the Catholic Church for the mentality that led to the cruel murder of Jean Calas, a Protestant merchant who was tortured to death in 1761 on the fallacious charge that he had murdered his son to prevent him from converting to Catholicism. Voltaire demanded that Christians learn complete tolerance: "It does not require any great art of studied elocution to prove that Christians ought to tolerate one another. I will go even further and say that we ought to look upon all men as our brothers. What! call a Turk, a Jew, a Siamese, my brother? Yes, of course; for are we not all children of the same father, and the creatures of the same God?" Voltaire returned to this theme in his *Philosophical Dictionary* (1764): "Of all religions, Christians ought doubtless to inspire the most tolerance, although hitherto the Christians have been the most intolerant of men." By the end of the eighteenth century, many other philosophes adopted Voltaire's theme. Moses Mendelssohn, the great Jewish philosopher of the Enlightenment, published a powerful plea for the freedom of conscience, the toleration of minorities, and the separation of church and state—*Jerusalem* (1783). Mendelssohn also served as the model for the title character in Lessing's passionate call for toleration, *Nathan the Wise* (1779).

The criticism that the philosophes leveled upon Christianity became so widespread that some historians have called the eighteenth century an age of modern paganism. However, the Enlightenment was not simply an atheist campaign. Some of the most distinguished philosophes were churchmen, such as the Anglo-Irish philosopher George Berkeley, an Anglican bishop. The institutional hostility of the Catholic Church to the Enlightenment did not stop many individual Catholic churchmen from being enthusiastic participants. One study of the *Encyclopédie* has shown that, in some regions of France, priests bought the majority of copies. Pope Benedict XV was an intellectual himself, a friend of Montesquieu and Voltaire. In 1744 he permitted the publication of Galileo's condemned works; in 1757 he stopped enforcing the decrees against books teaching the heliocentric theory of the universe. Many philosophes sought to reconcile Christianity and science, theology and reason, as Leibnitz did in *Théodicée*.

Most of the Enlightenment skeptics retained some form of belief in God, if only as an "Omniscient Architect" or "Designing Deity," terms favored by Montesquieu in *The Spirit of the Laws*. The most widespread form of belief balancing rationalism and skepticism with a belief in a supreme being is known as Deism (sometimes Theism, the term Voltaire preferred). Deism was neither a structured religion nor a coherent body of religious beliefs. Instead it was an individualistic blend of reason, skepticism, and moral virtue combined with a rejection of religious intolerance, dogmatic belief, and powerful ecclesiastical institutions. A large percentage of the eighteenth-century elite favored deism over organized religion, including not only French intellectuals such as Voltaire, Rousseau, and Montesquieu, but also such prominent colonial figures as Benjamin Franklin, George Washington, and Thomas Jefferson.

The Enlightenment and Government

The Enlightenment had equally grave implications for the monarchical governments of the Old Regime. The same application of skepticism and rationalism, the same search for natural laws, meant criticism of monarchy and aristocratic privilege. Rousseau, for example, bluntly styled himself "Jean-Jacques Rousseau, enemy of kings" and did not hesitate to sign letters to Frederick the Great that way. Diderot was more dramatic with his hostility: "Let us strangle the last king with the guts of the last priest!" Voltaire, who had good reasons to despise the powerful, treated them to the same acidic ridicule in *Candide* as churchmen received. When Candide and a companion arrived in a new kingdom, for example, they "asked one of the lords-in-waiting how he should behave in saluting His Majesty; should he fall on his knees or should he grovel, should he put his hands on his head or his behind, or should he just lick the dust off the floor . . . ?"

The criticism of a monarch who could imprison authors without a trial was a risky business. Voltaire's stay in the Bastille and Diderot's in the dungeon at Vincennes are only two of the most famous examples of the attempts to control troublesome writers. A study of French records has shown that the police kept thorough files on French authors; fully 10 percent of all writers in 1750 had spent some time in prison, usually the Bastille. The police used royal *lettres de cachet* to pursue such critics of the government, especially pamphleteers. Authors risked public whippings or even life sentences to the galleys for publishing their ideas. And the works of even the most famous writers were regularly censored by many authorities. Rousseau's *Emile*, for example, was not only condemned by the Catholic Church and placed on the Index of prohibited books, but it was also condemned by the Sorbonne (University of Paris), the General Assembly of the Clergy, and the Parlement of Paris. Fortunately for Rousseau, only his book was burnt in a public ceremony.

Consequently, early eighteenth-century writers sought indirect ways, such as Voltaire's satires, to make their point. When Archbishop François Fénelon wanted to criticize the king, he hid his satire in the form of an ancient epic. Fénelon's *Télémaque* reports the travels of the son of the Homeric hero, Ulysses; by describing Telemachus's visits to strange lands, Fénelon could comment on many forms of government and hide his comments on France. The book was banned and consigned to public fires anyway. Montesquieu similarly disguised his first critical comments in an epistolary novel (a novel in the form of letters), *The Persian Letters* (1721). These fictional letters were purportedly written by Persian visitors to Europe, whose naive comments hid barbs. One letter, for example, explains that the king of Spain owns many gold mines, but the king of France (who owns none) is richer because he has found a way to make unlimited money from the vanity of his subjects: He sells them offices, titles, and honors.

One strong criticism of government occurred naturally to writers—attacking censorship. Claude Helvétius, a rich government official under Louis XV, made one of the most vigorous attacks in 1758. His *De l'esprit* ("Essays on the Mind") was blunt: "To limit the press is to insult the nation; to prohibit the reading of certain books is to declare the people to be either fools or slaves." His book was condemned by the parlement and burnt by the public executioner in 1759. In England, where the tolerance of ideas was slightly greater—but censorship was practiced nonetheless—even jurists gave the philosophes some support. William Blackstone, a judge, a member of parliament, and one of the founders of modern university training in law, published four volumes of the extremely influential *Commentaries on the Laws of England* (1765–69). He cautiously concluded: "The liberty of the press is indeed essential to the nature of a free state, but this consists in laying no previous restraints upon publication, not in the freedom from censure for criminal matter when published."

As with the parallel battle against religious intolerance, not everyone agreed with the attack upon censorship. Conservatives rallied to the defense of the government, just as they stood by the church. Samuel Johnson, a journalist and lexicographer, is a good example. Johnson was a deeply conservative man who despised writers such as Voltaire and Rousseau and thought it a splendid idea that writers of their sort should be sent to penal colonies. And he stoutly defended censorship: "No member of society has a right to teach any doctrine contrary to what society holds to be true."

As the Enlightenment progressed, political writers became bolder in their criticism. The opposition of Louis XV, the French courts, and the Catholic Church did not stop the publication of the *Encyclopédie*. Its essay on "Government" shows how radical the criticism had become. It stated that society exists under a civil constitution that invests rulers with their power, but those rulers are "bound therein by the laws of nature and by the law of reason." Nature and reason both dictated that the "purpose in any form of government [is] the welfare" of civil society. Thus, the bold argument continued, society should expect "to abrogate laws that are flaws in a state" and even to revoke "the allegiance and the jurisdiction in which they are born," by changing the government.

Such ideas were not new to the Enlightenment. The English political theorist John Locke had made eloquent statements of them in the late seventeenth century, especially in his *Second Treatise on Civil Government* (1690).

Voltaire returned to France from his exile in England (1726–29) filled with similar willingness to write of his opposition to absolutism. His *Philosophical Letters* (1734) praised the English for their form of government and suggested it as a model for the rest of Europe. "The English nation," he wrote, "is the only one of earth that has successfully regulated the power of its kings by resisting them; and which, after repeated efforts, has established that beneficial government under which the Prince . . . is restrained from doing ill."

Baron Montesquieu, however, produced the most widely studied political analysis of the era (see docu-

◆ DOCUMENT 20.4 ◆

Montesquieu: Law, Liberty, and Government

The Spirit of the Laws

Law in general is human reason inasmuch as it governs all the inhabitants of the earth: the political and civil laws of each nation ought to be only the particular cases in which human reason is applied. . . .

There are three species of government: republican, monarchical, and despotic. . . . A republican government is that in which the body, or only a part of the people, is possessed of the supreme power; monarchy, that in which a single person governs by fixed and established laws; a despotic government, that in which a single person directs everything by his own will and caprice. . . .

There is no word that admits of more various significations, and has made more varied impressions on the human mind, than that of Liberty. . . . Political liberty does not consist in an unlimited freedom. . . . Liberty is a right of doing whatever the laws permit. . . .

It is necessary from the very nature of things that power should be a check to power. A government may be so constituted, as no man shall be compelled to do things which the law does not oblige him, nor forced to abstain from things which the law permits. . . .

In every government there are three sorts of power: the legislative, the executive in respect to things dependent on the law of nations; and the executive in regard to matters that depend on the civil law. . . . When the legislative and executive powers are united in the same person, or in the same body of magistrates, there can be no liberty.

Montesquieu, Baron de. *The Spirit of the Laws,* trans. Thomas Nugent. Cincinnati: Clarke, 1873.

ment 20.4). His *Spirit of the Laws* stands as the founding work of modern comparative government. Montesquieu adopted the ancient political observation—used by both Aristotle and Cicero—that three basic forms of government exist: a republic, in which the people or their representatives govern; a mixed monarchy, in which a king reigns with constitutional limits and aristocratic checks upon his power; and a despotism, in which the monarch holds unchecked, absolute power. Montesquieu contended that none of these was a perfect, universal form of government because governments should be appropriate to local conditions. He proposed features of the ideal government, however, such as "liberty," which he carefully defined: "Liberty does not consist in an unlimited freedom. . . . Liberty is a right of doing whatever the laws permit."

This line of reasoning led Montesquieu to state two of the most famous political theories of the eighteenth century: (1) the theory of the separation of powers and (2) the theory of checks and balances. Montesquieu first argued that the centers of power within the state—the executive, the legislative, and the judicial powers—should not be held by the same person or institution. "When the legislative and executive powers are united in the same person . . . there can be no liberty." He then added that these separated centers of power should check and balance each other: "Power should be a check to power." Such ideas had many dramatic implications for the eighteenth century. They meant, for example, that powerful institutions controlled by the aristocracy, such as the French parlements, must check the potential despotism of a king.

By the late eighteenth century, the Enlightenment produced even more radical political arguments. Tom Paine, the son of a quiet English Quaker family who became an active participant in both the American and the French revolutions, wrote passionate pamphlets and carefully reasoned multivolume works of political theory. One of his pamphlets, *Common Sense* (1776), attacked monarchical government and advocated a republic—arguments aimed at the British colonies in America. His *Rights of Man* (1791–92) defended the legislation of the French Revolution, attacked monarchical government, and called on the English to overthrow George III. The government of Britain indicted him for treason.

Jeremy Bentham took Enlightenment political and social thought in yet another direction. Bentham was a lawyer with a comfortable inherited income that allowed him to pursue his writing, which he deeply imbued with Enlightenment attitudes. He saw his writings as "an attempt to extend the experimental method of reasoning from the physical branch (sciences) to the moral." His *Principles of Morals and Legislation* (1789) called for rationalist legislation, favoring the least possible legislation and the least possible government. "Every law," Bentham believed, "is an evil, for every law is an infraction of liberty." This reasoning contained the germ of one of the dominant political gospels of the nineteenth century, classical liberalism.

Perhaps the most radical political theorist of the Enlightenment was Jean-Jacques Rousseau, a Franco-Swiss philosophe who never experienced the comfortable life that Montesquieu, Voltaire, and Bentham knew. Rousseau was the son of a watchmaker and a pastor's daughter. He was born in austere, Calvinist Geneva where stern laws regulated behavior. His mother died in the week of his birth, and his father deserted him as a child, fleeing imprisonment for dueling. Rousseau was raised by his mother's strict religious family and apprenticed to an engraver, but he ran away from Geneva at sixteen. During the remainder of his youth, Rousseau wandered as a vagabond. He survived as a beggar, domestic servant, tutor, music teacher, and the kept lover of an older woman. When he settled in Paris in 1744, he had a hatred of the rich but gave no signs of converting this into literary fame. Some of Rousseau's revolutionary anger showed in an early essay, the *Discourse on the Origin of Inequality* (1755). His concern was not "natural" inequality among individuals, but "moral or political inequality, because it depends on . . . the consent of mankind." The discourse went on to demand nothing less than the complete reorganization of society to eliminate inequalities based upon factors such as rank or race. Before the *Discourse* was finished, Rousseau attacked the concept of private property, which he considered "the worst of our institutions."

> The first man who, after fencing in a piece of ground, took it into his head to say: *This is mine*, and found people simple enough to believe him, was the true founder of civil society. How many crimes, wars, murders, how many miseries and horrors would not have been spared the human race by him who, pulling up the stakes or filling in the ditch, had cried out to his fellow men: Take care not to listen to this impostor; you are lost if you forget that the fruits belong to all and the earth to none.

The same passion characterized Rousseau's more complex masterpiece, *The Social Contract* (1762). It opened with one of the most famous sentences of the Enlightenment: "Man is born free, but is everywhere in chains." The great human emancipation that Rousseau desired led him to propose an ideal government that mixed democracy and authoritarianism. Rousseau, the enemy of kings, admired democracy and stimulated its growth in Europe with sentences such as: "No man has a natural authority over his fellow men." This reasoning led Rousseau to state the right of people to use force to resist forced obedience to authority: "As soon as [a people] can throw off its yoke, and does throw it off, it does better; for a people may certainly use, for the recovery of their liberty, the same right that was employed to deprive them of it." Rousseau also believed, however, that democracy would only work with "a people who were Gods." He criticized democracy because "it is contrary to the natural order" that a minority should always be governed by a majority. Thus, he introduced the concept of an abstract force, called "the general will," which would compel all members of society to desire the common good. Paradoxically, Rousseau's ideas thus encouraged both a democratic-egalitarian attack upon the Old Regime and a form of absolutism, the very concept of which had led to the initial Enlightened critiques of government.

The Spread of Rationalism

The Enlightenment had a tremendous impact on Western civilization because it spread skepticism and rationalism to many fields of human activity. Even the study of history felt the influence of these doctrines. Gibbon's *The Decline and Fall of the Roman Empire,* for example, showed the advantages of a reasoned study of the sources. The Neapolitan Enlightenment offered similar lessons in history. Giambattista Vico's *Principles of a New Science* (1725) urged scientific standards: Scholars should seek "the universal and eternal principles (such as every science must have)." Another Neapolitan historian, Pietro Giannone, suggested that this meant historians must write "histories of the kingdom" that contained more than the "lives of the kings." So Giannone began his masterwork with the words, "The history of the Kingdom of Naples which I am undertaking will not deafen readers' ears with the clash of arms and the din of battle. . . . This is to be a civic history."

Another leader of the Enlightenment in Italy, Cesare Beccaria, applied the scientific standards of careful observation and reasoning to another human activity, the punishment of crimes. Beccaria, a wealthy Milanese noble, studied prison conditions in Milan, and he was horrified by the conditions he discovered: Criminal charges were brought in secret, the accused had few opportunities to offer a defense and produce evidence, trials held before a jury were rare, torture was used both to determine guilt and to punish it, barbarous physical punishments such as branding and mutilation were commonplace, and people were executed for minor crimes. Beccaria's *Treatise on Crimes and Punishment* (1764) marked the beginning of modern criminology, and it led to more humane standards in European civilization. His argument was simple: "It is better to prevent crimes than to punish them" (see document 20.5). Therefore, he said, "Every punishment that does not arise from absolute necessity is tyrannical." Beccaria accepted pre-

---

◈ DOCUMENT 20.5 ◈

Beccaria: Penal Reform

Cesare Beccaria (1738–1794) was a Milanese nobleman and a leader of the Italian Enlightenment. His Tratto dei Delitti e delle Pene (Treatise on Crime and Punishment, 1764), *from which the following excerpt is taken, advocated many fundamental reforms such as the abolition of both torture and capital punishment.*

Of the Right to Punish: Every act of authority of one man over another, for which there is not an absolute necessity, is tyrannical. It is upon this that the sovereign's right to punish crimes is founded; that is, upon the necessity of defending the public liberty, entrusted to his care, from the usurpation of individuals. . . .

Of the Intent of Punishments: . . . [I]t is evident that the intent of punishments is not to torment a sensible being, nor to undo a crime already committed. Is it possible that torments and useless cruelty, the instrument of furious fanaticism or the impotency of tyrants, can be authorized by a political body? Can the groans of a tortured wretch recall the time past or reverse the crime he has committed?

The end of punishment, therefore, is no other than to prevent the criminal from doing further injury to society and to prevent others from committing the same offense. . . .

Of Torture: The torture of a criminal during his trial is a cruelty consecrated by custom in most nations. It is used with the intent of either making him confess his crime, or explaining some contradictions, or discovering his accomplices, or for some kind of metaphysical and incomprehensive purgation of infamy. . . . The very means employed to distinguish the innocent from the guilty will most effectually destroy all difference between them.

Beccaria, Cesare. An Essay on Crimes and Punishments. London: J. Almon, 1785.

---

ventive punishments—to stop a criminal from committing the same act again or to inhibit someone else from committing that crime—but he argued forcefully against any form of torture. However, he found it "a cruelty consecrated by custom in most nations."

One of the most far-reaching Enlightenment criticisms of the human condition focused on the inequality of women. The word *feminism* did not yet exist—it was a nineteenth-century coinage—and no organized campaigns for women's rights had been established. But several philosophes shaped these later developments by challenging accepted attitudes about the inferiority of women. A few prominent philosophes, such as Condorcet and Holbach, championed the equality of women, but most leaders of the Enlightenment did not. Instead, a few educated women, despite lacking the advantages of their famous colleagues, began to publish their own reasoned arguments about the condition of the sexes. It is indicative of the status of women that one of the most forceful works, an English pamphlet entitled *Woman Not Inferior to Man*, was published anonymously in 1739 by an author known only as "Sophia, A Person of Quality" (see document 20.6). "Everyone who has but a degree of understanding above the idiot," Sophia wrote, can "observe the universal prevalence of prejudice and custom in the minds of Men." Sophia did not mince words: Men exercised a "tyrannical usurpation of authority" over women.

The most influential advocate of the equality of the sexes, and one of the most important founders of feminist thought, was another Englishwoman—Mary Wollstonecraft. Wollstonecraft, the daughter of an alcoholic and abusive father, learned to support herself despite having only a limited education. She and her sister directed a school near London, and this led Wollstonecraft to begin writing texts and tracts on education. Success introduced her to literary circles in London, where she met radical writers who encouraged her to continue her writing. She practiced some of her radical ideas in her own life, living with a man and having a child outside marriage. Wollstonecraft found only limited happiness, however, and once attempted to drown herself in the Thames River.

From these poignant experiences, Mary Wollstonecraft found the materials for her masterwork, *A Vindication of the Rights of Woman* (1792). She, too, constructed her argument for women in the language of the Enlightenment. "In what," she asked, does human "pre-eminence over the brute creation consist? The

---

◈ DOCUMENT 20.6 ◈

Sophia's *Woman Not Inferior to Man*

"Sophia, A Person of Quality" was the pseudonym of an unknown author who anonymously published a forceful pamphlet on the equality of women in 1739. This work, Woman Not Inferior to Man, or A Short and Modest Vindication of the Natural Right of the Fair Sex to a Perfect Equality of Power, Dignity, and Esteem with Men, *employed many of the basic concepts of the Enlightenment, as the following excerpt shows.*

If a celebrated Author had not already told, that *there is nothing in nature so much to be wonder'd at as THAT WE WONDER AT ALL,* it must appear to every one, who has but a degree of understanding above the idiot, a matter of the greatest surprize, to observe the universal prevalence of prejudice and custom in the minds of the *Men.* One might naturally expect to see those lordly creatures, as they modestly stile themselves, everywhere jealous of superiority, and watchful to maintain it. Instead of which, if we except the tyrannical usurpation of authority they exert over us *Women,* we shall find them industrious in nothing but courting the meanest servitude. Was their ambition laudable and just, it would be consistent in itself, and this consistency would render them alike imperious in every circumstance, where authority is requisite and justifiable: And if their brutal strength of body entitled them to lord it over our nicer frame, the superiority of reason to passion, might suffice to make them blush to submit that reason to passion, prejudice, and groundless custom. If this haughty sex would have us believe they have a natural right of superiority over us, why do not they prove their charter from nature, by making use of reason. . . .

What I have hitherto said, has not been with an intention to stir up any of my own sex to revolt against the *Men,* or to invert the present order of things, with regard to *government* and *authority.* No, let them stand as they are: I only mean to show my sex, that they are not so despicable as the *Men* would have them believe themselves.

answer is clear . . . in Reason." Because women possessed reason as well as men, they were equally preeminent and should be treated that way: "[I]f they be really capable of acting like rational creatures, let them not be treated like slaves." And she proclaimed her own, unequivocal stand, unwilling to submit to domination by men: "I love man as my fellow; but his scepter, real or usurped, extends not to me, unless the reason of an individual demands my homage; and even then the submission is to reason, and to not to man."

CHAPTER 21

THE FRENCH REVOLUTION AND NAPOLEON, 1789–1815

CHAPTER OUTLINE

The end of the eighteenth century brought extraordinary upheaval. The French Revolution (1789–99) challenged the institutions of the Old Regime and provoked bitter struggles in which millions of people died. The turmoil in France gave way to a general European conflict (1792–1815) as great coalitions formed to halt the spread of revolution. The revolutionary government survived these attacks until 1799 when one of its own military heroes, Napoleon Bonaparte, seized power and created an authoritarian government. In a series of brilliant campaigns he extended French rule over much of Europe until he was defeated by the combined armies of a European coalition.

Chapter 21 surveys this upheaval, starting with its origins in the economic and social problems of the Old Regime. The French attempt to address those problems led to a series of revolutionary governments that abolished the monarchy, the aristocracy, and the established church. A revolutionary bill of rights and an idealistic constitution promised an age of liberty and equality, and the revolutionary government fulfilled much of this promise by abolishing slavery and by emancipating religious minorities. The French Revolution, however, is a complex, paradoxical subject. The story of great accomplishment is also a story of great violence. The revolution produced dictatorial governments and public executions, so many people remember the revolution as a "reign of terror." One of the best known passages in English literature, the opening of Charles Dickens's *A Tale of Two Cities* (1859), summarizes this revolutionary duality: "It was the best of times, it was the worst of times . . . it was the spring of hope, it was the winter of despair."

The Origins of the French Revolution

The French Revolution grew from the combination of an intractable economic crisis and the inability of the government to govern. King Louis XVI could neither raise taxes nor pay his bills. A recession and falling prices hurt farmers and workers. Manufacturing suffered in competition with the English, especially in the textile industry. Unemployment reached dangerous levels, passing eighty thousand in Paris in December 1788 (approximately one-third of the adult workforce), while poor harvests in 1787–88 produced shortages of wheat, which rose in price to record levels by mid–1789. The price of bread in Paris, normally eight or nine sous for a four-pound loaf, hit 14.5 sous.

Ominous signs were evident in 1788–89 that France was a volatile society. Bread riots occurred in many districts. Some villages refused to ship their grain. In towns, crowds, often led by women, attacked granaries, mills, and bakeries. The crowds typically forced sales at "the just price" (an old Christian idea); in Rouen, for example, they cut the price of bread in half.

Historians generally agree that such troubles became a revolution when four overlapping movements converged: (1) An aristocratic revolution had been building for many years, as aristocrats used institutions such as the parlements to thwart the king, especially on tax reform. This revolution forced Louis XVI to hold elections for the Estates General in 1789. (2) A bourgeois revolution challenged the aristocratic leadership of the reform movement and sought to limit aristocratic control of high government offices. (3) A peasant revolution went beyond disturbances over grain and became an armed uprising against the remnants of feudalism. This rebellion connected the common people to the reformers and made it extremely difficult for Louis XVI to act against them. (4) An urban working-class revolution turned the fury of the crowd to large political targets. The revolution of the crowd pressed reformers to extend the revolution.

The Estates General and the Beginning of the Revolution

Faced with bankruptcy, Louis XVI promised his critics in November 1787 that he would hold elections for the Estates General (the first since 1614) within five years. Under continuing pressure, Louis finally agreed that representatives from each of the three estates (the clergy, the aristocracy, and all others) that comprised the population of France (see chapter 17) could assemble in May 1789. His decision launched the first modern political debate in French history (see illustration 21.1). Should the third estate (97 percent of the popu-

Illustration 21.1

〽️ **The Three Estates.** Cartoons are often effective political tracts. The message of this one is clear and revolutionary: The two privileged estates, the clergy and the aristocracy, are crushing the common man, who must support them and the boulder of taxation.

lation) have more deputies than the others? Should the three estates meet together or separately? Such issues produced a flood of political pamphlets. The most famous of these was written by a provincial priest, the abbé Emmanuel Sieyès (1748–1836), who defended the third estate in a work entitled *What Is the Third Estate?* Sieyès's answer was "Everything!" The aristocracy, he added, was like "some horrible disease eating the living flesh of some unfortunate man."

Louis XVI agreed to double the representation of the third estate, but he insisted upon preserving traditions—the estates would meet separately. He permitted freedom of the press for the elections and asked that each district submit statements of their grievances (*cahiers des doléances*). Most cahiers condemned absolutism and praised constitutional monarchy; many pledged loyalty to Louis XVI, but none acknowledged his "divine right." They called for a French parliament to control taxation and legislation. The cahiers attacked hated aspects of the Old Regime (such as the arbitrary royal power of arrest by *lettres de cachet*) and demanded new freedoms (such as freedom of the press). Each cahier also expressed the interests of the estate that produced it. The first estate, for example, wanted clerical control of education, denounced immorality in the press, and objected to the toleration of Protestantism.

The Estates General met in Versailles, a short walk from the royal palace. It opened with a royal speech asking for new taxes. The deputies of the third estate, chiefly lawyers, rejected holding such discussions in separate meetings, and they asked other deputies to join them in legislating reforms. Nine priests agreed, and the combined group proclaimed itself the French National Assembly. A political revolution had begun. The deputies were locked out of their meeting hall, so they assembled at a nearby indoor tennis court and swore not to adjourn without preparing a constitution. Within a few days, 612 of 621 deputies of the third estate had signed the Tennis Court Oath; 149 priests and a few nobles joined them.

The king naturally resisted these events. He did not panic because he had learned from dealing with the parlements that he could suspend their business, transfer the meeting to a distant province, or even arrest troublesome leaders. Thus, he simply declared the decisions of the third estate illegal. He offered the hope of a constitution, with important reservations. "The King wills," he said, "that the traditional distinctions between the three orders of the state should be preserved in its entirety." Deputies of the defiant third estate chose to continue the National Assembly. As one liberal deputy, the Count de Mirabeau (1749–91), said, "We shall not leave our places except by the power of bayonet." Louis considered using the army but his ability to use French troops against the National Assembly was uncertain. Few were stationed in Versailles, and their loyalty was dubious. One regiment had refused to fire on demonstrators and another had vowed not to act against the third estate. So Louis called in German and Swiss reinforcements from the provinces (foreigners constituted 25 percent of his army). He still felt confident enough to do nothing when the National Assembly discussed a constitution. The revolution, however, quickly passed beyond his ability to control it.

The Revolutionary Crowd: The Bastille and the Great Fear

The political revolution begun by the aristocracy and expanded by the deputies of the third estate changed in July 1789, driven by crowds of commoners in both town and country. The revolutionary crowd ("the mob" to hostile observers) has been the subject of historical controversy. Some authors depict the crowds as purely destructive and conclude that they were comprised of criminals, vagabonds, and the unemployed. Edmund Burke, the most eloquent enemy of the revolution, called the crowd "a band of cruel ruffians and assassins." Recent study, however, has shown that the revolution-

ary crowds were comprised of wage earners, journeymen, artisans, and shopkeepers (see table 21.1).

The Parisian crowd changed the revolution in July 1789. The price of bread, fear of foreign troops, concern that the National Assembly would be closed, and the agitation of revolutionary orators (notably Camille Desmoulins, a twenty-nine-year-old radical lawyer) created a volatile situation. On July 11, the king dismissed his most popular advisor, Jacques Necker alarming moderates. Parisians burned the customs gates to the city, as a protest against the tariffs that they blamed for the high price of bread and wine. The next day, German soldiers fired on a crowd, and a riot followed. On the morning of July 14, eight thousand people attacked a royal barracks and took thirty-two thousand muskets and twelve artillery pieces. They used those arms later that day in the most famous act of the revolutionary crowd—the attack on the Bastille. The Bastille was a formidable fortress, towering nearly one hundred feet over eastern Paris. It was less important for the seven prisoners it held than as a symbol of despotism, in which such famous prisoners as Voltaire had been confined. (Studies have found that 10 percent of all French writers of the eighteenth century were locked up in the Bastille at least once.) Perhaps more important, it held five tons of gunpowder, defended by only eighty-two French soldiers and thirty-two Swiss. During a four-hour battle on July 14 (which became a French national holiday), one soldier and ninety-eight civilians were killed. The victorious crowd, which included many cabinetmakers and cobblers but no lawyers (see table 21.1), finished the day with an act that led to their image as a blood-thirsty mob: the brutal murder of the governor of the Bastille. Louis XVI spent the day hunting; his diary entry for July 14 read: "Nothing." The next day, stunned by the news from Paris, he went to the National Assembly and promised to withdraw the provincial troops.

Neither the king nor the National Assembly had adjusted to the insurrection in Paris when similar events occurred in rural France. The rural disturbances of July and August 1789, known as "the great fear," were a response to rumors. Some rumors held that the king wished to liberate the peasantry but expected them to take the lead. Worse rumors held that aristocrats, frustrated by events in Versailles, were preparing some terrible revenge or that armies of vagrants (whose numbers were high) were to be set loose on the peasantry. Peasants armed themselves in self-defense. When brigands did not appear, the frightened population turned their anxiety on the chateaux of their seigneurs. Some aristocrats were forced to renounce their feudal

TABLE 21.1

The Social Composition of Revolutionary Groups

Arrests at the Bastille (1789)		Emigrés (1789–99)	
Trade category	**Percentage**	**Class category**	**Percentage**
Furniture trades	17.1	Third estate	58.0
Building trades	14.2	(Peasantry	19.4)
Clothing trades	10.1	(Workers	14.3)
Metal workers	10.1	Clergy	25.2
Transport trades	6.8	Nobility	16.8
Food Trades	5.3		
Other	36.4		

Deputies in the convention (1792–95)		Jacobin clubs (1793–95)	
Profession	**Percentage**	**Profession**	**Percentage**
Lawyers	47.7	Shopkeepers	45.0
Businessmen	8.9	Farmers	9.6
Clergy	7.3	Businessmen	8.2
Civil servants	6.8	Lawyers	6.8
Medicine	6.1	Other professions	6.9
Farmers	5.1	Civil servants	6.7
Other	18.1	Other	16.8

Note: Total percentage may exceed 100 because of rounding.

Source: Colin Jones, ed., *The Longman Companion to the French Revolution* (London: Longman, 1988), pp. 120, 168, 186, 199; and George Rudé, *The Crowd in the French Revolution* (Oxford: Oxford University Press, 1959), pp. 246–48.

rights. In other places, peasants burned the records of the feudal dues that they owed, and sometimes the chateau as well.

The Legislative Revolution of the National Assembly, 1789–91

The actions of the Parisian crowd and the peasantry had two important effects on the National Assembly (also called the Constituent Assembly because it was writing a constitution). First, they strengthened the assembly because the king could not suppress it without fear of violence. Second, the rebellions encouraged the deputies to extend the revolution (see chronology 21.1).

A legislative revolution began on "the night of August 4th." Debates on the great fear led to a remarkable scene: Some aristocrats proposed ending their own privileges. Without preparation or committee studies, the deputies voted a series of decrees that began with: "The National Assembly completely abolishes the feudal regime." The night of August 4 marked the end of feudal servitude and taxes, the feudal rights of the aristocracy (such as hunting on peasant farmland), the manorial courts of aristocratic justice, "tithes of every description" owed to the Catholic Church, and the sale of public offices, which were opened to all citizens.

Three weeks later, the National Assembly adopted another historic document, a French bill of rights named the Declaration of the Rights of Man (see document 21.1). It promised freedom of religion, freedom of speech, freedom of the press, due process of law, and the prohibition of cruel and unusual punishment. It did not grant equal rights to religious minorities (Protestants received this in December 1789; Jews had to wait until September 1791), freedom for the black slaves in French colonies (adopted in February 1794, see illustration 21.2), or equal rights for women

---

❖ CHRONOLOGY 21.1 ❖

May 1789	Opening of the Estates General
The National Assembly (1789–91)	
June 1789	Third estate proclaims the National Assembly
June 1789	Tennis Court Oath not to disperse
July 1789	Fall of the Bastille
July 1789	Beginning of "the great fear" in rural France
August 1789	Abolition of feudalism, tithes, venal offices
August 1789	Declaration of the Rights of Man
October 1789	Women's march on Versailles
November 1789	Nationalization of church property
December 1789	Civil equality of Protestants
February 1790	Suppression of monasteries
March 1790	Abolition of the *lettres de cachet*
May 1790	Nationalization of royal land
June 1790	Nobility abolished
July 1790	Civil Constitution of the Clergy
June 1791	Chapelier Law outlaws unions and strikes
June 1791	Louis XVI's flight to Varennes and arrest
July 1791	Massacre on the Champ de Mars
July 1791	Law against seditious meetings
September 1791	Emancipation of Jews
September 1791	Constitution of 1791 adopted
September 1791	Declaration of the Rights of Woman
The Legislative Assembly (1791–92)	
November 1791	Decree against émigrés
November 1791	Decree against nonjuring priests
August 1792	King's powers suspended
August 1792	Prussia invades France
September 1792	Legalization of divorce
September 1792	September massacres
September 1792	Battle of Valmy
September 1792	French monarchy abolished

(which the revolution never accepted, see document 21.2)—but in 1789 it was the greatest statement of human rights in Europe.

Louis XVI rejected the August reforms. This action defended tradition, but it angered the National Assembly and the people of Paris. The people forced the issue. Their fears of a royal counterrevolution were exacerbated by the food crisis. The harvest of 1789 was good, but a late season drought had slowed the work of the water-powered mills that ground grain into flour. Thus, August and September 1789 again witnessed bread riots led by the women of Paris.

Historians call those days on which the action of the crowd changed the course of events "revolutionary *journées*" ("revolutionary days"). The angry housewives and working women of Paris led such a journée on October 5, 1789. Their target was the king. When Louis blocked the August reforms, talk circulated in Paris about a march to Versailles to bring him to Paris. On the rainy Monday morning of October 5, the women of Paris did just that. A procession of several thousand set out for Versailles, chanting "Let's fetch the baker!" A few hours later, a reluctant Lafayette led the National Guard to support them. After a small clash on the grounds of the royal palace, Louis XVI agreed to accept the August decrees and to move into his Tuileries Palace (today the Louvre Museum) in Paris.

The National Assembly moved to Paris, too, confident that it now controlled France. The deputies deprived the king of the right to dismiss them or to veto the constitution they were writing. Their effort to shackle royal power included one mistake: They excluded royal ministers from the assembly. This blocked the evolution of a cabinet system of government and the principle of ministerial responsibility to parliament.

The move to Paris stimulated the growth of political clubs (the precursors of political parties), which became one of the distinguishing features of the revolution. These clubs had roots in the salons of the Old Regime, organizations such as Masonic lodges, and the excited political meetings of 1788–89. They became the voice of Parisian radicalism and then the center of revolutionary power. One of the most influential clubs was the Cordeliers, named for a Catholic order whose

◆ DOCUMENT 21.1 ◆

The Declaration of the Rights of Man, 1789

1. Men are born and remain free and equal in rights. Social distinctions can be based only upon public utility.

2. The aim of every political association is the preservation of the natural and imprescriptable rights of man. These rights are liberty, property, security, and resistance to oppression.

3. The source of all sovereignty is essentially in the nation; no body, no individual can exercise authority that does not proceed from it in plain terms.

4. Liberty consists in the power to do anything that does not injure others. . . .

5. The law has the right to forbid only such actions as are injurious to society. . . .

6. Law is the expression of the general will. All citizens have the right to take part personally, or by their representatives, in its formation. It must be the same for all, whether it protects or punishes. . . .

7. No man can be accused, arrested, or detained except in the cases determined by the law. . . .

8. The law ought to establish only penalties that are strictly and obviously necessary. . . .

9. Every man being presumed innocent until he has been pronounced guilty. . . .

10. No one should be disturbed on account of his opinions, even religious. . . .

11. The free communication of ideas and opinions is one of the most precious rights of man; every citizen then can freely speak, write, and print, subject to responsibility for the abuse of this freedom. . . .

14. All the citizens have the right to ascertain, by themselves or by their representatives, the necessity of the public tax, to consent to it freely. . . .

17. Property being a sacred and inviolable right, no one can be deprived of it, unless a legally established public necessity evidently demands it, under the condition of a just and prior indemnity.

Anderson, Frank M., ed. *The Constitutions and Other Select Documents Illustrative of the History of France, 1789–1907*. Minneapolis: 1908.

---

monastery it rented. The Cordeliers included three of the most prominent radicals of the city: Camille Desmoulins (the orator who helped to precipitate the attack on the Bastille), Jean-Paul Marat (a physician whose radical newspaper, the *Friend of the People*, had shaped the journée of October 5), and Georges Danton (a radical lawyer who had married into middle-class wealth and purchased a venal office in the royal courts). The most important club, the Jacobins, drew their name from a rented Jacobin convent and their membership from Parisian small businessmen (see table 22.1). The Jacobins were especially influential because their membership included more than two hundred deputies. Jacobins ranged from moderates such as Lafayette to radicals such as Robespierre, but the latter soon predominated. In the first year, the club grew to more than twelve hundred members and 150 affiliated provincial clubs. The term *Jacobinism* soon entered political discourse to identify their militant ideas and actions.

Pushed by these radical clubs, the National Assembly continued its revolutionary legislation. Its attention soon fell on the Catholic Church, which seemed to hold an answer to the economic crisis. In November 1789 the revolutionary, and nonreligious, bishop of Au-

tun, Charles Talleyrand, convinced the assembly to "put at the disposal of the nation" all lands belonging to the church. This confiscated a huge amount of land—typically 20 percent of the farm land in a region, although it reached 40 percent in some areas. The assembly then sold interest-bearing bonds, called *assignats*, secured by this land. The assignats gradually circulated as revolutionary paper money. The notes could be redeemed for land and the value of the land was sufficient to cover them, but the public had little confidence in paper money, so assignats depreciated in value. By late 1792 inflation had taken 40 percent of their value.

Other legislation on the church followed. The loss of its lands and the abolition of the mandatory tithe left the church with limited income. This led the assembly to create a new relationship between the church and the state, known as the Civil Constitution of the Clergy of July 1790. The Civil Constitution converted priests into state employees and doubled their salaries, but it cut the number, income, and powers of the aristocratic bishops by changing their posts into elective state offices. Clerics had to swear loyalty to the constitution or be removed from office. By mid-1791, 60 percent of French priests (the "juring," or constitutional, clergy)

Illustration 21.2

/// **The Revolution and Equality.** At its most idealist stage, the French Revolution emancipated Protestants, Jews, and slaves. In this illustration, the revolution is glorified for proclaiming "all mortals are equal." The scales of justice find a white man and a black man to be precisely equal. The emancipated slave holds a copy of the *Declaration of the Rights of Man*, while the devils of inequality are driven away.

had accepted this arrangement; more than 95 percent of the bishops refused.

The legislative revolution proceeded rapidly. The assembly addressed the economic crisis by abolishing internal tariffs (October 1790), nationalizing royal land (May 1790), and creating a land tax (November 1790). It sought governmental efficiency by reorganizing local government (December 1789) by abolishing the parlements (September 1790). It decreed the civil equality of Protestants (December 1789) and ex-slaves (May 1791). And it continued to attack the elites of the Old Regime: The assembly abolished monasteries and most religious orders (February 1790) and then the nobility (June 1790). One of its most far-reaching reforms, however, restricted the rights of workers. The Chapelier Law of June 1791 abolished the guilds and outlawed trade unions, shaping French labor history for nearly a century.

One omission in this torrent of reform was women's rights, despite the active role of women in the revolution. The pamphlet campaign of early 1789 had included women's grievances; one petition to the king, for example, had called for educational and economic opportunities. A few women in religious orders had voted for representatives of the first estate. More than a dozen women had been among the conquerors of the Bastille. Women had led demonstrations over bread and the march on Versailles. They had formed political clubs, such as Théroigne de Méricourt's Friends of the

Law, which was denied affiliation by the Cordeliers. And when the Declaration of the Rights of Man failed to mention women, Olympe de Gouges responded with a brilliant manifesto entitled *Declaration of the Rights of Women* (1791). "Man, are you capable of being just?" she asked (see document 21.2). Although a few men, such as Condorcet, responded supportively, the answer remained no. Traditional attitudes about the role of women in society persisted, fears about the subservience of women to the church abounded, and a multitude of arguments (such as the lesser education of women) were advanced to perpetuate male dominance. Soon, the revolutionaries even closed women's clubs.

In September 1791 the National Assembly produced the first written constitution in French history. This document incorporated many of the decrees of the previous months. The Declaration of the Rights of Man formed the preamble. Louis XVI retained power as a constitutional monarch, but most power was vested in a unicameral parliament called the Legislative Assembly, which he could not dissolve. Elections were complicated. Adult male citizens were divided into "active" citizens (who got to vote, based on how much tax they paid) and "passive" citizens (who had full civil rights, but no vote). Elections were indirect: Active citizens chose representatives who met to elect deputies. This allowed 4.3 million people to vote, fewer people than had voted for the Estates General but higher percentage than the electorate for the House of Commons in Britain.

◈ DOCUMENT 21.2 ◈

The Revolution and Women's Rights

Olympe De Gouges's *Declaration of the Rights of Woman*, 1791

Olympe de Gouges (1748–93) was the illegitimate daughter of a provincial butcher. She ran away with a soldier at age sixteen and wound up as a writer in Paris. She supported the revolution and founded a club for women that Robespierre closed. Her opposition to Robespierre and her opposition to the execution of Louis XVI sent her to the guillotine in 1793. Compare the words of her articles with the similar ones in the Declaration of the Rights of Man.

Man, are you capable of being just? It is a woman who poses the question; you will not deprive her of that right at least. Tell me, what gives you sovereign empire to oppress my sex?

1. Woman is born free and lives equal to man in her rights. . . .

4. Liberty and justice consist of restoring all that belongs to others; thus, the only limits on the exercise of the natural rights of woman are perpetual male tyranny; these limits are to be reformed by the laws of nature and reason. . . .

10. No one is to be disquieted for his very basic opinions; woman has the right to mount the scaffold; she must equally have the right to mount the rostum.

The Committee of General Security Rejects Women's Rights, 1793

Should women exercise political rights and meddle in affairs of government? To govern is to rule the commonwealth by laws, the preparation of which demands extensive knowledge, unlimited attention and devotion, a strict immovability, and self-abnegation . . . . Are women capable of these cares and of the quality they call for? In General, we can answer no. . . .

[W]omen's associations seem dangerous. If we consider that the political education of men is at its beginning, that all its principles are not developed, and that we are still stammering the word liberty, then how much more reasonable is it for women, whose moral education is almost nil, to be less enlightened concerning principles?

Gouges, Olympe de. *Declaration of the Rights of Woman.* 1791.

Levy, Darline G., Applewhite, Harriet B., and Johnson, Mary D., ed. *Women in Revolutionary Paris, 1789–1795.* Urbana: University of Illinois Press, 1979.

Before the Constitution of 1791 took effect, another dramatic event changed the course of the French Revolution. On June 20, 1791, Louis XVI fled for the eastern frontier. A postmaster recognized the king, and at the village of Varennes the National Guard arrested him. Louis XVI returned to Paris as a prisoner. "There is no longer a king in France," he said. His flight to Varennes led to talk of abolishing the monarchy and creating a republic. For more than a year after the king's arrest, however, the revolutionary government allowed an aristocrat to continue publishing a royalist newspaper on his behalf.

◈

Europe and the Revolution

The arrest of Louis XVI accelerated the growth of counterrevolutionary opinion. The most dramatic expression of this in France had been emigration from the country. The émigrés (those who fled) had been led by the king's younger brother and future successor, the count of Artois, who left in July 1789. Each major event of the revolution increased the number of émigrés. The total ultimately reached 104,000. Adding twenty-five thousand people who were deported (chiefly nonjuring priests), 2 percent to 3 percent of the population left France. Most émigrés came from the third estate, but priests and aristocrats fled at higher rates (see table 21.1). In contrast, counterrevolutionary emigration to Canada during the American Revolution took 3 to 5 percent of the population. The émigrés concentrated in Koblenz and other towns near the border where they sought assistance from the crowned heads of Europe, aided rebellions in southern France, and built ties to nonjuring priests, especially in western France where a bitter civil war would soon be fought.

The émigrés got little help at first. European opinion was divided, but it was generally more favorable to the revolution than to émigré nobles. The English poet

William Wordsworth summarized the enthusiasm of the educated classes in a few lines of poetry: "Bliss was it in that dawn to be alive, But to be young was very heaven!" Such opinions were not limited to intellectuals. Charles James Fox, a leader of the Whig Party in Britain, called the revolution "much the greatest event that ever happened, and much the best."

The earliest opponent of the French Revolution was King Charles IV of Spain who was horrified by the treatment of the Catholic Church, but Spain was too weak to intervene. Catherine the Great of Russia dreaded the menace of French revolutionary ideas, but she was too far away to act, except against her own intelligentsia. The Habsburg emperors Joseph II and Leopold II carefully watched events in France because their sister, Marie Antoinette, was the queen and a target of popular abuse, but they initially accepted French reforms.

The most thoughtful critic of the revolution was Fox's rival in the House of Commons, Edmund Burke. Burke became one of the founders of modern conservatism with his attack on the revolution, *Reflections on the Revolution in France* (1790). "France," he wrote, "by the perfidy of her leaders, has utterly disgraced the tone of lenient council." The revolution was an "undignified calamity." The most influential early enemy of the revolution was Pope Pius VI who chiefly directed his anger at the Civil Constitution because it removed the church from papal control. In April 1791 he sent the encyclical letter *Caritas* to French bishops, forbidding the oath to the constitution. That oath, Pius insisted, was "the poisoned fountainhead and source of all errors." The French assembly answered by annexing the papal territory of Avignon (once the seat of the medieval papacy). Soon the French ambassador at Rome had been murdered, Parisian crowds had burnt the pope in effigy, and Pius VI had become a leader of the European counterrevolution.

The arrest of the French royal family at Varennes persuaded Leopold II to help his sister and her family. In July 1791 he sent a circular letter to the monarchs of England, Spain, Prussia, Naples, Sardinia, and Russia, urging them to join him in a protest to the French. He wanted "to vindicate the liberty and honor of the most Christian King and his family and to limit the dangerous extremes of the French revolution." Most rulers were unwilling to act. King George III of Britain abstained because the revolution weakened France, and he felt it was divine retribution for the French intervention in the American Revolution. The only ruler who joined Leopold II was King Frederick William II of Prussia. Together they issued the Brunswick Manifesto (1792) denouncing "the anarchy in the interior of France." Soon they would invade France.

European opinion gradually became polarized. As a Dutch conservative wrote in 1791, two parties were forming in all nations. One, a party of popular sovereignty and democratization, attacked all governments "except those arising from the free consent of those who submit to it." The other party held traditional values and, therefore, counterrevolutionary sentiments. It accepted government "by one or several persons over the mass of the people, a government of divine origin and supported by the church." The French Revolution was only the largest part of a democratic revolution that included liberal Polish nobles struggling against Russian influence; English dissenters campaigning for parliamentary reform; Rhineland Jews seeking emancipation; Irish peasants dreaming of French aid against the English; and Dutch, Belgian, and Swiss "patriots" who revived earlier rebellions.

The Legislative Assembly and the Wars of the Revolution

Elections for the Legislative Assembly took place in the aftermath of the flight to Varennes and the promulgation of *Caritas* and the Brunswick Manifesto. The new assembly of 745 deputies left a permanent mark on political discourse as a coincidence of its seating arrangement in a semicircular amphitheatre. As a speaker faced the assembled deputies, conservative members who defended the king sat on the right side. This group, led by members of the Feuillant Club, became the Right. On the left wing sat the radical members from the Jacobin and Cordeliers clubs. Less militant revolutionaries, who later became known as the Girondins (because many came from the region of the Gironde), sat in the middle. Thus was born the political vocabulary of "left," "right," and "center."

International tension distracted the Legislative Assembly from further reform. Instead, the assembly adopted legislation against the émigrés, branding those who did not return as conspirators. In February 1792 the state seized their property. Similar decrees against nonjuring priests followed in November 1792. Such legislation worsened French relations with the Austro-Prussian alliance. In March 1792 a belligerent, counterrevolutionary Francis II had succeeded to the Habsburg throne. By this time, the Girondins, whose foreign policy was more radical than their revolutionary aims, dominated the French assembly. They argued that war with the counterrevolutionaries would rally the French to defend the revolution, test the sympathies of Louis XVI, and export the revolution to other peoples. The leading Girondist, Jacques Brissot, said simply: "War is a blessing to the nation." Francis II and Brissot had led their countries to war by April 1792.

A Prussian army invaded eastern France in August 1792 and won several victories, but the course of the war shifted in September when a French army under General Charles Dumouriez defeated the Prussians in an artillery duel near the town of Valmy, bolstering republican enthusiasm. In the words of the German poet Johann von Goethe, the battle of Valmy meant that "here and today begins a new age in the history of the world." This was poetic exaggeration, but it made a point: The allies would not quickly crush the French Revolution. A few weeks later, Dumouriez and an army of forty-five thousand underscored that point by marching into Habsburg lands on France's northern border (today's Belgium) and winning a decisive victory at the town of Jemappes.

The War of 1792 grew into the War of the First Coalition (1793–95) when Britain, Spain, and Russia joined the alliance against the revolution, which had become passionately antimonarchical. Though this seemed like one of the most unevenly matched wars in history, the French not only survived it, but they also occupied the lowlands, the German Rhineland, and Northern Italy. They were able to do so because the revolution, among its other accomplishments, transformed the nature of modern warfare.

France had a larger population than most of her rivals, and in the early years of the revolution high unemployment made recruitment easy. The army grew from 180,000 men in 1789 to 650,000 in 1793. Then in August 1793 the assembly decreed universal military conscription (the *levée en masse*), placing the entire nation "in permanent requisition for army service." France soon had an unprecedented one million men in uniform. A conscript army of this size could not function according to the time-honored rules of European warfare. Though armed with the proceeds of revolutionary confiscations, it could feed itself only by living off the lands it conquered. Moreover, tactics had to be revised because intensive training had become impossible. Under reforms adopted by "the organizer of victory," Lazare Carnot, the French infantry advanced in deep columns instead of the traditional line, taking advantage of its superior numbers and revolutionary enthusiasm to overwhelm more disciplined enemies.

◆

The First Republic: The Convention

The War of 1792 changed the revolution and led to the abolition of the monarchy and the creation of a republic. Once again, the Parisian crowd took the initiative. Austro-Prussian threats on Louis XVI's behalf inspired demonstrations against the king, including an attack on the Tuileries Palace. The Legislative Assembly then suspended Louis's remaining powers and reenacted all legislation he had vetoed. Then, in "the revolution of August 10th" the assembly decided to create a new legislature. It would be called the Convention in honor of the Constitutional Convention recently held in America. Representatives to the Convention would be elected by universal manhood suffrage, and they would write a more democratic constitution. Among its final acts, the Legislative Assembly moved Louis XVI to a royal prison and urged the Convention to abolish the monarchy.

The late summer of 1792 also saw ominous hints of revolutionary authoritarianism. The assembly sent commissioners into provincial France hoping to rally support, but their powers often created opposition. Then the assembly required a loyalty oath of all government employees, and it gave those who refused two weeks to leave the country. Other laws permitted searches of homes for arms and counterrevolutionary suspects. The attack on the Catholic Church also continued. All surviving Catholic associations (such as teaching orders) were abolished, religious processions and public ceremonies were prohibited, and divorce was legalized.

This same period witnessed one of the worst atrocities of mob violence, known as the September Massacres. The allied invasion, the implications of the Brunswick Manifesto, and the defection of people such as Lafayette (seen as proof of widespread treason) created fears of a conspiracy linking the internal and external enemies of the revolution. The resultant panic was like the great fear of 1789, but this time the target was suspected enemies rather than châteaux. There were sixty-five lynchings around France. In Paris, the result was a massacre. During the first week the government did nothing for five days while the mobs slaughtered eleven hundred inmates, three-fourths of whom were nonpolitical prisoners such as common criminals and prostitutes.

Elections for the Convention thus took place in volatile circumstances. The 749 new deputies were chiefly lawyers (47.7 percent); fifty-five were priests and several others were former aristocrats, including Louis's revolutionary cousin, the former duke of

Illustration 21.3

///// **The Execution of Louis XVI.** The French republic, proclaimed in 1792, convicted the former Louis XVI of treason for the crime of plotting with the foreign powers that had invaded France. He was executed in January 1793 in a large public square, located at the end of the former royal gardens. In this illustration the crowd is shown the head of the king. The square where the guillotine stood, previously known as "Place Louis XV" and renamed "Place de la Revolution," is today known by the peacemaking name of "Place de la Concorde."

Orléans, now called Philippe Egalité (see table 21.1). The deputies were young—two-thirds were under age forty-four. No faction held a majority, but universal suffrage and the war produced a radical body. Jacobins and their allies, called *Montagnards* (mountain dwellers) because they sat in the upper levels, accounted for 40 percent of the seats; their ranks included a Parisian delegation led by such radicals as Danton, Marat, and Robespierre. The Girondins and their allies, led by Brissot and Roland, fell to less than 25 percent. The first year of the Convention was a struggle for predominance between these two factions, and the Jacobins won.

The Convention proclaimed a new order during its first week. Deputies voted unanimously to abolish the monarchy and create a republic. A committee began work on a new constitution, to be submitted to the people for ratification. When the Convention later invented a new calendar, this week in September would begin the new year, and September 1792 started Year I of the republican era.

The success of republican armies in 1792–93 meant that the greatest issue before the Convention became the fate of Louis XVI. A committee recommended that he be tried for treason, based upon his secret contacts with the governments that had invaded France. The trial of the king before the Convention began in December. Few doubted his guilt, revealed by his secret correspondence, and the deputies convicted him by a vote of 683–0. The debate over his sentence, however, caused bitter divisions. Jacobins advocated the normal death penalty. Passionate speakers insisted that "[k]ings are in the moral order what monsters are in the natural." Many leaders of the revolution, such as the abbé Sieyès, favored execution; even the king's cousin voted with the regicides. Louis XVI was condemned by a vote of 387–334 and beheaded on the guillotine in January 1793 (see illustration 21.3).

War consequently dominated the life of the Convention (1792–95) but deputies still aspired to reform society. Noteworthy laws envisioned schools open to all citizens. Robespierre, who had long championed the rights of minorities, scored his greatest triumph with the abolition of slavery in French colonies (February 1794), pushing the republic far ahead of Britain or the United States. The Convention's constitution, adopted in June 1793 and known as the Constitution of the Year I, summarized much of this egalitarian idealism. It began with an expanded version of the Declaration of the Rights of Man; stating, "The aim of society is the common welfare." That led to a constitutional assertion (Article Twenty-one) of the welfare state: "Every French citizen has a right to existence. . . . Public assistance is a sacred debt . . . Society owes subsistence to its unfortunate citizens, either in providing work for them, or in assuring the means of existence for those who are unable to work."

Civil War and the Reign of Terror

Whatever the intentions and accomplishments of the Convention, it is chiefly remembered for one of the most horrifying periods of modern history, the Reign of Terror (1793–94), when thousands of people were publicly executed. At the same time, a bloody civil war took tens of thousands of lives. The central issue in both tragedies was whether the revolution or the counterrevolution would prevail.

The crisis began with the war against the European coalition. In early 1793 the Austrians defeated the armies of General Dumouriez in the Austrian Netherlands and moved toward the French frontier. While the French braced themselves for an invasion, Dumouriez stunned them by defecting to the allies, making military catastrophe seem imminent. In addition to the Austrians on the northern frontier, Prussians were besieging French forts in the east, Italian troops were invading from the southeast, the Spanish army had crossed the southern border, and the English navy was threatening several ports. In Paris, many people agreed that the war effort required desperate measures.

The Convention's efforts to defend France, however, enlarged the problem. Plans to draft 300,000 men produced antidraft riots across France, chiefly in the west. This, plus continuing food shortages, the execution of the king, and the dechristianization of France, created opposition to the republic. By March 1793 peasant rebels in the Atlantic region of the Vendée had won several battles against the government. The Convention soon had to take units of the regular army from the frontier to combat the Vendéens, who now called themselves the Royal Catholic Army. Resistance to the Convention spread quickly, particularly to cities that resented the centralized control of Paris. In May 1793 moderates in Lyons overthrew the Jacobin municipal government. Their federalist revolt soon reached Marseilles and Toulon, and by the summer of 1793 the fed-

Illustration 21.4

Toussaint Louverture. Pierre Toussaint Louverture (c. 1743–1803), the son of African slaves, led the greatest slave rebellion in modern history. His insurrection (1791–93) won freedom for Haitian slaves and led to the creation of the first black republic. Although Toussaint joined with French revolutionary forces in fighting the British, Napoleon sought to restore slavery in Haiti. A French army captured Toussaint and brought him to France, where he died in prison.

eralists were as great a problem as the Royal Catholic Army. When the new government of Lyons executed the deposed Jacobin mayor, the Convention sent an army to besiege the city.

Ironically, the republic also faced an uprising from people who felt that the revolution had not yet gone far enough. The French colony of Saint Domingue (today Haiti) faced a slave rebellion supported by the English and the Spanish. This uprising produced one of the greatest black heroes of the resistance to slavery, François Toussaint, known as Pierre Toussaint Louverture (see illustration 21.4). Toussaint was an educated

❖ DOCUMENT 21.3 ❖

Robespierre: The Revolution and Its Ideals, 1794

It is time to define clearly the goal of the Revolution and the end which we wish to reach. . . . What is the goal toward which we strive? The peaceful enjoyment of liberty and equality . . .

We wish an order of things where all the base and cruel passions are chained, all generous and beneficent passions aroused by the laws . . . where distinctions are born only of equality itself; where the citizen is obedient to the magistrate, the magistrate to the people, and the people to justice; where the country assures the well-being of each individual . . .

What kind of government can realize these wonders? Only a democratic or republican government: these two words are synonymous, in spite of the abuses of popular usage. . . .

[W]hat is the fundamental principle of democratic or popular government. . . ? It is virtue; I speak of the public virtue which produced so many marvels in Greece and Rome, and which ought to produce even more astonishing ones in republican France; of that virtue which is nothing else but love of the country and its laws. . . .

If the force of popular government in peace is virtue, that of popular government in revolution is both *virtue and terror;* virtue, without which terror is deadly; terror, without which virtue is powerless. Terror is nothing but prompt, severe, inflexible justice; it is then an emanation of virtue.

Robespierre, Maximilien. *"Discours et rapports a la convention"* (Paris: 1965). In Wallace Adams, ed., *The Western World,* vol. 2. New York: Dodd, Mead, 1970.

ex-slave who had risen to the powerful position of steward on a large plantation before joining the rebellion. His abilities were so highly regarded that when the Convention abolished slavery (February 1794), the deputies offered Toussaint the rank of general to join them; he accepted because the British and the Spanish kept slavery.

The context of the Reign of Terror, therefore, was a desperate fight to save the republic and the revolution. The men of the Convention, who had executed Louis XVI, were also fighting for their lives, and they chose harsh measures. The revolution had already turned toward authoritarianism under the Legislative Assembly. The Convention went much further, reducing newly won liberties to a Jacobin dictatorship. Enactment of the constitution was postponed and severe laws adopted. Advocacy of a monarchical restoration and economic crimes such as hoarding were made capital crimes, to be tried before a special Revolutionary Tribunal. The freedom of the press to criticize the revolution was curtailed. A Law of Suspects expanded police powers, allowing the arrest of anyone "who by their conduct, their connections, their remarks, or their writings show themselves the partisans of tyranny or . . . the enemies of liberty." And a twelve-person executive committee with ill-defined powers, called the Committee of Public Safety, was created.

The Committee of Public Safety defended the revolution ferociously. In June 1793 the Convention was purged of moderate deputies, chiefly Girondins. A Reign of Terror, directed against spies, traitors, counter-revolutionaries, profiteers, hoarders, and corrupt officials had begun. Leaders of the Convention spoke with extraordinary candor. Danton called for them to "drink the blood of the enemies of humanity." Louis Saint-Just, an uncompromising twenty-six-year-old terrorist, was even more chilling: "Punish not only traitors, but even the indifferent." Maximilien Robespierre soon dominated the Committee of Public Safety (see document 21.3). The puritanical provincial lawyer who had built his career as an opponent of capital punishment and a defender of human rights led a terror that he defined as "nothing but prompt, severe, inflexible justice." The instrument of this severe justice was the guillotine, a machine for human decapitation. The guillotine became a gruesome symbol of the terror, crudely called "the republican razor" or "the widow" (because it made so many). It had been introduced, however, by a physician, Dr. Joseph Guillotin, as a humanitarian form of swift execution, in contrast to the horrible tortures employed by the Old Regime such as being broken on the wheel or drawn and quartered.

The Reign of Terror lasted for thirteen months, from June 1793 until July 1794. During those months,

TABLE 21.2
The Reign of Terror, 1793–94

Executions by the Paris Revolutionary Tribunal			Total executions in France		
Class category	Number	Percentage	Class category	Number	Percentage
Nobles	533	19.4	Nobles	1,156	8.2
Clergy	240	8.7	(Old	878	6.2)
Middle class	1,443	52.6	(Robe	278	2.0)
(Upper	903	32.9)	Clergy	920	6.5
(Lower	540	19.7)	Middle class	3,452	24.6
Workers	478	17.4	(Upper	1,964	14.0)
Unknown	53	1.9	(Lower	1,488	10.6)
Total	2,747		Workers	4,389	31.2
			Peasants	3,961	28.1
			Unknown	200	1.4
			Total	14,078	

Source: Donald Greer, *The Incidence of the Terror during the French Revolution: A Statistical Interpretation* (Cambridge, Mass.: Harvard University Press, 1935), p. 164; Colin Jones, ed., *The Longman Companion to the French Revolution* (London: Longman, 1988), p. 120.

tribunals around France ordered an estimated fourteen thousand to seventeen thousand executions; the most famous, the Revolutionary Tribunal of Paris, accounted for more than twenty-seven hundred (see table 21.2). The overwhelming majority of the executions (71 percent) were in regions of civil war, especially the Vendée; of those, 75 percent were rebels caught with weapons in their hands. Despite stereotypes in popular literature, most of the people executed were workers (31 percent) and peasants (28 percent), not aristocrats (8 percent) or priests (7 percent). The revolutionary tribunals acquitted many people. The tribunal at Marseilles, for example, acquitted more than 50 percent of the accused and sentenced 31 percent to death. The Parisian tribunal sent many famous figures to the guillotine: Members of the royal family (such as the duke of Orléans), leaders of the Old Regime (Malesherbes), noted scholars (the distinguished chemist Antoine Lavoisier), leading Girondins (Brissot), and feminists (Olympe de Gouges) all died there.

The civil war was especially bloody. Lyons was conquered, with ruthless reprisals, in October 1793; more than sixteen hundred people were executed. The Vendéen counterrevolution dragged on for years with enormous casualties and mass executions of rebels. One ferocious representative of the revolution in the Vendée—Jean-Baptiste Carrier—drowned prisoners in the Loire River by the hundreds, proclaiming, "We shall turn France into a cemetery rather than fail in her regeneration." A minimum of eighty thousand Vendéens died; some estimates for the civil war put the dead at more than 200,000. (By contrast, total war-related deaths during the American Revolution were fewer than ten thousand; in the American Civil War, more than 600,000.)

The Thermidorean Reaction and the Directory, 1794–99

The Reign of Terror reached its peak in December 1793–January 1794, when 49 percent of the executions (mostly in the west) occurred. In Paris, however, the Jacobin dictatorship accelerated the terror in June and July 1794, accounting for 57 percent of the executions there. Like the god Saturn in classical mythology, the revolution consumed its own children; even Danton was executed. Revulsion and fear then produced a conspiracy against Robespierre. The Convention ended the terror by arresting him in what is called the Thermidorean reaction (named for the date in the republican calendar). Robespierre attempted suicide, but he, Saint-Just, and other leading Jacobins went to the guillotine.

During 1794–95, the Convention labored to remove the more extreme aspects of the Jacobin dictatorship, starting with the abolition of the Jacobin clubs. The tribunals were closed and prisoners were released. The Law of Suspects was repealed and new judicial guarantees instituted. The Convention recalled deputies who had been purged. To placate federalists, the powers of the central government were reduced. An amnesty was offered to all rebels who laid down their arms. Freedom of religion was gradually restored, with churches separated from state control. Following these efforts to restore order, the Convention wrote a new constitution to keep it. The Constitution of the Year III (1795) was the third in the short history of the revolution. It, too, began with a declaration of rights, which was significantly renamed the Declaration of the Rights and Duties. Article One stated a right of security alongside liberty and equality.

France remained a republic with a broad suffrage including most (male) citizens, but it was constituted with safeguards, such as the separation of powers. A bicameral legislature, for example, included a lower house that introduced all legislation and an upper house with the power to block it. As a further safeguard, the upper house was a Council of Ancients, whose 250 members had to be at least forty years old—a reaction to the fact that in 1793 Robespierre had been thirty-five years old, Danton thirty-four, and Saint-Just twenty-six. The new government was called the Directory because the constitution also created an executive branch with that name. The Directory had five members, chosen by the legislature from among its own members and prohibited from succeeding themselves.

The Convention bequeathed great difficulties to the Directory. Economic problems were so severe that government ministers were given salaries measured in wheat because the currency was so unstable. Royalism was resurgent, and in some regions this had produced a "white (the symbol of royalism) terror" against former Jacobins. Simultaneously, however, new militants demanded further revolution. Gracchus Babeuf, a radical journalist, founded the Conspiracy of Equals in 1795, to restore the Constitution of the Year I and to create greater egalitarianism. Babeuf's manifesto bluntly proclaimed, "In a true society, there should be neither rich nor poor."

The Directory preserved the moderate republic by using the army against royalists, executing extremists such as Babeuf, and repudiating much of the national debt. It won a final victory in the Vendée in 1796 but became increasingly conservative when elections in 1797 returned only thirteen of the surviving 216 members of the Convention. The Directory was soon characterized by the return of individuals who had gone into hiding or fled the country. Talleyrand became foreign minister in July 1797; Sieyès became a director in 1799. The Directory thus attempted to stand in the political center, dreading both Jacobinism and royalism. It was a republic that distrusted republicanism, reflecting French exhaustion and apathy. This made it vulnerable to conspiracies, as Talleyrand realized when he attended a meeting of the directors, and guards confiscated his cane as a potential weapon. "It appears to me," he said, "that your government is terribly afraid of being poked with a stick." He was not surprised when the Directory fell in a military coup d'état in 1799.

The Revolutionary Wars and the Rise of Napoleon

Napoleon Bonaparte was born the second son of a minor Italian noble on the island of Corsica. The family became French when Louis XV bought Corsica from the republic of Genoa, whose government had become exasperated with Corsican rebellion. Napoleon's father had accepted the French occupation, a French patent of nobility, and a position in the government of Corsica. This enabled him to send the nine-year-old Napoleon to the Royal Military Academy for sons of the aristocracy in 1778. The poor, skinny, provincial Bonaparte was unpopular, but he was a good student. His mathematic skills determined his future: The artillery needed officers who could calculate trajectories. He graduated two years early, in 1785, and became a lieutenant in the royal artillery.

Napoleon harnessed his high intelligence to hard work. "Work is my element," he later wrote in a diary. He proved this as a young officer by working eighteen hours per day, typically eating only one meal and sleeping four or five hours. He kept these habits as emperor; on the two nights before his victory at Austerlitz (1805), Bonaparte slept a total of three hours. This trait enabled him to issue more than eighty thousand written orders in his fifteen-year reign, an average of fifteen documents per day. Even "the love of a woman," he noted at age twenty-two, "is incompatible with one's life work."

Lieutenant Bonaparte was a political radical. He had read the philosophes and admired Rousseau. He had contempt for the church and hatred for kings: "There are few of them who have not merited dethronement," he wrote. When the revolution began, he

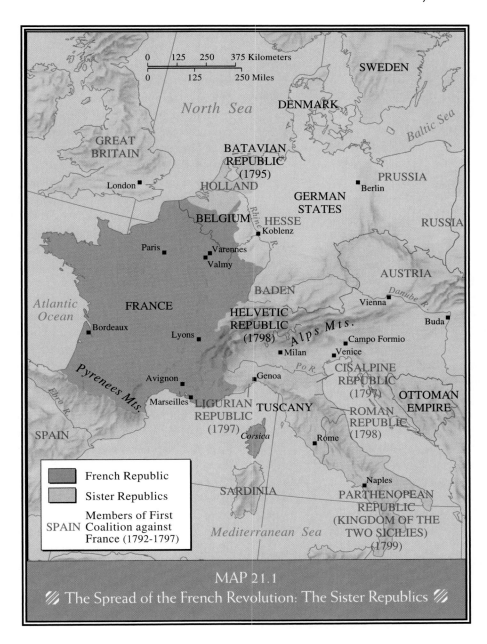

MAP 21.1

〆 The Spread of the French Revolution: The Sister Republics 〆

joined the Jacobin club. His revolutionary politics and the emigration of royalist officers led to Napoleon's rapid promotion. Then, in 1793, Napoleon found himself in the right place at the right time. Returning from Corsica to the south of France shortly after the people of Toulon had turned their port over to the British, Napoleon was placed in command of the artillery. In three months, Napoleon had forced the British to withdraw. Toulon capitulated to the army of the republic, and Napoleon became a general at age twenty-five. The fall of Robespierre resulted in Napoleon's imprisonment for Jacobinism, but the republic needed successful generals and soon restored his rank. When royalist demonstrations in Paris threatened the Direc-

tory, General Bonaparte used his artillery, loaded with small balls (the size of grapes), on the crowd. By killing demonstrators with "a whiff of grapeshot," he preserved the government, won powerful friends, and received his choice of commands.

French armies were in a strong position in 1795. The lowland provinces of modern Belgium had been taken from the Austrians and annexed to France. The coalition had collapsed over the division of Poland. A peace treaty with Prussia had given France the left bank of the Rhine River and recognized a French claim to Holland. The Dutch had been given their own republic, the first of several "sister republics" in western Europe created by French armies (see map 21.1). Spain

TABLE 21.3

The Military Campaigns of Napoleon, 1796–1815

Decisive battle	States at war	Army size	Losses
Italian campaign			
Arcola	France	20,000	4,500
(1796)	Austria	17,000	7,000
Egyptian campaign			
Pyramids	France	25,000	300
(1798)	Turks	21,000	5,000
Italian campaign			
Marengo	France	28,000	7,000
(1800)	Austria	31,000	14,000
War of Third Coalition			
Austerlitz	France	73,200	9,000
(1805)	Austria	85,400	27,000
Jena	France	96,000	5,000
(1806)	Prussia	53,000	25,000
Friedland	France	80,000	8,000
(1807)	Russia	60,000	20,000
Austrian campaign			
Wagram	France	170,000	32,000
(1809)	Austria	146,000	40,000
Russian campaign			
Borodino	France	133,000	30,000
(1812)	Russia	120,000	44,000
Battle of the Nations			
Leipzig	France	195,000	73,000
(1813)	Allies	365,000	54,000
The 100 days			
Waterloo	France	72,000	32,000
(1815)	Allies	120,000	22,000

hero who would liberate Italy and unify the small Italian states into a strong modern state. In October 1797 Francis I signed the Treaty of Campo-Formio, accepting French expansion and the sister republics. Other sister republics soon followed, in Switzerland (the Helvetian republic), central Italy (the Roman republic), and southern Italy (the Neapolitan, or Parthenopean republic).

Napoleon next sought a strategy to use against the British. He chose to challenge their global position by invading Egypt—a threat to British control of the Mediterranean and to British India. He arrived there in 1798 with an army of thirty-eight thousand and a corps of archeologists who helped found the study of Egyptology. A sweeping victory in the battle of the Pyramids gave him Cairo, but a British fleet commanded by Horatio Nelson destroyed the French fleet at the battle of Aboukir Bay.

When Napoleon Bonaparte returned to France in 1799, he was a national hero and he was dangerous. He combined aristocratic birth with a Jacobin youth. He had won great battles against foreign enemies and had saved the Directory from its royalist enemies. Now he delivered learned lectures on ancient Egypt and met with prominent scholars. Politicians soon had visions of the "man on horseback" saving France from the Directory, and Napoleon seized that opportunity. He overthrew the Directory in a military coup d'état in Brumaire (November) 1799. The coup had the support of several leaders of the Directory, notably Sieyès (the dominant director), Napoleon's brother Lucien (president of the legislature), and the unscrupulous minister of police, Joseph Fouché (a mathematics teacher who had been a Jacobin during the Reign of Terror and a leader of the Thermidorean reaction). Napoleon blithely announced that "the Revolution is at an end," and within one month he had produced the Constitution of the Year VIII (1799), dissolving the republic.

had left the war against France and Britain had no troops on the continent. Victory in the Vendée freed French armies.

Napoleon decided to force the Austrians to accept peace by driving them from northern Italy. His victory at the battle of Arcola (November 1796), where the Austrians lost more than 40 percent of their army, did just that (see table 21.3). Within a few months, Napoleon had created two sister republics in Italy—the Ligurian republic (formerly Genoa) and the Cisalpine republic (Lombardy, Modena, and part of Venetia). Italian nationalists began to dream that Bonaparte was the

France under Napoleon

The Constitution of 1799 created the Consulate, an authoritarian regime with some democratic elements. It put executive power in the hands of three consuls but added that "the decision of the First Consul (Napoleon) shall suffice." Legislative power was fragmented among many bodies: one to draft bills, a separate body to debate them, another to vote on them, and a fourth to rule on the constitutionality of these acts. All were elected by universal manhood suffrage, but it was diluted by three stages of indirect voting: voters chose representatives, who chose representatives, who chose a list of representatives from which the first consul named the legislators. Even with such restrictions, Napoleon permitted only "a single party and a single will."

The nearest approach to popular sovereignty in Napoleonic government was the plebiscite. Some legislation, such as the constitution itself, was submitted to a direct vote of adult men. A plebiscite of February 1800 ratified the Constitution of 1799 by a reported vote of three million to fifteen hundred. Electoral fraud, directed by Lucien Bonaparte as minister of the interior, doubled the favorable vote. The actual vote fell far below the turnout in 1793; in Paris only 23 percent voted. It is also noteworthy that Napoleon enforced the constitution before holding the plebiscite.

Napoleon's reign, from 1799 to 1814, mixed such techniques with a refined Old Regime despotism and revolutionary reformism. The trend of his regime, however, was unmistakably toward dictatorship. "Liberty," he said, "is a need felt by a small class of people. . . . [T]herefore, it may be repressed with impunity." He produced his second constitution in 1802, awarding himself the consulate for life. Two years later, his third constitution (France's sixth of the revolutionary era) created an hereditary empire and reduced the legislative bodies to mere ornaments. He celebrated with an elaborate coronation, crowning himself at Notre Dame Cathedral in December 1804.

Napoleon was not a simple counterrevolutionary, but he used his autocratic powers to undo some of the works of the French Revolution. He restricted divorce to preserve the traditional family. He legalized slavery again, hoping to boost the economy of Caribbean colonies. Denouncing the "pretensions of gilded Africans," he imprisoned Toussaint Louverture, who died in a French jail in 1803. And Bonaparte reestablished nobility as an honor for his generals and civil servants. Whereas Louis XVI had named approximately ten nobles per year, Napoleon averaged one a day.

Despotism was evident from the beginning of Napoleon's rule. In January 1800 he closed sixty of the seventy-three newspapers in France, and he soon shut others. "Three hostile newspapers," Napoleon told his staff, "are more to be feared than a thousand bayonets." Next he added censorship of the theatres. Then he took control of all printing, requiring the submission of all manuscripts to the government for prior censorship. Bonapartist thought control even reached into the mails. He instructed postmasters to open letters and take notes for him. Fouché's police enforced such regulations. Although he could sometimes be lenient, Napoleon usually dealt harshly with his opponents. He ended Vendéen resistance by ordering an army "to burn down two or three large villages as a salutary example." He jailed political prisoners, including many former Jacobin colleagues, without a trial. A plot against him in 1804 led him to execute a dozen people, including a member of the royal family, the duke d'Enghien, whom Napoleon seized by invading a neutral country.

Napoleon never silenced all of his critics. A remarkable example of defiance was given by Germaine de Staël, Necker's brilliant daughter, who called Napoleon "Robespierre on horseback." She organized a Parisian salon, with participants ranging from royalists to Jacobins, as a center of criticism. Napoleon was a misogynist who referred to women as "machines for making babies," but Madame de Staël fascinated him, and he merely banished her from Paris. She continued to insist that defending freedom in France was more important than winning foreign wars.

A balanced portrait of Napoleon must also see an enlightened side to his despotism. He tried to reunite France by welcoming home émigrés willing to accept his regime, and many aristocrats accepted the amnesty of 1802 to serve Napoleon. A similar compromise reestablished the Catholic Church. Napoleon had no religious faith himself, and his motive was purely pragmatic. He deposed one pope in 1798 and imprisoned another in 1809. He felt, however, that "[r]eligion is excellent stuff for keeping the common people quiet." This led him to negotiate the Concordat of 1801 with Pope Pius VII, recognizing Catholicism as "the religion of the vast majority of French citizens" and permitting it to be "freely practised." This treaty cost the Vatican many concessions. Pius VII accepted the confiscation of church lands, agreed that priests would be salaried employees of the state, permitted Napoleon to name French bishops, and even allowed a clerical "oath of fidelity" to the government.

In reestablishing Catholicism, Napoleon preserved the revolutionary protection of religious minorities. Protestants received their own state charter in 1802. Jews obtained new guarantees of their emancipation, although this did not prevent outbreaks of anti-Semitism in eastern France. Napoleon's attitudes toward Jews were sometimes suspect, but his defense of Jewish emancipation made France a center of nineteenth-century toleration. The Jewish population of Paris, which had been fewer than five hundred in 1789, reached three thousand in 1806, a tribute to his comparative toleration. And Napoleon carried Jewish emancipation into regions that his armies conquered, especially in western Germany.

Napoleon even enhanced some ideas of the revolutionary era. He completed a Jacobin project for the codification of French laws, producing the Civil Code (known as the Napoleonic Code) of 1804, then codes of commercial law (1807) and penal law (1810). The codes eliminated scores of antiquated laws, perpetuated much revolutionary legislation, and standardized the laws. Among the most far-reaching elements of the codes were detailed laws of private property, which protected people who had acquired property during the revolution. The Napoleonic Code was also bluntly paternalistic, explicitly treating women as subordinates of men and blocking their emancipation throughout the nineteenth century.

Napoleon also revived the revolutionary effort to expand education. A national school system existed, but only on paper. Napoleon considered the schools, like the churches and the law, to be instruments of social stability. "My principle aim," he said, "is to secure the means for directing political and moral opinion." Thus he provided the widest educational opportunity in the world, but his schools operated with "military discipline."

Napoleon's greatest accomplishment as the heir of the French Revolution was to sustain and expand a democratic meritocracy, often called "the career open to talent." In a world still characterized by corporate society, the Napoleonic Empire offered great opportunities for the able, whatever their social origin or religion. Bright students from poor backgrounds could rise to the top. No institution provided greater opportunities than his army, where soldiers could rise rapidly through the ranks despite humble origins. In one of Napoleon's favorite clichés, every soldier had a field marshal's baton in his napsack. His closest marshal, Joachim Murat, was the son of an innkeeper. In an act that would have been unthinkable under the monarchy, Murat married Napoleon's sister Caroline and became king of Naples. Other marshals were born the sons of a cooper, a miller, a mason, and a stableboy.

The Napoleonic Wars

Napoleon devoted most of his time to war; he stayed in France for only one-third of the days in his reign. When he became First Consul in 1799, France was at war with the remnants of the Second Coalition. France still relied on the numerical strength provided by the levée en masse, but battles were comparatively small. Napoleon's victory at Arcola, for example, had matched twenty thousand French soldiers against seventeen thousand Austrians. During the next fifteen years, Napoleon fought nearly permanent war against Europe. His armies occupied Madrid, Rome, Vienna, Berlin, and Moscow. This required the standing conscription of young Frenchmen, usually for five years. By 1814 he had drafted 2.6 million men and led more than one million of them to their death.

These huge numbers help to explain Napoleon's victories. The revolutionary army at Valmy had numbered only fifty-nine thousand. By the time of the Third Coalition (1805–07), Napoleon often sent 100,000 men into a battle, and that number soon seemed small. Much of his success came from having the largest army, or from maneuvering until he obtained numerical superiority. When he had the advantage, Napoleon was ruthless. The Prussians learned this at the battle of Jena (1806): A French army of ninety-six thousand crushed a Prussian force of fifty-three thousand, then pursued them relentlessly. Napoleon lost 5.2 percent of his army while the Prussians lost 47.2 percent. When Napoleon lost such advantages, he began to lose battles. Numbers alone do not account for Napoleon's military reputation, however. His skillful use of artillery, especially concentrated artillery firing rapidly (versus the accepted wisdom of conserving ammunition), won some battles. His use of elite cavalry units as shock troops to attack infantry won others. But his military greatness was less a matter of brilliant strategies than inspired opportunism.

As warfare changed from formal engagements of small professional armies to the ruthlessness of mass armies, other changes followed. In 1793 the Austrian army in the Netherlands had paid rent to Dutch farmers for permission to camp in their fields. Later, the retreating Austrians found themselves pushed against the Rhine River without sufficient money to pay for ferry service across the river; instead of seizing the ferries, the Austrians awaited the French and surrendered. In contrast, Napoleon encountered a different psychology of war when he invaded Russia in 1812. The Russians used a "scorched earth" strategy: They burnt the farms and fields of the Russian peasantry instead of leaving food supplies for the French.

By 1805 Napoleon faced a Third Coalition of Britain, Austria, and Russia. He prepared for an invasion of England until October 1805, when Admiral Horatio Nelson's fleet destroyed the French fleet near the Spanish coast off Cape Trafalgar, depriving Napoleon of the naval power needed for an invasion. Napoleon thereupon marched his army into central Europe and won

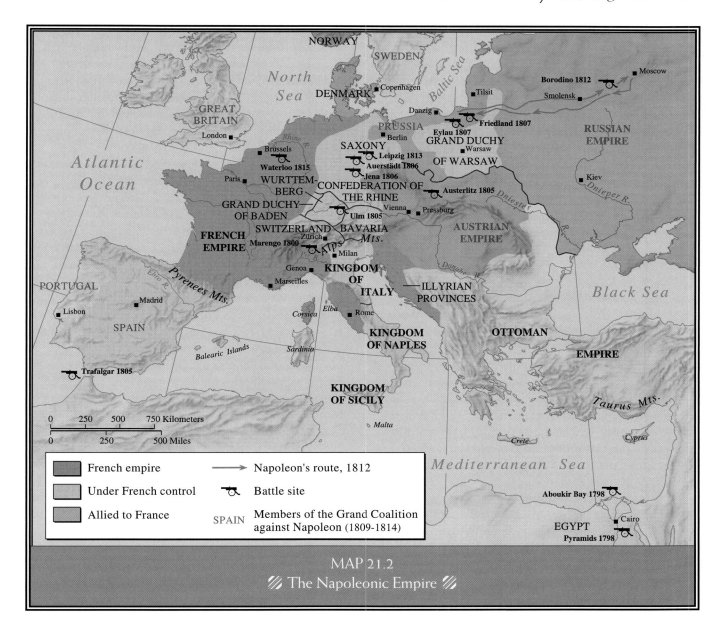

MAP 21.2

The Napoleonic Empire

major victories over the Austrians at Ulm (October 1805) and combined Austro-Russian forces at Austerlitz (December 1805). Napoleon was so proud of his great victory at Austerlitz that he adopted all children of the French soldiers killed in that battle, promising that the government would support them, educate them, and find husbands for the daughters and jobs for the sons. He then pressed his troops on, and they defeated the Prussians, who had belatedly joined the coalition, at Jena (October 1806) and the retreating Russians at Friedland (June 1807). In less than two years of fighting, Napoleon had gained control of central Europe.

Napoleon exploited his victories to redraw the map of Europe (see map 21.2). He abolished the Holy Ro-

man Empire, reducing Francis I to emperor of Austria. In 1806 he amalgamated western Germany into a puppet state called the Confederation of the Rhine. Holland was made a kingdom and given to his brother, Louis Bonaparte. The territory that Prussia had seized in the second and third partitions of Poland was taken from her to form another client state, the grand duchy of Warsaw. Italy was divided into three regions: Northern Italy became the Kingdom of Italy, with Napoleon as the nominal king; central Italy was directly annexed to France; and southern Italy became the Kingdom of Naples, with Napoleon's brother-in-law, Murat, named king. Territory along the Adriatic Coast (previously governed by Venice) and the northern coast of

Germany were also directly annexed to France. Spain was given to another brother, Joseph Bonaparte.

By 1810 most of Europe was under Napoleon's control, with Portugal, Britain, Scandinavia, Russia, and most of the Balkans remaining free. Prussia and Austria retained their independence, but they faced numerous controls. Prussia, for example, was limited to an army of forty-two thousand men and was made to host a French garrison. Austria, after attempting a Fourth Coalition and suffering another defeat at Wagram in 1809, was bound to France by a marriage in 1810 between Napoleon and Francis's teenaged daughter, Maria Louisa. As an angry Russian aristocrat said in the opening sentence of Leo Tolstoy's *War and Peace*, the great cities of Europe "are now just family estates of the Buonapartes."

Napoleon tried to fight Britain with economic warfare. His Berlin Decree of 1806 ordered the cessation of all commerce and communication with Britain. This plan, known as the Continental System, failed because it required more cooperation than Napoleon could compel. The loss of easy access to inexpensive English manufactures caused some Europeans to defy the Continental System. When Czar Alexander I of Russia refused to cooperate, Napoleon decided to invade Russia. He did so despite unresolved difficulties in western Europe, where the Spanish resistance to Joseph Bonaparte had already created an independent Cortes (1810) and produced a liberal constitution (1812). The Spanish had received the support of a British army commanded by Sir Arthur Wellesley. Spanish and British armies were already pushing back the French in Wellesley's brilliant Peninsular Campaign, which would earn him the title of the duke of Wellington.

Napoleon's Grande Armée of 600,000 men nonetheless invaded Russia in June 1812 and won several initial battles. This included the bloodiest battle of the nineteenth century, at Borodino where forty-four thousand Russians were killed in a single day. (In contrast, fifty-five thousand Americans were killed in the decade of the Vietnam War.) Russian armies, however, typically retreated without permitting decisive engagements, following the scorched earth strategy of Marshal Mikhail Kutuzov. Even when Moscow fell to Napoleon, the Russians refused peace negotiations and set fire to their own city. Napoleon, the author of the maxim that "an army marches on its stomach," found himself with an impossibly long supply line and few prospects for survival by plunder, as the winter neared.

His only choice was to retreat, which exposed his army to attacks from the rear, the tactic with which he had devastated opponents. He retreated, leaving nearly 300,000 French soldiers dead in Russia, with another 200,000 taken prisoner. Viewed from the other side of the field, this was an epic triumph, celebrated by Tolstoy in *War and Peace* (1866) and by Peter Tchaikovsky in *The 1812 Overture*.

Napoleon's defeat in Russia led directly to the collapse of his empire. Just as 1812 became a year celebrated in Russian patriotism, 1813 became a triumphal year of German nationalism. Frederick William III of Prussia immediately joined the Russians and urged Germans to unite against Napoleon. The leading statesman of the new allied coalition was the Austrian foreign minister, Prince Klemens von Metternich, who brought Austria into the war against France after Napoleon had rejected the generous offer of peace based upon the "natural frontiers" of France (shrinking the country back to the Rhine River).

The war in central Europe involved immense armies, especially in a decisive battle near the city of Leipzig (Saxony) in October 1813. This engagement, known as the *Völkerschlact* (the Battle of the Nations) to German patriots, saw the allies produce combined forces of 365,000 men, nearly double Napoleon's army and ten times the size of typical armies in the 1790s. Napoleon was thoroughly beaten (see illustration 21.5). Shortly thereafter, allied armies poured into France from several directions. They occupied Paris in March 1814, and Napoleon abdicated a few days later. The victorious allies granted France a lenient peace treaty, the Peace of Paris (1814), restoring the frontiers of 1792. Napoleon was exiled to the Italian island of Elba in comfortable conditions, and the Bourbon family was restored to the throne of France. The new king, Louis XVIII, was the brother of Louis XVI; he had survived the revolution by joining the émigrés in 1791. (He skipped the title of Louis XVII in deference to the son of Louis XVI, who had died in prison.)

In the following year, Napoleon escaped from Elba and with the support of his veterans seized control of France for a brief reign known as "the 100 days." Alarmed, the British and the Prussians joined forces under the duke of Wellington and defeated him at Waterloo, just south of Brussels, Belgium, on June 18, 1815. The Napoleonic era was over, but the emperor lived on until 1821, exiled to house arrest on the remote British island of St. Helena in the south Atlantic.

Illustration 21.5

Two Views of the Napoleonic Wars. The great neoclassical painter Jacques-Louis David became court painter to Napoleon and created several immense canvases glorifying his regime. None was greater propaganda than his "Napoleon Crossing the Alps" en route to his victory in Italy, following the path of earlier conquerers whose names are immortalized in Alpine stone. The heroic rider astride a fiery charger is far from the truth, however. Napoleon chose a cautious crossing of the Alps on the back of a sure-footed burro.

The white stallion remains, but little of the romantic heroism seen in David's painting survives in Ernest Meissonier's "The French Campaign, 1814." Here, a somber emperor leads an exhausted army that had been beaten repeatedly for two years.

CHAPTER 22

INDUSTRIALIZATION AND THE SOCIAL AND ECONOMIC STRUCTURE OF EUROPE

CHAPTER OUTLINE

◆◆◆◆◆◆◆◆◆◆◆◆◆◆◆◆◆◆◆◆

The industrialization of Europe began in the late eighteenth century and by 1900 had dramatically transformed the economy and social structure. Chapter 22 looks at this process. It begins with two demographic changes associated with industrialization: a population explosion and urbanization. A "vital revolution" was the product of changes in European agriculture that allowed a larger population to be fed. After analyzing these changes, the chapter then focuses on the industrialization of Great Britain, often called the industrial revolution. It starts with handcraft manufacture and cottage industry, then explains the impact of the steam engine. This leads to a discussion of the most important elements of early industrialization: the iron and coal industries, textile manufacturing, and the railroads.

After examining the positive and negative sides of life in the new urban world, the chapter focuses on the changing class structure of Europe with special attention to the new middle class and the urban working class. It then discusses the impact of industrialization on women, children, and the family. Analysis of these questions permits an introduction to what has been called the standard of living debate: Did the conditions of daily life improve or deteriorate during industrialization?

The chapter ends by tracing the spread of industrialization across Europe, stressing the "take-off period" of industrial growth during the mid-nineteenth century, followed by the "second industrial revolution" in which German industrial output began to match and even outstrip that of Great Britain.

The Population Explosion

One of the most important developments in modern European history was a dramatic increase in population during the eighteenth and nineteenth centuries. The population of Europe had been slowly rising for centuries, but severe checks, caused by poor diet and

TABLE 22.1

The European Population Explosion, 1700–1900

The data in this table reflect historical boundaries at the date shown and therefore are not perfectly comparable. For example, the population of Alsace-Lorraine is included in France in 1800 and in Germany in 1900.

State	1700 Population (in millions)	1800 Population (in millions)	Growth, 1700–1800 (in percent)	1900 Population (in millions)	Growth, 1800–1900 (in percent)
France	17.3	26.9	55.5	39.0	45.0
European Russia	17.0	29.0	70.6	106.2	266.2
Germany	13.5	18.5	37.0	56.4	204.9
Italy	13.0	18.1	39.2	33.4	84.5
Austria-Hungary	11.0	15.0	36.4	25.9	72.7
United Kingdom	8.9	16.2	82.0	41.5	156.2
Spain	7.5	10.5	40.0	18.1	72.4
Portugal	2.0	2.8	40.0	5.4	92.9
Sweden	2.0	2.3	15.0	5.1	121.7
Netherlands	1.9	2.1	10.5	5.1	142.9
Denmark	1.3	1.9	46.2	2.6	36.8
Switzerland	1.2	1.7	41.7	3.3	94.1
Belgium	a	a		6.7	
Ottoman Empire in Europe	6.4	11.5	79.7	4.8	

Source: Calculated from data in Jack Barbuscio and Richard M. Dunn, *European Political Facts, 1648–1789* (London: Macmillan, 1984), pp. 335–53; Chris Cook and John Paxton, *European Political Facts, 1848–1918* (London: Macmillan, 1978), pp. 213–32; A. Goodwin, ed., *The New Cambridge Modern History* (Cambridge: Cambridge University Press, 1965), 8:714–15; B. R. Mitchell, *European Historical Statistics, 1750-1970* (London: Macmillan, 1975), pp. 19–24.

a. Part of the Austrian Empire. No separate data available.

nutrition, epidemic disease, primitive medical care, warfare, and repressive government, had limited that growth. Great Britain offers a vivid illustration. After William the Conqueror won control of England in 1066, he ordered a survey of his new realm; the resultant Domesday Survey (1086) determined that England had a population of 3.5 million. A good estimate of England in 1750 is a population of 6.5 million, which meant an increase of three million people in seven hundred years, an average growth rate of less than 1 percent per decade.

In contrast to that history of slow population growth, what happened during the late eighteenth century and the nineteenth century must be called a population explosion. A continent inhabited by perhaps 110 million people in 1700 became a continent of 423 million people in 1900. This near quadrupling of Europe meant a growth rate of nearly 10 percent per decade, compared with the historic pattern of less than 1 percent. Britain, where the European population explosion began, provides the best illustration of this growth. Beginning in 1750, the British isles experienced three consecutive decades of 6 percent population growth, followed by stunning decennial increases of 9 percent,

11 percent, 14 percent, and 18 percent. The astonishing population boom meant that a country that had grown by three million people over seven hundred years then grew by eleven million people in one hundred years.

The British population explosion continued into the nineteenth century and became a widespread (although not universal) European phenomenon (see table 22.1). During the eighteenth century, population growth in most of the major states of Europe was approximately 35 percent to 40 percent—36 percent in the Austrian Empire, 37 percent across the Germanic states of central Europe, 39 percent in the Italian states, and 40 percent in Spain. France, the most populous and most powerful state of western Europe, experienced a slightly faster rate of growth (55 percent) but did not approach the remarkable 82 percent growth in Britain. In the nineteenth century, the rate of growth in Austria, Italy, and Spain increased to 70–85 percent, but the British rate of growth had soared to more than 150 percent, causing the population density to surpass one hundred inhabitants per square mile in large portions of Europe (see map 22.1). Only Germany and Russia—where population growth was more than 200 percent—

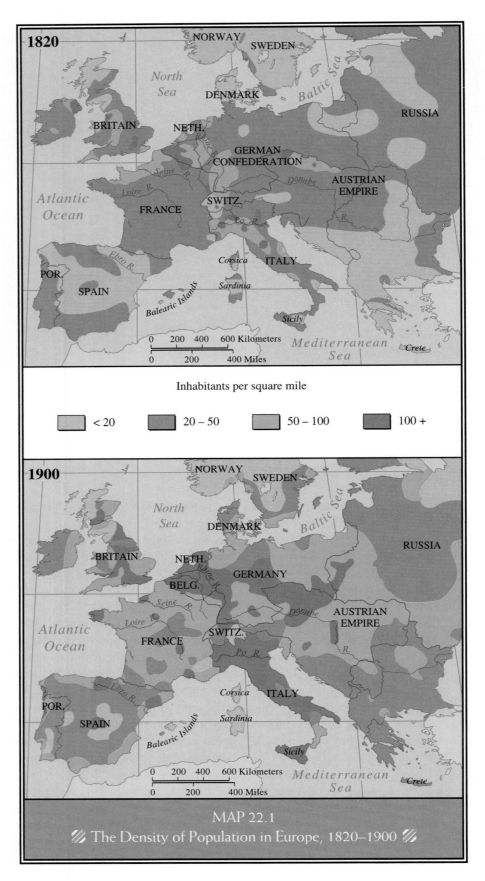

1820

Inhabitants per square mile

< 20   20 – 50   50 – 100   100 +

1900

MAP 22.1
The Density of Population in Europe, 1820–1900

kept up with Britain. France, which pioneered modern birth control practices, did not experience such a dramatic population explosion, and the nineteenth-century growth rate there (45 percent) was lower than that of the eighteenth century (55 percent).

The beginning of this population explosion so shocked one English economist, the Reverend Thomas Malthus, that he wrote the most famous book about population ever published, *An Essay on the Principle of Population* (1798), warning about the dangers of this trend. Malthus argued that unchecked population growth tended to increase at a geometric rate (one, two, four, eight, sixteen, thirty-two), while the means of subsistence to support those people increased only at an arithmetic rate (one, two, three, four, five, six). The contrast between these two rates, known as the Malthusian principle, prompted the pessimistic conclusion that, without some preventive restraints on population increase, the future of humankind would be a story of catastrophic checks on population.

The Vital Revolution

The conquest of the biological old regime, through the improvement of diet and the conquering of disease, amounts to a great vital revolution. The vital revolution that began in the late eighteenth century and extended through the twentieth century is arguably the most important revolution in modern history, even when compared with famous political and economic revolutions. Demographers measure the vital revolution with a variety of statistics, but the most important are straightforward: the birthrate and the death rate. The population of Europe had grown very slowly for centuries for the simple reason that the birthrate and the death rate remained similar. If one studies the birth and death data for early eighteenth-century Britain, the balance of the biological old regime becomes clear. In 1720, the birthrate per ten thousand people (314) and the death rate (311) were almost identical. Then in 1730, the death rate (349) exceeded the birthrate (339) and that pattern continued in 1740. Thus, for the first generation of the century, the biological old regime kept a virtually even balance between births and deaths. Beginning in 1750, however, British birthrates remained steady at a high level (between 366 and 377 per ten thousand) for decades, while the death rate plummeted, hitting 300 in 1770, then falling to 211 by 1820. The huge gap between 366 births and 211 deaths per ten thousand population is the demographer's measure of the vital revolution, the source of the population explosion, and the pattern that frightened Malthus.

The European death rate, especially the infant mortality rate, had remained frightfully high during the eighteenth century, and in many years the death rate surpassed the birthrate. Studies of regions of Europe that had higher birthrates than Britain did—such as Lombardy in northern Italy—have shown that great increases in the number of births did not necessarily produce a significant population increase. If the twin guardians of the biological old regime, diet and disease, were not beaten, the death rate simply consumed the higher birthrate. The vital revolution of the late eighteenth century owed more to the improvement of diet than to the conquest of disease: The benefits of the Columbian exchange, such as the potato and the agricultural revolution meant that Europe could feed a larger population. The great medical advances of the vital revolution mostly came in the nineteenth and twentieth centuries, although the slow conquest of smallpox had begun with Mary Wortley Montagu and Edward Jenner in the eighteenth century.

The Urbanization of Europe

The vital revolution led to the urbanization of European civilization. For more than two thousand years, the greatest centers of European civilization—from ancient Athens and Rome through the Italian city-states of the Renaissance to London and Paris in the Old Regime—had been its cities. By 1750 European cities had been growing in size and numbers for centuries. But the eighteenth century was not yet an urban society; in every country, the majority of the population lived on farms and in small villages.

The British census of 1850 found that more than 50 percent of the population lived in towns and cities, making Britain the first predominantly urban society in history. The early nineteenth century was consequently a period of remarkable urban growth. Between 1750 and 1800, nineteen towns in Europe doubled in size, and fifteen of them were located in Britain. No town in France, none in the Italian states, nor any in Russia grew so rapidly, but in northern England—from Lancashire in the west, across the midlands to Yorkshire in the east—seven towns doubled in size. And the impact of the population explosion was just beginning. During the next half-century, 1800–50, seven British cities (five of them in northern England) tripled in size, some nearly quintupling.

British cities were not huge by twenty-first century standards, but they were astonishing by contemporary standards because the population explosion had not yet transformed the continent. The port of Liverpool, a

◣ TABLE 22.2 ◢
The Major Cities of Europe, 1800–1900

British cities are highlighted in bold-faced type. Note the importance of British cities in the data for 1850, a date often chosen as the point at which Britain had become a predominantly industrial society.

Europe in 1800		Europe in 1850		Europe in 1900	
City	Population	City	Population	City	Population
London	1,117,000	**London**	2,685,000	**London**	6,586,000
Paris	547,000	Paris	1,053,000	Paris	2,714,000
Naples	427,000	St. Petersburg	489,000	Berlin	1,889,000
Moscow	250,000	Naples	449,000	Vienna	1,675,000
Vienna	247,000	Vienna	444,000	St. Petersburg	1,267,000
St. Petersburg	220,000	Berlin	419,000	Moscow	989,000
Amsterdam	201,000	**Liverpool**	376,000	Hamburg	931,000
Lisbon	180,000	Moscow	365,000	Budapest	732,000
Berlin	172,000	**Glasgow**	357,000	**Liverpool**	704,000
Dublin	165,000	**Manchester**	303,000	**Manchester**	645,000
Rome	163,000	Madrid	281,000	Warsaw	638,000
Madrid	160,000	**Dublin**	272,000	Brussels	599,000
Palermo	139,000	Brussels	251,000	Naples	564,000
Milan	135,000	Milan	242,000	Madrid	540,000
Venice	134,000	Lisbon	240,000	Barcelona	533,000
Hamburg	130,000	**Birmingham**	233,000	Amsterdam	511,000
Barcelona	115,000	Amsterdam	224,000	Munich	500,000
		Edinburgh	202,000	Milan	493,000

Source: B. R. Mitchell, *European Historical Statistics, 1750–1970* (London: Macmillan, 1975), pp. 76–78; Chris Cook and John Paxton, *European Political Facts, 1848–1918* (London: Macmillan, 1978), pp. 213–32.

town that had become prosperous during the slave trade, grew so fast in the early nineteenth century that it surpassed such capital cities as Moscow and Madrid in size (see table 22.2). In 1850 the British isles contained seven cities larger than Rome, the historic center of Europe. Nearly a quarter of the British population lived in metropolitan areas of 100,000 or more, while only 4.6 percent of France and 2.3 percent of Spain lived in such urban regions. The great Swiss cities of Geneva (31,000) and Zürich (17,000) were suddenly smaller than British towns such as Bradford (104,000). In 1800, two of the ten largest cities in Europe (London and Dublin) were in the United Kingdom; by 1850, four of the ten largest (London, Liverpool, Glasgow, and Manchester) were in the U.K.

When the effects of the population explosion reached continental Europe, so did urbanization. Just as Manchester, Birmingham, Leeds, and Sheffield had exploded from regional towns into major urban centers,

new cities grew in Europe. Essen, in the Ruhr valley of western Germany, changed from a small town of 4,000 people in 1800 into a sprawling city of 295,000 at the start of the twentieth century. The transformation of Łodz (Poland) was even more dramatic: A village of 200 people in 1800 became a city of 315,000 in 1900. By 1900 only three of the largest cities in Europe were in Britain.

The Agricultural Revolution

The first explanation of the vital revolution was an improved food supply. Although the nineteenth century still experienced famines in some regions (especially Russia) and occasional disasters such as the potato famine of the 1840s, the pattern of regular subsistence crises that characterized early modern history ended by the middle of the nineteenth century. The average European diet was poor by twenty-first century standards, but it had significantly improved since the eighteenth century, producing better general health, greater resistance to disease, and higher rates of healthy reproduction.

The improved food supply is best seen in late eighteenth-century Britain, where the population explosion began. Despite restrictive tariffs on grain imports known as the Corn Laws, Britain imported an increasing amount of food after 1780, and this provided partial support for a larger population. British grain imports stood at 200,000 tons in 1780, rising to 3.7 million tons in 1800, and then 7.5 million tons in 1840. At the same time, the improvements in British internal transportation—canals, toll roads, and railroads—reduced food prices in urban areas. Food shipment also improved as new technology allowed the preservation of food for transportation, beginning with the adoption of a sterile canning process that a Parisian chef, François Appert, had invented for Napoleon's armies in 1804.

The greatest source of an improved food supply in Britain, however, was an increase in British harvests so significant that historians have called it an agricultural revolution. The agricultural revolution involved both extensive use of land (more acres planted) and intensive use of the land (higher yields per acre). The stimulus to both developments was simple: Grain prices rose with the population, previous bad harvests had left few grain reserves, and a generation of war with France sometimes interrupted the importation of grain (which fell from 4.6 million tons to 2.9 million tons in the years following 1810).

Extensive use of the soil provides obvious possibilities. Land could be reclaimed by draining marshes and wetlands, such as the fens of eastern England or the marshes of central Italy. In other regions of Europe, especially Scandinavia and eastern Europe, sparsely populated woodlands and wildernesses could be cleared and planted. Wherever the science of agronomy established modern crop rotation, the tradition of leaving fields lie fallow every third year could be abandoned. This alone produced a 10 percent increase in arable land in some regions.

The most impressive side of the agricultural revolution—more intensive use of the land—achieved an unprecedented rise in European productivity. Scientific farming, such as improved understanding of fertilizers, significantly improved the harvest per acre. The beginnings of modern farm mechanization—from Jethro Tull's development of seed drills to replace the manual broadcasting of seeds to Andrew Meikle's invention of

the threshing machine in 1784—produced more efficient harvests. Such developments increased the ratio of grain harvested to grain sown. In Britain, the wheat harvest went from a yield of 7-to-1 to a ratio of 10.6 to 1; at that rate, the British harvest was nearly twice as productive per acre as the rest of Europe and three times as successful as farming in eastern Europe.

New crops were also an important part of the agricultural revolution. The introduction of winter crops in some regions, the continuing arrival of new American crops from the Columbian exchange, and the steady acceptance of root crops (such as the potato and the sugar beet) greatly changed European diets. The potato grew in more northerly climates and poorer soils than most grains; it had a three-to-four-month cycle to harvest, compared with ten months for many grains; and a single crop yielded twice as much nutrition per acre as grains did. Consequently, by the early 1840s, one-third of the population of England and one-half of Scotland lived on the potato. Even higher rates of potato consumption were found in Ireland and parts of Germany.

The Controversy over Enclosure

Clearing forests or swamps and harvesting more crops per acre were not the only changes by which the agricultural revolution fed the growing population of the British isles. The greatest source of new acreage being farmed resulted from a controversial political decision known as enclosure. This term simply means the enclosing of farm land within fences. The laws of enclosure, however, had more profound results than that description suggests, leading some historians to argue that it was a necessary condition for industrialization. By ancient tradition, most villages in Britain reserved a portion of local land called the commons for the use of all residents. No one could plant crops on the commons, but anyone could graze animals, forage for food (such as berries or acorns), and gather firewood there. Enclosure of the commons within fences meant that the land could be plowed to increase the national grain production, but the traditional rights of citizens ended, forcing many of them off the land. Enclosure in a larger sense ended the open field system of agriculture, in which the land was divided into numerous small strips. In 1700, 50 percent of English farmland, and most continental farmland, was in open field strips. By 1850 virtually all of rural Britain was enclosed.

Each enclosure required an act of Parliament, and four thousand such acts of enclosure were voted between 1750 and 1850, although a General Enclosure Act of 1801 served as a model for most others. By these acts, the commons lands were sold in some villages and distributed among the landowners in others. This led to the consolidation of individual strips into single farms and the failure of small farms where the owners had depended upon the commons. The resulting farms were larger than the sum of the strips because they incorporated the paths that had separated the strips, and they became larger yet as uncompetitive small farms were absorbed. By the early nineteenth century, two-thirds of British farmland was in large estates. Enclosure raised agricultural production as well as controversy. The benefits were larger than simply that more land was put under the plow and therefore more food was produced. Enclosure of the commons meant the segregation of herds of livestock, reducing disease transmission and permitting selective breeding. The breeding experiments conducted with sheep by Robert Bakewell, for example, saw the average weight of sheep brought to market rise from twenty-eight pounds in 1710 to eighty pounds in 1795. Larger farms encouraged crop rotation because the entire acreage did not have to be planted in the same subsistence grain for the farm family. Consolidation of the open field strips meant that farm equipment did not have to be moved great distances.

Enclosure provoked opposition because of the human effects on the rural population. Marginal farmers suffered worst. Without strips of common farmland, many families could not survive by agriculture. Others faced failure because they had depended upon the commons to graze a pig or a few geese. As one angry poet put it, "The law locks up the man or woman who steals the goose from off the Common; But leaves the greater villain loose who steals the common from the goose." Historians have debated the amount of suffering caused by enclosure, and they have generally agreed that it is a question of long-term gains for most of society versus short-term suffering for much of society.

Handcraft, Cottage Industry, and the Steam Engine

The agricultural revolution, the vital revolution, and the population explosion of late eighteenth- and nineteenth-century Europe were all important factors in making possible a dramatic transformation of the European economy known as industrialization, in which manufactured goods began to replace agriculture as the dominant sector of the economy. Large-scale factory production began to replace handcraft manufacture; machinery and inanimate power sources began to replace human labor. Such large-scale industrialization did not happen suddenly or universally—factories, traditional production, and agriculture coexisted within a country, and usually within a region. Nonetheless, industrialization was such a dramatic change that contemporaries and historians (especially in Britain) have sometimes called it the industrial revolution.

The pressure of growing population demanded (and rewarded) great increases in the production of essential goods, such as the woolen and cotton textiles needed for clothing. Such goods had long been made by traditional handwork methods of spinning thread and weaving cloth. This handwork production of textiles had spawned a form of manufacturing known as cottage industry, in which entrepreneurial middlemen engaged people to produce textiles in their homes (hence "cottage industry"), provided them with raw materials, paid them for finished work, then transported the goods to town for sale. This form of employment in home spinning and weaving lasted throughout the nineteenth century in some regions, but beginning in the mid-eighteenth century, technological innovations replaced human skills and power with machines. Industrialization was the broad process by which machines, operated by hundreds of people in urban factories, replaced the production of handcraft workers in small shops and cottages.

The age of industrialization was opened by a single new technology—the steam engine, which provided the power source for the innovations that followed. The principle of steam power was not new. It had been known in the ancient world and had long been the subject of study and experimentation. No single person invented the steam engine, although popular culture in English-speaking countries credits James Watt, while the French credit Denis Papin. In reality, the steam engine was the culmination of the work of many people. The first effective machines were developed in the 1770s by Watt, a maker of precision instruments for scientists at the University of Glasgow.

The initial use of the steam engine was in mining. Steam-powered pumps such as the Newcomen Engine could remove water from mine shafts that passed below the water table. This permitted much deeper mining, which in turn facilitated vastly greater coal extraction; the coal then could be burned to operate more steam engines. As coal became more plentiful and less expensive, and as steam engine technology proved successful, the engine found other applications. Steam-powered bellows at forges changed metallurgy, producing more

Illustration 22.1

〰 **A Coal Mine during Early Industrialization.** Coal was the primary new power source of industrialization. Pumps driven by steam engines, such as the Newcomen Engine, made it possible to tunnel below the water table. Note the use of child and female labor in much of this mine to cart coal in narrow spaces: It was usually cheaper to use children than pit-ponies.

⊠ TABLE 22.3 ⊠				
European Coal Production, 1820–50				
The data in this table are national outputs of coal in millions of tons.				
Country	1820	1830	1840	1850
Austria	.1	.2	.5	.9
Belgium	a	2.3	3.9	5.8
Britain	17.7	22.8	34.2	50.2
France	1.1	1.8	3.0	4.4
German states	1.3	1.8	3.9	6.9

Source: B. R. Mitchell, *European Historical Statistics, 1750–1970* (London: Macmillan, 1975), pp. 360–61.

a. Belgium was not independent in 1820.

and finer steel. Steam-powered mills for grinding grains or sugar freed millers from dependence upon rivers. Experiments applied steam power to transportation, including the first steam automobile (1769), steamboat (1783), and railroad locomotive (1804). The locomotive was the perfect symbol of the steam revolution because it was merely a giant steam engine with wheels attached.

The Age of Iron and Coal

Industrialization quickly came to depend upon plentiful resources of iron, from which the machinery of steam technology was made, and coal, with which it was powered. Both iron and coal had been mined in Europe for centuries, but the scale of this mining was small. The total European output of pig iron in 1788 was approximately 200,000 metric tons, of which the British mined 69,000 tons. Most countries produced so little iron that they kept no national records of it. Coal mining was a similarly small-scale industry.

Great Britain had the good fortune to possess exceptionally rich deposits of both natural resources. When the steam engine permitted—then demanded—greater coal mining, Britain exploited those resources (see illus-

tration 22.1) to become the world's first industrial power and to establish an enormous lead in industrial might (see table 22.3). During the French Revolution and the Napoleonic Wars, the British output of pig iron tripled to 248 metric tons; with peace, the output tripled again by the early 1830s. In 1850 Britain smelted 2.3 million metric tons of iron, more than one-half of the total supply of iron in the world (see illustration 22.2). British coal mining similarly overwhelmed the rest of the world. In 1820 the Austrian Empire mined 100,000 tons of coal and the German states slightly more than 1 million tons; Britain mined 17.7 million tons. Twenty years later, Austria and the German states had tripled their output but that was barely one-tenth of Britain's 34.2 million tons of coal. By midcentury, Britain mined more than two-thirds of the world's coal. Consequently, the British also generated more steam power than all of continental Europe combined. The British dominance in coal, iron, and steam production built an industrial leadership so great that Britons naturally spoke of their "industrial revolution" (see map 22.2).

The Machine Age and the Textile Factory

The availability of inexpensive steam power and iron for machinery led to an age of remarkable inventiveness. In the century between 1660 and 1760, the British government had registered an average of six new patents per year; applications of steam technology drove that average to more than two hundred patents per year in the 1770s, more than five hundred per year in the 1790s, and nearly five thousand per year by the 1840s. The British inventions of the early industrial age

Illustration 22.2

🖉 **The Coalbrookdale Ironworks at Night.** Nothing better symbolized the powerful changes of early industrialization than a large ironworks with its great coke furnaces stoked. Such ironworks were typically located on a country river, where wood, coal, and water were plentiful. This painting depicts the most important early ironworks, Abraham Darby's works in central England.

were not the result of excellent technical schools; continental schools such as the Schemnitz Academy in Hungary or the École des Ponts et Chaussées (the first engineering school) in France were far superior. Most British inventions were the inspiration of tinkerers and artisans. One of the most important inventors of the early industrial age, Richard Arkwright, was a semiliterate barber with an exceptional mechanical aptitude.

The earliest beneficiary of the new technology was the textile industry. Woolen goods had been a basic British export for centuries; in the early eighteenth century woolens accounted for 25 percent to 33 percent of export revenue. Cotton goods were a newer export, produced from raw cotton imported from Britain's American colonies. In 1700 textile manufacturing had not changed much from medieval industry. Fibers were spun into thread by hand, perhaps with a spinning wheel, perhaps with simpler tools such as the distaff. The threads were then woven into cloth on handlooms. Spinning was usually done by women (hence the terms *spinster* or *distaff side*); weaving, by men. The entire handcraft process fitted comfortably into a rural cottage.

The new technology of the steam age soon threatened cottage industry. Machines first changed the spinning of thread: James Hargreaves's spinning jenny allowed one person to spin thread onto multiple spindles, producing ten times as much thread—soon one hundred times as much thread—as a good manual spinner. Arkwright's water frame mechanized the spinning of threads to produce stronger thread with less labor. The spinning mule of 1779 combined the spinning jenny, the water frame, and the steam engine to produce forty-eight spindles of high-quality thread

simultaneously. Looms were also mechanized: The mechanical improvement of John Kay's flying shuttle loom allowed one person to do the work of two, and Edmund Cartwright patented the first steam-powered loom in 1785.

The consequence of this new technology was the textile factory. There, the steam engine could be linked to the spinning mule, to the power loom, or to banks of dozens of each. All goods, from raw cotton to coal, could be delivered to a single, convenient site, chosen for inexpensive transportation costs such as proximity to mines, location on a river, or nearness to a great harbor. Instead of having the looms of cottage industry scattered around the countryside, they were now grouped together in a single building or factory complex, where an overseer could control the pace and quality of work. Steam-powered textile machinery produced high-quality cloth in vast quantities.

The first steam loom factory opened at Manchester, in northern England, in 1806. By 1813 there were 2,400 power looms operating in Britain, concentrated in Lancashire, the Midlands, and Yorkshire. A decade later, there were more than 10,000 textile factories using power looms in Britain; at midcentury, 250,000. The resultant change in the scale of textile manufacturing was even greater than those numbers suggest. Whereas a master weaver with thirty years of experience could produce two bolts of cotton cloth a week on a handloom, a fifteen-year-old boy at a power loom could produce seven bolts. Britain dominated global commerce in textiles, especially in the British Empire and Latin America, and British merchants began to dream of the day they could sell a shirt to everyone in China.

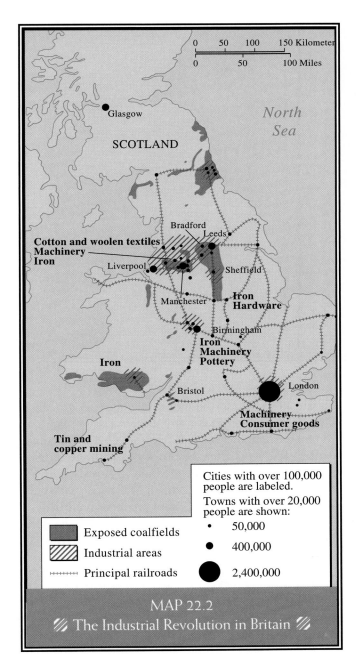

MAP 22.2

🏭 The Industrial Revolution in Britain 🏭

Map labels:
North Sea
Glasgow
SCOTLAND
Bradford
Leeds
Cotton and woolen textiles
Machinery
Iron
Liverpool
Sheffield
Manchester
Iron Hardware
Birmingham
Iron Machinery Pottery
Iron
Bristol
London
Machinery Consumer goods
Tin and copper mining

0   50   100   150 Kilometers
0   50   100 Miles

Cities with over 100,000 people are labeled.
Towns with over 20,000 people are shown:
• 50,000
● 400,000
⬤ 2,400,000

▨ Exposed coalfields
▨ Industrial areas
┼┼┼┼ Principal railroads

The Railroad Age

The new economy required improved transportation. Food had to be transported to factory towns in far greater quantities. Iron, coal, machinery, raw wool, and cotton had to be brought together. Manufactured goods had to be distributed. People had to be moved in large numbers. The railroad solved these problems, but the first steam locomotive was not built until 1804, and the first public railway—the Stockton-to-Darlington Railway—did not open until 1825. Railroads were the culmination of industrialization in Britain, not a cause of it.

Transportation in Britain had improved significantly in the century before 1825. The trip between London and Edinburgh that took twelve days in 1734 required four days in 1762 and forty hours on the eve of the railroad age. The chief developments in eighteenth-century transportation involved canal, road, turnpike, and bridge building. Britain had two thousand kilometers of canals in 1700 and sixty-five hundred kilometers in 1830. Transportation on rivers and these canals was the most efficient means of moving great weights, such as shipments of iron and coal. The development of canals serving Manchester cut the cost of coal to factory owners by 50 percent in the late eighteenth century, so the textile boom there owed more to waterways than to railways. Canals and rivers, however, had one major drawback: They sometimes froze in the winter, ending the distribution of goods.

Many technical advances made the British transportation system the best in Europe. An ironmaster named Abraham Darby III, whose family had built the world's largest blast furnaces and foundry, constructed the world's first iron bridge, a 295-foot-long "wonder of the age" that amazed gawking tourists and changed transportation. Similarly, a Scottish engineer named John MacAdam improved roads—subsequently called macadamized roads—by cambering them for drainage and paving them with crushed stones. (The black-topped road treatment known as macadam was named in his honor, but it was not yet in use.) The improvement in highway transportation was so dramatic that the coach companies began to remove the qualification "God Willing" from their time schedules.

The railroad was the culmination of these trends and was so successful that it ended the age of canals and coaching. Railroads began with an old idea borrowed from the coal mines. Since the seventeenth century, collieries had used wooden rails to guide horse-drawn coal wagons; by the 1760s many mines were switching to cast iron rails. Richard Trevithick, an

The woolen industry, which had older traditions, resisted the innovations that transformed the cotton industry and mechanized more slowly. Most wool remained handloomed in 1840. Cotton, however, was a new industry without such resistance to change. It even attracted innovation, such as patents to make cotton velvet, to create ribbed cloth for stockings, or to print patterns on cotton cloth. Consequently, cottons surpassed woolens as Britain's foremost export in 1803; by 1830 cotton—a plant not native to the British isles—accounted for more than 50 percent of Britain's foreign trade income and more than half of the world's cotton cloth came from Britain.

❧ TABLE 22.4 ❧

The Beginning of the Railroad Age in Europe, 1825–50

	Railway lines open, in kilometers					
Country	1825	1830	1835	1840	1845	1850
United Kingdom	43	157	544	2,411	4,081	10,662
Austrian Empire	n.a.	n.a.	n.a.	144	728	1,357
France	n.a.	31	141	410	875	2,915
German States	n.a.	n.a.	6	469	2,143	5,856
Italian States	n.a.	n.a.	n.a.	20	152	620
Russia	n.a.	n.a.	n.a.	27	144	501
Spain	n.a.	n.a.	n.a.	n.a.	n.a.	28
Total continent	n.a.	31	167	1,421	4,772	12,362
Total Europe	43	188	711	3,832	8,853	23,024
Percent in United Kingdom	100	84	77	63	46	46

Source: B. R. Mitchell, *European Historical Statistics 1750–1970* (London: Macmillan, 1975), pp. 581–82.
n.a. = Not available.

English mining engineer, won the race to develop the first practical vehicle to carry passengers and goods, by designing a high-pressure steam engine in 1800. In early 1804 Trevithick's locomotive, riding on colliery iron rails, pulled five wagons containing seventy passengers and ten tons of iron ore, for a distance of 9.5 miles at a speed of nearly five miles per hour.

George Stephenson, an inventor who had devised the miner's safety lamp, built on Trevithick's work to start the age of railroad service. Stephenson built the forty-three kilometer Stockton-to-Darlington in the early 1820s to serve the heavy industries of the midlands—so the first train became known as Stephenson's Rocket. He then turned to a more important line, a railroad linking the mills of Manchester with the port of Liverpool. Many people opposed this development, and dire predictions were made of the impact of railroads: The smoke and sparks from coal-burning locomotives would kill flora and fauna, start wildfires, and destroy foxhunting. When the Liverpool-Manchester line opened in 1830, however, it carried 445,000 passengers and ninety-eight thousand tons of goods in its first full year. Stephenson's railroad was so successful that, of the twenty-nine stage coach services between Manchester and Liverpool in 1830, only one remained in business in 1832.

On the continent, where rapid industrialization did not begin until after the end of the Napoleonic Wars in 1815, a railroad-building boom that started in the late 1830s supported industrialization. For much of the mid-nineteenth century, Britain kept a huge lead in railroad lines, as it did in iron, coal, steam, and textiles. Ten years after the Stockton-Darlington line opened, no railroads had been built in Austria, the Italian states, Russia, or Spain; all of the German states combined contained only six kilometers of railroad track (see table 22.4). Railroads were already changing the continental economy, however. A railway connecting the Belgian seaport of Antwerp with the Rhine River port of Cologne was inaugurated in 1843; this Iron Rhine became one of the world's industrial arteries and made Antwerp the third largest port in the world (after London and New York).

The Urban World

The impact of industrialization upon European society was most vivid in the growing cities. The population explosion, the decline in agricultural employment, the rise of the factory system, and the improvements in transportation combined to uproot thousands of people. Young adults, and sometimes whole families, found themselves so desperate for employment that they chose migration to the growing factory towns.

Unprecedented growth changed the nature of cities and urban life, but there was a range of types of towns and cities. Older towns often still stood within their medieval defensive walls. The urban and the rural were intertwined in such towns, sometimes with farmland within the walls and usually with important farming surrounding the town. Urban families often still had gardens or even orchards. Livestock lived inside the towns, and it was not unusual to see a pig wandering the streets. A 1786 census of Hanover—an important German capital and the home of the English royal family—found 365 head of cattle living within the town walls, but no sidewalks, paved streets, or sewer system. This remained true of the new industrial towns: Transplanted animals lived alongside uprooted workers in the shadow of the factory.

The modern city emerged painfully during the late eighteenth and nineteenth centuries. London began the habit of numbering street addresses and invented sidewalks in the 1760s. Watt developed steam heating for his office, and his steam pipes were the first central heating. Experiments with the newly plentiful supply of coal led William Murdock to the invention of indoor lighting—the burning of coal gas to provide better illumination than candles did. By 1807 the city of London was installing Murdock's gaslights on the streets; by 1820 gaslights were common in the homes of the well-to-do. The 1820s also saw London and Paris invent new public transportation systems: the horse-drawn omnibus, soon supplemented by urban railroads. The French Revolution led to a big change in city life—the invention of the restaurant, a result of the emigration of aristocrats who left behind many unemployed chefs. In 1789 Paris had only one restaurant (as distinct from inns or cafes); in 1804 there were more than five hundred and the institution was spreading. By the middle of the nineteenth century, the manufacturing economy had created vast department stores (such as the Bon Marché in Paris) and even arcade-shopping centers (such as the Galleria in Milan).

Urban life during industrialization was not entirely rosy. The industrial and manufacturing towns such as Manchester, Essen, and Łodz initially grew too fast for amenities to keep pace with the population (see document 22.1). Housing, fresh water, sewers, and sanitation were dangerously inadequate. An attractive environment (such as trees or clean air) or convenient services (such as shops or schools) were rarer. Many contemporaries recorded their horror at the sight of factory towns. Charles Dickens depicted Manchester as a dreadful place blackened by the soot of ubiquitous coal burning. Elisabeth Gaskell, who rivaled Dickens for vivid details, described the nightmare of life in such conditions. In *Mary Barton* (1848), she depicted the

◈ DOCUMENT 22.1 ◈

Charles Dickens Describes Conditions in Manchester

Observers were often startled by living conditions in the early industrial revolution, and many of them wrote vivid descriptions of what they had seen. The most famous include an unattractive portrait of Manchester in Charles Dickens's novel Hard Times *(1854)*

Coketown [Manchester] . . . was a town of red brick, or of brick that would have been red if the smoke and ashes had allowed it; but as matters stood it was a town of unnatural red and black, like the painted face of a savage. It was a town of machinery and tall chimneys, out of which interminable serpents of smoke trailed themselves forever and ever, and never got uncoiled. It had a black canal in it, and a river that ran purple with ill-smelling dye, and vast piles of buildings full of windows where there was a rattling and a trembling all day long, and where the piston of the steam engine worked monotonously up and down like the head of an elephant in a state of melancholy madness. It contained several large streets all very like one another, and many small streets still more like one another, inhabited by people equally like one another, who all went in and out at the same hours, with the same sound upon the same pavements, to do the same work, and to whom every day was the same as yesterday and tomorrow, and every year the counterpart of the last and the next.

Dickens, Charles. *Hard Times.* New York: T. L. McElrath, 1854; and Tocqueville, Alexis de. *Journeys to England and Ireland.* 1835.

squalid conditions of life in a slum cellar, where starvation and typhus competed for the lives of a family sleeping on beds of damp straw.

Even the old cities could not keep up with their growth. In the Westminster district of London, residents living within one block of Parliament complained to the government in 1799 about the stinking odor of their street, which had not been cleaned of horse and human waste in six months. In that same district of the richest city on Earth, air pollution was so terrible during hot weather that Parliament usually voted for an early summer recess. But those who went north for the

Illustration 22.3

Middle-Class Comfort. Views of European life during industrialization vary sharply depending upon the social class perspective of the observer. The middle class grew significantly in size and prosperity during the nineteenth century, and middle-class views such as this sentimental English print of a holiday dinner recall that progress. The life of the servants (the largest form of employment for women) depicted here was not so rosy, but it was markedly more comfortable than industrial work.

summer, as the poet laureate Robert Southey did, might not escape deplorable conditions. The air in Edinburgh was so bad, Southey claimed, that "you might smoke bacon by hanging it out of the window." Much of nineteenth-century urban history thus became the story of urban renewal. Paris became a much more pleasant city with the construction of the comprehensive sewer system that Victor Hugo described as a central setting of *Les Misérables.* In 1800 Paris had a total of twenty kilometers of sewers; by the late nineteenth century, more than two thousand kilometers. Paris was also a model of urban renewal above ground. In the 1850s and 1860s a government plan devised by Baron Georges Haussmann tore down many of the dark buildings and narrow streets surviving from medieval Paris and replaced them with the broad boulevards and graceful residences of a "city of light."

Changing Class Structures

The beginning of the industrial age changed the social order of the city as much as its physical appearance. Industrialization created a new elite, of wealth. This was a wealth based on capital, not land; a wealth of merchants, manufacturers, industrialists, and financiers. The British social critic Thomas Carlyle called them "Captains of Industry"; others referred to "Lords of the Loom," "Railroad Kings," and a dozen similar titles. Heavily industrialized regions, such as Alsace, created a wealthy new aristocracy. The Koechlin family of Mulhouse went from the comfortable life provided by a successful weaver in a cottage industry to the immense wealth of factory owners within a single generation. The leading families of this industrial bourgeoisie formed an elite different from the landed aristocracy. During the nineteenth century, this small social group, together with older elites of middle-class wealth (such as mercantile and banking wealth) and members of the educated professions (such as physicians, lawyers, teachers, and journalists) would challenge the political dominance of the Old Regime alliance of monarchy, aristocracy, and established churches. For the members of the prosperous middle class, the age of industrialization was an exciting and comfortable epoch (see illustration 22.3).

The new bourgeoisie may have been the most influential class in the changing society of the industrial age, but it was relatively small. A larger change in the social structure was the rapid growth of a class of urban workers who operated the steam engines, power forges, spinning mules, power looms, and trains. These men and women of the working class—or the proletariat, as this social class was frequently called—often formed the majority of a town's population. A study of the social structure in Belgium textile towns found that approximately half of the population was employed as spinners or weavers in the new factories. But a textile town might still have a quarter of its population employed in agriculture, including both farmers who lived in the town and agricultural laborers, or a quarter engaged in the traditional artisanal trades and crafts of the guilds. The educated professions, the industrial middle class, and the traditional upper classes of wealth remained small—less than 5 percent of the population.

Illustration 22.4

🖉 **Women Workers.** Women worked in many occupations before industrialization—in the rural family economy, in cottage industry, in family-run shops, in domestic service—but the factory system put a sharp new focus on the role of women in the economy. Many occupations were entirely feminized, often be- cause employers felt justified in paying women less than half of a man's wage. In the contemporary illustration here, women in an English pen-grinding factory appear to constitute 100 percent of the workforce.

Age, Gender, and the Family

The new industries initially favored the employment of men in all jobs, but the textile mills adopted the sexual division of labor that had typified cottage industry: Women did most of the spinning and men did most of the weaving. Many employment traditions quickly broke down, however. Machines often required few skills or little strength to make superior textiles; factory owners often favored women and children for wage la- bor because they worked for less than men. Women soon held the majority of the jobs in textile mills, and some occupations became feminized jobs, held only by women (see illustration 22.4). Some factory owners spoke of a woman's dexterity and many thought (often erroneously) of women as a less truculent labor force. However, low wages remained the decisive factor. A study of women workers in London in 1848, for exam- ple, found that women earned 34 percent of men's wages. When Parliament investigated working condi- tions, factory owners candidly admitted that they pre- ferred women because they could pay them less and because women would work hard to provide for their children. As one mill owner testified, women "are atten- tive, docile . . . and are compelled to use their utmost exertions to procure the necessities of life." But this low-paid existence was so precarious that thousands of women were forced into prostitution to survive, a plight dramatized by the character of Fantine in Victor Hugo's *Les Misérables* (1832) but visible to any contem- porary on the streets.

Whether the factory hired men, women, or chil- dren, factory employment changed the family econ- omy. Instead of a husband, wife, and children working together—at different tasks on a farm, in domestic production, or in a shop—factory employment split the family apart in individual employment for individual wages. As factory wages remained low, such employ- ment led all family members to take full-time employ- ment, and it encouraged large families in which children went to work at an early age. Economic histo- rians label the new arrangement a "family wage econ- omy" in which family members pool their earnings from different jobs.

Not all towns became centers of textile manufac- turing or heavy industry. Older towns, such as York, England, still prospered on traditional handcraft man- ufacturing and as commercial and marketing centers. The social structure in such towns was different,

✖ TABLE 22.5 ✖

The Labor Force in York, England, 1851

Labor category	Percentage of men	Percentage of women
Agriculture	9.9	2.1
Building trades	11.9	0.1
Craft manufacturing/shops	42.7	29.9
Domestic service	3.5	58.9
Factory manufacturing	8.9	1.1
Public service/professions	9.4	5.8
Transportation	7.6	1.6
Other	6.1	0.4
Number in labor force	11,225	5,129
Percentage of labor force	68.6	31.4

Source: Louise A. Tilly and Joan W. Scott, *Women, Work, and Family*
© 1987. Reprinted by permission of Taylor & Francis, Inc./Routledge, Inc.
(New York, N.Y.: Routledge, 1978), p. 86.

especially when considering gender. Women constituted nearly one-third of the labor force in York in 1851 (a typical figure for the nineteenth-century economy), but barely 1 percent of working women held jobs in factory manufacturing (see table 22.5). Far more women—30 percent of working women—worked in traditional handcraft manufacturing and small shops. But the majority of the working women of York labored in the century's chief occupation for women, domestic service. The middle-class prosperity of industrialization, and the low wages paid to women of the working class, created a market in which all members of the middle class were expected to keep household servants and even members of the lower middle class, such as shopkeepers, could afford a cook or a maid. Across Europe, the unmarried daughters of the lower classes filled these posts; they often did so eagerly because a servant's post meant a more comfortable life than factory work did.

Although working women faced terrible exploitation during industrialization, the treatment of working children was even worse. In the agricultural society of the Old Regime, children had worked as part of the family economy, and they had begun farm work at an early age. Urban children had traditionally left home to become apprentices in their early teens, and some trades took children at an earlier age. But none of these experiences prepared observers for the exploitation of children in the early industrial age.

Children were employed in mining as young as five to seven years old. Mine owners argued that children were needed because their size enabled them to fit into tight places. Often, however, they were used for tasks such as sorting coal or even to replace the ponies that pulled ore carts (see illustration 22.1). Furthermore, small wages were as important as small size. Studies of child labor during industrialization have found that these practices accounted for 15 percent to 20 percent of mining labor. It was unhealthy, dangerous work, and hundreds of children died in the mines each year. In 1838, for example, 122 British workers under the age of eighteen died in the mines; fourteen were preteenage children who died by falling down mineshafts, fifteen died in mine collapses, thirteen died in gas explosions, three drowned, and four were crushed by trams.

The factory age expanded this use of child labor. Factories such as Josiah Wedgwood's famous pottery typically employed as much as 30 percent of their labor force in workers under the age of eighteen. The textile mills pushed that policy to new extremes. Studies have found that the early British cotton mills averaged 40–50 percent of their labor force under the age of eighteen; the worst offenders relied upon children for 70–80 percent of their labor and strict discipline to keep the children docile. A study of child labor in France in the 1840s (see table 22.6) found that textile mills employed more than 72 percent of all child labor in France, and both the cotton and woolen industries still relied upon children for nearly 20 percent of their labor force. European society initially permitted this treatment of children because the prevalent political philosophy (classical liberalism) and economic theory (laissez-faire capitalism) both insisted that governments not intervene in the economic process or regulate industries.

The Standard of Living Debate

The subject of the exploitation of women and children in the industrial economy raises one of the most heated debates in modern historical scholarship, a controversy known as the standard of living debate. On one side of this debate, social historians depict the ghastly living and working conditions of workers in the early industrial age; on the other side, economic historians show a steady improvement in the cost of living and the standards of living for the working class. The optimists look back at the new industrial towns and see affordable workers' cafes in the bright illumination of Murdock's gaslights. When the pessimists look back, they smell

TABLE 22.6

Child Labor in the French Textile Industry, 1845

Industry	Children employed	Children as a percentage of that industry's labor force	Percentage of all child labor employed in that industry
Cotton	44,828	18.3	31.2
Woolen	26,800	18.6	18.7
Cotton blend	11,038	23.9	7.7
Silk	9,326	5.6	6.5
Hemp and flax	7,232	12.8	5.0
Wool and silk	4,765	12.5	3.3
Textile total	103,989	——	72.4

Source: Lee S. Weissbach, *Child Labor Reform in Nineteenth Century France* (Baton Rouge, La.: Louisiana State University Press, 1989), p. 19. Reprinted by permission of the publisher.

the stench of uncollected refuse in the streets and the foul dampness in typhus-infected cellar bedrooms. Both viewpoints contain an important historical truth, and the debate is not resolved. The optimistic version rests chiefly on tables of economic data, and the pessimistic version stresses the testimony of people who lived through industrialization.

The early critics of industrialization were numerous. They ranged from England's greatest romantic poet, William Wordsworth, who wrote in 1814, "I grieve, when on the darker side of this great change I look," to the cofounder of Marxist socialism, Friedrich Engels. Engels, the son of a rich German industrialist, lived in Manchester and studied manufacturing there in 1844. His conclusion was brutal: "I charge the English middle class with mass murder." The contemporary British historian who coined the name *industrial revolution* also reached a shocking conclusion; he called industrialization "a period as terrible as any through which a nation ever passed."

The anger of such critics has derived chiefly from the conditions in the new factories and factory towns. Life in that world had an undeniably grim side. Conditions in textile factories were so bad that another poet, William Blake, named them "dark Satanic mills." These unregulated workplaces had terrible safety standards; with no guards on the new machinery, mutilating accidents were common. Factories were unbearably hot, so men, women, and children often worked stripped to the waist. But the environment was hardly erotic: Machines filled the air with a deafening roar, the nose with overheating grease, and the eyes and lungs with cotton

dust. This combination gave Manchester the world's highest rate of bronchial ailments, a life expectancy sharply below the national average, and a horrifying infant mortality rate of 50 percent.

Jobs in these dreadful conditions also required workers to adapt to a new discipline (see document 22.2). Most workers came from the countryside, where they were accustomed to agricultural work defined by the rhythms of nature—the seasons, daylight, weather—or to such self-disciplined labor as spinning or weaving at home. Factory work was a regime of rules enforced by an overseer, regimentation by the clock or the pace of a machine. Typical industrial work rules forbade talking or singing. Fines for misbehavior were deducted from wages. The first large spinning factory in England fired an average of twenty workers per week and averaged a 100-percent turnover within one year. One of the most famous novels of the nineteenth century, Gustave Flaubert's *Madame Bovary*, ends with the thought that life in the dark, Satanic mills was appropriate punishment for sin. The protagonist of the novel, Emma Bovary, commits adultery and then suicide. Her relatives refuse to accept the care of Emma's orphaned daughter; the child is punished for the shame of Emma's behavior by being sent to earn her living in a cotton mill.

Other contemporaries defended the conditions of industrialization. Frederick Eden began the optimistic tradition with his defense of agricultural enclosures in *The State of the Poor* (1797). Eden acknowledged that the consolidation of farms might hurt small farmers and farm laborers, but he argued that the difficult

❖ DOCUMENT 22.2 ❖

Work Rules in a Prussian Factory, 1844

Good order and harmony must be looked upon as the fundamentals of success, and therefore the following rules shall be strictly observed. . . :

(1) The normal working day begins at all seasons at 6 AM precisely and ends, after the usual break of half an hour for breakfast, an hour for dinner and half an hour for tea, at 7 PM. . . . Workers arriving two minutes late shall lose half an hour's wages; whoever is more than two minutes late may not start work until after the next break. . . .

(2) When the bell is rung to denote the end of the working day, every workman . . . shall leave his workshop and the yard, but is not allowed to make preparations for his departure before the bell rings. Every breach of this rule shall lead to a fine of five silver groschen. . . .

(3) No workman . . . may leave before the end of the working day without having first received permission from the overseer. . . .

(4) Repeated irregular arrival at work shall lead to dismissal. . . .

(6) No worker may leave his place of work otherwise than for reasons connected with his work.

(7) All conversation with fellow-workers is prohibited. . . .

(9) Every worker is responsible for cleaning up his space in the workshop. . . .

(12) It goes without saying that all overseers and officials of the firm shall be obeyed without question and shall be treated with due deference. Disobedience will be punished by dismissal. . . .

Pollard, Sidney, and Holmes, Colin, eds. *Documents of European Economic History,* 3 vols. New York: St. Martin's, 1968.

❖ DOCUMENT 22.3 ❖

Andrew Ure: The Factory System, 1835

Andrew Ure (1778–1857) was a Scottish chemist and the author of several reference books about chemistry, mining, and manufacturing. He wrote The Philosophy of Manufactures *(1835) to respond to the criticism of factory conditions.*

In my recent tour, continued during several months, through the manufacturing districts, I have seen tens of thousands of old, young, and middle-aged of both sexes—many of them too feeble to get their daily bread by any of the former modes of industry—earning abundant food, raiment, and domestic accommodation without perspiring at a single pore, screened meanwhile from the summer's sun and the winter's frost, in an apartment more airy and salubrious than those of the metropolis, in which our legislative and fashionable aristocracies assemble. In those spacious halls, the benign power of steam summons around him his myriads of willing menials, and assigns to each the regulated task, substituting for painful muscular effort on their part the energies of his own gigantic arm and demanding in return only attention and dexterity to correct such little aberrations as casually occur in his workmanship. . . . Such is the factory system, replete with prodigies in mechanics and political economy, which promises in its future growth to become the great minister of civilization.

Ure, Andrew. *The Philosophy of Manufactures.* London: C. Knight, 1835.

straits that they faced were "but temporary" and they must be balanced against "the greater good which may be expected from the improvement." Early champions of industry went further in their defense of the factory system. Andrew Ure, a Scottish scientist angered at the criticism of industrialization, wrote a thoroughly optimistic book in 1835, entitled *The Philosophy of Manufactures* (see document 22.3). To Ure, the factory system was nothing less than "the great minister of civilization." He found workers to be "willing menials" who were "earning abundant food, raiment, and domestic accommodation without perspiring at a single pore."

Economic historians have shown much data to support the optimistic view that industrialization improved life for most people. The most obvious argument is that of the conquest of the biological old regime and the significantly increased life expectancy. Newborn infants in 1700 had an average life expectancy of less than forty years; by 1824 it had reached fifty years. Witnesses might describe terrible living conditions during industrialization, but increased life expectancy must prove that conditions had improved in some substantial ways.

Wages of workers did not improve greatly, and in some preindustrial occupations—such as a handloom weaver—they declined severely. But the data show a general pattern of improvement. Whereas a carpenter working in the London region had to work thirteen or fourteen days in 1800 to earn enough money to buy a suit, the same carpenter's wages in 1830 bought a suit in seven or eight days. Industrialization also provided luxuries that workers previously could not afford. By the 1840s railway expansion led to inexpensive excursion tickets. Railroads reinforced the rigid social structure of nineteenth- century Europe by segregating passengers according to the class of tickets they bought, but the existence of cheap second- or third-class tickets led to the birth of the working-class holiday. For the first time, most of the population of London could afford a day trip to the seashore. Workers had little leisure time to enjoy this benefit, but inexpensive travel allowed more than one-third of the total population of Great Britain to visit the world exposition in London in 1851.

From the British Industrial Revolution to Continental European Industrialization

British industrialization dwarfed the manufactures of any other country in the late eighteenth and early nineteenth century, but Britain was not unique in experiencing industrial development. In the textile industry, for example, Belgium had been an important manufacturer of cloth for centuries and rapidly industrialized following the British example. Textile towns such as Manchester developed across Europe, from Mulhouse in Alsace to Łodz in Poland. Many regions experienced their own industrial revolutions. Industrialization in the Rhône valley of southeastern France, for example, assured predominance in the manufacture of silk. Mechanical and chain-driven looms came into use there in the 1770s, although they had been known in China for centuries. By the 1780s, more than 23 percent of the population of Lyons worked in the silk industry. The delicacy of silk work delayed the development of a power silk loom, but when one was developed in the mid-nineteenth century, Lyons remained the center of silk manufacturing because it was located near the rich coal fields of St. Etienne.

The industrialization of continental Europe was slowed by the French Revolution and the Napoleonic Wars. Postwar economic problems were severe, and Europe remained in a depression until 1820. Governments hurried to demobilize their expensive armies, and this left hundreds of thousands of veterans unemployed. Jobs were scarce because governments also canceled wartime contracts for food, uniforms, and equipment, leading to the dismissal of agricultural, textile, and metallurgical workers. Most governments were deep in war debt; Prussia, for example, could barely pay the interest on war loans. Governments promised to cancel the war taxes needed for big armies, but that created the combination of high debt and reduced revenue when governments needed huge sums of money to rebuild the regions devastated by war. Roads and bridges required immediate attention to support the recovery of commerce. Consequently, Britain enjoyed a long lead in industrialization.

Nevertheless, Europe experienced steady industrialization in the early nineteenth century. Traditional textile regions, such as Alsace and Normandy in France, rapidly adapted to the age of the spinning mule and the power loom. A study of the Alsatian textile industry has shown its expansion from a total of 48,000 spindles in 1812 to 466,000 spindles in 1828. There were only 426 power looms in Alsace in 1827, but more than 18,000 in 1856. The strength of continental textiles in the nineteenth century is shown by the English language, which borrowed European words for textiles: Elegant Jacquard silks came from Lyons, and sturdy cotton denim came "from Nîmes" (*de Nîmes* in French).

Another sign of continental industrialization was the beginning of the railroad age in the 1830s and 1840s. The French opened a small line in 1828 to connect the coal fields of St. Etienne with the national canal and river system, but they were slow to build a large railroad network. No passenger service was established between Paris and Lyons until the 1850s. In most countries, the first tracks were laid in the 1830s or 1840s. Progressive statesmen such as Count Camilio Cavour of Piedmont-Sardinia made their reputations as early champions of the railroad. Cavour was convinced that "their economic importance will be from the outset magnificent," and by 1850 the Italian states had more miles of track than Russia and Spain combined.

The country that most profited from the beginning of continental industrialization was Prussia. This was partly the result of Prussian military success,

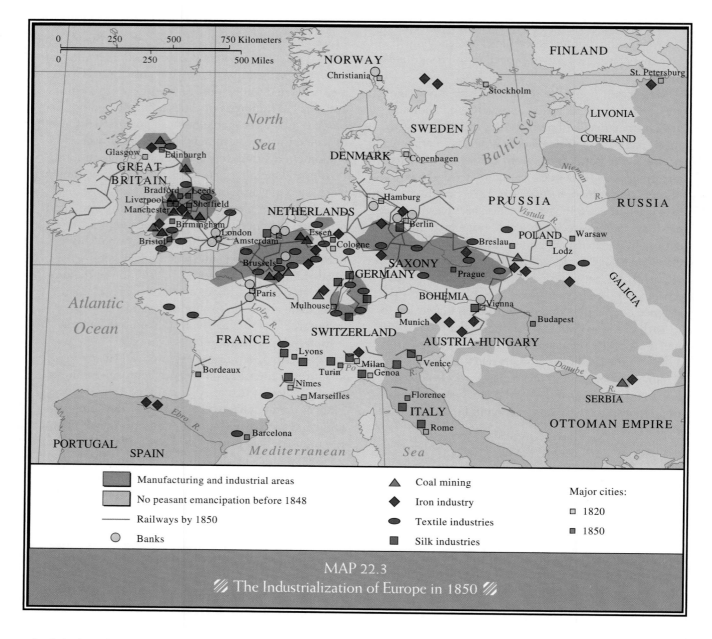

MAP 22.3

The Industrialization of Europe in 1850

Legend:
- Manufacturing and industrial areas
- No peasant emancipation before 1848
- Railways by 1850
- Banks
- Coal mining
- Iron industry
- Textile industries
- Silk industries
- Major cities:
  - 1820
  - 1850

which led to the annexation of rich mineral deposits. The wars of Frederick the Great had acquired the coal fields of Silesia and the defeat of Napoleon brought Prussia the iron and coal deposits of the Rhineland. The Prussian government also encouraged industrialization. Karl Freiherr vom Stein reorganized the government after the catastrophic loss to Napoleon in 1806. Stein secured the abolition of serfdom in 1807, and the emancipation edict had far-reaching economic provisions that opened landownership and granted the aristocracy freedom to choose any occupation. Friedrich von Motz, the Prussian minister of finance in the 1820s, presided over a similar modernization that included the abolition of internal tariffs; free trade treaties with neighboring German states;

and finally the formation of the *Zollverein,* a customs union that propelled Prussia toward the economic leadership of central Europe. King Frederick William IV encouraged industrialization by his love of trains when the emperor of Austria detested railroads and impeded their construction.

The European Industrial "Take-Off"

Economic historians use the term *take-off phase* to describe the period when a nascent industrial economy begins to expand rapidly. For much of western and central Europe, the take-off of industrialization occurred in the middle of the nineteenth century (see map 22.3).

ℵ TABLE 22.7 ℵ

The Take-Off of Heavy Industry in Europe, 1851–69

The data in this table show that Britain was already heavily industrialized in 1851, but none of the other great powers were. The data summarize output in millions of metric tons and show growth in percent. Note that the huge growth in iron and coal output in France and the Germanic states of central Europe—their industrial take-off—still left them far behind British production. Note also the comparison between French industrialization and German industrialization, which is much more rapid; this contrast had great implications for the balance of power on the continent.

Country	Output in 1851		Output in 1860		Output in 1869		Growth Percentage 1851–69	
	Iron	Coal	Iron	Coal	Iron	Coal	Iron	Coal
Austria	.5	1.0	n.a.	3.2	.7	6.6	40.0	560.0
Britain	9.7	50.2	8.2	81.3	11.7	109.2	20.6	118.9
France	1.8	4.4	3.0	8.3	3.1	13.5	72.2	202.3
Zollverein	.8	7.8	1.3	16.7	3.1	34.3	287.5	339.7

Source: Compiled from data in B. R. Mitchell, *European Historical Statistics, 1750–1970* (London: Macmillan, 1975), pp. 360–61, 387.

The word *capitalism* was coined during this mid-century generation, and Karl Marx published his famous critique of industrial capitalism, *Das Kapital.* The British celebrated their new society in a spectacular world's fair in London, known as the Crystal Palace Exhibition (1851), which showed the world the latest technical and mechanical wonders. Not surprisingly, some historians call this period the "age of capital."

Industrialization did not spread evenly across Europe, and the great powers did not industrialize in the same ways. Nor did the take-off phase mean that continental production caught up to Britain in a single generation. Between 1851 and 1869, British heavy industry continued to grow at a steady rate; iron production increased by 20 percent and coal production by 119 percent (see table 22.7). The French growth rate in iron production tripled British growth and nearly doubled it in coal. However, in 1869 French iron production remained barely one-fourth of the British rate and coal production one-eighth. Prussia and the smaller German states of the Zollverein increased iron and coal production at rates that suggest the terms *industrial revolution* and *take-off phase.* Both iron and coal production nearly quadrupled within a generation. German rates did not yet threaten British leadership, but the Zollverein had passed French production and the rate of production portended a future Anglo-German rivalry.

The continental industrial take-off can also be seen in the expansion of railroad networks. The midcentury was an age of railway construction across the continent. Austria, Belgium, Italy, and Spain all built large national

systems. Russia remained backward; in 1850 tiny Belgium had a larger railroad network. By 1870 a Russian building program had added more than ten thousand kilometers of track, but that meant that a country of more than twenty-two million square kilometers was served by half as much railroad as Great Britain, a country of 300,000 square kilometers. France and Germany both neared the size of the British network in 1870, but they, too, were much larger.

Such data show that France industrialized at a significant pace but never experienced the exponential rate of change that characterized the British industrial revolution or German industrialization. No population explosion occurred in France, and the government never completely abandoned the mercantilist tradition of a centrally directed economy. The mid-century government of Napoleon III encouraged the industrial take-off with institutions such as the Crédit Foncier, which provided low-interest business loans. A Railroad Law of 1857 guaranteed the interest payments of private railroad bonds, so investors could not lose. This law so stimulated railroad building that a system with 2,915 kilometers of track in 1850 grew to 16,465 kilometers before 1870.

German industrial development varied regionally, with the greatest strength concentrated in Prussia and the Rhineland. The German take-off was rapid. Between 1851 and 1857, the number of Prussian joint-stock companies, and their total capitalization, tripled. Prussian legislation encouraged British-style laissez-faire capitalism. New mining laws, for example, ended

Illustration 22.5

The Krupp Works at Essen. The Krupp family have been armaments makers at Essen, in the Ruhr River valley of western Germany, since the sixteenth century. The Krupp Works pioneered modern steel manufacturing. Under Alfred Krupp (1812–87), "the cannon king," the firm contributed significantly to German unification; under his son Fritz (1854–1902), the Krupp Works became the largest steel works in the world.

state control of coal mines, broke the powers of the miners' guild, and cut the taxes on mines by 50 percent. Prussian coal production sharply increased. The Krupp Works of Essen showed the similar growth of the metallurgical industry. Krupp had been a small, and nearly bankrupt, iron foundry with seven employees when it began to manufacture ordnance in 1847. Alfred Krupp won the firm's first government contract in 1859, and within a decade the Krupp Works became the largest arms manufacturer in central Europe, with iron and steel mills that made it one of the largest industrial combines in the world (see illustration 22.5).

CHAPTER 23

DAILY LIFE IN THE NINETEENTH CENTURY

CHAPTER OUTLINE

◆◆◆◆◆◆◆◆◆◆◆◆◆◆◆◆◆◆◆◆◆

This chapter examines the dramatic changes in the daily life of Europeans during industrialization. The biggest changes were so dramatic that they constitute a vital revolution. In 1800 the average European had a life expectancy at birth of about thirty-five years, but a boy born in 1900 could expect fifty years and his sister fifty-two years. Chapter 23 discusses this great change. Historians attribute 15 percent of all European deaths during the eighteenth century to smallpox; in a typical year, smallpox, typhus, and typhoid accounted for 35 percent of all deaths. By the early twentieth century, these diseases caused less than 1 percent of deaths in the most advanced regions of Europe. Similarly, the typical adult man of 1800 stood about 5′1″ tall, but in the early twentieth century the average reached 5′6″. The history of this vital revolution often receives less attention than the actions of princes, popes, and presidents, but no leader affected daily life as much as the conquest of disease and the improvement of diet did.

Chapter 23 also looks at the stages of the life cycle. It begins with birth and shows the falling birthrate caused by growing acceptance of birth control. For youth, the nineteenth century meant the beginning of compulsory education. The next great stage in life, marriage, increasingly began at a later age and produced a smaller family than the Old Regime had experienced. Even as basic an aspect of daily life as human sexuality changed during the nineteenth century, and the chapter considers such attitudes as the double standard and new laws regarding sexuality.

◇

European Demography and the Increase in Life Expectancy

Nineteenth-century demography is a good illustration of historical perspective: The subject looks very different if viewed from the perspective of the early eighteenth century or the early twenty-first century. The life expectancy of a European male born today is seventy-two to seventy-four years; females average seventy-eight to eighty-one years. (The figures for the United States are seventy-two and seventy-nine years, respectively.) Typical rates for 1750 ranged between twenty-eight and thirty-three years. Thus, a mean life expectancy of fifty years seems short or long, depending upon one's perspective. The benefits arrived unequally, and many regions did not experience them until the twentieth century. Scandinavians already expected fifty-five to sixty years of life for a child born in 1900, while Russians still lived in a biological old regime with life expectancies of thirty to thirty-five years (see table 23.1). Life expectancy also varied by social class; the wealthy usually lived longer than laborers did. A study conducted for the British parliament in 1842 found that in Manchester the average age at death was thirty-eight for professionals, twenty for shopkeepers, and seventeen for the working class.

A study of improving life expectancy starts with the decreasing death rate. The annual mortality rate in the eighteenth century was usually above thirty deaths per one thousand population; it reached thirty-five to thirty-six deaths per one thousand in England in the 1740s. This means that 3 percent of the population died each year. That rate plummeted during the nineteenth century. The lowest mortality rate in Europe on the eve of World War I was a Danish rate of 13.2 per thousand. (Rates today are near twelve per thousand.) The worst rates were in southern and eastern Europe: Spain had a death rate of 22.8 per thousand and Russia, 29.0, and both represented significant improvements over eighteenth-century rates. The unhealthy environment of cities meant that rates there resembled rural eighteenth-century rates; mortality in Moscow and St. Petersburg was 30–35 per one thousand in the 1880s. Paris (24.4), Berlin (26.5), and Vienna (28.2) also had high death rates.

The falling mortality rate chiefly resulted from declining infant and childhood mortality. A study of Dutch demography has found more than 23 percent of all deaths in Holland in 1811 were infants below the age of one; 41 percent of the dead were younger than ten. Such figures fell sharply. French rates fell from 16.2 percent of all infants dying in the year of their birth (1840) to 11.1 percent (1910); British rates fell from 15.4 percent (1840) to 10.5 percent (1910). These rates, too, were worse in southern and eastern Europe. Russian infant mortality was horrifying—51.9 percent between 1864 and 1879 and 30.5 percent on the eve of

TABLE 23.1

Life Expectancy in the Nineteenth Century

Country	Period	Male life expectancy at birth (in years)	Female life expectancy at birth (in years)
England and Wales	1838–54	39.9	41.8
	1901–10	48.5	52.3
	1989	72.0	78.0
Denmark	1835–44	42.6	44.7
	1911–15	56.2	59.2
	1989	72.0	79.0
France	1817–31	38.3	40.8
	1908–13	48.4	52.4
	1989	72.0	80.0
Germany	1871–81	35.5	38.4
	1910–11	37.4	50.6
	1989	71.5	78.1
Italy	1876–87	35.1	35.4
	1901–11	44.2	44.8
	1989	73.0	80.0
Russia	1896–97	31.4	33.3
	1989	64.0	74.0
Spain	1900	33.8	35.7
	1910	40.9	42.5
	1989	74.0	80.0
Sweden	1816–40	39.5	43.5
	1901–10	54.5	56.9
	1989	74.0	81.0
United States	1989	72.0	79.0

Source: André Armengaud, "Population in Europe, 1700–1914," in *The Industrial Revolution*, edited by C. Cipolla (London: Collins, 1973), p. 36; *The World Almanac and Book of Facts 1991* (Mahwah, N.J.: World Almanac Books, 1990) pp. 684–770.

World War I. (The U.S. rate is poor today, but it barely surpasses 1 percent for the total population.) Infant mortality rates remained high in cities. Madrid and Bucharest both had rates of 21 percent in 1909; Moscow, nearly 32 percent. In the prosperous west, rates were high in manufacturing towns. Roubaix, a French textile center, had an infant mortality rate nearly twice the national average. Death rates remained terrible throughout the years of childhood. In 1897 nearly 50 percent of the children born in rural Russia died before age five, and 68.7 percent did not reach ten. As terrible as such numbers seem, they nevertheless represented significant improvement by comparison to the eighteenth century. In 1750 the death rate in London for children before age five had been more than 75 percent; in 1914 only 15 percent of English children died

Illustration 23.1

Typhus and Warfare. Dreadful military hygiene meant that eighteenth- and nineteenth-century armies regularly lost more soldiers to typhus than they did on the battlefield. Typhus was a febrile disease, spread by the bite of a body louse that thrives in poor sanitary conditions. It was commonly found in armies, jails, and slums. In this illustration, Napoleon's army in Spain during the Peninsular War (1808–14) is stricken with typhus.

before their fifth birthday. The important facts, therefore, are the decline of infant mortality and the consequent increase in life expectancy.

Disease in Nineteenth-Century Europe

The foremost explanation of falling death rates lies in the history of contagious disease. One study has suggested that diseases explain 94 percent of all European deaths in the year 1850. The dominion of disease included wars; typhus killed more of Napoleon's soldiers than Wellington's army or the Russian army did (see illustration 23.1). That pattern remained true across the century: Typhus, typhoid, cholera, and smallpox killed more soldiers than enemy fire did. As late as the Boer War (1899–1902), the British army lost 6,425 soldiers in combat and 11,327 soldiers to disease. Contagious diseases killed more people than heart attacks or cancer did, because fewer people lived long enough to experience degenerative problems. At midcentury, even measles killed more people than cancer did. In 1848 the British deaths from diseases carried by microorganisms stood at 1,296 per 100,000 population (see table 23.2); today's death rate for acquired immune deficiency syndrome (AIDS, 8.6), cancer (199.2), and heart disease (311.9) combined do not reach half of that 1848 rate for contagious diseases.

In the late eighteenth century, European civilization had begun the conquest of contagious diseases, but the lesson of smallpox vaccination was learned very slowly. In Jenner's homeland, less than 1 percent of the population was vaccinated in 1801. Bavaria adopted compulsory vaccination in 1807, and the British government required it in 1835, but many states were slower (see illustration 23.2). Vaccination of all Germans became mandatory in 1874, during the smallpox epidemic of 1870–75, which killed more than 500,000 people in Europe. The Vatican outlawed vaccination, and Catholic states suffered higher death rates. Spain did not require vaccination until 1902, but the new policy did not come in time to prevent thirty-seven thousand Spanish smallpox deaths between 1901 and 1910. Even these numbers seem small compared with the horrors of public health in Russia. Four hundred thousand Russians died of smallpox in 1901–10, and one Orthodox sect still fought against vaccination, calling the resultant smallpox scar "the mark of the Anti-Christ." In contrast, Denmark recorded only thirteen smallpox deaths during that decade, and Sweden became the first country ever to go through an entire year (1895) with no smallpox deaths.

Tragedies such as the smallpox epidemic of 1870–75, or the Spanish and Russian crises of 1901–10, are noteworthy facts, but the virtual disappearance of smallpox in Denmark and Sweden is more important in understanding the nineteenth century as an age both of disease and the conquest of it. Childhood diseases—such as measles, whooping cough, and scarlet fever—account for less than 0.1 percent of deaths in the Western world today, but they remained virulent killers during the nineteenth century. An outbreak of scarlet fever killed nearly twenty-thousand children in Britain in 1840. The inhabitants of Denmark's Faeroe Islands suffered badly in 1846 because they had experienced sixty-five years without a case of the measles. No one had acquired immunity to the disease in childhood, and when a worker brought measles to the islands, 78 percent of the population (6,100 people) caught the disease and 106 adults died.

The most persistent epidemic disease of nineteenth-century Europe was cholera, an acute diarrheal disease usually transmitted through contaminated drinking water. Major epidemics swept Europe repeatedly—in 1817–23, 1826–37, 1846–63, 1865–75, and 1881–96. They typically arrived from India, where cholera was endemic along the Ganges River. That path of infection, combined with poor public health standards, meant that Russia suffered terribly from cholera. One study has found that Russia endured fifty-eight years of cholera

ℵ TABLE 23.2 ℵ

The Death Rate in England from Infectious Diseases, 1848–1901

Disease	1848 deaths per million population	1901 deaths per million population	Percentage change
Airborne diseases	7,259	5,122	−29.4
Tuberculosis (respiratory)	2,901	1,268	−56.3
Bronchitis, pneumonia, influenza	2,239	2,747	+22.7
Scarlet fever and diphtheria	1,016	407	−59.9
Whooping cough	423	312	−26.2
Measles	342	278	−18.7
Smallpox	263	10	−96.2
Ear, pharynx, larynx infections	75	100	+33.3
Water- and food-borne diseases	3,562	1,931	−45.8
Cholera, diarrhea, dysentery	1,819	1,232	−32.3
Typhoid and typhus	990	155	−84.3
Tuberculosis (nonrespiratory)	753	544	−27.8
Sexually transmitted diseases	50	164	+228.0
Syphilis	50	164	+228.0
Other diseases attributable to microorganisms			
Convulsions and teething	1,322	643	−52.4
Appendicitis and peritonitis	75	86	+14.7
Puerperal fever	62	64	+3.2
All others	635	458	−27.9
Total attributable to microorganisms	12,965	8,468	−34.7
Other death rates	8,891	8,490	−4.5
Heart diseases	698	1,673	+139.7
Cancer	307	844	+174.9
Violence	761	640	−15.9

Note: Data for 1848 are an average for the period 1848–54.

Source: Calculated from data in Thomas McKeown, *The Modern Rise of Population* (London: Academic Press, 1976), pp. 54–55, 58, 60, 62.

Illustration 23.2

▨ **Smallpox Vaccination.** If historians periodized the past on the basis of daily life instead of war and revolution, modern history would not start with dates such as the French Revolution (1789) or the defeat of Napoleon (1815). A more important date would be 1796, when Edward Jenner successfully vaccinated a young boy against smallpox. The gradual acceptance of vaccination during the nineteenth century—such as in this French scene of 1820—led to the total elimination of smallpox, a scourge that had killed more people than wars and revolutions combined.

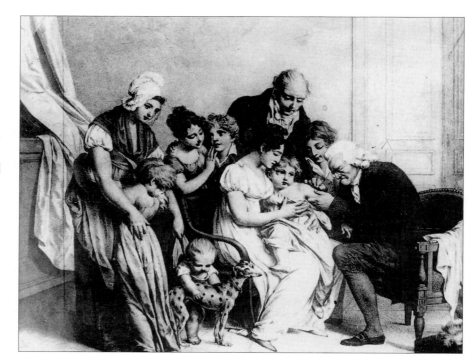

Annual income in marks (1 mark = 25¢)	Number of people	Percentage who caught cholera	Percentage who died
800–1,000	28,647	11.4	6.2
1,000–2,000	32,848	10.0	5.5
2,000–3,500	14,544	4.7	2.7
3,500–5,000	6,125	4.0	2.2
5,000–10,000	5,649	3.1	1.6
10,000–25,000	3,328	1.8	1.0
25,000–50,000	1,182	1.7	1.1
50,000+	834	0.6	0.5

✕ TABLE 23.3 ✕

The Hamburg Cholera Epidemic of 1892

Source: Richard J. Evans, *Death in Hamburg* (Oxford: Oxford University Press, 1987), p. 408. Used by permission of the publisher.

epidemic between 1823 and 1926. In that century, 5.5 million Russians contracted cholera and 2.1 million of them died.

A cholera epidemic of 1831–33 was especially severe. It initially moved from India to Persia to Russia. The Russian army sent to suppress the Polish revolution of 1830–31 carried cholera into central Europe. This biological tax on military action took 1,835 lives in Berlin (nearly 1 percent of the population) before moving westward. The epidemic reached Glasgow (population 202,000) in February 1832, and before it left, 1.6 percent of the city had died. When the epidemic struck Paris, it killed 2.5 percent of the population (19,000 people). If a catastrophe had that impact on New York City in 1990, it would kill 183,000 people in ten months.

Such numbers were basic facts of life in the nineteenth century. London had 20,000 cholera deaths in 1849–53, chiefly because the city dumped untreated sewage into the Thames River and collected drinking water nearby. Between 1853 and 1856, cholera killed 52,000 people in Britain and 140,000 in France, not counting 18,000 Anglo-French soldiers who died of cholera during the Crimean War. After an English doctor, John Snow, proved that cholera was spread by contaminated water, sewer systems and water filtration plants spared Britain and France the worst ravages of later epidemics. This lesson, like smallpox vaccination, was only accepted slowly, however. Snow's message might have prevented the epidemic of 1884–85, which killed more than 120,000 people in Spain, or the epidemic of 1892–93, which ravaged the German port of Hamburg, killing 8,600 people in a few months (see

table 23.3). A study of the Hamburg epidemic has highlighted the correlation between social class and disease: The higher a person's annual income, the lower the chance of catching cholera or of dying from it. The poor died at a rate twelve to thirteen times higher than the rich did. Both Hamburg and its more affluent suburb of Altona took their water from the same source, but Altona had a filtration system. Hamburg had a death rate of 13.4 per thousand; Altona, 2.1. The rich and famous did die—the composer Peter Tchaikovsky died later in that same epidemic—but the public health standards for their neighborhoods spared them much of the suffering found in cities.

Medicine, Public Health, and the Conquest of Disease

In 1800 the medical profession was virtually powerless to prevent diseases, the foremost exception being Jenner's smallpox vaccine, announced in 1798. Physicians had no power over infectious diseases because they did not know what caused them. They also had limited ability to control pain or to perform surgery because they lacked anesthetic drugs. During the vital revolution of the nineteenth century, those facts changed: Scientists proved the germ theory of disease transmission (which led to antiseptic surgery and to the conquest of many infectious diseases) and they discovered effective anesthetics. Nothing in all of modern history is more important than these facts for the improved quality of daily life.

The germ theory of disease transmission held that organisms invisible to the naked eye caused contagious diseases. These microorganisms (a term coined in 1880) might be spread by air (as was smallpox), by water or food (as was cholera), or by sexual intercourse (as was syphilis). The germ theory had been proposed by a Roman physician in the first century B.C., but physicians repeatedly rejected it in favor of other theories, such as the humoral theory (humors in the body were unbalanced) of the ancient world. The microscope revealed the existence of microorganisms in the seventeenth century, but scientists still favored the miasmal theory of diseases, which stressed vapors arising from the ground. The medical establishment remained so reluctant to accept the germ theory that in 1892 a German physician drank a beaker full of cholera bacteria to prove that microorganisms did not cause the disease. He did not die, but his theories did.

The germ theory was important for several reasons. First, it led to greater cleanliness, thereby reducing disease transmission. Without the knowledge that invisible organisms transmitted disease, no need existed for antiseptic conditions. Without antisepsis, doctors' offices, hospitals, and surgeries were deadly places. Hospitals packed fifty or sixty people into shared wards, where they also shared diseases. Surgeries had walls and floors impregnated with the waste of recent operations, the floors typically sprinkled with sawdust to soak up the mess. Surgeons wore frock coats, spattered with the blood of their patients; they tied whipcord, used to sew incisions shut, to their buttonholes, where it dangled in the blood of other patients. Doctors treated one patient after another often without washing their hands, and surgeons operated without washing their implements. Not surprisingly, survival rates were low. Even maternity wards were deadly, often having a 25 to 30 percent death rate for new mothers from puerperal fever, spread by physicians who performed examinations with unwashed fingers. General infections were so common that they were simply called "hospital disease." As Florence Nightingale later lamented, "The very first requirement in a hospital is that it should do the sick no harm."

The research of French chemist Louis Pasteur and German physician Robert Koch convinced the medical world to accept the germ theory of disease transmission. Pasteur's early work proved that microorganisms in the environment caused fermentation in beverages and the decay of organic matter. This knowledge led Pasteur, Koch, and others to the identification of the bacilli causing various diseases and then to the creation of vaccines against them. Pasteur's research showed how to keep dairy products and beer fresh by eliminating microorganisms (through "pasteurization") and led to a vaccination against rabies. Koch conducted similar work on tuberculosis, and in 1882 he isolated the bacillus of the disease that had killed an encyclopedia full of the creative artists of the nineteenth century, including the English romantic poet John Keats (at twenty-five), the Polish pianist Frederic Chopin, the French painter Paul Gaugin, and the Italian violinist Nicolo Paganini.

Even before Pasteur's proof of the germ theory, a few physicians had called for antiseptic medicine without being able to prove their case. The greatest early champion of antisepsis was Dr. Ignaz Semmelweiss, whose ideas earned him the nickname "the savior of mothers" and the scorn of his colleagues. Semmelweiss was an assistant in Vienna's maternity clinic in the 1840s. He observed high rates of puerperal fever among women whose doctors treated patients in other parts of the hospital, and this convinced him that simple cleanliness could reduce the death rate. Semmelweiss asked that doctors wash their hands in a chloride of lime solution before delivering a baby. He required such antisepsis in the Viennese delivery ward in 1847, and within a few weeks the death rate from puerperal fever fell from 18 percent to 2 percent. Semmelweiss could not demonstrate why antisepsis succeeded, however, and the medical profession rejected his conclusion; the savior of mothers was branded a charlatan and driven from his job after he also supported the revolution of 1848. The Medical Association of Vienna proclaimed it "time to stop all this nonsense about chlorine handwash" and abandoned his innovation. Semmelweiss died in a straitjacket during the same year that a British surgeon became famous for demonstrating the success of antisepsis.

Joseph Lister became the father of antisepsis instead of Semmelweiss. Lister had been studying wounds when he read Pasteur's work and concluded that microorganisms caused the infections he saw. He tested carbolic acid as a cleansing agent to kill such organisms in a successful experiment in 1865. His essay "On the Antiseptic System of Treatment in Surgery" (1867) quickly led to a decline in operating room deaths from 45 percent to 15 percent. Clean rooms, the storage of surgical threads in antiseptics, and a pump to spray a carbolic acid mist across the surgery (see illustration 23.3) won rapid acceptance, though simpler forms of antisepsis took a surprisingly long time to arrive. An American surgeon introduced rubber gloves (originally intended to protect his hands from the carbolic acid) in 1889; a Polish doctor began to use gauze facemasks and

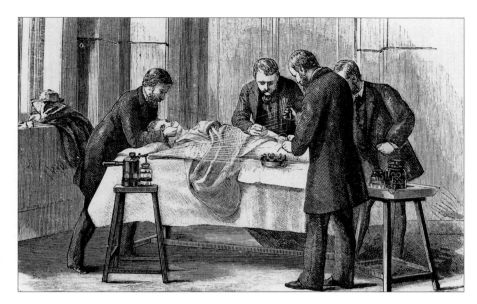

Illustration 23.3

Antiseptic Surgery. Joseph Lister experimented with carbolic acid in surgery to apply Louis Pasteur's germ theory of disease transmission. Lister's carbolic acid spray, shown here, effectively prevented infection during surgery and began the age of antiseptic medicine. Note, however, that in this 1882 surgery the physicians still wear their street clothes and do not use face masks or surgical gloves.

a German doctor suggested the steam sterilization of instruments in 1896.

Pasteur, Koch, Semmelweiss, Lister, and others greatly improved the human condition, but none of their work was more welcomed than were the discoveries of anesthetics. Untreatable pain was a fact of life in 1800. The agony of being fully conscious in a dentist's chair, in a delivery room, or on a surgical table was one of the nightmares of existence before 1846 (see document 23.1). Before the discovery of anesthetics, patients might have been drugged with alcohol or opium, but they were more often expected to bite down on a bullet. The greatest skill of a surgeon was speed in cutting the body.

Sir Humphrey Davy, a British chemistry professor, discovered the anesthetic property of nitrous oxide (laughing gas) in 1800. His laboratory assistant, the distinguished chemist and physicist Michael Faraday, discovered the similar properties of ether in 1815. No medical application was made of these discoveries until dentists began experimenting with ether and chloroform in the 1840s. Dental success led in 1846 to the first major surgery (a leg amputation) performed on a patient under anesthesia. British physicians began to campaign for the adoption of anesthesia in 1847. Professor James Young Simpson, a Scottish obstetrician, introduced the use of anesthesia in childbirth and campaigned in the British medical journal, the *Lancet,* for the adoption of his procedure. The medical profession accepted anesthetics in surgery at once but resisted them in the delivery ward. Many still held that the agony of childbirth was God's will in telling Eve "in sorrow thou shalt bring forth children."

Food and the Vital Revolution

The vital revolution of the nineteenth century was not simply a history of medical science. The increased availability of food and the improvement of diet also played a significant role. Well-fed people resist illness better and live longer. The average European diet of 1850 or 1890 was neither as diverse nor as nutritious as the diet most Europeans enjoy today, and it appears dreadful to most modern readers. However, historical perspective again demands that one compare it with the diet of earlier centuries; seen in that context, the nineteenth-century diet represented a significant improvement.

The simplest proof that the European diet improved during the nineteenth century is that Europeans grew taller. At the beginning of the century, the average soldier—selected for good health and strength—stood between 5'1" and 5'2" tall. Napoleon conquered Europe with warriors of that stature. To be sure, there were variations in height. The aristocracy had a much better diet and already stood closer to 5'6". The average height of west European soldiers did not reach 5'6" until 1900, when some countries produced averages of 5'7". This growth can be explained only by dietary changes. No institution kept similar records of the height of women across the century, but the average height was clearly below 5' in 1800 and across that line by 1900.

Dietary improvements arrived slowly, with significant variations by social class. A study of the Belgian city of Antwerp in 1850 found that the population of

◆ DOCUMENT 23.1 ◆

Life in a World Without Anesthesia

A Writer Describes Her Mastectomy (1811)

My dearest Esther,—and all my dears to whom she communicates this doleful ditty, will rejoice to hear that this resolution [to have surgery] once taken, was firmly adhered to, in defiance of a terror that surpasses all description, and the most torturing pain. Yet—when the dreadful steel was plunged into the breast—cutting through veins—arteries—flesh—nerves—I needed no injunctions not to restrain my cries. I began a scream that lasted unintermittingly during the whole time of the incision—and I almost marvel that it rings not in my ears still! so excruciating was the agony. When the wound was made, and the instrument was withdrawn, the pain seemed undiminished, for the air that suddenly rushed into those delicate parts felt like a mass of minute but sharp and forked poniards, that were tearing the edges of the wound—but when I again felt the instrument, describing a curve, cutting against the grain if I may so say, while the flesh resisted . . . I thought I must have expired. . . . The instrument this second time withdrawn, I concluded the operation over—Oh, no! presently the terrible cutting was renewed—and worse than ever. . . .

To conclude, the evil was so profound, the case so delicate, and the precautions necessary for preventing a return so numerous, that the operation, including the treatment and the dressing, lasted 20 minutes! a time, for sufferings so acute, that was hardly supportable—however, I bore it with all the courage I could exert, and never moved, nor stopt them, nor resisted.

Burney, Fanny. *Selected Letters and Journals*, ed. Joyce Hemlow. Oxford, England: Oxford University Press, 1986.

mal products in 1850—a big change from eighteenth-century averages. Similar studies of the German diet in the mid-nineteenth century found an average of 1.3 ounces of meat per day, little if compared with today but an amount that would have indicated prosperity in the eighteenth century. An increased consumption of fruits and vegetables came more slowly; they typically remained expensive, or seasonal, food for most people. The introduction of canned foods for Napoleon's army did not yield widespread improvements until the 1850s and 1860s. It also did not initially offer great availability of canned fruit or vegetables, because demand was highest for canned meats and canning was expensive.

Most studies of food consumption show steady improvement across the nineteenth century. A study of workhouse diets in Britain, for example, found that men received 2,350 calories in the 1880s–1890s, an improvement of nearly 20 percent from the 1830s. Thus, the poorest level of British society, whom the government treated with intentional stringency, ate better, too. Similarly, a study of German diets found that by 1910 per capita meat consumption had reached 4.5 ounces per day. Even if much of this came in tin cans, or much of it were horse meat (a habit promoted in European armies), this average would have seemed utopian in the eighteenth century.

The chief explanation for this improvement is that food prices declined significantly. The age of free trade ended tariffs on food and permitted the importation of cheaper food from around the world. In London, for example, the Napoleonic Wars had kept the price of a loaf of bread—then a four-pound loaf—artificially high at eleven to seventeen pence and it had fallen to a range of eight to twelve pence in peacetime under the Corn Laws. The repeal of the Corn Laws in 1846 produced a price of seven to eight pence per loaf, dropping to an average of five to six pence for the years 1895–1914. Thus, even if a worker's wages remained unchanged during the entire century, in 1900 they bought nearly three times as much bread as they had in lean years at the start of the century and nearly twice as much bread as they had under the Corn Laws.

Technology also drove down food prices. Vacuum canning, refrigeration, and steam ships enabled Europeans to exploit the agricultural wealth of Argentina, Australia, Canada, and the United States. The cost of shipping goods fell sharply. A study of French costs has shown that shipping goods by sea in 1825 added six centimes to the price for every kilometer that a ton of food was shipped, and once these goods reached France, highway transportation added thirty-three cen-

eighty-eight thousand people still received two-thirds of its calories from carbohydrates, mostly from bread (see table 23.4). Workers and the poor received 75 percent or more of their calories from bread. August Bebel's study of the German diet in the 1880s found a similar situation, although more calories came from potatoes.

The people of Antwerp received 10 percent of their calories from meat and nearly a quarter from ani-

⧊ TABLE 23.4 ⧊

The Average Daily Diet at Antwerp in the 1850s

Product	Consumption (per capita, per day)	Number of calories	Calories (as a percentage of total)
Animal products			
Butter	32 grams	240	10.6
Eggs	0.348 grams	26	1.1
Meat	104 grams	234	10.3
Salt fish	12 grams	32	1.4
Total		532	23.4
Beverages			
Beer	0.367 liters	163	7.2
Coffee	12 grams	12	0.5
Gin	0.015 liters	40	1.8
Wine	0.015 liters	12	0.5
Total		227	10.0
Carbohydrates			
Potatoes	700 grams	490	21.6
Rye flour	45 grams	140	6.2
Wheat flour	284 grams	880	38.8
Bread subtotal		1,020	45.0
Total		1,510	66.6

Source: Adapted from data in Catharina Lis, *Social Change and the Labouring Poor: Antwerp, 1770–1860* (New Haven, Conn.: Yale University Press, 1986), p. 182.

times for every kilometer a ton was carted. In 1905, when steamships had replaced sails, sea transportation had fallen to 2.4 centimes (a decrease of 58 percent); railroads had similarly replaced horse-drawn carts, and land transportation had fallen to 5.4 centimes (a decrease of 84 percent). Thus, foreign food fell simply because bringing it to market cost less. This competition drove down the price of locally produced food.

Data showing total consumption in a nation, or data divided to state average consumption, can be misleading. Individual consumption still varied greatly by social class. A study of the English diet in 1900 has suggested that a typical working-class family of four had a weekly food budget of fifteen shillings (about $3.75), while a middle-class family spent fifteen shillings per person. Well-to-do families, who took pride in lavish entertaining, spent thirty shillings per person. Working-class meals still consisted chiefly of starches, with few fruits or vegetables; meat chiefly came at a special Sunday meal, with occasional supplements such as bacon, sausage, or rabbit.

In contrast, food was a status symbol for the middle classes, the material proof of their success in reaching a standard of living previously limited to the wealthy.

Overeating became a conspicuous social process; obesity, a mark of distinction. Standards of both manly and womanly appearance favored robust figures showing that a person did not live on a modest budget. One of the best-selling books of the 1890s was an advice manual for women entitled *How to Become Pleasingly Plump*. Many public figures at the turn-of-the-century cast such large shadows. The prime minister of Britain on the eve of World War I, Sir Henry Campbell-Bannerman, weighed nearly 280 pounds, and his wife was almost as obese. They ate four meals every day, such as the prime minister's regular favorite: a bowl of mutton-broth soup, a fish course of either herring or salmon, then a roast lamb, followed by a grouse, and culminating in multiple desserts, usually an apple tart with fresh strawberries, then gingerbread and butter. His predecessor at the start of the century, the marquess of Salisbury, was only slightly smaller.

The health risks of a working-class diet were different from those of middle class overeating. The foremost problem (beyond obtaining sufficient food) was the adulteration of food. As Europe changed from an agricultural society, in which people produced the food that they ate, to an urban society, in which people purchased their food in markets, unscrupulous merchants exploited the unregulated economy to sell adulterated food. A parliamentary commission found that bread often contained chalk, plaster of Paris, sand, or lime. Powdered clay was mixed with cocoa, ground nut shells with pepper. Sulfuric acid was added to gin, producing a drink with a memorable bite. Sugar was debased with a dried residue from soap boilers. Parliament concluded that 62 percent of all food sold in London was corrupted. The problem was not limited to British cities, and many countries debated pure food laws versus pure capitalism before accepting the government regulation of food, drink, and drugs. The Dutch pioneered such legislation in 1829, and regulations against adulterated food soon followed in France, Belgium, Prussia, and Spain. British merchants continued to insist upon an unregulated market until scandals forced pure food legislation in 1860 and 1872.

The adulteration of food made people initially skeptical of altered or synthetic foods, which began to appear in the nineteenth century. Only after large advertising campaigns did people begin to accept pasteurized milk in which microbes had been killed by sterilization. Two American chemists synthesized a compound in 1879 and accidentally discovered that it was extremely sweet tasting; their "saccharin" was an effective sugar substitute, but people who knew about the corruption of sugar with soap wastes were reluctant to accept a sugar containing no sugar. One of the first successful substitute foods—often called by the German term *Ersatzessen*—was a flour made from potatoes instead of grains. Margarine, the most widely used ersatz food, was invented in a French laboratory in 1869, in response to a contest sponsored by Napoleon III to discover an affordable substitute for butter. The prize-winning recipe was a mixture of beef fat and ground cow's udders. This may seem a scant improvement on the outlawed adulteration, but it was just a short step to the use of vegetable oil instead of rendered beef fat, to create the commercially successful margarines sold to the urban working class.

Drink and Drugs in the Nineteenth Century

The nineteenth century was an age of high consumption of alcohol—compared with the late twentieth century, but not with the eighteenth century—plus consumption of opium and cocaine, both of which were legally available. The ravages caused to the human body by excessive alcohol or drugs were poorly understood, and physicians regularly prescribed narcotics as painkillers; some even recommended heavy alcohol consumption. Governments did little to control alcohol or opium sales in 1800. Laissez-faire capitalism, which opposed government restrictions on the market, perpetuated that situation. Furthermore, alcohol taxes kept most governments in business. In 1870 Britain had virtually no income tax but raised 35 percent of its total revenue on alcohol taxes. In Ireland, 54 percent of all government revenue was raised by taxes on alcohol. End-of-the-century Russia raised even more income through a government monopoly on vodka.

Heavy drinking was socially acceptable. William Pitt the Younger frequently addressed Parliament while drunk; on important occasions, he stepped behind the speaker's chair and induced vomiting before making a critical speech. Even the more puritanical Gladstone drank a sherry mixture in Parliament, to ease his way through three-hour speeches. Another prime minister made himself light-headed with ether before speaking, and a fourth took a jolt of opium dissolved in alcohol. If the rich and powerful behaved that way, it is hardly surprising that people who lived in a world of epidemic disease, short life expectancy, seventy-to-eighty-hour workweeks, no welfare legislation or retirement, and minimal diets found solace and sociability in cafes, pubs, and beer halls.

A variety of records reveal the extent of nineteenth-century drinking. The Antwerp study found that beer consumption in the 1820s averaged two bottles per day (twenty-three ounces) for every man, woman, and child in the population, plus approximately one bottle of wine and one bottle of gin each per month; by the 1850s nearly 10 percent of all calories consumed in the city came from alcohol. A similar survey of France in 1900 found a per capita annual consumption rate of 180 liters of wine (240 standard bottles), 27 liters of beer (more than three cases of 12-ounce bottles), and 4.7 liters of distilled spirits (more than 5 bottles of alcohol). Those averages include the entire population. If one excludes children below the age of fourteen (more than 30 percent of the population in 1900), every adult in France had to consume 325 bottles of wine per year; clearly, a significant portion of the population drank more than a bottle per day, all year long, much of it distilled to make a rough brandy. A study of Russia found that spending on vodka exceeded total spending for education, books, oil, gifts, priests, the poor, weddings, and funerals, which may explain why the government chose to tax vodka instead of books.

Such drinking led to efforts to control sales of alcoholic beverages. The first European temperance society was organized in Ireland in 1818, and such groups

TABLE 23.5
Opium Use in England, 1827–77

Year	Opium imports (in tons)	Total home consumption (in tons)	Home consumption (per 1,000 population in pounds)
1827	56.6	8.5	1.31
1837	40.3	18.5	2.48
1847	n.a.	23.0	2.67
1857	68.2	28.0	2.92
1867	136.8	n.a.	n.a.
1877	303.7	n.a.	n.a.

n.a. = Not available.

Source: Condensed from data in Virginia Berridge and Griffith Edwards, *Opium and the People: Opiate Use in Nineteenth Century England* (New Haven, Conn.: Yale University Press, 1987), tables 1–2, pp. 272–74.

spread across the British Isles during industrialization. Many motives could be discerned behind the temperance campaign: Some reformers were motivated by religious morality and saw drinking as sinful; others acted from the perspective of social class—sometimes to help families in poverty, sometimes in fear of the poor and crime, sometimes angry about alcohol and absenteeism from work. Although the upper classes were notoriously heavy drinkers, most reformers agreed with employers that drink was "the curse of [the] working class." British law regulated the opening hours of alehouses in 1828 and began the licensing of pubs in 1830. Scottish clergymen won the first prohibition of alcohol—no sales on Sundays—in 1853.

By the time that temperance leagues became active in European cities, advocates of social control were also becoming concerned about opium and cocaine. Opium, has been used medicinally since ancient Mediterranean civilizations; one of the oldest known Egyptian papyri praises its painkilling powers. A Swiss physician popularized medical opium in the sixteenth century in a compound he named laudanum ("highly praised"). Laudanum, a tincture of opium dissolved in alcohol, became a basic medication, and by 1800 it was widely consumed by all who could afford it.

Britain imported tons of opium every year. Most of this stock was reexported to the Far East, where the British were the world's pushers—they had used opium addiction as a means of opening oriental markets and they fought two Opium Wars (1839–42 and 1856–58) to keep their drug markets open. Even subtracting the

reexportation of opium, the British home market was enormous. Domestic consumption grew from 8.5 tons of opium in 1827 to 30.5 tons in 1859, spawning a network of respectable importers, auctioneers, brokers, and merchants (see table 23.5). British governments shared in this lucrative trade through an opium tariff until 1860. The abolition of the tariff cut the price of opium to approximately one shilling (twenty-five cents) per ounce, roughly an agricultural laborer's weekly wages in 1860.

Opium was initially a drug of the educated and upper classes, because of its cost and its circulation by physicians. In the early nineteenth century, addiction was far more common among famous writers than criminals or the poor. Virtually the entire literary community of romanticism used opium. Thomas de Quincey became famous for a book entitled *Confessions of an English Opium Eater* (1856), which bluntly said, "Thou hast the keys of paradise, O just, subtle, and mighty opium!" Coleridge became renowned for a poem ("Kubla Kahn") that he composed after an opium-induced fantasy. Byron took a brand of laudanum called the Black Drop and satisfied references to it appear in his writing. Shelley used opium to relieve stress. Keats consumed such large quantities that he even considered using it for suicide. Elizabeth Barrett Browning's spinal problems made her dependent on a daily dose of opium, and her husband concluded that "sleep only came to her in a red hood of poppies." Sir Walter Scott began taking huge quantities during an illness and wrote at least one of his novels under its influence. Similar lists could be drawn of political figures (the friends of George IV often found him stupefied by opium) or even famous preachers (William Wilberforce was an addict because of his ulcer medication). This situation lasted until the Pharmacy Act of 1868 introduced the first restrictions because the government feared that workers were starting to use opium for its pleasure-giving properties. Further restrictions appeared in the 1890s when the government began to fear that immigrants, especially the Chinese, congregated in "opium dens" and plotted crimes.

The Life Cycle: Birth and Birth Control

The subject of human reproduction led to much controversy during the nineteenth century. The century witnessed a significant decline in the birthrate, which is explained by a variety of birth control practices. Physicians, churches, and governments generally opposed the circulation of birth control information and the use of contraceptives, however; they considered them immoral and made them illegal in most places.

The search for a reliable means of birth control is as old as human records, and discussions of it are found in pre-Christian records. The early church opposed contraception and medieval canon law forbade it, but ideas about avoiding pregnancy nonetheless circulated in popular culture. The population explosion that began in the late eighteenth century persuaded nineteenth-century reformers to circulate birth control information. These neo-Malthusians proposed a variety of (semi-reliable) means of contraception: the insertion of a barrier (such as a sponge) as a rudimentary form of the diaphragm; the use of simple chemical douches (such as vinegar), as a rudimentary spermicide; and the practice of male withdrawal before ejaculation, modestly described by the Latin term *coitus interruptus*. Condoms made from animal membranes had been tried for centuries, and a reusable condom of vulcanized rubber (hence its nickname) was clandestinely marketed in the 1870s, although the modern, thinner condom made of latex was not invented until after World War I.

Such methods of contraception—plus abortion, infanticide, and abandonment—were first used on a scale large enough to check population growth in France. The French birthrate in 1810 was 317 births per ten thousand population, 15 percent lower than the rate in Britain (375 per ten thousand); the rate in the German states was even higher (395 per ten thousand). The difference between the French and the Anglo-German

birthrates widened during the nineteenth century, even when the British birthrate started falling. By 1910 the French birthrate (202 per ten thousand) was 26 percent below the British rate (272 per ten thousand) and 32 percent below the German rate (298 per ten thousand). By the early twentieth century, the French had reached zero population growth (a balance between births and deaths), despite the opposition of leaders who foresaw the depopulation of France. This trend, combined with other demographic data, leaves no doubt that the French were practicing birth control on a significant scale.

British radicals tried to spread such information. Richard Carlile, a tinsmith and printer, published a manual in 1838, entitled *Every Woman's Book,* advocating the use of a sponge barrier. It and an American manual, *Fruits of Philosophy* (1832), which advocated a vinegar douche, were censored, and some booksellers were imprisoned, but their ideas circulated. In 1877 Annie Besant, a preacher's wife and campaigner for unpopular causes, and Charles Bradlaugh, a social reformer, defied the courts and sold 125,000 copies of these reprinted works. Besant summarized the various methods of birth control in *The Law of Population* (1877), which conservatives branded as "a dirty, filthy book . . . that no human would allow on his table . . . and no decently educated English husband would allow even his wife to have" (see document 23.2). Besant was sentenced to six months in prison, but the verdict was overturned on a technicality.

Similar controversies developed in many countries. Dr. Alleta Jacobs, the first woman physician in the Netherlands, opened the world's first birth control clinic in Amsterdam in 1882, despite great opposition from the medical profession. In other countries, radical feminists, such as Dr. Madeleine Pelletier in France, made the control of reproduction an essential element of women's rights. Pelletier even published one of the first works claiming the right to abortion. By the end of the century, information about both birth control and abortion circulated widely. A study of Spain has found significant use of contraception in the cities, especially in Catalonia. A study of a Berlin working-class clinic in 1913 found that 64 percent of the women used birth control.

Historical data on abortions are among the least reliable evidence confronting historians, but provocative records survive on this controversial subject. A study of abortion in France in the late nineteenth century concluded that approximately 250,000 abortions per year were performed there. It was illegal to perform or to

❖ DOCUMENT 23.2 ❖

Birth Control Advice in Victorian England

Annie Besant Surveys Birth Control Options (1877)

All thinkers have seen that since population increases more rapidly than the means of subsistence, the human brain should be called in to devise a restriction of the population, and so relieve man from the pressure of the struggle for existence. . . . Malthus proposed . . . the delay of marriage. . . . [But] the more marriage is delayed, the more prostitution spreads. . . . Later, thinkers, recognizing at once the evils of over-population and the evils of late marriage . . . have advocated early marriages and small families. . . . [Yet] how is this duty to be performed?

The check we will take first is 'natural laws'. . . . Women are far less likely to conceive midway between the menstrual periods than either immediately before or after them.

The preventive check so generally practiced in France . . . consists simply in the withdrawal of the husband previous to the emission of the semen, and is, of course absolutely certain as a preventive . . . .

The preventive check advocated by Dr. Knowlton is, on the other hand, entirely in the hands of the wife. It consists in the use of the ordinary syringe immediately after intercourse, a solution of sulphate of zinc, or of alum, being used instead of water. There is but little doubt that this check is an effective one . . . [but] there are many obvious disadvantages connected with it as a matter of taste and feeling. The same remark applies to the employment of the *baudruche*, a covering used by men of loose character as a guard against syphilitic diseases, and occasionally recommended as a preventive check.

The check which appears to us to be preferable, as at once certain, and in no sense grating on any feeling of affection or of delicacy, is that recommended by Carlile many years ago in his *Every Woman's Book*. . . . To prevent impregnation, pass to the end of the vagina a piece of fine sponge. . . .

There is a preventive check attempted by many poor women which is most detrimental to health, and should therefore never be employed, namely, the too long persistence in nursing one baby in the hope of thereby preventing the conception of another. Nursing does not prevent conception. . . .

Another class of checks is distinctly criminal, i.e., the procuring of abortion. Various drugs are taken by women with this intent, and too often their use results in death, or in dangerous sickness.

Besant, Annie. *The Law of Population*. London: Freethought Publishing Company, 1877; and Carlile, Richard. *Every Woman's Book, or What is Love?* London: 1838.

obtain an abortion throughout those years, but only one hundred to two hundred French women were convicted of the crime each year. Physicians' records from small villages show varying local rates, from 3 percent to 18 percent of all pregnancies ending in abortion. In contrast, fully 40 percent of the working-class women interviewed in Berlin in 1913 admitted that they had at least one abortion; the entire group had terminated almost one-third of their pregnancies by abortions. The means of abortion that they reported were startling: One simply "jumped off chairs and stools." Another "sent for a [chemical] remedy that was advertised in the newspaper." And a third "poked around with a quill a little bit until blood came." Descriptions of similar means of aborting unwanted pregnancies occur in late nineteenth-century novels, such as Zola's grim portrayal of peasant life in France, *The Land* (1887). Such sources suggest that many abortions were performed by midwives (see illustration 23.4). Despite the medical, legal, social, and religious obstacles, European women practiced birth control and abortion on a large enough scale during the nineteenth century to sharply lower European birthrates (see table 23.6).

The increasing use of birth control did not mean that social problems associated with child birth, such as illegitimacy, abandonment, and infanticide, disappeared. Illegitimacy began to increase in the late eighteenth century and grew during the nineteenth century, until 8 percent of all European births in the 1880s were illegitimate. This pattern varied regionally, with the highest national averages being found in Germanic central Europe. Austria, Germany, Denmark, and Scandinavia had a combined illegitimate birthrate above 10 percent, with the highest figure being in Austria (14.9

Illustration 23.4

Abortion. Abortion was both illegal and widely practiced in the nineteenth century. Although little reliable data exists, hundreds of thousands of abortions clearly were being performed with relatively few trials taking place. As this turn-of-the-century caricature bluntly suggests, women knew where to find a local "angel-maker."

percent in 1889). Much lower rates were found in regions with early marriages (such as Serbia, which reported 1.1 percent illegitimacy) or the strictest sexual mores (such as Ireland, which reported 2.7 percent). Conversely, where late marriages were the norm, illegitimacy rose. A demographic study of rural Portugal found that, in villages where landless peasants could not marry until late in life, illegitimacy reached as high as 73 percent of all births. As the data for Ireland and Austria show, national religions were not the determining factor in illegitimate births.

Infanticide and the abandonment of newborn infants (often the same thing) remained serious social problems as they had been in the Old Regime. In Britain, the law stated that infanticide must be treated as murder, but it also said "it must be proved that the entire body of the child has actually been born into the world in a living state" before the child was legally alive and the act was legally murder. Killing an infant as it

emerged from the womb thus received some legal protection, and it was a horrifying, but not uncommon, urban experience of mid-Victorian England to find dead babies in the streets, in trash heaps, or in rivers. Abandonment was sufficiently common in Victorian England that George Eliot (the pseudonym of Mary Ann Evans) could make it a central element of *Adam Bede* (1859) and make the mother who left her child to die in the woods (Hetty Sorrel) a sympathetic character.

In France, infanticide was so common that at least one thousand women were indicted for it every year from the 1840s to the 1880s; annual arrests did not fall below five hundred until 1901. One study estimates that the crime reached its nineteenth-century peak at 12 percent of all births in 1862–63. In the years 1817–20, the abandonment of babies at Paris hospitals equaled one-third of the births recorded in the city, although many of these infants were undoubtedly brought to Paris from the countryside. The abandon-

TABLE 23.6

The Declining Birthrate in Europe, 1840–1914

| Year | Births per one thousand population | | | |
	England	France	Germany	Russia
1840	32.0	27.9	36.4	n.a.
1850	n.a.	26.8	37.2	n.a.
1860	35.6	26.2	36.4	49.7
1870	34.6	25.9	38.5	49.2
1880	33.6	24.6	37.6	49.7
1890	30.4	21.8	35.7	50.3
1900	28.7	21.3	35.6	49.3
1910	25.1	19.6	29.8	45.1
1914	23.8	18.1	26.8	43.1
Percentage decline from 1840 to 1914	–25.6	–35.1	–26.4	–13.3

Source: B. R. Mitchell, *European Historical Statistics, 1950–1970* (London: Macmillan, 1975), pp. 105–20.

n.a. = Not available.

ment of babies at public institutions in France reached a recorded peak of 164,319 in 1833. Thus, abandonment of infanticide may have claimed 40 percent of all babies in some years.

Abandonment was most common in regions where effective contraception was not well known, especially in eastern Europe. Catherine the Great had established foundling homes in Moscow and St. Petersburg, but abandoned babies soon overflowed these institutions, which then became processing centers for shipping unwanted babies to the countryside. In the 1830s the foundling home of St. Petersburg had twenty-five thousand children on its rolls with five thousand being added each year; by the 1880s the home in St. Petersburg was receiving nine thousand abandoned newborns per year and the home in Moscow, seventeen thousand. The problem was most urgent for the large numbers of women who were domestic servants in the cities—25 percent of women in Moscow, 37 percent in St. Petersburg. Marriage was difficult for these women and economic survival virtually impossible if they lost their posts, as they would if they had a child. Children who reached the foundling homes suffered terribly: Between 75 percent and 90 percent of them died each year. Similar patterns existed in western Europe, and critics were not totally wrong when they called foundling homes a system of "legalized infanticide."

The Life Cycle: Youth

No stage of the life cycle experienced a more dramatic change in daily life than the young did. The history of childhood and adolescence in nineteenth-century Europe saw the conquest of contagious ("childhood") diseases, which changed childhood from a world in which 50 percent of the population died to one where less than 10 percent did; the emergence of the idea that youth was a distinct phase of life and the consequent new attitudes and laws about different treatment of the young; and the industrial revolution, which changed the primary activities of the young, first shifting their economic roles and later requiring schooling instead of work.

The British led Europe toward a new legal treatment of the young by defining new borders between youth and adulthood. Nineteenth-century laws limited the maximum number of hours that children could work and the minimum number of years that they must attend school; laws defined the age at which the young could consent to sex or to marriage and the age at which they could be sentenced to death. For most of the nineteenth century, the age of sexual consent for girls was twelve; a reform of British criminal law in 1875 raised this to thirteen (the French standard), and another reform in 1885 set the age of consent at sixteen. A study of French criminal justice has shown that, despite such early ages of consent, the single most common felony against persons in the late nineteenth century was the molestation of young girls. The young similarly received at least nominal protection in penal law. For most of the century, British prison populations were segregated by gender, social class, and types of crimes committed, but they were not segregated by age; a ten-year-old thief would be imprisoned with adult criminals. British penal reforms of 1854 created reformatories for youthful offenders, with fifteen being considered the age of adulthood. A Children's Act of 1908 created separate prisons (borstals) for the young and set the age of adulthood (for hanging, for example) at sixteen, to match the sexual statutes.

Industrialization and urbanization transformed the economic life of the young. For many, life shifted from being farm workers in a household economy, or urban apprentices already separated from their families, to working in mines and factories and contributing to a family wage economy. By the 1840s child labor had become so common that governments began to regulate it. In France, for example, 18 percent to 24 percent of all workers in textile factories were children, and the

⚐ TABLE 23.7 ⚐
The Rise of Universal Education in Europe, 1849–1914

Country	Primary pupils		University students	
	Number (year)	Number (year)	Number (year)	Number (year)
Austria	1,450,000 (1850)	4,691,000 (1910)	11,439 (1850)	39,416 (1910)
Britain	278,000 (1850)	6,295,000 (1910)	n.a.	n.a.
France	3,322,000 (1850)	5,049,000 (1910)	n.a.	41,190 (1910)
Germany	n.a.	n.a.	21,432 (1880)	70,183 (1910)
Hungary	18,000 (1850)	2,549,000 (1910)	838 (1850)	12,951 (1910)
Italy	1,025,000 (1861)	3,473,000 (1910)	6,504 (1861)	26,850 (1910)
Ottoman Empire	5,000 (1858)	2,000,000 (1895)	n.a.	n.a.
Russia	n.a.	1,835,000 (1891)	n.a.	13,033 (1891)
Spain	1,005,000 (1855)	1,526,000 (1908)	7,528 (1857)	20,497 (1914)

Source: Data drawn from B. R. Mitchell, *European Historical Statistics, 1750–1970* (London: Macmillan, 1975), pp. 750–73; Chris Cook and John Paxton, *European Political Facts, 1848–1918* (London: Macmillan, 1978), pp. 307–15, J. Scott Keltie, ed., *Statesman's Yearbook* (London: Macmillan, 1891), pp. 855–56.
n.a. = Not available.

law limited children below the age of twelve to eight hours of work per day.

The Old Regime legacy of children working at an early age in agriculture, factories, mines, or apprenticeships left little room for universal education. A study of French schooling in the early nineteenth century found that more than fifteen thousand towns (40 percent of the communities in France) had no schools whatsoever. A study of Russia on the eve of emancipation (1861) found that 0.8 percent of the population was attending school. The German states had long been the leaders of European education because they had a tradition of compulsory education. In the 1850s nearly 95 percent of Prussian adults had received at least eight years of primary education; by the 1890s virtually 100 percent of German children received a primary education.

Most of Europe did not copy the German principle of compulsory education until the late nineteenth century. In 1850 the combined elementary school enrollments in Hungary, Portugal, and the Ottoman Empire amounted to fewer than 100,000 pupils—fewer than 5,000 in all of the Turkish provinces, only 18,000 in Portugal. The Ferry laws of the late 1870s and early 1880s in France gave Europe another model: mandatory, free, secular, universal education in state-run schools. British education, shaped by the Forster elementary education reforms of Gladstone's "great ministry" (1868–74), provided a competing model that encouraged private, fee-paying schools. By 1914

schooling had replaced disease as the basic fact of childhood. British primary school enrollments increased twentyfold, from 278,000 in 1850 to 6.3 million in 1910 (see table 23.7).

Compulsory education, like other social changes, often conflicted with traditional values and behavior. Just as conservatives opposed some of the new medical practices, such as vaccination and anesthesia, and they fought against birth control and abortion, many conservatives opposed compulsory education (see document 23.3). They argued that state-run schools gave the government too much power or that the family would be weakened. Religious leaders inveighed against the "godless school." Such arguments slowed, or blocked, universal education in some countries. The Spanish accepted only a minimum of universal education: The Moyano Education Law of 1857, which remained the basis of Spanish education until the 1960s, made schooling obligatory only until age nine and provided free schooling only for the poor.

The life of schoolchildren in the nineteenth century consisted chiefly of the memorization of facts. As Mr. Gradgrind, a teacher in Charles Dickens's *Hard Times* (1854), explained, "Now what I want is Facts. . . . Facts alone are wanted in life." There remained some variation about which facts pupils must memorize, but little doubt existed about this form of education. Girls and boys received different schooling, with boys being groomed for higher education and girls usually denied

◈ DOCUMENT 23.3 ◈

Conservative Arguments Against Compulsory Public Education

The French Ministry of Education, under the direction of a historian named Victor Duruy, did much to modernize education during the 1860s. Duruy gave libraries to primary schools, improved the salaries of teachers, sharply increased the number of schools for girls, expanded adult education, and reformed teacher training. Duruy supported the ideas of free and compulsory education, but he was a generation ahead of his time; conservative opposition to compulsory schooling was too strong, and such laws were not adopted until the 1880s. The following document was prepared in Duruy's Ministry of Education to summarize the conservative arguments.

The arguments against obligatory education can be listed under seven different headings:

    1. It is a limitation upon paternal authority. The State has no right to intervene in the family to diminish the power of its head.

    2. The obligation of a father to send his son to a public school cannot be reconciled with freedom of conscience, because the child is vulnerable to a religious education contrary to the faith which his father wishes to give him.

    3. It is a diminution of the resources of the family: the child of the poor person performs a host of small jobs which attenuate misery for them both. Thus the government intervenes in the workplace . . . and reduces productivity.

    4. Making education obligatory gives the government the sort of power which it should not have.

    5. Given the present state of the schools, it is economically impossible to open them to all children.

    6. The forced presence in the schools of children who refuse to learn and disrupt other students will destroy discipline.

    7. Finally, compulsory education, if it is not also free education, will create a heavy new tax on peasants and workers.

French Ministry of Education Yearbook (1863), trans. Steven C. Hause. In M. Chaulanges et all, eds., *Textes historiques, 1848–1871: le milieu du XIXe siècle.* Paris: Delagrave, 1975.

such preparation. Private (tuition paying) schools often stressed religious studies, while state schools in both the French and German models insisted upon strictly secular education. The master of a famous British school for the elite, Rugby School, stated his mission this way: "It is not necessary that this should be a school of 300 or 100, or of 50 boys, but it is necessary that it should be a school of Christian gentlemen." The French Ministry of Education, in contrast, removed Christianity from the classroom and the curriculum, teaching instead a secular moral philosophy. Most schools taught a little mathematics, more history (especially the national history), some geography (particularly as colonial empires grew), little literature, less science (sometimes omitted entirely), and a great deal of Latin and Greek, which were requirements for higher education. Classics remained the key to a university education throughout the century; although Oxford and Cambridge relaxed their Greek requirement at the turn of the century, proficiency in Latin remained *sine qua non* (indispensable) at universities well into the twentieth century.

    The foremost consequence of compulsory education laws was the birth of nearly universal literacy. The vast majority of Europeans were illiterate in 1800. This varied somewhat from one region to another, differed for men and for women, and followed the standards of social class or occupation, but the result was usually the same: Most people could neither read nor write. Studies of marriage records—by checking the signatures on wedding certificates—reveal the scope of illiteracy (see table 23.8). In 1800, 53 percent of the women married in England signed with an "X." As late as 1870, 58 percent of Italian men and 77 percent of Italian women still married with an "X." Other studies have shown how illiteracy varied by a family's social position or occupation. A study of French army recruits in the 1830s found that illiteracy was rare among the sons of professionals (less than 1 percent) or civil servants (2.4 percent), but high among the sons of factory workers (58.9 percent), peasants (83.5 percent), or domestic servants (96.0 percent). Similar variations occurred within the regions of a country. A study of Italian illiteracy in 1911 found it low in the more prosperous north (Piedmont, 11 percent; Lombardy, 13 percent) but high in the poorer south (Sicily, 58 percent; Calabria, 70 percent).

The Life Cycle: *Marriage and the Family*

European law in the nineteenth century still permitted marriages at an early age. British law allowed girls to

TABLE 23.8

The Decline of Illiteracy in Europe, 1800–1910

The figures in this table are the percentage of newlyweds signing wedding certificates with an "X."

	England		France	
Date	Men	Women	Men	Women
1800	n.a.	53	72	n.a.
1820	n.a.	n.a.	46	65
1830	n.a.	n.a.	n.a.	n.a.
1840	33	49	n.a.	n.a.
1850	31	36	n.a.	n.a
1860	26	36	30	45
1870	20	27	27	40
1880	14	19	16	25
1890	7	8	8	14
1900	3	3	5	6
1910			3	4

Source: *Statesman's Yearbook* (London: Macmillan, passim); Hartmut Kaelble, *Industrialization* (New York: St. Martin's, 1986), pp. 90–91.

n.a. = Not available.

[a] Italy did not yet exist as a unified country.

TABLE 23.9

Marriage Patterns in Nineteenth-Century Europe

Mean Age at Marriage in Belgium, 1800

Occupation	Men	Women
Artisans	26.8	26.6
Farmers	30.6	27.8
Servants	26.3	27.3
Shopkeepers	26.0	24.1
Spinners	29.9	29.8
Weavers	25.6	23.9
Others	32.1	27.5

Mean Age at Marriage in Württemberg, 1880–1914

Occupation	Men	Women
Agriculture	32.8	29.4
Metal worker	32.2	27.4
Textile worker	32.8	30.1

Source: Belgian data from Myron P. Gutman, *Toward the Modern Economy: Early Industry in Europe, 1500–1800* (New York, N.Y.: Knopf, 1988), p. 169; German data from Heilwig Schomerus, "The Family Life-Cycle: A Study of Factory Workers in Nineteenth Century Württemberg," in Richard J. Evans and W. R. Lee, eds., *The German Family: Essays on the Social History of the Family in Nineteenth and Twentieth Century Germany* (Totowa, N.J.: Barnes and Noble, 1981), p. 183.

marry at twelve and boys at fourteen for most of the century. Orthodox canon law accepted marriage at thirteen for girls and fifteen for boys. Literature from the era reminds readers that early marriages did occur, such as the nurse in Pushkin's *Eugene Onegin* (1832) who married at thirteen. The history of European marriage during the nineteenth century, however, is different from what the law permitted (see table 23.9). Marriage generally occurred much later—at, or after, age twenty-five—and the average age at marriage increased, reaching into the thirties in some regions. Women typically married at a younger age than men did.

The average age at marriage in Britain in the early nineteenth century was approximately twenty-five for women and twenty-six for men. A study of Belgium in 1800 found a range of marital ages for men of roughly twenty-five to thirty-two, depending upon their occupation; the same data found women marrying at twenty-four to thirty. The latest averages were in Ireland, where marriage was traditionally linked to sufficient landholding to support a family. The potato famine of the 1840s taught the tragedy of having a family but no ability to feed it. One-fourth of the popula-

tion of Ireland during the late nineteenth century never married, and those who did, married at an age of economic security: thirty-eight for men and thirty for women.

A dramatic contrast to these marital patterns existed in eastern Europe. A study comparing Sweden and Serbia in 1900 found huge differences for people in their twenties. Only 8 percent of Swedish men and 20 percent of Swedish women were married at age twenty to twenty-four, but the Serbian figures were 50 percent for men and 84 percent for women. The Serbian pattern also characterized nineteenth-century Russia, where the average age at marriage in the 1830s was eighteen for both sexes. Serfs could not postpone marriage until they possessed land of their own unless they planned never to marry. Even after emancipation, most Russian peasants in 1868 were married by age twenty. These marital patterns, like those in Ireland or Württemberg, appear to have been a direct result of the economic condition of the population.

The institution of marriage changed during the nineteenth century. One aspect of this change was the

◆ TABLE 23.10 ◆

Family Size in Württemberg in the 1850s and 1860s

Occupation of father	Percentage of families				
	0 children	1–3 children	4–6 children	7–9 children	10 or more children
Agricultural	31.3	33.6	22.8	7.2	4.8
Metal industry	17.1	59.9	17.1	2.9	2.9
Textile industry	21.4	32.2	25.0	14.2	7.2

Source: Heilwig Schomerus, "The Family-Life-Cycle: A Study of Factory Workers in Nineteenth Century Württemberg," in Richard J. Evans and W. R. Lee, eds., *The German Family: Essays on the Social History of the Family in Nineteenth and Twentieth Century Germany* (Totowa, N.J.: Barnes and Noble, 1981), p. 185.

transition from an agricultural economy to an industrial economy, which broke down the historic pattern of a household economy in which a husband and wife shared the labor of farm or shop, creating instead a family wage economy in which a husband and wife typically worked at separate jobs and pooled their wages to maintain the home. Other important changes in marriage were appearing by the end of the nineteenth century, largely the result of the successes of the women's movement. The historic pattern of patriarchal marriage—of a husband's authority and a wife's obedience—a pattern sanctified by law, religion, and custom, was breaking down. Married women were winning fundamental economic rights, such as the control of their own property or wages, beginning with the British Married Women's Property Acts of 1857–82. The breakdown of the paternalistic marriage, which has continued during the twentieth century, soon touched all aspects of family life, such as control of the children.

A third fundamental change in the nature of marriage, the legal right to end the marriage, developed during the nineteenth century. The French Revolution instituted divorce, but that law was repealed by the restored monarchy. The Prussian legal code of 1794 made divorce comparatively easy there, and Bismarck imposed divorce on Catholic Germany during the *Kulturkampf* of the 1870s. Legislation of 1857 in Britain and 1884 in France permitted divorce, and Scandinavian countries adopted similar statutes. Men and women (but significantly more women) increasingly exercised this right during the late nineteenth century. British divorces climbed from 178 per year in the late 1850s to surpass 1,000 for the first time in 1906. Divorce rates rose more rapidly in France. The first full year of divorce (1885) saw 4,000 marriages dissolved, and that

number doubled by 1895, tripled by 1905. By the early twentieth century both France and Germany were seeing 15,000 divorces per year. Such figures do not compare with the "divorce revolution" of the late twentieth century, but the social trend was clear, as the Catholic Church argued in blocking divorce in Italy and Spain.

The combination of later marriage, the increased use of birth control, and the legalization of divorce meant that the average size of European families declined. The economic system no longer rewarded large families when children were obliged to attend school. The vital revolution that conquered many childhood diseases meant that parents could be confident of children surviving into adulthood without having ten or twelve of them. Whereas ten or more children had been a common family size during the Old Regime, less than 10 percent of the population now had such large families. By the 1850s German peasants averaged four or fewer children; even textile workers had smaller families (see table 23.10). Families continued to shrink during the nineteenth century. Completed family size for all British marriages of the 1860s included four children; for marriages in the early twentieth century, the average had fallen to two children.

A typical household of nineteenth-century Europe still retained some characteristics of the Old Regime, however. A household still meant all of the people who lived together under a common roof, and that included servants, apprentices, or boarders. A study of Nottingham in midcentury found that more than 20 percent of households contained a lodger, and well-to-do families had an average of two servants. Most of these domestic servants were unmarried women, and such service was the largest source of employment for women during the century. More than 700,000 women worked as servants in mid-Victorian Britain, nearly twice as many as labored in textile industries, or twenty times as many as were engaged in all forms of education. Even middle-class families could afford at least one servant because the wages paid were shockingly low.

A study of Austrian household structure illustrates how nineteenth-century families became smaller, but household size remained large. Viennese census data reveal that a typical master baker and his wife had five children. But their household contained eighteen residents: six journeymen bakers, two shopgirls, and the family's three domestic servants. In another illustration, a widowed textile manufacturer in his sixties lived in a household of nine people: his two sons who had become his partners in their thirties and still lived at home, his five household servants, and his coachman.

Sexual Attitudes and Behavior in the Nineteenth Century

The nineteenth century lingers in popular memory as an age of prudery and puritanical restrictions. To describe a person or an idea as "Victorian" is to connote repressive attitudes about human sexuality commonly associated with the era. This stereotype of Victorianism contains much truth. Respectable women who consulted a physician normally went with a chaperon; they would point out their ailments on a doll rather than touch themselves. Gynecological examinations were performed only in extreme cases, and genteel opinion held that women should endure much pain before submitting to the indignity of a pelvic exam. Prudishness governed polite conversations. The words for bodily functions (sexual or not) were unacceptable, and this ban forbade such outrages to delicate ears as to sweat, which was deemed much too animalistic. Decent people did not refer to legs—a word thought to inflame sexual passions—but to limbs. This taboo included the legs on furniture, and truly respectable families placed a cloth skirt around a piano, lest the sight of its limbs provoke prurient thoughts. This puritanism culminated in Lady Gough's Book of Etiquette, which stated the moral principle that books in a family library must be organized so that those written by men not lay next to those written by women—unless the authors were married.

This image of the nineteenth century contains much truth, but it hides truth as well. The early nineteenth century, when fashionable dress at continental balls permitted the exposure of a woman's breasts, did not correspond to the prudery of later years. Many people believed that foreign countries teemed with a sexuality unknown at home (as the British viewed France), although that may reveal more about their own behavior away from home. The upper classes, including Queen Victoria's family, did not behave by the standards of middle-class Victorianism. Victoria's predecessor on the throne, William IV, lived with a mistress for twenty years and had ten illegitimate children with her; Victoria's husband, Prince Albert, was the child of a broken marriage; and Victoria's heir, the future Edward VII, had a legion of lovers, from a famous actress to a duchess who always curtsied before climbing into the royal bed. Such exceptions to the Victorian stereotype were widespread: Nude bathing at the seashore was commonplace for most of the nineteenth century and the mid-Victorian House of Commons declined to outlaw it in 1857. Somehow bourgeois prudery coexisted with startling exceptions, such as permitting Lewis Carroll to enjoy the hobby of photographing naked young girls, including the Alice for whom Alice in Wonderland was written.

Historians have studied many aspects of human sexuality hidden by the stereotype of Victorianism. Subjects such as the double standard, prostitution, venereal disease, and homosexuality have all drawn the attention of social historians. The double standard behind Victorianism is clear. Sometimes it was a matter of hypocrisy: the governing and opinion-making classes said one thing in public and behaved differently in private. During Napoleon III's Second Empire, for example, the government of France stoutly defended public morality. When Gustave Flaubert published Madame Bovary (1857), which dared to suggest that a respectable married woman might choose to commit adultery, the government immediately indicted Flaubert for outraging public morals. The public agreed so heartily that when Edouard Manet first exhibited "Olympia," destined to become one of the most noted paintings of the century but depicting a nude woman reclining in bed, guards had to be hired to protect it from vigilante moralists. The private morality of the Bonaparte family was somewhat different from their public standard, and they welcomed the friendship of Flaubert. The emperor was as lusty as Edward VII, and his biography is filled with episodes such as the costume ball at which he found one of his mistresses, a teenaged countess who wore a transparent costume.

Another variant of the sexual double standard expected different behavior from men and women. Unmarried women were expected to remain virginal until marriage; unmarried men were assumed to be sexually

◆ DOCUMENT 23.4 ◆

A British Prostitute Describes Her Life (1849)

Henry Mayhew was a journalist in London, well known to his contemporaries as a comic writer; he was one of the founding editors of Punch. *Mayhew is better remembered by scholars today for his serious side, shown in a series of sensitive articles about the daily life of the poor. These articles were collected in several volumes under the title* London Labour and London Poor *(1851–62). The following excerpt is one of Mayhew's most moving. He originally published it in* The Morning Chronicle *in 1849, under the title "Prostitution among Needlewomen."*

She told her tale with her face hidden in her hands, and sobbing so loud that it was difficult to catch her words . . . .

I used to work at "slop work"—at the shirt [handsewing] trade—the fine full-fronted white shirts; I got 2 1/2 pence each for them [approximately 5¢]. . . . By working from five o'clock in the morning to midnight each night I might be able to do seven in the week. That would bring me in 17 1/2 pence for my whole week's labor. Out of this the cotton must be taken, and that came to 2 pence every week, and so left me 15 1/2 pence to pay rent and living and buy candles with. I was single and received some little help from my friends; still it was impossible for me to live. I was forced to go out of a night to make my living. I had a child and it used to cry for food. So, as I could not get a living for him and myself by my needs, I went into the streets and made a living that way. . . .

My father was an independent preacher, and I pledge my word that it was the low price paid for my labor that drove me to prostitution. I often struggled against it, and many times I have taken my child into the streets to beg rather than I would bring shame on myself and it any longer. I have made pin cushions and fancy articles—such as I could manage to scrape together—and taken them into the streets to sell, so that I might get an honest living, but I couldn't. Sometime I should be out all night in the rain, and sell nothing at all, me and my child together. . . . I was so poor I couldn't have even a night's lodging on credit. One night in the depth of winter his legs froze to his side . . . .

[A]t last I left the 'house' [workhouse] to work at umbrella covering. . . . I then made from 3 shillings to 4 shillings a week [36–48 pence, 75¢–$1], and from that time I gave up prostitution. . . . Had I remained at shirt making, I must have been a prostitute to this day.

---

active. Adultery was a serious crime for married women but less so for men. Flaubert probably would not have been arrested had his novel been *Doctor Bovary*, describing the adultery of a prominent man. The respectable double standard even taught that women did not have sexual urges. As late as 1905 an Oxford physician could seriously testify that nine out of ten women disliked sex, and the tenth was invariably a harlot.

Given the double standard of sexual behavior, the late age of marriages, and the desperate economic situation of women from the lower classes, it is not surprising that prostitution thrived during the nineteenth century. Legal and open prostitution was a striking feature of European cities, and some authors have claimed that, in periods of economic distress, prostitution became the largest single form of women's employment. Women (frequently servants) who had been seduced and left with a child had little legal support (they could not even sue to prove paternity in most countries) and usually no economic support. The situation was even worse for rape victims who found many respectable jobs closed to them. Even widows could be driven to consider prostitution by their economic plight. Single factory workers, trying to live on a fraction of a man's wages, faced few alternatives to supplementing their wages through prostitution.

The London police estimated that six thousand full-time prostitutes worked in the city in the 1860s and twenty-five thousand in Britain; reformers claimed that the true number was ten times higher (see document 23.4). The number of prostitutes was much higher if one includes the thousands of working women driven to supplement their wages by part-time prostitution. The data behind such assertions are notoriously variable. The number of women who registered with the Parisian police as legal prostitutes increased from 1,293 in 1812 to 6,827 in 1914, and police records show that 10,000 to 30,000 Parisian women were arrested each year for unregistered prostitution. The police estimated 34,000 prostitutes in Paris in the 1850s, 35,000 to

40,000 at the turn-of-the-century. Similar estimates for Germany range from 100,000 to 330,000 women in 1914. All such numbers must be treated with caution: Some Victorian moralists counted any unmarried woman living with a man as a prostitute.

Britain, France, and Italy all enacted state-regulated prostitution. Most German states permitted municipal brothels, although after 1871 Berlin tried to eliminate them. Governments accepted regulated prostitution because it helped to control venereal diseases in naval bases and army garrisons. Prostitutes were required to have regular medical examinations and receive treatment for VD. Laws such as the British Contagious Diseases Acts of 1864 and 1866 gave the police exceptional powers to arrest any woman who was unescorted in public and to order her to have a medical examination. This abuse of women, combined with the moral opposition to prostitution and the desire to help prostitutes, led to abolitionist campaigns, such as Josephine Butler's, which won the suspension of the Contagious Diseases Acts in 1883 and their repeal in 1886. Women, typically Protestant reformers who linked moral reforms with feminism, launched abolitionist campaigns in many countries, as Avril de Sainte Croix did in France and Emilie de Morsier did in Switzerland.

Governments were right to worry about VD rates. The rate of infection and the death rate for syphilis in the 1890s were both higher than the rates for AIDS in the 1990s (see illustration 23.5). One French study found that the leading cause of death in Europe was tuberculosis (which killed 150,000 per year) but syphilis was a close second (140,000), killing three times as many people as cancer did (40,000). In Britain, where Lord Randolph Churchill demonstrated the universality of VD by slowly dying from syphilis in public, nearly 7,000 people died of VD in 1901—a death rate of 16.4 per 100,000 population (the death rate for AIDS in the United States was 8.6 per 100,000 in 1989). A German medical study of 1900 estimated even higher rates of infection there and asserted that 50 percent of German men had a venereal disease, usually gonorrhea, and 20 percent had syphilis.

European laws to regulate prostitution or to control VD were mild compared with the draconian laws against homosexuality. All sexual acts between men were illegal in most countries, and sexual intercourse between men (usually called buggery or sodomy in the nineteenth century) was often a capital crime. Dutch law allowed the execution of convicted homosexuals in 1800, and twenty-two trials had taken place for the crime in 1798, but imprisonment or banishment was

Illustration 23.5

Venereal Disease. Syphilis was an incurable and often fatal disease throughout the nineteenth century, killing far more Europeans in the 1890s than AIDS killed in the 1990s. There were an estimated 43,000 AIDS deaths in the United States in 1995, compared with 140,000 syphilis deaths in Europe in 1895. European alarm in the 1890s produced the engraving entitled "The Two Faces of Love," which uses striking imagery to warn of sexual dangers.

the usual punishment. There were seventeen convictions for homosexuality at Amsterdam in the decade 1801–10, and none resulted in an execution. Sexual intercourse between men remained a capital crime in Britain until 1861, and one or two men were hanged for it annually in the early nineteenth century. Gay men thus faced extreme dangers from blackmailers, as happened to Lord Castlereagh; the pressure led to his suicide in 1822. Others, such as the notoriously bisexual Lord Byron, fled the country.

The nineteenth-century reforms of sexual statutes typically perpetuated the criminalization of homosexuality but reduced the penalties. The penal code of the German Empire forbade "unnatural vice" between men, but sentences ranged from one day to five years. British law remained more severe. The Criminal Law Amendment Act of 1885 allowed life imprisonment for homosexuality, but it also created the lesser crime of "gross indecency," for which men could be sentenced to two years of hard labor. When that statute was reformed in 1912, it permitted the flogging of homosexuals without a jury trial. These statutes remained in force until 1967. Such statutes did not even mention lesbianism, an unthinkable subject to most Victorian legislators.

The criminalization of homosexuality led to dramatic scandals and trials at the turn of the twentieth century. The most famous trial involved a celebrated Irish writer, Oscar Wilde. Wilde was arrested following an acrimonious and public battle with the marquess of Queensbury (a bully chiefly remembered for formulating the rules of boxing), the father of his lover. Wilde was convicted in 1895 and imprisoned until 1897, an experience that he related in *Ballad of Reading Gaol* (1898). The government could have indicted many other prominent homosexuals—such as the members of the Bloomsbury set (named for a district of London), which included the economist John Maynard Keynes, the biographer Lytton Strachey, and the novelist E. M. Forster—but the government would have been obliged to arrest several of its own members.

A larger scandal over homosexuality occurred in Germany, where the central figures were not intellectuals but the commanders of the German army, members of the imperial government, and close associates of Kaiser Wilhelm II. The policy of the German army was to court-martial homosexuals if they had been publicly identified. That policy led to two dramatic trials in 1903–06, at which several officers were named, including the commander of the royal guard who was a member of the royal family. This led to the public admission that Prince Friedrich Heinrich of Prussia was gay. The German press then began a flamboyant investigation of homosexuality in the army and the government. The press soon focused on the kaiser's closest friend, Prince Philipp zu Eulenburg, an ambassador and a member of the House of Lords. When a police investigation began, the Berlin vice squad quickly identified several hundred prominent aristocrats, officers, and officials as known homosexuals, including General Kuno Count von Moltke, the military commandant of Berlin. The result was another wave of courts-martial in 1907–09. The German public soon received admissions of homosexuality from a long list of public figures, ranging from the director of the state theater to the royal equerry. As the number of homosexuals in royal and military circles became clear, one segment of the German press turned to homophobic attacks, using the affectionate nicknames that lovers revealed at trials. At the peak of this scandal, a prominent general died of a heart attack while dressed in a ballerina's tutu, to the cruel delight of political cartoonists.

The German scandals had tragic results for the individuals involved and dangerous implications for society. Kaiser Wilhelm II blamed the entire experience neither on the criminalization of homosexuality nor on the men who had broken his laws, but on the machinations of "international Jewry." He reached this bizarre and ominous conclusion because the journalist who had exposed Eulenburg was Jewish. It was equally ominous that the scandals, and the homophobic attacks, encouraged aggressive militarism, as a proof of masculinity, in Germany.

CHAPTER 24

THE DEFENSE OF THE OLD REGIME, 1815–48

The coalition that defeated Napoleon in 1812–15 supported monarchy and the institutions of the Old Regime. During the next generation (1815–48), victorious conservatives tried to restore their world. Chapter 24 examines this era, often called the age of Metternich in honor of its leading conservative statesman. It starts with monarchists reasserting the Old Regime at the peace congress of 1815 (the Congress of Vienna). Next the chapter looks at the postwar conservative alliance and its "congress system" designed to preserve that order.

The restoration of the Old Regime was widely resisted. A variety of political movements, from liberal reformism to socialist revolution, challenged the old order. These movements are discussed as are the revolutions that they encouraged, such as the liberal-national revolutions of the 1820s and a wave of revolutions in 1830–32. The chapter goes on to examine the success of the conservative order by exploring the differing conditions of autocratic monarchy in Russia, the victories of liberalism in Britain, and the delicate compromise between monarchism and liberalism reached in France.

The Congress of Vienna and the Restoration of the Old Order

A Quadruple Alliance of Russia, Prussia, Austria, and Britain was needed to defeat Napoleon. Armies of these allies reached Paris in 1814. Napoleon received a generous settlement in return for his unconditional abdication. He kept the title of emperor (with an annual income of two million French francs) and received the Italian island of Elba to govern. Similar leniency characterized the treaty given to France, the Treaty of Paris, which restored the Bourbon monarchy. The eldest brother of Louis XVI thus returned to Paris "in the baggage of the allies." He took the title of Louis XVIII, in

Illustration 24.1

The Congress of Vienna. The peace congress following the defeat of Napoleon was also one of the most glittering assemblies in the history of the European nobility. The statesmen portrayed here redrew the map of Europe in between balls, while other aristocrats celebrated in a party that lasted for months. Prince Metternich, who dominated European affairs for the next generation, is the dandy in tight white breeches standing at left. Lord Castlereagh, whose party life would soon lead him to suicide, is seated at center with legs crossed. Prince Talleyrand sits at right with his arm on the table and his crippled foot hidden.

respect for Louis XVI's son who had died in prison. The allies considered Louis XVIII a member of the counter-revolutionary coalition, so France lost recently annexed territory (such as Belgium) but kept the borders of 1792 without losing older provinces (such as Alsace).

These treaties were secondary issues to the allies, who wanted to reconsider the entire map of Europe and restore the prerevolutionary order. Representatives from hundreds of states assembled in Vienna in 1814 for this peace congress and to celebrate the end of the revolutionary era (see illustration 24.1). The decisions of the Congress of Vienna were made by the four strongest allies. The most influential statesman was the foreign minister of Austria, Prince Klemens von Metternich. He was a native of the Rhineland, and he had been raised in the French language, which he spoke at home; Metternich only entered Austrian service after a French army drove him from his Rhenish estates in 1794. His ideas, however, won the confidence of the emperor of Austria, Francis I; they agreed that revolu-

tionary ideas were "moral gangrene." Francis trusted Metternich to maintain a world with "no innovations" (see document 24.1). Enlightenment was so unwelcome, wrote the poet Heinrich Heine, that he should be remembered as "Prince Mitternacht" (midnight).

The allies shared variants of Metternichian conservatism. Britain was represented by the foreign secretary of a conservative government, Viscount Castlereagh. He was such a forceful spokesman for the aristocratic cause that the poor of London lined the streets to cheer his funeral procession. Prussia was represented by Prince Karl von Hardenberg who earned a reputation for liberalism for Prussian domestic reforms but who defended Prussian interests and international order with tenacity. The czar of Russia, Alexander I, the most complex and intelligent monarch of the age, often chose to represent Russia in negotiations himself. These counts, viscounts, dukes, and princes stated a guiding philosophy for the Congress of Vienna: the principle of legitimacy. Every province in Europe should be returned to

◆ DOCUMENT 24.1 ◆

Metternich: The Conservative's Faith (1820)

Prince Klemens von Metternich (1773–1859) was the Austrian foreign minister for nearly half a century, from 1809 to 1848. He was the most influential statesman in post-Napoleonic Europe, and he shaped the peace treaties of 1815, the postwar alliance system, and the antiliberal domestic policies of the age. The following document, which he sent to the emperors of Austria and Russia in 1820, explains his conservative values and his reasons for his policies.

Kings have to calculate the chances of their very existence in the immediate future; passions are let loose and league together to overthrow everything which society respects as the basis of its existence: religion, public morality, laws, customs, rights, duties are all attacked, confounded, overthrown, or called in question. The great mass of people are tranquil spectators of these attacks and revolutions. . . . It is principally the middle class of society which this moral gangrene has affected, and it is only among them that the real heads of the party [of revolution] are found. . . .

We are convinced that society can no longer be saved without strong and vigorous resolutions on the part of the Governments. . . in establishing the principle of *stability*, [which] will in no wise exclude the development of what is good, for stability is not immobility. . . .

Union between the monarchs is the basis for the policy which must now be followed to save society from total ruin. . . : Respect for all that is; liberty for every Government to watch over the well-being of its own people; a league of all Governments against all factions in all states; contempt for the meaningless words which have become the rallying cry of the factious; . . . refusal on the part of every monarch to aid or succour partisans under any mask whatever. . . .

We are certainly not alone in questioning if society can exist with the liberty of the press. . . . Let the monarchs in these troublous times be more than usually cautious. . . .

Metternich, Klemens von. *Memoirs of Prince Metternich,* 5 vol., trans. Mrs. Alexander Napier. New York: Scribner's, 1880–1882.

its legitimate ruler, and the people of each province should be restored to their place in the legitimate (Old Regime) social order.

In theory, the doctrine of legitimacy meant the recreation of pre-1789 frontiers, monarchies, and social systems—the divinely ordained order. In reality, the decisions made at Vienna stemmed from self-interest (see map 24.1). Compensation was a truer name for the philosophy of the congress, and the four allies each annexed territory without a pretense of legitimacy. Whole regions of Europe—such as Belgium, Genoa, Lombardy, Norway, Poland, and Saxony—became the pawns of the great powers. Russia kept Finland (which it had annexed during the war) and gained most of Poland. The Russian concession to legitimacy was to give "Congress Poland" its own constitution. Prussia annexed half of neighboring Saxony and several small states in the Rhineland. This changed the course of European history because an enlarged Prussia acquired great industrial potential and a presence in western Europe.

Britain and Austria demanded compensation to balance the gains of the Prussians and Russians. This led to

a two-against-two stalemate until the four powers asked a fifth diplomat to join them—Louis XVIII's foreign minister, Prince Charles-Maurice de Talleyrand. Talleyrand had served the Old Regime as a bishop, the French Revolution as a legislator, and Napoleon as a diplomat, so he was comfortable when self-interest was more important than principle. He supported Britain and Austria, so they, too, received compensation. The British took new colonies in Africa, Asia, and the Americas plus strategic islands, such as Malta; they also insisted that a friendly state (but not a great power) control the lowlands from which an invasion of England might be launched. Consequently, the predominantly Protestant, Dutch-speaking Netherlands annexed the Catholic, predominantly French-speaking region of Belgium. The Habsburgs had previously ruled this region (then known as the Austrian Netherlands), so Austria took compensation in northern Italy: Lombardy and the Republic of Venice.

Even after their mutual aggrandizement, the great powers did not follow the principle of legitimacy. They did not resurrect the Holy Roman Empire, which had confederated two hundred German states in central

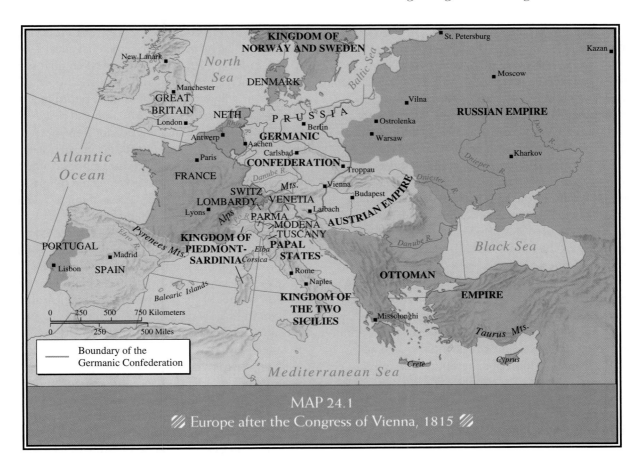

MAP 24.1

🎟 Europe after the Congress of Vienna, 1815 🎟

Europe until Napoleon abolished it in 1806. Instead, the allies restored only thirty-nine German states, linked in a loose German Confederation with a weak Diet at Frankfurt. The dispossessed rulers kept their titles, their personal estates, and good reasons to doubt the meaning of legitimacy. Italians had their own reasons to question the validity of that principle. Lombards and Venetians discovered that they were legitimate Austrians; the Genoese learned that their historic government was not legitimate because it had been a republic; and others, such as the Tuscans, found that their legitimate rulers were members of the Habsburg family.

Napoleon Bonaparte escaped from his lenient exile on Elba in March 1815 and returned to France during these negotiations. Louis XVIII fled and his army defected to Napoleon, but the allies rejected Napoleon's claim to the throne and assembled armies in Belgium under the duke of Wellington, who had defeated Napoleon's armies in Spain. A combination of British and Prussian armies defeated Napoleon outside Brussels at Waterloo, and his reign of one hundred days ended with harsher settlements. Napoleon became a British prisoner of war, and they held him under house arrest on the island of St. Helena until his death in 1821. A

Second Peace of Paris made the French pay for accepting Napoleon's return. France lost more Rhineland territory to Prussia and more of Savoy to the Kingdom of Piedmont-Sardinia, had to pay an indemnity of 700 million francs, and endured the military occupation of northeastern France until it was paid.

The Conservative Alliance and the Congress System

After the difficult negotiations at Vienna and the shock of the Hundred Days, the allies resolved to protect their newly restored order. Alexander I, who was attracted to religious mysticism, proposed a Holy Alliance in which they would pledge to act according to the teachings of the Bible. Most statesmen agreed with Castlereagh that this was "sublime nonsense" (one called it a "holy kiss"), but they promised to act "conformably to the words of the Holy Scriptures." In case that did not work, they also renewed the Quadruple Alliance against French armies and French ideas. Austria, Britain, Prussia, and Russia pledged "to employ all their means to prevent the general tranquility from again being disturbed."

The allies also protected the conservative order by planning regular meetings to discuss international problems. This led to a series of small congresses, also shaped by Metternich, during the next decade. In 1818 a congress met at Aachen to recognize that the French had paid the indemnity and to welcome the government of Louis XVIII into a Quintuple Alliance to maintain the status quo. A more important congress met in 1820 at Troppau, where the three eastern powers (Austria, Prussia, and Russia) adopted the Troppau Protocol, asserting the right of the allies to intervene in smaller countries if the conservative order were threatened. A congress of 1821 used this principle to justify an Austrian invasion of the Italian states to suppress radical rebels. The congress system faced a difficult decision in 1822 when a liberal revolution occurred in Spain. The Troppau Protocol called for armed intervention to crush the revolution, but that meant a French invasion of Spain. The allies decided that they were less afraid of a French army than of a French constitution and accepted the ironic position of cheering French military victories.

Protecting the Old Order: Religion

The conservatism of the post-1815 world is especially clear in the religious revival of that era. After an age in which philosophes satirized churches and the educated classes became skeptics, after a revolution in which churches were closed and their property seized, after an economic revolution that dechristianized many workers, and after a cynical conqueror imprisoned the pope and used religion as an instrument of political policy, many Christians were eager for their own restoration of old values and institutions.

The Vatican was a leader of the new conservatism. Pope Pius VII had slept in French jails during the revolutionary era and now retaliated against French ideas. He restored the Jesuit order, reestablished the Inquisition, and reconstituted the Index of prohibited books. Catholics were forbidden to believe that the Earth rotated around the Sun or to read Gibbon's *The Decline and Fall of the Roman Empire*. In the papal states, Pius annulled Napoleonic laws of religious toleration and reintroduced persecution of the Jews, who were returned to the ghetto and compelled to attend mass once a week. Pius ended freedom of speech and the press, outlawing statements of heresy, radicalism, or immorality. His criminal code permitted torture but outlawed vaccinations and street lighting as radical innovations.

Pope Pius VIII continued this effort to return to the Old Regime. As he explained in the encyclical *Traditi humilitati nostrae* (1829), the church must combat secularizatism in all its forms, including public schools, civil marriage, and divorce. Catholics must return to a religion based upon faith and Christian mysteries. A leading Catholic intellectual, the viscount René de Chateaubriand, had championed this in *The Genius of Christianity* (1802). Christians, Chateaubriand argued, must reject rationalism because it rejected religious mysteries: "It is a pitiful mode of reasoning to reject whatever we cannot comprehend."

Even political liberals embraced religious conservatism in some countries. In Spain, liberals fought an obsessively religious monarch, King Ferdinand VII, who was so devout that he personally embroidered robes for statues of the Virgin Mary in Spanish shrines. Yet Spanish liberals shared his religious beliefs. When they imposed a constitution in 1820, they rejected religious freedom. Article 12 said simply, "The religion of the Spanish nation is, and shall be perpetually, Apostolic Roman Catholic, the only true religion. The nation protects it by wise and just laws and prohibits the exercise of any other religion whatsoever."

A somewhat different conservatism characterized Protestantism. Evangelical churches (especially Pietists in Lutheran countries and Methodists elsewhere) denounced the evils of the modern world and taught obedience to established authority, as did the Vatican. Methodist governing statutes stated: "None of us shall, either in writing or in conversation, speak lightly or irreverently of the government." Prince Metternich could not have said it better. Even hymns could be counterrevolutionary: "The rich man in his castle, The poor man at the gate, God created both of them, And ordered their estate." An evangelical "awakening" swept Britain, the north German states, and Scandinavia and even won converts in such Catholic regions as Belgium, Switzerland, and France. This development was so important that some historians have argued that the spread of Methodism in the British working class was a reason why Britain never experienced a major revolution during industrialization.

Protestants stressed another element in conservatism: Puritanical restrictions upon behavior. Evangelicals insisted upon strict sexual morality, campaigned for the prohibition of alcoholic beverages, and fought blasphemous language. The most famous illustration of the Protestant effort to supervise morals is the work of Dr. Thomas Bowdler and his sister Harriet. The Bowdlers worked so avidly to censor immoral literature that they left their name behind for expurgated (*bowdlerized*) works. They abridged Shakespeare to produce *The Family Shakespeare* in 1818. The bowdlerized Shakespeare eliminated all passages that might "raise a blush on the cheek of modesty," such as Hamlet's famous remarks to Ophelia about sex.

Protecting the Old Order: The Law

Historians often characterize Metternichian government as an effort to curb dissent. Every state in Europe adopted such legislation as a bulwark against revolution. Freedom of the press and freedom of speech were the first targets. Russian restrictions were so severe that writers spoke of a "censorship terror." Two of the greatest figures of Russian literature, Alexander Pushkin and Fyodor Dostoevski, were exiled—Pushkin for writing "Ode to Liberty" and Dostoevski for belonging to a radical organization. In Scandinavia, the tales of Hans Christian Andersen were banned for corrupting the youth; Dante's *The Divine Comedy* was forbidden in Prussia because the title seemed blasphemous to a censor.

Such counterrevolutionary legal restrictions did not stop with obvious political targets; they also had profound effects on individual families. In France, for example, the government sought to rebuild the traditional family. The chief legal expression of this effort was the repeal of the divorce law adopted during the French Revolution. As Louis de Bonald, a philosopher of monarchism, explained: "Just as political democracy allows the people, the weak part of political society, to rise against the established power, so divorce, veritable domestic democracy, allows the wife, the weak part, to rebel against marital authority. In order to keep the state out of the hands of the people, it is necessary to keep the family out of the hands of wives and children." Metternich adopted similarly motivated family legislation in Austria. A Marriage Law of 1820, for example, forbade marriage by beggars, people receiving relief, the unemployed, and migrants; it also required a "marriage permit," without which servants, journeymen, and day laborers could not marry.

The policy of social control made schools another favorite target of conservative governments. Metternich's regulations for schools, announced at Karlsbad in 1819 (see document 24.2), put German universities under the control of a government commissioner, fired liberal professors, and closed student clubs. Francis I liked this policy; as he told a group of teachers in 1821: "I do not need scholars but obedient citizens." The arbitrary arrest and trial of teachers followed. In Prussia the

---

◆ DOCUMENT 24.2 ◆

The Karlsbad Decrees, 1819

Supervision of Universities

1. The sovereign [of each German state] shall choose for each university an extraordinary commissioner. . . . The duty of this commissioner shall be . . . to observe carefully the spirit with which the professors and tutors are guided in their public and private lectures; . . . to give the instruction a salutary direction, suited to the future destiny of the students. . . .

2. The governments of the states . . . reciprocally engage to remove from their universities and other establishments of instruction, professors and other public teachers against whom it may be proved, that . . . in abusing their legitimate influence over the minds of youth . . . they shall have shown themselves incapable of executing the important functions entrusted to them. . . .

3. . . . [L]aws . . . against secret or unauthorized associations at the universities shall be maintained in all their force and vigor.

Press Censorship

1. . . . [N]o writing appearing in the form of a daily paper or periodical pamphlet . . . shall be issued from the press without the previous consent of the public authority.

"Karlsbad Decrees." *The Annual Register* (1819). London: J. Dodsky, 1820.

---

harassment of liberal professors became a police recreation. This regulation of the schools reached its nadir when Friedrich Froebel opened the first kindergarten in 1837. Froebel believed that preschool children could learn through games and activities. The Prussian government, however, deemed this a revolutionary principle that undermined the authoritarian model of education. Kindergartens were outlawed.

German education laws provided a model for other countries. Shortly after the promulgation of the Karlsbad Decrees, Alexander I adopted a similar program. His instructions for the University of Kazan (1820) eliminated free speech and freedom of inquiry: "No harmful or seductive literature or speeches in any form shall be permitted to spread through the university." Alexander, like Francis I, thought that "[t]he soul of

Illustration 24.2

⚹ **The Peterloo Massacre.** Under the provisions of the Six Acts, the British government had the right to close political meetings, by force if necessary. In the most outrageous application of the law, depicted here, British cavalry use sabres to break up a meeting at Manchester in 1819. Note the crowd being attacked: Both men and women are present, and all are dressed very well.

education, and the prime virtue of the citizen, is obedience." His restrictions did not surpass the zeal of the French. In 1816 the government expelled the entire student body of their elite engineering school, the *Ecole polytechnique* (including Auguste Comte, a founder of sociology), for radicalism. Such attitudes also reached England, where one M.P. denounced plans for more schools by arguing that education only taught the masses "to despise their lot in life instead of making them good servants; instead of teaching them subordination, it would render them fractious[,] . . . insolent to their superiors."

The most severe Metternichian restrictions were the political use of the police and judiciary. Modern police forces did not exist in 1815, but the revolutionary era had taught many lessons about policing. Metternich had observed the methods of the French police, such as keeping files on suspects, organizations, or periodicals. He and Count Joseph Sedlnitzky founded one of the first effective police systems, using these bureaucratic techniques. Sedlnitzky merged the police and postal service, so letters could be read before delivery, and used internal passports to limit the movement of people and ideas within the empire.

In Britain, the counterrevolutionary policies of Lord Liverpool's government (1812–27) rivaled those in more despotic states. A Habeus Corpus Suspension Act denounced "a traitorous conspiracy" of radicals and authorized the arrest of "such persons as his majesty shall suspect are conspiring." A Seditious Meetings Act re-

stricted the right of assembly by requiring prior approval for meetings of fifty or more people. A set of repressive laws, collectively called the Six Acts, forbade the publication of anything the government considered seditious, authorized arbitrary searches and seizures, banned many political meetings, and taxed newspapers to make them too expensive for most of the public. The Liverpool government did not hesitate to use the British army against workers, as it did during the Spa Fields (London) Riot of 1816. This policy led to tragedy at Manchester in 1819, when sixty thousand workers assembled in St. Peter's Fields to listen to reform speakers. The Fifteenth Hussars (heroes of the battle of Waterloo) cleared the field with drawn sabers; they killed eleven people, wounded more than four hundred, and provided an ironic name for their heroism: the Peterloo massacre (see illustration 24.2).

British conservatives used the judiciary as effectively as the Austrians used the police. More than two hundred crimes were punishable by death, and these laws were often used for political effects, such as controlling workers. In 1833 the courts taught a lesson to workers by executing a nine-year-old apprentice for stealing two pence (about four cents) worth of ink from his master's shop. British judges more often solved political problems by ordering the transportation of troublesome people to penal colonies in Australia. Irish nationalists and labor militants were especially liable to receive such sentences. One of the first efforts to organize a labor union in Britain resulted in the transportation of six farm workers (the Tolpuddle martyrs) in 1834 for taking a secret oath. The conditions of penal servitude were harsh and included corporal punishment; one Irish nationalist received one hundred lashes for singing a rebel song.

Challenges to the Old Order: The '-isms'

The changes that had shaken Europe in the generation before 1815—the intellectual ferment of the Enlightenment, the political upheaval of the French Revolution, the social transformation of industrialization—had all produced pressures to reform the Old Regime. After 1815 these ideas of change began to crystallize into political doctrines (or ideologies). These new doctrines are known as the "-isms" because they took names ending in *ism*, a linguistic vogue that began with the word *liberalism* (coined in 1820), continued with the terms *nationalism* and *socialism* in the 1830s, and soon included such doctrines as radicalism, capitalism, Marxism, and feminism. These doctrines were sometimes compatible with each other and sometimes in conflict with each other, but they all called for changes in the Metternichian order.

The first of these doctrines, liberalism, was derived from the Latin word *liber* (free) to denote a doctrine about individual freedom. Early nineteenth-century liberalism (sometimes called classical liberalism to distinguish it from later liberalism) sought individual freedoms (such as freedom of speech), laws extending such liberty to more individuals (such as minorities), and the removal of impediments to liberty (such as laws favoring members of an established national church). To achieve such aims, liberals commonly demanded two fundamental documents: (1) a constitution establishing a representative government and specifying its powers, and (2) a bill of rights guaranteeing individual liberties. Few countries possessed such constitutions or bills of rights, and most monarchs opposed them. Liberals, therefore, were among the primary opponents of the Metternichian restoration.

A second ideology—nationalism—created additional problems for conservatives. This doctrine shifted discussion toward the collective rights of a nation. Nationalists asserted that it was possible to identify distinct nations, based upon shared characteristics such as language (see map 24.2). This nationalism is illustrated by a German song, Ernst Arndt's *Where Is the German's Fatherland?*: "Where is the German's Fatherland? Name me

at length that mighty land! 'Where'er resounds the German tongue, Where'er its hymns to God are sung.'" Other nationalists defined their nation by a shared culture, history, or religion. All advocated the creation of nation-states independent from foreign rule, uniting members of the nation in a single, self-governing state. Nationalists considered these objectives more important than the political rights that liberals sought. As a Rumanian nationalist said in the 1840s, "The question of nationality is more important than liberty. Until a people can exist as a nation, it cannot make use of liberty." One could be both a liberal and nationalist, seeking a nation-state that granted liberty, as Giuseppe Mazzini did in his movement called Young Italy (see document 24.3), but the two objectives often conflicted with each other.

Governments especially dreaded radicalism, the term they usually applied to democratic movements. Radicals endorsed liberalism but demanded more; whereas liberals were willing to accept a limited franchise, radicals called for a democratic franchise and sometimes for the abolition of monarchy. In the words of Mazzini, radicals "no longer believed in the sanctity of royal races, no longer believed in aristocracy, no longer believed in privilege." Radical movements, such as the Decembrists in Russia and the Chartists in Britain, however, made conservatives think of Robespierre and the guillotine.

The term *socialism* was also coined in the 1830s to identify doctrines stressing social and economic equality. Marxist socialism did not become a significant political philosophy until after midcentury, but many forms of pre-Marxist socialism existed. The earliest, known as utopian socialism, grew from critiques of industrial society. Robert Owen, the son of a poor Welsh artisan, made a fortune as a textile manufacturer and devoted his wealth to improving industrial conditions. He branded the factory system "outright slavery" and called for a new social order based on cooperation instead of competition. Owen applied his ideas to his own factories at New Lanark, Scotland, where he limited his profits and invested in building a comfortable life for his workers (see illustration 24.3). This won Owen an international reputation, but neither industrialists nor governments copied his ideas. Utopian socialism took different forms in France. The founder of French socialism, Count Henri de Saint-Simon, reversed the pattern of Owen's life: He was born to the nobility, squandered his fortune, and died in poverty. He was a hero of the American Revolution, a prisoner of the French Revolution, and a critic of the industrial revolution. He denounced all

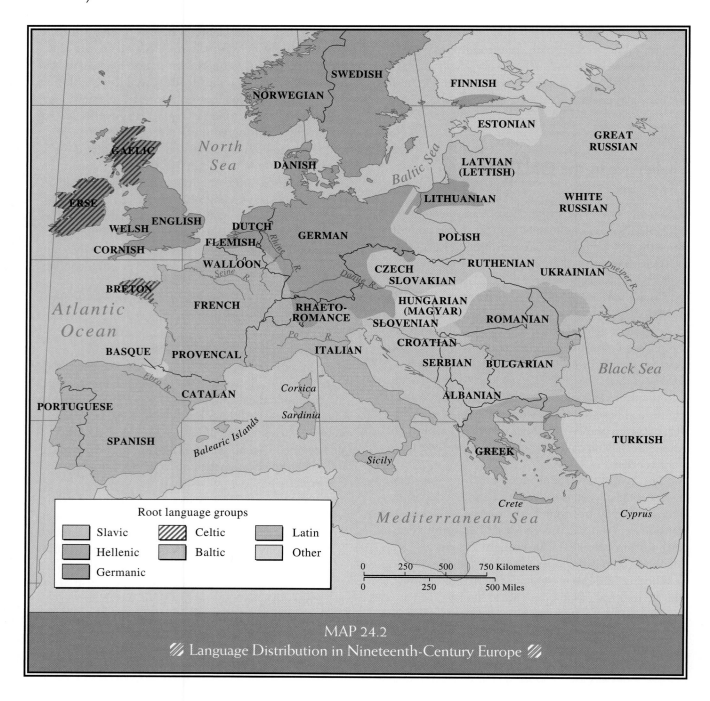

MAP 24.2

Language Distribution in Nineteenth-Century Europe

economies in which "man has exploited man" and called for a new order based upon the principle "from each according to his capacity, to each according to his productivity."

Charles Fourier proposed utopian communities, which he called phalansteries. Fourier envisioned an idealistic, but highly structured, society whose members shared labor and freedom. Other pioneers called for a cooperative socialism of workers, a Christian socialism based upon Jesus's devotion to the poor, or a democratic socialism, on the theory that the poor would have a majority in a true democracy and create a socialist society. The champion of democratic socialism was a French journalist, Louis Blanc, who developed the idea of a strong socialist state that regulated the economy and provided work for the unemployed in national workshops.

A final doctrine of social change, feminism, had not yet acquired that name (a late nineteenth-century coinage) but already called for reconsideration of the

◆ DOCUMENT 24.3 ◆

Mazzini: Instructions for Young Italy, 1831

Guiseppe Mazzini (1805–72) was one of the founders of Italian nationalism and the modern state of Italy. He greatly influenced nationalist thinking in many countries. Mazzini created a secret society, Young Italy, dedicated to the unification of all Italian states under a self-governing republic. His manifesto for Young Italy, from which the following excerpt is taken, was widely emulated.

Young Italy is a brotherhood of Italians who believe in a law of Progress and Duty, and are convinced that Italy is destined to become one nation. . . .

By Italy we understand —(1) Continental and peninsular Italy, bounded on the north by the Alps . . . and on the east by Trieste; (2) The islands proved Italian by the language of the inhabitants, and destined . . . to form a part of the Italian political unity.

Young Italy is Republican and Unitarian.

Republican because theoretically every nation is destined, by the Law of God and humanity, to form a free and equal community as brothers; and the republic is the only form of government that ensures this future. . . . Because our Italian tradition is essentially republican; our great memories are republican; the whole history of our national progress is republican; whereas the introduction of monarchy amongst us was coeval with our decay and consummated our ruin. . . .

Young Italy is Unitarian because without unity there is no true nation.

The means by which Young Italy proposes to reach its aim are education and insurrection, to be adopted simultaneously, and made to harmonize with each other.

Mazzini, Giuseppe. *Life and Writings.* London: Smith, Elder, 1880.

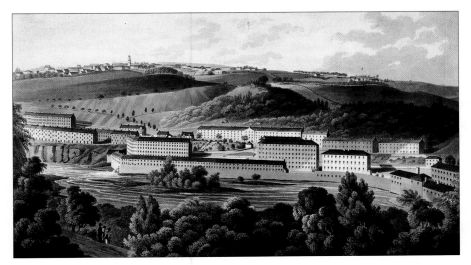

Illustration 24.3

▨ **Utopian Socialism at New Lanark.** The most successful of the utopian idealists was Robert Owen (1771–1858), an exceptionally able man who went to work in the cotton mills at age ten, was the manager of a mill by age nineteen, and was wealthy enough to buy the mills at New Lanark, Scotland, at twenty-nine. Owen devoted his wealth to creating the model community at New Lanark shown here. It provided unmatched working conditions and housing for workers, a nursery and school for their children, evening education for workers, and a cooperative store.

role of women in European society. Pioneers such as Mary Wollstonecraft and Olympe de Gouges had opened discussion of the woman question so effectively that the Metternichian reaction could not contain this debate. European legal systems, especially the Napoleonic Code, but also the British common law tradition and the Germanic Frederician Code, explicitly held women in an inferior position. The rights of women were exercised for them by men (their fathers, then their husbands). Women were expected to remain confined to limited spheres of activity—*Kinder, Kirche, Küche* (children, church, cooking) in a famous German cliché. Formal education (especially higher education) and educated occupations were closed to them. The legal condition of women within marriage and the family began with an obligation to obey their husbands, who legally controlled their wives' wages, children, and bodies. Divorce was illegal in many countries and rare everywhere (it required an act of parliament in Britain).

Illustration 24.4

Romanticism in Painting. This painting of the ruins of a medieval monastery in northern Germany expresses several of the themes of romanticism. The power of nature is vividly depicted (and felt?) in the stark force of winter and the weathering of the ruins. The viewer's focus is drawn, however, to the misty gothic architecture (pointed arches and portals typified late gothic churches) of a lost and moving past, which is presented with a strong dose of sentimentality.

Romanticism: European Culture in the Age of Metternich

The standards of neoclassical culture that had characterized the Old Regime did not survive into the postrevolutionary era. Even before the French Revolution, classicism had come under attack for its strict rules, formal styles, and stress upon reason. When the Congress of Vienna assembled in 1815, European high culture had become quite different. The new style, known as romanticism, reached its apogee in the age of Metternich and continued to be a force in European culture past midcentury.

Romanticism is difficult to define because it was a reaction against precise definitions and rules, and that reaction took many forms. The foremost characteristic of romanticism was the exaltation of personal feelings, emotions, or the spirit, in contrast to cold reason. The emphasis upon feelings led in many directions, from the passions of romantic love to the spirituality of religious revival. Other attitudes also characterized romanticism: a return to nature for themes and inspiration, the admiration of the Middle Ages instead of classical Greece and Rome, a fascination with the exotic and the supernatural, and the canonization of the hero or genius.

The emphasis upon feelings had begun in the late eighteenth century. Rousseau, one of the central figures of Enlightenment rationalism, was a transitional figure, a precursor of romanticism who argued, "To exist is to feel!" The greatest German poet, Johann von Goethe,

similarly bridged the change from the classical to the romantic. His short novel, *The Sorrows of Young Werther,* depicted feelings so strong that the protagonist's suicide began a vogue for melancholy young men killing themselves as Werther had, with moonlight falling across the last page of Goethe's book. The name of the school of German literature that evolved around Goethe, the *Sturm und Drang* ("storm and stress") movement, suggests the intensity of this emphasis upon feelings. Romanticism was the triumph of that emphasis. At the peak of romanticism, the British poet William Wordsworth simply defined poetry as "the spontaneous overflow of powerful feelings," and the landscape painter John Constable similarly insisted that "[p]ainting is another word for feeling."

The return to nature inspired much romantic poetry, especially Wordsworth's. It produced two generations of landscape painters, such as Constable and J. M. W. Turner, who found inspiration in natural scenery. This mood even extended to symphonic music, inspiring Beethoven's Sixth Symphony, known as the Pastoral Symphony. The romantic fascination with medieval Europe likewise had far-reaching influence. The most visible expression of it was a Gothic revival in architecture (see illustration 24.4). This produced both new construction in the flamboyant Gothic style of the late Middle Ages (such as the new Palace of Westminster, home of the British Houses of Parliament, built in 1836) and campaigns to preserve surviving Gothic masterpieces (such as Viollet-le-Duc's restoration of Notre Dame Cathedral in Paris). The same inspiration stimulated historical literature such as Hugo's *The Hunchback of*

Notre Dame, Sir Walter Scott's *Ivanhoe,* and Alexandre Dumas's *The Three Musketeers;* its most lasting effect on Western literature, however, was probably the invention of the Gothic horror story, a style made famous by Mary Shelley's *Frankenstein.*

Many of these themes made romanticism compatible with conservative political philosophy. The focus upon nature turned high culture toward the rural world, home of aristocratic power and the bastion of conservative sentiments. The focus upon the Middle Ages restored cultural emphasis upon a world of unchallenged monarchy and universal Christianity, instead of the republicanism, constitutionalism, and liberalism. The dethronement of rationalism and the recovery of emotion encouraged the revival of religions of faith, mystery, and miracle.

But another side of romanticism found a powerful voice in the liberal and national revolutions of the early nineteenth century. The revolutionary sympathies of some romantics can be seen in Eugène Delacroix's painting "Liberty at the Barricades"; the radical poems of Percy Bysshe Shelley; the angry novels of Victor Hugo, such as *Les Misérables;* and even Giuseppe Verdi's powerful opera *Rigoletto* (which depicts the scandalous behavior of a monarch). The link between romanticism and nationalism was especially strong because many nationalists built their philosophy upon the nation's shared culture. Many peoples found identity in folk tales, and their compilation (such as the work of the brothers Grimm in Germany) became a form of romantic nationalism. So did the recovery of the history of national minorities (as distinct from the history of their foreign government), as František Palacký did for the Czechs in his multivolume *History of Bohemia.* The strongest expression of romantic nationalism, however, was in music. All across Europe, nationalist composers drew inspiration from patriotic themes and folk music: Frédéric Chopin's *Polonaises* (Polish pieces), Bedrich Smetana's tone poems about Czech scenes (*Ma Vlast—My Country*), or Franz Liszt's *Hungarian Rhapsodies.*

Challenging the Old Order: Revolutions, 1815–25

Despite their precautions, the conservative forces in power after 1815 could not prevent revolutions. More than a dozen revolutions, from Portugal to Russia, took place in the decade following the Congress of Vienna, plus historic rebellions in the British and Spanish empires. Historians normally describe these upheavals as liberal-national revolutions because most rebellions sought national independence (in Serbia, Ireland, Greece, and Spanish America) or constitutional government (in Spain) or both (several Italian states).

Conservatives believed that these revolutions were nurtured and led by radical secret societies and used this to justify restricting civil rights. Such societies did exist, the most famous being an Italian society known as the Carbonari ("the charcoal burners"). Carbonari swore an oath to fight despotism and seek governments based on popular sovereignty, to oppose clericalism and seek secular institutions, and to challenge the foreign domination of the Italian states; in 1820 the Neapolitan chapter claimed 100,000 members. Similar societies existed in most countries—in the circles of Greek businessmen (the *Hetaires*), in Polish universities (Adam Mickiewicz founded his nationalist society at the University of Vilna in 1817), in the officer corps of the Russian army (the Society of the South in Ukraine and the Society of the North at St. Petersburg), in Masonic lodges in Spain, and among Napoleonic war veterans attending German universities who founded the *Burschenschaften.*

With or without the encouragement of such societies, political uprisings were frequent occurrences in the age of Metternich. While the Congress of Vienna met, a Serbian uprising against Ottoman Turkish rule began, the first in a series of Balkan revolts against the government in Constantinople. In 1816 Britain faced a slave rebellion in the Caribbean. A year later, a Carbonari-led liberal revolution was suppressed in the papal states. These uprisings provoked the conservative powers to adopt the Troppau Protocol in 1818, but barely two years later came the successful Spanish revolution (stimulated by King Ferdinand VII's abolition of the constitution of 1812 and by the impact of wars of independence in Spanish America), which was a nagging problem for the congress system in 1820–23. In 1820 revolutions also broke out in Portugal and Naples (both seeking constitutions), then at Palermo, in Sicily. Congresses of 1821 and 1822 sent Austrian armies to fight liberals in Italy, and French troops into Spain. By 1823 the conservative alliance had defeated the Spanish and Italians, treating the defeated rebels with savage cruelty; in Italy, captured rebels had their right hands cut off before being sent to Austrian dungeons. The British opposed the application of the Troppau Protocol elsewhere. The British navy supported the Monroe Doctrine (proclaimed by the United States to block allied intervention in America), so most of Latin America won its independence from Spain. As the British foreign secretary bragged to Parliament, "I have called the New World into existence to redress the balance of the old."

Illustration 24.5

🌊 **The Greek Revolution.** The Greek revolution of 1821–30 (or the Greek War of Independence) was one of the most successful nationalist uprisings of the Metternichian era, in part because philhellenism swept the educated classes in western countries, encouraging governments to support the Greeks. One moment of the Greek revolution became especially well-known in western Europe: the Turkish siege and assault on the Greek fortress of Missolonghi, which guarded the mouth of the Gulf of Corinth. Lord Byron, the noted English romantic poet, was devoted to the Greek cause and died at Missolonghi in 1824. Eugène Delacroix devoted one of the most famous paintings of Romanticism to the battle, "Greece in the Ruins of Missolonghi," shown here, in 1826.

The conservative alliance broke apart over the revolutions in the Balkans, where the Ottoman Empire was slowly disintegrating. Revolutions broke out in Serbia, Greece, and the Rumanian provinces of Moldavia and Wallachia (on the border of Russia), but it was the Greek revolution of 1821–27 that broke the Metternichian alliance (see illustration 24.5). After the Serbs won autonomy in their revolution, a Greek congress at

Epidaurus declared independence in 1822. According to the principles of the Troppau Protocol, the great powers should have supported the legitimate Turkish government. Metternich was almost alone in favoring that policy. Romantic philhellenism stimulated a pro-Greek policy in Britain and France, and for once governments agreed with the radical Shelley who wrote: "We are all Greeks. Our laws, our literature, our religion, our arts, have their roots in Greece." Russian policy was less sophisticated but more adamant: The Ottoman Empire deserved no help from the Holy Alliance because it was not a Christian state.

The Greeks won their independence in a long, brutal war that still echoes in Graeco-Turkish enmity. Greek Orthodox clergymen proclaimed a "war of extermination" against Islamic infidels, leading to the killing of twenty-five thousand civilians within six weeks; the sultan proclaimed an Islamic Holy War that produced forty thousand civilian corpses. Along the way, the patriarch of the Orthodox Church was hanged and his body thrown into the Bosphorus. This killing did not end until Britain, France, and Russia broke with Metternich and intervened in 1827. The counterrevolutionary alliance collapsed (there were no full congresses after 1822) because self-interest had prevailed over doctrine; ironically, the most conservative state in Europe had caused this.

Autocracy in Romanov Russia

The czar of Russia held enormous power in Metternichian Europe. No monarch had contributed more to the defeat of Napoleon Bonaparte: Napoleon's Grand Armée had perished in Russia in 1812, and Russian troops had occupied Paris in 1814. The czar's support had sustained the congress system, and his defection during the Greek revolution had destroyed it.

Russian internal affairs were less simple. The enigmatic Alexander I had come to the throne in 1801 at the age of twenty-four, after the assassination of his father, in which Alexander may have been involved. He was a tall and handsome youth who favored skin-tight uniforms; he had become overweight by 1815, but his vanity and his robust sexuality (which ranged from his sister to religious mystics) put him in corsets instead of loose-fitting clothes. This same Alexander was considered the most intelligent monarch of the age by both Thomas Jefferson and Napoleon Bonaparte (excepting himself). Alexander held more absolute power than anyone else in Europe and with it came the opportunity to propel Russia into the modern age by timely reforms (such as the abolition of serfdom) or to become the champion of the Old Regime. Alexander considered both.

Many historians describe Alexander I as the hope of Russian liberalism. He received a liberal education from his tutor, and he began his reign closely associated with a liberal adviser, Michael Speranski. Speranski was the son of a priest; his brilliance at school earned him a government job and caught the interest of the czar. He was a good administrator, well organized and able to write clear prose, who mixed liberal sentiments with bureaucratic caution. Speranski swayed Alexander to consider reforms. He founded four new universities (doubling the total in the empire), at Kazan, Kharkov, Warsaw, and St. Petersburg. He gave the Poles a constitution and allowed them to reopen their parliament (the *Sejm*). This led to a constitution for Finland and to discussions about a Russian constitution with Speranski. Alexander also restrained the persecution of minority religions and proclaimed religious toleration. Most important, he abolished serfdom in his Baltic provinces between 1816 and 1819 while hinting that this was a pilot project for the emancipation of all Russian serfs.

Alexander I remained, however, an autocrat unchecked by a constitution, an independent judiciary, or a parliament. He was a monarch closer to eighteenth-century enlighted despotism than to nineteenth-century liberalism, presiding over the most feudal economy in the world. He held conquered peoples against their will, no matter how generously he treated them. In his later years, Alexander preferred reactionary advisers. He yielded to their contempt for Speranski and banished his friend to Siberia (although he later made him governor-general of that province). In his place, Alexander entrusted Russian domestic policy to a leading reactionary, Alexis Arakcheyev. Arakcheyev was a cruel and arrogant man unlikely to abolish serfdom; he once ordered a young serf flogged to death because she did a poor job at her sweeping. Alexander also capitulated to religious conservatives and abandoned the policy of toleration, which they considered "a sin against the Holy Ghost." Religious repression resumed in 1821.

Alexander's death in 1825 precipitated a crisis in Russia. He had no children who could inherit the throne, so it should have passed to his eldest brother, Constantine, the governor-general of Poland; but Constantine had renounced his right to the throne in 1822. This brought to the throne Alexander's youngest brother, Nicholas, whose training (by a sadistic military

tutor) had been for military command, not for government. The accession of Nicholas I in December 1825 precipitated a rebellion led by liberal army officers. These Decembrists wanted to abolish the monarchy, write a constitution, and free the serfs, but their poorly organized revolt was quickly crushed. Nicholas found that many of the Decembrists were nobles who had been his friends (including two princes and a major general), but he responded harshly nonetheless. Five were hanged and 121 others were sentenced to hard labor in Siberia. The episode left the czar bitter and even less tolerant of liberalism.

Restrictive legislation was severely tightened under Nicholas I. He created a new branch of the government, the Third Section, to centralize the police. The head of the Third Section, General Alexander Benckendorff, vigorously enforced a Censorship Law forbidding all publications not "useful or at least harmless." The law even banned works considered "full of grammatical errors." Nicholas I relied upon the Ministry of Education to control minorities; the educational system became an instrument for the "russification" of minorities and the submission of everyone to the authority of the church and the state. This policy was summarized in a famous slogan: "Autocracy! Orthodoxy! Nationality!"

Historians sometimes contrast the repressive regime of Nicholas I with the liberal flirtations of Alexander I. More than seven hundred peasant uprisings occurred during his reign, and Nicholas repressed them with the same anger that he had shown the Decembrists. His eagerness to use the Russian army earned him the nickname "the gendarme of Europe." But contrasts are never as simple as they seem. Just as Alexander had shown an attachment to autocracy by entrusting the government to Arakcheyev, Nicholas I showed at least a mild interest in reform by recalling Speranski from Siberia and allowing him to finish his codification of Russian law.

The Liberal-Monarchical Compromise in France

The Bourbon Restoration of 1814–15 required a delicate compromise between Metternichian conservatism and deeply rooted French liberalism. Allied armies could put Louis XVIII on the throne, but the Bourbons could lose it again if Napoleon were correct when he jibed that they "had learned nothing and forgotten nothing" during the revolutionary era. The Bourbon compromise rested upon Louis's acceptance of a constitution and parliament. Louis insisted that his "constitutional charter" was a royal gift to the nation (not their natural right) and that the Bourbons still had a divine right to the throne; in return, the charter also included the liberal principles of equality before the law, freedom of religion, and freedom of the press (see document 24.4). This constitution created a Chamber of Deputies, elected by eighty-eight thousand well-to-do men (0.3 percent of the population), of whom fifteen thousand (0.06 percent) were eligible to be candidates. This contrasted with the French republic of 1792 with its universal manhood suffrage and Britain where 2.5 percent of adult men voted in 1815. The most democratic states in Europe were Norway and Sweden, where 10 percent voted, yet France remained decidedly more liberal than Austria, Prussia, Russia, or Spain, where there were no parliaments.

Reactionary nobles hated this compromise and favored a Metternichian, or even Russian government. These ultraroyalists (or "ultras") were led by Louis XVIII's younger brother, the count of Artois. The ultras had returned to France from twenty years in exile, determined to revive the Old Regime. They relied upon Louis's having no surviving sons, so Artois would inherit the throne (see genealogy 24.1). This prompted Louis to remark presciently that the fate of the Bourbon Restoration depended upon his outliving his brother. The French compromise seemed vulnerable during the first year of the Bourbon Restoration. Revenge against the supporters of previous regimes saw prominent supporters of Napoleon executed, peerages revoked, officers court-martialed, and government employees fired. The worst outrage was a vigilante bloodbath, known as "the white terror," directed against republicans and Protestants. More than two hundred people were killed in the white terror in the south of France. Louis XVIII, however, prevented the ultras from gaining control of the government and from returning to former owners the lands taken during the French Revolution. The successful peasant and middle-class proprietors who had purchased this "national property" received constitutional guarantees that their land was inviolable. Louis preserved his moderate compromise until 1820, when the son of Artois (and the heir to the throne) was assassinated. The king—tired, obese, sixty-five, and suffering from a bad case of the gout—then capitulated to many of the ultras' demands. French censorship became so strict that authors could be imprisoned if their books "cast disfavor" on the government; the police received the power to make arrests based solely upon suspicion;

❖ DOCUMENT 24.4 ❖

A Compromise Constitution: The French Charter of 1814

Louis, by the grace of God, King of France. . . .

Divine Providence, in recalling us to our estates after a long absence, has laid upon us great obligations. . . . A constitutional charter was called for by the actual conditions of the kingdom; we promised it . . . although all authority in France resides in the person of the king. . . .

Public Law of the French

1. Frenchmen are equal before the law, whatever may be their titles. . . .

2. They contribute without distinction, in proportion to their fortunes, towards the expenses of the state.

3. They are all equally admissible to civil and military employments.

4. Their personal liberty is likewise guaranteed. . . .

5. Every one may profess his religion with equal freedom, and shall obtain for his worship the same protection.

6. Nevertheless, the Catholic, Apostolic, and Roman religion is the religion of the state. . . .

8. Frenchmen have the right to publish and to have printed their opinions, while conforming with the laws which are necessary to restrain abuses of that liberty.

9. All property is inviolable. . . .

Form of the Government of the King

13. The person of the King is inviolable and sacred. His ministers are responsible [to him]. To the King alone belongs the executive power.

14. The King is the supreme head of the state, commands the land and sea forces, declares war, makes treaties.

Anderson, Frank M., ed. *The Constitutions and Other Select Documents Illustrative of the History of France, 1789–1907.* Minneapolis: 1908.

---

and the Sorbonne was placed under the control of a bishop and liberal professors were fired. The electorate for the Chamber of Deputies was sharply reduced, while the rich were given a second vote.

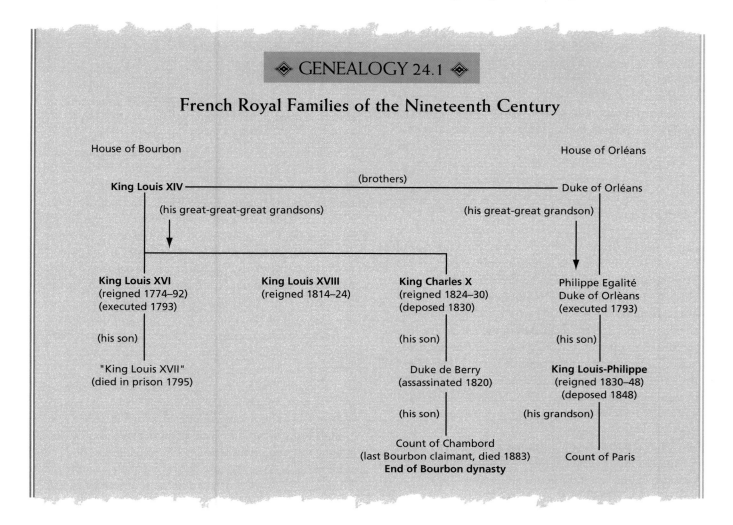

◈ GENEALOGY 24.1 ◈

French Royal Families of the Nineteenth Century

House of Bourbon   House of Orléans

(brothers)

King Louis XIV ———————————————— Duke of Orléans

(his great-great-great grandsons)   (his great-great grandson)

King Louis XVI
(reigned 1774–92)
(executed 1793)

King Louis XVIII
(reigned 1814–24)

King Charles X
(reigned 1824–30)
(deposed 1830)

Philippe Egalité
Duke of Orlèans
(executed 1793)

(his son)   (his son)   (his son)

"King Louis XVII"
(died in prison 1795)

Duke de Berry
(assassinated 1820)

King Louis-Philippe
(reigned 1830–48)
(deposed 1848)

(his son)   (his grandson)

Count of Chambord
(last Bourbon claimant, died 1883)
End of Bourbon dynasty

Count of Paris

The breakdown of Louis XVIII's compromise worsened in 1824, when Artois came to the throne as King Charles X. Historians have characterized Charles as a blind reactionary, an image that contemporary cartoonists fostered by drawing the king with his crown covering his eyes. Charles earned this image when he named the leading ultra, Count Jean-Baptiste Villèle, premier. Villèle's government adopted a Law of Indemnity (1825) to repay aristocrats who had lost land during the revolution and a Law of Sacrilege, making irreligion a capital crime.

Such extreme conservatism ended middle-class, liberal acceptance of the compromise and precipitated a revolution in 1830 that drove Charles X from the throne. When Charles tried to keep ultras as his ministers without the support of the Chamber of Deputies, elections in May 1830 showed that even rich voters opposed him. Then Charles responded in July 1830 with strict decrees known as the July Ordinances, tightening

censorship further, dissolving the chamber again, and reducing electoral eligibility once more. The July Ordinances provoked a vehement reaction in the Parisian press. Adolphe Thiers, the editor of a liberal newspaper and a future president of France, drafted a protest stating, "The government has violated legality and we are absolved from obedience." The Chamber agreed that the king had violated the constitution, but newspapermen and politicians did not overthrow the king. Their anger became a revolution when radical insurgents took to the streets of Paris. After a few incidents of rioting (such as breaking windows in government buildings), crowds built barricades across the streets in working-class districts. Charles X, who had learned a lesson from the execution of his eldest brother, fled into exile.

The revolution of 1830 ended the rule of the Bourbon dynasty and removed the ultras from power, but France remained a monarchy. The liberal opponents of Charles X agreed upon his cousin, Louis-Philippe, the duke of Orleans, as a new king. Louis-Philippe possessed moderate liberal credentials. He had initially supported the French Revolution and served in its armies, then fled France during the Reign of Terror. His father had even served in the Convention and voted for the execution of Louis XVI. Louis-Philippe had courted the liberal opposition during the restoration and convinced many of them that he represented "the republic in a single individual."

The Orleanist Monarchy, also called the July Monarchy (1830–48), began with a liberalized constitution but few dramatic changes. Louis-Philippe expanded voting rights from 90,000 to 170,000 (0.5 percent of the nation). He relaxed censorship but still tried to control the press. He brought new social strata into the government, but that chiefly meant that an elite of wealth was joined to that of the aristocracy. Louis-Philippe did select many of his chief ministers, such as Thiers and the historian François Guizot from middle-class liberals, but they were cautious men who feared democracy. Guizot became the chief architect of the Orleanist version of the French compromise, and he achieved greater success than Louis XVIII in creating a liberal constitutional monarchy comparable to the government in Britain.

The July Monarchy became so reknowned for supporting banking, business, and industrial interests that it was also called "the Bourgeois Monarchy." One of France's keenest political observers during the 1840s, Alexis de Tocqueville, saw this at once: "Posterity will perhaps never know to what degree the government of this time is a capitalist enterprise in which all action is taken for the purpose of profit."

Orleanist sympathies for business and industry had two important consequences. France experienced an important era of banking growth, railroad building, and industrial expansion after 1830, and the new regime deserves credit for its role in French industrialization and modernization. Simultaneously, however, the workers, shopkeepers, and students who had formed the crowds that drove Charles X into exile realized that the revolution of 1830 had made little difference in their existence. So France experienced further upheavals. In 1834, Louis-Philippe needed a tenth of his army to control a silk weavers' strike in Lyon. In 1835 an embittered radical built an "infernal machine" of twenty-five rifles in an iron rack and fired them with a single trigger. He killed eighteen people in a royal procession but only bruised the king. While France remained prosperous, such assaults remained isolated events; in the mid-1840s, however, a severe depression led to yet another French revolution.

The Revolutions of 1830

Metternich once observed that when Paris caught a cold, Europe sneezed. In 1830 that meant revolutions across Europe (see chronology 24.1). The sneezing began in August 1830 with unrest in the Belgian provinces of the Kingdom of the Netherlands. The French-speaking, Catholic population of Belgium was larger than the Dutch-speaking, predominantly Calvinist population of Holland. The king was Dutch, the capital was Amsterdam, officeholders were chiefly Dutch, and national institutions predominantly Dutch. As a Belgian nationalist asked in the summer of 1830, "By what right do two million Dutchmen command four million Belgians?" The Belgian revolution of 1830 followed the French pattern: An insurrection of workers forced the issue, but the educated elite seized control of the situation. A national congress proclaimed Belgian independence in October 1830, but reluctant, middle-class Belgians supported the revolution only after the Dutch army bombarded Antwerp.

Though Louis-Philippe gave the Belgians military assistance, they won their independence at the negotiating table. The British sympathized with Belgian nationalism but feared French influence. When the Belgians accepted a German prince (an uncle of Queen Victoria) as their ruler instead of a French king, British support assured Belgian independence. Belgium adopted a liberal constitution, more advanced than either the British or French constitutions, in 1831. It guaranteed freedom of the press and freedom of religion, then promised many other "inviolable" individual liberties (such as the right of association in unions), and it promoted secularization by establishing civil marriage.

Insurrection spread across Europe from France and Belgium. German antitax and food riots in 1830 revealed dissatisfaction with Metternichian Germany, but they produced no major revolution. A few smaller states, notably Saxony (1831), Brunswick (1832), and Hanover (1833), granted constitutions. Metternich considered granting a constitution in Austria, but the emperor Francis I insisted that he would tolerate "no innovation," so Metternich used the Germanic Confederation to stop the revolutions and to impose a new series of repressive laws, known as the Six Articles.

The revolution of 1830 reached Poland a few weeks after crossing the Rhine. The Polish November Rising did not seek a constitution (which already existed), but an end to Russian rule. It began with a Polish army mutiny provoked when the czar prepared to send

◈ CHRONOLOGY 24.1 ◈

The Revolutions of 1830

Dates	Country	Events	Results
July 1830–August 1830	France	Paris rebels over "July Ordinances," 1830; King Charles X abdicates	Revised constitution, 1830; King Louis-Philippe, 1830
August 1830–December 1832	Belgium	Brussels rebels against Dutch rule, 1830; Belgian declaration of independence, 1830; Belgian constitution, 1831	Dutch army shells Antwerp, French army expels Dutch army from Belgium, 1832; London Conferences recognize Belgium, 1830–32
September 1830–June 1832	German states	Rulers dethroned, 1830; constitutions granted, 1831	Metternichian "Six Articles" restore old order, 1832
November 1830–February 1832	Poland	Revolt versus Russia, 1830; *Sejm* declares Polish independence, 1831	Russian army suppresses revolt, 1831; Polish constitution abolished, 1832
February 1831–January 1832	Italian states	Administrative concessions by pope	Austrian army suppresses revolt, 1831–33
1831	Switzerland	Demonstrations in Swiss cities, 1831	Ten cantons adopt liberal constitutions, 1831–33

units to crush the French and Belgian revolutions. The *Sejm* declared Polish independence in January 1831. Nicholas decided that "the Poles must be made happy in spite of themselves" and sent a Russian army of 115,000 to teach them happiness. After the defeat of the Polish army at Ostrolenka and the fall of Warsaw, Poland was reunited with Russia. Nicholas I then exacerbated Polish nationalism with his retribution: Military tribunals convicted eighty thousand Poles of rebellion and the army marched them to Siberia in chains; a program of Russification ended all official use of the Polish language and closed the universities at Warsaw and Vilna; the Polish army, the Polish constitution, and the Polish Diet were all abolished.

Historians do not normally list Britain among the revolutions of 1830. Nonetheless, Britain experienced revolutionary activity in 1830–32. Rural violence, known as the Captain Swing Riots, began in Kent and covered southeastern Britain. Farm workers protested their poverty by burning hayricks and smashing the new threshing machines (the name *Captain Swing* came from the swinging flail used in hand threshing). More

riots followed at Bristol, Nottingham, and Derby in 1831. The British may have avoided a revolution when Parliament conceded reforms that the liberal middle classes wanted, thus preventing the alliance of propertied classes with revolutionary workers that had toppled Charles X in France. Thomas Macaulay, an eloquent leader of British liberalism, warned Parliament that "great and terrible calamities" were imminent. The House of Commons, Macaulay insisted, must "reform that you may survive." Parliament did adopt a series of historic reforms, which perpetuated its image as a model of representative government—notably the Reform (of Parliament) Bill of 1832, the Factory Act of 1833 (regulating hours and conditions), and the Abolition of Slavery Act of 1834.

The revolutions of 1830 are important for additional reasons beyond the struggles for national independence or liberal constitutions. They showed the beginnings of important new social movements that would shape the nineteenth century. The best known of these is the rise of working class radicalism; the events of 1830 (especially in Paris) provided a preview

◆ DOCUMENT 24.5 ◆

Feminists Proclaim a Women's Revolution of 1830

An Appeal to Women

At the moment when all peoples are aroused in the name of Liberty and the proletariat calls for its own emancipation, shall we women remain passive spectators of this great moment for social emancipation that is taking place before our eyes?

Is our condition so happy that we ourselves have no demands to make? Until now woman has been exploited and tyrannized. This tyranny, this exploitation must cease. We are born free, like man, and half the human race cannot, without injustice, be in servitude to the other half. . . .

We demand equality in marriage. We prefer celibacy to slavery!

. . . Liberty, equality—that is to say, a free and equal chance to develop our faculties: this is the victory we must win, and we can succeed only if we unite in a single group. Let us no longer form two camps—that of the women of the people and that of privileged women. Let our common interests unite us.

Bell, Susan G., and Offen, Karen M. eds. *Women, the Family, and Freedom: The Debate in Documents*, vol.1. Stanford, Calif.: Stanford University Press, 1983.

---

of subsequent risings. Other movements, such as the early campaign for women's rights, also received a stimulus from the revolutions of 1830 (see document 24.5). In France, for example, the revolution led to the foundation of a feminist newspaper entitled *La Femme libre* (the Free Woman), which asked, "Shall we women remain passive spectators of this great moment for social emancipation that is taking place before our eyes?" The combination of the revolution of 1830 and the utopian socialism of men such as Charles Fourier (who promised women an equal role) encouraged French feminism in the 1830s and 1840s. This group included Jeanne Deroin, a self-educated teacher and journalist who later became the first French woman to run for office; Eugénie Niboyet, whose Protestant zeal for moral reform led her to socialism and then to feminism; and Flora Tristan, whose Fourierism made her an advocate of equal rights for women.

◆ TABLE 24.1 ◆

The British Aristocracy in the Early Nineteenth Century

I. The Nobility
   A. Temporal lords: 326 families, with 8,000 members, ranked:
      4 princes and princesses of royal blood
      19 dukes and duchesses
      18 marquesses and marchionesses
      103 earls and ladies
      22 viscounts and vicountesses
      160 barons and baronesses
   B. Spiritual lords: 26 archbishops and bishops
II. The Lesser Nobility
   A. Baronets: 540 families with hereditary titles "Sir" and "Lady"
   B. Knights: 350 families with nontransmittable titles "Sir" and "Lady"
   C. The gentry: 6,000 families of landowning "squires"
   D. Gentlemen: 20,000 families with inherited income and coats of arms

---

The Advance of Liberalism in Britain

Historians usually cite Britain as the homeland of nineteenth-century liberalism and contrast it to the Metternichian reaction in central Europe. Truth exists in this contrast, but it should not obscure the strength of conservatism in post-1815 Britain. The landed aristocracy still dominated politics and society (see table 24.1). They composed less than 0.002 percent of the population but received more than 29 percent of the national income. Dukes, earls, and viscounts filled the cabinet. The House of Commons was elected by less than 3 percent of the population. If liberal reforms succeeded in that house, the House of Lords still held an aristocratic veto. The patronage system allowed this elite to perpetuate aristocratic domination of army and navy commands, the diplomatic corps, high government posts, and the leadership of the Church of England.

The English record on minority nationalism resembled that of Metternich and Nicholas I. An Act of Union of 1801 had absorbed Ireland into the United Kingdom, and the Protestant ascendancy of the eighteenth century had transferred landownership and political power in Ireland to the Protestant minority. The Catholic peasantry faced poverty and famine; suffering was so severe that some Irish nationalists have accused the British of genocide. Even British visitors to the Irish countryside were horrified by the suffering. Sir Walter Scott wrote of his 1825 visit: "Their poverty has not been exaggerated: it is on the extreme verge of human misery." Twenty years later, conditions were even worse, and during the potato famine of 1845–48, Ireland lost more than 25 percent of its population—experiencing more than 1 million deaths and losing 1.5 million refugees in a population of 8 million. Starving peasants ate their domestic pets.

Ireland needed a great defender, but the first parliamentary champion of Ireland could not take his seat in the House of Commons because British law excluded Catholics from office. Daniel O'Connell was a Jesuit-educated member of the Catholic gentry. He demanded the repeal of the Act of Union and the treatment of Ireland "not as a subordinate province, but . . . as a separate and distinct country." Lawful repeal was hardly likely. O'Connell could attract 100,000 people to a rally, but the House of Commons stood against him by 529–34. His experiences in the French Revolution, however, had convinced O'Connell of the horror and futility of revolution, and he continued to work for a parliamentary victory and reject violence.

Early nineteenth-century Britain was not yet a model of liberal democracy. However, Parliament accepted some important reforms between 1832 and 1846. Members did not democratize Britain, displace the governing elite, or encompass the radical agenda, but they made Britain the liberal leader of Europe. The reform of Parliament in 1832 illustrates the nature of British liberal reform (see map 24.3). It had been discussed since the 1780s, but little had been achieved except outlawing the sale of seats in the House of Commons (1809). The Reform Bill of 1832, won by the moderate liberals in a Whig government, enfranchised the new business and industrial elite, expanding the electorate from 2.1 percent of the population to 3.5 percent. The bill abolished "rotten boroughs" such as Old Sarum, the ruins of a medieval town that had no residents but still sent two members to Parliament. This eliminated fifty-six constituencies whose 111 seats were transferred to manufacturing towns such as Birmingham and Manchester, neither of which had representation in Parliament before 1832.

Liberal industrial reforms were modest in their range, but they pioneered European regulatory legislation. A Factory Act of 1833 established a maximum working day in textile mills for young children (nine hours) and for teenagers (twelve hours, or seventy-two hours per week) and planned for inspectors to enforce

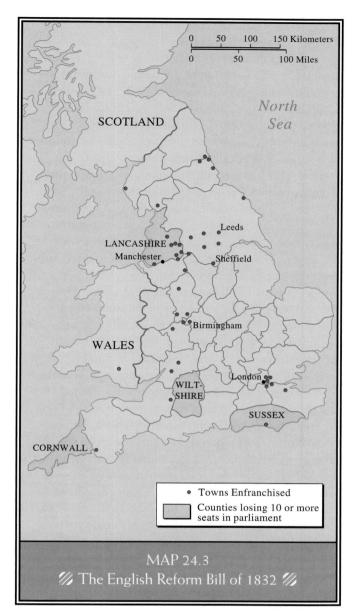

MAP 24.3
The English Reform Bill of 1832

• Towns Enfranchised

Counties losing 10 or more seats in parliament

these terms. The Factory Act of 1844 extended the regulatory principle to women working in the textile mills, limiting their daily work to twelve hours and their Saturday work to nine hours (a sixty-nine-hour week) and added the requirement of protective screening around machinery. Further regulatory legislation followed: a Mines Act (1842) prohibited underground work for boys under age ten and for all women; the Ten Hours Act (1847) lowered the workday for women and teenaged boys to ten hours (a fifty-nine-hour week) without provisions for enforcement. These laws have been controversial. Laissez-faire liberals opposed them, arguing that the state had no right to interfere with private business, while feminists have questioned the different treatment of men and women as paternalistic.

Another controversial form of liberal legislation involved the emancipation of the religious minorities—everyone who was not a member of the established Church of England. In 1815 only Anglicans could be elected to Parliament, command in the army, or enroll at Oxford; this intentional discrimination was created by a series of laws called the Test Acts. Unlike the French, who had promised religious freedom in the Constitutional Charter of 1814, or the Belgians, who provided a model of toleration in their Constitution of 1831, the British relaxed religious discrimination so slowly that it survived into the late nineteenth century. Parliament granted nonconforming Protestants ("dissenters," such as Methodists and Presbyterians) equal opportunity in 1828. In the same year, County Clare (Ireland) forced a larger reconsideration by electing O'Connell to Parliament, although Catholics were still excluded. Many conservatives considered Catholic emancipation to be a "suicidal measure" and fought bitterly against it, but after a conservative hero, the duke of Wellington, accepted the idea, the Tories made it law in 1829. The Catholic Emancipation Act did not end religious discrimination in British laws. The new oath of office still required M.P.s to swear "on the true faith of a Christian." This excluded Quakers (who would not swear), plus Jews and Atheists (who were not Christians). Parliament debated Jewish emancipation, but four separate bills failed between 1830 and 1836. Even when a London constituency elected a Jewish M.P in 1847 (Lionel Rothschild, of the famous banking family), Parliament refused to seat him. The debate on Jewish rights showed how far Britain remained from the liberal ideal: A majority still believed in such anti-Semitic clichés as Jewish collective responsibility for the crucifixion.

Another reform debate introduced Parliament to an issue that would demand attention for more than a century—women's rights. Although Queen Victoria sat on the throne, the women of her nation had no legal identity apart from their husbands or fathers. The law treated them as minor children and in some cases lumped them together with criminals and the insane. Husbands owned and controlled their property. Husbands exercised legal control of children. A father sentenced to prison could specify that his children be raised by his mistress instead of the children's legal mother. Cultural attitudes sustained this treatment, and most women accepted it. In a best-selling book of 1842, for example, a woman tried to teach young women "to be content to be inferior to men" (see document 24.6).

◆ DOCUMENT 24.6 ◆

A Conservative Woman's View of the Role of Women, 1842

Sarah Ellis was the devout wife of an English missionary to Polynesia who later served as secretary of the London Missionary Society. She wrote extensively on women and founded a school for girls to apply the principles in her books and teach them to the lower classes. The following excerpt is taken from her book entitled The Daughters of England, *published in London in 1842.*

As women, then, the first thing of importance is to be content to be inferior to men—inferior in mental power, in the same proportion that you are inferior in bodily strength. . . .

For a man it is absolutely necessary that he should sacrifice the poetry of his nature for the realities of material and animal existence; for women there is no excuse—for women, whose whole life from the cradle to the grave is one of feeling rather than action; whose highest duty is so often to suffer and be still; whose deepest enjoyments are all relative; who has nothing, and is nothing, of herself. . . . For woman, who, in her inexhaustible sympathies can live only in the existence of another, and whose very smiles and tears are not exclusively her own. . . .

Our moral worth or dignity depends upon the exercise of good taste. . . . It is strictly in subservience to religion that I would speak of good taste as being of extreme importance to women. . . .

Love is woman's all—her wealth, her power, her very being. Man, let him love as he may, has ever an existence distinct from that of his affections. He has his wordly interests, his public character, his ambition, his competition with other men—but woman centers all that in one feeling. . . . In woman's love is mingled the trusting dependence of a child, for she ever looks up to a man as her protector, and her guide . . . would she not suffer to preserve him from harm?

Ellis, Sara. "The Daughters of England" (London, 1842). In Patricia Hollis, ed., *Women in Public, 1850–1900. Documents of the Victorian Women's Movement.* London: 1979.

Queen Victoria gave scant help to the campaigns to change such attitudes and laws. She once wrote: "The Queen is most anxious to enlist everyone who can speak or write to join in checking this mad, wicked folly of 'Women's Rights' . . . *with all its attendant horrors. . . .* [I]t is a subject which makes the Queen so *furious* that she cannot contain herself." Ironically, the force of her example as a strong woman simultaneously served to advance the cause of emancipation, which she opposed.

The first changes in the legal restrictions on women resulted from the work of an outraged individual instead of a women's movement. Caroline Norton, the wife of an M.P., had an intimate friendship with a Whig prime minister, Lord Melbourne. This so enraged her husband (a confessed adulterer) that he sued the prime minister for alienation of his wife's affections. Caroline Norton then discovered she would not be allowed any role or representation in the trial because the law considered her interests to be represented by her husband. The suit failed, and the Nortons separated (she could not even divorce her husband), with the law awarding custody of their children to the father. Caroline Norton thereupon launched a pamphlet campaign that led to the Infant Custody Act of 1839, giving mothers limited rights over their infant children to age seven. Her role in the evolution of women's rights did not stop with that victory. She came from a talented family (her grandfather was the dramatist Richard Sheridan), and she supported herself comfortably by writing. In the 1850s her husband, now badly debt-ridden, legally seized all of her royalties as his property, and Caroline Norton became a central figure in the campaign to obtain a Married Woman's Property Act.

Other issues received more attention than women's rights, both from contemporaries and subsequent historians. The chief interest of middle-class liberals was the repeal of the Corn Laws, the high tariffs on imported grain that kept the price of bread high, the landowning-class prosperous, and workers hungry. Repeal, however, would produce cheaper bread, healthier workers (who still relied on starches for 50 percent of their total calories), and business profits (because workers need not be paid so much if bread were not dear). To win repeal, British liberals (led by Manchester business interests) founded the Anti-Corn Law League, which became the international model of a political lobbying group. At the same time, a parallel campaign of working-class radicals known as the Chartist movement (named for the National Charter of 1838) outlined a democratic program: universal manhood suffrage, the secret ballot, the abolition of property qualifications to serve in Parlia-

ment, the payment of salaries to M.P.s (so the poor could serve), the creation of equal-sized constituencies, and annual elections.

The fate of these two campaigns shows the cautious approach of European liberals. The leaders of the repeal campaign, John Bright (the M.P. son of a cotton-mill owner) and Richard Cobden (a wealthy Manchester textile factory owner), succeeded by courting conservatives. They convinced moderate Tories, led by Sir Robert Peel (now dubbed Re-Peel), to adopt free trade as economic orthodoxy. The same coalition, however, would not accept Chartism. The Chartists included radicals such as Feargus O'Connor, a newspaper editor whose willingness to consider violence frightened both the conservative government and the liberals who claimed to be his allies. Although Chartism summarized most elements of modern democracy, it did not come close to adoption.

International Liberalism and Slavery

Nothing better illustrates the strength of conservative regimes and the weakness of liberal reformers in Metternichian Europe than the persistence of serfdom in eastern Europe and slavery in European colonies. In 1700 virtually every state in Europe had practiced one of these forms of enslavement in some part of its territory. Britain had no serfs at home but had built slave economies in America. France had both serfdom at home and slavery in its colonies. Most of Russia, Prussia, and Austria lived in serfdom. During the Enlightenment, three important states abolished serfdom: Savoy, Baden, and Denmark. The abolition of serfdom during the French Revolution led to the spread of this idea to Switzerland, Poland, Prussia, and Bavaria. The French abolition of colonial slavery did not, however, persuade other slave states to follow, though Denmark and Britain both ended their slave trades, and the United States stopped the importation of new African slaves.

Abolitionists thus faced a great task in 1815. They won a few victories between 1815 and 1848, but millions of people in Western civilization remained in slavery or serfdom throughout the age of Metternich. Alexander I abolished serfdom in his Baltic provinces, and the revolutions of 1830 ended serfdom in several German states. At the beginning of 1848, however, feudal obligations still restricted peasants in the Austrian and the Hungarian portions of the Habsburg Empire, in a dozen German states (including Saxe-Coburg-Gotha, the homeland of Queen Victoria's consort), in the

Danubian provinces, and in Russia. The campaign against colonial slavery also made some progress yet left millions of people in bondage. The Congress of Vienna adopted a proclamation ending the slave trade in principle, but the same treaties accepted the existence of colonial slavery and returned lost colonies to Denmark, France, the Netherlands, and Spain knowing that these were to be slave economies. Europe then ignored the agreement ending the slave trade. The growing love of sweet foods demanded great quantities of cane sugar from Caribbean plantations, where sugar often accounted for 90 percent of the exports. Few people paused with the poet William Cowper, who wrote, "Think how many backs have smarted/For the sweets your cane affords." Thus, Bourbon France shipped more than 125,000 new slaves to the Caribbean between 1814 and 1831, and other slave states behaved similarly. In 1828 alone, 100,000 more African slaves were shipped to the Americas, despite the closing of the market in British colonies and the United States.

The Spanish revolution of 1820 led to a victory for abolitionism when the Spanish colonies won independence. The revolutionaries did not plan to end slavery at first, but Simon Bolivar realized that liberating slaves would increase his chances of victory. Bolivar adopted military manumission (freeing the slaves in areas conquered) in his campaigns after 1815, and his speech to the revolutionary congress of 1821 led to a Manumission Law. Bolivar thus doubly earned the nickname "El Libertador" (the liberator), by freeing a region from Spain and a class from slavery, but slavery persisted in those Spanish territories that did not win independence. Coffee and sugar plantations in Cuba required more than 200,000 slaves and those in Puerto Rico, 17,500.

Abolitionists won another important victory in British colonies. The British antislavery movement, led by Quakers and other Dissenters, had been gaining strength since the late eighteenth century. They found an effective leader in William Wilberforce, an M.P. and the head of an Anglican evangelical sect. Wilberforce founded the Antislavery Society with the aim of abolishing all slavery, and his movement flooded Parliament with petitions. In its first year, the Antislavery Society opened 220 local chapters and submitted 825 petitions, with hundreds of thousands of signatures. Abolitionism gained strength during the turbulent years of 1830–32, when many members of Parliament feared a revolution in Britain. At that moment, the British Caribbean experienced another slave rebellion (the third since 1815). On Christmas Day 1831, more than 20,000 Jamaican slaves revolted. The British army quelled the revolt, but 14 whites and 200 slaves were killed, while 312 more slaves were executed later. The message from Jamaica, alongside the news from Paris, Brussels, and the Kentish countryside, persuaded the Whig government to abolish slavery in the British colonies in 1834.

CHAPTER 25

EUROPE IN AN AGE OF NATIONALISM, 1848–70

CHAPTER OUTLINE

◆◆◆◆◆◆◆◆◆◆◆◆◆◆◆◆◆◆◆◆◆

Chapter 25 looks at the turbulent epoch following the years of Metternichian-enforced stability. It begins with the revolutions of 1848, revolutions that convulsed two dozen countries, ended the Orleanist monarchy in France, and brought down the government of Metternich in Austria. The revolutions of 1848 achieved important reforms but did not fulfill the dreams of nationalist and republican revolutionaries. The Old Regime—and conservatism—survived: Europe in 1870 was still governed by monarchs. Radicals had achieved little democratization, but gradual liberalization was under way in Victorian Britain and Alexander II made a dramatic attempt to modernize Russia by abolishing serfdom.

Greater change came on the battlefield. Europe experienced five wars between 1854 and 1870: the Crimean War, the War of Italian Unification, and three wars for the unification of Germany that ended in a decisive struggle between France and Prussia. This chapter describes how the modern states of Germany and Italy emerged from these conflicts, and it analyzes the internal developments that made unification possible.

The Origins of the Revolutions of 1848

The event that conservatives had feared for a generation (and which Marxists predicted for the next century)—widespread revolutions—swept Europe in 1848 (see chronology 25.1). Governments fell in France, the Italian states, the German states, and the Austrian Empire; revolutionary turmoil lasted for two years. Liberals and nationalists initially won great victories. Constitutions, bills of rights, even republics sprang up. Enthusiasm for national autonomy, independence, or unification was so universal that the revolutionary period became known as "the springtime of peoples." The alliance of nationalism and liberalism drove monarchs to abdicate and sent their ministers into exile. The king of France and Guizot and

◈ CHRONOLOGY 25.1 ◈

The Revolutions of 1848

Dates	Country	Revolutionary events	Outcome
January 1848–May 1848	Naples	Revolt in Sicily, short-lived constitution and independence	Revolt crushed
February 1848–June 1849	France	Revolt in Paris, abdication of king and formation of republic	Second Republic overthrown by President Louis-Napoleon
March 1848–August 1849	Piedmont-Sardinia	Constitution granted and war declared on Austria	Austrian victories force king to abdicate; constitution endures
March 1848–August 1849	Austria	Emperor abdicates and Metternich flees, constitutions in Austria and Hungary, nationalist uprisings	Austrian and Russian armies suppress all revolutions
March 1848–July 1849	Vatican states	Pope Pius IX grants constitution, but Mazzini proclaims republic	French troops crush the republic and restore the pope
March 1848–August 1849	Venice	Demonstrations drive out Austrian army, republic proclaimed	Republic capitulates to Austrian army
March 1848–December 1848	Prussia	Revolution in Berlin, king grants constitution	King dismisses assembly, keeps constitution
March 1848	Lombardy	Revolution in Milan forces Austrian evacuation	Austrian reconquest
March 1848–June 1849	Germany	National assembly in Frankfurt abolishes confederation and debates German unity	Assembly fails to create unity, dismissed by army

the emperor of Austria and Metternich were all driven from the stage of international politics. By 1850, however, the revolutions of 1848 had collapsed in the face of military repression. Some constitutions survived, as did a few revolutionary accomplishments, but counterrevolutionary governments dominated the 1850s.

Historians have explained the revolutions of 1848 in many ways. Liberals have stressed the repressive nature of government in the Metternichian era. More conservative historians have blamed the discontent of the intelligentsia, calling 1848 a "revolt of the intellectuals." Others have noted the willingness of the newly influential middle classes (such as bankers, manufacturers, merchants, and professionals) to accept revolutionary change because they had few attachments to the aristocratic regime. Marxists have pointed to the importance of the growing urban laboring class living in poverty, while social historians have examined urbanization (many cities doubled in size between 1800 and 1848) and found an array of problems in housing, public health, and crime.

One of the more convincing explanations of the origins of the revolutions has come from economic historians. In the late 1840s Europe simultaneously experienced the last great subsistence crisis as a result of agricultural failure and the first severe depression of the industrial age. Crop failures meant expensive bread (which had also preceeded the French Revolution); the downturn in the business cycle meant high unemployment (see illustration 25.1).

The agricultural crisis began with the potato famine of 1845. Ireland suffered horribly from this catastrophe, and all regions that depended upon the potato as a staple of the diet (such as the German states) had problems. Grain famines followed in 1846 and 1847, causing hardship for many people and mortal danger for some. In the Alsatian industrial center of Mulhouse, for example, the price of bread increased 67 percent during this crisis; in some German states, the price of staple foods rose between 250 percent and 450 percent. The depression of the 1840s multiplied the suffering and political agitation that grows when food

Illustration 25.1

▨ **The Depression of the 1840s.** Europe suffered one of the worst depressions of the industrial age during the mid- and late 1840s. Unemployment reached frightening levels in many occupations, and crops failed in several regions. This combination produced some of the last widespread food riots in European history. This German illustration depicts bread riots in Berlin in the spring of 1847; families sack a local bakery. Note the prominent role of women.

does not. The member states of the Zollverein experienced a mild depression in textiles, but a collapse in business and banking. Between August 1847 and January 1848, 245 firms and 12 banks failed in Prussia alone. France experienced a fearful collapse of the textile industry; consumption of cotton fell by 30 percent, reducing output to the lowest level in the industrial era. The human meaning of such numbers was reduced incomes or unemployment while the price of food was skyrocketing. In Silesia, one of the hardest hit regions in Prussia, an estimated 75 percent of the population sought poor relief. In Paris, unemployment exceeded 40 percent in most trades and ranged between 50 percent and 75 percent in the worst cases. An angry Parisian radical summarized the situation: "While half of the population of Paris dies of starvation, the other half eats for two."

The revolutions of 1848 began in the homeland of revolution—France. The constitutional monarchy of Louis-Philippe had evolved into an alliance of moderate conservatives and moderate liberals that the premier, François Guizot, considered "the golden mean." Guizot's perfect balance allowed 0.7 percent of the population to vote in 1845 while preserving the status quo for the propertied classes of landlords and capitalists. During the winter of 1847–48, his opponents tried a truly French form of protest: the banquet. Respectable middle-class critics of the regime organized large dinners and added inflammatory political oration to the menu. The campaign culminated in a great banquet scheduled for Paris in late February 1848, but the

Guizot government prohibited that assembly. Critics of the regime met nonetheless, to march to their locked banquet hall. Workers and students swelled the parade, and by nightfall barricades were again appearing on the streets of Paris (see illustration 25.2). Louis-Philippe dismissed Guizot, and when that did not placate the demonstrators, he fled the country. Republicans, led by a radical deputy named Alexandre Ledru-Rollin, seized the Hôtel de Ville (the town hall), proclaimed the Second Republic, and named a provisional government.

The French revolution of 1848 did not immediately fall into the hands of moderates as had the revolution of 1830. Republicans kept control but were soon divided between those who favored Ledru-Rollin's democratic program (universal manhood suffrage, parliamentary government, a cabinet responsible to a majority) and social radicals who demanded help for workers and the poor. Ledru-Rollin had more support, so the provisional government concentrated on political change: It abolished "all forms of monarchy," all titles of nobility, and laws restricting political activity. In contrast, it attempted only one idea for what radicals called "the social republic," Louis Blanc's National Workshops. The workshops were a relief plan for the unemployed. (The government's first assignment for relief workers was to remove the barricades.) Democratic elections in April 1848 gave moderate republicans a large majority; shortly thereafter, it curtailed support for workers.

The immediate consequence was an insurrection in June 1848. Workers, fearful that the counterrevolution

Illustration 25.2

🖎 **Barricades in Paris.** One of the characteristic features of revolutions in modern France has been the construction of barricades closing streets—mounds constructed from nearby vehicles, trees, furniture from surrounding buildings, and paving stones from the streets. Barricades such as the one shown here gave revolutionaries a strong position to confront government troops, and the neighboring buildings could hide snipers or provide objects to drop on soldiers.

had begun and remembering how monarchists had stolen the revolution of 1830, called for popular action. The republican government answered the demonstrations of "the June days" by giving General Louis Cavaignac dictatorial powers. Cavaignac unleashed the army on Paris and reduced unemployment with killings, arrests, and deportations. Others saw his accomplishment as ending a workers' uprising and preserving the republic. The assembly adopted a radical constitution in November 1848 and achieved a few legislative triumphs, such as the abolition of slavery in French colonies. But it had permanently alienated one of its strongest constituencies, the working class. The Second Republic managed to elect one president, but it never elected another.

The Spread of Revolution in 1848: "The Springtime of Peoples"

The February revolution in Paris encouraged March revolutions in many places (see map 25.1). It first stimulated demonstrations in the towns of the Rhineland,

such as Heidelberg. German radicals raised posters announcing that "[o]ur brothers in France have bravely led the way" and calling on Germans to follow. In many of the smaller German states, rulers quickly capitulated. Monarchs named liberal governments in Baden, Württemberg, and Saxony. The king of Bavaria abdicated. Revolution spread throughout the German Confederation in March 1848, changing central Europe so much that Germans thereafter described the "pre-March" (*Vormärz*) era as an antediluvian past.

The German revolutions of 1848 centered on three cities: Berlin, Vienna, and Frankfurt. In Berlin, liberal demonstrations led to the building of barricades. King Frederick William IV sent the army into the streets and their brutality made the liberal cause more popular. The dead included several women, the "amazons of the German revolution" and harbingers of a women's rights movement. Frederick William considered all-out war on the revolution but capitulated to it instead of leading to a bloodbath. Within a few days he abolished censorship, called elections for a new Diet (the United Landtag), and promised a liberal constitution. His "beloved Berliners," however, did not quit the barricades until he

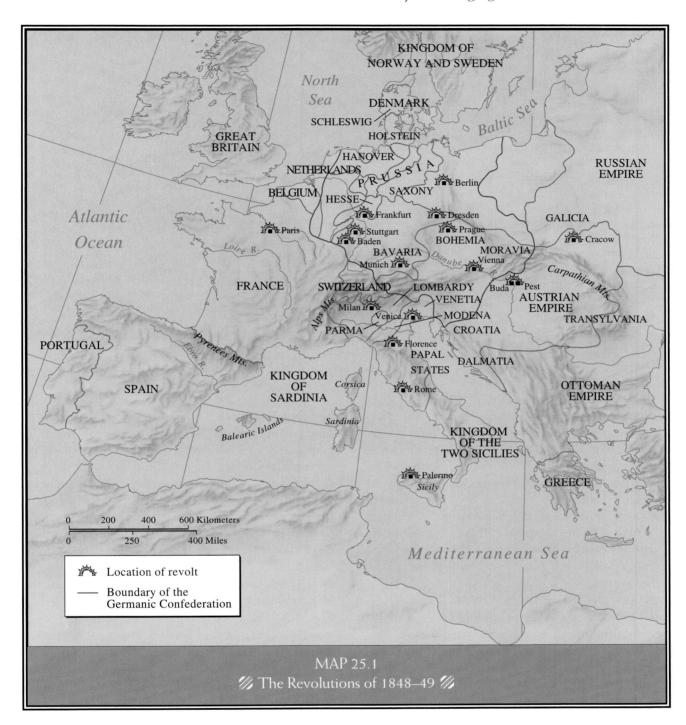

MAP 25.1

/// The Revolutions of 1848–49 ///

had withdrawn the army and joined them in saluting the bodies of the rebels.

In Vienna, Prince Metternich also resisted demands for liberalization and soon had more problems than he could handle. The most ominous was the awakening of nationalism throughout the empire, especially Hungarian nationalism, led by Lajos Kossuth. Kossuth was a reforming journalist who had spent four years in prison for political crimes and had been elected to the Hungarian Diet in 1847. When the news from Paris reached Buda (still a separate town from Pest), Kossuth inflamed opinion with a patriotic speech demanding Hungarian autonomy. By 1849, he was the leader of an insurrection that declared Hungarian independence. The Hungarian rebellion encouraged the other peoples of the Habsburg Empire to seek freedom. In April 1848,

Illustration 25.3

The Flight of Metternich. Nothing better symbolized the initial victories of the revolutions of 1848 than the flight of Prince Metternich. In mid-March, 1848, students and professors from the University of Vienna assembled outside the provincial parliament to chant "Down with Metternich." When they were joined by large numbers of workers, the army fired on them, killing five people. A riot followed and Metternich, who found himself friendless within the government, fled the country. This contemporary Austrian cartoon ridicules the flight of the frightened statesman.

Czech patriots led by the historian František Palacký won a separate Parliament for Bohemia. Similar claims quickly arose in Moravia (another Czech province), in Galicia (a predominantly Polish province in the north), in Dalmatia (a mixed Slavic province on the Adriatic coast), in Croatia (a southern province), and in Transylvania (a predominantly Rumanian province in the east). In the eastern half of the empire, these nationalist expectations were complicated by the claim of the Hungarians to exercise the full sovereignty previously held by the Austrians.

A liberal revolution also occurred in Vienna in March 1848. After one day of fighting between the army and demonstrators, Metternich fled to exile (see illustration 25.3), leaving the Austrian government in the hands of a feeble-minded emperor, Ferdinand I, and an intimidated group of advisers. After two more days of demonstrations, Ferdinand promised press freedom, a constitution, and an Austrian Parliament; he and the royal court then abandoned Vienna to the liberals. The liberal revolutionaries achieved two lasting successes in Austria—the abolition of serfdom and the granting of civil rights to Jews, who were allowed for the first time to live in the cities, enter the professions, and to marry freely.

The liberal victories in Prussia and Austria encouraged German nationalists to dream of a parallel triumph to unify the German states. They faced many problems, however, starting with disagreements among themselves. Many nationalists favored a comprehensive German nation-state—their "Germany" stretched "Wher'er is heard the German tongue!" This *grossdeutsch* (large German) nationalism was important to Austrians, who thought that Germany included the Habsburg Empire. *Grossdeutsch* nationalism, however, threatened the non-German peoples of that empire, who feared their treatment as minorities in an even larger and stronger German state. Pragmatic nationalists favored a *kleindeutsch* (little German) solution that excluded Habsburg lands or included only the German portion of them. Prussians, the rivals of Austrians for leadership of Germany, generally favored *kleindeutsch* nationalism, because it meant the exclusion or dismemberment of Austria.

The home of German nationalism during the revolutions of 1848 was the free city of Frankfurt, the seat of the German Confederation. Revolutionaries in many states called for a national Parliament to replace the confederation's Diet, and elections for the Frankfurt Parliament took place across Germany in April 1848. More than eight hundred members of this "parliament of professors" (although bureaucrats and lawyers were more numerous) met at the Paulskirche in Frankfurt. Under the leadership of a liberal lawyer from Hesse, Heinrich von Gagern, the Frankfurt Parliament produced fervent rhetoric, but not a treasury, an army, or effective leadership of German nationalism. Liberals wrote an idealistic constitution for unified Germany. It stripped the nobility of privileges, opening the bureaucracy and the officer corps to commoners; it abolished the pillory, branding, and other forms of corporal punishment; it proclaimed "The Fundamental Rights of the German People," including civil liberties; and it promised free state education. The pressure of nonvoting women "observer-delegates," championing the program of a German feminist newspaper, the *Frauenzeitung* (the Women's Newspaper), did not persuade the men of 1848 to add women's rights.

Another dramatic chapter in the springtime of peoples began in the Italian states. Sicily rose against its Neapolitan monarch, for its fifth insurrection in eighteen years. When revolution shook the Austrian Empire, the Habsburg provinces in northern Italy joined in the claims of minority peoples. When news of Metternich's departure reached Milan, barricades appeared in the streets. In a battle known as "the five glorious days," the Lombards expelled the Austrian garrison from Milan. The news from Milan and Vienna inflamed all of northern Italy. While the fighting continued in Lombardy, rebels led by Daniele Manin proclaimed the end of Austrian rule at Venice and formed a republic. On the other side of Lombardy, King Charles Albert of Piedmont-Sardinia supported the revolution rather than face upheaval at Turin. As the Austrian army retreated from Milan, Piedmont declared war on Austria. In central Italy, rebels drove out pro-Austrian rulers and adopted constitutions.

The refusal of Pope Pius IX to join the Italian war led to a democratic insurrection at Rome in November 1848 in which the pope's prime minister and personal confessor were both killed. Pius fled Rome, and revolutionaries abolished his temporal powers. The Roman republic attracted two of the heroes of Italian nationalism: Giuseppe Mazzini (the theorist who had created Young Italy) and Giuseppe Garibaldi (a Genoese radical who became the most famous general of the Italian wars). Despite papal threats to excommunicate all voters, they organized the Roman republic as a "pure democracy." One of Garibaldi's first acts was to abolish the Jewish ghetto and emancipate Roman Jews. Like the emancipation of the serfs in Germany, the emancipation of the Jews became one of the lasting accomplishments of the Italian revolution of 1848.

In mid-1848, the age of Metternich seemed over at Turin, Milan, Venice, and Rome. Austrian revolutionaries planned to grant Lombardy its independence. While constitutional governments were still being formed, however, an Austrian general dramatically changed events. Count Joseph Radetzky, the Austrian chief-of-staff during the Napoleonic Wars, commanded the garrison driven from Milan. Radetzky regrouped his forces and crushed a combined Italian army in the battle of Custozza (July 1848). The outcome at Custozza (a village in Venetia) left few doubts: Revolutionaries could not defeat determined professional armies, and they could not drive the Austrians from Italy.

The French, German, and Italian revolutions were the most significant upheavals of 1848, but important changes occurred in many countries, often when alert monarchs voluntarily introduced liberal innovations. In Denmark, a new king (Frederick VII) came to the throne in 1848 and launched a reform program culminating in the Danish constitution of 1849. Frederick accepted constitutional limits on his powers, a strengthened Parliament, widespread manhood suffrage (15 percent of the population voted in 1850 versus 4 percent in Britain), guarantees of civil liberties, and the emancipation of religious minorities. In the Netherlands, King William II agreed to liberal constitutional revision. The Dutch liberals, led by a noted constitutional jurist, Johan Thorbecke, won new parliamentary authority at the expense of the throne, including the principle of ministerial responsibility to a majority in Parliament.

The Conservative Counterrevolution, 1849–52

Most of the changes made during the revolutions of 1848 did not survive for long. Conservatives, typically led by army commanders, went on the counteroffensive in 1849 and reasserted principles of the Old Regime. Constitutions and reforms were nullified; royal authority reasserted. Pius IX summarized conservative sentiment in December 1848: "We . . . declare null and of no effect, and altogether illegal, every act" of the governments of 1848. The end of slavery in French colonies, the abolition of serfdom in Germany, and the emancipation of Jews in Italy remained a legacy of the revolutionary moment, but few of the governments and none of the republics of 1848 endured. The Italian republics at Venice and at Rome fell in 1849; the French Second Republic became so conservative that it helped to suppress the Roman republic and was itself overturned in 1851. The nationalist fires of 1848 turned to ashes everywhere. By 1850 a Neapolitan radical concluded, "The concept of nationality sufficed to bring about the insurrection, but it was not enough to bring victory." Alexis de Tocqueville had foreseen such problems in early 1848. "In a rebellion, as in a novel," he said, "the most difficult part to invent is the end."

Armies ended most of the revolutions. A cheery German prince summarized the situation in late 1848: "It takes soldiers to put democrats in their place." Europe had briefly been led by revolutionaries: Ledru-Rollin in Paris, Mazzini and Garibaldi in Rome, Manin in Milan, and Kossuth in Buda. At the end of the day, the true victors were generals such as Cavaignac in France and Radetzky in Austria. By 1850 Kossuth would be in prison and his radical colleagues in exile. Manin spent the rest of his life in Paris; Ledru-Rollin and Mazzini found exile in London; Garibaldi became a citizen of the United States and spent the early 1850s as a candle maker on Staten Island. Radetzky, meanwhile, ended his days as the governor-general of Lombardy and Venetia.

The military conquest of the revolution began in Prague in June 1848. The enraged army commander of Bohemia, Prince Alfred zu Windischgrätz, whose wife had been killed in riots there, ignored his orders and bombarded the city. Windischgrätz subdued Prague, then turned his armies on the Hungarians and took Buda and Pest a few weeks later. One month after the shelling of Prague, Radetzky (also resisting imperial instructions) defeated the Piedmontese at Custozza. Windischgrätz led a polyglot imperial army against Vienna in late October 1848 and shelled his third capital into submission. The army then peremptorily executed the leaders of the government, including Robert Blum, the leader of the Saxon revolution who was visiting Vienna as the vice president of the Frankfurt Parliament. The generals entrusted the Austrian Empire to a reactionary aristocrat, Prince Felix Schwarzenberg, the brother-in-law of Windischgrätz and a member of Radetzky's staff. Schwarzenberg and the generals arranged for the mentally deficient emperor Ferdinand to abdicate and for his son to renounce the throne. This brought the emperor's eighteen-year-old grandson, Franz Joseph, to the throne. The new emperor reigned for an exceptionally long time (from 1848 to 1916) and became the sentimental symbol of the twilight of an empire. In 1848 he was simply the pawn of counterrevolutionaries who asserted that he was not bound by concessions that he had not personally made.

The military counterrevolution in Austria stiffened the will of King Frederick William IV of Prussia. A few days after the bombardment of Vienna, he again sent the army into Berlin. Under the shrewd leadership of a conservative minister of the interior, Baron Otto von Manteuffel, the Prussian counterrevolution took a more moderate form than the Austrian reaction. The revolu-

tionary Parliament was dismissed, but Manteuffel appeased liberals by persuading the king to grant his promised constitution with a bicameral legislature. Manteuffel understood that constitutions could be conservative weapons, too. Thus, the Prussian Constitution of 1850 restated the principle of divine right and protected the Hohenzollern family by reserving crown domains that produced a huge income. The Prussian army remained an unrestricted state within the state. The government depended upon the support of the king, not the Parliament. The lower house of that Parliament (the *Landtag*) was elected by a broad manhood suffrage, but the electorate was subdivided (by taxes paid) into three classes, each of which elected one-third of the deputies.

The defeat of the revolution in Vienna and Berlin doomed the national revolution at Frankfurt. In March 1849 the desperate delegates offered the crown of a unified Germany to Frederick William. Under pressure from conservatives, he rejected "a crown from the gutter," which would make him "the serf of the revolution." Austria and Prussia recalled their delegates, and the city of Frankfurt refused to host the assembly any longer. A rump Parliament briefly met in Stuttgart, but the Württemberg army disbanded it. Prince Schwarzenberg seized the opportunity to block all manifestations of nationalism. He particularly tried to kill the *kleindeutsch* vision of Germany, which elevated Prussia at the expense of Austria. His greatest victory came at the expense of the Prussians who were obliged in 1850 to disavow a *kleindeutsch* union and to accept the recreation of the Austrian-dominated German Confederation, in an agreement known to Austrians as the Olmütz Convention and to Prussians as the "humiliation of Olmütz."

None of these counterrevolutionary victories was as startling as the events in France. General Cavaignac had demonstrated the limits of the French revolution in June 1848 by using the army against protesting workers. In December 1848 he sought the presidency of the republic against Ledru-Rollin. French voters, however, spurned both men in favor of an aspirant monarch. Prince Louis-Napoleon Bonaparte, the nephew of Napoleon Bonaparte, won more than 70 percent of the votes; he had far greater name-recognition in provincial France (where most voters were still illiterate), and his name stood for order after revolutionary chaos and it evoked the glorious triumphs of his uncle.

Louis-Napoleon proceeded to create an authoritarian regime. In short order, Louis-Napoleon reintroduced censorship, restricted universal suffrage, outlawed politi-

Illustration 25.4

▨ **The Triumph of Reaction.** Few events better symbolized the defeat of the liberal-national revolutions of 1848 than one in Paris, where the revolution had begun. The barricades of 1848 had sometimes been built using nearby trees, and the French republic had converted this fact into a great symbolic act—the planting of new "Liberty Trees" along the boulevards. In 1850–51, the conservative government of Louis-Napoleon Bonaparte made its own symbolic statement by removing the Liberty Trees, shown here. This act made a philosophical statement and also denied his opponents the materials for building barricades.

cal clubs, gave the Catholic Church control of French education, and arrested radicals. One of the founders of French feminism, Jeanne Deroin, had dared to run for office in 1849, after the assembly had laughed at her petitions; Louis-Napoleon restored order by throwing her in prison. He also demonstrated how far the republic had changed from its radical origins by sending the French army to Rome to fight on the side of counterrevolution and restore Pope Pius IX to temporal authority. In June 1849 another rising of Parisian workers provoked more severe reponses.

By December 1851 the Second Republic cast only a pale shadow of the liberal-democratic program of 1848, and President Bonaparte ended the pretense by overthrowing the republic in a military coup d'état. He created a Second Empire with himself as Emperor Napoleon III (honoring Napoleon and his son as predecessors). The French Second Empire (1852–70) began as a counterrevolutionary regime well suited to the Europe of Nicholas I, Schwarzenberg, and Pius IX. Yet Napoleon III differed from them in significant ways. He shaped France into a unique blend of Caesarism and modern democracy. The French Second Empire was an authoritarian regime—at its best a modern form of enlightened despotism, at its worst a hint of the modern police state. On one hand, Napoleon III gave a significant boost to the modernization of the French economy and a great assist to the industrialization of France, while remaining sensitive to the condition of workers, whose rights he expanded. On the other hand, a Law of Suspects (1858) allowed the government to banish or imprison anyone previously convicted of a political offense, including virtually all of the leaders of 1848; under this act, more than five hundred republicans were transported to Algeria. Although Napoleon III tried to reshape his regime into a "liberal empire" in the 1860s and allowed an opposition party, republicans never forgot that he was the "despicable assassin of the republic." No one branded him more effectively than Victor Hugo (who sat in the legislature of 1848). From exile, Hugo published a political diatribe entitled *Napoleon the Little,* taunting him as "this mummer, this dwarf, this stunted Tiberius." A fairer judgment would remember both sides of this complex man; but few understood him, and many agreed with Bismarck's remark that Napoleon III was "the sphinx without a riddle."

The Labor Movement and the Rise of Socialism

Even while victorious counterrevolutionaries dreamt of restoring the old order, the social and economic transformation of industrialization created great pressures for the social changes that they resisted. One of the foremost consequences of industrialization was the rise of a labor movement expressing the needs of the industrial working class (often known as the proletariat). The dreadful working and living conditions associated with industrialization were well known by midcentury, but neither conservative governments (typically dominated by great landowners) nor their liberal opposition (typically dominated by industrialists and manufacturers) did much to address the problem. Consequently, labor unrest and labor movements grew. These took two different forms: (1) associations of workers in the trade unions, seeking to persuade employers to grant better wages and working conditions, and (2) political movements, usually socialist, seeking to create governments that would govern in the interest of the laboring class.

Trade union movements grew slowly because they were illegal. In some countries, the legislation abolishing the monopolies of medieval guilds (such as the Chapelier Law of 1791 in France) also blocked unions. The traditional privileges of guilds survived in parts of Europe, however. German governments were still trying to legislate the principle of *Gewerbefreiheit* (the freedom to practice an occupation) in the 1850s; Denmark, Sweden, and Russia adopted such laws in the 1860s. In other countries, legislation explicitly banned trade unions, as a series of Combination Acts did in Britain. Changes in the Combination Acts in 1824–25 permitted the first legal unions, although they could neither strike nor restrain business. Other laws also restricted workers, as the "Tolpuddle martyrs" discovered in 1834 when they were convicted of the crime of taking a secret union oath. Nonetheless, British trade unionism grew during the 1840s, and the prosperity of the 1850s accelerated this growth (see document 25.1). The Amalgamated Society of Engineers, a union of mechanics founded in 1850, created a model of successful organization, based on collecting dues and offering services. Such unions of skilled labor (sometimes called "the labor aristocracy") flourished during the 1850s and 1860s, culminating in a potentially powerful alliance of unions—the Trades Union Congress—founded in 1868.

Continental Europe trailed Britain in labor organization. The revolutions of 1848 stimulated a German labor movement, but few organizations survived the political repression of the 1850s. It was the late 1860s before stronger unions appeared in Germany, and these were created by the workers' political movement. A variety of workers' societies, such as traditional journeymen's societies (*compagnonnages*), competed in France despite the Chapelier Law. Napoleon III felt paternalistic sympathy for French workers and approved liberal laws of 1864–68 legalizing their associations. When he died in exile years later, representatives of labor unions were the only French delegation at Napoleon III's funeral.

A second workers' movement, focusing on political activity, developed alongside trade unionism. This

---

◆ DOCUMENT 25.1 ◆

The Program of an Early Trade Union: The Drapers, 1845

A draper is a dealer in cloth, such as the cloth that might be used for curtains (or "drapes"). Sometimes the term also included dealers in clothing and other dry goods. As a consequence of the industrialization of textile manufacturing, there was a great expansion of the drapers' business and rapidly changing conditions of work. Drapers consequently made one of the first efforts to found a union during the industrial age. The following is the program of the drapers' union of 1845 in Britain.

The object of this association shall be to obtain an abridgment of the hours of business in the linen and woolen drapery, silk mercing, hosiery, haberdashery, lace and other trades, with a view to the physical and moral and intellectual improvement of those engaged therein:

1. by appealing to the public to abstain from shopping in the evening, by means of public meetings, sermons, lectures, tracts, and the press.
2. by representing to employers the evils arising from late hours of business and the advantage which would accrue from closing their shops at an early hour.
3. by impressing upon the minds of assistants the importance of using the time at their disposal in the improvement of their mental faculties, by the aid of literary institutions, lectures, and libraries, and by urging upon them the desirableness and advantages of industry in business, correctness of behavior, and intellectual acquirements.
4. by employing only such means as are of a peaceful and conciliatory nature, and by refusing to sanction or adopt any measure having a tendency to coerce or injure the interests of employers. . . .

"Rules of the Metropolitan Draper's Association" (London, 1845). In Ludwig Schaefer et al., eds., *Problems in Western Civilization*. New York: Scribner's, 1965.

❖ DOCUMENT 25.2 ❖

The Communist Manifesto

The history of all hitherto existing society is the history of class struggles. . . . The modern bourgeois society, that has sprouted from the ruins of feudal society, has not done away with class antagonisms. It has but established new classes, new conditions of oppression, new forms of struggle in place of the old ones. . . . The epoch of the bourgeoisie possesses, however, this distinctive feature: it has simplified class antagonisms. Society as a whole is more and more splitting up into two great hostile camps, into two great classes directly facing each other: Bourgeoisie and Proletariat. . . .

All property relations in the past have continually been subject to historical change. . . . The French Revolution, for example, abolished feudal property. . . . In this sense, the theory of the Communists may be summed up in the single sentence: Abolition of private property. . . . Do you mean the property of the petty artisan and of the small peasant, a form of property that preceded the bourgeois form? There is no need to abolish that. . . . Communism deprives no man of the power to appropriate the products of society; all that it does is to deprive him of the power to subjugate the labor of others by means of such appropriation. . . .

[I]n the most advanced countries the following [program] will be pretty generally applicable:

1. Abolition of property in land and application of all rents of land to public purposes.
2. A heavy progressive or graduated income tax.
3. Abolition of all right of inheritance. . . .
5. Centralization of credit in the hands of the State, by means of a national bank with State capital and an exclusive monopoly.
6. Centralization of the means of communication and transport in the hands of the State.
7. . . . [F]actories and instruments of production owned by the State. . . .
8. Equal liability of all to labor. . . .
10. Free education for all children in public schools.

Marx, Karl, and Engels, Friedrich. *The Communist Manifesto.* London: 1888.

---

movement encompassed a wide range of political doctrines, from the radical democracy of Chartism to the anarchism of Pierre-Joseph Proudhon and Mikhail Bakunin. Socialism began to emerge as the dominant philosophy of the workers' movement in the 1860s, and Marxism slowly became the dominant form of socialism. Karl Marx was born to a comfortable middle-class Jewish family that had converted to Lutheranism because of the legal requirements for Marx's father to practice law in Trier. At the University of Berlin, Marx became an enthusiastic student of G. W. F. Hegel, the German idealist philosopher who deemphasized the individualism of liberal philosophy and taught the preeminence of the state. Marx was deeply impressed with Hegelianism and adopted many of Hegel's concepts of the state and power, as well as his dialectic method of argument. Marx planned to become a philosophy professor, but his membership in a radical student organization during the age of Metternich closed that career to him. A brief stint as a journalist, which introduced Marx to industrial conditions, ended when censors closed his newspaper. Marx, already radicalized, began a life in exile. In France he learned revolutionary politics; in London he studied capitalist economics. By the 1850s Marx had already published several socialist works, and he had collaborated with Friedrich Engels (a factory owner's son) on *The Communist Manifesto* (1848), a concise statement of the theory of class struggle (see document 25.2). They wrote: "The history of all hitherto existing society is the history of class struggles." Only by overthrowing bourgeois society could peasants and industrial workers achieve social justice—hence their slogan, "Workers of the world, unite!" By the 1860s Marx—still in exile—was seeking to unite and direct European socialism through the International Workingman's Association, founded in London in 1864. This association (later called the First International) assembled leaders of the workers' movement in annual congresses and kept them informed of events in other countries.

Marxist socialism was only one variant in the emerging working-class political movement of the 1860s. Although it was the strongest version of revolutionary socialism (which accepted the violent overthrow of the government as the means to power), it faced much competition from advocates of evolutionary socialism (who believed that democratic elections would lead to socialism and therefore opposed violent revolution). Marx had little influence in Britain and was virtually unknown in France. He was not even dominant in his native Germany, where Ferdinand Lassalle had more influence. Lassalle, a successful lawyer and spellbinding orator, had organized workers at Leipzig in 1862 and created a national Workers Association in 1863. His theory of state socialism, in which governments would adopt socialist programs without being overthrown by a Marxist revolution, initially appealed to German workers, but Lassalle died in a duel in 1864. A more radical workers' party appeared in 1868, organized by Wilhelm Liebknecht and August Bebel. However, their first party congress, held at Eisenach in 1869, showed that socialism remained close to radical republicanism; the Eisenach program sought democratic reforms, not revolution.

Mid-Victorian Britain

If industrial conditions were heading toward revolution, the revolution would logically be expected to come in Great Britain, the birthplace of industrial society. The British census of 1851 showed the changes associated with the industrial revolution; more than 50 percent of the population lived in towns and cities, making Britain the first urban society in history. Comparative data show how unusual Britain was: The French census of 1851 found only 25.5 percent of the population in towns; the Spanish figure (1857) was 16.2 percent; and the Austrian figure (1857), 8.5 percent.

Despite the pressures of urbanization and industrialization, Britain had avoided revolution in 1848. Historians have explained this in many ways. Some have stressed the role of working-class religions (especially Methodism) that inculcated values such as the acceptance of one's social position and obedience to one's superiors. Charles Dickens put this into a prayer: "O let us love our occupations . . . and always know our proper stations." Others have extended this view to stress the importance of deference to the leadership of the upper class. As the constitutional scholar Walter Bagehot put it, "The English constitution in its palpable form is this: the mass of the people yield obedience to a select few." Economic historians have insisted that the answer is simpler: The working-class standard of living was steadily improving. A more traditional view stresses the importance of timely, but gradual, liberal reforms.

Yet mid-Victorian Britain faced problems. The kind of nationalist rebellion that struck central Europe might have occurred in Ireland, for the Irish problem was as severe as the plight of Czechs or Hungarians. The potato blight of the 1840s led to terrible famine and widespread unrest. The British responded by passing repressive laws. When the moderate Daniel O'Connell died in 1847, the leadership of Irish nationalism passed briefly to the Young Ireland movement, founded on the Mazzinian model by William Smith O'Brien. O'Brien tried to raise an insurrection at Tipperary in July 1848, but he failed and was sentenced to penal transportation to Tasmania. In the 1850s one of O'Brien's associates, James Stephens, founded the Irish Republican Brotherhood as a secret society dedicated to armed rebellion. Stephens's republican rebels became better known as the Fenians (honoring ancient Gaelic warriors, the Fianna). The Fenians planned an uprising in 1867 (for which they pioneered fund-raising among Irish immigrants in America) but were thwarted by informers.

In domestic affairs, Parliament advanced cautiously toward liberal-democratic government. This evolution extended civil rights to British Jews through the Jewish Disabilities Act of 1858, a generation after Catholic emancipation. The House of Lords had blocked Jewish (and atheist) emancipation on the argument that Britain was a Christian state and must therefore have a Christian Parliament. In typical British gradualism, Jewish emancipation provided only equal political rights; Oxford and Cambridge remained closed to them until a further reform in 1871.

The women's rights campaign also made historic progress during the 1850s. Parliament had briefly addressed this subject after Caroline Norton's struggle to win the Infant Custody Act of 1839, but no government adopted the principle of women's rights. In the 1850s another energetic woman with high political connections, Barbara Bodichon, resumed the campaign for the rights of married women. Bodichon had been one of the first women to attend Bedford College at the University of London. She managed her own school for women and there encountered the burden that the law placed upon a married woman. Bodichon published a pamphlet to educate the public: *A Brief Summary in Plain Language of the Most Important Laws of England Concerning Married Women* (1854). "A man and wife are one person in law," she explained. "The wife loses all her rights as a single woman, and her existence is . . . absorbed in that of her husband" (see document 25.3). That loss of legal identity was so complete that if a woman had her purse stolen, the thief could only be arrested for stealing the

❖ DOCUMENT 25.3 ❖

Barbara Bodichon: The Status of Married Women, 1854

A man and wife are one person in law; the wife loses all her rights as a single woman, and her existence is, as it were, absorbed in that of her husband. He is civilly responsible for her wrongful acts, and in some cases for her contracts; she lives under his protection or cover, and her condition is called coverture.

In theory, a married woman's body belongs to her husband; she is in his custody, and he can enforce his rights by a writ of habeas corpus; but in practice this is greatly modified. . . .

A man may not lend, let out, or sell his wife; such transactions are considered as being against public decency, and they are misdemeanors.

A wife's personal property before marriage [such as stock, shares, money in hand, money at bank, jewels, household goods, clothes, etc.] becomes absolutely her husband's, unless when settled in trust for her, and he may assign or dispose of it at his pleasure, whether he and his wife live together or not. . . .

Neither the Courts of Common Law nor of Equity have any direct power to oblige a man to support his wife. . . .

Money earned by a married woman belongs absolutely to her husband. . . .

The legal custody of children belongs to the father. During the lifetime of a sane father, the mother has no rights over her children, except limited power over young infants, and the father may take them from her and dispose of them as he sees fit. . . .

Bodichon, Barbara. "A Brief Summary in Plain Language of the Most Important Laws of England Concerning Married Women" (London, 1854). In Patricia Hollis, eds., *Women in Public, 1850–1900. Documents of the Victorian Women's Movement*. London: 1979.

---

property of her husband. Bodichon undertook a petition campaign and gathered tens of thousands of signatures that encouraged Parliament to take a first (and naturally, partial) step toward equal rights, the Married Women's Property Act of 1857. Encouraged by this progress and by the Matrimonial Causes Act of 1857 (which created Britain's first divorce courts), Bodichon devoted her resources to financing *The Englishwoman's Journal* (1858), which became the leading voice of British feminism.

The most debated mid-Victorian reform was electoral. Radicals had been disappointed in 1832, and in the 1850s they mounted another campaign to expand the electorate. John Bright produced a list of seventy-one constituencies with a population equal to metropolitan Manchester, noting that those boroughs held 117 seats in parliament to Manchester's 3. Several bills to expand the franchise or to redistrict seats failed during the next decade, until reform won a surprising champion—Benjamin Disraeli, a leader of the Tory Party. Disraeli concluded that "change is inevitable" and decided that it would be best if a conservative government arranged this "leap in the dark."

Disraeli's Reform Bill of 1867 doubled the electorate from approximately one million (4.2 percent of the population) to two million. It enfranchised urban males who paid £10 per year in rent. It also adjusted the overrepresentation of England (which held 72 percent of the seats in the kingdom) and the underrepresentation of cities; it denied rural workingmen the vote and explicitly excluded women by giving the vote to "every man." The debate included the first introduction of women's suffrage, however, championed by the liberal philosopher John Stuart Mill. Mill advocated women's suffrage in a speech insisting that the infringement of women's rights was "repugnant to the . . . principles of the British constitution." His motion received seventy-three votes in a house of 658 members, but that defeat led to the formation of suffrage societies in Birmingham, Manchester, and Edinburgh within the year. Two years later, Parliament accepted a partial form of women's suffrage when the Municipal Corporations Act (1869) allowed single women to vote in municipal elections.

❖

The Crimean War, 1853–56

Between 1815 and 1853, the Metternichian balance of power had given Europe a degree of stability in international affairs and a general peace among the great powers. Then, in 1853–56, Europe witnessed the first war

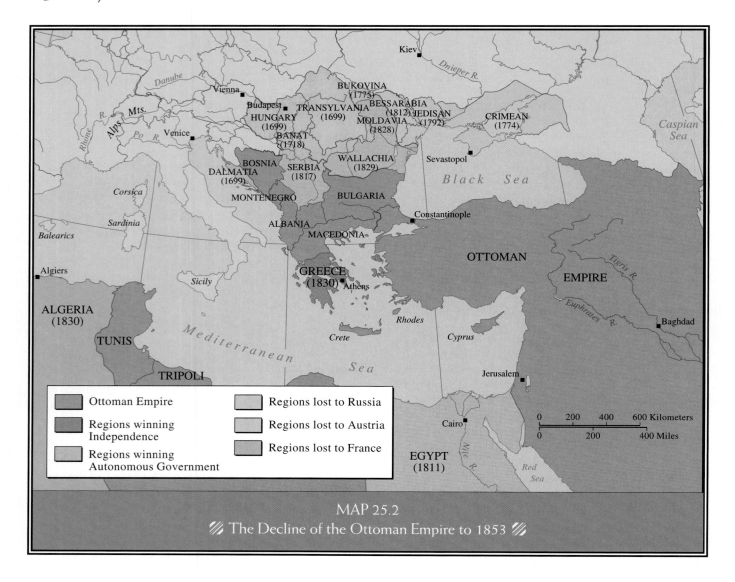

MAP 25.2

The Decline of the Ottoman Empire to 1853

among the great powers since the defeat of Napoleon. The Crimean War, was fought around the Black Sea (chiefly on the Russian peninsula of the Crimea). It demonstrated two important changes in the post-Metternichian world. First, the public discussion of international politics had changed. Ideology no longer defined relations—the politics of self-interest did. The Metternichian system had (in theory) united the great powers to defend the status quo; during the Crimean War, the great powers were candidly motivated by national interests, and they were willing to fight for them. As the nationalist foreign secretary of Britain, Lord Palmerston, told Parliament, "We have no eternal allies and we have no perpetual enemies. Our interests are eternal and perpetual, and these interests it is our duty to follow."

The second change in post-Metternichian power politics had more frightening implications: The

Crimean War gave the world its first glimpse of war in the industrial age, teaching lessons that were amplified during the 1860s by the American Civil War and the wars of German unification. Metallurgical advances, the factory system using interchangeable parts, and steam-powered transportation industrialized war.

The Crimean War originated in the eastern question, the complex issue of the survival of the Ottoman Empire. In the late seventeenth century, the Ottoman Empire had encompassed all of southeastern Europe, almost to the gates of Vienna (see map 25.2). By the end of the Napoleonic Wars, the Ottomans had lost vast territories to the Habsburg Empire (including both Hungary and Transylvania) and to the Russian Empire (which annexed the Crimea in 1783 and Bessarabia in 1812). In the 1850s Sultan Abdul Mejid ruled the eastern Mediterranean, the Balkans, the Middle East, and most of northern Africa. His authority was weak in many regions: Egypt had won autonomy in 1811, Serbia in 1817, and the provinces of Moldavia and Wallachia (the Danubian provinces) followed in 1829; Greece won independence in 1830. The European powers disagreed on the fate of the Ottoman Empire. Russia, coveting further expansion, favored the dismemberment of the empire; the British, fearing Russian ambitions, were determined to protect their naval superiority in the Mediterranean and the land routes to India by keeping "the sick man" alive. These interests defined the alliances of the Crimean War: Britain and the Ottoman Empire (joined by France and later Piedmont-Sardinia) fought Russia.

The immediate origins of the war were in the politics of 1848. A Russo-Ottoman dispute began when the sultan accepted revolutionary refugees fleeing the Russian army. A Franco-Russian dispute followed when Napoleon III tried to build his reputation as a defender of the Catholic Church by obtaining from Abdul Mejid the right to protect Catholic interests in Jerusalem. Nicholas I wanted similar rights to protect Orthodox interests, but the British and French blocked him. Such conflicts came to a head in May 1853 when an angry Nicholas instructed the Russian army to occupy Moldavia and Wallachia, provoking Britain and France to send a joint fleet to protect the sultan.

Fighting began when the Russian navy destroyed the Ottoman fleet off Sinope on the south shore of the Black Sea in November 1853. The Anglo-French fleet then entered the Black Sea (closed to warships by international convention) and declarations of war followed. In the autumn of 1854 the western allies landed armies on the Crimean peninsula. The French and British defeated the Russian army in several battles (including the battle of Balaclava, made famous by Tennyson's description of "the charge of the light brigade") and forced them to take refuge in the besieged city of Sebastopol. More than 250,000 soldiers died in the Crimea, but both sides suffered more from disease (especially cholera) than from fighting.

Britain and France won the most important battles of the Crimean War in part because their soldiers carried weapons with a range of one thousand yards while the Russian army still used smoothbore muskets with a range of two hundred yards. The large-scale use of rifles whose barrels were machined to close tolerances marks the beginning of industrialized warfare. It was made possible by the French invention of the Minié ball (1849), a conical bullet for rifled barrels that could be mass-produced. The next step in the industrializa-

tion of warfare came when an American, Samuel Colt, used automatic milling machines to produce interchangeable parts for the firearms themselves. His display at the Crystal Palace Exhibition of 1851 convinced the British to build an arms plant using mass-production techniques at Enfield in suburban London. The Enfield rifle and the Minié ball revolutionized warfare. The Crimean War showed the need for modern transport as well. Russian logistics depended upon 125,000 wooden carts pulled by draft animals, and it soon became obvious that they could not provide enough fodder for their support. The lesson was not lost on the more efficient armies of the 1860s, which learned to use railroads to transport both men and material.

The Crimean War was not fought to a decisive conclusion. Several events brought it to a victorious end for the allies: Piedmont-Sardinia (whose government wanted the friendship of Britain and France) joined the war against Russia; Austria (whose government feared Russian advances in the Balkans) threatened to do the same; and Nicholas I died. A peace conference at Paris in early 1856 quickly settled matters: Russia conceded some Danubian territory, promised to respect the integrity of the Ottoman Empire, and acquiesced in the neutralization of the Black Sea.

Russia in the Alexandrine Age

The thirty-seven-year-old Czar Alexander II who came to the throne of Russia in 1855 differed greatly from his father. He had spent a happier childhood, raised by humane tutors without the military discipline imposed on Nicholas. Alexander's personality was complex. He was an ascetic who sometimes slept on straw on stone floors. He had high moral aspirations and once spent a night locked in solitary confinement in one of his prisons to understand the conditions there. As crown-prince he joined the government commission studying the "flogging gentry." He seemed well suited to be the man who freed more than twenty million people from serfdom and earned the nickname "the czar liberator." Yet his morals permitted him to take young girls as mistresses, and his reforms were insufficient to prevent six assassination attempts in four years.

Alexander II assumed the throne in 1855, determined to emancipate the serfs (see table 25.1). One of his first acts was a manifesto giving the aristocracy a pragmatic explanation: "I am convinced that . . . it is better to begin to destroy serfdom from above than to wait for that time when it begins to destroy itself from

✠ TABLE 25.1 ✠

Serfs and Peasants in Imperial Russia, 1858

Peasant population	1858 Census
Serfs on private-owned estates	20,173,000
Serfs on imperial lands	2,019,000
Total serfs	22,192,000
Peasants on state lands	18,308,000
Peasants from state lands working in factories and mines	616,000
Peasants from state lands allowed to work in private factories	518,000
Peasants freed by military service	1,093,000
Total peasants	20,535,000

Source: P. I. Lyashchenko, *History of the National Economy of Russia* (New York: Macmillan, 1949) and Francis Conte, ed., *Les Grands dates de la Russie et de l'URSS* (Paris: Larousse, 1990), p. 131.

below." The thirty-year reign of Nicholas I had seen 556 serf rebellions, an average of more than one uprising per month; in the first years of Alexander's reign, the rate increased to 80 peasant rebellions per year. In 1857 the new czar named a secret committee, headed by his liberal adviser Nikolai Milyutin, to prepare for emancipation. Alexander II followed the advice of the Milyutin Commission and issued an edict (*ukase*) of emancipation in March 1861 on the same day that Abraham Lincoln took the oath of office as president of the United States. The details of emancipation were so complex that they required nearly five hundred pages. The basic provision ended serfdom, freeing 22,192,000 people, the majority of the Russian peasantry. Another obliged the serf-owners (most of whom opposed emancipation) to give the serfs land as a part of the emancipation. Serfs obtained "the full rights of free rural inhabitants," their homes, and arable land. Landowners, however, kept title to the land until the former serfs gradually paid for it. In the interim, the imperial government compensated landowners with bonds, and former serfs were obliged, through collective village obligations, to make the redemption payments on these bonds. Until the completion of redemption payments, peasants owed some labor to their landlords and shared their village's obligation. Emancipation began with enlightened principles but perpetuated involuntary servitude (see document 25.4).

Alexandrine liberalism went beyond the emancipation edict of 1861. Alexander II did not grant a constitution or a parliament, but his reforms made them logical expectations. In 1864 he created elective district assemblies (*zemstva*) with powers of local government. The *zemstva* were chosen by a three-class franchise similar to the voting for the Prussian *Landtag*, and legislation had to win the approval of the provincial governor, but this still left the assemblies a role in public health, education, and transportation. Educational reforms flowed from local self-government. Between the creation of the *zemstva* in 1864 and the end of Alexander's reign in 1881, 14,500 new schools opened in Russia. The tsar encouraged this trend by extending freedom to the universities. In 1864 the imperial government also reformed the judiciary and the criminal code. The new edicts, based on the principle of equality before the law, created an independent judiciary with a professional bar, abolished corporal punishment, and introduced the jury system in criminal cases.

The reforms of 1861–65 whetted the Russian appetite for further liberalization. During the remaining sixteen years of his reign, Alexander disappointed those who wanted more. He granted self-government to the cities in 1870 and reformed the army, reducing the term of service from twenty-five years to nine in 1874. But his liberalism stopped short of full westernization. He brought Russian institutions near to the level of the Austrian Empire, but not to Anglo-French standards. He began the economic modernization of his empire but did not bring it into the industrial age. A tragedy of historical development is that those who begin to modernize a backward country often awaken expectations that they cannot fulfull. The czar liberator became caught in this trap of rising expectations. He ameliorated the strict rule of Poland and amnestied thousands

A Radical Prince Describes the World of Serf-owning Aristocrats

Prince Peter Kropotkin (1842–1921) was born to the Russian nobility and spent his childhood in luxury. He became a geographer of distinction, known for his exploration of Siberia. Kropotkin slowly turned to social criticism, however, attacking the world into which he had been born. He entered radical politics in western Europe and spent several years in French prisons for his anarchism.

Wealth was measured in those times by the number of "souls" that a landed proprietor owned. So many "souls" meant so many male serfs: women did not count. My father, who owned nearly twelve hundred souls, in three different provinces, and who had, in addition to his peasants' holding, large tracts of land which were cultivated by these peasants, was accounted a rich man. He lived up to his reputation, which meant that his house was open to any number of visitors, and that he kept a very large household. We were a family of eight, occasionally ten or twelve; but fifty servants at Moscow, and half as many more in the country, were considered not one too many. Four coachmen to attend a dozen horses, three cooks for the masters and two more for the servants, a dozen men to wait upon us at dinner-time (one man, plate in hand, standing behind each person seated at the table), and girls innumerable in the maid-servants' room—how could any one do with less than this?

Kropotkin, Peter. *Memoirs of a Revolutionist*. Boston: Houghton Mifflin, 1899.

of his father's Polish political prisoners, yet confronted a major Polish revolution in 1863. He reopened universities and granted them greater freedom, yet they became centers of intellectual discontent pressing for more reforms. Alexander liberalized the press laws and harvested radical criticism. He emancipated the serfs but still faced peasant rebellions (one occurred in Kazan as early as April 1861). Revolutionaries repeatedly tried to kill him. They ultimately succeeded, and the reign that had begun with such promise ended with his blood on the pavement.

◆

The Unification of Italy: The *Risorgimento*

No event of the Crimean War was more surprising than the declaration of war on Russia by Piedmont-Sardinia, a distant state with no direct interests at stake. That decision was the carefully calculated work of the Piedmontese premier, Count Camillo di Cavour, the foremost architect of Italian unification. Cavour was a wealthy landowner with an advanced education in engineering and an admiration for England, which he knew much better than Sicily or Calabria. He was a short, plump, florid-faced man, a constantly cheerful hard worker who began the day at 5 A.M. His skills combined the pragmatism of the engineer and business executive with the cynical dexterity of the diplomat. Cavour had long advocated the liberalization of Italy. He meant the term broadly: Scientific agriculture, modern banking, railroad building, and free trade capitalism were as important as secularized institutions, a free press, and representative government. He became prominent in 1847 when he founded a newspaper, *Il Risorgimento* (the Revival), to champion Italian independence and progressive reforms. The newspaper became the leading voice of liberal-nationalism, making its title a synonym for the process of unification.

The revolutions of 1848 convinced most observers that rebellion in the streets would not drive the Austrians out of Italy. The leadership of a strong state, plus foreign assistance, would be needed. Both seemed distant during the reaction of 1849. In the south, Ferdinand of Naples was arresting, imprisoning, and torturing more than twenty thousand of his citizens. In Lombardy and Venetia, Marshal Radetzky dispensed the justice of the military tribunal—a few executions, many floggings, more imprisonments, thousands of exiles. Pope Pius IX, proscribed seven thousand people and executed priests with republican sympathies. Only in Piedmont, where King Charles Albert had abdicated in favor of his son, King Victor Emmanuel II, did the liberalism of 1848 survive. Victor Emmanuel kept the constitution (the *Statuto*) that his father had granted, despite an Austrian offer to cancel Piedmont's war indemnity if he abrogated the document. In 1850, Victor Emmanuel promulgated the Siccardi Laws, written by Cavour, limiting the powers of the Catholic Church by abolishing church courts, permitting civil marriage, and restricting the number of church holidays. This version of separation of church and state, which Cavour called "a free church in a free state," persuaded nationalists such as Garibaldi and Manin to recognize

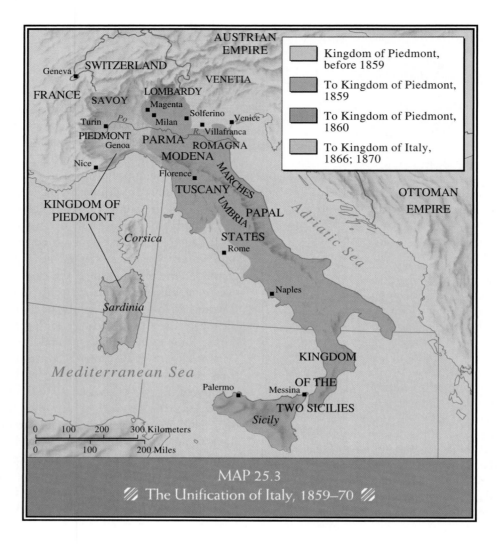

MAP 25.3

▨ The Unification of Italy, 1859–70 ▨

Legend:
- Kingdom of Piedmont, before 1859
- To Kingdom of Piedmont, 1859
- To Kingdom of Piedmont, 1860
- To Kingdom of Italy, 1866; 1870

the leadership of Piedmont. Cavour became premier in 1852 and kept that post for the rest of the decade, culminating in his leadership of Piedmont during a war of unification in 1859 (see map 25.3).

Cavour prepared for the war of 1859 by courting Britain and France. After sending the Piedmontese contingent to the Crimea in 1855, he raised the Italian question at the Paris Peace Conference of 1856. Cavour next sought an alliance with Napoleon III. He sent his teenaged cousin (and lover), the Countess Virginie di Castiglione, to become Napoleon's mistress and an Italian secret agent. He even profited from the attempt of a disgruntled nationalist, Felice Orsini, to kill Napoleon. The emperor seemed chastened by Orsini's conspiracy, as if embarrassed that he had slighted the Italian cause; he allowed Orsini to make a series of patriotic pronouncements ("So long as Italy is enslaved, death is a blessing.") before sending him to the guillotine. Cavour won his French alliance in 1858. He and Napoleon III

met covertly at the mineral springs resort of Plombières (eastern France) and reached a secret agreement. Napoleon pledged a French army of 200,000 men (larger than the entire Piedmontese army) "to drive the Austrians out of Italy once and for all and to leave them without an inch of territory south of the Alps." Cavour promised to return to France the province of Savoy (lost in 1815) and the coastal region of Nice, although his own mother was a Savoyard and Garibaldi had been born in Nice. In addition, Piedmont-Sardinia pledged 10 percent of its annual budget to pay the French war costs.

The Italian War of 1859 needed little provocation. Cavour mobilized the Piedmontese army, and the Austrians demanded that he demobilize it. When Cavour refused, the Austrians invaded Piedmont (April 1859) to teach him a lesson. This gave Napoleon III an excuse to send the French army to protect Piedmont. Bloodless revolutions soon drove pro-Austrian rulers from the small central Italian states. Allied armies entered Lombardy in June 1859 and forced the Austrians to retreat after the battle of Magenta (a village near Milan), which gave its name to a purplish-red color as a result of the quantity of blood spilled there. After another bloody but inconclusive battle, at Solferino in eastern Lombardy, the Austrian army retreated into a defensive complex of fortresses known as the Quadrilateral, and Napoleon III (who had seen battle for the first time) withdrew in nausea. More than seventy-five thousand soldiers were killed in less than two months of fighting, forty thousand of them in a single day at Solferino, and Napoleon III was not the only person horrified at the spectacle of industrialized armies slaughtering each other. J. Henri Dunant, a wealthy Swiss banker traveling in northern Italy, witnessed the battle of Solferino. The sight of the wounded, left to die in piles on the battlefield, so shocked Dunant that he devoted himself to creating an international organization to care for wounded soldiers. His efforts led to an international conference at Geneva and the (first) Geneva Convention (1864) in which twelve European states accepted Dunant's proposed relief society, the International Red Cross. In one of the final tragedies of Solferino, Dunant spent his entire fortune on this effort and lived thereafter in poverty, although he shared the first Nobel Peace Prize in 1901.

After the battle of Solferino, Napoleon III sought peace with the Austrians without consulting Victor Emmanuel II. Napoleon and Franz Joseph met privately at Villafranca (a village in Venetia) in July 1859 and agreed upon terms: Austria would keep Venetia but cede Lombardy to France, which could, in turn, give it to Piedmont. Victor Emmanuel accepted this agreement, despite the fury of Cavour, and yielded Nice and Savoy to France after plebiscites in the central states (Parma, Modena, Romagna, and Tuscany) made it clear that they would join Lombardy in merging with Piedmont. Before this new Italian state could be organized, another uprising began in Sicily. Garibaldi, as impetuous and idealistic as he had been in 1848, seized the initiative. With the connivance of Cavour, he raised a volunteer army of 1,067 men, dressed them in red woolen shirts, and launched an invasion of Sicily (see document 25.5). Garibaldi's red-shirts (also known as "the 1000") evaded the Neapolitan navy, trekked overland across Sicily, and were received as liberators in Palermo after defeating the Neapolitan army and setting up a provisional government. Garibaldi next crossed to the mainland, where the Neapolitan army dissolved, allowing the red-shirts to enter Naples.

◆ DOCUMENT 25.5 ◆

Garibaldi Calls Italians to Arms, 1860

Italians! The Sicilians are fighting against the enemies of Italy, and for Italy. It is the duty of every Italian to succour them with words, money, arms, and, above all, in person.

The misfortunes of Italy arise from the indifference of one province to the fate of others.

The redemption of Italy began from the moment that men of the same land ran to help their distressed brothers.

Left to themselves, the brave Sicilians will have to fight, not only the mercenaries of the Bourbon [of the government of Naples], but also those of Austria and the Priest of Rome.

Let the inhabitants of the free provinces lift their voices in behalf of their struggling brethren, and impel their brave youth to the conflict.

To arms! Let me put an end, once and for all, to the miseries of so many centuries. Prove to the world that it is no lie that Roman generations inhabited this land.

The Annual Register: 1860. London: J. G. and F. Rivington, 1861.

Garibaldi planned to continue his march northward to take Rome, believing that "[t]he Vatican is a dagger in the heart of Italy," and an uprising to support him began in the papal states in September 1860.

Cavour seized the opportunity provided by Garibaldi's victories to unite northern and southern Italy. Using the Roman rebellion as an excuse to intervene, Cavour sent Piedmontese armies into the papal states where they won rapid victories. After plebiscites in Sicily, southern Italy, and central Italy favored union with the north, the Kingdom of Italy was proclaimed in March 1861. Victor Emmanuel became the first king of Italy, and the *Statuto* provided the basis of an Italian constitution, including a parliamentary government elected by limited suffrage (2 percent of the population). The new kingdom did not include Venetia (which was still Austrian) or Rome (where the French army remained). Garibaldi attempted another uprising in 1862 to annex Rome as the natural capital of Italy, but he was beaten in a small skirmish and retired to his farm, where he plowed fields behind a team of jackasses he named Napoleon III, Pius IX, and Immaculate Conception. In one sense, the new Italy also included few Italians; barely 2 percent of the population spoke the Italian language, and most of the nation spoke local dialects. As one wit observed, because Italy now existed it would be necessary to invent the Italians.

Bismarck and the Unification of Germany

Following the revolutions of 1848, Germany remained a loose confederation of thirty-nine independent states: one empire (Austria), five kingdoms (Prussia, Bavaria, Württemberg, Saxony, and Hanover), one princedom (Hesse), and an assortment of grand duchies, duchies, principalities, and free cities. Although the Habsburgs had long dominated central European affairs, the leadership of the German states was shifting to Prussia for many reasons. The expansion of Prussia at Vienna in 1815 had affirmed Prussian dominance of northern Germany. The German states north of the Main River were also oriented toward Prussia by the confessional division of Germany into a Protestant north and Catholic south. States such as Hanover (95.7 percent Protestant), Hesse (83.1 percent), Mecklenburg (99.3 percent), and Saxony (98.1 percent) were more comfortable with Lutheran Prussia than with Catholic Austria; many of their leaders had been educated at the Protestant universities of Jena and Berlin. Industrial leadership and command of the Zollverein also made Prussia the economic leader of central Europe. German liberals preferred Prussian to Austrian leadership. Neither could be mistaken for a radical republic, but the Prussian record of reforms, from Stein and Hardenburg in 1807 to the constitution of 1850 (with an elective Landtag), was more appealing than the oppression of Metternich or Schwarzenberg.

The Prussian domination of Germany ultimately depended upon the army. Prussia, alone among the great powers, had not gone to war since the defeat of Napoleon, so statesmen did not appreciate the importance of Prussian army reforms undertaken by Gerhard von Scharnhorst and Count von Gneissenau after 1806. They had made all Prussian men liable for military service between ages twenty and thirty-nine, including a well-organized system of reserve duty that made the army potentially much larger than its apparent size. They had also adopted the revolutionary principle of

commissioning and promoting officers on the basis of ability, abolishing the aristocratic monopoly of rank (yet perpetuating some exclusions, such as Jews), and had created schools in which to train officers and a General Staff to provide the army with organization and planning. The Prussian General Staff had been quick to learn the lessons of war in the industrial age; they had, in the words of the nationalist historian Heinrich von Treitschke, "faith in the God who made iron."

The international tensions of the 1850s convinced the new king of Prussia, William I, that further reforms of the army were in order. In 1859 William named a new minister of war, General Albert von Roon, to supervise those reforms; Roon, in turn, selected a friend, General Helmuth von Moltke, to serve as chief of the general staff. Roon and Moltke needed a great deal of money for this undertaking, but their attempt to get financing precipitated a constitutional battle with the Landtag, where a liberal majority claimed the constitutional right to approve such expenditures. Roon fulminated that "in the sewer of doctrinaire liberalism, Prussia will rot without redemption," but the liberals held out. The constitutional battle over the Prussian budget lasted for nearly three years before a desperate king selected another of Roon's friends, Otto von Bismarck, to head the government. Bismarck was a hotheaded and mistrustful Junker who had followed a civil service career to ambassadorial posts in Frankfurt, St. Petersburg, and Paris. He was also a brilliantly pragmatic conservative who favored *Realpolitik* (a policy of realism) to defend the old order. As Bismarck put it, he "listened for the footsteps of God through history, and tried to grab hold of His coattails." Bismarck's *Realpolitik* made him at times a virtual dictator, led Prussia into three wars during the 1860s, and shoved German liberals into outer darkness; but at the end of his term as chancellor, a Prussian-dominated Germany was the strongest state in Europe.

Bismarck defeated the Landtag liberals by ignoring them and the constitution. He decided that "necessity alone is authoritative" and acted without legislative approval. Bismarck levied taxes, collected revenue, and spent money—all without legislation, without a budget, and without accounting. Roon and Moltke acquired breech-loading rifles (Johann von Dreyse's "needle gun") and Krupp cannons; these weapons soon acquired substantial real estate. "Better pointed bullets than pointed speeches," Bismarck felt. He explained his audacity in one of the most famous speeches of the century. He told a Landtag committee that it was the army that made Prussia great, not liberal ideals.

◆ DOCUMENT 25.6 ◆

Bismarck's "Iron and Blood" Speech on the Military Budget, 1862

Our blood is too hot; we prefer armor too heavy for our slight body, but we should put it to use nevertheless. The eyes of Germany are not fixed on Prussia's liberalism, but upon her power. Bavaria, Württemberg, and Baden may choose the liberal path. No one for that reason will allot Prussia's role to them. Prussia must gather up her strength and hold it in readiness for the favorable moment—a moment which has already been let pass on several occasions. Prussia's borders under the Treaty of Vienna are not suitable for a healthy national life. The great questions of the day will not be decided by speeches and the decisions of a parliamentary majority—that was the mistake of 1848 and 1849—but by iron and blood.

Kohl, H., ed. *"Die politischen Reden des Fursten Bismarck"* (Stuttgart, 1892). In Ludwig Schaefer et al., eds., *Problems in Western Civilization.* New York: Scribner's, 1965.

"The great issues of the day," he said defiantly, "will not be decided by speeches and the decisions of a parliamentary majority—that was the mistake of 1848 and 1849—but by iron and blood" (see document 25.6). These words stuck. Bismarck became "the Iron Chancellor" and Germany became a land of "iron and blood" instead of liberalism.

Bismarckian diplomacy and the Prussian army created a *kleindeutsch* Germany between 1864 and 1870 (see map 25.4). Bismarck first won the friendship of Czar Alexander II of Russia by helping him during the Polish revolution of 1863. He next positioned Prussia as the defender of German nationalism by supporting the confederation in a dispute with Denmark over two duchies, Schleswig and Holstein, located at their common border. In a dispute over the inheritance of these provinces, the German Confederation endorsed the claim of a German prince and in July 1863 called for the use of force against Denmark. Within a year Bismarck had produced an anti-Danish alliance with Austria and a war with Denmark. The Danes held out for five months before surrendering Schleswig and Holstein. Bismarck did not free the duchies; instead, he ne-

gotiated the Convention of Gastein (August 1865) by which Holstein became Austrian and Schleswig, cut off by Austrian territory, became Prussian. This difficult situation soon provided the disputes that led to a war between Austria and Prussia.

Bismarck prepared Prussia for a war with Austria by the skillful diplomacy that made him the most renowned statesman of the late nineteenth century. Two months after his treaty with Austria, Bismarck held anti-Austrian negotiations with Napoleon III at Biarritz on the southwestern coast of France. Using vague assurances of fair compensation to France (perhaps in Belgium, perhaps in Luxembourg, perhaps on the Rhineland frontier), Bismarck won a promise of French neutrality in the event of an Austro-Prussian War plus French help in making a similar deal with Italy. The Biarritz agreement of October 1865 was followed by a Prusso-Italian alliance (April 1866); Italy would help Prussia in a war with Austria in return for Venetia. Confident that he had secured the sympathies of Russia, France, and Italy, Bismarck provoked the Austrians into war, much as Napoleon III and Cavour had done in 1859.

By June 1866 Austria and Prussia were fighting an unexpectedly lopsided Seven Weeks' War (see table 25.2). Moltke directed a Prussian army whose needle-guns enabled them to fire five to seven times per minute from crouching or lying positions; the Austrians used muzzle-loading guns that required soldiers to remain standing while firing two or three rounds per minute. Moltke had also learned the lessons of the American Civil War on the use of railroads to mobilize large armies. The first advantage meant that Austria suffered four times as many casualties as Prussia; the second enabled Moltke to move a fresh army into a decisive battle at the Bohemian town of Königgrätz. The Austrians, whose introduction to industrialized warfare cost them more than twelve thousand men per week, surrendered shortly after the battle of Königgrätz (also known as the battle of Sadowa, for a neighboring village). Europe had entered a new age of warfare. As one military observer of the wars of German unification put it, "The armies taking the field today differ from those commanded by the Duke of Wellington [in 1815] as much as the latter differed from the Roman legions."

The stunning Prussian victory over Austria changed the balance of power in Europe. By the Treaty of Prague (August 1866), the Habsburg Empire gave Venetia to Italy and acquiesced in a Prussian reshaping of Germany. Franz Joseph had to swallow his own Olmütz. The confederation, the last remnant of centuries of Austrian hegemony in central Europe, was

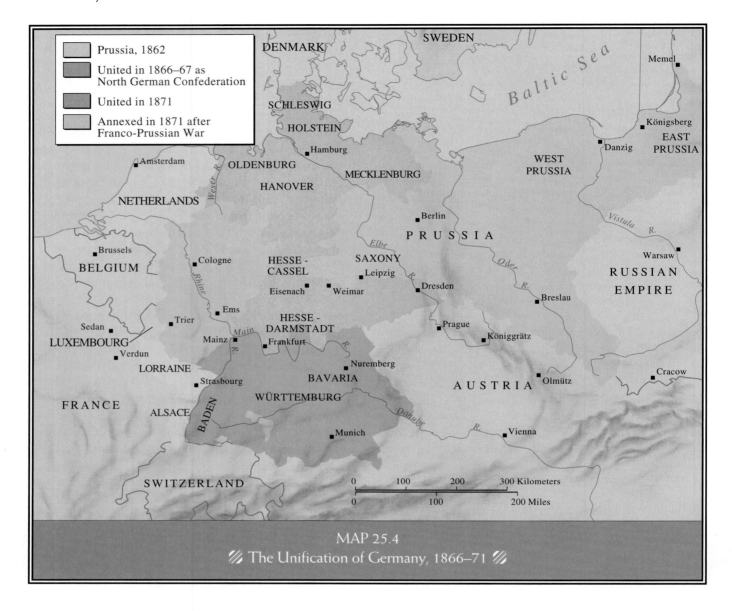

MAP 25.4

The Unification of Germany, 1866–71

abolished. Several of the north German states (including Hanover) were absorbed into an enlarged Prussia. All other German states north of the Main River (including Saxony) were brought into a new confederation under Prussian domination, the North German Confederation. A few southern states (Baden, Württemberg, and Bavaria) retained their independence, although Bismarck brought them into the Zollverein and military alliances with Prussia.

Bismarck resisted the desires of army leaders and the king to annex Austrian territories because he wanted Austrian support in the future. Franz Joseph had other urgent problems. Fearing that civil war could follow the humiliation of Königgrätz, the Austrian government reached a compromise (*Ausgleich*) negotiated by the Hungarian statesman Francis Deák. Deák, a

moderate liberal who had resisted Kossuth's radicalism in 1848–49, sought only the restitution of the ancient Hungarian constitution granting self-government in domestic affairs. In accepting the *Ausgleich* of 1867, the Austrians converted the empire into a dual monarchy known as the Austro-Hungarian Empire. Vienna continued to control the western half of the empire, but the Magyars now controlled the east, cheerfully accepting the task of keeping the Slavic peoples of the empire subordinated.

The Seven Weeks' War created a crisis in Franco-Prussian relations. One month after the battle of Königgrätz, Napoleon III reminded Bismarck of their Biarritz agreement. He requested, for the promised compensation, that France receive her eastern frontiers of 1814 plus additional territory such as Luxembourg.

◼ TABLE 25.2 ◼

Human Losses in the Wars of German Unification, 1864–71

Danish War (1864)		Seven Weeks' War (1866)		Franco-Prussian War (1870–71)	
Country	Losses	Country	Losses	Country	Losses
Austria	1,100	Italy	11,197	France	580,000
Prussia	2,423	Prussia	22,376		
Allied total	3,523	Allied total	33,573	Prussia	130,000
Denmark	11,000	Austria	87,844		
		German allies	24,628		
		Allied total	*112,472*		

Source: Calculated from data in Chris Cook and John Paxton, *European Political Facts, 1848–1918* (London: Macmillan, 1978), p. 177.
Note: Losses include the category of prisoners of war.

Bismarck categorically refused such compensation as offensive to German nationalism, intentionally angering the French as he had recently provoked the Austrians. Poor relations deteriorated into a Franco-Prussian War because of a dispute over Spain. In September 1868 the Spanish army overthrew the corrupt regime of Queen Isabella and created a liberal regime based on a newly elected Córtes. The Córtes created a constitutional monarchy but had difficulty finding a member of the European royalty to accept the throne. Finally, in the summer of 1869, Prince Leopold of Hohenzollern-Sigmaringen, a relative of King William I of Prussia, accepted the Spanish throne. The candidacy of a Hohenzollern prince alarmed the French, who envisioned allied armies on their southern and eastern borders, and they demanded that Leopold withdraw. The French applied diplomatic pressure and blocked the Hohenzollern candidacy in June 1870, but this episode led to a Franco-Prussian War in July. At a meeting between William I and the French ambassador at the resort town of Bad Ems (Hesse), the ambassador pressed the king to disavow the candidacy and to promise that it would never be revived. William reported the incident to Bismarck in a telegram that became known as the Ems Dispatch. Bismarck edited the telegram to make it seem like an arrogant French insult, then released the text to the nationalist press, hoping to goad the French into war. He succeeded; France declared war two days later.

The Franco-Prussian War of 1870–71 again demonstrated the superiority of the Prussian army and the advantages of the industrial age. General von Moltke used railroads and the telegraph to mobilize his armies with remarkable efficiency. The German invasion first drove the French army out of their frontier province (Alsace). Then, after less than a month of war, Prussian armies won a crushing victory at Sedan (September 1870) and took the emperor prisoner. Despite these defeats, France did not capitulate quickly. Forcing a French surrender required a four months' siege of Paris, which held out despite Krupp artillery shelling residential districts; Parisians lived on zoo animals, domestic pets, rats, and shoe leather before accepting an armistice in January 1871.

The surprising defeat of the French army, which Europeans had considered the successor to Napoleon I's armies, had tremendous consequences for Europe. France lost Alsace and part of adjacent Lorraine, accepted a proclamation of German unification (made at the French royal palace of Versailles), and endured a German triumphal march down the Champs Elysée. Bismarck's Frankfurt Peace Treaty also cost France a huge indemnity (five billion francs) and the military occupation of northeastern France until it was paid. For France, *l'annee terrible* (the terrible year) included another violent revolution and virtual civil war before the creation of the first enduring republic (the Third Republic) among the great powers. The Franco-Prussian War also led to the completion of Italian unification because the withdrawal of the French troops from Rome permitted the Kingdom of Italy to annex it. The greatest immediate effect, however, was Bismarck's merger of the North German Confederation and the south German states into the German Empire (known as the Second Reich, in recognition of the Holy Roman Empire, which Napoleon had abolished). This Germany, with its dominant army, its great industrial strength, and with royalism victorious over constitutionalism, had become the preeminent power on the continent of Europe.

CHAPTER 26

EUROPE IN THE BELLE ÉPOQUE, 1871–1914

Turn-of-the-century Europe is known as the Belle Époque (the beautiful era) because it was a period of unusual peace and prosperity compared with the preceding century or the following generation. For nearly half a century, between the Paris Commune of 1871 and the beginning of World War I in 1914, no European wars broke out among the great powers, no wave of revolutions arose. A long recession troubled people during the 1870s and 1880s, but the Belle Époque experienced nothing so severe as the great depressions of the 1840s or 1930s.

Chapter 26 examines Europe during this era of relative tranquility. It surveys the four greatest powers (the German Empire, the French Third Republic, Great Britain, and the Russian Empire) and draws some comparisons with other states. Each of the great powers made progress toward democratic societies, but the attitudes and institutions of the Old Regime still persisted. The chapter shows how reforms such as the creation of universal education in France by Jules Ferry, and the foundation of social security in Germany by Otto von Bismarck marked this democratic trend; however, it also shows a less democratic context, such as the Bismarckian attack on the Catholic Church during the *Kulturkampf*, the outbreak of the anti-Semitic Dreyfus affair in France, and the British refusal of home rule to the Irish. The final sections of the chapter discuss two of the major issues confronting European democracy during the Belle Époque: the growth of the labor movement and socialist political parties and the emergence of feminism as a mass movement. Workers, women, and minorities all demanded a share in the emerging democracy.

◇

The German Empire, 1871–1914

The Prussian victory in the Franco-Prussian War enabled Bismarck to bring the south German states (Baden, Bavaria, and Württemberg) into a union with

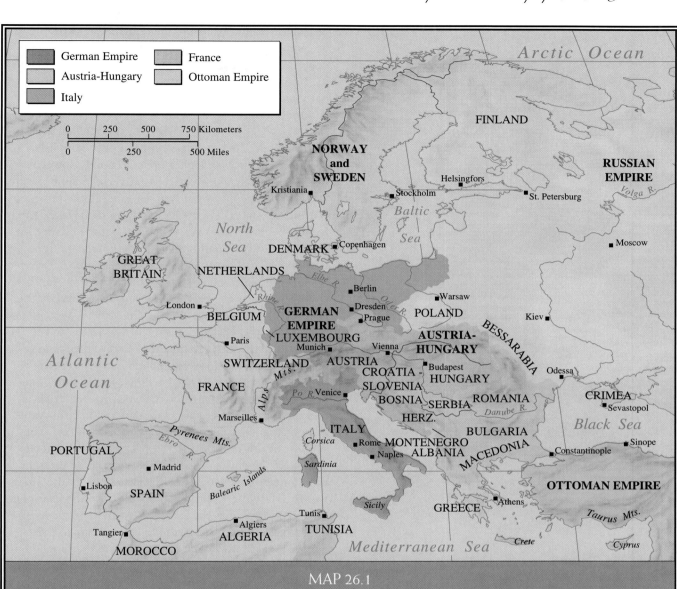

German Empire
Austria-Hungary
Italy
France
Ottoman Empire

0   250   500   750 Kilometers
0   250   500 Miles

MAP 26.1
Europe in 1871

the Prussian-dominated North German Confederation. The result was the German Empire (called the Second Empire, or Second *Reich*). Unquestionably the most powerful state on the continent, it stretched from the newly annexed French provinces of Alsace and Lorraine in the west to the Lithuanian frontier on the Baltic Sea (nine hundred miles away); its population roughly equaled France and Spain combined or Italy and Austria-Hungary combined. The German army had proven its mastery of the battlefield; German industry was beginning to demonstrate a comparable superiority. Just as the French had been forced to swallow German military leadership, the British increasingly lost ground

to German industrial might. Germany surpassed Britain in iron consumption by the late 1890s, then in coal consumption in the early twentieth century (see chart 26.1).

Although the German army and economy were the most modern in Europe, the government and its institutions remained rooted in the eighteenth century. Prussia had created Germany, and the German constitution (1871) showed the dominance of Prussia. The empire was a federal government of twenty-five unequal states. Many historic states survived with their monarchies intact but subordinated to the Prussian king, who was crowned emperor (*Kaiser*) of Germany. The empire thus

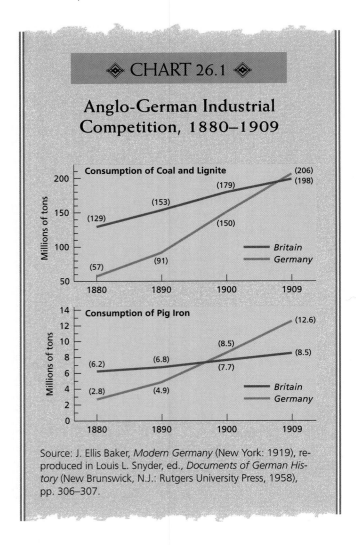

◈ CHART 26.1 ◈

Anglo-German Industrial Competition, 1880–1909

Consumption of Coal and Lignite

Millions of tons

(129) (153) (179) (206) — Britain
(57) (91) (150) (198) — Germany

1880 1890 1900 1909

Consumption of Pig Iron

Millions of tons

(6.2) (6.8) (7.7) (8.5) — Britain
(2.8) (4.9) (8.5) (12.6) — Germany

1880 1890 1900 1909

Source: J. Ellis Baker, *Modern Germany* (New York: 1919), reproduced in Louis L. Snyder, ed., *Documents of German History* (New Brunswick, N.J.: Rutgers University Press, 1958), pp. 306–307.

contained four kingdoms (Prussia, Bavaria, Saxony, and Württemberg), six grand duchies, five duchies, seven principalities, and three free cities. All states retained some sovereignty, with separate constitutions, taxes, and laws. The Bavarians even obtained "special rights" and kept their own postal service and diplomatic corps. An enlarged Prussia, however, encompassed 65 percent of all German territory, 62 percent of the population, and the richest economic areas (the Saar, the Ruhr, and Upper Silesia). The Prussian-dominated imperial government controlled the army, decisions of war or peace, and such central economic institutions as banking and the railroads.

The emperor of Germany (the king of Prussia, William I) held genuine power under the new constitution, which was significantly less democratic than the regimes in Britain and France. The emperor named a chancellor—the architect of unification, Prince Bismarck—to direct the government. The chancellor

never needed to be elected; he remained responsible to the emperor (who could dismiss him at any time) and could govern without the support of a legislative majority. Bismarck held office without leading any political party and without a parliamentary majority. He frankly admitted that his primary job was to preserve the monarchy: "The Prussian crown must not allow itself to be thrust into the powerless position of the English crown." The German legislature contained a lower house (the *Reichstag*), elected by universal manhood suffrage (at age twenty-five), and an upper house representing the states. The Reichstag's approval was needed for new legislation or a new budget, but the chancellor could perpetuate an old budget indefinitely and ignore the Reichstag. This constitution was a compromise between eighteenth-century absolutism and nineteenth-century popular sovereignty, a fact underscored by the absence of any German bill of rights.

During the "founding years" of the 1870s and 1880s, Bismarck built an alliance of conservative interests to support his government and battle its enemies. By 1879 he had gained the backing of the landowning aristocracy, the growing class of wealthy industrialists, and the supporters of militarism and nationalism—an alliance that set the direction of German history. The support of this coalition enabled Bismarck to fight the *Reichsfeinde* (enemies of the empire), whom he thought threatened the new empire. His target during the 1870s was the Catholic Church. The battle with the Catholic Church is known as the *Kulturkampf* (the struggle for civilization). The roots of the *Kulturkampf* lay in the confessional division of Germany and in the reinvigoration of the papacy under Pope Pius IX. The new empire held a Protestant (mostly Lutheran) majority, dominated by a Protestant state and monarch, but included a large Catholic minority. Pius IX made religion a major issue in Germany when he wrote the militant Syllabus of Errors and led the Vatican Council (1869–70) to state the doctrine of papal infallibility. The syllabus opposed cooperation with Protestantism and resisted the power of the state. Bismarck insisted that all Germans must accept the primacy of the German state, not of the church. Between 1872 and 1875, Prussia adopted a series of "May laws" increasing state control in matters previously left to churches and expelling clerics who lacked state certification. By 1876 no Catholic bishops were left in Prussia (outside of prison) and fourteen hundred parishes were vacant.

Bismarck ended the *Kulturkampf* in the late 1870s to shift his attention to socialism after Pius IX was succeeded by the more conciliatory Leo XIII and elections gave the Social Democratic Party (SPD) nearly 10 percent of the vote. An Anti-Socialist Law of 1878 prohibited socialist meetings, closed socialist newspapers, restricted socialist fund-raising, and permitted the harassment of the leaders of the SPD. Because the Second Reich had no bill of rights, this was all legal under German law. When trade union membership and socialist votes continued to increase, Bismarck changed his tactics. Concluding that "[s]omething positive should be done to remove the causes for socialism," he borrowed some of the legislative ideas that made socialism appealing. The deeply conservative Bismarck became one of the founders of the welfare state, telling the Reichstag that the state had "the duty of caring for its helpless fellow-citizens," adding that "[i]f someone objects that this is socialism, I do not shrink from it in the least." German health insurance began in 1883, workers' accident compensation insurance in 1884, and old age and disability pensions in 1889. These programs were kept small by granting pensions at age sixty-five when the average life expectancy at birth was forty-one. (Life expectancy did not reach sixty-five until the 1940s.)

The death of Kaiser William I in 1888 nearly led to the liberalization of Germany, a course favored by his son, Frederick III. Frederick reigned for only a few weeks, however, before dying of throat cancer at age fifty-seven, and his son, Kaiser William II, led Germany in a different direction. William II (often known by the German form of his name, Wilhelm) came to the throne at twenty-nine. He had no links to the dreams of 1848, the constitutional crisis of the 1850s, or the wars of the 1860s. Born with a deformed arm as the consequence of a forceps delivery, he was aggressive and arrogant to hide his insecurity. Bismarck tried to restrain the impulsive young emperor: "The Kaiser is like a balloon. If you don't hold fast to the string, you never know where he'll be off to." William II, however, decided in 1890 to retire the aging old chancellor. This episode, known as "the dropping of the pilot" (see illustration 26.1) clearly reflected the young emperor's intention to rule personally. In William's words, "If Frederick the Great had had such a chancellor, he would not have been Frederick the Great."

The leaders of Wilhelmine Germany were consequently men of less ability than Bismarck. They attempted to set a new course in the 1890s but accomplished little change in domestic affairs. Their greatest task was often to restrain the undemocratic instincts of the kaiser. William summarized his political sentiments when he attended a colonial exposition and observed a crude display of an African king's hut with the skulls of

Illustration 26.1

The End of the Bismarckian Era. Otto von Bismarck was the dominant statesman in Europe for nearly thirty years. In 1890 the thirty-one-year-old Kaiser William II ended that era by dismissing the seventy-five-year-old Bismarck; the German chancellor served at the pleasure of the monarch, not the Parliament. The cartoon shown here, from the British magazine *Punch,* summarized that event with a famous nautical metaphor, "the dropping of the pilot." During the next generation, the German ship of state lacked such a skilled hand at the helm.

his rivals posted outside: "If only I could see the Reichstag stuck up like that!"

The strongest chancellor of Wilhelmine Germany, Count Bernhard von Bülow, maintained the Bismarckian conservative coalition by giving higher agricultural tariffs to the Junkers and larger military contracts to industrialists. Bülow directed German energies to "world policy" (*Weltpolitik*). With the enthusiasm of the emperor and the energy of a strong minister of the navy, Admiral Alfred von Tirpitz, the Bülow government (1900–09) undertook a major arms race (especially in naval construction), the extension and consolidation of a German colonial empire (reluctantly begun by Bismarck), and the assertion of German leadership in global issues.

The French Third Republic

The war of 1870–71 destroyed the French Second Empire as it created the German Second Empire. Napoleon III was taken prisoner at Sedan in September 1870. When the news reached Paris, a bloodless revolution announced the creation of a Third Republic (honoring the predecessors of 1792 and 1848). The Third Republic became the first republic in European history to last long enough to offer a viable alternative to monarchy. Despite its rocky start, and a history filled with crises, the French Third Republic survived a generation longer than imperial Germany did.

Gambetta's provisional government of 1870 was replaced by an elected assembly after the capitulation of Paris in January 1871, when Bismarck allowed an armistice for the French to elect a new government to negotiate a peace treaty. Republicans and Parisians wanted to fight to the bitter end, while monarchists and the provinces favored peace. A majority of the nation would have voted against monarchy if that were the issue, but they accepted monarchist representatives as the price of peace. A French National Assembly chose Adolphe Thiers, a leader of the Orleanist monarchy and a critic of Napoleon III, as its executive. His government negotiated the Frankfurt Peace Treaty of May 1871, which cost France Alsace, much of Lorraine, and a five-billion-franc war indemnity (one billion dollars).

While the monarchist government of Thiers deliberated in suburban Versailles, Paris elected a municipal government, known as the Paris Commune of 1871, which denied the authority of the Versailles government. The Commune was a mixture of republicans, socialists, and anarchists. It did not last long enough to prepare a full program, but the Communards favored decentralized government, the separation of church and state, and a variety of social programs. Although it became a famous symbol in socialist literature, the Commune never even seized the Bank of France or the Stock Exchange. It (and smaller communes in other cities) survived only for a few weeks from March to May 1871 before falling in a bloody civil war. Thiers used the French army to attack Paris (while the German army watched), and Versailles troops fought Communards street-by-street, executing anyone who was armed. The Communards responded with a similar ferocity, executing hostages (including the archbishop of Paris) and destroying monarchist monuments. The Versailles army destroyed the Commune in a week of street fighting, known as "the bloody week." Under the direction of a candidly cruel general, the Marquis de Gallifet, the army began to punish the city. Gallifet felt justified in executing anyone who had stayed in Paris during the Commune, and he set such examples as executing wounded prisoners (wounds were evidence of being involved in the fighting) or white-haired prisoners (who were thought old enough to have fought in the revolution of 1848, too). The monarchical revenge upon Paris killed ten times as many Parisians (an estimated twenty-five thousand) as the Reign of Terror had guillotined there (twenty-six hundred). An additional forty thousand military trials produced ten thousand sentences of imprisonment or deportation to a penal colony.

Following this civil war, the French had great difficulty in agreeing upon a government during the 1870s. The National Assembly held a monarchist majority, split among supporters of three royal families: the Bourbon legitimists, who wanted to crown the grandson of Charles X; the Orleanists, who favored the grandson of Louis Philippe (see genealogy 24.1); and the Bonapartists, who supported Napoleon III or his son. While these factions squabbled, by-elections filled vacant seats with republicans, until even Thiers admitted that France must become a republic. The constitutional laws of the Third Republic were finally adopted in 1875. Monarchist deputies tried to make the new regime conservative, to guard against democracy and to provide for a future monarchical restoration. The constitution created a strong lower house of Parliament (the Chamber of Deputies), which was elected by universal manhood suffrage, and balanced it with an upper house (the Senate) elected indirectly. The head of the government (the premier) needed the support of a majority in the Chamber of Deputies.

In the late 1870s and the 1880s, republicans created many of the basic laws and institutions of modern France. Moderates led by a quiet lawyer named Jules Ferry and radicals led by the more flamboyant Georges Clemenceau compromised on an initial program. The Ferry laws of the early 1880s created one of the basic institutions of democracy—a public school system that was free, secular, and compulsory. This legislation opened secondary schools to women and to children of the poorer classes. While the population of France increased by less than 8 percent between 1883 and 1913, secondary school enrollment grew by 106 percent. The number of girls in secondary education grew from 11,100 to 55,700. The new school system was secular because republicans recognized that the church remained allied with the monarchy against democracy. As Gambetta once put it, "Clericalism, there is the enemy." Whereas 44 percent of all French children (60 percent of all girls) were educated by the church in 1876, less than 1 percent (0.05 percent of all boys) were in 1912. The same sentiment also led to secular hospitals, civil marriage and burial, and divorce. Clemenceau campaigned for the separation of church and state, plus other radical innovations such as an income tax and welfare legislation (see document 26.1), but most republicans still resisted such reforms.

A conservative reaction against this republicanism swept France in the late nineteenth century. A popular minister of war, General Georges Boulanger, became the symbolic leader of this reaction, and monarchists, nationalists, and Catholics rallied to "Boulangism," hoping that he would overthrow the republic. Boulangists won many seats in Parliament in the late 1880s and taught the world a lesson in electoral demagoguery, but the general, fearing conspiracy charges against him, fled the country and committed suicide. Right-wing enemies of the republic resumed the attack in the 1890s, when several republican politicians were involved in corruption surrounding a failed French attempt to build a canal across the isthmus of Panama.

The Panama Canal scandal of 1892–93 awakened one of the ugliest elements in European antidemocratic politics, anti-Semitism. Anti-Semitism remained widespread in the late nineteenth century, and newspapers and political parties blatantly called themselves anti-Semitic. Vienna elected an anti-Semite, Karl Lueger, as its mayor, and he fired Jewish officials and segregated the schools. In Germany, an Anti-Semite Party elected deputies to the Reichstag in every election from 1887 to 1912 and held eleven to sixteen seats after 1893. In Russia, the pogroms (direct attacks on Jewish communities) killed thousands and led millions to flee the country.

French anti-Semitism produced the most dramatic human rights battle of the nineteenth century—the Dreyfus affair. The French army was one of the few European armies of the 1890s to open its officer corps to Jews, and Captain Alfred Dreyfus was one of three hun-

◆ DOCUMENT 26.1 ◆

Clemenceau's Radical-Democratic Program, 1881

Article 1. Revision of the constitution. Abolition of the Senate and the Presidency. . . .

Article 2. Individual freedom. Liberty of the press, of meetings, of association, guaranteed by the constitution. . . .

Article 3. Separation of church and state. Suppression of state aid for churches. . . .

Article 4. The right of children to a full education. Secular, free, obligatory education.

Article 5. Reduction of the term of military service. Obligatory military service for all citizens. . . .

Article 6. Judicial system free and equal for all. Judges elected for short terms. . . . Abolition of the death penalty.

Article 7. Sovereignty of universal suffrage. . . . [S]horter terms of office for elected officials. . . .

Article 9. Autonomy for local governments. Town governments to control their own administration, finances, police. . . .

Article 11. Tax reform. . . . Suppression of indirect consumption taxes. Progressive taxes on capital or income.

Article 13. Legalization of divorce.

Article 14. Reduction in the length of the working day. Suppression of work by children younger than fourteen. . . . Creation of retirement savings for the aged and the injured.

Article 15. Revision of labor laws. . . . Responsibility of employers for work-related accidents, guaranteed by insurance.

Clemenceau, Georges. "Cahier des électeurs," trans. Steven C. Hause. *La Justice,* November 19, 1881.

dred French Jewish officers in the 1890s. Dreyfus was serving as an artillery expert on the French General Staff in 1894 when French counterintelligence found evidence that artillery secrets from the General Staff were reaching the Germans. Bigoted officers convicted Dreyfus of treason and sentenced him to solitary imprisonment on Devil's Island (off the northern coast of South America), although they never possessed a shred of evidence against him (see illustration 26.2). When evidence of Dreyfus's innocence began to accumulate in

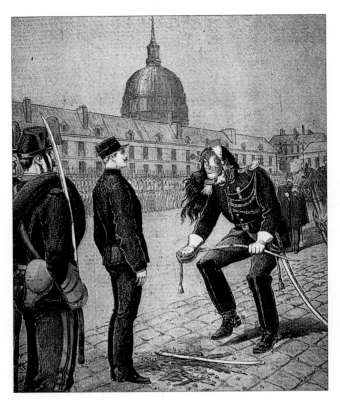

Illustration 26.2

🥀 **The Dreyfus Affair.** The 1894 court-martial of Captain Alfred Dreyfus, a Jewish officer on the French General Staff, led to the most passionate human rights debate of the nineteenth century in 1898–99, when the innocence of Captain Dreyfus was discovered but the army refused to reconsider its verdict. The debate between the defenders of Dreyfus and the defenders of the army awakened some of the most vehement anti-Semitism of the century. Here Dreyfus is stripped of his rank and watches his sword being broken before being sent to Devil's Island.

Illustration 26.3

🥀 **Hubertine Auclert.** Auclert founded the women's suffrage movement in France in the 1880s. Her most famous demonstration—depicted here in an error-filled contemporary sketch—was to invade a polling place on election day in 1908, smash a ballot box to the ground, and trample on men's votes. The woman with upraised arm at left is Auclert.

the late 1890s, Dreyfusards organized to free him. An anti-Dreyfusard coalition of monarchists, Catholics, nationalists, militarists, and anti-Semites defended the army and its verdict. French anti-Semitism remained a nasty element throughout the Dreyfus affair, but the battle came to focus on the issues of justice and individual rights balanced against the interests of the state. The fight continued until a second court-martial reconvicted Dreyfus in 1899, and an outraged president of the republic pardoned him.

The immediate importance of the Dreyfus affair was that it led to electoral victories for the republicans, radicals, and socialists who defended Dreyfus. This made the left-wing majority feel strong enough to return to its reform agenda. In 1905 they separated church and state, ending both state financial support for, and state regulation of, the churches. In 1906

Clemenceau became premier for the first time (at age sixty-five) and created the first Ministry of Labor, which he entrusted to a socialist. In 1907 feminists won one of their foremost goals, a married women's property act known as the Schmahl Law for the woman who had campaigned for it. The radicals also laid the basis of the French welfare system. Earlier governments had established state aid for neglected children (1889) and a medical assistance program (1893). Republicans now provided state support for hygienic housing (1902), needy children (1904), the aged and the infirm (1905–06), retirement pensions (1910), and large families (1913).

Such reforms still left a large democratic agenda on the eve of World War I. Despite feminist electoral violence by Hubertine Auclert and Madeleine Pelletier in 1908 (see illustration 26.3) and the peaceful demonstrations of hundreds of thousands of suffragists, women's suffrage remained far from acceptance. Despite greater labor violence and equally large demonstrations, the forty-hour workweek remained a utopian dream. Despite their electoral successes, the Radicals were unable to win a majority for proportional representation, the right of government employees to strike, a graduated income tax, maternity leaves for new mothers, or the abolition of the death penalty. Simply debating such issues, however, made France a leader of European democratic thought.

Late Victorian and Edwardian Britain

Great Britain also remained a leader in the evolution of liberal-democratic institutions. Smaller states were often pioneers in adopting radical reforms—as the Scandinavian states were with women's rights—but Britain and France defined the model of parliamentary democracy for the great powers. The British model remained one of gradual evolution, but the years before 1914 witnessed two important periods of rapid change.

The first period of intensive reform came during a Liberal government of 1868–74, elected after the expansion of the franchise in 1867. The leader of this government was one the greatest figures of nineteenth-century liberalism, William E. Gladstone. Gladstone had been elected to Parliament at twenty-two, following a brilliant career at Oxford in which he had won first-class honors in two separate fields. He began his career as a cabinet minister at thirty-four and served as an M.P. for more than sixty years. Gladstone served four terms as prime minister of Britain, beginning with his "great ministry" (1868–74) and ending with a cabinet in his eighties (1892–94). He brought to government a religious scholar's moralistic temperament that made him resemble an Old Testament patriarch. Gladstone supported his moralism with an intellect that dominated Parliament. He could speak for three hours without a break or summarize an arduous debate with a long quotation in untranslated Latin, leaving few M.P.s to match him.

Gladstone's great ministry adopted nearly a dozen major reforms. He did not attempt another expansion of the franchise (although that was on his agenda) or to give women the vote (which was not in his plans). He did, however, enhance British democracy with a Secret Ballot Act of 1872. The Elementary Education Act of 1870 (known as the Forster Act for its author, William Forster) made primary schooling available to all children in England and Wales, from age five to thirteen. In contrast to the Ferry laws in France, the Forster Act subsidized private, tuition-paying schools and created state schools only, as Forster put it, "to complete the present voluntary system, to fill up the gaps." In Britain as in France, adult illiteracy quickly fell, from 20 percent of adult males (1870) to 2 percent (1900). Gladstone similarly opened higher education. A University Tests Act (1871) abolished religious barriers to enrollment at Oxford and Cambridge, permitting Catholics, Jews, and nonbelievers to matriculate. At the same time, two colleges at Cambridge were opened to women, although women remained ineligible for degrees until after World War I.

Gladstone's government also tackled army reform, judicial reform, trade union rights, the civil service, and the Irish question. The sale of commissions as officers in the army was abolished, and the term of military enlistment was reduced from twelve years to six. Judicial reforms ended imprisonment for debt and created appellate courts. Workers won the complete legalization of unions and the recognition of their right to strike, but not the right to picket their employers. Civil service reforms created a modern bureaucracy by abolishing the patronage system of giving jobs to friends and supporters in favor of competitive examinations for all posts except those in the Foreign Office. Gladstone's great ministry also began to address the Irish question. An Irish Land Act gave some protection to Irish farmers who rented lands and could be evicted after poor harvests. Gladstone also disestablished the Church of Ireland (the Anglican Church in Ireland), meaning that the people of Ireland (90 percent Catholic) were no longer required to provide tax support for a Protestant state church. Such reforms built cooperation between the Liberal Party and Irish M.P.s, who pressed Gladstone to take the next logical step—grant the Irish home rule in domestic matters.

The end of Gladstone's great ministry returned to office his long-time rival, the conservative prime minister Benjamin Disraeli. In contrast to Gladstone's sober strengths, Disraeli sparkled with wit and style. He derided Gladstone's much-praised oratory as "harebrained chatter." Disraeli had flirted with reforms in his earlier career, but in his second term as prime minister (1874–80), he steered a more traditional course, satisfying conservatives opposed to liberal reformism. As one conservative essayist, Thomas Carlyle, had summarized the attack on Gladstonian liberalism: Britain was a nation of "mostly fools" and it was dangerous to "believe in the collective wisdom of individual ignorance." Disraeli shrewdly turned the government's attention away

⚑ TABLE 26.1 ⚑

The Democratization of the British Electorate, 1831–86

Year	England and Wales Eligible voters	Percentage of total population	Scotland Eligible voters	Percentage of total population	Ireland Eligible voters	Percentage of total population	United Kingdom Eligible voters	Percentage of total population
1831	435,000	3.1	5,000	0.2	76,000	0.9	516,000	2.1
1833	656,000	3.5	64,000	2.7	92,000	1.2	812,000	3.4
1866	1,054,000	5.3	105,000	3.4	205,000	3.5	1,364,000	4.7
1868	1,960,000	9.8	236,000	7.7	222,000	3.8	2,418,000	8.4
1883	2,618,000	10.1	310,000	8.3	224,000	4.3	3,152,000	9.0
1885	4,380,000	16.9	551,000	14.7	738,000	14.3	5,669,000	16.3

Source: Compiled from data in Chris Cook and Brendan Keith, *British Historical Facts, 1830–1900* (London: MacMillan, 1975), pp. 115, 232–33.

from domestic issues and aimed for British success in foreign and colonial affairs.

Gladstone returned to his reform agenda in a second ministry (1880–85) after shocking conservatives by introducing campaigning to British politics; he toured the nation and appealed directly to the voters. This time Gladstone sought democratization and Irish home rule. His Representation of the People Bill (1884) extended the vote in rural Britain and brought the kingdom closer to the universal manhood suffrage that existed in France and Germany (see table 26.1). Domestic servants were still denied the vote, as were all women.

The Irish question presented greater difficulties. Home rule had become the objective of Irish politicians in the 1870s when Isaac Butt, a lawyer and the son of a Protestant clergyman, had formed a coalition of Catholics and Protestants to seek it. When Butt's movement won the support of most Irish M.P.s in 1874, it became the Irish Home Rule League. A few years later, the league found a popular successor to Butt in Charles Stewart Parnell, a Protestant landowner who had entered Parliament in 1875 at twenty-nine. Parnell managed to unite Irish nationalists, including the more militant and republican Fenians; the British increased his popularity by imprisoning him and watching while he organized a farmers' rent strike from his cell. Parnell denounced revolutionary violence in 1882, after the assassination in Dublin of the two leading cabinet members for the government of Ireland, an act known as the Phoenix Park murders. Parnell and his followers developed nonviolent tactics such as the boycott of uncooperative landlords; the name of that tactic came from a campaign in which no servants, no farm workers, no shopkeepers, not even a postman would acknowledge the existence of a landlord in County Mayo named Charles Boycott.

Gladstone adopted the cause of home rule in 1886 and introduced the first Home Rule Bill with a three-and-one-half-hour speech at the age of seventy-seven. This issue shattered the Liberal Party. Ninety-two Liberal M.P.s, led by the prominent Liberal spokesman of the 1840s, John Bright, and Bright's protégé, a wealthy manufacturer from Birmingham, Joseph Chamberlain, left the party and formed their own faction, the Unionists. Gladstone strove to build a majority in favor of home rule but suffered another setback when Irish M.P.s were divided by a scandal over Parnell's love affair with the wife of another M.P. Gladstone defended Parnell, observing that "I have known eleven prime ministers, ten of whom were adulterers," but Parnell's career, and the chances for home rule, were ruined. Gladstone obtained the prime ministry for the fourth time in 1892. He introduced a second Home Rule Bill a few months later (1893), and his Liberal majority carried it through the House of Commons. A decade of debate, however, had entrenched conservative opposition to home rule. An aggressive Tory M.P. who had once led the progressive wing of the party, Lord Randolph Churchill, fought Gladstone under the slogan "Home Rule Means Rome Rule." This campaign encouraged resistance in the Protestant population of northern Ireland, where militants warned that "Ulster will fight." Such passions led the conservative majority in the House of Lords to crush the second Home Rule Bill, 419–41.

◆ DOCUMENT 26.2 ◆

Lloyd George The "People's Budget"

The provision for the aged and deserving poor—was it not time something was done? It is rather a shame that a rich country like ours—probably the richest in the world, if not the richest the world has ever seen—should allow those who toiled all their days to end in penury and possibly starvation. It is rather hard that an old workman should have to find his way to the gates of the tomb, bleeding and footsore, through the brambles and thorns of poverty. We cut a new path for him. . . : There are many in the country blessed by Providence with great wealth, and if there are amongst them men who grudge out of their riches a fair contribution towards the less fortunate of their fellow countrymen they are very shabby rich men.

We propose to do more by means of the Budget. We are raising money to provide against the evils and suffer-ings that follow from unemployment. We are raising money for the purpose of assisting . . . to provide for the sick and the widows and orphans. . . .

Some of our critics say, "The taxes themselves are unjust, unfair, unequal, oppressive—notably so the land taxes. . . ." They are now protesting against paying their fair share of the taxation of the land, and they are doing so by saying, ". . . You are putting burdens upon the people which they cannot bear." Ah! they are not thinking of themselves. Noble souls! . . . [W]e were so impressed by this tearful appeal that at last we said, "We will leave [small landowners] out."

George, Lloyd. In *The Times*, July 31, 1909

The early twentieth century witnessed a second period of radical reform in Britain, comparable to Gladstone's great ministry. The Liberal Party built a new majority in 1905, sometimes supported by the twenty-nine M.P.s of the new Labour Party, which had been organized in 1906 by a Scottish miner, Keir Hardie, and a Scottish journalist, Ramsay MacDonald. One of the first legislative actions of the new government, the Trades Disputes Act of 1906, responded to labor's greatest grievance. Gladstone's Trades Disputes Act of 1871 had given legal recognition to unions, and they had gradually gained such rights as picketing. In 1901, however, the House of Lords had rendered a dramatically antilabor ruling in a legal case known as the *Taff Vale Railway Company v. Amalgamated Society of Railway Servants.* The *Taff Vale* ruling held that a union could be sued for the actions of its members and that a union could be held liable for a company's losses during a strike. The Liberal government of 1906 repaid labor support by overturning the *Taff Vale* decision and restoring the right to strike and picket, through the Trade Disputes Act.

The Liberal coalition found its radical voice in David Lloyd George, who typified the changing nature of liberalism from a laissez-faire doctrine of noninterventionist government to an activist doctrine of governmental intervention to protect the vulnerable. A

Welsh lawyer possessed of a charming yet ferocious mastery of debate, Lloyd George drafted the government's economic policies as chancellor of the exchequer (minister of finance) and led Britain into the age of welfare legislation. A Workmen's Compensation Act (1906) greatly expanded benefits; an Old Age Pensions Act (1909) replaced the workhouse system; and the National Insurance Act (1912) introduced health and unemployment insurance. The cornerstone of the liberal welfare state was the budget that Lloyd George introduced in 1909. The "people's budget" attacked the conservative tradition that the state could spend large sums for military preparations (such as large new battleships) but not for social welfare (see document 26.2). Lloyd George further angered conservatives by proposing to pay for these expenditures by taxes on the rich.

The Lloyd George budget led to the democratization of Parliament (by ending the power of the House of Lords to block legislation) and therefore to hopes for a third Home Rule Bill. The Lords, which remained an unelected body defending the interests of the landed aristocracy, traditionally held the power to veto any legislation except a budget. Lloyd George, however, had presented them with an irresistible target. The House of Lords vetoed the People's Budget of 1909, creating a constitutional crisis and exposing itself to a Liberal assault. The Liberal government turned to the new king, George V (reigned 1910–36), and asked him to support them in defending the prerogatives of the House of Commons. George V reluctantly promised to ennoble four hundred commoners (enough new peers to create a Liberal Party majority in the House of Lords) if the Conservative nobles did not back down. Forced to choose between surrendering their obstructionist power and the prospect of Lloyd George selling hundreds of titles to the highest radical bidder, the Tories capitulated. The result was the Parliament Act of 1911. The House of Lords surrendered its claim to power over the budget and lost its absolute veto over all legislation. The Lords retained a suspensive veto; they could delay a law by vetoing it for two consecutive years, but they could not block a bill on its third passage of the Commons.

This democratization of Parliament raised Irish hopes for home rule because they still had the support of a liberal majority in the House of Commons. When the third Home Rule Bill sailed through the House of Commons in 1912, again to be vetoed in the House of Lords, it seemed certain that Ireland would receive self-government in 1914. Protestants in northern Ireland warned of civil war. Ironically, a war of another kind blocked home rule: World War I began in 1914, shortly before home rule would have become law, and Liberals suspended the issue until the war's end. The Irish felt betrayed by the British political system and would rise up during the war in the Easter Rebellion of 1916.

Though the Irish did not win self-government until 1920, the Liberals had tried harder on their behalf than they had for women's rights. The first women's suffrage debate in Parliament (1867) and the right of women to vote in local elections (1869) had arrived before the first Home Rule Bill (1886), but neither of the major parties was willing to adopt the cause of votes (or candidacy) for women. Gladstone consciously chose to exclude women's suffrage from his electoral reform bill (1884). Thus, as suffragism became a widespread issue across Europe, Britain seemed scarcely closer to change in 1906 than thirty years earlier.

Imperial Russia on the Eve of Revolution

The Russian Empire remained markedly different from Britain, France, and Germany in the late nineteenth century. Despite the abolition of serfdom in 1861, Russian society was more typical of the Old Regime than of the industrialized liberal democracies of western Eu-

rope. Ninety percent of the population still lived in a rural world. Urbanization was so slight in 1870 that capitals such as Helsinki (twenty-six thousand) or Kiev (seventy-one thousand) remained mere towns. Despite the reforms of the Alexandrine age, Russia remained a peasant society ruled by aristocratic landowners unrestrained by a parliament, a constitution, or a bill of rights. The distribution of land at emancipation had not created a class of peasant landowners with small farms. More than 80 percent of the peasant land in Russia was owned communally (although some regions, such as Lithuania, had significant private ownership). These communal farms of the late nineteenth century fell short of western standards; a study of 1900 found that 83 percent of all peasants still used wooden plows.

Russian backwardness produced many tragedies, such as the killing of Alexander II in 1881. An old witticism of European statecraft said that Russia was "an absolute monarchy tempered by regicide." That remark became somewhat less amusing after 1879, when a group of radicals founded a revolutionary society named the People's Will (*Narodnaia Volia*). Their program resembled democratic socialism in the west (a Russian Parliament, universal suffrage, freedom of speech and the press, peasant ownership of the land, and worker control of the factories), but their chief activity was assassination. The People's Will made five unsuccessful attempts to kill Alexander II, including burrowing under railroad tracks to blow up his train, before succeeding on their sixth attempt.

The murdered czar's son, Alexander III (reigned 1881–94), had the Romanov family's extraordinary height (6′6″ in a world where the average height was below 5′6″) and exceptional strength (he once intimidated a statesman at the dinner table by tying a piece of silverware into a knot) but none of the liberal sentiments that had made his father the most significant Russian reformer of the century. Alexander III's mind had been shaped by his chief adviser, Konstantin Pobedonostsev, a deeply conservative, antidemocratic man who opposed the westernization of Russia as destructive of national traditions. His official position as procurator of the holy synod (minister of religion) enabled him to state the regime's philosophy. He taught that popular sovereignty was "among the falsest of political principles" and that universal suffrage was "a fatal error, and one of the most remarkable in the history of mankind" (see document 26.3). Pobedonostsev and the head of the secret police, Vyacheslav Plehve, presided over a police state that cracked down on dissident groups. They tightened censorship, established firmer control over schools, and reduced the independence of

❖ DOCUMENT 26.3 ❖

Pobedonostsev: Conservative Critique of Democracy, 1898

Konstantin Pobedonostsev expressed his opposition to the liberalization of Russia in his memoirs, published after Count Sergei Witte had begun to lead Russia toward westernization.

Among the falsest of political principles is the principle of the sovereignty of the people, the principle that all power issues from the people, and is based upon the national will—a principle which has unhappily become more firmly established since the time of the French revolution. From it proceeds the principle of parliamentarianism, which, today has deluded much of the so-called "intelligentsia," and has unfortunately infatuated certain foolish Russians. It continues to maintain its hold on many minds with the obstinacy of a narrow fanaticism, although every day its falsehood is exposed more clearly to the world. . . .

What is this freedom by which so many minds are agitated, which inspires so many insensate actions, so many wild speeches, which leads the people so often to misfortune? In the democratic sense of the word, freedom is the right to political power, or, to express it otherwise, the right to participate in the government of the state. This universal aspiration for a share in government has no constant limitations, and seeks no definite issue, but incessantly extends. . . . Forever extending its base, the new democracy now aspires to universal suffrage—a fatal error, and one of the most remarkable in the history of mankind. . . . In a Democracy, the real rulers are the dexterous manipulators of votes. . . . [T]hey rule the people as any despot or military dictator might rule it.

Pobedonostsev, Konstantin. *Reflections of a Russian Statesman.* London: Robert Long, 1898.

---

the judiciary. Russification was again imposed on minorities. Jews suffered especially severe restrictions, but Catholics in Poland and small sects, such as the "Old Believers," also endured harassment. Nearly eight thousand trials of political opponents were held in the 1880s. Alexander II's reforms were diluted, and two-thirds of the eligible voters for the *zemstva* were disenfranchised; turn-of-the-century St. Petersburg thus had an electorate of seven thousand men in a population of 1,267,000 (0.6 percent).

The repressive regime of Alexander III, Pobedonostsev, and Plehve provoked a revolutionary opposition. Populist movements, collectively known as the *Narodniki,* continued the Russian tradition of peasant socialism and assassinations, although the government broke up the most militant terrorist groups. Early industrialization in Moscow and St. Petersburg led some dissidents to Marxism. George Plekhanov began to introduce Marxism into Russia in the 1880s, and imperial censors assisted him by permitting the publication of *Das Kapital,* reasoning that it was too boring to be a threat.

Alexander III died of natural causes in 1894, bringing to the throne his son, the last czar of Russia, Nicholas II. Nicholas was a more sensitive and intelligent man than his father, but less forceful and resolute. He was fortunate to inherit a capable statesman, Count

Sergei Witte, whom Alexander had named minister of finance in 1892. Witte's tenure in that post and subsequent leadership as prime minister marked the first sustained effort to bring Russia into the industrial age. He pressed the cause of economic westernization with a vigor unseen since Peter the Great, arguing that an unindustrialized Russia would be unable to compete in the European state system. During the 1890s Witte's view of Russia's future supplanted Pobedonostsev's slavophilic insistence upon guarding Russia's separate historic evolution.

The Russia of the 1890s had far to go before it could compete with western Europe. The empire had a large labor supply, but restraints remained upon its mobility, because of the obligation of former serfs to help their commune repay the redemption bonds given to the landowners at the time of emancipation. Nearly 10 percent of the imperial budget depended upon these redemption payments, and rural communities kept a maximum working population in the fields. Factories consequently remained few in number and small in size before the expansion of the 1890s. A study of Ukraine has shown that factories tripled their average workforce (to forty-six hundred workers) during that decade. Russian agriculture had the potential to feed this urban population and to raise capital by exporting surpluses, but it remained too backward to fulfill the promise. At the turn-of-the-century (1898–1902), Russian farmers produced an average yield of 8.8 bushels of grain per acre, whereas British farmers supported an urban population by producing 35.4 bushels per acre. As late as 1912 the entire Russian Empire contained a total of 166 tractors.

Sergei Witte addressed Russian backwardness in several ways. Taxes on the sale of alcoholic spirits provided the largest source of revenue, so Witte built a state monopoly on such sales. He put the Russian currency (the ruble) on the gold standard, to enhance credit with foreign lenders. Russia already carried a large national debt, which amounted to 5.5 billion rubles in 1891—nearly six times the annual budget of the empire. Such debt had become so integral to European economics that Russia was still repaying Dutch loans of 1778 and 1815 and devoted nearly 27 percent of its budget to loan repayments. Witte believed that "[n]o country has ever developed without foreign capital" and sought new loans. He used this investment to found a national bank, provide state aid in building factories, and construct the Russian railroad system. Witte created a system of state-controlled (60 percent ownership) railways. He doubled the total of working track in Russia during the 1890s, including the construction of the Trans-Siberian Railroad, a five-thousand-mile link between Moscow and the Pacific port of Vladivostok. The cost of this program, however, was a national debt so severe that state supported progress in other areas was impossible.

Industrialization increased political discontent. The living and working conditions that characterized early industrialization everywhere increased the revolutionary violence that Russia had experienced for a generation. Attempted assassinations became a regular feature of Russian politics. During the 1890s two prime ministers, an education minister, a provincial governor, and an uncle of the czar were among those killed. With no Parliament, underground radical parties flourished. Plekhanov organized the Russian Social Democratic Party in 1898, and agrarian radicals from the populist tradition created a competing organization, the Socialist Revolutionary Party, in 1901. This underground—largely led by people from educated, middle-class backgrounds—became more complex in 1903 when the Social Democrats held a party congress in London and split in two. That congress marked the emergence of Lenin in Russian politics. Lenin (the adopted name of a lawyer born Vladimir Ulyanov) was radicalized by the execution of his older brother for plotting against the czar. Arrested in 1895 and sent to Siberia for spreading propaganda in St. Petersburg, Lenin reached

Switzerland in 1900 and there published a revolutionary newspaper, *Iskra* (the Spark), to be smuggled into Russia. He joined Plekhanov (also an intellectual living in exile) in building the Social Democratic Party, but he soon rejected Plekhanov's idealistic socialism in favor of a more revolutionary doctrine. Lenin called for a small party of revolutionary leaders instead of a mass movement. In a clever propaganda stroke, Lenin named his small faction of the party the Bolsheviks (the majority), branding the more numerous supporters of Plekhanov the Mensheviks (the minority).

In addition to the underground activities of the Social Democrats and the Social Revolutionaries, open opposition existed to czarist autocracy among liberal-democratic westernizers. This movement drew its strength from the intelligentsia, the liberal professions, educated urban circles, and *zemstvo* workers who combined to organize the Union of Liberation in 1903. This group was a nascent liberal political party, critical of autocracy and calling for a constitution, a parliament, and a bill of rights.

Russia experienced a major revolution in 1905. Crushing defeat in the Russo-Japanese War of 1904–05, (see chapter 27), led to this revolt. In mid-1904, Plehve was killed in a terrorist bombing. A few weeks later, *zemstvo* delegates assembled for a congress in St. Petersburg and asked Nicholas II to call a Russian Parliament. During the winter of 1904–05, as the Russian army suffered reverses in the Orient, strikes and demonstrations began. A turning point came in January when an Orthodox missionary to the working-class slums of St. Petersburg, George Gapon, led a protest march to deliver a petition to Nicholas II. Gapon (known as Father Gapon, although he had not completed his study for the priesthood) had been organizing illegal trade unions since 1903 and had recently led his followers out on strike. Their petition to the czar called for Russian democracy and help for workers and peasants. Before marchers could reach the royal palace, however, the army fired upon them. Seventy marchers were killed and 240 wounded in this "Bloody Sunday" massacre. Gapon escaped to London but was assassinated there. Strikes, demonstrations, and a naval mutiny (aboard the battleship *Potemkin* in the Black Sea) followed.

Nicholas II vacillated in response to the revolution of 1905. Count Witte was not a great champion of liberalism, but he was a pragmatist. He encouraged the czar to concede, and he drafted the documents (the August Manifesto and the October Manifesto) in which Nicholas did so. The August Manifesto promised a limited Parliament (the *Duma*) to be elected by limited suffrage. When unrest continued and a general strike was called, Nicholas II granted further concessions in the October Manifesto: a Russian constitution, a Duma with significant legislative powers, and virtually universal suffrage. The Russian Constitution of 1906 did not mark the complete surrender of autocracy. It opened with a section entitled "On the Nature of the Supreme Autocratic Power." Article Four of that section stated: "Supreme autocratic power belongs to the Emperor of All the Russias. To obey his power, not only through fear but also by conscience, is commanded by God Himself." Subsequent articles gave the czar the sole right to introduce legislation, an absolute veto over any work of the Duma, and the power to name or dismiss the government. Nicholas II nonetheless detested the constitution and soon fired Witte for leading him to it.

Four turbulent Dumas met under this constitution. The first two lasted for a few months in 1906 and 1907 before the czar prorogued them. Nicholas II decreed a new electoral law in 1907, giving greater representation to the wealthy, so the Third Duma (1907–12) obtained a conservative majority. Even middle-class liberals, organized as the Constitutional Democratic Party (known by a Russian abbreviation, the Kadets) under the leadership of Professor Paul Milyukov, opposed this government, angry that meaningful reform moved at a maddeningly slow pace. Nicholas II had promised in 1904 a program of accident and illness insurance for workers. That idea, the first piece of Russian welfare legislation, led to a draft policy in 1905, a proposal to the Duma in 1908, study by a special committee in 1910–11, and debate by the Duma in 1912.

The dominant political figure of the Duma was the new prime minister (1906–11), Peter Stolypin, a conservative noble who had won favor for his role in suppressing the revolution in the provinces. Stolypin was not a simple antiparliamentary reactionary. He accepted the Duma and the principle of liberal modernization, but within the context of strictly enforced law and order. He met radical extremism with state extremism, and Russia saw both in large quantities. Historians have estimated that seventeen thousand terrorist assassinations (in twenty-three thousand attempts) took place between 1905 and 1914. Any official was a target. In a single day, attempts were made on every policeman walking the streets of Warsaw and Lodz; on another, one-fourth of the police force of Riga was killed. Terrorists still favored bombs and even used small children to deliver them; the youngest arrested was an eleven-year-old girl who had been paid fifty kopecks (approximately twenty-five cents) for the job.

Stolypin responded with both state violence and noteworthy reforms. He allowed instant trials in the field and the execution of sentences on the spot. Suspected terrorists were hanged in such numbers that the noose became known as a "Stolypin necktie." At the same time, however, he liberalized censorship, expanded education, and defended freedom of religion. Perhaps the most important idea of Stolypin's government was support for peasant landownership. This program created a class of nine million landowning peasants in Russia by 1914. No legislation could save Stolypin, however. He was the most hated man in Russia, and he was shot to death (by an assassin who could have killed the czar instead) at the Kiev Opera House in 1911. This level of hatred and violence did not augur well for the solution of Russia's manifold problems, and time was running out. Stolypin's successors were increasingly consumed by foreign problems in the Balkans, problems that would soon lead to another war, another disastrous defeat, and another violent revolution.

Belle Époque Democracy around Europe

The great powers of Europe were significantly more democratic in 1914 than they had been in 1870. The French had abolished monarchy and created the first enduring republic among the great powers, with a parliamentary democracy based upon universal manhood suffrage and ministerial responsibility. The British had undertaken two periods of democratization when Gladstone more than doubled the electorate in 1884 and Lloyd George had broken the power of the House of Lords in 1911. The newly unified Germany was significantly less democratic than Britain and France—lacking such features as ministerial responsibility—but it had constitutional government that included a Parliament elected by universal manhood suffrage. Even the most autocratic state, Russia, advanced toward the democratic model in the constitution of 1906 and the creation of the Duma elected by universal suffrage. Europe was clearly moving toward an age of mass participation in politics.

Many of the other states of Europe shared in this trend. Newly unified Italy shared the Piedmontese constitution and parliamentary government on the west European model. Post-Risorgimento Italy began with a limited franchise on the British model and democratized further in the 1880s. A similar pattern of

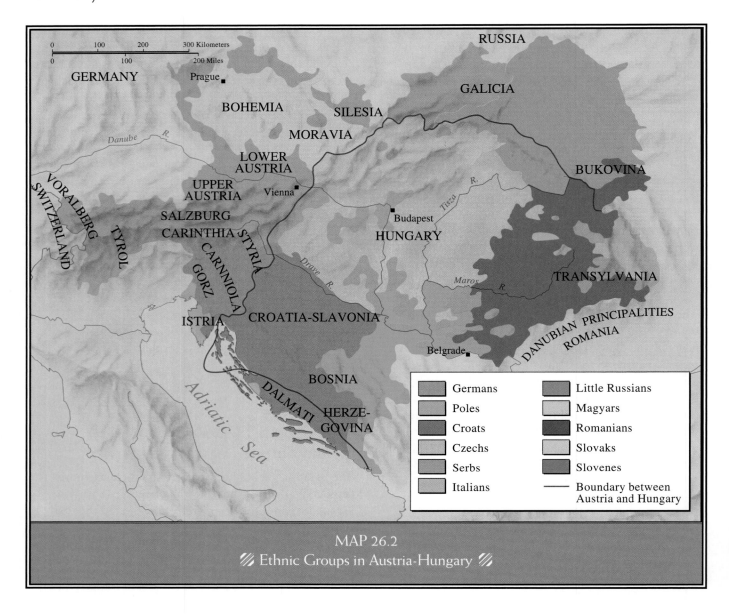

MAP 26.2

▨ Ethnic Groups in Austria-Hungary ▨

gradual democratization existed in many of the smaller states of western Europe. In Belgium, for example, a period of reform in the 1890s led to the direct election of the upper house of Parliament—a reform comparable to French democratization of the Senate in the 1880s and to the British restriction of the House of Lords in 1911. In 1899 Belgium became one of the European pioneers of proportional representation, an advanced form of democratic election in which smaller parties and minorities had a greater chance of being elected. In Scandinavia, the trend toward democracy was even stronger. Norway, which became independent from Sweden in a peaceful agreement of 1905, adopted universal manhood suffrage and a pioneering form of women's suffrage in 1907. The Swedes also adopted universal manhood suffrage and the Finns, women's suf-

frage. Even Ottoman Turkey received a constitution from the Sultan, creating a bicameral legislature, in 1876; Turkish democracy, like German or Russian democracy, was limited yet a dramatic advance from the government of earlier generations.

The pattern of evolving democracy could not hide many European political problems, however. Nationalism was perhaps the most severe, troubling governments across Europe—from the Irish question in Britain to the Polish problem in Russia and Pan-Slavic nationalism in the Balkans. No government faced a more severe challenge than the dual monarchy of Austria-Hungary, which had emerged from the *Ausgleich* of 1867. This empire was an anachronism in 1900, a multinational state held together by historic obedience to the Habsburg monarchy (see map 26.2). According

Illustration 26.4

░░ **The Second Industrial Revolution.** European industrial growth in the late nineteenth century was characterized by the growth of new industries such as the chemical industry, by the increasing use of steel instead of iron, and by the arrival of new sources of power such as electricity. The era of practical electrical power began in the 1880s, but steam remained the dominant source of power into the twentieth century. This photograph of a German factory shows a moment in the transition to electrical power: Light bulbs are being mass-produced, but they are still being handmade by glass-blowers, then individually inspected.

to the census of 1910, the dominant German population of Austria constituted less than 24 percent of the total population, and the Magyar population of Hungary added slightly more than 20 percent; that is, the majority of the people living in the Austro-Hungarian Empire were neither Austrian nor Hungarian. More than 10 percent of the empire was Polish, inhabiting the northeastern provinces of Galicia and Silesia. The northwest contained a large Czech population (nearly 13 percent) in the provinces of Bohemia and Moravia; adjacent regions in the Hungarian portion of the empire held large Slovak, Ruthenian, and Romanian populations (16 percent of the empire). In the south, the Habsburgs still governed an Italian minority (2 percent) and expansion into the Balkans had acquired a large population of southern Slavs—Slovenes, Croats, Bosnians, and Serbs—(nearly 13 percent). The ethnic mixture of the empire was further complicated by religious divisions: Slightly more than three-fourths of the population were Catholic (including splinter churches), with large minorities of Protestants and Orthodox Christians (nearly 9 percent each) plus significant populations of Jews (4 percent) and Moslems (more than 1 percent, concentrated in the Balkans). The Jewish population of the Austro-Hungarian Empire represented more than 26 percent of the world population, second only to Russia's 37 percent; Vienna had a Jewish population of 175,000 and Budapest was the largest Jewish city on earth with 203,000 Jews (23 percent of the city). The ethnic divisions of the empire made the dual monarchy a volatile society, and the consequences of this would soon be tragedy for Europe.

◆

The Rise of Trade Unionism and Socialism

In addition to nationalism, the Belle Époque faced the problem of responding to the consequences of continuing industrialization. A second industrial revolution during the later nineteenth century shared many characteristics of early industrialization. It saw rapid population growth, steady urbanization, and an agricultural revolution sufficient to feed the cities. But many changes also were evident in the new industrialization. The European economy overcame the dominance of Britain. Germany (and the United States) matched British industrialization, and many countries were sufficiently industrialized to compete effectively. The foci of industrialization also changed: Steel replaced iron at the center of heavy industry, electricity began to replace steam as the source of industrial power, and new industries such as the chemical industry challenged the preeminence of textiles (see illustration 26.4).

The population boom that accompanied industrialization affected the entire continent of Europe, but it had special importance in central Europe. In 1800 the states that later formed Germany had a combined population of 18.5 million people. This was larger than the population of the Austrian Empire, the Italian states, or even Great Britain, but it provided few competitive advantages. France dwarfed the German states with a population of 26.9 million. By 1900, however, the German Empire had experienced the population explosion and grown to 56.4 million, while neighboring France had no such population boom and numbered only 39 million people. Much of the economic history, and the political history, of the nineteenth century is contained in this demographic data: France was 45 percent larger than Germany at the start of the century, but Germany was 45 percent larger than France at the end of the century.

This population trend was especially vivid in the urbanization of Germany. In 1880 Britain remained the only country in the world where a majority of the population lived in towns and cities. Belgium, which had led early industrialization on the continent, was drawing close at 43 percent urban, but both France and Germany remained merely one-third urban. By the early years of the twentieth century, Germany had changed into an urban society. In 1800 Berlin's 172,000 people had made it the largest city in the German states; in 1910 unified Germany contained seventeen cities larger than Berlin had been, including the industrial cities of Essen and Duisberg in the Rhineland that had grown from sleepy villages of 4,000 people into capitals of heavy industry with populations over 200,000.

As in Britain, the continuing population explosion and urbanization in Europe were made possible by dramatic improvements in the food supply. For most of the continent, the historic epoch of subsistence and periodic famine had ended. A significant part of the increased food supply was the result of the success of industrialization. The development of inorganic fertilizers greatly increased food production in countries—such as Germany—that possessed a strong chemical industry. The revolution in farm machinery also expanded European production. French farmers, for example, were conservative and slow to accept new machinery. Yet between 1888 and 1908 French agriculture changed from a national total of two hundred reaping machines and fifty harvesters to fifteen thousand reaping machines and twenty-five thousand harvesters.

The European food supply also profited greatly from importation. Vast tracts of rich virgin soil were being plowed in Argentina, Australia, Canada, Russia, and the United States. The acceptance of food in tin cans, the invention of ammonia-based refrigeration, and the availability of quick and inexpensive steam shipping brought the harvest of the world to the tables of Europe. Grain from the American Middle West cost 53¢ per bushel to ship from Chicago to London in 1870; by 1919 that price had fallen to 16¢ per bushel. The price of wheat in Europe consequently tumbled from $1.50 per bushel in 1870 to 85¢ per bushel in 1900.

The greatest stimulus to the second industrial revolution came from new materials, new energy, and new

TABLE 26.2

European Steel Production, 1871–1911

Country	Output of steel in tons		
	1871	1891	1911
Austria-Hungary	36,000	495,000	2,174,000
Belgium	n.a.	222,000	2,028,000
Britain	334,000	3,208,000	6,566,000
France	80,000	744,000	3,837,000
Germany	143,000	2,452,000	14,303,000
Italy	n.a.	76,000	736,000
Luxembourg	n.a.	111,000	716,000
Russia	7,000	434,000	3,949,000
Spain	n.a.	90,000	323,000
Sweden	9,000	172,000	471,000

Source: Compiled from data in B. R. Mitchell, *European Historical Statistics, 1750–1970* (London: Macmillan, 1975), pp. 399–401.

industries. Steel became the symbol of the new industrialization (see table 26.2). The making of steel—distinguished from iron by a higher carbon content—has been known since ancient times. It was preferred for its hardness, its strength in relation to weight, and its plasticity, but the process required to adjust the carbon content in steel had been too expensive for widespread use. In the 1850s a British metallurgist named Henry Bessemer invented a simpler process for making steel. By sending a blast of air through molten iron, Bessemer was able to heat iron to the point where it obtained the desired carbon content. By the 1870s Bessemer's "blast furnaces" were being widely adopted in industrial countries because governments craved steel for heavy artillery, railroads, and warships. In 1871 the total European output was less than 1 million tons of steel; in 1913 tiny Luxembourg alone produced 1.3 million tons of steel. Britain had entered the steel age with the continuing advantage of plentiful iron and coal plus the pioneering role in blast furnace development. But Britain did not start with an insurmountable lead. Germany, which also possessed abundant iron and coal, closed the production gap in the 1880s and passed Britain in steel production in the 1890s. By the start of the twentieth century, Germany produced 20 percent more steel than Britain. In 1911 Germany produced as much steel as Britain, France, and Russia combined, and on the eve of World War I, German steel production stood at eighteen times the European total of 1870. The second industrial revolution had broken the industrial dominance of Britain.

The German leadership of the second industrial revolution was even more notable in chemical industries. Chemical engineering shaped late nineteenth-century industrialization just as mechanical engineering had shaped early industrialization. The initial importance of chemistry came in the textile industry: The manufacture of cotton cloth required large quantities of alkalis, sulfuric acid, and dyes, and the expansion of textile manufactures necessitated expansion of chemical industries. Many noted chemical industries, such as Friedrich Bayer's company in Germany, originated in support of the textile industry. Bayer developed synthetic dyes from coal tar to replace the natural dyes used to color cloth; his aniline dyes permitted a vast range of new, durable colors in clothing and became a tremendous commercial success. Bayer and Company soon diversified and developed other products, such as the first aspirin, patented in 1899.

One of the consequences of this continuing industrialization and urbanization was that the largest social issue confronting governments was the question of the working class. Most workers lived arduous lives and had many valid grievances. Rapid urbanization had produced dreadful living conditions in working-class slums. The importation of cheap food improved the diet of most workers, but it also led to the depression of 1873–94 with periodic high unemployment. A study of the London working class in 1887 found that 52.3 percent of the population experienced short-term unemployment and 30.1 percent of the population was unemployed for twelve weeks or more. Governments slowly emulated the Bismarckian welfare laws of the 1880s and offered workers some measure of unemployment insurance, accident compensation, health care, or retirement benefits, but the welfare state was still in a rudimentary form and provided limited security. Working conditions were deplorable in many occupations. The coal miners and steel workers whose labor sustained heavy industry had life expectancies ten years less than other men; those who operated a Bessemer blast furnace frequently died in their thirties. Most jobs required a minimum of five-and-one-half ten-hour days per week, and many expected six twelve-hour days (see table 26.3). Minimum wage legislation, overtime pay, and paid vacations did not exist.

Trade unions grew quickly under these conditions, as a new wave of unionization spread from the skilled crafts to less skilled occupations. By the early twentieth century, the leading industrial states (Britain, Germany, and the United States) each counted more than a million union members (see table 26.4). In Britain, more

TABLE 26.3

The Average Workweek of the 1890s

Occupation	Hours in Britain	Hours in France
Baker	70	78–96
Brickmaker	54–69	96–108
Chemical worker	53–70	64.5–72
Construction	50–55	72–48
Foundry	48–72	72–84
Metalworker	54	63–66
Miners	42.5–55	51–60
Paper worker	66–78	63
Printer	53–54	60
Railway ticket agent	56–62	90–96
Railway guard	64–70	96–108
Restaurant waiter	96	101
Textile worker	56	66–72
Tailor	54–96	66–96

Source: Gary Cross, *A Quest for Time: The Reduction of Work in Britain and France, 1840–1940* (Berkeley, Calif.: University of California Press, 1989), p. 235. Used by permission of the publisher.

than 20 percent of the adult population belonged to unions in 1913. Elsewhere, lesser industrialization and restrictive legislation kept union membership smaller. Spanish unions included only 0.02 percent of the population in 1889 and 0.2 percent in 1910. Two patterns were clear: Only a minority of workers belonged to unions, but their numbers were growing significantly. As their membership grew, trade unions called strikes to win improved conditions. Turn-of-the-century France experienced an average of nearly 1,000 industrial strikes per year, reaching a peak of 1,319 strikes involving 509,274 strikers in 1906. A study of these strikes has found that 56 percent sought higher wages, 15 percent sought shorter working hours, 13 percent sought the rehiring of fired workers, and 4 percent sought the abolition of certain work rules. By the eve of World War I, Britain, France, and Germany were each losing nearly five million working days to strikes every year; Europe was entering an age of mass participation more direct than the trend toward democratization.

Governments responded to trade union militancy with restrictive legislation and the use of force. In Britain, the Masters and Servants Act (1867) made any breach of contract a criminal instead of a civil offense; the Criminal Law of 1871 created a new category of crime—conspiracy—for acts committed by more than one person and included collective acts that were not crimes for individuals; and the Protection of Property

◾ TABLE 26.4 ◾
The Growth of Union Membership in the Early Twentieth Century

Country	Union membership 1890	1900	1905	1910	1913
Britain	1,576,000	2,022,000	1,997,000	2,565,000	4,135,000
Germany	344,000	851,000	1,650,000	2,435,000	3,024,000
United States		869,000	1,959,000	2,184,000	2,753,000
France			203,000	358,000	400,000
Russia			123,000		
Austria-Hungary	47,000	135,000	482,000		
Sweden		180,000		136,000	
Belgium	13,000	43,000		116,000	
Spain	3,000			41,000	

Source: Compiled from data in Edwin R. A. Seligman, ed., *Encyclopedia of the Social Sciences* (New York, N.Y.: Macmillan, 1937), 8:9–41.

Act (1875) set stiff criminal penalties for compelling a person to commit (or not commit) an act such as joining a strike. Armed with such legislation, and the pro-management sentiments that produced it, governments did not hesitate to use military force against disruptive workers in Britain or France just as in Russia. Unemployed workers demonstrated in central London in the fall of 1887. The government responded by banning labor marches. When workers persisted, they were met by armed police in the "bloody Sunday" clash of November 1887. Three of the unemployed were killed and several hundred injured. Similarly, strikes by coal miners in the Ruhr valley in 1889 led to violent clashes (known as the Herne riots) when the German government called out two battalions of infantry and a squadron of cavalry to oppose the strikers. French troops fired on strikers at the northern industrial town of Fourmies in 1891, killing nine and wounding thirty-five; the conservative government responded to the massacre by arresting Karl Marx's son-in-law, who had spoken there two days earlier, for inciting a riot. At Lodz (in Russian Poland), forty-six workers were killed in a clash in 1892; ninety-two died in a confrontation in Sicily in 1893. And Georges Clemenceau, who had risen to political prominence as a democratic radical and friend of workers, did not hesitate to call out the troops against French strikers in 1906; he even seemed to relish being called "the number one cop in France."

Workers responded with another form of mass politics—supporting political parties that promised to create governments sympathetic to them. This converted socialism from a theory into a mass movement.

Socialist parties were typically led by intellectuals who combined a program of political democracy with social benefits. The Austrian Socialist Party was led by a physician, the Belgian Socialist Party by a lawyer, and the French and German parties by professors. The foremost French socialist, Jean Jaurès, began his career by writing a Latin dissertation to earn a professorship at the University of Toulouse. The clearest example of middle-class intellectuals shaping socialism was the Fabian Society founded in Britain in 1883. Its leaders were a novelist (H. G. Wells), a dramatist (George Bernard Shaw), and a brilliant couple (Sidney and Beatrice Webb) who founded both a university (the London School of Economics) and several periodicals. Such leaders espoused democratic socialism and believed they would ultimately win an electoral majority. They called for radical democracy similar to the Chartist program of the 1830s or the advanced constitutions of 1848; universal suffrage (often including women's suffrage), secret ballots, salaried representatives, and proportional representation were typical political objectives. The eight-hour working day, government regulation of working conditions, and free medical care were typical social goals of democratic socialism.

All over Europe, however, democratic socialists contended with Marxists for control of working-class political movements. Philosophical disputes, such as the abolition of private property, separated these two wings of the socialist movement. The greatest of these disagreements involved the seizure of power. Marxists expected the working-class victory to come through violent revolution. "Force," Marx and Engels wrote, "is

Illustration 26.5

▨ **The Growth of Socialist Parties.** By the early twentieth century, socialist parties such as the SFIO in France and the SPD in Germany were winning dozens of seats in Parliament and growing rapidly. These parties contained an unresolved conflict between their evolutionary, democratic wing and their revolutionary, Marxist wing—a dichotomy well symbolized in this photo of Rosa Luxemburg, a leading militant in the SPD, giving a public speech. Note that on her right is a portrait of Ferdinand Lassalle, a pioneer of moderation, and on her left is a portrait of Karl Marx, the strongest voice of revolutionary socialism.

the midwife of every old society pregnant with a new one." Democratic socialists rejected revolution and believed that they could achieve their objectives through elections. The greatest philosophic rejection of Marxism was advanced by a German socialist, Edouard Bernstein. He was driven into exile by Bismarck's harassment of socialists in the 1880s and edited a newspaper in Zürich where he developed his socialism in contact with British democratic socialists. During the 1890s he lived in London and wrote *Evolutionary Socialism* (1899) to demonstrate the errors of *The Communist Manifesto* and to advocate gradual, democratic socialism. Marx's theory of revolution, Bernstein wrote, was "a mistake in every respect."

Divisions within the socialist movement initially produced competing socialist parties in many countries, but political realism soon obliged socialists to contain their disagreements within a unified party. Thus, French evolutionary socialists (led by Jaurès) and French Marxists (led by Jules Guesde) created a unified party, known by the French initials SFIO, in 1905. British socialists, from the Fabians to the Marxist Social Democratic Federation, combined to create the Labour Party in 1906. Followers of Marx and Bernstein learned to live together within the SPD (see illustration 26.5). Collaboration allowed ideological debates at the congresses of the international movement known as the Second International (1889–1914), but it also led to electoral success. Bismarck's fears notwithstanding, few socialists could be found in European parliaments in the 1880s, but they were among the largest parties in 1914.

The German SPD held more than 25 percent of the seats in the Reichstag, making it the second largest party; French socialists were the second largest block in the fragmented Chamber of Deputies with 22 percent of the seats. And in the 1914 elections the Swedish Socialist Party showed that evolutionary socialists might be right: It became the largest party in Parliament with eighty-seven seats against eighty-six conservatives.

The Growth of Women's Rights Movements

Industrialization stimulated other movements. None had more far-reaching importance than the women's rights movement. Industrialization contributed to the rise of feminism by transforming the roles of women in Western societies. It broke down the traditional household economy in which women labored at home, sharing in agricultural duties or the work of a family-run shop, plus non-wage-paying work such as spinning yarn or making candles. That economic model yielded to a family wage economy in which women (and children) provided less home labor and more wage-earning labor. Families increasingly bought their yarn or ready-made clothing, candles, or vegetables; women increasingly worked outside the home to pay for them.

A study of women in the French labor force reveals these momentous changes in the lives of women. In

1872 less than 25 percent of the total female population of France worked for wages. In 1906 nearly 40 percent of the total female population (54 percent of women age twenty to sixty and 60 percent of women in their early twenties) worked for wages. Furthermore, the work women did was changing. The largest employers remained agriculture, the textile industry, and domestic service, but governments were opening white-collar positions (typically in postal and telephone services), the age of the department store was creating sales positions, the needs of businesses were opening secretarial and clerical jobs, and compulsory education laws were providing teaching jobs.

Women's employment varied across Europe—Russian law closed the civil service to women whereas a Swedish law of 1864 opened all employment to women—but the impact was similar. Educated and energetic women in increasing numbers (although still a minority of women) demanded equality with men. Conservatives, and some men who thought themselves radicals, resisted equality as staunchly as they resisted the demands of workers. Pope Leo XIII's encyclical letter *Rerum Novarum* was clear on the subject of working women: "Women are not suited for certain occupations; a woman is by nature fitted for home-work, and it is that which is best adopted at once to preserve her modesty and promote the good bringing up of children and the well-being of the family."

The women's rights movement was relatively small in the 1870s, but militants articulated comprehensive programs. The leading French militant of the 1870s, Hubertine Auclert, summarized such a program for her organization, *Droit des femmes* (Women's Rights): "The ultimate objective of *Droits des femmes* is: The perfect equality of the two sexes before the law and in morality" (see document 26.4). Feminists (a term that Auclert pioneered in the 1880s) debated priorities, but comprehensive programs soon resembled Auclert's: full political rights, open education and careers, equal civil rights, and equal pay.

Leagues with such programs existed in most of western and northern Europe by the end of the 1870s, though pioneering feminists favored a strategy of starting with limited programs and postponing the issue of women's suffrage. Louise Otto-Peters, the founder of the German women's rights movement, focused on civil rights. The generation of German feminists that followed her, such as Anita Augsburg and the General Federation of German Women's Associations, also began with limited demands. Not until the early twentieth century did women's rights advocates in most countries begin to seek political rights. Augsburg reached this

<hr />

◆ DOCUMENT 26.4 ◆

Hubertine Auclert: The Equality of the Sexes, 1877

Hubertine Auclert (1848–1914) was a daughter of prosperous farmers, who inherited enough money to devote her life to a political cause. She founded the women's suffrage campaign in France and organized demonstrations on behalf of women's rights. During the 1880s she edited the leading newspaper of militant feminism in France, La Citoyenne. *Frustrated by the rate of progress, she considered violent protest in the early twentieth century but kept faith in democratic programs like the following.*

The ultimate objective of *Droit des femmes* is: The perfect equality of the two sexes before the law and in morality.

PROGRAM: *Droit des femmes* will seek, from the beginning and by all means in its power:

1. The accession of women, married or not, to full civil and political rights, on the same legal conditions as apply to men.
2. The reestablishment of divorce.
3. A single morality for men and for women; whatever is condemned for one cannot be excusable for the other.
4. The right for women to develop their intelligence through education, with no other limitation than their ability and their desire.
5. The right to knowledge being acquired, the free accession of women to all professions and careers for which they are qualified at the same level as applies to men (and after the same examination).
6. The rigorous application, without distinction by sex, of the economic formula: Equal Pay for Equal Work.

Hause, Steven C. *Hubertine Auclert: The French Suffragette.* New Haven: Yale University Press, 1987.

<hr />

position in 1898 but did not create her suffrage league (the German Union for Women's Suffrage) until 1902. A similar situation existed in Italy, where Maria Mozzoni fought for civil and economic rights but avoided suffragism. In France, the suffrage campaigns of Auclert during the 1880s attracted only a handful of followers. The women's rights majority there, led by Léon Richer and Maria Deraismes, the founders of the French League for the Rights of Women, favored programs like Otto-Peters', concentrating upon civil and legal rights.

The strongest movement developed in Britain. Women in England and Wales won the vote and eligibility for office at the local level in 1869, and they pressed, with growing militancy, for full political rights for the next fifty years. Between 1870 and 1914 approximately three thousand women were elected to local boards and councils in Britain, but these offices were chiefly on school boards and social agencies dealing with infant mortality or unsanitary housing—positions considered a natural part of "women's sphere." British women, led by Lydia Becker and Millicient Garrett Fawcett, organized the first large suffrage movement and won support in the House of Commons. Though they obtained majorities—but not the support of either major party—in the House of Commons, the conservative majority in the House of Lords blocked the reform.

The women's suffrage movement in Britain became one of the most radical movements in Europe in the early twentieth century. Fawcett, the widow of a radical M.P. who shared many of his parliamentary duties because of his blindness, presided over the unification of several suffrage leagues into a National Union of Women's Suffrage Societies in 1897. It grew from sixteen founding societies to more than four hundred in 1913. Even during this period of rapid growth, militant suffragists formed new organizations to attempt more radical tactics than Fawcett used. They were dubbed "suffragettes" by a newspaper hoping to ridicule the movement, but militants accepted the label and made it famous. The most famous suffragettes, Emmeline Pankhurst and her daughters, Christabel and Sylvia, founded the Women's Social and Political Union (WSPU) in 1903 and led it to violent tactics (against property, not people) such as smashing store windows. Emmeline Pankhurst decided that they "had to do as much of this guerilla warfare as the people of England would tolerate." That decision had dreadful results: When arrested, she (and several other strong women) infuriated the government by going on a hunger strike. When hunger strikers suffered declining health, the government chose to force feed them (see document 26.5). This sequence of events culminated in the notorious Cat-and-Mouse Act of 1913—suffragist prisoners would be released until they recovered.

Despite the remarkable example of the WSPU, moderation characterized the struggle for women's suffrage in most of Europe. Large suffrage movements had developed by 1914, but they did not adopt WSPU tactics. A few militants, such as Auclert and Pelletier in France, briefly attempted violent demonstrations but found no support. Instead, the movements in France, Germany, Italy, and Russia chose campaigns of respectable moderation. Their organizations grew large by 1914 (the French Union for Women's Suffrage had twelve thousand members in seventy-five regional chapters), but none won the vote.

◆ DOCUMENT 26.5 ◆

Sylvia Pankhurst Describes the Treatment of Suffragette Prisoners: Force-Feeding

Emmeline Pankhurst (1858–1928) was the daughter of a wealthy Manchester cotton magnate who married a radical lawyer and joined the first labor party. Her two daughters, Christabel (1880–1958) and Sylvia (1882–1960), joined her in a life of political activism. In the following excerpts from her memoirs, Sylvia Pankhurst talks about the treatment of suffragette prisoners.

The government was not slow to take advantage of the new tactics to inflict harsher punishments. . . . These women should not be permitted to terminate their imprisonment by the hunger strike, as thirty-seven had already done. . . . The Home Secretary ordered the medical officer to feed them forcibly by means of a rubber tube passed through the mouth or nose into the stomach. . . . Mrs. Leight had been handcuffed for upwards of thirty hours, the hands fastened behind during the day and in front with the palms outward at night. Only when the wrists had become intensely painful and swollen were the irons removed. On the fourth day of her fast, the doctor had told her that she must either abandon the hunger strike or be fed by force. She protested that forcible feeding was an operation, and as such could not be performed without a sane patient's consent; but she was seized by the wardresses and the doctor administered food by the nasal tube. This was done twice daily, from 22 September till 30 October. All her companions were forcibly fed.

Pankhurst, Sylvia. *The Suffragette Movement.* London: Longmans, 1931.

Feminists also concentrated on other targets. Many favored modernization of legal codes, such as the Napoleonic Code in France or the Pisanelli Code in Italy, that made wives subordinate to husbands. The most basic reform sought was a Married Woman's Property Act, such as the British had adopted in stages between 1856 and 1882, and several countries (chiefly in Scandinavia) followed. French women obtained this right with the Schmahl Law of 1907; German women did not win it before the war. Most women's rights advocates also sought the legalization of divorce. This was permissible in the German Lutheran tradition and had been established in British law in 1857. The campaign was more difficult in Catholic countries because Pope Leo XIII stongly opposed divorce and issued an encyclical in 1880 stating that "[d]ivorce is born of perverted morals." French women won a limited form of divorce in 1884; Spanish and Italian women did not. Women's rights advocates generally had more success in seeking educational opportunities. The University of Zürich became the first to open to women (1865) and other Swiss universities followed in the 1870s. Russian women briefly won a series of university rights but they were rescinded in 1881 because of the involvement of some women in radical political groups. Germany, home of the most highly praised and emulated universities of the late nineteenth century, resisted higher education for women. The state of Baden was the most progressive, offering women a secondary school curriculum to prepare for universities in 1893 and then opening higher education to them in 1900. The Prussian Ministry of Education was more conservative and perpetuated a secondary school curriculum stressing "Household Arts" to teach "feminine precision, neatness, and patience" while denying young women the prerequisites for entering universities. The distinguished University of Berlin thus remained closed to women until 1908. In 1914 German universities enrolled a combined total of slightly more than four thousand women, who formed 6.2 percent of the student population. The situation was only slightly better for women in France, where 4,254 women students (10.1 percent of enrollment) studied in 1913.

European Culture During the Belle Époque

The Belle Époque was a period of great cultural creativity, but no single style dominated the arts and typified the era. Unlike the baroque and classical styles of the eighteenth century, or the romanticism of the early nineteenth century, no style summarizes the cultural trends of the era. Instead, the Belle Époque was an age of vitality expressed in conflicting styles. In painting, the realism of 1870 gave way to a succession of new styles, such as impressionism, fauvism, cubism, and expressionism. Realism lingered in novels and drama of social comment (such as Emile Zola's novels of ordinary life in France or Henrik Ibsen's plays of angry social criticism), a style known as naturalism, but poetry evolved into an introverted and sometimes mystical style called symbolism. Music, architecture, philosophy, sculpture, and the decorative arts produced no style that dominated the era.

The best remembered cultural style of the Belle Époque was impressionism, a style of painting that originated in France in the 1860s–1880s. Impressionism produced several of the greatest artists of the century, such as Claude Monet, whose painting entitled *Impression: Sunrise* (1874) led to the name. And impressionism influenced the other arts, from music (Debussy is sometimes called an impressionist) to poetry (the symbolist poets are also called impressionists). But the Belle Époque was an era of so much change that it cannot be called the "age of impressionism."

Belle Époque architecture illustrates both the jumble of cultural styles and the emergence of the dramatically new. Late nineteenth-century architecture first suggests an age of revivalism, because almost all past styles were exploited: Bavarians built another great castle in neorococo style, the most noted new building in central Vienna (a theater) was in neobaroque style, the Hungarian Parliament on the banks of the Danube in Budapest was neo-Gothic, the most discussed new church of the age in Paris was neoromanesque, the Dutch national museum built in Amsterdam was neo-Renaissance, and the vast Gum Department Store in Moscow was neoclassical. Despite this cacophony of styles of the past, an exciting architecture of the twentieth century began to emerge in the closing years of the nineteenth. The French built the tallest structure on earth for their world's fair of 1889 (the centennial of the revolution), and they built the Eiffel Tower in structural steel. By the 1890s this use of steel and the American-born style of building skyscrapers by attaching a masonry exterior to a metal frame had begun a profound change in the appearance of cities. Walter Gropius, a German architect who had tremendous influence on the visual arts of the new century, built the first steel frame building with glass walls in 1911.

The birth of the twentieth century seen in architecture had parallels throughout the arts. Startling innovators broke with tradition. In music, the rejection of the nineteenth-century symphonic heritage led after 1900 to efforts to compose atonal music, culminating in 1914 with Arnold Schonberg's system of composing to destroy the feeling of tonality. Other composers, such as Igor Stravinsky, boldly created dissonant harmonies. Such music so offended traditional tastes that performances were sometimes met with howls of protest from the audience; the first performance of Stravinsky's ballet *The Rite of Spring* provoked a riot in Paris in 1913. Horrified traditionalists even saw the rules of dancing begin to break down as free dance abolished the following of steps or prescribed positioning.

The breakdown of traditional styles was especially controversial in the visual arts where the popularity of photography and the cinema pressed painters to find artistic expression that these new arts could not rival. The nonrepresentational styles of painting that emerged still evoke hostility from traditionalists a century later. The most inventive artist of the twentieth century, Pablo Picasso, began his career producing works of emotional realism, but after 1904 he pioneered a style known as cubism in which shapes and structures (such as the human face) were simplified into geometric outlines. Picasso pushed the breakdown of realism so far that a face might have two eyes on the same side of the nose. Denounced for his nonrepresentational styles, Picasso responded that his art was "a lie that tells the truth." Painting was no longer a simple depiction of the physical world; it revealed hidden truths about a two-faced world.

European thought during the Belle Époque followed a similar course. The most influential works of the era drew upon the new discipline of psychology. Novelists from Feodor Dostoevski (whose *The Brothers Karamazov* appeared in 1879–80), through Joseph Conrad (whose *Lord Jim* appeared in 1900), to Marcel Proust (whose first volume of *Remembrance of Things Past* appeared in 1913) relied upon psychological detail and insight. The inner life of characters and their subconscious motivation gained emphasis as central features of the novel. Psychology also reshaped European philosophy. Friedrich Nietzsche, a pastor's son who reacted against the piety of his home, was such a brilliant student that he became a professor at the University of Basel at age twenty-four. Nietzsche wrote with psychological insight about the sublimation of passions and instincts, the relativity of morals, and what he called "the will to power." He had contempt for contemporary cultural and moral values and, in works such as *Thus Spoke Zarathustra* (1883), argued that "God is dead" and Christianity is based on the mentality of slaves. Such arguments did not have much immediate impact, but they grew increasingly influential in European thought.

Perhaps the most influential thinkers of the Belle Époque were two scientists: Sigmund Freud, the Austrian neurologist who founded the science of psychoanalysis and Charles Darwin, the English Naturalist who developed the theory of evolution by Natural Selection. Freud's study of psychoneuroses in the 1890s led him to an analytic technique of the "free association" of thoughts, a process that he named "psychoanalysis." This, in turn, led him to the analysis of dreams. *The Interpretation of Dreams* (1900) stated his first model of the workings of the mind, a model that evolved into a description of three competing subconscious elements of the mind: the ego, the superego, and the libido (or id). Freud's attention to the libido as the seat of emotional (and especially sexual) urges led to his famous stress upon sexual explanations (especially those with origins in infantile sexuality) in *Three Contributions to the Sexual Theory* (1905). Many of Freud's theories have been controversial, and some are simply wrong, but Freud's impact upon European thought has been so enormous that he remains the most influential author of his era.

Darwin had presented his theories in two controversial works, *On the Origin of Species* (1859), which demonstrated how natural selection worked, and *The Descent of Man* (1871), which applied evolution to humanity. The theory of evolution—that plants and animals naturally experience a process of gradual change into a more complicated or advanced state—was advanced by many scientists. Darwin's greatest contribution was to demonstrate natural selection as the means of evolution. He first did this by studying the evolution of the beaks of birds in the Galapagos Islands, showing how the environment favored certain shapes of beaks, thus birds with such an advantage were naturally selected for survival and reporduction. Darwin's application of evolution to human history was enormously controversial because it conflicted with the biblical account of human origins, but scientists steadily accepted his theory. Social theorists in many fields soon appropriated (and misappropriated) Darwin's ideas. The most wide-spread derivation during the belle époque was known as "social darwinism." This doctrine applied a crude version of natural selection to human society and then asserted that certain people were suited for dominance and they would triumph, following what Herbert Spencer called "the survival of the fittest." Such social darwinism was used to justify the class system, unregulated capitalist competition, racism, and imperialism.

CHAPTER 27

IMPERIALISM, WAR, AND REVOLUTION, 1881–1920

CHAPTER OUTLINE

Chapter 27 looks at three great experiences that shaped European (and global) history in the twentieth century: (1) the new imperialism (1881–1914), in which the great European powers seized control of most of Africa and much of Asia; (2) World War I (1914–18), which destroyed the last monarchical empires of the Old Regime; and (3) the Russian Revolution (1917–20), which posed a new and powerful form of mass politics to compete with democracy.

The chapter begins with the background to these great events during two generations of peace. It examines the Bismarckian alliance system, which divided Europe into two opposing sides, and the militarism and arms race, which made this division so dangerous. Although it was an era of peace among the European great powers, the same powers fought dozens of imperial wars of conquest and annexed empires around the world. During the new imperialism, they seized control of nearly 25 percent of the planet. The discussion of World War I shows how it introduced Europe to a century of "total war"—in both its destructive battles and life on the home front. The final section focuses on the Russian Revolution of 1917. This wartime revolution established Lenin's Communist government in Russia, a regime that introduced Europe to twentieth century totalitarianism.

The Bismarckian System of Alliances, 1871–90

The German victory in the Franco-Prussian War led to the creation of a unified German Empire so strong, both militarily and economically, that it dominated Europe, yet Chancellor Otto von Bismarck still feared French revenge. After 1871 he aimed to protect Germany by negotiating treaties that would guarantee the support of the other powers and deny France potential allies. He achieved both goals through a web of alliances collectively known as the Bismarckian system, with which he dominated European diplomacy for twenty years (1871–90). Bismarck's accomplishment radically altered European statecraft. Whereas the Metternichian system had kept the peace by a delicate balance of power in which none of the great powers became too dominant and none felt too threatened, the Bismarckian system kept peace through the lopsided superiority of the German alliances and the comparative weakness of France.

French nationalists nonetheless dreamt of the day of revenge—*la revanche*—on Germany, the day when the republic would reclaim "the lost provinces" of Alsace and Lorraine, whose borders were marked on the maps of French schools in a deep black. Realistic nationalists such as the hero of 1870, Léon Gambetta, understood that Germany had become too powerful to fight alone. The French must wait for *revanche*; in Gambetta's words, they should "[t]hink of it always, speak of it never." Despite a war scare in 1875 and a tense period during the Boulangist nationalism of the late 1880s, no French government planned a war of revenge.

The first treaty in Bismarck's alliance system was the Three Emperors' League (*Dreikaiserbund*) of 1873, an outgrowth of state visits exchanged by William I of Germany, Franz Joseph of Austria-Hungary, and Alexander II of Russia. The *Dreikaiserbund* represented an amicable understanding (an entente) among recent rivals who shared a belief in monarchical solidarity. (France remained the only republic in monarchical Europe.) The king of Italy soon embraced this counterrevolutionary league, siding with Germany despite the debt Italians owed to the French from their wars of unification. The British remained outside this league, favoring a policy of continental nonalignment that came to be called splendid isolation.

The development of the Bismarckian system accelerated as a result of warfare in the Balkans in 1875–78, which convinced Bismarck to seek more formal treaties. The provinces of Bosnia and Herzegovina (see map 27.1) rebelled against Turkish rule in 1875, and the Principality of Serbia intervened to support them. The Serbs had won autonomous government in their rebellion of 1817 and had become the center of Pan-Slavism, an ardent nationalism dedicated to the unity of the southern Slavs. The insurrection against the Ottoman Empire next spread to Bulgaria in 1876, and the Turks responded with violent repression known in the European press as "the Bulgarian horrors." This enlarged Balkan war forced the European powers to address a

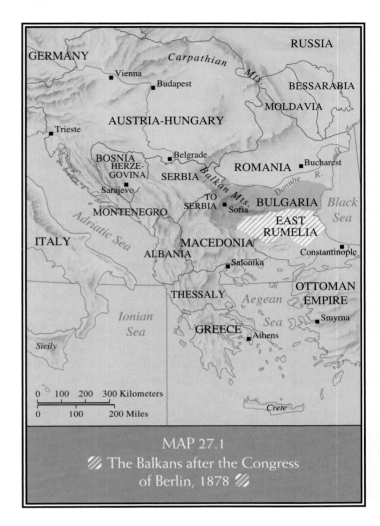

MAP 27.1
The Balkans after the Congress of Berlin, 1878

problem that had come to be called the eastern question. This was the question of the survival of the Ottoman Empire—still known as "the sick man of Europe"—and the fate of territories under the control of Constantinople. The eastern question posed the danger of Austro-Russian conflict because both governments coveted Ottoman territory in the Balkans. To avoid such a confrontation, Bismarck adopted the role of "the honest broker" of the eastern question and presided over the Congress of Berlin (1878) to end the fighting. The British endorsed the congress because it served their policy of preserving the Ottoman Empire rather than dismantling it. The Berlin settlement placated Turkish honor by returning some territory lost in the fighting, and it awarded Balkan territory to both the Russians (Bessarabia) and the Austrians (Bosnia-Herzegovina). Bismarck bought French backing with support for colonial expansion. The Slavic nationalist movements of the Balkans—both Serbian and Bulgarian—were not satisfied: Serbs won their independence but Pan-Slavs saw Bosnia lost to Austria; the Bulgarians won independence but lost much territory promised to them in a preliminary treaty, the Treaty of San Stefano.

The Balkan crisis of 1875–78 drove Bismarck to negotiate a close military alliance with Austria-Hungary known as the Dual Alliance (1879), which became the new cornerstone of his alliance system. The Habsburg prime minister and foreign minister was a Hungarian, Count Julius Andrássy, who held no grudge against Germany for the war of 1866. Secret terms of the Dual Alliance promised each country military assistance if they were attacked by Russia and guaranteed neutrality if either were attacked by any other country. Bismarck labored simultaneously to retain Russian friendship by preserving and strengthening the Three Emperors' League; he understood that "[i]n a world of five powers, one should strive to be *a trois*" (on the side with three). Italy, motivated by a growing colonial rivalry with France in north Africa, joined the Dual Alliance in 1882, converting the pact into the Triple Alliance. Germany thus acquired explicit security against France, although Bismarck publicly presented the treaty as merely a bulwark of the monarchical order. To underscore his desire for Russian friendship, Bismarck later negotiated another Russo-German treaty known as the Reinsurance Treaty (1887). This document gave a German pledge not to support Austrian aggression against Russia, and it was accompanied by significant German investment in Russian industrial development. Both governments reiterated their devotion to the status quo. Finally, Bismarck orchestrated a series of secondary treaties, such as the Mediterranean Agreements (1887), which involved other governments (including Britain and Spain) in the defense of the status quo. The network of his treaties became so complex that Bismarck enjoyed the self-bestowed image of being a juggler who could keep five balls in the air at once.

The New Imperialism, 1881–1914

The great powers exploited the European peace to annex large empires around the world. In 1871 only 10 percent of Africa had fallen under European control. Britain held the Cape Colony in South Africa and a few strips of West Africa. France had seized Algeria in 1830 and had long controlled part of West Africa including Senegal, while Portugal retained southern colonies dating back to the fifteenth and sixteenth centuries, but most of the continent remained self-governing. By 1914 Europeans claimed virtually the entire continent,

leaving independent only Liberia (under American influence) and Ethiopia (claimed by Italy but unconquered) (see map 27.2). The new imperialism had also ended self-government in the Pacific by 1914. There, the Japanese, who took the Ryuku Islands in 1874 and Formosa in 1895, and Americans, who took Hawaii in 1898 and part of Samoa in 1899, joined Europeans in building oceanic empires. Simultaneously, Britain and Russia expanded in southern Asia, Britain and France occupied most of Southeast Asia, and all of the industrial powers (including Japan and the United States) menaced China. Empires were growing so fast that a leader of British imperialism, Colonial Secretary Joseph Chamberlain, gloated, "The day of small nations has long passed away. The day of empires has come."

Europeans had been claiming empires around the world for centuries. Britain, France, Spain, Portugal, Denmark, and the Netherlands all held colonies taken before the nineteenth century. According to an estimate made in 1900, the frontiers of Russia had been advancing into Asia (much as the United States pushed westward) at the rate of fifty-five square miles per year since the sixteenth century. In the century between the 1770s and the 1870s, Russia fought six wars against the Ottoman Empire and four wars against Persia, in the course of which the czars annexed the Crimea, Georgia, and Armenia, then advanced into south Asia and prepared to take Afghanistan. Newly unified Italy and Germany were eager—against Bismarck's better judgment—to join this club. As Kaiser Wilhelm II said in a speech of 1901, echoing Bülow's *Weltpolitik*, Germans also expected "our place in the sun."

Europeans had previously built colonial empires, sending colonists to live in distant colonies. The new imperialism of 1881–1914 included little colonialism. Europeans sent soldiers to explore and conquer, officials to organize and administer, missionaries to teach and convert, and merchants to develop and trade, but few families of colonists. When Germany annexed African colonies in the 1880s, more Germans chose to emigrate to Paris (the capital of their national enemy) than to colonize Africa.

Earlier empires had also been based on mercantilist commerce. Colonies might provide such diverse goods as pepper, tulip bulbs, opium, or slaves, but they were expected to strengthen or to enrich the imperial state. Economic interests still drove imperialism, but the motor had changed. Imperialists now sought markets for exported manufactures, especially textiles. They dreamt, in the imagery of one British prime minister, of the fortunes to be made if every Oriental bought a woolen nightcap. The rise of trade unions inspired in-

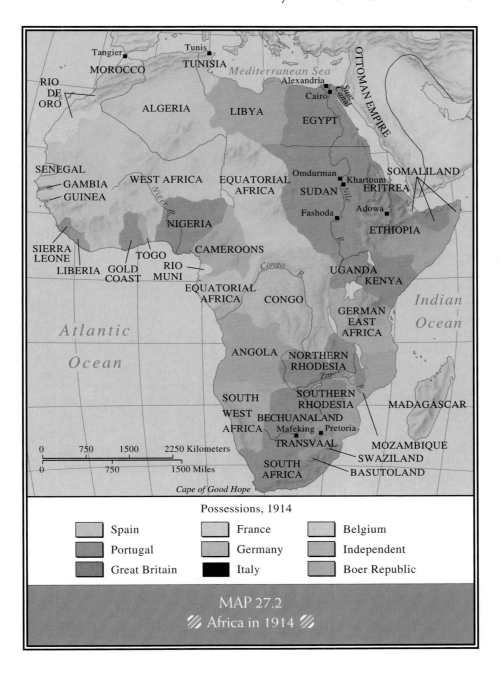

Possessions, 1914

Spain	France	Belgium
Portugal	Germany	Independent
Great Britain	Italy	Boer Republic

MAP 27.2
Africa in 1914

dustrialists to covet cheaper, more manageable, colonial labor. Financiers needed to find markets for investing the capital accumulating from industrial profits. As a leading French imperialist, Jules Ferry, said, "Colonial policy is the daughter of industrial policy" (see document 27.1). The new imperialism, however, cannot be explained entirely by economics. Colonies cost imperial governments sums of money for military, administrative, and developmental expenses that far exceeded the tax revenues they produced. Many private enterprises also lost money on imperialism. In the early twentieth century, the five largest banks in Berlin ap-

pealed to the government to stop acquiring colonies because they were losing ventures. Individual investors usually lost money in colonial stocks; they frequently paid neither dividends nor interest and were sold as patriotic investments. Some businesses, and the elites who controlled them, did make great profits from captive markets; textile towns and port-cities prospered in this way and championed imperialism. A few individuals made staggering fortunes overseas, as Cecil Rhodes did in the African diamond fields. Rhodes was a struggling cotton farmer who bought a diamond claim and hired Africans to work it. When he died, he was considered

◆ **DOCUMENT 27.1** ◆

Jules Ferry: French Imperialism (1885)

Jules Ferry (1832–1893) was a wealthy middle-class lawyer who served as premier of France in the 1880s. He was a moderate republican and one of the founders of the Third Republic. His greatest accomplishments came in the creation of the French educational system, but he also became a leading champion of imperialism. The following document is excerpted from one of his parliamentary speeches.

Our colonial policy . . . rests upon our economic principles and interests, on our humanitarian visions of order, and on political considerations. . . .

[Interruptions by hecklers: "Yes, 20,000 corpses!" and "Ten thousand families in mourning!"]

Why have colonies from an economic standpoint? . . . [C]olonies are, for wealthy countries, an advantageous investment. France, which has exported a great amount of capital abroad, must consider this aspect of the colonial question. There is, however, another point, even more important: . . . For countries like France, devoted to exports by the nature of their industry, the colonial question is a question of markets. . . .

Gentlemen, there is a second point, a second set of ideas, that I must also raise: the humanitarian and civilizing side of imperialism. The honorable Camille Pelletan [another deputy] scoffs at this point. . . . He asks, "What is this civilization that one imposes with cannon shells?" . . . One must answer that superior races have rights with regard to the inferior races. They have rights because they have duties. They have the duty to civilize the inferior races. . . . Can anyone deny that it was good fortune for the people of equatorial Africa to fall under the protection of France and Britain?

. . . I add that French colonial policy . . . is inspired by another truth which you must reflect upon: a navy such as ours cannot survive with the shelters, defenses, supply bases. Just look at the map of the world. . . . No warship, no matter how perfectly organized, can carry more than a fourteen day supply of coal, and a warship short of coal is only a derelict on the high seas.

Journal officiel de la république française. Debates of July 28, 1885. Trans. Steven C. Hause. Paris: Imprimerie des journaux officiels.

---

the richest man on earth. His power was so enormous that a colony was named for him (Rhodesia, today Zimbabwe), and his fortune was so immense that it endowed the famous Rhodes scholarships to Oxford. Not surprisingly, Rhodes was an ardent imperialist who lamented that he could not annex the stars. Even the fantasy of striking it as rich as Rhodes, however, cannot fully explain why governments ran deficits to pay for empire.

The new imperialism must also be understood in terms of nationalism, militarism, and racism (see illustration 27.1). Imperialist politicians insisted that empire was the measure of a nation's greatness. Nationalist organizations, such as the Pan-German League, pressed their government to take more territory. It would "awaken and foster the sense of racial and cultural kinship" of Germans to know that their country occupied a city on the coast of China. Journalists, teachers, and scholars promoted similar attitudes about the greatness of empire. As a Cambridge historian wrote in 1883, "[T]here is something intrinsically glorious in an empire 'upon which the sun never sets.' " Even Cecil Rhodes in-

sisted that his motives began with his nationalism. "I contend," he wrote, "that we [the British] are the first race in the world, and the more of the world we inhabit, the better it is for the human race. I believe it to be my duty to God, my Queen, and my Country to paint the whole map of Africa red [the color typically used to depict British colonies], red from the Cape to Cairo."

Militarism was also a significant factor in imperialism. The conquest of distant lands required larger armies and bigger budgets. Decoration, promotion, and territory were more easily won against preindustrial armies. Lord Kitchener became famous for commanding the outnumbered army that conquered the Sudan in 1896–98. Kitchener's army of twenty-five thousand defeated an army of fifty thousand because they were equipped with Maxim (machine) guns, which enabled them to kill large numbers of Sudanese with relative ease; at the decisive battle of Omdurman, Kitchener's forces suffered five hundred casualties and killed more than fifteen thousand Sudanese—"giving them a good dusting" in Kitchener's words. Thus, while the nine-

So kolonisiert der Deutsche,

So kolonisiert der Engländer,

Illustration 27.1

Imperialism. The German satirical review *Simplicissimus* published this commentary in 1904: German imperialism is seen to be an extension of German militarism, whereas British imperialism is seen to be an extension of British capitalism. (The captions read, "This is the way the German colonizes. This is the way the Englishman colonizes." The sign on the tree says, "It is forbidden to dump trash or snow here.") Other drawings in the series depicted French soldiers making love to native women and a Belgian roasting an African over an open fire and preparing to eat him.

teenth century appears to be an age of peace for Britain when viewed in a European context, it was an epoch of constant warfare when viewed in a global context.

In addition to economic and political explanations of imperialism, Western cultural attitudes are also important. These range from religion and humanitarianism to social Darwinism and racism. Christian missionaries formed the vanguard of imperialist intervention in Africa and Asia. They were successful in some regions: Nigeria and Madagascar, for example, are both more than 40 percent Christian today. In other regions, people resisted Christianity as an imperialist intervention; as one Indian put it, "Buddha came into our world on an elephant; Christ came into our world on a cannonball." Missionaries also taught Western attitudes and behavior, such as denouncing the depravity of seminudity in tropical climates. Textile manufacturers were not alone in concluding that "[b]usiness follows the Bible." Europeans also justified imperialism by speaking of humanitarianism. Some used crude stereotypes about abolishing cannibalism or moralistic arguments about ending polygamy; others took pride in the campaign to end the slave trade, which Europeans had done so much to develop. More educated arguments cited the abolition of practices such as *Suttee* in India (the tradition by which a widow threw herself on her husband's funeral pyre) or the benefits of Western medicine.

Humanitarian justifications for imperialism were often cloaked in terms such as the French doctrine of *la mission civilatrice* or the title of Rudyard Kipling's poem "The White Man's Burden" (1899). Such terms suggested the social Darwinian argument that Western civilization was demonstrably superior to others, and this led to the simple corollaries that (1) in Jules Ferry's words, "superior races have rights with regard to inferior races" and (2) they had a duty to help "backwards" peoples. Kipling, for example, urged advanced states: "Fill full the mouth of Famine/And bid the sickness cease." Even humanitarianism thus contained an element of the racism common in imperialism. Europeans had often viewed colonial peoples as heathens or savages. Late nineteenth-century social Darwinism worsened such stereotypes with the pseudoscientific notion that all races were locked in a struggle for survival, a struggle to be won by the fittest. Imperialists cheerfully concluded that their own nation would win this struggle. A president of the United States spoke of his desire to help his "little brown brothers" (the people of the Philippines). A czar of Russia joked about going to war with "little yellow monkeys" (the Japanese, who promptly defeated the Russians). By the early twentieth century, Western racism was so unchallenged that a major zoo exhibited an African in a cage alongside apes.

The Scramble for Africa

Historians often cite the French occupation of Tunis in 1881 as the beginning of the new imperialism. French pride had been hurt by the events of 1870–71, and it had received another blow in 1875 when the British purchased control of the Suez Canal (built by the French in the 1860s) from the khedive of Egypt. Bismarck used the distrust generated by the Suez issue to reawaken Anglo-French rivalry. At the Congress of Berlin in 1878, he encouraged the French to claim Tunis, and the congress approved. Jules Ferry, who became premier of France in 1880, used the excuse of raids by Tunisian tribes into Algeria to proclaim a French protectorate over Tunis—an act that promptly benefited Bismarck by driving the Italians into the Triple Alliance. The British responded by using nationalist riots as an excuse to extend their control of Egypt in 1882. They bombarded Alexandria, occupied Cairo, and placed Egypt under the thumb of a British consul. Nationalist rebellion moved south to the Sudan in 1883. It acquired a religious fervor from an Islamic leader known as the Mahdi (messiah); the mahdists defeated several British garrisons, notably the forces of General Gordon at Khartoum (1885), and sustained an autonomous government until Kitchener's victory at Omdurman a decade later.

Anglo-French imperialism in North Africa provoked a race among European governments, known as "the scramble for Africa," to claim colonies in sub-Saharan Africa. In the five years between 1882 and 1887, Europeans claimed more than two million square miles of Africa. (The United States today totals less than 3.7 million square miles.) In 1884 alone, Germany took more than 500,000 square miles as German Southwest Africa (today Namibia), Cameroon, and Togo; two years later, they added nearly 400,000 square miles as German East Africa (today Tanzania). The largest single claim, nearly a million square miles of central Africa known as the Congo, was taken by King Leopold II of Belgium in 1885. Leopold then founded a company that brutally exploited the Congo as a gigantic rubber plantation, under the ironic name of the Congo Free State. But even land grabs that huge could not compete with the British and French empires; by 1914 Great Britain and France each controlled approximately five million square miles of Africa.

The scramble for Africa had repercussions in European diplomacy, chiefly the reopening of the colonial rivalry between Britain and France. After General Kitchener's victory at Omdurman, his troops confronted a small French exploratory mission, the Marchand mission, which had camped on the upper Nile at the Sudanese town of Fashoda. Kitchener and Marchand both claimed Fashoda, but the size of Kitchener's forces obliged the French to leave. The Fashoda crisis showed that France remained vulnerable in 1898.

In the following months, however, the vulnerability of British diplomatic isolation was exposed by Britain's involvement in the Boer War (1899–1902). The Boers, white settlers of mixed Dutch and Huguenot descent, had created a republic, the Transvaal, in Bantu territory north of the Britain's Cape Colony in South Africa. The British annexed the Transvaal in 1877, but a revolt in 1880–81 earned the Boers autonomy under the strong leadership of President Paul Kruger. Tensions remained high, however, especially after the discovery of vast deposits of gold in the Transvaal. An Anglo-Boer war broke out in 1899. The Boers won initial victories, besieged the British at Mafeking and Ladysmith, and earned international sympathy, especially after the British placed 120,000 Boer women and children in concentration camps (the first use of this term) to limit support for Boer guerrillas and twenty thousand died, chiefly from disease. Massive British reinforcements under General Kitchener reversed the course of the war in 1900, lifting the siege of Mafeking, capturing the Boer capital of Pretoria, and again annexing the Transvaal. The Boer leaders continued resistance in two years of guerrilla fighting before accepting the British victory in the Treaty of Vereeniging in 1902.

The Boer War was the largest imperial war in Africa, but it should not distract attention from the wars of African resistance to imperialism. The British annexation of the Transvaal, for example, led them into the Zulu War of 1879, which showed that a poorly equipped African army could defeat Europeans. The Ashanti tribes of West Africa, in what is now Ghana, resisted the British in four wars during the nineteenth century, three of them fought between 1873 and 1896. The Ashanti, too, won battles against the British. The French likewise experienced defeats in fighting two Dahomeyan wars (in today's Benin); the Mandingo tribes (in today's Ivory Coast) resisted French occupation of the interior for thirteen years (1885–98) making a great hero of their chief, Samory. The Hereros (Bantu tribes of southwest Africa) and the Hottentots withstood the German army for nearly six years (1903–08). They did not capitulate until the Germans had reduced the Herero population from eighty thousand to fifteen thousand. The Ethiopians threw out European invaders; Emperor Menelik II resisted an Italian occupation in 1896, and his forces annihilated an Italian army in the massive battle (more than 100,000 combatants) of Adowa.

Europeans eventually won most imperial wars. The advantage of modern armament is sufficient explanation, as Kitchener demonstrated in the bloody engagement on the plains of Omdurman. In the blunt words of one poet, "Whatever happens we have got/The Maxim Gun, and they have not." Europeans also held a numerical advantage whenever they chose to use it; defeats usually summoned reinforcements that Africans could not match, as the Bantus, the Zulus, and the Boers learned. The Italian army was outnumbered by eighty thousand to twenty thousand at Adowa. If Italy had wanted Ethiopia badly enough to obtain a four-to-one advantage (the Italian army and militia of the 1890s numbered nearly three million men), they, too, might have won. Europeans also succeeded in imperial conquests because of biological and medical advantages. Westerners had an advantage in nutrition that translated into larger, healthier armies, and invaders carrying smallpox, whooping cough, or the measles sometimes carried a biological weapon better than gunpowder. Conversely, African diseases (especially malaria) had long blocked European penetration of the continent. When the French occupied Tunis in 1881, malaria took twenty-five times as many soldiers as combat did. Europeans knew that quinine, derived from the bark of the cinchona tree, prevented malaria, and scientists isolated the chemical in 1820, but not until the late nineteenth century did they synthesize quinine in adequate quantities to provide an inexpensive daily dose for large armies. Such scientific conquests made possible the military conquest of Africa.

Imperialism in Asia and the 'Opening of China'

Europeans began their conquests in Asia in the early sixteenth century. By the late nineteenth century (see map 27.3), Britain dominated most of south Asia (today's India, Pakistan, Sri Lanka, and Bangladesh) and Australasia (Australia and New Zealand). They had begun to expand into Southeast Asia, annexing much of Burma (now Myanmar) in 1853. This led them into competition with the French who landed troops in Annam (Vietnam) in 1858. Most of the East Indies had been claimed by the Dutch (the Dutch East Indies,

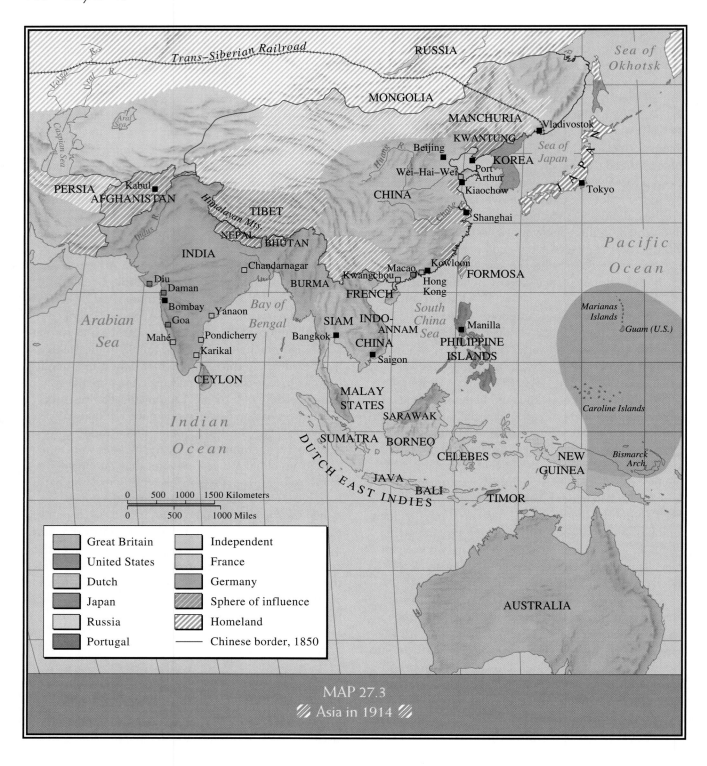

Legend:

Great Britain	Independent
United States	France
Dutch	Germany
Japan	Sphere of influence
Russia	Homeland
Portugal	Chinese border, 1850

MAP 27.3

Asia in 1914

today Indonesia) or the Spanish (the Philippines) for centuries. China and Japan had largely resisted Western penetration, except for toeholds such as Hong Kong, which the British leased in 1841.

The new imperialism refreshed the European appetite for Asia. Between 1882 and 1884 the French subjugated the region of modern Vietnam, and their expedition continued until Cambodia (1887) and Laos (1893) were combined with Annam to form French Indo-China. This prompted the British to complete their annexation of Burma (1886) and to reach south for the Malay States (today Malaysia), which became a British-run federation in 1896. By the turn of the century, only Siam (Thailand) remained independent in the entire subcontinent, and Siamese freedom depended upon Anglo-French inability to compromise. Most of Southeast Asia had been under the loose suzerainty of the Manchu dynasty of China, and the European conquests of 1882–96 exposed the vulnerability of that regime. Japan's easy military victory in the Sino-Japanese War of 1894–95—the result of a decade of rivalry over Korea, which Japan seized in 1894—underscored that lesson. The Treaty of Shimonoseki ended that war, with China granting independence to Korea and ceding the province of Kwantung (west of Korea) and the island of Formosa (Taiwan) to Japan.

Europeans could not resist exploiting the infirmity of the Chinese Empire. Their initial intervention, however, was against the Japanese, who were obliged to return Kwantung to China. Then, in 1896, the Russians extracted a treaty allowing them to build the Trans-Siberian Railway across the Chinese province of Manchuria to the port of Vladivostok. Shortly thereafter, the Russians simply occupied Manchuria. In early 1897 the Germans followed the Japanese and Russians into China by occupying the northern port city of Kiaochow after two German missionaries had been killed in that region. These events launched another imperialist scramble, this time known as "the opening of China." Unlike their outright annexation of land in Africa, European governments used the genteel device of pressing the Manchu government to sign ninety-nine-year "leases" to "treaty ports" along the coast of China. During 1898 the Germans extracted a lease to Kiaochow, the Russians to the Liaodong peninsula and Port Arthur, the French to Kwangchow in the south (near to Indo-China), and the British to both Wei-Hai-Wei in the north and Kowloon (near Hong Kong) in the south.

While Europeans were extracting leases to Chinese territory, another war shifted imperialist attention further east, to the islands of the Pacific Ocean. The Spanish-American War of 1898—chiefly fought in the Caribbean, following a Cuban insurrection against Spanish rule in 1895—completed the collapse of the Spanish colonial empire. The victorious United States, which had won an important naval victory against the Spanish at Manila, claimed the Philippine archipelago (the largest Spanish colony) and fought a three-year war (1899–1901) to subdue Filipino nationalists. The United States chose to follow European imperialism and established an American government for the islands. This stimulated a race to claim the remaining islands of the Pacific. Germany and the United States, both eager for bases to support global fleets, led this rush. Between 1899 and 1914 Germany claimed dozens

of north Pacific islands (such as the Mariana Islands, the Caroline Islands, and the Marshall Islands, which would become famous battlegrounds of World War II). The United States took Hawaii (1898), Guam (1898), and Wake Island (1900), while joining Germany and Britain in dividing the Samoan Islands (1899). By 1914 no self-governing atoll survived in the Pacific.

The Asian resistance to Western imperialism, like the African resistance, was repeatedly expressed with arms. The opening of China in 1898 precipitated a turbulent period in Chinese history that included an uprising against foreigners, the Boxer Rebellion (1900–01). The Boxers, the European name for a paramilitary organization of Chinese nationalists who hoped to expel all foreigners from China, began the uprising by attacking Christian missionaries and their converts. Violence spread to Beijing, culminating in the murder of the German ambassador and a siege of Western legations. A multinational expedition put down the Boxer Rebellion and conducted punitive missions into provincial China.

Japan provided the most successful opposition to European imperialism in Asia. European intervention against the Japanese in 1895, followed by provocations such as the Russian occupation of Manchuria, lease to Port Arthur, and penetration of Korea led to the Russo-Japanese War of 1904–1905. The Japanese attacked Port Arthur in February 1904, trapping the entire Russian Pacific fleet except for the ships icebound at Vladivostok. A few weeks later, the Japanese army landed in Korea, advanced into Manchuria, and defeated the Russian army. In the spring of 1905, a Russian European fleet reached the Orient only to be destroyed (thirty-three of forty-five ships were sunk) in the battle of Tsushima Strait between Japan and Korea.

Resistance to European imperialism went beyond the Indo-Chinese wars of the 1880s, the Boxer uprising of 1900, and the Japanese victory of 1904–05. Well-organized nationalist movements appeared in the early twentieth century. In 1908, for example, a group of moderate nationalists wrote a constitution for the Indian National Congress (later, the Congress Party), calmly stating their objective of winning self-government by constitutional means. The African National Congress (ANC) of South Africa originated at a similar meeting in 1912. Many of the nationalists who would lead the twentieth-century resistance to Western imperialism emigrated to Europe where they received formal and informal educations in dealing with European governments. Ho Chi Minh, the leader of Vietnamese armed resistance to French, Japanese, and American imperialism, lived in France as a young man;

there he joined in the foundation of the French Communist Party. Perhaps the most impressive resistance to imperialism was begun by an Indian lawyer, Mohandas Gandhi. Gandhi began his career as a lawyer defending Indian laborers in South Africa in 1889. There he developed a policy of nonviolent resistance known by the Sanskrit word *Satyagraha*. Despite harassment, beatings, and imprisonment, Gandhi stood with the moral force of *Satyagraha* and gained a global reputation. When the frustrated British deported him to India, Gandhi brought passive resistance to Indian nationalism.

The Diplomatic Revolution, 1890–1914

Imperial rivalries strained the Bismarckian system in Europe, but his network of alliances survived until Kaiser Wilhelm II sent Bismarck into retirement in 1890. The young emperor followed the advice of one of Bismarck's rivals, Baron Fritz von Holstein, to revise the Bismarckian system because Bismarck's promises to Russia risked losing the close alliance with Austria. Despite repeated Russian requests, the kaiser therefore decided not to renew the Reinsurance Treaty of 1887, and it lapsed three months after the dismissal of Bismarck. Instead, Wilhelm expanded the Triple Alliance in 1891, giving larger promises of support to Austria-Hungary and Italy. The consequence of the lapsing of Reinsurance Treaty was Franco-Russian friendship. One year after Bismarck's departure, a French fleet paid a symbolic visit to the Russian port of Kronstadt (near St. Petersburg) and Franco-Russian negotiations began; French pledges of loans to help industrialize Russia quickly led to the August Convention of 1891, an informal guarantee of cooperation. Avid French diplomacy expanded this into a military treaty, the Franco-Russian Alliance of 1894. Through this pact, the czar pledged to use the full Russian army against Germany, if Germany invaded France; the reciprocal French promise gave Russia security against Austria and Germany. To be ready for war, both sides also pledged to mobilize their armies as soon as any member of the Triple Alliance began mobilization.

The 1890s witnessed a further weakening of the German position as a result of deteriorating Anglo-German relations. The rise of Germany as an industrial power caused a rivalry for markets and aroused hostile public opinion in both countries. The jingoistic press contributed significantly to the worsening relations. The trade rivalry made the British question their tradi-

tion of free trade, and newspapers were soon denouncing goods "Made in Germany." German imperialism and German sympathy for the Boers (the kaiser sent a notorious telegram of encouragement to President Kruger in 1896) worsened relations further. German colonies contributed to the emergence of a larger problem: the German decision to build a great navy. Through the efforts of Admiral von Tirpitz, Germany adopted an ambitious Naval Law in 1898 and expanded that construction program with a second Naval Law in 1900. The British, who had long counted upon "ruling the waves" as their insurance against invasion, had adopted a vigorous naval building policy in 1889 known as "the two-power standard"; that is, they would build a navy equal to the combined forces of any two rivals. This policy, in combination with the German naval laws, led Europe to a dangerous arms race.

When the Fashoda crisis rekindled Anglo-French colonial disputes in 1898, some British statesmen, led by Joseph Chamberlain, argued that the government must abandon splendid isolation and enter the European alliance system. Chamberlain suggested resolving Anglo-German differences and negotiating an Anglo-German alliance, but his unofficial talks with minor diplomats in 1898–1901 failed to persuade either Prime Minister Salisbury or Chancellor von Bülow, and they were flatly rejected by the kaiser. The French foreign minister who yielded to Britain in the Fashoda crisis, Théophile Delcassé, responded by seizing the opportunity to open Anglo-French negotiations over their generations of colonial differences. By skillfully expanding colonial negotiations, Delcassé became the architect of a diplomatic revolution that ended British isolation and the hegemony of the Triple Alliance. His greatest accomplishment was an Anglo-French agreement of 1904 known as the Entente Cordiale (cordial understanding). The entente was not a military treaty comparable to the Triple Alliance or the Franco-Russian Alliance. It simply resolved colonial disputes: France recognized British preeminence in Egypt, and Britain accepted the French position in Morocco. Starting with this *quid pro quo*, the two governments were able to end squabbles around the globe.

The German reaction to the Entente Cordiale was to provoke an international crisis over Morocco in 1905. Germany, which had a growing commercial interest in Morocco, had been excluded from talks on the subject, although Delcassé had conducted subsequent negotiations on Morocco to acquire the support of Spain (by giving up the Moroccan coast opposite Spain) and of Italy (by backing an Italian claim to Tripoli). The Moroccan Crisis (later called the first Moroccan Crisis) resulted from a state visit by Kaiser Wilhelm II to Tangier, Morocco, where he made a strong speech in defense of Moroccan independence. When Delcassé proposed that some territorial concession be made to Germany to recognize the French position in Morocco, the kaiser refused. This confrontation led, at the invitation of the sultan of Morocco, to an international conference at Algeciras (Spain) in 1906, where Delcassé's diplomacy succeeded again, although he was driven from office in France by fears that he was dangerously provoking Germany. The crisis strengthened the Entente Cordiale and prompted closer Anglo-French military conversations; and when a vote was taken at Algeciras, only Austria supported Germany. The survival of the entente cordiale convinced the Reichstag to adopt a third Naval Law in 1906, but that in turn frightened the British enough to negotiate their territorial disputes with Russia in south Asia (Persia and Afghanistan). The Russians recognized the need for this in the aftermath of their defeat in 1905; the resultant Anglo-Russian Entente of 1907 divided Persia into spheres of influence and exchanged a Russian agreement to stay out of Afghanistan in return for British support for Russian naval access to the Mediterranean. This entente combined with the Entente Cordiale to create the Triple Entente. The Triple Entente did not include the explicit military provisions of the Triple Alliance, but Britain, France, and Russia soon entered into talks to plan military cooperation. Whereas French diplomats once worried about their isolation by Bismarck, the diplomatic revolution made Germans speak angrily of their *Einkreisung* (encirclement) by hostile competitors.

The Eastern Question and the Road to War

This division of Europe into two competing alliances meant that virtually any local crisis could precipitate a general war. Europe held several grave local problems, but the worst remained the eastern question. Bismarck's Congress of Berlin in 1878 had not settled this issue; it had merely temporized by placating the great powers; it did nothing to resolve Balkan nationalist claims or to settle the internal problems of the Ottoman Empire. Fighting resumed in the Balkans in the 1880s and had become severe in 1885 when Bulgarian nationalists in East Rumelia sought unity with Bulgaria, and Serbia went to war to prevent the creation of a large Bulgaria on its frontier. Fighting broke out twice in the 1890s,

then two more times in the early twentieth century before the next major crisis, known as the Balkan crisis of 1908. The crisis began with a long-simmering rebellion of westernizers inside the Ottoman Empire, known as the Young Turk rebellion; the victorious Young Turks won numerous concessions from the Sultan and exposed the weakness of the government in Constantinople to resist changes.

Almost constant crises wracked the Balkans from 1908 to 1914. Austria-Hungary, which had established a claim to Bosnia and Herzegovina in 1878, took advantage of the Ottoman crisis to annex the two provinces in 1908. This act outraged Pan-Slav nationalists in Serbia who had long seen Serbia as "the Piedmont of the Balkans" and anticipated a merger with Bosnia in a union of the southern Slavs (the Yugo Slavs in the Serbian language). After the annexation, Slavic nationalists turned increasingly to revolutionary societies, such as the Black Hand, to achieve unity. The 1911 statutes of the Black Hand stated the danger bluntly: "This organization prefers terrorist action to intellectual propaganda." The Habsburg monarchy was soon to discover that this was not an idle threat. None of the European powers was pleased by the annexation of Bosnia, but none intervened to prevent it.

The continuing weakness of the Ottoman Empire, militancy of Balkan nationalism, and reluctance of the great powers to intervene led to a succession of crises. In 1911 a second Moroccan crisis occurred, in which Germany sent the gunboat *Panther* to Morocco to protect German interests and the French conceded territory in central Africa to resolve the dispute. In 1912 a war broke out in North Africa, in which Italy invaded Tripoli to acquire their compensation for French gains in Morocco. Later that year, open warfare began in the Balkans when Serbia, Montenegro, Bulgaria, and Greece joined to attack the Ottoman Empire and detach some of the few remaining Turkish provinces in Europe; the Italians soon joined this First Balkan War (1912–13) by invading the Dodecanese Islands off the coast of Turkey. After the Turks had conceded territory to all of the belligerents, they quarreled among themselves; several states fought Bulgaria in the Second Balkan War (1913) to redivide the spoils, but nationalist ambitions were still unsatisfied.

Militarism and the European Arms Race

Imperial competition, alliance system rivalries, and the Balkan crises were all happening in an age of militarism.

⚓ TABLE 27.1 ⚓

The European Army Buildup, 1879–1913

Country	1879		1913	
	Standing army in peacetime	Fully mobilized army for war	Standing army in peacetime	Fully mobilized army for war
Austria-Hungary	267,000	772,000	800,000	3,000,000
Britain	136,000	600,000	160,000	700,000
India	200,000		249,000	
France	503,000	1,000,000	1,200,000	3,500,000
Germany	419,000	1,300,000	2,200,000	3,800,000
Russia	766,000	1,213,000	1,400,000	4,400,000

Europe in 1900 was the scene of a heated arms race, sustained by a mentality that glorified military action. When Bismarck negotiated the Triple Alliance in 1879, the typical great power army was smaller than 500,000 men; by 1913 the average exceeded one million men, with mobilization plans for armies of three million to four million men (see table 27.1). The naval construction race between Britain and Germany was the most costly part of the arms race. The industrial age had made it possible to build enormous, steam-powered, steel battleships, equipped with long-range artillery. These dreadnoughts (from the expression "Fear God and Dread Nought") were staggeringly expensive. The construction of submarine fleets added significantly to the total (see illustration 27.2). Before the shipbuilding mania of the 1890s, Britain had an annual naval budget of £13.8 million. This took more than 15 percent of government revenues, or more than twice the amount spent on education, science, and the arts combined (£6.1 million). Then, between 1890 and 1914, annual British naval expenditures more than tripled to £47.4 million. (The total revenue raised by the British income tax in 1913 was £44 million.) The German naval budget, meanwhile, almost quintupled from £4.6 million (1871) to £22.4 million (1914).

Few people yet understood the implications of this marriage between militarism and industrialization. Cavalry troops wearing brightly colored eighteenth-century uniforms and sabres remained the image of a heroic army, although a more accurate image of an army in 1900 portrayed its machines: rapid-firing heavy artillery and machine guns such as the Maxims that had slaughtered the Sudanese. And no army could be

Illustration 27.2

▨ **The Arms Race.** This 1909 photograph of British submarines in the Thames River near Westminster Palace (the seat of Parliament) conveys an eerie foreshadowing of the war. It was intended to show British naval might protecting freedom, a justification for the vast expenses of naval construction. Viewed in retrospect, it is an ironic and tragic scene because the naval competition led to German submarines, which were effective in choking British shipping.

stronger than the chemical industry that stood behind it; mass armies, and the total war that they implied, only became possible when chemists devised ways to manufacture millions of tons of explosives.

The arms race was accompanied by a popular militarism glorifying war. "Eternal peace is a dream, and not even a beautiful one," held one famous general. A book entitled *Germany and the Next War* (1911) insisted that "war is a biological necessity." Writers everywhere popularized such attitudes. In the words of an Italian journalist, "We wish to glorify war—the only health-giver of the world." Or, in those of an American philosopher, "War is a school of strenuous life and heroism." Militaristic governments produced elaborate plans for possible wars. German planners, for example, were ready for an invasion of the British Isles or of Texas (supporting a Mexican invasion of the southwestern United States), although they naturally lavished their most meticulous attention, such as the creation of precise railroad timetables, on plans to invade France.

The most famous peacetime war plan was the Schlieffen Plan, named for the general who devised it in 1892 in response to the Franco-Russian rapprochement and the fear that Germany might have to fight a war on two fronts at once. Schlieffen reasoned that the Russians would be slow to mobilize, but the French, able to employ modern communications and transportation, would be an immediate threat. The Schlieffen Plan therefore directed the German army to begin any war by concentrating all possible forces against the French; a rapid victory there would permit defeating the Russians afterward. To win that rapid victory over the French, the plan proposed to start any war (without regard to where it originated) by invading neutral Belgium. As the German strategist Karl von Clausewitz had explained a century earlier, "The heart of France lies between Brussels and Paris." The German plan for marching to Brussels and then pivoting southward was so precise that it included a timetable for each day's progress, culminating in a triumphal parade through Paris on day thirty-nine. French war planners also believed that the next war would be decided by a rapid offensive. Their 1913 regulations were straightforward: "The French army, returning to its tradition, henceforth admits no law but the offensive." It was expounded through a document known as Plan XVII, drafted by French generals for the reconquest of Alsace and Lorraine. Most of the French army was to be concentrated on the eastern frontier and then march into Alsace, but French planners so poorly understood what an industrial war would be like that they rejected camouflage uniforms for their great offensive and dressed soldiers in bright red trousers.

The Balkan Crisis of July 1914

Europeans little recognized the gravity of their situation in the early twentieth century; their rivalries for markets and empire, their nationalist ambitions and hatreds, their alliances and battle plans, their militarism, and their crude social Darwinian belief in "the survival of the fittest" all threatened the devastation of their civilization. Putting the matter most succinctly, Winston Churchill noted, "Europe in 1914 was a powderkeg where everybody smoked." When yet another Balkan crisis occurred in the summer of 1914, European governments precipitated a monstrously destructive war, known to contemporaries as "the Great War" and to later generations as World War I. Some historians have called it "the suicide of the old Europe."

The Balkan crisis of 1914 began in the Bosnian city of Sarajevo. A nineteen-year-old Serbian nationalist and member of the Black Hand, Gavrilo Princip, assassinated the heir to the Habsburg throne, the archduke Franz-Ferdinand, during a state visit to Sarajevo in late June. The Austrian government blamed the Serbian government, which knew of the planned assassination and did not stop it, for the murder. After securing a promise that their German allies would support them in a confrontation with Serbia—a pledge known as "the blank check"—the Austrians sent a forty-eight-hour ultimatum to Serbia: The government must dissolve nationalist societies, close nationalist periodicals, end anti-Austrian propaganda, fire anti-Austrian members of the government, allow Austrian investigation of the crime inside Serbia, and arrest officials implicated. The Russian government meanwhile warned that it would not tolerate an Austrian invasion of Serbia. The Russians, too, received assurances that their allies, the French, would support them—President Poincaré of France was visiting Russia during the crisis and stood by France's staunchest ally. When Serbia accepted most, but not all, of the ultimatum, the Austrians declared war on July 28, 1914, exactly one month after the assassination in Sarajevo; they bombarded the Serbian capital, Belgrade (which sat at the border), on the next day.

The Third Balkan War quickly became a general European war. The Russians responded to it by ordering the mobilization of their army. Germany, whose war plans were predicated upon the Russians being slow to mobilize, demanded that the Russian army

Illustration 27.3

💯 **War Enthusiasm.** The beginning of World War I was greeted with remarkable public enthusiasm. Cheering crowds volunteered to fight and hailed departing soldiers. One of the most memorable photographs of this war fever was taken in Munich on the day that war was declared, August 2, 1914. Holding his hat near the center of the happy crowd is Adolf Hitler, who soon joined a Bavarian regiment and fought in the war. The photographer, Heinrich Hoffmann, later became Hitler's court photographer.

stand down. When the Russians did not, the German army invaded Belgium. This violation of the international treaty on Belgian neutrality ("a scrap of paper" in the phrase of the chancellor Bethmann-Hollweg of Germany) led the British to recognize that their interests were on the side of the French. For centuries, British policy had opposed the dominance of the lowlands (from where an invasion might be launched) by any strong power—by Spain, later by France, or now by Germany. European declarations of war rained down in the first days of August, until the members of the Triple Alliance, (except Italy) and the Triple Entente were at war with each other over a crisis of Balkan nationalism. As the British foreign secretary observed, after a long cabinet meeting had chosen war and the streetlights of London were being extinguished for daybreak, "The lights are going out all over Europe." That somber statement was a good metaphor for the four years of darkness that followed; at the time, however, public opinion greeted the war with great enthusiasm (see illustration 27.3) and brisk sales were made of French (or German) dictionaries for "the stroll to Paris" (or Berlin). Only limited expressions of antiwar sentiment were heard after Jean Jaurès, the leading socialist proponent of organizing workers against war, was assassinated on July 31 (three days after the assassination of Franz-Ferdinand and the day before mobilization of the French and German armies).

Other belligerents entered the war slowly. The Ottoman Empire, whose continuing collapse in the Balkans had been such a factor in the coming of the war, followed its close ties with Germany and its historic rivalry with Russia into the war in October 1914. Italy remained neutral, declaring that the Triple Alliance was binding only if Germany or Austria were invaded, not when they invaded small neighbors. The Italians then negotiated with both sides and eventually joined the entente powers in 1915, when a secret Treaty of London promised them significant territorial compensation at the expense of the Habsburg Empire. The United States likewise remained neutral despite significant pro-British sentiment. Although a dispute over submarine warfare clouded German-American relations, President Woodrow Wilson kept the country out of war and contributed to efforts for a negotiated peace until entering the war on the side of the entente powers in 1917.

World War I: From the Invasion of Belgium to a World War

The decisive theatre of the war was the western front in France and Belgium, although the largest armies met on the eastern front and fighting reached into the Middle East, Africa, and the Pacific Islands. More than sixty million men were mobilized to fight, including millions of Africans, Indians, Canadians, Australians, and Americans. The French, for example, conscripted 519,000 Africans to fight in Europe. By 1917 the belligerents included Japan and China (both on the side of the west-

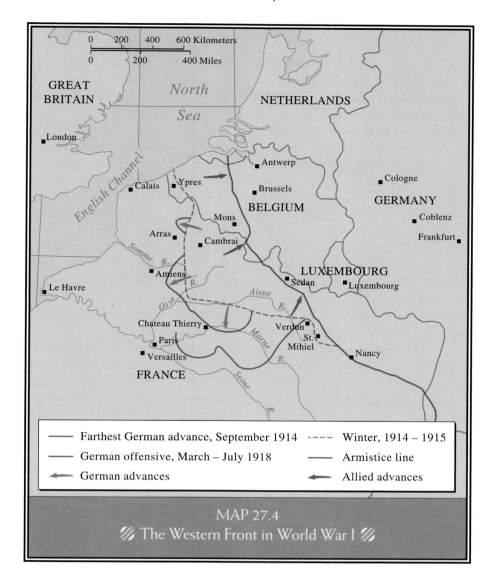

MAP 27.4

The Western Front in World War I

ern Allies), Turkey (on the side of Germany and the Central Powers), and many smaller states supporting the western Allies. For example, the governments of Siam, Liberia, and Peru all found reasons to declare war on Germany.

Fighting in the west nearly resulted in a German victory in 1914. The Schlieffen Plan led to the German occupation of Brussels on the sixteenth day of the war, and a German army of 1.5 million men pushed far into France by the thirty-fifth day (see map 27.4). Simultaneously, the French invasion of Alsace and Lorraine (the battle of the Frontiers) failed and the French were driven back with heavy losses. In early September, the German army stood within a few miles of Paris. Victory seemed imminent, and the chief of staff, General Helmuth von Moltke (nephew of the Moltke of the 1860s), sent part of the army to the eastern front to protect

Prussia. In a week of desperate fighting along the Marne River, in which the military governor of Paris (General Joseph Gallieni) gambled the city's garrison, which he shuttled to the front in Parisian taxicabs, the French stopped the German advance and forced the invaders to retreat to more defensible positions. Victory at the Marne saved France at a horrifying price. Of 1.3 million French field troops at the start of the war, more than 600,000 were killed, wounded, or taken prisoner in one month of fighting. The casualty rate among infantry officers reached two-thirds. The aftermath of the battle of the Marne was a different war: After a "race to the sea" stretched the opposing armies from the English Channel to Switzerland, they fought a defensive war in which massive battles hardly budged the opposing army. By late 1914 both armies had dug into fixed positions and faced each other from a system of earthen trenches. (Trenches were typically seven to eight feet deep and six to seven feet wide, dug in parallel lines with connecting lateral trenches; they were often filled with mud, standing water, vermin, or the unburied dead; and despite timbering, tended to collapse.) Despite staggering casualty rates, the line did not move more than ten miles in the next three years.

In the east, Russian armies engaged the Austrian army in Galicia and invaded East Prussia, while most of the German army participated in the Schlieffen Plan in the west. They won some initial victories in Galicia, but the German and Austrian armies soon defeated the poorly equipped and commanded Russians. An outnumbered German army, led by a Prussian aristocrat and veteran of the wars of unification, General Paul von Hindenburg, and a young staff officer who had distinguished himself in the west, General Erich von Ludendorff, stopped the Russian invasion at the battle of Tannenberg in August 1914, taking more than 100,000 prisoners. Two weeks later, Hindenburg's army defeated the Russians again at the battle of the Masurian Lakes, taking another 125,000 captives and driving a demoralized enemy from Prussia. The Russian defeat was so complete that the commander shot himself, whereas Hindenburg became a national hero who would be elected president of Germany in 1925. Large armies and vast territory still protected the czarist government, but the first year of fighting cost nearly one million soldiers plus all of Poland and Lithuania. The Russians recovered sufficiently to stage a great offensive against the Austrians in 1916 (the Brusilov Offensive), but that campaign cost one million men and worsened demoralization. Subsequent losses were so enormous (more than 9 million Russian military casualties, including 1.7 million deaths, plus 2.2 million civilian deaths) that in early 1918 a revolutionary government negotiated a separate peace in the Treaty of Brest-Litovsk, surrendering vast territories in order to leave the war.

By 1915 secondary fronts had expanded the European conflagration into a world war. In the first weeks of the war, British and French colonial armies conquered most of the German colonies in Africa. In southern Europe, Italy joined the western Allies in 1915, and the Italian front witnessed two years of indecisive fighting. In late 1917 the Italians were badly defeated by forces under General Ludendorff at the battle of Caporetto, but that action came too late to change the outcome of the war. In the Balkans, the Serbians initially held out against the Austrians, but the Balkan war quickly expanded: Turkey joined the Central Powers in 1914, and Bulgaria followed in 1915. Romania joined the western Allies in 1916. Turkish participation led to bloody fighting in the Middle East. A Russo-Turkish War nearly annihilated the Armenians who were caught between them; in 1915 the Turks accused the Armenians of pro-Russian sympathies and began their forced eviction, a death march known as the Armenian Massacre. The British intervened in the Middle Eastern front (upon the advice of Winston Churchill) and in 1915 made a landing at Gallipoli, a peninsula in the Aegean Sea near the narrow passage of the Dardanelles. This ill-conceived attempt to open the straits and supply the Russians ended in 1916 with heavy British losses and a Turkish victory that established the reputation of Mustapha Kemal (later known as Attaturk), who became the first president of the postwar Turkish republic. Britain countered by aiding an Arab revolt whose success (such as the campaign led by Colonel T. E. Lawrence in Arabia) hastened the Ottoman collapse.

An important part of World War I took place at sea, but it was not the anticipated duel of dreadnoughts. Both sides were extremely cautious with their expensive super-battleships and rarely sent them to fight. Of fifty-one British, French, and German dreadnoughts afloat in 1914, only two were sunk during the entire war. The British failed to win a decisive victory against the German fleet at Jutland in May 1916, but they effectively blockaded Germany, allowing only 10 percent of prewar imports to reach shore. The German navy scored its own dramatic successes with submarines. Between late 1916 and late 1917, German submarines sank more than eight million tons of Atlantic shipping, threatening the British food supply but contributing to the American entry into the war on Britain's side. In 1915 German submarines sank passenger liners with Americans aboard and American ships carrying goods to Britain. Sentiment boiled over when the *Lusitania*, a passenger liner en route from New York to England with a cargo that included arms, went down with 139 Americans aboard. Germany placated American opinion with a promise not to sink passenger liners but withdrew that promise to resume unrestricted submarine warfare in 1917; four days after that announcement, the United States broke relations with Germany and, two months later, entered the war.

Trench Warfare and the Machine Gun

World War I was ultimately decided on the western front. There, Britain, France, and Germany fought a war of attrition in which hundreds of thousands of men

◆ DOCUMENT 27.2 ◆

Robert Graves: Life in the Trenches

Robert Graves was a British poet and author who was nineteen when World War I began. He first won fame for his autobiography, published in the 1920s, that covered the war years. This excerpt is from that autobiography, entitled Goodbye to All That.

After a meal of bread, bacon, rum, and bitter stewed tea sickly with sugar, we went . . . up a long trench to battalion headquarters. The trench was cut through red clay. I had a torch [flashlight] with me which I kept flashed on the ground. Hundreds of field mice and frogs were in the trench. They had fallen in and had no way out. The light dazzled them and we could not help treading on them.

. . .

The trench was wet and slippery. The guide was giving hoarse directions all the time. "Hole right." "Wire high." "Wire low." "Deep place here, sir." "Wire low." I had never been told about the field telephone wires. They were fastened by staples to the side of the trench, and when it rained the staples were always falling out and the wire falling down and tripping people. . . . The holes were the sump-pits used for draining the trenches. We were

now under rifle fire. . . . The rifle bullet gave no warning. . . . [W]e learned not to duck to a rifle bullet, because once it was heard it must have missed. . . . In a trench the bullets, going over the hollow, made a tremendous crack. Bullets often struck the barbed wire in front of the trenches, which turned them and sent them spinning in a head-over-heels motion. . . .

Our guide took us up to the front line. We passed a group of men huddled over a brazier. They were wearing waterproof capes, for it had now started to rain, and cap-comforters, because the weather was cold. They were little men, daubed with mud. . . . We overtook a fatigue-party struggling up the trench, loaded with timber lengths and sandbags, cursing plaintively as they slipped into sumpholes and entangled their burdens in the telephone wire. Fatigue parties were always encumbered by their rifles and equipment, which it was a crime ever to have out of reach. . . . [W]e had to stand aside to let a stretcher-case past.

Graves, Robert. *Goodbye to All That*. London: Cape, 1923.

died in offensives that failed to break the stalemate. Heavy artillery bombardment could not produce a breakthrough: Krupp guns virtually leveled the fortifications at Verdun without producing a breakthrough. The German introduction of poison gas (such as phosgene and mustard gas) at the battle of Ypres (Belgium) in 1915 and the British use of the first tanks in 1916 could not break the defensive lines. Two of the most murderous battles of human history were fought on this front in 1916—the German offensive at Verdun and an Anglo-French counterattack along the Somme River— but neither battle broke the defensive positions. The fighting around Verdun cost France 542,000 casualties and Germany 434,000, shifting the lines only slightly. The French commander at Verdun, General Henri Pétain, became famous for claiming that the Germans "shall not pass" and a national hero when they did not. (Pétain's reputation, like Hindenburg's, suffered greatly when he became a postwar head of state.)

Even while the carnage at Verdun continued, the British and French began their own offensive on the Somme River. After seven days and nights of artillery

bombardment on the German trenches (see document 27.2), Allied soldiers went "over the top," walking toward the German lines, with sixty-six pounds of equipment strapped to their backs. They marched into a storm of machine gun fire, and by nightfall 40 percent of the British frontline troops and 60 percent of their officers were dead. In one day of fighting, the bloodiest day in the history of the British army, they suffered twenty thousand deaths (compared with an American death toll of fifty-eight thousand in the entire Vietnam War). When the Allies finally stopped their attack, they had pushed the German lines back a maximum of seven miles, at the combined cost of 1.2 million casualties.

The Home Front

Civilian populations suffered terribly during the war. Seven million civilians were killed, and in several countries (especially in the Balkans and eastern Europe) more civilians were killed than soldiers. Civilian populations that were spared direct contact with the fighting

<table>
<tr><th colspan="4">★ TABLE 27.2 ★

Life on the Home Front in World War I</th></tr>
</table>

Wartime Inflation in the Prices of Consumer Goods			
	Prices as a percentage of 1913 prices		
Country	1914	1917	1919
France	102	262	357
Germany	106	179	415
Great Britain	100	206	242
Italy	96	299	364

Source: *History of the World Economy in the Twentieth Century*, vol. 2: Gerd Hardach, *The First World War, 1914–1918* (Berkeley, Calif.: University of California Press, 1977), pp. 119, 172.

typically endured lesser hardships. The war brought martial law in many countries (starting with Germany), press censorship and the jailing of journalists (including a cabinet minister in France), harassment of foreigners and pacifists, suspension of many peacetime activities (British schools even canceled cricket), and dreadful propaganda (such as reports that the Germans were bayoneting babies in Belgium). Transportation, food, clothing, and fuel were requisitioned, regulated, or rationed by governments. The scarcity and inflated prices of daily necessities frequently left the home front as hungry as the army. The war doubled the price of consumer goods in Britain, tripled prices in France, and quadrupled those in Germany (see table 27.2). The Allied blockade made the situation so bad in Germany that even the invention of *ersatz* foods (substitute foods, often adulterated) left the people with less than half of the nutrition in their prewar diet. During "the turnip winter" of 1916–17, much of the population survived on that humble tuber. In Russia, the scarcity of food and fuel was so severe that it was a major factor in the outbreak of revolution in 1917.

The war also led to dramatic changes on the home front. The most important change resulted from the mobilization of so many men to fight. In France, 43 percent of all adult men were conscripted, a total of 8.4 million men over five years. (All of the powers, except Britain, drafted their armies before the war; Britain was forced to end the volunteer army in 1916 when the death rate became too high to replace with volunteers.) To replace conscripted soldiers in their peacetime jobs, the French government welcomed 184,000 colonial workers into France, creating immigrant communities

that would later become controversial. The principal solution for the labor shortage, however, was the recruitment of women. The war sharply increased the percentage of women in the labor force (especially in Britain and France), and it put women into jobs from which they had previously been excluded. In France, for example, women had constituted more than 35 percent of the prewar workforce. Then the French state railroads increased women workers from six thousand to fifty-seven thousand. The Ministry of Education added thirty thousand women in secondary education. Banks, businesses, and the government all hired women to replace men on clerical and secretarial staffs. The largest opening for women, however, was in munitions factories, which employed fifteen thousand women in 1915 and 684,000 in 1917 (see document 27.3). Without such women workers, armies could not have continued to fight. The women received less pay than the men they replaced (and typically lost their jobs at the war's end), but they contributed significantly to the long-term evolution of women's rights.

Exhaustion and Armistice, 1917–18

By 1917–18 Europe was exhausted. Combat deaths were approaching eight million; total war deaths, fifteen million. Britain also experienced rebellion at home in 1916: P. H. Pearse and the *Sinn Fein* (Gaelic for "ourselves alone") led an unsuccessful Irish nationalist uprising known as the Easter Rising. Pearse and others were executed, and many Irish nationalists were imprisoned, although only temporarily halting the Irish Revolution that produced a larger Anglo-Irish War in 1919–21 and Irish independence. The Russian Revolution of 1917, meanwhile, devastated that country. Before the war in the west ended, the revolution brought about the abolition of the Romanov monarchy, the execution of Czar Nicholas II, and a separate peace treaty with Germany. Also in 1917 fully half of the units of the French army mutinied. Twenty thousand men deserted, more refused to fight, and discipline was not restored until three thousand soldiers (often chosen by lot) had been executed—more than the total executed on the guillotine in Paris during the French Revolution. Similar demoralization (but not mutiny) took root in the British army after their commander, Sir Douglas Haig, ordered another offensive in Flanders, known as the battle of Ypres; 400,000 Britons died in that campaign. In Germany, where the civilian government was directed by the army high command (and the virtual dictatorship of General Ludendorff), the Allied blockade was

Sylvia Pankhurst: The Situation of Women War Workers

Propaganda was insistent to get women into the munition factories, and every sort of work ordinarily performed by men. The sections clamouring for the military conscription of men saw in the industrial service of women a means to their end. Feminists who were advocates of Conscription for men believed themselves adding to the importance of women by demanding that women also should be conscripts. . . .

From all over the country we cited authentic wage scales: Waring and Gillow paying 3½ d. an hour to women, 9d. to men for military tent making; the Hendon aeroplane works paying women 3d. per hour, at work for which men got 10d. per hour; women booking clerks at Victoria Station getting 15s. a week, though the men they replaced got 35s.; and so on, in district after district, trade after trade. . . .

Firms like Bryant and May's, the match makers, were now making munitions. Accustomed to employ large numbers of women and girls at ill-paid work, they knew by long experience that piece rates would secure them a higher production than could be induced by a bonus. Without a care for pre-war standards, in a trade new to their factory, they had fixed for munition work, often perilous and heavy, similar sweated piece rates to those paid for matches. . . .

Pankhurst, Sylvia. "The Home Front" (London: 1932). In Brian Tierney and Joan Scott, *A Documentary History of Western Societies,* vol. 2. New York: McGraw-Hill, 1984.

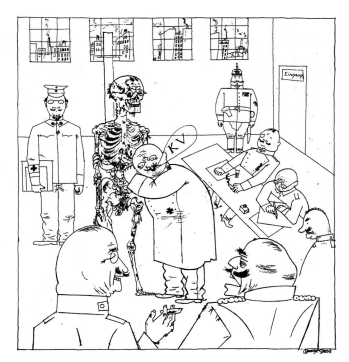

Illustration 27.4

The Rise of Antiwar Sentiment. The German artist George Grosz was one of the most caustic social critics of the early twentieth century. In this pen-and-ink drawing of 1916 entitled "The Faith Healers," he attacked the German army, whose officers are seen declaring that a decaying corpse is still "fit for active duty" (KV). Note the stereotype of smug commanders in the foreground and, through the windows, Grosz's assertion that big business and industry stood right behind the army.

bringing the nation to the brink of starvation, and discontent was so severe that defiant strikes and sabotage became widespread in early 1918. In Berlin alone, more than 250,000 workers refused to continue; their strike soon ended, but revolutionary conditions did not. Antiwar sentiment developed in many places (see illustration 27.4).

The last months of the war brought one more epic tragedy to the world. A virulent form of influenza struck in the trenches of the western front and flourished when soldiers carried it home. Before the pandemic ended in 1919, it had become the greatest public health disaster of modern history. More than two billion people worldwide contracted the disease, and somewhere between twenty-two million and thirty million people died from it—twice as many as died in the fighting. The disease spread from France to Spain, where it killed an estimated eight million Spaniards (more than 40 percent of the 1910 population) and acquired the name of the Spanish influenza. Returning British colonial troops spread the disease in India, where an estimated twelve million people perished from it. In the United States, 500,000 deaths made this flu the worst plague in American history. By comparison, AIDS killed 125,000 in its first decade.

Among the states fighting on the western front, Germany most severely felt the exhaustion of war in 1918. The Allied naval blockade and the American entry into the war left little doubt that Germany was defeated, although the fighting had not been pushed onto German soil. As the army neared collapse, the German

TABLE 27.3

Losses in World War I, 1914–18

Country	Total men mobilized	Combat deaths	Percentage of forces killed	Military casualties	Percentage of forces wounded	Civilian deaths	Total war dead	Percentage population killed
Austria-Hungary	7,800,000	1,200,000	15.4	7,000,000	90.0	300,000	1,500,000	5.2
Belgium	267,000	14,000	5.2	93,000	34.8	30,000	44,000	0.6
British Empire	8,900,000	947,000	10.6	3,200,000	35.2	30,000	977,000	2.4
France	8,400,000	1,400,000	16.2	6,200,000	73.2	40,000	1,440,000	3.6
Germany	11,000,000	1,800,000	16.1	7,100,000	64.9	760,000	2,560,000	3.8
Italy	5,600,000	460,000	8.2	2,200,000	39.1	n.a.	n.a	
Russia	12,000,000	1,700,000	14.2	9,200,000	76.3	2,000,000	3,700,000	2.4
Serbia	707,000	125,000	17.7	331,000	46.8	650,000	775,000	17.6
Ottoman Empire	2,900,000	325,000	11.4	975,000	34.2	2,200,000	2,525,000	10.1
United States	4,740,000	115,000	2.4	204,000	6.7		115,000	0.1

Source: Calculated from data in Chris Cook and John Paxton, *European Political Facts, 1848–1918* (London: Macmillan, 1978), pp. 188–89, 213–32; William L. Langer, ed., *An Encyclopedia of World History* (Boston, Mass.: Houghton-Mifflin, 1968), 976; *The World Almanac and Book of Facts, 1997* (Mahwah, N.J.: World Almanac Book, 1996), p. 184.

generals called for an armistice in mid-1918. In early November, the German navy at Kiel mutinied rather than continue fighting and revolution spread to Munich (where a short-lived socialist republic of Bavaria was proclaimed) and other cities. Two days later, Kaiser Wilhelm II abdicated and fled to Holland. While militant socialists (known as the Spartacists, after an ancient Roman slave rebellion) led by Karl Liebknecht and Rosa Luxemburg sought to establish a communist regime in Berlin, a hastily formed republican government led by Matthias Erzberger met the Allied commander in chief, French Marshal Ferdinand Foch, in a railroad boxcar outside Compiègne, France, and accepted strict Allied terms (which made further fighting impossible) for an armistice. The fighting stopped at a symbolic moment—the eleventh hour of November 11th.

The human cost of the war was staggering, and grim numbers only sketch its outlines (see table 27.3). More than sixty million soldiers were mobilized to fight, and nearly fifteen million people were killed (eight million military and seven million civilians), not counting the tens of millions who fell to the Spanish influenza and other war-related diseases. Most of the great powers saw between one-third to three-fourths of all military forces suffer war wounds and 10 percent to 17 percent killed. A generation of young European men was lost.

The Russian Revolution: The February Revolution

The most important wartime consequence of the war took place in Russia in 1917–20. A revolution in 1917 (the February revolution) ended the Romanov monarchy, and a second revolution a few months later (the Bolshevik, or October, revolution) brought Lenin and the Bolsheviks to power. A subsequent civil war (1918–20) led to the creation of a communist state.

The government of Nicholas II already faced extreme difficulties on the eve of World War I. The peasant majority of the nation had never achieved the economic freedom or landownership implicit in the emancipation of 1861. A growing working class, created by the beginnings of Russian industrialization, was enduring conditions as bleak as those in England in the 1840s. Minority populations such as the Poles felt the nationalist ambitions for self-rule that had swept Europe, while minority religions, especially the Jews, detested the regime that persecuted them. Much of the intelligentsia aspired to the individual rights and representative government they saw in western Europe.

Added to these problems, World War I was a catastrophe for Russia. The Russian army's inferior preparation and equipment led to shocking defeats. In 1915 the army suffered shortages of rifles, ammunition, and

TABLE 27.4

The Cost of Basic Russian Consumer Goods, 1914–17

The 1914 ruble equaled 100 kopecks or 50 cents.

Commodity	April 1914	April 1917
Sack of potatoes	1 ruble	7 rubles
Sack of wheat flour (c. 36 pounds)	2.5 rubles	16 rubles
Pound of meat	10 kopecks	70 kopecks
Lard	12 kopecks	90 kopecks
One pair of shoes	5–8 rubles	40 rubles
One cubic meter of firewood	3 rubles	20 rubles

Source: Marc Ferro, *La Révolution de 1917*, vol. 1 (Paris: Flammarion, 1967), and Francis Conte, *Les Grands dates de la Russie et de l'URSS* (Paris, Larousse, 1990), p. 175.

clothing; conscripts were even sent into battle without equipment. Army morale collapsed. On the home front, a shortage of skilled labor, caused by an ill-planned mobilization, led to shortages of critical supplies and chaos in their transportation and distribution. The cost of basic consumer goods rose dramatically as the government printed worthless money to pay for the war; a pound of meat and a sack of potatoes each increased by 700 percent (see table 27.4). Food shortages became severe because peasants refused to sell grain for paper money. The government seemed mired in scandals and corruption, of which the influence of Grigori Rasputin (a religious mystic who was close to the royal family, especially the czarina), and his dramatic assassination by a group of prominent aristocrats, most aroused criticism. Russia had no stable government: Four prime ministers were dismissed in slightly more than two years, and the czar remained at the front with his army. Even moderates in the Duma expressed outrage at the incompetence and repressiveness of the government. Paul Milyukov, Kadets, put it bluntly: "How did Russia get here? Stupidity or treason?" In 1916 real wages fell by approximately 20 percent, prompting more than fourteen hundred strikes in Russian cities. Sporadic mutinies began in the demoralized army. An imperial decree ordered conscription of 400,000 people for civilian labor, and violent resistance broke out, especially in southern portions of the empire. By winter, bread was becoming scarce in major cities.

The February Revolution of 1917 began, like many rebellions of the Old Regime, when food shortages made life intolerable for urban workers. The year began with fifty thousand workers striking in Petrograd (formerly St. Petersburg), and the number grew to eighty thousand in the next month. Demonstrations and bread riots, led by women as they had been in the French Revolution, occurred in early March 1917 (February in the old Russian calendar). By March 10th Petrograd was in the grip of nearly general strikes, and Nicholas II ordered the army to "end them tomorrow." After officers ordered soldiers to fire on the crowd on March 11, killing 150 civilians, discontented soliders of the Petrograd garrison mutinied on March 12 and joined the demonstrators. The czar tried to suspend the Duma, but parliamentary leaders refused to disband. The revolutionary tide in Petrograd was rapidly passing by the Duma, however, and the mutineers elected a competing body, a council (*soviet*) of soldiers, which joined with a soviet of labor deputies, led by Alexander Kerensky (a socialist lawyer), to set up an alternative government. On March 13 the Petrograd soviets called on soldiers throughout the army to elect their own soviets to take control from imperial officers, and the fate of the regime was settled.

On March 15, 1917, six days after the first protest marches and four days after the army fired on the crowd, Czar Nicholas II abdicated for himself and for his son, passing the throne to his brother, the grand duke Michael, who also refused the crown. Leaders of the Duma, the Petrograd Soviet, and the Zemstva assumed power and announced a Provisional Government headed by Prince Georgi Lvov, a liberal aristocrat and Kadet who presided over the national union of Zemstva. This government included democratic centrists such as Lvov and Milyukov and democratic socialists such as Kerensky, but none of the leading Bolsheviks, who were returning from exile and attacking the government in their newspaper, *Pravda*, which circulated openly in Russia. The Provisional Government, under Lvov and soon under Kerensky, won international praise for its democratic program—an amnesty for political crimes, a constitutional assembly elected by universal suffrage, equal rights for minorities, and full civil liberties—but it remained a severely divided coalition. Lenin (who was in exile in Zurich) urged the soviets to withdraw their support from the government, and conservatives (many of whom rallied behind the Cossack commander of the Petrograd garrison, General Lavr Kornilov) considered a coup d'état to forcibly suppress the Bolsheviks.

During its brief existence, the Provisional Government faced numerous problems. It remained at war with Germany, and the governments of Britain, France, and the United States (whose help Russia desperately needed) all wanted it to remain part of the wartime coalition that could now be described as a democratic alliance against autocracy. The Provisional Government may have sealed its own fate in April 1917 when Foreign Minister Milyukov reaffirmed the Russian promise to the Allies to remain in the war, in a document known as the Milyukov Note. Nor did the government have an easy solution for the shortages of food and other critical supplies. In the spirit of a democratic revolution, the Provisional Government recognized the independence of Poland and Finland, established the eight-hour workday and granted freedom of religion, but the war never allowed it to consolidate a hold on Russian public popularity. The Petrograd Soviet of Workers' and Soldiers' Deputies, meanwhile, still held the backing of those critically important groups, while the continuation of the war caused support for the Provisional Government to dwindle rapidly.

The October Revolution of 1917

The most tenacious opposition to the Provisional Government came from Lenin and his supporters in the Bolshevik faction of revolutionary socialism. Lenin had spent the war in exile in Switzerland until his clandestine return (aided by the Germans, who hoped his politics would weaken Russia) in April 1917. He expounded a simple, yet highly effective program (see illustration 27.5) known as the April Theses: (1) immediate peace, even at the cost of a harsh German treaty; (2) immediate redistribution of land to the peasants; (3) transfer of political power from the Provisional Government to the soviets; and (4) transfer of the control of factories to committees of workers. The promises of the April Theses (especially peace) contrasted vividly with the policies of the Provisional Government (especially the Milyukov Note). Lenin's program of land and peace first won the Bolsheviks a majority on the Moscow Soviet and made Lenin's foremost lieutenant, Leon Trotsky (whose real name was Lev Bronstein), the head of the Petrograd Soviet by the early autumn of 1917. Trotsky, a Ukrainian Jewish peasant who had entered radical politics as a teenager, was a leader of the revolution of 1905, and one of the most effective leaders of the Bolshevik revolution.

Even with the appeal of the April Theses, the Bolsheviks had the support of only a small minority of Rus-

Illustration 27.5

Lenin Exhorting the Crowd. Among the strongest weapons that Lenin and the Bolsheviks had against Kerensky and the Provisional Government was the simple call for peace, a weapon that could be used in repeated speeches in the street. This photograph of Lenin addressing the revolutionary crowd in Moscow later became famous because of a secondary detail: The figure standing on the steps and facing the camera is Trotsky, who was edited out of most subsequent versions of this picture to hide his prominence in the revolution.

sians. When the Petrograd Soviet of Workers' and Soldiers' Deputies held a Panrussian Congress in June and July 1917, only 105 of 822 delegates were Bolsheviks, who were far outnumbered by both Mensheviks and rural radicals just among the revolutionary parties. Lenin and Trotsky responded by forming a Military Revolutionary Committee to prepare for a second Russian revolution of 1917 and created their own military force—the Red Guards—composed of soldiers from the Petrograd garrison and armed workers, forces that were essential in open battles against Kornilov's troops. A Bolshevik party congress held in August 1917 resolved upon the conquest of power by an armed insurrection, though most of the party was unprepared for action. Lenin and Trotsky won the backing of the party's leadership (the Central Committee) after the Russian army suffered more reverses, and they orchestrated a minutely planned coup to seize power in Petrograd in early November (October in the old-style calendar). Two days of violent fighting gave the Bolsheviks control of the Winter Palace and then of Petrograd. The Bolshevik revolution spread to Moscow on the third day, and within a week soviets of workers and

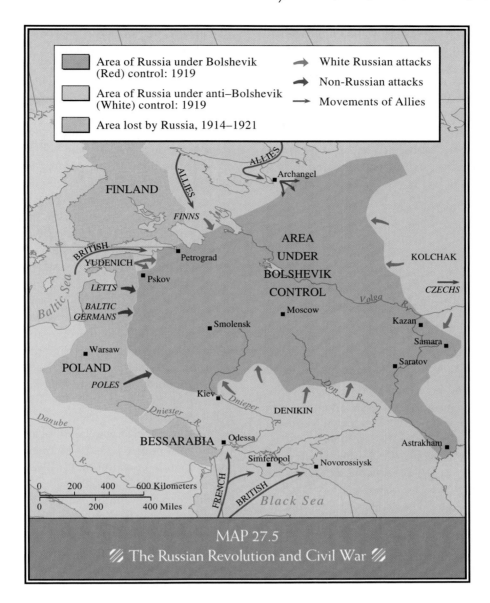

Legend:
- Area of Russia under Bolshevik (Red) control: 1919
- Area of Russia under anti–Bolshevik (White) control: 1919
- Area lost by Russia, 1914–1921
- → White Russian attacks
- → Non-Russian attacks
- → Movements of Allies

ALLIES
FINLAND
Archangel
FINNS
BRITISH
YUDENICH
Petrograd
Pskov
LETTS
Baltic Sea
BALTIC GERMANS
Warsaw
POLAND
POLES
Smolensk
Moscow
AREA UNDER BOLSHEVIK CONTROL
Volga R.
KOLCHAK
CZECHS
Kazan
Samara
Saratov
Kiev
Dnieper
Dniester R.
BESSARABIA
Odessa
DENIKIN
Don R.
Astrakham
Danube R.
Simferopol
Novorossiysk
FRENCH
BRITISH
Black Sea

0 200 400 600 Kilometers
0 200 400 Miles

MAP 27.5
The Russian Revolution and Civil War

soldiers held Moscow, Smolensk, and Kazan (see map 27.5).

An All-Russian Congress of Soviets immediately endorsed the Bolshevik revolution and approved a new government, which Lenin organized with himself at its head. This Council of Commissars (later called the Politburo) included Trotsky as commissar (minister) of foreign affairs and his bitter rival, Joseph Dzhugashvili, known as Stalin ("the man of steel"), as commissar for the nationalities. Stalin, the son of a Georgian shoemaker, was one of the few Bolshevik leaders who could honestly claim to be a member of the working class. He had entered an Orthodox seminary at age twenty, but had been expelled for his Marxism, and before the war he had been arrested six times and twice sent to Siberia for revolutionary politics. The Council of Commisars

acted quickly to consolidate the Bolshevik position by issuing Lenin's decrees on peace and land. Although the decree on peace secured much support, elections for a constituent assembly gave the Bolsheviks only 25 percent of the vote. The council responded by creating a new secret police, known as the Cheka, to fight opponents of the revolution. The Cheka, which was not greatly different from the czarist secret police, laid the basis for the new regime to become a police state. And it showed that Lenin meant his words of 1902: "We have never rejected, and cannot reject, terror." Not surprisingly, Lenin and Trotsky closed the constituent assembly in January 1918, on the second day of its meetings.

Lenin and Trotsky fulfilled their promise to bring peace. The high command of the German army agreed to talks at Brest-Litovsk (today in Belarus) in December 1917. They presented Russia with severe terms (far more severe than the treaty later given to defeated Germany) and the Treaty of Brest-Litovsk (March 1918) showed that Lenin and Trotsky were determined to have peace. They gave up Finland, the Baltic States, Poland, White Russia (Belarus), Ukraine, and Bessarabia. When the Germans capitulated to the Western allies in November, however, Russia repudiated the treaty.

Civil War, 1918–20

The Bolshevik seizure of power in late 1917 did not give them control of the entire Russian Empire. They had begun as a small faction in Russian politics, and they won control in Petrograd because they were well organized, had the will to act (and to act ruthlessly), and understood that land and peace were more popular than parliamentary democracy. "No amount of political freedom," Lenin noted, "will satisfy the hungry." The Bolshevik government, however, faced opposition in many regions of the empire, often from larger and more popular forces. The result was a Russian civil war that continued long after the end of the world war.

When the civil war began, the Bolsheviks (renamed the Communist Party in 1918) had sufficient forces for a coup d'état but not for a war. However, they faced civil war on several fronts. They shifted the capital from Petrograd to Moscow, a city less vulnerable to foreign-supported armies, as they faced early defeats. White (anti-Bolshevik) forces soon controlled Siberia (where they installed Admiral Alexander Kolchak as their ruler), the southern regions around Kazan, and Ukraine, where the Cossacks joined the anti-Bolshevik coalition. Trotsky, named commisar for war, organized a volunteer (later conscript) army known as the Red Army to fight the counterrevolutionary Whites, and brutal civil war soon stretched across the Russian Empire. It included a war with the Cossacks in southern Russia, wars of independence in Ukraine and the Baltic states, intervention by several of the western Allies, campaigns in the Caucasus that led to the secession of south Asian provinces, and even war in the Far East, where the Japanese invaded Russia. The intervention of the western Allies scored some brief success in Ukraine, where they supported early victories by General Anton Deniken. The Americans staged a landing at Archangel, and the British and French briefly supported a puppet

government of Northern Russia at Archangel, but neither the British nor the Americans were willing to accept significant involvement in the war. For a while this produced a bizarre situation in which German anti-Bolsheviks fought together with western Allies, but western forces withdrew from Russia in September 1919.

A Communist victory in the civil war was complete in most regions by 1920. The Whites were poorly coordinated among the many fronts, badly divided in their plans for Russia, and heavily dependent upon the western world. The western Allies, however, were simply too exhausted by the years of fighting Germany to be interested in another prolonged battle. Shortly after they stopped supplying the Whites, the Red Army won the civil war. Ukraine (1919) and the Caucasian states (1920) were annexed again, although the Baltic states (Estonia, Latvia, and Lithuania) kept their independence. The most famous episode of the civil war did not occur on a battlefield: In the summer of 1918, the Communist government ordered the execution of Nicholas II and his family (who had been held prisoner at Ekaterinburg, on the Asian side of the Ural Mountains) when it appeared possible that White armies of Kolchak might liberate them.

During the civil war, Lenin began to consolidate Communist power. In 1918 a Congress of Soviets adopted a new constitution for Russia (the country did not become the Union of Soviet Socialist Republics [USSR], or Soviet Union, until 1922). The constitution attempted to create a "dictatorship of the proletariat," including one-party government and restrictions on freedoms of speech, press, and assembly. The government, now led by a five-man Politburo, demonstrated the police powers of this dictatorship after a socialist woman attempted to assassinate Lenin in 1918: Thousands of critics of the regime were killed in a policy called "the red terror," a grim introduction to the authoritarian violence that Europe would face during most of the twentieth century. The most far-reaching policy of the new Communist state had global implications. In the spring of 1919 Lenin created the Third International (the Comintern, 1919–43) to link Communist parties in all countries and to support revolutions around the world. Revolutionary situations existed in many war-weary countries, such as the Spartacist revolt in Berlin in early 1919. Béla Kun, a protegé of Lenin, established a short-lived Bolshevik government in Hungary later in 1919. These events alarmed anti-communist capitals around the world and led to a postwar "Red scare" in many countries.

CHAPTER 28

EUROPE IN AN AGE OF DICTATORSHIP, 1919–39

An old Europe lay in ruins in 1919. Five years of world war had swept away four empires: the Russian, German, Habsburg, and Ottoman. A dozen new states appeared, chiefly in central and eastern Europe, stretching from Finland in the north to Turkey in the south. The war also destroyed monarchy as the dominant form of European government, and it burdened the new democratic governments with great problems.

Chapter 28 looks at Europe in the generation after World War I. It begins with the peace settlement reached at Paris in 1919 and the problems that this peace bequeathed to the next generation. Next, it examines postwar problems (such as the reconstruction of devastated areas) and attitudes (such as conservative desires to preserve the old Europe) that derived from the war. Subsequent sections discuss the problems of postwar democracies, such as the Great Depression of the 1930s, and the controversial governments (such as the Popular Fronts in France and Spain) that tried to address them. The chapter then examines the rise of dictatorships as the typical form of European government. Separate sections focus on the forms of dictatorship in Fascist Italy, Nazi Germany, and Communist Russia.

◇

The Peace of Paris, 1919–20

The fighting in World War I ended with the Compiègne armistice of November 1918, which disarmed Germany to make further combat impossible. Similarly, the Paris Peace Conference, which assembled in January 1919, disarmed German diplomacy; a German delegation was allowed to come to Versailles but not to negotiate. (The Allies held separate conferences for each of the defeated powers at palaces around Paris; peace with Germany was planned at the royal palace in suburban Versailles.) The German republic, founded

Lost immediately after World War I

- By Russia
- By Germany
- By Bulgaria
- By Austria–Hungary

MAP 28.1

Europe in 1919

after the abdication of Kaiser Wilhelm II, could only hope that the treaty would be based on the idealistic Fourteen Points stated in early 1918, in a speech by U.S. president Woodrow Wilson (who had endorsed "peace without victory" as late as 1916). Although dozens of states sent diplomats to Paris, the basic elements of the treaties were negotiated among representatives of the "Big Four" wartime allies—chiefly by Wilson, Premier Georges Clemenceau of France, and

Prime Minister David Lloyd George of Britain, and sometimes including Premier Vittorio Orlando of Italy. This was similar to the situation at Vienna in 1815 (where France had initially been excluded from negotiations among the four victorious great powers), with an important exception: One of the great powers that had fought long for the allied cause, Russia, was an excluded pariah state in 1919, governed by Communist revolutionaries who had negotiated a separate peace.

The most important authors of the postwar world were Clemenceau and Lloyd George, neither of whom felt bound by Wilson's program. Lloyd George had run for reelection in the Khaki Election of December 1918 promising to punish German "war criminals" and saying "I'll hang the Kaiser!" Clemenceau scoffed at Wilsonian idealism with snide reminders that even God presented only ten Commandments; Europe, he added on another occasion, might consider Wilsonian moral leadership when he ended racial segregation in the United States. Unlike the situation at Vienna in 1815, the Allies were never so divided that they invited Germany to participate in negotiations. German diplomats had their first formal meeting with Allied diplomats in May 1919, when a draft treaty was presented to them; Clemenceau introduced the treaty by saying, "The time has come to settle accounts" (see illustration 28.1). The Germans, given no chance to negotiate compromises, bitterly called the treaty a *diktat* (a dictated peace) but nonetheless signed it in June 1919; the German response to the peace treaty (in contrast to the French response to the Frankfurt Treaty of 1871) became one of the most severe problems of the following generation and a major factor in the resumption of war in 1939.

The Versailles Treaty returned Alsace and Lorraine to France, awarded frontier territory to Belgium, restored to Denmark land lost in the war of 1864, and made major concessions to Poland (see map 28.1). The most controversial decision gave part of western Prussia to the reborn state of Poland (which Prussia had played a leading role in destroying in the eighteenth century); this created a Polish Corridor to the Baltic Sea, but it isolated East Prussia as an exclave surrounded by Poland and it fostered German hatred of the treaty similar to the French reaction to the loss of Alsace in 1871. Germany was also stripped of all colonies and Russian territory annexed by the Treaty of Brest-Litovsk in 1918. The Saar River basin, a coal-rich region in the Rhineland, was detached from Germany; France was given control of the Saar mines for fifteen years, after which a plebescite would determine the status of the region. The German army was limited to 100,000 men (intentionally smaller than the Polish army). Germany was denied heavy artillery, submarines, and an air force, and the entire Rhineland was demilitarized.

The most controversial section of the Versailles Treaty was Article 231, known as "the war guilt clause." This article made Germany accept responsibility for causing the war. On this basis, the German nation was to pay reparations for all civilian damage caused by the war (in contrast to the indemnity payments that France

Illustration 28.1

The Versailles Peace Treaty. The peace treaty with Germany in 1919 was severe, although no worse than the treaties imperial Germany imposed on France in 1871 or Russia in 1918. From the German point of view, shown in this contemporary cartoon, the Big Three (from the left, Wilson, Clemenceau, and Lloyd George) were executing Germany.

had been made to pay in 1815 and 1871)—a subject destined to become another of postwar Europe's greatest controversies. When critics asked Clemenceau if he thought that future historians would conclude that Germany had caused the war, he answered that they certainly would not conclude that Belgium had invaded Germany in 1914. As a concession to Wilson and to ensure the enforcement of the treaty, the Allies also created a permanent international assembly known as the League of Nations—whose founding covenant spoke of reducing armaments and ending war but established few instruments of enforcement. The Versailles Treaty was thus an awkward compromise among the victors, and it remained controversial among them (especially in Britain), so they never did a good job of enforcing it.

The secondary treaties signed at Paris registered the collapse of two great empires, recognized more than a dozen new countries, and addressed territorial problems that would remain unresolved throughout the twentieth century. The Habsburg monarchy had broken apart in mid-1918, creating separate states of Austria and Hungary. Minority populations of the empire joined Poland (Upper Silesia) and Romania (Transylvania) or the newly created states of Czechoslovakia and Yugoslavia. The Treaty of St. Germain with Austria recognized these changes as a *fait accompli* and also obliged the Austrians to cede the frontier territory of the south Tyrol and the Istrian Peninsula to Italy (as promised in the Treaty of London), although Orlando walked out of the conference to protest other "unredeemed promises" of territory, such as the town of Fiume on the Adriatic. The once mighty Habsburg Empire, which had dominated central Europe for centuries, was reduced to an Austria 12 percent of its size in 1914, left with a population of six million, and forbidden to unite with Germany. The Hungarians were made to accept the Treaty of Trianon, by which they lost 75 percent of their prewar territory. Serbia, whose Pan-Slavic nationalism had done so much to provoke the war (and had suffered so much during the war), was rewarded with the creation of Yugoslavia, which included Montenegro, part of Macedonia, Bosnia and Herzegovina, Croatia, and Slovenia.

The Treaty of Sèvres (1920), which made peace with Turkey, bequeathed the twentieth century some of its most difficult problems. Turkey received much harsher treatment than Germany had in the Versailles Treaty; the powerless sultan lost all non-Turkish portions of the former Ottoman Empire, but these territories did not become independent. Greece claimed most of European Turkey and part of the Turkish coast, Italy took Rhodes and several other Mediterranean islands, and the entire Middle East was detached from Turkey. Turkish nationalists, led by Atatürk, fought many of these losses and won a new treaty in 1923.

Economic Recovery and the Reconstruction of Europe in the 1920s

The cost of World War I cannot be measured precisely. More than eight million soldiers and seven million civilians had died in the fighting; counting war-related epidemics, roughly twenty million Europeans had perished. France and Germany lost approximately 10 percent of their labor force; Britain lost one-third of all men aged fifteen to twenty-four in the 1911 census. The casualties rate in some armies surpassed 50 percent of all personnel. The German and the Austro-Hungarian armies each reported more than five million war wounds. The French wounded included 740,000 crippled men, *mutilés de guerre,* who would be living reminders of the war for fifty years. The British

TABLE 28.1
Industrial Recovery after World War I

Output of crude steel (*in thousands of metric tons*)

Country	1913	1919	1923	1928
Belgium	2,467	334	2,297	3,905
France	4,687	1,293	5,222	9,479
Germany	17,609	8,710	6,305	14,517

Output of coal (*in thousands of metric tons*)

Country	1913	1919	1923	1928
Belgium	24,371	18,483	22,922	27,587
France	40,844	22,441	38,556	52,440
Germany	277,342	210,355	180,474	317,136

Source: B. R. Mitchell, *European Historical Statistics, 1750–1970* (London: Macmillan, 1975), pp. 362–65, 400, 430.

needed forty-eight new mental hospitals just to house the sixty-five thousand cases of acute shell shock. Little wonder that a British novelist, D. H. Lawrence, wrote, "We have all lost the war. All Europe." The living and the dead alike were a "lost generation."

Economic data show similar devastation. The economic cost of World War I still cannot be counted (veterans and widows still receive benefits), and even the direct costs, such as government spending and property destroyed, can only be estimated. Postwar calculations translate into nearly 100 trillion late twentieth-century dollars. Economic historians have shown what this meant in local cases: six percent of all Belgians lost their homes, the nation lost 75 percent of its railroad cars, and farmers lost two-thirds of all pigs in prewar totals. The devastation in France was even worse. The fighting had laid waste to more than six thousand square miles of northeastern and eastern France; nine thousand small factories and five thousand large factories were destroyed, as were fifteen hundred miles of railroad and thirty-three thousand miles of highway. Europe needed nearly a decade of peace merely to approach 1913 levels of production (see table 28.1). This slow recovery permitted the United States to achieve dominance in the global economy. While France mined 7 million tons of coal in 1924, the United States mined 485 million tons; while Germany produced 9 million tons of steel that year, the United States produced 45 million tons. By 1929 the United States accounted for 34.4 percent of global industrial production, while Britain, France,

Illustration 28.2

/// **The German Inflation of 1923.** One of the worst inflation crises in European history hit Germany in 1923. Prices skyrocketed and paper money lost its value overnight. Some businesses started the day with a schedule of how prices would rise during the day, and others charged people at the end of a service (such as a movie or a bus ride) instead of at the start because the price would be higher. This photo shows the nadir of a collapsing currency: A woman uses worthless paper money to light her stove.

and Germany combined accounted for 25.7 percent. Debt slowed the recovery. Governments had financed the war by borrowing rather than taxing. The French government, for example, had a total wartime income of $5.1 billion but spent $32.9 billion. British and German debts were even worse. Germany had contracted loans totaling 98 billion gold marks (approximately $25 billion) and that indebtedness still left a deficit of nearly $8 billion. The combined effect of such staggering debts plus the immensity of the reparations payments led many economists to conclude, as John Maynard Keynes did in *The Economic Consequences of the Peace,* that Allied economic expectations were unrealistic.

Postwar conditions worsened these problems. Fighting the war on credit had led to runaway inflation. Prices increased by 264 percent in Italy and by 302 per-

cent in Germany during the war, and the end of fighting did not stabilize them. Germany endured another 162 percent increase in prices in 1920–21, and the worst was yet to come: In 1922–23 inflation made the German mark (valued at twenty-five cents in 1913) virtually worthless (see illustration 28.2). The price of bread went from 0.63 marks per loaf in 1918 to 250 marks in January 1923, then 3,465 marks in July, 1.5 million marks in September, and 201 billion marks for a loaf in November. This inflation devastated German society almost as badly as German arms had devastated Belgium. Unemployment posed other problems. It had stood at 3 percent before the war, but the demobilization of armies left millions of veterans jobless. Unemployment hit 15 percent in 1921 and stayed above 10 percent for years. Having seen the role of disgruntled soldiers in the Bolshevik revolution, governments were eager to remedy this situation. Many nations adopted their first unemployment compensation laws because conservatives wanted to help veterans; Italy did so in 1919, and Austria and Britain followed in 1920.

The Conservative Reaction of the 1920s

One widely shared postwar mood was a desire to recover the remembered tranquillity of antediluvian Europe. In an awkward American coinage, people wanted a "return to normalcy." This led to conservative electoral victories in many countries. British voters dismissed their wartime leader, Lloyd George, and gave the Tories a huge victory in 1924. The French sent Clemenceau into retirement and elected a Chamber of Deputies so full of veterans that it was called the "horizon blue" assembly (because of their uniform color). Conservative Catholic parties won landmark victories in Belgian elections of 1919 and 1921 and in Austrian elections of 1920 and 1923.

The conservative reaction typically encompassed efforts to guard morality. This led to the prohibition of alcoholic beverages in the United States and Bolshevik Russia and to lesser restrictions on drink (commonly the perpetuation of wartime regulations) around Europe. The French continued a ban on certain alcoholic beverages, and the British strictly regulated the hours when they could be sold (ending early and interrupting sales during the day). Many countries imposed higher taxes on alcohol, on the theory that people would accept "sin taxes." And most of Europe, which had

◆ DOCUMENT 28.1 ◆

Pope Pius XI: Marriage, Birth Control, Abortion, and Divorce

Pius XI (served 1922–39) was a conservative pope. His encyclical Casti connubi (1930), from which the following excerpts are taken, gave the first comprehensive statement of the church's position of many issues concerning the family.

Domestic . . . order includes both the primacy of the husband with regard to the wife and children, the ready subjection of the wife and her willing obedience, which the Apostle commends in these words: "Let women be subject to their husbands as to the Lord, because the husband is the head of the wife, as Christ is the head of the Church." This subjection, however, does not deny or take away the liberty which fully belongs to the woman. . . .

First consideration is due to the offspring, which many have the boldness to [avoid] . . . by frustrating the marriage act. . . . But no reason, however grave, may be put forward by which anything intrinsically against nature may become conformable to nature and morally good. Since, therefore, the conjugal act is destined primarily by nature for the begetting of children, those who in exercising it deliberately frustrate its natural power and purpose sin against nature and commit a deed which is shameful and intrinsically vicious. . . .

Another very grave crime is to be noted, Venerable Brethren, which regards the taking of the life of the offspring hidden in the mother's womb. Some wish it to be allowed and left to the will of the father or the mother; others . . . ask that the public authorities provide aid for these death-dealing operations. . . . Venerable Brethren, however much we may pity the mother whose health or even life is gravely imperiled in the performance of a duty allotted to her by nature, nevertheless what could ever be a sufficient reason for excusing in any way the direct murder of the innocent?

The advocates of the neo-paganism of today . . . continue by legislation to attack the indissolubility of the marriage bond, proclaiming the lawfulness of divorce. . . . Opposed to all these reckless opinions, Venerable Brethren, stands the unalterable law of God, fully confirmed by Christ, a law that can never be deprived of its force by the decrees of men, the ideas of a people, or the will of any legislator: "What God hath joined together, let no man put asunder." . . .

Pius Xi, "Casi Connubi." In Anne Fremantle, *The Papal Encyclicals.* New York: Putnam, 1956.

---

allowed the consumption of narcotic drugs during the prewar Belle Époque, joined in an international convention against drugs in 1925.

More countries rewrote their laws on sexuality and reproduction, marriage and divorce. Pope Pius XI stated strict standards for Catholics in 1930, in the encyclical *Casti connubi* (see document 28.1). He opposed birth control, abortion, and divorce; birth control, for example, was branded "criminal abuse" and "intrinsically vicious." Many governments, motivated by population losses as much as by morality, outlawed birth control or abortion. The French banned both (and information about them) in 1920. Madeleine Pelletier, the prewar feminist who had championed women's right to have abortions, was jailed in an asylum under these laws and died there. Ireland made it a felony to sell, import, or advertise any birth control device. Mussolini criminalized abortion in 1930, although Italian women still obtained 500,000 illegal abortions annually. Britain was an unusual exception where an abortion law of 1929 al-

lowed the operation until the twenty-eighth week of pregnancy. Few European governments followed Pius's urging to outlaw divorce, which was still a relatively uncommon phenomenon. British courts, for example, granted a total of 3,747 divorces in 1920. However the details varied, the postwar mood of moral reform was larger than a Christian religious revival. At the Islamic southeastern edge of Europe, Atatürk reformed Turkish marital law and outlawed polygamy.

Casti connubi also restated traditional views of the position of women. It instructed Catholics to accept "the primacy of the husband" and "the ready subjection of the wife" who must obey him. Many governments saw an economic benefit in this. War work by millions of women had encouraged feminists to believe that women would soon win equality in jobs and wages. They did not. Fewer Frenchwomen were working in 1921 than had been in 1906, despite the loss of 1.4 million male workers in the war. In Britain, 750,000 women lost their jobs in the first year of peace; by 1923 women were a

TABLE 28.2

The Decline of Infant Mortality in Europe, 1900–40

Deaths of infants under one year of age, as a percentage of live births

Year	Britain	France	Germany	Russia
1900	15.4	16.0	22.9	25.2
1910	10.5	11.1	16.2	27.1
1920	8.0	12.3	13.1	n.a.
1930	6.0	8.4	8.5	n.a.
1940	5.7	9.1	6.4	n.a.

n.a. = not available.

Source: B. R. Mitchell, *European Historical Statistics, 1750–1970* (London: Macmillan, 1975), pp. 130–31.

smaller portion of labor unions than they had been in 1913, though nearly one million British workers had been lost. This pattern was repeated across the continent. Although most of the major powers granted women's suffrage during or after the war, old attitudes about women remained strong.

The Changing Conditions of Life in Europe

Although Europe endured tragic difficulties following World War I, seeing the era solely in terms of its problems would be misleading. Historians must keep many perspectives on the past. Cultural historians, for example, explore the mixture of vitality and decadence known in America as "the roaring twenties." The Weimar Republic is a tragic failure in the history of democracy, but its vigorous cultural history fascinates historians who look at expressionist painting, Bauhaus architecture, or the novels of Thomas Mann instead of dictatorship and depression. Historians of popular culture find an exciting interwar world by considering the impact of the automobile (private autos in use in Britain rose from 79,000 in 1919 to 2,034,000 in 1939), aircraft (British Imperial Airways began overseas passenger service in 1924 and the German Lufthansa airline started service in 1926), or the telephone (introduced in London in 1879 and still limited to an elite of 10,000 homes in Britain on the eve of the war, the two millionth phone was installed in Buckingham Palace in 1931). Historians of science treat epochal developments in physics, where scientists such as Albert Ein-

stein, Max Planck, Enrico Fermi, and Ernest Rutherford transformed understanding of the physical world; the atom, long considered the indivisible basis of all matter, was first split in 1932.

Among the many differences from the past that are examined by social historians of the early twentieth century, the most notable may be the dramatic decline in infant mortality rates (see table 28.2). Under the biological old regime, between 20 percent and 30 percent of all babies never reached their first birthday. By 1940 most of Europe had a rate below 10 percent as a result of the accelerated conquest of epidemic diseases. The death rate from diphtheria for British children fell by 49 percent, measles by 76 percent, and scarlet fever by 83 percent. Hundreds of thousands of Europeans who would have died of contagious diseases in the nineteenth century now reached adulthood. In 1921, two French scientists developed a vaccine against tuberculosis, the greatest scourge of Belle Époque Europe. The most remarkable life-saving discoveries of the interwar era—the antibiotic treatment of wounds and diseases—did not have a great impact until the generation of World War II. Two of the twentieth century's most important Nobel Prizes in Medicine were awarded to men whose work contributed greatly to the conquest of disease: Scottish bacteriologist Alexander Fleming in 1945 and German chemist Gerhard Domagk in 1939. (The Nazi government made Domagk decline the prize, however.) Domagk's work led to the development of sulfa drugs, a treatment nontoxic to humans yet powerful in combating infectious diseases. Fleming discovered penicillin in 1928, though its development was left to others (Ernst Chain and Sir Howard Florey shared the 1945 Nobel Prize) and the drug was not synthesized until the war. Such "miracle drugs" were first used experimentally in 1932; penicillin saved thousands of soldiers in World War II and became widely available after the war.

European Culture after the Deluge

The Great War caused deep cultural despair in Europe. It spawned pessimism in some people, cynical frivolity in others; bitterness in many, spiritual barrenness in most. In the imagery of the Irish poet William Butler Yeats:

> Things fall apart; the centre cannot hold;
> Mere anarchy is loosed upon the world.
> The blood-dimmed tide is loosed, and everywhere
> The ceremony of innocence is drowned;
> The best lack all conviction, while the worst
> Are full of passionate intensity.

This postwar mood produced the absurdities of dadaism and surrealism, the alienated literature of modernism, and ubiquitous antiwar sentiments. Dada was the response of iconoclastic intellectuals—an intentionally meaningless art, an anarchistic "anti-art." According to the Dadaist Manifesto of the Roumanian poet Tristan Tzara, European culture should abandon everything from logic to good manners and teach spontaneous living. The more sophisticated doctrine of surrealism also purged reason from art, replacing it with images from the subconscious, as painters such as Rene Magritte and Marcel Duchamp demonstrated.

The masterpieces of literary modernism showed similar responses to the war. The poetry of T. S. Eliot, such as *The Wasteland* (1922), stated a disillusioned lament for European civilization and asked "what branches grow out of this stony rubbish?" Another of the great works of modernism, James Joyce's *Ulysses* (1922), broke down the logical structure of the novel and fashioned a story about the commonplace events of a single day, verbalized in an inventive but sometimes incoherent form called stream of consciousness. *Ulysses* focused on the postwar mood of Leopold Bloom who, like Europe, had become bitter and dispirited.

The creative artist who best typified the postwar despair of European culture was Franz Kafka, an Austrian-Czech writer so powerful that his name became an adjective. The kafkaesque world is incomprehensible yet menacing; complex, bizarre, absurd, and ominous. Kafka wrote of people so alienated that one of them awakens to find himself transformed into a large insect; of people held in a prison where preposterous commands are tattooed onto their bodies; of a person brought to a bizarre trial in which the charges are never specified; of someone hired for a frustrating job that seems to have neither instructions nor anyone to explain it.

One of the central themes of this postwar mood was anger at war and the society that produced it or profited from it. Erich Maria Remarque, a German writer who later joined a flood of intellectual emigres to America, penned one of the most famous antiwar novels ever written, *All Quiet on the Western Front* (1929), describing the experiences of a group of schoolboys in the dehumanizing life of the trenches. Jaroslav Hasek's *Good Soldier Schweik* (1923) made fun of armies and officers (Hasek used some of his own commanders' names) by showing how easily everyone is fooled by a soldier acting stupid. Wilfred Owen's posthumously published poetry (he was killed in France one week before the armistice) described the suffering of the common soldier and burned with loathing for the war. Vera Brittain, a British volunteer nurse during the war, used her experiences to write of pacifism with such conviction that she became an officer of the Women's International League of Peace and Freedom. George Grosz, a German graphic artist embittered by the war, used savage caricature to attack the government, the military, and the classes that prospered while others suffered.

Ironically, the most important development in European culture in the early twentieth century was not linked to World War I and the postwar despair. A cultural revolution had begun in the early years of the century, and it triumphed dramatically in the 1920s and 1930s. The new technologies of radio and motion pictures led to the democratization of culture, the creation of mass culture. Two French chemists, Louis and Auguste Lumière, presented the first public showing of a motion picture in 1895, a one-minute film of workers leaving their factory. The first narrative film, the American-made *The Great Train Robbery*, appeared in 1903, and the silent film industry was born in the following decade. The commercial exploitation of the Lumière brothers' "cinematograph" was achieved by Charles Pathé, the first movie mogul, who made Paris the world center of the motion picture industry in the years before 1914. Although the center of the industry had shifted to Hollywood by the 1920s, booming film industries developed in interwar Europe. The British, French, and German industries each were producing more than one hundred feature films per year by the early 1930s.

An Italian inventor, Guglielmo Marconi, launched the world into the age of broadcasting in 1895, shortly before the Lumières showed the first film. Marconi's "wireless telegraphy" did not develop as rapidly as the cinema did, but individual radio transmissions in Europe and America began in the decade before the war. The first broadcast of a program of music occurred at Graz (Austria) in 1908, and the world's first station broadcasting regularly scheduled radio programs began its transmissions in Pittsburgh in 1920. That same year, the British government created a broadcasting monopoly, the BBC (British Broadcasting Company, later Corporation), and it produced the first European daily programming in 1922. Radio, like the movies, became widespread in interwar Europe. By 1930–31 radio reached most households in western and central Europe; there was a radio set for every 12 people in Britain, one per 15 in Germany.

European Democracy after World War I

Most of Europe lived under parliamentary democracy in 1920 but under authoritarianism in 1939. The era began with popularly elected parliaments in the new states of eastern Europe, from the Finnish and Estonian assemblies of 1919 to the Turkish republic of 1922 and the Greek republic of 1924.

The enthusiasm for democracy included an expansion of its definition. Between 1915 and 1922, eighteen European countries gave women the right to vote in national elections. The trend began in Scandinavia, where Norway had led the way before the war. Denmark enfranchised women in 1915, with Finland (1917) and Sweden (1918) following. The idea then took root in the new regimes of Eastern Europe and in the Austrian and German republics. Ironically, women's suffrage found less acceptance in western Europe. Britain only allowed women to vote at the age of thirty until an equal franchise law was passed in 1928 (see illustration 28.3). In France, a conservative Senate blocked women's suffrage in 1922 and prevented women from voting until 1944. Belgium, Italy, Portugal, and Switzerland (the last state in Europe to accept women's suffrage) also rejected enfranchisement. A second expansion of democracy was proportional voting to give representation to minorities. Under traditional procedures, a group receiving 10 percent of the vote seldom won an election; advocates of proportional representation said that group deserved 10 percent of the seats in a legislature. Belgium had employed pro-

Illustration 28.3

Women's Suffrage. Women won the right to vote in many European states during or immediately after the world war—including the Soviet Union (1917), Britain (1918), and Germany (1918), but not France or Italy. Here British women protest that they did not receive the right to vote until age thirty.

portional representation since 1899, and varieties of that system were adopted in France, Germany, and Italy at the end of the war.

Despite such trends, democracy did not flourish during the interwar years. By 1939 more than a dozen parliamentary democracies had been replaced by dictatorships. The newly independent states were especially vulnerable. General Jozef Pilsudski used the Polish army to hold dictatorial power for nearly fifteen years after his coup d'état of 1926. Monarchies abolished political freedoms in Yugoslavia and Albania. In Hungary, Admiral Miklos Horthy governed (from 1920 to 1944) as the regent for a vacant monarchy; he retained a Parliament, but curtailed the electoral process, held a veto over legislation, and created an anachronistic upper house of Parliament controlled by nobles.

As the failed democracies of eastern Europe suggest, the era between 1919 and 1945 became an age of dictatorship. The Communist dictatorship of Joseph Stalin in the Soviet Union (ruled 1924–53); the Nazi dictatorship of Adolf Hitler in Germany (ruled 1933–45); the Fascist dictatorship of Benito Mussolini in Italy (ruled 1922–45); the military dictatorships of General Primo de Rivera (ruled 1922–30); General Francisco Franco in Spain (ruled 1936–75);

and Antonio Salazar in Portugal (ruled 1926–68); and the wartime dictatorship of Marshal Henri Pétain in France (ruled 1940–45) are the characteristic regimes of the era. World War II accelerated this trend, and by 1941 only five parliamentary democracies survived in Europe: Britain, Ireland, Iceland, Sweden, and Switzerland.

German Democracy in the 1920s: The Weimar Republic

After the abdication of Kaiser Wilhelm II in 1918, a provisional government held elections for a constituent assembly to meet in the Saxon city of Weimar and create a German republic. This provisional government put down the Sparticist revolt of German Communists at Berlin in January 1919 and accepted the responsibility for signing the Versailles Treaty in June 1919. Consequently, the Weimar Republic began life in the summer of 1919 detested by both the communist left and the nationalist right. The Weimar constitution contained universal suffrage, proportional representation, popular referenda, the abolition of aristocratic privilege, and basic individual freedoms. It entrusted the government to a chancellor, who needed the support of a majority in the Reichstag, but it also created a seven-year presidency with special powers to suspend the constitution during emergencies.

Right-wing opposition to the Weimar Republic flourished immediately and dominated the early 1920s. Paramilitary leagues of war veterans, known as the *Freikorps* (Free Corps), remained a violent factor in German politics. Extremists assassinated the socialist premier of Bavaria in 1919, then Matthias Erzberger (who had bravely accepted the job of signing the Versailles Treaty) in 1921, and Walter Rathenau (the foreign minister) in 1922. *Freikorps* troops supported monarchists in seizing control of Berlin in the Kapp *Putsch* (coup) of 1920, and the German army refused to fire on them; the *Putsch* was only blocked by a general strike of Berlin workers. Nationalists blamed republicans for a supposed civilian betrayal of the German army in 1918—the "stab-in-the-back" (or *Dolchstoss*) myth of the German defeat—even though their military hero, General Ludendorff, had been the person who admitted that military victory was impossible and called for peace. Ludendorff participated in what became the most famous right-wing conspiracy of the 1920s, the Munich Beer Hall *Putsch* of November 1923. This attempted coup introduced the world to Adolf Hitler and his small National Socialist German Workers' Party

---

◆ DOCUMENT 28.2 ◆

Hitler: Anti-Semitism in *Mein Kampf* (1925)

The first part of Mein Kampf *from which the following excerpt is taken, was written during Hitler's imprisonment and published in 1925. It provided unmistakable indications of his racist thoughts and intentions. Hitler asserted that the Jews were lowest of all the races, who destroyed the civilization of other races; they were responsible for World War I and for the Bolshevik revolution.*

There were few Jews in Linz. In the course of the centuries their outward appearance had become Europeanized and had taken on a human look; in fact, I even took them for Germans. . . .

Then I came to Vienna. . . . Once, as I was strolling through the Inner City, I suddenly encountered an apparition in a black caftan and black hair locks. Is this a Jew? was my first thought. . . . The longer I stared . . . the more my question assumed a new form: Is this a German?

The cleanliness of this people, moral and otherwise, I must say, is a point in itself. By their very exterior you could tell that these were no lovers of water, and, to your distress, you often knew it with your eyes closed. . . .

I became acquainted with their activity in the press, art, literature, and the theater. . . . Nine-tenths of all literary filth, artistic trash, and theatrical idiocy can be set to their account. . . .

Then a flame flared up within me. . . . Hence, today I believe that I am acting with the will of the Almighty Creator: by defending myself against the Jew, I am fighting for the work of the Lord.

Hitler, Adolph. *Mein Kampf*. Boston: Houghton Mifflin, 1943.

("Nazi" as a contraction). The Beer Hall *Putsch* was easily stopped and Hitler was convicted of high treason and sentenced to prison for five years, where he dictated *Mein Kampf* (My Struggle) before his early release (see document 28.2). Hitler's book was a muddle of hatreds (of Communism, Jews, the Versailles Treaty, democracy, and the Weimar Republic), stating the right-wing agenda; initially it found few readers.

The success of parliamentary democracy in Germany depended upon winning the support of the middle classes and the peasantry away from the alternatives proposed by nationalists or communists. Many Germans were alienated, however, by the economic catastrophes of the early 1920s. The imperial government had destroyed the value of the mark by its vast borrowing and the reckless printing of money. Territorial losses and reparations payments compounded the problem. The inflation of 1922–23 destroyed the savings, pensions, and income of millions of Germans. Consequently, the German middle class, especially the lower middle class, never developed fond ties to the Weimar government.

The German republic did recover and prosper after 1924. A coalition of moderate socialists, democrats, and the Catholic Party (the *Zentrum*) brought stability to the government. An international agreement, the Dawes Plan (1924), readjusted reparations and created a stable currency. Industrial production rose. A strong and capable foreign minister, Gustav Stresemann, risked the ire of nationalists by pursuing conciliatory policies. Stresemann, the brilliant son of an innkeeper, had risen in politics as Ludendorff's protégé and had been an ardent nationalist and imperialist, but he reconsidered his beliefs during the right-wing violence of the early 1920s, especially after the murders of Erzberger and Rathenau. His cooperation with the French foreign minister Aristide Briand restored normal peacetime conditions. Briand had risen in French politics as a socialist ally of Jean Jaurès, but socialists expelled him from the party for accepting a cabinet post in a bourgeois government, and he began a long career as a centrist. Between 1906 and 1932 he held twenty-six cabinet appointments. As the leading voice of postwar French foreign policy, Briand twice (1924 and 1929) agreed to ease reparations payments. Briand and Stresemann negotiated the Locarno Treaty (1925), reaffirming the Franco-German frontier drawn in the Versailles Treaty. Stresemann led Germany into the League of Nations (1926) as the equal of Britain and France. In short, peace and prosperity seemed possible when Stresemann and Briand shared the 1926 Nobel Peace Prize for creating the "spirit of Locarno."

Postwar Recovery in Britain and France

The older democracies also experienced difficult times in recovering stability. Britain and France struggled with economic problems, faced social unrest, and turned to conservative governments for most of the 1920s.

At the end of the war, the British government had addressed two of its greatest prewar problems: women's rights and the government of Ireland. Lloyd George's Representation of the People Act (1918) gave women the vote at age thirty, and the Equal Franchise Act (1928) finally granted women suffrage on the same basis as men. In 1919 the American-born Lady Nancy Astor became the first woman to sit in the House of Commons; by 1929 there were 69 women candidates and 14 women M.P.s (of 615 seats). British women won other important rights in the Sex Disqualification Act of 1919 (which abolished gender barriers to universities, the professions, and public positions) and the Law of Property of 1926 (which gave all women the right to hold and dispose of property on the same terms as men). Important as this legislation was, it fell short of full equality for women, as dismissed war workers learned. Even those women who kept their jobs in the 1920s and 1930s still worked for less than half of a man's wages, and that situation was not improving. Working women's percentage of men's earnings was 48.2 percent in 1924 and 48.1 percent in 1935.

The British addressed the Irish question with mixed success. Three years after the Easter Rebellion of 1916, Irish nationalists again rebelled against British rule. In a treaty of 1921, twenty-six (largely Catholic) counties of Ireland gained independence as the Irish Free State, although six other counties (with a large Protestant population) in the northern region of Ulster remained a part of the United Kingdom. This agreement precipitated an Irish civil war between protreaty and antitreaty forces; protreaty forces that accepted the border dividing Ireland won. (The continuing acceptance of this treaty and this border led to the reopening of the Irish question in 1969 when a militant minority of the Irish Republican Army (IRA), known as the Provos, began a terrorist campaign intended to end the union of Britain and Northern Ireland and to reunite the north with the south.)

The most severe problem that interwar Britain faced was neither the woman question nor the Irish question. It was economics. Prewar unemployment had been 3.3 percent, and it remained low until soldiers and women workers were demobilized. Unemployment hit 14.8 percent in 1921 and stayed above 10 percent for the remainder of the decade. Productivity stood at a fraction of prewar levels, many of which (such as coal production) were never reached again. The cost of living in 1921 had risen to four times the level of 1914. By 1922 marches of the unemployed and hungry had become a common feature of British daily life. And the home of capitalist free trade orthodoxy watched as its imports doubled its exports.

Britain was one of the most heavily unionized states in the world, with 30 percent of workers belonging to trade unions in 1921. The miners' unions were especially militant, and they led major strikes in 1919 and 1921. Though elections in early 1924 created a short-lived Labour Party government in which Ramsay MacDonald became Britain's first socialist prime minister, angry workers obtained little welfare legislation except the Pension Act of 1925. MacDonald, the illegitimate son of a farm laborer and a servant, had risen through self-education to become the leading theorist of British socialism. He rejected Marxist doctrines of class warfare and violent revolution and believed in an evolutionary, democratic socialism as "the hereditary heir of liberalism." After MacDonald granted diplomatic recognition to the USSR, however, the evolutionary process restored conservatives to power, and Stanley Baldwin (the son of a rich industrialist) formed his second government. Social unrest worsened under both governments. Mine owners lowered wages and lengthened the working day, leading to another wave of strikes, which culminated in the general strike (when all workers were expected to leave their jobs) of 1926. More than 2.5 million workers in a labor force of 6 million walked out. The Baldwin government, fearful of the revolutionary potential of the general strike, made enough concessions to bring back moderate workers. With the general strike beaten, conservatives quickly passed the Trade Disputes Act of 1927 limiting the right to strike. General strikes, sympathy strikes, and strikes in many occupations (such as the police) became illegal.

The postwar government in France was a similar conservative coalition, led by Raymond Poincaré. Poincaré, educated as both an engineer and a lawyer, had held elective office since the 1880s, culminating in the wartime presidency. As premier in the early 1920s, Poincaré concentrated upon the rebuilding of France and a nationalist agenda. He expected the strict enforcement of the Versailles Treaty and ordered a military occupation of the Ruhr (permitted by the reparations agreement) when Germany defaulted on payments in 1923. French conservatives supported Poincaré in treason trials of wartime pacifists, the dissolution of the militant confederation of trade unions (the CGT), aid to big business and the peasantry, and concessions to the Catholic Church. During the mid- and late 1920s, Briand persuaded the conservative coalition to relax its anti-German nationalism, and Poincaré acquiesced in this policy to concentrate upon economic recovery. French problems were so bad that Poincaré

asked and received the right to solve them by decrees without a vote of the Chamber of Deputies. He stabilized the French franc in 1926–28 by devaluing it to 20 percent of its prewar value. This meant that the government repudiated 80 percent of its foreign debt written in francs, chiefly war bonds. When Poincaré retired in 1929, his accomplishments included a stable currency, a growing economy, record industrial production, and the reconstruction of most war-damaged regions. Briand had simultaneously won guarantees of peace. Many resentments simmered below the surface, but France appeared to have made a strong recovery.

The Great Depression of the 1930s

By 1928 Europe had largely recovered from the ravages of World War I. Total productivity stood 13 percent above the 1913 level, slightly stronger in western Europe (16 percent). The year 1929, however, marked the beginning of the worst economic depression of the twentieth century. This crisis began in the United States with the collapse of stock market values known as the Wall Street Crash, and it spread into a global collapse in 1929–32. Most of Europe felt the depression begin in 1930, and it soon became the deepest of the industrial age, comparable only to the depression of the 1840s, which contributed to the outbreak of the revolutions of 1848. The collapse of the American stock values, the loss of American credit, the recall of American loans, the rise of American tariffs, and the withering of exports to America caused deep declines in European production and frightening levels of unemployment. As unemployment rose, small shops went bankrupt; as world trade collapsed, big industries such as shipbuilding closed down. In 1931, when banks could not obtain repayment of outstanding loans, a wave of bank failures swept Europe. After a great Austrian bank, the Kredit-Anstalt, failed, much of the banking system of eastern and central Europe collapsed, and the wave of bank closings reached back to the United States. Most of Europe was still struggling to recover from this cycle when World War II began in 1939.

The most dramatic measure of the crisis of the 1930s is in unemployment data (see table 28.3). Despite the recovery of the late 1920s, Europe had not returned to the low levels of joblessness seen in 1913–14 (3–4 percent), but no one was prepared for the catastrophic unemployment of the 1930s. Most of Europe had double-digit unemployment in 1930, then rates above 20 percent in 1931–32. Many countries, how-

✠ TABLE 28.3 ✠
Unemployment During the Great Depression, 1930–39

	Percentage of labor force unemployed			
Year	United States	Britain	Germany	Netherlands
1930	7.8	14.6	15.3	9.7
1931	16.3	21.5	23.3	18.1
1932	24.9	22.5	30.1	29.5
1933	25.1	21.3	26.3	31.0
1934	20.2	17.7	14.9	32.1
1935	18.4	16.4	11.6	36.3
1936	14.5	14.3	8.3	36.3
1937	12.0	11.3	4.6	29.2
1938	18.8	13.3	2.1	27.2
1939	16.7	11.7	n.a.	21.8

Source: *Annuaire statistique de la Société des Nations, 1939–1940* (Geneva: League of Nations, 1940), pp. 70–71.

n.a. = not available

ever, experienced 30 percent jobless rates; the Dutch lived with unemployment averaging 31.7 percent for seven years (1932–38).

The Great Depression tested the Western world's belief in liberal-democratic government and capitalist economics. Many countries abandoned democracy in favor of authoritarian leadership; many surviving democracies (such as France and the United States) found that they must provide their citizens with significantly higher levels of welfare benefits. All countries (including Britain, France, and the United States) abandoned some classic precepts of market capitalism, such as free trade; many adopted the eighteenth-century economics of autarchy (self-sufficiency).

Britain illustrates the severity of the crisis. The National Insurance Act of 1911 gave Britain the largest unemployment insurance program in Europe, but it covered fewer than two-thirds of British workers and provided only fifteen weeks of benefits. (German unemployment legislation, by comparison, covered less than half of the labor force.) When unemployment in old industrial centers reached horrendous proportions, as it did in the Welsh coal-mining town of Merthyr Tydfil (62 percent in 1934) and the English shipbuilding town of Jarrow (68 percent in 1934), such insurance was insufficient. A National Coalition government of all major parties (1931–35) adopted drastic measures. They abandoned the gold standard, devalued the pound by nearly 30 percent, adopted protective tariffs (including a new

Corn Law in 1932), cut the wages of government employees (such as teachers and soldiers), and reduced unemployment benefits.

This produced a volatile situation in Britain. Riots in London, Liverpool, and Glasgow greeted the announced economies in 1931. Part of the royal navy mutinied. The crime rate soared. (The burglary rate for stores and shops in 1938 was 556 percent of the rate in 1900.) The unemployed marched on Parliament—one protest was known as the Jarrow Marches because much of that town marched to London in 1936 when unemployment there hit 96 percent, closing virtually every store in the town. British democracy survived, but not without enduring the birth of fascist and racist movements such as Sir Oswald Mosley's British Union of Fascists.

The French Third Republic came even closer to collapsing. French unemployment quintupled in 1932 and passed 1.3 million in early 1933. The government, long considered unstable, became a series of short-lived cabinets: four different cabinets in 1930, three in 1931, five in 1932, four in 1933, and four in 1934. As one wit observed, tourists went to London to see the changing of the guard and to Paris to see the changing of the government. The Stavisky affair of 1933–34 showed that the French government was as corrupt as it was ineffectual. This scandal began when Alexandre Stavisky, a Ukrainian-born swindler, confessed to selling fraudulent bonds with the assistance of prominent politicians.

Stavisky's death in a reported suicide and the dubious nature of investigations created a volatile antiparliamentary mood in France. Several far right-wing leagues—such as Colonel de la Rocque's *Croix de feu* (The Fiery Cross) and Pierre Taittinger's *Jeunesses Patriotes* (Young Patriots)—had flourished during the depression, and their members seized upon the Stavisky scandal as the excuse for anti-parliamentary riots in the central Paris in February 1934. Thousands of right-wing demonstrators battled with police in an attempt to attack the Chamber of Deputies. The republic survived the Stavisky riots, but fifteen people were killed and more than one thousand injured.

Léon Blum and the Popular Front in France

The depression, the Stavisky affair, and the February 1934 riots led, paradoxically, to a strengthening of the Third Republic, because they frightened political leaders into creating a powerful coalition called the Popular Front (1936–38). The parties of the French left had long fought each other, but fears of a fascist *Putsch* united them. Moderate democrats (called the Radical Party) led by Edouard Daladier, democratic socialists, trade unionists, and even Communists (frightened by the spread of fascism, which was strongly anti-Communist) supported the Popular Front under the leadership of Léon Blum, the head of the Socialist Party. Blum, a Jewish intellectual and a distinguished jurist, had entered politics at the time of the Dreyfus affair. He fought against both Poincaré's conservatism and French Communism while rebuilding the democratic socialist (SFIO) party during the 1920s. When the 1934 riots alarmed France about the strength of fascism there, Blum took the lead in creating the Popular Front and brought it to victory in the 1936 parliamentary elections, becoming the first Jewish prime minister in French history.

Léon Blum held office for only one year before the Popular Front began to crumble, but he achieved Europe's most profound response to the depression: a workweek of forty hours, paid annual vacations of four weeks, a 12 percent raise for workers and civil servants, and acceptance of collective bargaining. Under Blum's direction, France also abandoned some aspects of capitalist economics: he nationalized the Bank of France and parts of the armaments industry, and undertook government regulation of basic food prices. The Blum government also restored a degree of order in France and calmed the worst fears of industrialists by ending the wave of sit-down strikes and factory occupations that had swept the country and by agreeing not to nationalize most industries. When Blum proposed further financial reforms in 1937, however, the Radical Party deserted the Popular Front, and Blum was obliged to resign, to the cheers of many conservatives who felt "Better Hitler than Blum."

The Spanish Second Republic and the Spanish Civil War

Spain entered the twentieth century in an age of governmental instability under a constitutional monarchy (1874–1923) that lasted until General Primo de Rivera created a military dictatorship (1923–30). The Spanish Second Republic was created in 1931 after Primo de Rivera allowed local elections, which produced an outpouring of support for a republic.

The Spanish republic of 1931 was among the frailest of Europe's parliamentary democracies, and it faced many threats. A regional revolt broke out in 1934 when Catalonia proclaimed itself independent. The republic was also internally divided between groups of moderate, Catholic republicans led by Prime Minister Alcalá Zamora and groups of more radical, anticlerical republicans led by Manuel Azaña. Its radical constitution alarmed landowners, who feared nationalization of property; the leaders of the church, who resisted its program of secularization; and the army, whose officer corps was greatly reduced by forced retirements at half-pensions. These groups formed the nucleus of a resurgent right-wing in Spanish politics. Primo de Rivera's son launched a Spanish fascist movement known as the Falange in 1933; it later stopped using the word *fascist*, but it remained emphatically antidemocratic. The program of the Falange was clear: "Our State will be a totalitarian instrument. . . . We shall immediately abolish the system of political parties."

The crisis of Spanish democracy culminated in the Spanish Civil War of 1936–39. War began with the revolt of army units stationed in Spanish Morocco and spread to garrison towns in Spain. The Falange joined General Francisco Franco in forming a coalition of Nationalists seeking to abolish the Second Republic and restore traditional order to Spain. A similar coalition of Loyalists, including Catalan rebels, defended the republic. The Loyalists held most of the great cities of Spain, such as Madrid and Barcelona, but the Nationalists held most of the military strength. Franco was the son of a naval paymaster, educated in a military academy, and made his reputation in colonial wars in the 1920s; his reckless bravery in combat (perhaps a compensation for his insecurity at standing only 5'3") made him the youngest general in Europe (at thirty-three) in 1926. His mixture of nationalism, military dictatorship, Falangist fascism, monarchism, and clericalism did not precisely fit the mold of fascist movements elsewhere, but it won the military support of both Mussolini, who sent Franco seventy-five thousand soldiers, and Hitler during the civil war. The Soviet Union similarly aided the republic. General Franco, proclaimed chief of the Spanish state by the insurgents in late 1936, led the Nationalist armies in the steady destruction of the republic and Basque and Catalan separatist regimes. The civil war ended in 1939 after Barcelona fell to an assault by allied Nationalist and Italian troops and Madrid surrendered. Three years of fighting had killed more than 700,000 people in combat and at least 100,000 civilians. General Franco replaced the republic with a dictatorship that lasted until his death in 1975.

The Global Struggle for Freedom from Europe

The most ironic problem confronting the European democracies was that they opposed self-government outside of Europe. Native leaders, nationalist organizations, and armed uprisings already characterized the global resistance to imperialism before 1914. The success of Japanese arms in 1905 and Chinese revolutions in 1900 and 1911 inspired Asian nationalists, just as the Young Turk Revolution of 1908 and the Arab Revolt of 1916 stirred the Islamic world. By 1919 most regions of the world heard voices such as that of the Bengali poet Rabindranath Tagore, who won the Nobel Prize in Literature for the simple force of lines such as his prayer, "My father, let my country awake."

World War I exposed the vulnerability of European armies and eroded the moral position of Western propaganda. The Allies had proclaimed that they were fighting to make the world "safe for democracy." They had promised peace based upon principles such as "national self-determination" (in the words of Wilson's Fourteen Points), and they recruited millions of Africans and Asians to serve Europe under these banners. India alone sent 1.3 million soldiers and replacement laborers to aid Britain; Algeria, Indochina, and West Africa sent 650,000 to France. A few colonial voices had questioned the war, as John Chilembwe did in East Africa. He simply asked why Africans were "invited to shed our innocent blood in this world's war." (Chilembwe wound up being shot by the police.) Most

nationalists, including Ghandi, stood by their wartime governments until 1918, hoping that their loyalty would be rewarded. But World War I did not bring democracy or national self-determination to Africa and Asia. Instead, it created new colonies (especially in the Middle East) through the League of Nations mandate system. Before the ink had dried on the peace settlements, nationalists again challenged European imperialism. An Egyptian nationalist party, the *Wafd*, led an insurrection in 1919 and thereafter combined passive resistance and terrorism until the British granted them independence in 1922. A Syrian national congress proclaimed independence from France in 1920, and a similar congress at Nablus in 1922 called for the independence of Transjordan and Palestine from Britain. The French rejected Syrian independence and took Damascus by force; they then faced a decade of Druse rebellion and an all-out war in 1925–27. The British granted Transjordan autonomy in 1923 and independence in 1928, but they kept control of Palestine, where the question of a Jewish state was already an explosive issue. The British had promised "a national home for the Jewish people" in the Balfour Declaration of 1917, but immigration led to anti-Jewish riots in 1921 and 1929. The British backed down and curbed immigration in 1930. A Pan-Arab Congress of 1937 called for Palestinian independence and condemned the projected Jewish state, but neither Palestinians nor Zionists would accept British compromises.

Anti-imperialism took a different form in India. Ghandi began his civil disobedience movement in April 1919 and the noncooperation movement in 1920. He was jailed in 1922 but still insisted upon nonviolence: "I discovered in the earliest stages that pursuit of the truth did not admit of violence being inflicted upon one's opponent, but that he must be weaned from error by sympathy and patience." The Indian nationalist movement, known as the Congress, grew increasingly radical yet accepted Ghandi's doctrines. By the 1930s Ghandi had become such a revered leader that when he announced a "fast unto death" the British capitulated to his demands in six days.

Other patterns of anti-imperialism flourished in the Far East. A scholarly Buddhist monk, U Ottama, led Burmese resistance to Britain by blending religious revival and nationalism. Islam similarly strengthened nationalism in the East Indies; on the island of Java (today, Indonesia), the Sarekat Islam had 2.5 million members opposing the Dutch in 1919. When Asian nationalist movements did not ally with such religious revivals, they often found secular support in newly formed Communist parties. The Indonesian Communist Party, organized in 1920, was typical; it drew more members by linking poverty with opposition to the Dutch than by linking poverty to Marxist-Leninist analysis. In French Indochina, Ho Chi Minh (a pseudonym meaning "He Who Enlightens") likewise found supporters for his Vietnamese Young League of Revolutionaries by uniting nationalism and communism.

Mussolini and Fascist Italy, 1919–39

The Italian constitutional monarchy survived World War I, although the king held little power. Victor Emmanuel III (reigned 1900–47), the grandson of the monarch of the *Risorgimento*, remained a figurehead monarch throughout the Fascist era. Italians had been slowly creating a parliamentary democracy, although they were accustomed to fewer civil liberties than existed in Britain or France. An electoral law of 1912 introduced universal manhood suffrage and another gave proportional representation (but not yet women's suffrage) in 1919.

Italy had candidly fought World War I for territorial compensation. It had quit the Triple Alliance and joined the Allies for the deal they offered in the Treaty of London: Italy would annex the frontier province of the Tyrol, the Istrian Peninsula at the head of the Adriatic Sea, the Dalmatian coast opposite Italy, and an African colony. When Premier Vittorio Orlando asked for this territory at the peace conference, however, President Wilson, who had not participated in the London Treaty, insisted that those regions be distributed on the basis of nationality. Consequently, Italy received only the southern Tyrol and Istria; the town of Fiume and the Adriatic coast became part of Yugoslavia. Angry Italian nationalists, the irredentists, continued to demand the unredeemed territories.

Italy paid heavily for its new territory. In addition to 500,000 combat deaths, 2.2 million military casualties, and the devastation of Venetia, the war brought a huge national debt, 400 percent inflation (see table 28.4), massive unemployment, and violent social unrest. The combination of embittered nationalism and economic hardship produced many authoritarian movements in Europe; in Italy, it led to the Fascist dictatorship. Benito Mussolini founded the Italian Fascist movement at Milan in 1919. Mussolini, the son of a radical blacksmith who had named him in honor of Benito Juárez (the Mexican anticlerical), had been an elementary school teacher, a trade union organizer, and a socialist journalist before the war. At the start of the

TABLE 28.4

Inflation and the Cost of Living in Italy, 1914–21

Year	Cost of living index	Annual inflation rate (in percent)
1914	100.0	——
1915	107.0	7.0
1916	133.9	25.1
1917	189.4	41.4
1918	264.1	39.4
1919	268.1	1.5
1920	352.3	31.4
1921	416.8	18.3

Source: Instituto centrale di statistica, *Sommario di statistiche storiche italiane, 1861–1955* (Rome: 1955), p. 172.

fighting, he converted to vehement nationalism; he served as a private until being wounded and discharged. At the end of the war, he organized angry unemployed veterans at Milan into the *Fascio di Combattimento* ("Combat Group"). These black-uniformed street fighters embraced his program of strict discipline and authority. They accepted an ancient Roman symbol of such authority, the *Fasces* (a bundle of rods bound around an axe), which led to their name *Fascisti*, or Fascists; they accepted funding from large landowners and industrialists to use violence to break up trade union meetings, beat up striking workers, and terrorize peasants. During the Italian "red scare" of the *biennio rosso* (1918–20), Mussolini built Fascist popularity by a mixture of extreme nationalism and violent anti-Bolshevism. Between 1919 and 1921 the Black Shirts progressed from bullies into killers. They believed, as Mussolini put it, that "a certain kind of violence is moral."

In 1921 Mussolini organized Fascism as a political party, and his doctrine (see document 28.3) provides the model for understanding the varieties of European fascism in the interwar years. The essential element of Fascism was a political program vehemently opposed to all other forms of government. It was a counterrevolutionary revolution, opposed to the revolutionary tradition of 1789 (which encouraged liberal-democratic forms of parliamentary government across Europe) and equally opposed to the new revolutionary tradition of 1917 (which stimulated socialist or communist forms of government)—yet it was not a reactionary demand to

◈ DOCUMENT 28.3 ◈

Mussolini's Explanation of Fascism (1932)

Fascism . . . was born of the need for action, and it was itself from the beginning practical rather than theoretical; it was not merely another political party but, even in the first two years, in opposition to all political parties. . . . The necessity for action did not permit research or any complete elaboration of doctrine. The battle had to be fought . . . against Liberalism, Democracy, Socialism, and the Masons. . . .

Fascism . . . believes neither in the possibility nor the utility of perpetual peace. It thus repudiates the doctrine of Pacifism. . . . War alone brings up to its highest tension all human energy and puts the stamp of nobility upon the peoples who have the courage to meet it. . . .

Fascism [is] the complete opposite of . . . so-called scientific and Marxian socialism. . . . Fascism, now and always, believes in holiness and in heroism; that is to say, in actions influenced by no economic motive, direct or indirect. . . .

. . . After Socialism, Fascism combats the whole complex system of democratic ideology, and repudiates it. . . . Fascism denies that the majority, by the simple fact that it is a majority, can direct society . . . [and] it affirms the inequality of mankind, which can never be permanently levelled. . . . Fascism denies, in democracy, the absurd conventional untruth of political equality. . . . Fascism has taken up an attitude of complete opposition to the doctrines of Liberalism, both in the political field and the field of economics [Capitalism]. . . .

The foundation of Fascism is the conception of the State, its duty and its aim. Fascism conceives of the State as an absolute, in comparison with which individuals or groups are relative. . . . Whoever says Fascism implies the State.

Mussolini, Benito [actually written by Giovanni Gentile]. *The Political and Social Doctrine of Fascism.* London: Hogarth Press, 1933.

return to monarchical authority. The Fascist alternative offered a strong authoritarian government (which became totalitarian government) buttressed with nationalism and militarism. Fascist totalitarianism, soon established with local variations in many European countries, was similar to Communist totalitarianism in creating a one-party state, headed by a single leader with dictatorial powers, maintained in power by a secret police and the use of violence, and unrestrained by constitutional laws, liberties, and thoughts of human rights. It differed from Communist totalitarianism by stressing nationalism instead of internationalism, by rejecting class conflict (old aristocrats and wealthy bourgeois could both flourish), and by preserving capitalist concepts such as private property.

Mussolini's variety of Fascism produced a less totalitarian dictatorship than subsequent varieties (especially Nazi Germany). He packaged his antiparliamentary, anticommunist nationalism in a rhetoric about heroism, courage, and sacrifice. He created a cult of leadership around himself in the role of *Il Duce* (the leader) and promised leadership that would change the peace treaty and the economic crisis. This attracted enough votes under proportional representation to elect Mussolini and thirty-four supporters to the Chamber of

Deputies in 1921. Mussolini won less than 10 percent of the vote, yet he successfully exploited Italian troubles and government weakness to gain dictatorial powers in 1922. This began with the "march on Rome" in October 1922, when Mussolini led thousands of Fascists in a demonstration seeking his appointment as premier. "Either they will give us the government or we shall seize it," Mussolini said. When armed Fascists seized arsenals, railroad stations, and telephone and telegraph offices, the king relented and appointed Mussolini to office. Within one month, he persuaded Parliament to give him dictatorial powers for one year, to restore economic order without the delays of the democratic process. Mussolini used his power to pack the courts, the administration, and local government with his supporters; simultaneously he browbeat the king into naming a Fascist majority in the Italian Senate. As his dictatorial powers neared their expiration, Mussolini issued a new electoral law, the Acerbo Law of 1923, that abolished proportional representation and awarded 67 percent of the Chamber of Deputies to the party with the most votes, even if it only obtained one-fourth of the votes.

Mussolini and the Fascist Party built their dictatorship on the parliamentary elections of 1924. They exploited their control of the courts and local government, used direct intimidation and violence as needed, and relied on outright fraud in counting the votes. This combination earned the Fascists a two-thirds majority in Parliament and a Fascist government. When a leader of the Socialist Party, Giacomo Matteotti (whose book *The Fascisti Exposed* had detailed Fascist political violence), denounced this undemocratic seizure of power, Fascist thugs kidnapped him and stabbed him to death. When socialist, liberal, and Catholic deputies walked out of Parliament in a protest known as the Aventine Secession, the Fascist majority permanently expelled them. Critical journalists were jailed.

The Fascist dictatorship in Italy quickly uprooted democratic society. All opposition parties—monarchical, democratic, Catholic, and socialist—were abolished, creating a one-party state. Universal suffrage was abolished and voting was defined by the amount of taxes paid. A Fascist Grand Council named members of Parliament and voters ratified their selections. Mussolini kept the power to govern by decree. Strict press censorship was installed. All local officials were made appointive. A secret police (the OVRA) cracked down on opponents of the regime, armed with a law permitting capital punishment for political offenses. Despite such powers, Mussolini never created a total dictatorship because he never broke the independent power of the army, the Catholic Church, or the wealthy upper classes.

The Fascist regime focused its attention on economic recovery, and it had noteworthy successes although problems remained. Mussolini abandoned capitalism in favor of state planning and state intervention, but he kept private property and profit. These steps never achieved the self-sufficient economy he sought. The Battle for Wheat increased farm acreage and production, but Italy remained dependent on imports. Unemployment was cut sharply by extending education, expanding the army, and hiring thousands for public works projects (such as draining swamps to become farmland). Labor unrest was controlled by abolishing trade unions and outlawing strikes; management was regulated and made to accept state arbitration. To keep a tranquil economy and state direction of it, Mussolini created what he called "the corporate state." All occupations were organized into "syndicates" (a syndicate even existed for intellectuals); groups of syndicates were linked as "corporations." Representatives of occupations met in a quasi-legislative body called the National Council of Corporations. The council and a Ministry of Corporations theoretically directed the economy, but the corporate state never had perfectly defined powers. It generally supported propertied interests and management, and its biggest creation was a bloated bureaucracy.

◆

Hitler and Nazi Germany, 1928–39

Adolph Hitler and the Nazi Party similarly exploited the legacies of World War I—angry nationalism and economic crisis—in Germany. Like Mussolini and the Fascists, they mixed the legitimate political process with violence to seize power, destroy democracy, and build a dictatorship.

The Nazis remained a small and ineffective party during the Weimar recovery of the mid-1920s. In the parliamentary elections of 1928, the Nazi Party had a membership of 100,000 and received a meager 2.6 percent of the votes cast. The party attracted some support for its strident nationalism and denunciation of the Versailles Treaty, but its growth chiefly came during economic crisis. Although the full name of the party (German National Socialist Workers' Party) suggests that it was a working-class party, most urban workers voted against the Nazis; instead, the Nazis drew their electoral strength from small farmers and the lower middle class occupations known as the *Mittelstand* (chiefly small shopkeepers, artisans, and retail merchants). Such groups had suffered greatly in the nation's ordeal since 1914, were strongly nationalistic, vulnerable to economic crises, and without strong voices in the political process. When the depression hit Germany in 1930, many people saw a solution in strong leadership.

Adolph Hitler seized power through the political crisis of the German depression. Reichstag elections in 1930 showed frightened voters seeking new solutions: Both the Communist Party and the Nazi Party registered large gains, with Hitler now leading a delegation of 107 deputies. Part of this electoral success stemmed from the effectiveness of Nazi propaganda, managed by Josef Goebbels and presented in spell-casting oratory by Hitler. Goebbels, the chief author of fulsome Nazi propaganda images of a tall, blond, Aryan race of supermen, was himself a short and dark-haired man with a withered foot from childhood polio. In addition to artful propaganda, Nazi success resulted from using the intimidation and violence that Mussolini had taught. Nazi stormtroops—at first the brown-shirted SA (short for *Sturmabteilungen*, literally "storm troopers") and later Heinrich Himmler's black-shirted SS (short for *Schutzstaffel* or "defense echelon")—fought street battles, especially against leftists. The growth in Nazi popularity persuaded Hitler to run for the presidency of Germany in 1932, but he was overwhelmingly beaten (twenty million to thirteen million votes) by the eighty-five-year-old incumbent Field Marshal von Hindenburg. In two separate Reichstag elections that year, the Nazis polled 37 percent and 33 percent of the popular vote but became the largest party in a fragmented Reichstag. Party membership stood at 849,000 in a population of 66 million.

Hitler became chancellor of Germany by gaining the support of Reichstag conservatives led by Franz von Papen, a Catholic aristocrat and former General Staff officer who had married into one of the wealthy industrial families of the Saar. Von Papen had dedicated his political career to preserving the leadership of the Junker and industrial elites, and he believed that Hitler would do this. When Hitler became chancellor in early 1933, his lieutenant, Hermann Göring (a World War I fighter pilot and hero who had won the Iron Cross), became minister of the interior with control of the police. Hitler immediately called Reichstag elections. The Nazis increased their electoral violence, harassing opponents, intimidating voters, and even burning the Reichstag building. The Reichstag fire was blamed on Communists and used to justify the suspension of civil liberties, including both freedom of speech and the press. Nazi violence achieved 44 percent of the votes and a parliamentary majority through the alliance with von Papen. This Reichstag voted Hitler dictatorial powers for five years in the Enabling Act of March 1933, which allowed him to change the constitution and to promulgate laws with the Reichstag's approval. (Similar Enabling Laws had been used to deal with the economic crisis and Ruhr invasion of 1923.) Hitler used these powers to begin a policy that he called *Gleichschaltung* (coordination); this simply meant the consolidation of a lasting Nazi dictatorship. In the first few months of the *Gleichschaltung*, the Nazis created a secret police force (the Gestapo), a law permitting the arrest of dissenters, secret trials in People's Courts, and the first concentration camps (Dachau, near Munich, and Buchenwald, near Weimar) for the detention of political opponents. Elective local governments, labor unions, other political parties, the upper house of Parliament, the presidency, and civil liberties were all abolished. Nazi violence also increased. On "the Night of the Long Knives" in June 1934, Himmler (a frail and sickly man with an enormous drive for power) directed the SS in the murder of approximately one thousand people—opponents of the Nazis and unreliable party members, including the leaders of the SA.

Nazi persecution of the Jews (approximately 1 percent of the German population) began almost immediately. The purge of the bureaucracy ousted Jewish civil servants, professors, and public school teachers. A government-backed boycott closed many Jewish businesses. The Nuremberg Laws of 1935 (and 250 supplemental decrees) defined Jews as anyone having one Jewish grandparent (increasing the number of Jews to 2.5 million, or 4 percent of the population). These decrees stripped Jews of their citizenship, forbade intermarriage, barred them from many occupations, and restricted where they could live. Discrimination and harassment turned to violence in the late 1930s, and 72 percent of German Jews fled the country before emigration became impossible. On the *Kristallnacht* ("night of the broken glass," named for thousands of broken windows) in November 1938 (see illustration 28.4), the SS launched a pogrom. Rioters killed approximately one hundred Jews, trashed more than 7,000 businesses (completely destroying 815 shops), and burned 191 synagogues. More than twenty thousand Jews were arrested in the following weeks, and many of them were sent to concentration camps such as Dachau.

Nazi persecution was not limited to the Jews. Political opponents were the first to suffer under the new police state. Communists were rounded up and interred in March 1933 (barely one month after Hitler became chancellor) and the arrest of leading socialists followed in April 1933; high office was no protection, as the prime minister of Oldenburg (arrested in early March) discovered. Between July 1933 and April 1935, Nazi campaigns were launched against homosexuals, gypsies, the handicapped, and members of several religious sects, especially the Jehovah's Witnesses. A law of 1933, for example, permitted the government to order the sterilization of the handicapped (and several other groups), starting a campaign that culminated in Operation T4, begun in 1939, to "grant mercy death" to the handicapped. The Nazi attempt to exterminate members of such groups, especially Jews, in the concentration camps (for which the word *genocide* was coined) did not begin until after World War II had started.

Nazi social policy also affected women and children, schools and churches. Nazi policy toward women, for example, sought their return to the supposed traditional "women's place": *Kinder, Kirche, Küche* (children, church, kitchen). This led to efforts to drive women out of the workplace and higher education. The first Nazi economic plan, for example, sought to cut the employment of women by 200,000 per year, while educational policy cut the enrollment of women in German universities from 18,315 in 1932 to 5,447 in

Illustration 28.4

///// **Nazi Anti-Semitism.** Anti-Semitism was a central element of Nazi doctrine long before the party came to power, and this led to anti-Semitic policies from the earliest days of the regime. One of the most ominous moments came on November 9, 1938, known as the *Kristallnacht* ("night of the broken glass"). Nazi hooligans attacked Jews (killing more than one hundred), burnt synagogues, and trashed more than seven thousand Jewish businesses—whose broken windows, shown here, gave *Kristallnacht* its name.

1939. The regime strongly encouraged motherhood, which had long been a central theme of the Nazi program. This led to pronatalist policies ranging from grants for large families and strict laws against abortions to punishments for remaining unmarried. World War II later changed many of these policies, bringing women back into the workplace and the universities, but Nazi ideology remained antifeminist.

Hitler, like Mussolini, kept a capitalist economy in the narrow sense that it accepted private property and individual profit; however, he quickly converted Germany to a government-planned and -directed economy. The Nazi Four Year Plan of 1936 outlined German autarchy—a self-sufficient economy. Some industries, such as the Krupp Works and IG Farben, willingly collaborated with the Nazi plan and profited from government backing (and slave labor). Self-sufficiency made striking progress in some fields, such as gasoline production, which was 44 percent synthetic by 1938. Some industries, such as Ruhr coal, profited from Nazi help, such as forced labor, yet kept independent policies.

Nazi economic policies ended German unemployment. The unemployment rate of 30.1 percent in 1932 hit 4.6 percent in 1937, while the rest of the industrialized world remained in double digits. This was achieved through compulsory programs: conscription for military service, employment in state-funded armaments industries, drafted labor in public works projects (such as building the highway system known as the autobahn), and labor camps for young men and women. The regime financed this with other extreme measures: renouncing reparations payments, forcing involuntary

loans to the government, and confiscating Jewish wealth (initially a 20 percent tax on Jewish property in 1938). Dictatorship thus achieved a form of recovery. Coal production, which stood at 110 million tons in 1933, reached 188 million tons in 1939 (a 71 percent increase); steel production rose from 7.6 million tons to 23.7 million tons (a 212 percent increase).

Stalin and Soviet Communism, 1924–39

Among the dictatorships that characterized Europe in the 1930s, none was more harshly totalitarian than the dictatorship that Joseph Stalin built in the Soviet Union. Historians cannot say with certainty how many people died as a consequence of Stalin's horrifying policies of the 1920s and 1930s, but numbers between ten million and twenty million are usually suggested.

After a decade of war, revolution, and civil war, the Russian economy lay in ruins in 1921. The output of mining and heavy industries stood at 21 percent of the prewar level, compared with figures closer to 50 percent in Belgium, France, or Germany—Russian pig iron production in 1921, for example, amounted to 100,000 tons, compared with 4.2 million tons in 1913. Exports (and the capital that they raised) had virtually ceased, standing at 1.3 percent of the 1913 total. To address this crisis, Lenin and the Politburo leadership adopted a New Economic Policy (NEP) that mixed communist theories of state ownership and planning with capitalist theories of private ownership and the free market. The

NEP, Lenin explained, was a matter of taking one step backward to take two steps forward. Under the NEP, 98 percent of heavy industry, factory manufacturing, mining, and public services were state-owned; simultaneously, however, 90 percent of handicraft manufacturing, small shops, and agriculture remained privately owned. At the time of Lenin's death, 54 percent of all Soviet income still came from the private sector.

Lenin died in 1924 following his third stroke and a period of speechless incapacitation. He had favored Trotsky to succeed him, but Stalin used his leadership post in the Communist Party and maneuvering in the Politburo to isolate Trotsky. During a period of collective leadership in the mid-1920s, Trotsky was edged out of the Politburo (1925), out of the party (1927), and out of the country (1929); a Stalinist agent assassinated him in Mexico in 1940. After defeating Trotsky, Stalin then used an ideological battle to divide the Politburo and purge other leaders. The issues were the NEP and Stalin's doctrine known as "socialism in one country." Stalin asserted that the Soviet Union could create a Communist society alone; the NEP should be retained as the first step. His rivals on the left wing of the Politburo (whom he branded "left deviationists") backed Trotsky's idea of "permanent revolution"—work for revolution everywhere and continue it in Russia by ending the NEP. Stalin won this argument, and the left deviationists were ousted. In 1927, however, Stalin turned against his supporters in that fight; he purged them as "right deviationists" because they still supported the NEP. By 1928 Stalin's dictatorial power was unchallenged. He then announced his "new socialist offensive," borrowing ideas from the left deviationists and abolishing the NEP.

One of the foremost attributes of Stalin's dictatorship was the police state. The czarist secret police and the Bolshevik Cheka (reorganized as the OGPU in 1922) formed the basis of Stalin's secret police, known by a series of Russian acronyms, beginning as the NKVD (from 1926) and ending up as the KGB (from 1954). Under Feliks Dzerzhinsky and Nikolai Yezhov, the Soviet secret police became one of the most feared institutions in the world. The Bolsheviks had already established Holmogor concentration camp in Siberia for political prisoners in 1921 and had begun to use such camps (*gulags*) for forced labor in 1923. Stalin expanded this into an immense network of prison camps—named the *Gulag Archipelago* by Nobel Prize–winning novelist Alexandr Solzhenitsyn (see document 28.4). Many details about the *gulags* remain unclear, but more than ten million people were sent to such notorious camps as Kolyma or Magadan in eastern

---

◆ DOCUMENT 28.4 ◆

Life in the Stalinist Police State

Alexandr Solzhenitsyn Describes Being Arrested

Alexandr Solzhenitsyn is a Russian writer who won the Nobel Prize for literature in 1970. He served eight years in a concentration camp for the crime of criticizing Stalin in a letter to a friend.

For several decades political arrests were distinguished in our country precisely by the fact that people were arrested who were guilty of nothing and were therefore unprepared to put up any resistance whatsoever. There was a general feeling of being destined for destruction, a sense of having nowhere to escape. . . . People leaving for work said farewell to their families every day, because they could not be certain they would return at night. . . .

By and large, the [police] had no profound reasons for their choice of whom to arrest and whom not to arrest. They merely had over-all assignments, quotas for a specific number of arrests. These quotas might be filled on an orderly basis or wholly arbitrarily. . . .

The majority [of those arrested] sit quietly and dare to hope. Since you aren't guilty, then how can they arrest you? . . . Others are being arrested en masse, and that's a bothersome fact, but in those cases there is always some dark area: "Maybe *he* was guilty." . . . Why, then, should you run away? After all, you'll only make your situation worse; you'll make it more difficult for them to sort out the mistake. . . .

Once a person was arrested, he was never released; and [there was] the inevitability of a tenner, a ten-year sentence.

Mandelstam, Nadezhda. *Hope Against Hope,* trans. Max Hayward. London: Collins & Harvill, 1971; and Solzhenitsyn, Alexandr. *The Gulag Archipelago,* trans. Thomas Whitney. New York: Harper & Row, 1973.

Siberia. Prisoners in the *gulag* labored at preposterous tasks such as building a railroad across the Arctic. At Pelvozh camp on the Arctic Circle, prisoners slept four men to a straw pallet, with three feet of space each; they worked fourteen-hour shifts through the Siberian winter (except when the temperature fell below minus

✖ TABLE 28.5 ✖

Soviet Industrialization Under the Five-Year Plan, 1928–32

Output	1928 total	Target in the plan	1932 total
Gross industrial production (in billions of 1927 rubles)	18.3	43.2	43.3
Consumer goods production (in billions of 1927 rubles)	12.3	25.1	20.2
Gross agricultural production (in billions of 1927 rubles)	13.1	25.8	16.6
Hard coal production (in millions of tons)	35.4	75.0	64.3
Iron ore production (in millions of tons)	5.7	19.0	12.1
Steel production (in millions of tons)	4.0	10.4	5.9
Electricity generated (in billions of kilowatt hours)	5.1	22.0	13.4

Source: Alec Nove, *An Economic History of the USSR* (London: Penguin, 1969, 1982), p. 192.

fifty degrees Fahrenheit), dressed in light clothing and felt boots, and were fed a diet of approximately one thousand calories per day.

Stalin used these instruments of terror to build the Communist state. He ended the NEP and its privately owned shops and farms. The nationalization of this property (a process called collectivization) led to bitter fights, especially with the successful class of landowning peasants known as the *kulaks*. There were approximately twenty-five million peasant farms in the Soviet Union in 1928, with a livestock population of twenty-eight million pigs and sixty-six million cattle. By 1932 collectivization had created 250,000 large state farms (*sovkhoz*), where the government employed peasant workers to farm state land, and collective farms (*kolkhoz*), where state land was leased to a peasant community that farmed it as a collective enterprise. The kulaks resisted collectivization by burning crops, smashing farm implements, and slaughtering livestock. Thus, in 1934 the Soviet livestock population had plummeted to eleven million pigs and thirty-three million cattle. Stalin answered with a brutal repression aimed at nothing less than "the liquidation of the kulak class." Between five million and six million peasants (chiefly in Ukraine and the Caucasus) were executed in their villages or died in the *gulags*; another four million died in the famine of 1933, a direct consequence of collectivization.

Stalin used the grains and profits of collectivized agriculture to feed and finance the forced industrialization of the Soviet Union. He placed the economy under a central planning office (*Gosplan*) that drafted a series of Five Year Plans directing the creation of an industrial economy. The first Five Year Plan (1928–32)

encompassed the collectivization of agriculture and rapid industrialization (see table 28.5). The cost of these plans in human suffering was horrifying, but they accomplished the goal of industrialization (although they did not meet their production targets in heavy industry). Russia had lagged far behind western Europe throughout the nineteenth century; by 1940, however, the Soviet Union had the third largest industrial economy in the world (behind the United States and Germany), and at Stalin's death in 1953 it stood second. The same Five Year Plans that starved the kulaks increased Soviet coal production from 36 million tons (1928) to 166 million tons (1940), steel production from 4 million tons to 18 million tons. Production often fell short of Gosplan's targets (leading to the purge of "plan wreckers"), and both efficiency and quality suffered, but Stalin made the Soviet Union into an industrial power.

Simultaneously, Stalin relied on police terror to maintain his dictatorship. He began a new series of purges directed by Yezhov in 1936, which grew into the Great Terror (1936–39). This purge struck millions of members of the Communist Party, including virtually all surviving leaders of the Bolshevik revolution of 1917. Many of Stalin's old comrades, such as Nikolai Bukharin, the intellectual leader of the right deviationists, were convicted in public "show trials" after confessing to absurd charges such as being Nazi agents. In 1937 the purge decimated the officer corps of the Red Army, including the chief of staff and seven leading generals. By the end of the Great Terror, approximately one million people had been killed (including both Bukharin and Yezhov) and eight million to ten million sent to the *gulags*.

CHAPTER 29

EUROPE IN AN AGE OF TOTAL WAR: WORLD WAR II, 1939–45

CHAPTER OUTLINE

◆◆◆◆◆◆◆◆◆◆◆◆◆◆◆◆◆◆◆◆◆◆◆

Europe had lived through a generation of enormous suffering between 1914 and 1939, but the worst was yet to come when the age of total war culminated in the largest war in history. Between 1939 and 1945, World War II killed an estimated forty million Europeans, most of them noncombatants; the global total neared sixty million. The Soviet Union, which had suffered millions of deaths in World War I, the Russian Revolution and Civil War, and then in Stalin's terror of the 1930s, now endured an estimated twenty-five million deaths. Simultaneously, in one of the most horrifying chapters in human history, Nazi Germany attempted the complete extermination of the Jews of Europe; nearly eleven million people, including six million Jews, died in German death camps. World War II ended with enormous civilian casualties as a result of the aerial bombardment of major cities. The most ominous bombing came in the events that ended the war in Asia: the detonation of atomic bombs over the Japanese cities of Hiroshima and Nagasaki.

Chapter 29 covers the events of World War II beginning with its origins in the Peace of Paris of 1919 and the European diplomatic crises of the 1930s. It concludes with the diplomatic conferences at the end of the war (no formal peace conference was held), the world's discovery of the Holocaust in Europe, and the war crimes trials (the Nuremberg Trials) of 1945–46. Most of the chapter is devoted to the events of the war in Europe, from the German invasion of Poland in September 1939 to the unconditional surrender of Nazi Germany in May 1945. World War II was a worldwide war, however, so the chapter also surveys the course of the war in Asia and the Pacific.

❖

The Long Armistice and the Origins of World War II

The two world wars of the twentieth century were closely related to each other, with the second originating in the disputed outcome of the first. Winston Churchill, whose history of World War II won him the Nobel Prize in literature, saw the wars as a new Thirty Years' War, interrupted by a long armistice in which weary and devastated countries rebuilt their capacity to fight. The peace settlements that ended World War I, and the bitter nationalism that these treaties produced, linked the two wars. Opposition to the peace treaties was especially strong in the dictatorships that emerged during the 1920s and the 1930s, and in some cases the treaties were a significant factor in the rise of dictatorship. Defeat gave German territory to France, Belgium, Denmark, and Poland (see map 28.1); moreover, German nationalists were outraged by the war guilt clause, reparations payments, military restrictions, and the demilitarization of the Rhineland. Defeat similarly cost Russia Finland, the Baltic states, Poland, and Bessarabia; the loss of these buffers on Russia's western frontier produced anxiety in the Kremlin because neighboring states were vehemently anti-Communist. Victory failed to satisfy Italian nationalists because the treaties had denied Italy some of the territory that the Allies had promised as compensation for Italian participation in the war. Even in victorious Britain and France, many asked if World War I had been worth the cost; many British and American critics of the treaties opposed French efforts to enforce the treaty, making the campaign of German and Italian critics easier.

Battles over the peace treaties began as the ink on them dried. In 1919 alone, six armed disputes broke out over territorial settlements in Europe. The new state of Czechoslovakia and the reborn state of Poland fought over a frontier district, as did Austria and Hungary, both now small remnants of the once vast Habsburg Empire. Italian nationalists occupied the town of Fiume on the Yugoslavian border, which had been denied to Italy in the peace treaty. Thus, when the League of Nations was formally organized in January 1920, it inherited a host of problems spawned by the Peace of Paris.

The gravest issue of the early 1920s was the Versailles Treaty's provision for reparations payments by Germany to fund the reconstruction of war-torn Belgium and France. A series of Allied conferences labored to refine this question, but repeated German failures to make payments produced the first severe postwar crisis in 1923 when the Weimar government did not deliver

in-kind payments of timber. The frustrated Poincaré government in France, supported by the Belgians but not by the British or the Americans, insisted upon enforcing the treaty to occupy part of western Germany and extract in-kind payments (especially coal) directly. This led to a Franco-Belgian occupation of the Ruhr valley in January 1923, to a rupture of cooperation among the former western allies, and to a German campaign of noncooperation. To encourage noncooperation, the Weimar government paid striking workers by simply printing new money, therefore fueling the devastating inflation of 1923. The occupation of the Ruhr failed to provide France with reparations and cost the French hostile international opinion; Britain and America organized to save the German economy through the Dawes Plan and the French retreated.

A more optimistic mood characterized Franco-German relations during the later 1920s, the result of good relations between Briand and Stresemann. This short-lived period of hope produced its most noteworthy success in the Locarno Treaty of 1925 in which France, Belgium, Germany, Britain, and Italy guaranteed the western borders of Germany (thereby gaining German acceptance of the retrocession of Alsace and Lorraine to France) and established arbitration treaties to resolve future disputes. In the same spirit, Briand and Stresemann collaborated to secure German admission to the League of Nations in 1926. At its most idealistic moment, the "spirit of Locarno" stretched to create the idealistic Kellogg-Briand Pact (or the Pact of Paris) of 1928, in which the powers accepted a proposal by U.S. secretary of state Frank B. Kellogg for the renunciation of aggressive war. Although ratified by many states and embraced by the League of Nations, this toothless treaty contained no means of enforcement, not even trade sanctions. Dawes received the Nobel Peace Prize in 1925, Briand and Stresemann shared the prize for 1926, and Kellogg received it in 1929, but these awards were a measure of the world's hopes for peace in Europe, not a measure of success.

The most insistent challenge to the peace treaties of 1919 initially came from Italy. Mussolini was in power for less than a year when he attempted to annex the island of Corfu (off the coast of Albania and Greece) in mid-1923, only to be forced to back down by British pressure. He had better fortune in advancing Italian irredentist nationalism by resolving the Fiume question in a 1924 treaty with Yugoslavia, which recognized the Italian annexation of the town. An Italo-Albanian agreement of 1926 made the small Balkan state a virtual protectorate of Fascist Italy, a preliminary step in the annexation of Albania in early 1939. In 1928 Mussolini negotiated treaties of friendship with two countries with which he envisioned future wars—Ethiopia and Greece. Ethiopia was especially important to Italian nationalists because it had been the site of the humiliating colonial defeat of 1896 (the battle of Adowa) and had been an important Italian claim denied at Paris in 1919. In 1934 Mussolini used the excuse of border clashes between Ethiopia and the Italian colony of Somaliland to resume the attempted conquest. An Italian invasion of Ethiopia in 1935 led the League of Nations to declare Italy an aggressor state and to apply economic sanctions such as an embargo on selling military goods or giving financial assistance to Italy. The League, however, could not agree upon severe sanctions (such as shutting off Mussolini's oil supplies) and thus gave little effective support to Ethiopia, which was formally annexed by Italy in 1936. The western weakness in dealing with the Ethiopian question was a sign that the western powers lacked the resolution to stop aggression in Europe.

Nazi Germany exploited the western irresolution. Hitler was a product of World War I, and his efforts to abrogate the Versailles Treaty led to World War II. For most of the 1930s, the victors did nothing to stop him. Hitler had made his intentions clear in *Mein Kampf* and in German political debate; within weeks of coming to power in 1933, he showed his determination to change the 1919 settlement by walking out of disarmament negotiations and the League of Nations. The most fateful western inaction came in early 1935 when Hitler bluntly renounced the disarmament provisions of the treaty and reintroduced military conscription. The disarmament clauses had permitted Germany only a small army (seven divisions in 1933) and no air force or submarines. France, and perhaps Poland, could have withstood that Germany. Nazi conscription and construction, however, built a German army of fifty-two divisions by 1939, backed by a *Luftwaffe* (air force) of more than four thousand planes and a navy with fifty-four submarines. Hitler found battlefield training for this army by sending units to fight in the Spanish Civil War. The *Luftwaffe*, for example, polished the dive-bombing tactics that it would use in World War II by bombing the Basque town of Guernica. Fascist cooperation in Spain led to an Italo-German alliance of 1936, which Mussolini dubbed the Axis. The Anti-Comintern Pact (1936) expanded this alliance to include Japan, and the Pact of Steel (1939) tightened the Axis.

Hitler's second great challenge to the Versailles Treaty came eleven months later, in early 1936, when he renounced the Locarno Treaty and ordered the remilitarization of the Rhineland. The French army could

have stopped this, but the French and the British governments were indecisive and bickering over the Ethiopian question. France had a caretaker government on the eve of the most important election of the interwar era—the depression election of Léon Blum's Popular Front government; Britain had a newly elected Conservative government unwilling to send British soldiers to the continent again or to support sanctions in the League of Nations. Consequently the World War I allies did nothing to stop the remilitarization of the Rhineland, and Hitler (whose rearmament had only just begun) won a risky gamble.

His victories in 1935–36 encouraged Hitler to overthrow the rest of the Versailles restrictions and to plan the expansion of Germany. Hitler outlined his war plans to German military leaders in 1937. The record of that meeting, known as the Hossbach Memorandum, reveals Hitler's thinking: "The German racial community," he said, must have *Lebensraum* ("living space"), and he projected a new European war before 1943 (see document 29.1).

Hitler achieved most of his territorial goals without war (see map 29.1). A plebiscite in the Saar in 1935 restored that region to Germany by an overwhelming vote, lending some international credence to Hitler's demands for revision of the Versailles Treaty. He did not seek further territory, however, until March 1938, when he annexed Austria, an act that he preferred to call the *Anschluss* (union), which had been forbidden by the treaty. After promising to respect Austrian independence and then browbeating the chancellor of Austria, Kurt von Schuschnigg, into disbanding Austrian militias and granting an amnesty to Austrian Nazis, Hitler used the excuse of Austrian unrest (largely provoked by Austrian Nazis) to invade that country. The Austrians did not offer military resistance, and the western powers again did nothing. (France was again in the midst of a ministerial crisis, and the British were disposed to accept the *Anschluss*.) In a sham plebiscite, 99.75 percent of Austrians were reported to support the annexation, not counting the votes of, among others, concentration camp internees.

Shortly after the annexation of Austria, Hitler returned to his oratorical theme of "protecting the 10 million Germans living outside the Reich" and reopened the question of Czechoslovakia. He demanded that the Czechs cede to Germany the Sudetenland, a border region of western Bohemia that contained a German population (2.8 million Germans compared with 700,000 Czechs) plus Czechoslovakia's natural defenses (the Sudeten mountains and frontier fortresses) and much of

❖ DOCUMENT 29.1 ❖

The Hossbach Memorandum on the German Need for War, 1937

After World War II, the Allies searched German archives for documents to be used in the Nuremberg war crimes trials. The chief document used by prosecutors to prove that Hitler intended war is known as the Hossbach Memorandum, named for the colonel who took minutes at the meeting. The memorandum records a discussion at a conference between Hitler and German military leaders in November 1937.

The Führer initially said that the subject matter of today's conference was of such high importance that further detailed discussion would probably take place in Cabinet sessions. However, he, the Führer, had decided not to discuss this matter in the larger circle of the Reich Cabinet because of its importance. . . .

The Führer then stated: The aim of German policy is the security and the preservation of the nation, and its propagation. This is, consequently, a problem of space. The German nation is composed of 85 million people, which . . . form a homogeneous European racial body which cannot be found in any other country. On the other hand, it justifies the demand for larger living space (*Lebensraum*) more than for any other nation. . . . The Ger-

man future is therefore dependent exclusively on the solution of the need for *Lebensraum*. . . .

The German question can be solved only by way of force, and this is never without risk. The battles of Frederick the Great for Silesia, and Bismarck's wars against Austria and France had been a tremendous risk. . . . If we place the decision to apply force with risk at the head of the following exposition, we are only left to reply to the questions "when" and "how."

The rearming of the German Army, the Navy, and the Air Force, as well as the formation of the Officers' Corps, are practically concluded. Our material equipment and armaments are modern, with further delay the danger of their becoming out-of-date will increase. . . . In comparison with the rearmament of other nations, which will have been carried out by that time, we shall begin to decrease in relative power. . . . It is certain, however, that we can wait no longer.

Nürnberg War Crimes Trials Documents. Nazi Conspiracy and Aggression, vol. 3. Washington, DC: U.S. Government Printing Office, 1946–1948.

---

its industry. When Hitler stated this claim as giving the Sudetenland "the right of self-determination," the prime minister of Britain, Neville Chamberlain, agreed to meet with him to discuss the Czech question. Although Hitler made clear his intention to annex the Sudetenland, British and French (but not the Czech) diplomats prepared for the Munich Conference of October 1938 with Hitler. There, Chamberlain and the French premier, Edouard Daladier, agreed to the annexation of the Sudetenland and pressured the Czech government of President Edvard Benes (who thereafter resigned) into accepting it. The effect was to reduce Czechoslovakia to a Nazi client state. In early 1939 Czechoslovakia was abolished, most of it (Bohemia and Moravia) becoming a German protectorate.

The western capitulation to Hitler's demands at Munich became known as a policy of appeasement—appeasing dictators by surrendering to their demands. A 1938 newsreel records the return of Prime Minister Chamberlain from Munich and clarifies his policy: A pleased Chamberlain waves the Munich agreement and proclaims that he has won "peace in our time." Public

opinion in both Britain and France shared in the sense of relief that a war, fought over "far-off countries of which we know little" (such as Serbia in 1914), had been avoided. To Chamberlain's opponents, led by Winston Churchill, Chamberlain and Daladier had made craven concessions to avoid fighting.

World War II began when Hitler sought to revise the eastern border of Germany, where the Polish Corridor and the free city of Danzig separated East Prussia from the rest of Germany. This, Hitler told the world, was his last territorial demand in Europe. Stalin neither believed this nor waited for further Anglo-French concessions. He answered western appeasement with the Nazi-Soviet Nonaggression Treaty, also known as the Molotov-Ribbentrop Pact for the foreign ministers who signed it. Germany and the Soviet Union promised not to attack each other and to remain neutral in a war with a third party. They sealed the bargain with secret provisions of the treaty reprising the eighteenth-century partition of Poland. Germany would take the western two-thirds while the Soviet Union absorbed eastern Poland and the Baltic republics. This treaty stunned

MAP 29.1

The Road to War, 1936–39

Legend:

Germany

German advances:

Reoccupied Rhineland, March 1936

Annexed Austria, March 1938

Annexed Sudetenland, October 1938

Occupied Bohemia and Moravia, March 1939

Annexed Memel, March 1939

Italy

Annexed Albania, April 1939

Poland and Hungary

Annexed Czech territory, 1938 and 1939

( ) Former independent nations: Albania, Austria, and Czechoslovakia

opinion worldwide—Joachim von Ribbentrop, after all, was also the author of the largest anti-Communist alliance in the world, the Anti-Commintern Pact linking Germany, Italy, and Japan. The stunned silence did not last. A few days after concluding this treaty, Hitler used a dispute over Danzig as his excuse to send an army of 1.25 million men into Poland. Two days after the invasion began in September 1939, Britain and France declared war on Germany.

The Years of Axis Conquest, 1939–42

The war in Poland showed that technology had again changed warfare. The use of tanks and airplanes to support an invading army created a powerful offensive force, in contrast to the defensive war of barbed wire and machine guns fought in 1914–18. Even the infantry had changed, with mechanized units able to move rapidly. The German army (the *Wehrmacht*) possessed another major advantage: It was more than twice as large as the Polish army, and twenty-two divisions could not stop fifty-four. The *Luftwaffe* destroyed most of the Polish air force on the ground in the first hours of the war, and the *Wehrmacht* swept across Poland so fast that the campaign was called a *Blitzkrieg* (lightning war). The Germans reached Warsaw in barely one week, after a time-warp spectacle of Polish cavalry on horseback, with sword and lance, fighting in the same campaign that introduced German *Panzer* tanks. The opening days of the campaign presented one of the most hellish aspects of total war—the attack upon civilian populations. Göring ordered the "saturation bombing" of Warsaw, and the Polish capital was pounded into submission by *Luftwaffe* "dive-bombers" (*Stukas*), which dove toward the city with nerve-shattering whistles mounted in the wings. During a four-week battle, the *Luftwaffe* leveled 15 percent of all buildings and killed forty thousand civilians. After two weeks of the German devastation of Warsaw, Stalin sent the Red Army into eastern Poland, as foreseen in the Nazi-Soviet Pact and as a precaution against German seizure of the rich oil resources of Galicia and Romania. German and Russian armies met in central Poland during the third week of the war; a few days later, independent Poland had disappeared (see map 29.2). Sixty thousand Polish dead and 200,000 Polish wounded were just the beginning of Polish suffering. Approximately six million Poles would die before the war's end, including more than three million Polish Jews. Fleeing to the Russian sector gave no safety; when a Polish army tried this, the Red Army executed forty-two hundred Polish officers in the Katyn Forest massacre.

World War II seemed to have ended before it could spread. Italy and the United States declared neutrality. Britain (sitting behind the traditional security of the English Channel) and France (sitting behind the supposed security of the Maginot Line fortifications built across eastern France in the 1920s and 1930s) found themselves in a "phony war," sarcastically called the *Sitzkrieg* (sitting war). Stalin took advantage of this moment to annex the Baltic states and then, in November 1939, to attack Finland. The Finns held out for weeks behind exceptional fortifications devised by their commander, General Karl von Mannerheim, who refused to concede territory to the Russians, even after Stalin bombed Helsinki: "We shall fight to the last old man and the last small child. We shall burn our forests and houses . . . and what we yield will be cursed by the scourge of God." The Finns hoped for western aid that never arrived. The League of Nations expelled the USSR, and many countries sent limited supplies and sympathy, but the Finns were forced to surrender in March 1940 (after the Russian manpower advantage reached fifty-to-one) and to yield frontier territory.

The war continued in the west in 1939–40, but it was hidden from sight, on the high seas. Britain's lifeline remained, as it had been in World War I, on the Atlantic. German submarines (*Unterseeboots* or U-boats) had nearly beat the British in the first war, and an experienced U-boat commander, Admiral Karl Doenitz, now headed the German navy. However, Hitler (like Napoleon before him) had paid far less attention to naval preparation for war than he lavished on his army, leaving Doenitz a total submarine fleet of only fifty-six vessels in 1939. Doenitz launched total war on the seas (including orders to attack passenger ships in convoy for Britain), and the battle of the Atlantic began shortly after the invasion of Poland. A British liner was sunk by a German U-boat on the first day of the war, and "wolf-pack" U-boat tactics sank nineteen ships in two weeks, forty before the fall of Poland. In two shocking episodes for British morale, a U-boat sank a major British aircraft carrier (with the loss of 514 men) in September, and another snuck into the British base at Scapa Flow and sank the battleship *Royal Oak.* By spring, Doenitz's men had sunk 688,000 tons of merchant shipping. As the German U-boat fleet increased, so did the toll in the battle of the Atlantic. By 1942 it had reached 14 million tons.

The *Sitzkrieg* ended in April 1940, when Germany attacked Denmark (with whom it had a nonaggression treaty) on the flimsy pretext that the Danes would not be able to defend themselves against an Allied attack, but in reality because it was the first step in controlling Scandinavian iron and steel. The surprised Danes could offer no resistance, and units of the Nazi army reached Copenhagen in only a few hours, forcing the king to capitulate within twenty-four hours of the start of the war. On the same day as the Danish campaign, units of the *Luftwaffe* occupied the airports at Oslo and other major towns, and the German navy entered every major fjord on the Norwegian coast. The Norwegians—who had housed and fed thousands of German children during the starvation in the closing phase of World War I—were as astonished as the Danes had been. The king of Norway and the government fled to the north, and Britain and France landed a few troops there, but the Allies (and a Norwegian government in exile) were soon forced to evacuate. German conquest had reached the Arctic Circle. A Nazi sympathizer agreed to lead a collaborationist government, and Major Vidkun Quisling thereby made his last name a synonym for traitor.

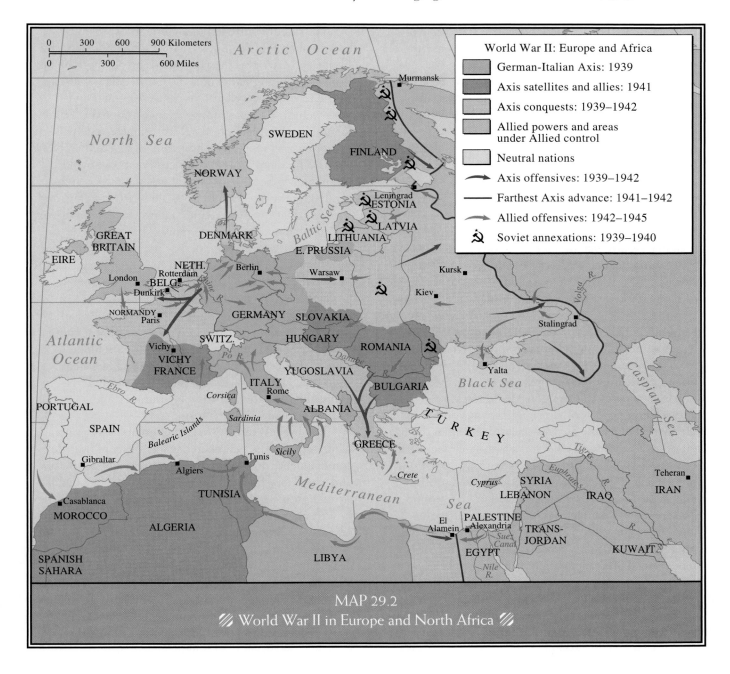

MAP 29.2
World War II in Europe and North Africa

The *Blitzkrieg* came to western Europe in May 1940 with a German assault (a 4 A.M. sneak attack) on the Low Countries (as a way of flanking the fortifications of the French Maginot Line) and then on northern France. The great cities of Amsterdam, Antwerp, and Brussels all suffered bombardment; the great port-city of Rotterdam (despite being declared an open city) was virtually flattened in withering *Stuka* attacks, which reduced two square miles of the city center (including twenty-five thousand private residences) to rubble. The destruction of Rotterdam convinced the British Royal Air Force (RAF) to bring the same sense of total war to German cities, and this strategy would devastate Germany later in the war. The Dutch army suffered 100,000 casualties (25 percent of the army) in just five days of fighting, enough to force a surrender. The queen, and a government in exile, managed to escape to Britain, leaving the Dutch under the brutal rule of a Nazi governor, Arthur Seyss-Inquart, a meek little man who plundered the country for nearly five years and sent more than five million Dutch citizens to forced labor in Germany. (Seyss-Inquart would be executed as a war criminal in 1946.) A simultaneous *Panzer* attack on Belgium sliced between France and Belgium, and Brussels fell. The

Belgians, who had endured more than four years of bloodletting without yielding in 1914–18, surrendered to the Nazis in one week.

The British had sent a large expeditionary force (the BEF) to the continent, but this army was cut off and trapped near the coast of the English Channel at Dunkirk (the northernmost port in France), with its entire left flank exposed by the fall of Belgium and the *Luftwaffe* pounding it at will. Facing almost certain catastrophe, the British chose to evacuate the BEF. In one of the most important retreats in military history, the British used every available boat (mostly civilian) from the English coast to ferry their army back across the channel. Nearly 340,000 men (including 140,000 French and Belgian soldiers) abandoned their equipment and the continental war, but thanks to the armada of nine hundred small craft (and Hitler's strange decision to halt the *Panzer* assault at Dunkirk), they survived to fight Germany on more favorable terms.

A vulnerable and demoralized France faced the Nazi *Blitzkrieg* without the allies of 1914. Although the French army of 800,000 regular forces and 5.5 million trained reserves had been considered the strongest army in Europe, it took no significant action against Germany during the *Sitzkrieg*, instead sitting in the Maginot fortications and awaiting a German attack. Many of the strongest units of the French army were lost in the debacle in Belgium, however, and much of the French air force had been destroyed on the ground in a Nazi preemptive attack. Then, two days after the Dunkirk evacuation, 120 divisions of the *Wehrmacht* poured into northern France, outflanking the Maginot Line instead of challenging it. *Blitzkrieg* shattered quickly assembled French lines, as the Nazis drove past Sedan, site of the German victory of 1870, and Verdun, symbol of French resistance in 1916. By mid-June (after less than two weeks of fighting), the French army was in chaos and Paris, without significant defenses, was evacuated by the government to spare it the fate of Warsaw and Rotterdam. With the fall of France seeming imminent, Mussolini declared war on Britain and France, invading the Riviera with an army of 400,000 men. France had been routed, and when the government turned to Marshal Henri Pétain, the hero of Verdun, he immediately surrendered. A gleeful Hitler accepted the French surrender in Compiègne, signed in exactly the same railroad boxcar where Imperial Germany had capitulated in 1918 (which Hitler ordered taken back to Berlin as a tourist attraction). The *Wehrmacht* staged a victory parade down the Champs Elysées and hung a giant Nazi banner from the Eiffel Tower.

The fall of France led to a German peace much harsher than the Versailles Treaty. Germany reannexed Alsace and Lorraine, then occupied the northern half of France (including Paris) plus the entire Atlantic coast; all the territory was placed under a German military government. This partition of France ended the Third Republic, which had often been a troubled regime but had pioneered republican government in a monarchical world. The rump state of southern France, known as Vichy France because its capital was the spa of Vichy, was led by the eighty-four-year-old Marshal Pétain and a former conservative premier, Pierre Laval, who served as Pétain's most important deputy. They replaced French constitutional democracy with an authoritarian government that had no constitution, collaborated with the Third Reich, and launched a Fascist National Revolution. Vichy France changed the national motto of "Liberty, Equality, Fraternity" to "Work, Family, Fatherland" and demonstrated the end of liberty by sending leaders of the Third Republic, such as Léon Blum, to German concentration camps. Pétain and Laval emulated the Nazi *Gleichschaltung*, seen in restricted freedoms, the regulation of basic institutions, and institutionalized anti-Semitism.

The highest ranking leader to escape was General Charles de Gaulle, who had been an obscure brigade commander in 1939 and whose government post was undersecretary for war in June 1940. De Gaulle had favored fighting to the bitter end, but when Pétain chose to surrender de Gaulle fled to London, where he organized a government in exile known as Free France. On his first day in London he addressed a famous radio appeal to the French people: "Has the last word been said? Has all hope disappeared? Is this defeat definitive? No! Believe me." This powerful broadcast (reproduced on clandestine posters around France) sealed de Gaulle's wartime leadership—by 1941, some forty-five thousand French troops from the Dunkirk evacuation and French colonies had rallied to him—although the British and Americans tried to replace him.

The first German defeat came when Hitler turned his attention to Britain in the summer of 1940. To prepare for an invasion of Britain, the *Luftwaffe* contested the RAF for control of the skies over the English Channel. The future of Britain, and perhaps of Europe, rested with approximately five thousand pilots during this battle of Britain and with an untested British invention—radar—which enabled them to spot planes seventy-five miles away from the coast of England (see illustration 29.1). The *Luftwaffe* sent as many as twenty-one hundred planes over England, greatly outnumbering RAF defenses. During July 1940 the British lost

Illustration 29.1

The Battle of Britain. The first defeat that Nazi Germany suffered, and the first turning point in the course of the war in Europe, came in an air war fought over Britain in the summer of 1940. The German *Luftwaffe*, with twenty-eight hundred aircraft, was asked to win control of the skies in preparation for an invasion of England, but the Royal Air Force (RAF), with seven hundred fighters, prevented them from doing so. In this photo, RAF pilots have just received a radar warning of approaching bombers and run to their Hurricane fighters to intercept the German planes.

nearly half of the RAF, but they shot down German planes at a higher rate and denied them control of the skies. Hitler dared not risk sending an invasion armada to sea. As the new prime minister of Britain, Winston Churchill, put it, "Never . . . was so much owed by so many to so few."

The battle of Britain entered a horrifying second phase in September 1940. Hitler decided to break British morale by obliterating London in terrorizing bomber raids called the *Blitz*. Twenty-three consecutive days of bombing rained nearly twenty thousand tons of bombs down on the city, destroying more than 450,000 private homes and killing thirty thousand civilians but failing to break the British will. Nothing symbolized British resistance better than the leadership of Churchill, one of the greatest wartime leaders in European history. Churchill was the descendant of an eighteenth-century military hero and the son of a prominent Conservative M.P. and a wealthy American mother. He worked exceptionally hard, but he had an infuriating personality, few friends, and a record of political failure. But Winston Churchill possessed a rare eloquence that summoned up resistance to the Nazis. In his maiden speech as prime minister, he had told the nation he had nothing to offer "but blood, toil, tears, and sweat." But, he soon added, if the nation paid that price, "should the British Empire last for a thousand years, people would say 'This was their finest hour.'"

The battle of Britain drew the United States closer to the war. President Roosevelt was sympathetic, and he inched America toward intervening against the steady

opposition of isolationists. In the aftermath of the Dunkirk evacuation Roosevelt sent $43 million worth of surplus arms (such as 600,000 rifles) to Britain. In August he struck a "destroyers for bases deal" to protect Atlantic shipping by sending fifty-one aging American destroyers to Britain. The conservative U.S. Congress limited arms sales by a strict "cash-and-carry" policy, but Roosevelt fought this short-sighted policy and called upon Congress to aid threatened democracies. The fruit of Roosevelt's efforts was the Lend-Lease Act of March 1941, which empowered the president to send arms to any nation deemed "vital to the defense of the United States." Congress initially authorized an appropriation of $7 billion for Lend-Lease arms (which grew to $50 billion during the war) and supplies began to flow from "the arsenal of democracy" to the enemies of Hitler. Then, in August 1941, FDR and Churchill met on a warship off Newfoundland and agreed upon the Atlantic Charter, a statement of war aims and postwar plans comparable to the Fourteen Points of World War I. They renounced territorial gain, called for "the destruction of Nazi tyranny," and spoke of human rights.

Despite victory in the battle of Britain, 1941–42 was a dark time for opponents of the Axis. An Italian invasion of Egypt (from their colony in Libya) threatened the Suez Canal and Middle Eastern oil supplies; both targets were so important that when British defenders drove the Italians from Egypt, Hitler reinforced the Axis effort with an elite German *Panzer* army known as the Afrika Korps, commanded by an exceptional tank commander, General Erwin Rommel, who forced

Illustration 29.2

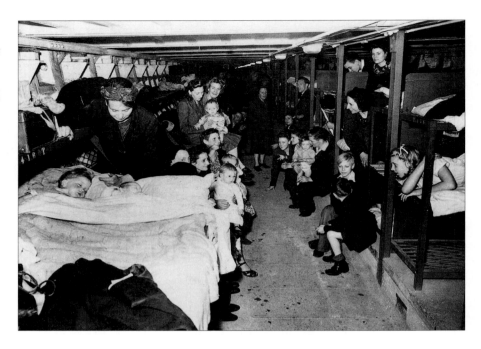

/// **The Home Front.** In total war there was scant respect for the distinction between a "battle front" and a "home front"—and civilian populations suffered terrible attacks in many countries. One of the most famous attacks on civilian centers was the German bombing of London, known as "the Blitz." During the German air raids, many British families took refuge in makeshift quarters, such as those shown in this photograph, set up in the tunnels of the London subway system.

the British to retreat. By June 1942 the Afrika Korps was threatening to take the Suez Canal. Simultaneously, Italian armies invaded Greece (October 1942) and opened war in the Balkans. The *Wehrmacht* also entered this theater, supporting the Italians in Greece and then invading Yugoslavia. Belgrade (severely bombed by the *Luftwaffe* in punishment for continued resistance) and Athens both fell to German occupation. The war in the Balkans continued as a guerrilla war, however, and Yugoslav partisans led by Joseph Broz (known as "Tito") never surrendered. The Balkan theater saw some of the most ferocious combat of World War II, and Yugoslavia (a nation of 14 million people in the 1930s) would lose 1.5 million to 2 million people.

The most important theater of World War II in Europe was the eastern front. Hitler, like Napoleon before him, turned from his failure to invade England and attacked Russia. This was the logical culmination of Hitler's determination to gain *Lebensraum* in the east, a calculation eased by his racist conviction of Slavic inferiority. In June 1941 he launched Operation Barbarosa, hitting the Soviet Union along a two-thousand-mile front in three massive offensives—toward Leningrad, Moscow, and Kiev. Finland resumed its war with the Soviet Union in the north while Hungary and Romania supported Germany in the south. The Nazi *Blitzkrieg* again won quick victories. Soviet armies were in disarray, partly because of Stalin's purge of army commanders in the 1930s and partly because of Stalin's belief that Hitler would not attack him. (The USSR was still

shipping food and military aid to Germany in the spring of 1941.) By autumn the *Wehrmacht* had penetrated hundreds of miles into the Soviet Union. In the north they laid siege to Leningrad and subjected it to the treatment that obliterated Warsaw, Rotterdam, and Belgrade. In the center, German bombers hit Moscow in the first weeks of the war, and German armies drew within sight of the city by late fall (see illustration 29.2). In the south, the *Wehrmacht* overran the Ukraine, taking Minsk, Kiev, and Odessa and finally planting the Swastika on the banks of the Black Sea, as they had hung it from the Eiffel Tower and the Parthenon. Hitler seemed near to dominion over continental Europe. His empire stretched from the Arctic Circle in Norway to the desert of western Egypt, from the French Pyrenees to the Crimea. But he had opened Pandora's box; for the next three years, 90 percent of German deaths would happen on the eastern front.

World War II on the Home Front

Life on European home fronts during the Second World War was naturally austere. The British, who imported much of their food, faced strict rations of basic foods (such as meat, butter, sugar, eggs, and tea), the total loss of many foreign foods (such as oranges, bananas, and chocolate), and reliance upon foods not previously eaten (such as shark and whale). Rationing identity cards were issued in September 1939 (during the Polish campaign), and the first rationing began in January 1940. Britons would live with rationing for the next fourteen years—a period long past the end of the war being required to rebuild the economy. Many families dug up their lawn or flowers to plant vegetables, and towns in Britain (as in many other countries) matched that effort by ploughing public parks or athletic playing fields; the moat around the Tower of London, for example, was converted to such a garden. Families in the south of England also learned to live without their children; 1.5 million children were moved outside German bombing range, many to refuge in Canada and the United States. The government curtailed free-market capitalism in favor of a regulated economy. Strikes were outlawed, the workweek increased to fifty-four hours, and the Ministry of Labor received the power to reassign workers to different jobs. The war effort also demanded much higher taxes. With one-third of all men between the ages of sixteen and sixty-four serving in uniform, women again entered the workforce at much higher levels, not only in factory jobs but also in a wide range of replacement positions (such as the police force, which lost much personnel to the military).

Domestic conditions were worse in the theaters of war. Russia suffered enormously from total war. Civilian populations overrun by the German army endured severe privation and frequent atrocities; these people had scarcely recovered from the suffering of forced collectivization and a subsequent famine in the 1930s. For those caught directly in the fighting, the meaning of total war was abundantly clear: The three million people of Leningrad endured a German siege lasting 890 days, and 600,000 of them died of starvation.

Civilian resistance in Britain and the Soviet Union contrasted with the collaboration of defeated countries such as Vichy France. The Nazi puppet government of Pétain and Laval sent more than one million Frenchmen to forced labor in Germany and arranged the Nazi requisition of three million tons of wheat and one million tons of meat. Conditions in France deteriorated so far that even wine was rationed. An underground resistance movement, composed of many separate groups (chiefly Communist, but with a large Catholic element) was collectively known as the *Maquis* or the French Forces of the Interior (FFI). Approximately 2 percent of the population took the risks of espionage, sabotage, or simple defiance, but the *Maquis* made a significant contribution to later stages of the war. Similar resistance movements existed in all occupied countries, with especially active movements in the mountain regions of Greece and Yugoslavia.

Hitler initially strove to cushion most of the German civilian population from the impact of the war because he feared the collapse of the home front, which had been a significant factor in the German defeat in 1918. Thus military deferments remained common until 1942. Rationing was introduced in August 1939, but the level was kept unusually high (a weekly supply of one pound of meat, five pounds of bread, twelve ounces of cooking fat, twelve ounces of sugar, and one pound of ersatz coffee per person), largely through food supplies plundered abroad. Behind such comforts, however, hid a nightmarish expression of Nazi total war at home: a euthanasia program to eliminate "useless mouths," launched at the start of the war. Between 100,000 and 200,000 of the elderly, the severely ill, the handicapped, the mentally ill, and even severely injured World War I veterans were put to death by the government with the willing cooperation of doctors, nurses, and hospital administrators. Only when Clemens von Galen, the bishop of Münster, courageously protested in 1941 did the government suspend the program (planning to resume it after victory), fearing a propaganda catastrophe if army units learned of the program of euthanasia for crippled veterans.

The Global War

The European war had been preceded by an Asian war, which began when Japan invaded China in 1937 (see map 29.3). The Japanese had been building an Asian empire for half a century. While acquiring Formosa (won in the Sino-Japanese War of 1895), Korea (won in the Russo-Japanese War of 1904–05), and Manchuria (occupied in 1931), Japanese nationalists developed the dream of a Greater East Asia Co-Prosperity Sphere—a slogan to cover Japanese conquest and dominance of East Asia. A second Sino-Japanese War began in 1937, and by the end of that year the Japanese Empire stretched across China as far south as Shanghai. In the course of this conquest, the Japanese army committed some of the most ruthless atrocities of the age of total war. The "rape of Nanking," which followed the conquest of that city, included the massacre of approximately 300,000 Chinese civilians, often in extremely cruel ways such as using live people for bayonet practice. (The name of this brutality was not misplaced: The Japanese army made rape an organized aspect of warfare, victimizing perhaps eighty thousand women in Nanking.) After the fall of France in June 1940, the Japanese army landed forces in French Indochina and

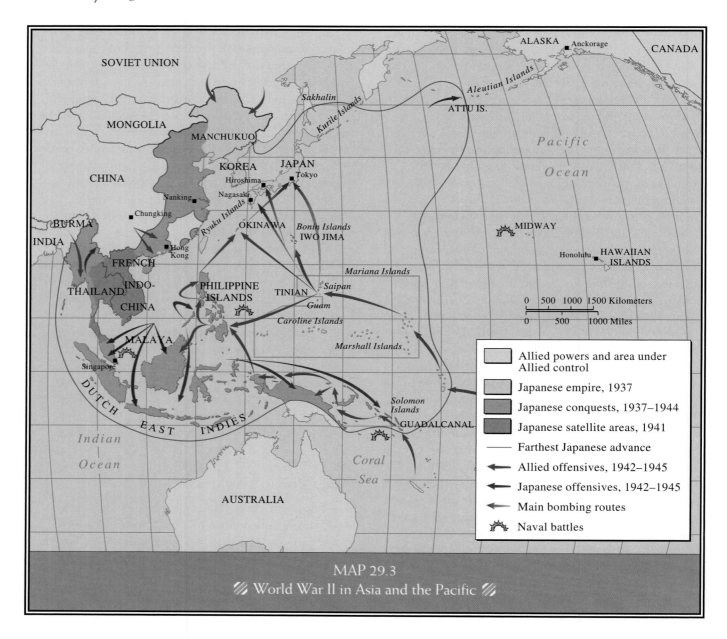

MAP 29.3
World War II in Asia and the Pacific

began the expansion of the co-prosperity sphere into Southeast Asia, where they hoped to obtain war materials. The further expansion meant a collision with the British Empire, which stretched across Asia from India to Singapore to Australia. Japanese expansion similarly menaced American territories in the Pacific, stretching from Hawaii to the Philippine Islands.

Britain and the United States were both drawn into the Asian war by Japanese attacks in December 1941. Japanese-American relations had deteriorated during the war in China. American sympathies for the Chinese government of Generalissimo Chiang Kai-Shek led to the prohibition of exporting war materials to Japan. Protests, warnings, and recriminations crossed the Pa-

cific Ocean in 1940–41. In July 1941 the military dictatorship of Japan resolved to establish the Greater East Asia Co-Prosperity Sphere "no matter what international developments take place." A few weeks later, all armed forces in the Philippine Islands were placed under the command of General Douglas MacArthur to ready them for war, and President Roosevelt froze Japanese assets in the United States. Trade between the two countries ceased. In August 1941 Roosevelt warned Japan against any further expansion in Asia saying that the United States would "take immediately any and all steps necessary" to protect its interests. Japan responded with a surprise attack on the home base of the U.S. navy at Pearl Harbor (near Honolulu, Hawaii) on

December 7, 1941. The attack crippled the U.S. Pacific Fleet, destroying 19 warships and 150 naval aircraft and causing three thousand American casualties. Denouncing "a date which will live in infamy," the United States declared war on Japan. As the Japanese had made simultaneous attacks upon British forces in Asia (notably in Hong Kong and Malaya), the British also declared war. Germany and Italy then declared war on the United States, linking the Asian and European wars into World War II.

In the six months following Pearl Harbor, the Japanese won important victories across Southeast Asia. They invaded the Philippines in late December 1941, drove General MacArthur to retreat, and won control of the islands in March 1942, taking a large army captive on the peninsula of Bataan. Another Japanese army drove the British out of Hong Kong in December 1941, and a third successfully invaded Burma in January 1942, cutting off British forces, which retreated to the stronghold of Singapore, but the Japanese took that city after a two-week siege in February 1942. Sixty thousand British prisoners of war fell to the Japanese. Allied armies were beaten in Indonesia in March 1942, and by spring the Japanese Empire stretched from the gates of India almost to the international dateline, from Korea almost to Australia.

The turning point of the war in Asia came in a series of air-sea battles in the Pacific in 1942. In the battle of the Coral Sea (May 1942), the first naval battle ever fought between ships so distant that they could not see each other, the United States stopped the Japanese advance and probably saved Australia and New Zealand. In the battle of Midway (May-June 1942)—named for the U.S.-held Midway Islands, northwest of Hawaii and at the approximate midpoint of the Pacific—a U.S. fleet under Admiral Chester Nimitz fought one of the largest naval engagements in history, inflicting heavy losses on the Japanese and forcing Admiral Yamamoto to retreat. By the summer of 1942, the war in the Pacific had become a succession of island-hopping—amphibious invasions slowly driving toward Japan. After victories by British armies in Burma and Australian armies in New Guinea, Allied forces under Admiral Lord Louis Mountbatten slowly defeated the Japanese armies of Southeast Asia. The United States dislodged the Japanese from Guadalcanal (in the Solomon Islands) in early 1943 and began the reconquest of the Philippines. Bloody fighting followed on many islands, especially in the Marshall Islands and Guam in 1944 and on Okinawa in 1945, but an invasion of Japan also awaited.

Allied Victory in Europe, 1942–45

The turning point of the war in Europe also came in 1942. British armies in North Africa under the command of Field Marshal Montgomery stopped the advance of the Afrika Korps in the battle of El Alamein. While the German army regrouped, an Anglo-American army of 100,000 men, under the command of General Dwight D. Eisenhower, landed in French North Africa in November 1942—less than a year after Hitler had declared war on the United States. This amphibious operation required 850 ships and was at that time the largest such landing in history. Caught between the armies of Eisenhower and Montgomery, the Axis armies in North Africa suffered a series of defeats, and the last Axis troops in North Africa surrendered in May 1943.

Even before the victory in Africa, Roosevelt and Churchill had met at the Casablanca Conference of January 1943 and decided that the next stage of the war in Europe would be the invasion of Italy, "the soft under-belly of Europe" in Churchill's words. The Allies began bombing raids over Sicily and combined British, Canadian, and American armies, commanded by Eisenhower, invaded in July. Palermo fell in two weeks and the Allies began bombing Naples, but before they could cross to the Italian peninsula, Mussolini was deposed in a sudden coup, ending twenty-one years of Fascist rule in Italy and dissolving the Fascist Party. As the British and American armies made their first landings near Naples, Italy unconditionally surrendered in September 1943. German armies still occupied Milan, Rome, and Naples, and the Italian campaign therefore became a slow battle up the peninsula in 1943–45, speeded by a landing behind German lines at Anzio in early 1944. Rome did not fall until June 1944. As the German army began to pull out of Italy, Mussolini was captured by Italian anti-Fascists while attempting to escape to Switzerland and was shot without a trial.

While the victories in North Africa and Italy were important steps in the defeat of the Axis, the decisive theater of the war was the eastern front. The German invasion of Russia had been stopped by the winter of 1941–42 and the determined defense of Moscow led by General Georgi Zhukov. Zhukov was the son of illiterate peasants and had a gruff and unsophisticated style, but he was one of the first commanders to master tank warfare. He so distinguished himself in saving Moscow that Stalin sent him to Leningrad, where he ordered that the city be defended street by street and that officers who retreated be shot. German assaults (which cost them 200,000 soldiers) and bombardment failed to

Illustration 29.3

D-Day. The turning point of World War II on the western front came on June 6, 1944, when the Allies staged the greatest amphibious landing in history, along the shores of northern France. Landing craft such as the one shown in this photograph put an army of more than 150,000 men ashore in the first day, losing slightly more than 2,000 killed.

break Leningrad. When the siege ended in early 1943, half of the population of Leningrad had died.

The turning point of World War II in Europe came in southern Russia. The *Wehrmacht* had already lost nearly two million men on the eastern front before the Red Army began to counterattack in the winter of 1942–43. A campaign on the Volga River at Stalingrad was the beginning of the end for Nazi Germany, an epic battle comparable to Verdun in the First World War. The Red Army encircled a German army of 300,000 men at Stalingrad and relentlessly attacked in horrifying conditions where temperatures reached minus forty-nine degrees Fahrenheit. When the Germans gave up in February 1943, a veteran army that had sped across Belgium and Holland was reduced to ninety-one thousand starving, frostbitten prisoners of war, only six thousand of whom eventually survived Russian imprisonment. After the battle of Stalingrad, the *Wehrmacht* attempted another offensive, the largest tank battle in history—the battle of Kursk, a rail center south of Moscow. This nine-day battle involved more than two million combatants, five thousand planes, and six thousand tanks. The *Wehrmacht* lost badly, as the Red Army threw seemingly endless numbers of men and equipment into the battle. Then began a long German retreat. The Russian army recaptured Smolensk in

September 1943, liberated Kiev in November, and crossed the frontier into Poland in January 1944.

The Allies had long planned to open a western front against Germany. Stalin pressed this policy to reduce the burden of the eastern front, where Russian deaths had passed the ten million mark. The western Allies responded with Operation Overlord, a plan to invade northern France with a combined army of five divisions (two British, two American, and one Canadian), commanded by General Eisenhower. They prepared elaborately, staging men and materiel in southern England and conducting bombing raids over Germany. The RAF struck Berlin with nine hundred tons of bombs in March 1943, then concentrated on the industrial Rhineland. The bombing of Essen cut the output of the Krupp armaments complex by 65 percent.

The result was the largest amphibious invasion in history, landing on the shores of Normandy on D-Day, June 6, 1944 (see illustration 29.3). An armada of five thousand ships landed 150,000 soldiers (plus thousands of vehicles and tons of supplies) on the French coast. In less than two weeks, these numbers reached nearly 500,000 soldiers and 90,000 vehicles. The Normandy landings led to a rapid breakthrough by Allied tank forces, and by midsummer Germany clearly had lost the second battle of France, permitting armies of the

British Empire, the Free French, and the United States to press into western Germany while the Russians invaded eastern Germany. This reverse precipitated an attempt to assassinate Hitler by a conspiracy within the *Wehrmacht*. The plot involved several senior officers, but the central figure was Colonial Claus von Stuaffenberg, who carried a bomb into a conference among Hitler and his military advisers. Hitler survived and the conspirators were brutally executed (Hitler filmed their deaths for evening entertainment).

Hitler responded to the reverses of June–July 1944 with one last surprise: a wave of rocket attacks whose technology presaged the cold war and the space race. A German research program (which included many scientists who would later contribute to the space race of the 1950s and 1960s, such as Dr. Wernher von Braun) at Peenemünde, on the Baltic coast, achieved significant advances in rocketry. The results were the V-1 rockets — flying bombs with a ton of explosives traveling 370 miles per hour—which hit London in the summer of 1944, and more sophisticated V-2 rockets, which struck London and Antwerp that autumn. V-1 and V-2 attacks delivered more than seventy thousand tons of explosives to Britain, approximately four times the amount that the *Luftwaffe* dropped in 1940; the rockets killed nearly eight thousand people but had little effect on the course of the war.

Allied armies reached Paris in August 1944 and speeded the liberation of France by making further landings in the south of France. Lyons, Brussels, and Antwerp were all liberated in September 1944, and western armies crossed into western Germany in that same month. The Allies officially recognized Charles de Gaulle's government of liberated France in October. Although the *Wehrmacht* staged a strong counteroffensive through the Ardennes forest in December 1944, the Nazi regime was crushed between western and Soviet armies. The Red Army had reached Warsaw in July 1944 and a Polish uprising joined in throwing off the Nazi occupation. The Russian army, however, waited for the Nazis to crush the Polish resistance (with 245,000 Poles killed) before advancing on Warsaw (because Stalin reasoned that Polish resistance to a German occupation could easily become Polish resistance to a Russian occupation). As France was being freed in the west, Russian troops were crossing into East Prussia. The Red Army approached Berlin in early 1945 (see illustration 29.4), just as the U.S. army was crossing the Rhine River. With the war nearly over, Allied bombers delivered a horrifying final blow, a last testament to the

Illustration 29.4

Victory on the Eastern Front. The turning point of the war in eastern Europe had come in 1943 when the USSR won the battle of Stalingrad. For the next two years, the Red Army under Marshal Zhukov pressed into central Europe in a campaign that culminated in the Soviet capture of Berlin in April–May 1945. In this photo, Zhukov (front, lower right) and his staff stand on the steps of the ruined Reichstag, now covered in Russian graffiti.

nature of total war: The historic Saxon city of Dresden, known as "the Florence of Germany," was subjected to two days of nightmarish bombing, killing more than 130,000 civilians.

Mussolini and Hitler died one day apart in April 1945. While Il Duce was killed by Italian partisans, der Führer committed suicide in the ruins of Berlin a day later. Hitler's war had cost Germany more than three million combat deaths; more than twice that number of Russian soldiers had died, compared with a combined total of approximately one million British, French, and American troops (see table 29.1). Roosevelt also died in April, a few days before the unconditional surrender of

TABLE 29.1

The Estimated Casualties of World War II

Country	Killed in combat	Wounded	Civilians killed	Total killed
Allied casualties				
Australia	23,000–26,000	39,000–180,000		23,000–26,000
Belgium	8,000–10,000	56,000	60,000–76,000	68,000–86,000
Britain	244,000–264,000	370,000	60,000–93,000	304,000–357,000
Canada	32,000–37,000	53,000		32,000–37,000
China	1.3 million–2.2 million	1.8 million		1.3 million–2.2 million plus
Denmark	3,000–4,000		2,000–3,000	5,000–7,000
France	200,000–400,000	400,000	200,000–350,000	400,000–750,000
Greece	17,000–74,000	47,000	325,000–391,000	342,000–465,000
India	24,000–32,000	64,000		24,000–32,000
Netherlands	7,000	3,000	200,000	207,000
New Zealand	11,000	17,000		11,000
Norway	1,000–2,000		7,000–8,000	8,000–10,000
Poland	123,000–600,000	530,000	5 million plus	about 6 million
United States	292,000	670,000	6,000	298,000
USSR	6.0 million–7.5 million		2 million–9 million plus	8 million–20 million
Yugoslavia	305,000–410,000	425,000	1.2 million	1.5 million–1.6 million
Axis casualties				
Bulgaria	7,000–10,000		10,000	17,000–20,000
Finland	79,000–82,000		2,000–11,000	81,000–93,000
Germany	3.3 million–4.4 million		780,000 plus	4.1 million–5.2 million
Hungary	140,000–180,000		280,000–290,000	420,000–470,000
Italy	78,000–162,000		146,000	224,000–308,000
Japan	1.2 million–2.0 million		280,000 plus	1.5 million–2.3 million
Romania	300,000–350,000		200,000	500,000–550,000

Source: Adapted from data in Louis L. Snyder, ed., *Louis L. Snyder's Historical Guide to World War II* (Westport, Conn.: Greenwood, 1982), p. 126.
Note: Figures show range from lowest to highest estimates. German data include Austria. Holocaust victims are counted in homeland civilians.

Germany on V-E Day (Victory in Europe Day). Finishing the war in Asia thus fell to Roosevelt's vice president, Harry S. Truman.

President Truman took the painful decision to use the atomic bomb on Japan to avoid the frightful costs of invading Japan. In the late 1930s experiments with splitting the atom had begun to convince physicists around the world of the potential of a weapon based on nuclear fission. In 1939 a group of distinguished European émigré scientists (notably Enrico Fermi, Leo Szilard, and Albert Einstein) at American universities began to worry that Nazi Germany might be working on such an atomic bomb. This resulted in a historic letter from Albert Einstein to President Roosevelt explaining these possibilities. FDR responded with top-secret

(even from Congress) funding of the Manhattan Project to construct a nuclear fission bomb. An international team of scientists, many of them Jewish refugees driven from Europe by Nazi racial policies, and all of them fearful that Werner Heisenberg and other German scientists were ahead of them, succeeded in the summer of 1945. The first atomic bomb exploded at a desert site near Alamogordo, New Mexico. It generated the explosive power of twenty thousand tons of TNT, vaporized all surrounding equipment, and startled even its inventors. J. Robert Oppenheimer, the director of the Manhattan Project laboratory, was moved to recall a line of Hindu scripture, "I am become Death, the destroyer of worlds." The European war had already ended, and the awesome new weapon quickly ended

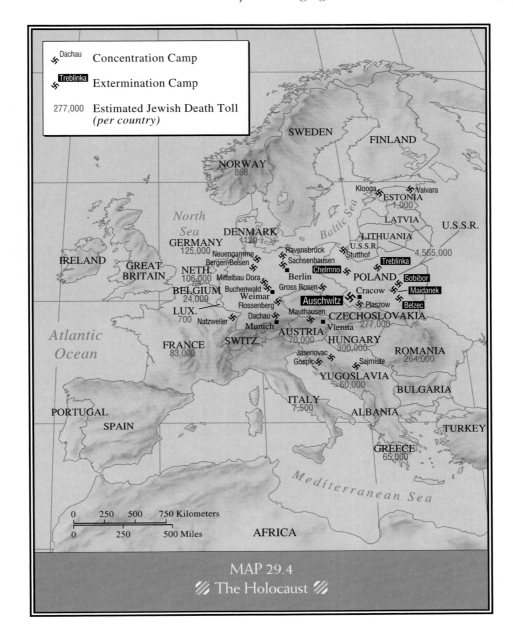

Concentration Camp — Dachau

Extermination Camp — Treblinka

277,000 — **Estimated Jewish Death Toll** *(per country)*

MAP 29.4
The Holocaust

the Asian war. The United States bombed the Japanese city of Hiroshima on August 6, 1945, killing 68,000 people instantly and nearly 100,000 over time. A second A-bomb, dropped on Nagasaki three days later, killed another 35,000 and convinced the Japanese to surrender.

The Holocaust, 1941–45

In 1945 the world learned the details of a crime as incredible as was the destructive force of the atomic bomb: During the war, the Nazis had used their concentration camps for the systematic murder of millions of people. Rumors of Nazi horrors had circulated earlier, but they had not been widely known and they did not provoke Allied governments to act. The original network of camps (see map 29.4), including Dachau (near Munich), Buchenwald (near Weimar), and Sachsenhausen (near Berlin), expanded during the war, especially in Poland, the site of such notorious camps as Auschwitz (near Cracow) and Treblinka (near Warsaw). In a speech to the Reichstag in January 1939, Hitler had warned that the Jewish race in Europe would be exterminated in the next world war. Hitler's psychotic anti-Semitism culminated in a grotesque plan to "purify Aryan blood,"

Illustration 29.5

Nazi Concentration Camps. One of the first concentration camps liberated by Allied armies was Bergen-Belsen in northwestern Germany, a camp originally opened in 1941 for Allied prisoners of war but converted by Himmler into a camp for Jews from western Europe (including Anne Frank) in 1943. When the British army entered Bergen-Belsen in April 1945, they found thousands of unburied bodies (shown here) and, as the BBC reported, thousands of "scarcely human, moaning skeletons" who had been without food or water for five days.

known as the Final Solution (*Endlösung*). The Final Solution was mass murder; approximately eleven million people were killed in the Nazi camps. Gypsies, homosexuals, Communists, the handicapped, the mentally ill, and members of sects such as the Jehovah's Witnesses were all marked for extermination, and they died in large numbers—from 5,000 German and Austrian homosexuals to 200,000 gypsies. Millions of Poles and Soviet prisoners of war (both nations were *Untermenschen*, or subhumans, in the Nazi racial cosmology) also perished in the German concentration camps. But the Final Solution was aimed first at the Jews, nearly 6 million of whom were killed (two-thirds of all European Jews), including 1.5 million children (see illustration 29.5).

Under the direction of Himmler, Reinhard Heydrich, and Adolph Eichmann, the concentration camps became a universe of slave labor and starvation, then of brutality so savage that it included medical experimentation on live people and ultimately factories for the efficient killing of people. Nazi officials had begun to discuss "a complete solution of the Jewish question" in 1941, and the concentration camps started to become death camps that year. Then in January 1942, fifteen leading Nazi officials met at Wannsee, in suburban Berlin, to plan genocide; in the Wannsee Protocol, they pledged to achieve the Final Solution. This led to grisly experimentation to find an efficient means of committing genocide: Sobibor killed 200,000–250,000 people by carbon monoxide poisoning, before the managers of the Auschwitz-Birkenau complex discovered the efficiencies of Zyclon-B (a form of Prussic acid) for gassing inmates. Poison gas was typically administered to

groups of people locked into large rooms made to resemble showers; great furnaces were built to burn the bodies. More than 1.1 million people were killed in this way at Auschwitz, and meticulous Nazi bureaucrats kept detailed records of their murders. At his postwar trial, the Nazi commandant of Auschwitz, Rudolf Hoess, calmly described the entire procedure (see document 29.2).

The Holocaust witnessed heroism amid the horror. Fascist Italy joined in anti-Semitic legislation (such as a 1938 law forbidding intermarriage with Jews) and had interned foreign-born Jews, but Mussolini resisted genocide and refused to deport forty-four thousand Jews to the death camps, enabling 85 percent of Italian Jews to survive the war. Although Vichy France similarly collaborated by deporting foreign-born Jews, a heroic Protestant village in southern France, Le Chambon, led by Pastor André Tromé, saved five thousand Jews by hiding them, and a Capuchin monk at Marseille, Marie Benoît, saved four thousand by providing papers allowing them to escape. Danes ferried Jews to safety in Sweden so effectively that seven thousand Danish Jews escaped and only fifty-one died in the camps. A single Swedish diplomat, Raoul Wallenberg, organized a system that saved ten thousand Budapest Jews. (In a tragic irony, Wallenberg himself died in Soviet captivity.) A German businessman, Oscar Schindler, saved Jews from Auschwitz by taking them to work in his factory. Jewish self-defense also had notable moments: In April 1942 the Jewish ghetto of Warsaw fought back and killed five thousand German soldiers.

❖ DOCUMENT 29.2 ❖

The Commandant of Auschwitz Confesses

Rudolf Hoess (1900–47) was a decorated World War I veteran who spent much of the 1920s in prison for killing a teacher who had insulted the memory of a Nazi hero. He joined the SS and spent his career working in the concentration camps, rising from a corporal at Dachau to be the commandant of Auschwitz (1940–43). Under his supervision, 2.5 million inmates were executed, and Hoess earned an SS commendation for efficiency. At his trial he gave a remarkably calm and detailed confession of his life as a mass murderer.

In the summer of 1941—I can no longer remember the exact date—I was suddenly summoned to the Reichsführer SS [Himmler] in Berlin directly by his adjutant's office. Contrary to his normal practice, he received me without his adjutant being present and told me, in effect:

"The Führer has ordered the final solution of the Jewish question and we—the SS—have to carry out this order. The existing extermination centers in the east are not in a position to carry out the major operations which are envisaged. I have, therefore, earmarked Auschwitz for this task, both because of its favorable communications and because the area envisaged can be easily sealed off and camouflaged. . . .

"You will maintain the strictest silence concerning this order, even vis-à-vis your superiors. After your meeting with Eichmann [Himmler's SS assistant] send me the plans for the proposed installations at once. The Jews are the eternal enemies of the German people and must be exterminated. Every Jew we can lay our hands on must be exterminated. . . .

Shortly afterwards, Eichmann came to see me in Auschwitz. . . . We discussed how the extermination was to be carried out. Gas was the only feasible method, since it would be impossible to liquidate by shooting the large numbers envisaged, and shooting would place too heavy a burden on the SS men who had to carry it out, particularly in view of the women and children involved.

Eichmann informed me of the method of killing by exhaust fumes from vans, which had been implemented in the east hitherto. However, it was out of the question to use it in Auschwitz on the mass transports that were envisaged. . . . My deputy . . . [had] used gas to exterminate the Russian prisoners of war. He crammed individual cells with Russians and, protected by gas masks, hurled Zyclon-B into the cells which caused death immediately. . . . During Eichmann's next visit, I reported to him about this use of Zyclon-B and we decided to employ this gas for the future mass extermination program. . . .

Auschwitz reached its high point in the spring of 1944. . . . A triple track railway line leading to the new crematoria enabled a train to be unloaded while the next one was arriving. . . . All four crematoria operated at full blast. . . . The last body had hardly been pulled from the gas chambers and dragged across the yard behind the crematorium, which was covered in corpses, to the burning pit, when the next lot were already undressing in the hall for gassing.

Hoess, Rudolph. Nuremburg testimony. In J. Noakes and G. Pridham, eds. *Nazism, 1919–1945. A History in Documents and Eyewitness Accounts,* vol. 2. New York: Schocken, 1988.

❖

Conference Diplomacy and Peace in Europe in 1945

No peace or treaty ended World War II in Europe. Churchill, Stalin, and Roosevelt had prepared for Germany's unconditional surrender at a series of summit conferences during the war. The Tehran Conference of 1943, for example, projected new frontiers for Poland and discussed the dismemberment of Germany. The Dumbarton Oaks Conference (in Washington, D.C.) planned an international organization—the United Nations (UN)—to keep the peace. Churchill and Stalin met in Moscow in 1944 and agreed to divide eastern

Europe into "spheres of influence"; the USSR would be preeminent in Romania and Bulgaria and have influence in Hungary and Yugoslavia.

The most important wartime conference took place in early 1945 in the Russian resort town of Yalta, on the Crimean peninsula. Churchill, Roosevelt, and Stalin agreed to divide Germany into four zones of military occupation, with France administering the fourth. They pledged the "complete disarmament, demilitarization, and dismemberment" of Germany, including the right of occupying powers to remove German wealth, such as dismantling factories. The Potsdam Conference (in suburban Berlin in the summer of 1945) finalized the partition of Germany. The Allies agreed that Germans must "atone for the terrible crimes committed under the leadership of those whom, in the hour of their success, they openly approved and blindly obeyed." The boundary between a reduced Germany and a recreated Poland would be defined by two rivers, the Oder-Neisse Line. Much of historic Prussia thus became part of Poland.

The Potsdam Protocol also stated the right of the victors to hold trials of war criminals. Similar trials had been planned after World War I, when the Allies had drawn up a list of 890 people to be tried, beginning with Kaiser Wilhelm II. But the trials begun at Leipzig in 1921 collapsed when the German high court accepted the exculpatory plea of individuals who were "just following orders." The Potsdam Protocol avoided this problem by chartering an Allied tribunal to sit at Nuremberg and by defining the crimes that would come before it (see document 29.3). This included "crimes against humanity" for acts committed against civilian populations. Twenty-two Nazi leaders were accordingly tried at the Nuremberg Trials of 1945–46, and twelve were sentenced to death. Hitler, Goebbels, and Himmler were all dead, but Göring and Ribbentrop were among the prominent Nazis at Nuremberg. Others were tried in the east, and war crimes trials continued in the postwar era: Israel convicted and executed one of the architects of the Holocaust, Adolf Eichmann, in 1962; a French court convicted the Gestapo chief in Lyons (Klaus Barbie) as late as 1987, then tried a Vichy police official, Maurice Papon, in 1997. Similar trials (and informal revenge) covered the war zone. In France, eight hundred Vichy collaborationists were executed during the Liberation. The hero of World War I, Marshal Pétain, was convicted of treason for his collaboration with the Nazis; although de Gaulle spared Pétain's life in respect for his age and his historic role in World War I, Pierre Laval was executed. No court applied the Nuremburg precedent to other conflicts until 1996 when the United Nations began war crimes trials for atrocities committed in the Bosnian War.

An international conference at San Francisco in 1945 adopted the Dumbarton Oaks plan and founded the United Nations, to replace the League of Nations (which had been so ineffectual in preventing World War II) and "to save succeeding generations from the scourge of war." Fifty-one countries (excluding the Axis powers) committed themselves to the idea of "collective security." The UN Charter created a General Assembly, to represent all countries and to debate international issues. Primary responsibility for keeping

◆ DOCUMENT 29.3 ◆

The Charter of the Nuremberg Tribunal (1945)

The following acts, or any of them, are crimes coming within the jurisdiction of the Tribunal for which there shall be individual responsibility:

(a) **Crimes against peace.** Namely, planning, preparation, initiation, or waging of a war of aggression or a war in violation of international treaties, agreements, or assurances, or participation in a common plan or conspiracy for the accomplishment of any of the foregoing.

(b) **War crimes.** Namely, violations of the laws or customs of war. Such violations shall include, but not be limited to, murder, ill treatment, or deportation to slave labor or for any other purpose of civilian population of or in occupied territory, murder or ill treatment of prisoners of war or persons on the seas, killing of hostages, plunder of public or private property, wanton destruction of cities, towns, or villages, or devastation not justified by military necessity.

(c) **Crimes against humanity.** Namely, murder, extermination, enslavement, deportation, and other inhumane acts committed against any civilian population before or during the war or persecutions on political, racial, or religious grounds in execution of or in connection with any crime within the jurisdiction of the Tribunal, whether or not in violation of the domestic law of the country where perpetrated . . .

The fact that the defendant acted pursuant to order of his government or of a superior shall not free him from responsibility but may be considered in mitigation of punishment if the Tribunal determines that justice so requires.

Potsdam Protocol, Article 6. In U.S. Department of State, *Bulletin*, 13:320 (August 12, 1945): 224.

the peace, however, was given to a Security Council with five permanent members (the United States, the USSR, Britain, France, and China) and six elected members. The Security Council chose a secretary-general, the chief administrative officer of the UN who could bring issues to the council but had little power to act. Many UN bodies were subsequently created, be-

◆ DOCUMENT 29.4 ◆

The Universal Declaration of Human Rights, 1948

Preamble

Whereas recognition of the inherent dignity and of the equal and inalienable rights of all members of the human family in the foundation of freedom, justice, and peace in the world,

Whereas disregard and contempt for human rights have resulted in barbarous acts which have outraged the conscience of mankind. . . .

Now, therefore, the General Assembly *proclaims this universal declaration of human rights* as a common standard of achievement for all peoples and all nations. . . .

Article 1. All human beings are born free and equal in dignity and rights. They are endowed with reason and conscience and should act towards one another in a spirit of brotherhood.

Article 2. Everyone is entitled to all the rights and freedoms set forth in this Declaration, without distinction of any kind, such as race, color, sex, language, religion, political or other opinion, national or social origin, property, birth, or other status. . . .

Article 3. Everyone has the right to life, liberty and security of person.

Article 4. No one shall be held in slavery or servitude. . . .

Article 5. No one shall be subjected to torture or cruel, inhuman or degrading treatment or punishment.

Article 6. Everyone has the right to recognition everywhere as a person before the law.

Article 7. All are equal before the law and are entitled without discrimination to equal protection.

Brownlie, Ian, ed. *Basic Documents of Human Rights.* Oxford: Clarendon, 1992.

---

ginning with an International Court of Justice. The charter of the UN had tried to launch the postwar era on a positive note, and this led to the adoption in 1948 of the Universal Declaration of Rights, the first effort in history to state minimal human rights for the world (see document 29.4).

CHAPTER **30**

THE SOCIAL AND ECONOMIC STRUCTURE
OF CONTEMPORARY EUROPE

CHAPTER OUTLINE

The twentieth century opened with both the economic structures and the social structures of Europe in the middle of a continuing historic change. Chapter 30 surveys these changes, beginning with a study of the population of Europe—one of the most important indicators of socioeconomic change since the middle of the eighteenth century. The chapter shows how the population growth of the previous two centuries continued but slowed greatly by the end of the twentieth century. It also looks at continuing urbanization, a trend that made Europe a predominantly urban civilization. The study of population also explains how Europe changed from a society that lost millions of emigrants in 1900 to a society attracting millions of immigrants.

The twentieth century began with a mixed economy of agriculture and industry, in which industrialization was the dominant trend. Agriculture steadily shrank as a segment of the European economy until it employed less than 10 percent of the population of western Europe at the end of the century. The triumph of the industrial economy did not last long, however, as a third sector of the economy—the service sector—became dominant. The chapter traces some of the implications of these changes, such as the shifting role of the young, the elderly, and women in the economy.

Chapter 30 concludes with a look at social changes. It explains how the vital revolution of modern history accelerated, reducing the mortality rate so much that the average life expectancy of Europeans grew from forty-five years in 1900 to seventy-five years in 1990. It also examines changes in the family, such as earlier marriage, smaller family size, and divorce. To explain these changes, the chapter considers the controversial history of birth control and abortion.

	TABLE 30.1		
The Growth of European Population, 1700–1990			
Country	Estimated population in 1700 (in millions)	Census population c. 1900 (in millions)	Census population c. 1990 (in millions)
France	19.3	38.5	57.7
Germany	13.5	56.4	81.1
Italy	13.0	32.5	57.8
Spain	7.5	18.6	39.1
Britain	6.4	37.0	58.0
Russia	16.0	126.4	149.0
Europe	110	423	501

The Population of Twentieth-Century Europe

At the beginning of the modern era in the early eighteenth century, Europe had an estimated population of slightly more than 100 million persons. By the late twentieth century, Europe numbered more than 500 million inhabitants—approximately twice the population of the United States. Most of that population growth came during the population explosion that began in the mid-eighteenth century and continued during the nineteenth century. In 1900 the population of Europe stood at 423 million, meaning that three-fourths of Europe's modern growth had occurred before the twentieth century (see table 30.1). In the late twentieth century, the rate of growth began to drop sharply, although the full impact of that trend will not be seen until the early twenty-first century (because demographic totals are often seen a generation after the start of a trend).

The population history of the major states of Europe underscores modern political history. In 1700 France possessed a great demographic advantage over all of its rivals in western and central Europe; France was nearly 50 percent larger than all German states added together and three times as populous as Great Britain. By the start of the twentieth century, France had less than three-fourths of the population of unified Germany and approximately the same population as Britain. The population explosion had quadrupled Germany and quintupled Britain while not quite doubling the population of France. The reunified Germany of 1990 remains the largest state in the European Union (EU) with a population of eighty-one million; Britain, France, and Italy each number approximately fifty-eight million, slightly more than 70 percent of the size of Germany. In the 1980s and 1990s, however, birthrates in Europe fell precipitously—which demographers are calling a "baby bust"—meaning that these relationships will be changed in the early twenty-first century. The birthrate in Germany dropped below a level that would sustain the same population total (demographers use a rate of 2.1 children per woman), so Germany is expected to be smaller in 2025 than in 2000, whereas France will grow slightly. Such trends raise complex questions about the balance of power within Europe and the continued preeminence of Europe as a center of world power. (Will smaller populations be an advantage or a disadvantage?)

The European population explosion of the eighteenth and nineteenth centuries shaped the important trend of urbanization. During the eighteenth century, Europe had been a rural society, with the vast majority of the population living on farms and in small villages. By 1850 Britain had become the first country in history to have the majority of its population living in cities. Although much of Europe still remained rural in 1900, nineteenth-century Europe had become an urban civilization. Population migration from agricultural communities had made London and Paris the largest cities on Earth, and it had created dozens of large cities from small towns (see illustration 30.1).

Illustration 30.1

/// **Urbanization.** The concentration of population in large metropolitan regions, which had begun in late eighteenth-century Britain and had characterized many regions in the nineteenth century, continued throughout the twentieth century. At the start of the century, Europe contained half a dozen congested cities of more than one million population. This 1910 photograph of central London shows what *congested* meant before the automobile dominated cities.

The twentieth century saw the trend toward urbanization continue. By 1950 the majority of the population of western and central Europe lived in cities. Metropolitan Paris (the region containing the city and its suburbs) quadrupled in size during the twentieth century, growing from 2.3 million people in 1900 to 8.7 million in 1991. Yet Paris is far from the most dramatic example. Milan grew nearly tenfold, from 493,000 in 1900 to 4.7 million in 1991; Moscow, center of the post–World War II communist empire, went from less than 1 million to more than 10 million (see table 30.2).

Despite the dramatic urbanization seen in these figures, European growth was moderate compared with the global trend. No longer are London and Paris the largest cities on Earth; London ranked seventeenth in 1991, Paris nineteenth. Tokyo, Mexico City, São Paulo, and Seoul are nearly twice the size of London or Paris. No European city (and only one American city, New York) ranks in the world's ten largest cities. In many ways, the European city representative of global trends is Athens, which has exploded from a national capital of 111,000 in 1900 to a rambling metropolitan region of 3.7 million in 1991, nearly 50 percent of the Greek population. (By comparison, Paris contains 15 percent of the population of France.)

Twentieth-century European urbanization, like so many historic patterns, has not been the same in western and eastern Europe. On the eve of World War II, the population of Romania was still 82 percent rural, a figure more typical of the eighteenth century in western or central Europe. As late as 1970, Hungary and Romania remained less than 50 percent urban. Even in 1985 Albania, Yugoslavia, and Romania were still less than 50 percent.

Urbanization has not been the only important trend in European population migration. The twentieth century began with Europe losing millions of people through emigration to other parts of the world. Between 1871 and 1914, Sweden lost 1.5 million emigrants—chiefly to the United States—which accounted for more than one-third of the population of Sweden in 1870. Over that same time period, more than 3.2 million people (chiefly Irish) left Great Britain; the richest state in the world lost nearly 8 percent of its 1901 population to emigration. More than 2 million people (chiefly Jews) fled Russia during the revolution of 1905 and its aftermath. Italian population loss was perhaps the most striking. In the early 1880s Italy lost a million people every five years; by the early 1890s Italy was losing a million people every three years; and in the first decade of the twentieth century, a million more people left Italy every eighteen months. By 1913 the rate of Italian exiles had reached nearly 900,000 per year. This meant that Italy was losing 2.5 percent of its total population every year, roughly the equivalent to losing the entire population of Rome (542,000), Venice (161,000), and Florence (135,000) annually.

The twentieth century thus began with Europe losing 1.3 million people per year. Some fled to avoid religious persecution, others to avoid conscription into

❦ TABLE 30.2 ❦
The Growth of European Cities, 1900–91

The data reflect the total metropolitan region.

City	1991 population (in millions)	1991 population density per square mile
Moscow	10.4	27,562
London	9.8	10,429
Paris	8.7	20,185
Essen	7.5	10,585
Milan	4.7	13,806
St. Petersburg	4.7	33,614
Madrid	4.5	68,385
Barcelona	4.2	48,584
Manchester	3.8	11,287
Athens	3.5	30,237
Rome	3.0	43,949
Berlin	3.0	11,026
Naples	3.0	48,032
Kiev	2.8	45,095
Lisbon	2.4	n.a.
Vienna	2.3	n.a.
Budapest	2.3	16,691

Source: All 1991 data from U.S. Department of Commerce calculations, reprinted in *The World Almanac and Book of Facts 1993* (Mahwah, N.J.: World Almanac Books, 1992), p. 818.

n.a. = Not available.

❦ TABLE 30.3 ❦
Commonwealth Immigration into Britain

Annual net commonwealth immigration

Year	West Indies	India	Pakistan and Bangladesh
1960	49,700	5,900	2,500
1961	66,300	23,750	25,100
1962	35,041	22,100	24,943
January–June	31,800	19,050	25,080
July–December	3,241	3,050	−137
1972	1,176	3,634	−3,515

Source: Adapted from data in David Butler and Anne Sloman, eds., *British Political Facts, 1900–1975*, 4th ed. (London: Macmillan, 1975), p. 268.

monarchical armies, but most emigrants left for greater economic opportunities. Millions of Europeans lived in such poverty in 1900 that flight to the Americas, Australia, or the scattered corners of European empires was preferable to hunger at home. World War I nearly stopped European emigration, and in the 1920s many states (led by the United States) adopted much stricter policies on accepting immigrants. Although emigration increased during some crises—especially Germans during the 1930s and many nations in the decade following World War II—by the end of the century, Europe's migration pattern had completely reversed the pattern of 1900. Millions of non-Europeans sought to immigrate to Europe because economic opportunity was much greater there.

Much of the late twentieth-century immigration into Europe has its origins in the history of European colonial empires and in the age of decolonization that followed World War II. The end of empire forced imperialist governments to reintegrate European-born colonists and their descendants; the Franco-Algerian War of 1954–62, for example, led more than one million *pieds noirs* (French colonists in Algeria) to return to France in the 1960s. In many cases, the indigenous population of European colonies had the legal right to migrate to the imperial state or had legal preference in normal immigration. For example, after the Dutch East Indies won their independence as Indonesia in 1949, the Netherlands absorbed 300,000 immigrants from their former colony. The independence of the *maghreb* (the Arabic term for north Africa—Morocco, Algeria, and Tunisia) from France resulted in an influx of millions of north Africans starting in the late 1960s and peaking in the 1980s. Until strict—and often racially motivated—immigration controls were adopted by Britain in mid-1962, hundreds of thousands of south Asians (chiefly from India and Pakistan) and blacks from the West Indies migrated to Britain (see table 30.3). These migrations of non-Europeans into Europe reversed long-standing patterns of population movement; in the case of Britain, for example, the largest group of immigrants had remained Irish through the 1960s.

France provides a dramatic illustration of this transformation of European population. By 1982 immigrants formed nearly 7 percent of the population of France; counting the families of immigrant workers, France was more than 8 percent immigrant. At the start of the twentieth century, less than 3 percent of the population of France was foreign-born, and nearly 90 percent of the immigrants came from Europe—chiefly Belgians and Italians who found work across the border. By the end of the century, immigration had quadrupled and most French immigrants were Algerians (22 percent) and Moroccans (12 percent). Nearly half of all French immigrants came from Africa; meanwhile, Italian and Belgian immigration into France fell to less than one-sixth of its previous rate. The wars and revolutions of twentieth-century Europe also shifted millions of people across national frontiers, such as the repatriation of 1.2 million Greeks from Turkey after World War I, the migration of 200,000 Magyars from Transylvania to Hungary in the 1920s, or the flight and expulsion of nearly 7.5 million Germans from Eastern Europe after World War II. But none of these migrations changed Europe as profoundly as the arrival of millions of non-Europeans as a result of decolonization.

Another important form of migration accompanied European prosperity in the late twentieth century. The United Nations estimated in 1973 that the Common Market states plus Austria, Norway, Sweden, and Switzerland included 7.5 million foreign workers. West Germany, for example, held 2.6 million "guest workers" (*Gastarbeiter*) who constituted 12 percent of the German labor force. Nearly 20 percent of those workers came from Turkey, a figure that surpassed one-third by the late 1980s. The Turkish population of Germany passed two million in the 1990s. Although their guest-worker status (and an extremely strict German citizenship law of 1913) denied them the rights of immigrants, a study in 1977 found that one-fourth of all German guest workers had resided there for at least a decade. The foreign-born population of Germany again increased dramatically after the collapse of the Soviet bloc in 1989. Tens of thousands of ethnic Germans returned (claiming citizenship under the 1913 law), hundreds of thousands of refugees arrived (for example, 320,000 Bosnians fled the Yugoslav War), and tens of thousands of Soviet Jews were granted residence. These trends, along with the strict laws and a plummeting birthrate, combined in the late 1990s to create a situation in which more than 20 percent of the babies born in Germany were born to non-Germans.

The immigration trends of the late twentieth century led to tense political situations in many European countries. Most European states had defined their identity in images shaped by nineteenth-century nationalism: A shared language, religion, culture, and history created a nation-state. Many states now confronted the reality of cultural diversity.

TABLE 30.4

The Decline of Agricultural Employment, 1920–60

Country	Percentage of labor force engaged in agriculture		
	c. 1910–11:	c. 1930–31:	c. 1960–61:
Austria	53.1	31.7	18.4
Britain	8.6	6.0	3.6
France	41.0	35.6	20.0
Germany	37.8	29.0	13.4 (West)
Ireland	42.9	25.3 (Northern)	13.0 (Northern)
		52.1 (republic)	48.6 (republic)
Italy	55.4	35.5	29.0
Russia			23.5

Source: Calculated from tables in B. R. Mitchell, *European Historical Statistics, 1750–1970* (London: Macmillan, 1975), pp. 153–63.

Economic Structures: The Decline of Agriculture

Agriculture dominated the economy of eighteenth-century Europe but began to lose that preeminence during the industrialization. Nineteenth-century industrialization, however, should not obscure the persistence of agricultural society. Just as the European political history of 1900 depicts the progress of democracy as well as the persistence of monarchical government and aristocratic privilege, the European economic history of 1900 must show the progress of industry alongside a surviving agricultural society. In Eastern Europe, where industrialization had not yet advanced greatly, the huge majority of the population was still engaged in agriculture. In France, a major industrial power, less than one-third of the labor force worked in industrial occupations. Even Germany, the greatest industrial power-house of the continent, had less than half of its population engaged in the industrial workforce (see table 30.4).

Despite the strength of agricultural society at the beginning of the twentieth century, a trend was clear: Agriculture was steadily employing fewer people, producing a smaller share of the gross national product (GNP). On the eve of the First World War, many states, including Austria and Italy, still found the majority of their population on the farm. By 1930 comparatively few regions—such as Ireland, eastern Europe, and the Balkans—still had such rural economies. Some of those areas remained strongly agricultural long after World War II. In Ireland, nearly 50 percent of the population was engaged in agriculture as late as 1960, but the European trend was clear: In Russia, where 75 percent of the population had been employed in agriculture at the beginning of the century, less than 25 percent were employed there by 1960; in Britain, a scant 3.6 percent of the population lived by agriculture in 1960.

Although agriculture was no longer at the center of the European economy and employed comparatively few people, late twentieth-century European agriculture was neither weak nor unimportant. In France, where the agricultural economy was especially persistent, peasant farmers still formed 35 percent of the labor force at the end of World War II, declining to 13 percent in 1970 and to 8 percent in 1980. Three million people left French farming between 1945 and 1980, but French agricultural production increased during that period, because of modern machinery and farming methods. When 35 percent of the French labor force was engaged in farming, fewer than 30,000 tractors were in use; by 1967, there were more than 1.1 million. With less than 10 percent of the population engaged in agriculture in the 1980s, France was nonetheless the second largest food exporter in the world.

Continuing Industrialization

The decline of an agriculture-dominated economy in twentieth-century Europe corresponded to continuing industrialization. Most of Europe was highly industrialized by the late twentieth century, even if compared with the most advanced economies of 1900. In 1980, for example, industrial output in Czechoslovakia, Poland, or Spain far exceeded the British standard of 1900; Italian output more than tripled that standard.

The data on industrialization also reveal the strength of the European great powers. The British, who had the dominant economy of 1900, continued to expand their industrial output during the twentieth century despite the century's multiple catastrophes. British industrialization increased by 27 percent from 1900 to the eve of World War I; by more than one-third from 1900 to 1928, despite the consequences of World War I; by more than three-fourths from 1900 to 1938, despite the Great Depression of the 1930s; by more than double between 1900 and 1953, despite World War II; and by more than fourfold by the late twentieth cen-

tury. Germany, which had been challenging British leadership in 1900, surpassed British output before World War I and remained the dominant industrial economy in Europe until World War II. Although the divided and devastated Germany fell behind in the years following World War II, by 1963 West German industrial output matched the British and within a decade far exceeded it; and the combined output of West and East Germany in the 1980s doubled British production. France, whose industrial output had never approached British levels during the nineteenth century, did not reach the Anglo-German levels of 1900 until the mid-1950s. A French industrial resurgence after 1960, however, brought France close to British levels: French industrial output had stood at 41 percent of British output at the beginning of World War II, but it reached 82 percent of British output in 1980. Italy achieved a comparable industrial boom expanding from 18 percent of Britain's production in 1913 to 72 percent in 1980. Put differently, Britain had begun the nineteenth century with a dominant lead in European industrial production, and then Britain and Germany had begun the twentieth century with such dominance, but by the end of the twentieth century, many European states had industrialized to competitive levels with Britain and Germany (see table 30.5).

Industrial data also underscore the change in European political and military power during the twentieth century. Imperial Russian industrialization had been meager before World War I; in the late 1920s the USSR still managed only 53 percent of British output, or 46 percent of German output. Before the death of Stalin in 1953, however, the Soviet Union had significantly surpassed the industrial production of either Britain or West Germany; by 1963 Soviet output was more than Britain and Germany combined, and by 1980 it nearly equaled Britain, Germany, France, and Italy combined.

Similar economic data provide a different perspective if historians seek to illustrate the standard of living instead of political and military power. Combining agricultural and industrial output into a figure for gross national product and then considering population to determine the GNP per capita, neither the Soviet Union nor the west European powers can match the accomplishment of Sweden. Although the Swedes had only 52 percent of the per capita GNP in Britain at the start of the twentieth century, they had surpassed the British by 1950 (partly by avoiding participation in the world wars) and had become 20 percent more prosperous than Britain and 17 percent more prosperous than West Germany in 1980.

❧ TABLE 30.5 ❧

The Growth of European Industrial Output, 1913–80

	Percentage of British industrial output in 1900			
Country	1913	1938	1953	1980
Britain	127	181	258	441
France	57	74	98	362
Germany	138	214	224	747
West Germany			180	590
East Germany			44	157
Italy	23	46	71	319
Spain	11	14	22	156
Sweden	9	21	28	83
Soviet Union	n.a.	152	328	1630

Source: Adapted from data in Paul Bairoch, "International Industrialization Levels from 1750 to 1980," *Journal of European Economic History*, 11 (1982), pp. 299, 331; and Gerold Ambrosius and William H. Hubbard, *A Social and Economic History of Twentieth Century Europe* (Cambridge, Mass.: Harvard University Press, 1989), p. 187.

n.a. = Not available

The economic evolution of the twentieth century also requires a global perspective on European industrial might. On the eve of World War I, nearly 58 percent of the world's total industrial production came from Europe, with Britain holding a global share of 14 percent and Germany 15 percent. Europe still produced more than 50 percent of the world's industrial output on the eve of World War II. By 1980 European production had fallen to 44 percent, and Japanese production (9.1 percent) nearly equaled British (4.0 percent) and German production (5.3 percent) combined. The United States, which represented 32 percent of global production in 1913, still accounted for 31.5 percent in 1980, although that stable share is distorted by the post–World War II rise to nearly 45 percent of global production (1953) while Europe had still not recovered from wartime devastation.

The relative decline in European industrial output in the late twentieth century raises several related issues. The European economy came to be dominated by a new sector, neither industrial nor agricultural. In the course of this transition to a postindustrial economy, Europe (and the United States) deindustrialized their economies to a significant degree, allowing uncompetitive industries to close and many forms of traditional industrial production to go overseas (especially to Asian countries) where production costs (especially labor) were much lower. By the 1990s many industrial and manufacturing sectors (including such traditional measures of economic might as steel and textiles) existed in which Western countries could import goods cheaper than manufacturing them. No image of the European economy of 2000 would have been more startling to Europeans of 1900 than the contrast between the powerful look of the smokestacks of heavy industry and the stark reality of deindustrialization (see illustration 30.2).

The Service Economy

By the end of the nineteenth century, the focus on industrial production no longer presented a complete picture of European economies and social structures. A third sector of the economy had emerged, and by the second half of the twentieth century it had grown to be as important as industrial employment. By 1980 this third sector, called the service sector, dominated the economy of Western Europe (see table 30.6). In 1910 industry employed 41 percent of the population compared with 30 percent for agriculture. In 1980 the service economy employed 55 percent of the labor force of Western Europe while industry had declined to 39 percent and agriculture took only 6 percent. In 1910 Europeans had expected a continually expanding industrialization; in 1980 Europe had a postindustrial economy. The service sector did not dominate any East European economy at the time of the revolutions of

Illustration 30.2

/// **The Industrial Economy.** At the beginning of the twentieth century, heavy industry was the source of a nation's power and wealth. This view (above) of the Krupp Works at Essen in 1912 was a fair representation of the great strength of the German economy, and the dream of the future for less developed economies.

At the end of the twentieth century, heavy industry was in sharp decline throughout the Western world, and many of the old centers of industrial and manufacturing wealth had experienced the shock of deindustrialization and unemployment. This image (left) of late twentieth-century deindustrialization shows Bristol in the 1960s.

1989, although East Germany (41 percent service to 49 percent industry) and Czechoslovakia (41 percent service to 48 percent industry) were drawing close.

The service sector, also called the tertiary sector, had always existed; it had chiefly been a relatively small, but necessary, companion to the industrial economy. The simplest distinction between industrial employment and service employment is that the former produces material goods and the latter produces customer services. Industrial employment includes most

❧ TABLE 30.6 ❧

The Socioeconomic Structure of Twentieth-Century Europe

	Percentage of working population													
Country	1910			1930			1950			1960			1980		
	Ag.	Ind.	Ser.	Ag.	Ind.	Ser.	Ag.	Ind.	Ser.	Ag.	Ind.	Ser.	Ag.	Ind.	Ser.
Britain	9	52	40	6	46	48	5	49	46	4	48	48	3	42	56
France	41	33	26	36	33	31	27	36	37	22	39	39	8	39	53
Germany	37	41	22	29	40	31	23	43	38	14	48	38	4	46	50
Greece	50	16	34	54	16	30	51	21	28	56	20	24	37	28	35
Italy	55	27	18	47	31	22	42	32	26	31	40	29	11	45	44
Poland	77	9	14	66	17	17	54	26	20	48	29	23	31	39	30
Sweden	49	32	19	39	36	25	21	41	38	14	45	41	5	34	61

Note: Data for Greece and Poland for 1910 are post–World War I data, c. 1920. Data for Germany for 1950, 1960, and 1980 are for West Germany only.

Ag. = Agriculture; Ind. = Industry; Ser. = Service.

jobs in fields such as manufacturing, heavy industry, mining, construction, and energy. It is typically manual labor—blue-collar work—paid by hourly or daily wages. The service sector has long included such smaller categories as banking and insurance, commerce and trade, journalism and communications, and a growing list of public employees. Employment in the service sector often requires more education and rarely requires physical labor; it is usually white-collar work performed in offices (see illustration 30.3). Service employees typically (but not universally) receive an annual or monthly salary, however many hours they work, frequently adding up to better total compensation.

One of the areas of most rapid growth in the service economy of the twentieth century has been government employment. This category is much larger than the image of anonymous bureaucrats filling the offices of a national capital. Millions of public school teachers or postal workers are also employees of the tertiary sector. The French Ministry of Education employed 121,000 people in 1896 and more than 1 million people in 1984; in the same years, the French Ministry of Posts grew from 70,000 workers to 513,000. Thus, in a century during which the population of France increased by less than 44 percent, employees in one ministry increased by 768 percent and in another by 639 percent. The police, the judicial system, and—a natural consequence of taxing to finance all of the others—the Ministry of Finance also grew much faster than population did.

The service sector was already an important part of the European economy at the start of the twentieth century, but it was clearly tertiary. In 1910, for example, 41 percent of German labor was employed in industry, 37 percent in agriculture, and 22 percent in service. The service sector accounted for 26 percent of employment in France and only 18 percent of employment in Italy that year. European employment data for 1930 show that different economies coexisted in Europe: Poland remained a traditional, rural economy with 66 percent of the population employed in agriculture; Germany remained a strongly industrial economy, with 40 percent of employment there, 29 percent in agriculture, and 31 percent in service; Britain revealed the emerging pattern of the twentieth-century economy with only 6 percent of labor in agriculture and slightly more workers in the service sector (48 percent) than the industrial (46 percent).

The growth of the tertiary economy chiefly occurred after World War II. By 1980, 61 percent of all workers in Sweden were in the service sector. More than 50 percent of employment in Britain, France, and Germany were in service. Meanwhile agricultural employment had fallen to less than 10 percent of the labor force in Britain (3 percent), Germany (4 percent), Sweden (5 percent), France (8 percent), and Austria (9 percent). Thus, industrial employment still remained important in all European economies, but nowhere did it account for a majority of the labor force, as it had in Britain in 1910 (52 percent). In some

Illustration 30.3

The Service Economy. The biggest change in Western economies during the twentieth century was the growth of a third sector of the economy, neither agricultural nor industrial, which became the dominant sector of European economies after World War II. This service economy depicted itself—as in this photograph from the early days of the computer revolution in the 1960s—as the modern and efficient sector of the economy, as compared with the smokestack economy of heavy industry and large factories. (Note that men work with the office computer at this date.)

In 1967 the French director Jacques Tati made a film (part of the service economy) about the cold, impersonal nature of life in the service economy. The story of *Playtime* involves visitors to Paris who see only the business and office world, encountering the beautiful, historic Paris only through pictures on post cards. In this scene, Tati makes fun of the impersonal, labyrinthine office of cubicles.

economies, industrial employment was declining: In Britain it fell from 49 percent in 1950 to 42 percent in 1980; in Sweden, from 45 percent in 1960 to 34 percent in 1980.

Age, Gender, and the Labor Force

Economists who study the economic vitality of a society use an index called the participation rate to measure the volume and distribution of labor in an economy.

Changes in the components of the participation rate tell historians much about a changing society. The total participation rate merely counts all employed persons plus all part-time workers, expressed as a percentage of the population. As a healthy economy grows, so does the participation rate. This simple index provides economic historians with a long perspective on the twentieth century. In 1900 Europe had experienced a generation of internal peace and had a generally solid economy; the participation rate was high. Between

1910 and 1950 Europe was devastated by multiple catastrophes—World War I, the Russian Revolution, the Great Depression, the Spanish Civil War, World War II, the Holocaust—and European economies suffered terribly. The internal peace of the cold war and the economic miracle between 1950 and the Revolutions of 1989, however, overcame the catastrophes of the first half of the century to build a stronger economy. Economists claim that the prosperity of 1990 rests on a stronger economy than the prosperity of 1910 by showing that the participation rate had grown, despite the collapse of 1910–50, and by correlating participation with productivity.

This arcane tool of economic analysis is more interesting to historians who ask "Who is participating in the economy? Who is working and who is not?" Between 1870 and 1940, for example, age became a significant factor in the changing participation rate. Compulsory education laws subtracted millions of teenagers from the labor force, thereby reducing the participation rate. The economic role of older ages has also affected the participation rate. In 1900 few programs guaranteed a paid retirement, so many people remained in the labor force beyond age sixty-five, thereby keeping the participation rate higher. Put differently, the compulsory education laws and the welfare programs of the twentieth century have sharply changed the answer to the question "Who works?"

At the same time that the economic participation rate was being reduced by new social attitudes toward age, the labor movement succeeded in its long battle to reduce the workweek. Full-time employment in 1900 typically meant a six-day, fifty-five-hour workweek; many occupations still expected sixty to seventy-two hours per week. When European countries began to regulate the workweek, standards set in the 1920s were usually close to a forty-eight-hour week; only during the massive unemployment of the Great Depression of the 1930s did countries start to adopt the century-old labor dream of a forty-hour workweek. During the European prosperity of the late twentieth century, workers in many countries of the European Union (led by Belgium and Sweden) obtained workweeks of thirty-five to forty hours.

The twentieth-century labor movement also won paid vacations. Norway introduced the first paid vacations, guaranteeing all workers two weeks by a 1919 law. Several other Western countries—including Britain and France—adopted this concept in the 1930s. It became the universal standard in postwar Europe as well as the minimum standard, because France and the Scandinavian countries increased paid vacations to three weeks. After 1970 the same prosperity that allowed workweeks of less than forty hours provided minimum paid vacations of four weeks in EU countries, while the most progressive granted five or six weeks.

The consequence of this century of transforming traditional labor was to cut both its participation rate and its productivity rate. Economic historians estimate that the annual total number of hours worked by each individual worker has been cut in half. Despite all the changes that achieved this—won by the young, the elderly, and the labor movement—other factors were so dramatic that the total participation rate and total productivity increased. One final economic trend explains this apparent paradox: the growing, and changing, employment of women.

Throughout modern history, working women have been a large and essential part of the European economy, although not always in ways that were noted in economic statistics. In the household economy of the eighteenth century, women worked alongside men in farms or shops. In the family wage economy of the industrial era, women entered the wage-earning labor force and their numbers in economic statistics grew significantly. At the start of the twentieth century, women formed 30 percent to 35 percent of the salary and wage-earning labor force in western Europe. Those percentages did not shift dramatically for most of the twentieth century, although historical circumstances sometimes caused noteworthy trends. For example, much greater employment of women was evident during both world wars and for brief postwar periods when large numbers of men were lost. (In the USSR, the death rate in World War II so reduced the postwar labor pool that women remained employed at a high rate for the entire next generation.) The employment of women sometimes fell sharply as a consequence of conservative social policy based on the theory that women belonged in the home; Mussolini, for example, managed to reduce women's share of jobs from 32 percent in 1910 to 23 percent in 1930. Despite such secondary trends, the foremost trend was that the employment of women did not significantly change between 1910 and 1970 (see table 30.7). In the first two-thirds of the century, it rose just 3 percent in Britain and 2 percent in Sweden, while falling 3 percent in France and 6 percent in Italy.

In the last third of the twentieth century, the employment of women in western Europe changed significantly. Between 1970 and 1990 women went from 32 percent of the British labor force to 44 percent; that is,

TABLE 30.7

Woman in the European Labor Force, 1910–90

Country	Women as a percentage of total labor force				
	c. 1910	c. 1930	c. 1950	c. 1970	c. 1990
Britain	29.5	29.8	30.8	32.4	43.5
France	36.7	36.6	33.9	33.2	42.3
Germany	30.7	35.6	36.3	37.4	40.8
Italy	31.6	22.6	25.1	25.1	34.5
Sweden	27.8	31.0	26.4	29.8	47.8

Source: Compiled from data in B. R. Mitchell, *European Historical Statistics, 1750–1970* (London: Macmillan, 1975), pp. 153–63, and *The Information Please Almanac, Atlas, and Yearbook 1994* (Boston, Mass.: Houghton Mifflin, 1994), p. 136.

the number of women employed grew by more than one-third. The growth in the employment of women was equally dramatic in France and Italy, and it was very marked in Sweden, where women went from 30 percent of the labor force to 48 percent—meaning that the number of working women grew by more than 60 percent in one generation. This transformation of the labor market was most dramatic in regions where women previously had limited access to jobs. Women accounted for only 18 percent of the Greek labor force in 1961 and nearly doubled that share to 32 percent in a single decade. In Hungary, the employment of women nearly doubled between 1945 and 1980. As late as 1960, women provided 52 percent of all labor on Soviet collective farms and produced 76 percent of all medical doctors in the USSR. A generation later, in 1987, these numbers had declined to 43 percent of agricultural labor and 69 percent of physicians.

The high levels of the employment of women in the twentieth century are especially noteworthy because the two greatest job markets for women in the nineteenth century—domestic service and the textile industry—both collapsed. The role of textiles in west European industry shrank by 75 percent between 1901 and 1975. Nonetheless, the participation of women in the labor force increased, and the explanation involves several factors. The nineteenth-century and early twentieth-century economy had a limited variety of jobs available to women—typically jobs deemed similar to a woman's role in housework, as both domestic service and textile work illustrate. Much of the

explanation, therefore, is found in a new range of employment available to women. War work—demonstrating that women could effectively perform many jobs previously denied to them—was important in this trend but is insufficient to explain it, as the postwar demobilization of women suggests. The rise of the service economy was probably more important. Millions of new jobs were being created, without a tradition of being held by only one gender; so many new jobs were being created that the demand for workers virtually required the participation of women in the economy, especially in government and business offices. At the same time, demographic changes facilitated the participation of women. As the birthrate fell sharply, women spent far less of their lives in child care, thereby making them available for employment. At the same time that the service economy was booming and families were shrinking, a reinvigorated women's rights movement in the late twentieth century effectively advocated the equal treatment of women. This meant that women were not only entering new types of jobs, but they also were obtaining more jobs requiring skill or education. It did not mean, however, that women acquired economic equality in the late twentieth century; women were still typically concentrated in lower-level positions, earning lower wages than men.

The Vital Revolution of the Twentieth Century: Mortality and Life Expectancy

The twentieth century witnessed dramatic demographic changes, continuing the vital revolution that began in the eighteenth century and flourished during the nineteenth century. None of these changes was more important for understanding life in the modern world than the falling death rate and the increase in life expectancy. In 1900 many regions of Europe—from Spain in the west to Poland in the east—had an annual death rate of twenty-five to thirty deaths per thousand population (and some regions and subcultures had even higher rates). In the worst areas, including much of Russia, the rate was normally greater than thirty per thousand. In the healthiest areas of western and northern Europe, mortality generally ranged between fifteen and twenty per thousand. By the 1930s, however, the death rate had fallen below twenty per thousand in all corners of the continent; by the 1960s many countries were reporting mortality figures below ten per thousand (see table 30.8).

TABLE 30.8

The Twentieth-Century Decline in Death Rates

Death rates per 1,000 population

Country	1910	1930	1960	1990
England	13.8	12.0	11.8	11.2
France	18.2	15.7	11.2	9.3
Germany	16.6	11.0	11.4	11.2
Italy	19.2	14.1	11.7	9.4
Russia	28.2	17.8	7.2	16.0
Spain	22.5	16.6	8.7	8.5
Sweden	13.9	11.6	10.0	11.0
United States	14.7	11.3	9.3	8.6

Source: B. R. Mitchell, *European Historical Statistics, 1750–1970* (London: Macmillan, 1975), pp. 127–32; B. R. Mitchell, *The Fontana Economic History of Europe: Statistical Appendix, 1920–1970* (London: Collins, 1974), pp. 28–34; *The World Almanac and Book of Facts 1995,* (Mahwah, N.J.: World Almanac Books, 1994), pp. 740–839, 959; *Information Please Almanac, Atlas, and Yearbook 1994* (Boston, Mass.: Houghton Mifflin, 1994), p. 135; U.S. Bureau of the Census, *Historical Statistics of the United States* (Washington, D.C.: Government Printing Office, 1960), p. 28.

TABLE 30.9

The Twentieth-Century Decline in Infant Mortality

Deaths of Infants under one year old, per 1,000 live births

Country	1900	1950	1990
England	154	30	7
France	160	52	7
Germany	229	55 (West)	7
		72 (East)	
Italy	174	64	8
Poland	a	108	13
Russia	252	81	27
Sweden	99	21	6

Source: B. R. Mitchell, *European Historical Statistics, 1750–1970* (London: Macmillan, 1975), pp. 127–32; B. R. Mitchell, *The Fontana Economic History of Europe: Statistical Appendix, 1920–1970* (London: Collins, 1974), pp. 28–34; *The World Almanac and Book of Facts 1995* (Mahwah, N.J.: World Almanac Books, 1994), pp. 740–839, 959; *The World Almanac and Book of Facts 1997* (Mahwah, N.J.: World Almanac Books, 1996), p. 964; *Information Please Almanac, Atlas and Yearbook 1994* (Boston, Mass.: Houghton Mifflin, 1994), p. 135.

n.a. = Not available.

The vital revolution of modern European history chiefly rested upon a decline in infant mortality, and that trend accelerated dramatically in the twentieth century (see table 30.9). In 1900 Europeans expected at least 15 percent of newborn children to die within the first year of life. In prosperous Germany, the rate for infant mortality was 23 percent; in Russia, more than 25 percent. As late as the 1920s, advanced countries such as France (12 percent) and Germany (13 percent) still had high rates. Between 1920 and 1950, the infant death rate was cut in half, then halved again between 1950 and 1970, and finally halved once more between 1970 and 1990. Thus, the century witnessed the infant mortality rate in England fall from 15.4 percent to 0.7 percent, and in Germany from 22.9 percent to 0.7 percent.

The sharp decline in infant mortality explains much, but not all, of the decline in death rates. The vital revolution of the twentieth century also saw the population cohort aged sixty-five years or older grow steadily. The combination of better diet and nutrition, better sanitation and public health standards, and greatly improved medical knowledge and health care delivery systems improved prospects for all. The consequence was a remarkable increase in life expectancy. In Great Britain in 1901—in the most prosperous society in Europe—a newborn baby boy had a life expectancy of slightly more than forty-five years. A century later, the estimated life expectancy of a newborn had grown to more than seventy-five years, an additional thirty years of life or a 67 percent increase in expectation. If the twenty-first century continues similar wonders, centenarians could become commonplace, perhaps the expectancy at birth. Even without such developments, increased life expectancy has created a significantly older society. In 1910 only 6–7 percent of the population of Europe was age sixty-five or older; in the 1980s western and northern Europe had 12 percent to 17 percent of the population in that age cohort.

The Life Cycle: Marriage and Divorce

Although many of the demographic trends of modern history find their explanation in subjects such as diet or disease, some important explanations must come from human behavior rooted in institutions such as marriage and the family. Both institutions changed significantly during the twentieth century.

During the eighteenth and nineteenth centuries, economic restraints created a trend toward marriage at a later age. Couples did not marry without a steady job or a plot of land; many waited until they had accumulated savings or property. By the start of the twentieth century, the average age at which British men married had passed twenty-six years. For Irish men, the age was past thirty. Women in both societies married at a slightly younger age. The trend toward later marriage continued into the twentieth century, and on the eve of World War I British men were typically marrying at twenty-seven or twenty-eight. In the postwar years, however, that trend began to change, and age at marriage began to fall. By the 1960s British men were marrying a full three years younger, at twenty-four or twenty-five; British women at twenty-two or twenty-three. In western Europe only 2 or 3 percent or marriages involved teenaged women. In Belarus, however, 26 percent of all marriages involved teenaged girls and 3 percent involved girls fifteen or younger. Poland reported 22 percent and Bulgaria 38 percent of all marriages involved teenaged girls.

If the trend toward younger ages at marriage in western Europe, and very young marriages in the east, had appeared in an earlier century, it would have had a significant impact on European population because the number of childbearing years within marriage would have increased. At the start of the twentieth century, the average woman had fourteen to fifteen childbearing years within marriage. By the 1980s, however, that number had fallen below five years, despite younger marriages. Much of the explanation for this phenomenon has come from the restriction of childbearing years through the use of artificial birth control. Another part of the explanation is that the earlier marriages in the twentieth century were not necessarily longer marriages because divorce often truncated marriages during the childbearing years.

In 1900 divorce remained illegal in some countries (such as Italy and Spain), difficult to obtain in some (such as Britain), and only recently adopted in others (such as France). As twentieth-century society accepted divorce, it witnessed both the spreading legalization of divorce and the exponential growth of the rate at which marriages were dissolved (see table 30.10). Even the most devoutly Catholic states of Europe accepted divorce by the end of the century. Public support in a referendum of 1970 led to the legalization of divorce in Italy, although the law there remains cautious and requires a three-year separation before a divorce is granted. The Spanish republic introduced divorce in

TABLE 30.10
Divorce in Europe, 1910–90

Country	Number of divorces in 1910	Number of divorces in 1990	Divorces as a percentage of marriages (1990)
Britain	701	165,700	41
France	15,125	106,096	31
Germany	13,008	128,729	30
Italy	0	30,778	8
Russia	n.a.	n.a.	42
Sweden	n.a.	n.a.	44

Source: Priscilla Robertson, *An Experience of Women*, (Philadelphia, Pa.: Temple University Press, 1982), p. 250; Roderick Phillips, *Untying the Knot: A Short History of Divorce* (Cambridge: Cambridge University Press, 1991), pp. 185–86; *The Economist*, December 25, 1993; Martha Cronin and Julia Nasser, "Number of Marriages and Divorces in E.C. Countries," *Europe* (June 1992), p. 4; *Information Please Almanac, Atlas, and Yearbook 1994* (Boston, Mass.: Houghton Mifflin, 1994), p. 839.

n.a. = Not available

1932, but it remained legal in Spain only until Franco revoked it in 1938. Divorce was not reinstituted there until 1981, but Spain then adopted a liberal divorce law. The last Western nation to prohibit divorce was Ireland, where the constitution expressly banned it; a referendum in 1995—the closest vote in Ireland's history—amended the constitution to permit divorce. In other countries, the divorce rate grew rapidly. By 1990, 30 percent of marriages ended in divorce in France and Germany, and more than 40 percent were dissolved in Britain, Denmark, Russia, and Sweden. The trend was vivid in post–World War II Britain: In 1950, there were 11.5 marriages and 0.4 divorces per one thousand population, a marriage to divorce ratio of 29-to-1; that ratio steadily fell to 9-to-1 in 1960 and to less than 3-to-1 in 1980. Approximately one-fourth of British divorces ended marriages before they had lasted five years, and the majority of divorces ended marriages shorter than ten years. Divorce thus significantly reduced childbearing to less than fifteen years within marriage.

Childbirth, Birth Control, and Abortion

Despite the pattern of earlier marriages, the birthrate also fell sharply during the twentieth century (see table 30.11). The German birth rate of 28.2 births per thousand population in 1910 dropped to 11.4 per thousand

TABLE 30.11

The Decline in European Birthrates, 1910–90

Country	Birth rates per 1,000 population			
	1910	1930	1960	1990
England	24.2	15.3	17.9	13.9
France	18.8	17.0	18.0	13.5
Germany	28.2	16.3	18.0	11.4
Italy	32.0	24.5	18.6	9.8
Russia	44.2	43.4	22.4	12.7
Spain	31.3	27.6	21.4	10.2
Sweden	23.7	14.4	14.5	14.5

Source: B. R. Mitchell, *European Historical Statistics, 1750–1970* (London: Macmillan, 1975), pp. 127–32; B. R. Mitchell, *The Fontana Economic History of Europe: Statistical Appendix, 1920–1970* (London: Collins, 1974), pp. 28–34; *The World Almanac and Book of Facts 1995* (Mahwah, N.J.: World Almanac Books, 1994), pp. 740–839, 959; *Information Please Almanac, Atlas, and Yearbook 1994* (Boston, Mass.: Houghton Mifflin, 1994), p. 135; U.S. Bureau of the Census, *Historical Statistics of the United States* (Washington, D.C.: Government Printing Office, 1960), p. 23.

in 1990, a remarkable 60 percent fall in the birthrate. In England, the rate fell from 28.6 per thousand in 1900 to 12.9 per thousand in 1994, a fall of 55 percent. The Russian birthrate fell by more than 71 percent between 1910 and 1990.

By the late twentieth century, the birthrate in most of western Europe had fallen below the level needed to sustain population. Demographers estimate that an unchanging population requires 2.1 children born per woman in the population. (The global rate has fallen sharply, from 5.0 in the early 1950s to 2.8 in 1997.) In the late 1980s only two states (Ireland and Spain) in the European Union reached 2.1; Germany had the extraordinarily low rate of 1.3 children per woman. By the 1990s the European Union average had fallen again, to 1.4, and Catholic Italy had the lowest rate in the world for 1997, 1.2. Birthrates so low raise the strong possibility that, despite greater longevity and immigration pressures, Europe could lose population in the twenty-first century. Demographers—who have called this striking new development the "baby bust" (in contrast to the post–World War II period of high birthrates, known as the "baby boom")—have recently calculated that, if Europe could restore a rate of 2.1, the continent would still have lost 24 percent of its current population by 2060.

One natural consequence of the low birthrate was that family size became much smaller during the twentieth century. During the eighteenth and nineteenth centuries, the average family size in western and central Europe had been close to five persons. This remained true in Victorian Britain during the industrial revolution, when family size had averaged 4.75 members. Significant regional variation was evident in family size, with larger families being typical of rural communities and smaller families found in towns. The falling birthrates of the twentieth century rapidly reduced average family size. In Vienna, family size fell from 4.7 in 1890 to 4.1 in 1910, then to 3.2 in 1934, and down to 2.3 in 1961. Berlin and Hamburg both had averages of 1.9 in 1993, whereas communities of fewer than five thousand people held average families of 2.6 members. In Italy, average family size remained 4.3 members as late as 1951, when one-third of all Italian families contained five or more members. By 1980 the average Italian family had 2.8 members in the prosperous north and 3.3 members in more rural south; less than 15 percent of Italian families had five or more members. By the 1990s Italy had become the state most likely to experience a population decline in the twenty-first century.

The decline in twentieth-century birthrates and family size happened despite changing sexual attitudes that tolerated illegitimate births. In 1990 more than one-fourth of all births in Great Britain were illegitimate and 44.7 percent of births in Denmark were outside of marriage; a century earlier, Victorian Britain had low social tolerance of illegitimacy and the rate had been 5 percent. Even in Catholic countries, the stigma previously attached to having children outside of marriage has diminished. In conservative Ireland, 12 percent of 1990 births were illegitimate. In France, the number reached 26.3 percent in 1990 and passed one-third in 1995. The French showed the new social acceptability of unmarried childbirth in 1996 when the nation celebrated with President Jacques Chirac the illegitimate birth of his first grandchild. Although some parts of Europe maintained strict attitudes toward illegitimacy in the 1990s—such as Greece, where the rate was 2.1 percent—traditional sexual morality did not keep the birthrate low in Europe.

The most important explanation of falling birthrates has been the widespread practice of birth control. Information about contraception, and contraceptive devices, remained illegal in most of Europe well into the twentieth century. In the 1920s some countries (led by France) adopted stiff new prohibitions to recover population losses during World War I, but champions of women's rights in some Western countries challenged this trend. Aletta Jacobs still maintained the world's first birth control clinic, which she had opened in Amsterdam in 1878. A paleobotanist at the University of London, Marie Stopes, in 1921 opened the first British birth control clinic—the Mothers' Clinic for Constructive Birth Control. Stopes's *Contraception: Its Theory, History, and Practice* was published in 1923, and she continued to fight for easy public access to contraceptives as president of the Society for Constructive Birth Control.

Strong opposition existed to birth control clinics and contraceptives in the interwar years. Pronatalist governments, such as the conservative coalition led by Raymond Poincaré in France, the Fascist government of Benito Mussolini in Italy, and the Nazi regime in Germany, all strove to defend motherhood and to increase the population. The Vatican strongly supported this position in 1930 when Pope Pius XI issued the first encyclical opposed to birth control, *Casti connubi*. Pius XI left no doubt about the correct moral position for Catholics: "Any use whatsoever of matrimony exercised in such a way that the [sex] act is deliberately frustrated in its natural power to generate life is an offense against the law of God and of nature, and those who indulge in such are branded with the guilt of a grave sin." Some Catholic states responded to *Casti connubi*. The Irish not only outlawed birth control, but they also deemed a felony the importing, selling, or advertising of any birth control device or any birth control instructions (such as Marie Stopes's book).

European birthrates, however, show that millions of people, including Catholics, defied both church and state and practiced birth control. Birth control advocates, often led by champions of women's rights, won changes in restrictive laws after World War II. Postwar scientists also changed the nature of contraception. The principle behind oral contraceptives—changing a woman's balance of hormones—was well understood in the 1940s, and supplementary hormone pills were developed and tested in the 1950s. The first oral contraceptive, Enovid, was marketed in the United States in 1960, and "the pill" was introduced in Britain as Conovid in 1961. France legalized contraceptives in 1967; although conservative governments restricted this law in many indirect ways, the French nation voted with their bodies. An International Conference on Population held in 1994 estimated that France had the highest rate of contraception in the world. Eighty percent of all married Frenchwomen used contraceptives, while a rate of 70 percent to 80 percent was reported in many other countries (including the United States).

Spain legalized contraceptives after the death of General Franco, and 500,000 Spanish women began using the pill in the first three years that it was legal. After a long and passionate debate, Ireland legalized contraceptives in 1985 for people over the age of eighteen. And the government of Ireland even began to provide free contraceptives (although not condoms) to recipients of government-supported health care.

Conservatives, led by the Vatican, did not abandon the battle against birth control information and devices. When the birth control pill became popular in many Western countries in the late 1960s, Pope Paul VI reiterated the church's total opposition to birth control in his 1968 encyclical *Humanae vitae* (Of Human Life). Despite the clear evidence that Catholics accepted and used birth control, Pope John Paul II continued the strenuous rejection of all contraceptives in policy statements of 1987 and 1995. As late as 1995 John Paul II's encyclical, *Evangelium vitae* (The Gospel of Life), forcefully asserted that birth control was one of modern society's "crimes against life" and "a significant cause of grave moral decline."

The most controversial check on population growth, however, was not birth control but abortion. Abortion had long been illegal but had nonetheless been widely practiced in most of Europe. Pope Pius IX had denounced abortion and made it an excommunicatory sin in 1870. British laws of 1803 and 1861 had expressly outlawed abortion, providing penalties up to life imprisonment. The same statutes also criminalized many forms of assisting an abortion, such as sharing an abortifacient medication. The criminal code of newly unified Germany in 1871 made abortion a serious crime with five-year prison sentences. The French legislation of 1920 that targeted birth control also tightened the laws against abortion, establishing large new fines and longer prison sentences for performing an abortion, having an abortion, or providing information about abortion. Under those statutes, a prominent French feminist who had long championed a woman's right to control her own body, Dr. Madeleine Pelletier, was imprisoned (and died) in a mental asylum in 1939. Mussolini promulgated strict anti-abortion legislation in 1930, branding abortion a crime against "the health of the race." The foremost exception to the strict laws against abortion came in the Soviet Union, where Lenin's government legalized abortion in 1920. The decree required all physicians to perform an abortion if a pregnant woman requested it during the first two-and-one-half months of pregnancy. Stalin, however, revoked this decree and recriminalized abortion in 1936.

TABLE 30.12

Legal Abortions, 1990

Rate of legal abortions performed per 1,000 population

Country	1989
Bulgaria	16.1
Czechoslovakia	10.3
Hungary	8.8
Sweden	4.3
Denmark	4.1
United States	3.9
Norway	3.8
Britain	3.1
France	2.9
Italy	2.9
Poland	2.1
West Germany	1.0

Percentage of pregnancies terminated by abortion

Country	1990
USSR	54.9
United States	29.7
Denmark	27.0
Sweden	24.9
Britain	18.6

Source: Rates per thousand calculated using data from the *Demographic Yearbook*, reported in *Information Please Almanac, Atlas, and Yearbook 1994* (Boston, Mass.: Houghton Mifflin, 1994), pp. 130–31, 135; rates of pregnancies terminated by abortion from Michael Wolff and others., *Where We Stand* (New York: Bantam, 1992), pp. 253, 264.

The changing attitudes in post–World War II Europe led to the reversal of the legislation outlawing abortion (see table 30.12). Shortly after Stalin's death, the Soviet Union relegalized abortion in 1955. Abortion became legal in Britain in 1968, and nearly 24,000 legal abortions were performed that year. In the next twenty years, the number of legal abortions performed in Britain grew nearly eightfold, reaching 184,000 in 1990. At that rate, nearly 20 percent of all pregnancies in Britain ended in an abortion. By the 1970s the legalization of abortion had become a trend in Europe. Simone Veil, the minister of health, persuaded Jacques Chirac's conservative government to legalize abortion in France in 1974. A French endocrinologist, Etienne Baulieu, developed an abortifacient drug known as RU 486, and in 1980 it became widely available there. Ital-

ian voters went to the polls in the spring 1981 referendum and approved abortion by a two-to-one margin, despite papal opposition calling abortion murder. Belgium legalized abortion in 1990. Although Ireland did not legalize abortion, a controversial case in 1995 allowed Irish clinics to assist Irish women to obtain abortions abroad.

The highest rates of abortion were typically found in the Soviet Union and the states of eastern Europe. Bulgaria had an abortion rate more than four times as high (per one thousand population) as the United States did. And in 1990, 55 percent of all pregnancies in the Soviet Union were terminated by a legal abortion, in part because contraceptives remained largely unavailable. Romania, however, forbade abortions under the dictatorship of Nicolae Ceausescu and did not legalize them until he was deposed in 1989. And in Poland, where the Catholic Church played an important role in both the revolution of 1989 and the election of Lech Walesa to the presidency, abortion was again outlawed.

The Continuing Vital Revolution

The vital revolution of modern European history is chiefly explained in terms of diet and disease (see chapters 17 and 22). Twentieth-century European history—with its larger population, lower death rates, longer life expectancy, smaller families, and reduced agricultural sector of the economy—must return to these factors for explanations.

To understand the role of food in the vital revolution of the twentieth century, one must resolve a puzzle: Between 1900 and 1990 the population of Europe increased from 423 million to 501 million, while agricultural employment declined dramatically—from 32 percent of the population in Austria to 9 percent, from 41 percent of the population in France to 8 percent—and the amount of land devoted to agriculture decreased (by 15 percent in western Europe). Whereas the vital revolution of the eighteenth century had led to extensive use of the land—such as clearing forests, draining swamps, and enclosing common lands — to feed a growing population, the vital revolution of the twentieth century fed a growing (albeit more slowly) population with less land and fewer workers.

Grain has long been the key to understanding agriculture and the diet, and studies of grain production show the success of European agriculture during the twentieth century. Total European production (excluding Russia) of all grains—wheat, rye, barley, oats, and corn—stood at slightly less than 100 million tons in 1900. Good harvests preceded World War I, and production had grown by nearly 25 percent in 1913, before plummeting during the war. The European grain harvest reached prewar levels by 1929–30 but had only slightly exceeded them when World War II devastated agriculture and reduced production far below 1900 levels. In 1945, war-torn Europe produced less than 70 million tons. Between World War II and 1980, however, European agriculture experienced a miracle comparable to that of European industry. Total grain production nearly quadrupled, surpassing 250 million tons in the late 1970s. The average diet of twentieth-century Europeans is thus much healthier, and food costs were a much smaller percentage of the average person's income at the end of the twentieth-century than they were at the start. The agricultural miracle and its contribution to the vital revolution are the result of a tremendous investment in agronomy. The mechanization of agriculture—the widespread use of machinery such as tractors, harvesters, and threshers—has transformed farming and required fewer people to produce more food. On the eve of World War II, fewer than 300,000 tractors were being used in all of European farming; in 1980, the total was more than 8 million. Although many environmental problems have been attributed to them, the use of chemicals—both for fertilizing the soil and as pesticides—have performed an even larger part in increasing the yield per acre. The success of biologists in developing new strains of crops or new breeds of animals has also greatly improved food production. A United Nations study of agriculture in Czechoslovakia between 1948 and 1978 shows how much these things have transformed agriculture. In the traditional Czech agriculture that persisted in 1948, the UN calculated that the chief production factors were natural soil fertility, climatic conditions, and ground preparation; these variables explained 80 percent of the harvest size. In the modernized Czech agriculture of 1978, the UN concluded that the most important variables were fertilization, seed quality, and the use of pesticides—which accounted for 65 percent of harvest size.

While the success of European agriculture is important, the foremost factor in understanding the vital revolution of the twentieth century has been the conquest of disease. In 1901 the largest cause of death was respiratory diseases, including influenza and pneumonia, which appeared on 16.8 percent of all death certificates. Tuberculosis (7.5 percent) or cholera (7.3 percent) killed almost as many people as heart disease (9.9 percent). Childhood diseases such as whooping cough, measles, scarlet fever, and smallpox were still more significant causes of death (5.9 percent) than cancer (5.0 percent). By 1990 British deaths from infectious disease had fallen from 49.9 percent to 0.4 percent. Smallpox had ceased to exist as an epidemic disease, and zero deaths were reported attributable to cholera, typhoid, diphtheria, or scarlet fever. Whooping cough and measles killed a total of eight children, compared with more than twenty thousand in 1901.

The conquest of epidemic disease had begun at the end of the eighteenth century with Jenner's smallpox vaccination. It made significant progress during the second half of the nineteenth century when Pasteur established the germ theory of disease transmission and biochemists such as Pasteur and Robert Koch began the slow process of finding vaccines that could protect people from other infectious diseases. Nonetheless, the twentieth century dawned on a world still in the grip of epidemic disease. The nineteenth century ended with yellow fever and malaria still preventing the construction of the Panama Canal, and the bubonic plague remained a rare but virulent killer that ravaged both Honolulu and San Francisco. The twentieth century began with a typhoid epidemic in New York (1903), a polio epidemic in Sweden (1905), 1.3 million deaths from bubonic plague in British India (1907), virtually annual cholera epidemics in Russia (until 1926), and a British report that the Anglo-Boer War in South Africa (1899–1902) had a British death rate from disease five times higher than the death rate from enemy fire. The association of war and disease would persist in World War I. Tetanus spread through the trenches of the western front in 1915, a typhus epidemic took 150,000 lives in Serbia in 1915 and another killed 3 million people in Russia beginning in 1917. The Spanish influenza pandemic of 1919 became the most horrifying disease since the Black Death. Though it originated elsewhere, the disease took its name from the fact that nearly 80 percent of the Spanish population became infected. In two years, according to conservative estimates, it killed twenty-two million people worldwide, more than twice the number of combat deaths that occurred in World War I. In short, infectious disease was still a catastrophic feature of life in the early twentieth century. Some diseases, such as malaria in Italy and cholera in Russia, remained endemic. Some, such as polio, came in frightening epidemics (such as the one that crippled

Franklin Roosevelt). And some, such as influenza and venereal diseases, were universal pandemics that few could escape.

But the twentieth century also began with dramatic medical progress. The first Nobel Prizes were awarded in 1901, and the prize in physics went to Wilhelm Roentgen for the discovery of X-rays while the first prize in medicine went to a bacteriologist in Koch's Berlin laboratory for the discovery of the diphtheria antitoxin, which became a universal childhood inoculation of the twentieth century. In 1909 another German scientist, Paul Ehrlich, opened research into a new family of drugs—antibacterial therapeutic drugs—with his development of an arsenic-based treatment for syphilis named Salvarsan. Syphilis had been one the greatest scourges of the Belle Époque, killing more Europeans per year than AIDS did at the end of the century. Salvarsan cut the syphilis infection rate in western Europe by more than 50 percent before the First World War, although its application was restricted by moralists who denounced the drug for encouraging sin.

Many of the most deadly diseases of European history gradually fell to the laboratory work of microbiologists, biochemists, and pathologists. After diphtheria and syphilis, yellow fever, typhus, tetanus, scarlet fever, bubonic plague, malaria, measles, and polio were all conquered or contained in Europe. Perhaps the most historic moment in this conquest of disease came in 1979 when the World Health Organization (WHO) announced that smallpox, the dreaded disease that had formerly killed tens of thousands of Europeans every year, had been totally eradicated. The last case of smallpox, WHO reported, had passed without transmission in 1977. Smallpox can, however, be revived because the governments of the United States and Russia have both stored samples of the smallpox virus.

The identification of the bacteria and viruses responsible for contagious diseases, and the development of vaccines and drug therapies stand at the center of the vital revolution of the twentieth century. No element of this story is more dramatic than the discovery of the powerful drugs that became available after 1945, popularly known as the miracle drugs. Their discovery began in the late 1920s when Scottish physician and bacteriologist Alexander Fleming discovered penicillin and accelerated in 1935 when German pathologist Gerhard Domagk reported the discovery of the first antibacterial drug in a group called sulfa drugs. Many scientists contributed to the understanding and development of these miracle drugs. A French-American bacteriologist, René Dubos, developed the technique for isolating antibacterial agents in 1939. An Australian-born British pathologist, Sir Howard Florey, developed Fleming's penicillin into a powerful drug in 1940. Shortly thereafter, Selman Waksman, an American microbiologist, introduced one of the strongest miracle drugs—streptomycin—in 1944. During the late 1940s, a dozen new drugs followed from this collective effort. Thus, for much of the late twentieth century, miracle drugs such as penicillin seemed to hint at the complete conquest of disease. That optimism had faded by the 1990s, however, as viruses evolved that were resistant to many antibiotics. The fight against contagious diseases was not the only great medical contribution to the vital revolution of the twentieth century—a century that saw such remarkable procedures as open-heart surgery, a range of organ transplantation, and even successes with artificial organs.

CHAPTER 31

EUROPE IN THE AGE OF THE COLD WAR, 1945–75

CHAPTER OUTLINE

◆◆◆◆◆◆◆◆◆◆◆◆◆◆◆◆◆◆◆◆

Europe was again a devastated continent in 1945 with homes, industries, transportation systems, and entire cities in ruins. Chapter 31 begins by describing the territorial changes that resulted from World War II, the devastation in Europe caused by the war, and the years of austere living that Europeans faced to rebuild. The steady economic recovery of Western Europe, with aid from the U.S. Marshall Plan, produced growing prosperity in the late 1950s and the 1960s. The West German economy recovered at such a fast rate that it became know as the "economic miracle."

At the same time that Western Europe experienced this recovery, it confronted a global rivalry between the two strongest victors in World War II—the Soviet Union and the United States. This struggle never led to a shooting war between the rivals, but confrontations in the age of atomic weapons were so menacing, and small regional crises so frequent that the rivalry was called the cold war. The chapter describes the European tension and crises—chiefly the creation of Communist satellite states in Eastern Europe and threats elsewhere, especially over Berlin—that led to the beginning of the cold war in the late 1940s, and it describes the confrontations of the cold war during the 1950s and 1960s.

As the great powers of Europe recovered and survived the fears of a Communist takeover, the new democracies evolved in different ways. The British, under Prime Minister Clement Attlee, developed the welfare state; the French, following the ideas of Jean Monnet, developed a new form of capitalism within a planned economy; and the Germans, under the leadership of Konrad Adenauer, created a successful democracy in contrast to the failed Weimar democracy of the 1920s. The chapter ends with decolonization, the dismantling of ancient colonial empires; the beginning of European economic unity with the creation of the European Economic Community (EEC); and the steady calming of the cold war in Europe, during a period of détente.

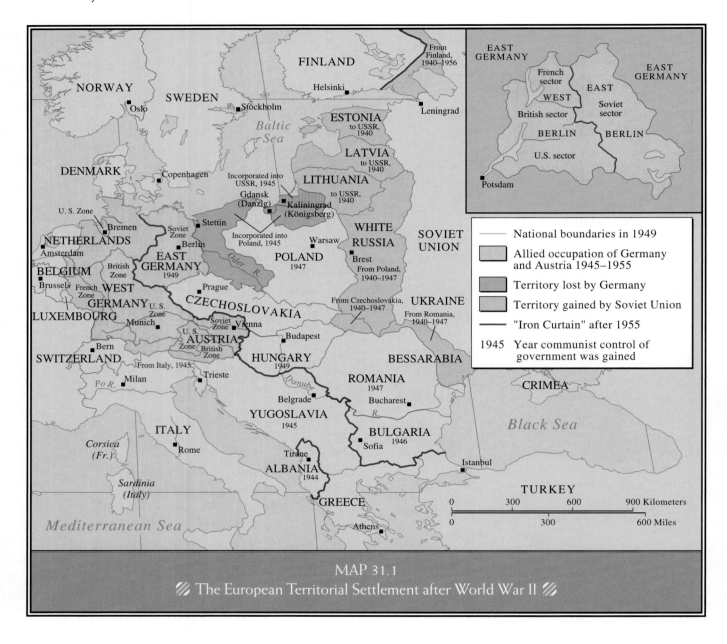

MAP 31.1

The European Territorial Settlement after World War II

Postwar Europe

No peace conference was held at the end of World War II, no treaty drawn up with the Axis powers. The map of postwar Europe was the consequence of Allied wartime conferences at Tehran, Yalta, and Potsdam and the political realities of the military situation in 1945 (see map 31.1). Germany was reduced in size and partitioned into four zones of military occupation. East Prussia, the isolated exclave of prewar Germany that had been cut off by the Polish Corridor, was taken from Germany and divided by Poland and the USSR; the Soviet annexation converted the Prussian city of Königsberg into the Soviet city of Kaliningrad and the

Polish annexation included the former free city of Danzig, now the Polish city of Gdansk. The eastern frontier of Germany was moved westward, to a line defined by the Oder and Neisse Rivers, giving Poland thousands of square miles of Prussia (roughly historic Silesia and Pomerania) and converting the German cities of Stettin and Breslau into the Polish cities of Szczecin and Wroclaw. In the west, France reacquired Alsace and Lorraine; in the north, Denmark recovered Schleswig. The initial division of Germany was into three zones of military occupation, under the British, American, and Russian armies. In the west, Britain and the United States shared their zones with France (which Stalin had refused to do), creating a four-power

Illustration 31.1

Reconstruction of a Devastated Europe. For the second time in thirty years, Europeans faced the task of rebuilding war-ravaged cities, industries, and infrastructure in the late 1940s.

A photograph like this one could have been taken in dozens of European cities from Rotterdam to Leningrad. It shows the center of Nuremburg, Germany at the time of the war crimes trial.

occupation. The city of Berlin, although located deep in the Soviet zone of occupation, was likewise divided into sectors administered by the great powers.

The territorial changes were less dramatic in the remainder of Europe. Austria was again detached from Germany; like Germany, it was divided into zones of occupation. Austria, Czechoslovakia, Hungary, Yugoslavia, and Romania were all restored to their approximate frontiers of 1919. The most important changes in eastern Europe involved the march of the Soviet Union westward. The Baltic states of Estonia, Latvia, and Lithuania (annexed in 1939) remained part of the USSR, as did slices of eastern Poland (much of White Russia, or Belarus), Czechoslovakia (much of Ruthenia), and Romania (the province of Bessarabia). This reversed the perspective of the Peace of Paris: The 1919 treaties had created a "cordon sanitaire" of small east European states as a barrier to the spread of Bolshevism, but eastern Europe now stood as a buffer zone protecting an expanded Soviet Union from western militarism and anticommunism.

The territorial changes of 1945 led to a period of great migration, especially of the German population now scattered in many states. More than eight million Germans left Poland and the Baltic states for Germany; they were joined by nearly three million Germans driven out of Czechoslovakia (chiefly the Sudeten Germans), by more than a million Germans fleeing the Soviet zone of occupied Germany, and by nearly another million Germans from Hungary, Yugoslavia, and Romania. Approximately thirteen million Germans were uprooted in the period 1945–47. Similarly, some 3.5 million Poles moved into the territory newly acquired from Germany and 1.5 million Poles fled the territory acquired by the USSR. Hundreds of thousands of Italians (leaving the Istrian Peninsula, which was now Yugoslavian), Turks (driven from Bulgaria), and Ukrainians (leaving Poland for Ukraine) shared this experience.

The Austerity of the 1940s and the Economic Recovery

Much of Europe lay in ruins in 1945. Great cities from London and Antwerp to Dresden and Leningrad were devastated (see illustration 31.1). Ninety-five percent of

TABLE 31.1

Food Production in Postwar Europe

Country	Millions of metric tons of		
	Wheat	Sugar beets	Milk
France			
1938	9.8	8.0	13.8
1945	4.2	4.5	7.9
Italy			
1938	8.2	3.3	n.a.
1945	4.2	0.4	n.a.
Poland			
1938	2.2	3.2	10.3
1945	0.8	3.5	2.8
Russia			
1938	40.8	16.7	29.0
1945	13.4	5.5	26.4

Source: B. R. Mitchell, *European Historical Statistics, 1750–1970* (London: Macmillan, 1975), passim.
n.a. Not available.

Berlin was in rubble, and forty percent of all German housing was damaged or destroyed. Much of the surviving productive capacity of Germany was dismantled and shipped to Russia. European transportation had collapsed amidst bombed out ports, rails, roads, and bridges. In Holland, 60 percent of the transportation network was destroyed, industrial output amounted to only 25 percent of the 1939 level, and thousands of acres of farmland lay flooded. As millions of war refugees spread across the continent, tuberculosis and malnutrition stalked displaced persons everywhere.

The primary characteristic of postwar Europe was the austere existence of the survivors. The European production of bread grains in 1945 stood at 50 percent of the prewar level. Food was rationed in most of Europe; bread was rationed in Britain although it had not been rationed during the war. The wheat crop in France for 1945 totaled 4.2 million tons, compared with 9.8 million tons in the last year of peace (1938) (see table 31.1). The United Nations estimated that 100 million people were receiving fifteen hundred calories or fewer per day. Governments tried to control prices, but scarcity caused inflation. Between 1945 and 1949, prices tripled in Belgium and quintupled in France. Hungary suffered perhaps the worst inflation in world history, and the national currency was printed in 100 trillion pengo notes. Blackmarkets selling food,

fuel, and clothing flourished. Simultaneously, military demobilization created widespread unemployment.

The recovery of Europe in the late 1940s and early 1950s relied upon planned economies and foreign aid. Jean Monnet, a distinguished French economist and civil servant, became the father of European mixed economics that relied upon state planning, such as his Monnet Plan of 1947. UN agencies such as the World Bank and the United Nations' International Children's Emergency Fund (UNICEF) channeled assistance to Europe, but the United States played the greatest role. In June 1947 Secretary of State George C. Marshall proposed a program of American aid to Europe. Between 1948 and 1952 the Marshall Plan sent $13 billion to Europe, with Britain ($3.2 billion), France ($2.7 billion), and Germany and Italy ($1.4 billion each) receiving the most. The USSR rejected aid. During 1948 West European industrial production reached 80 percent of its 1938 level in most countries (60 percent in Holland and West Germany). European economies showed signs of recovery but shortages, unemployment, and austerity continued in the early 1950s. By 1957, however, Prime Minister Harold MacMillan of Britain could say that "most of our people have never had it so good."

Eastern Europe and the Origins of the Cold War, 1945–49

The Red Army occupied vast regions of central and eastern Europe in 1945. Russia had survived its third invasion from the west in modern times, outlasting Hitler just as it had survived Napoleon and the kaiser. The Soviet war effort had taken two or three times as many lives (as many as twenty million to twenty-five million people in the largest estimates) as British, French, German, and American deaths combined. Stalin, who ruled the USSR until his death in 1953, concluded that he must exploit the vacuum in Europe to guarantee Russian security.

The summit conferences at Moscow, Yalta, and Potsdam gave the Soviet Union a strong position in Eastern Europe. Churchill had recognized Romania and Bulgaria as falling in the Soviet "sphere of influence," and the USSR had been conceded the occupation of the eastern one-third of Germany. In Yugoslavia, managed elections of 1945 (in which all opposition parties abstained) gave 90 percent of the vote and the presidency to the hero of the resistance (and prewar secretary general of the Communist Party), Marshal Tito, who held that office until his death in 1980. Multiparty democracies were announced in Poland, Czechoslovakia, and Hungary, and Communist parties formed a strong minority in each state. These democracies bore the burdens of postwar austerity during 1945–47, and each was so fragile that the Communist Party—backed by the Red Army—could seize control of the government. Poland, Czechoslovakia, and Hungary all fell to such Stalinist coups in 1947–49.

A dramatic example of the Communist takeover in Eastern Europe occurred in Czechoslovakia in 1948. Edouard Beneš, the prewar president of Czechoslovakia and head of the government in exile during the war, returned to Prague to lead a provisional government and he was reelected president of the republic. Free parliamentary elections in 1946 gave Czech Communists 38 percent of the vote and 114 seats; their four strongest rivals (Catholic, democratic, and socialist parties) won 178 seats. This produced a coalition government with a Communist prime minister, Klement Gottwald, plus Communist management of key ministries such as the Ministry of the Interior. The Gottwald government attempted to nationalize several Czech industries, just as socialists were doing in Britain and France; Gottwald followed Soviet orders and refused to accept Western aid, such as the Marshall Plan, for the rebuilding of Czechoslovakia. These policies led to bitter disputes with more conservative coalition partners, conflict that Gottwald resolved in early 1948 by staging a coup d'état, naming a Communist government, and blocking elections. This coup included the mysterious death of Czechoslovakia's most prominent statesman, Foreign Minister Jan Masaryk, whose fall from a high window was labeled a suicide by the government; many other non-Communists were purged from high office. Managed elections then named Gottwald president, from which position he solidified a Communist dictatorship. A new Czech Constitution of 1948 proclaimed a People's Democratic Republic on Soviet lines.

Similar coups created Communist states in Hungary and Poland, where Communist-led provisional governments and the presence of the Red Army facilitated the takeover. In Hungary, free elections and a secret ballot in September 1945 gave the Communist Party only 22 percent of the vote (the third highest share) and 70 seats in parliament, far behind a Smallholders Party (an anticommunist party) which garnered 57 percent of the vote and 245 seats. Charges of a conspiracy and "plotting against the occupying forces" were brought against leaders of the new republic, who

were rapidly purged. This led to new elections in 1947 and a reported 95.6 percent vote for a Communist coalition. A Soviet-inspired constitution of 1949 proclaimed Hungary a People's Republic.

The Communist position in Poland was strong in 1945 because many non-Communist leaders had been killed in the Warsaw uprising of 1944. Two competing governments-in-exile claimed to represent Poland, one that spent the war in Moscow, another in London. When the Red Army liberated Poland, Stalin installed the pro-Soviet government in the Polish town of Lublin, and it formed the basis of the postwar compromise government. The Communist-led provisional government did not hold elections until 1947, when its coalition received 80.1 percent of the vote and Western protests arose that the elections had not been fair. In a pattern similar to the events in Hungary and Czechoslovakia, the government nationalized land and industries, fought with the Catholic Church, punished collaborators (more than one million people were disenfranchised), adopted a new constitution, and purged the party. Although other parties continued to exist, the Communist government won a reported 99.8 percent of the vote in the elections of 1952.

The creation of Communist dictatorships allied to the Soviet Union provoked a strong reaction in the West. Winston Churchill, a lifelong anti-Communist, sounded the alarm against Soviet expansionism in a speech delivered at a small college in Missouri in March 1946. Churchill said that "an iron curtain has descended across the Continent," and the term *Iron Curtain* became the Western world's cold war symbol for the border between the democratic West and the Communist East (see document 31.1).

The West first confronted Communist expansionism in the Balkans. Greece had been a scene of intense partisan fighting throughout the war. The Greek resistance was predominantly composed of Communists (similar to the situation in Yugoslavia and, to a slightly lesser degree, France), whereas the government of Greece was a monarchy. The conflict between the resistance and the government produced sporadic fighting in 1944–45 and degenerated into a Greek Civil War (1946–49), widely seen as an attempted coup d'état by Greek Communists. This civil war focused western attention on the Balkans (including the vulnerability of Turkey and the strait linking the Black Sea and the Mediterranean). The geopolitical importance of this region plus growing western anxieties about Communist expansionism led President Truman to announce aid to Greece and Turkey in 1947. This policy became the

◈ DOCUMENT 31.1 ◈

Churchill: An "Iron Curtain" in Europe, 1946

A shadow has fallen upon the scenes so lately lightened, lighted by the Allied victory. Nobody knows what Soviet Russia and its communist international organization intends to do in the immediate future, or what are the limits, if any, to their expansive and proselytizing tendencies.

I have a strong admiration and regard for the valiant Russian people and for my war-time comrade, Marshal Stalin. There is deep sympathy and good-will in Britain—and I doubt not here also—toward the peoples of all the Russias. . . . We understand the Russian need to be secure on her western frontiers by the removal of all possibility of German aggression. We welcome Russia to her rightful place among the leading nations of the world. . . .

It is my duty, however . . . to place before you certain facts about the present position in Europe.

From Stettin in the Baltic to Trieste in the Adriatic, an iron curtain has descended across the Continent. Behind that line lie all the capitals of the ancient states of central and eastern Europe. Warsaw, Berlin, Prague, Vienna, Budapest, Belgrade, Bucharest, and Sofia, all these famous cities and the populations around them lie in what I might call the Soviet sphere, and all are subject, in one form or another, not only to Soviet influence but to a very high and in some cases increasing measure of control from Moscow.

Police governments are pervading from Moscow. . . . The communist parties, which were very small in all these eastern states of Europe, have been raised to preeminence and power far beyond their numbers and are seeking everywhere to obtain totalitarian control.

Churchill, Winston. Speech at Fulton, Missouri, March 5, 1946. *Current History,* April 1946, pp. 358–361.

Truman Doctrine: The United States would "support free peoples who are resisting attempted subjugation by armed minorities or by outside pressures." The Truman Doctrine of aid to threatened countries blended with the Marshall Plan for aid in economic recovery; humanitarian assistance and military assistance were intertwined instruments of the cold war. American aid contributed significantly to the victory of the Greek monarchy over Communist guerrilla forces in 1949.

The most dramatic American intervention in the early days of the cold war came in the Berlin Airlift of 1948. To protest the increasing merger of the British and American zones of West Germany (dubbed "Bizonia" in 1946), the Soviet Union began to interfere with western access to Berlin and in July 1948 sealed off the city by closing all land access through the Soviet zone of East Germany. The United States considered opening the route to Berlin by force but instead chose "Operation Vittles"—daily flights of assistance to sustain a city of two million. The Berlin Airlift delivered more than eight thousand tons of food and supplies daily, with British and American flights landing every five minutes around the clock until the Soviet Union lifted its blockade in the spring of 1949.

NATO and the Warsaw Pact: Containment and Confrontation

The Truman Doctrine and the policy of the "containment" of Communism within the countries where it had been established soon prompted military alliances. Britain, France (where the government was doubly nervous because French Communists won more than 25 percent of the votes, making it the largest party in Parliament), and the Benelux states had signed a defensive treaty in March 1948. The blockade of Berlin and the Czech coup of 1948 led to the expansion of this alliance in 1949 into the North Atlantic Treaty Organization (NATO). Italy, Portugal, Norway, Denmark, Iceland, Canada, and the United States joined the original Allies in a twelve-member alliance that stationed American forces throughout Europe. Greece and Turkey were added to NATO in 1949. When a reunited West Germany joined the alliance in 1955, the Soviet Union countered by forming the Warsaw Pact, an alliance linking the USSR, East Germany, Poland, Czechoslovakia, Hungary, Romania, Bulgaria, and Albania. Members of the Warsaw Pact pledged to respond to aggression against any member; although such preparations never led to war between NATO and Warsaw Pact nations, this proviso was used by the USSR to send troops into member states where the Communist government was being challenged. Throughout the cold war, NATO and the Warsaw Pact kept large armed forces facing each other, with thousands of American and Soviet troops stationed in allied

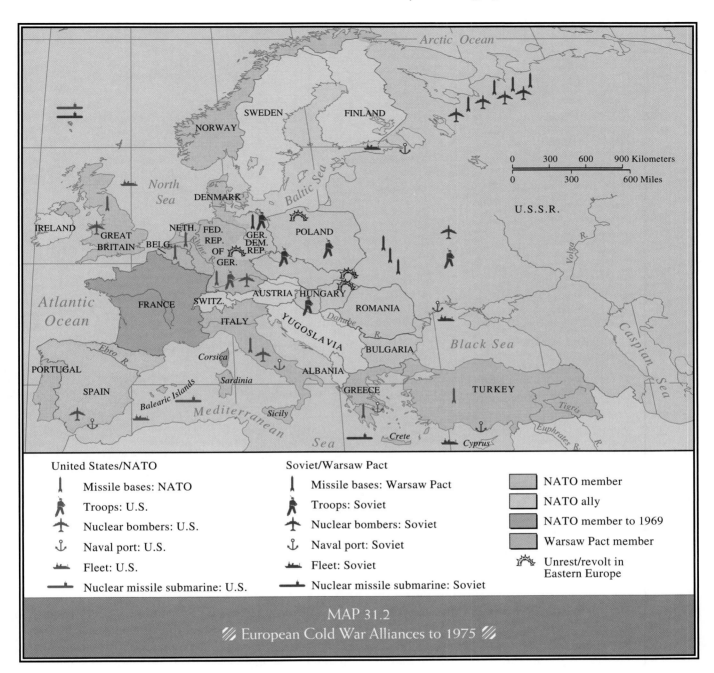

United States/NATO

Missile bases: NATO
Troops: U.S.
Nuclear bombers: U.S.
Naval port: U.S.
Fleet: U.S.
Nuclear missile submarine: U.S.

Soviet/Warsaw Pact

Missile bases: Warsaw Pact
Troops: Soviet
Nuclear bombers: Soviet
Naval port: Soviet
Fleet: Soviet
Nuclear missile submarine: Soviet

NATO member

NATO ally

NATO member to 1969

Warsaw Pact member

Unrest/revolt in Eastern Europe

MAP 31.2
European Cold War Alliances to 1975

countries, with nuclear weapons (see map 31.2 and chronology 31.1).

The cold war was much larger than a European struggle. Dozens of global crises threatened to bring the two sides to combat. The most dangerous of these crises occurred in Asia. In 1949 Mao Zedong's Chinese Communists won the war for control of China that they had begun in the 1930s. Mao took Beijing and drove his nationalist opponents, led by Chiang Kai-Shek, off the mainland to the island of Formosa (now called Taiwan). In early 1950 the U.S. Pacific Fleet pa-

trolled the waters around Taiwan to prevent a Communist invasion. A few weeks later Mao and Stalin agreed upon a Sino-Soviet Alliance. And a few weeks after that, the armies of Communist North Korea invaded the south of that partitioned country and captured the capital city of Seoul. The United Nations adopted a resolution to send troops to Korea to block aggression—a resolution made possible because the Soviet delegate was boycotting the UN Security Council meeting and therefore not present to cast a veto. President Truman sent the U.S. army (commanded by the

---

◈ CHRONOLOGY 31.1 ◈

The Cold War in Europe, 1945–75

1946 Churchill's "Iron Curtain" speech on the division of Europe

1946 Civil war in Greece, Communist guerrillas against monarchist government

1947 United States announces Truman Doctrine of aid against Communist takeovers

1948 Communist coup seizes power in Czechoslovakia

1948 The Marshall Plan for American aid for European recovery

1948 Soviet blockade of Berlin circumvented by Berlin Airlift

1949 Creation of North Atlantic Treaty Organization (NATO) alliance linking United States, Canada, and Western Europe

1949 Communists seize power in Hungary

1949 Three western zones of occupation united to form Federal Republic of Germany

1951 USSR explodes its first atomic bomb

1953 Death of Stalin and rise of Khrushchev

1953 Uprising in East Germany suppressed

1955 West Germany joins NATO

1955 Soviet Union organizes Warsaw Pact of East European states

1956 Uprisings in Poland and East Germany suppressed

1957 Soviet launching of *Sputnik* begins space race

1961 USSR achieves first manned space flight

1961 Berlin Crisis and construction of the Berlin Wall to block emigration

1962 United States forces USSR to withdraw missiles in Cuban Missile Crisis

1962 Solzhenitsyn reveals details of the Soviet gulag

1963 Partial Test Ban Treaty signed, beginning relaxation of cold war tensions

1966 France withdraws from NATO command

1968 Nuclear Nonproliferation Treaty Signed

1968 USSR and Warsaw Pact nations suppress Czech liberalization

1969 United States puts astronauts on moon

1970 Rioting in Poland over austerity program

1970 Heads of West Germany and East Germany hold first official meeting

1972 President Nixon visits Moscow and signs Strategic Arms Limitation Talks Treaty

1973 West Germany and East Germany both join the UN

1975 Helsinki accords on human rights mark age of détente

---

hero of the Pacific theatre of World War II, General Douglas MacArthur) to South Korea to join UN contingents from several countries, in the small portion of the Korean peninsula around Pusan still held by the South Koreans. After a UN counteroffensive, including an amphibious landing at Inchon, the North Korean army was driven back across the border (the thirty-eighth parallel) and MacArthur drove deep into North Korea, reaching the border of Manchuria. Then, in November 1951, Mao responded with Chinese "volunteers" to help the North. The Korean War (1950–53), which had begun with a near victory by North Korea and led to great danger of another world war, resulted in a stalemate and a ceasefire, perpetuating both the division of Korea and cold war anxieties.

The most frightening aspect of such cold war confrontations was the constant threat of nuclear war. The United States remained the only state with the atomic bomb for just four years (1945–49), until the Soviet Union, with significant assistance from atomic spies, detonated its first nuclear bomb. For the next quarter-century, the United States and the USSR engaged in a nuclear arms race that constantly increased the destructive power of both sides. The United States exploded the world's first hydrogen bomb, many times more destructive than the atomic bombs used on Hiroshima and Nagasaki, in 1952 but held this lead for only a few months. The arms race then shifted to the technology of delivering nuclear bombs. The United States tested the first Intermediate Range Ballistic Missile (IRBM) soon became commonplace. President John F. Kennedy committed the United States to win the space race by putting the first people on the moon, and by 1969 the United States succeeded in sending Apollo astronauts to the moon.

While the space race glamorized one aspect of the cold war arms race, the United States quietly took the lead in another technology capable of raining atomic bombs on the Soviet Union by building a fleet of nuclear submarines with atomic missiles aboard. By the early 1970s technology had produced the MIRV, a hydra-headed missile that could deliver separate bombs (multiple independent reentry vehicles in the cold war lexicon) to several cities from one missile. Both sides stockpiled nuclear weapons and their delivery systems long after they attained the capacity to obliterate civilization. Simultaneously, both sides developed the philosophy of using nuclear weapons. The United States, for example, threatened the use of nuclear weapons to force negotiations to end the Korean War and again in 1962 to force the USSR to withdraw its missiles from Cuba. And both sides seriously discussed such strategies as "massive retaliation" with nuclear bombs instead of fighting traditional ground wars. One of the keenest metaphors of the cold war appeared on the cover of a scientific journal: a clock showing that the human race had reached one minute before midnight.

The nuclear arms race and the space race were enormously expensive, which would ultimately have much to do with the end of the cold war. An early sign that this was an extremely expensive burden for the USSR came in 1959, when Stalin's successor, Nikita Khrushchev, proposed the concept of "peaceful coexistence" (see document 31.2). Many in the West doubted Khrushchev's sincerity (he had recently made another speech, taunting the West with the message, "We will bury you!"), and few were yet willing to gamble on a relaxation of cold war preparedness. Many Europeans would favor peaceful coexistence by the late 1960s, when it came to be called a policy of relaxed tensions (*detente* in the French vocabulary of diplomacy).

As the nuclear balance-of-power became a balance-of-terror, the cold war became a delicate stalemate. The NATO allies restrained themselves from direct interventions in Communist countries, although discontent with Communist rule provided opportunities. A workers' revolt in East Berlin was put down by force in 1953, beginning an era of uprisings behind the Iron Curtain. A Hungarian rebellion in 1956 led to fighting in the streets of Budapest and the creation of reformist government under Imre Nagy. Nagy pledged to withdraw

Illustration 31.2

⫸ **The Space Age.** The space age began in October 1957 when the USSR successfully launched the first artificial satellite (*Sputnik*) into orbit around the Earth. In this photo, visitors to the Brussels World's Fair in 1958 flock to see *Sputnik* on exhibit.

capable of carrying bombs long distances, in 1953, and both sides developed Intercontinental Ballistics Missiles (ICBMs) that could reach each other's cities.

The nuclear arms race shared much of its technology with a simultaneous space race between the USSR and the United States. The space age—and an era of Soviet superiority in space—began in 1957 when a Russian rocket carried the first artificial satellite, *Sputnik*, into orbit (see illustration 31.2). A month later, the Soviets launched a second satellite sending a dog into space and safely retrieving it. When President Eisenhower rushed an American rocket to show the world that the United States did not lag far behind, it exploded a few feet off the ground and became known as the American "Dudnik." The Soviet lead in the space race continued into the 1960s when the USSR sent the first person into outer space, the cosmonaut Yuri Gagarin. The U.S. space program of the 1960s showed that this "missile gap" was narrowing; launches of American astronauts and Soviet cosmonauts into space

◆ DOCUMENT 31.2 ◆

Nikita Khrushchev: "Peaceful Coexistence," 1959

Nikita Khrushchev often used the annual party congress of the Communist Party to make dramatic speeches. At the congress of 1956, he opened the age of destalinization in Russia in a speech attacking "the crimes of the Stalin era." In 1959, at the Twentieth Party Congress, he declared that the basis of foreign policy should be the "peaceful coexistence" of states with differing social systems, inviting a détente in cold war tensions. Western nations did not start to trust this concept for another decade.

We all of us well know that tremendous changes have taken place in the world. Gone, indeed, are the days when it took weeks to cross the ocean from one continent to the other or when a trip from Europe to America, or from Asia to Africa, seemed a very complicated undertaking. The progress of modern technology has reduced our planet to a rather small place; it has even become, in this sense, quite congested. And if in our daily life it is a matter of considerable importance to establish normal relations with our neighbors in a densely inhabited settlement, this is so much more necessary in the relations between states, in particular states belonging to different social systems. . . . What then remains to be done? There may be two ways out: either war—and war in the rocket H-bomb age is fraught with the most dire consequences for all nations—or peaceful coexistence. . . .

The problem of peaceful coexistence between states with different social systems has become particularly pressing. . . . The Soviet people have stated and declare again that they do not want war. If the Soviet Union and the countries friendly to it are not attacked, we shall never use any weapons either against the United States or against any other countries. . . . Precisely because we want to rid mankind of war, we urge the Western powers to peaceful and lofty competition.

Krushchev, Nikita. "On Peaceful Coexistence." In Ludwig Schaefer et al., eds., *Problems in Western Civilization*. New York: Scribner's, 1965.

Hungary from the Warsaw Pact and to become neutral. A few weeks later, the Red Army invaded Hungary. The Soviet intervention led to the flight of 200,000 Hungarians to the west, 25,000 casualties in combat, and 2,000 executions (including Nagy) in reprisal. The NATO powers still chose not to go to war over Hungary. Similarly, the Soviet Union did not intervene in Western wars, such as the Anglo-French invasion of Egypt in 1956 (an attempt to keep control of the Suez Canal) known as the Suez War. When the United States later fought a second Asian war based on the policy of containing the spread of Communism, the Vietnam War (1965–75), the USSR and China gave assistance to North Vietnam and to the Communist guerrilla armies of the Viet Cong, but they both refrained from directly entering the war.

◆

The USSR under Stalin and Khrushchev, 1945–64

No country suffered more severely from World War II than the Soviet Union. In the western quarter of the country, more than seventy thousand villages were classified as "destroyed." In a war zone of 800,000 square miles (Germany and Poland combined occupy only 210,000 square miles), 50 percent of all residences and eighty thousand schools were lost. Twenty-five million dead overshadows every other tragedy in a century of megadeath, and it explains why Stalin demanded postwar security for the USSR.

Stalin began the reconstruction of the Soviet Union by plundering defeated Germany. The Yalta and Potsdam agreements recognized a Soviet right to reparations from Germany and permitted Stalin to collect them "in kind." This meant the confiscation and shipment to the USSR of billions of dollars worth of surviving German industry. Recovery was entrusted to the state planning agency, Gosplan, which drafted a Five Year Plan for 1946–50. With severe enforcement, the Soviet Union exceeded the production quotas set in this plan. Stalin promised that Soviet output would triple prewar levels, and by 1960 that standard had been met, although agricultural recovery was slower. Ironically, the speed of the Russian recovery increased cold war tensions because it underscored the enormous potential of the Soviet Union. And when the USSR launched *Sputnik* into orbit, no one could doubt Soviet technical potential.

Soviet security and recovery both rested upon Stalin's dictatorship. His brutality had not diminished with age, and in 1948 he ordered another purge. The new repression was conducted by his senior lieutenant, Georgi Malenkov, and the head of his secret police, Lavrenti Beria. It did not match the Great Terror of the 1930s, but it took a terrifying toll, especially on Soviet cultural life, where writers and filmmakers were prominent victims. The purges then moved through the military, the bureaucracy, and the Communist Party. Anti-Semitism was a common feature of the purges. This culminated in the so-called Doctors' Plot of 1952 when Stalin accused Jewish physicians in the Kremlin of poisoning Soviet leaders.

When Stalin died of a cerebral hemorrhage in early 1953, Malenkov and Beria claimed power. Despite the idealistic constitution of 1936, the USSR had no formal system for the transfer of power. Senior leaders feared that the rule of Malenkov or Beria meant continued terror. The army arrested and shot Beria on a charge of "plotting to restore Capitalism"; his secret police was reorganized as the KGB. Malenkov was dismissed from office, but to show that Stalinism had ended, he was merely sentenced to end his career as the manager of a hydroelectric plant in provincial Kazakhstan.

After a period of "collective leadership," Nikita Khrushchev emerged as Stalin's successor. Khrushchev, the son of a Ukrainian miner, had joined the Communist Party as an illiterate worker in 1918. He rose rapidly under Stalin's regime and participated in some of its crimes during the 1930s, but his dictatorship differed from Stalinist bloodletting. At the Communist Party Congress of 1956, Khrushchev announced a program of change and openly attacked Stalin. He denounced "the crimes of the Stalin era," and, as symbols of destalinizaion, Khrushchev removed Stalin's body from public display and renamed Stalingrad as Volgograd. Three years later, at another party congress, he made his famous call for relaxed economic controls and peaceful coexistence with the West. Westerners were startled by Khrushchev's crude style. For many, the enduring image of Nikita Khrushchev was a fat man in a rumpled suit, banging his shoe on a podium and shouting. Soviet dissidents still faced harassment and the *gulag* under Khrushchev, and when he fell in 1964, the Soviet Union remained a dictatorship. However, Khrushchev had taken the first steps toward the age of détente.

◈

Great Britain: Clement Attlee and the Birth of the Welfare State

In contrast to Eastern Europe and the Soviet Union, postwar Western Europe experienced the recovery of parliamentary democracy. Britain, France, the Benelux countries, Italy, the Scandinavian states, and even the reunited zones of western Germany were stable democracies by the 1950s. Spain and Portugal kept their prewar autocratic governments, but these fell after the death of Franco (1975) and Salazar (1970). The postwar Western democracies were more than mere restorations, however, and several governments expanded the European definition of democracy.

Postwar Britain led the evolution of European democracy by founding the modern welfare state. The British electorate rejected Winston Churchill's conservative government in 1945 (much as the French had rejected Clemenceau after World War I or the Russians would reject Gorbachev after the revolutions of 1989), giving the Tories only 39.9 percent of the vote in parliamentary elections. The new prime minister, Clement Attlee, received an overwhelming majority in Parliament (393–213) with which to enact socialist plans for a welfare state. Attlee had been born to an upper-class family and sensitized to the needs of the poor through social work in the East End of London. After World War I he became a lecturer at the London School of Economics, a nondogmatic socialist, and a leading Labour M.P. His government planned a new British democracy based on two broad policies: (1) the adoption of welfare legislation by which the state provided all citizens with basic services "from the cradle to the grave" and (2) the "nationalization of leading elements" of the British economy, on the theory that state profits would pay for welfare services. Attlee's welfare program derived from an idealistic wartime plan, the Beveridge Report of 1942, which called for government insurance to protect the nation. The Beveridge Report laid the basis for the National Health Act (1946) and the National Insurance Act (1946), laws that promised "a national minimum standard of subsistence" to everyone. In return for a regular payroll deduction, all citizens received sick leave benefits, retirement pensions, maternity benefits, unemployment compensation, widow's and orphan's allowances, and medical care. One of the first reforms of the welfare state was a program to provide British schoolchildren (many of whom had poor nutrition from years of privation) with free milk at school, and this image did much to popularize the welfare state (see illustration 31.3). Beveridge, Attlee, and the minister for health and housing, Aneurin Bevan, gave Western Europe the model for a democratic welfare state.

The Labour government also carried out the second half of its program, the nationalization of key in-

Illustration 31.3

 The Welfare State. The British lived with food rationing until 1954. To improve the health of British children, the postwar Labour government in 1946 included a provision for free milk for schoolchildren in the welfare program it introduced. This photo shows boys at a grammar school in Manchester taking their daily milk break. Such programs were a dramatic success at improving the children's health, but they also became a visible symbol of the welfare state. When Margaret Thatcher set out to dismantle the welfare state, free milk was one of her first targets.

dustries. This had been a central objective of European socialists since the late nineteenth century and a cornerstone of Labour programs since 1918. The idea had gained respectability in the 1920s when a conservative government had created the British Broadcasting Corporation as a state corporation. Nationalization gained further appeal during the depression of the 1930s when big business was widely blamed for the terrible unemployment. The Attlee government compensated the owners of private firms that were nationalized into "public corporations," and the Tory Party made only limited protests when Attlee nationalized the Bank of England in 1945 and civil aviation in 1947 (creating the parent corporation of British Air). Conservatives more vigorously contested the nationalization of the coal mines (1946) and the iron and steel industries (1950); when Churchill returned to power in 1951, his government allowed most of Labour's nationalizations to stand, denationalizing only iron and steel and road haulage. A broad conservative attack on the policies of the Attlee years did not come until the Margaret Thatcher era, beginning in 1979, when both denationalization and the dismantling of the welfare state defined her government.

Subsequent Labour governments under Harold Wilson (1964–70 and 1974–76) expanded the new sense of British democracy by legislating equal rights: The Race Relations Act (1965) outlawed racial discrimi-

nation, and the Sexual Offenses Act (1967) legalized homosexual acts by consenting adults. An Abortion Act (1967), an Equal Pay Act (1970), and the Equal Opportunities Act (1975) legislated the three chief aims of the women's rights movement. These Labour reforms of the Wilson era survived Thatcher's conservatism better than Attlee's reforms.

The French Fourth Republic: Jean Monnet and the Planned Economy

The reestablishment of a French republic also involved the rejection of a famous wartime leader. General de Gaulle's provisional government, which returned in the aftermath of D-Day, prepared the constitution of a Fourth Republic. De Gaulle feared a Communist coup in France because many of the leaders of the wartime Resistance had been Communists. To block the Communists, De Gaulle chose dramatic steps: He adopted the socialist program of nationalization that Léon Blum had begun in the 1930s. The state now took control of energy and the utilities (gas, oil, and coal); most insurance companies and banking; and some prominent industrial companies, such as Renault and Air France. Twenty percent of the French economy had been nationalized by the late 1940s—a program of conservative nationalization even larger than the Labour Party's efforts in Britain.

Charles de Gaulle also gave women the vote because he believed a common stereotype holding that women would vote conservatively, as their priests directed. While this was an important step in equal rights for women, it did not lead to a large role for women in French politics; until the socialist parliamentary victory in the spring of 1997, France remained nearly last among European states in electing women. (The French did, however, accept a woman as prime minister—Edith Cresson in the 1980s—long before Germany or the United States accepted a woman at the head of government.) De Gaulle's concession of the vote thus did not convince all French women that they had yet won equality. One prominent intellectual, Simone de Beauvoir, responded with a landmark manifesto of women's rights, *The Second Sex* (1949), showing that women were "still bound in a state of vassalage" (see document 31.3). The late twentieth-century reinvigoration of feminism throughout the Western world owed much to de Beauvoir's book, and the next generation of feminists hailed her as "the mother of us all."

The French postwar elections divided power among three parties, each with 25 percent of the seats: a Catholic party (the MRP), the socialist party of Léon Blum (who had survived Nazi imprisonment), and the Communist Party (which was popular because of its role in the wartime resistance). When each of these parties rejected de Gaulle's ideas for a strong presidency (designed to suit his own leadership), he retired in anger to write his war memoirs. The French consequently created a parliamentary democracy known as the Fourth Republic (1946–58), which greatly resembled the Third Republic (1871–1940). When the wars of decolonization—especially the Algerian War (1954–62)—destroyed the Fourth Republic in 1958, de Gaulle returned to politics and created his strong presidential government in the constitution of the Fifth Republic.

The greatest French contribution to postwar democracy was neither De Gaulle's concept of a presidential republic nor his specific accomplishments such as women's suffrage (which most of Europe had granted before he did). It was, instead, a democratic version of economic planning. Jean Monnet never led the government, but his Plan for Modernization and Equipment (1946), embodied in the First Plan (1947–53) and the Second Plan (1954–57), shaped the French postwar recovery. He created an "indicative plan" that set goals in important sectors (such as mining or transportation)

◆ DOCUMENT 31.3 ◆

De Beauvoir: Emancipation of the "Second Sex"

Simone de Beauvoir (1908–86) was the daughter of a respectable bourgeois family who rebelled against the standards of her world. She became a leader of Parisian intellectual society, a novelist, and a philosopher closely associated with Jean-Paul Sartre and the school of existentialist philosophy, which held that people create their identity through acts of will throughout their existence.

French Law no longer lists obedience among the duties of a wife, and every Frenchwoman now has the right to vote; but these civil liberties remain only theoretical while they are not accompanied by economic freedom. A woman supported by a man—a wife or a mistress—is not emancipated from him because she has a ballot in her hand; if customs now constrain her less than before, this has not profoundly changed her situation; she is still bound in a state of vassalage. It is through paid employment that women have covered most of the distance separating them from men; nothing else can guarantee her freedom. Once woman ceases to be a parasite, the system based on her dependence falls apart; there is no longer any need for men to mediate between women and the universe.

Beauvoir, Simon de. *Le Deuxieme Sexe*. Vol. 2, *L'Expérience vecue*. Excerpt trans. Steven C. Hause. Paris: Gallimard, 1950.

and then provided government assistance to private businesses in reaching those goals. The plan was not compulsory, and it did not create government control over private firms. Monnet thus pioneered the "mixed economy," combining elements of capitalist and noncapitalist economics. French steel output doubled between 1950 and 1960, wheat output doubled between 1950 and 1962, and other governments soon followed Monnet.

As the French economy recovered, France became more conservative. The popularity of the Communist Party declined sharply, from 25 percent of the seats in Parliament in 1945 to 5 percent in 1988. The governments of the 1950s were so conservative that they even changed the traditional French insistence upon secular

Illustration 31.4

The Berlin Wall. Berlin remained at the center of the cold war in Europe and was the issue in a heated East-West dispute of 1960–61. This Berlin crisis saw renewed Soviet claims to the city and threats to close access to it. When President Kennedy and other Western leaders stood firm, the Soviet response was to close the border between East and West Germany. A wall was constructed through the center of Berlin in August 1961. In this photo, the wall curves around the historic Brandenburg Gate with winged victory riding in a chariot atop it. The gate was in the Soviet zone, where the "shoot-to-kill" area near the wall is clearly visible.

education; the Barange Law (1951) gave state aid to Catholic schools. When Charles de Gaulle founded the Fifth Republic in 1958, the conservative coalition in France—known as Gaullism—won a solid majority of electoral support and retained power throughout the 1960s and 1970s. Gaullist conservatives, however, did not try to reprivatize the nationalized sectors of the economy, to abandon the state direction of a mixed economy, or to dismantle the growing welfare state. Gaullists extended French welfare benefits several times, especially in the 1970s when they expanded a state-run system of old age pensions for the entire nation.

The Federal Republic of Germany: Konrad Adenauer and the Economic Miracle

The rebirth of German democracy followed a more difficult course. The four-power occupation of Germany created conflicting administrations. In the Soviet zone, the revived German Communist Party, led by survivors from the Weimar Republic such as Walter Ulbricht,

failed to win a majority in the elections of 1946 but took control of the government with Soviet approval. By 1948 the Soviet zone was a one-party state at the center of the cold war, and millions of East Germans were emigrating to the West. The flood of refugees going west became so embarrassing that in 1961 Ulbricht closed the border. He erected a dramatic barrier in Berlin: the Berlin Wall—a brick, concrete, barbed wire, and machine gun impediment to travel—which became the most vivid symbol of the Iron Curtain (see illustration 31.4).

The Western powers slowly united their zones. Britain and the United States began the economic merger of their zones in 1946; when the French accepted German unity, the allies created the German Federal Republic (West Germany) in May 1949. The allies required that the Federal Republic's constitution (known as the *Grundgesetz*, or basic law) protect regional rights, create authority without authoritarianism, and include a liberal bill of rights.

The leading founder of the Federal Republic of Germany was Konrad Adenauer, a lawyer who had served as mayor of Cologne and a deputy during the Weimar Republic. Adenauer had survived the Nazi era in an early retirement, and he had twice been arrested by the Gestapo. He founded a conservative party, the Christian Democratic Union (CDU), which was heavily Catholic but nevertheless tried to avoid the confessional identity of the old Center Party. The CDU stood for anticommunism, free-enterprise economics, and social conservatism, but Adenauer, like many British and French conservatives, defended the welfare state and drew on Bismarck's example in the 1880s to advocate "socially responsible" capitalism.

The CDU mixture of conservatism and socialism won a narrow plurality of the votes for the German parliament (the *Bundestag*) in 1949 elections; the party expanded that margin to win every national election of the 1950s and the 1960s. Adenauer won the chancellorship of West Germany by a single vote by allying with a moderate third party (the Free Democrats) against a strong Social Democratic Party. Adenauer's personality was more authoritarian than democratic, but his fourteen-year chancellorship (1949–63) firmly established the Federal Republic as a Western democracy. Because of his influence, the capital of the new republic was situated in the small (100,000 population in 1939) Rhineland manufacturing town of Bonn where he had been a student, and the Federal Republic was sometimes called the Bonn republic.

The greatest accomplishment of the Bonn republic was an economic recovery called the *Wirtschaftswunder* ("economic miracle"). The *Wirtschaftswunder* owed much to American policy: Germany was included in the Marshall Plan of 1948 and was given $3.5 billion by 1961. Much of the credit for the recovery also belongs to the finance minister in Adenauer's cabinet, Ludwig Erhard. Erhard was a professor of economics at the University of Munich and the principal author of the CDU program linking free-enterprise economics with social welfare. He presided over a monetary policy that penalized savings and favored the purchase of commodities. His demand-driven economy created a huge increase in production (see table 31.2). German steel production had been 13.7 million tons in 1910, and East and West Germany together produced only 13.1 million tons in 1950. By 1960 West Germany alone produced 34.1 million tons. Translated into a consumer economy, this meant that West Germany manufactured only 301,000 automobiles in 1950 but more than 3 million in 1960. This rapid growth of production virtually eliminated unemployment, which fell below 1 percent. Credit for this prosperity also belongs to the generation of workers who lived with long workweeks (typically forty-eight hours) and low wages (twenty-five cents per hour

❧ TABLE 31.2 ❧ The German Economic Miracle, 1945–69			
Product	1949	1959	1969
Pig iron (1,000 tons)	7,140	21,602	33,764
Steel (1,000 tons)	9,156	29,435	45,316
Natural gas (million cubic meters)	534	388	8,799
Private cars (1,000s)	104	1,503	3,380
Electricity (million kilowatt hours)	40.7	106.2	226.1

Source: B. R. Mitchell, *European Historical Statistics, 1750–1990* (London: Macmillan, 1975), pp. 372, 395, 467, 481.

in the 1950s—less than half of the American standard). In return for social benefits, such as four to six weeks of paid vacation per year, Germany obtained great labor peace: During the first decade of the twentieth century, Germany had lost an annual average of 6.5 million working days to strikes; during the 1960s, West Germany lost an average of 0.3 million working days.

Europe and the World: The Age of Decolonization, 1945–75

When World War II ended, Europe still held vast colonial empires. Most of Africa, the Middle East, South and Southeast Asia, the East Indies and Pacific Oceania, and the Caribbean remained under imperial rule. Movements for national independence had begun in many areas before the war. After the war, the imperial powers learned that they could not keep their empires even by fighting major wars. The resulting breakup of European colonial empires, called decolonization, is one of the most important themes of twentieth-century world history. As one non-Western nationalist put it, decolonization changed "the international structure more profoundly than did the two terrible world wars." That change happened rapidly. Most of South Asia and the East Indies (more than 500 million people) won self-government between 1946 and 1950. Most of Africa (more than thirty countries) won independence between 1956 and 1966.

Three major patterns of decolonization emerged in the 1940s: (1) the pattern set by the British in India (granted independence in 1947) showed that Europeans could end imperialism when convinced that they must do so or pay a terrible price; (2) the pattern set by the French in the Brazzaville Conference of 1944 showed that some governments would struggle to retain empires; and (3) the pattern set by the people of the Dutch East Indies (1945–49) showed that colonial peoples could win their independence by force.

The British acceptance of decolonization began with the election of the Attlee government in 1945. Labour Party doctrine had included colonial independence since a 1926 program denounced the empire as "based on the absolute subjection of the native population." British economic weakness and war weariness also made resistance unlikely. Gandhi's continued campaign of nonviolent resistance (*Satyagraha*), massive demonstrations, and the astute political leadership of Jawaharlal Nehru won Indian independence in 1947. The most difficult issue facing the British was not granting independence (they realized that they had little choice), but the conditions of it: Conflicts between the Moslem and Hindu populations of India led to its partition into a largely Hindu India (with Nehru as its first prime minister) and a largely Moslem Pakistan, a bitter parting that led to violence in 1946–48 and to India-Pakistan Wars in 1965, 1971, and 1984.

The French began the postwar era struggling to retain their colonial empire, instead of withdrawing as the British were obliged to do in India and Palestine. A French effort to block decolonization started with the doctrine of assimilation. Advocates of assimilation believed that colonial peoples could be integrated (assimilated) into a French-speaking, French-cultured civilization in which both the metropolitan and the overseas territories were principal parts. That philosophy shaped both the Brazzaville Conference, where the French promised "the material and moral development of the natives" but not independence, and the colonial provisions in the constitution of the Fourth Republic (1946): France and her colonies formed an indissoluble French Union. So the French fought independence. While the British were granting independence to Burma (1947), the French were resisting a proclamation of independence in neighboring Vietnam. During the next generation, independent Burma produced a secretary-general of the United Nations, U Thant, while Vietnam fought nineteen years of war against France (1946–54) and the United States (1965–75).

The Indonesian pattern of guerrilla warfare became one of the predominant features of decolonization. Two days after the surrender of Japan in 1945 Indonesian leaders proclaimed a republic of Indonesia under the presidency of Achmed Sukarno, who had led resistance since 1927. When the Dutch refused independence, they had to fight an Indonesian People's Army until accepting independence four years later (see map 31.3). Variations of this pattern were repeated in all European empires. The French fought Ho Chi Minh's Vietminh forces in Vietnam until withdrawing after a shocking defeat at Dienbienphu in 1954. The British fought the Mau Mau movement of Jomo Kenyatta in Kenya from 1948 to 1957. The last country to accept decolonization, Portugal, battled guerrilla warfare in Mozambique until 1975.

Decolonization became intertwined with the cold war. The Soviet Union realized that the peoples of Africa and Asia were fighting their mutual enemies, so Moscow supported movements of national liberation. Some independence leaders were Communists, such as Ho Chi Minh, one of the founders of the French Communist Party. Some liberation movements hid an uncomfortable alliance between Communist elements and nationalists; this happened in the Dutch East Indies, where the leadership was anti-Communist and later conducted a bloody purge of Communists. The United States and the European imperial powers often reacted to decolonization as if it were only a theater of the cold war where the policy of containment applied. This led to further Western hostility to many independence movements and was a major factor for American involvement in Vietnam.

The turning point in decolonization came between 1957 and 1962. During those years both Britain and France acknowledged the end of their empires, and more than two dozen countries gained their independence. France had lost the disastrous war in Vietnam in 1954. Britain and France had suffered further embarrassment in the Suez War of 1956. In 1957 the British West African colony of Gold Coast had become the independent state of Ghana under the leadership of Kwame Nkrumah (see map 31.4). In 1958 he led the first conference of independent African states in condemning Western colonialism and racism. Two years later, the United Nations adopted a Declaration against Colonialism stating that the ideals of the World War II Allies, embodied in the UN Charter and the UN Declaration of Human Rights, must apply to the peoples of Africa and Asia, too (see document 31.4). The remain-

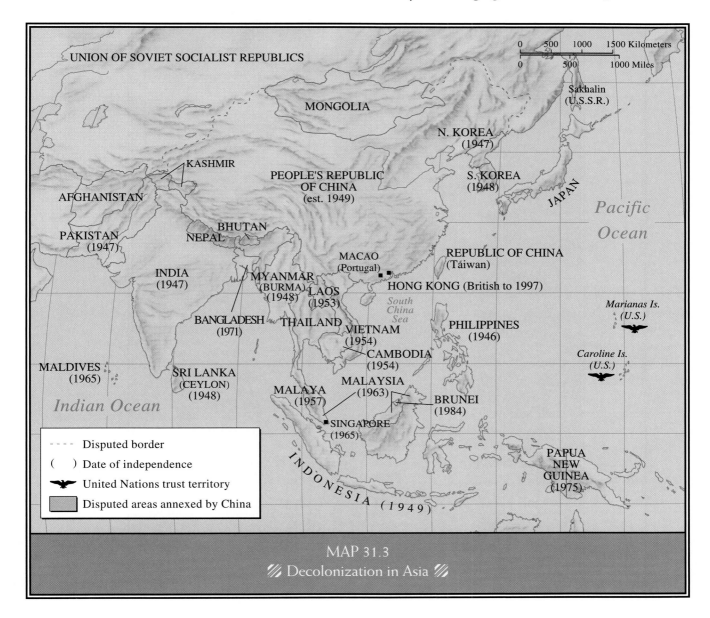

MAP 31.3
Decolonization in Asia

ing European empires (Belgium, Britain, France, Portugal, and Spain), plus the United States, did not support this resolution, but they could not overcome global support for it.

Conservative governments in Britain and France, long the staunchest imperialists, recognized that the age of empire—or "the great western party," as one black leader termed it—was over. Prime Minister Harold MacMillan acknowledged this in a 1960 speech discussing the "wind of change" blowing across the African continent. His Tory government of 1957–64 granted Ghana, Kenya, Nigeria, and four other territories independence. President de Gaulle, who had coura-

geously granted Algerian independence at the risk of French civil war, presided over the independence of thirteen more French African colonies between 1958 and 1962.

The European Economic Community, 1945–75

The most historic trend in postwar Europe may not have been reconstruction and prosperity, the revival of democratic government, the cold war between the

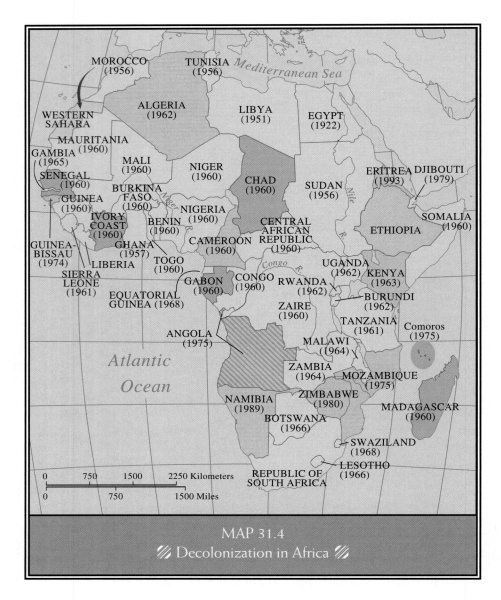

MAP 31.4
Decolonization in Africa

West and the Soviet bloc, or even the age of decolonization, but the progress toward European unity.

Postwar cooperation began with the negotiation of free trade agreements. A 1948 treaty linked Belgium, Luxembourg, and the Netherlands in the Benelux Customs Union. The Organization for European Economic Cooperation (OEEC) united sixteen non-Communist states, from Iceland and Scandinavia in the north to Turkey and Iberia in the south, for the distribution of American aid from the Marshall Plan. The OEEC sparked debates about European unity, especially after the selection of Paul-Henri Spaak of Belgium as the first president of its council. Spaak called for political institutions to accompany economic unity, and a 1949 treaty founded the Council of Europe to begin such cooperation.

Meaningful economic integration began in 1950. The foreign minister of France, Robert Schuman, introduced a new plan devised by Monnet: pooling coal and steel resources under an international authority to speed recovery. Britain—in a fateful decision that long separated the British from the evolution of European unity—rejected the Schuman Plan, but France, West Germany, Italy, and the Benelux states created the European Coal and Steel Community in 1951. Monnet, a strong advocate of a United States of Europe, became the first president of the Coal and Steel Community. Despite appeals by Schuman and Monnet, British conservatives still refused to join, so the six continental states chose "to create Europe without Britain."

The Paris Treaty of 1951 that created the Coal and Steel Community also contained plans for a European

◈ DOCUMENT 31.4 ◈

The United Nations Declaration
Against Colonialism (1960)

The General Assembly, mindful of the determination proclaimed by the peoples of the world in the Charter of the United Nations to reaffirm faith in fundamental human rights, in the dignity and worth of the human person, in the equal rights of men and women and of nations large and small, and to promote social progress and better standards of life in larger freedom . . . declares that:

1. The subjection of peoples to alien subjugation, domination, and exploitation constitutes a denial of fundamental human rights, is contrary to the Charter of the United Nations and is an impediment to the promotion of world peace and cooperation.

2. All peoples have the right to self-determination; by virtue of that right they freely determine their political status and freely pursue their economic, social, and cultural development.

3. Inadequacy of political, economic, social or educational preparedness should never serve as a pretext for delaying independence.

4. All armed action or repressive measures of all kinds directed against dependent peoples shall cease in order to enable them to exercise peacefully and freely their right to complete independence.

United Nations. *Official Records of the General Assembly.* December 14, 1960. Resolution 1514. New York: United Nations.

Parliament to sit in Strasbourg, and the six members added other supranational institutions such as the European Court of Human Rights (1953), a dedication to human rights that would later become one of the hallmarks of European unity when other states sought to join. (Even if it were in Europe, the United States would be ineligible for membership because the widespread application of the death penalty in America violates the European standard of human rights.) When the Coal and Steel Community prospered, this persuaded "the Six" to begin to discuss a common market for all goods. The Rome Treaties of 1957 then created the European Economic Community (the EEC)—often called the Common Market—in which the Six accepted the gradual elimination of tariffs (1959–68) among themselves and a common tariff policy toward other countries.

The EEC enjoyed economic advantages during the recovery of the 1950s and the prosperity of the 1960s. Its success was so clear that seven other countries (Austria, Denmark, Norway, Portugal, Sweden, Switzerland, and a reluctant Britain) formed a similar organization, the European Free Trade Association (EFTA) in 1959. The EEC, however, moved more quickly to economic and political cooperation than the EFTA did, and by the early 1960s EEC membership clearly was highly desirable. Greece obtained associate status in the EEC

in 1961, with limited trade benefits, and Turkey followed in 1963. Britain, Ireland, and Norway then applied for full membership. President de Gaulle—who had never forgiven Britain and America for their treatment of him during World War II and who believed that the British were unwilling to surrender any measure of sovereignty to a continental organization—vetoed British entry into the Common Market, however, leading the EEC to table all applications. Instead of expanding, the EEC chose to tighten its internal unity, and the EEC, the European Coal and Steel Community, and other organizations linking the Six were merged to form the European Community (EC) in 1967.

Charles de Gaulle remained an obstacle to expansion of the EC until his retirement in 1969, but the Six voted for expansion immediately after his departure. The EC accepted all four applications, but Norwegians rejected membership in a national referendum (53–47 percent), so the Six became the Nine. The British, whose relations with Europe had been troubled for a generation, reconsidered their membership and demanded new terms for entry into the EC. They joined in 1973, but domestic opinion still demanded concessions; after winning some agreements, the British supported membership in a national referendum in 1975. Most of non-Communist Europe then began to line up for entry into the European Community.

◆

The Cooling Down of the Cold War: *Ostpolitik* and Détente, 1965–75

The cold war in Europe began to end in the mid-1960s, and both the Soviet and American alliance systems began to weaken. A growing rift between the USSR and China opened in the 1960s, and the USSR denounced Chinese policy as "anti-Leninist" and branded Mao a dictator. The chill worsened when the Chinese detonated their first H-bomb in 1967, and frontier incidents became common in the late 1960s. Simultaneously, American alliances were strained by the protracted Vietnam War, which was widely denounced in Europe.

The diplomatic consequences of these events were enormous, and new policies emerged during the late 1960s and early 1970s. President de Gaulle of France and Chancellor Willy Brandt of West Germany led Europe into this new era—de Gaulle by distancing France from the Western alliance in the late 1960s and Brandt by normalizing relations with Eastern Europe in the early 1970s. These changes initially discomfitted American governments, but they helped to change American policy. President Lyndon B. Johnson and Secretary Leonid Brezhnev cautiously accepted arms control negotiations in the late 1960s, and this produced a series of important treaties in the 1970s. The next president of the United States, Richard M. Nixon, carried this policy to dramatic lengths in improving relations with the USSR and Maoist China, despite his career-long image as a dedicated anticommunist.

Charles de Gaulle opened the decade of diplomatic change in 1966 with a dramatic announcement that France was quitting its role in the NATO alliance and that NATO must leave French soil. De Gaulle also had a vision behind his actions. He visited the USSR and Eastern Europe in 1967 to promote his vision of "Europe to the Urals." This was not his most startling idea. The French tested their first atomic bomb in 1966 and their first H-bomb in 1968, and de Gaulle then proclaimed an independent French *force de frappe* (nuclear striking force) that was aimed at *toutes azimuths* (all points of the compass).

Willy Brandt's role in the diplomatic revolution had a more pacific tone. Brandt was shaped by his wartime experience as a refugee from Nazi Germany. He became famous as the mayor of West Berlin (1957–66) at the height of the cold war, leading that isolated city during confrontations over the Berlin Wall. Brandt then became the head of the West German socialist party and led the SPD to electoral victory. As chancellor of West Germany, he introduced his own dramatic policy known as *Ostpolitik* (eastern policy). He improved relations between the two Germanys by visiting the DDR in 1970 and shaking hands with the Communist prime minister. He signed treaties with both the Soviet Union and Poland, guaranteeing Germany's postwar frontiers, especially the Oder-Neisse Line that left much of prewar Germany inside Poland. He then negotiated a series of treaties between the two Germanys, culminating in a 1972 treaty permitting both states to enter the United Nations. *Ostpolitik* won Brandt the Nobel Peace Prize, but he resigned in 1974 when a spy scandal revealed that a member of his staff was an East German agent.

These European changes encouraged the improvement in Soviet-American relations known as *détente* (the relaxation of tension). Arms control negotiations with the USSR were controversial in the United States, and conservatives had fought against President John F. Kennedy's Test Ban Treaty (1963) in which both sides promised not to test nuclear weapons in the atmosphere, in outer space, or under the oceans. The French and Chinese nuclear explosions of 1967 persuaded Washington and Moscow to resume negotiations for the nuclear nonproliferation treaty of 1968, and this treaty encouraged the United States and the USSR to open larger Strategic Arms Limitation Talks (SALT) in 1969. Anti-Communist conservatives in America fought this policy, but it succeeded when a conservative anti-Communist adopted it. Richard Nixon, who placated anti-Communists by waging vigorous war in Asia, followed the left-wing policy of détente to new relations with the Soviet Union. Nixon and Brezhnev exchanged state visits in the early 1970s and signed a series of arms treaties, beginning with the SALT treaty of 1972. A vivid symbol of the age of détente came in the summer of 1975 when American and Russian spacecrafts docked together in outer space, but Nixon provided an even more dramatic symbol in his Chinese policy. He accepted Communist Chinese membership in the UN, flew to Beijing to meet with Chairman Mao, agreed that Taiwan was part of China, and posed for photographs atop the Great Wall of China. The cold war was ending.

◆

An Era of Unrest and Violence, 1968–75

Although the cold war was less heated in 1970 than it had been in the 1950s, Europe faced other violence. The war in southeast Asia, which had been a battleground for thirty years, formed an important background for the violence of 1968–75. Fighting in Vietnam reduced the global prestige of the United States to its lowest level since World War II. Student and leftwing demonstrations in the great cities of Europe protested American militarism. Simultaneously, American military prestige suffered in 1968 when the Viet Cong's Tet (the lunar new year) Offensive overran American positions and took the fighting into the cities of South Vietnam. American moral leadership suffered when the U.S. army began a war crimes trial of American officers for killing 567 civilians in the village of My Lai in 1969, and the evidence led to the conviction of Lt. William Calley. Such events produced great turbulence in American society, and the late 1960s and early 1970s witnessed vehement student protests on university campuses, race riots in American cities, a police riot in Chicago, an antiwar march on Washington, D.C., the assassination of two American political leaders (the Reverend Dr. Martin Luther King, Jr., and Senator Robert F. Kennedy), and the use of armed troops against protesters, resulting in the killing of four students at Kent State University.

One consequence of these events for Europe was that the United States lost much of its authority to oppose the Soviet Union when a crisis occurred in Czechoslovakia. In January 1968 the Czech Communist Party selected a liberal reformer, Alexander Dubček, for the leadership post of first secretary of the party. Dubček proposed political and economic liberties to humanize communist society. The enthusiastic Czech response to Dubček's brand of socialism led to an optimistic period known as the Prague Spring, but the reforms and the optimism were both short-lived. Brezhnev ordered an invasion of Czechoslovakia in August 1968. An occupying force of 200,000 Soviet and Warsaw Pact troops encountered Czech protests, and 650,000 soldiers were ultimately needed to end the demonstrations, oust Dubček, and install a pro-Moscow government (see illustration 31.5).

Militant student protests in European universities, the rise of European terrorist movements, and the rebirth of violent nationalist movements also characterized the era. The largest European student protest occurred in Paris in the spring of 1968. Demonstrations at the University of Paris (which had an enrollment of 160,000) were part of an international youth rebellion of the late 1960s that had produced major outbreaks from the University of California to the University in Berlin a few weeks earlier. Many issues angered students, but in most protests they denounced American

imperialism in Asia and the autocratic administration of their campus. The demonstrations at Paris became a global symbol of a near revolution sparked by students, as many of the revolutions of 1848 had been. They began with disputes on the suburban campus at Nanterre, then closed the Sorbonne, and grew into riots in central Paris. Once again, barricades closed streets in Paris. On one night, an estimated twenty-five thousand students fought the police. The events of May 1968 assumed greater importance when industrial workers called a general strike to support the students and paralyzed much of France. The strikes and riots soon ended, but they led to the resignation of President de Gaulle a few months later.

Student protests were not the most violent legacy of the late 1960s and early 1970s. More fearsome was the rebirth of terrorism in European politics. Some terrorist movements had roots in the extreme left-wing politics of the era, including the Baader-Meinhof gang in West Germany (whose actions included setting fire to a Berlin department store) and the Red Brigades in Italy (who assassinated prominent individuals, such as the president of Fiat motors, and terrorized more by shooting people in the kneecap). International politics, particularly the Middle Eastern question, was an even greater source of terrorism. In 1972 alone, international terrorists high-jacked a German jetliner, attacked Jewish athletes at the Munich Olympic games, and sent letter bombs to businessmen in several countries.

A continuing part of the new violence in European politics was the escalation of nationalist terrorism. Basque nationalists sought independence from Spain by assassinations such as the bombing death of Spanish premier Luis Carrero Blanco in 1973. Corsican nationalists fought for independence from France by bombing public buildings. The most uncompromising terrorist movement in Europe was Irish. Sectarian violence between Catholics and Protestants in Northern Ireland killed eight people in Belfast in August 1969, and the British government responded with troops to maintain order. This revived the Irish Republican Army (IRA), which hoped to drive the British out of Ulster and reunite Northern Ireland with the Republic of Ireland. The British government, however, was intransigent. In 1971 the British proclaimed emergency powers of detention and arrest and curtailed civil rights; in early 1972 Britain suspended the government of Northern Ireland and established direct rule by London. Later in 1972 British troops fired upon Catholic rioters in Londonderry, killing thirteen people in the "Bloody Sunday Massacre." By early 1973 the IRA had opened the

Illustration 31.5

Rebellion in the Soviet Bloc. Throughout the cold war, the Soviet Union faced the problem of discontent in its satellite states in Eastern Europe. Major uprisings in East Germany in 1953, Hungary in 1956, and Czechoslovakia in 1968 were put down by force. This photo shows a scene from the Soviet-led Warsaw Pact invasion of Czechoslovakia: A Soviet tank has come under attack and crashed into a building in central Prague.

biggest terrorist campaign in postwar European history. A series of pub bombings in Guildford and Birmingham shocked British opinion by killing nearly thirty people in 1974, but London became the favorite IRA target. Bombs exploded there in law courts and at tourist attractions; later, the IRA would bomb a major department store during Christmas shopping, launch a mortar assault on the prime minister's residence at 10 Downing Street, attempt to assassinate the prime minister with a hotel bombing during a party conference, and set off an enormous explosion in the financial district. The first five years of public riots, sectarian assaults, vigilante justice, police and military repression, and terrorist attacks killed more than one thousand people.

CHAPTER 32

THE NEW BELLE ÉPOQUE: DEMOCRACY AND PROSPERITY SINCE 1975

CHAPTER OUTLINE

◆◆◆◆◆◆◆◆◆◆◆◆◆◆◆◆◆◆◆◆◆◆

Chapter 32 examines contemporary Europe since the mid-1970s. The year 1975 was not an abrupt turning point in Western history, as 1914 or 1939 had been, but the events of the mid-1970s showed that the cold war was ending and a prosperous new Europe was emerging. The chapter begins by looking at this peace and prosperity, including signs of progress toward the ages-old dream of European unity. One element of European progress was the rise of women to real political power, and the chapter next looks at Great Britain under Margaret Thatcher, who introduced Europe to a firm, conservative reevaluation of that prosperity.

The most dramatic changes resulted from the collapse of the Communist regimes in the Soviet Union and Eastern Europe. Chapter 32 shows the background discontent such as the rise of the Solidarity movement in Poland, the revolution that Mikhail Gorbachev brought to the USSR, and the upheavals in Eastern Europe known as the revolutions of 1989. Two other historic events followed the collapse of Communist governments: the reunification of Germany and the Yugoslav Wars of 1991–99.

◈

European Peace and Prosperity

During 1975 two dramatic events gave Europe greater hope for an age of peace. The first was the end of the Vietnam War. This conflict, the last stage of thirty years of fighting to drive Japanese, then French, and finally American armies out of Southeast Asia, ended in April 1975 with the evacuation of the last American officials from South Vietnam and the fall of the Saigon government. Although this long war ended in Communist expansion, it did not greatly worsen cold war relations; instead, it allowed them to improve, especially in Europe where the war had been widely opposed.

Illustration 32.1

💥 **The Age of Détente.** Willy Brandt, the chancellor of West Germany, was perhaps the most influential statesman in launching the age of détente in the early 1970s. Brandt repeatedly made friendly overtures to the states of Eastern Europe, especially to East Germany and Poland—a policy known as *Ostpolitik*. He not only negotiated treaties that improved relations, but he also made a series of symbolic gestures, as seen in this photo, taken during a state visit to Poland: Brandt is silently contemplating a monument to the victims of the Warsaw ghetto, killed by Germans.

Despite the conflict in Southeast Asia, détente between east and west—which Chancellor Willy Brandt of West Germany had launched with his *Ostpolitik* of the early 1970s (see illustration 32.1)—had grown; the end of the war permitted even better relations among the United States, Western Europe, the USSR, and China. Détente culminated in the Helsinki Accord of 1975, in which thirty-five nations guaranteed the frontiers of 1945, renewed their support for the United Nations and the peaceful resolution of crises, swore respect for "the sovereign equality and individuality" of all states, expanded economic cooperation, renounced the threat or use of force, and pledged respect for human rights (see document 32.1). Like most idealistic treaties—such as the UN Declaration of Human Rights of 1946, the Geneva Conventions, the Kellogg-Briand Pact of 1928, the League of Nations Charter of 1920, and the Hague Treaties of 1899 and 1906—the Helsinki Accord contained no mechanism to enforce its principles during crises, yet still promoted hope. Westerners acclaimed a treaty that obliged the USSR to honor human rights; but Soviet leader Leonid Brezhnev believed that the document still permitted actions such as the invasion of Afghanistan.

By the late 1970s Western Europe had also developed a booming economy, which created a standard of living comparable to that in the United States. Recovery from the devastation of World War II had been largely completed by the late 1950s, and thriving European economies began to catch up with the United States during the 1960s. West Germany had become the most prosperous country in Europe, with a GNP

larger than France or Britain. The economic miracle of Ludwig Erhart and Konrad Adenauer created the fastest growing economy in German history. The German model of labor relations, in which labor, management, the government, and public opinion shared a strong consensus on supporting a welfare state and promising job security in return for strike- and strife-free production, resulted in a rapidly growing economy. German unemployment fell so low that foreign guest workers (*Gastarbeiter*) from Turkey and other Mediterranean countries were needed to fill jobs. The German domestic market absorbed most of this production during the 1960s, but Germany increased exports by 1,300 percent during the 1970s. The other EEC states also began exporting more goods. French agriculture prospered so well that France became the world's second largest food exporter. By the end of the 1970s the European Union had become a major economic competitor of the United States. By 1990 GNP per capita in France ($16,000) and Germany ($18,500) neared that in the United States ($19,800).

Widespread prosperity had two important consequences in Western Europe: (1) it stimulated closer economic unity, a trend that had been slowly progressing for twenty-five years, and (2) it facilitated larger commitments to the welfare state. For the first of these trends, the mid-1970s were an important turning point. The European Community (the EC—the association that grew out of the EEC in 1967, tightening the linkage of France, West Germany, Italy, and the Benelux countries), was the highest degree of European economic integration ever achieved. Negotiations to ex-

The Helsinki Accord, 1975

The Conference on Security and Cooperation in Europe produced the most idealistic international agreement of the cold war. Thirty-five countries signed the Final Act of this conference, which became known as the Helsinki Accord.

The participating states will respect human rights and fundamental freedoms, including the freedom of thought, conscience, religion or belief, for all without distinction as to race, sex, language or religion.

They will promote and encourage the effective exercise of civil, political, economic, social, cultural, and other rights and freedoms all of which derive from the inherent dignity of the human person and are essential for his free and full development.

Within this framework the participating states will recognize and respect the freedom of the individual to profess and practice, alone or in community with others, religion or belief acting in accordance with the dictates of his own conscience.

The participating states on whose territory national minorities exist will respect the rights of persons belonging to such minorities to equality before the law, will afford them the full opportunity for the actual enjoyment of human rights and fundamental freedoms and will, in this manner, protect their legitimate interests in this sphere.

Helsinki Accord. *New York Times,* August 2, 1975.

pand the EC revived in the 1970s, and plans were drafted for adding Britain, Ireland, Denmark, and Norway as the first step toward the economic union of all of non-Communist Europe (see chronology 32.1). The most important (and sometimes the most troublesome) of these states, Britain, finally joined the EC in 1973. In several cases, membership treaties were submitted for public approval in a referendum. A negative vote in Norway kept that country out of the European Community, but British membership was reaffirmed in a public vote in 1975, encouraging a generation of EC growth (see map 32.1). The death of General Franco (1975) and the subsequent election of a democratic government in Spain (1977), plus free elections in Portugal (1975) that freed Iberia from the authoritarian

governments of the 1930s, allowed the EC to accept both Iberian states, bringing membership to twelve. Under the leadership of Jacques Delors, who presided over the European Commission in Brussels for ten years (1985–95), and Helmut Kohl, who strongly supported closer unity, Europe moved toward a federal unity and oversaw the transformation of the European Community EC into the European Union (EU) in 1991, when the Maastricht summit outlined a treaty to open European frontiers and establish a single market. By the mid-1990s, the European Union had grown to fifteen members with the addition of Sweden, Finland, and Austria. The fall of the Communist bloc led to a wave of applications from Eastern Europe, and in 1997 plans were adopted for the eventual membership of Estonia, Poland, the Czech Republic, Hungary, and Slovenia; other Eastern European applications (plus one from Turkey) have been put on a slower track.

As the European Union grew, so did its institutions. The first direct elections for the European Parliament in Strasbourg were held in 1979, and a woman, Simone Veil of France, was chosen as its first president. An agreement signed that same year created an integrated monetary system to control exchange rates, the first step toward a common European currency known as the Euro, launched for banks in 1999 and scheduled to replace European currencies such as the German mark and the French franc (but not the British pound) in 2001.

The Maastricht Treaty of 1991 created a closer union by opening national frontiers (in 1992) for the free movement of goods, workers, students, or investments. The European Convention on Human Rights quickly became another important part of the European Union because all potential members were required to subscribe to it and accept the jurisdiction of the European Court of Human Rights. The strict human rights standards for membership create an obstacle to joining the EU for several countries—laws allowing capital punishment or evidence of the use of torture can exclude a country.

The closer federation planned at Maastricht was so controversial that many governments held referenda to gain public approval of the treaty. In France, long a leader in the drive toward greater unity, a referendum of September 1992 only approved of the Maastricht Treaty by the narrow margin of 51–49 percent. Prime Minister Thatcher of Britain was the leading critic of the European Union. She attacked the Brussels bureaucracy of "Eurocrats," the plans for a common currency, the Union's common social policy (which she de-

◈ CHRONOLOGY 32.1 ◈

The Growth of European Union Since 1975

1975   British referendum accepts EC membership

1975   Greece, Spain, and Portugal apply for EC membership

1979   First direct elections to the European Parliament in Strasbourg

1979   Simone Veil elected first president of the European Parliament

1979   The EC creates the European Monetary System (EMS) and European Currency Unit (ECU)

1981   Greece begins five-year phased entry into the EC as tenth member

1983   Governments of the ten EC members sign the Solemn Declaration on unity

1984   European Parliament adopts treaty on creating the European Union (EU)

1985   Spain and Portugal accepted into the EC as eleventh and twelfth members

1985   Single European Act sets 1992 as date for open frontiers and single market

1986   Single European Act adopted in parliaments of all twelve member states

1987   Turkey applies for membership in the EC

1988   Delors Plan outlines closer economic unity and a common currency

1989   EC adopts draft Charter of Fundamental Social Rights

1989   Austria applies for membership in the EC

1990   Cyprus and Malta apply for EC membership

1991   Sweden applies for membership in the EC

1992   Single European Act and Maastricht Treaty create open frontiers and single market: EC becomes the EU

1992   Norway and Finland apply for EU membership

1992   Twelve members of the EU agree to negotiations to expand to sixteen members

1992   Switzerland applies for EU membership

1994   Sweden, Finland, and Austria reach agreements to join the EU

1995   Norwegian national referendum again rejects EU membership

1997   EU adopts plan for Estonia, Poland, Czech Republic, Hungary, and Slovenia to join

1997   Membership plans for Latvia, Lithuania, Slovakia, Romania, Bulgaria, and Turkey postponed

---

nounced as a backdoor route for socialism into Britain), the increasing role of the European Parliament at Strasbourg (at the expense of Britain's Parliament), and the apparent birth of a European "superstate."

The second trend encouraged by the new prosperity was the growth of the welfare state and social benefits. Most West European governments, following such examples as Swedish state socialism or the policies of Attlee's Britain, devoted a significant share of new wealth and production to public services and benefits. In West Germany, both the socialist governments of Willy Brandt (1969–74) and Helmut Schmidt (1974–82) and the conservative government of Helmut Kohl (1982–98) accepted high tax rates as the price of social cohesion. And the benefits of European prosperity have been great: Britain, France, and Germany all established workweeks below thirty-eight or thirty-nine hours for full pay. Britain, France, Germany, and Italy all guaranteed employees and workers a minimum of five to six weeks of paid vacation per year—compared with the

two weeks standard in the United States and Japan. German workers had the most exceptional treatment: a minimum of fifty-eight paid days off (eleven-and-one-half weeks) per year in combined vacation days and paid holidays. France and Italy established age sixty for retirement at full pay, with age fifty or fifty-five the standard in some occupations. In 1996 Germans were guaranteed 52 weeks of unemployment compensation, or 128 weeks after age fifty-four, at 60 percent of salary. All EU countries except Luxembourg granted pregnant women a minimum of three months of paid maternity leave, with Denmark granting six months. Many countries, led by France, have given free tuition to state universities to all students. And the entire EU is committed to free, or low cost, medical care for all; some states, led by Germany, include free nursing home care for the elderly.

The price of such benefits has been high taxation. European taxation has been so high that in the late 1980s it consumed one-third to one-half of the GNP

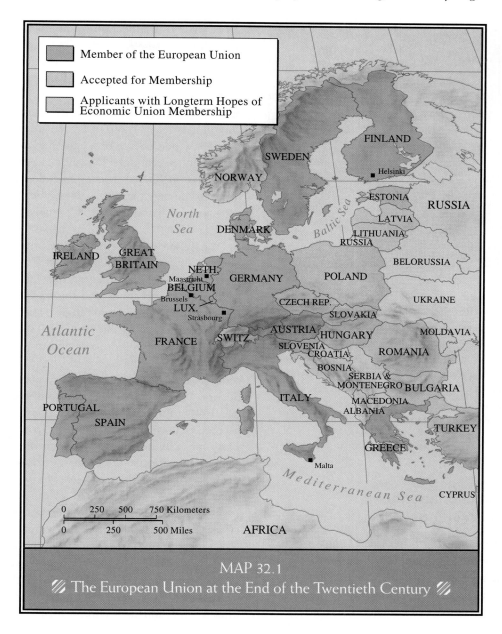

Member of the European Union

Accepted for Membership

Applicants with Longterm Hopes of Economic Union Membership

MAP 32.1

The European Union at the End of the Twentieth Century

in Britain, France, and Germany and more than 55 percent in Sweden. And it has been growing: French government spending grew from 44 percent in 1987 to 52 percent in 1995. Although most of the taxation that supports this social system comes from indirect taxes—especially a Value Added Tax (VAT) hidden in the cost of goods—Europeans do notice the cost of these benefits. The unemployment of German workers, for example, is supported by a 3.25 percent payroll deduction from workers' gross income, matched by a 3.25 percent payment by employers; the lesser benefit in the United States is supported by a 2.3 percent tax on payroll, paid by employers. European con-

servatives such as Helmut Kohl of Germany tried to reduce spending on social services during the late 1980s and the 1990s, but they accepted both the welfare state and the taxation needed to finance it. Even the socialist president of France, François Mitterand (served 1981–95), who defended the welfare commitment, faced hard fiscal decisions and his government adopted many conservative policies. The French public, however, has been one of the staunchest constituencies for protecting the welfare state. When the conservative government proposed reduced services in 1997, French socialists under Lionel Jospin won an upset parliamentary victory.

Illustration 32.2

⚡ **The Conservative Revolution.** Margaret Thatcher, the first woman to become prime minister of Britain, was one of the strongest and most successful prime ministers in British history. She was the driving force behind a conservative revolution that dismantled much of the welfare state and the nationalized economy created by the Labour government after World War II. Here, she celebrates her landslide electoral victory of 1983, which created the overwhelming majority in Parliament to adopt her program.

Margaret Thatcher and the Conservative Revolution

European history was facing other great changes in the mid-1970s. The most important harbinger of the new Europe could be seen in Britain in 1975. In February 1975 Britain's Conservative Party elected Margaret Thatcher, a former minister of education, to lead the party (see illustration 32.2). That event was a landmark in European history for two reasons: (1) never in the history of parliamentary democracy had one of the great powers chosen a woman to lead them, and (2) her policies provided the first vigorous challenge to the growth of the welfare state. These dramatic changes began in 1979 when Thatcher became the first woman prime minister in British history, a post she held for the longest period of any modern prime minister. Her success began an era of women reaching the top in European politics (see chronology 32.2). In 1980 Norway elected a woman prime minister, Iceland a woman president, and Portugal a woman prime minister. By the 1990s even Ireland (1990), France (1991), and Turkey (1993) had elected women as either prime minister or president. Simultaneously, European women gained a

larger share of political power at lower levels. No country, however, has a Parliament in which 50 percent of the representatives are women. Sweden, where women won 41 percent of the seats in Parliament in 1994 has the highest rate; Greece (5.3 percent) has the lowest percentage. Despite the presence of a woman at 10 Downing Street, Britain had been among the nations with a low percentage of women in Parliament during the Thatcher years; the landslide Labour victory of Tony Blair in 1997, however, included 102 women M.P.s in the new majority—far higher than the participation of women in France, Germany, or the United States.

Thatcher was not born to the British political elite. She was the daughter of a successful small-town grocer who twice was elected mayor. Her father was also a Methodist lay preacher, and she was raised in strict family virtues drawn from religion as well as business. It was less typical of families in the 1930s that Thatcher's parents encouraged her to be ambitious and to develop her intelligence. She attended Oxford University as a scholarship student and chemistry major during the Second World War, was drawn to British politics in the late 1940s, and soon studied law to advance that career. Elected to Parliament in 1959, she rose in Conservative Party ranks by becoming an expert on social issues, such as education and welfare, which were often deemed the appropriate subjects for women in politics. When Edward Heath formed a Conservative government in 1970, Margaret Thatcher became minister of education and science, the only woman in the cabinet.

Thatcher built her reputation during Heath's troubled Tory government. Conservatives struggled to restrict the power of the trade unions with only limited success. Strikes by tens of thousands of dockworkers, miners, and industrial workers protested plans to curb wages or union powers. Simultaneously, the Heath government faced a worsening of the Irish question. Sectarian riots, police battles, and terrorist bombing became commonplace in the early 1970s. The Conservative government responded by suspending the powers of the provincial government and Parliament in Northern Ireland, establishing direct British rule of the province, escalating the number of troops sent to maintain order, and finally governing under state of emergency decrees that suspended many liberties. Amidst these crises, the British public lost confidence in the government, and Margaret Thatcher emerged as the strongest Tory leader. She had the strength to champion the conservative program of severe budget cuts even when they were immensely unpopular. As minister of education she eliminated a national program of free

---

◈ CHRONOLOGY 32.2 ◈

The Acceptance of Women in Political Leadership, 1974–94

1974 Barbara Castle becomes Britain's first secretary of state for social security

Simone Veil becomes France's minister for health

Eva Kolstad becomes president of Norway's Liberal Party

Françoise Giroud becomes France's first minister for women's affairs

1975 Margaret Thatcher becomes first woman to lead a major British political party

1976 Mairead Corrigan and Betty Williams of Northern Ireland share Nobel Peace Prize

Françoise Giroud becomes France's minister of culture

Yelena Bonner is cofounder of Helsinki Human Rights Group in the USSR

1979 Margaret Thatcher becomes first woman prime minister of Britain

Petra Kelly is cofounder of West Germany's environmentalist Green Party

Louise Weiss becomes senior member elected to the European Parliament

1980 Maria de Lourdes Pintasilgo briefly serves as Portugal's first woman prime minister

Vigdis Finnbogadottir elected first woman president of Iceland

Gro Brundtland becomes first woman prime minister of Norway

1981 Karin Ahrland becomes Sweden's minister for public health

Shirley Williams is cofounder of Britain's Social Democratic Party

1982 Gertrud Sigurdsen becomes Sweden's minister for public health

Anna-Greta Leijon becomes Sweden's minister of labor

1983 Petra Kelly is elected Green Party member of West German Parliament

1985 Melina Mercouri becomes Greece's minister of culture

1986 Anita Gradin becomes Sweden's minister for foreign trade

1987 Anita-Greta Leijon becomes Sweden's minister of justice

Margaret Thatcher is first modern prime minister to win three consecutive terms

1990 Mary Robinson elected first woman president of Ireland

1991 Edith Cresson becomes first woman premier of France

1992 Betty Boothroyd becomes first woman Speaker of Britain's Parliament

1993 Tansu Çiller becomes first woman prime minister of Turkey

1997 Labour landslide includes 102 women M.P.s

---

school milk for small children to make this point. In British popular culture she became "Thatcher, Thatcher, Milk Snatcher," but in conservative circles she became the leader of the future. She appealed to many conservatives because she embodied and defended their sense of "Victorian virtues." As Thatcher put it, "I was brought up to work jolly hard. We were taught to live within our income, that cleanliness is next to godliness. We were taught self-respect. You were taught tremendous pride in your country." After Heath had lost the parliamentary elections of 1974, Thatcher challenged him for the leadership of the Conservative Party in 1975 and won. She became prime minister in 1979, following a campaign in which she promised to restore many aspects of the nineteenth-century laissez-faire liberal economics of free enterprise. "Free choice is ultimately what life is about," she proclaimed.

The Thatcher government of 1979–90 introduced Britain (and Europe) to strict fiscal conservatism. Thatcher championed monetarist economics that called for limiting the money supply to curb inflation. She coupled this with a promise to reduce taxes. The Conservative government honored this promise in one sense but violated it in another: It cut income taxes, but it raised indirect taxes, especially the national sales tax known as the VAT. Thatcher cut top income tax rates from 83 percent to 60 percent in 1979 and reduced them to 40 percent in 1979; the rate paid by average taxpayers fell from 33 percent to 30 percent and then to 25 percent. When she tried in 1990 to compensate for this huge loss of government revenue by instituting another regressive tax called the Poll Tax, antitax demonstrations drove her from office.

This conservative revolution necessitated severe reductions in government spending, especially in the budgets that Thatcher knew well—education and welfare services. Thatcher asserted that the cradle-to-grave welfare state that had evolved out of the Beveridge Plan and the Attlee reforms of the 1940s cost more than the nation could pay. The demographic portrait of the nation—greater longevity, lower employment, and lower birthrates—meant that the costs of the welfare state, which stood at 25 percent of the budget in 1979 and rose to 31 percent by 1988 (chiefly because of retirement pensions and the high cost of benefits in a period of high unemployment), would continue to rise. The Thatcher government cut some benefits directly, chiefly housing benefits, and curtailed others by taxing them or not raising them to match inflation. Her monetarism and budget cuts lowered inflation (5 percent), increased unemployment (12.7 percent), reduced public services, and caused vehement public debate.

Simultaneously, Thatcher aimed to increase the private sector of the British economy by selling off some previously nationalized enterprises. (Ten percent of the British national economy was state-run in 1979.) This policy of privatization eliminated state monopolies in some areas and sold state-run enterprises in others. This extended a cycle in British history; the Labour Party had begun nationalizations in 1945. Two of the most controversial nationalizations were privatized by Conservatives in 1951 (iron and steel) and a Labour government of 1967 made a few gestures toward the party's historic commitment. (Ironically, Thatcher's privatizations happened at the same time that François Mitterand's socialist government in France was undertaking new nationalizations in 1981–82.) Thatcher now sold nationalized coal, gas, oil, and steel interests such as the leading gasoline company, BP.

The Thatcher government also adopted a tough policy toward labor unions and public employees. Employment Acts in 1980, 1982, and 1988, plus a Trade Union Act of 1984, changed labor relations in Britain and weakened trade unions. These laws continued a century-long battle over union powers, redefining the right to strike (by requiring a membership ballot before a strike), restricting the right to picket, making unions liable for strike damages, and curtailing union monopolies known as closed shops. These restrictions were backed by the courts and grew stronger when unions became reluctant to strike.

Margaret Thatcher imposed her policies on a sometimes nervous conservative government with a forceful, intransigent style of leadership that belied generalizations about women leaders. Her tough policies and tougher style (especially in her dealings with the Soviet Union) earned her the nickname of "the Iron Lady." Thatcher also demonstrated her hard-line style during her chief foreign policy crisis. In the spring of 1982 Argentina invaded the Falkland Islands, a small British colony in the south Atlantic, claiming that they formed a historic part of the Argentine state. Against the strong opposition of the Labour Party and many members of her own party, Thatcher insisted upon taking back the Falklands by war. One month after the Argentine occupation, British troops stormed the islands and reclaimed them after a three-week land battle and several bloody encounters at sea. A year later, the Iron Lady was reelected with an overwhelming majority.

Discontent in Eastern Europe and the Rise of Solidarity

The peoples of eastern Europe demonstrated their hostility to Communist dictatorship on many occasions after 1945. Antigovernment demonstrations in East Berlin in 1953, an anti-Soviet rebellion in Hungary in 1956, and the Prague Spring reform movement in Czechoslovakia in 1968 were the most dramatic outbursts against the Soviet system. The frustration in Eastern Europe grew from the desire for both western freedoms and western material conditions. The standard of living in the east was far below conditions in the west, so daily frustrations compounded the discontent.

The Soviet Union had used force to suppress East Europe protest movements, asserting a right to intervene in neighboring states. This Soviet policy was known as the Brezhnev Doctrine in analogy to the Monroe Doctrine by which the United States intervened in neighboring states of Latin America. The Helsinki Agreement of 1975, however, contained Soviet guarantees of human rights. This inspired dissidents in several of the Soviet satellites. Czech intellectuals, led by the playwright Vaclav Havel, created a civil rights movement known as Charter 77. Their manifesto charged that the Czech government violated the human rights promised at Helsinki. The campaign was short-lived. Havel, whose satirical plays had been banned since 1968, and five other civil rights activists were jailed in 1979 for the crime of subversion.

Illustration 32.3

The Solidarity Movement in Poland. The founder and president of the workers' movement known as *Solidarnosc* (Solidarity), which played a major role in the fall of the Communist government in Poland, was a thirty-seven-year-old electronics technician and electrical worker at the state shipyards in Gdansk named Lech Walesa. He expressed the grievances of shipbuilders so effectively that he became a national symbol of Solidarity's resistance to the government. Here, Walesa addresses dockworkers in Gdansk in 1980; three years later he won the Nobel Peace Prize.

Poland witnessed the most successful challenge to Communist dictatorship in Eastern Europe. The Poles had resisted in 1956; worker protests in Poznan led to more than one hundred killings. Food riots were put down in 1970 and new strikes were suppressed in 1976, yet Poland still became the home of sustained protests in the 1980s. Rising food prices in 1980 led workers in Gdansk to strike. The movement spread among Polish industries, building a network of unions known as the Solidarity movement (*Solidarnosc*). Solidarity was the first independent trade union in the Soviet bloc, and it grew to ten million members. Under the leadership of Lech Walesa, a Gdansk shipyard electrician (see illustration 32.3), Solidarity strikers issued a dramatic list of demands (see document 32.2) and won changes in the government, increased wages, and most of their demands. Within a few months, however, a military government took power and banned the union.

The USSR warned Poland in 1981 to crack down on counterrevolution, and Poland was put under martial law with civil liberties suspended. Troops fired on strikers, killing seven. Walesa and thousands of strikers were imprisoned. Walesa won international support, however, including a Nobel Peace Prize (1983). The election of a Polish-born pope who supported Solidarity—John Paul II, the first non-Italian pope in 455 years—greatly strengthened the movement. Poland had re-

mained strongly Catholic during the Communist regime, and Pope John Paul II's 1979 visit to Poland had strengthened the will to resist the government. In part because NATO governments warned the Soviet Union that intervention in Poland under the Brezhnev Doctrine would end détente, the movement survived in a delicate compromise with the Communist regime during the 1980s.

The Soviet Union of the post-Stalin era had its own dissident movement. Khrushchev's destalinization allowed enough freedom for dissident writers to risk criticism of the regime. In 1962 Alexander Solzhenitsyn was allowed to publish a novel entitled *A Day in the Life of Ivan Denisovitch*, which exposed conditions in the Soviet *gulag*. Solzhenitsyn's criticism of continuing censorship led to the banning of his subsequent books, which appeared in the West and circulated in the USSR in *samizdat* (clandestinely printed) form. His Nobel Prize in Literature (1970) gave Solzhenitsyn the stature to publish a massive history of Stalin's terror, *The Gulag Archipelago* (1973–75), which led the frustrated Soviet regime to deport him to the West. Other distinguished dissidents included the physicist considered the father of the Russian hydrogen bomb, Andrei Sakharov, who championed international arms control and Soviet civil rights so persistently that he won the Nobel Peace Prize in 1975.

◆ DOCUMENT 32.2 ◆

Demands of the Solidarity Workers in Poland, 1980

Striking ship-workers at Gdansk confronted the Communist government with the following demands in August 1980.

1. Acceptance of free trade unions independent of the Communist Party.
2. A guarantee of the right to strike and of the security of strikes and those aiding them.
3. Compliance with the constitutional guarantee of freedom of speech, the press and publication.
4. A halt in repression of the individual because of personal conviction.
5. Guaranteed automatic increases in pay on the basis of increases in prices and the decline of real income.
6. A full supply of food products for the domestic market, with exports limited to surpluses.
7. The selection of management personnel on the basis of qualifications not party membership.
8. Privileges of the secret police, regular police and party apparatus are to be eliminated by equalizing family subsidies, abolishing special stores, etc.

9. Reduction in the age of retirement for women to 50 and for men to 55, or after 30 years of employment in Poland for women and 35 years for men, regardless of age.
10. Conformity of old-age pensions and annuities with what has actually been paid in.
11. Improvements in the working conditions of the health service to insure full medical care for workers.
12. Assurances of a reasonable number of places in day-care centers and kindergartens for the children of working mothers.
13. Paid maternity leave for three years.
14. A decrease in the waiting period for apartments.
15. A day of rest on Saturday.

Solidarity. "Demands of the Solidarity Workers in Poland." *New York Times*, August 28, 1980.

Discontent in the USSR worsened after the Red Army invaded neighboring Afghanistan in 1979. The Kremlin sought to prevent the establishment of a militant Islamic government on its southern border, adjacent to Soviet republics with a large Islamic population. A minor military campaign to install a friendly government in Kabul, however, soon grew into the Soviet Union's Vietnam. Forty thousand troops were needed in the first month, as the Red Army encountered fierce resistance from Afghan rebels, the *mujahedeen*. As the war became a frustrating, no-win stalemate, the USSR met the same international hostility that the Vietnam War caused the United States. A conference of thirty-six Islamic states condemned the Soviet Union. The United Nations voted a resolution denouncing the war. A planned Soviet showcasing of Communist society, the 1980 Olympic Games, was boycotted by the United States, West Germany, and Japan. Internal dissent also increased. Sakharov and his wife, Yelena Bonner, were so troublesome to the regime that they were exiled to a Russian city closed to foreigners.

◆

The Gorbachev Revolution in the USSR, 1985–89

The turning point for the USSR and Eastern Europe came in 1985 when a youthful reformist and westernizer, Mikhail Gorbachev, became the head of the Soviet Union following a succession of ineffective, elderly, doctrinaire leaders (see illustration 32.4). Gorbachev was the son of Russian peasants. He joined the Communist Party at twenty-one, rose to membership in the Supreme Soviet at thirty-nine, reached a cabinet post at forty-seven, and in 1980 became the youngest member of the Politburo at forty-nine. Gorbachev emerged as one of the energetic leaders of the Politburo during the rudderless period following the death of Leonid Brezhnev in 1982. The Soviet Union was widely considered a gerontocracy, and three aging heads of government died in quick succession between 1982 and 1985. The instability of this period encouraged the Politburo to accept the fifty-four-year-old Gorbachev as first secretary.

Illustration 32.4

///// The Gorbachev Revolution.
Mikhail Gorbachev, who became general
secretary of the Communist Party of the
Soviet Union in 1985, was the leading
figure in the revolutions of 1989. His determined efforts to reform the USSR and
Eastern Europe created the environment
in which Communist governments were
toppled, and this made him enormously
popular across Europe, as this 1987
photo of his state visit to Prague shows.
Note that Gorbachev (smiling at center)
seems much happier than the man with
the forced smile behind him, Gustav
Husak, the president of Czechoslovakia.
Gorbachev won the Nobel Peace Prize
for 1990; Husak was deposed.

Gorbachev had served as minister of agriculture
from 1978 and knew that Soviet farming was failing. In
1981 Brezhnev had been forced to acknowledge the
regime's economic failure before the Central Committee; food production had fallen to dangerously low levels for three consecutive years and stood at an
embarrassing 30 percent of the planned harvest. The
Soviet Union could not feed itself and imported forty-
three million tons of grain, much of it coming from the
United States. Simultaneously, the war in Afghanistan
was a great drain on Russian finances and morale. In
1982 the Politburo decided to seek economic stability
by curtailing the enormously expensive arms race with
the West. A few months later, however, President
Ronald Reagan of the United States announced plans
for a new weapons system, the Strategic Defense Initiative, that theoretically would provide a missile shield
for the United States. This plan, soon dubbed "star
wars," required vast new spending to develop antimis-
sile technology. Reagan, who considered the USSR "the
Evil Empire" and "the focus of all evil in the modern
world," was willing to spend the United States deeply
into debt to combat the Soviet Union. By 1985 the
United States had become a debtor nation, but Mikhail
Gorbachev came to power with another great concern
to add to the human rights pressures, the antiwar
mood, and the economic failures of the Soviet Union.

In his first weeks in power, Gorbachev launched a
liberalizing revolution. He retired older leaders and

hard-liners while promoting reformers and westernizers
such as Eduard Schevardnadze, who replaced an old-
line Communist, Andrei Gromyko, as foreign minister.
Within one year, Gorbachev had changed 70 percent
of all cabinet ministers and 50 percent of the higher administration. The Gorbachev revolution was characterized by two objectives: *glasnost* (openness) and *perestroika*
(restructuring). *Glasnost* meant a freer political and cultural life in which criticism of the party and state were
possible; Gorbachev even allowed television broadcasts
depicting the quagmire in Afghanistan and its increasing casualty rate. *Perestroika* meant reforming political
and economic structures to create more democracy and
efficiency (see document 32.3).

Gorbachev's two doctrines also led to a "détente offensive" to persuade the West to curtail the cold war
and its costly arms race. To prove his earnestness, he
announced a unilateral freeze on medium range missiles
during his first month in office. In September 1985 the
USSR offered a 50 percent cut in arms in return for a
Western cut in the star wars program. Many Western
leaders, led by Margaret Thatcher, were greatly impressed by this beginning, and European opinion soon
strongly favored the curtailment of cold war military
expenditures. In the fall of 1985 more than 100,000
people demonstrated in London to stop these ruinous
expenses, and Gorbachev received popular greetings
during visits to the West. Reagan and Gorbachev held
six hours of face-to-face meetings in Geneva, but Rea-

◈ DOCUMENT 32.3 ◈

Mikhail Gorbachev: *Perestroika* and *Glasnost* (1987)

What is perestroika? What prompted this idea of restructuring?

At some stage—this became particularly clear in the latter half of the seventies—something happened that was at first sight inexplicable. The country began to lose momentum. Economic failures became more frequent. Difficulties began to accumulate and deteriorate, and unresolved problems to multiply. . . .

The 27th Congress of the Communist Party of Soviet Union [1986] . . . was a courageous congress. We spoke openly about the short-comings, errors, and difficulties. . . .

The main idea . . . was the development of democracy. It is the principal guarantee of the irreversibility of perestroika. The more socialist democracy there is, the more socialism we will have. This is our firm conviction, and we will not abandon it. We will promote democracy in the economy, in politics and within the Party itself. . . .

The greatest difficulty in our restructuring effort lies in our thinking, which has been molded over the past years. Everyone, from General Secretary [Gorbachev] to worker, has to alter this thinking. . . . We have to overcome our conservatism. . . .

The new atmosphere is, perhaps, most vividly manifest in glasnost. We want more openness about public affairs in every sphere of life. . . . Truth is the main thing. Lenin said: More light! Let the Party know everything. . . . Glasnost is a vivid example of a normal and favorable spiritual and moral atmosphere in society, which makes it possible for people to understand better what happened to us in the past, what is taking place now . . . and, on this basis of this understanding, to participate in the restructuring effort. . . .

Gorbachev, Mikhail. *Perestroika: New Thinking for Our Country and the World.* New York: Harper & Row, 1987. Copyright © Mikhail Gorbachev.

gan refused to back down from his star wars program, even when Gorbachev offered to eliminate all nuclear arms by the year 2000.

The Communist Party Congress of 1986 heard Gorbachev denounce the stagnation of the Brezhnev era (1964–82), much as Khrushchev had attacked Stalin thirty years earlier. The congress endorsed Gorbachev's program, and for the next four years an astonished world watched historic changes unfold. Gorbachev scored his first successes by responding to his human rights critics. During 1986 prominent dissidents such as Sakharov were gradually released from confinement. Anatoly Shcharansky was freed from his thirteen-year sentence to a prison camp for his campaign to help Russian Jews emigrate. In 1987 Gorbachev denounced Stalin's terror and praised Khrushchev's report on the crimes of the Stalin era; he most shocked devout Communists by admitting that Lenin had relied upon terror, too. A few months later, Gorbachev announced that the Soviet Union would withdraw its army of 120,000 men from Afghanistan. By early 1988 he was promising religious freedom.

Gorbachev's campaign for *perestroika* also stunned the Western world. In 1987 he unveiled a startling plan to dismantle the one-party political system by allowing multiple candidates and a secret ballot. He explained that the Communist Party bore much of the blame for Russian economic stagnation and that only greater democracy could revitalize the USSR. Soviet police even tolerated a few limited demonstrations, chiefly by Baltic and south Asian peoples. More surprisingly, Gorbachev told a nation accustomed to policies defined by the tenets of Marxism-Leninism that he wanted "socialism extricated from the slag heap of dogma."

Gorbachev increased the pace of democratization in 1988. A special congress of the Communist Party voted a remarkable agenda: the enlargement of *glasnost* and *perestroika*, the reform of the judicial system, a war on bureaucratic intransigence, greater rights for minority nationalities, and the rehabilitation of Stalin's opponents purged in the 1930s. Legislation began to transfer decision making from the central government to the local level, while reducing government guarantees and financing. At this point, the speed of change began to exceed Gorbachev's control of it. A blunt-talking champion of reform, Boris Yeltsin, pushed him to go further, faster. Yeltsin's criticism of Gorbachev had led to his dismissal as Moscow party head in 1987 and then to Yeltsin's resignation of his Politburo membership. When Yeltsin called for a multiparty system of government, more than ten thousand people turned out in the streets of Moscow to support him. When Gorbachev created a new congress and held the first free elections in the history of the USSR in March 1989, Yeltsin, like Andrei Sakharov, was one of the first deputies elected to it. By early 1990 the Communist Party had lost its control of the state, multiparty politics had been legalized, and a Russian presidency created. The Gorbachev revolution had gone beyond Gorbachev. He no longer had a strong constituency of supporters inside the Soviet Union. Ardent Communists began to detest him for destroying Communism, but ardent reformers wanted leaders who would go much further. Revolutions often consume individuals who stand between the extremes, and Gorbachev was now a centrist. On May Day 1990 he was publicly booed by thousands of demonstrators, chiefly hard-line Communists and staunch Russian nationalists. Before the month was over, Yeltsin was elected to the presidency instead of Gorbachev.

The Revolutions of 1989 in Eastern Europe

The Gorbachev revolution in the USSR led directly to the breakup of the Communist bloc in Eastern Europe and to the dissolution of the Soviet Union itself. The Warsaw Pact had been renewed only a few weeks before Gorbachev came to power in 1985. But four years later, the revolutions of 1989 (see chronology 32.3) ended the Soviet Empire in Eastern Europe and redrew the map of Europe with few shots being fired (see map 32.3). Two years later, the USSR itself dissolved into more than a dozen republics.

The revolutions of 1989 began in Poland and Hungary. The Solidarity movement, which had been struggling with the Communist government of Poland for nearly a decade, finally won legal recognition in January 1989. The union movement used that new status and its vast popularity to press the government to extend *perestroika* in Poland by liberalizing the political system. The government, whose only signals from

Moscow were to accept restructuring, capitulated to Solidarity in a series of April meetings and agreed to free elections for the upper house of Parliament. Lech Walesa called those meetings "the beginning of the road to democracy." That agreement guaranteed the Communist Party a large block of seats whatever the outcome of the voting, but Polish voters gave Solidarity a landslide victory (80 percent of the vote) in June 1989. In the *Sejm*, the nonelected lower house of the Polish Parliament, the agreement gave the Communist Party 38 percent of the seats and Solidarity 35 percent. The two houses would together elect the president of Poland. The Polish elections of 1989–90 ended a generation of Communist government in Poland. Solidarity candidates won 96 percent of the seats in the upper house. In elections to the *Sejm*, many prominent Communists who were unopposed still could not win the 50 percent of the vote needed for election. Lech Walesa, the shipyard electrician and chief founder of Solidarity, won the presidency of Poland in 1990 with 75 percent of the vote. The new government immediately launched plans for the difficult transition to a market economy.

The Hungarian revolution of 1989, in contrast, began among reformers within the Communist Party. The government announced in January that Hungarian *perestroika* would allow multiple political parties, and it backed that announcement with a new constitution ending the Communist Party's monopoly of political power. Communist reformers were so determined to end the postwar regime that they abolished their party in October 1989 and tried to reorganize themselves as a socialist party in hopes of surviving free elections. None of their decisions was more popular than the January 1990 Hungarian-Soviet agreement for the withdrawal of all Soviet troops stationed on Hungarian soil. None was a more powerful symbol than the June 1990 reopening of the Budapest Stock Exchange. But the most momentous decision of Hungarian reformers came in May 1989, when the government opened the border between Austria and Hungary, demolishing fortifications and removing barbed wire. This breech in the Iron Curtain allowed East Europeans free access to Western Europe. Communist states slower to embrace change now faced the prospect that thousands of their citizens might flee to the West.

The most dramatic of the revolutions of 1989 occurred in East Germany. The DDR remained a strict Communist dictatorship under Erich Honecker, the aging leader who had supervised the construction of the

The Revolutions of 1989 in Eastern Europe

USSR

January	Coal miners in Ukraine defy government and strike
February	Gorbachev withdraws last Soviet troops from Afghanistan
March	Elections for new Parliament give landslide victory to reformers
	Government admits that Nazi-Soviet Treaty of 1939 planned Baltic annexation
	Estonia, Latvia, Lithuania, Armenia, Azerbaijan, Georgia, and Ukraine demand autonomy
September	Azerbaijan becomes first republic of USSR to declare its independence
December	Lithuania changes constitution and abolishes Communist monopoly of power
	Presidents Gorbachev and Bush meet in Malta and declare the cold war over

Poland

January	Government legalizes Solidarity and multiple trade unions
February	Solidarity enters negotiations for reform of Polish political system
March	Government agrees to multiple party political system and calls elections
June	First free Polish elections after World War II give sweeping victory to Solidarity
August	Poland ends forty years of Communist rule
September	New Polish government launches plans for transition to market economy

Hungary

January	Reforms permit multiple political parties
March	Draft constitution ends dominance of Communist Party
September	Government violates treaties and allows massive transit of East Germans to West
October	Reformers abolish Communist Party and regroup as Socialist Party
	Parliament democratizes constitution and calls elections

East Germany

September	Hundreds of thousands of East Germans flee to West through Hungary
October	Gorbachev visits East Germany and encourages liberalization
	Mass demonstrations of New Forum in Leipzig and other cities
	President Erich Honecker forced to resign amid growing demonstrations
November	Government allows citizens to visit West without visas; thousands cross borders
	Demonstrating crowds begin to demolish the Berlin Wall
December	East German government resigns and free elections scheduled for early 1990

Czechoslovakia

October	Government troops crush student demonstrations in Prague and arrest dissidents
	Gorbachev urges Czech government to accept need for restructuring
	Civic Forum leads demonstrations in Prague, demands resignation of government
November	Entire Czech government resigns but demonstrations and strikes continue
December	Non-Communist cabinet installed in the Velvet Revolution
	Czech Parliament approves Western-style democracy and names dissident president
	Slovaks open question of cession to create separate state of Slovakia

Romania

December	Secret police shoot demonstrators seeking ethnic and religious freedom in Timisoara
	Units of army join demonstrators as National Salvation Front against Ceausescu dictatorship
	Ceausescu arrested, tried, and executed by provisional government

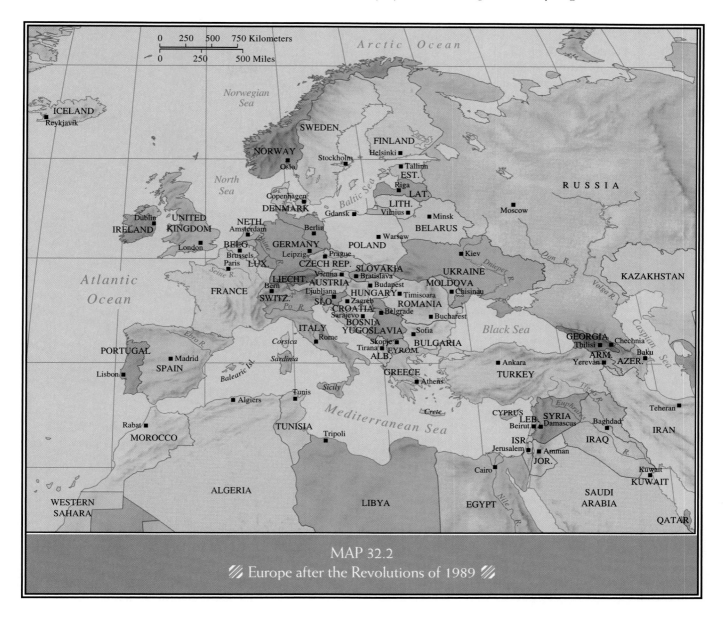

MAP 32.2

Europe after the Revolutions of 1989

Berlin Wall a generation earlier. Honecker, the son of a militant coal miner in the Saar, had been a Communist since the Weimar Republic and had spent ten years in Nazi prisons. He had been a leading organizer of the postwar Communist Party, who rose to become the head of state security in 1958, and had served as party leader since 1971. Honecker had followed a policy of severe domestic repression and a strictly controlled economy. He was personally responsible for an order that border guards shoot to kill anyone seeking to flee to the West, and in February 1989 he had confidently predicted that the Berlin Wall would remain standing for one hundred years.

Erich Honecker vigorously resisted reform of the Communist regime and fought against the idea of *perestroika.* The tightly bottled-up discontent of East Germans became clear in the late summer of 1989, following the Hungarian decision to open their Austrian border. By West German law, all East Germans who came to the West received automatic citizenship, but the Iron Curtain had kept that number small. Suddenly, thousands of East Germans exploited Hungarian liberalization to visit there and then cross into the West; seven thousand people fled on the first night that the border was open, and sixty thousand went to the West in the first month. The DDR was soon losing three hundred citizens—chiefly the young, the skilled, and the educated—per hour. The Honecker government denounced Hungary and called for another Warsaw Pact invasion.

Illustration 32.5

The End of the Berlin Wall. The Berlin wall, constructed in 1961 (see illustration 31.4), was the foremost symbol of the Iron Curtain separating East and West, the palpable image of the cold war. The opening of the Berlin Wall in November 1989—a delirious occasion to the people in this photo—quickly became the symbol of the revolutions of 1989 and the fall of Communism.

As East German Communists tried to close this border, they soon faced demonstrations in favor of reform. Leipzig became known as the *Heldenstadt* (city of heroes) as thousands of people took to the streets, marching in defiance of a heavy military presence, standing up to the threat of tanks. Honecker seriously considered turning the army loose on the crowds. At that moment, Gorbachev visited East Berlin (October 1989) and was received by crowds chanting, "Gorby, Gorby, make us free." Gorbachev, who had already publicly reversed the Brezhnev Doctrine, told Honecker that the Warsaw Pact would not act against reformers, and he urged the East Germans to choose liberalization instead of civil war. When Honecker did not unleash the army, his regime collapsed. He was forced to resign as party leader, and he was later indicted for the crimes of the Communist era. In November the East German Politburo was replaced and plans

were announced for free elections. On midnight of November 9–10, the new government opened the border between East Berlin and West Berlin at the Brandenburg Gate. A carnival atmosphere enveloped Berlin—the symbolic city of the cold war—as thousands of people walked freely into the West, and others danced atop the Berlin Wall (see illustration 32.5). Berlin thus provided the most symbolic moment of the revolutions of 1989, as German crowds began to tear down sections of the hated wall. In the new spirit of the free-market economy, the Berlin Wall ended its days broken into small fragments and sold as tourist souvenirs.

The revolution of 1989 in Czechoslovakia became known as the Velvet Revolution because it, too, was a nonviolent transition, but it did not seem that way at the beginning. Encouraged by events in the Soviet Union, university students in Prague began demonstrations at the start of the school year in October. The

Communist government initially felt strong and the first demonstrations were met with force and arrests. The Czech dissident movement had for a long time drawn its leaders from the intelligentsia who had supported the Prague Spring in 1968, drafted Charter 77 in 1977, and then grouped themselves together under the leadership of Vaclav Havel in the Civic Forum. After Gorbachev visited Prague in October 1989, the Civic Forum resumed the demonstrations, and this time they were backed by a widespread strike of workers. The Czechoslovak Communist Party initially agreed to surrender its monopoly on power and to include non-Communists in the government, but the tempest of *perestroika* could not be contained with such limited concessions. Negotiations with leaders of the Civic Forum produced an agreement to abolish controls on the press and TV, release political prisoners, and end the Marxist control of universities. Demonstrations continued, however, and within a few weeks, the Communist government resigned. The Parliament hurriedly adopted a democratic system of government and scheduled elections; in the interim, it named Havel president of Czechoslovakia. Havel negotiated the withdrawal of the Soviet army and led Civic Forum to victory in the first free elections in June 1990. Like all of the states breaking away from their Communist past, Czechoslovakia faced great problems, including one that was especially urgent: Slovakian leaders representing the eastern portion of the country asked to separate a Czech state (the western provinces of Bohemia and Moravia) and a Slovak state.

Only in Romania did the revolution of 1989 result in a bloody conflict. The struggle began in the Transylvanian town of Timisoara, one of the centers of the Hungarian minority population, which numbered two million. A Hungarian Protestant clergyman in Timisoara, Lazlo Tökés, had become a champion of religious and ethnic freedom there. In December 1989 the government of dictator Nicolae Ceausescu ordered Tökés deported; when he refused to leave, an attempt to arrest him precipitated a demonstration of ten thousand people in Timisoara. The Romanian security police fired on the demonstrating crowds, killing several hundred people. Romanians responded with anti-Ceausescu demonstrations in Bucharest, and the Romanian army refused to break them up. When Ceaucescu declared martial law, units of the army joined the demonstrators. Two weeks of fighting between the army and the security police, who remained loyal to Ceausescu, killed an estimated ten thousand to eighty thousand. Ceausescu was caught, given a two-hour trial, and executed that same day.

The Breakup of the Soviet Union, 1989–91

Nationalist unrest in the USSR had become open in the late 1980s. In the north, the Baltic states (Estonia, Latvia, and Lithuania) began to challenge Moscow. In 1988 the Estonians amended their constitution to permit a local veto of Soviet laws. When Gorbachev rejected this degree of autonomy, 60 percent of the entire population of Estonia (a nation of only 1.5 million) signed a petition demanding self-rule. In the south, the neighboring Asian republics of Armenia and Azerbaijan quarreled over territory and the treatment of each other's minority population. Only an old-fashioned intervention by the Red Army in September 1988 prevented open war.

The Soviet Union began to break up in 1989. There were riots against the central government in Georgia in April, the Lithuanian legislature voted for independence in May, workers struck for local self-government in the Ukraine in July, demonstrations in all of the Baltic states called for independence in August, and Azerbaijan delivered the first formal declaration of independence in September. By the end of the year, the Estonian government had adopted a Declaration of Sovereignty, and the Lithuanian legislature had disavowed their 1940 treaty of annexation and restored their 1938 constitution, thereby abolishing the Communist monopoly of power. In early 1990 all three Baltic republics formally proclaimed their independence. Once again, revolutionary events were racing past Gorbachev's ability to manage them. He tried to block Baltic secession but a new Lithuanian president—until recently a dissident professor of music—and a Lithuanian army of fifteen hundred men refused to back down. Gorbachev made a desperate attempt to stand against the breakup of the Soviet Union by ordering an army crackdown in the Baltic states. When the Red Army fired on a protesting crowd in Lithuania, thirteen people were killed; 100,000 then turned out in Moscow to protest and Gorbachev was beaten by the openness he had fostered. Lithuania was allowed to hold a referendum in February 1991, and 91 percent of the electorate backed independence. The trend became so powerful that two months later a similar referendum was held in Georgia (Stalin's birthplace), and 90 percent voted for independence. Before the year had ended, fifteen of the Soviet republics had chosen self-rule, including the Baltic states and the European republics of Belarus (a state of predominantly White Russian population located on the eastern border of

Poland), Moldova (a largely Romanian population located on the Romanian border), and Ukraine. These six newly independent states formed a solid belt stretching from the Baltic Sea to the Black Sea, separating Russia from Europe.

While the Soviet Union broke apart, the traditional Communist regime of Russia itself also collapsed. Between late 1989 and early 1991, Russia experienced constant change. Gorbachev announced a new agricultural plan to break up the collective farms and a new economic plan that introduced television advertising. Unions were given the right to strike and promptly tried it. The KGB announced that it disavowed its previous terrorism. Shevardnadze acknowledged that the Soviet invasion of Afghanistan had been illegal. The Red Army withdrew from most of Eastern Europe, slowed only by limited finances for housing them in the Soviet Union. After 100,000 public demonstrators demanded a multiparty democracy within the Russian Federation, the Communist Party agreed to end its monopoly on political power. In one of the bluntest rejections of Communism, the Russian Parliament voted in March 1990 to approve of private property, in September 1990 to allow religious freedom, and in May 1991 to give all Russian citizens freedom of travel, including abroad. The Soviet archives were opened and confessions poured out—from the calculation that Stalin's terror had killed twenty million people to the admission that the Soviet Union had been responsible for the Katyn Massacre of Polish officers during World War II. The city of Leningrad reverted to its historic name, St. Petersburg. Thousands of other institutions and towns simply took down the portrait, or pulled down the statue, of Lenin, or any other symbol of the regime (see illustration 32.6).

This stunning collapse of the USSR provoked conservative, anti-*perestroika* Communists to attempt a coup d'état in August 1991. Advocates of the old regime, including several leaders of the army and the KGB, held Mikhail Gorbachev under house arrest and tried to seize centers of power such as the Parliament building in Moscow. Reformers, such as Yeltsin and the mayor of St. Petersburg, resisted the coup and used the army (which did not support the conspiracy) to bombard the conspirators into submission. Boris Yeltsin, standing atop a tank and exhorting the crowd to stand up to the conspirators, became the leader of the new Russia. While the ruins of the Russian Parliament still smoldered, Yeltsin shut down all offices of the Communist Party, purged hard-liners from the government, and suspended newspapers that had been sympathetic to

the coup, such as *Pravda*. Crowds in Moscow vandalized the KGB building with impunity. Less than two weeks later, in September 1991, Parliament voted the dissolution of the USSR. Gorbachev remained in office until resigning in December 1991. His farewell speech did not regret his historic role. "The old system," he said, "fell apart."

One of the most important consequences of the Gorbachev revolution and the revolutions of 1989 was the end of the cold war. From Gorbachev's first days in office, he tried to find ways to reach a historic agreement with the United States; by late 1988 the toughest conservative in Europe, Margaret Thatcher, did not hesitate to say that she believed that the West could trust Gorbachev and deal with him when he offered to reduce Soviet military expenditures and to end the arms race. Gorbachev won popularity in Europe with his repeated proposals to reduce Soviet military strength, but the United States under President Reagan at first declined to join in arms and expenditure reductions. World opinion, however, gradually sensed that the cold war was ending. When Gorbachev and Reagan met at Reykjavik, Iceland, in 1986, the United States still insisted upon building the new generation of star wars weapons. But when the two heads of state met in the Washington summit of 1987, Reagan agreed to cut nuclear arsenals and Gorbachev accepted unbalanced terms: Over the next three years, the USSR would dismantle 1,752 missiles and the United States, 859. During 1989–91, numerous arms reduction treaties and summit meetings underscored the conclusion that the age of the cold war was over. When Gorbachev met U.S. President George Bush on the island of Malta in late 1989, phrase makers concluded that the cold war had lasted "from Yalta to Malta." A few months later, Mikhail Gorbachev won the Nobel Peace Prize for 1990.

Helmut Kohl and the Reunification of Germany, 1989–90

Two dramatic consequences quickly flowed from the collapse of the Soviet bloc: (1) in October 1990 the two Germanys reunited, when the German Democratic Republic (East Germany) joined the Federal Republic of Germany, and (2) in December 1990 Yugoslavia began to break apart and fell into an internecine civil war (1991–99), which killed hundreds of thousands and left Yugoslavia divided into six states.

Illustration 32.6

The Fall of the Soviet Union. With the fall of the Soviet Union in 1991, one of the most widely repeated scenes was the destruction of the icons of the Communist regime. Hundreds of monumental statues of Lenin and Stalin were toppled, but none of these acts better symbolized the end of Communism than the one shown here: A fourteen-ton statue of Felix Dzerhinsky (the founder of the Soviet secret police) is lowered outside of the KGB headquarters in Moscow.

The Bonn Constitution of West Germany, adopted in 1949, had encompassed the dream of a reunified Germany. Its preamble stated that "the entire German people is called upon to achieve by self-determination the unity and freedom of Germany." The cold war postponed the German dream of reunification to a distant future. The USSR uncompromisingly opposed any possibility of a strong, unified Germany near its frontiers. Many Westerners privately preferred the division of Germany; it had facilitated the postwar Franco-German rapprochement and the progress toward the European Union. Most Germans had accepted the reality of two Germanys—West Germans helped by their prosperity and East Germans by their comparative success within the Eastern bloc. The formal recognition of division, the absence of a German problem on his frontier, and the successful arms negotiations of the age of détente, had been essential factors in facilitating the Gorbachev revolution—as important as the victory of American technology and spending to win the arms race or the unyielding pressure for human rights and freedom from within.

When the revolutions of 1989 upended the long-standing political realities in central Europe, the chancellor of West Germany was given the unexpected opportunity to become the Bismarck of the twentieth century. Helmut Kohl was an unlikely man for this comparison, but he succeeded in the role with remarkable ease. Kohl, like Adenauer before him, came from a conservative Catholic family from the Rhineland. He was the first chancellor from the generation too young to have had an active role in World War II, being fifteen when the war ended. Kohl had taken a Ph.D. in political science and immediately entered local politics as a pragmatic, rather than ideological, conservative. By 1976, he had become the leader of the German conservative party, the Christian Democratic Union. In 1982 he engineered the ouster of the socialist chancellor, Helmut Schmidt, by persuading a small third party, the Free Democrats, to abandon their coalition with Schmidt and form a new majority with Kohl and the CDU. Kohl promised "a government of the middle" and followed a moderate course. He embraced the

German model for social peace and economic growth (requiring more concessions to labor and more support of the welfare state than British or American conservatives would accept). In European policy, he was one of the chief advocates of the European Union and, in foreign policy, one of the chief defenders of NATO and close ties to the United States. By 1989 he had achieved a long tenure as chancellor but had not given any signs that he would preside over one of the most important accomplishments of twentieth-century German history.

When the events of October-November 1989 reopened the German question, Helmut Kohl seized the opportunity with surprising speed. On the night that the DDR opened the Berlin Wall and joyous Berliners celebrated in the streets, Kohl made a simple speech nearby: "We are, and we remain, one nation." Kohl promptly produced, and the Bundestag ratified, a Ten-Point Plan for German Unity in November 1989. Point ten was clear: "We are working for a state of peace in Europe in which the German nation can recover its unity in free self-determination." The speed of Kohl's action surprised many, but he argued that something must be done to slow the torrent of East Germans migrating to the West—500,000 immigrants arrived in November alone. World leaders could only respond as the surprised George Bush did: "We're pleased." A few weeks later, in January 1990, Gorbachev acknowledged that reunification was probable.

The East German government initially hesitated, and the prime minister of the DDR spoke of plans for a commission to study the possibilities, but the sentiment of public opinion was overwhelming. Demonstrations in East Germany denounced the old regime—especially after revelations of the activities of the *Stasi,* the former secret police—and hard-liners were forced to resign. East German elections of March 1990 settled the question. No party received an absolute majority, but 48 percent voted for a party backing immediate unification and nearly 70 percent voted for parties favoring some form of unification. The Communist Party received 16 percent of the vote. This election led directly to negotiations for unification. Helmut Kohl pressed for immediate action, and within a few weeks, the two Germanys had agreed upon a common currency and economic policy, although this typically meant that West German standards prevailed or difficult problems were postponed. More than eight thousand state-run businesses in the DDR would be privatized. Institutions in the East would be transformed; universities, for example, were given West German administrators who

closed most programs in Marxism-Leninism and reduced programs in Russian language and studies.

The negotiations between the Federal Republic and the DDR were expanded into the "two-plus-four negotiations" in May 1990, bringing together the two Germanys and the four powers that had divided Germany in 1945 (Britain, France, Russia, and the United States). In these talks, the four powers accepted German reassurances about the international aspects of the new Germany. A Russo-German Treaty of July 1990 and a Treaty of Final Settlement on Germany in September 1990 stated the terms: Germany could unite and remain within NATO, but the German government must (1) reduce its standing army to fewer than 400,000 troops; (2) renounce all nuclear, chemical, and biological weaponry; and (3) provide financial assistance to Russia for the repatriation of the Soviet army. While those details were still being worked out, the two Germanys formed an economic merger based on the West German mark. Then, in October 1990, forty-five years after the postwar partition, a unified Germany of nearly eighty million population was created by the DDR joining the Federal Republic. The first all-German elections in nearly sixty years followed in December 1990, with Helmut Kohl becoming the first chancellor of the new state. The Bundestag voted in 1991, by a narrow margin, to return the capital of Germany to Berlin in a twelve-year transition.

The Yugoslav War, 1991–99

While Germans were celebrating their union to the tune of Beethoven's "Ode to Joy," Yugoslavia was fragmenting into six states in an internecine war. Yugoslavia had been created at the Paris Peace Conference of 1919, according to the principle of "the national self-determination of peoples," by merging the independent states of Serbia and Montenegro with provinces taken from the defeated Austro-Hungarian Empire. Although Yugoslavia ("the land of the southern slavs") had been a dream of Slavic nationalists, it had always been a delicate federation of several different peoples (chiefly Slovenes, Croatians, Bosnians, Serbs, Albanians, and Macedonians) who practiced several different religions (chiefly Roman Catholicism in Slovenia and Croatia, Islam in Bosnia and Kosovo, and Orthodox Christianity in the other regions) and who spoke languages different enough to require different alphabets.

Yugoslavia and the western Balkans had long been a powder keg of bitter rivalries, many of which had

Illustration 32.7

⚏ **War Crimes.** The Yugoslav War of 1991–95 produced evidence of terrible war crimes, which persuaded the United Nations to establish the first war crimes tribunal to sit since the crimes of the Holocaust were tried at Nuremberg in 1945–46. The Hague Tribunal found evidence of crimes committed by all sides in the Yugoslav War, but most of the evidence involved Serbian atrocities. This photograph shows one section of a mass grave near the town of Vukovar, where Croatian civilians were massacred by Serbs.

been exacerbated by questions of collaboration with the Nazis during World War II. The forceful personality of President Tito—a Croatian who had been the leader of the predominantly Serbian resistance to Nazism—had held Yugoslavia together as a federation of equals. His refusal to follow Moscow as a satellite of the Soviet Union had earned Yugoslavia massive Western assistance, which helped to sustain his regime. His successors were less able to follow these policies. Regional nationalism increased after Tito's death in 1980, despite Yugoslavia's rotating presidency, which gave each major ethnic group a turn at leadership. The Albanian minority rioted in 1981, seeking independence. Widespread unrest was evident among the Muslim population of Bosnia in 1983. Croatian terrorists conducted a bombing campaign in 1985.

The collapse of the Yugoslav Communist Party in the revolution of 1989 worsened the federation's crisis of nationalist regionalism. Without the strong central authority that had held the federated republics together, political power passed to local authorities during 1990. The two most westernized republics, Slovenia and Croatia, held free elections in the spring of 1990. Slovenia, the most prosperous portion of Yugoslavia, adopted a declaration of sovereignty a few weeks later, and by the end of the year a public referendum had approved secession from Yugoslavia. Croatia meanwhile prepared a new constitution that asserted the right to secede. Stimulated by these developments, the Serbian minority population in the non-Serbian republics of Croatia and Bosnia formed separatist groups that claimed the right of self-government.

The Yugoslav crisis became the Yugoslav War in 1991. Slovenia and Croatia each proclaimed their independence from Yugoslavia in July. The Serbian minority in Croatia (especially those concentrated in a region that the Serbs called Krajina) resisted this declaration and announced the secession of some districts that would join the neighboring republic of Bosnia. Serbia, the largest state of Yugoslavia, controlled the military and intervened on behalf of the Serbian minority. The Yugoslav air force bombed Zagreb, the capital of Croatia, in October 1991, and a few days later the Yugoslav army besieged and shelled the picturesque Croatian town of Dubrovnik on the Adriatic Coast. In November the Croatian city of Vukovar surrendered to Serbian forces; shortly thereafter, the first stories of war atrocities—the murder of Croatian civilians in Vukovar—began to reach the West (see illustration 32.7). By the end of 1991 the president of Yugoslavia announced that the country had ceased to exist. In early 1992 the European Union recognized the independence of Slovenia, Croatia, and Bosnia, and the United Nations accepted all three as members. Simultaneously, the republics of Serbia and Montenegro announced their merger as the new Republic of Yugoslavia.

Outsiders seemed powerless to prevent an expansion of the Yugoslav War. The European Union, the United Nations, and the United States applied many forms of pressure—an embargo on arms shipments to the Balkans, a larger embargo against the new Yugoslavia and its expulsion from UN membership, repeated cease-fire negotiations, the proclamation of safe zones, and the intervention of UN peacekeeping forces to protect civilians. But a long and brutal war had begun. Serbia did not take a direct role in the fighting, but the Serbian minority in Croatia and Bosnia was so well equipped that it conducted the war without the Yugoslav army.

In 1992 the chief theater of the Yugoslav War became Bosnia. Bosnia was an ethnically mixed region composed chiefly of Bosnian Muslims (more than 40 percent), Serbian Orthodox Christians (more than 30 percent), and Croatian Catholics (less than 20 percent). The capital of Bosnia, Sarajevo, had been considered a model city of different peoples living together harmoniously when it hosted the winter Olympic games in 1984. The Bosnian declaration of independence, however, had prompted a furious offensive—often centered on the siege and bombardment of Sarajevo—by the Bosnian Serbs, who proclaimed their own government led by a militant Serbian nationalist, Radovan Karadzic. For the next three years, the Bosnian Serbs, with support from Yugoslavia, conquered most of Bosnia in fighting so ferocious that it shocked the rest of the world. The Bosnian Serb army, commanded by General Ratko Mladic, devastated the city of Sarajevo in constant bombardments. In the villages of Bosnia, Mladic imposed a policy of "ethnic cleansing"—driving all non-Serbs from an area. The war in Bosnia produced the worst atrocities in Europe since World War II. By late 1992 accusations of extreme abuses in Serbian detention camps, including the execution of three thousand people in one camp, reached the West. They were followed by a litany of horrors alleged against the Serbs—from the intentional mass rape of Bosnian women as an instrument of policy to the mass execution of all Bosnian Muslim men taken captive. International opinion became so outraged at the continuing atrocities in the Balkans that the United Nations established the first international war crimes tribunal since the Nuremberg Trials of 1945–46. The Hague Tribunal returned indictments against Croatians and Bosnian Muslims as well as Serbs, but most of the indictments and the gravest accusations were against Bosnian Serbs, whose head of state (Karadzic) and military leader (Mladic) were both indicted *in absentia*.

The first effective cease-fire of the Yugoslav War produced a delicate peace agreement in 1995. The gradual arming of Croatia had produced significant military victories against the Serbs, an international Islamic coalition had begun to support Bosnia, and the United States had even bombed Serbian positions. In November 1995 the presidents of Serbia, Croatia, and Bosnia met in Dayton, Ohio, and signed a peace agreement brokered by the United States. Bosnian Serbs served in the Serbian delegation, but Radovan Karadzic could not negotiate alongside the other heads of government because the Bosnian Serbs were not recognized as an independent government and Karadzic remained under indictment for war crimes. The Dayton Accord dealt chiefly with Bosnia: It would remain a single state within its previous borders, but it would contain two entities—a Bosnian-Croatian federation and a Bosnian Serb republic (see map 32.3). These two would have a single central government at Sarajevo. To maintain this unusual arrangement, NATO agreed to send sixty thousand peacekeeping troops to Bosnia for one year. By 1998, fighting had shifted to Kosovo, where Albanians and Serbs fought.

A third phase of the Yugoslav War was fought in 1999 in the Serbian province of Kosovo, a region of great patriotic importance to Serbs but populated by an overwhelming majority of Albanian Muslims. This time the western powers did not hestitate as they had in Bosnia, and NATO intervened to protect the Kosovar Albanians. As tens of thousands of them fled the province and renewed stories of war crimes circulated, NATO attacked Serbia from the air, forcing the Serbian army to withdraw.

AUSTRIA

HUNGARY

0   50   100   150 Kilometers

0   50   100 Miles

Maribor

Kranj
Ljubljana

SLOVENIA

ROMANIA

Zagreb

CROATIA

Osijek

VOJVODINA

Rijeka

Vukovar

Novi Sad

K r a j i n a

Sava
R.

Banja
Luka

SERB
REPUBLIC

Belgrade

Danube

R.

Y U G O S L A V I A

Tuzla

Drina R.

Zenica

SERBIA

FEDERATION
OF BOSNIA AND
HERZEGOVINA

Sarajevo

Pale

Split

Mostar

SERB
REPUBLIC

A d r i a t i c   S e a

Leskovac

MONTENEGRO

KOSOVO

Dubrovnik

Pristina

Titograd

Pec

Skopje

MACEDONIA

ALBANIA

Bitola

GREECE

Serb Republic

Croat-Muslim Federation

Dayton Agreement Line

MAP 32.3

The Yugoslav War, after the Dayton Accord of 1995

SUGGESTED READINGS

❖❖❖❖❖❖❖❖❖❖❖❖❖❖❖❖❖❖❖❖

Chapter 1

General histories of the ancient Near East include A. B. Knapp, *The History and Culture of Ancient Western Asia and Egypt* (1987), W. von Soden, *The Ancient Orient* (1994), and C. Burney, *The Ancient Near East* (1977).

On Mesopotamia, see A. L. Oppenheim, *Ancient Mesopotamia*, 2d. ed. (1977) and H. Crawford, *Sumer and the Sumerians* (1991). A leading authority on post-Sumerian Mesopotamia is H. W. F. Saggs. His works include *The Babylonians* (1995), *Everyday Life in Babylonia and Assyria* (1965), and *The Might That Was Assyria* (1984).

A general survey of the prehistoric world is provided by T. Champion, C. Gamble, S. Shennan, and A. Whittle, *Prehistoric Europe* (1984). The problem of human origins is discussed in R. Leakey, *The Making of Mankind* (1981) and in P. Mellars and C. Stringer, *The Human Revolution* (1989). M. Ehrenberg, *Women in Prehistory* (1989) and F. Dahlberg, ed., *Woman the Gatherer* (1981) describe the role of women in prehistoric society. For the Neolithic revolution, see N. Cohen, *The Food Crisis in Prehistory: Overpopulation and the Origins of Agriculture* (1977), G. Barker, *Prehistoric Farming in Europe* (1984), and A. Whittle, *Neolithic Europe: A Survey* (1985).

General surveys of ancient Egypt include C. Aldred, *The Egyptians* (1984), B. J. Kemp, *Ancient Egypt* (1989), and C. Hobson, *The World of the Pharaohs* (1987). An unusually rich literature also can be found on Egyptian social history. See B. G. Trigger, B. J. Kemp, D. O'Connor, and A. B. Lloyd, *Ancient Egypt, A Social History* (1983), G. Robins, *Women in Ancient Egypt* (1993), and J. White, *Everyday Life in Ancient Egypt* (1963). The best book on the pyramids is I. E. S. Edwards, *The Pyramids of Egypt*, rev. ed. (1974). On religion, see J. Cerney, *Ancient Egyptian Religion* (1979).

Several works deal with the other peoples of the eastern Mediterranean and Near East. G. Herm, *The Phoenicians: The Purple Empire of the Ancient World* (1975) emphasizes commerce and expansion, while the development of the alphabet is covered by D. Diringer, *The Alphabet* (1975).

Many histories of ancient Israel have been written. See the fundamental J. Bright, *A History of Israel*, 3d ed. (1981), J. M. Miller and J. H. Hayes, *A History of Ancient Israel and Judah* (1986), and M. Grant, *The History of Ancient Israel* (1984). Social history and institutions are covered by N. P. Lemche, *Ancient Israel: A New History of Israelite Society* (1988). The literature on religion is enormous, but the following are useful as general studies: Y. Kaufmann, *The Religion of Israel* (1960), H. Ringgren, *Israelite Religion* (1966), and D. R. Hillers, *Covenant: The History of a Biblical Idea* (1969).

Chapter 2

J. B. Bury and R. Meiggs, *A History of Greece to the Death of Alexander the Great*, 4th ed. (1975) has held up well as the standard survey of Greek history, but N. G. L. Hammond, *A History of Greece to 322 B.C.*, 3d ed. (1986) is a venerable competitor.

On Minoan civilization, see S. Hood, *The Minoans: The Story of Bronze Age Crete* (1971). The best studies of Mycenaean Greece are L. W. Taylor, *The Mycenaeans*, rev. ed. (1983) and J. T. Hooker, *Mycenaean Greece* (1976), but several good surveys of early Greek history as a whole can be found, including M. I. Finley, *Early Greece: The Bronze and Archaic Ages*, 2d ed. (1982), and R. Drews, *The Coming of the Greeks* (1988), which describes the migrations. On Homer and the Homeric Age, see J. Griffin, *Homer* (1980). C. Starr, *The Economic and Social Growth of Early Greece, 800–500 B.C.* (1977) and C. Roebuck, *Economy and Society in the Early Greek World* (1984) are good on the early period. V. Hanson, *Warfare and Agriculture in Classical Greece* (1983) deals with hoplite warfare and and its purposes. Political development is described by W. G. Forest, *The Emergence of Greek Democracy* (1966). A. J. Graham, *Colony and Mother City in Ancient Greece*, rev. ed. (1984) describes the process of colonization.

W. Guthrie, *The Greeks and Their Gods* (1965) and W. Burkert, *Greek Religion* (1985) are general studies of Greek religious beliefs. The role of athletics in the Greek world is described by D. Sansone, *Greek Athletics and the Genesis of Sport* (1988).

Studies on politics are heavily weighted toward Athens. See A. Jones, *Athenian Democracy* (1975), and J. Ober, *The Athenian Revolution* (1996). R. Hopper, *Trade and Industry in Classical Greece* (1979) covers economic development. Social history, too, is based heavily on Athenian sources. See T. B. L. Webster, *Everyday Life in Classical Athens* (1969), and S. C. Humphreys, *The Family, Women, and Death* (1983). Slavery is covered in Y. Garlan, *Slavery in Ancient Greece* (1988). The best general work on Greek women is probably the early chapters of S. Pomeroy, *Goddesses, Whores, Wives, and Slaves* (1975), which also covers the Hellenistic and Roman periods. The complex issue of homosexuality is examined by K. Dover, *Greek Homosexuality* (1978) and E. Cantarella, *Bisexuality in the Ancient World* (1992).

The best studies of Sparta are P. Catledge, *Sparta and Laconia: A Regional History, 1300–362 B.C.* (1979) and W. Forrest, *A History of Sparta, 950–121 B.C.*, 2d ed. (1980).

Herodotus remains indispensable for the Persian War and for much else about the ancient world. A. Burn, *Persia and the Greeks: The Defense of the West*, rev. ed. (1984) is a fine modern study.

Any study of the Peloponnesian Wars must begin with Thucydides, but the modern works by D. Kagan are indispensable: *Outbreak of the Peloponnesian War* (1969), *The Archidamian War* (1974), *The Peace of Nicias and the Sicilian Expedition* (1981), and *The Fall of the Athenian Empire* (1987).

Chapter 3

The standard survey of Greek literature is A. Lesky, *History of Greek Literature* (1966). For Greek drama, see A.W. Pickard-Cambridge, *The Dramatic Festivals of Athens*, 2d ed. (1968), and H.C. Baldry, *The Greek Tragic Theater* (1971). Studies on the development of historical writing include J. A. S. Evans, *Herodotus* (1982) and K. Dover, *Thucydides* (1973). Surveys of Greek art include M. Robertson, *A History of Greek Art*, 2 vols. (1975) and J. Boardman, *Greek Art* (1985) and A. W. Lawrence, *Greek Architecture*, rev. ed. (1983). W. K. C. Guthrie, *A History of Greek Philosophy*, 6 vols. (1962–81) is a comprehensive survey of the subject.

Substantial literature exists on politics after the Peloponnesian Wars. On Athens in the fourth century B.C., see J. Ober, *Mass and Elite in Democratic Athens* (1989) and J. Cargill, *The Second Athenian League* (1981); for Sparta, P. Cartledge, *Agesilaos and the Crisis of Sparta* (1987). The standard work on Thebes is J. Buckler, *The Theban Hegemony, 371–362 B.C.* (1980). For the rise of Macedon, see E. Borza, *In the Shadow of Olympus: The Emergence of Macedon* (1990), and R. Errington, *A History of Macedonia* (1990). The career of Philip II is covered in N. Hammond, *Philip of Macedon* (1994). Modern biographies of Alexander the Great include N. G. L. Hammond, *Alexander the Great* (1981), and Peter Green, *Alexander of Macedon* (1991).

The best general survey of Hellenistic civilization is probably F. W. Wallbank, *The Hellenistic World* (1993). Studies of individual kingdoms include N. G. L. Hammond and F. Wallbank, *A History of Macedonia*, vol. 3, 336–167 B.C. (1988), H. I. Bell, *Egypt from Alexander the Great to the Arab Conquest* (1948), and O. Morkholm, *Antiochus IV of Syria* (1966). B. Bar-Kochva, *The Seleucid Army* (1976) is the most current treatment of military affairs. The dislocation of the Greeks and their impact on Egypt is discussed in A. K. Bowman, *Egypt after the Pharaohs* (1986) and N. Lewis, *Greeks in Ptolemaic Egypt* (1986).

For Hellenistic social and economic history, begin with M. Rostovtzeff, *Social and Economic History of the Hellenistic World*, 3 vols., 2d ed. (1953), supplemented by M. I. Finley, *The Ancient Economy*, 2d ed. (1985). S. B. Pomeroy, *Women in Hellenistic Egypt* (1984) is a valuable study. For slavery, see the appropriate sections of W. L. Westerman, *The Slave Systems of Greek and Roman Antiquity* (1955).

Good surveys of Hellenistic higher culture include M. Hadas, *Hellenistic Culture: Fusion and Diffusion* (1959) and J. Onians, *Art and Thought in the Hellenistic Age* (1979). G. E. R. Lloyd, *Greek Science after Aristotle* (1973) is an outstanding survey. The best survey of Hellenistic art is J. J. Pollitt, *Art in the Hellenistic Age* (1986). A. A. Long, *Hellenistic Philosophy* (1974) is the standard survey in its field. L. Martin, *Hellenistic Religions: An Introduction* (1987) is a useful survey. Jewish resistance to hellenizing tendencies is discussed by V. Tcherikover, *Hellenistic Civilization and the Jews* (1959) and M. Hengel, *Judaism and Hellenism* (1974). B. Bar-Kochva, *Judas Maccabeus* (1988) deals with the Maccabean revolt.

Chapter 4

The best surveys of Rome under the republic are H. H. Scullard, *History of the Roman World, 753–146 B.C.* (1978) and M. H. Crawford, *The Roman Republic*, 2d ed. (1993). For the Etruscans, see M. Pallottino, *The Etruscans*, rev. ed. (1975). Roman relations with and other early Italians are covered by J. C. Meyer, *Pre-Republican Rome* (1983). E. Salmon, *The Making of Roman Italy* (1985) examines Roman expansion in the peninsula. F. Adcock, *The Roman Art of War under the Republic*, rev. ed. (1963) describes the development of the Roman military system.

K. D. White, *Roman Farming* (1970) is a thorough treatment of this important subject. Many of the works on religious and social history cover both the republic and the empire; see J. Liebeschutz, *Continuity and Change in Roman Religion* (1979), J. Balsdon, *Life and Leisure in Ancient Rome* (1969), J. Balsdon, *Roman Women*, rev. ed. (1974), F. Dupont, *Daily Life in Ancient Rome* (1994), J. F. Gardner, *Women in Roman Law and Society* (1986), and S. Dixon, *The Roman Family* (1992). The struggle of the orders and the evolution of Roman law are covered by R. Mitchell, *Patricians and Plebians: The Origins of the Roman State* (1990), and H. Jolowicz and B. Nicholas, *Historical Introduction to Roman Law* (1972).

Roman expansion under the republic is described by R. M. Errington, *The Dawn of Empire: Rome's Rise to World Power* (1971), and W. V. Harris, *War and Imperialism in Republican Rome* (1979), while J. Lazenby, *Hannibal's War: A Military History of the Second Punic War* (1978) provides a detailed account of the most important of the Carthaginian wars. A broader treatment of the crisis is found in B. Caven, *The Punic Wars* (1980). The best works on Roman expansion in the east are E. S. Gruen, *The Hellenistic World and the Coming of Rome*, 2 vols. (1984) and A. N. Sherwin-White, *Roman Foreign Policy in the Near East* (1984). For Spain, see L. Curchin, *Roman Spain: Conquest and Assimilation* (1991). The Roman method of securing frontiers is dealt with by S. L. Dyson, *The Creation of the Roman Frontier* (1985).

Chapter 5

The best general works on the crisis of the late republic are R. Syme, *The Roman Revolution*, rev. ed. (1960) and M. Beard and M. Crawford, *Rome and the Late Republic* (1985). For the underlying social crisis, see K. Hopkins, *Conquerors and Slaves* (1978), P. A. Brunt, *Social Conflicts in the Late Republic* (1971), and C. Nicolet, *The World of the Citizen in Republican Rome* (1980). D. Stockton, *The Gracchi* (1979) and A. H. Bernstein, *Tiberius Sempronius Gracchus: Tradition and Apostasy* (1978) are standard works on the reformers. A. Keaveney, *Sulla: The Last Republican* (1983) deals with a reformer of a different kind. A. Eckstein, *Senate and Generals* (1987) analyzes the role of the army in Roman domestic and foreign affairs. E. S. Gruen, *The Last Generation of the Roman Republic* (1971) provides an overview of the end. The best work on Caesar is M. Gelzer, *Caesar: Politician and Statesman* (1968). A. H. N. Jones, *Augustus* is a good short summary.

For surveys on the history of the early Roman Empire, see C. Wells, *The Roman Empire* (1984), P. Garnsey and R. Saller, *The Roman Empire: Economy, Society, and Culture* (1987), and J. Wacher, *The Roman Empire* (1987).

The most useful survey of Roman art is D. E. Strong, *Roman Art* (1976). On architecture, see J. B. Ward-Perkins, *Roman Imperial Architecture* (1981). R. M. Ogilvie, *Roman Literature and Society* (1980) offers a broad general survey.

The economy of the Roman Empire is covered by R. Duncan-Jones, *The Economy of the Roman Empire: Quantitative Studies*, 2d ed. (1982). T. Frank, *An Economic Survey of Ancient Rome*, vols. 2–5 (1933–40) is uneven but still useful. A number of excellent works are available on social history, including R. MacMullen, *Roman Social Relations, 50 B.C. to A.D. 284* (1981), P. Garnsey, *Social Status and Legal Privilege in the Roman Empire* (1970), R. P. Saller, *Personal Patronage under the Early Empire* (1982), and K. Bradley, *Slaves and Masters in the Roman Empire* (1988). Town life is memorably described by J. Carcopino, *Daily Life in Ancient Rome*, rev. ed. (1975) and by T. Africa, *Rome of the Caesars* (1965).

Chapter 6

J. Lebreton and J. Zeiller, *History of the Primitive Church*, 3 vols. (1962) is a survey of early church history from the Catholic point of view. H. Lietzmann, *History of the Early Church*, 2 vols. (1961) offers a Protestant point of view. Works on the origins and spread of Christianity include T. Barnes, *Christianity and the Roman Empire* (1984), S. Benko, *Pagan Rome and Early Christians* (1985), W. Frend, *The Rise of Christianity* (1984), and R. Mac-Mullen, *Christianizing the Roman Empire* (1984). The lives of both Christian and pagan women are explored in G. Clark, *Women in Late Antiquity: Pagan and Christian Life Styles* (1993).

A rich literature exists on the Roman army and the problem of imperial defense. See L. Keppie, *The Making of the Roman Army* (1984), and J. B. Campbell, *The Emperor and the Roman Army* (1984). Strategy and policy are covered in E. Luttwak, *The Grand Strategy of the Roman Empire from the First Century A.D. to the Third* (1976), and S. L. Dyson, *The Creation of the Roman Frontier* (1985).

The broader subject of Rome's decline and the collapse of the west was first described in E. Gibbon, *The Decline and Fall of the Roman Empire* (1776). More modern surveys include A. H. M. Jones, *The Decline of the Ancient World* (1966), A. H. M. Jones, *The Later Roman Empire* (1964), F. Walbank, *The Awful Revolution* (1969), and A. Cameron, *The Later Roman Empire* (1993). On Diocletian's reforms, see S. Williams, *Diocletian and the Roman Recovery* (1985) and T. D. Barnes, *The New Empire of Diocletian and Constantine* (1982); for Constantine, R. MacMullan, *Constantine* (1969) and M. Grant, *Constantine the Great: The Man and His Times* (1993). The last years of the Roman west are described by E. A. Thompson, *Romans and Barbarians* (1982), and A. Ferrill, *The Fall of the Roman Empire: The Military Explanation* (1983).

The religious and intellectual life of the fourth and fifth centuries is described by P. Brown, *The World of Late Antiquity* (1971). His *Augustine of Hippo* (1969) is also the best biography of that central figure. On St. Benedict and the beginnings of western monasticism, see O. Chadwick, *The Making of the Benedictine Ideal* (1981).

Chapter 7

Brief introductions to Byzantine history may be found in J. Norwich, *Byzantium: The Early Centuries* (1989), S. Runciman, *Byzantine Civilization* (1956), H. Haussig, *A History of Byzantine Civilization* (1971), and C. Mango, *Byzantium: The Empire of New Rome* (1980). R. Browning, *Justinian and Theodora*, 2d ed. (1987) is the standard treatment of the reign. For church history, see J. Hussey, *The Orthodox Church in the Byzantine Empire* (1986). The early history of the Slavs is covered by Z. Vana, *The World of the Ancient Slavs* (1983), and A. Vlasto, *The Entry of the Slavs into Christendom* (1970).

Surveys dealing with the early history of Islam include G. von Grunebaum, *Classical Islam: A History, 600–1250* (1970), H. Kennedy, *The Prophet and the Age of the Caliphates: The Islamic Near East from the Sixth to the Eleventh Centuries* (1986), and J. Saunders, *A History of Medieval Islam* (1965). For social history in the Islamic world, see E. Ashtor, *A Social and Economic History of the Near East in the Middle Ages* (1976) and M. Ahsan, *Social Life under the Abbasids* (1979). Islamic art and architecture are covered by O. Graber, *The Formation of Islamic Art*, 2d ed. (1987). The best introductions to Muslim thought are O. Leamon, *An Introduction to Medieval Islamic Philosophy* (1985) and M. Fakhry, *History of Islamic Philosophy*, 2d ed. (1983).

The best surveys of Europe in the early Middle Ages are R. Collins, *Early Medieval Europe, 300–1000* (1991), and J. Wallace-Hadrill, *The Barbarian West*, rev. ed. (1985). On the papacy in this period, see J. Richards, *The Popes and the Papacy in the Early Middle Ages* (1979). For the invasions and their impact, see L. Musset, *The German Invasions* (1975), W. Goffart, *Barbarians and Romans, A.D. 418–554: The Techniques of Accommodation* (1980), and P. Geary, *Before France and Germany* (1988). On England, F. Stanton, *Anglo-Saxon England*, rev. ed. (1947) is comprehensive. For Ireland as a center of missionary Christianity, see L. Bitel, *Isle of the Saints: Monastic Settlement and Christian Community in Early Ireland* (1990).

The standard surveys of Carolingian history are H. Fichtenau, *The Carolingian Empire* (1957), D. Bullough, *The Age of Charlemagne* (1966), and J. McKitterick, *The Frankish Kingdoms under the Carolingians, 751–987* (1983). For Charlemagne, see H. Loyn and R. Percival, *The Reign of Charlemagne* (1976). Carolingian society is described in P. Riché, *Daily Life in the World of Charlemagne* (1978) and in S. Wemple, *Women in Frankish Society: Marriage and the Cloister* (1981). The Carolingian Renaissance is described in P. Riché, *Education and Culture in the Barbarian West: From the Sixth through the Eighth Century* (1976).

Chapter 8

The age of the great raids is surveyed by G. Barraclough, *The Crucible of Europe: The Ninth and Tenth Centuries in European History* (1976) and E. James, *The Origins of France: From Clovis to the Capetians* (1982). For the Vikings, see G. Jones, *A History of the Vikings*, rev. ed. (1984) and F. Logan, *The Vikings in History*, 2d ed. (1991). In P. Suger and others, *A History of Hungary* (1990), chapters 1–3 deal with the Magyars and early Hungary in general. Military issues are covered by P. Contamine, *War in the Middle Ages* (1984) and J. Beeler, *War in Feudal Europe* (1991). Three outstanding studies on the emergence of medieval institutions in general are R. W. Southern, *The Making of the Middle Ages*, rev. ed. (1973), M. Bloch, *Feudal Society* (1961), and G. Duby, *The Early Growth of the European Economy: Warriors and Peasants from the First to* the *Twelfth Century* (1974). For feudalism, see F. Ganshof, *Feudalism* (1952). More suggested readings on the evolution of feudalism and chivalry and readings on the life and work of a medieval manor are found in chapter 11.

The Celtic portion of the nonfeudal world is covered in D. Walker, *Medieval Wales* (1990), R. Davies, *Domination and Conquest: The Experience of Scotland and Wales* (1990), and A. Cosgrove, ed., *A New History of Ireland, 1169–1534*, vol. 2 (1993). The best work on medieval Spain is J. O'Callaghan, *Medieval Spain* (1975).

A vast literature can be found on the feudal monarchies. For England, see R. Brown, *The Normans and the Norman Conquest*, 2d ed. (1986), and R. Frame, *The Political Development of the British Isles, 1100–1400* (1990). W. L. Warren, *Henry II* (1973) is a good biography. D. C. Holt, *Magna Carta* (1965) deals with the circumstances surrounding that extraordinary document. R. Turner, *King John* (1994) provides a balanced view of a controversial figure. Developments in France are covered by J. Dunbabin, *France in the Making, 843–1180* (1985) and E. M. Hallam, *Capetian France, 987–1328* (1980). For feudalism in Germany, see B. Arnold, *German Knighthood 1050–1300* (1985). H. Fuhrmann, *Germany in the High Middle Ages c. 1050–1250* (1986) provides a good general account of feudal Germany. On Hildegard of Bingen, see S. Flanagan, *Hildegard of Bingen* (1989).

Chapter 9

The Cluniac movement is covered by H. E. J. Cowdrey, *The Cluniacs and the Gregorian Reform* (1970). On the background of the investiture crisis, see K. Morrison, *Tradition and Authority in the Western Church 300–1140* (1969). A number of studies on the evolution of the medieval papacy are also useful, including C. Morris, *The Papal Monarchy* (1989), and I. Robinson, *The Papacy* (1990). For the issue of clerical celibacy, see A. Barstow, *Married Priests and the Reforming Papacy* (1982).

W. Ullman, *Law and Politics in the Middle Ages* (1975) discusses the development of canon law. Monastic reform is described in B. Bolton, *The Medieval Reformation* (1983). On the great cathedrals see G. Duby, *The Age of the Cathedrals: Art and Society, 980–1420* (1981).

Works that deal with the Iberian reconquest include G. Jackson, *The Making of Medieval Spain* (1971), and A. Mackay, *Spain in the Middle Ages* (1977). The Normans in Sicily and elsewhere are the subject of J. le Patourel, *The Norman Empire* (1976), D. Douglas, *The Norman Achievement* (1969), and R. Brown, *The Normans* (1983). The literature on the Crusades is rich. H. E. Mayer, *The Crusades* (1972) and J. Riley-Smith, *The Crusades: A Short History* (1987) are good surveys. There is also a multivolume work, edited by K. M. Setton, *A History of the Crusades* (1955–77). Medieval attitudes toward the Jews are covered by R. Chazan in *European Jewry and the First Crusade* (1987), *Church, State, and the Jew in the Middle Ages* (1980), and *Daggers of Faith: Thirteenth Century Christian Missionizing and Jewish Response* (1989). J. Marcus, *The Jew in the Medieval World* (1972) is a broad general survey. For attitudes toward homosexuals, see J. Boswell, *Christianity, Social Tolerance, and Homosexuality* (1980).

General surveys of medieval thought are provided by D. Knowles, *The Evolution of Medieval Thought* (1962) and A. Murray, *Reason and Society in the Middle Ages* (1978). For the intellectual re-

newal of the twelfth century and the crisis it provoked, see the classic by C. H. Haskins, *The Renaissance of the Twelfth Century* (1957). For the heresies of the twelfth century, see R. I. Moore, *The Origins of European Dissent* (1977), and J. Strayer, *The Albigensian Crusades* (1971). For the Inquisition, B. Hamilton, *The Medieval Inquisition* (1981), while the rise of the mendicant orders is described by R. Brooke, *The Coming of the Friars* (1975). The classic work on medieval universities is H. Rashdall, *The Universities of Europe in the Middle Ages*, 3 vols. (1936), but see also A. Cobban, *The Medieval Universities* (1975) and S. Ferruolo, *The Origin of the Universities* (1985). For scholasticism, see J. W. Baldwin, *The Scholastic Culture of the Middle Ages, 100–1300* (1971). The best analysis of Aquinas's thought is in F. Copleston, *Aquinas* (1965); whose *A History of Philosophy*, vols. 2 and 3 (1963) provide a useful analysis of the other scholastics including Scotus and Ockham.

Chapter 10

For medieval technology, see L. White, *Medieval Technology and Social Change* (1962), J. Gimpel, *The Medieval Machine* (1976), and J. Langdon, *Horses, Oxen, and Technological Innovation* (1986). B. Slicher van Bath, *Agrarian History of Western Europe: A.D. 500–1850* (1963), C. Cipolla, *Before the Industrial Revolution: European Society and Economy, 1000–1700* (1976), G. Hodgett, *A Social and Economic History of Medieval Europe* (1974), and G. Duby, *The Early Growth of the European Economy: Warriors and Peasants from the Seventh to the Twelfth Century* (1978) provide broad general surveys of agricultural developments. The standard work on the revival of trade is R. S. Lopez, *The Commercial Revolution of the Middle Ages, 950–1350* (1970).

On the Italian cities, see J. K. Hyde, *Society and Politics in Medieval Italy, 1000–1350* (1973), D. Waley, *The Italian City Republics* (1969), D. Herlihy, *Cities and Society in Medieval Italy* (1980), and G. Tabacco, *The Struggle for Power in Medieval Italy, 400–1400* (1989).

Most studies of town life focus on the later Middle Ages and Renaissance when documentation became more consistent, but many of their conclusions are valid for earlier periods as well. The basic social structures had changed little since the thirteenth century. J. Gies and F. Gies, *Life in a Medieval City* (1969) offers a good, popular portrait of urban life. Among the better monographs are M. Howell, *Women, Production, and Patriarchy in Late Medieval Cities* (1986), D. Nicholas, *The Domestic Life of a Medieval City: Women, Children, and the Family in Fourteenth-Century Ghent* (1985), and a host of works on the Italian towns, including D. Herlihy, *The Family in Renaissance Italy* (1974), S. Cohn, *The Laboring Classes in Florence* (1980), F. Kent, *Neighbors and Neighborhoods in Renaissance Florence: The District of the Red Lion in the Fifteenth Century* (1982), and D. Romano, *Patricians and Popolani: The Social Foundations of the Venetian Renaissance State* (1987).

Chapter 11

A basic work, J. C. Russell, *The Control of Late Ancient and Medieval Populations* (1985), covers diet, disease, and demography. For the role of epidemic disease, see W. H. McNeill, *Plagues and Peoples* (1976). S. Rubin, *Medieval English Medicine* (1974), B. Rowland, *Medieval Woman's Guide to Health* (1981).

For castles, see W. Anderson, *Castles in Europe* (1970), N. J. G. Pounds, *The Medieval Castle in England and Wales: A Social and Political History* (1990). Medieval concepts of the social order are studied in G. Duby, *The Three Orders: Feudal Society* (1980). An immense literature exists on chivalry and the life of the knightly classes. S. Reynolds, *Kingdoms and Communities in Western Europe, 900–1300* (1984), and G. Duby, *The Chivalrous Society* (1977). M. Keen, *Chivalry* (1984) is the standard work on the subject. On noble marriages, see G. Duby, *The Knight, the Lady, and the Priest* (1984); on tournaments, R. Barber and J. Barker, *Tournaments: Jousts, Chivalry and Pageants in the Middle Ages* (1988).

The rural economy and village life are described in G. Duby, *Rural Economy and Country Life in the Medieval West* (1968), G. Homans, *English Villagers in the Thirteenth Century* (1975), H. S. Bennett, *Life on an English Manor: A Study of Peasant Conditions* (1960), and the best-selling E. Le Roy Ladurie, *Montaillou* (1978). For the lowest levels of the social order, see M. Mollat, *The Poor in the Middle Ages* (1986). The standard work on family structure, marriage patterns, inheritance, and similar questions is D. Herlihy, *Medieval Households* (1985). B. Hanawalt, *The Ties That Bind: Peasant Families in Medieval England* (1986) provides a vivid and insightful picture of English peasant life. On women in various social settings, see M. Labarge, *A Small Sound of the Trumpet: Women in Medieval Life* (1986), and S. Shahar, *The Fourth Estate: A History of Women in the Middle Ages* (1983). On children, P. Ariés, *Centuries of Childhood* (1962) has proved controversial. See also D. Herlihy, "Medieval Children," in *Essays on Medieval Civilization*, ed. B. Lackner and K. Philip (1978). For the common practice of abandonment, see J. Boswell, *The Kindness of Strangers: The Abandonment of Children in Western Europe from Late Antiquity to the Renaissance* (1989).

Chapter 12

Attempts to understand the later Middle Ages should begin with the classic J. Huizinga, *The Waning of the Middle Ages* (1949). B. Tuchman, *A Distant Mirror: The Calamitous Fourteenth Century* (1980) is a popular, best-selling, and memorable vision of the age. R. Gottfried, *The Black Death* (1983) is the most recent account of the plague. W. H. McNeill, *Plagues and Peoples* (1976) discusses the impact of epidemic disease in general. H. Miskimin, *The Economy of Early Renaissance Europe, 1300–1460* (1975) is the best study of economic matters, but see also J. Hatcher, *Plague, Population, and the English Economy, 1348–1550* (1977) and G. Huppert, *After the Black Death: A Social History of Early Modern Europe* (1986). M. Mollat and P. Wolff, *The Popular Revolutions of the Late Middle Ages* (1973) surveys both peasant and urban revolts.

A general work that covers military innovations in the later Middle Ages is P. Contamine, *War in the Middle Ages* (1984). On the evolution of the ship, see R. Unger, *The Ship in the Medieval Economy* (1980) and the profusely illustrated R. Gardner and others, eds., *Cogs, Caravels and Galleons* (1994).

For the tribulations of Russia, begin with D. Morgan, *The Mongols* (1986). I. Grey, *Ivan III and the Unification of Russia* (1964) is a brief biography of the founder of the Muscovite state. For Poland, see N. Davies, *Poland: God's Playground* (1981). The standard work on the Ottomans is H. Inalcik, *The Ottoman Empire: The Classical Age* (1973). S. Runciman, *The Fall of Constantinople 1435* (1965) is excellent.

The best accounts of the Hundred Years' War are E. Perroy, *The Hundred Years' War* (1951) and C. Allmand, *The Hundred Years'*

War: England and France at War, c. 1300–1450 (1988). M. Warner, *Joan of Arc: The Image of Female Heroism* (1981) is the best study of "The Maid." On the Hundred Years' War in Spain, see the pertinent chapters of J. O'Callaghan, *Medieval Spain* (1975) and J. N. Hillgarth, *The Spanish Kingdoms, 1250–1516*, vol. 1 (1978).

Chapter 13

The best survey of fifteenth-century Spain is J. Hillgarth, *The Spanish Kingdoms, 1250–1516*, vol. 2 (1978). See also P. Liss, *Isabella the Queen* (1992). Henry Kamen, *The Spanish Inquisition* (1997). On France, J. Major, *Representative Institutions in Renaissance France, 1421–1559* (1960) is an outstanding monograph. P. M. Kendall, *Louis XI: The Universal Spider* (1971) and R. Knecht, *Francis I* (1982) are good biographies. For Burgundy, see R. Vaughan, *Valois Burgundy* (1975). The best study of the War of the Roses is J. Gillingham, *The War of the Roses* (1981). *The Reign of Henry VI* (1981), *Edward IV* (1974), and *Richard III* (1982) by C. Ross are sound biographies as is S. Chrimes, *Henry VII* (1972). F. Boulay, *Germany in the Later Middle Ages* (1983) surveys the later empire. F. L. Carsten, *Princes and Parliaments in Germany: From the Fifteenth to the Eighteenth Century* (1963) is a classic study of representative institutions. For eastern Europe, see the collection of essays by A. Maczak and others, *East-Central Europe in Transition from the Fourteenth to the Seventeenth Century* (1986), and R. Crummey, *The Formation of Muscovy, 1304–1613* (1987).

L. Martines, *Power and Imagination: City-States in Renaissance Italy* (1988) is an excellent survey of the Italian cities and their cultural preoccupations; G. Brucker, *Renaissance Florence*, 2d ed. (1983) remains the best general treatment of Florence. Two outstanding introductions to Renaissance humanism are C. Nauert, *Humanism and the Culture of Renaissance Europe* (1995) and D. Kelley, *Renaissance Humanism* (1991).

Useful collections of essays on various aspects of the humanist program are found in A. Rabil, ed., *Renaissance Humanism: Foundations, Forms, and Legacy*, 3 vols. (1988) and C. Trinkhaus, *The Scope of Renaissance Humanism* (1983). Humanist ideas on rhetoric and education are explored by J. Siegel, *Rhetoric and Philosophy in Renaissance Humanism* (1968), P. Grendler, *Schooling in Renaissance Italy, 1300–1600* (1989), and A. Grafton and L. Jardine, *From Humanism to the Humanities: Education and the Liberal Arts in Fifteenth- and Sixteenth-Century Europe* (1988). See also M. King, *Women in the Renaissance* (1991). On the dissemination of humanism to northern Europe, see R. Weiss, *The Spread of Italian Humanism* (1964) and the collection of essays by A. Goodman and A. MacKay, *The Impact of Humanism on Western Europe* (1990). E. Eisenstein, *The Printing Press as an Agent of Change*, 2 vols. (1978) examines the impact of the printing press. On Erasmus, see R. Bainton, *Erasmus of Christendom* (1969) and J. Tracy, *Erasmus of the Low Countries* (1996).

E. Cochrane, *Historians and Historiography in the Italian Renaissance* (1981) is a good survey of an important topic. Among the immense literature on Machiavelli and Guicciardini, J. R. Hale, *Machiavelli and Renaissance Italy* (1960), F. Gilbert, *Machiavelli and Guicciardini* (1965) remain especially useful. F. Hartt, *History of Italian Renaissance Art* (1979) is an introductory survey to an immense topic. K. Clark, *The Art of Humanism* (1983) is a brief but provocative essay.

Chapter 14

The problems of the late medieval church are best summarized in F. Oakley, *The Western Church in the Later Middle Ages* (1979). A study of the papacy at Avignon is Y. Renouard, *The Avignon Papacy, 1305–1403* (1970). On the Great Schism, see W. Ullmann, *Origins of the Great Schism* (1949). The conciliar movement is analyzed in F. Oakley, *Natural Law, Conciliarism, and Consent in the Late Middle Ages* (1984). A good survey of the papacy is J. A. F. Thompson, *Popes and Princes, 1417–1517: Politics and Polity in the Late Medieval Church* (1980). A. Kenny, *Wyclif* (1985) is a good introduction to the English heretic. For Hus and the Hussites, see M. Spinka, *John Hus: A Biography* (1979) and H. Kaminsky, *A History of the Hussite Revolution* (1967).

Good biographies of Luther include R. Bainton, *Here I Stand: A Life of Martin Luther* (1950), the more modern J. Kittelson, *Luther the Reformer* (1986), and the revisionist work by H. Oberman, *Luther: Man between God and Devil* (1992).

G. H. Williams, *The Radical Reformation* (1962, 1991) is a comprehensive account that covers Anabaptists, Spiritualists, and Antitrinitarians. See also the shorter M. Mullett, *Radical Religious Movements in Early Modern Europe* (1980). The most accessible biography of Zwingli is probably G. Potter, *Zwingli* (1976). A. McGrath, *A Life of John Calvin* (1990) is a good introduction. See also the brilliant, if somewhat difficult, study by W. Bousma, *John Calvin* (1988) and W. Monter, *Calvin's Geneva* (1967). On the English Reformation, the interpretation of G. Dickens, *The English Reformation* (1964) has been challenged, among others, by J. J. Scarisbricke, *The Reformation and the English People* (1984). The best biography of Henry VIII remains J. J. Scarisbricke, *Henry VIII* (1968); for Cranmer, see D. MacCulloch, *Thomas Cranmer* (1996). The most reliable study on Mary is by D. Loades, *The Reign of Mary Tudor* (1979).

Good surveys of the Catholic Reformation include G. Dickens, *The Counter Reformation* (1969), M. O'Connell, *The Counter Reformation, 1559–1610* (1974), and L. Chatellier, *The Europe of the Devout: The Catholic Reformation and the Formation of a New Society* (1989). See also the important revisionist interpretation of J. Delumeau, *Catholicism from Luther to Voltaire* (1977).

On the consequences of reform, G. Strauss, *Luther's House of Learning* (1978) has proved as controversial as the views of Delumeau. For the effect of the Reformation on women and the family, see S. Ozment, *When Father's Ruled: Family Life in Reformation Europe* (1983), M. Wiesner, *Working Women in Renaissance Germany* (1986), L. Roper, *Work, Marriage, and Sexuality: Women in Reformation Augsburg* (1985), and J. Irwin, *Womanhood in Radical Protestantism, 1525–1675* (1989). For popular culture and its struggles, see P. Burke, *Popular Culture in Early Modern Europe* (1978), and M. Mullett, *Popular Culture and Popular Protest in Late Medieval and Early Modern Europe* (1986). B. Levack, *The Witch-Hunt in Early Modern Europe* (1987) is a broad survey of the witch persecutions.

Chapter 15

Standard introductions to the history of European expansion overseas are J. H. Parry, *The Age of Reconnaissance: Discovery, Exploration, and Settlement, 1450–1650* (1963, 1981) and G. Scammell,

The World Encompassed: The First European Maritime Empires, c. 800–1650 (1981). Portuguese expansion is described in B. Diffie and G. Winius, *Foundations of the Portuguese Empire, 1415–1580* (1979) and C. R. Boxer, *The Portuguese Seaborne Empire, 1415–1825* (1969). Among the best biographies of Columbus are S. Morison, *Admiral of the Ocean Sea: A Life of Christopher Columbus* (1942) and F. Fernández-Armesto, *Columbus* (1991). The best overall descriptions of the Spanish imperial system are still C. H. Haring, *The Spanish Empire in America* (1947), and C. Gibson, *Spain in America* (1966).

The standard biography of Charles V is K. Brandi, *The Emperor Charles V* (1939). M. Rady, *The Emperor Charles V* (1988) is a brief, but useful, handbook. For good general histories of Spain in the sixteenth and seventeenth centuries, see J. H. Elliott, *Imperial Spain* (1963) and J. Lynch, *Spain under the Habsburgs*, vol. 1, 2d ed. (1981). Good studies of Philip II and his reign include H. Kamen, *Philip of Spain* (1997), P. Pierson, *Philip II of Spain* (1975), and G. Parker, *Philip II* (1978).

The best surveys of the French Wars of Religion are probably M. Holt, *The French Wars of Religion* (1993) and J. H. M. Salmon, *Society in Crisis: France in the Sixteenth Century* (1975). The best account of the revolt of the Netherlands is G. Parker, *The Dutch Revolt* (1977), but see also P. Geyl, *The Revolt of the Netherlands*, 2d ed. (1966) and A. Duke, *Reformation and Revolt in the Low Countries* (1990). English foreign policy in this era is described by R. B. Wernham, *Before the Armada* (1966). A vast literature exists on the Spanish Armada of 1588. The classic G. Mattingly, *The Armada* (1959) and C. Martin and G. Parker, *The Spanish Armada* (1988) are excellent. On Elizabeth I, see W. MacCaffrey, *Elizabeth I* (1993), and S. Bassnett, *Elizabeth I: A Feminist Perspective* (1988). The most reliable treatment of the Thirty Years' War is G. Parker, *The Thirty Years' War* (1984). For Gustav Adolph, see M. Roberts, *Gustavus Adolphus and the Rise of Sweden* (1975). The literature on the English civil wars is enormous. Begin with L. Stone, *The Causes of the English Revolution* (1972) and C. Russell, *The Causes of the English Civil War* (1990), then see R. Ashton, *The English Civil War: Conservatism and Revolution, 1604–1649* (1976) and M. Kishlansky: *The Rise of the New Model Army* (1979). Among the better works on Cromwell are C. Hill, *God's Englishman: Oliver Cromwell and the English Revolution* (1976), and R. Howell, *Cromwell* (1977).

To understand the military history of the sixteenth and seventeenth centuries, begin with J. R. Hale, *War and Society in Renaissance Europe, 1450–1620* (1985) and two enlightening special studies, G. Parker, *The Army of Flanders and the Spanish Road, 1567–1659* (1972) and J. Guilmartin, *Gunpowder and Galleys: Changing Technology and Mediterranean Warfare at Sea in the Sixteenth Century* (1975). G. Parker, *The Military Revolution: Military Innovation and the Rise of the West, 1500–1800* (1988) provides a global perspective.

Chapter 16

Good surveys of the scientific revolution include A. R. Hall, *The Revolution in Science, 1500–1700* (1983), and A. Debus, *Man and Nature in the Renaissance* (1978). For the occult and hermetic traditions, see W. Shumaker, *The Occult Sciences in the Renaissance: A Study in Intellectual Patterns* (1985). Medieval ideas on cosmology may be found in P. Duhem, *Medieval Cosmology: Theories of Infinity, Place, Time, Void, and the Plurality of Worlds* (1985), a condensation of the ten-volume original. For astrology, see E. Garin, *Astrology in the Renaissance: The Zodiac of Life* (1983).

Copernicus stands at the beginning of modern cosmology. See E. Rosen, *Copernicus and the Scientific Revolution* (1984) and T. Kuhn, *The Copernican Revolution: Planetary Astronomy in the Development of Western Thought* (1971). A. Koestler, *The Sleepwalkers: A History of Man's Changing Vision of the Universe* (1959) is a broad, often ironic, survey. A vast literature exists on Galileo; the works of S. Drake, *Galileo at Work: His Scientific Biography* (1978), *Galileo* (1980), and *Galileo: Pioneer Scientist* (1990) are standards. On Newton, see R. Westfall, *The Life of Isaac Newton* (1993). The development of medicine is surveyed by W. Wightman, *The Emergence of Scientific Medicine* (1971). M. Jacobs, *The Cultural Meaning of the Scientific Revolution* (1988) and L. Schiebinger, *The Mind Has No Sex? Women in the Origins of Modern Science* (1989) are useful essays on science as an intellectual movement.

On the expansion of the northern powers, see C. R. Boxer, *The Dutch Seaborne Empire, 1600–1800* (1965) and R. Davis, *English Overseas Trade, 1500–1700* (1973). J. Israel, *The Dutch Republic: Its Rise, Greatness, and Fall, 1477–1806* (1995) is a monumental survey, and S. Schama, *The Embarrassment of Riches: An Intepretation of Dutch Culture in the Golden Age* (1987) is an ambitious study of Dutch culture.

J. Black describes military changes in *European Warfare, 1660–1815* (1994) and *A Military Revolution? Military Change and European Society, 1550–1800* (1991). On the reorganization of the state in France, see M. Greengrass, *France in the Age of Henri IV: The Struggle for Stability* (1984), and D. Parker, *The Making of French Absolutism* (1983). See also R. Knecht, *Richelieu* (1991), and the insightful essay by J. H. Elliott, *Richelieu and Olivares* (1984). J. Collum, *The State in Early Modern France* (1995) is a recent overview. J. B. Wolf, *Louis XIV* (1968) and O. Bernier, *Louis XIV* (1988) are good studies of the Sun King. For a survey of the German-speaking states, see M. Hughes, *Early Modern Germany, 1477–1806* (1992). The standard work on the Austrian Empire is R. J. W. Evans, *The Making of the Habsburg Monarchy, 1550–1700* (1979); on Prussia, see F. Carsten, *The Origins of Prussia* (1954) and H. Rosenberg, *Bureaucracy, Aristocracy, and Autocracy: The Prussian Experience, 1660–1815* (1966). Good studies of Peter the Great include M. Anderson, *Peter the Great* (1978), and the popular R. Massie, *Peter the Great* (1980). For the English politics, see R. Hutton, *The Restoration: A Political and Religious History of England and Wales, 1658–1667* (1985) and J. R. Jones, *Country and Court: England, 1658–1714* (1978). R. Hutton, *Charles II* (1989) is a good biography.

Chapter 17

For broad overviews of the eighteenth-century economy, see J. H. Clapham and others, eds., *The Cambridge Economic History of Europe*, 10 vols. (1941–89) and C. Cipolla, ed., *The Fontana Economic History of Europe*, 6 vols. (1972–76). Compare these with the more recent R. Floud and D. McCloskey, eds., *The Economic History of Britain since 1700*, 2 vols. (1993), which is highly statistical, and C. H. Lee, *The British Economy since 1700* (1986), which gives a broader view. R. Forster, ed., *European Society in the Eighteenth Cen-*

tury (1967) is an exceptional collection of contemporary readings on both social and economic topics.

Chapter 18

For a general social history of the Old Regime, the masterwork is F. Braudel, *Civilization and Capitalism, 15th–18th Century*, 3 vols., especially vol. 1, *The Structures of Everyday Life* (1985). For demographic studies and population, see M. W. Flinn, *The European Demographic System, 1500–1820* (1981), the standard work on western Europe; M. Anderson, *Population Change in Northwestern Europe, 1750–1850* (1988); For sickness and disease, see the pertinent chapters in W. McNeill, *Plagues and Peoples* (1976), the pioneering work in this field; For the history of the family, see M. Anderson, *Approaches to the History of the Western Family* (1980), an excellent introduction; The most helpful general works for the history of women included an excellent anthology by S. G. Bell and K. M. Offen, eds., *Women, the Family, and Freedom*, 2 vols. (1983), B. Anderson and J. Zinsser, *A History of Their Own: Women in Europe from Prehistory to the Present*, 2 vols. (1988).

Chapter 19

Good survey histories of the Old Regime can be found in W. Doyle, *The Old Order, 1660–1800* (1978), M. S. Anderson, *Europe in the Eighteenth Century*, 2d ed. (1976), I. Woloch, *Eighteenth-Century Europe* (1982), G. Rudé *Europe in the Eighteenth Century: Aristocracy and the Bourgeois Challenge* (1972), and O. Hufton, *Europe: Privilege and Protest, 1730–1789* (1980). The volumes in *The Rise of Modern Europe* series edited by W. Langer are now dated but remain helpful on many subjects; see W. L. Dorn, *Competition for Empire, 1740–1763* (1940) and L. Gershoy, *From Despotism to Revolution, 1763–1789* (1944).

Chapter 20

For overviews of the Enlightenment, see the works of P. Gay, especially his *The Enlightenment: An Interpretation*, 2 vols. (1966–69) and *The Party of Humanity: Essays in the French Enlightenment* (1964); N. Hampson, *The Enlightenment* (1968); E. Cassirer, *The Philosophy of the Enlightenment* (1951); and P. Hazard, *European Thought in the Eighteenth Century from Montesquieu to Lessing* (1963). See also the essays in R. Porter and M. Teich, eds., *The Enlightenment in National Context* (1981); R. Anchor, *The Enlightenment Tradition* (1967); J. Cottingham, *The Rationalists* (1988).

Chapter 21

One of the best overviews of the era remains R. R. Palmer, *The Age of the Democratic Revolution, 1760–1800*, 2 vols. (1959–64); the classic French account, sympathetic to the revolution, is G. Lefebvre, *The French Revolution*, 2 vols. (1962), which has been challenged by more recent works such as F. Furet, *Interpreting the French Revolution* (1981) and W. Doyle, *The Oxford History of the French Revolution* (1988). Good recent introductions include D. Sutherland, *France, 1789–1815* (1985), M. Vovelle, *The Fall of the French Monarchy, 1787–1792* (1984), and A. Forrest, *The French Revolution* (1995). For an overview of arguments about the revolution see F. Kafker and J. Laux, *The French Revolution: Conflicting Interpretations*, 4th ed. (1989).

Chapter 22

For the industrial revolution, see the older, but still classical, work by P. Mantoux, *The Industrial Revolution in the Eighteenth Century* (1961); T. S. Ashton, *The Industrial Revolution* (1948), a brief introduction, stressing the human side; D. Landes, *The Unbound Prometheus: Technological Change and Industrial Development in Western Europe from 1750 to the Present Day* (1969); P. Dean, *The First Industrial Revolution* (1965); E. A. Wrigley, *Continuity, Chance, and Change: The Character of the Industrial Revolution in England* (1988); and R. M. Hartwell, ed., *The Causes of the Industrial Revolution* (1967), an anthology presenting several conflicting perspectives. For industrialized Britain, see J. H. Clapham, *An Economic History of Modern Britain*, 3 vols. (1926–39), and F. Crouzet, *The Victorian Economy* (1982).

For continental and comparative industrialization, see A. Milward and S. Saul, *The Economic Development of Continental Europe*, 2 vols. (1977–79); T. Kemp, *Industrialization in Nineteenth-Century Europe* (1985); C. Trebilcock, *The Industrialization of the Continental Powers, 1780–1914* (1981); W. O. Henderson, *The Industrial Revolution in Europe* (1961) and *The Industrialization of Europe, 1780–1914* (1969); F. Crouzet, *Britain Ascendant* (1990), on the continental effort to catch up; P. O'Brien and C. Keyder, *Economic Growth in Britain and France, 1780–1914* (1978); J. H. Clapham, *The Economic Development of France and Germany, 1815–1914* (1936); C. Kindleberger, *Economic Growth in France and Britain* (1964); and A. L. Dunham, *The Industrial Revolution in France, 1815–1848* (1955).

Chapter 24

For general works on this period, the most recent surveys are R. Gildea, *Barricades and Borders* (1987), which covers the period 1800–1914; F. Ford, *Europe, 1780–1830* (1989); E. J. Hobsbawm, *The Age of Revolution* (1978); and T. Hamerow, *The Birth of a New Europe* (1983), which covers the entire nineteenth century. Valuable older studies include F. Artz, *Reaction and Revolution, 1814–1832* (1968) and W. Langer, *Political and Social Upheaval, 1832–1852* (1969), from the "Rise of Modern Europe" series.

Chapter 25

For surveys of the period, see E. J. Hobsbawm, *The Age of Capital, 1848–1875* (1979), the second volume of his history of modern Europe; the volume of the *New Cambridge Modern History* edited by J. P. T. Bury, *The Zenith of European Power, 1830–1870* (1964); R. Binkley's volume in the *Rise of Modern Europe* series, *Realism and Nationalism, 1852–1871* (1963).

Chapter 26

The most recent surveys of this period are E. J. Hobsbawm, *The Age of Empire, 1875–1914* (1987) and N. Stone, *Europe Transformed,*

1878–1919 (1984); see also C. Hayes, *A Generation of Materialism, 1871–1900* (1941); O. Hale, *The Great Illusion, 1900–1914* (1971), in the *Rise of Modern Europe* series; and F. H. Hinsley, ed., *Material Progress and World-Wide Problems, 1870–1898* (1962), in the *New Cambridge Modern History* series. B. Tuchman, *The Proud Tower* (1966) is a highly readable overview of the period 1890–1914.

Chapter 27

For European imperialism, see T. Pakenham, *The Scramble for Africa, 1876–1912* (1991); D. Gillard, *The Struggle for Asia, 1828–1914* (1977).

For the debate over the origins of World War I, see J. Joll, *The Origins of the First World War* (1992) and L. Lafore, *The Long Fuse* (1965), both good syntheses.

For World War I, see B. Tuchman, *The Guns of August* (1962), for the opening phase of the war; M. Ferro, *The Great War, 1914–1918* (1978), for a good short history. For surveys of the Russian Revolution, see R. Pipes, *The Russian Revolution* (1990), a vigorously hostile account; J. Reed, *Ten Days That Shook the World* (1935), a highly sympathetic contemporary account; E. H. Carr, *The Bolshevik Revolution, 1917–1923*, 3 vols. (1950–53), for an exceptionally detailed investigation.

Chapter 28

For surveys of the interwar period, see R. Sontag, *A Broken World, 1919–1939* (1971), for political detail, and C. Kindleberger, *The World in Depression, 1929–1939* (1986), for economics.

Chapter 29

For overviews of the wartime era, see G. Wright, *The Ordeal of Total War, 1939–1945* (1968), a comprehensive survey in the Rise of Modern Europe series; G. Weinberg, *A World at Arms* (1994), a massive and up-to-date general history; and E. Hobsbawm, *The Age of Extremes* (1996), helpful for putting the war into context.

Chapter 30

For general economic histories of the twentieth century, see C. Cipolla, ed., *The Fontana Economic History of Europe*, especially vol. 5: *The Twentieth Century* and vol. 6: *Contemporary Economies* (1976); M. M. Poston, D. C. Coleman, and P. Mathias, eds., *The Cambridge Economic History*, especially vols. 7 and 8 (1978); S. Clough, T. Moodie, and C. Moodie, eds., *Economic History of Europe: Twentieth Century* (1969).

Chapter 31

For overviews of the period, see E. Hobsbawm, *The Age of Extremes* (1994) and A. W. De Porte, *Europe between the Superpowers: The Enduring Balance* (1986).

PHOTO CREDITS

◆◆◆◆◆◆◆◆◆◆◆◆◆◆◆◆◆◆◆◆◆

GLOSSARY

❖❖❖❖❖❖❖❖❖❖❖❖❖❖❖❖❖❖❖❖

Chapter 1

Biological Old Regime.   The natural restrictions on population size and living conditions in the age before the Industrial Revolution, such as widespread undernourishment, famine, and unchecked disease.

Clientage.   A system of mutual dependency in which a powerful individual protects the interests of others in return for their political or economic support. It may exist with or without legal sanction, and has long been a basic institution in many societies.

Demography.   The statistical study of populations through data such as birth and death rates, censuses, or marriage rates.

Extended Family.   A family unit containing not only the nuclear family, but other relatives (siblings, parents, etc.) living under the same roof.

Matrilineal.   Inheritance of property, and sometimes the family name, through the female line.

Monotheism.   Belief in the existence of only one god, as opposed to **Polytheism,** or the belief in many.

Neolithic Revolution.   The transition to the "new stone age" involving the domestication of animals, the development of agriculture, and the extensive use of basketry and pottery.

Nuclear Family.   The basic family unit of mother, father, and their children.

Paleolithic.   The "old stone age" before the invention of agriculture. Tools were made of stone and people lived by hunting and gathering.

Slave.   A person who is the chattel property of another and therefore without rights.

Debt Slavery   is the practice of enslaving someone to satisfy a debt, often for a fixed period of time.

Chapter 2

Democracy.   Rule by the people. In Greek terms, this meant government by the entire body of male citizens as opposed to by a small group of wealthy aristocrats. Slaves, women, and resident aliens were excluded.

Hoplites.   Armored spearmen trained to fight shoulder to shoulder in a rectangular formation that was normally eight ranks deep.

Polis.   The Greek city-state, composed in theory of those who shared a common ancestry and worshipped the same gods. It was the basis of Greek life and values in the Classical Age.

Trireme.   The dominant warship of the Classical Age. It was propelled by three ranks of oars supplemented by square sails, and had a metal prow for ramming opponents.

Tyrant.   A ruler who, though sometimes legitimately elected, ignored the laws and institutions of his polis and governed as a dictator.

Zoroastrianism.   A Persian religion based upon the conflict between a god of good (Ahura Mazda) and a god of evil (Ahriman). Its duallism influenced later Christian thought.

Chapter 3

Epistemology.   In philosophy, the study of how human knowledge is acquired.

Hellenistic.   The Greek culture of the fourth through the first centuries B.C., based not on the polis, but on the great empires founded by Alexander the Great's commanders.

Pharisees.   A Jewish sect that demanded strict observance of the religious laws and opposed the introduction of Greek customs and ideas by their rivals, the **Sadducees.**

Platonic Idealism (Realism).   Plato's theory that ideas or forms are real and intelligible, and that they exist independently of appearances discernible to the senses.

Sophists.   Teachers of rhetoric who held that individual experience, based primarily on the senses, was the only basis for knowledge, and that all teachings were therefore relative.

Syllogism.   A form of argument, common to much of western thought, that reasons: if all A is B, and all C is A, then all C must be B.

Teleological.   Relating to the assumption that things can best be understood in relation to their end or purpose. In ethics, the principle that actions must be judged in terms of the result they are intended to produce.

Chapter 4

Censor.   The official responsible for conducting the **Census** which ranked each citizen's property qualifications. In later years the censor acquired substantial authority over public morals and religious observances as well.

Consul. The highest office in the Roman state. Consuls served one-year terms and could succeed themselves only after the passage of ten years. They commanded the army and, in civil matters, their edicts had the force of law.

Familia. In Roman Law, the entire household headed by a *Paterfamilias,* or father, including his nuclear family, dependent relatives, and slaves.

Partible Inheritance. The legal requirement that all property be distributed equally among an individual's heirs. It is the opposite of **Nonartible Inheritance,** which permits all of the property in an estate to be passed to a single heir, often the eldest son.

Patricians. The hereditary aristocracy of the Roman Republic. Only they could hold office as magistrates or serve in the Senate.

Plebeians. The lower class of Roman citizens. They could vote and, after the so-called struggle of the orders, served in the Plebeian Assembly and were represented to the Senate by Tribunes.

Proconsul. A consul whose authority was extended for the duration of a military campaign, normally in a distant province.

Chapter 5

Pax Romana. The Roman Peace. A long period of peace within the empire established by Augustus. It did not preclude revolts within individual provinces or conflicts with the Germanic tribes and other outsiders.

Latifundia. Large, self-sufficient estates that dominated the economic life of the western Roman empire. In the late Republic they were usually worked by slaves, who were gradually replaced by tenants (*coloni*) under the empire.

Codex. A manuscript volume of pages, usually bound in leather. It began to replace the scroll in the first century A.D.

Coloni. Tenants on a Roman estate or *latifundia.* Under the early empire *coloni* were normally free citizens who leased their land and returned a percentage of their yield to the estate.

Equestrians. A new social class that emerged after the Punic Wars. Most were merchants or financiers who, while rich enough to fight on horseback (hence the term "equestrian"), lacked the political privileges of the Patricians.

Imperator. Originally a military title, it was adopted by Vespasian as a symbol of ultimate power. The origin of the title "emperor."

Insulae. The large, tenement-like apartment houses in which most urban Romans lived.

Publicani, or **Publicans.** Tax farmers who purchased the right to levy provincial taxes at auction in return for a percentage of the funds to be raised.

Chapter 6

Arianism. The doctrine, advanced by Arius and accepted by many of the Germanic tribes, that Christ was a created being, neither fully God, nor fully man. The orthodox view in both the Eastern and Western churches is that Christ is both fully God and fully man.

Cataphracti. Armored heavy cavalry first commonly used under Diocletian. They became the dominant branch of the Roman army after the battle of Adrianople in 378.

Command Economy. An economic system in which the government sets wages and prices and attempts to regulate production.

Decurians. In the late Roman empire, members of the urban elite who monopolized most city offices, but who also paid many of the costs of government.

Forced Requisitions. The practice of confiscating food, draft animals, and other private property to support the army in a particular region.

Monasticism. The practice of living in a secluded community under the rule of religious vows.

Paganism. A generic term for all those who had not been converted to Christianity. It is derived from the Latin word *pagani,* a slang term for rustics.

Predestination. The doctrine, advanced by Augustine, that God selects those who will be saved. **Double Predestination** holds that God also selects those who will be damned. (see also Chapter Fourteen)

Tetrarchy. The system introduced by Diocletian under which the empire was ruled by two caesars and two augusti.

Chapter 7

Epiboli. The Byzantine system whereby all of the members of a community were required to pay the taxes of those unable to do so.

Iconoclasm. The belief that images should be destroyed because they are contrary to God's commandment.

Shahada. The Muslim profession of faith: "There is no God but God and Mohammed is his prophet."

Shar'ia. A way of life wholly commanded by God. The religious goal of pious Muslims.

Jihad. A holy war fought against the enemies of *al-Islam.*

Caliph. The chief civil and religious ruler in Islamic society.

Allod. A freehold property, normally unencumbered by feudal dues or other obligations.

Carolingian Minuscule. A style of handwriting developed in the Carolingian renaissance that became the basis of most modern hands.

Salic Law. The law of the Salian, or "salty" Franks that became the basis of succession in the Frankish kingdoms and later in

France. It demanded partible inheritance and in later years was said to forbid the succession of women.

Chapter 8

Comitatus.   The Latin term for a war band bound to their chieftain by oaths of loyalty.

Custom of the Manor.   The collective record of contractual obligations within a manor, including the dues and services owed by each tenant to the lord. It was usually preserved in the form of an oral tradition until the fourteenth century.

Fief.   The landed property granted to a warrior in return for his promise of military service. It was sometimes called a **Benefice,** but this term more commonly refers to property granted for the support of a cleric.

Feudalism.   A social and economic system based upon grants of land offered in exchange for military service.

Homage.   The formal expression of loyalty offered by a vassal to his lord.

Private Jurisdiction.   The right of a vassal to establish courts of law within his fief. It was normally granted by a lord as part of the feudal contract.

Manor.   An estate whose inhabitants are the legal subjects of its lord or owner. In most cases, manorialism involves some form of tenancy. Peasants hold land and a cottage in return for specified dues and services.

Subinfeudation.   The process by which vassals grant a portion of their fiefs to vassals of their own, thereby creating subtenants who owe homage to them rather than to the original tenant-in-chief.

Tenement, or Tenure.   Property held by a peasant within the manor.

Vassal.   The party to a feudal agreement who receives a fief in return for military service. Though subordinate to a lord, all vassals were by definition members of the feudal elite.

Chapter 9

Dominium.   The theory that the church, and in particular the pope, has authority over secular rulers.

Gothic.   A style of medieval architecture characterized by pointed arches, extensive carving, and sometimes by flying buttresses.

Hildebrandine Reformation.   The movement for papal reform that grew out of the Cluniac movement, for which Hildebrand of Soana (Pope Gregory VII) has been given too much credit.

Investiture.   The process by which rank or office is bestowed. In the Middle Ages, **Lay Investiture** meant the granting of ecclesiastical rank or authority by lay people.

Mendicant Orders.   Religious societies, the first of which were founded in the thirteenth century. Their members were bound by vows and were expected to live by begging. Collectively called **Friars,** they included the Dominicans and the Franciscans.

Nominalism.   The theory that universals are not real, but *nomina* or "names" that reflect little more than linguistic convention.

Romanesque.   A style of architecture that featured massive vaulting and round arches. It generally preceeds the Gothic.

Scholasticism.   The thought of the medieval schools and universities. It attempted to solve theological and philosophical problems through the application of Aristotelian logic.

Universals.   Those qualities and categories held by philosophical realists to have objective reality of their own (e.g., redness, justice, beauty, etc.).

Chapter 10

Agricultural Specialization.   The practice of cultivating those crops for which a given estate is best suited. It is the opposite of **Subsistence Farming,** which seeks to grow everything that the inhabitants of a farm or estate may need.

Commune.   A government of citizens and its institutions, as opposed to one controlled by a bishop or feudal lord. In some medieval towns the commune at first grew in parallel with the government of the lord and then supplanted it.

Signorie.   In some Italian cities, the name of the elected council that governed the town, combining legislative and executive authority.

Ghetto.   Part of a city in which members of a minority group live as a result of social, religious, or economic discrimination. Originally, the district of Venice to which Jews were confined.

Guild.   An association of craftsmen or merchants whose purpose was to guarantee quality, set prices, and provide for the general welfare of its members. In some cities, citizens had to be guild members.

Hanse.   In North Germany, a league of cities formed to protect their commercial and military interests.

Militia.   The citizen-soldiers of a medieval city.

Monoculture.   Primary reliance on a single crop by a farm or manor. The ultimate form of agricultural specialization.

Rentiers.   Townspeople who live primarily from the proceeds of rented or leased property. They were an important segment of the elite in most medieval towns.

Vendetta.   A feud or private war, usually between two clientage groups or factions within a town or among the landed nobility.

Chapter 11

Chivalric Romance.   An epic, often recited in poetic or musical form by troubadours, which glorified the chivalric values of bravery, loyalty, and courtesy.

Domus. In southern Europe, an entity composed of the family (usually extended), the household, and the physical property from which both took their name.

Entail. A legal restriction placed upon an inheritance to prevent future generations of heirs from alienating or otherwise disposing of property against the wishes of the original holder.

Lent. The six-and-a half week period of fasting and penitence from Ash Wednesday to Easter during which Christians were supposed to refrain from eating meat.

Lineage. The concept of a family name and family identity handed down from generation to generation. More common in southern than in northern Europe, it was often based upon the *domus* or the possession of some other landed estate.

Midwife. A woman trained to assist in childbirth. In medieval and early modern times, university-trained physicians did not normally practice obstetrics.

Primogeniture. Inheritance of all or most of an estate by the eldest son.

Tournament. A contest between knights that attempted to mimic the conditions of feudal warfare in a controlled, ritualized setting.

Wardship. The placement of orphans (and their assets) under the guardianship of an individual or of the courts. In medieval and early modern times the practice was largely restricted to the wealthier classes.

Chapter 12

Bastion Trace. A system of fortification based upon a series of bastions or projections connected by walls and manned by artillery. Ideally, every part of a bastion trace could be covered by defending fire.

Bundschuh. The peasant boot, bound with laces. German peasants took it as symbol of social revolt during the fifteenth century, hence the term **Bundschuh revolts.**

Forest Laws. Laws passed to prevent peasants from hunting, fishing, or gathering firewood in forests claimed by the lords

Ghazis. Muslim raiders, primarily of Turkish origin, who raided the Byzantine Empire and other Christian states. They were in some respects the Muslim equivalent of crusaders.

Regency. The period during which an individual or group of individuals is appointed to rule on behalf of a prince who is either a minor or incapacitated.

Soldier. A warrior who receives a cash payment or *solde* for fighting, as opposed to one who serves in return for land or in the discharge of some non-monetary obligation.

Chapter 13

Classicism. The admiration (and emulation) of the styles, aesthetics, and thought of the "classical" civilization of ancient Greece and Rome.

Domain. Land, properties, rents, and income-producing rights that are the personal property of a ruler. **Domain Revenues** are those derived from the domain as opposed to those derived from taxation.

Enclosure. The process by which landowners deprived peasants of a village's common lands and seized them for their own use.

Humanism. The study of Greek and Roman classics with the intention of applying their teachings to life in the present.

Neoplatonism. A philosophical school founded originally in Hellenistic Alexandria and revived during the Renaissance. Its chief concern was achieve knowledge of the Platonic forms.

Perpetual Taxes. Taxes that may be collected each year without further permission from a representative body. In the medieval and early modern period, most taxes required a special and separate vote each time they were levied.

***Pomest'e* System.** In Muscovy, the system by which the Tsar granted land directly to cavalrymen in return for military service, thereby creating a kind of "service nobility" that was separate from the traditional *boyars.*

Serfdom. A form of servitude in which tenants are regarded as the property of an estate. Unlike slaves, they cannot be sold as individuals, but they lack all other rights and may be sold as part of the property on which they live.

Chapter 14

Anticlericalism. Opposition to the influence and special privileges of the clergy or to the existence of the clergy as an organized hierarchy.

Conciliarism. The theory that the rulings of a council of the church are superior to those of any pope, and that a council may depose an unworthy pope if necessary.

Mysticism. The effort to achieve personal union with God through ecstatic contemplation.

Popular Culture. The culture that springs from the interests, activities, and entertainments of the people rather than from the received traditions of the cultural elite.

Possessionist Controversy. The dispute between Spiritual or Observant Franciscans and Conventual Franciscans over whether it was permissible for the order to hold property.

Transubstantiation. The doctrine that the substance of the bread and wine in Communion are converted by consecration to the body and blood of Christ, though their appearance or "accidents" remains the same.

Witchcraft. In the sixteenth century, a body of practices that included magic, the casting of spells, and usually Satanism, or devil-worship.

Chapter 15

Administrative Devolution. The process by which early modern rulers assigned military and administrative functions to private contractors in an attempt to save money.

Cuius regio, eius religio. The principle that the religion of an area may be determined by its ruler.

Encomienda. An institution in which Spanish kings placed newly converted subjects under the "protection" of a Christian lord who was supposed to defend them and see to their religious instruction in return for certain dues and payments.

Military Contractors. Entrepreneurs who contracted to provide a fixed number of fully equipped troops, and sometimes to lead them, in return for pay. Ships were often contracted on a similar basis in time of war.

Proprietary Colonies. Overseas colonies granted to a private individual (a Captain or Lord Proprietor) whose responsibility it was to settle and defend them.

Puritans. A party of English Protestants which demanded simplicity in church ceremonies and a high standard of moral conduct.

Chapter 16

Absolutism. A political doctrine that asserts the unrestrained power of a monarch, who is usually considered to hold sovereignty by divine will.

Chartered Companies. Companies of merchants chartered by the crown to conduct business in specified areas overseas (e.g. The East India Company). Such companies often maintained their own armies and fleets of warships.

Cosmology. The study of the universe as an ordered whole.

Experimentalism. The idea, supported by Francis Bacon, Galileo, and others that experiment can determine the validity of a scientific theory, and that, conversely, theories should be experimentally verifiable.

Heliocentric Theory. The theory, originally developed by such ancient thinkers as Eratosthenes and Aristarchus of Samos, that the planets revolve around the sun. Revived by Copernicus in the sixteenth century it was accepted by Kepler and Galileo.

Hermetic Tradition. A body of occult literature, supposedly derived from ancient Egypt, that concerned itself with natural magic, alchemy, and related subjects.

Magic. A science or pseudo-science that attempts to manipulate the supposed relationships among phenomena or natural objects for the magician's ends.

Oligarchy. A form of government in which power is in the hands of a relatively small group of people, usually wealthy ones.

Chapter 17

Corporative Society. Term to describe the highly stratified social structure of Europe during the Old Regime, with the population in most countries divided into separate legal bodies (most often called estates) each with separate rights, duties, and laws. Also called the *Ständestaat*.

Elbe-Trieste Line. An imaginary diagonal line, drawn on the map of Europe between the mouth of the Elbe River on the North Sea and the town of Trieste at the head of the Adriatic Sea; used by historians as a general line separating western and eastern Europe.

Gentry. A portion of the land-owning upper class, deemed people of "gentle" birth (gentlemen and women), holding a privileged position but not always part of the titled aristocracy (as in England).

Mercantilism. The predominant economic theory of the Old Regime, holding that states should seek self-sufficiency in resources and manufactured goods and thus import little; to achieve this end, the state regulated trade, granting monopolies and regulating manufactures and trade.

Nobility of the Robe. A branch of the nobility in many countries (especially France), composed of families who had recently acquired noble status through service to the monarch, typically as judges; in contrast to the older "nobility of the sword," ennobled for military service.

Old Regime. Term used to describe the period before the French Revolution of 1789 – roughly the 17th and 18th centuries – and its institutional structure of monarchy, aristocracy, and state religions.

Triangular Trade. A pattern of Old Regime commerce, following a triangle across the Atlantic Ocean: European manufactured goods were taken to Africa, slaves from Africa were shipped to the Americas, and American agricultural goods (especially sugar and tobacco) went to Europe.

Chapter 18

Columbian Exchange. The reciprocal introduction of unknown plants, animals, and microorganisms into Europe and the Americas following the voyages of Columbus, such as the arrival of the first potatoes in Europe or the first sheep in the Americas.

Eendemic Disease. A disease located only in specific regions, such as malaria, which is native to warm, swampy regions.

Foundlings. Unwanted newborn babies, abandoned by their parents at high rates during the Old Regime, sometimes in the open with the expectation of death, sometimes at churches or hospitals, with modest prospects of survival.

Germ Theory. The theory of disease transmission holding that invisible microorganisms such as bacteria and viruses spread disease.

Inoculation. A medical procedure which intentionally introduces a mild dose of a disease, such as smallpox, into a patient to build antibodies against that disease and acquire future immunity.

Patriarchal Family. The typical structure of families during the Old Regime, in which authority—domestic, legal, and economic authority—was vested in the husband/father and obedience was expected from the wife/children.

Puerperal Fever. The greatest cause of death among pregnant women during the Old Regime (also known as "child-bed fever") in which the absence of aseptic methods during delivery led to acute infections.

Chapter 19

Cabinet System. A form of government that began to emerge in the 18th century, in which a "cabinet" of advisers to the monarch assumes responsibility for a branch of the bureaucracy, with each adviser serving as "minister" in charge of one specialty (e.g., finance). The cabinet stands collectively as "the government."

Civil Code. A codified body of civil law, addressing private issues such as property law or marriage, as distinct from criminal law or constitutional law; especially found in regions who inherited their legal traditions from the Roman Empire.

Enlightened Despotism. An interpretation of the rule of some Old Regime monarchies, suggesting that a monarch retained the absolute power of a despot yet chose to adopt some advanced reforms deemed "enlightened."

Josephinism. An Austrian religious policy, similar to Gallicanism in France, in which the monarch contested the authority of the papacy over the Catholic Church in their lands, hoping to shape a national Catholicism more obedient to the throne.

Parlements. The high courts in Old Regime France, dominated by aristocrats who owned their offices and used the courts to check the powers and policies of the king.

Republic. A form of government without a monarch, in which sovereignty rests with the people (or some portion of them) and public business is conducted by representatives of the people, usually elected to an assembly such as a parliament or diet.

State Service. A doctrine especially strong in Eastern Europe, by which the aristocracy accepted a duty to serve the monarch in a variety of posts, such as the officer corps and the bureaucracy, but in return received an aristocratic monopoly over such positions.

Ukase. The Russian term for a royal decree that has the force of law without being approved by any legislative body.

Chapter 20

Baroque. The predominant style in European arts during 17th century and early 18th century, which appealed to the emotions and spirituality through the ornately decorated and the extravagantly expressed.

The Enlightenment. Term to describe European thought in the "Age of Reason" extending from the late 17th century to the late 18th, when philosophes stressed the need to be skeptical about all received knowledge and apply rationalism to test its validity.

Gallicanism. Doctrine supporting French kings in creating a virtually autonomous Catholic Church in France, in which the monarch named cardinals and bishops and decided if papal decrees would apply.

Natural Laws. Universal, immutable laws believed to exist in the natural world (such as the law of gravity), in contrast to laws promulgated by rulers. Leaders of the Enlightenment believed that natural laws of human behavior existed and awaited discovery or articulation.

Philosophes. A French term, much broader than the English equivalent (philosophers), used to identify the influential thinkers, writers, scientists, and reformers of the Enlightenment.

Rationalism. The belief, widely held during the Enlightenment, that all knowledge should be based upon human reason and rational proof, rather than accepted on other standards, such as faith.

Salon. A social gathering held in a private home where notable literary, artistic, and political figures discussed the issues of the day with other well-born or well-educated guests; typically organized and hosted by women who thereby played a central role in the shaping and transmission of ideas.

Chapter 21

Cahiers. The political pamphlets produced in France in 1788–1789 to express the grievances which the Estate General should address.

Continental System. Napoleon's economic plan to close European markets to the British and weaken the British economy, begun in the Berlin Decree of 1806.

Coup d'état. The overthrow of a government by force, such as Napoleon's seizure of power in Brumaire (which became a synonym for a coup) 1799.

Émigrés. French term for people who emigrate from their homeland, especially those (such as aristocrats) who fled the French Revolution.

Great Fear. Rural disturbances in France during the summer of 1789 in which peasants, frightened by rumors of violence against them, turned on local aristocrats and forced them to renounce their feudal rights.

Jacobins. Radical leaders of the French Revolution who drew their name from a former monastery where they met; they initially championed constitutional freedoms and a republic instead of a monarchy, but later directed the reign of terror.

Passive Citizens. The portion of the population of France, under the Constitution of 1791, who enjoyed all civil rights of citizenship but did not pay enough taxes to qualify for the right to vote or hold office.

Reign of Terror. The thirteen-month period of the French Revolution during 1793–1794 when radical revolutionaries held a virtual dictatorship and executed thousands of opponents of the regime, most famously 2.700 people executed on the guillotine in Paris.

Thermidorean Reaction The overthrow of the reign of terror, the execution of its leaders, and the establishment of a conservative republic during the summer of 1794, named for the mid-summer month in the revolutionary calendar.

Chapter 22

Agricultural Revolution. The significant improvement of European agriculture, beginning in 18th century Britain, where more intensive and extensive use of the soil sharply improved the food supply, sustaining population growth.

Cottage Industry. A traditional form of handcraft manufacture of textiles in rural regions during the Old Regime; spinning and weaving were done by individuals in their homes, typically with raw materials provided by a middleman who bought the finished cloth and marketed it.

Enclosure. The process of enclosing open fields of farm land, often shared for common use, within walls or fences and assigning them to a single owner, especially in Britain, 1700–1850; the change led to greater agricultural production, but to the failure of many small farmers.

Family Wage Economy. Economists' term to describe the relationship of working families to the economy during industrialization; low wages dictated that all members of a family work at wage-paying jobs away from home and pool their earnings.

Industrial Revolution. General term for the transformation of an economy from a predominantly rural and agricultural base to a predominantly urban and industrial-manufacturing base; specific term for the first such transformation, which occurred in Britain c. 1750–1850.

Laissez-faire Capitalism. The economic doctrine advocated by manufacturers and industrialists, especially in Britain, during the industrial revolution; it held that governments should not regulate the economy, but leave individuals free to act as they saw best.

Take-off Phase Economists' term for the period when a nascent industrial economy begins to expand rapidly, leading to an industrial society.

Vital Revolution A major demographic shift in which the death rate declined sharply and life expectancy steadily increased, due to the steady improvement of diet and the gradual conquest of contagious disease.

Zollverein Prussian-led customs union linking states of northern Germany in the early 19th century which promoted free trade, stimulating economic development and enhancing the Prussian position in Germany.

Chapter 23

Adulterated Food. A widespread scandal of the unregulated economy of the 19th century, in which many foods were mixed with cheap extenders in order to increase profits, such as putting powdered clay in cocoa.

Antisepsis. A medical term, coined after acceptance of the germ theory of disease transmission, to describe conditions in which the growth and multiplication of microorganisms has been inhibited; initially achieved by Joseph Lister's use of a carbolic acid mist.

Cholera. An acute diarrheal disease caused by microorganisms usually transmitted through contaminated drinking water which was the most persistent epidemic disease of 19th century Europe.

Double Standard. A widespread Victorian attitude about human sexuality, imbedded in the law as well as in middle class standards, in which different sexual behavior was expected of (and allowed to) men and of women

Laudanum. The Latin name ("highly praised") for a tincture of opium dissolved in alcohol, which was an unregulated and a very widely consumed pain killer until the drug laws of the 20th century.

Neo-Malthusians. Reformers who advocated birth control and education about it as a means of curbing the population explosion, improving the life of women, and easing the economic burden on poor families.

Vaccination. A form of inoculation against smallpox developed by Edward Jenner in 1796, in which people were administered a small amount of cowpox virus which conferred immunity to smallpox. Widespread use of the technique gradually led to the elimination of smallpox.

Victorianism. A term used to imply a stereotype of 19th century prudery and repressiveness about human sexuality.

Chapter 24

Congress System. The system of regular meetings of leaders of the great powers following the Congress of Vienna, in an effort to cooperate in maintaining the international order established at Vienna.

Corn Laws. British laws regulating, through high tariffs, the importation of corn (grain) into Britain, in order to protect the interests of land owners.

Feminism. The modern name for the 19th-century doctrine and movement for the equal rights of women; the doctrine sought integral equality, but initially stressed economic, educational, legal, and political rights.

Habeas Corpus. The traditional Latin words ("you shall have the body") at the start of a writ; the right of habeas corpus is the right of a citizen to obtain such a writ as protection against illegal imprisonment.

Legitimacy. The doctrine stated by the victorious allies of 1814–15 for the restoration of the old order in Europe after Napoleon's conquests; it asserted that every region had a "legitimate" ruler who should be restored to the throne, such as Bourbon restoration in France.

Liberalism. The name coined in the early 19th century for the political and economic doctrine that emphasized individual freedoms (such as free speech in politics and free trade in economics) and opposed state restrictions of such liberties; sometimes called "classical liberalism" to distinguish it from later versions of liberalism.

Nationalism. The political doctrine developed in the 19th century to assert the collective rights of a nation, which was understood to be defined by a shared language, culture, history or religion; the doctrine initially sought the independence and the unity of a nation.

Romanticism. The European cultural reaction to the neoclassicism of the 18th century—a rejection of strict artistic rules and an artistic rediscovery of feelings, emotions, and the spirit in contrast to strict reason.

Socialism. A group of political and economic doctrines that stressed the creation of social and economic equality; 19th century varieties included Christian, democratic, revolutionary, and utopian doctrines.

Chapter 25

Anarchism. A political theory asserting that all forms of government are unnecessary and should be abolished, to be replaced by a society based on cooperation and free association.

Barricades. A characteristic feature of urban riots and revolutions, especially in France; residents of a district close streets by building mounds of overturned vehicles, furniture from nearby buildings, and trees, defying the government to attack them.

Class Struggle. A central theory of Marxism, in which inevitable conflict between social classes (such as the property owning *bourgeoisie* and the laboring *proletariat*) explains great historical changes.

Combination Acts. A type of legislation (association laws in many countries) by which governments limited the right of citizens to combine (or associate) in groups, such as clubs, political parties, or trade unions; governments required authorization for such groups, declaring some illegal.

Deference. The central concept in many interpretations of Victorian Britain: that the mass of the population recognized the superior position of the upper classes and deferred to their leadership.

Intelligentsia. Intellectuals from many different fields who collectively form an elite, and sometimes act as the vanguard of artistic, political, or social movements.

Marxism. A radical form of socialism propounded by Karl Marx, encompassing a broad social, economic, and political critique of capitalist society and advocating a workers' revolution to seize power and institute dramatic reforms such as the abolition of private property.

Realpolitik. German term meaning "a policy of realism," used to describe political policies developed on pragmatic or opportunistic grounds rather than being defined by ideology or a predetermined program.

Chapter 26

Bolshevik(s). Russian word meaning "member of the majority," appropriated by Lenin in 1903 to identify his supporters within the Russian social democratic party, although they were actually a minority; later used as a synonym for Communist.

Commune. The smallest territorial division in the administrative structure of France, roughly equivalent to a town; the term has been borrowed to describe famous municipal governments, notably the radical Paris Commune of 1871.

Home Rule. The political doctrine holding that the citizens of a region (or country, or colony) should be allowed to govern themselves, especially in local matters; often used specifically for the campaign (c. 1870–1914) for the devolution of the government of Ireland.

Impressionism. Avant-garde style of painting originating in France in 1860s–1880s that sought to represent the overall visual impression that a subject made rather than to create a detailed reproduction of the subject.

Papal Infallibility. The Roman Catholic doctrine, promulgated by the Vatican Council of 1869–1870, that the pope infallibly expresses the will of God, when he speaks (1) "*ex cathedra*" (from the throne of St. Peter's) and (2) on matters of faith and morals.

Pogrom. Russian term for an organized, officially tolerated, attack upon members of a minority; especially attacks on Jewish communities.

Second Industrial Revolution. A stage in the industrialization of the western civilization, reached by the most advanced states (such as Britain and Germany) in the late 19th century, when steel began to replace iron at the center of heavy industry, electricity to replace steam as a power source, and the chemical industry challenged the preeminence of textiles.

Social Darwinism. A nineteenth social theory which used a crude version of Darwin's principle of natural selection (usually called "survival of the fittest") to justify the dominance of some social groups, supporting such ideas as the class system and doctrines of racial superiority.

Suffragists. Advocates of women's rights who focused on political rights, especially an equal right of women to vote and hold public office; the most militant in tactics were sometimes called suffragettes.

Chapter 27

Dictatorship of the Proletariat. Marxist-Leninist term for the phase of the class struggle following the defeat by the bourgeoisie by the proletariat; the dictatorship is seen as an inevitable but temporary stage, giving way to a classless society.

Eastern Question. Name used in the 19th and early 20th centuries to refer to the dangerous weakness of the Ottoman Empire and the many rivalries to acquire Ottoman territory, especially in the Balkans.

Entente. A French word used in the language of diplomacy to describe a close understanding between two governments, a closer relationship than *detente* (a relaxation of conflict) but not as close as an alliance; most famously used to describe the Anglo-French understanding of 1904.

Ersatz **Food.** German term to describe substitute foods developed to replace those that are too expensive (eg, margarine to replace butter), unhealthy (eg, saccharin to replace sugar), or unavailable (eg, chickory to replace coffee during World War One).

Home Front. Term for the civilian population behind the military lines (the front) during wartime, especially the two world wars; used to explore the civilian condition and role during wartime, such as the role of women in war production or the suffering of non-combattants.

Satyagraba. The sanskrit word used by Ghandi to describe his policy of nonviolent resistance to European imperialism.

Soviet. Russian word meaning "council," used to describe the revolutionary groups of soldiers and workers who wished to direct their own affairs.

Trench Warfare. The form of fighting that characterized most of World War One on the western front. Armies on both sides dug long, narrow trenches as defensive positions from which to fight and fortified them with barbed wire and machine-gun emplacements, making attacks very costly.

Chapter 28

Collectivization. Communist economic policy in which the ownership of the land and the means of production and distribution are transferred from individual to collective (state) ownership.

Depression. Economic term for a period of severe and prolonged decline in economic activity, typically characterized by a slump in production, high unemployment, and declining prices.

Fascism. A nationalist and militarist political doctrine rejecting both the liberal-democratic tradition of representative government and socialist or communist alternatives to it, in favor of an authoritarian (or totalitarian) government controlled by a strong leader, a single party, and strong police, unrestrained by constitutional laws or bills of rights.

Gulag. Russian acronym for concentration camps ("labor camps") created by the Soviet regime, administered by the secret police.

Kulaks. Russian term for the land-owning peasants eliminated by the collectivization of agriculture.

Lost Generation. Term originally used in post-World War One Europe by Gertrude Stein to describe the young generation that had experienced the devastation of the war and consequently showed emotional, cultural, and political instability afterwards.

Popular Front. A coalition of political parties of the left and left-center, such as the governments of France and Spain in 1936 which united democrats, socialists, and communists.

Reparations. Postwar compensation demanded of defeated states by the victors in order to repair damage done by a war or recover its costs, as distinguished from indemnity payments which punish a defeated state for the conflict whatever the damages.

Surrealism. An early 20th century trend in western art and literature which sought to replace rational imagery by expressing the subconscious mind in seemingly irrational juxtapositions of images.

Chapter 29

Aryans. The peoples of south Asia who spoke the parent language of the Indo-European family of languages and descendant peoples; term converted in Nazi propaganda to mean non-Jewish Caucasians.

Blitzkrieg. German military term ("lightning war") for a rapid and powerful offensive campaign intended to produce an equally rapid victory; especially the Nazi offensives in the early phases of World War Two.

Crimes against Humanity. Category of crimes of total war against civilian populations, including extermination, enslavement, and other inhumane acts; one of the categories of international crimes established by the Nuremberg Tribunal.

Genocide. The deliberate and systematic murder, or attempted murder, of all members of a perceived genus, such as all members of a race, religion, or nation; especially the Nazi attempt to exterminate all the Jews of Europe in the Holocaust.

Home Front. The civilian region of a country at war, behind the lines of combat.

Isolationism. The diplomatic policy of a powerful state (as opposed to small neutral states) not to participate in major international events, organizations, and especially commitments such as alliances; often used to refer to the policy of Britain in the 1880s–90s or the US in the 1920s–30s.

Nuclear Fission. Term in physics for splitting the nucleus of heavy atoms (such as uranium atoms) into two nuclei, thereby releasing great amounts of energy; the scientific principle behind the atomic bomb.

Sphere of Influence. Term in diplomacy for the claim of a strong state to exercise significant authority in a weaker region without fully annexing it; used to describe claims in 19th century imperialism and the cold war.

Total War. A war in which all of a society's resources are dedicated to war, all possible weapons developed and used, all possible personnel conscripted and used, all parts of enemy territory become part of the war zone, and all behavioral scruples may be abandoned.

Chapter 30

Baby Boom. The dramatic upswing in the birth rate in the western world during the generation following World War II.

Deindustrialization. One of the major trends of post-1945 European economic history, in which heavy industry and manufacturing account for a steadily smaller percentage of the economy.

Economic Miracle. Term for the dramatic European economic recovery after World War Two, especially the German recovery known as the *Wirtschaftswunder.*

Guest Workers. Term for the immigrant labor force in some European countries (especially Germany), where they are not citizens and have no rights as citizens or as immigrants.

Mixed Economy. A national economy, especially in Europe during the Cold War, which combines elements of capitalism with elements of state-planned economies, such as French *dirigisme.*

Participation Rate. Measurement used by economists to study what segments of the population are employed in the economy; used especially to evaluate the role of the youth or the aged, the comparative role of men and women, and the effects of policies such as retirement of workers.

Service Economy. A "tertiary sector" in the economic analysis of modern economies, comprised of those occupations not engaged in agriculture or industry, a sector in which workers provide a service instead of a product; including occupations such as teachers, bankers, journalists, and civil servants.

Urbanization. The growth of towns and cities, and the evolution of an urban-centered civilization; in Europe, a centuries old pattern of the shift of wealth, population, political power, and cultural focus to the cities which accelerated rapidly in the 19th century.

Chapter 31

Cold War. The global conflict between the United States and its western allies in NATO and the Soviet Union and its communist allies in the period between World War Two and the collapse of the Soviet system, 1945–1989; characterized by constant war-readiness but not combat.

Containment. The policy adopted by the United States and its western allies of blocking the spread of communism by confronting it in every region where it seemed to be spreading from communist states; stated in the Truman Doctrine and first applied to conflict in Greece and Turkey.

Decolonization. The breakup of European colonial empires and the granting (or winning) of independence to colonized countries around the world, following World War Two, 1945–1975.

Détente. French term (literally, relaxation or an easing) used in the language of diplomacy to describe improving relations between rivals after a period of conflict; specifically applied to the easing of the Cold War beginning in the late 1960s and early 1970s.

Iron Curtain. Image created by Winston Churchill in a 1946 speech to portray the division of Europe into a democratic west and a communist east, separated by impenetrable barrier maintained by the Red Army.

Nationalization. An economic policy in states with socialist and mixed economies, in which some sectors of the economy (such as railroads and airlines) are acquired by the state and operated in the public interest rather than for private profit.

Planned Economy. An economy in which the government develops a plan to sponsor growth and development (by regulations or benefits) instead of an unregulated free economy; includes early-modern mercantilist economies, war-time managed economies, communist economies, and mixed economies.

Welfare State. A country with, or a policy of, state-provided social services and benefits (especially for the poorest citizens), such as free medical care, free public education, unemployment and accident insurance, paid vacations and retirement pensions.

Chapter 32

Destalinization. A policy of admitting the "crimes of the Stalin era" in communist states, such as the secret police terror and the gulag system, and attempting some degree of liberalization of the totalitarian regime; begun by Khrushchev in 1956, culminating in Gorbachev's reforms.

Ethnic Cleansing. Violent policy of converting an ethnically-mixed region into one with a homogeneous population by any means necessary, including the terrorizing of civilian populations by planned mass rapes, forced expulsion of people from their homes, or massacres; specifically used in Yugoslav wars of 1990s, chiefly by Serbians in Bosnia.

Euro. The international currency adopted by the European Union to replace local currencies such as the German mark and the French franc and thereby increase European economic efficiency across borders.

Glasnost. Russian word meaning "openness," used by Gorbachev to describe the freer cultural and political society he proposed to build in the USSR; linked to the policy of *perestroika.*

Monetarism. Economic theory that holds that increases in the supply of money in circulation leads to inflation; revived by conservative economists in the late 20th century as a component of laissez-faire capitalism.

Perestroika. Russian word meaning "restructuring," used by Gorbachev to describe the political and economic reforms that he proposed to introduce into the USSR to create more democracy and efficiency.

Privatization. An economic policy of selling state-owned enterprises and returning them to the privately owned sector of the economy; the opposite (and the undoing) of nationalization.

Value Added Tax. A form of indirect taxation (also called VAT), hidden in the cost of goods and services in Europe by adding a portion of the tax at each stage of production and distribution; the largest source of government revenue in some countries.

INDEX

◆◆◆◆◆◆◆◆◆◆◆◆◆◆◆◆◆◆◆◆◆◆◆

What the Bible
says about the

Church of Christ

Dave Miller, Ph.D.

Apologetics Press, Inc.
230 Landmark Drive
Montgomery, Alabama 36117-2752

© Copyright 2007
ISBN: 978-1-60063-001-9

Library of Congress Cataloging-in-Publication

Dave Miller (1953 -)

What the Bible says about the Church of Christ/Dave Miller

Includes bibliographic references

ISBN: 978-1-60063-001-9

1. Comparative religion. 2. Christian theology. I. Title

280—dc22   2007929504

DEDICATION
To Deb—
whose positive influence on my
life has been inestimable, profound, and eternal.

TABLE OF CONTENTS

Chapter 1

FORETOLD AND FOUNDED

If you were to open your Bible and begin reading, you would quickly come to understand how the Universe got here, including the Earth, and how we human beings came into existence. You would read about the first two human beings, Adam and Eve, and how they disobeyed God's directive to them, thereby introducing sin into the world. This circumstance becomes the central concern of the rest of the Bible: human sin and God's intention to atone for that sin so that humans can be reconciled to Him through the forgiveness of their sins.

Something had to be done about human sin. God loves people in spite of their sin. Neither His love nor His justice would let that be the end of the matter. Being perfect, holy, and unable to allow sin to go unresolved

(Habakkuk 1:13), God had already devised a wonderful plan to make it possible for Adam, Eve, and all people since them to be forgiven of sin. Consequently, the Old Testament is riddled with references to God's eternal and ultimate plan to redeem people from their disobedience to His will. It turns out that, due to the foreknowledge of God, this divine intention was formulated **in eternity** before the sin of Adam and Eve (Ephesians 3:9-11). God knew that humans would violate His will, so He preplanned a means by which they could be forgiven if they would choose to do so. This plan entailed the sending of Himself, in the person of His Son, to be offered as a perfect sacrifice for human sin (Hebrews 9:26-28).

Genesis 3:15

Anticipation of this amazing plan of redemption is detected repeatedly in the Old Testament. Even on the occasion when sin first entered the world, God offered a glimpse of His intention in His remarks to the snake through whom Satan had worked his seductive ploy: "And I will put enmity between you and the woman, and between your seed and her Seed; He shall bruise your head, and you shall bruise His heel" (Genesis 3:15). What did God mean by this statement?

He meant that trouble would always exist between Satan (including those who follow him), and those who follow God. From the Garden until now, Satan tries to get people to disobey God. The righteous people and the unrighteous have always been at odds with each other. But God explained how He would handle this trouble: "He shall bruise your head, and you shall bruise His heel." He meant that even though Satan would do everything possible to get people to sin, and to stop God from saving people from their sin, God would still make a way for people to be forgiven. He would send Jesus to live a sinless life, and then to die for everybody's sin.

When Jesus died on the cross, His horrible suffering constituted the "heel bruising" accomplished by Satan. But His death was the right sacrifice that would allow God to forgive sin without violating His nature. Christ's death on the cross satisfied the justice and wrath of God, enabling Him to forgive the sinner. The cross amounted to the crushing of Satan's head—in the sense that people do not have to be consigned to the final abode of Satan—hell. Now people can escape the power of Satan (Acts 26:18). The death of Jesus on the cross destroyed Satan's efforts to prevent people from having access to forgiveness (Hebrews 2:14). People still have to exercise their free will and **choose** to follow God. They have to follow God's Word in order to avoid sinning. But the atoning act of Jesus on the cross enabled God to frustrate the activity of Satan and to forgive those who choose to live life in harmony with His will.

Genesis 12:3

Another recorded mention of God's intention to redeem humans came when God spoke to a man named
Abram who lived in Ur—a highly advanced civilization
for its day. God made the following declaration to him:
"Get out of your country, from your family and from your
father's house, to a land that I will show you. I will make
you a great nation; I will bless you and make your name
great; and you shall be a blessing. I will bless those who
bless you, and I will curse him who curses you; and in
you all the families of the earth shall be blessed" (Genesis 12:1-3). God fulfilled the first two promises when
He multiplied Abraham's offspring to form the nation of
Israel (Deuteronomy 1:10; 26:5), and when He brought
the descendents of Abraham, the Israelites, into the land
of Canaan (Joshua 11:23). But the third promise (i.e., "in
your seed all the nations of the earth shall be blessed")
was fulfilled in the arrival of Jesus into the world, as Paul
explained: "Now to Abraham and his Seed were the
promises made. He does not say, 'And to seeds,' as of
many, but as of one, 'And to your Seed,' who is Christ"
(Galatians 3:16).

Predictions about the coming of Christ to Earth abound
in the Old Testament. In fact, it has been estimated that
there are over 300 distinct prophecies in the Old Testament that have been literally fulfilled in Christ. The fact
that Jesus is God is so important to Christianity that to

reject it is to reject the whole Christian religion and to rob Christianity of its power. Most people in Christendom recognize this truth and acknowledge that without Christ, there is no Christianity.

What is so surprising is that Christendom has largely failed to see the comparable importance assigned by Scripture to **the church**. This failure has made itself visible in the very existence of multiple churches and different denominations—a circumstance in direct conflict with the will of Christ (see Appendix A). The majority view seems to be that one can embrace Christ before and without any connection to any church.

Ephesians 3

But as one goes through the Old Testament, one is struck with the fact that even as God predicted the coming Christ, He likewise offered glimpses of the kingdom of Christ—the church of Christ—and how it would be linked to Christ and His atoning work at the cross. Indeed, before Adam and Eve lived in the Garden of Eden together; before the skies, seas, and land were populated by birds, fish, and animals; before the Sun, Moon, and stars were situated in the Universe; and before our planet Earth was but a dark, watery, formless mass—God purposed to bring into being **the church of Christ**.

Scripture describes this divine intention as "eternal." Central to the great purposes of God from eternity has been **both** the sending of His Son **and** the creation of the church of Christ—the blood-bought body of Jesus and living organism of the redeemed. Read Paul's statement: "To the intent that now unto the principalities and powers in heavenly places might be known **by the church** the manifold wisdom of God, according to **the eternal purpose** which he purposed in Christ Jesus our Lord" (Ephesians 3:10-11, emp. added). It is difficult for human beings to understand "eternal." There are times when the notion of "everlasting" is abbreviated—like Jonah 2:6 where Jonah said he was in the fish's stomach "forever." It must have seemed like it to him. So the word can be used in a limited way. In Philemon 15, Paul said that once Onesimus returned, he would be with Philemon *aionion*—"forever." But the context limits the meaning to just until he dies.

But when we speak of deity or the church, we are talking about **everlasting, eternal, forever**. Hebrews 12:28 asserts confidently: "Wherefore we receiving a kingdom which..." will someday end? No! Rather, "a kingdom that is unshakable," destined to be around forever—an **eternal** institution. No wonder Daniel was informed: "The saints of the most high shall take the kingdom and possess the kingdom forever, even **forever and ever**" (Daniel 7:18, emp. added). With that grand purpose in mind, God gradually began predicting (through promise and prophecy) the eventual accomplishment of that purpose.

The Prophets

Some 750 years before Christ came to Earth, Isaiah announced the eventual establishment of the "Lord's house" in the "last days" in Jerusalem (Isaiah 2:1-4). At about the same time, Micah preached basically the same message (Micah 4:1-3). Some 500 years before Christ, Daniel declared to a pagan king that during the days of the Roman kings, the God of heaven would set up a kingdom that would never be destroyed (Daniel 2:44). He also stated that the "Son of man" would pass through the clouds, come to the Ancient of Days, and be given an indestructible kingdom (Daniel 7:13-14). Thus, the church, which existed first in purpose in the mind of God, now existed in promise and prophecy in the utterances of His spokesmen.

With the appearance of John the Baptizer and Jesus on the Earth, the church of Christ entered a new phase of existence. Now, more than ever before, the kingdom was presented with a sense of immediacy, nearness, and urgent expectation. Now, God's workers actively prepared for its immediate appearance. John exclaimed: "[T]he kingdom of heaven is at hand" (Matthew 3:2). Jesus echoed precisely the same point: "[T]he kingdom of heaven is at hand" (Matthew 4:17). As John made preparations for the Lord (Matthew 3:3), so the Lord made preparations for the kingdom. He announced His intention personally to establish His church (Matthew

16:18). He declared that it would occur during the lifetime of His earthly contemporaries, and that, in fact, some were standing in His presence who would not die before they would see the kingdom of God come with power (Mark 9:1). [NOTE: As it turned out, among the apostles, only Judas died before the kingdom came.]

Just prior to His departure from Earth, Jesus further noted that the apostles would be witnesses of His death and resurrection, and would preach repentance and re- mission of sins in His name among all nations, beginning at Jerusalem. He would even send the promise of the Father upon them, which would entail being "endued with power from on high" (Luke 24:46-49). This power was to be equated with Holy Spirit immersion (Acts 1:4-5,8).

Now that the kingdom had existed in **purpose, prom- ise**, and **prophecy**, as well as in **preparation**, the time had come for the church to come forth in **perfection**. After urging the apostles to "wait in Jerusalem," Jesus ascended into a cloud and into heaven (Acts 1:9). The apostles returned to Jerusalem and for ten days awaited the fulfillment of the Savior's words.

Acts 2: The Hub of the Bible

Then it happened. The year was approximately A.D. 30. The place was the city of Jerusalem (Acts 1:8,12,19)—just as Isaiah predicted (Isaiah 2:3). The time was the "last days" (Acts 2:16-17)—just as Isaiah predicted (Isaiah 2:2), during the time of the Roman kings (specifically, Tiberius: Luke 3:1)—just as Daniel predicted (Daniel 2:44). With stunning splendor, after centuries of eager anticipation, God poured out His Spirit upon the Twelve on the first Pentecost after Christ's resurrection (Acts 2:2-4)—just as Joel predicted (Joel 2:28ff.). This miraculous outpouring enabled these one dozen "ambassadors" (2 Corinthians 5:20) to present a stirring defense of Christ's resurrection, convicting some in the audience with the guilt of the crucifixion. Peter then detailed the conditions of forgiveness and the terms of entrance into the kingdom of Christ (Acts 2:37-38)—just as Jesus predicted (Matthew 16:19; 18:18).

The church of Christ was now perfected into existence on the Earth—just as Jesus predicted (Matthew 16:18; Mark 9:1). She consisted of approximately 3,000 members—all of Jewish descent (Acts 2:41). From this moment forward, the kingdom of Christ on the Earth was a reality. From this point forward in the New Testament, the church/kingdom is always spoken of as being in existence (e.g., Acts 14:22; Romans 14:17). To its Jewish citizens were added the first Gentile converts, when those of the household of Cornelius obeyed the same terms of entrance that their Jewish counterparts had obeyed some ten to fifteen years earlier (Acts 10:47-48). By the cross, Christ had made "in Himself one new man from the two, thus making peace, and that He might reconcile them both to God in one body" (Ephesians 2:15-16).

In his great writing on the church of Christ, Paul in Ephesians insisted that the church of Christ is the body of Christ over which Jesus now reigns and rules from heaven (1:20-23). He further insisted that Jesus is the "head" of this body (1:22), and that "there is one body" (4:4). Yet Christendom has made mockery of these foundational premises of Christ's religion by founding and fashioning many churches with differing names, creeds, and doctrines. Two points are clear: (1) if Christ approves of multiple churches, then being the Bridegroom (Mark 2:19-20), He is a polygamist; and (2) if "one church is as good as another," and the church is so unimportant that mere human beings are permitted to found them, then the New Testament endorses a decapitated Gospel in which the head of the body (Christ) is disconnected from His body.

Churches of Christ are those who conform themselves to the teaching of the Bible regarding the founding of Christ's church. If they are genuinely the church of Christ, they are indistinguishable from the church of the Bible.

Chapter 2

DOCTRINE/CREED

Faithful churches of Christ, like the church we read about in the New Testament, manifest a conspicuous absence of denominational trappings. New Testament churches of Christ have no official creeds, church manuals, or confessions of faith to which members must subscribe. There are no synods, councils, or governing bodies handing down official decrees to churches. The only authoritative document that governs belief and practice is the Bible. Once the New Testament was completely revealed by the Holy Spirit, the Bible became God's complete revelation to humans. Thus, the Bible presents itself as the inspired, inerrant, infallible Word of God—the only reliable and authoritative guide to get humans from this life to heaven (1 Thessalonians 2:13; 2 Timothy 2:15; 2 Peter 3:16).

The 66 books of the Bible, written by some 40 men over a period of 1,600 years, are the product of the Holy Spirit, Who empowered the writers to pen only what God wanted written (2 Samuel 23:2; 1 Corinthians 2:9-13; 2 Timothy 3:16-17; 1 Peter 1:10-12; 2 Peter 1:20-21). The Bible is thus verbally inspired of God, inerrant, and all-sufficient. [NOTE: For an excellent discussion of the inspiration of the Bible, see Butt, 2007.]

In order to understand God's Word, one must "rightly divide" it or "handle it aright" (2 Timothy 2:15). Churches of Christ recognize that it records three distinct periods of human history. The Patriarchal period extended from the Creation to the cross of Christ and was addressed to all people prior to Mt. Sinai, and only Gentiles from Mt. Sinai to the cross. The Mosaic period, on the other hand, refers to the period that began when God gave the Old Covenant (Law of Moses) to the nation of Israel at Mt. Sinai (about 1500 B.C.). This period of Bible history came to a close at the death of Christ when Jesus "nailed" the Old Law to the cross and took it out of the way (Colossians 2:14; Hebrews 9:15-17).

It would be extremely difficult, if not impossible, to grasp many of the details of New Testament Christianity if a person does not understand these biblical distinctions. In any given passage, one must recognize who is being addressed and which laws apply to whom. For example, mechanical instruments of music in worship are often defended on the grounds that "David used them." But David was a Jew (neither a Gentile nor a Christian) who lived under the Law of Moses and was not subject to the regulations of the New Covenant of Christ. Another example is the failure to understand the importance of water baptism on the grounds that "the thief on the cross did not have to be baptized." Yet, the thief also lived under a different law before Christ's New Testament came into effect. He was not subject to the command to be baptized for the remission of sins (see Appendix B).

Faithful churches of Christ accept the Bible as their only guide in spiritual matters. Indeed, it is "the perfect law of liberty" (James 1:25) that contains "all things that pertain to life and godliness" (2 Peter 1:3). No additions are permissible (Galatians 1:6-9).

REFERENCE

Butt, Kyle (2007), *Behold the Word of God* (Montgomery, AL: Apologetics Press).

Chapter 3

ENTRANCE REQUIREMENTS

The entrance requirements for the church of Christ are unlike any other institution on Earth. Just before He left the planet, Christ Himself articulated them in what is often referred to as the "Great Commission": Matthew 28:18-20, Mark 16:15-16, and Luke 24:46-47.

The Great Commission

Jesus lived prior to the establishment of His church and the Christian religion. Therefore, one must go to the book of Acts to see the outworking of Jesus' instructions regarding how to enter the church of Christ.

Acts

As reported early in the book of Acts, the church had its beginning on the first Pentecost after Christ's resurrection. Observe what people in the first century did to become a member of the church of Christ. In Acts 2, after listening to the preaching of the Gospel, the people were so convicted by the message that they were "cut to the heart" (Acts 2:37). They then asked the apostles what they needed to do. Peter responded: "Repent and be baptized every one of you in the name of Jesus Christ, for the remission of your sins" (Acts 2:38). This was in fulfillment of Jesus' own words in Mark 16:16: "He who believes and is baptized will be saved."

The exact same procedure is depicted over and over again in Acts, earning for this inspired record the label—"the book of conversions." Acts 8:12-13 records that "when they believed Philip as he preached the good news of the kingdom of God and the name of Jesus Christ, they were baptized, both men and women. Simon himself believed and was baptized." In the same chapter, Philip preached Jesus to the Ethiopian eunuch. After hearing Philip's preaching about Jesus, they came to a body of water, and the eunuch said: "See, here is water. What hinders me from being baptized?" Philip said he could if he believed (Acts 8:36ff.).

In Acts 10, Cornelius heard the message, believed, and was baptized (vss. 47-48). In Acts 16, Lydia listened to the message, believed, and was baptized (vss. 14-15). In the same chapter, the Philippian jailer heard the Word of the Lord and was immediately baptized the same hour of the night (vss. 33-34). In Acts 18:8, many of the Corinthians heard the Word, believed, and were baptized. In Acts 19:4-5, some of the citizens of Ephesus listened to Paul's preaching, believed, and were baptized. Paul, himself, in Acts chapters 9 and 22, heard the Word and was baptized to have his sins washed away (9:18; 22:16). The same "pattern" of conversion is repeated over and over again in Acts. Examine the following chart:

Great Commission	Matthew 28:19-20	Mark 16:15-16	Luke 24:46-47	Romans 10:9

Acts	Believe	Repent	Confess	Baptized	Saved
2:37-38 Jews	pricked	repented		baptized	remission
8:12-13 Samaritans	believed			baptized	
8:36-39 Eunuch	believed		confessed	baptized	rejoiced
9:6,9,18; 22:16 Saul	trembled	sorrow	confessed	baptized	sins washed
10:43,48; 11:14,17-18 Cornelius	believed	repented		baptized	saved/life
16:14-15 Lydia	heart opened			baptized	faithful
16:31-34 Jailer	believed	washed stripes		baptized	rejoiced
17:12 Bereans	believed				
18:8 Corinthians	believed			baptized	saints 1 Cor. 1:2
19:2-5,18 Ephesians	believed	confessed evil deeds		baptized	in Christ Eph. 1:3

Notice that this chart pinpoints only the explicit indications of what first-century people did to be saved. By allowing the Bible to speak for itself unfettered by human theology, one can quickly surmise the divine entrance requirements of the church of Christ.

Rome, Corinth, Galatia, Colossae, and Beyond

The rest of the New Testament confirms these procedures for becoming a Christian. Everyone who became a Christian did so in precisely the same manner. Paul reminded Roman Christians that on the day they were baptized, they were baptized into Christ, into His death, and were made free from sin to live a new life: "[D]o you not know that as many of us as were baptized into Christ Jesus were baptized into His death? Therefore we were buried with Him through baptism into death, that just as Christ was raised from the dead by the glory of the Father, even so we also should walk in newness of life" (Romans 6:3-4). He told the Corinthians that on the day they were baptized, they were baptized into the one body, which is the church of Christ (1 Corinthians 12:13). He told the Galatians that when they were baptized, they were baptized into Christ, and thus "put on" Christ, that is, they were **clothed** with Him (3:27). He told the Colossians that it was at the point of baptism that their sins had been cut off as a sort of spiritual circumcision (2:11-12). Peter added his support to this same understanding by declaring that one is **saved** at the moment of baptism, for it is at **that point** that the benefits of the **resurrection of Christ** are applied to the believer (1 Peter 3:21).

Hear, Believe, Repent, Confess, Be Baptized

Notice from these Scriptures that in the first century, a person became a Christian in the same way and at the same moment that he became a member of the church of Christ. Upon hearing the gospel message of salvation and God's will for their life, first-century people who were receptive to the message were made aware of their horribly sinful condition. They recognized the purpose of Jesus' atoning sacrifice through His death upon the cross. This realization caused them to believe (have faith) in God, in Jesus as the Son of God, and in the New Testament expression of the will of God. After all, "faith comes by hearing, and hearing by the word of God" (Romans 10:17). This belief/faith then lead those individuals to repent of their sins. Jesus Himself had stated: "[B]ut unless you repent you will all likewise perish" (Luke 13:3,5). These now penitent believers were then required to confess that Jesus is the Christ, the Lord, the Son of God. Paul insisted: "[I]f you **confess with your mouth the Lord Jesus** and believe in your heart that God has raised Him from the dead, you will be saved. For with the heart one believes unto righteousness, and **with the mouth confession is made unto salvation**"

(Romans 10:9-10, emp. added). Then these now penitent, confessing believers were baptized—immersed in
water (see Appendix C)—with the understanding that
the blood of Christ was contacted in the act of baptism,
and that as they rose from the waters of baptism, they
were forgiven of sin and added to the church by Christ
(cf. Hebrews 10:22). Peter had announced on the day
of Pentecost: "Repent, and let every one of you be
baptized in the name of Jesus Christ for the remission
of sins" (Acts 2:38). These first-century people did not
become Christians and then "join the church of their
choice." When they were baptized for the remission of
sins, they were **simultaneously** added to the church of
Christ by Jesus Himself (cf. Acts 2:41, KJV; 1 Corinthians
12:13; Ephesians 5:26). Believe, repent, confess, and be
immersed—simple!

Summary

So much diversity and widespread misconception
exists. Most religious groups teach salvation is solely by
faith, without any further acts of obedience. They say
that all you have to do is "accept Jesus as your savior,"
which means saying, "I believe in Jesus Christ, I accept
Him into my heart as my personal savior." Denominationalism teaches that **at that moment** the person is
forgiven of sin and he becomes a Christian. While the
New Testament certainly teaches that a non-Christian
must **believe**, as noted above, it also teaches the ne-

cessity of repentance, confession, and baptism. In fact, the apostle Paul stated that his sins were washed away and he "called on the name of the Lord" **in the act of baptism** (Acts 22:16; see Appendix C). Most people in the religious world believe that a person is forgiven of sins **before** being immersed. But, once again, that is a departure from New Testament teaching. The church of Christ practices the entrance requirements set forth in the New Testament.

Chapter 4

STRUCTURE/ORGANIZATION

The organizational structure of the church of Christ comes from the arrangement given in the New Testament. Each local congregation is independent and autonomous. There is no hierarchy or denominational headquarters. Churches of Christ have no synods, councils, or conventions that establish policy or provide governing guidelines. Every single local congregation is self-governing and completely autonomous.

Christ the Head

The first century New Testament churches were organized first and foremost with Jesus as the head (Colossians 1:18). After all, He stated that He would build **His** church (Matthew 16:18). So the church belongs to Him, and only He has the right to structure the church.

Only He has the right to function as head. Churches of Christ recognize that no human may rightly substitute for Christ and act as head of the church on Earth.

Elders

Under the authority of Christ as the Chief Shepherd (1 Peter 5:4), a qualified group of men serves as the earthly overseers or managers of the local congregation (1 Timothy 3:1-7; Titus 1:5-9). Three terms are used in the New Testament to identify and describe these men and their role. One of the terms is typically translated into English as elder or presbyter. The second term is translated pastor or shepherd. [NOTE: The name "pastor" did not refer to a preacher in the New Testament, but to an elder.] The third term is translated as bishop or overseer. All three terms are used interchangeably (Acts 20:17,28; Titus 1:5,7; 1 Peter 5:1-4). They refer to a single "office," position, or function (1 Timothy 3:1). Elders' authority extends only to the congregation where they are members. A **plurality** of elders is necessary for each single congregation—in harmony with New Testament practice (e.g., Acts 14:23; 20:17; Philippians 1:1; Titus 1:5). These men function as the overseeing authorities in the local church. As the overseers of the congregation, they "admonish" (1 Thessalonians 5:12), "take care of" (1 Timothy 3:5), "rule over" (Hebrews 13:7), "watch for souls" (Hebrews 13:17), and "feed" or "shepherd" the membership (Acts 20:28; 1 Peter 5:2).

Deacons

Working under the oversight of the elders, another group of men serve as deacons. Like the elders, they too must meet the qualifications laid out in Scripture (1 Timothy 3:8-13). Whereas the elders are the spiritual overseers of the souls of the members of the local congregation, the deacons are assigned responsibilities and tasks that involve serving the needs of the congregation (cf. Acts 6:1-6). Their assigned areas of work and ministry enable the shepherds to concentrate on the spiritual condition of the members.

Preachers/Evangelists and Teachers

In addition to the elders and deacons (Philippians 1:1), churches of Christ have preachers or evangelists who proclaim the Gospel, the good news (Ephesians 4:11; 2 Timothy 4:5; James 3:1). They have the responsibility to declare the whole counsel of God (Acts 20:27)—teaching and preaching Christian doctrine to non-Christian and Christian alike. They serve under the authority of the elders. They are joined by other members of the local congregation, both men and women, who act as Bible class teachers, also instructing members in the faith. Female Bible teachers teach women and children (Titus 2:4). All of the members participate together in the work and worship of the church in an effort to glorify God in their lives.

Summary

Many changes have been made since the first century in church government and organization. Faithful churches of Christ avoid the ecclesiastical hierarchy and denominational trappings typical of many churches. In summary, in accordance with the simple structure of Christ's church according to the New Testament, churches of Christ have elders who shepherd the flock, deacons who minister to the congregation, preachers and evangelists who preach the Gospel, Bible class teachers, and all other members of the local congregation who work and worship under the oversight of the elders. Who are the churches of Christ? They are **those churches that follow this simple New Testament format**.

Chapter 5

NAMES

As one takes Bible in hand and reads about the church of the New Testament, the terminology used to refer to Christ's church becomes readily apparent. Churches of Christ endeavor to conform themselves to this scriptural terminology. They attempt to confine themselves to the names and designations that have been given by Christ through the Holy Spirit. Even the name "churches of Christ" (Romans 16:16) is the result of this intention to "call Bible things by Bible names," as well as to "speak where the Bible speaks and be silent where the Bible is silent."

Names for the Church

Churches of Christ have insisted through the years that the designation "church of Christ" is not a formal or official designation (like "Baptist Church" or "Methodist Church"). It is not a denominational identifier. Rather, it is to be understood in the same way that the New Testament uses several other expressions to refer to the collective group of Christians: "church of God" (1 Corinthians 1:2), "church of the living God" (1 Timothy 3:15), "the temple of God" (1 Corinthians 3:16), "body of Christ" (Ephesians 4:12), "the church" (Acts 8:1—the most prominent expression), "the kingdom" (Matthew 16:19), "the kingdom of God" (Mark 9:1; John 3:5), "the kingdom of heaven" (Matthew 18:3), "the kingdom of His dear Son" (Colossians 1:13). "Churches of Christ" (Romans 16:16) is simply a plural form of the singular concept.

In the New Testament, these expressions are not intended to be formal denominational titles. Rather, they are **descriptions**. Churches of Christ have so intended their use of the name "church of Christ." They have insisted that any of the above expressions are scriptural and may be used. In contrast, the New Testament grants no sanction to refer to the church of the New Testament as the Baptist, Methodist, Presbyterian, Episcopal, Lutheran, or Pentecostal church. These are **manmade** designations that spotlight mere humans or favorite doctrines, rather than giving honor to the Founder and Owner of the church.

Since Jesus promised to build **His** church (Matthew 16:18), and since He paid for His church with His **own** blood (Acts 20:28), and since He is the **head** of that body (Ephesians 1:22-23; Colossians 1:18), then the church belongs to **Him** and wears **His** name (even as individuals who are saved bear the name "**Christ**ian"). Even the designation "church of God" refers to God the Son. Jesus is now reigning and ruling over His kingdom, the church (Acts 2:30,33; Ephesians 1:22). He will turn the kingdom over to His Father when He returns at the end of time (1 Corinthians 15:24). Until then, the church is unquestionably intended in the New Testament to be associated in name with Christ. Hence, "churches of Christ" is simply the most expedient way to emphasize to the world that the church is Christ's, she belongs to Him, she is **Christ's** church, i.e., the church of Christ. Thus, she wears the name of her Head, Owner, and Savior— Christ (Daniel 7:14; Ephesians 4:12; Revelation 11:15).

No wonder Paul wrote in his remarks to the church at Ephesus:

- "to Him be glory **in the church** by Christ Jesus" (Ephesians 3:21)
- "as **the church** is subject to Christ" (Ephesians 5:24)
- "just as Christ also loved **the church** and gave Himself **for her**, that He might sanctify and cleanse her with the washing of water by the

word, that He might present her to Himself a
glorious church" (Ephesians 5:25-27)

These verses clarify forcefully the relationship that
exists between Christ and the church. The church (the
bride) is to wear the name of the bridegroom (Jesus),
even as women today take the name of their husband
when they marry. But Jesus has only one bride—not
multiple ones as existing today in the denominational
world. Interestingly, many churches of Christ over the
years have placed on their church building sign, "The
Church of Christ Meets Here," in order to emphasize to
the public that the **people**, not the building, make up
the church, which, in turn, **belongs to Christ**.

Names for the Members of the Church

The same may be said with regard to the names that
God wants individual members of the church to wear.
In Isaiah 62:2, the prophet foretold that God, with His
own mouth, would give a name to His people. We find
the fulfillment of that prophecy in Acts 11:26. **The name**
that God wants individual members of His church to
wear is the name "Christian" (Acts 26:29; 1 Peter 4:16).
Again, this name is the name that indicates that one
belongs to Christ. Beyond this central name, the New
Testament uses several secondary names to describe
Christians. Romans 1:7 uses the term "saints," while Acts
5:14 uses the term "believer." Other passages refer to
"disciples" (Acts 20:7), which means "learners," "saints"

(1 Corinthians 1:2), "brothers" (1 Corinthians 15:1), "sons of God" (Romans 8:14), "children of God" (1 John 3:1), and "priests" (1 Peter 2:9). These are **scriptural** names. Churches of Christ use all of them, though priority is given to the name Christian.

Churches of Christ have also avoided using many of the religious titles that are commonly used in Christendom. The denominational concept of a **clergy** is foreign to the New Testament. Preachers in the New Testament were merely Christians who prepared themselves to preach. They were not set apart as a special class of religious people. They did not receive special titles like "reverend" or "pastor" or "father" (Matthew 23:9). The term "pastor" is used in the New Testament to refer to one who has been appointed to serve as an elder or shepherd along with other men. This office was distinct from the role of the preacher. Churches of Christ have sought to avoid using names that are manmade, or that serve only to cultivate the praise of men, when, in fact, all praise belongs to God (Luke 4:8).

Summary

New Testament truth on the matter of names is simple. Contrary to that New Testament pattern, many churches and individuals have taken the name of a man or a particular doctrine and applied that name to themselves—names that are conspicuously absent from the New Testament. Surely, God is not pleased with man-

made names. Surely, God will not sanction or extend
His grace to groups and individuals who have chosen
to stray from His will and His pattern for religion. Those
who formulate for themselves their own religions, their
own churches, and their own names, surely displease
God since He has already given the names He expects
the church to use. Indeed, down through the annals of
human history, the Bible records that God has never
accepted human invention in religion (Matthew 15:9).

So who are the churches of Christ? They are **those
churches that wear the name of Christ**—individually
and collectively. As the apostle Peter stated: "Neither is
there salvation in any other, for there is **no other name**
under heaven given among men by which we must be
saved" (Acts 4:12, emp. added). "If any man suffers as
a **Christian**, let him not be ashamed; but let him glorify
God **in this name**" (1 Peter 4:16, emp. added).

Chapter 6

WORSHIP

Churches of Christ seek to worship God in harmony with the worship specifications given in the New Testament. Even as God has always explained to humans throughout Bible history how they are to worship Him (e.g., Genesis 4:3-5), so the New Testament provides specific instructions that indicate how God wants to be worshipped in the Christian age.

Sunday

In the first century, Christians met for worship on the first day of the week—Sunday. Sunday is pinpointed in New Testament Christianity as the special day on which Christians gather together to worship God (Acts 20:7). Christians are required by God to attend these worship assemblies on a regular basis, since the Bible teaches the necessity of assembling with other Christians for mutual edification (Hebrews 10:25). Jesus referred to the church when He said, "Seek first the kingdom of God" (Matthew 6:33). Putting the church first in life necessarily entails regularly meeting with fellow Christians for worship on Sunday.

Lord's Supper

In harmony with New Testament practice, churches of Christ observe the Lord's Supper, also called "communion" (1 Corinthians 10:16). In keeping with Acts 2:46 and 20:7, as well as 1 Corinthians 11:20-34 and 16:1-3, the Lord's Supper is observed **every first day of the week**. This observance is in keeping with Jesus' own instructions (Matthew 26:26-29), and thus consists of every Christian partaking of both the fruit of the vine (grape juice) and unleavened bread. These symbols represent the shed blood and crucified body of Christ. Christians sit quietly and meditate on the sacrifice of Christ.

Singing

In the realm of music, churches of Christ follow the expressed directives of the New Testament. Ephesians 5:19 reads: "[S]peaking to one another in psalms and hymns and spiritual songs, singing and making melody in your heart to the Lord." Colossians 3:16 states: "Let the word of Christ dwell in you richly in all wisdom, teaching and admonishing one another in psalms and hymns and spiritual songs, singing with grace in your hearts to the Lord." New Testament instructions for musical worship are that simple and unencumbered. There is no authority in the New Testament for playing musical instruments in worship to God—which would constitute a manmade addition to pure, spiritual worship. Nor does the New Testament give authority for performance groups like choirs and praise teams. The music in the New Testament is very clearly **congregational**, **vocal singing**. Churches of Christ endeavor to conform themselves to this simple specification.

Giving

In addition, every first day of the week churches of Christ contribute a percentage of their income to a general treasury so that the church may carry on its work. Paul instructed the church at Corinth: "Now concerning the collection for the saints, as I have given orders to the churches of Galatia, so you must do also: On the first day of the week let each one of you lay something aside, storing up as he may prosper, that there be no collections when I come" (1 Corinthians 16:1-2). Whereas tithing is an Old Testament command given to the Jews (e.g., Malachi 3:8), a requirement not directed to Christians in the New Testament, churches of Christ encourage each other simply to give liberally, in keeping with New Testament injunction: "But this I say: He who sows sparingly will also reap sparingly, and he who sows bountifully will also reap bountifully. So let each one give as he purposes in his heart, not grudgingly or of necessity; for God loves a cheerful giver" (2 Corinthians 9:6-7). The collected funds are then used to carry on the work of the local church.

Prayer

Churches of Christ also give serious attention to prayer. The New Testament has much to say about prayer in the life of the faithful Christian (e.g., Ephesians 6:18; Philippians 4:6; 1 Thessalonians 5:17; James 5:13). Even as the early church gave herself continually to prayer, churches of Christ include this feature of worship in their worship assemblies (Acts 2:42; 1 Timothy 2:1-8).

Preaching, Teaching, Bible Reading

A final avenue of worship through which churches of Christ approach God in their corporate assemblies is through preaching, teaching, Bible study, and Scripture reading. When the church listens to and contemplates the meaning of the Scriptures, he or she is receiving direct information from God. Christians honor God when they are receptive to His admonitions issued through His Word. Consequently, a preacher will typically preach a gospel sermon to the congregation at some point in the service. A designated member may read a passage from the Bible to the entire assembly (1 Timothy 4:13).

In these ways, Christians worship God by encountering Him in His Word.

Summary

Luke summarized the worship of the first church of Christ in these words: "And they continued steadfastly in the apostles' doctrine and fellowship, in the breaking of bread, and in prayers" (Acts 2:42). Churches of Christ endeavor to emulate these avenues of worship in their own assemblies, by continuing in the apostles' doctrine (teaching, preaching, and examining doctrinal truth), fellowship (weekly contributions to the work of the church), the breaking of bread (the Lord's Supper), and in prayers. As noted above, they also engage in congregational singing at every service. The public worship assemblies of faithful churches of Christ employ these five acts of worship—without modification or human addition.

The worship of churches of Christ is extremely simple and unpretentious—free from the hype and glitter that bored humans frequently fabricate. Faithful churches of Christ have restored simple New Testament worship in their congregations. They meet together every first day of the week and commune together around the Lord's Table; they sing psalms, hymns, and spiritual songs together; they contribute a percentage of their income to carry on the work of the church; they pray together; and they study the Word of God together.

Chapter 7

WORK AND PURPOSE

Churches of Christ recognize that the unique mission of the church is to bring glory to God (1 Corinthians 6:20). Peter explained: "If anyone speaks, let him speak as the oracles of God. If anyone ministers, let him do it as with the ability which God supplies, **that in all things God may be glorified through Jesus Christ**, to whom belong the glory and the dominion forever and ever. Amen" (1 Peter 4:11, emp. added). This task is accomplished through essentially three avenues of activity.

Evangelism

First, churches of Christ place a high priority on spreading the Gospel of Christ to the human race (Matthew 28:18-20; Mark 16:15-16; Luke 24:46-47; Acts 8:4; Romans 10:14; Philippians 2:15-16; Hebrews 5:12-14).

This prime directive stems from the fact that, as noted earlier, after Jesus' crucifixion and resurrection, He issued to His apostles what some have called the "Great Commission." The apostles, and by implication all Christians since, are to go into the whole world and preach the Gospel to every creature (Mark 16:16). This objective is accomplished in many ways. Some churches support fulltime missionaries in foreign fields. Others harness mass media by producing television and radio programs, Internet Web sites, newspaper advertisements, or mass mail outs. Some go door-to-door and speak with their neighbors.

Edification

Second, churches of Christ try to keep their members faithful (Romans 14:19; 15:1-3; Ephesians 4:12; Jude 20-24). Edification, which refers to building up the body of Christ, is generally accomplished by providing members with a strong program of Bible study. Bible classes, with teachers for all age groups, are typically held on Sunday mornings and Wednesday nights. Other forms of encouragement to sustain members spiritually include gospel meetings, seminars, retreats, lectureships, and other means of strengthening the saints.

Benevolence

Third, churches of Christ seek to manifest a benevolent spirit to society. Assistance is given to the poor and those who are struggling with the physical necessities of life (Matthew 25:31-46; Galatians 6:10; James 2:1-17). Even as Jesus placed a high priority on being compassionate towards the needy, so faithful churches of Christ strive to assist their fellowman with their basic needs.

These three avenues serve to summarize the basic work of the church. In short, churches of Christ attempt to achieve complete conformity to the will of Christ (Matthew 22:37-38; 2 Corinthians 5:9; 10:5; Ecclesiastes 12:13).

Chapter 8

CONCLUSION

Churches of Christ today possess as a conscious, deliberate intention to be reproductions of the church of Christ that is described in the New Testament. Members of churches of Christ are certainly not perfect. As in the first century, churches of Christ are composed of imperfect people. But the superstructure of the New Testament church has been set in place. Therefore, it is possible for anyone to be **simply a Christian**—a member of the church we read about in the New Testament—**the church of Christ**.

That's not to say that all groups who wear the name "church of Christ" are following the New Testament portrait of the church. A church may have a scriptural name without engaging in scriptural worship. Some churches of Christ have followed the road to apostasy by restructuring the church and making unscriptural changes. Such churches cannot be endorsed, even though they continue to wear the name "church of Christ."

Nevertheless, every reader of this book can be a member of the New Testament church. You do not have to settle for a manmade denomination. Study for yourself what the **New Testament** says about the church of Christ. If you conform yourself to the teaching of the New Testament by obeying the gospel plan of salvation, then you, too, can be simply a member of the church of Christ.

Appendix A

NEW TESTAMENT CHRISTIANITY VS. DENOMINATIONALISM

What is a "denomination"? Does God approve of denominations? These extremely significant and critical questions deserve answers from the Word of God.

When we go to the New Testament and examine God's Word with a view toward ascertaining what His will is with regard to religion, we find that there is a clearly defined system of religion—**God's** religion—in the New Testament. It is the religion of Christ that has come to be called Christianity. We also find that Satan does everything he can to blur the distinctions that God wants observed. We should not be surprised at that. Think about the great hoaxes that have been perpetrated upon mankind. For instance, the doctrine of evolution is almost universally believed by the scientific elite of many societies. So it is with many political, philosophical, and religious systems of thought like Communism, Buddhism, and Hinduism. Those who have examined the evidence—objective truth—on these matters know that those systems of thought simply are not true. Yet large numbers of people adhere to them.

In 2 Corinthians 2:11, Paul spoke about the fact that Satan endeavors to take advantage of people. He said that we should not let Satan take advantage of us, "for we are not ignorant of his devices." The word "devices" means "schemes." We must be aware of the fact that Satan uses deceitful, deceptive ploys in an effort to trick people to get them to believe and practice various things that simply are not true. In a similar statement, Paul used the phrase "wiles of the devil" (Ephesians 6:11). Most people are oblivious to this fact. Many people do not even believe that Satan exists—anymore than they believe that God exists. Yet if the New Testament is true, it is clear there is a Satan, and he will do all he can to fool, trick, and deceive people. He wants to obscure distinctions that God wants observed—distinctions that are scriptural and biblical.

It is clear that this is the case with **denominationalism**. Consider the following dictionary definitions (American..., 2000, p. 485). The term "denominate" means "to give a name to; designate." "Denomination" is "[a] large group of religious congregations united under a common faith and name and organized under a single administrative and legal hierarchy; a name or designation, especially for a class or group." "Denominator" refers to "[t]he expression written below the line in a common fraction that indicates the number of parts into which one whole is divided." "Denominationalism" is "[t]he tendency to separate into religious denominations; sectarianism." Think about these meanings for just a moment. The very word "denomination" refers to a named or designated division. Denominationalism occurs when religious people and groups divide and segregate themselves on the basis of different designations or church affiliations and different doctrines.

Have you gone to the New Testament and read Jesus' prayer for unity in John chapter 17? There He prayed **against** religious division, and prayed to God that believers in Christ would be unified! Paul made the same point to the church of Christ in Corinth: "I beseech you brothers by the name of our Lord Jesus Christ that you all speak the same thing and that there be no divisions among you" (1 Corinthians 1:10). Here is a passage that says denominations are not even to exist! "Let there be no divisions among you." If a denomination is a "designated division," then denominationalism is clearly unscriptural! It is against the will of Christ. The passage continues, "but that you be perfectly joined together in the same mind and in the same judgment."

I assure you, I have nothing against any particular religious group. I have no biases or prejudices against any one church or denomination. But we must go to Scripture and be objective in our appraisal of New Testament truth. It is clear when we go to the Bible that denominationalism, though viewed innocently by millions of people worldwide, is an approach to religion that is out of harmony with New Testament teaching. **God does not want denominations to exist**. He wants all of us to understand His will in the New Testament, and then to bring our lives into conformity and our spirits into submission to that will.

"One Body" = One Church

In Ephesians 1:22-23, the body of Christ is referred to as the church, and later we are told that there is only one (4:4). Those two passages alone should cause us to recognize that the existence of denominations is out of harmony with God's will. Ephesians 4:4 says there is one body. That body is the church of our Lord. He established it; He built it; He purchased it with His own blood (Acts 20: 28). If there is only one church, God is not pleased with the division, the named designations, of competing churches with various names, doctrines, and practices.

In 1 Timothy 3:15, Paul wrote to Timothy that he might know how to conduct himself in the house of God, which is the church of the living God. Most people just do not realize that New Testament truth is that simple, that plain, and that uncomplicated. The denominationalism that has gripped western civilization is so entrenched and so entangled in the minds of people that they seem to be unable to detach themselves from it, and to go back to the New Testament to get a clear conception of the New Testament church. They seem unable or unwilling to embrace pure New Testament teaching and to repudiate all denominationalism.

Pluralism: "Live and Let Live," "I'm Okay, You're Okay"

Our society says, "People ought to be free to believe what they want. Don't be judgmental. You don't have any right to say they are wrong." But such propaganda is unbiblical. **God** has a right. He is the Creator, and He said in His Word that we must know His truth, we must be right about that truth, and we must obey that truth (Hebrews 5:9). Jesus said, "If you love Me, keep My commandments" (John 14:15). He also said, "[Y]ou shall know the truth, and the truth shall make you free" (John 8:32). Paul spoke about the time when people would refuse to hear healthy teaching (2 Timothy 4:3). But God wants all men to be saved and to come to the knowledge of the truth (1 Timothy 2:4).

The Scriptures make clear that God never has and never will sanction the present blurring of the distinction between the New Testament church and the manmade, counterfeit churches that exist in abundance. Many seem oblivious to the fact that no denominations can be found in the Bible. They appear unaware of the fact that the Bible describes a single church—Christ's church.

The only hope of any individual is to be in the one true church living faithfully in accordance with God's desires. The New Testament teaches that we must stay with **God's** words. We are not free to deviate, or to believe and practice whatever **we** choose (2 John 9; 1 Corinthians 4:6; Galatians 1:8). In the final analysis, denominationalism is what results when humans assert their own religious inclinations, formulate their own religious doctrines, and originate their own churches. Solomon's words ought to cause every single person to refrain from affiliation with denominationalism: "Every word of God is pure. He is a shield to those who put their trust in Him. Do not add to His words lest He reprove you and you be found a liar" (Proverbs 30:5-6).

The truth continues to be that denominations are manmade divisions, unmitigated departures from the faith. Denominationalism is about the best thing Satan has come up with to subvert the truth of the Bible and to bring otherwise religious people under his influence. The world religions, as well as those who embrace humanistic philosophies like atheism, by definition, have rejected the one true God and have capitulated to Satan. So where do you suppose Satan is going to focus the brunt of his assault upon the Earth? The more he is able to muddy the waters and to obscure the certainty of the truth, the more chance he has of luring people into his clutches.

CONCLUSION

If one could be just a Christian in the first century without being affiliated with any denomination, then one can be simply a New Testament Christian today. If denominations were not created by God, but have, in fact, come into existence **since** the first century, then to participate in and support denominations is to promote that which God did not create. It is to give sanction to mere manmade invention, and to tamper with the divine system originated by God and Christ. It is to subject oneself to the eventual wrath of God, for Jesus Himself declared: "Every plant which My heavenly Father has not planted will be uprooted" (Matthew 15:13).

If we would truly fathom that the church of Christ is distinctive, exclusive, and unique; if we would truly view fraternization with the denominations as traitorous; if we would love the genuine body of Christ with the same fervency and jealousy with which Jesus loves her; then we would be in a position to proclaim with Paul: "Unto

Him be glory in the church by Christ Jesus throughout all ages, world without end" (Ephesians 3:21).

REFERENCE

American Heritage Dictionary of the English Language (2000), (Boston, MA: Houghton Mifflin), fourth edition.

Appendix B

THE THIEF ON THE CROSS

Legion are those who dismiss water baptism as pre-requisite to salvation on the grounds that "the thief on the cross was not baptized." The thought is that since the thief was suspended on the cross when Jesus said to him, "Today you will be with Me in paradise" (Luke 23:43), he was being pronounced as saved by Christ without being required to be baptized. As one well-known preacher put it, "There was no water within 10 miles of the cross." Please give consideration to two important observations.

First, the thief may well have been baptized **prior** to being placed on the cross. Considerable scriptural evidence points to this conclusion (Matthew 3:5-6; Mark 1:4-5; Luke 3:21; 7:29-30). If he was, in fact, baptized, he would have been baptized with the baptism administered by John the Baptizer. John's baptism was temporary (i.e., in force only during his personal ministry, terminating at the death of Christ). However, even John's baptism was "for the remission of sins" (Mark 1:4) and, hence, essential for salvation for those to whom it was addressed. John's baptism, like the one administered by Jesus while He was on Earth (John 3:22,26; 4:1-2), was unique and temporary. It was addressed **only** to Jews, and only to the Jews who populated the vicinity of **Jerusalem and Judea**. It was designed to prepare the **Jewish** people for the arrival of the Messiah. But John's baptism must not be confused with **New Testament** baptism that is addressed to everybody, and that did not take effect until **after** the cross of Christ. If the thief was a Jew, and if he already had submitted to John's baptism, there would have been no need for him to be re-baptized. He simply would have needed to repent of his post-baptism thievery and acknowledge his sins—which the text plainly indicates that he did.

Second, and most important, the real issue pertains to an extremely crucial feature of Bible interpretation. This hermeneutical feature is so critical that, if a person does not grasp it, his effort to sort out Bible teaching, in order to arrive at correct conclusions, will be inevitably hampered. This principle was spotlighted by Paul when he wrote to Timothy and told him he must "rightly divide the word of truth" (2 Timothy 2:15). In other words, if one simply takes the entire Bible—all 66 books—and treats them as if everything that is said applies directly and equally to everyone, his effort to be in harmony with God's Word will be hopeless and futile. For example, if a person turned to Genesis 6 and read where God instructed Noah to build a boat, if he did not study enough to determine whether such instruction applied to himself, he would end up building his **own** boat—the entire time thinking that God wanted him to do so! The Bible is literally filled with commands, instructions, and requirements that were **not intended to be duplicated** by people living today. Does God forbid you and me from eating a certain fruit (Genesis 2:17; 3:3)? Are we to refrain from boiling a baby goat in its mother's milk (Exodus 23:19)? Does God want you and me to offer our son as a burnt offering (Genesis 22:2)? Are we commanded to load up and leave our homeland (Genesis 12:1)? Moving to the New Testament, does God want you to sell everything you have and give it to the poor (Matthew 19:21)? Does God expect you to leave everything, quit your job, and devote yourself full time to spiritual pursuits (Matthew 4:20; 19:27; Mark 10:28; Luke 5:28)? Does God intend for you to "desire spiritual gifts" (1 Corinthians 14:1), i.e., seek to possess miraculous abilities? The point is that the entire Bible applies to the entire human race. However, careful and diligent study is necessary to determine **how** it applies. We must understand the biblical distinction between the application of the **principles** of the Bible and the **specific details**.

Here, then, is the central point as it pertains to the relevance of the thief on the cross: Beginning at Creation, all humans were amenable to the laws of God that were given to them at that time. Bible students typically call this period of time the Patriarchal Dispensation. During this period, which lasted from Creation to the cross, non-Jews were subject to a body of legislation passed down by God through the fathers of family clans (cf. Hebrews 1:1). In approximately 1500 B.C., God removed the genetic descendants of Abraham from Egyptian bondage, took them out into the Sinai desert, and gave them their own law code (the Law of Moses). Jews were subject to that body of legal information from that time until it, too, was terminated at the cross of Christ. The following passages substantiate these assertions: Matthew 27:51; Romans 2:12-16; Galatians 3:7-29; Ephesians 2:11-22; Colossians 2:11-17. The book of Hebrews addresses this subject extensively. To get to the heart of the matter quickly, read especially Hebrews 9:15-17. When one "correctly handles the Word of truth," one sees that the Bible teaches that when Christ died on the cross, Patriarchal and Mosaic law came to an end. At that point, all humans on the planet became amenable to **the law of Christ** (cf. Galatians 6:2). The law of Christ consists strictly of information that is intended to be in effect **after** the death of Christ. It includes **some** of the things that Jesus and His disciples taught while He was still on Earth. But as regards the **specifics** of salvation, one must go to Acts 2 and the rest of the New Testament (especially the book of Acts) in order to determine what one must do today to be saved. Beginning in Acts 2, the new covenant of Christ took effect, and every single individual who responded correctly to the preaching of the Gospel was **baptized in water in order to be forgiven of sin by the blood of Christ.** Recall the chart on page 21. Every detail of an individual's conversion is not always mentioned, but a perusal of the book of Acts demonstrates decisively that water immersion was a **prerequisite** to forgiveness, along with faith, repentance, and confession of the deity of Christ (Acts 2:38,41; 8:12,13,16,36-38; 9:18; 10:47-48; 16:15,33; 18:8; 19:5; 22:16).

The thief was not subject to the New Testament command to be baptized into Christ's death (Romans 6:3-4), just as Moses, Abraham, and David were not amenable to it. They all lived **prior** to the cross under different law codes. They could not have been baptized into Christ's death—**because He had not yet died!** The establishment of the church of Christ and the launching of the Christian religion did not occur until **after** Christ's death, on the day of Pentecost in the year A.D. 30 in the city of Jerusalem (Acts 2). An honest and accurate appraisal of the biblical data forces us to conclude that the thief on the cross is not an appropriate example of how people are to be saved this side of the cross.

Appendix C

THE ESSENTIALITY OF BAPTISM

Several aspects of the New Testament as it relates to baptism merit special consideration in this book. Why? Because it constitutes a fundamental difference between the churches of Christ and the denominational world at large.

The New Birth

A major cleavage within Christendom pertains to **when** the new birth occurs. Most of Christendom maintains that a person is born again, and thus has sin washed away by the blood of Christ, when that person "accepts Jesus Christ as his personal savior." By this expression it is meant that a person must mentally/orally decide to embrace Christ as the Lord of his life. Hence, the new birth is seen simply as a determination of the will—a moment in time when the person accepts Christ in his mind and couples that decision with an oral confession.

The passage in the New Testament that alludes specifically to being born again pertains to a conversation that Jesus had with a high-ranking Jewish official:

> There was a man of the Pharisees named Nicodemus, a ruler of the Jews. This man came to Jesus by night and said to Him, "Rabbi, we know that You are a teacher come from God; for no one can do these signs that You do unless God is with him." Jesus answered and said to him, "Most assuredly, I say to you, unless one is **born again**, he cannot see the kingdom of God." Nicodemus said to Him, "How can a man be born when he is old? Can he enter a second time into his mother's womb and be born?" Jesus answered, "Most assuredly, I say to you, **unless one is born of water and the Spirit**, he cannot enter the kingdom of God. That which is born of the flesh is flesh, and that which is born of the Spirit is spirit. Do not marvel that I said to you, 'You must be **born again**.'" (John 3:1-7, emp. added).

In an effort to avoid identifying "water" (vs. 5) as water baptism, many within Christendom in the last half century have proposed a variety of novel interpretations. For example, some have proposed that "water" is a reference to the Holy Spirit. While it is certainly true that John uses the word water symbolically to represent the Spirit later in his book (7:38-39), that fact had to be explained by the inspired writer. However, in chapter three the normal, literal meaning is clearly in view, not only because water baptism throughout the New Testament is consistently associated with the salvation event (e.g., Acts 2:38; 8:12-13,36-38; 9:18; 10:47-48; 16:15,33; 18:8; 19:5; 22:16; Romans 6:3-4; Galatians 3:27; Colossians 2:12; Hebrews 10:22; 1 Peter 3:21), but even in this context, 18 verses later, the term clearly has a literal meaning: "Now John also was baptizing in Aenon near Salim, because there was much **water** there" (John 3:23). Additionally, if water in John 3:5 is an allusion to the Holy Spirit, the result would be nonsensical: "unless one is born of the Spirit and the Spirit."

Another quibble offered in an effort to avoid the clear import of John 3:5 is that "water" is a symbol for the blood of Jesus. Of course, no rationale exists for making such a connection. Elsewhere John refers explicitly to water and blood, but clearly distinguishes them from each other in their import (1 John 5:6).

Perhaps the most popular notion, advanced only in recent years, is that water is a reference to the "water," i.e., amniotic fluid, that accompanies the physical birth of a child. However, this novel concept likewise fails to fit the context of Jesus' remarks. In fact, Nicodemus thought Jesus was referring to physical birth ("mother's womb"). But Jesus corrected his misconception and contrasted such thinking with the intended meaning of "water and Spirit." Indeed, Jesus would not have told Nicodemus that he needed to be born physically ("water"). He would not have included the act of physical birth in His listing of prerequisites to entering the kingdom. That would make Jesus say that before a person can enter the kingdom he or she must first be a person! What would be the point of stating such a thing? Perhaps to make certain that everyone knows that **non**-humans, or perhaps animals, cannot enter the kingdom?! Later in the same chapter, did John baptize near Salim "because there was much amniotic fluid there" (vs. 23)?

If one cares to consult the rest of the New Testament in order to allow the Bible to be its own best interpreter, and in order to allow the Bible to harmonize with itself, additional passages shed light on the meaning of John 3:5. According to the rest of the New Testament, spiritual **conception** occurs when the Gospel (i.e., the seed of the Holy Spirit—Luke 8:11) is implanted in the human heart/mind (James 1:18; 1 Corinthians 4:15; Ephesians 6:17; 1 Peter 1:23). The Word of God, in turn, generates penitent faith in the human heart (Romans 10:17) that leads the individual to obey the Gospel by being baptized in water (Mark 16:16; Acts 2:38; Hebrews 10:22). The resulting condition of the individual is that he or she is now a child of God, a citizen of the kingdom, and member of the church of Christ (Matthew 28:19-20; Galatians 3:26-27; Romans 6:4).

Additional verses in the New Testament clarify and cinch this meaning of John 3:5, pinpointing the meaning of the "new birth," while also allowing us to understand the activity of the Holy Spirit in the act of conversion. Consider the following chart (Jackson, 1988):

John 3:5	Spirit	Water	Kingdom
1 Corinthians 12:13	Spirit	Baptized	Body
Ephesians 5:26	Word	Washing/Water	Cleansed Church
Titus 3:5	Renewal of Spirit	Washing of Regeneration	Saved by Mercy

These verses demonstrate that God achieves conversion through the gospel message authored by the Holy Spirit. When a person comes to an understanding (Acts 8:30) of the gospel message, his penitent faith leads him to submit to water immersion for the remission of sins (Acts 8:36,38; 10:47). The result of his obedient response to the Gospel is that he is saved and cleansed from past sin and instantaneously placed into the kingdom of Christ.

Notice that submission to the divine plan of salvation does not mean that humans save themselves by effecting their own salvation. Their obedience does not earn or merit their forgiveness. Rather, the terms or conditions of salvation are stipulated **by God**—not by humans—and are a manifestation of **His** mercy! When people submit to the terms of entrance into the kingdom of Christ, they are saved by the blood of Jesus and the grace of God—not their own effort! Water immersion is not to be viewed as a "work of righteousness which we have done" (Titus 3:5). When we submit to baptism, we are being saved by "the kindness and love of God our Savior" (Titus 3:4). We are being saved "according to His mercy" (Titus 3:5).

Is Baptism a Symbol?

The design of water baptism in the New Testament is unquestionably to allow for the sinner's sins to be removed by the blood of Jesus. This purpose is variously described as "to be saved" (Mark 16:16), "for the remission of sins" (Acts 2:38), to "put on Christ" (Galatians 3:27), to "enter the kingdom of God" (John 3:5), to "wash away your sins" (Acts 22:16), to place one "into one body" (1 Corinthians 12:13) and "into Christ" (Romans 6:3). These are parallel expressions that pinpoint the same design.

In an effort to avoid the clear import of such verses, some theologians have concocted the notion that water baptism is a **post**-salvation action that **follows** the forgiveness of sins. Christendom, almost in its entirety, insists that remission of sin is imparted to the sinner at the very moment the sinner "believes" (i.e., accepts Jesus as personal Savior). This reception of Christ is an internal, mostly intellectual/mental decision in which the individual makes a genuine commitment to receive Jesus as Lord.

In his book *How To Be Born Again*, Billy Graham articulated the viewpoint espoused by the bulk of Christendom: "All you have to do to be born again is to repent of your sins and believe in the Lord Jesus as your personal Lord and Savior" (1977, p. 156). He stated further: "Faith is trust, an act of commitment, in which I open the door of my heart to Him" (p. 160); "It means a single, individual relinquishment of mind and heart toward the one person, Jesus Christ" (p. 161); "Conversion occurs when we repent and place our faith in Christ" (p. 162). Near the close of his book, Graham summarized the prevailing view of when forgiveness occurs:

> Make it happen **now**. ...If you are willing to repent for your sins and to receive Jesus Christ as your Lord and Savior, you can do it now. At this moment you can either bow your head or get on your knees and say this little prayer which I have used with thousands of persons on every continent: O God, I acknowledge that I have sinned against You. I am sorry for my sins. I am willing to turn from my sins. I openly receive and acknowledge Jesus Christ as my Savior. I confess Him as Lord. From this moment on I want to live for Him and serve Him. In Jesus' name. Amen. ...If you are willing to make this decision and have received Jesus Christ as your own Lord and Savior, then you have become a child of God in whom Jesus Christ dwells. ...You are born again (pp. 168-169, emp. in orig.).

Mr. Graham leaves no doubt as to his view of when forgiveness of sins occurs, and that it occurs before and without water baptism.

Another popular Christian writer, Max Lucado, expressed the same viewpoint in his book, *He Did This
Just for You*:

> Would you let him save you? This is the most important
> decision you will ever make. Why don't you give your
> heart to him right now? **Admit** your need. **Agree** with
> his work. **Accept** his gift. Go to God in prayer and tell
> him, *I am a sinner in need of grace. I believe that
> Jesus died for me on the cross. I accept your offer
> of salvation*. It's a simple prayer with eternal results
> (2000, p. 50, italics and emp. in orig.).

Lucado then followed this statement with a "response
page" that provided the reader with the opportunity to
make the decision that he (Lucado) had just advocated.
The page, titled "Your Response," includes the statement,
"I believe that Jesus Christ is the Son of the Living God.
I want him to be the Lord of my life," and is followed
by two blank lines, one for the reader to sign his or her
name, and the other to record the date (p. 51).

These two widely recognized figures are sufficient to
establish the point: most within Christendom believe that
salvation occurs **prior** to water baptism. The Protestant
world has insisted that water baptism is a secondary and
subsequent action to salvation. But if this is the case,
what then is the purpose of baptism? Various religion-
ists have maintained that it serves as "an outward sign
of an inward grace." That is, since a person already has
received the saving grace of God by which sins have

been cleansed, baptism serves the purpose of providing an **outward** demonstration or public declaration that the person has already been saved. The claim is that baptism is a **symbol**—a visible expression of the forgiveness already received at the point of faith.

Perhaps the reader would be shocked to find that the Bible nowhere articulates this unbiblical—albeit provocative—concept. It is the figment of someone's vivid imagination that has been taken up and repeated so often that it "sounds biblical," even when it is not. When Ananias prodded Paul to "arise and be baptized, and wash away your sins, calling on the name of the Lord" (Acts 22:16), he said nothing about an alleged **symbolic** (versus actual) cleansing or **post**-forgiveness washing. He uttered not one word that would lead the unbiased reader to even remotely conclude that Paul's sins were washed away **before** he was baptized in water.

The grammar that the Holy Spirit selected by which to express Himself is very often a key to allowing the Bible to interpret itself. In Acts 22:16, the grammar militates against the denominational interpretation that so often is imposed on Paul's baptism. The Holy Spirit utilized two participles and two verbs in verse 16 that clarify His intended meaning:

- *anastas* is an aorist **active** participle: "having arisen" or "rising"
- *baptisai* is an aorist **middle** imperative verb: "get yourself baptized"
- *apolousai* is also an aorist **middle** imperative verb: "get your sins washed away"
- *epikalesamenos* is an aorist **middle** participle: "you will have been calling"

An adverbial participle is a participle that is used as an adverb to modify the verb. "Calling" is an adverbial participle of manner. It shows the **manner** in which the main verbs are accomplished. The verbs ("baptized" and "wash away sins")—joined by the coordinate conjunction "and" (*kai*)—are "causative middles" (Robertson, 1934, p. 808) in the aorist tense, and so relate to the aorist middle of the participle that follows ("calling"). Hence, a literal translation would be: "Having arisen, get yourself baptized and get your sins washed away, and you will have been calling on the name of the Lord." In other words, Ananias was telling Paul that the way to accomplish "calling on the Lord" was to be baptized and have his sins washed away.

But doesn't the Bible teach that baptism is, in fact, a **symbol**? Doesn't baptism have "symbolic" significance? Yes, the Bible assigns symbolic significance to baptism in regard to at least three distinct features.

Romans 6:3-18

In a context dealing with the power of the Gospel to counteract sin (5:20), Paul addressed the potential misconception that some may form in thinking that the continued indulgence in sin might be justified in order to allow grace to flourish (6:1). When the Romans became Christians, they died to sin (vs. 2). Thus, they should no more have continued a sinful lifestyle, than a physically deceased person could continue living physically. In arguing his point, Paul informed the Romans that water baptism symbolizes the death, burial, and resurrection of Jesus. He used the term "likeness" (and later "form") to pinpoint this symbolism:

> Or do you not know that as many of us as were baptized into Christ Jesus were baptized into His death? Therefore we were buried with Him through baptism into death, that just as Christ was raised from the dead by the glory of the Father, even so we also should walk in newness of life. For if we have been united together in the likeness of His death, certainly we also shall be in the likeness of His resurrection, knowing this, that our old man was crucified with Him, that the body of sin might be done away with, that we should no longer be slaves of sin. For he who has died has been freed from sin (Romans 6:3-8).

When the believing, penitent non-Christian allows him or herself to be lowered into the watery grave of baptism, a parallel to Christ's redemptive work is taking place. Baptism is into Christ's **death** because that is where He shed His blood on our behalf. The atoning activity of Christ was achieved in His death, burial, and resurrection. Consequently, the alien sinner taps into that redemptive power in the act of water immersion. The "newness of life" **follows**—not precedes—baptism (vs. 6). The "old man of sin," the "body of sin," is eliminated in the waters of baptism. Being immersed in water—"buried in baptism" (vs. 4)—is equivalent to "you obeyed from the heart that **form** of doctrine to which you were delivered" (vs. 17). Only **then**, i.e., in the act of emulating Jesus' atonement in the waters of baptism, is one "set free from sin" (vs. 18). To summarize, notice that seven significant achievements occur at the point of water immersion: (1) baptized into Christ; (2) baptized into Christ's death; (3) newness of life; (4) united in His death; (5) old man/body of sin crucified/done away; (6) no longer slaves of sin; and (7) freed from sin.

Colossians 2:11-13

A second depiction of baptism as a symbol is seen in Paul's identification of a link between baptism and the Old Testament practice of circumcision. God introduced the rite of circumcision into His covenant relationship with Abraham (Genesis 17:10ff.). This surgical procedure was strictly a **physical** feature of the Abrahamic covenant sustained by God with the **physical** descendants of Abraham, i.e., the Israelites. In this sense, it did not pertain ultimately to one's **spiritual** standing with God (1 Corinthians 7:19). In contrasting and comparing Christianity with various unacceptable religions and philosophies, Paul used the physical rite of Jewish circumcision as a parallel to water baptism:

> In Him you were also circumcised with the circumcision made without hands, by putting off the body of the sins of the flesh, by the circumcision of Christ, buried with Him in baptism, in which you also were raised with Him

through faith in the working of God, who raised Him from the dead. And you, being dead in your trespasses and the uncircumcision of your flesh, He has made alive together with Him, having forgiven you all trespasses (Colossians 2:11-14).

One must be very careful to allow the text to express itself with regard to the intended symbolism, refraining from drawing unintended points of comparison. The point that Paul was making is the idea that as skin was cut off in the act of circumcision, so sins are cut off at baptism—**skin** vs. **sin**!

Paul underscored this meaning by alluding to the fact that baptism in water involves a burial followed by a resurrection—being "raised" (vs. 12). Twelve verses later, he again referred to this rising from the waters of baptism: "If then you were **raised** with Christ..." (3:1, emp. added). The conclusion is unmistakable: being buried/lowered into the waters of baptism, and then being raised from those waters, is the point at which sin is removed from the sinner—in the same way that flesh was removed from the body in the act of circumcision.

In fact, Paul presented precisely the same case to the Colossians that he presented to the Romans. Note carefully the points of comparison in the following chart:

Romans 6	Colossians 2/3
"we died" (6:2)	(3:3) "you died"
"we died with Christ" (6:8)	(2:20) "you died with Christ"
"buried with Him/baptism" (6:4)	(2:12) "buried with Him/baptism"
"Christ raised from dead" (6:4)	(2:12) "raised Him from dead"
"Walk in newness of life" (6:4)	(3:1) "Seek things above"
"be dead to sin" (6:11)	(3:5) "put to death your members"
"live any longer in it" (6:2)	(3:7) "when you lived in them"

Both passages teach that people are dead in sin and lost until they access the benefits of the death of Christ by being buried in water baptism. At that point, a person becomes dead to sin in the mind of God. Coming up out of the waters of baptism is a type of resurrection that signals a change in the way that person now lives life.

1 Peter 3:20-22

Peter added a third instance of baptism's symbolic value.

For Christ also suffered once for sins, the just for the unjust, that He might bring us to God, being put to death in the flesh but made alive by the Spirit, by whom also He went and preached to the spirits in prison, who formerly were disobedient, when once the Divine longsuffering waited in the days of Noah, while the ark was being prepared, in which a few, that is, eight souls, were saved through water. There is also an antitype which now saves us—baptism (not the removal of the filth of the flesh, but the answer of a good conscience toward God), through the resurrection of Jesus Christ, who has gone into heaven and is at the right hand of God, angels and authorities and powers having been made subject to Him (1 Peter 3:18-22).

Peter made a powerful point of comparison. The antediluvian people had the opportunity to hear God's will for their lives. Noah preached to them (2 Peter 2:5), perhaps for over a century (Genesis 6:3). But the day came when God brought the Flood waters upon the Earth, drowning the entire human population with the exception of only eight individuals. Peter noted that those eight people were "saved by (i.e., *dia*—**through**) water," i.e., through the medium of water. In other words, God used water as the dividing line between the lost and the saved. The water was the medium that separated the eight members of Noah's family from the rest of humanity. He then compared—not the ark—but those Flood waters with the water of baptism. The water of baptism is the dividing line that God has designated to distinguish between the lost person and the saved person.

But does that mean that H_2O is the **cleansing agent**? Of course not. Such a conclusion is unwarranted, and would certainly contradict other clear biblical testimony. Salvation is dependent upon and accomplished by means of the atoning work of Jesus Christ on the cross—His death, burial, and resurrection (1 Corinthians 15:1-4). Likewise, immersion must be preceded by faith, repentance, and confession of the deity of Christ. But

Peter included this very point in his discussion. When one removes the parenthetical material from the verse, the interplay between baptism and Christ's redemptive activity is clearly seen: "There is also an antitype which now saves us—baptism, through the resurrection of Jesus Christ." "Resurrection" is the figure of speech known as synecdoche in which the part is put in place of the whole. "Resurrection" includes the entire atoning event of Jesus—death, burial, and resurrection. Hence, Peter attributed one's salvation to Christ's work on the cross—but the application of this salvific achievement to the sinner occurs **at the point of baptism**.

Summary

The Bible is its own best interpreter. It teaches that baptism is, indeed, a symbol. **But what does baptism symbolize?** It symbolizes: (1) Christ's death, burial, and resurrection; (2) the act of "cutting off" in circumcision; and (3) the waters of the Flood. How could anyone get out of this that **baptism symbolizes past forgiveness** that was achieved **prior** to being immersed? The honest exegete is forced to conclude that the Bible nowhere expounds such a notion. The symbolism associated with water baptism further verifies the essentiality of immersion as a mandatory prerequisite to forgiveness. We dare not go beyond what is written (1 Corinthians 4:6), since it is by Jesus' words that we will be judged (John 12:48).

Christ at the Door of Your Heart?

One of the most familiar expressions uttered within Christendom is: "Christ stands at the door of your heart." Many have been the preachers who have urged their hearers to "invite Jesus into their hearts" in order to be forgiven of sin and made a Christian. Someone said if you repeat a statement enough times, people will come to accept it on the basis of sheer repetition and familiarity. The admonition that "Christ stands at the door of your heart" has been repeated so frequently that, for many, to question it is unthinkable. One would think that since this approach to salvation is so widespread, and the expression is so predominant, that surely the statement can be found in Scripture—even if only in so many words. How disturbing to realize that **the statement is not found in Scripture** and that the Bible simply does not teach this doctrine!

The phraseology is reminiscent of Revelation 3:20—the passage usually quoted to support the idea of Christ standing at the door of one's heart. But observe the context. Revelation chapters two and three consist of seven specific mini-letters directed to the seven churches of Christ in Asia Minor near the end of the first century. At the outset, one must recognize that Revelation 3:20 is addressed to **Christians**—not non-Christians on the verge of conversion.

Second, the verse is found among Christ's remarks to the church in Laodicea. Jesus made clear that the church had moved into an unfaithful condition. They were **lost**. They were unacceptable to God since they were "lukewarm" (3:16). They had become unsaved since their spiritual condition was "wretched and miserable and poor" (3:17). Thus, in a very real sense, Jesus had abandoned them by removing His presence from their midst. Now He was on the outside looking in. He still wanted to be among them, but the decision was up to them. They had to recognize His absence, hear Him knocking for admission, and open the door—all of which is figurative language to say that they must **repent** (3:19). They would have to return to the obedient lifestyle so essential to receiving God's favor (John 14:21,23).

This means that Revelation 3:20 **in no way** supports the idea that non-Christians merely have to "open the door of their heart" and "invite Jesus in" with the assurance that the moment they mentally/verbally do so, Jesus will come into their heart and they will be simultaneously saved from all past sin and counted as Christians! The **context** of Revelation 3:20 shows that Jesus was **seeking readmission into an apostate church**.

"But doesn't the Bible teach that Christ does come into a person's heart?" Yes. But not the way the religious world suggests. Ephesians 3:17 states that Christ dwells in the heart **through** faith. Faith can be acquired only by hearing biblical truth (Romans 10:17). When that biblical truth is **obeyed**, the individual is "saved by faith" (Hebrews 5:9; James 2:22; 1 Peter 1:22; et al.). So Christ enters our lives when we "draw near with a sincere heart in full assurance of **faith**, having our hearts sprinkled from an evil conscience [i.e., when we **repent** of our sins] and our bodies washed with pure water [i.e., when we are **baptized** in water]" (Hebrews 10:22). Here is the New Testament (i.e., non-denominational) way to accept Christ.

Calling on the Lord

Considering how many people within "Christendom" teach that an individual can be saved merely by professing a belief in Christ, it is not surprising that skeptics claim that the Bible contradicts itself in this regard. Although Peter and Paul declared, "Whoever calls on the name of the Lord shall be saved" (Acts 2:21; Romans 10:13; cf. Joel 2:32), skeptics quickly remind their readers that Jesus once stated: "Not everyone who says to Me, 'Lord, Lord,' shall enter the kingdom of heaven, but he who does the will of My Father in heaven" (Matthew 7:21; cf. Luke 6:46). Allegedly, Matthew 7:21 clashes with such passages as Acts 2:21 and Romans 10:13 (see Morgan, 2003; Wells, 2001). Since many professed Christians seem to equate "calling on the name of the Lord" with the idea of saying to Jesus, "Lord, I receive You," Bible critics feel even more justified in their pronouncement of "conflicting testimonies." How can certain professed followers of Christ claim that they were saved by simply "calling out to Christ," when Christ Himself proclaimed that a mere calling upon Him would not save a person?

The key to understanding correctly the phrase "calling on the name of the Lord" is to recognize that more is involved in this action than a mere verbal petition directed toward God. The "call" mentioned in Acts 2:21, Romans 10:13, and Acts 22:16 (where Paul was "calling on the name of the Lord"), is not equated with the "call" ("Lord, Lord") Jesus spoke of in the Sermon on the Mount (Matthew 7:21).

First, it is appropriate to mention that even in modern times, to "call on" someone frequently means more than simply making a request for something. When a doctor goes to the hospital to "call on" some of his patients, he does not merely walk into the room and say, "I just wanted to come by and say, 'Hello.' I wish you the best. Now pay me." On the contrary, he involves himself in a service. He examines the patient, listens to the patient's concerns, gives further instructions regarding the patient's hopeful recovery, and then oftentimes prescribes medication. All of these elements may be involved in a doctor "calling upon" a patient. In the mid-twentieth century, it was common for young men to "call on" young ladies. Again, this expression meant something different than just "making a request" (Brown, 1976, p. 5).

Second, when an individual takes the time to study how the expression "calling on God" is used throughout Scripture, the only reasonable conclusion to draw is that, just as similar phrases sometimes have a deeper meaning in modern America, the expression "calling on God" often had a deeper meaning in Bible times. Take, for instance, Paul's statement recorded in Acts 25:11: "I appeal unto Caesar." The word "appeal" (*epikaloumai*) is the same word translated "call" (or "calling") in Acts 2:21, 22:16, and Romans 10:13. But, Paul was not simply saying, "I'm calling on Caesar to save me." As James Bales noted:

> Paul, in appealing to Caesar, was claiming the right of a Roman citizen to have his case judged by Caesar. He was asking that his case be transferred to Caesar's court and that Caesar hear and pass judgment on his case. In so doing, he indicated that he was resting his case on Caesar's judgment. In order for this to be done Paul had to submit to whatever was necessary in order for his case to be brought before Caesar. He had to submit to the Roman soldiers who conveyed him to Rome. He had to submit to whatever formalities or procedure Caesar demanded of those who came before him. All of this was involved in his appeal to Caesar (1960, pp. 81-82, emp. added).

Paul's "calling" to Caesar involved his submission to him. "That, in a nutshell," wrote T. Pierce Brown, "is what 'calling on the Lord' involves"—obedience (1976, p. 5). It is not a mere verbal recognition of God, or a verbal petition to Him. Those whom Paul (before his conversion to Christ) sought to bind in Damascus—Christians who were described as people "who call on Your [Jehovah's] name"—were not people who only prayed to God, but those who were serving the Lord, and who, by their obedience, were submitting themselves to His authority (cf. Matthew 28:18). Interestingly, Zephaniah 3:9 links one's "calling" with his "service": "For then I will restore to the peoples a pure language, that they all may call on the name of the Lord, to serve Him with one accord" (emp. added). When a person submits to the will of God, he accurately can be described as "calling on the Lord." Acts 2:21 and Romans 10:13 (among other passages) do not contradict Matthew 7:21, because to "call on the Lord" entails more than just pleading for salvation; it involves submitting to God's will. According to Colossians 3:17, every single act a Christian performs (in word or deed) should be carried out by Christ's authority. For a non-Christian receiving salvation, this is no different. In order to obtain salvation, a person must submit to the Lord's authority. This is what the passages in Acts 2:21 and Romans 10:13 are teaching; it is up to us to go elsewhere in the New Testament to learn **how** to call upon the name of the Lord.

After Peter quoted the prophecy of Joel and told those in Jerusalem on Pentecost that "whoever calls on the name of the Lord shall be saved" (Acts 2:21), he told them how to go about "calling on the name of the Lord." The people in the audience in Acts 2 did not understand Peter's quotation of Joel to mean that an alien sinner must pray to God for salvation. [Their question in Acts 2:37 ("Men and brethren, what shall we do?") indicates such.] Furthermore, when Peter responded to their question and told them what to do to be saved, he did not say, "I've already told you what to do. You can be saved by petitioning God for salvation through prayer. Just call on His name." On the contrary, Peter had to explain to them what it meant to "call on the name of the Lord." Instead of repeating this statement when the crowd sought further guidance from the apostles, Peter commanded them, saying, "Repent, and let every one of you be baptized in the name of Jesus Christ for the remission of sins" (2:38). Notice the parallel:

Acts 2:21 = Acts 2:38

Acts 2:21	Whoever	calls	on the name	of the Lord	shall be saved
Acts 2:38	every one of you	repent and be baptized	in the name	of Jesus Christ	for the remission of sins

Peter's non-Christian listeners learned that "calling on the name of the Lord for salvation" was equal to obeying the Gospel, which approximately 3,000 did that very day by repenting of their sins and being baptized into Christ (2:38,41).

But what about Romans 10:13? What is the "call" mentioned in this verse? Notice Romans 10:11-15:

> For the Scripture says, "Whoever believes on Him will not be put to shame." For there is no distinction between Jew and Greek, for the same Lord over all is rich to all who call upon Him. For "whoever calls on the name of the Lord shall be saved." How then shall they call on Him in whom they have not believed? And how shall they believe in Him of whom they have not heard? And how shall they hear without a preacher? And how shall they preach unless they are sent? As it is written: "How beautiful are the feet of those who preach the gospel of peace, who bring glad tidings of good things!" (emp. added).

Although this passage does not define precisely what is meant by one "calling on the name of the Lord," it does indicate that an alien sinner cannot "call" until after he has heard the Word of God and believed it. Such was meant by Paul's rhetorical questions: "How then shall they call on Him in whom they have not believed? And how shall they believe in Him of whom they have not heard?" Paul's statements in this passage are consistent with Peter's proclamations in Acts 2. It was only after the crowd on Pentecost believed in the resurrected Christ Whom Peter preached (as is evident by their being "cut to the heart" and their subsequent question, "Men and brethren, what shall we do?") that Peter told them how to call on the name of the Lord and be saved (2:38).

Perhaps the clearest description of what it means for an alien sinner to "call on the name of the Lord" is found in Acts 22. As the apostle Paul addressed the mob in Jerusalem, he spoke of his encounter with the Lord, Whom he asked, "What shall I do?" (22:10; cf. 9:6). The answer Jesus gave Him at that time was not "call on the name of the Lord." Instead, Jesus instructed him to "arise and go into Damascus, and there you will be told all things which are appointed for you to do" (22:10). Paul (or Saul—Acts 13:9) demonstrated his belief in Jesus as he went into the city and waited for further instructions. In Acts 9, we learn that during the next three days, while waiting to meet with Ananias, Paul fasted and prayed (vss. 9,11). Although some today might consider what Paul was doing at this point as "calling on the name of the Lord," Ananias, God's chosen messenger to Paul, did not think so. He did not tell Paul, "I see you have already called on God. Your sins are forgiven." After three days of fasting and praying, Paul still was lost in his sins. Even though he obviously believed at this point, and had prayed to God, he had yet to "call on the name of the Lord" for salvation. When Ananias finally came to Paul, he told him: "Arise and be baptized, and wash away your sins, calling on the name of the Lord" (22:16). Ananias knew that Paul had not yet "called on the name of the Lord," just as Peter knew that those on Pentecost had not done so before his command to "repent and be baptized." Thus, Ananias instructed Paul to "be baptized, and wash away your sins." The participle phrase, "calling on the name of the Lord," describes what Paul was doing when he was baptized for the remission of his sins. Every non-Christian who desires to "call on the name of the Lord" to be saved, does so, not simply by saying, "Lord, Lord" (cf. Matthew 7:21), or just by wording a prayer to God (e.g., Paul—Acts 9; 22; cf. Romans 10:13-14), but by obeying God's instructions to "repent and be baptized...in the name of Jesus Christ for the remission of your sins" (Acts 2:38).

This is not to say that repentance and baptism have always been (or are always today) synonymous with "calling on the name of the Lord." Abraham was not baptized when he "called upon the name of the Lord" (Genesis 12:8; cf. 4:26), because baptism was not demanded of God before New Testament times. And, as I mentioned earlier, when the New Testament describes people who were already Christians as "calling on the name of the Lord" (Acts 9:14,21; 1 Corinthians 1:2), it certainly does not mean that Christians continually were being baptized for the remission of their sins after having been baptized to become a Christian (cf. 1 John 1:5-10). Depending on when and where the phrase is used, "calling on the name of the Lord" includes: (1) obedience to the gospel plan of salvation; (2) worshiping God; and (3) faithful service to the Lord (Bates, 1979, p. 5). However, it never is used in the sense that all the alien sinner must do in order to be saved is to cry out and say, "Lord, Lord, save me."

Thus, the skeptic's allegation that Matthew 7:21 contradicts Acts 2:21 and Romans 10:13 is unsubstantiated. And, the professed Christian who teaches that all one must do to be saved is just say the sinner's prayer, is in error.

REFERENCES

Bales, James (1960), *The Hub of the Bible—Or—Acts Two Analyzed* (Shreveport, LA: Lambert).

Bates, Bobby (1979), "Whosoever Shall Call Upon the Name of the Lord Shall be Saved," *Firm Foundation*, 96:5, March 20.

Brown, T. Pierce (1976), "Calling on His Name," *Firm Foundation*, 93:5, July 20.

Graham, Billy (1977), *How to Be Born Again* (Waco, TX: Word Books).

Jackson, Wayne (1988), "The New Birth: What is It?" *Christian Courier*, 24/4:14.

Lucado, Max (2000), *He Did This Just for You* (Nashville, TN: Word).

Morgan, Donald (2003), "Biblical Inconsistencies," [On-line], URL: http://www.infidels.org/library/modern/donald_morgan/inconsistencies.shtml.

Robertson, A.T. (1934), *A Grammar of the Greek New Testament* (Nashville, TN: Broadman).

Wells, Steve (2001), *Skeptic's Annotated Bible*, [On-line], URL: http://www.Skepticsannotatedbible.com.